The Norton Anthology of World Literature

SECOND EDITION

VOLUME B

100–1500

John Bierhorst

Jerome Wright Clinton
PROFESSOR OF NEAR EASTERN STUDIES, PRINCETON UNIVERSITY

Robert Lyons Danly
LATE OF THE UNIVERSITY OF MICHIGAN

Kenneth Douglas
LATE OF COLUMBIA UNIVERSITY

Howard E. Hugo
LATE OF THE UNIVERSITY OF CALIFORNIA, BERKELEY

F. Abiola Irele
PROFESSOR OF AFRICAN, FRENCH, AND COMPARATIVE LITERATURE,
THE OHIO STATE UNIVERSITY

Heather James
ASSOCIATE PROFESSOR OF ENGLISH, UNIVERSITY OF SOUTHERN CALIFORNIA

Bernard M. W. Knox
DIRECTOR EMERITUS, CENTER FOR HELLENIC STUDIES

John C. McGalliard
LATE OF THE UNIVERSITY OF IOWA

Stephen Owen
PROFESSOR OF CHINESE AND COMPARATIVE LITERATURE,
HARVARD UNIVERSITY

P. M. Pasinetti
PROFESSOR OF ITALIAN AND COMPARATIVE LITERATURE EMERITUS, UNIVERSITY OF CALIFORNIA,
LOS ANGELES

Lee Patterson
F. W. HILLES PROFESSOR OF ENGLISH, YALE UNIVERSITY

Indira Viswanathan Peterson
PROFESSOR OF ASIAN STUDIES, MOUNT HOLYOKE COLLEGE

Patricia Meyer Spacks
EDGAR F. SHANNON PROFESSOR OF ENGLISH, UNIVERSITY OF VIRGINIA

William G. Thalmann
PROFESSOR OF CLASSICS, UNIVERSITY OF SOUTHERN CALIFORNIA

René Wellek
LATE OF YALE UNIVERSITY

The Norton Anthology of World Literature

SECOND EDITION

Sarah Lawall, *General Editor*

PROFESSOR OF COMPARATIVE LITERATURE AND ADJUNCT PROFESSOR OF
FRENCH, UNIVERSITY OF MASSACHUSETTS, AMHERST

Maynard Mack, *General Editor Emeritus*

LATE OF YALE UNIVERSITY

VOLUME B

100–1500

W·W·NORTON & COMPANY · *New York* · *London*

Editor: Peter J. Simon
Developmental Editor: Carol Flechner
Associate Managing Editor: Marian Johnson
Production Manager: Diane O'Connor
Editorial Assistant: Isobel T. Evans
Project Editors: Candace Levy, Vivien Reinart, Carol Walker, Will Rigby
Permissions Manager: Nancy Rodwan
Assistant Permissions Manager: Sandra Chin
Text Design: Antonina Krass
Art Research: Neil Ryder Hoos
Maps: Jacques Chazaud

The text of this book is composed in Fairfield Medium
with the display set in Bernhard Modern.
Composition by Binghamton Valley Composition.
Manufacturing by R. R. Donnelley & Sons.
Cover illustration: *Portrait of Sung Jen-tsung.* Collection of the National Palace Museum, Tai-
pei, Taiwan, Republic of China.

The Library of Congress has cataloged another edition as follows:

The Norton anthology of world literature / Sarah Lawall, general editor; Maynard
Mack, general editor emeritus. —2nd ed.
    p.   cm.
Includes bibliographical references and index.
Contents: v. A. Beginnings to A.D. 100—v. B. A.D. 100–1500—v. C. 1500–1650—v.
D. 1650–1800—v. E. 1800–1900—v. F. The twentieth century.
ISBN 0-393-97764-1 (v. 1)—ISBN 0-393-97765-X (v. 2)
    1. Literature—Collections. I. Lawall, Sarah N. II. Mack, Maynard, 1909–

PN6014.N66 2001
808.8—dc21   2001030824

ISBN 0-393-97756-0 (pbk.)

W. W. Norton & Company, Inc., 500 Fifth Avenue, New York, NY 10110
www.wwnorton.com

W. W. Norton & Company Ltd., Castle House, 75/76 Wells Street, London W1T 3QT

1 2 3 4 5 6 7 8 9 0

Contents

China's "Middle Period"

The Rise of Islam and Islamic Literature 1419

The Golden Age of Japanese Culture 2143

Preface

The first edition of the *Norton Anthology of World Literature* to appear in the twenty-first century offers many new works from around the world and a fresh new format that responds to contemporary needs. The global reach of this anthology encompasses important works from Asia and Africa, central Asia and India, the Near East, Europe, and North and South America—all presented in the light of their own literary traditions, as a shared heritage of generations of readers in many countries, and as part of a network of cultural and literary relationships whose scope is still being discovered. With this edition, we institute a shift in title that reflects the way the anthology has grown. The initial *Norton Anthology of World Masterpieces* (1956) aimed to present a broader "Western tradition of world literature" in contrast to previous anthologies confined to English and American works; it focused on the richness and diversity of Western literary tradition, as does the Seventh Edition of 1999. The present volume, which derives from the "Expanded" edition of 1995, contains almost all the texts of the Seventh Edition and also thousands of pages from works around the globe; it now logically assumes the broader title of "World Literature." In altering the current title to *The Norton Anthology of World Literature,* we do not abandon the anthology's focus on major works of literature or a belief that these works especially repay close study. It is their consummate artistry, their ability to express complex signifying structures, that gives access to multiple dimensions of meaning, meanings that are always rooted in a specific setting and cultural tradition but that further constitute, upon comparison, a thought-provoking set of perspectives on the varieties of human experience. Readers familiar with the anthology's two volumes, whose size increased proportionally with the abundance of new material, will welcome the new boxed format, in which each of the earlier volumes is separated into three slim and easily portable smaller books. Whether maintaining the chronological structure of the original boxed set or selecting a different configuration, you will be able to consult a new Web site, developed by Norton specifically for the world-literature anthologies and containing contextual information, audiovisual resources, exploratory analyses, and related material to illustrate and illuminate these compelling texts.

The six volumes represent six consecutive chronological periods from approximately 2500 B.C. to the present. Subsequently, and for pedagogical reasons, our structure is guided by the broad continuities of different cultural traditions and the literary or artistic periods they recognize for themselves. This means that chronology advises but does not dictate the order in which works appear. If Western tradition names a certain time slot "the Renaissance" or "the Enlightenment" (each term implying a shared set of beliefs), that designation has little relevance in other parts of the globe; similarly, "vernacular literature" does not have the same literary-historical status in all traditions; and "classical" periods come at different times in India, China, and Western Europe. We find that it is more useful to start from a tradition's own sense of itself and the specific shape it gives to the community memory embodied as art. Occasionally there are displacements of absolute chronology: Petrarch, for example, belongs chronologically with Boccaccio and Chaucer, and Rousseau is a contemporary of Voltaire. Each can be read as a new and dissonant voice within his own century, a foil and balance for accepted ideas, or he can be considered as part of a powerful new consciousness, along with those indebted to his thought and example. In the first and last volumes of the anthology, for different pedagogical purposes, we have chosen to present diverse cultural traditions together. The first section of the first volume, "The Invention of Writing and the Earliest Literatures," introduces students to the study of world literature with works from three different cultural traditions—Babylonian, Egyptian, Judaic—each among the oldest works that have come down to us in written form, each in its origins reaching well back into a preliterate past, yet directly accessible as an image of human experience and still provocative at the beginning of the twenty-first century. The last volume, *The Modern World: Self and Other in Global Context,* reminds us that separation in the modern world is no longer a possibility. Works in the twentieth century are demonstrably part of a new global consciousness, itself fostered by advances in communications, that experiences reality in terms of interrelationships, of boundaries asserted or transgressed, and of the creation of personal and social identity from the interplay of sameness and difference. As teachers, we have tried to structure an anthology that is usable, accessible, and engaging in the classroom—that clarifies patterns and relationships for your students, while leaving you free to organize selections from this wealth of material into the themes, genres, topics, and special emphases that best fit your needs.

Changes in this edition have taken several forms. Most visibly, there are many new selections to spark further combinations with works you have already been teaching and to suggest ways of extending your favorite themes with additional geographic, gendered, chronological, or cultural perspectives. Thus the volume on the twentieth-century adds five important Latin American authors who are pivotal figures in their own time and with an established international stature that, in a few cases, is just beginning to be recognized in the United States. In fiction, there is Juan Rulfo, whose landmark novel *Pedro Páramo* is at once an allegory of political power in modern Mexico and a magical narrative that introduced modernist techniques to Latin American fiction, and Clarice Lispector, the innovative Brazilian novelist and short-story writer who writes primarily about women's experience and is internationally known for her descriptions of psychological states of mind. In poetry, the vehicle for political and cultural revolution in so many European and Latin American countries, we introduce the Nicaraguan Rubén Darío, a charismatic diplomat-poet at home in Europe and Latin America who created the image of a Spanish cultural identity that included his own Indian ancestry and counteracted prevailing images of North American dominance. After Darío there is Alfonsina Storni, the Argentinian poet who was as well known in the 1920s and 1930s for her independent journal articles and her feminism as for the intensely personal poetry that assures her reputation today. Finally, the Nobel Prize winner and Chilean activist Pablo Neruda, who reinvigorated the concept of public poet and became the best-known Latin American poet of the twentieth century, is represented by selections from various periods and styles of his work—in particular, the epic vision of human history taken by many to be his crowning achievement, *The Heights of Macchu Picchu*. Works by all five authors add to our representation of Spanish and Latin American literature, but their importance is not limited to regional or cultural representation. Each functions within a broader framework that may be artistic convention; national, ethnic, or class identity; feminist or postcolonial perspectives; or a particular vision of human experience. Each resonates with other works throughout the volume and is an opportunity to enrich your world-literature syllabus with new comparisons and contrasts.

Many of the new selections draw attention to historical circumstances and the texture of everyday life. Biographical tales from records of the ancient Chinese historian Ssu-ma Ch'ien give a glimpse of contemporary attitudes and ideals, as does the dedicated historian's poignant *Letter in Reply to Jen An,* written after his official punishment by castration. Entries in Dorothy Wordsworth's *Grasmere Journals* express the very personal world of the intimate journal, and Virginia Woolf's passionate analysis of the woman writer's position, in *A Room of One's Own*, combines autobiography with essay and fiction. Still other texts focus on specific historical events or issues but employ fictional techniques for greater immediacy. There is a thin line between fiction and autobiography in Tadeusz Borowski's terrifying Holocaust story *Ladies and Gentlemen, to the Gas Chamber.* Nawal El Saadawi's chilling courtroom tale *In Camera* uses the victim's shifting and fragmented perspectives to evoke the harsh realities of twentieth-century political torture and repression. Zhang Ailing's novella of a difficult love, *Love in a Fallen City,* depicts the decline of traditional Chinese society and concludes with the Japanese bombing of Hong Kong in World War II, while Anita Desai's *The Rooftop Dwellers* follows the struggles of a single woman in Delhi to make a career for herself in the face of social disapproval and family pressure. African American realist author Richard Wright, describes an adolescent crisis related to specific social images of manliness in *The Man Who Was Almost a Man.* Yet there are always different ways of presenting historical circumstances and dealing with the questions they raise. A play from Renaissance Spain, Lope de Vega's *Fuente Ovejuna,* is a light romantic comedy that draws heavily on dramatic conventions for its humor; yet it is also set during a famous peasant uprising whose bloodshed, political repercussions, and torture of the entire citizenry are represented in the course of the play. Readers who follow historical and cultural themes throughout the anthology will find much provocative material in these diverse new selections.

In renewing this edition, we have taken several routes: introducing new authors (many previously mentioned); choosing an alternate work by the same author when it resonates with material in other sections or speaks strongly to current concerns; adding small sections to existing larger pieces in order to fill out a theme or narrative line, or to suggest connections with other texts; and grouping several works to bring out new strengths. Three stories by the African writer Bernard Dadié appear here for the first time, as do the romantic adventures of Ludovico Ariosto's epic parody *Orlando Furi-*

oso, an African tale by Doris Lessing—*The Old Chief Mshlanga*—and Alice Munro's complex evocation of childhood memories *Walker Brothers Cowboy.* Among the alternate works by existing authors, we present Gustave Flaubert's great realist novel *Madame Bovary,* James Joyce's Dublin tale *The Dead,* and William Faulkner's *The Bear,* the latter printed in its entirety to convey its full scope as a chronicle of the legacy of slavery in the American South. New plays include Bertolt Brecht's drama *The Good Woman of Setzuan* and William Shakespeare's *Othello* as well as *Hamlet;* each has its own special resonance in world literature. Derek Walcott is represented by a selection of his poetry, including excerpts from the modern epic *Omeros.* Five more magical tales are added to the *Thousand and One Nights* and three new essays from Montaigne, including his memorable *To the Reader.* Six new tales from Ovid (in a new translation by Allen Mandelbaum) round out a set of myths exploring different images of love and gender, themes that reappear in two of the best-known lays of Marie de France, *Lanval* and *Laüstic,* as well as in Boccaccio's famous "Pot of Basil" and the influential tale of patient Griselda and her tyrannical husband, all presented here. From Chaucer, there is the bawdy, popular *Wife of Bath's Tale,* and from the *Heptameron* of Marguerite de Navarre fresh tales of love and intrigue that emphasize the stereotyping of gender roles. To *The Cherry Orchard* by Anton Chekhov, we add his famous tale of uncertain love *The Lady with the Dog.* New selections from Books 4 and 8 of John Milton's *Paradise Lost* depict the drama of Satan's malevolent entry into Paradise, Adam and Eve's innocent conversation, and the angel's warning to Adam. Finally, the poignant tales of Abraham and Isaac and of Jacob and Esau (Genesis 22, 25, 27) are added to the Old Testament selections, as well as the glorious love poetry of the Song of Songs; and Matthew 13 [Why Jesus Teaches in Parables] is included among the selections from the New Testament.

Two founding works of early India, the *Rāmāya°na* and the *Mahābhārata,* are offered in greatly increased selections and with new and exceptionally accessible translations. Readers can now follow (in a new translation by Swami Venkatesananda) the trajectory of Rāma's exile and life in the forest, the kidnapping of his wife Sītā, and ensuing magical adventures up to the final combat between Rāma and the demon king Rāva°na. A lively narrative of the *Mahābhārata's* civil war (in a new translation by C. V. Narasimhan) unfolds in sequential excerpts that include two sections of special interest to modern students: the insulted Draupadī's formal accusation of the rulers in the Assembly Hall and the tragic story of the heroic but ill-fated warrior Kar°na.

To increase our understanding of individual authors' achievement, we join to the Indian Rabindranath Tagore's story *Punishment* a selection of the Bengali poems with which he revolutionized literary style in his homeland, and to the Chinese Lu Xun's two tales, examples of his poetry from *Wild Grass.* Rousseau's *Confessions* gain historical and psychological depth through new passages that shed light on his early years and on the development of his political sympathies.

The epic poetry that acts as the conscience of a community—*The Iliad, The Mahābhārata,* the *Son-Jara,* among others—has long been represented in the anthology. It has been our practice, however, to minimize the presence of lyric poetry in translation, recognizing—as is so cogently argued in the "Note on Translation," printed at the end of each volume—that the precise language and music of an original poem will never be identical with its translation and that short poems risk more of their substance in the transfer. Yet good translations often achieve a poetry of their own and occupy a pivotal position in a second literary history; thus the Egyptian love songs, the Chinese *Classic of Poetry* (*Book of Songs*), the biblical Song of Songs, and the lyrics of Sappho, Catullus, Petrarch, Rumi, and Baudelaire have all had influence far beyond the range of those who could read the original poems. Some poetry collections—like the Japanese *Man'yōshū* and *Kokinshū*—are recognized as an integral part of the society's cultural consciousness, and others—notably, the European Romantics—embody a sea change in artistic and cultural consciousness.

New to this edition is a series of poetry clusters that complement existing collections and represent a core of important and influential poetry in five different periods. You may decide to teach them as part of a spectrum of poetic expression or as reference points in a discussion of cultural consciousness. Thus a newly translated series of early hymns by the Tamil Śaiva saints exemplifies the early mystical poetry of India, while the multifarious vitality of medieval Europe is recaptured in poems by men and women from Arabic, Judaic, Welsh, Spanish, French, Provençal, Italian, English, and German traditions. Those who have taught English Romantic poetry will find both contrast and comparison in Continental poets from France, Italy, Germany, Spain, and Russia, many of whom possess lasting influence in nineteenth- and twentieth-century literature. Symbolism, whose insights into the relation of language and reality have permeated modern poetry and linguistic theory, is represented by the great nineteenth-century poets Charles Baudelaire, Stéphane Mallarmé, Paul Verlaine, and Arthur Rimbaud. Finally, a cluster of Dada-Surrealist poems that range from slashing, rebellious humor to ecstatic love introduces the free association and dreamlike structures of this visionary movement, whose influence extends around the world and has strong links to modern art and film.

How to choose, as you turn from the library before you to the inevitable constraint of available time? There is an embarrassment of riches, an inexhaustible series of options, to fit whatever course pattern you wish. Perhaps you have already decided to proceed by theme or genre, in chronological order or by a selected comparative principle; or you have favorite titles that work well in the classroom, and you seek to combine them with new pieces. Perhaps you want to create modules that compare ideas of national identity or of bicultural identity and shifting cultural paradigms, that survey images of gender in different times and places or that examine the place of memory in a range of texts. In each instance, you have only to pick and choose among a variety of works from different countries, languages, and cultural backgrounds. If you are teaching the course for the first time or wish to try something different, you may find what you are looking for in the sample syllabi of the *Instructor's Guide* or on the new Web site, which will also contain supporting material such as maps, time lines, and audio pronunciation glossaries, resource links, guides to section materials, various exercises and assignments, and a series of teaching modules related to specific works. Throughout, the editors (who are all practicing teachers) have selected and prepared texts that are significant in their own area of scholarly expertise, meaningful in the larger context of world literature, and, always, delightful, captivating and challenging to students.

Clearly one can parcel out the world in a variety of ways, most notably geopolitical, and there is no one map of world literature. In order to avoid parochialism, some scholars suggest that we should examine cultural activity in different countries at the same period of time. Others attempt to deconstruct prevailing literary assumptions (often selected from Western literary theory) by using history or cultural studies as a framework for examining texts as documents. "Global" literary studies project a different map that depends on one's geopolitical view of global interactions and of the energies involved in the creation and dissemination of literature. *The Norton Anthology of World Literature*, Second Edition, takes a different point of departure, focusing first of all on literary texts—artifacts, if you will, that have a special claim on our attention because they have been read over a great period of time and are cherished by a wide variety of readers. Once such texts have been proposed as objects of knowledge—and enjoyment, and illumination— they are available for any and all forms of analysis. Situating them inside larger forms of textuality—linguistic, historical, or cultural—is, after all, an inevitable part of the meaning-making process. It is the primary task of this anthology, however, to present them as multidimensional objects for discussion and then to let our readers choose when and where to extend the analysis.

From the beginning, the editors of *The Norton Anthology of World Literature* have always balanced the competing—and, we like to think, complementary—claims of teaching and scholarship, of the specialist's focused expertise and the generalist's broader perspectives. The founding editors set the example, which guides their successors. We welcome three new successor editors to this edition: William G. Thalmann, Professor of Classics at the University of Southern California; Lee Patterson, Professor of English at Yale University; and Heather James, Associate Professor of English at the University of Southern California. Two founding editors have assumed Emeritus status: Bernard M. W. Knox, eminent classical scholar and legendary teacher and lecturer; and P. M. Pasinetti, who combines the intellectual breadth of the Renaissance scholar with a novelist's creative intuition. We also pay tribute to the memory of Robert Lyons Danly, translator and astute scholar of Japanese literature, whose lively interventions have been missed since his untimely death in 1995. Finally, we salute the memory of Maynard Mack, General Editor and presiding genius from the first edition through the Expanded Edition of 1995. An Enlightenment scholar of much wisdom, humanity, and gracefully worn knowledge, and a firm believer in the role of great literature—world literature—in illuminating human nature, he was also unstintingly dedicated to this anthology as a teaching enterprise. To him, therefore, and on all counts, we dedicate the first millennial edition of the anthology.

Acknowledgments

Among our many critics, advisers, and friends, the following were of special help in providing suggestions and corrections: Joseph Barbarese (Rutgers University); Carol Clover (University of California, Berkeley); Patrick J. Cook (George Washington University); Janine Gerzanics (University of Southern California); Matthew Giancarlo (Yale University); Kevis Goodman (University of California at Berkeley); Roland Greene (University of Oregon); Dmitri Gutas (Yale University); John H. Hayes (Emory University); H. Mack Horton (University of California at Berkeley); Suzanne Keen (Washington and Lee University); Charles S. Kraszewski (King's College); Gregory F. Kuntz; Michelle Latiolais (University of California at Irvine); Sharon L. James (Bryn Mawr College); Ivan Marcus (Yale University); Timothy Martin (Rutgers University, Camden); William Naff (University of Massachusetts); Stanley Radosh (Our Lady of the Elms College); Fred C. Robinson (Yale University); John Rogers (Yale University); Robert Rothstein (University of Massachusetts); Lawrence Senelick (Boston University); Jack Shreve (Alleghany Community College); Frank Stringfellow (University of Miami); Nancy Vickers (Bryn Mawr College); and Jack Welch (Abilene Christian University).

We would also like to thank the following people who contributed to the planning of the Second Edition: Charles Adams, University of Arkansas; Dorothy S. Anderson, Salem State College; Roy Anker, Calvin College; John Apwah, County College of Morris; Doris Bargen, University of Massachusetts; Carol Barrett, Austin Community College, Northridge Campus; Michael Beard, University of North Dakota; Lysbeth Em Berkert, Northern State University; Marilyn Booth, University of Illinois; George Byers, Fairmont State College; Shirley Carnahan, University of Colorado; Ngwarsungu Chiwengo, Creighton University; Stephen Cooper, Troy State University; Bonita Cox, San Jose State University; Richard A. Cox, Abilene Christian University; Dorothy Deering, Purdue University; Donald Dickson, Texas A&M University; Alexander Dunlop, Auburn University; Janet Eber, County College of Morris; Angela Esterhammer, University of Western Ontario; Walter Evans, Augusta State University; Fidel Fajardo-Acosta, Creighton University; John C. Freeman, El Paso Community College, Valle Verde Campus; Barbara Gluck, Baruch College; Michael Grimwood, North Carolina State University; Rafey Habib, Rutgers University, Camden; John E. Hallwas, Western Illinois College; Jim Hauser, William Patterson College; Jack Hussey, Fairmont State College; Dane Johnson, San Francisco State University; Andrew Kelley, Jackson State Community College; Jane Kinney, Valdosta State University; Candace Knudson, Truman State University; Jameela Lares, University of Southern Mississippi; Thomas L. Long, Thomas Nelson Community College; Sara MacDonald, Sterling College; Linda Macri, University of Maryland; Rita Mayer, San Antonio College; Christopher Morris,

Norwich University; Deborah Nestor, Fairmont State College; John Netland, Calvin College; Kevin O'Brien, Chapman University; Mariannina Olcott, San Jose State University; Charles W. Pollard, Calvin College; Pilar Rotella, Chapman University; Rhonda Sandford, Fairmont State College; Daniel Schenker, University of Alabama at Huntsville; Robert Scotto, Baruch College; Carl Seiple, Kutztown University; Glenn Simshaw, Chemeketa Community College; Evan Lansing Smith, Midwestern State University; William H. Smith, Piedmont College; Floyd C. Stuart, Norwich University; Cathleen Tarp, Fairmont State College; Diane Thompson, Northern Virginia Community College; Sally Wheeler, Georgia Perimiter College; Jean Wilson, McMaster University; Susan Wood, University of Nevada, Las Vegas; Tom Wymer, Bowling Green State University.

Phonetic Equivalents

for use with the Pronouncing Glossaries preceding most
selections in this volume

a as in *cat*
ah as in *father*
ai as in *light*
ay as in *day*
aw as in *raw*
e as in *pet*
ee as in *street*
ehr as in *air*
er as in *bird*
eu as in *lurk*
g as in *good*
i as in *sit*
j as in *joke*
nh a nasal sound (as in French *vin, vẽ)*
o as in *pot*
oh as in *no*
oo as in *boot*
oy as in *toy*
or as in *bore*
ow as in *now*
s as in *mess*
ts as in *ants*
u as in *us*
zh as in *vision*

The Norton Anthology of World Literature

SECOND EDITION

VOLUME B

100–1500

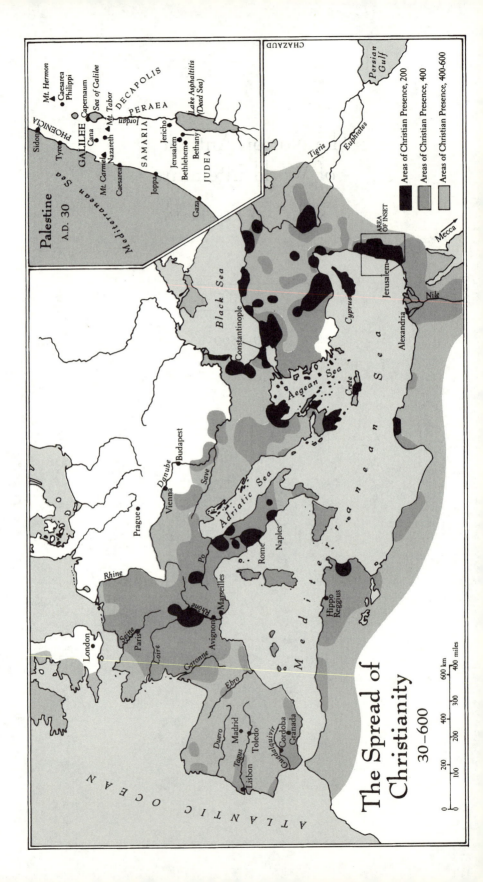

The Spread of Christianity
30–600

Areas of Christian Presence, 200
Areas of Christian Presence, 400
Areas of Christian Presence, 400–600

Palestine
A.D. 30

PHOENICIA
Sidon
Tyre
Mt. Hermon
Caesarea Philippi
Capernaum
Sea of Galilee
GALILEE
Cana
Mt. Tabor
Mt. Carmel
Nazareth
DECAPOLIS
PERAEA
Jordan
SAMARIA
Caesarea
Joppa
Jericho
Jerusalem
Bethlehem
Bethany
JUDEA
Lake Asphaltitis
(Dead Sea)
Gaza
Mediterranean Sea

CHAZAUD
Persian Gulf
Tigris
Euphrates
AREA OF INSET
Jerusalem
Nile
Mecca
Alexandria
Cyprus
Crete
Aegean Sea
Black Sea
Constantinople
Mediterranean Sea
Adriatic Sea
Save
Danube
Budapest
Vienna
Prague
Po
Rome
Naples
Hippo Reggius
Marseilles
Rhine
Rhône
Avignon
Paris
Seine
Loire
Garonne
London
Ebro
Duero
Madrid
Tagus
Toledo
Lisbon
Guadalquivir
Cordoba
Granada
ATLANTIC OCEAN

0   100   200   300   400   600 km
0   100   200   300   400 miles

From Roman Empire to Christian Europe

In the last years of Augustus's life, in the Roman province of Judea, there was born to Joseph, a carpenter of Nazareth, and his wife, Mary, a son who was in the tradition of the Hebrew prophets but was also the bearer of a message that was to transform the world. His life on earth was short; it ended in the agony of crucifixion in about his thirty-third year. This event is a point of intersection of three of the main lines of development of the ancient world—Hebrew, Greek, and Latin—for this Hebrew prophet was executed by a Roman governor, and his life and teachings were written down in the Greek language. These documents became the sacred texts of a church that, at first persecuted by and then triumphantly associated with Roman imperial power, outlasted the destruction of the empire and ruled over a spiritual empire that still exists.

The teaching of Jesus was revolutionary not only in terms of Greek and Roman feeling but also in terms of the Hebrew religious tradition. The Hebrew idea of a personal God who is yet not anthropomorphic, who is omnipotent, omniscient, and infinitely just was now broadened to include among His attributes an infinite mercy that tempered the justice. Greek and Roman religion was outward and visible, the formal practice of ritual acts in a social context; Christianity was inward and spiritual, the important relationship being that between the individual soul and God. All human beings were on an equal plane in the eyes of their Creator. This idea ran counter to the theory and practice of an institution basic to the economy of the ancient world, slavery. Like the earlier Hebrew prophets, Jesus was rejected by his contemporaries, as prophets have always been, and his death on the Cross and resurrection provided his followers and future converts with an unforgettable symbol of a new dispensation, the son of God in human form suffering to atone for the sins of humanity, the supreme expression of divine mercy. This conception is the basis of the teaching of Paul, the apostle to the Gentiles, who in the middle years of the first century A.D. changed Christianity from a Jewish sect to a worldwide movement with flourishing churches all over Asia Minor and Greece—and even in Rome. The burden of his teaching was the frailty and corruption of this life and world and the certainty of resurrection. "For this corruptible must put on incorruption, and this mortal must put on immortality" (1 Corinthians 14.53). To those who had accepted this vision, the secular materialism that was the dominant view in the new era of peace and progress guaranteed by the stabilization of Roman rule was no longer tenable.

In any case, the stability of Roman rule did not outlast the reign of the philosopher emperor Marcus Aurelius, who died in A.D. 180. His son and successor, Commodus, was assassinated in 192, and for years rival military commanders fought for mastery of the empire. In the years between 218 and 268 there were more than fifty claimants to the imperial power; one short-lived emperor after another was killed by his own troops, while new and formidable enemies—the Goths to the north and the Persians to the east—invaded and plundered the Balkan and eastern provinces. The empire seemed to be on the brink of collapse, but a succession of soldier emperors reestablished central power and secured the frontiers. This success was won at tremendous cost, however; the economic resources of the empire were drained to pay and equip the armies, and inflation caused by government debasement of the gold and silver currency undermined the economic system. Under Diocletian (ruled 284–305) there was an ineffectual attempt to fix the maximum price of all goods and a successful consolidation of the emperor's powers as the rule of a semidivine despotic monarch.

Through all the years of turmoil the Christian church, often persecuted by the imperial authorities—by Nero in the first century, by Marcus Aurelius and, more severely, by Diocletian in the third—was growing in numbers and influence, its network of religious communities organized by bishops. After Diocletian's retirement from power in 305 a new civil war began; the victor, Constantine, declared himself a Christian and enlisted the support of the Church in his reorganization of the empire.

In the course of the long series of defensive wars on the frontiers it had become clear that Rome could no longer serve as the strategic center of the empire; it was too far away from the endangered areas on the northern and eastern frontiers. It had also become clear that the western and eastern halves of the empire needed separate administrative and military organization, and under Diocletian such a system was established. The two halves of the empire were in any case distinct cultural and linguistic entities: Latin and Greek. This was also true of the Christian church. Constantine established a new capital for his reign on the site of the Greek city Byzantium and renamed it Constantinople. By the time one of his successors, Theodosius, made Christianity the official religion of the Roman empire in 391, the two halves of the empire were to all intents and purposes separate states.

They were to have separate destinies. In the east the imperial power based on the capital founded by Constantine maintained a Greek-speaking Christian empire for many centuries until, after fighting a long losing battle against the advance of Islam, the city fell to the Ottoman Turks in 1453. But in the west, collapse came much sooner. In 410 Rome fell to Alaric at the head of an army of Visigoths; many of the western provinces had already been overrun by new peoples moving south. But the Church survived, to convert the conquerors to the Christian religion and establish the cultural and religious foundations of the European Middle Ages.

FURTHER READING

Jaroslav Pelikan, *The Excellent Empire: The Fall of Rome and the Triumph of the Church* (1987), is a collection of brilliant essays by a famous historian of the Christian church on Gibbon's *Decline and Fall*, the early centuries of the Church, and St. Augustine. For a critical assessment of Constantine by a noted historian of Rome, see Ramsay MacMullen, *Constantine* (1969); Michael Grant, *Constantine the Great* (1994), is also recommended. Averil Cameron, *The Later Roman Empire* (1993), is a basic source for the study of "late antiquity" (Diocletian to Constantine) by a well-known specialist on the period. F. W. Walbank, *The Awful Revolution: The Decline of the Roman Empire in the West* (1969), provides a detailed but lucid analysis of the crisis and collapse of Roman imperial power—Gibbon's "awful Revolution."

TIME LINE

TEXTS	CONTEXTS
100 The four **Gospels** of the life and sayings of Jesus and the Acts of the Apostles are complete	
	117–138 Hadrian emperor
	131–134 Jewish revolt against Roman rule; Jews expelled from Palestine in 134
	138–161 Antoninus Pius emperor
	161–180 Marcus Aurelius emperor
	ca. 200–300 Systematic effort by the Roman empire to destroy Christianity fails
	284–305 Diocletian emperor
	303–311 Last persecution of Christians
	312–337 Constantine I emperor
	313 Constantine issues Edict of Milan, declaring toleration of all religions
	330 Constantine moves capital of the Roman empire to Byzantium, renaming the city Constantinople
367 Final canon of the New Testament of the Bible is established	
387 Augustine baptized as a Christian	
	391 Christianity becomes official religion of the Roman empire; pagan religions outlawed
ca. 393–405 Jerome translates the Bible into Latin	
	395 The Roman empire is permanently divided into the Eastern empire, based in Constantinople, and the Western empire, based in Rome

Boldface titles indicate works in the anthology.

TIME LINE

TEXTS	CONTEXTS
397 Augustine begins *Confessions*	
	410 Rome sacked by Alaric and the Visigoths
	455 Rome invaded by Vandals
	476 Last emperor of the Western empire is deposed by Odoacer, king of Heruli

Boldface titles indicate works in the anthology.

THE BIBLE: THE NEW TESTAMENT
ca. first century

When Jesus was born in the Roman province of Judea, there were four languages spoken in the area, a consequence of its complicated history. Classical Hebrew, the language of the sacred books of the Jews, was understood by educated people, especially the priestly caste, but the general population spoke Aramaic. This was a Semitic language close to classical Hebrew—the relationship has been compared with that between Portuguese and Spanish—but different enough to necessitate an Aramaic paraphrase of the sacred texts for use in the synagogue. Aramaic was the language in which Jesus preached to crowds and conversed with his disciples; the last words he spoke in agony on the cross were Aramaic: *Eli, Eli, lama sabachthani?* ("My God, my God, why hast thou forsaken me?").

But Judea, like all of the territory conquered by Alexander the Great, had come under Macedonian-Greek rule by the beginning of the second century B.C., and many Jews, especially those of the upper and educated classes, had learned Greek, an entry to the new administrative, commercial, and cultural milieux of the Hellenistic empires. Finally, in the last half of the first century B.C. Judea became a Roman province, and Latin (the language of the Roman governor and the military establishment) became the language of government. Most cultured Romans, however, knew Greek, and Greek remained the lingua franca of the educated classes all over the huge territory now called the Middle East.

If the disciples of Jesus were to obey his command "Go ye into all the world, and preach the gospel to every creature" (Mark 16.20), they would have to use Greek outside the Aramaic-speaking world. And it is in Greek that the four Gospels (the word is an Old English translation of the Greek for "good news") were written, probably some forty to sixty years after Jesus' death. They must have been based on the oral teaching of the original disciples, and the first three (selections from which are printed here) were clearly designed with an eye to different readerships. The Gospel according to Matthew, for example, has a Jewish public in mind; one of its main concerns is to convince its readers not only that Jesus was the legitimate heir to the throne of the royal house of David but also that Jesus was the king, the Messiah, announced by the Hebrew prophets. Mark, on the other hand, is clearly written with a Gentile audience in mind and pays particular attention to the needs of the Roman reader, translating Aramaic words and even explaining that the courtyard into which the Roman soldiers took Jesus after he was condemned was the place the Romans called the *praetorium*. And the Gospel according to Luke is obviously addressed to cultured Greek readers; it makes very few references to the Hebrew prophecies and is in fact dedicated to a Greek called Theophilos.

These three Gospels contain a central core of identical material that must come from an earlier source now lost (it is known as the Q document). The fourth Gospel, that of John, draws on different sources and also has greater theological density than the other three. The collection known to Christians as the New Testament was formed by combining the four Gospels with another book by Luke, The Acts of the Apostles, which is an account of Paul's missionary journeys to the cities of Greece and Asia Minor. Added to this were letters of Paul and others to the Christian communities in such cities as Corinth, Thessalonica, and Rome and the book called Revelation, a vision of the end of the world and the second coming of Jesus.

There were, of course, many other documents that gave accounts of the life and teaching of Jesus, but this particular collection contained those judged most reliable by the Church authorities and was declared canonical some time in the third century. Latin translations of the Greek texts were made for the use of the Churches of the Western Roman empire, but there was no official version until in 382 Pope Damasus commissioned a scholar called Jerome to produce a correct translation. It soon became known as the Vulgate—the "common" or "popular" version. This was the text used and quoted by Augustine, and with some revisions over the centuries, the one that remained in use in the Christian churches of the west through the Middle Ages.

Recommended reading is Bruce M. Metzger, *The New Testament, Its Background, Growth, and Content* (1965), and the relevant chapters in Robert Alter and Frank Kermode, eds., *The Literary Guide to the Bible* (1987). For a translation in modern English, with commentary, see *The New Oxford Annotated Bible* (1975), edited by Herbert E. May and Bruce Metzger.

THE BIBLE: THE NEW TESTAMENT[1]

Luke 2

[The Birth and Youth of Jesus]

2. And it came to pass in those days, that there went out a decree from Cæsar Augustus, that all the world[2] should be taxed. (And this taxing was first made when Cyrenius was governor of Syria.) And all went to be taxed, every one unto his own city. And Joseph also went up from Galilee, out of the city of Nazareth, into Judæa, unto the city of David, which is called Bethlehem; (because he was of the house and lineage of David:) to be taxed with Mary his espoused wife, being great with child. And so it was, that, while they were there, the days were accomplished that she should be delivered. And she brought forth her firstborn son, and wrapped him in swaddling clothes, and laid him in a manger; because there was no room for them in the inn. And there were in the same country shepherds abiding in the field, keeping watch over their flock by night. And, lo, the angel of the Lord came upon them, and the glory of the Lord shone round about them: and they were sore afraid. And the angel said unto them, Fear not: for, behold, I bring you good tidings of great joy, which shall be to all people. For unto you is born this day in the city of David a Saviour, which is Christ[3] the Lord. And this shall be a sign unto you; ye shall find the babe wrapped in swaddling clothes, lying in a manger. And suddenly there was with the angel a multitude of the heavenly host praising God, and saying, Glory to God in the highest, and on earth peace, good will toward men. And it came to pass, as the angels were gone away from them into heaven, the shepherds said one to another, Let us now go even unto Bethlehem, and see this thing which is come to pass, which the Lord hath made known unto us. And they came with haste, and found Mary, and Joseph, and the babe lying in a manger. And when they had seen it, they made known abroad the saying which was told them concerning this child. And all they that heard it wondered at those things which were told them by the shepherds. But Mary kept all these things, and pondered them in her heart. And the shepherds returned, glorifying and praising God for all the things that they had heard and seen, as it was told unto them. And when eight days were accomplished for the circumcising of the child, his name was called JESUS, which was so named of the angel[4] before he was

---

1. The King James Version.   2. The Roman empire.   3. Anointed (Greek); used of kings, priests, and the deliverer promised by the prophets.   4. In the Annunciation to Mary (Luke 1.31). *Jesus* is a form of the name Joshua, which means "he shall save."

conceived in the womb. And when the days of her purification according to the law of Moses were accomplished, they brought him to Jerusalem, to present him to the Lord; (as it is written in the law of the Lord, Every male that openeth the womb[5] shall be called holy to the Lord;) and to offer a sacrifice according to that which is said in the law of the Lord, A pair of turtledoves, or two young pigeons. And, behold, there was a man in Jerusalem, whose name was Simeon; and the same man was just and devout, waiting for the consolation of Israel: and the Holy Ghost was upon him. And it was revealed unto him by the Holy Ghost, that he should not see death, before he had seen the Lord's Christ. And he came by the Spirit into the temple: and when the parents brought in the child Jesus, to do for him after the custom of the law, then took he him up in his arms, and blessed God, and said, Lord, now lettest thou thy servant depart in peace, according to thy word: for mine eyes have seen thy salvation, which thou hast prepared before the face of all people; a light to lighten the Gentiles,[6] and the glory of thy people Israel. And Joseph and his mother marvelled at those things which were spoken of him. And Simeon blessed them, and said unto Mary his mother, Behold, this child is set for the fall and rising again[7] of many in Israel; and for a sign which shall be spoken against; (yea, a sword shall pierce through thy own soul also,) that the thoughts of many hearts may be revealed. And there was one Anna, a prophetess, the daughter of Phanuel, of the tribe of Aser: she was of a great age, and had lived with an husband seven years from her virginity; and she was a widow of about fourscore and four years, which departed not from the temple, but served God with fastings and prayers night and day. And she coming in that instant gave thanks likewise unto the Lord, and spoke of him to all them that looked for redemption in Jerusalem. And when they had performed all things according to the law of the Lord, they returned into Galilee, to their own city Nazareth. And the child grew, and waxed strong in spirit, filled with wisdom: and the grace of God was upon him. Now his parents went to Jerusalem every year at the feast of the passover. And when he was twelve years old, they went up to Jerusalem after the custom of the feast. And when they had fulfilled the days, as they returned, the child Jesus tarried behind in Jerusalem; and Joseph and his mother knew not of it. But they, supposing him to have been in the company, went a day's journey; and they sought him among their kinsfolk and acquaintance. And when they found him not, they turned back again to Jerusalem, seeking him. And it came to pass that after three days they found him in the temple, sitting in the midst of the doctors,[8] both hearing them, and asking them questions. And all that heard him were astonished at his understanding and answers. And when they saw him, they were amazed: and his mother said unto him, Son, why hast thou thus dealt with us? behold, thy father and I have sought thee sorrowing. And he said unto them, How is it that ye sought me? wist ye not that I must be about my Father's business? And they understood not the saying which he spake unto them. And he went down with them, and came to Nazareth, and was subject unto them: but his mother kept all these sayings in her heart. And Jesus increased in wisdom and stature, and in favour with God and man.

---

5. The firstborn son is believed to belong to God (Exodus 13.2). The purification laws are given in Leviticus 12.   6. Non-Jews.   7. The Greek word is the one always used for the resurrection of the dead. 8. Teachers, rabbis.

Matthew 5–7

[The Teaching of Jesus: The Sermon on the Mount]

5. And seeing the multitudes, he went up into a mountain: and when he was set, his disciples came unto him: and he opened his mouth, and taught them, saying, Blessed are the poor in spirit: for theirs is the kingdom of heaven. Blessed are they that mourn: for they shall be comforted. Blessed are the meek: for they shall inherit the earth. Blessed are they which do hunger and thirst after righteousness: for they shall be filled. Blessed are the merciful: for they shall obtain mercy. Blessed are the pure in heart: for they shall see God. Blessed are the peacemakers: for they shall be called the children of God. Blessed are they which are persecuted for righteousness' sake: for theirs is the kingdom of heaven. Blessed are ye, when men shall revile you, and persecute you, and shall say all manner of evil against you falsely, for my sake. Rejoice, and be exceeding glad: for great is your reward in heaven: for so persecuted they the prophets which were before you.

Ye are the salt of the earth: but if the salt have lost his savour, wherewith shall it be salted?[1] it is thenceforth good for nothing, but to be cast out, and to be trodden under foot of men. Ye are the light of the world. A city that is set on a hill cannot be hid. Neither do men light a candle, and put it under a bushel,[2] but on a candlestick; and it giveth light unto all that are in the house. Let your light so shine before men, that they may see your good works, and glorify your Father which is in heaven.

Think not that I am come to destroy the law, or the prophets: I am not come to destroy, but to fulfil. For verily I say unto you, Till heaven and earth pass, one jot or one tittle shall in no wise pass from the law, till all be fulfilled. Whosoever therefore shall break one of these least commandments, and shall teach men so, he shall be called the least in the kingdom of heaven: but whosoever shall do and teach them, the same shall be called great in the kingdom of heaven. For I say unto you, That except your righteousness shall exceed the righteousness of the scribes and Pharisees,[3] ye shall in no case enter into the kingdom of heaven.

Ye have heard that it was said by them of old time, Thou shalt not kill; and whosoever shall kill shall be in danger of the judgment: but I say unto you, That whosoever is angry with his brother without a cause shall be in danger of the judgment: and whosoever shall say to his brother, Raca,[4] shall be in danger of the council: but whosoever shall say, Thou fool, shall be in danger of hell fire.[5] Therefore if thou bring thy gift to the altar, and there rememberest that thy brother hath ought against thee; leave there thy gift before the altar, and go thy way; first be reconciled to thy brother, and then come and offer thy gift. Agree with thine adversary quickly, whiles thou art in the way with him; lest at any time the adversary deliver thee to the judge,

---

1. How can it regain its savor?   2. A household vessel with the capacity of a bushel.   3. A sect that insisted on strict observance of the Mosaic law. *Scribes:* the official interpreters of the sacred Scriptures. 4. Empty (Aramaic?).   5. The reference is to Jewish legal institutions. The penalties that might be inflicted for murder were death by the sword (a sentence of a local court, *the judgment*), death by stoning (the sentence of a higher court, *the council*), and the burning of the criminal's body in the place where refuse was thrown, Gehenna, which is hence used as a name for hell. Jesus compares the different degrees of punishment (administered by God) for the new sins, which he here lists, with the degrees of punishment recognized by Jewish law.

and the judge deliver thee to the officer, and thou be cast into prison. Verily I say unto thee, Thou shalt by no means come out thence, till thou hast paid the uttermost farthing.

Ye have heard that it was said by them of old time, Thou shalt not commit adultery: but I say unto you, That whosoever looketh on a woman to lust after her hath committed adultery with her already in his heart. And if thy right eye offend thee, pluck it out, and cast it from thee: for it is profitable for thee that one of thy members should perish, and not that thy whole body should be cast into hell. And if thy right hand offend thee, cut it off, and cast it from thee: for it is profitable for thee that one of thy members should perish, and not that thy whole body should be cast into hell. It hath been said, Whosoever shall put away his wife, let him give her a writing of divorcement: but I say unto you, That whosoever shall put away his wife, saving for the cause of fornication, causeth her to commit adultery: and whosoever shall marry her that is divorced committeth adultery.

Again, ye have heard that it hath been said by them of old time, Thou shalt not forswear thyself, but shalt perform unto the Lord thine oaths: but I say unto you, Swear not at all; neither by heaven; for it is God's throne: nor by the earth; for it is his footstool: neither by Jerusalem; for it is the city of the great King. Neither shalt thou swear by thy head, because thou canst not make one hair white or black. But let your communication be, Yea, yea; Nay, nay: for whatsoever is more than these cometh of evil.

Ye have heard that it hath been said, An eye for an eye, and a tooth for a tooth: but I say unto you, That ye resist not evil: but whosoever shall smite thee on thy right cheek, turn to him the other also. And if any man will sue thee at the law, and take away thy coat, let him have thy cloak also. And whosoever shall compel thee to go a mile, go with him twain. Give to him that asketh thee, and from him that would borrow of thee turn not thou away.

Ye have heard that it hath been said, Thou shalt love thy neighbour, and hate thine enemy. But I say unto you, Love your enemies, bless them that curse you, do good to them that hate you, and pray for them which despitefully use you, and persecute you; that ye may be the children of your Father which is in heaven: for he maketh his sun to rise on the evil and on the good, and sendeth rain on the just and on the unjust. For if ye love them which love you, what reward have ye? do not even the publicans[6] the same? And if ye salute your brethren only, what do ye more than others? do not even the publicans so? Be ye therefore perfect, even as your Father which is in heaven is perfect.

6. Take heed that ye do not your alms before men, to be seen of them: otherwise ye have no reward of your Father which is in heaven. Therefore when thou doest thine alms, do not sound a trumpet before thee, as the hypocrites do in the synagogues and in the streets, that they may have glory of men. Verily I say unto you, They have their reward. But when thou doest alms, let not thy left hand know what thy right hand doeth: that thine alms

---

6. The men who collected the taxes for the Roman tax-farming corporations; they were, naturally, universally despised and hated.

may be in secret: and thy Father which seeth in secret himself shall reward thee openly.

And when thou prayest, thou shalt not be as the hypocrites are: for they love to pray standing in the synagogues and in the corners of the streets, that they may be seen of men. Verily I say unto you, They have their reward. But thou, when thou prayest, enter into thy closet, and when thou hast shut thy door, pray to thy Father which is in secret; and thy Father which seeth in secret shall reward thee openly. But when ye pray, use not vain repetitions, as the heathen do; for they think that they shall be heard for their much speaking. Be not ye therefore like unto them: for your Father knoweth what things ye have need of, before ye ask him. After this manner therefore pray ye: Our Father which art in heaven, Hallowed be thy name. Thy kingdom come. Thy will be done in earth, as it is in heaven. Give us this day our daily bread. And forgive us our debts, as we forgive our debtors. And lead us not into temptation, but deliver us from evil: For thine is the kingdom, and the power, and the glory, for ever. Amen. For if ye forgive men their trespasses, your heavenly Father will also forgive you: but if ye forgive not men their trespasses, neither will your Father forgive your trespasses.

Moreover when ye fast, be not, as the hypocrites, of a sad countenance: for they disfigure their faces, that they may appear unto men to fast. Verily I say unto you, They have their reward. But thou, when thou fastest, anoint thine head, and wash thy face; that thou appear not unto men to fast, but unto thy Father which is in secret: and thy Father, which seeth in secret shall reward thee openly.

Lay not up for yourselves treasures upon earth, where moth and rust doth corrupt, and where thieves break through and steal: but lay up for yourselves treasures in heaven, where neither moth nor rust doth corrupt, and where thieves do not break through nor steal: for where your treasure is, there will your heart be also. The light of the body is the eye: if therefore thine eye be single,[7] thy whole body shall be full of light. But if thine eye be evil, thy whole body shall be full of darkness. If therefore the light that is in thee be darkness, how great is that darkness!

No man can serve two masters: for either he will hate the one, and love the other; or else he will hold to the one, and despise the other. Ye cannot serve God and Mammon. Therefore I say unto you, Take no thought for your life, what ye shall eat, or what ye shall drink; nor yet for your body, what ye shall put on. Is not the life more than meat, and the body than raiment? Behold the fowls of the air: for they sow not, neither do they reap, nor gather into barns; yet your heavenly Father feedeth them. Are ye not much better than they? Which of you by taking thought can add one cubit unto his stature? And why take ye thought for raiment? Consider the lilies of the field, how they grow; they toil not, neither do they spin. And yet I say unto you, That even Solomon in all his glory was not arrayed like one of these. Wherefore, if God so clothe the grass of the field, which today is, and tomorrow is cast into the oven, shall he not much more clothe you, O ye of little faith? Therefore take no thought, saying, What shall we eat? or, What shall we drink? or, Wherewithal shall we be clothed? (For after all these things do

7. Clear.

the Gentiles seek:) for your heavenly Father knoweth that ye have need of all these things. But seek ye first the kingdom of God, and his righteousness; and all these things shall be added unto you. Take therefore no thought for the morrow: for the morrow shall take thought for the things of itself. Sufficient unto the day is the evil thereof.

7. Judge not, that ye be not judged. For with what judgment ye judged, ye shall be judged: and with what measure ye mete, it shall be measured to you again. And why beholdest thou the mote that is in thy brother's eye, but considerest not the beam[8] that is in thine own eye? Or how wilt thou say to thy brother, Let me pull out the mote out of thine eye; and, behold, a beam is in thine own eye? Thou hypocrite, first cast out the beam out of thine own eye; and then shalt thou see clearly to cast out the mote out of thy brother's eye.

Give not that which is holy unto the dogs, neither cast ye your pearls before swine, lest they trample them under their feet, and turn again and rend you.

Ask, and it shall be given you; seek, and ye shall find; knock, and it shall be opened unto you: for every one that asketh receiveth; and he that seeketh findeth; and to him that knocketh it shall be opened. Or what man is there of you, whom if his son ask bread, will he give him a stone? Or if he ask a fish, will he give him a serpent? If ye then, being evil, know how to give good gifts unto your children, how much more shall your Father which is in heaven give good things to them that ask him? Therefore all things whatsoever ye would that men should do to you, do ye even so to them: for this is the law and the prophets.

Enter ye in at the strait gate: for wide is the gate, and broad is the way, that leadeth to destruction, and many there be which go in thereat: because strait is the gate, and narrow is the way, which leadeth unto life, and few there be that find it.

Beware of false prophets, which come to you in sheep's clothing, but inwardly they are ravening wolves. Ye shall know them by their fruits. Do men gather grapes of thorns, or figs of thistles? Even so every good tree bringeth forth good fruit; but a corrupt tree bringeth forth evil fruit. A good tree cannot bring forth evil fruit, neither can a corrupt tree bring forth good fruit. Every tree that bringeth not forth good fruit is hewn down, and cast into the fire. Wherefore by their fruits ye shall know them.

Not every one that saith unto me, Lord, Lord, shall enter into the kingdom of heaven; but he that doeth the will of my Father which is in heaven. Many will say to me in that day, Lord, Lord, have we not prophesied in thy name? and in thy name have cast out devils? and in thy name done many wonderful works? And then will I profess unto them, I never knew you: depart from me, ye that work iniquity.

Therefore whosoever heareth these sayings of mine, and doeth them, I will liken him unto a wise man, which built his house upon a rock; and the rain descended, and the floods came and the winds blew, and beat upon that house; and it fell not: for it was founded upon a rock. And every one that heareth these sayings of mine, and doeth them not, shall be likened unto a foolish man, which built his house upon the sand: and the rain descended,

---

8. A long piece of heavy timber, in contrast to a *mote,* a particle or speck.

and the floods came, and the winds blew, and beat upon that house; and it
fell: and great was the fall of it. And it came to pass, when Jesus had ended
these sayings, the people were astonished at his doctrine: for he taught them
as one having authority, and not as the scribes.

Luke 15

[The Teaching of Jesus: Parables]

15. Then drew near unto him all the publicans and sinners for to hear
him. And the Pharisees and scribes murmured, saying, This man receiveth
sinners, and eateth with them.

And he spoke this parable unto them, saying, What man of you, having a
hundred sheep, if he lose one of them, doth not leave the ninety and nine
in the wilderness, and go after that which is lost, until he find it? And when
he hath found it, he layeth it on his shoulders, rejoicing. And when he cometh home, he calleth together his friends and neighbours, saying unto them,
Rejoice with me; for I have found my sheep which was lost. I say unto you
that likewise joy shall be in heaven over one sinner that repenteth, more than
over ninety and nine just persons, which need no repentance.

Either what woman having ten pieces of silver, if she lose one piece, doth
not light a candle, and sweep the house, and seek diligently till she find it?
And when she hath found it, she calleth her friends and her neighbours
together, saying, Rejoice with me; for I have found the piece which I had
lost. Likewise, I say unto you, there is joy in the presence of the angels of
God over one sinner that repenteth.

And he said, A certain man had two sons: and the younger of them said
to his father, Father, give me the portion of goods that falleth to me. And he
divided unto them his living. And not many days after the younger son gathered all together, and took his journey into a far country, and there wasted
his substance with riotous living. And when he had spent all, there arose a
mighty famine in that land; and he began to be in want. And he went and
joined himself to a citizen of that country; and he sent him into his fields to
feed swine. And he would fain have filled his belly with the husks that the
swine did eat: and no man gave unto him. And when he came to himself, he
said, How many hired servants of my father's have bread enough and to spare,
and I perish with hunger! I will arise and go to my father, and will say unto
him, Father, I have sinned against heaven, and before thee, and am no more
worthy to be called thy son: make me as one of thy hired servants. And he
arose, and came to his father. But when he was yet a great way off, his father
saw him, and had compassion, and ran, and fell on his neck, and kissed him.
And the son said unto him, Father, I have sinned against heaven, and in thy
sight, and am no more worthy to be called thy son. But the father said to his
servants, Bring forth the best robe, and put it on him; and put a ring on his
hand, and shoes on his feet: and bring hither the fatted calf, and kill it; and
let us eat, and be merry: for this my son was dead, and is alive again; he was
lost, and is found. And they began to be merry. Now his elder son was in the
field: and as he came and drew nigh to the house, he heard musick and
dancing. And he called one of the servants, and asked what these things

meant. And he said unto him, Thy brother is come; and thy father hath killed the fatted calf, because he hath received him safe and sound. And he was angry, and would not go in: therefore came his father out, and intreated him. And he answering said to his father, Lo, these many years do I serve thee, neither transgressed I at any time thy commandment: and yet thou never gavest me a kid, that I might make merry with my friends: but as soon as this thy son was come, which hath devoured thy living with harlots, thou hast killed for him the fatted calf. And he said unto him, Son, thou art ever with me, and all that I have is thine. It was meet that we should make merry, and be glad: for this thy brother was dead, and is alive again; and was lost, and is found.

Matthew 13[1]

[Why Jesus Teaches in Parables]

13. The same day went Jesus out of the house, and sat by the sea side. And great multitudes were gathered together unto him, so that he went into a ship, and sat; and the whole multitude stood on the shore. And he spake many things unto them in parables, saying, Behold, a sower went forth to sow; and when he sowed, some seeds fell by the wayside, and the fowls came and devoured them up: some fell upon stony places, where they had not much earth: and forthwith they sprung up, because they had no deepness of earth: and when the sun was up, they were scorched; and because they had no root, they withered away. And some fell among thorns; and the thorns sprung up, and choked them: but other fell into good ground, and brought forth fruit, some a hundredfold, some sixtyfold, some thirtyfold. Who hath ears to hear, let him hear.

And the disciples came, and said unto him, Why speakest thou unto them in parables? He answered and said unto them, Because it is given unto you to know the mysteries of the kingdom of heaven, but to them it is not given. For whosoever hath, to him shall be given, and he shall have more abundance: but whosoever hath not, from him shall be taken away even that he hath. Therefore speak I to them in parables: because they seeing see not; and hearing they hear not, neither do they understand. And in them is fulfilled the prophecy of Esaias, which saith, By hearing ye shall hear, and shall not understand; and seeing ye shall see, and shall not perceive: for this people's heart is waxed gross, and their ears are dull of hearing, and their eyes they have closed; lest at any time they should see with their eyes, and hear with their ears, and should understand with their heart, and should be converted, and I should heal them. But blessed are your eyes, for they see: and your ears, for they hear. For verily I say unto you, That many prophets and righteous men have desired to see those things which ye see, and have not seen them; and to hear those things which ye hear, and have not heard them.

Hear ye therefore the parable of the sower. When any one heareth the word of the kingdom, and understandeth it not, then cometh the wicked one, and catcheth away that which was sown in his heart. This is he which

1. Verses 1–35.

received seed by the wayside. But he that received the seed into stony places, the same is he that heareth the word, and anon with joy receiveth it; yet hath he not root in himself, but dureth for a while: for when tribulation or persecution ariseth because of the word, by and by he is offended. He also that received seed among the thorns is he that heareth the word; and the care of this world, and the deceitfulness of riches, choke the word, and he becometh unfruitful. But he that received seed into the good ground is he that heareth the word, and understandeth it; which also beareth fruit, and bringeth forth, some a hundredfold, some sixty, some thirty.

Another parable put he forth unto them, saying, The kingdom of heaven is likened unto a man which sowed good seed in his field: but while men slept, his enemy came and sowed tares among the wheat, and went his way. But when the blade was sprung up, and brought forth fruit, then appeared the tares also. So the servants of the householder came and said unto him, Sir, didst not thou sow good seed in thy field? from whence then hath it tares? He said unto them, An enemy hath done this. The servants said unto him, Wilt thou then that we go and gather them up? But he said, Nay; lest while ye gather up the tares, ye root up also the wheat with them. Let both grow together until the harvest: and in the time of harvest I will say to the reapers, Gather ye together first the tares, and bind them in bundles to burn them: but gather the wheat into my barn.

Another parable put he forth unto them, saying, The kingdom of heaven is like to a grain of mustard seed, which a man took, and sowed in his field: which indeed is the least of all seeds: but when it is grown, it is the greatest among herbs, and becometh a tree, so that the birds of the air come and lodge in the branches thereof.

Another parable spake he unto them; The kingdom of heaven is like unto leaven, which a woman took, and hid in three measures of meal, till the whole was leavened.

All these things spake Jesus unto the multitude in parables; and without a parable spake he not unto them: that it might be fulfilled which was spoken by the prophet, saying, I will open my mouth in parables; I will utter things which have been kept secret from the foundation of the world.

Matthew 26[1]

[The Betrayal of Jesus]

26. * * * Then one of the twelve, called Judas Iscariot, went unto the chief priests, and said unto them, What will ye give me, and I will deliver him unto you? And they covenanted with him for thirty pieces of silver. And from that time he sought opportunity to betray him.

Now the first day of the feast of unleavened bread[2] the disciples came to Jesus, saying unto him, Where wilt thou that we prepare for thee to eat the passover? And he said, Go into the city to such a man, and say unto him, The Master saith, My time is at hand; I will keep the passover at thy house

---

1. Verses 14–75.   2. Passover, held in remembrance of the delivery of the Jews from captivity in Egypt (Exodus 12).

with my disciples. And the disciples did as Jesus had appointed them; and they made ready the passover. Now when the even was come, he sat down with the twelve. And as they did eat, he said, Verily I say unto you, that one of you shall betray me. And they were exceeding sorrowful, and began every one of them to say unto him, Lord, is it I? And he answered and said, He that dippeth his hand with me in the dish, the same shall betray me. The Son of man goeth as it is written of him: but woe unto that man by whom the Son of man is betrayed! it had been good for that man if he had not been born. Then Judas, which betrayed him, answered and said, Master, is it I? He said unto him, Thou hast said.

And as they were eating, Jesus took bread, and blessed it, and brake it, and gave it to the disciples, and said, Take, eat; this is my body. And he took the cup, and gave thanks, and gave it to them, saying, Drink ye all of it; for this is my blood of the new testament,[3] which is shed for many for the remission of sins. But I say unto you, I will not drink henceforth of this fruit of the vine, until that day when I drink it new with you in my Father's kingdom. And when they had sung an hymn, they went out into the mount of Olives. Then saith Jesus unto them, All ye shall be offended because of me this night: for it is written,[4] I will smite the shepherd, and the sheep of the flock shall be scattered abroad. But after I am risen again, I will go before you into Galilee. Peter answered and said unto him, Though all men shall be offended because of thee, yet will I never be offended. Jesus said unto him, Verily I say unto thee, That this night, before the cock crow, thou shalt deny me thrice. Peter said unto him, Though I should die with thee, yet will I not deny thee. Likewise also said all the disciples.

Then cometh Jesus with them unto a place called Gethsemane, and saith unto the disciples, Sit ye here, while I go and pray yonder. And he took with him Peter and the two sons of Zebedee,[5] and began to be sorrowful and very heavy. Then saith he unto them, My soul is exceeding sorrowful, even unto death: tarry ye here, and watch[6] with me. And he went a little farther, and fell on his face, and prayed, saying, O my Father, if it be possible, let this cup pass from me: nevertheless, not as I will, but as thou wilt. And he cometh unto the disciples, and findeth them asleep, and saith unto Peter, What, could ye not watch with me one hour? Watch and pray, that ye enter not into temptation: the spirit indeed is willing, but the flesh is weak. He went away again the second time, and prayed, saying, O my Father, if this cup may not pass away from me, except I drink it, thy will be done. And he came and found them asleep again: for their eyes were heavy. And he left them, and went away again, and prayed the third time, saying the same words. Then cometh he to his disciples, and saith unto them, Sleep on now, and take your rest: behold, the hour is at hand, and the Son of man is betrayed into the hands of sinners. Rise, let us be going: behold, he is at hand that doth betray me.

And while he yet spake, lo, Judas, one of the twelve, came, and with him a great multitude with swords and staves, from the chief priests and elders of the people. Now he that betrayed him gave them a sign, saying, Whom-

---

3. I.e., of the new covenant, or agreement. Jesus compares himself to the lamb that was killed at the Passover as a sign of the covenant between God and the Jews.   4. In Zechariah 13.7. *Be offended*: be made to stumble (literal translation of the Greek).   5. James and John.   6. Stay awake.

soever I shall kiss, that same is he: hold him fast. And forthwith he came to Jesus and said, Hail, master; and kissed him. And Jesus said unto him, Friend, wherefore art thou come? Then came they and laid hands on Jesus, and took him. And behold, one of them[7] which were with Jesus stretched out his hand, and drew his sword, and struck a servant of the high priest's, and smote off his ear. Then said Jesus unto him, Put up again thy sword into his place: for all they that take the sword shall perish with the sword. Thinkest thou that I cannot now pray to my Father, and he shall presently give me more than twelve legions[8] of angels? But how then shall the scriptures be fulfilled, that thus it must be? In that same hour said Jesus to the multitudes, Are ye come out as against a thief with swords and staves for to take me? I sat daily with you teaching in the temple, and ye laid no hold on me. But all this was done that the scriptures of the prophets might be fulfilled. Then all the disciples forsook him, and fled.

And they that had laid hold on Jesus led him away to Caiaphas the high priest, where the scribes and the elders were assembled. But Peter followed him afar off unto the high priest's palace, and went in, and sat with the servants, to see the end. Now the chief priests, and elders, and all the council, sought false witness against Jesus, to put him to death; but found none: yea, though many false witnesses came, yet found they none. At the last came two false witnesses, and said, This fellow said, I am able to destroy the temple of God, and to build it in three days. And the high priest arose, and said unto him, Answerest thou nothing? What is it which these witness against thee? But Jesus held his peace. And the high priest answered and said unto him, I adjure thee by the living God, that thou tell us whether thou be the Christ, the Son of God. Jesus saith unto him, Thou hast said: nevertheless I say unto you, Hereafter shall ye see the Son of man sitting on the right hand of power, and coming in the clouds of heaven. Then the high priest rent his clothes, saying, He hath spoken blasphemy; what further need have we of witnesses? behold, now ye have heard his blasphemy. What think ye? They answered and said, He is guilty of death.[9] Then did they spit in his face, and buffeted him; and others smote him with the palms of their hands, saying, Prophesy unto us, thou Christ, Who is he that smote thee?

Now Peter sat without in the palace: and a damsel came unto him, saying, Thou also wast with Jesus of Galilee. But he denied before them all, saying, I know not what thou sayest. And when he was gone out into the porch, another maid saw him and said unto them that were there, This fellow was also with Jesus of Nazareth. And again he denied with an oath, I do not know the man. And after a while came unto him they that stood by, and said to Peter, Surely thou also art one of them; for thy speech betrayeth thee.[10] Then began he to curse and to swear, saying, I know not the man. And immediately the cock crew. And Peter remembered the word of Jesus, which said unto him, Before the cock crow thou shalt deny me thrice. And he went out, and wept bitterly.

---

7. Peter.   8. A legion was a Roman military formation; its full complement was six thousand men.
9. Liable to the death penalty.   10. In other words, Peter's speech revealed his Galilean origin.

Matthew 27

[*The Trial and Crucifixion of Jesus*]

27. When the morning was come, all the chief priests and elders of the people took counsel against Jesus to put him to death: and when they had bound him, they led him away, and delivered him to Pontius Pilate the governor.[1]

Then Judas, which had betrayed him, when he saw that he was condemned, repented himself, and brought again the thirty pieces of silver to the chief priests and elders, saying, I have sinned in that I have betrayed the innocent blood. And they said, What is that to us? see thou to that. And he cast down the pieces of silver in the temple, and departed, and went and hanged himself. And the chief priests took the silver pieces, and said, It is not lawful for to put them into the treasury, because it is the price of blood. And they took counsel, and bought with them the potter's field,[2] to bury strangers in. Wherefore that field was called, The field of blood, unto this day. Then was fulfilled that which was spoken by Jeremy the prophet,[3] saying, And they took the thirty pieces of silver, the price of him that was valued, whom they of the children of Israel did value; and gave them for the potter's field, as the Lord appointed me.[4] And Jesus stood before the governor: and the governor asked him, saying, Art thou the King of the Jews? And Jesus said unto him, Thou sayest.

And when he was accused of the chief priests and elders, he answered nothing. Then said Pilate unto him, Hearest thou not how many things they witness against thee? And he answered him to never a word; insomuch that the governor marvelled greatly. Now at that feast the governor was wont to release unto the people a prisoner, whom they would. And they had then a notable prisoner, called Barabbas.[5] Therefore when they were gathered together, Pilate said unto them, Whom will ye that I release unto you? Barabbas, or Jesus which is called Christ? For he knew that for envy they had delivered him.[6]

When he was set down on the judgment seat, his wife sent unto him, saying, Have thou nothing to do with that just man: for I have suffered many things this day in a dream because of him. But the chief priests and elders persuaded the multitude that they should ask Barabbas, and destroy Jesus. The governor answered and said unto them, Whether of the twain will ye that I release unto you? They said, Barabbas. Pilate saith unto them, What shall I do then with Jesus which is called Christ? They all say unto him, Let him be crucified.[7] And the governor said, Why, what evil hath he done? But they cried out the more, saying, Let him be crucified.

When Pilate saw that he could prevail nothing, but that rather a tumult was made, he took water, and washed his hands before the multitude, saying, I am innocent of the blood of this just person: see ye to it. Then answered all the people, and said, His blood be on us, and on our children.

---

1. His official title was procurator of the province of Judea. Roman policy was to allow the Jews as much independence as possible (especially in religious matters), but only the Roman authorities could impose a death sentence.   2. A field that had been dug for potter's clay and thus was not worth very much as land.   3. Jeremiah.   4. Compare Zechariah 11.13: "And the Lord said unto me, Cast it unto the potter: a goodly price that I was prised at of them."   5. Under sentence of death for sedition and murder.   6. Delivered him to the Roman authorities.   7. The regular Roman punishment for sedition.

Then released he Barabbas unto them: and when he had scourged[8] Jesus, he delivered him to be crucified. Then the soldiers of the governor took Jesus into the common hall, and gathered unto him the whole band of soldiers. And they stripped him, and put on him a scarlet robe.

And when they had platted a crown of thorns, they put it upon his head, and a reed[9] in his right hand: and they bowed the knee before him, and mocked him, saying, Hail, King of the Jews! And they spit upon him, and took the reed, and smote him on the head. And after that they had mocked him, they took the robe off from him, and put his own raiment on him, and led him away to crucify him. And as they came out, they found a man of Cyrene,[1] Simon by name: him they compelled to bear his cross. And when they were come unto a place called Golgotha, that is to say, a place of a skull,

They gave him vinegar to drink mingled with gall:[2] and when he had tasted thereof, he would not drink. And they crucified him, and parted his garments, casting lots: that it might be fulfilled which was spoken by the prophet, They parted my garments among them, and upon my vesture did they cast lots.[3] And sitting down they watched him there; and set up over his head his accusation written, THIS IS JESUS THE KING OF THE JEWS. Then were there two thieves crucified with him, one on the right hand, and another on the left.

And they that passed by reviled him, wagging their heads, and saying, Thou that destroyest the temple, and buildest it in three days, save thyself. If thou be the Son of God, come down from the cross. Likewise also the chief priests mocking him, with the scribes and elders, said, He saved others; himself he cannot save. If he be the King of Israel, let him now come down from the cross, and we will believe him. He trusted in God; let him deliver him now, if he will have him: for he said, I am the Son of God. The thieves also, which were crucified with him, cast the same in his teeth. Now from the sixth hour there was darkness over all the land unto the ninth hour. And about the ninth hour Jesus cried with a loud voice, saying, Eli, Eli, lama sabachthani? that is to say, My God, my God, why hast thou forsaken me?[4] Some of them that stood there, when they heard that, said, This man calleth for Elias.[5] And straightway one of them ran, and took a sponge, and filled it with vinegar, and put it on a reed, and gave him to drink. The rest said, Let be, let us see whether Elias will come to save him.

Jesus, when he had cried again with a loud voice, yielded up the ghost. And, behold, the veil of the temple[6] was rent in twain from the top to the bottom; and the earth did quake, and the rocks rent; and the graves were opened; and many bodies of the saints which slept arose, and came out of the graves after his resurrection, and went into the holy city, and appeared unto many. Now when the centurion,[7] and they that were with him, watching Jesus, saw the earthquake, and those things that were done, they feared greatly, saying, Truly this was the Son of God. And many women were there beholding afar off, which followed Jesus from Galilee, ministering unto him: among which was Mary Magdalene, and Mary the mother of James and Joseph, and the mother of Zebedee's children. When the even was come, there came a rich man of Arimathæa, named Joseph, who also himself was

---

8. Whipped, a routine part of the punishment.   9. To represent the king's scepter.   1. On the coast of North Africa.   2. The Greek word translated *vinegar* describes a sour wine that was the regular drink of the Roman soldiery; the addition of bitter gall is further mockery.   3. It is generally agreed that this sentence is a late addition to the text.   4. The opening words of Psalm 22. Jesus spoke Aramaic, a language closely related to Hebrew.   5. The prophet Elijah.   6. The curtain that screened off the holy of holies.   7. The Roman officer in charge of the execution.

Jesus' disciple. He went to Pilate, and begged the body of Jesus. Then Pilate commanded the body to be delivered. And when Joseph had taken the body, he wrapped it in clean linen cloth, and laid it in his own new tomb, which he had hewn out in the rock: and he rolled a great stone to the door of the sepulchre, and departed. And there was Mary Magdalene, and the other Mary, sitting over against the sepulchre.

Now the next day, that followed the day of the preparation, the chief priests and Pharisees came together unto Pilate, saying, Sir, we remember that that deceiver said, while he was yet alive, After three days I will rise again. Command therefore that the sepulchre be made sure[8] until the third day, lest his disciples come by night, and steal him away, and say unto the people, He is risen from the dead: so the last error shall be worse than the first. Pilate said unto them, Ye have a watch:[9] go your way, make it as sure as ye can. So they went, and made the sepulchre sure, sealing the stone, and setting a watch.

Matthew 28

[*The Resurrection*]

28. In the end of the sabbath, as it began to dawn toward the first day of the week, came Mary Magdalene and the other Mary to see the sepulchre. And, behold, there was a great earthquake: for the angel of the Lord descended from heaven, and came and rolled back the stone from the door, and sat upon it. His countenance was like lightning, and his raiment white as snow: and for fear of him the keepers did shake, and became as dead men. And the angel answered and said unto the women, Fear not ye: for I know that ye seek Jesus, which was crucified. He is not here: for he is risen, as he said. Come, see the place where the Lord lay. And go quickly, and tell his disciples that he is risen from the dead; and, behold, he goeth before you into Galilee; there shall ye see him: lo, I have told you. And they departed quickly from the sepulchre with fear and great joy; and did run to bring his disciples word.

And as they went to tell his disciples, behold, Jesus met them, saying, All hail! And they came and held him by the feet, and worshipped him. Then said Jesus unto them, Be not afraid: go tell my brethren that they go into Galilee, and there shall they see me.

Now when they were going, behold, some of the watch came into the city, and shewed unto the chief priests all the things that were done. And when they were assembled with the elders, and had taken counsel, they gave large money unto the soldiers, saying, Say ye, His disciples came by night, and stole him away while we slept. And if this come to the governor's ears, we will persuade him, and secure you. So they took the money, and did as they were taught: and this saying is commonly reported among the Jews until this day.

Then the eleven disciples went away into Galilee, unto a mountain where

8. Guarded.   9. Police force.

Jesus had appointed them. And when they saw him, they worshipped him: but some doubted. And Jesus came and spake unto them, saying, All power is given unto me in heaven and in earth.

Go ye therefore, and teach all nations, baptizing them in the name of the Father, and of the Son, and of the Holy Ghost: teaching them to observe all things whatsoever I have commanded you: and, lo, I am with you always, even unto the end of the world. Amen.

AUGUSTINE
354–430

Aurelius Augustine was born in 354 in Tagaste, in North Africa. He was baptized as a Christian in 387 and ordained bishop of Hippo, in North Africa, in 395. When he died there in 430, the city was besieged by Gothic invaders. Besides the *Confessions* (begun in 397) he wrote *The City of God* (finished in 426) and many polemical works against schismatics and heretics.

He was born into a world that no longer enjoyed the "Roman peace." Invading barbarians had pierced the empire's defenses and were increasing their pressure every year. The economic basis of the empire was cracking under the strain of the enormous taxation needed to support the army; the land was exhausted. The empire was Christian, but the Church was split, beset by heresies and organized heretical sects. The empire was on the verge of ruin, and there was every prospect that the Church would go down with it.

Augustine, one of the men responsible for the consolidation of the Church in the West, especially for the systematization of its doctrine and policy, did not convert to Christianity until he had reached middle life. "Late have I loved Thee, O Beauty so ancient and so new," he says in his *Confessions*, written long after his conversion. The lateness of his conversion and his regret for his wasted youth were among the sources of the energy that drove him to assume the intellectual leadership of the Western church and to guarantee, by combating heresy on the one hand and laying new ideological foundations for Christianity on the other, the Church's survival through the dark centuries to come. Augustine had been brought up in the literary and philosophical tradition of the classical world, and it is partly because of his assimilation of classical literature and method to Christian training and teaching that the literature of the ancient world survived at all when Roman power collapsed in a welter of bloodshed and destruction that lasted for generations.

In his *Confessions* he set down, for the benefit of others, the story of his early life and his conversion to Christianity. This is, as far as we know, the first authentic ancient autobiography, and that fact itself is a significant expression of the Christian spirit, which proclaims the value of the individual soul and the importance of its relation with God. Throughout the *Confessions* Augustine talks directly to God, in humility, yet conscious that God is concerned for him personally. At the same time he comes to an understanding of his own feelings and development as a human being that marks his *Confessions* as one of the great literary documents of the Western world. His description of his childhood is the only detailed account of the childhood of a great man that antiquity has left us, and his accurate observation and keen perception are informed by the Hebrew and Christian idea of the sense of sin. "So small a boy and so great a sinner"—from the beginning of his narrative to the end Augustine sees individuals not as the Greeks at their most optimistic tended to see humanity, the center and potential masters of the universe, but as children, wandering in ignorance, capable of reclamation only through the divine mercy that waits eternally for them to turn to it.

In Augustine are combined the intellectual tradition of the ancient world and the religious feeling that was characteristic of the Middle Ages. The transition from the old world to the new can be seen in his pages; his analytical intellect pursues its odyssey through strange and scattered islands—the mysticism of the Manichees, the skepticism of the academic philosophers, the fatalism of the astrologers—until he finds his home in the Church, to which he was to render such great service. His account of his conversion in the garden at Milan records the true moment of transition from the ancient to the medieval world. The innumerable defeats and victories, the burning towns and ravaged farms, the bloodshed, dates, and statistics of the end of an era are all illuminated and ordered by this moment in the history of the human spirit. Here is the point of change itself.

Peter Brown, *Augustine of Hippo* (1967), is an authoritative and engrossing account of Augustine's career and major works. Warren Thomas Smith, *Augustine, His Life and Thought* (1980), gives a brief and readable overview of his biography, his times, and his intellectual development. Another introduction to Augustine's life and thought, with a substantial discussion of the *Confessions,* is James J. O'Donnell, *Augustine* (1985). Gillian Clark, *Augustine, the Confessions* (1993), is an excellent short guide to this work, with discussions of various literary and intellectual issues that it raises and particular attention to the historical context.

From Confessions[1]

FROM BOOK I

[*Childhood*]

What have I to say to Thee, God, save that I know not where I came from, when I came into this life-in-death—or should I call it death-in-life? I do not know. I only know that the gifts Your mercy had provided sustained me from the first moment: not that I remember it but so I have heard from the parents of my flesh, the father from whom, and the mother in whom, You fashioned me in time.

Thus for my sustenance and my delight I had woman's milk: yet it was not my mother or my nurses who stored their breasts for me: it was Yourself, using them to give me the food of my infancy, according to Your ordinance and the riches set by You at every level of creation. It was by Your gift that I desired what You gave and no more, by Your gift that those who suckled me willed to give me what You had given them: for it was by the love implanted in them by You that they gave so willingly that milk which by Your gift flowed in the breasts. It was a good for them that I received good from them, though I received it not *from* them but only through them: since all good things are from You, O God, and *from God is all my health.*[2] But this I have learnt since: You have made it abundantly clear by all that I have seen You give, within me and about me. For at that time I knew how to suck, to lie quiet when I was content, to cry when I was in pain: and that was all I knew.

---

1. Translated by F. J. Sheed.   2. Throughout the *Confessions* Augustine quotes liberally from the Bible; the quotations are set off in italics. When a quotation bears on Augustine's situation, it is annotated.

Later I added smiling to the things I could do, first in sleep, then awake. This again I have on the word of others, for naturally I do not remember; in any event, I believe it, for I have seen other infants do the same. And gradually I began to notice where I was, and the will grew in me to make my wants known to those who might satisfy them; but I could not, for my wants were within me and those others were outside: nor had they any faculty enabling them to enter into my mind. So I would fling my arms and legs about and utter sounds, making the few gestures in my power—these being as apt to express my wishes as I could make them: but they were not very apt. And when I did not get what I wanted, either because my wishes were not clear or the things not good for me, I was in a rage—with my parents as though I had a right to their submission, with free human beings as though they had been bound to serve me; and I took my revenge in screams. That infants are like this, I have learnt from watching other infants; and that I was like it myself I have learnt more clearly from these other infants, who did not know me, than from my nurses who did.

*   *   *

From infancy I came to boyhood, or rather it came to me, taking the place of infancy. Yet infancy did not go: for where was it to go to? Simply it was no longer there. For now I was not an infant, without speech, but a boy, speaking. This I remember; and I have since discovered by observation how I learned to speak. I did not learn by elders teaching me words in any systematic way, as I was soon after taught to read and write. But of my own motion, using the mind which You, my God, gave me, I strove with cries and various sounds and much moving of my limbs to utter the feelings of my heart—all this in order to get my own way. Now I did not always manage to express the right meanings to the right people. So I began to reflect [I observed that][3] my elders would make some particular sound, and as they made it would point at or move towards some particular thing: and from this I came to realize that the thing was called by the sound they made when they wished to draw my attention to it. That they intended this was clear from the motions of their body, by a kind of natural language common to all races which consists in facial expressions, glances of the eye, gestures, and the tones by which the voice expresses the mind's state—for example whether things are to be sought, kept, thrown away, or avoided. So, as I heard the same words again and again properly used in different phrases, I came gradually to grasp what things they signified; and forcing my mouth to the same sounds, I began to use them to express my own wishes. Thus I learnt to convey what I meant to those about me; and so took another long step along the stormy way of human life in society, while I was still subject to the authority of my parents and at the beck and call of my elders.

O God, my God, what emptiness and mockeries did I now experience: for it was impressed upon me as right and proper in a boy to obey those who taught me, that I might get on in the world and excel in the handling of words[4] to gain honor among men and deceitful riches. I, poor wretch, could not see the use of the things I was sent to school to learn; but if I proved

---

3. Words in brackets are the translator's.   4. The study of rhetoric, which was the passport to eminence in public life.

idle in learning, I was soundly beaten. For this procedure seemed wise to our ancestors: and many, passing the same way in days past, had built a sorrowful road by which we too must go, with multiplication of grief and toil upon the sons of Adam.

Yet, Lord, I observed men praying to You: and I learnt to do likewise, thinking of You (to the best of my understanding) as some great being who, though unseen, could hear and help me. As a boy I fell into the way of calling upon You, my Help and my Refuge; and in those prayers I broke the strings of my tongue—praying to You, small as I was but with no small energy, that I might not be beaten at school.[5] And when You did not hear me (*not as giving me over to folly*), my elders and even my parents, who certainly wished me no harm, treated my stripes as a huge joke, which they were very far from being to me. Surely, Lord, there is no one so steeled in mind or cleaving to You so close—or even so insensitive, for that might have the same effect— as to make light of the racks and hooks and other torture instruments[6] (from which in all lands men pray so fervently to be saved) while truly loving those who are in such bitter fear of them. Yet my parents seemed to be amused at the torments inflicted upon me as a boy by my masters, though I was no less afraid of my punishments or zealous in my prayers to You for deliverance. But in spite of my terrors I still did wrong, by writing or reading or studying less than my set tasks. It was not, Lord, that I lacked mind or memory, for You had given me as much of these as my age required; but the one thing I revelled in was play; and for this I was punished by men who after all were doing exactly the same things themselves. But the idling of men is called business; the idling of boys, though exactly like, is punished by those same men: and no one pities either boys or men. Perhaps an unbiased observer would hold that I was rightly punished as a boy for playing with a ball: because this hindered my progress in studies—studies which would give me the opportunity as a man to play at things more degraded. And what difference was there between me and the master who flogged me? For if on some trifling point he had the worst of the argument with some fellow-master, he was more torn with angry vanity than I when I was beaten in a game of ball.

*   *   *

But to continue with my boyhood, which was in less peril of sin than my adolescence. I disliked learning and hated to be forced to it. But I *was* forced to it, so that good was done to me though it was not my doing. Short of being driven to it, I certainly would not have learned. But no one does well against his will, even if the thing he does is a good thing to do. Nor did those who forced me do well: it was by You, O God, that well was done. Those others had no deeper vision of the use to which I might put all they forced me to learn, but to sate the insatiable desire of man for wealth that is but penury and glory that is but shame. But You, Lord, *by Whom the very hairs of our head are numbered*,[7] used for my good the error of those who urged me to study; but my own error, in that I had no will to learn, you used for my punishment—a punishment richly deserved by one so small a boy and so

---

5. Augustine recognizes the necessity of this rigorous training; that he never forgot its harshness is clear from his remark in the *City of God* (21.14): "If a choice were given him between suffering death and living his early years over again, who would not shudder and choose death?"   6. The instruments of public execution.   7. Who knows and attends to the smallest detail of each life (compare Matthew 10.30).

great a sinner. Thus, You brought good for me out of those who did ill, and justly punished me for the ill I did myself. So You have ordained and so it is: that every disorder of the soul is its own punishment.

To this day I do not quite see why I so hated the Greek tongue[8] that I was made to learn as a small boy. For I really liked Latin—not the rudiments that we got from our first teachers but the literature that we came to be taught later. For the rudiments—reading and writing and figuring—I found as hard and hateful as Greek. Yet this too could come only from sin and the vanity of life, because *I was flesh, and a wind that goes away and returns not.* For those first lessons were the surer. I acquired the power I still have to read what I find written and to write what I want to express; whereas in the studies that came later I was forced to memorize the wanderings of Aeneas[9]—whoever *he* was—while forgetting my own wanderings; and to weep for the death of Dido who killed herself for love,[1] while bearing dry-eyed my own pitiful state, in that among these studies I was becoming dead to You, O God, my life.

Nothing could be more pitiful than a pitiable creature who does not see to pity himself, and weeps for the death that Dido suffered through love of Aeneas and not for the death he suffers himself through not loving You, O God, Light of my heart, Bread of my soul, Power wedded to my mind and the depths of my thought. I did not love You and I went away from You in fornication:[2] and all around me in my fornication echoed applauding cries "Well done! Well done!" *For the friendship of this world is fornication against Thee:* and the world cries "Well done" so loudly that one is ashamed of unmanliness not to do it. And for this I did not grieve; but I grieved for Dido, slain as she sought by the sword an end to her woe, while I too followed after the lowest of Your creatures, forsaking You, earth going unto earth. And if I were kept from reading, I grieved at not reading the tales that caused me such grief. This sort of folly is held nobler and richer than the studies by which we learn to read and write!

But now let my God cry aloud in my soul, and let Your truth assure me that it is not so: the earlier study is the better. I would more willingly forget the wanderings of Aeneas and all such things than how to write and read. Over the entrance of these grammar schools hangs a curtain:[3] but this should be seen not as lending honor to the mysteries, but as a cloak to the errors taught within. Let not those masters—who have now lost their terrors for me—cry out against me, because I confess to You, my God, the desire of my soul, and find soul's rest in blaming my evil ways that I may love Your holy ways. Let not the buyers or sellers of book-learning cry out against me. If I ask them whether it is true, as the poet says, that Aeneas ever went to Carthage, the more ignorant will have to answer that they do not know, the more scholarly that he certainly did not. But if I ask with what letters the name Aeneas is spelt, all whose schooling has gone so far will answer correctly, according to the convention men have agreed upon for the use of letters. Or again, were I to ask which loss would be more

---

8. Important not only for gaining knowledge of Greek literature but also because it was the official language of the Eastern Roman empire. Augustine never really mastered Greek, though his remark elsewhere that he had acquired so little Greek that it amounted to practically none is overmodest.   9. Virgil's *Aeneid* 3. 1. *Aeneid* 4.   2. Here, metaphorically.   3. School was often held in a building open on one side and curtained off from the street.

damaging to human life—the loss from men's memory of reading and writing or the loss of these poetic imaginings—there can be no question what anyone would answer who had not lost his own memory. Therefore as a boy I did wrong in liking the empty studies more than the useful—or rather in loving the empty and hating the useful. For one and one make two, two and two make four, I found a loathsome refrain; but such empty unrealities as the Wooden Horse with its armed men, and Troy on fire, and Creusa's Ghost, were sheer delight.[4]

Give me leave, O my God, to speak of my mind, Your gift, and of the follies in which I wasted it. It chanced that a task was set me, a task which I did not like but had to do. There was the promise of glory if I won, the fear of ignominy, and a flogging as well, if I lost. It was to declaim the words uttered by Juno in her rage and grief when she could not keep the Trojan prince from coming to Italy.[5] I had learnt that Juno had never said these words, but we were compelled to err in the footsteps of the poet who had invented them: and it was our duty to paraphrase in prose what he had said in verse. In this exercise that boy won most applause in whom the passions of grief and rage were expressed most powerfully and in the language most adequate to the majesty of the personage represented.

What could all this mean to me, O My true Life, My God? Why was there more applause for the performance I gave than for so many classmates of my own age? Was not the whole business so much smoke and wind? Surely some other matter could have been found to exercise mind and tongue. Thy praises, Lord, might have upheld the fresh young shoot of my heart, so that it might not have been whirled away by empty trifles, defiled, a prey to the spirits of the air. For there is more than one way of sacrificing to the fallen angels. * * *

FROM BOOK II

[The Pear Tree]

I propose now to set down my past wickedness and the carnal corruptions of my soul, not for love of them but that I may love Thee, O my God. I do it for love of Thy love, passing again in the bitterness of remembrance over my most evil ways that Thou mayest thereby grow ever lovelier to me, O Loveliness that dost not deceive, Loveliness happy and abiding: and I collect myself out of that broken state in which my very being was torn asunder because I was turned away from Thee, the One, and wasted myself upon the many.

Arrived now at adolescence I burned for all the satisfactions of hell, and I sank to the animal in a succession of dark lusts: *my beauty consumed away,* and I stank in Thine eyes, yet was pleasing in my own and anxious to please the eyes of men.

My one delight was to love and to be loved. But in this I did not keep the measure of mind to mind, which is the luminous line of friendship; but from the muddy concupiscence of the flesh and the hot imagination of

---

4. *Aeneid* 2. **5.** Augustine was assigned the task of delivering a prose paraphrase of Juno's angry speech in *Aeneid* 1. In it she complains that her enemies, the Trojans under Aeneas, are on their way to their destined goal in Italy in spite of her resolution to prevent them. Rhetorical exercises such as this were common in the schools, because they served the double purpose of teaching both literature and rhetorical composition.

puberty mists steamed up to becloud and darken my heart so that I could not distinguish the white light of love from the fog of lust. Both love and lust boiled within me, and swept my youthful immaturity over the precipice of evil desires to leave me half drowned in a whirlpool of abominable sins. Your wrath had grown mighty against me and I knew it not. I had grown deaf from the clanking of the chain of my mortality, the punishment for the pride of my soul: and I departed further from You, and You left me to myself: and I was tossed about and wasted and poured out and boiling over in my fornications: and You were silent, O my late-won Joy. You were silent, and I, arrogant and depressed, weary and restless, wandered further and further from You into more and more sins which could bear no fruit save sorrows.

*   *   *

Where then was I, and how far from the delights of Your house, in that sixteenth year of my life in this world, when the madness of lust—needing no licence from human shamelessness, receiving no licence from Your laws—took complete control of me, and I surrendered wholly to it? My family took no care to save me from this moral destruction by marriage: their only concern was that I should learn to make as fine and persuasive speeches as possible.

*   *   *

Your law, O Lord, punishes theft; and this law is so written in the hearts of men that not even the breaking of it blots it out: for no thief bears calmly being stolen from—not even if he is rich and the other steals through want. Yet I chose to steal, and not because want drove me to it—unless a want of justice and contempt for it and an excess for iniquity. For I stole things which I already had in plenty and of better quality. Nor had I any desire to enjoy the things I stole, but only the stealing of them and the sin. There was a pear tree near our vineyard, heavy with fruit, but fruit that was not particularly tempting either to look at or to taste. A group of young blackguards, and I among them, went out to knock down the pears and carry them off late one night, for it was our bad habit to carry on our games in the streets till very late. We carried off an immense load of pears, not to eat—for we barely tasted them before throwing them to the hogs. Our only pleasure in doing it was that it was forbidden. Such was my heart, O God, such was my heart: yet in the depth of the abyss You had pity on it. Let that heart now tell You what it sought when I was thus evil for no object, having no cause for wrongdoing save my wrongness. The malice of the act was base and I loved it— that is to say I loved my own undoing, I loved the evil in me—not the thing for which I did the evil, simply the evil: my soul was depraved, and hurled itself down from security in You into utter destruction, seeking no profit from wickedness but only to be wicked.

There is an appeal to the eye in beautiful things, in gold and silver and all such; the sense of touch has its own powerful pleasures; and the other senses find qualities in things suited to them. Worldly success has its glory, and the power to command and to overcome: and from this springs the thirst for revenge. But in our quest of all these things, we must not depart from You, Lord, or deviate from Your Law. This life we live here below has its own attractiveness, grounded in the measure of beauty it has and its harmony with the beauty of all lesser things. The bond of human friendship is admirable, holding many souls as one. Yet in the enjoyment of all such things we commit sin if through immoderate inclination to them—for though they are good, they are of the lowest order of good—things higher and better are forgotten, even You, O Lord our God, and Your Truth and Your Law. These lower things have their delights but not such as my God has, for He made them all: *and in Him doth the righteous delight, and He is the joy of the upright of heart.*

Now when we ask why this or that particular evil act was done, it is normal to assume that it could not have been done save through the desire of gaining or the fear of losing some one of these lower goods. For they have their own charm and their own beauty, though compared with the higher values of heaven they are poor and mean enough. Such a man has committed a murder. Why? He wanted the other man's wife or his property; or he had chosen robbery as a means of livelihood; or he feared to lose this or that through his victim's act; or he had been wronged and was aflame for vengeance. Would any man commit a murder for no cause, for the sheer delight of murdering? The thing would be incredible. There is of course the case of the man [Catiline] who was said to be so stupidly and savagely cruel that he practised cruelty and evil even when he had nothing to gain by them. But even there a cause was stated—he did it, he said, lest through idleness his hand or his resolution should grow slack. And why did he want to prevent that? So that one day by the multiplication of his crimes the city should be his, and he would have gained honors and authority and riches, and would no longer be in fear of the law or in the difficulties that want of money and the awareness of his crimes had brought him. So that not even Catiline loved his crimes as crimes: he loved some other thing which was his reason for committing them.

What was it then that in my wretched folly I loved in you, O theft of mine, deed wrought in that dark night when I was sixteen? For you were not lovely: you were a theft. Or are you anything at all, that I should talk with you? The pears that we stole were beautiful for they were created by Thee, Thou most Beautiful of all, Creator of all, Thou good God, my Sovereign and true Good. The pears were beautiful but it was not pears that my empty soul desired. For I had any number of better pears of my own, and plucked those only that I might steal. For once I had gathered them I threw them away, tasting only my own sin and savouring that with delight; for if I took so much as a bite of any one of those pears, it was the sin that sweetened it. And now, Lord my God, I ask what was it that attracted me in that theft, for there was no beauty in it to attract. I do not mean merely that it lacked the beauty that there is in justice and prudence, or in the mind of man or his senses and vegetative life: or even so much as the beauty and glory of the stars in the heavens, or of earth and sea with their oncoming of new life to replace the generations that pass. It had not even that false show or shadow of beauty by which sin tempts us.

[For there *is* a certain show of beauty in sin.] Thus pride wears the mask of loftiness of spirit, although You alone, O God, are high over all. Ambition seeks honor and glory, although You alone are to be honored before all and glorious forever. By cruelty the great seek to be feared, yet who is to be feared but God alone: from His power what can be wrested away, or when or where or how or by whom? The caresses by which the lustful seduce are a seeking for love: but nothing is more caressing than Your charity, nor is anything more healthfully loved than Your supremely lovely, supremely luminous Truth. Curiosity may be regarded as a desire for knowledge, whereas You supremely know all things. Ignorance and sheer stupidity hide under the names of simplicity and innocence: yet no being has simplicity like to Yours: and none is more innocent than You, for it is their own deeds that harm the wicked. Sloth pretends that it wants quietude: but what sure rest is there save the Lord? Luxuriousness would be called abundance and completeness; but You are the fullness and inexhaustible abundance of incorruptible delight. Wastefulness is a parody of generosity: but You are the infinitely generous giver of all good. Avarice wants to possess overmuch: but You possess all. Enviousness claims that it strives to excel: but what can excel before You? Anger clamors for just vengeance: but whose vengeance is so just as Yours? Fear is the recoil from a new and sudden threat to something one holds dear, and a cautious regard for one's own safety: but nothing new or sudden can happen to You, nothing can threaten Your hold upon things loved, and where is safety secure save in You? Grief pines at the loss of things in which desire delighted: for it wills to be like to You from whom nothing can be taken away.

Thus the soul is guilty of fornication when she turns from You and seeks from any other source what she will nowhere find pure and without taint unless she returns to You. Thus even those who go from You and stand up against You are still perversely imitating You. But by the mere fact of their imitation, they declare that You are the creator of all that is, and that there is nowhere for them to go where You are not.

So once again what did I enjoy in that theft of mine? Of what excellence of my Lord was I making perverse and vicious imitation? Perhaps it was the thrill of acting against Your law—at least in appearance, since I had no power to do so in fact, the delight a prisoner might have in making some small gesture of liberty—getting a deceptive sense of omnipotence from doing something forbidden without immediate punishment. I was that slave, who fled from his Lord and pursued his Lord's shadow. O rottenness, O monstrousness of life and abyss of death! Could you find pleasure only in what was forbidden, and only because it was forbidden? * * *

[Student at Carthage]

I came to Carthage[6] where a cauldron of illicit loves leapt and boiled about me. I was not yet in love, but I was in love with love, and from the very depth of my need hated myself for not more keenly feeling the need. I sought some object to love, since I was thus in love with loving; and I hated security and a life with no snares for my feet. For within I was hungry, all for the want of that spiritual food which is Thyself, my God; yet [though I was hungry for want of it] I did not hunger for it: I had no desire whatever for incorruptible food, not because I had it in abundance but the emptier I was, the more I hated the thought of it. Because of all this my soul was sick, and broke out

6. The capital city of the province, where Augustine went to study rhetoric.

in sores, whose itch I agonized to scratch with the rub of carnal things—carnal, yet if there were no soul in them, they would not be objects of love. My longing then was to love and to be loved, but most when I obtained the enjoyment of the body of the person who loved me.

Thus I polluted the stream of friendship with the filth of unclean desire and sullied its limpidity with the hell of lust. And vile and unclean as I was, so great was my vanity that I was bent upon passing for clean and courtly. And I did fall in love, simply from wanting to. O my God, my Mercy, with how much bitterness didst Thou in Thy goodness sprinkle the delights of that time! I was loved, and our love came to the bond of consummation: I wore my chains with bliss but with torment too, for I was scourged with the red hot rods of jealousy, with suspicions and fears and tempers and quarrels.

I developed a passion for stage plays, with the mirror they held up to my own miseries and the fuel they poured on my flame. How is it that a man wants to be made sad by the sight of tragic sufferings that he could not bear in his own person? Yet the spectator does want to feel sorrow, and it is actually his feeling of sorrow that he enjoys. Surely this is the most wretched lunacy? For the more a man feels such sufferings in himself, the more he is moved by the sight of them on the stage. Now when a man suffers himself, it is called misery; when he suffers in the suffering of another, it is called pity. But how can the unreal sufferings of the stage possibly move pity? The spectator is not moved to aid the sufferer but merely to be sorry for him; and the more the author of these fictions makes the audience grieve, the better they like him. If the tragic sorrows of the characters—whether historical or entirely fictitious—be so poorly represented that the spectator is not moved to tears, he leaves the theatre unsatisfied and full of complaints; if he *is* moved to tears, he stays to the end, fascinated and revelling in it.

     ✻ ✻ ✻

Those of my occupations at that time which were held as reputable[7] were directed towards the study of the law, in which I meant to excel—and the less honest I was, the more famous I should be. The very limit of human blindness is to glory in being blind. By this time I was a leader in the School of Rhetoric and I enjoyed this high station and was arrogant and swollen with importance: though You know, O Lord, that I was far quieter in my behavior and had no share in the riotousness of the *eversores*—the Overturners[8]—for this blackguardly diabolical name they wore as the very badge of sophistication. Yet I was much in their company and much ashamed of the sense of shame that kept me from being like them. I was with them and I did for the most part enjoy their companionship, though I abominated the acts that were their specialty—as when they made a butt of some hapless newcomer, assailing him with really cruel mockery for no reason whatever, save the malicious pleasure they got from it. There was something very like the action of devils in their behavior. They were rightly called Overturners, since they had themselves been first overturned and perverted, tricked by those same devils who were secretly mocking them in the very acts by which they amused themselves in mocking and making fools of others.

---

7. I.e., his rhetorical studies. 8. *Eversores* is the Latin word that means "overturners": a group of students who prided themselves on their wild actions and lack of discipline.

With these men as companions of my immaturity, I was studying the books of eloquence; for in eloquence it was my ambition to shine, all from a damnable vaingloriousness and for the satisfaction of human vanity. Following the normal order of study I had come to a book of one Cicero, whose tongue[9] practically everyone admires, though not his heart. That particular book is called *Hortensius*[1] and contains an exhortation to philosophy. Quite definitely it changed the direction of my mind, altered my prayers to You, O Lord, and gave me a new purpose and ambition. Suddenly all the vanity I had hoped in I saw as worthless, and with an incredible intensity of desire I longed after immortal wisdom. I had begun that journey upwards by which I was to return to You. My father was now dead two years; I was eighteen and was receiving money from my mother for the continuance of my study of eloquence. But I used that book not for the sharpening of my tongue; what won me in it was what it said, not the excellence of its phrasing.

*   *   *

So I resolved to make some study of the Sacred Scriptures and find what kind of books they were. But what I came upon was something not grasped by the proud, not revealed either to children, something utterly humble in the hearing but sublime in the doing, and shrouded deep in mystery. And I was not of the nature to enter into it or bend my neck to follow it. When I first read those Scriptures, I did not feel in the least what I have just said; they seemed to me unworthy to be compared with the majesty of Cicero. My conceit was repelled by their simplicity, and I had not the mind to penetrate into their depths. They were indeed of a nature to grow in Your little ones.[2] But I could not bear to be a little one; I was only swollen with pride, but to myself I seemed a very big man. * * *

FROM BOOK V

[Augustine Leaves Carthage for Rome]

It was by Your action upon me that I was moved to go to Rome and teach there what I had taught in Carthage. How I was persuaded to this, I shall not omit to confess to you, because therein Your most profound depths and Your mercy ever present towards us are to be meditated upon and uttered forth. My reason for going to Rome was not the greater earnings and higher dignity promised by the friends who urged me to go—though at that time, these considerations certainly influenced my mind: the principal and practically conclusive reason, was that I had heard that youths there pursued their studies more quietly and were kept within a stricter limit of discipline. For instance, they were not allowed to come rushing insolently and at will into the school of one who was not their own master, nor indeed to enter it at all unless he permitted.

At Carthage the licence of the students is gross and beyond all measure. They break in impudently and like a pack of madmen play havoc with the

---

9. Style.   1. Only fragments of this dialogue remain. In it Cicero replies to an opponent of philosophy with an impassioned defense of the intellectual life.   2. Refers not only to the rhetorical simplicity of Jesus' teachings but also to his interest in teaching children; compare Matthew 19.14: "For of such is the kingdom of heaven."

order which the master has established for the good of his pupils. They commit many outrages, extraordinarily stupid acts, deserving the punishment of the law if custom did not protect them. Their state is the more hopeless because what they do is supposed to be sanctioned, though by Your eternal law it could never be sanctioned; and they think they do these things unpunished, when the very blindness in which they do them is their punishment, so that they suffer things incomparably worse than they do. When I was a student I would not have such habits in myself, but when I became a teacher I had to endure them in others; and so I decided to go to a place where, as I had been told by all who knew, such things were not done. But You, O my Hope and my Portion in the land of the living, forced me to change countries for my soul's salvation: You pricked me with such goads at Carthage as drove me out of it, and You set before me certain attractions by which I might be drawn to Rome—in either case using men who loved this life of death, one set doing lunatic things, the other promising vain things: and to reform my ways You secretly used their perversity and my own. For those who had disturbed my peace were blind in the frenzy of their viciousness, and those who urged me to go elsewhere savoured of earth. While I, detesting my real misery in the one place, hoped for an unreal happiness in the other.

Why I left the one country and went to the other, You Knew, O God, but You did not tell either me or my mother. She indeed was in dreadful grief at my going and followed me right to the seacoast. There she clung to me passionately, determined that I should either go back home with her or take her to Rome with me, but I deceived her with the pretence that I had a friend whom I did not want to leave until he had sailed off with a fair wind. Thus I lied to my mother, and such a mother; and so got away from her. But this also You have mercifully forgiven me, bringing me from the waters of that sea, filled as I was with execrable uncleanness, unto the water of Your grace; so that when I was washed clean, the floods that poured from my mother's eyes, the tears with which daily she watered the ground towards which she bent her face in prayer for me, should cease to flow. She would not return home without me, but I managed with some difficulty to persuade her to spend the night in a place near the ship where there was an oratory in memory of St. Cyprian, That night I stole away without her: she remained praying and weeping. And what was she praying for, O my God, with all those tears but that You should not allow me to sail! But You saw deeper and granted the essential of her prayer: You did not do what she was at that moment asking, that You might do the thing she was always asking. The wind blew and filled our sails and the shore dropped from our sight. And the next morning she was frantic with grief and filled Your ears with her moaning and complaints because You seemed to treat her tears so lightly, when in fact You were using my own desires to snatch me away for the healing of those desires, and were justly punishing her own too earthly affection for me with the scourge of grief. For she loved to have me with her, as is the way of mothers but far more than most mothers; and she did not realize what joys you would bring her from my going away. She did not realize it, and so she wept and lamented, and by the torments she suffered showed the heritage of Eve in her, seeking with sorrow what in sorrow she had brought forth. But when she had poured out all her accusation at my cruel deception, she turned once more to prayer to You for me. She went home and I to Rome. * * *

FROM BOOK VI

[*Worldly Ambitions*]

By this time my mother had come to me, following me over sea and land with the courage of piety and relying upon You in all perils. For they were in danger from a storm, and she reassured even the sailors—by whom travelers newly ventured upon the deep are ordinarily reassured—promising them safe arrival because thus You had promised her in a vision. She found me in a perilous state through my deep despair of ever discovering the truth. But even when I told her that if I was not yet a Catholic Christian, I was no longer a Manichean,[3] she was not greatly exultant as at some unlooked-for good news, because she had already received assurance upon that part of my misery; she bewailed me as one dead certainly, but certainly to be raised again by You, offering me in her mind as one stretched out dead, that You might say to the widow's son: *"Young man, I say to thee arise"*:[4] and he should sit up and begin to speak and You should give him to his mother.

*   *   *

Nor did I then groan in prayer for Your help. My mind was intent upon inquiry and unquiet for argumentation. I regarded Ambrose[5] as a lucky man by worldly standards to be held in honor by such important people: only his celibacy seemed to me a heavy burden. I had no means of guessing, and no experience of my own to learn from, what hope he bore within him, what struggles he might have against the temptations that went with his high place, what was his consolation in adversity, and on what joys of Your bread the hidden mouth of his heart fed. Nor did he know how I was inflamed nor the depth of my peril. I could not ask of him what I wished as I wished, for I was kept from any face to face conversation with him by the throng of men with their own troubles, whose infirmities he served. The very little time he was not with these he was refreshing either his body with necessary food or his mind with reading. When he read, his eyes traveled across the page and his heart sought into the sense, but voice and tongue were silent. No one was forbidden to approach him nor was it his custom to require that visitors should be announced: but when we came into him we often saw him reading and always to himself; and after we had sat long in silence, unwilling to interrupt a work on which he was so intent, we would depart again. We guessed that in the small time he could find for the refreshment of his mind, he would wish to be free from the distraction of other men's affairs and not called away from what he was doing. Perhaps he was on his guard lest [if he read aloud] someone listening should be troubled and want an explanation

---

3. Augustine had for nine years been a member of this religious sect, which followed the teaching of the Babylonian mystic Mani (216–277). The Manicheans believed that the world was a battleground for the forces of good and evil; redemption in a future life would come to the elect, who renounced worldly occupations and possessions and practiced a severe asceticism (including abstention from meat). Augustine's mother, Monica, was a Christian, and lamented her son's Manichean beliefs.   **4.** Luke 7.14, recounting one of Christ's miracles.   **5.** The leading personality among the Christians of the West; not many years after this he defied the power of Emperor Theodosius and forced him to beg for God's pardon in the church at Milan for having put the inhabitants of Thessalonica to the sword.

if the author he was reading expressed some idea over-obscurely, and it might be necessary to expound or discuss some of the more difficult questions. And if he had to spend time on this, he would get through less reading than he wished. Or it may be that his real reason for reading to himself was to preserve his voice, which did in fact readily grow tired. But whatever his reason for doing it, that man certainly had a good reason.

*   *   *

I was all hot for honors, money, marriage: and You made mock of my hotness. In my pursuit of these, I suffered most bitter disappointments, but in this You were good to me since I was thus prevented from taking delight in anything not Yourself. Look now into my heart, Lord, by whose will I remember all this and confess it to You. Let my soul cleave to You now that You have freed it from the tenacious hold of death. At that time my soul was in misery, and You pricked the soreness of its wound, that leaving all things it might turn to You, who are over all and without whom all would return to nothing, that it might turn to You and be healed. I was in utter misery and there was one day especially on which You acted to bring home to me the realization of my misery. I was preparing an oration in praise of the Emperor[6] in which I was to utter any number of lies to win the applause of people who knew they were lies. My heart was much wrought upon by the shame of this and inflamed with the fever of the thoughts that consumed it. I was passing along a certain street in Milan when I noticed a beggar. He was jesting and laughing and I imagine more than a little drunk. I fell into gloom and spoke to the friends who were with me about the endless sorrows that our own insanity brings us: for here was I striving away, dragging the load of my unhappiness under the spurring of my desires, and making it worse by dragging it: and with all our striving, our one aim was to arrive at some sort of happiness without care: the beggar had reached the same goal before us, and we might quite well never reach it at all. The very thing that he had attained by means of a few pennies begged from passers-by—namely the pleasure of a temporary happiness—I was plotting for with so many a weary twist and turn.

Certainly his joy was no true joy; but the joy I sought in my ambition was emptier still. In any event he was cheerful and I worried, he had no cares and I nothing but cares. Now if anyone had asked me whether I would rather be cheerful or fearful, I would answer: "Cheerful"; but if he had gone on to ask whether I would rather be like that beggar or as I actually was, I would certainly have chosen my own state though so troubled and anxious. Now this was surely absurd. It could not be for any true reason. I ought not to have preferred my own state rather than his merely because I was the more learned, since I got no joy from my learning, but sought only to please men by it—not even to teach them, only to please them. Therefore did You break my bones with the rod of Your discipline.

*   *   *

Great effort was made to get me married. I proposed, the girl was promised me. My mother played a great part in the matter for she wanted to have me

---

6. Probably the young Valentinian, whose court was at Milan.

married and then cleansed with the saving waters of baptism,[7] rejoicing to see me grow every day more fitted for baptism and feeling that her prayers and Your promises were to be fulfilled in my faith. By my request and her own desire she begged You daily with the uttermost intensity of her heart to show her in a vision something of my future marriage, but You would never do it. She did indeed see certain vain fantasies, under the pressure of her mind's preoccupation with the matter; and she told them to me, not, however, with the confidence she always had when You had shown things to her, but as if she set small store by them; for she said that there was a certain unanalyzable savor, not to be expressed in words, by which she could distinguish between what You revealed and the dreams of her own spirit. Still she pushed on with the matter of my marriage, and the girl was asked for. She was still two years short of the age for marriage[8] but I liked her and agreed to wait.

There was a group of us friends who had much serious discussion together, concerning the cares and troubles of human life which we found so hard to endure. We had almost decided to seek a life of peace, away from the throng of men. This peace we hoped to attain by putting together whatever we could manage to get, and making one common household for all of us: so that in the clear trust of friendship, things should not belong to this or that individual, but one thing should be made of all our possessions, and belong wholly to each one of us, and everybody own everything. It seemed that there might be perhaps ten men in this fellowship. Among us there were some very rich men, especially Romanianus, our fellow townsman, who had been a close friend of mine from childhood and had been brought to the court in Milan by the press of some very urgent business. He was strongest of all for the idea and he had considerable influence in persuasion because his wealth was much greater than anyone else's. We agreed that two officers should be chosen every year to handle the details of our life together, leaving the rest undisturbed. But then we began to wonder whether our wives would agree, for some of us already had wives and I meant to have one. So the whole plan, which we had built up so neatly, fell to pieces in our hands and was simply dropped. We returned to our old sighing and groaning and treading of this world's broad and beaten ways:[9] for many thoughts were in our hearts, but *Thy counsel standeth forever.* And out of Thy counsel didst Thou deride ours and didst prepare Thine own things for us, meaning to *give us meat in due season and to open Thy hands and fill our souls with Thy blessing.*

Meanwhile my sins were multiplied. She with whom I had lived so long was torn from my side as a hindrance to my forthcoming marriage. My heart which had held her very dear was broken and wounded and shed blood. She went back to Africa, swearing that she would never know another man, and left with me the natural son I had had of her. But I in my unhappiness could not, for all my manhood, imitate her resolve. I was unable to bear the delay of two years which must pass before I was to get the girl I had asked for in marriage. In fact it was not really marriage that I wanted. I was simply a slave to lust. So I took another woman, not of course as a wife; and thus my soul's disease was nourished and kept alive as vigorously as ever, indeed

---

7. He could not be baptized while living in sin with his mistress, a liaison that resulted in the birth of a son, Adeodatus, who later accompanied Augustine to Italy.   8. The legal age was twelve years; Augustine was in his early thirties.   9. Compare Matthew 7.13: "Broad is the way that leadeth to destruction," that is, to damnation.

worse than ever, that it might reach the realm of matrimony in the company of its ancient habit. Nor was the wound healed that had been made by the cutting off of my former mistress. For there was first burning and bitter grief; and after that it festered, and as the pain grew duller it only grew more hopeless. * * *

FROM BOOK VIII

[Conversion]

* * * Thus I was sick at heart and in torment, accusing myself with a new intensity of bitterness, twisting and turning in my chain in the hope that it might be utterly broken, for what held me was so small a thing! But it still held me. And You stood in the secret places of my soul, O Lord, in the harshness of Your mercy redoubling the scourges of fear and shame lest I should give way again and that small slight tie which remained should not be broken but should grow again to full strength and bind me closer even than before. For I kept saying within myself: "Let it be now, let it be now," and by the mere words I had begun to move toward the resolution. I almost made it, yet I did not quite make it. But I did not fall back into my original state, but as it were stood near to get my breath. And I tried again and I was almost there, and now I could all but touch it and hold it: yet I was not quite there, I did not touch it or hold it. I still shrank from dying unto death and living unto life. The lower condition which had grown habitual was more powerful than the better condition which I had not tried. The nearer the point of time came in which I was to become different, the more it struck me with horror; but it did not force me utterly back nor turn me utterly away, but held me there between the two.

Those trifles of all trifles, and vanities of vanities, my one-time mistresses, held me back, plucking at my garment of flesh and murmuring softly: "Are you sending us away?" And "From this moment shall we not be with you, now or forever?" And "From this moment shall this or that not be allowed you, now or forever?" What were they suggesting to me in the phrase I have written "this or that," what were they suggesting to me, O my God? Do you in your mercy keep from the soul of Your servant the vileness and unclean-ness they were suggesting. And now I began to hear them not half so loud; they no longer stood against me face to face, but were softly muttering behind my back and, as I tried to depart, plucking stealthily at me to make me look behind. Yet even that was enough, so hesitating was I, to keep me from snatching myself free, from shaking them off and leaping upwards on the way I was called: for the strong force of habit said to me: "Do you think you can live without them?"

But by this time its voice was growing fainter. In the direction toward which I had turned my face and was quivering in fear of going, I could see the austere beauty of Continence, serene and indeed joyous but not evilly, honorably soliciting me to come to her and not linger, stretching forth loving hands to receive and embrace me, hands full of multitudes of good examples. With her I saw such hosts of young men and maidens, a multitude of youth and of every age, gray widows and women grown old in virginity, and in them all Continence herself, not barren but the fruitful mother of children, her joys, by You, Lord, her Spouse. And she smiled upon me and her smile gave courage as if she were saying: "Can you not do what these men have done, what these women have done? Or could men or women have done such in themselves, and not in the Lord their God? The Lord their God gave me to them. Why do you stand upon yourself and so not stand at all? Cast yourself upon Him and be not afraid; He will not draw away and let you fall. Cast yourself without fear, He will receive you and heal you."

Yet I was still ashamed, for I could still hear the murmuring of those vanities, and I still hung hesitant. And again it was as if she said: "Stop your ears against your unclean members, that they may be mortified. They tell you of delights, but not of such delights as the law of the Lord your God tells." This was the controversy raging in my heart, a controversy about myself against myself. And Alypius[1] stayed by my side and awaited in silence the issue of such agitation as he had never seen in me.

When my most searching scrutiny had drawn up all my vileness from the secret depths of my soul and heaped it in my heart's sight, a mighty storm arose in me, bringing a mighty rain of tears. That I might give way to my tears and lamentations, I rose from Alypius: for it struck me that solitude was more suited to the business of weeping. I went far enough from him to prevent his presence from being an embarrassment to me. So I felt, and he realized it. I suppose I had said something and the sound of my voice was heavy with tears. I arose, but he remained where we had been sitting, still in utter amazement. I flung myself down somehow under a certain fig tree and no longer tried to check my tears, which poured forth from my eyes in a flood, *an acceptable sacrifice to Thee.* And much I said not in these words but to this effect: *"And Thou, O Lord, how long? How long, Lord; wilt Thou be angry forever? Remember not our former iniquities."*[2] For I felt that I was still bound by them. And I continued my miserable complaining: "How long, how long shall I go on saying tomorrow and again tomorrow? Why not now, why not have an end to my uncleanness this very hour?"

Such things I said, weeping in the most bitter sorrow of my heart. And suddenly I heard a voice from some nearby house, a boy's voice or a girl's voice, I do not know: but it was a sort of singsong, repeated again and again. "Take and read, take and read." I ceased weeping and immediately began to search my mind most carefully as to whether children were accustomed to chant these words in any kind of game, and I could not remember that I had ever heard any such thing. Damming back the flood of my tears I arose, interpreting the incident as quite certainly a divine command to open my book of Scripture and read the passage at which I should open. For it was part of what I had been told about Anthony,[3] that from the Gospel which he happened to be reading he had felt that he was being admonished as though what he read was spoken directly to himself: *Go, sell what thou hast and give to the poor and thou shalt have treasure in heaven; and come follow Me.*[4] By this experience he had been in that instant converted to You. So I was moved to return to the place where Alypius was sitting, for I had put down the Apostle's[5] book there when I arose. I snatched it up, opened it and in silence

1. A student of Augustine's at Carthage; he had joined the Manichees with Augustine, followed him to Rome and Milan, and now shared his desires and doubts. Alypius finally became a bishop in North Africa. 2. Compare Psalm 79.5–8; Augustine compares his spiritual despair with that of captive and subjected Israel.   3. The Egyptian saint whose abstinence and self-control are still proverbial; he was one of the founders of the system of monastic life.   4. Luke 18.22.   5. Paul.

read the passage upon which my eyes first fell: *Not in rioting and drunkenness, not in chambering and impurities, not in contention and envy, but put ye on the Lord Jesus Christ and make not provision for the flesh in its concupiscences.* [Romans 13.13.] I had no wish to read further, and no need. For in that instant, with the very ending of the sentence, it was as though a light of utter confidence shone in all my heart, and all the darkness of uncertainty vanished away. Then leaving my finger in the place or marking it by some other sign, I closed the book and in complete calm told the whole thing to Alypius and he similarly told me what had been going on in himself, of which I knew nothing. He asked to see what I had read. I showed him, and he looked further than I had read. I had not known what followed. And this is what followed: *"Now him that is weak in faith, take unto you."* He applied this to himself and told me so. And he was confirmed by this message, and with no troubled wavering gave himself to God's goodwill and purpose—a purpose indeed most suited to his character, for in these matters he had been immeasurably better than I.

Then we went in to my mother and told her, to her great joy. We related how it had come about: she was filled with triumphant exultation, and praised You who are mighty beyond what we ask or conceive: for she saw that You had given her more than with all her pitiful weeping she had ever asked. For You converted me to Yourself so that I no longer sought a wife nor any of this world's promises, but stood upon that same rule of faith in which You had shown me to her so many years before.[6] Thus You changed her mourning into joy, a joy far richer than she had thought to wish, a joy much dearer and purer than she had thought to find in grandchildren of my flesh.

FROM BOOK IX

[Death of His Mother]

* * * And I thought it would be good in Your sight if I did not dramatically snatch my tongue's service from the speech-market but quietly withdrew; but that in any event withdraw I must, so that youths—not students of Your law or Your peace but of lying follies and the conflicts of the law—should no longer buy at my mouth the tools of their madness. Fortunately it happened that there were only a few days left before the Vintage Vacation,[7] and I decided to endure them so that I might leave with due deliberation, seeing that I had been redeemed by You and was not going to put myself up for sale again. Our purpose therefore was known to You, but not to men other than our own friends. We had agreed among ourselves not to spread the news abroad at all, although, in our ascent from *the valley of tears and our singing of the song of degrees,* You had given us *sharp arrows* and *burning coals* against *cunning tongues* that might argue against us with pretended care for our interest, might destroy us saying that they loved us: as men consume food saying that they love it.

---

6. At Carthage, when Augustine was still a Manichee, Monica had dreamed that she was standing on a wooden ruler weeping for her son and then saw that he was standing on the same ruler as herself.   7. This grape-harvesting and wine-making holiday lasted from the end of August to the middle of October.

*   *   *

Furthermore that very summer, under the too heavy labor of teaching, my lungs had begun to give way and I breathed with difficulty,[8] the pain in my breast showed that they were affected and they no longer let me talk with any strength for too long at a time. At first this had disturbed me, because it made it practically a matter of necessity that I should lay down the burden of teaching, or at least give it up for the time if I was to be cured and grow well again. But when the full purpose of giving myself leisure to meditate on how You are the Lord arose in me and became a settled resolve—as you know, O my God—I actually found myself glad to have this perfectly truthful excuse to offer parents who might be offended and for their children's sake would never willingly have let me give up teaching. So I was full of joy, and I put up with the space of time that still had to run—I fancy it was about twenty days. But to bear the time took considerable fortitude. Desire for money, which formerly had helped me to bear the heavy labor of teaching, was quite gone; so that I should have [had nothing to help me bear it and so] found it altogether crushing if patience had not taken the place of covetousness. Some of Your servants, my brethren, may think that I sinned in this, since having enrolled with all my heart in Your service, I allowed myself to sit for so much as an hour in the chair of untruthfulness. It may be so. But, most merciful Lord, have You not pardoned and remitted this sin, along with others most horrible and deadly, in the holy water of baptism?

*   *   *

And now the day was come on which I was to be set free from the teaching of Rhetoric in fact, as I was already free in mind. And so it came about. You delivered my tongue as You had already delivered my heart, and I rejoiced and praised You, and so went off with my friends to the country-house.[9] The amount of writing I did there—the writing was now in your service but during this breathing-space still smacked of the school of pride—my books[1] exist to witness, with the record they give of discussions either with my friends there present or with Yourself when I was alone with You; and there are my letters to show what correspondence I had with Nebridius[2] while he was away.

*   *   *

When the Vintage Vacation was over I gave the people of Milan notice that they must find someone else to sell the art of words to their students, because I had chosen to serve You, and because owing to my difficulty in breathing and the pain in my lungs I could not continue my teaching. And in a letter I told Your bishop, the holy Ambrose, of my past errors and my present purpose, that he might advise me which of Your Scriptures I should especially read to prepare me and make me more fit to receive so great a grace. He told me to read Isaiah the prophet, I imagine because he more clearly

---

8. Because he not only lectured but also read aloud, as is suggested by his comments on Ambrose's silent reading (book 6).   9. At Cassiciacum, placed at his disposal by a friend.   1. While at Cassiciacum, Augustine wrote a book attacking the academic philosophers; a book on the happy life; and another entitled *De ordine*, a treatise on divine providence.   2. Nebridius came from Carthage to Milan with Augustine, shared his spiritual pilgrimage through the pagan philosophies and Manichean doctrines to become a Christian, and returned to Africa, where he died. Augustine's letters to Nebridius are still extant.

foretells the gospel and the calling of the gentiles[3] than the other Old Testament writers; but I did not understand the first part of this book, and
thinking that it would be all of the same kind, put it aside meaning to return
to it when I should be more practised in the Lord's way of speech.

When the time had come to give in my name for baptism, we left the
country and returned to Milan. Alypius had decided to be born again in You
at the same time, for he was already endowed with the humility that Your
sacraments require, and had brought his body so powerfully under control
that he could tread the icy soil of Italy with bare feet, which required unusual
fortitude. We also took with us the boy Adeodatus, carnally begotten by me
in my sin. You had made him well. He was barely fifteen, yet he was more
intelligent than many a grave and learned man. In this I am but acknowledging to You Your own gifts, O Lord my God, Creator of all and powerful
to reshape our shapelessness: for I had no part in that boy but the sin. That
he had been brought up by us in Your way was because You had inspired us,
no other. I do but acknowledge to You Your own gifts. There is a book of
mine called *De Magistro*:[4] it is a dialogue between him and me. You know,
O God, that all the ideas which are put into the mouth of the other party to
the dialogue were truly his, though he was but sixteen. I had experience of
many other remarkable qualities in him. His great intelligence filled me with
a kind of awe: and who but You could be the maker of things so wonderful?
But You took him early from this earth, and I think of him utterly without
anxiety, for there is nothing in his boyhood or youth or anywhere in him to
cause me to fear. We took him along with us, the same age as ourselves in
Your grace, to be brought up in Your discipline: and we were baptized, and
all anxiety as to our past life fled away. The days were not long enough as I
meditated, and found wonderful delight in meditating, upon the depth of
Your design for the salvation of the human race. I wept at the beauty of Your
hymns and canticles, and was powerfully moved at the sweet sound of Your
Church's singing. Those sounds flowed into my ears, and the truth streamed
into my heart: so that my feeling of devotion overflowed, and the tears ran
from my eyes, and I was happy in them.

It was only a little while before that the church of Milan had begun to
practice this kind of consolation and exultation, to the great joy of the
brethen singing together with heart and voice. For it was only about a year,
or not much more, since Justina, the mother of the boy emperor Valentinian,
was persecuting Your servant Ambrose in the interests of her own heresy:
for she had been seduced by the Arians.[5] The devoted people had stayed day
and night in the church, ready to die with their bishop, Your servant. And
my mother, Your handmaid, bearing a great part of the trouble and vigil, had
lived in prayer. I also, though still not warmed by the fire of Your Spirit, was
stirred to excitement by the disturbed and wrought-up state of the city. It

---

3. The appeal of Christ's apostles to peoples outside the Hebrew nation: "I am sought of them that asked
not for me; I am found of them that sought me not" (Isaiah 65.1).   **4.** *The Teacher,* written in Tagaste,
Africa, two years after Augustine's baptism and shortly after his return from Italy; it concerns teaching and
the thesis that only God is the cause for humankind's acquisition of learning and truth.   **5.** Members of
a sect who followed the doctrine of Arius (250–336) that the Son had not existed from all eternity and was,
therefore, inferior to the Father. At the Council of Nicaea (325) Arius and his followers were declared
heretical, but the Arian heresy remained a serious problem for the Church for many years. Justina demanded
that Ambrose allow the Arians to hold public services inside the walls of Milan.

was at this time that the practice was instituted of singing hymns and psalms after the manner of the Eastern churches,[6] to keep the people from being altogether worn out with anxiety and want of sleep. The custom has been retained from that day to this, and has been imitated by many, indeed in almost all congregations throughout the world.

At this time You revealed to Your bishop Ambrose in a vision the place where the bodies of the martyrs Protasius and Gervasius[7] lay hid, which You had for so many years kept incorrupt in the treasury of Your secret knowledge that You might bring them forth at the proper moment to check a woman's fury—the woman[8] being the ruler of the Empire! For when they were discovered and dug up and with due honor brought to Ambrose's basilica, not only were people cured who had been tormented by evil spirits—and the devils themselves forced to confess it—but also there was a man, a citizen well known to the city, who had been blind for many years: he asked what was the cause of the tumultuous joy of the people, and when he heard, he sprang up and asked his guide to lead him into the place. When he arrived there he asked to be allowed to touch with his handkerchief the place on which lay the saints, whose death is precious in Your sight. He did so, put the handkerchief to his eyes, and immediately they were opened. The news spread abroad, Your praises glowed and shone, and if the mind of that angry woman was not brought to the sanity of belief, it was at least brought back from the madness of persecution. Thanks be to my God! From what and towards what have You led my memory, that it should confess to You these great things which I had altogether forgotten? Yet even then, *when the odor of Thy ointments was so sweet smelling*, I did *not run after Thee:* and for this I wept all the more now when I heard Your hymns and canticles, as one who had then sighed for You and now breathed in You, breathed so far as the air allows in this our house of grass.[9]

You, Lord, who make men of one mind to dwell in one house brought to our company a young man of our own town, Evodius. He had held office in the civil service, had been converted and baptized before us, had resigned from the state's service, and given himself to Yours. We kept together, meaning to live together in our devout purpose. We thought deeply as to the place in which we might serve You most usefully. As a result we started back for Africa. And when we had come as far as Ostia[1] on the Tiber, my mother died. I pass over many things, for I must make haste. Do You, O my God, accept my confessions and my gratitude for countless things of which I say nothing. But I will not omit anything my mind brings forth concerning her, Your servant, who brought me forth—brought me forth in the flesh to this temporal light, and in her heart to light eternal. Not of her gifts do I speak but of Your gifts in her. For she did not bring herself into the world or educate herself in the world: it was You who created her, nor did her father or mother know what kind of being was to come forth from them. It was the scepter of

---

6. The Greek-speaking churches of the Eastern Roman empire; they split off from the Catholic Church in the ninth century.   7. Two beheaded skeletons discovered by Ambrose at Milan were identified as the relics of these saints; nothing certain is known about them, but they were said to have been martyred in the second century.   8. Justina.   9. Compare Isaiah 40.6–8: "All flesh is grass. . . . The grass withereth, the flower fadeth: but the word of our God will stand forever."   1. On the southwest coast of Italy; it was the port of Rome and the point of departure for Africa.

Your Christ, the discipline of your Only-Begotten, that brought her up in holy fear, in a Catholic family which was a worthy member of Your church. Yet it was not the devotion of her mother in her upbringing that she talked most of, but of a certain aged servant, who had indeed carried my mother's father on her back when he was a baby, as little ones are accustomed to be carried on the backs of older girls. Because of this, because also of her age and her admirable character, she was very much respected by her master and mistress in their Christian household. As a result she was given charge of her master's daughters. This charge she fulfilled most conscientiously, checking them sharply when necessary with holy severity and teaching them soberly and prudently. Thus, except at the times when they ate—and that most temperately—at their parents' table, she would not let them even drink water, no matter how tormenting their thirst. By this she prevented the forming of a bad habit, and she used to remark very sensibly: "Now you drink water because you are not allowed to have wine: but when you are married, and thus mistresses of food-stores and wine-cellars, you will despise water, but the habit of drinking will still remain." By this kind of teaching and the authority of her commands she moderated the greediness that goes with childhood and brought the little girls' thirst to such a control that they no longer wanted what they ought not to have.

Yet, as Your servant told me, her son, there did steal upon my mother an inclination to wine. For when, in the usual way, she was sent by her parents, as a well-behaved child, to draw wine from the barrel, she would dip the cup in, but before pouring the wine from the cup into the flagon, she would sip a little with the very tip of her lips, only a little because she did not yet like the taste sufficiently to take more. Indeed she did it not out of any craving for wine, but rather from the excess of childhood's high spirits, which tend to boil over in absurdities, and are usually kept in check by the authority of elders. And so, adding to that daily drop a little more from day to day—for he that despises small things, falls little by little—she fell into the habit, so that she would drink off greedily cups almost full of wine. Where then was that wise old woman with her forceful prohibitions? Could anything avail against the evil in us, unless Your healing, O Lord, watched over us? When our father and mother and nurses are absent, You are present, who created us, who call us, who can use those placed over us for some good unto the salvation of our souls. What did You do then, O my God? How did You cure her, and bring her to health? From another soul you drew a harsh and cutting sarcasm, as though bringing forth a surgeon's knife from Your secret store, and with one blow amputated that sore place. A maidservant with whom she was accustomed to go to the cellar, one day fell into a quarrel with her small mistress when no one else chanced to be about, and hurled at her the most biting insult possible, calling her a drunkard. My mother was pierced to the quick, saw her fault in its true wickedness, and instantly condemned it and gave it up. Just as the flattery of a friend can pervert, so the insult of an enemy can sometimes correct. Nor do You, O God, reward men according to what You do by means of them, but according to what they themselves intended. For the girl being in a temper wanted to enrage her young mistress, not to amend her, for she did it when no one else was there, either because the time and place happened to be thus when the quarrel arose, or because she was afraid that elders[2] would be angry because she had not told it sooner. But You, O Lord, Ruler of heavenly things and earthly, who turn to Your own purposes the very depths of rivers as they run and order the turbulence of the flow of time, did by the folly of one mind bring sanity to another; thus reminding us not to attribute it to our own power if another is amended by our word, even if we meant to amend him.

My mother, then, was modestly and soberly brought up, being rather made obedient to her parents by You than to You by her parents. When she reached the age for marriage, and was bestowed upon a husband, she served him as her lord. She used all her effort to win him to You, preaching You to him by her character, by which You made her beautiful to her husband, respected and loved by him and admirable in his sight. For she bore his acts of unfaithfulness quietly, and never had any jealous scene with her husband about them. She awaited Your mercy upon him, that he might grow chaste through faith in You. And as a matter of fact, though generous beyond measure, he had a very hot temper. But she knew that a woman must not resist a husband in anger, by deed or even by word. Only, when she saw him calm again and quiet, she would take the opportunity to give him an explanation of her actions, if it happened that he had been roused to anger unreasonably. The result was that whereas many matrons with much milder husbands carried the marks of blows to disfigure their faces, and would all get together to complain of the way their husbands behaved, my mother—talking lightly but meaning it seriously—advised them against their tongues: saying that from the day they heard the matrimonial contract read to them they should regard it as an instrument by which they became servants; and from that time they should be mindful of their condition and not set themselves up against their masters. And they often expressed amazement—for they knew how violent a husband she had to live with—that it had never been heard, and there was no mark to show, that Patricius[3] had beaten his wife or that there had been any family quarrel between them for so much as a single day. And when her friends asked her the reason, she taught them her rule, which was as I have just said. Those who followed it, found it good and thanked her; those who did not, went on being bullied and beaten.

Her mother-in-law began by being angry with her because of the whispers of malicious servants. But my mother won her completely by the respect she showed, and her unfailing patience and mildness. She ended by going to her son, telling him of the tales the servants had bandied about to the destruction of peace in the family between herself and her daughter-in-law, and asking him to punish them for it. So he, out of obedience to his mother and in the interests of order in the household and peace among his womenfolk, had the servants beaten whose names he had been given, as she had asked when giving them. To which she added the promise that anyone must expect a similar reward from her own hands who should think to please her by speaking ill of her daughter-in-law. And as no one had the courage to do so, they lived together with the most notable degree of kindness and harmony.

This great gift also, O my God, my Mercy, You gave to Your good servant, in whose womb You created me, that she showed herself, wherever possible,

---

2. Leaders of the Church.　　3. Augustine's father.

a peacemaker between people quarreling and minds at discord. For swelling and undigested discord often belches forth bitter words when in the venom of intimate conversation with a present friend hatred at its rawest is breathed out upon an absent enemy. But when my mother heard bitter things said by each of the other, she never said anything to either about the other save what would help to reconcile them. This might seem a small virtue, if I had not had the sorrow of seeing for myself so many people who—as if by some horrible widespreading infection of sin—not only tell angry people the things their enemies said in anger, but even add things that were never said at all. Whereas, on the contrary, ordinary humanity would seem to require not merely that we refrain from exciting or increasing wrath among men by evil speaking, but that we study to extinguish wrath by kind speaking. Such a one was she: and You were the master who taught her most secretly in the school of her heart.

The upshot was that toward the very end of his life she won her husband to You; and once he was a Christian she no longer had to complain of the things she had had to bear with before he was a Christian. Further, she was a servant of Your servants. Such of them as knew her praised and honored and loved You, O God, in her; for they felt Your presence in her heart, showing itself in the fruit of her holy conversation. She had been *the wife of one husband, had requited her parents, had governed her house* piously, *was well reported of for good works. She had brought up her children,*[4] being in labor of them as often as she saw them swerving away from You. Finally of all of us Your servants, O Lord—since by Your gift You suffer us to speak— who before her death were living together[5] after receiving the grace of baptism, she took as much care as if she had been the mother of us all, and served us as if she had been the daughter of us all.

When the day was approaching on which she was to depart this life—a day that You knew though we did not—it came about, as I believe by Your secret arrangement, that she and I stood alone leaning in a window, which looked inwards to the garden within the house where we were staying, at Ostia on the Tiber; for there we were away from everybody, resting for the sea voyage from the weariness of our long journey by land. There we talked together, she and I alone, in deep joy; and *forgetting the things that were behind and looking forward to those that were before,* we were discussing in the presence of Truth, which You are, what the eternal life of the saints could be like, *which eye has not seen nor ear heard, nor has it entered into the heart of man.* But with the mouth of our heart we panted for the high waters of Your fountain, the fountain of the life which is with You: that being sprinkled from that fountain according to our capacity, we might in some sense meditate upon so great a matter.

And our conversation had brought us to this point, that any pleasure whatsoever of the bodily senses, in any brightness whatsoever of corporeal light, seemed to us not worthy of comparison with the pleasure of that eternal Light, not worthy even of mention. Rising as our love flamed upward towards that Selfsame,[6] we passed in review the various levels of bodily things, up to the heavens themselves, whence sun and moon and stars shine upon this

---

4. Augustine is paraphrasing Paul's description of the duties of a widow, given in 1 Timothy 5.   5. Augustine and his fellow converts.   6. Reality, the divine principle. This ecstasy of Augustine and Monica is throughout described in philosophical terms, in which God is Wisdom.

earth. And higher still we soared, thinking in our minds and speaking and marveling at Your works: and so we came to our own souls, and went beyond them to come at last to that region of richness unending, where You feed Israel forever with the food of truth: and there life is that Wisdom by which all things are made, both the things that have been and the things that are yet to be. But this Wisdom itself is not made: it is as it has ever been, and so it shall be forever: indeed "has ever been" and "shall be forever" have no place in it, but it simply is, for it is eternal: whereas "to have been" and "to be going to be" are not eternal. And while we were thus talking of His Wisdom and panting for it, with all the effort of our heart we did for one instant attain to touch it; then sighing, and leaving the first fruits of our spirit bound to it, we returned to the sound of our own tongue, in which a word has both beginning and ending. For what is like to your Word, Our Lord, who abides in Himself forever, yet grows not old and makes all things new!

So we said: If to any man the tumult of the flesh grew silent, silent the images of earth and sea and air: and if the heavens grew silent, and the very soul grew silent to herself and by not thinking of self mounted beyond self: if all dreams and imagined visions grew silent, and every tongue and every sign and whatsoever is transient—for indeed if any man could hear them, he should hear them saying with one voice: We did not make ourselves, but He made us who abides forever: but if, having uttered this and so set us to listening to Him who made them, they all grew silent, and in their silence He alone spoke to us, not by them but by Himself: so that we should hear His word, not by any tongue of flesh nor the voice of an angel nor the sound of thunder nor in the darkness of a parable,[7] but that we should hear Himself whom in all these things we love, should hear Himself and not them: just as we two had but now reached forth and in a flash of the mind attained to touch the eternal Wisdom which abides over all: and if this could continue, and all other visions so different be quite taken away, and this one should so ravish and absorb and wrap the beholder in inward joys that his life should eternally be such as that one moment of understanding for which we had been sighing—would not this be: *Enter Thou into the joy of Thy Lord?* But when shall it be? Shall it be when *we shall all rise again* and *shall not all be changed?*[8]

Such thoughts I uttered, though not in that order or in those actual words; but You know, O Lord, that on that day when we talked of these things the world with all its delights seemed cheap to us in comparison with what we talked of. And my mother said: "Son, for my own part I no longer find joy in anything in this world. What I am still to do here and why I am here I know not, now that I no longer hope for anything from this world. One thing there was, for which I desired to remain still a little longer in this life, that I should see you a Catholic Christian before I died. This God has granted me in superabundance, in that I now see you His servant to the contempt of all worldly happiness. What then am I doing here?"

What answer I made, I do not clearly remember; within five days or not much longer she fell into a fever. And in her sickness, she one day fainted

---

7. Compare Luke 8.10: "Unto you it is given to know the mysteries of the kingdom of God: but to others in parables; that seeing they might not see, and hearing they might not understand."   8. Compare 1 Corinthians 15.52: "the trumpet shall sound, and the dead shall be raised incorruptible, and we shall be changed," referring to the Last Judgment.

away and for the moment lost consciousness. We ran to her but she quickly returned to consciousness, and seeing my brother and me standing by her she said as one wondering: "Where was I?" Then looking closely upon us as we stood wordless in our grief, she said: "Here you will bury your mother." I stayed silent and checked my weeping. But my brother said something to the effect that he would be happier if she were to die in her own land and not in a strange country. But as she heard this she looked at him anxiously, restraining him with her eye because he savored of earthly things, and then she looked at me and said: "See the way he talks." And then she said to us both: "Lay this body wherever it may be. Let no care of it disturb you: this only I ask of you that you should remember me at the altar of the Lord wherever you may be." And when she had uttered this wish in such words as she could manage, she fell silent as her sickness took hold of her more strongly.

But as I considered Your gifts, O unseen God, which You send into the hearts of Your faithful to the springing up of such wonderful fruits, I was glad and gave thanks to You, remembering what I had previously known of the care as to her burial which had always troubled her: for she had arranged to be buried by the body of her husband. Because they had lived together in such harmony, she had wished—so little is the human mind capable of rising to the divine—that it should be granted her, as an addition to her happiness and as something to be spoken of among men, that after her pilgrimage beyond the sea the earthly part of man and wife should lie together under the same earth. Just when this vain desire had begun to vanish from her heart through the fullness of Your goodness, I did not know; but I was pleased and surprised that it had now so clearly vanished: though indeed in the conversation we had had together at the window, when she said: "What am I still doing here?" there had appeared no desire to die in her own land. Further I heard afterwards that in the time we were at Ostia, she had talked one day to some of my friends, as a mother talking to her children, of the contempt of this life and of the attraction of death. I was not there at the time. They marveled at such courage in a woman—but it was You who had given it to her—and asked if she was not afraid to leave her body so far from her own city. But she said: "Nothing is far from God, and I have no fear that He will not know at the end of the world from what place He is to raise me up." And so on the ninth day of her illness, in the fifty-sixth year of her life and the thirty-third of mine, that devout and holy soul was released from the body.

I closed her eyes; and an immeasurable sorrow flowed into my heart and would have overflowed in tears. But my eyes under the mind's strong constraint held back their flow and I stood dry-eyed. In that struggle it went very ill with me. As she breathed her last, the child Adeodatus broke out into lamentation and we all checked him and brought him to silence. But in this very fact the childish element in me, which was breaking out into tears, was checked and brought to silence by the manlier voice of my mind. For we felt that it was not fitting that her funeral should be solemnized with moaning and weeping and lamentation, for so it is normal to weep when death is seen as sheer misery or as complete extinction. But she had not died miserably, nor did she wholly die. Of the one thing we were sure by reason of her character, of the other by the reality of our faith.

What then was it that grieved my heart so deeply? Only the newness of the wound, in finding the custom I had so loved of living with her suddenly snapped short. It was a joy to me to have this one testimony from her: when her illness was close to its end, meeting with expressions of endearment such services as I rendered, she called me a dutiful loving son, and said in the great affection of her love that she had never heard from my mouth any harsh or reproachful word addressed to herself. But what possible comparison was there, O my God who made us, between the honor I showed her and the service she had rendered me?

Because I had now lost the great comfort of her, my soul was wounded and my very life torn asunder, for it had been one life made of hers and mine together. When the boy had been quieted and ceased weeping, Evodius took up the psalter and began to chant—with the whole house making the responses—the psalm *Mercy and judgment I will sing to Thee, O Lord.*[9] And when they heard what was being done, many of the brethren and religious women came to us; those whose office it was were making arrangement for the burial, while, in another part of the house where it could properly be done I discoursed, with friends who did not wish to leave me by myself, upon matters suitable for that time. Thus I used truth as a kind of fomentation[1] to bring relief to my torment, a torment known to You, but not known to those others: so that listening closely to me they thought that I lacked all feeling of grief. But in Your ears, where none of them could hear, I accused the emotion in me as weakness; and I held in the flood of my grief. It was for the moment a little diminished, but returned with fresh violence, not with any pouring of tears or change of countenance: but I knew what I was crushing down in my heart. I was very much ashamed that these human emotions could have such power over me—though it belongs to the due order and the lot of our earthly condition that they should come to us—and I felt a new grief at my grief and so was afflicted with a twofold sorrow.

When the body was taken to burial, I went and returned without tears. During the prayers which we poured forth to you when the sacrifice of our redemption[2] was offered for her—while the body, as the custom there is, lay by the grave before it was actually buried—during those prayers I did not weep. Yet all that day I was heavy with grief within and in the trouble of my mind I begged of You in my own fashion to heal my pain; but You would not—I imagine because You meant to impress upon my memory by this proof how strongly the bond of habit holds the mind even when it no longer feeds upon deception. The idea came to me to go and bathe, for I had heard that the bath—which the Greeks call βαλανῖον[3]—is so called because it drives anxiety from the mind. And this also I acknowledge to Your mercy, O Father of orphans, that I bathed and was the same man after as before. The bitterness of grief had not sweated out of my heart. Then I fell asleep, and woke again to find my grief not a little relieved. And as I was in bed and no one about, I said over those true verses that Your servant Ambrose wrote of You:

> Deus creator omnium
> polique rector vestiens

---

9. Compare Psalm 101.1.   1. Soothing dressing for a wound.   2. Perhaps a communion service.
3. Augustine evidently derives *balaneion* ("bath") from the words *ballo* ("cast away") and *ania* ("sorrow").

diem decoro lumine,
noctem sopora gratia,

artus solutos ut quies
reddat laboris usui
mentesque fessas allevet
luctusque solvat anxios.[4]

And then little by little I began to recover my former feeling about Your handmaid, remembering how loving and devout was her conversation with You, how pleasant and considerate her conversation with me, of which I was thus suddenly deprived. And I found solace in weeping in Your sight both about her and for her, about myself and for myself. I no longer tried to check my tears, but let them flow as they would, making them a pillow for my heart: and it rested upon them, for it was Your ears that heard my weeping, and not the ears of a man, who would have misunderstood my tears and despised them. But now, O Lord, I confess it to You in writing, let him read it who will and interpret it as he will: and if he sees it as sin that for so small a portion of an hour I wept for my mother, now dead and departed from my sight, who had wept so many years for me that I should live ever in Your sight—let him not scorn me but rather, if he is a man of great charity, let him weep for my sins to You, the Father of all the brethren of Your Christ.

Now that my heart is healed of that wound, in which there was perhaps too much of earthly affection, I pour forth to You, O our God, tears of a very different sort for Your handmaid—tears that flow from a spirit shaken by the thought of the perils there are for every soul that dies in Adam.[5] For though she had been made alive in Christ, and while still in the body had so lived that Your name was glorified in her faith and her character, yet I dare not say that from the moment of her regeneration in baptism no word issued from her mouth contrary to Your Command. Your Son, who is Truth, has said: *Whosoever shall say to his brother, Thou fool, shall be in danger of hell fire;*[6] and it would go ill with the most praiseworthy life lived by men, if You were to examine it with Your mercy laid aside! But because You do not enquire too fiercely into our sins, we have hope and confidence of a place with You. Yet if a man reckons up before You the merits he truly has, what is he reckoning except Your own gifts? If only men would know themselves to be but men, so that he that glories would glory in the Lord!

Thus, my Glory and my Life, God of my heart, leaving aside for this time her good deeds, for which I give thanks to Thee in joy, I now pray to Thee for my mother's sins. Grant my prayer through the true Medicine of our wounds,[7] who hung upon the cross and who now sitting at Thy right hand makes intercession for us. I know that she dealt mercifully, and from her heart forgave those who trespassed against her: do Thou also forgive such trespasses as she may have been guilty of in all the years since her baptism, forgive them, Lord, forgive them, I beseech Thee: enter not into judgment with her. Let Thy mercy be exalted above Thy justice for Thy words are true

---

4. God, the creator of all things / and ruler of the heavens / you who clothe the day with the glory of light, / and the night with the gift of sleep, / so that rest may relax the limbs / and restore them for the day's work / relieve the fatigue of the mind / and dispel anxiety and grief (Latin).   5. That is, with the curse of Adam not nullified through baptism in Jesus Christ and conformity with his teachings.   6. From Matthew 5.22, Jesus' Sermon on the Mount. He is preaching a more severe moral code than the traditional one that whoever kills shall be liable to judgment.   7. Jesus.

and Thou hast promised that the merciful shall obtain mercy. That they should be merciful is Thy gift who *hast mercy on whom Thou wilt, and wilt have compassion on whom Thou wilt.*

And I believe that Thou hast already done what I am now asking; but be not offended, Lord, at the things my mouth would utter. For on that day when her death was so close, she was not concerned that her body should be sumptuously wrapped or embalmed with spices, nor with any thought of choosing a monument or even for burial in her own country. Of such things she gave us no command, but only desired to be remembered at Thy altar, which she had served without ever missing so much as a day, on which she knew that the holy Victim was offered; *by whom the handwriting is blotted out of the decree that was contrary to us,*[8] by which offering too the enemy was overcome who, reckoning our sins and seeking what may be laid to our charge, found nothing in Him, in whom we are conquerors. Who shall restore to Him his innocent blood? Who shall give Him back the price by which He purchased us and so take us from Him? To this sacrament of our redemption Thy handmaid had bound her soul by the bond of faith. Let none wrest her from Thy protection; let neither the lion nor the dragon[9] bar her way by force or craft. For she will not answer that she owes nothing, lest she should be contradicted and confuted by that cunning accuser: but she will answer that her debts have been remitted by Him, to whom no one can hand back the price which He paid for us, though He owed it not.

So let her rest in peace, together with her husband, for she had no other before nor after him, but served him, in patience bringing forth fruit for Thee, and winning him likewise for Thee. And inspire, O my Lord my God, inspire Thy servants my brethren, Thy sons my masters, whom I serve with heart and voice and pen, that as many of them as read this may remember at Thy altar Thy servant Monica, with Patricius, her husband, by whose bodies Thou didst bring me into this life, though how I know not.[1] May they with loving mind remember these who were my parents in this transitory light, my brethren who serve Thee as our Father in our Catholic mother, and those who are to be fellow citizens with me in the eternal Jerusalem,[2] which Thy people sigh for in their pilgrimage from birth until they come there: so that what my mother at her end asked of me may be fulfilled more richly in the prayers of so many gained for her by my Confessions than by my prayers alone.

*   *   *

---

8. Alludes to Christ's redemption of humanity from the curse of Adam through the Crucifixion. **9.** Compare Psalm 91.13: "Thou shalt tread upon the lion and the adder: the young lion and the dragon shalt thou trample under feet," which invokes God's protection of the godly." **1.** Augustine does not understand the seemingly miraculous process by which the fetus grows in the womb. **2.** I.e., heaven.

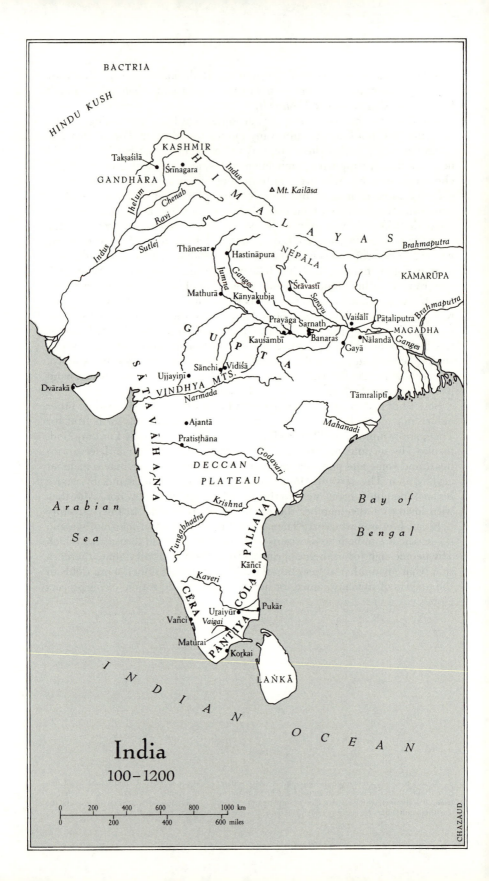

BACTRIA

HINDU KUSH

KASHMIR

Takṣaśilā
Śrīnagara
HIMALAYAS
Indus

GANDHĀRA

Jhelum
Chenab
Ravi

△ Mt. Kailāsa

Indus

Sutlej

Thānesar
Hastināpura
NEPĀLA
Brahmaputra

KĀMARŪPA

Jumna
Ganges
Śrāvastī

Mathurā
Kānyakubja
Sarayu

Prayāga Sarnath
Vaiśālī Pāṭaliputra Brahmaputra

Kauśāmbī
Banaras
Nālandā Ganges
MAGADHA

GUPTA

Gayā

SĀTAVĀHANA

Sānchi
Vidiśā
Ujjayinī
VINDHYA MTS.

Dvārakā
Narmada

Tāmraliptī

Ajantā

Pratiṣṭhāna
Mahanadi

DECCAN
PLATEAU
Godavari

Arabian

Krishna
Bay of

Sea
Tungabhadra
PALLAVA
Bengal

Kaveri
Kāñcī

CERA
CŌLA
Pukār

Vañci
Uraiyūr
Vaigai

Maturai
PĀNṬIYA
Korkai

LAŃKĀ

INDIAN

OCEAN

India
100–1200

0   200   400   600   800   1000 km
0   200   400   600 miles

CHAZAUD

India's Classical Age

The classical literature of India had its great flowering under the Guptas, who ruled over much of India from their north Indian capitals in Pāṭaliputra (modern Patna) and Ujjayinī (modern Ujjain) between 335 and 470. During the Gupta era Ujjayinī in the west and the seaport Tāmraliptī in the east were centers of a flourishing trade with Rome, China, and Southeast Asia. While Indian merchants voyaged on the seas to Java and other islands in the Indonesian archipelago, Chinese pilgrims traveled to the holy sites of Buddhism in the land of its birth. Ancient India's greatest achievements in mathematics, logic, and astronomy as well as in literature and the fine arts were made in this prosperous, cosmopolitan milieu, and the classical ideals expressed in the masterworks of the Gupta period continued to be influential well into the twelfth century and later.

Gupta classicism was closely connected with the development of Sanskrit as a literary language. *Saṃskṛta,* the very name of the language, means "perfected, classified, refined." Already by the end of the heroic age the veneration of the Vedic hymns had led to the ideal of Sanskrit as "correct speech," a speech that was fully codified and frozen in the *Aṣṭādhyāyī* (The Book of Eight Chapters [of the rules of grammar]) of Pāṇini, a pioneer in the science of linguistics. In the Indian view, Sanskrit's nature as a code and construct made it the ideal language for the classics, in contrast to the Prakrit (*prākṛta,* meaning "original" or "natural") dialects that were allowed to change and develop in the manner of "natural," spoken languages.

The Prakrit literature that developed around the second century was soon absorbed into the Sanskrit classical tradition. Until the development of the south Indian regional languages in the tenth and eleventh centuries, Tamil alone continued to nourish a classical tradition that was distinct from that of Sanskrit, in spite of the many features absorbed into Tamil civilization from centuries of interaction with Indo-Aryan culture and literature. The fifth-century *Cilappatikāram* (The Poem of the Anklet) is the oldest extant epic in Tamil. This classical poem, written at the court of a Cēra king, bears no resemblance whatsoever to the Indo-Aryan epics, although its author, Iḷaṅkōvaṭikaḷ, was a Jaina monk and the Tamil folk narrative on which the epic is based is heavily overlaid with Jaina doctrine.

Classical Sanskrit literature is permeated with the culture of the courts of ancient India. Learned poets (*kavi*) wrote poetry under the patronage of kings and recited their works at court for audiences of connoisseurs, known as *sahṛdaya* ("with heart," or responsive) or *rasika* ("enjoyer of aesthetic mood"). Whatever their specific subject matter, only works whose primary aim was to evoke an aesthetic response were admitted into the classical literary canon, and such works were called *kāvya,* "poetry" in the broadest sense of the word—that is, literature as art. *Kāvya* literature is governed by meticulously formulated norms and conventions that circumscribe the poet's freedom, at the same time putting at his or her disposal a rich array of traditional poetic means, along with the opportunity to refine on the achievements of the past.

The court epic, drama, short lyric, and narrative are the major genres of *kāvya.* The first of these, the *mahākāvya* ("great poem," or court epic), grew out of the older epics and bardic praise poems and treats the martial exploits of kings, warriors, and gods. Unlike the older narrative epics, however, the *kāvya* epics are made up of lyric stanzas, with elaborate figures of speech and a descriptive emphasis. The drama, or *nāṭya* (exemplified in plays: *rūpaka*, "representation"), is a more heterogeneous genre, employing prose and verse, in Sanskrit and Prakrit, and a somewhat wider range of characters than the court epic. In classical plays the warrior-king is portrayed as a romantic hero, and here, too, lyrical description dominates over dramatic action.

The short lyric poem (*muktaka*, "detached verse") is the quintessential genre of classical Sanskrit poetry. Sanskrit poets achieved their finest and most characteristic effects in poems of a single stanza divided into "quarters" (*pāda*), normally of equal length. The brevity of the form (the longest *kāvya* meter has only twenty-one syllables per verse quarter) combined with the complexities of the Sanskrit language and the rules of *kāvya* poetry results in miniature poems that are at once complex and extraordinarily compact, similar in effect to the miniature paintings produced at Indian courts in the seventeenth and eighteenth centuries. The *muktaka* genre encompasses the trenchant epigrams of Bhartṛhari, and Kālidāsa's idyllic verses on nature and love as well as the erotic vignettes of Amaru. Designated *subhāṣita* ("well-wrought verse"), the best stanzas of the classical poets—both men and women—were anthologized in such collections as the eleventh-century *Subhāṣitaratnakoṣa* (A Treasury of Well-Wrought Verse), to be memorized, recited, and savored by connoisseurs. Such poets as Bhartṛhari and Amaru, who specialized in particular themes, earned their own anthologies, organized into "centuries [of stanzas]," or *śataka*, perhaps on the model of earlier anthologies of Tamil and Prakrit lyric poetry.

From the earliest times India has been a vast storehouse of tales, many of which have traveled all over the world. Among the most widely known works in the narrative genre known as *kathā* or *ākhyāyikā* ("story") is the *Pañcatantra*, a Gupta-period collection of animal fables. The most popular of the later *kāvya* tale collections, however, is the Kashmirian poet Somadeva's eleventh-century *Kathāsaritsāgara* (Ocean to the Rivers of Story), a compendium in narrative verse of picaresque tales, tales of the marvelous, and romances. With its gentle but pointed satire of ancient Indian society and manners and its array of vivid, earthy characters, Sanskrit story literature presents a marked contrast to the sober elegance of the other *kāvya* genres.

The practice of *kāvya* literature seems always to have been correlated with an influential body of works on poetics. The first major work devoted solely to poetic theory is the seventh-century *Kāvyādarśa* (Mirror for Poetry), in which the south Indian writer on poetic theory Daṇḍin systematically discusses the figures of speech (*alaṃkāra*, literally "ornament") that differentiate poetry from ordinary discourse. An earlier concept, *rasa* or "aesthetic mood," remained the dominant theoretical framework for the aesthetics of drama and also influenced the criticism of the other *kāvya* genres. Finally, in the ninth century, the master critic Ānandavardhana expounded in his *Dhvanyāloka* (Light of Suggestion) the aesthetic ideal of *dhvani* ("poetic suggestion"; literally, "resonance") as the measure of the best kind of poetry in all the forms of *kāvya*. Besides poetic theory *kāvya* texts are keyed to technical treatises (*śāstra* or *sūtra*) in every branch of classical learning, ranging from Pāṇini's grammar and Vātsyāyana's *Kāmasūtra* (Treatise on Erotics) to the *Dharmaśāstra* of Manu (Manu's treatise on the religious law) and the *Arthaśāstra*, Kauṭilya's influential text on politics.

Reflecting the conservative values of courtly and learned elites, the masterworks of *kāvya* carry forward the idealization of *dharma* (religious duty), the first of the four aims of human endeavor enjoined for Hindu men and a seminal theme in the major texts of the heroic age, such as the *Rāmāyaṇa* and the *Bhagavad-Gītā*. In the classical texts, however, the concern with religious duty is offset by a more direct preoccupation with *artha* (wealth, politics, public life) and *kāma* (the realm of erotic pleasure and the emotions), the second and third aims, and their vision is of a life in which all four goals of action are harmoniously balanced. Like earlier epic heroes such as Arjuna and Rāma, the exemplary warriors and kings of the courtly literature combine sagelike self-control with more active, worldly, heroic traits, for in Hindu belief austerity is an essential means by which a person may attain the ultimate goal of life—

liberation (*mokṣa*) from the chain of birth and death in which souls are trapped because of the results of good and bad action (*karma*).

The philosophy of *karma*-rebirth implies fluid relationships among the human, animal, and divine worlds. In a universe where a king might be a divine incarnation, a god come down to earth (*avatāra*, "descent"), sages and holy people, who have amassed superhuman powers by exercising extraordinary self-control, represent the possibility of the ascent of human beings to godlike states; hence the great respect given to these gods-on-earth. As keepers of both sacred and secular learning, members of the brahman class, the highest of the four classes of Hindu society and the class to which most of the classical poets belonged, are naturally portrayed in a most favorable light in the works of the classical era. Certain genres, however, were allowed the privilege of satire and critique. The "Fool" of the Sanskrit drama is a dull-witted, gluttonous brahman; the story literature is full of corrupt monks and less-than-perfect religious figures; and the animal fables of the *Pañcatantra* offer an unvarnished picture of courtly intrigue.

Śakuntalā, the heroine of Kālidāsa's celebrated play *Śākuntala* (fourth century), a representative *kāvya* classic, reinforces the image of the ideal Hindu wife, a role already exemplified in the personality of the long-suffering Sītā in the *Rāmāyaṇa*. The indispensability of marriage for women in Hindu society, and their near-total dependence on the will of their husbands, dominates even this work with its explicit focus on the erotic aspect of gender relations. In the course of the play, Śakuntalā matures from a naive girl into the ideal wife: chaste, loyal, submissive, and willing to bear suffering patiently. However, the classical literature offers very different images of women as well. The Tamil epic *Cilappatikāram* portrays Kaṇṇaki as a woman whose chastity endows her with independent agency and superhuman power. Chaste though they may be, there is nothing submissive about the women of the Sanskrit story literature, a literature of the merchant-class milieu. Women are as often likely to be the protagonists of these stories as men, and they surpass men—very often, their own husbands—in wit, wisdom, resourcefulness, and the ability to act.

The hierarchy of gender roles is often reversed in the Sanskrit erotic lyrics, which also challenge the normative emphasis on female chastity by their sympathetic treatment of extramarital love. In the spectrum of female figures in classical literature, the courtesan, whose skill in the arts enables her to earn her own living and dispense with marriage, stands at the opposite end from the chaste wife. The courtesans of Sanskrit and Tamil literature are beautiful, intelligent, ruthless, and rapacious women; but there are also sympathetic potraits. Finally, in such characters as the female hermit Gautamī in *Śākuntala*, we have exemplars of women who, as religious contemplatives, are figures of authority and free agents on a par with their male counterparts.

The lives of many *kāvya* poets are shrouded in myth and legend. This is true even of Kālidāsa, the greatest poet, not only of the age of the Guptas but also of the entire *kāvya* tradition. Likewise, the identities of the royal patrons of early *kāvya*, except in the odd case, remain a matter for speculation. *Kāvya* is a poetry of universals and ideals, and its heroes and heroines are, by and large, types, not individuals. The early epic poetry, too, idealized and universalized its heroes. Whether the hero is a king, merchant, or brahman, and regardless of his distinctive virtues, the ideal personage of the classical literature must possess—to a greater or lesser degree—the generalized qualities of a *nāgaraka*, "citizen" or "courtier," the cultivated person of the courtly civilization. So, too, must the ideal *kāvya* heroine—whether she is a courtesan or a chaste wife—be beautiful and refined in the courtly manner.

Vātsyāyana devotes the opening section of the *Kāmasūtra* to the qualifications of the *nāgaraka* and his female counterpart. The gentleman is enjoined to equip his house (a pleasant villa surrounded by a garden) with the requisites of a cultivated life. These include "a box containing ornaments, and also a lute hanging from a peg made of the tooth of an elephant, a board for drawing, a pot containing perfume, and

some garlands of yellow amaranth flowers." All women, not just professional courtesans, are encouraged to learn the sixty-four arts, among which are enumerated
several kinds of verse making and "writing and drawing, and spreading and arranging
beds or couches of flowers, and scenic representation and stage playing." Life itself
is an art, and the ideal person is a *rasika*, or a *sahṛdaya*—one whose sensibility has
been cultivated to celebrate and respond to life as art. This aesthetic ideal, more than
any other trait, characterizes the literature of India's classical age.

FURTHER READING

The Literatures of India (1974), edited by Edward C. Dimock et al., contains good
introductions to the various genres of classical Sanskrit literature, and Daniel
H. H. Ingalls, *Sanskrit Poetry from Vidyākara's Treasury* (1968), offers an outstand-
ing introduction to *kāvya* poetry and its aesthetic. A. L. Basham, *The Wonder That
Was India* (1956), is the best study of India's classical civilization. For a history of
Sanskrit literature, see A. B. Keith, *History of Classical Sanskrit Literature*. The
Kāmasūtra may be consulted in Richard Burton's translation, *The Kama Sutra of
Vatsyayana* (1923). On women in classical civilization, see A. S. Altekar, *The Posi-
tion of Women in Hindu Civilization* (1938), and J. J. Meyer, *Sexual Life in Ancient
India* (1930).

PRONOUNCING GLOSSARY

The following list uses common English syllables and stress accents to provide rough equivalents of selected words whose pronunciation may be unfamiliar to the general reader.

ākhyāyikā: *ah-khyah'-yee-kah*

alaṃkāra: *uh'-luhng-kah-ruh*

Amaru: *uh'-muh-roo*

Ānandavardhana: *ah-nuhn-duh-vuhrd'-*
    huh-nuh

artha: *uhrt'-huh*

Arthaśāstra: *uhrt-huh-shahs'-truh*

Aṣṭādhyāyī: *uhsh'-tahdh-yah'-yee*

Bhagavad Gītā: *buh'-guh-vuhd gee'-taa*

Bharata: *buh'-ruh-tuh*

Bhartṛhari: *buhr'-tree-huh'-ree*

Cēra: *say'-ruh*

Cilappatikāram: *see-luhp'-puh-dee-*
    hah'-ruhm

Daṇḍin: *duhn'-deen*

Dharmaśāstra: *duhr'-muh-shahs'-truh*

dhvani: *dvuh'-nee*

Dhvanyāloka: *d-vuhn'-yah-loh'-kuh*

Gupta: *goop'-tuh*

Iḷaṅkōvaṭikaḷ: *ee-luhn'-goh-vuh-dee-*
    guhl

Jaina: *jai'-nuh*

Kālidāsa: *kah-lee-dah'-suh*

kāma: *kah'-muh*

Kāmasūtra: *kah-muh-soot'-ruh*

karma: *kuhr'-muh*

kathā: *kuht'-hah*

Kathāsaritsāgara: *kuht-hah'-suh-reet-*
    sah'-guh-ruh

Kauṭilya: *kow-teel'-yuh*

kavi: *kuh'-vee*

kāvya: *kahv'-yuh*

Kāvyādarśa: *kahv-yah-duhr'-shuh*

mahākāvya: *muh-hah-kahv'-yuh*

Manu: *muh'-noo*

mokṣa: *mohk'-shuh*

muktaka: *mook-tuh'-kuh*

nāgaraka: *nah'-guh-ruh-kuh*

nāṭya: *naht'-yuh*

Nāṭyaśāstra: *naht'-yuh-shahs'-truh*

pāda: *pah'-duh*

Pañcatantra: *puhn'-chuh-tuhn'-truh*

Pāṇini: *pah'-nee-nee*

Pāṭaliputra: *pah'-tuh-lee-poo'-truh*

prākṛta: *prah'-kree-tuh*

Rāmāyana: *rah-mah'-yuh-nuh*

rasa: *ruh'-suh*

rasika: *ruh'-see-kuh*

rūpaka: *roo'-puh-kuh*

sahṛdaya: *suh-hree'-duh-yuh*

Śākuntala: *shah-koon'-tuh-luh*

saṃskṛta: *suhms'-kree-tuh*

śāstra: *shah'-struh*

śataka: *shuh'-tuh-kuh*

śloka: *shloh'-kuh*

Somadeva: *soh'-muh-day'-vuh*

subhāṣita: *soob-hah'-shee-tuh*

Subhāṣitaratnakoṣa: *soob-hah'-shee-tuh-ruht'-nuh-koh'-shuh*

sūtra: *soo'-truh*

Tāmraliptī: *tahm'-ruh-leep'-tee*

Ujjayinī: *ooj'-juh-yee-nee*

Vātsyāyana: *vahts-yah'-yuh-nuh*

TIME LINE

TEXTS	CONTEXTS
ca. 2nd century The Sanskrit *Nāṭyaśāstra* of Bharata, the authoritative work on drama, poetry, and aesthetics, is completed	
2nd or 3rd century Viṣṇuśarman completes the Sanskrit animal tale collection *Pañcatantra*	
	335–470 The reign of the Gupta emperors in north India, an age of great achievement in arts, letters, science, international trade, and conquest • Indian civilization spreads to Southeast Asia
ca. 375–425 Kālidāsa, preeminent poet of the Gupta age, writes the play *Śākuntala* and other works in Sanskrit	
5th century The Sanskrit epigrams of Bhartṛhari are collected in the *Śatakatrayam* (The Anthology of Three Centuries)	
ca. 400–500 Tiruvaḷḷuvar composes the Tamil *Tirukkuraḷ*, a collection of ethical aphorisms • Vātsyāyana writes the Sanskrit *Kāmasūtra*, the authoritative treatise on the science of erotics	ca. 400–500 A great Buddhist monastery and university are founded in Nālandā in eastern India
	454 The Huns invade India
late 5th century The Jaina monk Iḷaṅkōvaṭikaḷ writes the *Cilappatikāram* (The Poem of the Anklet), an epic poem in Tamil concerning the heroic deeds and apotheosis of the chaste wife Kaṇṇaki	
7th century *Amaruśataka*	
600–700 The poet-leaders of the south Indian devotional *(bhakti)* movements dedicated to the god Śiva compose Tamil hymns praising the god	ca. 600–800 Pallava rulers of Kanchipuram in south India patronize populist religious movements and poetry in the Tamil language
	629–645 Chinese Buddhist pilgrim Hsuan-tsang visits India

Boldface titles indicate works in the anthology.

TIME LINE

TEXTS	CONTEXTS
	ca. 711–715 Arabs conquer the province of Sind in western India, bringing Islam to the region
ca. 800 Hindu philosopher Śaṅkara writes commentaries on the *Upaniṣads* and the **Bhagavad Gītā**	
900–1000 Māṇikkavācakar, preeminent devotional poet of south India, writes the *Tiruvācakam* (Sacred Utterance), a sequence of hymns to the Hindu god Śiva, in Tamil • The *Bhāgavata Purāṇa*, the Sanskrit sacred narrative (*purāṇa*) of the life and deeds of the god Krishna, is completed	
11th century Somadeva writes the Sanskrit compendium of stories called **Kathāsaritsāgara** (Ocean to the Rivers of Story) for Queen Sūryamatī of Kashmir	1000 The Cōḻa king Rajaraja I builds a great temple for the Hindu god Śiva at Tanjore in south India
12th century Kampaṉ authors the *Irāmāvatāram*, a version of the **Rāmāyaṇa** epic in Tamil • The Buddhist monk Vidyākara of Bengal (in eastern India) compiles the *Subhāṣitaratnakoṣa* (Treasury of Well-Turned Verse), an anthology of Sanskrit lyric poems • Cēkkiḻār completes the *Periyapurāṇam* (The Great Sacred History), a long poem on the lives of the Tamil saints who are devotees of Śiva • Jayadeva composes the Sanskrit lyric-dramatic poem *Gītagovinda* in Bengal, on Krishna's love for the herdswoman Rādhā, the central theme of later poetry about Krishna	ca. 1100–1200 Buddhist monuments are built at Angkor Wat in Cambodia

ca. 1193 Turkish warrior Qutb-ud-din Aibak captures the city of Delhi, initiating a period of several centuries of rule in north India by Delhi-based Muslim kings |

VIṢṆUŚARMAN
second or third century

The *Pañcatantra* (The Five Books *or* The Five Strategies), attributed to Viṣṇuśarman, is the best-known collection of folktales and animal fables in Indian literature. A Gupta-period work in the ornate classical *kāvya* style, the *Pañcatantra* went through many subsequent revisions. Translated into old Persian as early as the mid-seventh century and brought by the Arabs to Europe in the eighth, it is also the source of some of the best-known tales in Middle Eastern and European collections such as the *Thousand and One Nights*, the *Decameron*, the *Canterbury Tales*, Grimm's *Fairy Tales*, and the fables of La Fontaine and Aesop.

If the Buddhists used the animal fable as a vehicle for teaching religious and ethical values (see the *Jātaka*, p. 1002), the *Pañcatantra's* central concern is *nīti* ("conduct"), a term connoting a range of explicitly worldly values, most important among which are political expediency and social advantage. The work's prologue, in which we are told that the brahman scholar Viṣṇuśarman used the fables as a strategy to teach the science of politics to three dull-witted princes, affirms its affiliation with the world of kings and policymakers.

Each of the five books of the *Pañcatantra* begins with a frame story, whose characters tell each other stories illustrating the conduct appropriate to diverse social and political situations. The characters within these illustrative tales tell each other stories as well, and so on, until the nested tales eventually lead back to the frame story. The *Pañcatantra* is most probably the source from which the author of the *Thousand and One Nights* adopted the device of the emboxed story, which was eventually incorporated into the European tale collections, although it is in the *Pañcatantra*—and in classical Indian narrative literature in general—that the technique is found at its most complex. As in the Buddhist *Jātaka* tales, each tale in the *Pañcatantra* begins with a narrator reciting an epigrammatic verse that at once summarizes the tale's lesson and points to its subject matter, thus arousing the listener's curiosity. Stylistically, however, the ornate classical prose and elegant *kāvya* stanzas of the *Pañcatantra* are a far cry from the simpler Pali *Jātakas*.

While it is not certain that the *Pañcatantra's* author intended it, the word *tantra* in the work's title can mean "strategy" as well as "book." The main themes of the *Pañcatantra* are reflected in the titles of its five books; and at least in the case of the first four books, the book's main topic corresponds to one of the topics in the *Arthaśāstra* (Manual of Political Theory), the pre-eminent Gupta period treatise on political science. The frame narrative of Book I (*The Loss of Friends*) traces the sowing of dissension between the lion Rusty (Piṅgalaka), king of the beasts, and the mighty bull Lively (Saṃjīvaka), by the former's crafty counselors, the jackals Cheek (Karaṭaka) and Victor (Damanaka). Book II (*The Winning of Friends*) concerns the successful course of friendship among four animals of the forest. Book III (*Crows and Owls*) treats the war between the owls and crows, sworn enemies of each other. The processes by which the animals in these books make friends (*mitra*) and enemies (*para*) closely resemble the strategies of alliance and war Kauṭilya delineates for ancient Indian kings. Books IV and V (*Loss of Gains* and *Ill-Considered Action*) are more broadly concerned with strategies for worldly success.

Among the most appealing features of the *Pañcatantra* is its humorous and faithful portrayal of human nature in all its variety. As in other cultures, the animals of village and forest are assigned stereotypical human traits. Thus the lion, king of animals, is powerful and proud but easily duped; the jackal, like the European fox, is cunning and deceitful; the cat is a hypocrite. Charmingly appropriate names alert the reader to the salient traits of each animal character: the bull of the frame story of Book I is called Lively; the sage of the mouse-maid tale is Godly; and three temperamentally differentiated fish are Forethought, Readywit, and Fatalist.

The *Pañcatantra* bases its counsel on the premises that social life is both necessary and inevitable and that we must make the best of our condition as social beings. Unlike the epics, the animal stories teach not the Hindu ideals of behavior according to the code of *dharma*, but *nīti*, which, as noted earlier, broadly connotes worldly wisdom and the art of living in the world. The *Pañcatantra* views friendship properly contracted, maintained, and used as the sine qua non of social life, but it does not idealize friendship. The world of these stories is a cruel place in which the strong oppress those weaker than themselves, and yet the weak not only survive but triumph over adversity, provided they are intelligent, find the right allies, and have the will and ability to act.

The *Pañcatantra* stories do not offer simple solutions to life's dilemmas. To act wisely, one must exercise discrimination and judgment. Treachery awaits the unwary at every turn, and those who are gullible perish, but paranoia is equally dangerous, as the brahman's wife learns after she has killed the innocent mongoose (in *The Loyal Mungoose*). In her decision to stick to her own kind Mouse-maid (in *Mouse-Maid Made Mouse*) is motivated by a desire for emotional as well as social security in a hierarchically organized, minutely differentiated society. On the other hand, Creep the louse's friendship with Leap the flea (*Leap and Creep*) is doomed to disaster as much because of Creep's trusting a fool as her stepping over social boundaries. Indeed, the frame story of Book II, featuring the felicitous friendship of four such unlikely animals as a deer, a turtle, a mouse, and a crow, demonstrates that some difference is essential to really fruitful alliances. Then again, the whole of Book III (*Crows and Owls*) is devoted to the theme of unending strife between those who are "natural" enemies, such as owls and crows and the snake and the mongoose. The enduring popularity of the *Pañcatantra* animal stories—at home and abroad—is due at least in part to their complex mix of realism and optimism and their essentially pluralistic vision of social relations.

Arthur W. Ryder's translation of *The Pañcatantra* (1956) is faithful to the Sanskrit text, conveying in good measure the liveliness and wit of the original. For the history of the *Pañcatantra* and its transmission to the Middle East and Europe, see Maurice Winternitz, *A History of Indian Literature* (1963), and Joseph Jacobs, *History of the Aesopic Fable* (1889). Francis Hutchins offers a fine translation of the *Hitopadeśa*, with many illustrations, in *Animal Fables from India; Nārāyaṇa's Hitopadesha or Friendly Counsel* (1985).

PRONOUNCING GLOSSARY

The following list uses common English syllables and stress accents to provide rough equivalents of selected words whose pronunciation may be unfamiliar to the general reader.

Arthaśāstra: *uhrt-huh-shahs'-truh*

Bṛhatkathā: *bree-huht'-kuht-hah*

Damanaka: *duh-muh'-nuh-kuh*

Hitopadeśa: *hee-toh-puh-day'-shuh*

Jātaka: *jah'-tuh-kuh*

Karaṭaka: *kuh-ruh'-tuh-kuh*

Kathāsaritsāgara: *kuht-hah'-suh-reet-sah'-guh-ruh*

Kauṭilya: *kow-teel'-yuh*

Mūladeva: *moo'-luh-day'-vuh*

Nārāyana: *nah-rah'-yuh-nuh*

Pañcatantra: *puhn'-chuh-tuhn'-truh*

Piṅgalaka: *peen'-guh-luh-kuh*

Saṃjīvaka: *suhn-jee'-vuh-kuh*

Viṣṇuśarman: *veesh'-noo-shuhr'-muhn*

Yājñavalkya: *yahg-nyuh-vuhl'-kyuh*

From Pañcatantra[1]

From *Book I*

The Loss of Friends

*   *   *

"With no stranger share your house;
Leap, the flea, killed Creep, the louse."

"How was that?" asked Rusty. And Victor[2] told the story of

LEAP AND CREEP

In the palace of a certain king stood an incomparable bed, blessed with every cubiculary virtue. In a corner of its coverlet lived a female louse named Creep. Surrounded by a thriving family of sons and daughters, with the sons and daughters of sons and daughters, and with more remote descendants, she drank the king's blood as he slept. On this diet she grew plump and handsome.

While she was living there in this manner, a flea named Leap drifted in on the wind and dropped on the bed. This flea felt supreme satisfaction on examining the bed—the wonderful delicacy of its coverlet, its double pillow, its exceptional softness like that of a broad, Gangetic sand-bank, its delicious perfume.[3] Charmed by the sheer delight of touching it, he hopped this way and that until—fate willed it so—he chanced to meet Creep, who said to him: "Where do *you* come from? This is a dwelling fit for a king. Begone, and lose no time about it." "Madam," said he, "you should not say such things. For

The Brahman reverences fire,[4]
Himself the lower castes' desire;
The wife reveres her husband dear;
But all the world must guests revere.

Now I am your guest. I have of late sampled the various blood of Brahmans, warriors, business men, and serfs, but found it acid, slimy, quite unwholesome. On the contrary, he who reposes on this bed must have a delightful vital fluid, just like nectar. It must be free from morbidity, since wind, bile, and phlegm are kept in harmony by constant and heedful use of potions prepared by physicians. It must be enriched by viands unctuous, tender, melting in the mouth; viands prepared from the flesh of the choicest creatures of land, water, and air, seasoned furthermore with sugar, pomegranate, ginger, and pepper. To me it seems an elixir of life. Therefore, with your kind permission, I plan to taste this sweet and fragrant substance, thus combining pleasure and profit."

"No," said she. "For fiery-mouthed stingers like you, it is out of the question. Leave this bed. You know the proverb:

---

1. Translated by Arthur W. Ryder.   2. In the principal frame narrative of Book I, Victor the jackal tells this story to Rusty the lion.   3. This is a parody of the involved style of description found in the more ornate classical *kāvya* poems. *Gangetic:* of the Ganges River.   4. Refers to the sacred fire of Hindu ritual.

The fool who does not know
His own resource, his foe,
His duty, time, and place,
Who sets a reckless pace,
Will by the wayside fall,
Will reap no fruit at all."

Thereupon he fell at her feet, repeating his request. And she agreed, since courtesy was her hobby, and since, when the story of that prince of sharpers, Muladeva,[5] was being repeated to the king while she lay on a corner of the coverlet, she had heard how Muladeva quoted this verse in answer to the question of a certain damsel:

Whoever, angry though he be,
Has spurned a suppliant enemy,
In Shiva, Vishnu, Brahma,[6] he
Has scorned the Holy Trinity.

Recalling this, she agreed, but added: "However, you must not come to dinner at a wrong place or time." "What is the right place and what is the right time?" he asked. "Being a newcomer, I am not *au courant.*" And she replied: "When the king's body is mastered by wine, fatigue, or sleep, then you may quietly bite him on the feet. This is the right place and the right time." To these conditions he gave his assent.

In spite of this arrangement, the famished bungler, when the king had just dozed off in the early evening, bit him on the back. And the poor king, as if burned by a firebrand, as if stung by a scorpion, as if touched by a torch, bounded to his feet, scratched his back, and cried to a servant: "Rascal! Somebody bit me. You must hunt through this bed until you find the insect."

Now Leap heard the king's command and in terrified haste crept into a crevice in the bed. Then the king's servants entered, and following their master's orders, brought a lamp and made a minute inspection. As fate would have it, they came upon Creep as she crouched in the nap of the fabric, and killed her with her family.

"And that is why I say:"
With no stranger share your house, ...

and the rest of it. And another thing. My lord and king does wrong in neglecting the servants who are his by inheritance. For

Whoever leaves his friends,
Strange folk to cherish,
Like foolish Fierce-Howl, will
Untimely perish."

"How was that?" asked Rusty. And Victor told the story of

THE BLUE JACKAL

There was once a jackal named Fierce-Howl, who lived in a cave near the suburbs of a city. One day he was hunting for food, his throat pinched with

---

5. A hero in the well-known Sanskrit romance *Bṛhatkathā* (The Great Romance). See also *Kathāsaritsāgara* (p. 1345).   6. Gods of the Hindu triad. Shiva (Śiva) is the destroyer god. Vishnu (Viṣṇu) is the preserver god. Brahma is the creator god.

hunger, and wandered into the city after nightfall. There the city dogs snapped at his limbs with their sharp-pointed teeth, and terrified his heart with their dreadful barking, so that he stumbled this way and that in his efforts to escape and happened into the house of a dyer. There he tumbled into a tremendous indigo vat, and all the dogs went home.

Presently the jackal—further life being predestined—managed to crawl out of the indigo vat and escaped into the forest. There all the thronging animals in his vicinity caught a glimpse of his body dyed with the juice of indigo, and crying out: "What is this creature enriched with that unprecedented color?" they fled, their eyes dancing with terror, and spread the report: "Oh, oh! Here is an exotic creature that has dropped from somewhere. Nobody knows what his conduct might be, or his energy. We are going to vamoose. For the proverb says:

> Where you do not know
> Conduct, stock, and pluck,
> 'Tis not wise to trust,
> If you wish for luck."

Now Fierce-Howl perceived their dismay, and called to them: "Come, come, you wild things! Why do you flee in terror at sight of me? For Indra,[7] realizing that the forest creatures have no monarch, anointed me—my name is Fierce-Howl—as your king. Rest in safety within the cage formed by my resistless paws."

On hearing this, the lions, tigers, leopards, monkeys, rabbits, gazelles, jackals, and other species of wild life bowed humbly, saying: "Master, prescribe to us our duties." Thereupon he appointed the lion prime minister and the tiger lord of the bedchamber, while the leopard was made custodian of the king's betel,[8] the elephant doorkeeper, and the monkey the bearer of the royal parasol. But to all the jackals, his own kindred, he administered a cuffing, and drove them away. Thus he enjoyed the kingly glory, while lions and others killed food-animals and laid them before him. These he divided and distributed to all after the manner of kings.

While time passed in this fashion, he was sitting one day in his court when he heard the sound made by a pack of jackals howling near by. At this his body thrilled, his eyes filled with tears of joy, he leaped to his feet, and began to howl in a piercing tone. When the lions and others heard this, they perceived that he was a jackal, and stood for a moment shamefaced and downcast, then they said: "Look! We have been deceived by this jackal. Let the fellow be killed." And when he heard this, he endeavored to flee, but was torn to bits by a tiger and died.

> "And that is why I say:
> Whoever leaves his friends, ..."

and the rest of it."

*   *   *

FORETHOUGHT, READYWIT, AND FATALIST[9]

In a great lake lived three full-grown fishes, whose names were Forethought, Readywit, and Fatalist. Now one day the fish named Forethought

---

7. The king of the gods.   8. The leaves of this plant are chewed as a digestive and stimulant in India.
9. In the frame story Constance the plover tells this story to her mate, Sprawl.

overheard passers-by on the bank and fishermen saying: "There are plenty of fish in this pond. Tomorrow we go fishing."

On hearing this, Forethought reflected: "This looks bad. Tomorrow or the day after they will be sure to come here. I will take Readywit and Fatalist and move to another lake whose waters are not troubled." So he called them and put the question.

Thereupon Readywit said: "I have lived long in this lake and cannot move in such a hurry. If fishermen come here, then I will protect myself by some means devised for the occasion."

But poor, doomed Fatalist said: "There are sizable lakes elsewhere. Who knows whether they will come here or not? One should not abandon the lake of his birth merely because of such small gossip. And the proverb says:

> Since scamp and sneak and snake
> So often undertake
> A plan that does not thrive,
> The world wags on, alive.

Therefore I am determined not to go." And when Forethought realized that their minds were made up, he went to another body of water.

On the next day, when he had gone, the fishermen with their boys beset the inner pool, cast a net, and caught all the fish without exception. Under these circumstances Readywit, while still in the water, played dead. And since they thought: "This big fellow died without help," they drew him from the net and laid him on the bank, from which he wriggled back to safety in the water. But Fatalist stuck his nose into the meshes of the net, struggling until they pounded him repeatedly with clubs and so killed him.

"And that is why I say:

> Forethought and Readywit thrive;
> Fatalist can't keep alive."

*   *   *

From *Book III*

Crows and Owls

*   *   *

> "Though mountain, sun, and cloud, and wind
>   Were suitors at her feet,
> The mouse-maid turned a mouse again—
>   Nature is hard to beat."

"How was that?" asked Live-Strong. And Red-Eye told the story of

MOUSE-MAID MADE MOUSE[1]

The billows of the Ganges were dotted with pearly foam born of the leaping of fishes frightened at hearing the roar of the waters that broke on the rugged,

---

1. In the frame story of Book III, Red-Eye, the counselor of the king of the owls, tells this story to Live-Strong, the counsel of the king of the crows.

rocky shore. On the bank was a hermitage crowded with holy men devoting their time to the performance of sacred rites—chanting, self-denial, self-torture, study, fasting, and sacrifice. They would take purified water only, and that in measured sips. Their bodies wasted under a diet of bulbs, roots, fruits, and moss. A loin-cloth made of bark formed their scanty raiment.

The father of the hermitage was named Yajnavalkya. After he had bathed in the sacred stream and had begun to rinse his mouth, a little female mouse dropped from a hawk's beak and fell into his hand. When he saw what she was, he laid her on a banyan leaf, repeated his bath and mouth-rinsing, and performed a ceremony of purification. Then through the magic power of his holiness, he changed her into a girl, and took her with him to his hermitage.

As his wife was childless, he said to her: "Take her, my dear wife. She has come into life as your daughter, and you must rear her carefully." So the wife reared her and spoiled her with petting. As soon as the girl reached the age of twelve, the mother saw that she was ready for marriage, and said to her husband: "My dear husband, how can you fail to see that the time is passing when your daughter should marry?"

And he replied: "You are quite right, my dear. The saying goes:

> Before a man is gratified,
> These gods must treat her as a bride—
> The fire, the moon, the choir of heaven;
> In this way, no offense is given.
>
> Holiness is the gift of fire;   5
> A sweet voice, of the heavenly choir;
> The moon gives purity within:
> So is a woman free from sin.
>
> Before nubility, 'tis said
> That she is white; but after, red;   10
> Before her womanhood is plain,
> She is, though naked, free from stain.
>
> The moon, in mystic fashion, weds
> A maiden when her beauty spreads;
> The heavenly choir, when bosoms grow;   15
> The fire, upon the monthly flow.
>
> To wed a maid is therefore good
> Before developed womanhood;
> Nor need the loving parents wait
> Beyond the early age of eight.[2]   20
>
> The early signs one kinsman slay;
> The bosom takes the next away;
> Friends die for passion gratified;
> The father, if she ne'er be bride.
>
> For if she bides a maiden still,   25
> She gives herself to whom she will;
> Then marry her in tender age:
> So warns the heaven-begotten sage.

2. Eight indeed was considered a good age for marriage.

If she, unwed, unpurified,
Too long within the home abide,   30
She may no longer married be:
A miserable spinster, she.

A father then, avoiding sin,
Weds her,[3] the appointed time within
(Where'er a husband may be had)   35
To good, indifferent, or bad.

Now I will try to give her to one of her own station. You know the saying:

Where wealth is very much the same,
And similar the family fame,
Marriage (or friendship) is secure;
But not between the rich and poor.

And finally:

Aim at seven things in marriage;
All the rest you may disparage:

But

Get money, good looks,
And knowledge of books,
Good family, youth,
Position, and truth.

"So, if she is willing, I will summon the blessèd sun, and give her to him."
"I see no harm in that," said his wife. "Let it be done."

The holy man therefore summoned the sun, who appeared without delay,
and said: "Holy sir, why am I summoned?" The father said: "Here is a daughter of mine. Be kind enough to marry her." Then, turning to his daughter,
he said: "Little girl, how do you like him, this blessèd lamp of the three
worlds?"[4] "No, father," said the girl. "He is too burning hot. I could not like
him. Please summon another one, more excellent than he is."

Upon hearing this, the holy man said to the sun: "Blessèd one, is there
any superior to you?" And the sun replied: "Yes, the cloud is superior even
to me. When he covers me, I disappear."

So the holy man summoned the cloud next, and said to the maiden: "Little
girl, I will give you to him." "No," said she. "This one is black and frigid. Give
me to someone finer than he."

Then the holy man asked: "O cloud, is there anyone superior to you?" And
the cloud replied: "The wind is superior even to me."

So he summoned the wind, and said: "Little girl, I give you to him."
"Father," said she, "this one is too fidgety. Please invite somebody superior
even to him." So the holy man said: "O wind, is there anyone superior to
you?" "Yes," said the wind. "The mountain is superior to me."

So he summoned the mountain and said to the maiden: "Little girl, I give
you to him." "Oh, father," said she. "He is rough all over, and stiff. Please
give me somebody else."

---

3. Following the Indian tradition of arranged marriages, the father finds a suitable bridegroom for his
daughter.   4. That is, heaven, earth, and the underworld.

So the holy man asked: "O kingly mountain, is there anyone superior even to you?" "Yes," said the mountain. "Mice are superior to me."

Then the holy man summoned a mouse, and presented him to the girl, saying: "Little girl, do you like this mouse?"

The moment she saw him, she felt: "My own kind, my own kind," and her body thrilled and quivered, and she said: "Father dear, turn me into a mouse, and give me to him. Then I can keep house as my kind of people ought to do."

And her father, through the magic power of his holiness, turned her into a mouse, and gave her to him.

* * *

From *Book V*

Ill-Considered Action

* * *

> Let the well-advised be done;
> Ill-advised leave unbegun:
> Else, remorse will be let loose,
> As with lady and mungoose.

"How was that?" asked Jewel. And they told the story of

THE LOYAL MUNGOOSE[5]

There was once a Brahman named Godly in a certain town. His wife mothered a single son and a mungoose. And as she loved little ones, she cared for the mungoose also like a son, giving him milk from her breast, and salves, and baths, and so on. But she did not trust him, for she thought: "A mungoose is a nasty kind of creature. He might hurt my boy." Yes, there is sense in the proverb:

> A son will ever bring delight,
> Though bent on folly, passion, spite,
> Though shabby, naughty, and a fright.[6]

One day she tucked her son in bed, took a water-jar, and said to her husband: "Now, Professor,[7] I am going for water. You must protect the boy from the mungoose." But when she was gone, the Brahman went off somewhere himself to beg food,[8] leaving the house empty.

While he was gone, a black snake issued from his hole and, as fate would have it, crawled toward the baby's cradle. But the mungoose, feeling him to be a natural enemy, and fearing for the life of his baby brother, fell upon the vicious serpent halfway, joined battle with him, tore him to bits, and tossed the pieces far and wide. Then, delighted with his own heroism, he ran, blood

---

5. A band of judges tells this story to Jewel the merchant. A mungoose (mongoose) is a small mammal and a natural enemy of snakes, which it can kill and eat without harm to itself.   6. A great value is placed on sons in the Indian family.   7. Priestly brahmans study the *Vedas* and other ritual texts.   8. Brahmans are entitled to live on alms; those priests without ritual commissions are obliged to live by begging.

trickling from his mouth, to meet the mother; for he wished to show what he had done.

But when the mother saw him coming, saw his bloody mouth and his excitement, she feared that the villain must have eaten her baby boy, and without thinking twice, she angrily dropped the water-jar upon him, which killed him the moment that it struck. There she left him without a second thought, and hurried home, where she found the baby safe and sound, and near the cradle a great black snake, torn to bits. Then, overwhelmed with sorrow because she had thoughtlessly killed her benefactor, her son, she beat her head and breast.

At this moment the Brahman came home with a dish of rice gruel which he had got from someone in his begging tour, and saw his wife bitterly lamenting her son, the mungoose. "Greedy! Greedy!" she cried. "Because you did not do as I told you, you must now taste the bitterness of a son's death, the fruit of the tree of your own wickedness. Yes, this is what happens to those blinded by greed. For the proverb says:

> Indulge in no excessive greed
> (A little helps in time of need)—
> A greedy fellow in the world
> Found on his head a wheel that whirled."[9]

*   *   *

9. This verse is the come-on for the next story.

KĀLIDĀSA
fourth century

Kālidāsa, the author of the Sanskrit play *Abhijñānaśākuntala* (Śakuntalā and the Ring of Recollection, commonly referred to as *Śākuntala*), is India's preeminent classical poet. As with other great writers of the classical era, his life is clothed in popular legend, but royal inscriptions and other sources indicate that he flourished during the Gupta period, between 390 and 470, possibly in Ujjayinī (Ujjain), the Gupta capital in north India, where he may have served at the court of the greatest of the Gupta kings, Candragupta II (375–415), called Vikramāditya (Like the Sun in Valor).

Śākuntala is the most beloved of Indian plays. Sir William Jones's English translation (1789) created a sensation in Europe, especially in Germany, where it had a powerful impact on Goethe and the writers of the German Romantic movement. Rooted in the values of India's classical civilization, and at the same time articulating a profoundly human vision, this play about lovers parted and reunited transcends cultural particularities.

The plot, adapted from an older epic tale, is simplicity itself. On seeing the lovely maiden Śakuntalā in the enchanting setting of the woodland hermitage presided over by the sage Kaṇva, Duṣyanta (model king and romantic hero) inevitably falls in love with her. The young woman, daughter of a celestial nymph and a child of nature, returns his passion. Circumstances cause the lovers to part. A sage's curse and the loss of the king's signet ring result in the king's forgetting his liaison with Śakuntalā, and plunge her into further suffering, far away from her lover. The recovery of the ring jogs the king's memory, and now it is his turn to suffer, not knowing where to find his beloved. With the intervention of gods and sages, the lovers are reunited, together with their young son.

In Sanskrit dramaturgy, *Śakuntala* is a heroic romance (*nāṭaka*), a play about love between a noble hero and a beautiful woman. The *nāṭaka* is the most important of the ten types of plays (*rūpaka*, "representation") described in the classical texts on dramaturgy. While in some respects the play resembles the romantic comedies of the Western tradition, such as Euripides' *Alcestis* or Shakespeare's *Winter's Tale*, its cultural premises and aesthetic goals are entirely different from those of Greek or Shakespearean drama, following instead the canons of Bharata's *Nāṭyaśāstra* (ca. second century), the authoritative text on aesthetics and dramatic theory.

Some Sanskrit critics consider drama (*nāṭya*) to be the best of the *kāvya* genres, because it is most inclusive, or complete. Although rhythmic speech is the only expressive medium available to lyric poetry, with the occasional addition of music, drama has at its command both prose and lyric verse as well as an entire range of nonverbal expression. Hence it is also called, from the perspective of the audience, "poetry to be seen" (*dṛśyakāvya*), as opposed to other kinds of *kāvya* texts, which are "poetry to be heard" (*śravyakāvya*). From stage directions in the texts themselves and from ancient accounts and treatises on dramatic theory, we know that extensive use was made of stylized gesture, facial expression, eye movement, music, and dance in enacting the poetic text. Meaning was to be conveyed to the audience through *abhinaya*, acting conceived as a symphony of "languages," the verbal text being only one of them. The *Nāṭyaśāstra* treats dance, music, and poetry as aspects of dramatic action in the unified aesthetic of *rasa*, preserved in the major traditions of classical dance in India today.

In classical aesthetic theory, *rasa* signifies "sentiment" or "mood," the aesthetic experience evoked by the artistic depiction of human emotion. Sanskrit poetic theory distinguishes eight fundamental emotions (*bhāva*), expressed in eight major *rasas*, ranging from the erotic to the horrific. (Later tradition added "the calm" as a ninth.) According to Bharata, both text and performance are aimed at such emotional states, stimulating in readers and viewers their aesthetic flavor. This is not *actual* emotion but rather its universalized counterpart, to be conveyed through the stylized interplay of text, character, and the nuances of affect and response produced by the actors. Where real emotion limits by its particularity, *rasa* liberates the individual from the limitations of the everyday world, propelling him or her toward a higher apprehension of beauty, an experience of extraordinary universality.

Like all Sanskrit plays, *Śakuntala* ends in happiness and harmony because it must do so. The absence of tragedy sharply differentiates Sanskrit drama from Greek drama, its ancient counterpart in the Western tradition. Tragedy is impossible in the Hindu and Buddhist conceptual universes, in which time and life function as open-ended cycles and human beings are linked with nature and the cosmos through *karma*—impersonal networks of volition, action, and response. The characters of the Sanskrit drama, especially the hero and heroine, are types, not individuals. The universalization of emotion in aesthetic terms depends on the predictability of character and behavior; kings, sages, and beautiful women are defined by their social roles and dramatic personae and must look, speak, and behave in entirely recognizable ways. The individual will and personal destiny, which are essential to the notion of tragedy, have no place in this vision.

Performed at seasonal festivals and auspicious occasions such as weddings, the ancient dramas were regarded as rites of renewal and order. The goal of Sanskrit drama is to reestablish emotional harmony in the spectators by showing underlying correspondences that reconcile the apparent conflicts of existence. In *Śakuntala*, the realization of the play's dominant mood, the erotic *rasa*, turns on the tension between duty (*dharma*) and desire (*kāma*), traced through the relationship between the king and Śakuntalā. At first each acts impulsively, moved purely by passion. In the end, each is refined by duty and chastened by suffering. The king needs Śakuntalā, as she needs him, for both the reclusive life of the hermitage and the outwardly vital life of the court are, in reality, incomplete and sterile. The ideal life is the life of the golden mean, of mutually tempered duty and desire, of vitality shaped by self-control, of nature celebrated as culture's foundation and its complement. At the end of *Śakuntala*, through the intense, transporting savoring of *rasa*, we are to reach a state of integrity with ourselves and our world.

The curse and the loss and recovery of the ring, the "chance" events that guide the course of the plot, are Kālidāsa's invention, necessitated precisely by an ideal of plot that is not "action" in the Aristotelian sense but a chart of emotional interactions. We trace not the progression of external events but the finely calibrated play of suggested emotional states, through individual moments and "scenes" such as the one in which we observe the king watching Śakuntalā from his hidden vantage point, while the frightened young woman wards off an annoying bee. We must also remember that the full effect of the text is to be realized in performance, with the actors suggesting the transitory emotions of eagerness, fear, and nascent attraction, through dance, mime, gesture, the language of the eyes, and in the king's case, lyric verse. The verses and songs in *Śakuntala* embody moments of concentrated emotion in the progression of the plot.

The effectiveness of a Sanskrit play depends to a great extent on canonically required contrasts and complementarities among its diverse elements. The contrasts in Kālidāsa's play—between lyric verse and prose dialogue; the erotic and the heroic moods; the gluttonous buffoon and the disciplined king; the Sanskrit spoken by noblemen and the Prakrit dialects assigned to women, children, and male characters of the lower castes (including the buffoon who, although he is a high-caste brahman, normally speaks Prakrit)—are staples of Sanskrit dramatic theory. The play's plot, too, is analyzable according to the precisely delineated stages and junctures of the ideal dramatic plot according to Bharata. The contrasts in *Śakuntala*, however, transcend these traditional requirements. Court and hermitage, the active and the contemplative life, are pitted against each other, as are the domestic and public worlds and the emotional universes of women and men. The women's rites in Act IV contrast with the king's court of Act V; Duṣyanta moves freely between earthly and celestial hermitages, Indra's court in heaven, and his own on earth, paralleling the audience's movement, through the prologue, from the real world into the world of the theater.

Among the many excellences impossible to convey in translation are the limpid clarity and sweetness of Kālidāsa's language and the powerful imagery and formal perfection of his lyric verse. His genius shines equally in his deep feeling for nature and the delicate and personal sensibility he brings to the stereotyped characters and situations of his play. The comparison between women and nature is a commonplace of Sanskrit poetry, rooted in the notion of the relatedness of all life, but Śakuntalā's personal kinship with nature makes her unforgettable. Born of a nymph and a sage but reared by the *śakunta* birds of the forest, Kālidāsa's heroine expresses a touching love of the plants, birds, and deer of her adoptive father's hermitage. Act IV, in which the animals and plants bid farewell to the heroine as one of their own, is in the original a passage of haunting, lyrical beauty and affective power.

In contrast to the heroine, and similar to the other kings of Kālidāsa's poems and plays, Duṣyanta is an establishment figure, in whose persona the poet gathers up the conservative values of *dharma* and the royal ethic of action and protection. It is clear from the focus of the psychological plot, however, that the king's heroic persona is equally grounded in his vulnerability to the awakening of love and its permeation into the depths of his being. In Indian thought, with its framework of *karma* and rebirth, all learning is recognition or recollection, a recovery or retrieval, through memory, of lost knowledge and lost sensibilities. Memory can carry us back not only into the past in this life but to the pasts of all our previous lives. In this sense then, love is a union with our deepest selves. In the symbolic acts of recollection in the play, and in the very symbol after which the play is named, "the ring of recollection or recognition," Kālidāsa has given profound artistic expression to the Indian belief that memory and love have the power of making human lives whole.

Barbara Stoler Miller, ed., *Theater of Memory: The Plays of Kālidāsa* (1984), contains the best translations of Kālidāsa's three plays, along with an excellent introduction to Sanskrit drama and dramaturgy. A selection of the major Sanskrit plays is available in (adapted) translation in P. Lal, *Great Sanskrit Plays* (1964). In *Two Plays of Ancient India* (1968) J. A. B. van Buitenen has translated Śūdraka's *Mṛcchakaṭikā* (The Little Clay Cart) and Viśākhadatta's *Mudrārākṣasa* (Rākṣasa's Signet ring), major plays of the Gupta period, both very different from *Śākuntala*. For a comparative perspective, see Henry W. Wells, *The Classical Drama of India* (1963). Readers interested in Kālidāsa's lyric poems should consult the beautiful translations of the court epic *Kumārasaṃbhava* in Hank Heifetz, *The Origin of the Young God* (1985), and of the minor lyric poem *Meghadūta* in Leonard Nathan, *The Transport of Love* (1976).

PRONOUNCING GLOSSARY

The following list uses common English syllables and stress accents to provide rough equivalents of selected words whose pronunciation may be unfamiliar to the general reader.

Abhijñānaśākuntala: *uhb-hee-gnyah'-nuh-shah'-koon-tuh-luh*

Anasūyā: *uh-nuh-soo'-yah*

Aparājitā: *uh-puh-rah'-jee-tah*

aśoka: *uh-shoh'-kuh*

Ayodhyā: *uh-yodh'-yah*

Bhāratavarṣa: *bah'-ruh-tuh-vuhr-shuh*

cakravāka: *chuhk-ruh-vah'-kuh*

cakravartin: *chuhk'-ruh-vuhr-teen*

Candragupta: *chuhn'-druh-goop-tuh*

Caturikā: *chuh-too'-ree-kah*

Dakṣa: *duhk'-shuh*

Dhanamitra: *duh'-nuh-meet-ruh*

dṛśyakāvya: *dreesh'-yuh-kahv'-yuh*

Durvāsas: *door-vah'-suhs*

Duṣyanta: *doosh-yuhn'-tuh*

Haṃsapadikā: *huhm'-sah-puh-dee-kah*

Hastināpura: *huhs'-tee-nah-poo-ruh*

Jayanta: *juh-yuhn'-tuh*

Kālanemi: *kah'-luh-nay-mee*

Karabhaka: *kuh-ruh'-buh-kuh*

kṣatriya: *kshuh'-tree-yuh*

Mādhavya: *mahd'-huhv-yuh*

Madhukarikā: *muhd'-hoo-kuh-ree-kah*

Mārīca: *mah-ree'-chuh*

Marīci: *muh-ree'-chee*

Mitrāvasu: *meet-rah'-vuh-soo*

mokṣa: *mohk'-shuh*

Nāṭyaśāstra: *naht-yuh-shahs'-truh*

Parabhṛtikā: *puh'-ruh-bree-tee-kah*

Parivaha: *puh-ree'-vuh-huh*

Paulomī: *pow'-loh-mee*

Priyaṃvadā: *pree-yuhm'-vuh-dah*

Puru: *poo'-roo*

Raivataka: *rai'-vuh-tuh-kuh*

śakunta: *shuh-koon'-tuh*

Śākuntala: *shah-koon'-tuh-luh*

Śakuntalā: *shuh-koon'-tuh-lah*

śamī: *shuh'-mee*

Sānumatī: *sah'-noo-muh-tee*

Śāradvata: *shah'-ruhd-vuh-tuh*

Śārṅgarava: *shahrn'-guh-ruh-vuh*

Sarvadamana: *suhr'-vuh-duh-muh-nuh*

śirīṣa: *shee-ree'-shuh*

Somarāta: *soh-muh-rah'-tuh*

Somatīrtha: *soh-muh-teert'-huh*

śravyakāvya: *shruhv'-yuh-kahv'-yuh*

śṛṅgāra: *shreen-gah'-ruh*

Sūcaka: *soo'-chuh-kuh*

svabhāvokti: *svuh-bah'-voh-tee*

svarga: *svuhr'-guh*

svayaṃvara: *svuh-yuhm'-vuh-ruh*

Taralikā: *tuh-ruh'-lee-kah*

Triśaṅku: *tree-shuhn'-koo*

Triṣṭubh: *treesh'-toob*

Vasumatī: *vuh-soo'-muh-tee*

Vātāyana: *vah-tah'-yuh-nuh*

Vetravatī: *vay'-truh-vuh-tee*

vidūṣaka: *vee-doo'-shuh-kuh*

Viṣṇu: *veesh'-noo*

Viśvāmitra: *veesh-vah'-meet-truh*

yakṣī: *yuhk'-shee*

Śakuntalā and the Ring of Recollection[1]

CHARACTERS

Players in the prologue:
DIRECTOR: Director of the players and manager of the theater.
ACTRESS: The lead actress.

Principal roles:
KING: Duṣyanta, the hero; ruler of Hastināpura; a royal sage of the lunar dynasty of Puru.
ŚAKUNTALĀ: The heroine; daughter of the royal sage Viśvāmitra and the celestial nymph Menakā; adoptive daughter of the ascetic Kaṇva.
BUFFOON: Māḍhavya, the king's comical brahman companion.

Members of Kaṇva's hermitage:
ANASŪYĀ and PRIYAMVADĀ: Two young female ascetics; friends of Śakuntalā.
KAṆVA: Foster father of Śakuntalā and master of the hermitage; a sage belonging to the lineage of the divine creator Marīci, and thus related to Mārīca.
GAUTAMĪ: The senior female ascetic.
ŚĀRṄGARAVA and ŚĀRADVATA: Kaṇva's disciples.
Various inhabitants of the hermitage: a monk with his two pupils, two boy ascetics (named Gautama and Nārada), a young disciple of Kaṇva, a trio of female ascetics.

Members of the king's forest retinue:
CHARIOTEER: Driver of the king's chariot.
GUARD: Raivataka, guardian of the entrance to the king's quarters.
GENERAL: Commander of the king's army.
KARABHAKA: Royal messenger.
Various attendants, including Greco-Bactrian bow-bearers.

Members of the king's palace retinue:
CHAMBERLAIN: Vātāyana, chief officer of the king's household.
PRIEST: Somarāta, the king's religious preceptor and household priest.
DOORKEEPER: Vetravatī, the female attendant who ushers in visitors and presents messages.
PARABHṚTIKĀ and MADHUKARIKĀ: Two maids assigned to the king's garden.
CATURIKĀ: A maidservant.

City dwellers:
MAGISTRATE: The king's low-caste brother-in-law; chief of the city's policemen.

---

1. Translated by Barbara Stoler Miller.

POLICEMEN: Sūcaka and Jānuka.
FISHERMAN: An outcaste.

Celestials:
MĀRĪCA: A divine sage; master of the celestial hermitage in which Śakuntalā gives birth to her son; father of Indra, king of the gods, whose armies Duṣyanta leads.
ADITI: Wife of Mārīca.
MĀTALI: Indra's charioteer.
SĀNUMATĪ: A nymph; friend of Śakuntalā's mother Menakā.

Various members of Mārīca's hermitage: two female ascetics, Mārīca's disciple Gālava.
BOY: Sarvadamana, son of Śakuntalā and Duṣyanta; later known as Bharata.

Offstage voices:
VOICES OFFSTAGE: From the backstage area or dressing room; behind the curtain, out of view of the audience. The voice belongs to various players before they enter the stage, such as the monk, Śakuntalā's friends, the buffoon, Mātali; also to figures who never enter the stage, such as the angry sage Durvāsas, the two bards who chant royal panegyrics (*vaitālikau*).
VOICE IN THE AIR: A voice chanting in the air from somewhere offstage: the bodiless voice of Speech quoted in Sanskrit by Priyaṁvadā; the voice of a cuckoo who represents the trees of the forest blessing Śakuntalā in Sanskrit; the voice of Haṁsapadikā singing a Prakrit love song.

The setting of the play shifts from the forest hermitage (Acts I–IV) to the palace (Acts V–VI) to the celestial hermitage (Act VII). The season is early summer when the play begins and spring during the sixth act; the passage of time is otherwise indicated by the birth and boyhood of Śakuntalā's son.

Act I

The water that was first created,
the sacrifice-bearing fire, the priest,
the time-setting sun and moon,
audible space that fills the universe,
what men call nature,[2] the source of all seeds,   5
the air that living creatures breathe—
through his eight embodied forms,
may Lord Śiva come to bless you![3]

---

2. Here, earth.   3. This verse is a *nāndī* ("benedictory verse") recited at the beginning of a Sanskrit play, immediately after the preparatory rituals performed before a dramatic performance in ancient India. The benedictory verses of Sanskrit plays usually invoke the blessings of Śiva, dancer of the cosmic dance of creation and destruction as well as patron god of the drama. In this verse, Kālidāsa praises Śiva as the cosmic divinity pervading the universe in his eight manifest forms—the five elements (ether, air, fire, water, and earth), the sun and moon, and the sacrificing priest.

Prologue

DIRECTOR: [*Looking backstage.*] If you are in costume now, madam, please come on stage! 10

ACTRESS: I'm here, sir.[4]

DIRECTOR: Our audience is learned. We shall play Kālidāsa's new drama called *Śakuntalā and the Ring of Recollection*. Let the players take their parts to heart!

ACTRESS: With you directing, sir, nothing will be lost. 15

DIRECTOR: Madam, the truth is:

> I find no performance perfect
> until the critics are pleased;
> the better trained we are
> the more we doubt ourselves. 20

ACTRESS: So true . . . now tell me what to do first!

DIRECTOR: What captures an audience better than a song? Sing about the new summer season and its pleasures:

> To plunge in fresh waters
> swept by scented forest winds 25
> and dream in soft shadows
> of the day's ripened charms.

ACTRESS: [*Singing.*]

> Sensuous women
> in summer love
> weave 30
> flower earrings
> from fragile petals
> of mimosa
> while wild bees
> kiss them gently.[5] 35

DIRECTOR: Well sung, madam! Your melody enchants the audience. The silent theater is like a painting. What drama should we play to please it?

ACTRESS: But didn't you just direct us to perform a new play called *Śakuntalā and the Ring of Recollection?* 40

DIRECTOR: Madam, I'm conscious again! For a moment I forgot.

> The mood of your song's melody
> carried me off by force,
> just as the swift dark antelope
> enchanted King Duṣyanta. 45

[*They both exit; the prologue ends. Then the* KING *enters with his* CHARIOTEER, *in a chariot, a bow and arrow in his hand, hunting an antelope.*]

---

4. The prologues to many plays present the actress as the director's wife.   5. Such verses are sung by women in Prakrit and set to a melody, whereas the Sanskrit *kāvya* verses of the play are recited or sung to a simple tune that follows the rhythmic pattern of the verse quarter. The women's songs generally feature nature descriptions or the nuances of love in natural settings.

CHARIOTEER: [*Watching the* KING *and the antelope.*]

> I see this black buck move
> as you draw your bow
> and I see the wild bowman Śiva,
> hunting the dark antelope.[6]

KING: Driver, this antelope has drawn us far into the forest. There he   50
is again:

> The graceful turn of his neck
> as he glances back at our speeding car,
> the haunches folded into his chest
> in fear of my speeding arrow,   55
> the open mouth dropping
> half-chewed grass on our path—
> watch how he leaps, bounding on air,
> barely touching the earth.

> [*He shows surprise.*]
> Why is it so hard to keep him in sight?   60

CHARIOTEER: Sir, the ground was rough. I tightened the reins to slow
the chariot and the buck raced ahead. Now that the path is smooth,
he won't be hard to catch.

KING: Slacken the reins!

CHARIOTEER: As you command, sir. [*He mimes the speeding chariot.*]   65
Look!

> Their legs extend as I slacken the reins,
> plumes and manes set in the wind, ears angle back;
> our horses outrun their own clouds of dust,
> straining to match the antelope's speed.   70

KING: These horses would outrace the steeds of the sun.[7]

> What is small suddenly looms large,
> split forms seem to reunite,
> bent shapes straighten before my eyes—
> from the chariot's speed   75
> nothing ever stays distant or near.

CHARIOTEER: The antelope is an easy target now. [*He mimes the fixing
of an arrow.*]

VOICE OFFSTAGE: Stop! Stop, king! This antelope belongs to our hermitage! Don't kill him!

CHARIOTEER: [*Listening and watching.*] Sir, two ascetics are pro-   80
tecting the black buck from your arrow's deadly aim.

KING: [*Showing confusion.*] Rein in the horses!

CHARIOTEER: It is done!

> [*He mimes the chariot's halt. Then a* MONK *enters with* TWO PUPILS,
> *his hand raised.*]

---

6. The comparison is based on an ancient myth of Śiva's pursuit of the creator god Prajāpati, who had
taken the form of an antelope. The verse flatters the king.   7. The seven horses that draw the sun god's
chariot.

MONK: King, this antelope belongs to our hermitage.
Withdraw your well-aimed arrow! Your weapon should rescue vic- 85
tims, not destroy the innocent!
KING: I withdraw it. [*He does as he says.*]
MONK: An act worthy of the Puru dynasty's shining light!

> Your birth honors
> the dynasty of the moon![8] 90
> May you beget a son
> to turn the wheel of your empire![9]

THE TWO PUPILS: [*Raising their arms.*] May you beget a son to turn the
wheel of your empire!
KING: [*Bowing.*] I welcome your blessing. 95
MONK: King, we were going to gather firewood.[1] From here you can see
the hermitage[2] of our master Kaṇva on the bank of the Mālinī river.
If your work permits, enter and accept our hospitality.

> When you see the peaceful rites of devoted ascetics,
> you will know how well your scarred arm protects us.[3] 100

KING: Is the master of the community there now?
MONK: He went to Somatīrtha,[4] the holy shrine of the moon, and put
his daughter Śakuntalā in charge of receiving guests. Some evil
threatens her, it seems.
KING: Then I shall see her. She will know my devotion and commend 105
me to the great sage.
MONK: We shall leave you now.
[*He exits with his pupils.*]
KING: Driver, urge the horses on! The sight of this holy hermitage will
purify us.
CHARIOTEER: As you command, sir. [*He mimes the chariot's speed.*] 110
KING: [*Looking around.*] Without being told one can see that this is a
grove where ascetics live.
CHARIOTEER: How?
KING: Don't you see—

> Wild rice grains under trees 115
> where parrots nest in hollow trunks,
> stones stained by the dark oil
> of crushed iṅgudī nuts,[5]
> trusting deer who hear human voices
> yet don't break their gait, 120
> and paths from ponds streaked
> by water from wet bark cloth.[6]

CHARIOTEER: It is perfect.

---

8. Known as the "lunar dynasty," because it traces its descent to the moon god. 9. Any ancient Indian emperor is a *cakravartin*, a turner of the wheel of empire. 1. For the fire rituals and Vedic sacrifices performed at the hermitage. 2. It includes men and women and is organized like an extended family. 3. One of a king's chief duties is to protect hermits and ascetics. 4. A place of pilgrimage in western India. 5. These nuts are pressed by forest dwellers for oil. 6. Forest dwellers wear a cloth made of tree bark.

KING: [*Having gone a little inside.*] We should not disturb the grove!
Stop the chariot and let me get down! 125
CHARIOTEER: I'm holding the reins. You can dismount now, sir.
KING: [*Dismounting.*] One should not enter an ascetics' grove in hunt-
ing gear. Take these! [*He gives up his ornaments and his bow.*] Driver,
rub down the horses while I pay my respects to the residents of the
hermitage! 130
CHARIOTEER: Yes, sir! [*He exits.*]
KING: This gateway marks the sacred ground. I will enter.
[*He enters, indicating he feels an omen.*]

> The hermitage is a tranquil place,
> yet my arm is quivering . . .
> do I feel a false omen of love 135
> or does fate have doors everywhere?

VOICE OFFSTAGE: This way, friends!
KING: [*Straining to listen.*] I think I hear voices to the right of the grove.
I'll find out.
[*Walking around and looking.*]
Young female ascetics with watering pots cradled on their hips are 140
coming to water the saplings. [*He mimes it in precise detail.*] This
view of them is sweet.

> These forest women have beauty
> rarely seen inside royal palaces—
> the wild forest vines far surpass 145
> creepers in my pleasure garden.

I'll hide in the shadows and wait.
[ŚAKUNTALĀ *and her two friends enter, acting as described.*]
ŚAKUNTALĀ: This way, friends!
ANASŪYĀ: I think Father Kaṇva cares more about the trees in the her-
mitage than he cares about you. You're as delicate as a jasmine, yet 150
he orders you to water the trees.
ŚAKUNTALĀ: Anasūyā, it's more than Father Kaṇva's order. I feel a sis-
ter's love for them. [*She mimes the watering of trees.*]
KING: [*To himself.*] Is this Kaṇva's daughter? The sage does show poor
judgment in imposing the rules of the hermitage on her. 155

> The sage who hopes to subdue
> her sensuous body by penances
> is trying to cut firewood
> with a blade of blue-lotus leaf.

Let it be! I can watch her closely from here in the trees. 160
[*He does so.*]
ŚAKUNTALĀ: Anasūyā, I can't breathe! Our friend Priyaṁvadā tied my
bark dress too tightly! Loosen it a bit!
ANASŪYĀ: As you say. [*She loosens it.*]
PRIYAṀVADĀ: [*Laughing.*] Blame your youth for swelling your breasts.
Why blame me? 165
KING: This bark dress fits her body badly, but it ornaments her
beauty . . .

A tangle of duckweed adorns a lotus,
a dark spot heightens the moon's glow,
the bark dress increases her charm—   170
beauty finds its ornaments anywhere.

ŚAKUNTALĀ: [*Looking in front of her.*] The new branches on this mimosa tree are like fingers moving in the wind, calling to me. I must go to it! [*Saying this, she walks around.*]

PRIYAMVADĀ: Wait, Śakuntalā! Stay there a minute! When you stand   175 by this mimosa tree, it seems to be guarding a creeper.

ŚAKUNTALĀ: That's why your name means "Sweet-talk."[7]

KING: "Sweet-talk" yes, but Priyaṁvadā speaks the truth about Śakuntalā:

Her lips are fresh red buds,   180
her arms are tendrils,
impatient youth is poised
to blossom in her limbs.

ANASŪYĀ: Śakuntalā, this is the jasmine creeper who chose the mango tree in marriage,[8] the one you named "Forestlight." Have you for-   185 gotten her?

ŚAKUNTALĀ: I would be forgetting myself? [*She approaches the creeper and examines it.*] The creeper and the tree are twined together in perfect harmony. Forestlight has just flowered and the new mango shoots are made for her pleasure.   190

PRIYAMVADĀ: [*Smiling.*] Anasūyā, don't you know why Śakuntalā looks so lovingly at Forestlight?

ANASŪYĀ: I can't guess.

PRIYAMVADĀ: The marriage of Forestlight to her tree makes her long to have a husband too.   195

ŚAKUNTALĀ: You're just speaking your own secret wish. [*Saying this, she pours water from the jar.*]

KING: Could her social class be different from her father's?[9] There's no doubt!

She was born to be a warrior's bride,
for my noble heart desires her—   200
when good men face doubt,
inner feelings are truth's only measure.

Still, I must learn everything about her.

ŚAKUNTALĀ: [*Flustered.*] The splashing water has alarmed a bee. He is flying from the jasmine to my face. [*She dances to show the bee's*   205 *attack.*]

KING: [*Looking longingly.*]

7. The characters of the two friends correspond to their names: Anasūyā (Without Envy) is a serious, straightforward, decisive young woman, while Priyaṃvadā (Sweet Talker) loves to tease and laugh and has a way with words. As noted above, the women speak Prakrit, whereas the king and other upper-class male characters speak Sanskrit.   8. In calling the jasmine creeper *svayaṃvara-vadhū* ("bride by her own choice"), Anasūyā refers to the public ceremony called *svayaṃvara* ("choosing one's own bridegroom") in which women of the warrior class chose their own husbands, thus foreshadowing Śakuntalā's own action later in the play.   9. Marrying outside one's class in the fourfold Hindu scheme of classes (*varṇa*) is forbidden. As the sage Kaṇva's daughter, Śakuntalā would be a brahman, and the king, being of the *kṣatriya* (warrior) class, would not be allowed to marry her.

> Bee, you touch the quivering
> corners of her frightened eyes,
> you hover softly near
> to whisper secrets in her ear;
> a hand brushes you away,   210
> but you drink her lips' treasure—
> while the truth we seek defeats us,
> you are truly blessed.

ŚAKUNTALĀ: This dreadful bee won't stop. I must escape. [*She steps to one side, glancing about.*] Oh! He's pursuing me. . . . Save me! 215 Please save me! This mad bee is chasing me!

BOTH FRIENDS: [*Laughing.*] How can we save you? Call King Duṣyanta. The grove is under his protection.

KING: Here's my chance. Have no fear . . . [*With this half-spoken, he stops and speaks to himself.*] Then she will know that I am the king. 220 . . . Still, I shall speak.

ŚAKUNTALĀ: [*Stopping after a few steps.*] Why is he still following me?

KING: [*Approaching quickly.*]

> While a Puru king rules the earth
> to punish evildoers,
> who dares to molest   225
> these innocent young ascetics?

[*Seeing the* KING, *all act flustered.*]

ANASŪYĀ: Sir, there's no real danger. Our friend was frightened when a bee attacked her. [*She points to* ŚAKUNTALĀ.]

KING: [*Approaching* ŚAKUNTALĀ.] Does your ascetic practice go well?

[ŚAKUNTALĀ *stands speechless.*]

ANASŪYĀ: It does now that we have a special guest. Śakuntalā, go to 230 our hut and bring the ripe fruits. We'll use this water to bathe his feet.[1]

KING: Your kind speech is hospitality enough.

PRIYAMVADĀ: Please sit in the cool shadows of this shade tree and rest, sir.   235

KING: You must also be tired from your work.

ANASŪYĀ: Śakuntalā, we should respect our guest. Let's sit down. [*All sit.*]

ŚAKUNTALĀ: [*To herself.*] When I see him, why do I feel an emotion that the forest seems to forbid?

KING: [*Looking at each of the girls.*] Youth and beauty complement 240 your friendship.

PRIYAMVADĀ: [*In a stage whisper.*] Anasūyā, who is he? He's so polite, fine looking, and pleasing to hear. He has the marks of royalty.

ANASŪYĀ: I'm curious too, friend. I'll just ask him. [*Aloud.*] Sir, your kind speech inspires trust. What family of royal sages do you adorn? 245 What country mourns your absence? Why does a man of refinement subject himself to the discomfort of visiting an ascetics' grove?[2]

---

1. A traditionally mandated rite of hospitality.   2. Anasūyā uses the formal, florid style of courtly conversation.

ŚAKUNTALĀ: [*To herself.*] Heart, don't faint! Anasūyā speaks your thoughts.   250
KING: [*To himself.*] Should I reveal myself now or conceal who I am? I'll say it this way: [*Aloud.*] Lady, I have been appointed by the Puru king as the officer in charge of religious matters. I have come to this sacred forest to assure that your holy rites proceed unhindered.
ANASŪYĀ: Our religious life has a guardian now.   255
     [ŚAKUNTALĀ *mimes the embarrassment of erotic emotion.*]
BOTH FRIENDS: [*Observing the behavior of* ŚAKUNTALĀ *and the* KING; *in a stage whisper.*] Śakuntalā, if only your father were here now!
ŚAKUNTALĀ: [*Angrily.*] What if he were?
BOTH FRIENDS: He would honor this distinguished guest with what he values most in life.
ŚAKUNTALĀ: Quiet! Such words hint at your hearts' conspiracy. I won't   260
listen.
KING: Ladies, I want to ask about your friend.
BOTH FRIENDS: Your request honors us, sir.
KING: Sage Kaṇva has always been celibate, but you call your friend his daughter. How can this be?   265
ANASŪYĀ: Please listen, sir. There was a powerful royal sage[3] of the Kauśika clan . . .
KING: I am listening.
ANASŪYĀ: He begot our friend, but Kaṇva is her father because he cared for her when she was abandoned.   270
KING: "Abandoned"? The word makes me curious. I want to hear her story from the beginning.
ANASŪYĀ: Please listen, sir. Once when this great sage was practicing terrible austerities on the bank of the Gautamī river, he became so powerful that the jealous gods sent a nymph named Menakā to   275
break his self-control.[4]
KING: The gods dread men who meditate.
ANASŪYĀ: When springtime came to the forest with all its charm, the sage saw her intoxicating beauty . . .
KING: I understand what happened then. She is the nymph's daughter.   280
ANASŪYĀ: Yes.
KING: It had to be!

> No mortal woman could give birth to such beauty—
> lightning does not flash out of the earth.

     [ŚAKUNTALĀ *stands with her face bowed. The* KING *continues speaking to himself.*]
My desire is not hopeless. Yet, when I hear her friends teasing her   285
about a bridegroom, a new fear divides my heart.
PRIYAMVADĀ: [*Smiling, looking at* ŚAKUNTALĀ, *then turning to the* KING.]
Sir, you seem to want to say more.
     [ŚAKUNTALĀ *makes a threatening gesture with her finger.*]

---

3. Viśvāmitra, who was born in the warrior class but acquired the spiritual powers of a brahman sage.
4. A standard theme in classical Indian mythology, appearing in the narratives of the life of the Buddha as well. The gods feel threatened by the supernatural powers that ascetics amass through self-denial.

KING: You judge correctly. In my eagerness to learn more about your
pious lives, I have another question.
PRIYAMVADĀ: Don't hesitate! Ascetics can be questioned frankly.   290
KING: I want to know this about your friend:

> Will she keep the vow of hermit life
> only until she marries . . .
> or will she always exchange
> loving looks with deer in the forest?   295

PRIYAMVADĀ: Sir, even in her religious life, she is subject to her father,
but he does intend to give her to a suitable husband.
KING: [To himself.] His wish is not hard to fulfill.

> Heart, indulge your desire—
> now that doubt is dispelled,   300
> the fire you feared to touch
> is a jewel in your hands.

ŚAKUNTALĀ: [Showing anger.] Anasūyā, I'm leaving!
ANASŪYĀ: Why?
ŚAKUNTALĀ: I'm going to tell Mother Gautamī that Priyamvadā is talk-   305
ing nonsense.
ANASŪYĀ: Friend, it's wrong to neglect a distinguished guest and leave
as you like.[5]
[ŚAKUNTALĀ starts to go without answering.]
KING: [Wanting to seize her, but holding back, he speaks to himself.] A
lover dare not act on his impulsive thoughts!

> I wanted to follow the sage's daughter,   310
> but decorum abruptly pulled me back;
> I set out and returned again
> without moving my feet from this spot.

PRIYAMVADĀ: [Stopping ŚAKUNTALĀ.] It's wrong of you to go!
ŚAKUNTALĀ: [Bending her brow into a frown.] Give me a reason why!   315
PRIYAMVADĀ: You promised to water two trees for me. Come here and
pay your debt before you go! [She stops her by force.]
KING: But she seems exhausted from watering the trees:

> Her shoulders droop, her palms
> are red from the watering pot—   320
> even now, breathless sighs
> make her breasts shake;
> beads of sweat on her face
> wilt the flower at her ear;
> her hand holds back   325
> disheveled locks of hair.

Here, I'll pay her debt!
[He offers his ring. Both friends recite the syllables of the name on
the seal and stare at each other.][6]

---

5. Śakuntalā's failure here foreshadows her neglect of this duty and its consequences later in the play.
6. A clear indication that women were part of the literate courtly culture of classical India.

Don't mistake me for what I am not! This is a gift from the king to identify me as his royal official.

PRIYAMVADĀ: Then the ring should never leave your finger. Your word 330 has already paid her debt. [*She laughs a little.*] Śakuntalā, you are freed by this kind man . . . or perhaps by the king. Go now!

ŚAKUNTALĀ: [*To herself.*] If I am able to . . . [*Aloud.*] Who are you to keep me or release me?

KING: [*Watching* ŚAKUNTALĀ.] Can she feel toward me what I feel 335 toward her? Or is my desire fulfilled?

> She won't respond directly to my words,
> but she listens when I speak;
> she won't turn to look at me,
> but her eyes can't rest anywhere else. 340

VOICE OFFSTAGE: Ascetics, be prepared to protect the creatures of our forest grove! King Duṣyanta is hunting nearby!

> Dust raised by his horses' hooves
> falls like a cloud of locusts swarming
> at sunset over branches of trees 345
> where wet bark garments hang.

> In terror of the chariots, an elephant
> charged into the hermitage
> and scattered the herd of black antelope,
> like a demon foe of our penances— 350
> his tusks garlanded with branches
> from a tree crushed by his weight,
> his feet tangled in vines
> that tether him like chains.

[*Hearing this, all the girls are agitated.*]

KING: [*To himself.*] Oh! My palace men are searching for me and 355 wrecking the grove. I'll have to go back.

BOTH FRIENDS: Sir, we're all upset by this news. Please let us go to our hut.

KING: [*Showing confusion.*] Go, please. We will try to protect the hermitage. 360

[*They all stand to go.*]

BOTH FRIENDS: Sir, we're ashamed that our bad hospitality is our only excuse to invite you back.

KING: Not at all. I am honored to have seen you.

[ŚAKUNTALĀ *exits with her two friends, looking back at the* KING, *lingering artfully.*]

I have little desire to return to the city. I'll join my men and have them camp near the grove. I can't control my feelings for Śakun- 365 talā.

> My body turns to go,
> my heart pulls me back,
> like a silk banner
> buffeted by the wind. 370

[*All exit.*]

Act II

[*The* BUFFOON *enters, despondent.*]
BUFFOON: [*Sighing.*] My bad luck! I'm tired of playing sidekick to a
king who's hooked on hunting.[7] "There's a deer!" "There's a boar!"
"There's a tiger!" Even in the summer midday heat we chase from
jungle to jungle on paths where trees give barely any shade. We drink
stinking water from mountain streams foul with rusty leaves.   5
At odd hours we eat nasty meals of spit-roasted meat. Even at night
I can't sleep. My joints ache from galloping on that horse. Then at
the crack of dawn, I'm woken rudely by a noise piercing the forest.
Those sons of bitches hunt their birds then. The torture doesn't
end—now I have sores on top of my bruises. Yesterday, we lagged   10
behind. The king chased a buck into the hermitage. As luck would
have it, an ascetic's daughter called Śakuntalā caught his eye. Now
he isn't even thinking of going back to the city. This very dawn I
found him wide-eyed, mooning about her. What a fate! I must see
him after his bath. [*He walks around, looking.*] Here comes my   15
friend now, wearing garlands of wild flowers. Greek women carry his
bow in their hands.[8] Good! I'll stand here pretending my arms and
legs are broken. Maybe then I'll get some rest.
[*He stands leaning on his staff. The* KING *enters with his retinue, as
described.*]
KING: [*To himself.*]

My beloved will not be easy to win,
but signs of emotion revealed her heart—   20
even when love seems hopeless,
mutual longing keeps passion alive.

[*He smiles.*] A suitor who measures his beloved's state of mind by his
own desire is a fool.

She threw tender glances   25
though her eyes were cast down,
her heavy hips swayed
in slow seductive movements,
she answered in anger
when her friend said, "Don't go!"   30
and I felt it was all for my sake . . .
but a lover sees in his own way.

BUFFOON: [*Still in the same position.*] Dear friend, since my hands can't
move to greet you, I have to salute you with my voice.
KING: How did you cripple your limbs?   35
BUFFOON: Why do you ask why I cry after throwing dust in my eyes
yourself?

---

7. The brahman *vidūṣaka* (buffoon), though the king's constant companion, differs from him in every
respect, from his obsession with creature comforts and his cowardice to his coarse language. A caricature
of the learned brahman and Sanskrit scholar, the buffoon speaks only Prakrit and is incapable of versifying.
8. In Kālidāsa's plays the king's bow bearers are identified as *yavanī* ("Greek women"). North Indian kings
of the Gupta age and earlier employed Bactrian Greek women as bodyguards and bow bearers.

KING: I don't understand.

BUFFOON: Dear friend, when a straight reed is twisted into a crooked reed, is it by its own power, or is it the river current?[9] 40

KING: The river current is the cause.

BUFFOON: And so it is with me.

KING: How so?

BUFFOON: You neglect the business of being a king and live like a woodsman in this awful camp. Chasing after wild beasts every day 45
jolts my joints and muscles till I can't control my own limbs anymore. I beg you to let me rest for just one day!

KING: [To himself.] He says what I also feel. When I remember Kaṇva's daughter, the thought of hunting disgusts me.

> I can't draw my bowstring 50
> to shoot arrows at deer
> who live with my love
> and teach her tender glances.[1]

BUFFOON: Sir, you have something on your mind. I'm crying in a wilderness.[2] 55

KING: [Smiling.] Yes, it is wrong to ignore my friend's plea.

BUFFOON: Live long! [He starts to go.]

KING: Dear friend, stay! Hear what I have to say!

BUFFOON: At your command, sir!

KING: When you have rested, I need your help in some work that you 60
will enjoy.

BUFFOON: Is it eating sweets? I'm game!

KING: I shall tell you. Who stands guard?

GUARD: [Entering.] At your command, sir!

KING: Raivataka! Summon the general! 65

[The GUARD exits and reenters with the GENERAL.]

GUARD: The king is looking this way, waiting to give you his orders. Approach him, sir!

GENERAL: [Looking at the KING.] Hunting is said to be a vice,[3] but our king prospers.

> Drawing the bow only hardens his chest, 70
> he suffers the sun's scorching rays unburned,
> hard muscles mask his body's lean state—
> like a wild elephant, his energy sustains him.

[He approaches the KING.] Victory, my lord! We've already tracked some wild beasts. Why the delay? 75

KING: Mādhavya's[4] censure of hunting has dampened my spirit.

GENERAL: [In a stage whisper, to the BUFFOON.] Friend, you stick to your opposition! I'll try to restore our king's good sense. [Aloud.] This fool is talking nonsense. Here is the king as proof:

---

9. Like Shakespeare's fools, the buffoon likes to speak in riddles. 1. A comparison of women's eyes with the eyes of deer, conventional in Sanskrit poetry. 2. A paraphrase of the Sanskrit proverbial expression *araṇyaruditam* ("a cry in the wilderness"); this is an expression of his puzzlement at the king's behavior. 3. The censure of hunting in Hindu law reflects the influence of the theory of *karma* rebirth and the impact of nonviolent creeds. 4. The buffoon's.

A hunter's belly is taut and lean,   80
his slender body craves exertion;
he penetrates the spirit of creatures
overcome by fear and rage;
his bowmanship is proved
by arrows striking a moving target—   85
hunting is falsely called a vice.
What sport can rival it?

BUFFOON: [*Angrily.*] The king has come to his senses. If you keep chasing from forest to forest, you'll fall into the jaws of an old bear hungry
for a human nose . . .   90
KING: My noble general, we are near a hermitage; your words cannot
please me now.

Let horned buffaloes plunge into muddy pools!
Let herds of deer huddle in the shade to eat grass!
Let fearless wild boars crush fragrant swamp grass!   95
Let my bowstring lie slack and my bow at rest!

GENERAL: Whatever gives the king pleasure.
KING: Withdraw the men who are in the forest now and forbid my
soldiers to disturb the grove!

Ascetics devoted to peace   100
possess a fiery hidden power,
like smooth crystal sunstones
that reflect the sun's scorching rays.

GENERAL: Whatever you command, sir!
BUFFOON: Your arguments for keeping up the hunt fall on deaf ears!   105
[*The* GENERAL *exits.*]
KING: [*Looking at his* RETINUE.] You women, take away my hunting
gear! Raivataka, don't neglect your duty!
RETINUE: As the king commands!
[*They exit.*]
BUFFOON: Sir, now that the flies are cleared out, sit on a stone bench
under this shady canopy. Then I'll find a comfortable seat too.   110
KING: Go ahead!
BUFFOON: You first, sir!
[*Both walk about, then sit down.*]
KING: Mādhavya, you haven't really used your eyes because you haven't
seen true beauty.
BUFFOON: But you're right in front of me, sir!   115
KING: Everyone is partial to what he knows well, but I'm speaking about
Śakuntalā, the jewel of the hermitage.
BUFFOON: [*To himself.*] I won't give him a chance! [*Aloud.*] Dear friend,
it seems that you're pursuing an ascetic's daughter.
KING: Friend, the heart of a Puru king wouldn't crave a forbidden   120
fruit . . .

The sage's child is a nymph's daughter,
rescued by him after she was abandoned,

> like a fragile jasmine blossom
> broken and caught on a sunflower pod.   125

BUFFOON: [*Laughing.*] You're like the man who loses his taste for dates and prefers sour tamarind![5] How can you abandon the gorgeous gems of your palace?

KING: You speak this way because you haven't seen her.

BUFFOON: She must be delectable if you're so enticed!   130

KING: Friend, what is the use of all this talk?

> The divine creator imagined perfection
> and shaped her ideal form in his mind—
> when I recall the beauty his power wrought,
> she shines like a gemstone among my jewels.   135

BUFFOON: So she's the reason you reject the other beauties!

KING: She stays in my mind:

> A flower no one has smelled,
> a bud no fingers have plucked,
> an uncut jewel, honey untasted,   140
> unbroken fruit of holy deeds—
> I don't know who is destined
> to enjoy her flawless beauty.

BUFFOON: Then you should rescue her quickly! Don't let her fall into the arms of some ascetic who greases his head with ingudī oil!   145

KING: She is someone else's ward and her guardian is away.

BUFFOON: What kind of passion did her eyes betray?

KING: Ascetics are timid by nature:

> Her eyes were cast down in my presence,
> but she found an excuse to smile—   150
> modesty barely contained the love
> she could neither reveal nor conceal.

BUFFOON: Did you expect her to climb into your lap when she'd barely seen you?

KING: When we parted her feelings for me showed despite her modesty.   155

> "A blade of kuśa grass[6]
> pricked my foot,"
> the girl said for no reason
> after walking a few steps away;   160
> then she pretended to free
> her bark dress from branches
> where it was not caught
> and shyly glanced at me.

BUFFOON: Stock up on food for a long trip! I can see you've turned that ascetics' grove into a pleasure garden.   165

KING: Friend, some of the ascetics recognize me. What excuse can we find to return to the hermitage?

---

5. A fruit, the extract of which is used to flavor Indian sauces.   6. Used in Hindu sacred rites.

BUFFOON: What excuse? Aren't you the king? Collect a sixth of their
wild rice as tax!   170
KING: Fool! These ascetics pay tribute that pleases me more than
mounds of jewels.

> Tribute that kings collect
> from members of society decays,
> but the share of austerity   175
> that ascetics give lasts forever.[7]

VOICE OFFSTAGE: Good, we have succeeded!
KING: [Listening.] These are the steady, calm voices of ascetics.
GUARD: [Entering.] Victory, sir! Two boy ascetics are waiting near the
gate.   180
KING: Let them enter without delay!
GUARD: I'll show them in. [He exits; reenters with the boys.] Here you
are!
FIRST BOY: His majestic body inspires trust. It is natural when a king is
virtually a sage.[8]   185

> His palace is a hermitage
> with its infinite pleasures,
> the discipline of protecting men
> imposes austerities every day—
> pairs of celestial bards praise   190
> his perfect self-control,
> adding the royal word "king"
> to "sage," his sacred title.

SECOND BOY: Gautama, is this Duṣyanta, the friend of Indra?[9]
FIRST BOY: Of course!   195
SECOND BOY:

> It is no surprise that this arm of iron
> rules the whole earth bounded by dark seas—
> when demons harass the gods, victory's hope
> rests on his bow and Indra's thunderbolt.

BOTH BOYS: [Coming near.] Victory to you, king!   200
KING: [Rising from his seat.] I salute you both!
BOTH BOYS: To your success, sir! [They offer fruits.]
KING: [Accepting their offering.] I am ready to listen.
BOTH BOYS: The ascetics know that you are camped nearby and send
a petition to you.   205
KING: What do they request?
BOTH BOYS: Demons are taking advantage of Sage Kaṇva's absence to
harass us.[1] You must come with your charioteer to protect the her-
mitage for a few days!

---

7. The king values the sacred power that the sages amass through self-denial.   8. While Duṣyanta may
appear worldly to a modern audience, his sacred royal office, his respect for the sages, and his disciplined
adherence to the standards of dharma make him, in the sages' eyes, a person of tremendous self-
control.   9. His friendship with Indra underscores the king's status as the earthly counterpart of the king
of the gods.   1. The motif of a royal hero slaying demons who destroy the sacred rituals of forest sages,
as seen in the Rāmāyaṇa (p. 890), is traditional.

KING: I am honored to oblige. 210
BUFFOON: [*In a stage whisper.*] Your wish is fulfilled!
KING: [*Smiling.*] Raivataka, call my charioteer! Tell him to bring the
 chariot and my bow!
GUARD: As the king commands! [*He exits.*]
BOTH BOYS: [*Showing delight.*]

> Following your ancestral duties 215
> suits your noble form—
> the Puru kings are ordained
> to dispel their subjects' fear.

KING: [*Bowing.*] You two return! I shall follow.
BOTH BOYS: Be victorious! [*They exit.*] 220
KING: Mādhavya, are you curious to see Śakuntalā?
BUFFOON: At first there was a flood, but now with this news of demons,
 not a drop is left.
KING: Don't be afraid! Won't you be with me?
BUFFOON: Then I'll be safe from any demon . . . 225
GUARD: [*Entering.*] The chariot is ready to take you to victory . . . but
 Karabhaka has just come from the city with a message from the
 queen.
KING: Did my mother send him?
GUARD: She did. 230
KING: Have him enter then.
GUARD: Yes. [*He exits; reenters with* KARABHAKA.] Here is the king.
 Approach!
KARABHAKA: Victory, sir! Victory! The queen has ordered a ceremony
 four days from now to mark the end of her fast. Your Majesty will 235
 surely give us the honor of his presence.
KING: The ascetics' business keeps me here and my mother's command
 calls me there. I must find a way to avoid neglecting either!
BUFFOON: Hang yourself between them the way Triśaṅku[2] hung
 between heaven and earth. 240
KING: I'm really confused . . .

> My mind is split in two
> by these conflicting duties,
> like a river current split
> by boulders in its course. 245

[*Thinking.*] Friend, my mother has treated you like a son. You must
go back and report that I've set my heart on fulfilling my duty to the
ascetics. You fulfill my filial duty to the queen.
BUFFOON: You don't really think I'm afraid of demons?
KING: [*Smiling.*] My brave brahman, how could you be? 250
BUFFOON: Then I can travel like the king's younger brother.

---

2. A mythic king who was left suspended between heaven and earth in a contest of power between the
sage Viśvāmitra and the gods.

KING: We really should not disturb the grove! Take my whole entourage with you!

BUFFOON: Now I've turned into the crown prince!

KING: [To himself.] This fellow is absent-minded. At any time he may 255 tell the palace women about my passion. I'll tell him this: [Taking the BUFFOON by the hand, he speaks aloud.] Dear friend, I'm going to the hermitage out of reverence for the sages. I really feel no desire for the young ascetic Śakuntalā.

> What do I share with a rustic girl 260
> reared among fawns, unskilled in love?
> Don't mistake what I muttered
> in jest for the real truth, friend!

[All exit.]

Act III

[A disciple of KAṆVA enters, carrying kuśa grass for a sacrificial rite.]
DISCIPLE: King Duṣyanta is certainly powerful. Since he entered the hermitage, our rites have not been hindered.

> Why talk of fixing arrows?
> The mere twang of his bowstring
> clears away menacing demons 5
> as if his bow roared with death.

I'll gather some more grass for the priests to spread on the sacrificial altar. [Walking around and looking, he calls aloud.] Priyaṁvadā, for whom are you bringing the ointment of fragrant lotus root fibers and leaves? [Listening.] What are you saying? Śakuntalā is suffering 10 from heat exhaustion? They're for rubbing on her body? Priyaṁvadā, take care of her! She is the breath of Father Kaṇva's life. I'll give Gautamī this water from the sacrifice to use for soothing her.

[He exits; the interlude ends. Then the KING enters, suffering from love, deep in thought, sighing.]
KING:

> I know the power ascetics have
> and the rules that bind her, 15
> but I cannot abandon my heart
> now that she has taken it.

[Showing the pain of love.] Love, why do you and the moon both contrive to deceive lovers by first gaining our trust?

> Arrows of flowers and cool moon rays 20
> are both deadly for men like me—

the moon shoots fire through icy rays
and you hurl thunderbolts of flowers.

[*Walking around.*] Now that the rites are concluded and the priests
have dismissed me, where can I rest from the weariness of this   25
work? [*Sighing.*] There is no refuge but the sight of my love. I must
find her. [*Looking up at the sun.*] Śakuntalā usually spends the heat
of the day with her friends in a bower of vines on the Mālinī river-
bank. I shall go there. [*Walking around, miming the touch of breeze.*]
This place is enchanted by the wind.   30

> A breeze fragrant with lotus pollen
> and moist from the Mālinī waves
> can be held in soothing embrace
> by my love-scorched arms.

[*Walking around and looking.*]

> I see fresh footprints   35
> on white sand in the clearing,
> deeply pressed at the heel
> by the sway of full hips.

I'll just look through the branches. [*Walking around, looking, he
becomes joyous.*] My eyes have found bliss! The girl I desire is lying   40
on a stone couch strewn with flowers, attended by her two friends.
I'll eavesdrop as they confide in one another. [*He stands watching.*
ŚAKUNTALĀ *appears as described, with her two friends.*]
BOTH FRIENDS: [*Fanning her affectionately.*] Śakuntalā, does the breeze
from this lotus leaf please you?
ŚAKUNTALĀ: Are you fanning me?   45
[*The friends trade looks, miming dismay.*]
KING: [*Deliberating.*] Śakuntalā seems to be in great physical pain. Is
it the heat or is it what is in my own heart? [*Miming ardent desire.*]
My doubts are unfounded!

> Her breasts are smeared with lotus balm,
> her lotus-fiber bracelet hangs limp,   50
> her beautiful body glows in pain—
> love burns young women like summer heat
> but its guilt makes them more charming.

PRIYAMVADĀ: [*In a stage whisper.*] Anasūyā, Śakuntalā has been pining
since she first saw the king. Could he be the cause of her sickness?   55
ANASŪYĀ: She must be suffering from lovesickness. I'll ask her . . .
[*Aloud.*] Friend, I have something to ask you. Your pain seems so
deep . . .
ŚAKUNTALĀ: [*Raising herself halfway.*] What do you want to say?
ANASŪYĀ: Śakuntalā, though we don't know what it is to be in love,   60
your condition reminds us of lovers we have heard about in stories.
Can you tell us the cause of your pain? Unless we understand your
illness, we can't begin to find a cure.
KING: Anasūyā expresses my own thoughts.

ŚAKUNTALĀ: Even though I want to, suddenly I can't make myself tell   65
you.
PRIYAṀVADĀ: Śakuntalā, my friend Anasūyā means well. Don't you see
how sick you are? Your limbs are wasting away. Only the shadow of
your beauty remains . . .
KING: What Priyaṁvadā says is true: 70

> Her cheeks are deeply sunken,
> her breasts' full shape is gone,
> her waist is thin, her shoulders bent,
> and the color has left her skin—
> tormented by love,   75
> she is sad but beautiful to see,
> like a jasmine creeper
> when hot wind shrivels its leaves.

ŚAKUNTALĀ: Friends, who else can I tell? May I burden you?
BOTH FRIENDS: We insist! Sharing sorrow with loving friends makes it   80
bearable.
KING:

> Friends who share her joy and sorrow
> discover the love concealed in her heart—
> though she looked back longingly at me,
> now I am afraid to hear her response.   85

ŚAKUNTALĀ: Friend, since my eyes first saw the guardian of the hermits'
retreat, I've felt such strong desire for him!
KING: I have heard what I want to hear.

> My tormentor, the god of love,
> has soothed my fever himself,   90
> like the heat of late summer
> allayed by early rain clouds.

ŚAKUNTALĀ: If you two think it's right, then help me to win the king's
pity. Otherwise, you'll soon pour sesame oil and water[3] on my
corpse . . .   95
KING: Her words destroy my doubt.
PRIYAṀVADĀ: [In a stage whisper.] She's so dangerously in love that
there's no time to lose. Since her heart is set on the ornament of the
Puru dynasty, we should rejoice that she desires him.
ANASŪYĀ: What you say is true.   100
PRIYAṀVADĀ: [Aloud.] Friend, by good fortune your desire is in harmony
with nature. A great river can only descend to the ocean. A jasmine
creeper can only twine around a mango tree.
KING: Why is this surprising when the twin stars of spring serve the
crescent moon?[4]   105
ANASŪYĀ: What means do we have to fulfill our friend's desire secretly
and quickly?

---

3. Offerings to the dead in Hindu funeral rites. Śakuntalā and her friends have learned of the king's real
identity, because the hermits have asked him to guard their hermitage from demons.   4. The king refers
metaphorically to the two friends attending Śakuntalā as stars attending a young moon that is waning.

PRIYAMVADĀ: "Secretly" demands some effort. "Quickly" is easy.
ANASŪYĀ: How so?
PRIYAMVADĀ: The king was charmed by her loving look; he seems thin   110
these days from sleepless nights.
KING: It's true . . .

> This golden armlet
> slips to my wrist
> without touching the scars   115
> my bowstring has made;
> its gemstones are faded
> by tears of secret pain
> that every night wets my arm
> where I bury my face.   120

PRIYAMVADĀ: [Thinking.] Compose a love letter and I'll hide it in a
flower. I'll deliver it to his hand on the pretext of bringing an offering
to the deity.
ANASŪYĀ: This subtle plan pleases me. What does Śakuntalā say?
ŚAKUNTALĀ: I'll try my friend's plan.   125
PRIYAMVADĀ: Then compose a poem to declare your love!
ŚAKUNTALĀ: I'm thinking, but my heart trembles with fear that he'll
reject me.
KING: [Delighted.]

> The man you fear will reject you
> waits longing to love you, timid girl—   130
> a suitor may lose or be lucky,
> but the goddess always wins.

BOTH FRIENDS: Why do you belittle your own virtues? Who would
cover his body with a piece of cloth to keep off cool autumn moonlight?   135
ŚAKUNTALĀ: [Smiling.] I'm trying to follow your advice. [She sits
thinking.]
KING: As I gaze at her, my eyes forget to blink.

> She arches an eyebrow,
> struggling to compose the verse—
> the down rises on her cheek,   140
> showing the passion she feels.[5]

ŚAKUNTALĀ: I've thought of a verse, but I have nothing to write it on.
PRIYAMVADĀ: Engrave the letters with your nail on this lotus leaf! It's
as delicate as a parrot's breast.
ŚAKUNTALĀ: [Miming what PRIYAMVADĀ described.] Listen and tell me   145
this makes sense!
BOTH FRIENDS: We're both paying attention.
ŚAKUNTALĀ: [Singing.]

> I don't know
> your heart,

---

5. "Thrilling" of the cheek is held to be a sign of inner emotion which the actress is supposed to be able
to represent.

but day and night   150
for wanting you,
love violently
tortures
my limbs,
cruel man.   155

KING: [*Suddenly revealing himself.*]

Love torments you, slender girl,
but he completely consumes me—
daylight spares the lotus pond
while it destroys the moon.

BOTH FRIENDS: [*Looking, rising with delight.*] Welcome to the swift   160
success of love's desire!
[ŚAKUNTALĀ *tries to rise.*]
KING: Don't exert yourself!

Limbs lying among crushed petals
like fragile lotus stalks
are too weakened by pain   165
to perform ceremonious acts.

ANASŪYĀ: Then let the king sit on this stone bench!
[*The* KING *sits;* ŚAKUNTALĀ *rises in embarrassment.*]
PRIYAṀVADĀ: The passion of two young lovers is clear. My affection for
our friend makes me speak out again now.[6]
KING: Noble lady, don't hesitate! It is painful to keep silent when one   170
must speak.
PRIYAṀVADĀ: We're told that it is the king's duty to ease the pain of his
suffering subjects.
KING: My duty, exactly!
PRIYAṀVADĀ: Since she first saw you, our dear friend has been reduced   175
to this sad condition. You must protect her and save her life.
KING: Noble lady, our affection is shared and I am honored by all you
say.
ŚAKUNTALĀ: [*Looking at* PRIYAṀVADĀ.] Why are you keeping the king
here? He must be anxious to return to his palace.   180
KING:

If you think that my lost heart
could love anyone but you,
a fatal blow strikes a man
already wounded by love's arrows!

ANASŪYĀ: We've heard that kings have many loves. Will our dear   185
friend become a sorrow to her family after you've spent time with
her?
KING: Noble lady, enough of this!

Despite my many wives,
on two the royal line rests—   190

---

6. Śakuntalā's modesty and good breeding prevent her from making her own declaration of love.

sea-bound earth
and your friend.[7]

BOTH FRIENDS: You reassure us.
PRIYAMVADĀ: [*Casting a glance.*] Anasūyā, this fawn is looking for its
mother. Let's take it to her!   195
[*They both begin to leave.*]
ŚAKUNTALĀ: Come back! Don't leave me unprotected!
BOTH FRIENDS: The protector of the earth is at your side.
ŚAKUNTALĀ: Why have they gone?
KING: Don't be alarmed! I am your servant.

Shall I set moist winds in motion   200
with lotus-leaf fans to cool your pain,
or rest your soft red lotus feet[8]
on my lap to stroke them, my love

ŚAKUNTALĀ: I cannot sin against those I respect!
[*Standing as if she wants to leave.*]
KING: Beautiful Śakuntalā, the day is still hot.   205

Why should your frail limbs
leave this couch of flowers
shielded by lotus leaves
to wander in the heat?

[*Saying this, he forces her to turn around.*]
ŚAKUNTALĀ: Puru king, control yourself! Though I'm burning with   210
love, how can I give myself to you?
KING: Don't fear your elders! The father of your family knows the law.
When he finds out, he will not blame you.

The daughters of royal sages often marry
in secret[9] and then their fathers bless them.   215

ŚAKUNTALĀ: Release me! I must ask my friends' advice!
KING: Yes, I shall release you.
ŚAKUNTALĀ: When?
KING:

Only let my thirsting mouth
gently drink from your lips,   220
the way a bee sips nectar
from a fragile virgin blossom.

[*Saying this, he tries to raise her face.* ŚAKUNTALĀ *evades him with a
dance.*]
VOICE OFFSTAGE: Red goose,[1] bid farewell to your gander! Night has
arrived!

---

7. Royal polygamy was common in ancient India; it served to make and cement political alliances. Here
the king speaks of the conventional ideal of a ruler's two "chief queens": the royal consort, whose son will
inherit the kingdom, and the earth, personified as the king's spouse.   8. A common metaphor for feet in
Indian verse.   9. The *gāndharva* form of marriage, a secret marriage of mutual consent, was permitted
for the warrior class. By the beginning of Act IV this has taken place.   1. Also known as the sheldrake
(*cakravāka*). In Sanskrit poetry, separated lovers are symbolized by these birds, subject to a curse that
separates them from their mates every night.

ŚAKUNTALĀ: [*Flustered.*] Puru king, Mother Gautamī is surely coming 225
to ask about my health. Hide behind this tree!
KING: Yes.
[*He conceals himself and waits. Then* GAUTAMĪ *enters with a vessel
in her hand, accompanied by* ŚAKUNTALĀ's *two friends.*]
BOTH FRIENDS: This way, Mother Gautamī!
GAUTAMĪ: [*Approaching* ŚAKUNTALĀ.] Child, does the fever in your
limbs burn less? 230
ŚAKUNTALĀ: Madam, I do feel better.
GAUTAMĪ: Kuśa grass and water will soothe your body. [*She sprinkles*
ŚAKUNTALĀ's *head.*] Child, the day is ended. Come, let's go back to
our hut! [*She starts to go.*]
ŚAKUNTALĀ: [*To herself.*] My heart, even when your desire was within 235
reach, you were bound by fear. Now you'll suffer the torment of
separation and regret. [*Stopping after a few steps, she speaks aloud.*]
Bower of creepers, refuge from my torment, I say goodbye until our
joy can be renewed . . . [*Sorrowfully,* ŚAKUNTALĀ *exits with the other
women.*]
KING: [*Coming out of hiding.*] Fulfillment of desire is fraught with
obstacles. 240

> Why didn't I kiss her face
> as it bent near my shoulder,
> her fingers shielding lips
> that stammered lovely warning?

Should I go now? Or shall I stay here in this bower of creepers that 245
my love enjoyed and then left?

> I see the flowers her body pressed
> on this bench of stone,
> the letter her nails inscribed
> on the faded lotus leaf, 250
> the lotus-fiber bracelet
> that slipped from her wrist—
> my eyes are prisoners
> in this empty house of reeds.

VOICE IN THE AIR: King! 255

> When the evening rituals begin,
> shadows of flesh-eating demons swarm
> like amber clouds of twilight,
> raising terror at the altar of fire.

KING: I am coming. 260
[*He exits.*]

Act IV

[*The two friends enter, miming the gathering of flowers.*]
ANASŪYĀ: Priyaṁvadā, I'm delighted that Śakuntalā chose a suitable
husband for herself, but I still feel anxious.

PRIYAṀVADĀ: Why?
ANASŪYĀ: When the king finished the sacrifice, the sages thanked him
and he left. Now that he has returned to his palace women in the
city, will he remember us here?
PRIYAṀVADĀ: Have faith! He's so handsome, he can't be evil. But I don't
know what Father Kaṇva will think when he hears about what
happened.
ANASŪYĀ: I predict that he'll give his approval.
PRIYAṀVADĀ: Why?
ANASŪYĀ: He's always planned to give his daughter to a worthy hus-
band. If fate accomplished it so quickly, Father Kaṇva won't object.
PRIYAṀVADĀ: [Looking at the basket of flowers.] We've gathered enough
flowers for the offering ceremony.
ANASŪYĀ: Shouldn't we worship the goddess who guards Śakuntalā?
PRIYAṀVADĀ: I have just begun. [She begins the rite.]
VOICE OFFSTAGE: I am here!
ANASŪYĀ: [Listening.] Friend, a guest is announcing himself.
PRIYAṀVADĀ: Śakuntalā is in her hut nearby, but her heart is far away.
ANASŪYĀ: You're right! Enough of these flowers!
    [They begin to leave.]
VOICE OFFSTAGE: So . . . you slight a guest . . .

> Since you blindly ignore
> a great sage like me,
> the lover you worship
> with mindless devotion
> will not remember you,
> even when awakened—
> like a drunkard who forgets
> a story he just composed!

PRIYAṀVADĀ: Oh! What a terrible turn of events! Śakuntalā's distraction has offended someone she should have greeted. [Looking
ahead.] Not just an ordinary person, but the angry sage Durvāsas
himself cursed her and went away in a frenzy of quivering, mad
gestures. What else but fire has such power to burn?
ANASŪYĀ: Go! Bow at his feet and make him return while I prepare the
water for washing his feet!
PRIYAṀVADĀ: As you say. [She exits.]
ANASŪYĀ: [After a few steps, she mimes stumbling.] Oh! The basket of
flowers fell from my hand when I stumbled in my haste to go. [She
mimes the gathering of flowers.]
PRIYAṀVADĀ: [Entering.] He's so terribly cruel! No one could pacify
him! But I was able to soften him a little.
ANASŪYĀ: Even that is a great feat with him! Tell me more!
PRIYAṀVADĀ: When he refused to return, I begged him to forgive a
daughter's first offense, since she didn't understand the power of
his austerity.
ANASŪYĀ: Then? Then?
PRIYAṀVADĀ: He refused to change his word, but he promised that
when the king sees the ring of recollection, the curse will end. Then
he vanished.

ANASŪYĀ: Now we can breathe again. When he left, the king himself gave her the ring engraved with his name. Śakuntalā will have her own means of ending the curse.

PRIYAMVADĀ: Come friend! We should finish the holy rite we're performing for her.   55

[*The two walk around, looking.*]

Anasūyā, look! With her face resting on her hand, our dear friend looks like a picture. She is thinking about her husband's leaving, with no thought for herself, much less for a guest.

ANASŪYĀ: Priyamvadā, we two must keep all this a secret between us. Our friend is fragile by nature; she needs our protection.   60

PRIYAMVADĀ: Who would sprinkle a jasmine with scalding water?

[*They both exit; the interlude ends. Then a* DISCIPLE *of* KAṆVA *enters, just awakened from sleep.*]

DISCIPLE: Father Kaṇva has just returned from his pilgrimage and wants to know the exact time. I'll go into a clearing to see what remains of the night. [*Walking around and looking.*] It is dawn.

> The moon sets over the western mountain   65
> as the sun rises in dawn's red trail—
> rising and setting, these two bright powers
> portend the rise and fall of men.

> When the moon disappears, night lotuses
> are but dull souvenirs of its beauty—   70
> when her lover disappears, the sorrow
> is too painful for a frail girl to bear.

ANASŪYĀ: [*Throwing aside the curtain and entering.*][2] Even a person withdrawn from worldly life knows that the king has treated Śakuntalā badly.   75

DISCIPLE: I'll inform Father Kaṇva that it's time for the fire oblation. [*He exits.*]

ANASŪYĀ: Even when I'm awake, I'm useless. My hands and feet don't do their work. Love must be pleased to have made our innocent friend put her trust in a liar . . . but perhaps it was the curse of Durvāsas that changed him . . . otherwise, how could the king have   80 made such promises and not sent even a message by now? Maybe we should send the ring to remind him. Which of these ascetics who practice austerities can we ask? Father Kaṇva has just returned from his pilgrimage. Since we feel that our friend was also at fault, we haven't told him that Śakuntalā is married to Duṣyanta and is   85 pregnant. The problem is serious. What should we do?

PRIYAMVADĀ: [*Entering, with delight.*] Friend, hurry! We're to celebrate the festival of Śakuntalā's departure for her husband's house.

ANASŪYĀ: What's happened, friend?

PRIYAMVADĀ: Listen! I went to ask Śakuntalā how she had slept. Father   90 Kaṇva embraced her and though her face was bowed in shame, he

---

2. The *javanikā* ("impeller"), a curtain hung over two doors separating the backstage area from the stage of the ancient Indian playhouse. An agitated entrance was indicated when, as here, a character entered the stage by throwing aside the curtain.

blessed her: "Though his eyes were filled with smoke, the priest's oblation luckily fell on the fire. My child, I shall not mourn for you . . . like knowledge given to a good student I shall send you to your husband today with an escort of sages." 95

ANASŪYĀ: Who told Father Kaṇva what happened?

PRIYAMVADĀ: A bodiless voice was chanting when he entered the fire sanctuary. [Quoting in Sanskrit.]

> Priest, know that your daughter
> carries Duṣyanta's potent seed
> for the good of the earth— 100
> like fire in mimosa[3] wood.

ANASŪYĀ: I'm joyful, friend. But I know that Śakuntalā must leave us today and sorrow shadows my happiness.

PRIYAMVADĀ: Friend, we must chase away sorrow and make this hermit girl happy! 105

ANASŪYĀ: Friend, I've made a garland of mimosa flowers. It's in the coconut-shell box hanging on a branch of the mango tree. Get it for me! Meanwhile I'll prepare the special ointments of deer musk, sacred earth, and blades of dūrvā grass.[4]

PRIYAMVADĀ: Here it is! 110

[ANASŪYĀ exits; PRIYAMVADĀ gracefully mimes taking down the box.]

VOICE OFFSTAGE: Gautamī! Śārṅgarava and some others have been appointed to escort Śakuntalā.

PRIYAMVADĀ: [Listening.] Hurry! Hurry! The sages are being called to go to Hastināpura.

ANASŪYĀ: [Reentering with pots of ointments in her hands.] Come, 115
friend! Let's go!

PRIYAMVADĀ: [Looking around.] Śakuntalā stands at sunrise with freshly washed hair while the female ascetics bless her with handfuls of wild rice and auspicious words of farewell. Let's go to her together. 120

[The two approach as ŚAKUNTALĀ enters with GAUTAMĪ and other female ascetics, and strikes a posture as described. One after another, the female ascetics address her.]

FIRST FEMALE ASCETIC: Child, win the title "Chief Queen" as a sign of your husband's high esteem!

SECOND FEMALE ASCETIC: Child, be a mother to heroes!

THIRD FEMALE ASCETIC: Child, be honored by your husband!

BOTH FRIENDS: This happy moment is no time for tears, friend. 125

[Wiping away her tears, they calm her with dance gestures.]

PRIYAMVADĀ: Your beauty deserves jewels, not these humble things we've gathered in the hermitage.

[Two boy ascetics enter with offerings in their hands.]

BOTH BOYS: Here is an ornament for you!

[Everyone looks amazed.]

GAUTAMĪ: Nārada, my child, where did this come from?

FIRST BOY: From Father Kaṇva's power. 130

---

3. Here, the śamī tree, which Indians consider the repository of fire. 4. Materials prepared by women for the ritual of farewell to a young woman moving from her father's to her husband's home.

GAUTAMĪ: Was it his mind's magic?
SECOND BOY: Not at all! Listen! You ordered us to bring flowers from the forest trees for Śakuntalā.

> One tree produced this white silk cloth,
> another poured resinous lac to redden her feet— 135
> the tree nymphs produced jewels in hands
> that stretched from branches like young shoots.[5]

PRIYAMVADĀ: [Watching ŚAKUNTALĀ.] This is a sign that royal fortune will come to you in your husband's house.
[ŚAKUNTALĀ mimes modesty.]
FIRST BOY: Gautama, come quickly! Father Kaṇva is back from bath- 140 ing. We'll tell him how the trees honor her.
SECOND BOY: As you say.
[The two exit.]
BOTH FRIENDS: We've never worn them ourselves, but we'll put these jewels on your limbs the way they look in pictures.
ŚAKUNTALĀ: I trust your skill. 145
[Both friends mime ornamenting her. Then KAṆVA enters, fresh from his bath.]
KAṆVA:

> My heart is touched with sadness
> since Śakuntalā must go today,
> my throat is choked with sobs,
> my eyes are dulled by worry—
> if a disciplined ascetic 150
> suffers so deeply from love,
> how do fathers bear the pain
> of each daughter's parting?[6]

[He walks around.]
BOTH FRIENDS: Śakuntalā, your jewels are in place; now put on the pair of silken cloths. 155
[Standing, ŚAKUNTALĀ wraps them.]
GAUTAMĪ: Child, your father has come. His eyes filled with tears of joy embrace you. Greet him reverently!
ŚAKUNTALĀ: [Modestly.] Father, I welcome you.
KAṆVA: Child,

> May your husband honor you 160
> the way Yayāti honored Śarmiṣṭhā.
> As she bore her son Puru,[7]
> may you bear an imperial prince.

GAUTAMĪ: Sir, this is a blessing, not just a prayer.
KAṆVA: Child, walk around the sacrificial fires![8] 165
[All walk around; KAṆVA intoning a prayer in Vedic meter.[9]]

5. The verse suggests that Śakuntalā is a kinswoman of the tree goddesses (yakṣīs), worshiped in popular cults. Lac: a substance secreted by a species of beetle, used by Indian women as a cosmetic dye for coloring fingernails and toenails.   6. A celebrated passage, prized for its convincing portrait of an Indian father's sorrow at losing his daughter to another household.   7. Yayāti and Puru are ancestors of Duṣyanta.   8. Holy objects, persons, and places are honored by ritually walking around them.   9. The version of the Triṣṭubh meter used in the Vedic hymns, the oldest scriptures of the Hindu tradition.

> Perfectly placed around the main altar,
> fed with fuel, strewn with holy grass,
> destroying sin by incense from oblations,
> may these sacred fires purify you!

You must leave now! [*Looking around.*] Where are Śārṅgarava and   170
the others?
DISCIPLE: [*Entering.*] Here we are, sir!
KAṆVA: You show your sister the way!
ŚĀRṄGARAVA: Come this way!
> [*They walk around.*]
KAṆVA: Listen, you trees that grow in our grove!   175

> Until you were well watered
> she could not bear to drink;
> she loved you too much
> to pluck your flowers for her hair;
> the first time your buds bloomed,   180
> she blossomed with joy—
> may you all bless Śakuntalā
> as she leaves for her husband's house.

[*Miming that he hears a cuckoo's cry.*]

> The trees of her forest family
> have blessed Śakuntalā—   185
> the cuckoo's melodious song
> announces their response.

VOICE IN THE AIR:

> May lakes colored by lotuses mark her path!
> May trees shade her from the sun's burning rays!
> May the dust be as soft as lotus pollen!   190
> May fragrant breezes cool her way!

[*All listen astonished.*]
GAUTAMĪ: Child, the divinities of our grove love you like your family
and bless you. We bow to you all!
ŚAKUNTALĀ: [*Bowing and walking around; speaking in a stage whisper.*]
Priyaṁvadā, though I long to see my husband, my feet move with
sorrow as I start to leave the hermitage.   195
PRIYAṀVADĀ: You are not the only one who grieves. The whole her-
mitage feels this way as your departure from our grove draws near.

> Grazing deer
> drop grass,
> peacocks   200
> stop dancing,
> vines loose
> pale leaves
> falling
> like tears.   205

ŚAKUNTALĀ: [*Remembering.*] Father, before I leave, I must see my sister, the vine Forestlight.

KAṆVA: I know that you feel a sister's love for her. She is right here.

ŚAKUNTALĀ: Forestlight, though you love your mango tree, turn to embrace me with your tendril arms! After today, I'll be so far 210 away . . .

KAṆVA:

> Your merits won you the husband
> I always hoped you would have
> and your jasmine has her mango tree—
> my worries for you both are over. 215

Start your journey here!

ŚAKUNTALĀ: [*Facing her two friends.*] I entrust her care to you.

BOTH FRIENDS: But who will care for us? [*They wipe away their tears.*]

KAṆVA: Anasūyā, enough crying! You should be giving Śakuntalā courage! 220

[*All walk around.*]

ŚAKUNTALĀ: Father, when the pregnant doe who grazes near my hut gives birth, please send someone to give me the good news.

KAṆVA: I shall not forget.

ŚAKUNTALĀ: [*Miming the interrupting of her gait.*] Who is clinging to my skirt? 225

[*She turns around.*]

KAṆVA: Child,

> The buck whose mouth you healed with oil
> when it was pierced by a blade of kuśa grass
> and whom you fed with grains of rice—
> your adopted son will not leave the path. 230

ŚAKUNTALĀ: Child, don't follow when I'm abandoning those I love! I raised you when you were orphaned soon after your birth, but now I'm deserting you too. Father will look after you. Go back! [*Weeping, she starts to go.*]

KAṆVA: Be strong!

> Hold back the tears that blind 235
> your long-lashed eyes—
> you will stumble if you cannot see
> the uneven ground on the path.

ŚĀRṄGARAVA: Sir, the scriptures prescribe that loved ones be escorted only to the water's edge. We are at the shore of the lake. Give us 240 your message and return!

ŚAKUNTALĀ: We shall rest in the shade of this fig tree.

[*All walk around and stop;* KAṆVA *speaks to himself.*]

KAṆVA: What would be the right message to send to King Duṣyanta? [*He ponders.*]

ŚAKUNTALĀ: [*In a stage whisper.*] Look! The wild goose cries in anguish when her mate is hidden by lotus leaves. What I'm suffering 245 is much worse.

ANASŪYĀ: Friend, don't speak this way!.

> This goose spends
> every long night

in sorrow 250
without her mate,
but hope lets her
survive
the deep pain
of loneliness. 255

KAṆVA: Śārṅgarava, speak my words to the king after you present
Śakuntalā!

ŚĀRṄGARAVA: As you command, sir!

KAṆVA:

Considering our discipline,
the nobility of your birth 260
and that she fell in love with you
before her kinsmen could act,
acknowledge her with equal rank
among your wives—
what more is destined for her, 265
the bride's family will not ask.

ŚĀRṄGARAVA: I grasp your message.

KAṆVA: Child, now I must instruct you. We forest hermits know something about worldly matters.

ŚĀRṄGARAVA: Nothing is beyond the scope of wise men. 270

KAṆVA: When you enter your husband's family:

Obey your elders, be a friend to the other wives!
If your husband seems harsh, don't be impatient!
Be fair to your servants, humble in your happiness!
Women who act this way become noble wives; 275
sullen girls only bring their families disgrace.

But what does Gautamī think?

GAUTAMĪ: This is good advice for wives, child. Take it all to heart!

KAṆVA: Child, embrace me and your friends!

ŚAKUNTALĀ: Father, why must Priyaṁvadā and my other friends turn 280
back here?

KAṆVA: They will also be given in marriage. It is not proper for them
to go there now. Gautamī will go with you.

ŚAKUNTALĀ: [*Embracing her father.*] How can I go on living in a strange
place, torn from my father's side, like a vine torn from the 285
side of a sandalwood tree growing on a mountain slope?[1]

KAṆVA: Child, why are you so frightened?

When you are your husband's honored wife,
absorbed in royal duties and in your son,[2]
born like the sun to the eastern dawn, 290
the sorrow of separation will fade.

[ŚAKUNTALĀ *falls at her father's feet.*]
Let my hopes for you be fulfilled!

---

1. Śakuntalā's sorrow reflects the real world of every Indian bride as she permanently leaves the home of
her birth to join the extended family into which she has married.   2. The son, heir to the throne, will
ensure an honored place for Śakuntalā among the hitherto childless wives of King Duṣyanta.

ŚAKUNTALĀ: [*Approaching her two friends.*] You two must embrace me
together!
BOTH FRIENDS: [*Embracing her.*] Friend, if the king seems slow to   295
recognize you, show him the ring engraved with his name!
ŚAKUNTALĀ: Your suspicions make me tremble!
BOTH FRIENDS: Don't be afraid! It's our love that fears evil.
ŚĀRṄGARAVA: The sun is high in the afternoon sky. Hurry, please!
ŚAKUNTALĀ: [*Facing the sanctuary.*] Father, will I ever see the grove   300
again?
KAṆVA:

> When you have lived for many years
> as a queen equal to the earth
> and raised Duṣyanta's son
> to be a matchless warrior,   305
> your husband will entrust him
> with the burdens of the kingdom
> and will return with you
> to the calm of this hermitage.[3]

GAUTAMĪ: Child, the time for our departure has passed. Let your father   310
turn back! It would be better, sir, if you turn back yourself. She'll
keep talking this way forever.
KAṆVA: Child, my ascetic practice has been interrupted.
ŚAKUNTALĀ: My father's body is already tortured by ascetic practices.
He must not grieve too much for me!   315
KAṆVA: [*Sighing.*]

> When I see the grains of rice
> sprout from offerings you made
> at the door of your hut,
> how shall I calm my sorrow!

[ŚAKUNTALĀ *exits with her escort.*]
BOTH FRIENDS: [*Watching* ŚAKUNTALĀ.] Śakuntalā is hidden by forest   320
trees now.
KAṆVA: Anasūyā, your companion is following her duty. Restrain yourself and return with me!
BOTH FRIENDS: Father, the ascetics' grove seems empty without Śakuntalā. How can we enter?   325
KAṆVA: The strength of your love makes it seem so. [*Walking around
in meditation.*] Good! Now that Śakuntalā is on her way to her husband's family, I feel calm.

> A daughter belongs to another man—
> by sending her to her husband today,   330
> I feel the satisfaction
> one has on repaying a loan.

[*All exit.*]

---

3. It was a custom of Hindu kings (and commoners of the twice-born classes) to retire to the forest with
their wives to concentrate on the spiritual life.

Act V

[*The* KING *and the* BUFFOON *enter; both sit down.*]
BUFFOON: Pay attention to the music room, friend, and you'll hear the notes of a song strung into a delicious melody . . . the lady Haṁsapadikā is practicing her singing.
KING: Be quiet so I can hear her!
VOICE IN THE AIR: [*Singing.*]

> Craving sweet   5
> new nectar,
> you kissed
> a mango bud once—
> how could you
> forget her, bee,   10
> to bury your joy
> in a lotus

KING: The melody of the song is passionate.
BUFFOON: But did you get the meaning of the words?
KING: I once made love to her. Now she reproaches me for loving   15
Queen Vasumatī. Friend Mādhavya, tell Haṁsapadikā that her words rebuke me soundly.
BUFFOON: As you command! [*He rises.*] But if that woman grabs my hair tuft, it will be like a heavenly nymph grabbing some ascetic . . . there go my hopes of liberation![4]   20
KING: Go! Use your courtly charm to console her.
BUFFOON: What a fate!
[*He exits.*]
KING: [*To himself.*] Why did hearing the song's words fill me with such strong desire? I'm not parted from anyone I love . . .

> Seeing rare beauty,   25
> hearing lovely sounds,
> even a happy man
> becomes strangely uneasy . . .
> perhaps he remembers,
> without knowing why,   30
> loves of another life
> buried deep in his being.[5]

[*He stands bewildered. Then the* KING'S CHAMBERLAIN *enters.*]
CHAMBERLAIN: At my age, look at me!

> Since I took this ceremonial bamboo staff
> as my badge of office in the king's chambers   35
> many years have passed; now I use it
> as a crutch to support my faltering steps.

---

4. The buffoon is referring, in his own inimitable way, to the seduction of the ascetic by the courtesan and the thwarting of the former's quest for liberation from *karma* and rebirth. The buffoon's joke turns on the word *mokṣa*, which means "release," in the physical sense as well as in the spiritual one of liberation from *karma*.   5. Alludes to the power of art to revive buried memories of experiences from former lives.

A king cannot neglect his duty. He has just risen from his seat of
justice and though I am loath to keep him longer, Sage Kaṇva's
pupils have just arrived. Authority to rule the world leaves no time   40
for rest.

> The sun's steeds were yoked before time began,
> the fragrant wind blows night and day,
> the cosmic serpent always bears earth's weight,[6]
> and a king who levies taxes has his duty.   45

Therefore, I must perform my office. [*Walking around and looking.*]

> Weary from ruling them like children,
> he seeks solitude far from his subjects,
> like an elephant bull who seeks cool shade
> after gathering his herd at midday.   50

[*Approaching.*] Victory to you, king! Some ascetics who dwell in the
forest at the foothills of the Himālayas have come. They have women
with them and bring a message from Sage Kaṇva. Listen, king, and
judge!

KING: [*Respectfully.*] Are they Sage Kaṇva's messengers?   55
CHAMBERLAIN: They are.
KING: Inform the teacher Somarāta that he should welcome the ascet-
ics with the prescribed rites and then bring them to me himself. I'll
wait in a place suitable for greeting them.
CHAMBERLAIN: As the king commands. [*He exits.*]   60
KING: [*Rising.*] Vetravatī, lead the way to the fire sanctuary.
DOORKEEPER: Come this way, king!
KING: [*Walking around, showing fatigue.*] Every other creature is happy
when the object of his desire is won, but for kings success contains
a core of suffering.   65

> High office only leads to greater greed;
> just perfecting its rewards is wearisome—
> a kingdom is more trouble than it's worth,
> like a royal umbrella one holds alone.

TWO BARDS OFFSTAGE: Victory to you, king!   70
FIRST BARD:

> You sacrifice your pleasures every day
> to labor for your subjects—
> as a tree endures burning heat
> to give shade from the summer sun.

SECOND BARD:

> You punish villains with your rod of justice,   75
> you reconcile disputes, you grant protection—
> most relatives are loyal only in hope of gain,
> but you treat all your subjects like kinsmen.

---

6. According to Hindu mythology the earth rests on Śeṣa, the cosmic serpent. *Sun's steeds:* see n. 7, p.
1274.

KING: My weary mind is revived. [*He walks around.*]
DOORKEEPER: The terrace of the fire sanctuary is freshly washed and   80
the cow is waiting to give milk for the oblation. Let the king ascend!
KING: Vetravatī, why has Father Kaṇva sent these sages to me?

> Does something hinder their ascetic life?
> Or threaten creatures in the sacred forest?
> Or do my sins stunt the flowering vines?   85
> My mind is filled with conflicting doubts.

DOORKEEPER: I would guess that these sages rejoice in your virtuous
conduct and come to honor you.
> [*The ascetics enter;* ŚAKUNTALĀ *is in front with* GAUTAMĪ; *the* CHAM-
> BERLAIN *and the* KING'S PRIEST *are in front of her.*]
CHAMBERLAIN: Come this way, sirs!
ŚĀRNGARAVA: Śāradvata, my friend: 90

> I know that this renowned king is righteous
> and none of the social classes follows evil ways,
> but my mind is so accustomed to seclusion
> that the palace feels like a house in flames.

ŚĀRADVATA: I've felt the same way ever since we entered the city.   95

> As if I were freshly bathed, seeing a filthy man,
> pure while he's defiled, awake while he's asleep,
> as if I were a free man watching a prisoner,
> I watch this city mired in pleasures.

ŚAKUNTALĀ: [*Indicating she feels an omen.*] Why is my right eye   100
twitching?
GAUTAMĪ: Child, your husband's family gods turn bad fortune into
blessings! [*They walk around.*]
PRIEST: [*Indicating the* KING.] Ascetics, the guardian of sacred order
has left the seat of justice and awaits you now. Behold him!   105
ŚĀRNGARAVA: Great priest, he seems praiseworthy, but we expect no
less.

> Boughs bend, heavy with ripened fruit,
> clouds descend with fresh rain,
> noble men are gracious with wealth—   110
> this is the nature of bountiful things.

DOORKEEPER: King, their faces look calm. I'm sure that the sages have
confidence in what they're doing.
KING: [*Seeing* ŚAKUNTALĀ.]

> Who is she? Carefully veiled
> to barely reveal her body's beauty,   115
> surrounded by the ascetics
> like a bud among withered leaves.

DOORKEEPER: King, I feel curious and puzzled too. Surely her form
deserves closer inspection.
KING: Let her be! One should not stare at another man's wife!   120

ŚAKUNTALĀ: [*Placing her hand on her chest, she speaks to herself.*] My heart, why are you quivering? Be quiet while I learn my noble husband's feelings.

PRIEST: [*Going forward.*] These ascetics have been honored with due ceremony. They have a message from their teacher. The king should hear them! 125

KING: I am paying attention.

SAGES: [*Raising their hands in a gesture of greeting.*] May you be victorious, king!

KING: I salute you all! 130

SAGES: May your desires be fulfilled!

KING: Do the sages perform austerities unhampered?

SAGES:

> Who would dare obstruct the rites
> of holy men whom you protect—
> how can darkness descend 135
> when the sun's rays shine?

KING: My title "king" is more meaningful now. Is the world blessed by Father Kaṇva's health?

SAGES: Saints control their own health. He asks about your welfare and sends this message . . . 140

KING: What does he command?

ŚĀRṄGARAVA: At the time you secretly met and married my daughter, affection made me pardon you both.

> We remember you to be a prince of honor;
> Śakuntalā is virtue incarnate— 145
> the creator cannot be condemned
> for mating the perfect bride and groom.

And now that she is pregnant, receive her and perform your sacred duty together.

GAUTAMĪ: Sir, I have something to say, though I wasn't appointed to speak: 150

> She ignored her elders
> and you failed to ask her kinsmen—
> since you acted on your own,
> what can I say to you now? 155

ŚAKUNTALĀ: What does my noble husband say?

KING: What has been proposed?

ŚAKUNTALĀ: [*To herself.*] The proposal is as clear as fire.

ŚĀRṄGARAVA: What's this? Your Majesty certainly knows the ways of the world! 160

> People suspect a married woman who stays
> with her kinsmen, even if she is chaste—
> a young wife should live with her husband,
> no matter how he despises her.

KING: Did I ever marry you? 165

ŚAKUNTALĀ: [*Visibly dejected, speaking to herself.*] Now your fears are real, my heart!
ŚĀRṄGARAVA:

Does one turn away from duty in contempt
because his own actions repulse him?

KING: Why ask this insulting question? 170
ŚĀRṄGARAVA:

Such transformations take shape
when men are drunk with power.

KING: This censure is clearly directed at me.
GAUTAMĪ: Child, this is no time to be modest. I'll remove your veil.
Then your husband will recognize you. 175
[*She does so.*]
KING: [*Staring at* ŚAKUNTALĀ.]

Must I judge whether I ever married
the flawless beauty they offer me now?
I cannot love her or leave her, like a bee
near a jasmine filled with frost at dawn.

[*He shows hesitation.*]
DOORKEEPER: Our king has a strong sense of justice. Who else would 180
hesitate when beauty like this is handed to him?
ŚĀRṄGARAVA: King, why do you remain silent?
KING: Ascetics, even though I'm searching my mind, I don't remember
marrying this lady. How can I accept a woman who is visibly preg-
nant when I doubt that I am the cause? 185
ŚAKUNTALĀ: [*In a stage whisper.*] My lord casts doubt on our marriage.
Why were my hopes so high?
ŚĀRṄGARAVA: It can't be!

Are you going to insult the sage
who pardons the girl you seduced 190
and bids you keep his stolen wealth,
treating a thief like you with honor?

ŚĀRADVATA: Śārṅgarava, stop now! Śakuntalā, we have delivered our
message and the king has responded. He must be shown some proof. 195
ŚAKUNTALĀ: [*In a stage whisper.*] When passion can turn to this, what's
the use of reminding him? But, it's up to me to prove my honor now.
[*Aloud.*] My noble husband . . . [*She breaks off when this is half-
spoken.*] Since our marriage is in doubt, this is no way to address
him. Puru king, you do wrong to reject a simple-hearted person 200
with such words after you deceived her in the hermitage.
KING: [*Covering his ears.*] Stop this shameful talk!

Are you trying to stain my name
and drag me to ruin—
like a river eroding her own banks, 205
soiling water and uprooting trees?

ŚAKUNTALĀ: Very well! If it's really true that fear of taking another man's wife turns you away, then this ring will revive your memory and remove your doubt.

KING: An excellent idea!   210

ŚAKUNTALĀ: [*Touching the place where the ring had been.*] I'm lost! The ring is gone from my finger. [*She looks despairingly at* GAUTAMĪ.]

GAUTAMĪ: The ring must have fallen off while you were bathing in the holy waters at the shrine of the goddess near Indra's grove.

KING: [*Smiling.*] And so they say the female sex is cunning.   215

ŚAKUNTALĀ: Fate has shown its power. Yet, I will tell you something else.

KING: I am still obliged to listen.

ŚAKUNTALĀ: One day, in a jasmine bower, you held a lotus-leaf cup full of water in your hand.   220

KING: We hear you.

ŚAKUNTALĀ: At that moment the buck I treated as my son approached. You coaxed it with the water, saying that it should drink first. But he didn't trust you and wouldn't drink from your hand. When I took the water, his trust returned. Then you jested, "Every creature   225 trusts what its senses know. You both belong to the forest."

KING: Thus do women further their own ends by attracting eager men with the honey of false words.

GAUTAMĪ: Great king, you are wrong to speak this way. This child raised in an ascetics' grove doesn't know deceit.   230

KING: Old woman,

> When naive female beasts show cunning,
> what can we expect of women who reason?
> Don't cuckoos let other birds nurture
> their eggs and teach the chicks to fly?   235

ŚAKUNTALĀ: [*Angrily.*] Evil man! you see everything distorted by your own ignoble heart. Who would want to imitate you now, hiding behind your show of justice, like a well overgrown with weeds?

KING: [*To himself.*] Her anger does not seem feigned; it makes me doubt myself.   240

> When the absence of love's memory
> made me deny a secret affair with her,
> this fire-eyed beauty bent her angry brows
> and seemed to break the bow of love.[7]

[*Aloud.*] Lady, Dusyanta's conduct is renowned, so what you say is   245 groundless.

ŚAKUNTALĀ: All right! I may be a self-willed wanton woman! But it was faith in the Puru dynasty that brought me into the power of a man with honey in his words and poison in his heart. [*She covers her face at the end of the speech and weeps.*]

ŚĀRṄGARAVA: A willful act unchecked always causes pain.   250

> One should be cautious
> in forming a secret union—

7. Of the love god Kāma.

> unless a lover's heart is clear,
> affection turns to poison.

KING: But sir, why do you demean me with such warnings? Do you 255
trust the lady?
ŚĀRṄGARAVA: [*Scornfully.*] You have learned everything backwards.

> If you suspect the word of one
> whose nature knows no guile,
> then you can only trust 260
> people who practice deception.

KING: I presume you speak the truth. Let us assume so. But what could
I gain by deceiving this woman?
ŚĀRṄGARAVA: Ruin.
KING: Ruin? A Puru king has no reason to want his own ruin! 265
ŚĀRADVATA; Śārṅgarava, this talk is pointless. We have delivered our
master's message and should return.

> Since you married her, abandon her or take her—
> absolute is the power a husband has over his wife.

GAUTAMĪ: You go ahead. 270
[*They start to go.*]
ŚAKUNTALĀ: What? Am I deceived by this cruel man and then aban-
doned by you? [*She tries to follow them.*]
GAUTAMĪ: [*Stopping.*] Śārṅgarava my son, Śakuntalā is following us,
crying pitifully. What will my child do now that her husband has
refused her? 275
ŚĀRṄGARAVA: [*Turning back angrily.*] Bold woman, do you still insist
on having your way?
[ŚAKUNTALĀ *trembles in fear.*]

> If you are what the king says you are,
> you don't belong in Father Kaṇva's family—
> if you know that your marriage vow is pure,
> you can bear slavery in your husband's house. 280

Stay! We must go on!
KING: Ascetic, why do you disappoint the lady too?

> The moon only makes lotuses open,
> the sun's light awakens lilies— 285
> a king's discipline forbids him
> to touch another man's wife.

ŚĀRṄGARAVA: If you forget a past affair because of some present attachment, why do you fear injustice now?
KING: [*To the* PRIEST.] Sir I ask you to weigh the alternatives: 290

> Since it's unclear whether I'm deluded
> or she is speaking falsely—
> should I risk abandoning a wife
> or being tainted by another man's?

PRIEST: [*Deliberating.*] I recommend this . . . 295

KING: Instruct me! I'll do as you say.

PRIEST: Then let the lady stay in our house until her child is born. If you ask why: the wise men predict that your first son will be born with the marks of a king who turns the wheel of empire.[8] If the child of the sage's daughter bears the marks, congratulate her and welcome her into your palace chambers. Otherwise, send her back to her father.

KING: Whatever the elders desire.

PRIEST: Child, follow me!

ŚAKUNTALĀ: Mother earth, open to receive me!

[*Weeping,* ŚAKUNTALĀ *exits with the* PRIEST *and the hermits. The* KING, *his memory lost through the curse, thinks about her.*]

VOICE OFFSTAGE: Amazing! Amazing!

KING: [*Listening.*] What could this be?

PRIEST: [*Reentering, amazed.*] King, something marvelous has occurred!

KING: What?

PRIEST: When Kaṇva's pupils had departed,

> The girl threw up her arms and wept,
> lamenting her misfortune . . . then . . .

KING: Then what?

PRIEST:

> Near the nymph's shrine a ray of light
> in the shape of a woman carried her away.

[*All mime amazement.*]

KING: We've already settled the matter. Why discuss it further?

PRIEST: [*Observing the* KING.] May you be victorious! [*He exits.*]

KING: Vetravatī, I am bewildered. Lead the way to my chamber!

DOORKEEPER: Come this way, my lord! [*She walks forward.*]

KING:

> I cannot remember marrying
> the sage's abandoned daughter,
> but the pain my heart feels
> makes me suspect that I did.

[*All exit.*]

Act VI

[*The* KING's *wife's brother, who is city* MAGISTRATE, *enters with two policemen leading a* MAN *whose hands are tied behind his back.*]

BOTH POLICEMEN: [*Beating the* MAN.] Speak, thief! Where'd you steal this handsome ring with the king's name engraved in the jewel?

MAN: [*Showing fear.*] Peace, sirs! I wouldn't do a thing like that.

---

8. See n. 9, p. 1275.

FIRST POLICEMAN: Don't tell us the king thought you were some famous
   priest and gave it to you as a gift!   5

MAN: Listen, I'm a humble fisherman who lives near Indra's grove.

SECOND POLICEMAN: Thief, did we ask you about your caste?

MAGISTRATE: Sūcaka, let him tell it all in order! Don't interrupt him!

BOTH POLICEMEN: Whatever you command, chief!

MAN: I feed my family by catching fish with nets and hooks.   10

MAGISTRATE: [Mocking.] What a pure profession![9]

MAN:

> The work I do
> may be vile
> but I won't deny
> my birthright—   15
> a priest
> doing his holy rites
> pities the animals
> he kills.

MAGISTRATE: Go on!   20

MAN: One day as I was cutting up a red carp, I saw the shining stone
   of this ring in its belly. When I tried to sell it, you grabbed me. Kill
   me or let me go! That's how I got it!

MAGISTRATE: Jānuka, I'm sure this ugly butcher's a fisherman by his
   stinking smell. We must investigate how he got the ring. We'll go   25
   straight to the palace.

BOTH POLICEMEN: Okay. Go in front, you pickpocket!

   [All walk around.]

MAGISTRATE: Sūcaka, guard this villain at the palace gate! I'll report to
   the king how we found the ring, get his orders, and come back.

BOTH POLICEMEN: Chief, good luck with the king!   30

   [The MAGISTRATE exits.]

FIRST POLICEMAN: Jānuka, the chief's been gone a long time.

SECOND POLICEMAN: Well, there are fixed times for seeing kings.

FIRST POLICEMAN: Jānuka, my hands are itching to tie on his execution
   garland.[1] [He points to the MAN.]

MAN: You shouldn't think about killing a man for no reason.   35

SECOND POLICEMAN: [Looking.] I see our chief coming with a letter in
   his hand. It's probably an order from the king. You'll be thrown to
   the vultures or you'll see the face of death's dog[2] again . . .

MAGISTRATE: [Entering.] Sūcaka, release this fisherman! I'll tell you
   how he got the ring.   40

FIRST POLICEMAN: Whatever you say, chief!

SECOND POLICEMAN: The villain entered the house of death and came
   out again. [He unties the prisoner.]

MAN: [Bowing to the MAGISTRATE.] Master, how will I make my living
   now?   45

MAGISTRATE: The king sends you a sum equal to the ring. [He gives the
   money to the MAN.]

---

9. Because their profession involves taking animal life, fishermen rank low in the caste system.
1. Condemned prisoners were taken to their executions dressed in robes and garlands, in the manner of
sacrificial victims.   2. In Hindu myth two four-eyed dogs guard the path of the dead.

MAN: [*Bowing as he grabs it.*] The king honors me.

FIRST POLICEMAN: This fellow's certainly honored. He was lowered from the execution stake and raised up on a royal elephant's back.

SECOND POLICEMAN: Chief, the reward tells me this ring was special 50 to the king.

MAGISTRATE: I don't think the king valued the stone, but when he caught sight of the ring, he suddenly seemed to remember someone he loved, and he became deeply disturbed.

FIRST POLICEMAN: You served him well, chief! 55

SECOND POLICEMAN: I think you better served this king of fish. [*Looking at the fisherman with jealousy.*]

MAN: My lords, half of this is yours for your good will.

FIRST POLICEMAN: It's only fair!

MAGISTRATE: Fisherman, now that you are my greatest and dearest friend, we should pledge our love over kadamba-blossom wine. 60 Let's go to the wine shop!

[*They all exit together; the interlude ends. Then a nymph named SĀNUMATĪ enters by the skyway.*]

SĀNUMATĪ: Now that I've performed my assigned duties at the nymph's shrine, I'll slip away to spy on King Duṣyanta while the worshipers are bathing. My friendship with Menakā makes me feel a bond with Śakuntalā. Besides, Menakā asked me to help her daughter. 65 [*Looking around.*] Why don't I see preparations for the spring festival in the king's palace? I can learn everything by using my mental powers, but I must respect my friend's request. So be it! I'll make myself invisible and spy on these two girls who are guarding the pleasure garden. 70

[SĀNUMATĪ *mimes descending and stands waiting. Then a* MAID *servant named Parabhṛtikā, "Little Cuckoo," enters, looking at a mango bud. A* SECOND MAID, *named Madhukarikā, "Little Bee," is following her.*]

FIRST MAID:

> Your pale green stem
> tinged with pink
> is a true sign
> that spring has come—
> I see you, 75
> mango-blossom bud,
> and I pray
> for a season of joy.

SECOND MAID: What are you muttering to yourself?

FIRST MAID: A cuckoo goes mad when she sees a mango bud. 80

SECOND MAID: [*Joyfully rushing over.*] Has the sweet month of spring come?

FIRST MAID: Now's the time to sing your songs of love.

SECOND MAID: Hold me while I pluck a mango bud and worship the god of love. 85

FIRST MAID: Only if you'll give me half the fruit of your worship.

SECOND MAID: That goes without saying . . . our bodies may be separate, but our lives are one . . .[*Leaning on her friend, she stands and plucks a mango bud.*] The mango flower is still closed, but this broken stem is fragrant. [*She makes the dove gesture with her hands.*]   90

> Mango blossom bud,
> I offer you to Love
> as he lifts
> his bow of passion.
> Be the first   95
> of his flower arrows
> aimed at lonely girls
> with lovers far away!

[*She throws the mango bud.*]

MAGISTRATE: [*Angrily throwing aside the curtain and entering.*] Not now, stupid girl! When the king has banned the festival of spring,   100
how dare you pluck a mango bud!

BOTH MAIDS: [*Frightened.*] Please forgive us, sir. We don't know what you mean.

CHAMBERLAIN: Did you not hear that even the spring trees and the nesting birds obey the king's order?   105

> The mango flowers bloom without spreading pollen,
> the red amaranth buds, but will not bloom,
> cries of cuckoo cocks freeze though frost is past,
> and out of fear, Love holds his arrow half-drawn.

BOTH MAIDS: There is no doubt about the king's great power!   110

FIRST MAID: Sir, several days ago we were sent to wait on the queen by Mitrāvasu, the king's brother-in-law. We were assigned to guard the pleasure garden. Since we're newcomers, we've heard no news.

CHAMBERLAIN: Let it be! But don't do it again!

BOTH MAIDS: Sir, we're curious. May we ask why the spring festival   115
was banned?

SĀNUMATĪ: Mortals are fond of festivals. The reason must be serious.

CHAMBERLAIN: It is public knowledge. Why should I not tell them? Has the scandal of Śakuntalā's rejection not reached your ears?

BOTH MAIDS: We only heard from the king's brother-in-law that the   120
ring was found.

CHAMBERLAIN: [*To himself.*] There is little more to tell. [*Aloud.*] When he saw the ring, the king remembered that he had married Śakuntalā in secret and had rejected her in his delusion. Since then the king has been tortured by remorse.   125

> Despising what he once enjoyed,
> he shuns his ministers every day
> and spends long sleepless nights
> tossing at the edge of his bed—
> when courtesy demands that   130
> he converse with palace women,
> he stumbles over their names,
> and then retreats in shame.

SĀNUMATĪ: This news delights me.

CHAMBERLAIN: The festival is banned because of the king's melan- 135
choly.

BOTH MAIDS: It's only right.

VOICE OFFSTAGE: This way, sir!

CHAMBERLAIN: [*Listening.*] The king is coming. Go about your
business! 140

BOTH MAIDS: As you say.

[*Both maids exit. Then the* KING *enters, costumed to show his grief,
accompanied by the* BUFFOON *and the* DOORKEEPER.]

CHAMBERLAIN: [*Observing the* KING.] Extraordinary beauty is appealing
under all conditions. Even in his lovesick state, the king is wonderful
to see.

> Rejecting his regal jewels, 145
> he wears one golden bangle
> above his left wrist;
> his lips are pale with sighs,
> his eyes wan from brooding at night—
> like a gemstone ground in polishing, 150
> the fiery beauty of his body
> makes his wasted form seem strong.

SĀNUMATĪ: [*Seeing the* KING.] I see why Śakuntalā pines for him though
he rejected and disgraced her.

KING: [*Walking around slowly, deep in thought.*]

> This cursed heart slept 155
> when my love came to wake it,
> and now it stays awake
> to suffer the pain of remorse.

SĀNUMATĪ: The girl shares his fate.

BUFFOON: [*In a stage whisper.*] He's having another attack of his 160
Śakuntalā disease. I doubt if there's any cure for that.

CHAMBERLAIN: [*Approaching.*] Victory to the king! I have inspected the
grounds of the pleasure garden. Let the king visit his favorite spots
and divert himself.

KING: Vetravatī, deliver a message to my noble minister Piśuna: "After 165
being awake all night, we cannot sit on the seat of justice today. Set
in writing what your judgment tells you the citizens require and send
it to us!"

DOORKEEPER: Whatever you command! [*She exits.*]

KING: Vātāyana, attend to the rest of your business! 170

CHAMBERLAIN: As the king commands! [*He exits.*]

BUFFOON: You've cleared out the flies. Now you can rest in some pretty
spot. The garden is pleasant now in this break between morning cold
and noonday heat.

KING: Dear friend, the saying "Misfortunes rush through any crack" is 175
absolutely right:

> Barely freed by the dark force
> that made me forget Kaṇva's daughter,

> my mind is threatened by an arrow
> of mango buds fixed on Love's bow. 180

BUFFOON: Wait, I'll destroy the love god's arrow with my wooden stick.[3]
[Raising his staff, he tries to strike a mango bud.]
KING: [Smiling.] Let it be! I see the majesty of brahman bravery. Friend,
where may I sit to divert my eyes with vines that remind me of my
love? 185
BUFFOON: Didn't you tell your maid Caturikā, "I'll pass the time in the
jasmine bower. Bring me the drawing board on which I painted a
picture of Śakuntalā with my own hand!"
KING: Such a place may soothe my heart. Show me the way!
BUFFOON: Come this way! 190
[Both walk around; the nymph SĀNUMATĪ follows.]
The marble seat and flower offerings in this jasmine bower are cer-
tainly trying to make us feel welcome. Come in and sit down!
[Both enter the bower and sit.]
SĀNUMATĪ: I'll hide behind these creepers to see the picture he's drawn
of my friend. Then I'll report how great her husband's passion is.
[She does as she says and stands waiting.]
KING: Friend, now I remember everything. I told you about my first 195
meeting with Śakuntalā. You weren't with me when I rejected her,
but why didn't you say anything about her before? Did you suffer a
loss of memory too?
BUFFOON: I didn't forget. You did tell me all about it once, but then
you said, "It's all a joke without any truth." My wit is like a lump 200
of clay, so I took you at your word . . . or it could be that fate is
powerful . . .
SĀNUMATĪ: It is!
KING: Friend, help me!
BUFFOON: What's this? It doesn't become you! Noblemen never take 205
grief to heart. Even in storms, mountains don't tremble.
KING: Dear friend, I'm defenseless when I remember the pain of my
love's bewilderment when I rejected her.

> When I cast her away, she followed her kinsmen,
> but Kaṇva's disciple harshly shouted, "Stay!" 210
> The tearful look my cruelty provoked
> burns me like an arrow tipped with poison.

SĀNUMATĪ: The way he rehearses his actions makes me delight in his
pain.
BUFFOON: Sir, I guess that the lady was carried off by some celestial 215
creature or other.
KING: Who else would dare to touch a woman who worshiped her husband? I was told that Menakā is her mother. My heart suspects that
her mother's companions carried her off.
SĀNUMATĪ: His delusion puzzled me, but not his reawakening. 220
BUFFOON: If that's the case, you'll meet her again in good time.

---

3. It is clear in the original that the buffoon's staff parodies Indra's rod (a symbol of virility) and the phallic
arrows of the god of love.

KING: How?

BUFFOON: No mother or father can bear to see a daughter parted from her husband.

KING:

> Was it dream or illusion or mental confusion,   225
> or the last meager fruit of my former good deeds?
> It is gone now, and my heart's desires are
> like riverbanks crumbling of their own weight.

BUFFOON: Stop this! Isn't the ring evidence that an unexpected meeting is destined to take place?   230

KING: [Looking at the ring.] I only pity it for falling from such a place.

> Ring, your punishment is proof
> that your face is as flawed as mine—
> you were placed in her lovely fingers,
> glowing with crimson nails, and you fell.   235

SĀNUMATĪ: The real pity would have been if it had fallen into some other hand.

BUFFOON: What prompted you to put the signet ring on her hand?

SĀNUMATĪ: I'm curious too.

KING: I did it when I left for the city. My love broke into tears and   240 asked, "How long will it be before my noble husband sends news to me?"

BUFFOON: Then? What then?

KING: Then I placed the ring on her finger with this promise:

> One by one, day after day,   245
> count each syllable of my name!
> At the end, a messenger will come
> to bring you to my palace.

But in my cruel delusion, I never kept my word.

SĀNUMATĪ: Fate broke their charming agreement!   250

BUFFOON: How did it get into the belly of the carp the fisherman was cutting up?

KING: While she was worshiping at the shrine of Indra's wife, it fell from her hand into the Gaṅgā.[4]

BUFFOON: It's obvious now!   255

SĀNUMATĪ: And the king, doubtful of his marriage to Śakuntalā, a female ascetic, was afraid to commit an act of injustice. But why should such passionate love need a ring to be remembered?

KING: I must reproach the ring for what it's done.

BUFFOON: [To himself.] He's gone the way of all madmen . . .   260

KING:

> Why did you leave her delicate finger
> and sink into the deep river?

of course . . .

---

4. The Ganges River.

> A mindless ring can't recognize virtue,
> but why did I reject my love? 265

BUFFOON: [*To himself again.*] Why am I consumed by a craving for food?

KING: Oh ring! Have pity on a man whose hate is tormented because he abandoned his love without cause! Let him see her again!
[*Throwing the curtain aside, the maid* CATURIKĀ *enters, with the drawing board in her hand.*]

CATURIKĀ: Here's the picture you painted of the lady. [*She shows the* 270 *drawing board.*]

BUFFOON: Dear friend, how well you've painted your feelings in this sweet scene? My eyes almost stumble over the hollows and hills.

SĀNUMATĪ: What skill the king has! I feel as if my friend were before me.

KING:

> The picture's imperfections are not hers, 275
> but this drawing does hint at her beauty.

SĀNUMATĪ: Such words reveal that suffering has increased his modesty as much as his love.

BUFFOON: Sir, I see three ladies now and they're all lovely to look at. Which is your Śakuntalā? 280

SĀNUMATĪ: Only a dim-witted fool like this wouldn't know such beauty!

KING: You guess which one!

BUFFOON: I guess Śakuntalā is the one you've drawn with flowers falling from her loosened locks of hair, with drops of sweat on her face, 285 with her arms hanging limp and tired as she stands at the side of a mango tree whose tender shoots are gleaming with the fresh water she poured. The other two are her friends.

KING: You are clever! Look at these signs of my passion!

> Smudges from my sweating fingers 290
> stain the edges of the picture
> and a tear fallen from my cheek
> has raised a wrinkle in the paint.

Caturikā, the scenery is only half-drawn. Go and bring my paints!

CATURIKĀ: Noble Mādhavya, hold the drawing board until I come 295 back!

KING: I'll hold it myself. [*He takes it, the maid exits.*]

> I rejected my love when she came to me,
> and how I worship her in a painted image—
> having passed by a river full of water, 300
> I'm longing now for an empty mirage.

BUFFOON: [*To himself.*] He's too far gone for a river now! He's looking for a mirage! [*Aloud.*] Sir, what else do you plan to draw here?

SĀNUMATĪ: He'll want to draw every place my friend loved.

KING:

> I'll draw the river Mālinī 305
> flowing through Himālaya's foothills

where pairs of wild geese nest in the sand
and deer recline on both riverbanks,
where a doe is rubbing her left eye
on the horn of a black buck antelope   310
under a tree whose branches
have bark dresses hanging to dry.

BUFFOON: [*To himself.*] Next he'll fill the drawing board with mobs of
ascetics wearing long grassy beards.
KING: Dear friend, I've forgotten to draw an ornament that Śakuntalā 315
wore.
BUFFOON: What is it?
SĀNUMATĪ: It will suit her forest life and her tender beauty.
KING:

I haven't drawn the mimosa flower on her ear,
its filaments resting on her cheek,
or the necklace of tender lotus stalks,   320
lying on her breasts like autumn moonbeams.

BUFFOON: But why does the lady cover her face with her red lotus-
bud fingertips and stand trembling in fear? [*Looking closely.*] That
son-of-a-bee who steals nectar from flowers is attacking her face. 325
KING: Drive the impudent rogue away!
BUFFOON: You have the power to punish criminals. You drive him off!
KING: All right! Bee, favored guest of the flowering vines, why do you
frustrate yourself by flying here?[5]

A female bee waits on a flower,   330
thirsting for your love—
she refuses to drink
the sweet nectar without you.

SĀNUMATĪ: How gallantly he's driving him away!
BUFFOON: When you try to drive it away, this creature becomes   335
vicious.
KING: Why don't you stop when I command you?

Bee, if you touch the lips of my love
that lure you like a young tree's virgin buds,
lips I gently kissed in festivals of love,   340
I'll hold you captive in a lotus flower cage.

BUFFOON: Why isn't he afraid of your harsh punishment? [*Laughing,
he speaks to himself.*] He's gone crazy and I'll be the same if I go on
talking like this. [*Aloud.*] But sir, it's just a picture!
KING: A picture? How can that be?   345
SĀNUMATĪ: When I couldn't tell whether it was painted, how could he
realize he was looking at a picture?
KING: Dear friend, are you envious of me?

My heart's affection made me feel
the joy of seeing her—   350

---

5. The king's preoccupation with the bee recalls the events of Act I.

but you reminded me again
that my love is only a picture.

[*He wipes away a tear.*]
SĀNUMATĪ: The effects of her absence make him quarrelsome.
KING: Dear friend, why do I suffer this endless pain?   355

Sleepless nights prevent our meeting in dreams;
her image in a picture is ruined by my tears.

SĀNUMATĪ: You have clearly atoned for the suffering your rejection
caused Śakuntalā.
CATURIKĀ: [*Entering.*] Victory my lord! I found the paint box and   360
started back right away . . . but I met Queen Vasumatī with her maid
Taralikā on the path and she grabbed the box from my hand, saying,
"I'll bring it to the noble lord myself!"
BUFFOON: You were lucky to get away!
CATURIKĀ: The queen's shawl got caught on a tree. While Taralikā was   365
freeing it, I made my escape.
KING: Dear friend, the queen's pride can quickly turn to anger. Save
this picture!
BUFFOON: You should say, "Save yourself!" [*Taking the picture, he
stands up.*] If you escape the woman's deadly poison, then send   370
word to me in the Palace of the Clouds. [*He exits hastily.*]
SĀNUMATĪ: even though another woman has taken his heart and he
feels indifferent to the queen, he treats her with respect.[6]
DOORKEEPER: [*Entering with a letter in her hand.*] Victory, king!
KING: Vetravatī, did you meet the queen on the way?   375
DOORKEEPER: I did, but when she saw the letter in my hand, she turned
back.
KING: She knows that this is official and would not interrupt my work.
DOORKEEPER: King, the minister requests that you examine the contents of this letter. He said that the enormous job of reckoning the   380
revenue in this one citizen's case had taken all his time.
KING: Show me the letter! [*The girl hands it to him and he reads barely
aloud.*] What is this? "A wealthy merchant sea captain named
Dhanamitra has been lost in a shipwreck and the laws say that
since the brave man was childless, his accumulated wealth all   385
goes to the king." It's terrible to be childless! A man of such wealth
probably had several wives. We must find out if any one of his wives
is pregnant!
DOORKEEPER: King, it's said that one of his wives, the daughter of a
merchant of Ayodhyā, has performed the rite to ensure the birth of   390
a son.[7]
KING: The child in her womb surely deserves his parental wealth. Go!
Report this to my minister!
DOORKEEPER: As the king commands! [*She starts to go.*]
KING: Come here a moment!   395
DOORKEEPER: I am here.

---

6. Royal polygamy called for elaborate courtesies.   7. This rite (*puṃsavana*) is performed in the third
month of pregnancy.

KING: Is it his offspring or not?

> When his subjects lose a kinsman,
> Duṣyanta will preserve the estates—
> unless there is some crime. 400
> Let this be proclaimed.

DOORKEEPER: It shall be proclaimed loudly. [*She exits; reenters.*] The king's order will be as welcome as rain in the right season.

KING: [*Sighing long and deeply.*] Families without offspring whose lines of succession are cut off lose their wealth to strangers when 405 the last male heir dies. When I die, this will happen to the wealth of the Puru dynasty.

DOORKEEPER: Heaven forbid such a fate!

KING: I curse myself for despising the treasure I was offered.

SĀNUMATĪ: He surely has my friend in mind when he blames himself. 410

KING:

> I abandoned my lawful wife, the holy ground
> where I myself planted my family's glory,
> like earth sown with seed at the right time,
> ready to bear rich fruit in season.

SĀNUMATĪ: But your family's line will not be broken. 415

CATURIKĀ: [*In a stage whisper.*] The king is upset by the story of the merchant. Go and bring noble Mādhavya from the Palace of the Clouds to console him!

DOORKEEPER: A good idea! [*She exits.*]

KING: Duṣyanta's ancestors are imperiled. 420

> Our fathers drink the yearly libation
> mixed with my childless tears,
> knowing that there is no other son
> to offer the sacred funeral waters.

[*He falls into a faint.*]

CATURIKĀ: [*Looking at the bewildered KING.*] Calm yourself, my lord! 425

SĀNUMATĪ: Though a light shines, his separation from Śakuntalā keeps him in a state of dark depression. I could make him happy now, but I've heard Indra's consort consoling Śakuntalā with the news that the gods are hungry for their share of the ancestral oblations and will soon conspire to have her husband welcome his lawful 430 wife. I'll have to wait for the auspicious time, but meanwhile I'll cheer my friend by reporting his condition. [*She exits, flying into the air.*]

VOICE OFFSTAGE: Help! Brahman-murder![8]

KING: [*Regaining consciousness, listening.*] Is it Mādhavya's cry of pain? Who's there? 435

DOORKEEPER: King, your friend is in danger. Help him!

KING: Who dares to threaten him?

---

8. Murder of a brahman is among the most heinous sins.

DOORKEEPER: Some invisible spirit seized him and dragged him to the roof of the Palace of the Clouds.

KING: [*Getting up.*] Not this! Even my house is haunted by spirits.   440

> When I don't even recognize
> the blunders I commit every day,
> how can I keep track
> of where my subjects stray?

VOICE OFFSTAGE: Dear friend! Help! Help!   445

KING: [*Breaking into a run.*] Friend, don't be afraid! I'm coming!

VOICE OFFSTAGE: [*Repeating the call for help.*] Why shouldn't I be afraid? Someone is trying to split my neck in three, like a stalk of sugar cane.

KING: [*Casting a glance.*] Quickly, my bow!   450

BOW-BEARER: [*Entering with a bow in hand.*] Here are your bow and quiver.

> [*The* KING *takes his bow and arrows.*]

VOICE OFFSTAGE:

> I'll kill you as a tiger kills struggling prey!
> I'll drink fresh blood from your tender neck!
> Take refuge now in the bow Duṣyanta lifts   455
> to calm the fears of the oppressed!

KING: [*Angrily.*] How dare you abuse my name? Stop, carrion-eater! Or you will not live! [*He strings his bow.*] Vetravatī, lead the way to the stairs!

DOORKEEPER: This way, king.   460

> [*All move forward in haste.*]

KING: [*Searching around.*] There is no one here!

VOICE OFFSTAGE: Help! Help! I see you. Don't you see me? I'm like a mouse caught by a cat! My life is hopeless!

KING: Don't count on your powers of invisibility! My magical arrows will find you. I aim this arrow: 465

> It will strike its doomed target
> and spare the brahman it must save—
> a wild goose can extract the milk
> and leave the water untouched.[9]

> [*He aims the arrow. Then Indra's charioteer* MĀTALI *enters, having released the* BUFFOON.]

MĀTALI: King!   470

> Indra sets demons as your targets;
> draw your bow against them!
> Send friends gracious glances
> rather than deadly arrows!

---

9. The *haṃsa;* in Sanskrit poetry this bird is said to have the ability to separate milk from the water with which it has been diluted.

KING: [*Withdrawing his arrow.*] Mātali, welcome to great Indra's char- 475
ioteer!
BUFFOON: [*Entering.*] He tried to slaughter me like a sacrificial beast
and this king is greeting him with honors!
MĀTALI: [*Smiling.*] Your Majesty, hear why Indra has sent me to you!
KING: I am all attention. 480
MĀTALI: There is an army of demons descended from one-hundred-
headed Kālanemi, known to be invincible . . .
KING: I have already heard it from Nārada, the gods' messenger.
MĀTALI:

> He is invulnerable to your friend Indra,
> so you are appointed to lead the charge— 485
> the moon dispels the darkness of night
> since the sun cannot drive it out.

Take your weapon, mount Indra's chariot, and prepare for victory!
KING: Indra favors me with this honor. But why did you attack Māḍ-
havya? 490
MĀTALI: I'll tell you! From the signs of anguish Your Majesty showed,
I knew that you were despondent. I attacked him to arouse your
anger.

> A fire blazes when fuel is added;
> a cobra provoked raises its hood— 495
> men can regain lost courage
> if their emotions are aroused.

KING: [*In a stage whisper.*] Dear friend, I cannot disobey a command
from the lord of heaven. Inform my minister Piśuna of this and tell
him this for me: 500

> Concentrate your mind on guarding my subjects!
> My bow is strung to accomplish other work.

BUFFOON: Whatever you command!
[*He exits.*]
MĀTALI: Mount the chariot, Your Majesty!
[*The* KING *mimes mounting the chariot; all exit.*]

Act VII

[*The* KING *enters with* MĀTALI *by the skyway, mounted on a chariot.*]
KING: Mātali, though I carried out his command, I feel unworthy of
the honors Indra gave me.
MĀTALI: [*Smiling.*] Your Majesty, neither of you seems satisfied.

> You belittle the aid you gave Indra
> in face of the honors he conferred,
> and he, amazed by your heroic acts, 5
> deems his hospitality too slight.

KING: No, not so! When I was taking leave, he honored me beyond my heart's desire and shared his throne with me in the presence of the gods:

> Indra gave me a garland of coral flowers[1]
> tinged with sandalpowder from his chest,
> while he smiled at his son Jayanta,
> who stood there barely hiding his envy.

MĀTALI: Don't you deserve whatever you want from Indra?

> Indra's heaven of pleasures has twice
> been saved by rooting out thorny demons—
> your smooth-jointed arrows have now done
> what Viṣṇu once did with his lion claws.[2]

KING: Here too Indra's might deserves the praise.

> When servants succeed in great tasks,
> they act in hope of their master's praise—
> would dawn scatter the darkness
> if he were not the sun's own charioteer?

MĀTALI: This attitude suits you well! [*He moves a little distance.*] Look over there, Your Majesty! See how your own glorious fame has reached the vault of heaven!

> Celestial artists are drawing your exploits
> on leaves of the wish-granting creeper[3]
> with colors of the nymphs' cosmetic paints,
> and bards are moved to sing of you in ballads.

KING: Mātali, in my desire to do battle with the demons, I did not notice the path we took to heaven as we climbed through the sky yesterday. Which course of the winds are we traveling?
MĀTALI:

> They call this path of the wind Parivaha—
> freed from darkness by Viṣṇu's second stride,
> it bears the Gaṅgā's three celestial streams[4]
> and turns stars in orbit, dividing their rays.

KING: Mātali, this is why my soul, my senses, and my heart feel calm. [*He looks at the chariot wheels.*] We've descended to the level of the clouds.
MĀTALI: How do you know?
KING:

> Crested cuckoos fly between the spokes,
> lightning flashes glint off the horses' coats,
> and a fine mist wets your chariot's wheels—
> all signs that we go over rain-filled clouds.

---

1. The coral trees of heaven bear never-fading flowers.   2. In his incarnation as half man, half lion, the god Viṣṇu slew a demon.   3. The *kalpalatā* vine that grows in Indra's heaven.   4. In heaven the Ganges flows with three streams before descending to earth. As the cosmic strider, Viṣṇu scattered the darkness from heaven.

MĀTALI: In a moment you'll be back in your own domain, Your Majesty.
KING: [*Looking down.*] Our speeding chariot makes the mortal world
appear fantastic. Look!   50

> Mountain peaks emerge as the earth descends,
> branches spread up from a sea of leaves,
> fine lines become great rivers to behold—
> the world seems to hurtle toward me.

MĀTALI: You observe well! [*He looks with great reverence.*] The   55
beauty of earth is sublime.
KING: Mātali, what mountain do I see stretching into the eastern and
western seas, rippled with streams of liquid gold, like a gateway of
twilight clouds?
MĀTALI: Your Majesty, it is called the "Golden Peak," the mountain   60
of the demigods, a place where austerities are practiced to perfection.

> Mārīca, the descendant of Brahmā,
> a father of both demons and gods,
> lives the life of an ascetic here
> in the company of Aditi, his wife.   65

KING: One must not ignore good fortune! I shall perform the rite of
circumambulating the sage.
MĀTALI: An excellent idea!
[*The two mime descending.*]
KING: [*Smiling.*]

> The chariot wheels make no sound,
> they raise no clouds of dust,   70
> they touch the ground unhindered—
> nothing marks the chariot's descent.

MĀTALI: It is because of the extraordinary power that you and Indra
both possess.
KING: Mātali, where is Mārīca's hermitage?   75
MĀTALI: [*Pointing with his hand.*]

> Where the sage stands staring at the sun,
> as immobile as the trunk of a tree,
> his body half-buried in an ant hill,
> with a snake skin on his chest,
> his throat pricked by a necklace   80
> of withered thorny vines,
> wearing a coil of long matted hair
> filled with nests of śakunta birds.

KING: I do homage to the sage for his severe austerity.
MĀTALI: [*Pulling hard on the chariot reins.*] Great king, let us enter 85
Mārīca's hermitage, where Aditi nurtures the celestial coral trees.
KING: This tranquil place surpasses heaven. I feel as if I'm bathing in
a lake of nectar.
MĀTALI: [*Stopping the chariot.*] Dismount, Your Majesty!

KING: [*Dismounting.*] Mātali, what about you? 90
MĀTALI: I have stopped the chariot. I'll dismount too. [*He does so.*] This way, Your Majesty! [*He walks around.*] You can see the grounds of the ascetics' grove ahead.
KING: I am amazed!

> In this forest of wish-fulfilling trees 95
> ascetics live on only the air they breathe
> and perform their ritual ablutions
> in water colored by golden lotus pollen.
> They sit in trance on jeweled marble slabs
> and stay chaste among celestial nymphs, 100
> practicing austerities in the place
> that others seek to win by penances.

MĀTALI: Great men always aspire to rare heights! [*He walks around, calling aloud.*] O venerable Śākalya, what is the sage Mārīca doing now? What do you say? In response to Aditi's question about the 105 duties of a devoted wife, he is talking in a gathering of great sages' wives.[5]
KING: [*Listening.*] We must wait our turn.
MĀTALI: [*Looking at the* KING.] Your Majesty, rest at the foot of this aśoka tree. Meanwhile, I'll look for a chance to announce you to 110 Indra's father.
KING: As you advise . . . [*He stops.*]
MĀTALI: Your Majesty, I'll attend to this. [*He exits.*]
KING: [*Indicating he feels an omen.*]

> I have no hope for my desire.
> Why does my arm throb in vain? 115
> Once good fortune is lost,
> it becomes constant pain.

VOICE OFFSTAGE: Don't be so wild! Why is his nature so stubborn?
KING: [*Listening.*] Unruly conduct is out of place here. Whom are they reprimanding? [*Looking toward the sound, surprised.*] Who is 120 this child, guarded by two female ascetics? A boy who acts more like a man.

> He has dragged this lion cub
> from its mother's half-full teat
> to play with it, and with his hand 125
> he violently tugs its mane.

[*The* BOY *enters as described, with two female ascetics.*]
BOY: Open your mouth, lion! I want to count your teeth!
FIRST ASCETIC: Nasty boy, why do you torture creatures we love like our children? You're getting too headstrong! The sages gave you the right name when they called you "Sarvadamana, Tamer-of-everything." 130
KING: Why is my heart drawn to this child, as if he were my own flesh? I don't have a son. That is why I feel tender toward him . . .

---

5. In Gupta society, the sages were teachers of *dharma* and of the norms of behavior for women of the upper classes.

SECOND ASCETIC: The lioness will maul you if you don't let go of her
cub!
BOY: [*Smiling.*] Oh, I'm scared to death! [*Pouting.*]
KING:

> This child appears to be   135
> the seed of hidden glory,
> like a spark of fire
> awaiting fuel to burn.

FIRST ASCETIC: Child, let go of the lion cub and I'll give you another
toy!   140
BOY: Where is it? Give it to me! [*He reaches out his hand.*]
KING: Why does he bear the mark of a king who turns the wheel of
empire?

> A hand with fine webs connecting the fingers
> opens as he reaches for the object greedily,   145
> like a single lotus with faint inner petals
> spread open in the red glow of early dawn.

SECOND ASCETIC: Suvratā, you can't stop him with words! The sage
Mārkaṇḍeya's son left a brightly painted clay bird in my hut. Get it
for him!   150
FIRST ASCETIC: I will! [*She exits.*]
BOY: But until it comes I'll play with this cub.
KING: I am attracted to this pampered boy . . .

> Lucky are fathers whose laps give refuge
> to the muddy limbs of adoring little sons   155
> when childish smiles show budding teeth
> and jumbled sounds make charming words.

SECOND ASCETIC: Well, he ignores me. [*She looks back.*] Is one of the
sage's sons here? [*Looking at the* KING.] Sir, please come here! Make
him loosen his grip and let go of the lion cub! He's tormenting   160
it in his cruel child's play.
KING: [*Approaching the* BOY, *smiling.*] Stop! You're a great sage's son!

> When self-control is your duty by birth,
> why do you violate the sanctuary laws
> and ruin the animals' peaceful life,   165
> like a young black snake in a sandal tree?

SECOND ASCETIC: Sir, he's not a sage's son.
KING: His actions and his looks confirm it. I based my false assumption
on his presence in this place. [*He does what she asked; responding to
the* BOY'*s touch, he speaks to himself.*]

> Even my limbs feel delighted   170
> from the touch of a stranger's son—
> the father at whose side he grew
> must feel pure joy in his heart.

SECOND ASCETIC: [*Examining them both.*] It's amazing! Amazing!

KING: What is it, madam?   175
SECOND ASCETIC: This boy looks surprisingly like you. He doesn't even
know you, and he's acting naturally.
KING: [*Fondling the child.*] If he's not the son of an ascetic, what lineage does he belong to?
SECOND ASCETIC: The family of Puru.   180
KING: [*To himself.*] What? His ancestry is the same as mine . . . so this
lady thinks he resembles me. The family vow of Puru's descendants
is to spend their last days in the forest.

> As world protectors they first choose
> palaces filled with sensuous pleasures,   185
> but later, their homes are under trees
> and one wife shares the ascetic vows.

[*Aloud.*] But mortals cannot enter this realm on their own.
SECOND ASCETIC: You're right, sir. His mother is a nymph's child. She
gave birth to him here in the hermitage of Mārīca.   190
KING: [*In a stage whisper.*] Here is a second ground for hope! [*Aloud.*]
What famed royal sage claims her as his wife?
SECOND ASCETIC: Who would even think of speaking the name of a
man who rejected his lawful wife?
KING: [*To himself.*] Perhaps this story points to me. What if I ask the   195
name of the boy's mother? No, it is wrong to ask about another man's
wife.
FIRST ASCETIC: [*Returning with a clay bird in her hand.*] Look, Sarva-
damana, a śakunta! Look! Isn't it lovely?
BOY: Where's my mother?   200
BOTH ASCETICS: He's tricked by the similarity of names.[6] He wants his
mother.
SECOND ASCETIC: Child, she told you to look at the lovely clay śakunta
bird.
KING: [*To himself.*] What? Is his mother's name Śakuntalā? But   205
names can be the same. Even a name is a mirage . . . a false hope
to herald despair.
BOY: I like this bird! [*He picks up the toy.*]
FIRST ASCETIC: [*Looking frantically.*] Oh, I don't see the amulet-box on
his wrist!   210
KING: Don't be alarmed! It broke off while he was tussling with the lion
cub. [*He goes to pick it up.*]
BOTH ASCETICS: Don't touch it! Oh, he's already picked it up! [*With
their hands on their chests, they stare at each other in amazement.*]
KING: Why did you warn me against it?
FIRST ASCETIC: It contains the magical herb called Aparājitā,[7] honored   215
sir. Mārīca gave it to him at his birth ceremony. He said that if it fell
to the ground no one but his parents or himself could pick it up.

---

6. *Śakunta*, one of the Sanskrit and Prakrit words for "bird," is etymologically related to *Śakuntalā* (Woman
of the Birds), who was so named because she was found in the forest in the company of birds. Now her
son, Bharata, mistakes *śakunta* for *śakuntalā*. Like the women, the child speaks Prakrit, the "natural"
language, but once he has entered the social world of men he must speak Sanskrit.   7. Meaning "invincible" or "unvanquished."

KING: And if someone else does pick it up?
FIRST ASCETIC: Then it turns into a snake and strikes.   220
KING: Have you two seen it so transformed?
BOTH ASCETICS: Many times.
KING: [To himself, joyfully.] Why not rejoice in the fulfillment of my
heart's desire? [He embraces the child.]
SECOND ASCETIC: Suvratā, come, let's tell Śakuntalā that her penances   225
are over.
      [Both ascetics exit.]
BOY: Let me go! I want my mother!
KING: Son, you will greet your mother with me.
BOY: My father is Duṣyanta, not you!
KING: This contradiction confirms the truth.   230
      [ŚAKUNTALĀ enters, wearing the single braid of a woman in
      mourning.]
ŚAKUNTALĀ: Even though Sarvadamana's amulet kept its natural form
instead of changing into a snake, I can't hope that my destiny will
be fulfilled. But maybe what my friend Sānumatī reports is right.
KING: [Looking at ŚAKUNTALĀ.] It is Śakuntalā!

> Wearing dusty gray garments,   235
> her face gaunt from penances,
> her bare braid[8] hanging down—
> she bears with perfect virtue
> the trial of long separation
> my cruelty forced on her.   240

ŚAKUNTALĀ: [Seeing the KING pale with suffering.] He doesn't resemble
my noble husband. Whose touch defiles my son when the amulet is
protecting him?
BOY: [Going to his mother.] Mother, who is this stranger who calls me
"son"?   245
KING: My dear, I see that you recognize me now. Even my cruelty to
you is transformed by your grace.
ŚAKUNTALĀ: [To herself.] Heart, be consoled! My cruel fate has finally
taken pity on me. It is my noble husband!
KING:

> Memory chanced to break my dark delusion   250
> and you stand before me in beauty,
> like the moon's wife Rohiṇī
> as she rejoins her lord after an eclipse.

ŚAKUNTALĀ: Victory to my noble husband![9] Vic . . . [She stops when the
word is half-spoken, her throat choked with tears.]
KING: Beautiful Śakuntalā,   255

> Even choked by your tears,
> the word "victory" is my triumph
> on your bare pouting lips,
> pale-red flowers of your face.

---

8. A woman separated from her lover neglected her looks and wore her hair in a single braid.   9. The traditional formula for greeting a royal husband.

BOY: Mother, who is he?   260
ŚAKUNTALĀ: Child, ask the powers of fate!
KING: [*Falling at* ŚAKUNTALĀ's *feet.*][1]

> May the pain of my rejection
> vanish from your heart;
> delusion clouded my weak mind
> and darkness obscured good fortune—   265
> a blind man tears off a garland,
> fearing the bite of a snake.

ŚAKUNTALĀ: Noble husband, rise! Some crime I had committed in a
former life surely came to fruit and made my kind husband indifferent to me.   270
   [*The* KING *rises.*]
But how did my noble husband come to remember this woman who
was doomed to pain?
KING: I shall tell you after I have removed the last barb of sorrow.

> In my delusion I once ignored
> a teardrop burning your lip—   275
> let me dry the tear on your lash
> to end the pain of remorse!

   [*He does so.*]
ŚAKUNTALĀ: [*Seeing the signet ring.*] My noble husband, this is the ring!
KING: I regained my memory when the ring was recovered.   280
ŚAKUNTALĀ: When it was lost, I tried in vain to convince my noble
husband who I was.
KING: Let the vine take back this flower as a sign of her union with
spring.
ŚAKUNTALĀ: I don't trust it. Let my noble husband wear it!   285
   [MĀTALI *enters.*]
MĀTALI: Good fortune! This meeting with your lawful wife and the sight
of your son's face are reasons to rejoice.
KING: The sweet fruit of my desire! Mātali, didn't Indra know about all
this?
MĀTALI: What is unknown to the gods? Come Your Majesty! The sage   290
Mārīca grants you an audience.
KING: Śakuntalā, hold our son's hand! We shall go to see Mārīca
together.
ŚAKUNTALĀ: I feel shy about appearing before my elders in my hus-
band's company.   295
KING: But it is customary at a joyous time like this. Come! Come!
   [*They all walk around. Then* MĀRĪCA *enters with* ADITI; *they sit.*]
MĀRĪCA: [*Looking at the* KING.]

> Aditi, this is king Duṣyanta,
> who leads Indra's armies in battle;
> his bow lets your son's thunderbolt
> lie ready with its tip unblunted.   300

---

1. In Sanskrit poetry, the repentant lover, regardless of his rank, must fall at the feet of his beloved,
expressing his remorse and asking for her forgiveness.

ADITI: He bears himself with dignity.
MĀTALI: Your Majesty, the parents of the gods look at you with affection reserved for a son. Approach them!
KING: Mātali, the sages so describe this pair.

> Source of the sun's twelve potent forms,   305
> parents of Indra, who rules the triple world,
> birthplace of Viṣṇu's primordial form,
> sired by Brahmā's sons,[2] Marīci and Dakṣa.

MĀTALI: Correct!
KING: [Bowing.] Indra's servant, Duṣyanta, bows to you both.   310
MĀRĪCA: My son, live long and protect the earth!
ADITI: My son, be an invincible warrior!
ŚAKUNTALĀ: I worship at your feet with my son.
MĀRĪCA:

> Child, with a husband like Indra
> and a son like his son Jayanta,   315
> you need no other blessing.
> Be like Indra's wife Paulomī!

ADITI: Child, may your husband honor you and may your child live long to give both families joy! Be seated!
[All sit near MĀRĪCA.]
MĀRĪCA: [Pointing to each one.]

> By the turn of fortune,   320
> virtuous Śakuntalā, her noble son,
> and the king are reunited—
> faith and wealth with order.

KING: Sir, first came the success of my hopes, then the sight of you. Your kindness is unparalleled.   325

> First flowers appear, then fruits,
> first clouds rise, then rain falls,
> but here the chain of events is reversed—
> first came success, then your blessing.

MĀTALI: This is the way the creator gods give blessings.   330
KING: Sir, I married your charge by secret marriage rites. When her relatives brought her to me after some time, my memory failed and I sinned against the sage Kaṇva, your kinsman. When I saw the ring, I remembered that I had married his daughter. This is all so strange!

> Like one who doubts the existence   335
> of an elephant who walks in front of him
> but feels convinced by seeing footprints,
> my mind has taken strange turns.

MĀRĪCA: My son, you need not take the blame. Even your delusion has another cause. Listen!   340

---

2. These references establish Aditi and Mārīca's status as primordial parents of the universe and of the gods themselves.

KING: I am attentive.

MĀRĪCA: When Menakā took her bewildered daughter from the steps of the nymph's shrine and brought her to my wife, I knew through meditation that you had rejected this girl as your lawful wife because of Durvāsas' curse, and that the curse would end when you saw the ring. 345

KING: [Sighing.] So I am freed of blame.

ŚAKUNTALĀ: [To herself.] And I am happy to learn that I wasn't rejected by my husband without cause. But I don't remember being cursed. Maybe the empty heart of love's separation made me deaf 350 to the curse . . . my friends did warn me to show the ring to my husband . . .

MĀRĪCA: My child, I have told you the truth. Don't be angry with your husband!

> You were rejected when the curse 355
> that clouded memory made him cruel,
> but now darkness is lifted
> and your power is restored—
> a shadow has no shape
> in a badly tarnished mirror, 360
> but when the surface is clean
> it can easily be seen.

KING: Sir, here is the glory of my family! [He takes the child by the hand.]

MĀRĪCA: Know that he is destined to turn the wheel of your empire!

> His chariot will smoothly cross 365
> the ocean's rough waves
> and as a mighty warrior
> he will conquer the seven continents.
> Here he is called Sarvadamana,
> Tamer-of-everything; 370
> later when his burden is the world,
> men will call him Bharata, Sustainer.[3]

KING: Since you performed his birth ceremonies, we can hope for all this.

ADITI: Sir, let Kaṇva be told that his daughter's hopes have been ful- 375 filled. Menakā, who loves her daughter, is here in attendance.

ŚAKUNTALĀ: [To herself.] The lady expresses my own desire.

MĀRĪCA: He knows everything already through the power of his austerity.

KING: This is why the sage was not angry at me. 380

MĀRĪCA: Still, I want to hear his response to this joyful reunion. Who is there?

DISCIPLE: [Entering.] Sir, it is I.

MĀRĪCA: Gālava, fly through the sky and report the joyous reunion to

---

3. Bharata is to become the emperor after whom ancient India (Bhāratavarṣa) is named. Seven continents: those of the Hindu universe.

Kaṇva in my own words: "The curse is ended. Śakuntalā and her   385
son are embraced by Duṣyanta now that his memory is restored."
DISCIPLE: As you command, sir! [He exits.]
MĀRĪCA: My son, mount your friend Indra's chariot with your wife and
son and return to your royal capital!
KING: As you command, sir!   390
MĀRĪCA: My son, what other joy can I give you?
KING: There is no greater joy, but if you will:

> May the king serve nature's good!
> May priests honor the goddess of speech!
> And may Śiva's dazzling power   395
> destroy my cycle of rebirths!⁴

[All exit.]

---

4. All Sanskrit plays end with a traditional verse called *bharatavākya* ("the utterance of [the sage] Bharata"), in which the play's protagonist invokes the blessings of the gods on himself and the universal order.

BHARTṚHARI
fifth century

The *Śatakatrayam* (The Anthology of Three Centuries [i.e., three hundred poems]) of Bhartṛhari contains some of the most celebrated short lyric poems (*muktaka*) in classical Sanskrit literature. Although each of the three sections of the anthology is devoted to a different subject—political wisdom (*nīti*), erotic passion (*śṛṅgāra*), and world renunciation (*vairāgya*)—its epigrammatic stanzas are permeated by a perspective of wise counsel. Perhaps it is the philosophical tone of the poems that led to the identification of their author with the philosopher Bhartṛhari, who wrote the *Vākyapadīya*, an original treatise on metaphysics and the philosophy of language. All that can be said with certainty about the poet of the *Śatakatrayam*, however, is that he lived during the Gupta era, most likely in the fifth century, and that he was already a legend by the seventh century, when he is mentioned by the Chinese Buddhist pilgrim I-ching in his memoir of his travels in India.

The themes of the poems suggest that, like Kālidāsa, Bhartṛhari was a court poet, but there the similarity ends. Bhartṛhari's mordant lyrics reflect a sensibility very different from that of the greatest spokesman for the harmonious vision of the classical culture. The voice that comes across in these poems is that of a proud and bitter man who is painfully aware of life's indignities and of his vulnerability to the very things he despises. Although wise men are infinitely superior to kings, says Bhartṛhari, they are forced to depend on kings for their survival. The poet responds with withering sarcasm to the greed and sycophancy that he witnesses in the courts of the rich. But even a man who has mastered the desire for gold has no defense against the charm of beautiful women, which Bhartṛhari depicts as the most powerful obstacle standing between the wise man and the calm joy that characterizes liberation from *karma* and rebirth, the ultimate goal in the ancient Indian religions.

The wise man's dream in these poems is to find peace in a life of renunciation, to retire "to a sylvan silence, / o the forest where no echo sounds / of wicked men whose muddled minds / show their confusion—/ vile lords whose tongues stammer folly aloud, / confounded by disease of wealth." But no such peace is in store for the poet, who is deeply attracted by the very diversity of human experience: "In life as transient as a flashing glance, / I can choose no single course." The language, imagery, and structural strategies in the philosopher-poet's stanza poems mirror the deep conflicts and tensions in his personality, and his unique personal vision informs them, making them instantly recognizable as his. Two examples from the selections printed here will help illustrate their style and the ways in which the poems use and expand the structural and aesthetic possibilities of the *muktaka* genre.

kusumastabakasyeva   *dvayī vṛttir*   *manasvinaḥ*
As to a cluster of blossoms   two destinies   [belong to] a wise man:

mūrdhni vā   *sarvalokasya*
[it / he is] either at the crest   of the whole world,
    śīryate vana eva vā
    or [it / he] withers in the forest.

The effect here turns on a striking simile, the basic figure of speech in Sanskrit *kāvya* poetry, comparing the fate of blossoms to that of a wise man. The first half of the couplet establishes the comparison; the second deepens it in the punning, suggestive use of the phrases "crest / head / top of the world" (a mountain peak, or kingship), and "withers in the forest" (a literal withering as well as the life of ascetics in the forest). The riddlelike cerebral quality is softened by delicate imagery and suggestive overtones; both are equally essential to the epigrammatic effect. What begins as a simple simile ends as an elaborate conceit, bold, complex, and precise, in ways that delight the connoisseur of *kāvya*.

The second example, composed in *sragdharā*—the longest of the *kāvya* meters, with twenty-one syllables per verse quarter *(pāda)* in an identical pattern of short (˘) and long (−) syllables in all four *pādas*—illustrates the more complex effects within the symmetrical miniature frame of the lyric stanza.

1. **arthānām**   *īśiṣe tvaṃ*   *vayamapi*   *ca girām*   *īśmahe*
   Riches   you rule;   I, too,   of words   am master,
   yāvad **arthaṃ**
   with their infinite meanings.

2. *śūras tvam*   *vādidarpavyupaśamanavidhāv*
   Conquering hero (are) you;   in-opponent (debator)-pride-quelling-technique
   akṣayam pāṭavaṃ naḥ
   boundless (is) my skill.

3. *sevante tvāṃ dhanāḍhyā*
   (They) serve you, they who-are-blinded-by-wealth;
   matimalahataye   *māṃ api śrotukāmā*
   for-purifying-the-mind   there (are those who-) wish-to-hear me.

4. *mayy apy* **āsthā** *na te cet*   *tvayi mama nitarām*
   If for me you have no regard,   for you even greater,
   eva rājann **anāsthā**
   O king, (is) my disregard/absence.

The impact of this poem about poets and kings depends primarily not on one of the many precisely defined figures of speech *(alaṃkāra)* of Sanskrit *kāvya* but on the striking juxtaposition of antithetical statements within each quarter of the verse, the parallelism of the four *pādas*, and the resulting balance of elements in the poem as a whole. The richly varied linguistic texture of words in *kāvya* poems derives in part from the formal complexities of Sanskrit grammar and in part from the facility of the Sanskrit language to create new words by putting together other words to make compounds of any length, as in "in-opponent-pride-quelling-technique," above. Functioning like a code that must be deciphered, the compounds create complexity and ambiguity, as does the punning and balancing use of *artha* ("wealth" or "meaning") with *āsthā* ("regard") and *anāsthā* ("lack of regard" or "absence," "not staying").

Bhartṛhari's poems became the model for epigrammatic poetry, not only in Sanskrit but also in the classical traditions that developed from the tenth century onward in the regional languages of India. No later poet, however, has been able to match them in passion, ironic perspective, or eloquence.

For translations of a judicious selection of Bhartṛhari's poems, with an excellent introduction, see Barbara Stoler Miller, *The Hermit and the Love-Thief* (1978).

PRONOUNCING GLOSSARY

The following list uses common English syllables and stress accents to provide rough equivalents of selected words whose pronunciation may be unfamiliar to the general reader.

alaṃkāra: *uhl-uhng-kah'-ruh* Śatakatrayam: *shu'-tuh-kuh-truh-yuhm*

Bhartṛhari: *buhr'-tree-huh-ree* Śiva: *shee'-vuh*

dīpaka: *dee'-puh-kuh* sragdharā: *sruhg'-duh-rah*

Kālidāsa: *kah-lee-dah'-suh* śṛṅgāra: *shreen-gah'-ruh*

mokṣa: *mohk'-shuh* subhāṣita: *soo-bah'-shee-tuh*

saṃskṛta: *suhms'-kree-tuh* Vākyapadīya: *vahk'-yuh-puh-dee'-yuh*

From Śatakatrayam[1]

4

Wise men are consumed by envy,
kings are defiled by haughty ways,
the people suffer from ignorance.
Eloquence[2] is withered on my tongue.

7

A splendid palace, wanton maids,
and a white umbrella's[3] princely luster
are luxuries of wealth that survive
only while auspicious karma thrives.[4]
When this is exhausted then wealth,
like a string of pearls snapped
in violent games of love,[5]
is squandered—
falling in every dark direction.

11

A gem carved by the jeweler's stone,
a warrior-hero wounded at arms,
an elephant wasted by rut,
river banks dry in the sultry months,

---

1. Translated by Barbara Stoler Miller.   2. *Subhāṣita*, eloquent Sanskrit verse.   3. An emblem of kingship.   4. Wealth and position are thought to be good *karma*, being the result of good deeds done in past lives.   5. Evokes the erotic mood to point out the contrast between a life devoted to sensual pleasure and one devoted to virtuous conduct.

the moon in its final phase, a girl exhausted
by loveplay,
and men whose riches are spent in alms—
all are magnificent in their decline.[6]

34

Like clusters of blossoms,
wise men have two destinies:
to grace the summit of the world
or wither in the forest.

35

When silent, the courtier is branded dumb;
when eloquent, pretentious or a prating fool;
when intimate, presumptuous;
when distant, diffident;
when patient, pusillanimous;
when impetuous, ill-bred.
The rules of service are a mystery
inscrutable even to masters of wisdom.

70

Knowledge is man's crowning mark,
a treasure secretly buried,
the source of luxury, fame, and bliss,
a guru most venerable,
a friend on foreign journeys,
the pinnacle of divinity.
Knowledge is valued by kings beyond wealth—
when he lacks it, a man is a brute.

76

Armlets do not adorn a person,
or necklaces luminous as the moon;
or ablutions, or ointments,
or blossoms, or beautiful hair.
Eloquent speech that is polished[7] well
really adorns a person—
When other ornaments are ruined,
the ornament of speech is an enduring jewel.

85

Why all these words and empty prattle?
Only two worlds are worth a man's devotion:
the youth of beautiful women wearied by heavy breasts
and full of fresh wine's excitement,
or the forest.[8]

---

6. In a number of his poems, as here, Bhartṛhari illuminates unexpected commonalities among diverse phenomena; the figure of speech is appropriately called *dīpaka*, "the Illuminator."   7. *Saṃskṛta*, "refined" or "polished"; speech in the Sanskrit language.   8. This poem juxtaposes the pursuit of *kāma* ("pleasure") with that of *mokṣa* ("liberation"), which requires a person to renounce worldly life and retire to an ascetic life in the forest.

102

A melodious song,
a graceful form,
a sweet draught,
a heady fragrance,
then the touch of her breasts.
I whirl in sensations
which veil what is real.
I fall deceived by senses
cunning in seduction's art.

148

So I have roamed through perilous lands
in fruitless pursuit of reward,
relinquished my pride and my birthright
to fawn in futile servitude,
shamelessly eaten in other men's homes,
cowering like a common crow.
Greed, you gloated on my wretched deeds;
even now you will not rest content!

155

We savored no pleasure,
so we are consumed.
We practiced no penance,
so we are afflicted.
We did not elude time,
so we are pursued.
We did not wither craving,
so we are the wizened.

166

You are a king of opulence;
I am a master
of infinite words.
You are a warrior;
I hold a skill in eloquence
which subdues the fever of pride.
Men blinded by riches serve you;
but they desire to hear me
that their minds may be pure.
Since you have no regard for me,
the less have I for you,
O king—I am gone.

172

Should I sojourn in austerity
on the sacred river's bank,
or should I, in worldly fashion,
court women of high grace?
Or drink at streams of scripture

the nectar of rich verse?
In life as transient as a flashing glance,
I can choose no single course.

190
Earth his soft couch,
arms of creepers his pillow,
the sky his canopy,
tender winds his fan,
the moon his brilliant lamp,
indifference his mistress,
detachment his joy—
tranquil, the ash-smeared[9] hermit
sleeps in ease like a king.

191
Why do men need scriptures revealed, remembered,
recited in legend? Why tedious tomes of precepts?
Why the labyrinth of ritual acts
performed for reward in heaven's abode?
When compared with the fire ending time,
ending all the pain of worldly toil,
and leading men's souls into bliss,[1]
all these are the goods of haggling merchants.

9. Ascetics and worshipers of the god Śiva wear sacred ash on their bodies.   1. Even ritual acts, rewarded by finite periods in heaven, are frivolous when contrasted with the immeasurable bliss of *mokṣa* (liberation from *karma*), sole antidote to the terror of rebirth.

AMARU
seventh century

The *Amaruśataka* (Amaru's Century [of love poems]) is an anthology of more than one hundred *kāvya* poems attributed to Amaru, whom Indian tradition celebrates as a master of the short lyric (*muktaka*) genre. Of the historical Amaru we know next to nothing, although the name is surrounded by the usual quota of authorial legend. While the *Amaruśataka* appears to date from the seventh century, its author is one of the favorite poets of the influential ninth-century critic Ānandavardhana, and many of the Amaru poems eventually found their way into every major anthology of Sanskrit lyric poetry.

Amaru's lyrics are not the poems of a lover to his beloved, but evocations of the erotic mood (*śṛṅgāra rasa*), the supreme aesthetic mood in the Sanskrit *kāvya* lyric canon. Each poem is a microcosmic exploration of an aspect of the relationship between anonymous lovers. Many poems are presented in the voice of one or the other of the lovers; others are "spoken" by a narrator. Although the brevity of the verse form and the device of the lovers' voices reflect the influence of Prakrit and Tamil lyric poetry (second–third centuries), Amaru's poems are firmly situated in the classical aesthetic and courtly milieu of Sanskrit *kāvya*.

A full appreciation of Amaru's poems requires some knowledge of the conventions of the erotic *rasa*. The poems capture particular moments and stages in the progression of a love affair as schematized in the texts on poetic and dramatic theory as well as in the celebrated manual of erotics, the *Kāmasūtra* of Vātsyāyāna. The *nāyikā* (heroine) of each poem must be identified according to the several "types" into which women in love are classified in this literature, ranging from the *mugdhā* ("the timid, inexperienced heroine") to the *pragalbhā* ("the bold one"). Conventions govern the delineation of the emotional states and behavior of the hero (*nāyaka*) and heroine in each phase of the relationship and lead to further classification. A favorite theme of Amaru's is the description of the "angry heroine" (*māninī*), whose anger (*māna*) has been prompted by the hero's infidelity.

An important aspect of these love poems is the description of the physical aspects of lovemaking, especially in terms of the conventions of the *Kāmasūtra*, which specifies the strategies and accompaniments of passionate encounters, including the disarray of the bed and the art of etching "nail-marks of love"—on the woman's breasts. In classical aesthetic theory, the description of physical love serves as the necessary ground for the description of the psychological and emotional states that in turn serve as the vehicles for the reader's apprehension of the erotic mood.

According to the classical critics, Amaru excels in evoking a deeply satisfying aesthetic experience of the erotic *rasa* ("essence, flavor, mood"), which is the universalized essence of the emotion of love. For Ānandavardhana, Amaru's poems are proof that in the hands of a gifted poet a miniature stanza is no less capable of creating the full-blown aesthetic delight of mood than is a longer work such as a play—the difference between long poems and short being chiefly technique. Given the brief compass of the genre, poets of the short lyric must exploit to the utmost the suggestive powers of language, imagery, and poetic convention, as a brief examination of an Amaru poem will show.

1. *ekasmiñ śayane   parāṅmukhatayā   vītottaram*
   On the same bed,   turned away from the other,   without any answers
   tāmyator
   lying, suffering,

2. *anyonyaṃ hṛdayasthite'py   anunaye*
   each to the other in their hearts even though   (there was) making up,
   saṃrakṣator   gauravam
   as they guarded   pride,

3. *dampatyoḥ   śanakair apāṅgavalanān*
   of that couple   (upon) slowly glancing-sideways,
   miśrībhavaccakṣuṣor
   (ending in) meeting eyes,

4. *bhagno   mānakaliḥ*
   was shattered, the (lover's)   quarrel,-
   sahāsarabhasaṃ   vyāvṛttakaṇṭhagrahaḥ
   in-spontaneous-laughter,   with-enfolding-embraces.

This poem seeks to illuminate a specific moment in a love affair, here the end of a lovers' quarrel (*mānakaliḥ*, line 4). The entire poem is one long, complex sentence with its grammatical subject placed in the last line, a strategy enabled by the flexible word order in Sanskrit, in which, as in Latin, a word's grammatical function is indicated by built-in grammatical inflection. The sequence of "events" in the four lines (which are really quarter verses) maps the succession of emotional states through which the lovers pass, from silence and hurt pride to laughter and reconciliation. The sequence of emotions itself mirrors the lovers' physical movements, from lying with their backs turned to each other to the enfolding embraces at the end of the poem. The impasse of the first line is literally shattered by the denouement in the last, with the vivid turning point—the meeting of the eyes—placed at the end of line 3. The poem manages to imply the whole curve of feelings from hostility to passion in eighteen words—a delight for the connoisseur and at the same time accessible to anyone who has ever been in love.

According to Ānandavardhana the poem's effectiveness in evoking a nuance of the erotic *rasa* derives from the power of each of the elements in the poem (such as vocabulary, grammatical construction, connections with other poems, rhythm, imagery, and figures of speech) to create suggestions and resonances (*dhvani*) that go far beyond its primary function in the verse. The thirteenth-century commentator Arjunavarmadeva closes his explication of this verse with the observation that the special flavor of the "love-in-enjoyment" (*saṃbhoga*) aspect of the erotic mood in this verse arises from the progression it delicately and convincingly traces from lover's anger through a vignette of "love in separation" (*vipralambha*) to the union of eyes, arms, and hearts. Though the subtleties of Amaru's poems in the original remain the province of the connoisseur, the poems themselves offer rewarding reading to all who love lovers and love poems.

Daniel H. H. Ingalls's general introduction to *Sanskrit Poetry from Vidyākara's Treasury* (1968) is the best introduction to the aesthetics of the Sanskrit short lyric. In addition to translations of a number of love poems by Amaru and other authors, this volume also contains excellent sectional introductions that treat the conventions and classificatory schemes relating to love poetry. For Amaru in (rhymed) English verse, see John Brough, *Poems from the Sanskrit* (1968). In *Fires of Love, Waters of Peace* (1983) Lee Siegel offers lively translations and a comparison of Amaru and the philosopher poet Śaṃkara. Selected translations of Amaru may also be found in J. Moussaieff Masson and W. S. Merwin, *The Peacock's Egg* (1981).

PRONOUNCING GLOSSARY

The following list uses common English syllables and stress accents to provide rough equivalents of selected words whose pronunciation may be unfamiliar to the general reader.

Amaru: *uh'-muh-roo*

Amaruśataka: *uh'-muh-roo-shuh'-tuh-kuh*

Ānandavardhana: *ah'-nuhn-duh-vuhr'-duh-nuh*

Arjunavarmadeva: *uhr'-joo-nuh-vuhr-muh-day'-vuh*

Kāmasūtra: *kah-muh-soot'-ruh*

mānakali: *mah'-nuh-kuh-lee*

nāyikā: *nah'-yee-kah*

pragalbhā: *pruh-guhl'-bah*

saṃbhoga: *suhm-boh'-guh*

śṛṅgāra: *shreen'-gah-ruh*

vipralambha: *vee-pruh-luhm'-buh*

From Amaruśataka[1]

23

Lying on the same bed,
backs to each other,
without any answers,
holding their breaths,

even though making up   5
each to the other

---

1. Translated by Martha Ann Selby.

> was in their hearts,
>   each guarded their pride,
>
> but slowly,
>   each looked sideways,   10
> glances mingled
> and the quarrel
> exploded in laughter;
>   in enfolding embraces.

34

She's just a kid,[2]
    but I'm the one who's fainthearted.
She's the woman,
    but I'm the coward.
She bears that high, swollen set of breasts,   5
    but I'm the one who's burdened.
The heavy hips are hers,
    but I'm unable to move.

It's a wonder
how clumsy I've become   10
because of flaws
that shelter themselves
in another.

38

When anger
        was a crease in the brow
and silence
        a catastrophe,

When making up   5
        was a mutual smile
and a glance
        a gift,

now just look at this mess
that you've made of that love.   10

You grovel at my feet
and I berate you
and can't let my anger go.

57

My girl.
        Yes, lord?
Get rid of your anger, proud one.
        What have I done out of anger?
This is tiresome to me.   5
        You haven't offended me.

---

2. *Bālā*, a realistic epithet, because the inexperienced heroines of Sanskrit poems were teenage girls, generally several years younger than their lovers.

All offenses are mine.
So why are you crying yourself hoarse?
    In front of whom am I crying?
In front of me.   10
    So what am I to you?
You're my darling.
    No, I'm not.
    That's why I'm crying.

69

At first,
our bodies were as one.

Then
you were unloving,
but I still played the wretched mistress.   5

Now
you're the master
and I'm the wife.

What's next?

This is the fruit I reap   10
from our lives
as hard as diamond.

101

When my lover came to bed,
the knot[3] came untied
all by itself.

My dress,
held up by the strings of a loosened belt,   5
barely stayed on my hips.

Friend,
that's as much as I know now.

When he touched my body,
I couldn't at all remember   10
who he was,
who I was,
or how It was.

102

She's in the house.
She's at turn after turn.
She's behind me.
She's in front of me.

---

3. That is, of her garment, at the waist.

She's in my bed.   5
She's on path after path,
and I'm weak from want of her.

O heart,
there is no reality for me
other than she she   10
she she she she[4]
in the whole of the reeling world.

And philosophers talk about Oneness.[5]

4. The repetition of *sā* ("she") in the original is meant to create the effect of a sacred litany; a repeated
sacred chant *(mantra)*. **5.** The poet plays on the doctrine of the Vedanta philosophy, based on
the *Upaniṣads*, that the universe if pervaded by the "One," a single divine reality—which obviously, for
this lover, "she" is. Cf. John Donne's "The Sun Rising": "She's all states, and all princes I, / Nothing else
is."

SOMADEVA
eleventh century

Somadeva tells us that he wrote the *Kathāsaritsāgara* (Ocean to the Rivers of Story)
for the benefit of his patroness, Queen Sūryamatī of Kashmir, "to divert Her Majesty
for a while when her mind has been wearied by the continuous study of the sciences."
A Sanskrit *kāvya* work in narrative verse *(śloka)*, the *Kathāsaritsāgara* is based on a
much older tale collection called *The Great Romance (Bṛhatkathā)*, attributed to Guṇāḍhya. Guṇāḍhya's *Bṛhatkathā* has not survived, but the authors of Sanskrit story
literature from the seventh century onward acknowledge their debt to the lost work,
and the *Kathāsaritsāgara* was preceded by at least two north Indian versions of *The
Great Romance* in Sanskrit verse. True to its name, Somadeva's version has been the
preeminent repository of tales in Sanskrit literature, containing among its more than
350 stories not only individual tales but originally independent story collections, such
as *The Twenty-five Stories of the Ghoul (Vetālapañcaviṃśatikā)*, and *The Seventy Tales
of the Parrot (Śukasaptati)*. The charm of the *Kathāsaritsāgara's* stories, enhanced by
Somadeva's elegant verse, has delighted generations of Indian readers.

Like most Indian narratives, the *Kathāsaritsāgara* uses the device of nested tales
(see *Pañcatantra*, p. 1260). The main frame story traces the adventures of Naravāhanadatta, son of the legendary King Udayana, relating how he became king of the
Vidyādharas (aerial spirits). This central narrative is itself emboxed in a "tale about a
tale," which tells how *The Great Romance* came to be written. According to Somadeva,
it all began when the goddess Pārvatī cursed Puṣpadanta, a goblin attendant of her
husband (the great god Śiva). Puṣpadanta had overheard and broadcast the tales with
which Śiva had been entertaining his wife in their celestial abode. The goblin Mālyavān, who interceded for his friend, was similarly cursed. Both goblins would be reborn
on earth, and the curse of exile from heaven would be lifted only when each had
retold Śiva's stories to others on earth. All came about as predicted. Puṣpadanta told
the stories to a troll *(piśāca)* in the Vindhya forest. Mālyavān, born as Guṇāḍhya, the
court poet of King Sātavāhana, heard them from that troll, and related them to the
world in his *Bṛhatkathā*.

The Guṇāḍhya story is pervaded by Indian folklore and occult beliefs concerning
northwestern India and the Vindhya mountains in central India. In Somadeva's

version, Guṇāḍhya wrote *The Great Romance* in the forest, with his own blood, in the Paiśācī language ("trolls' tongue," identified as a northwestern Indo-Aryan dialect) and presented the work to his king, only to have it scorned and rejected on account of the barbarity of its language. The heartbroken Guṇāḍhya returned to the forest, where, weeping, he burned his manuscript, page by page, but only after reciting the contents of each page to the birds and beasts, who listened, enraptured. When this news was brought to the king, he relented, and ordered that the remainder of the manuscript be rescued and preserved in Sanskrit. His task on earth completed, Guṇ-āḍhya regained his celestial identity.

The main themes of the story of Prince Naravāhanadatta are the hero's acquisition of wealth and magical powers and his amorous adventures with a number of princesses and beautiful women, including his great love, the courtesan Madanamañcukā (Seat of the Love God). The many tales embedded in this frame story are told by the characters in the narrative to entertain their friends, lovers, and spouses, replicating the model provided by Śiva and the goddess as well as the goblins of the Guṇāḍhya story. In the *Kathāsaritsāgara* the fairy-tale–like quality of the stories is balanced by the witty social commentary and the vivid pictures that are painted of Indian society in the classical period.

Like the *Pañcatantra*, the stories of the *Kathāsaritsāgara* are concerned with *artha*, the second of the four major human pursuits, as the most important value in the context of social life. However, these tales focus on *artha* quite literally and specifically in the sense of "wealth," "profit," and "the success that wealth brings," rather than on political power and the means for acquiring such power. The majority of the heroes of the stories are merchants, bankers, and other experts in acquiring and keeping wealth, a category that includes rogues and thieves. The focus on the merchant class and on sea voyages in search of gold undoubtedly reflects the flourishing overseas commerce of Gupta and post-Gupta India as well as the worldly values cultivated in its prosperous, cosmopolitan cities. Although Naravāhanadatta is a prince, he is very different from the warrior heroes of the epics, and his very name, Gift of the God of Riches, is a name typical of the merchant community.

The tale included here, *The Red Lotus of Chastity*, is a microcosm of the Sanskrit story literature and its motifs and values. The story, which is similar to other tales about a test of conjugal fidelity in world literature (Shakespeare's *Cymbeline*, for instance), relates how the heroine Devasmitā secures the lasting love and admiration of her husband, Guhasena, by thwarting a plot hatched by some merchants (who receive help from two procuresses) to seduce her and humiliate her husband. Some of the favorite characters of the story literature are featured here: the adventurous young merchant, the beautiful and clever heroine, the corrupt nun-procuress and her crafty agent, the playboys who lust after an innocent man's wife. While virtue is rewarded and vice punished, the story revolves around the quest for gold and a woman's resourceful action in the face of a dilemma.

Guhasena is a typical hero of story literature: he knows the value of wealth and will travel to the ends of the earth to acquire it, but he is not greedy or crooked, rather, just the sort of man who is likely to be duped by scheming crooks in a foreign land. But the real hero of the story is Devasmitā. The combination of virtue, intelligence, courage, and wit in her character makes her the ideal woman of story literature, refreshingly different from women in the courtly and traditional genres. A woman who does not hesitate to elope with the man she loves, Devasmitā demands that her husband be faithful to her, even as she is to him. She immediately sees through the absurd stories cooked up by the procuresses, and the scheme whereby she gets her own back with the tricksters is testimony as much to her sense of humor as to her genius.

The stories in the *Kathāsaritsāgara* teem with colorful, earthy characters. In the Buddhist nun Yogakaraṇḍikā we have a distant forerunner of the hypocritical Tartuffe in Molière's play, and in the corrupt "holy" men and women we have early versions of the satirical portraits of monks and nuns in Chaucer. Both the nun and her help-mate Siddhikarī embody the qualities usually assigned to the courtesan and bawd in story literature—greed, rapacity, and hearts of stone. "Good" courtesans, such as Naravāhanadatta's lover Madanamañcukā, are considered to be admirable precisely because they defy the stereotype.

Storytelling ranks high among the pleasures depicted in Somadeva's stories, which brim with the enjoyment of life. Yet the recurrent theme of curses, rebirth, and the remembrance of past lives in these stories indicates that in Indian culture telling a tale is more than a pastime; it has, in fact, deep metaphysical implications. In India the gods themselves tell stories—and it is by telling and hearing stories that the sailors, goblins, and women of these stories overcome the curses that blind them to their own inner selves and thus gain access to memory, joy, and liberation at last from *karma*.

A complete translation of the *Kathāsaritsāgara*, with extensive notes bearing on comparative folklore is available in C. H. Tawney and N. M. Penzer, *The Kathā-saritsāgara or Ocean of the Streams of Story* (1880). For a thoughtful introduction to the Sanskrit story literature, and for excellent translations of selections from the *Kathāsaritsāgara* and two other Sanskrit narrative texts, see J. A. B. van Buitenen, *Tales of Ancient India* (1959).

PRONOUNCING GLOSSARY

The following list uses common English syllables and stress accents to provide rough equivalents of selected words whose pronunciation may be unfamiliar to the general reader.

Avīcī: *uh-vee'-chee*

Bṛhatkathā: *bree-huht'-kuh-thah*

Devasmitā: *day'-vuh-smee-tah*

Dhanadatta: *dhuh'-nuh-duht-tuh*

Dharmagupta: *dhuhr'-muh-goop-tuh*

Digambara: *deeg-uhm'-buh-ruh*

Guṇāḍhya: *goo-nah'-dh-yuh*

Kathāsaritsāgara: *kuh-thah'-suh-reet-sah'-guh-ruh*

Madanamañcukā: *muh-duh-nuh-muhn'-choo-kah*

Mālyavān: *mahl'-yuh-vahn*

Maṇibhadra: *muh'-neeb-huhd-ruh*

Naravāhanadatta: *nuh-ruh-vah'-huh-nuh-duht'-tuh*

Paiśācī: *pye'-shah-chee*

Pārvatī: *pahr'-vuh-tee*

piśāca: *pee-shah'-chuh*

Puṣpadanta: *poosh-puh-duhn'-tuh*

Śaktimatī: *shuhk'-tee-muh-tee*

Samudradatta: *suh-moo'-druh-duht-tuh*

Sātavāhana: *sah-tuh-vah'-huh-nuh*

Siddhikarī: *seed'-dhee-kuh-ree*

Śiva: *shee'-vuh*

Somadeva: *soh'-muh-day'-vuh*

Śukasaptati: *shoo-kuh-suhp'-tuh-tee*

Sūryamatī: *soor'-yuh-muh-tee*

Udayana: *oo-duh'-yuh-nuh*

Vetālapañcaviṃśatikā: *vay'-tah-luh-puhn'-chuh-veem-shuh-tee-kah*

Vidyādhara: *veed-yah'-dhuh-ruh*

Vindhya: *veen'-dh-yuh*

Yakṣa: *yuhk'-shuh*

Yogakaraṇḍikā:*yoh'-guh-kuh-ruhn'-dee-kah*

From Kathāsaritsāgara[1]

The Red Lotus of Chastity

In this world is a famous port, Tāmraliptī,[2] and there lived a rich merchant whose name was Dhanadatta. He had no sons, so he assembled many brahmins, prostrated himself before them, and requested: "See to it that I get a son!"

"That is not at all difficult," said the priests, "for the brahmins can bring about everything on earth by means of the scriptural sacrifices.[3]

"For example," they continued, "long ago there was a king who had no sons, though he had one hundred and five women in his seraglio. He caused a special sacrifice for a son to be performed, and a son was born to him. The boy's name was Jantu, and in the eyes of all the king's wives he was the rising new moon. Once when he was crawling about on all fours, an ant bit him on the thigh, and the frightened child cried out. The incident caused a terrific disturbance in the seraglio, and the king himself lamented—'My son! O my son!'—like a commoner. After a while, when the ant had been removed and the child comforted, the king blamed his own anxiety on the fact that he had only one son.

" 'There must be a way to have more sons,' he thought, and in his grief he consulted the brahmins. They replied: 'Indeed, Your Majesty, there is one way by which you can have more sons. Kill the son you have and sacrifice all his flesh in the sacred fire. When the royal wives smell the burning flesh, they will all bear sons.' The king had everything done as they said and got as many sons as he had wives.

"Thus with the help of a sacrifice," concluded the brahmins, "we can bring you, too, a son."

So at the advice of the brahmins, merchant Dhanadatta settled on a stipend for their sacerdotal services, and the priests performed the sacrifice for him. Subsequently a son was born to the merchant. The boy, who was given the name Guhasena, grew up in due time, and his father Dhanadatta was seeking a wife for him. And the merchant voyaged with his son to the Archipelago[4] to find a bride, though he pretended that it was just a business expedition. In the Archipelago he asked the daughter of a prominent merchant, Dharmagupta, a girl named Devasmitā, On-Whom-the-Gods-Have-Smiled, in marriage for his son Guhasena. Dharmagupta, however, did not favor the alliance, for he loved his daughter very much and thought that Tāmraliptī was too far away. But Devasmitā herself, as soon as she had set eyes on Guhasena, was so carried away by his qualities that she decided to desert her parents. Through a companion of hers she arranged a meeting with the man she loved and sailed off from the island at night with him and his father. On their arrival in Tāmraliptī they were married; and the hearts of husband and wife were caught in the noose of love.

Then father Dhanadatta died, and, urged by his relatives to continue his father's business, Guhasena made plans for a voyage to the island of

---

1. Translated by J. A. B. van Buitenen.   2. During the Gupta era, an important port on the Bay of Bengal, a center for north India's trade with south India and Southeast Asia.   3. That is, those described in the Vedas.   4. Islands of Southeast Asia and Indonesia.

Cathay.[5] Devasmitā, however, did not approve of his going, for she was a jealous wife and naturally suspected that he would love another woman. So with his relatives urging him on and his wife opposing, Guhasena was caught in the middle and could not get on with his business.

Thereupon he went to a temple and took a vow of fasting. "Let God in this temple show me a way out," he thought. Devasmitā came along, and she took the same vow. God Śiva[6] appeared to both of them in a dream. He gave them two red lotuses and spoke: "Each of you must keep this lotus in his hand. If one of you commits adultery while the other is far away, the lotus in the other's hand will wither away. So be it!" The couple woke up, and each saw in the other's hand the red lotus which was an image of the lover's heart.

So, carrying his lotus, Guhasena departed, and Devasmitā stayed home watching hers. Presently Guhasena reached Cathay and went about his business, trading in precious stones. But the lotus he carried around in his hands aroused the curiosity of four merchant's sons who noticed that the flower never seemed to fade. They tricked him into accompanying them home and gave him quantities of mead to drink; when he was drunk, they asked him about the lotus, and he told them. Calculating that the merchant's trade in precious stones would take a long time to be completed, the mischievous merchant's sons plotted together, and, their curiosity aroused, all four set sail at once for Tāmraliptī, without telling anybody, to see if they could not undo the chastity of Guhasena's wife. Reconnoitering in Tāmraliptī, they sought out a wandering nun,[7] Yogakaraṇḍikā, who lived in a Buddhist monastery. They ingratiated themselves with her and proposed, "Reverend Madam, if you can bring about what we wish, we shall reward you richly."

"Of course, you boys want some girl in town," said the nun. "Tell me. I shall see to it. I have no desire for money, because I have a clever pupil named Siddhikarī,[8] and thanks to her I have amassed a great fortune."

"How is that? You have acquired great wealth through the favor of your pupil?" the merchant's sons asked.

"If you are curious to hear the story, my sons," said the nun, "I shall tell you. Listen.

"Some time ago a merchant came to town from the North. While he was staying here, my pupil, in disguise, contrived to get herself employed in his house as a maid of all work; and as soon as the merchant had come to trust her, she stole all the gold he had in his house and sneaked away at dawn. A drummer[9] saw her leave town and, his suspicions aroused by her fast pace, started with his drum in his hand to pursue and rob her in turn. Siddhikarī had reached the foot of a banyan tree when she saw the drummer approach, and the cunning girl called out to him in a miserable voice: 'I have quarreled with my husband, and now I have run away from home to kill myself. Could you fasten the noose for me, my friend?'

" 'If she is going to hang herself, then why should I kill the woman?' thought the drummer, and he tied a noose to the tree. He stepped on his drum, put his head through the noose, and said, 'This is the way to do it.' The same instant Siddhikarī kicked the drum to pieces—and the drummer

---

5. Not China but an island in Southeast Asia or Indonesia.   6. Śiva, the destroyer god, one of the two great gods of Hinduism.   7. Buddhist monks and nuns must have no possessions and are required to live on alms, which they collect by wandering.   8. She Who Can Accomplish What One Desires.   9. A ḍomba, an executioner or low-caste functionary in cemeteries.

himself perished in the noose. But at that moment the merchant came looking for her, and from a distance he discerned the maid who had stolen his
entire fortune. She saw him come, however, and immediately climbed up
the tree and hid among the leaves. When the merchant came to the tree
with his servants, he saw only the drummer dangling from the tree, for Siddhikarī was nowhere in sight.

" 'Can she have climbed up the tree?' the merchant questioned, and immediately one of the servants went up.

" 'I have always loved you, and here you are, with me in a tree!' whispered
Siddhikarī. 'Darling, all the money is yours. Take me!' And she embraced
him and kissed him on the mouth and bit the fool's tongue off with her teeth.
Overcome with pain the servant tumbled out of the tree, spitting blood, and
cried something unintelligible that sounded like 'la-la-la.' When he saw him,
the merchant thought that the man was possessed by a ghost, and in terror
he fled home with his servants. No less terrified, Siddhikarī, my pupil,
climbed down from the top of the tree and went home with all the money."

The nun's pupil entered just as her mistress finished, and the nun presented her to the merchant's sons.

"But now tell me the truth," resumed the nun, "which woman do you want?
I shall prepare her for you at once!"

"Her name is Devasmitā," they replied, "Guhasena's wife. Bring her to bed
with us!" The nun promised to do so and gave the young men lodging in her
house.

The wandering nun ingratiated herself with the servants at Guhasena's
house by giving them delicacies and so on, and thus she gained entrance to
the house with her pupil. But when she came to the door of Devasmitā's
chambers, a dog which was kept on a chain at the door barked at her, though
never before had the bitch been known to bark. Then Devasmitā saw her,
and wondering who the woman was that had come, she sent a servant girl
to inquire and then herself conducted the nun into her chamber. When she
was inside, the nun gave Devasmitā her blessing, and after courteous amen-
ities for which she found a pretext, the wicked woman said to the chaste
wife: "I have always had a desire to see you, and today I saw you in a dream.[1]
That is why I have come to visit you. I see that you are separated from your
husband, and my heart suffers for you; if youth and beauty are deprived of
love's pleasures, they are fruitless."

With such talk the nun gained Devasmitā's confidence, and after having
chatted awhile she returned to her own home. The next day the nun took a
piece of meat covered with sneezing powder and went to Devasmitā's house.
She gave the meat to the dog at the door, and the animal at once swallowed
it. The sneezing powder caused the dog's eyes to run, and the animal sneezed
incessantly. Then the nun entered Devasmitā's apartment, and once she had
settled down to her hostess' hospitality, the shrew began to weep. Pressed
by Devasmitā she said, as if with great reluctance; "Oh, my daughter, go and
look outside at your dog; she is crying. Just now she recognized me from a
former life[2] when we knew each other, and she burst out in tears. Pity moved
me to weep with her."

Devasmitā looked outside the door and saw the dog which seemed to be

---

1. Holy persons are thought to have occult gifts, such as the ability to dream true events and interpret
them.   2. The memory of past lives is a gift, enabling the rememberer to make amends for evil deeds of
such lives.

weeping. "What miracle is this?" she wondered for the space of a moment. Then the nun said: "Daughter, in a former life both she and I were the wives of a brahmin. Our husband had to travel everywhere at the king's orders as his envoy, and while he was gone, I carried on with other men as I pleased, to avoid frustrating the senses and the elements. Our highest duty, you know, is to yield to the demands of sense and element. That is why I in this present life have the privilege of remembering past existences. But she in her ignorance guarded her chastity, and so she has been reborn a bitch, though she does remember her other life."

"What kind of moral duty is that?" thought Devasmitā, who was clever enough. "This nun has some crooked scheme afoot!" Then she said: "Reverend Madam, how long I have been ignorant of my real duty! You must introduce me to some handsome man!"

"There are some merchant's sons from the Archipelago who are staying in town," said the nun. "I shall bring them to you if you want."

Overjoyed the nun went home. And Devasmitā said secretly to her servant girls: "I am sure that some merchant's sons have seen the never-fading lotus which my husband carries in his hand, and out of curiosity they have asked him about it when he was drinking. Now the scoundrels have come here from their island to seduce me and have engaged that depraved nun as their go-between. Fetch me immediately some liquor loaded with Datura[3] drug and go and have a dog's-paw branding iron made." The maids did as their mistress told them, and one of them, at Devasmitā's instructions, dressed up as her mistress.

Meanwhile the nun selected one of the four merchant's sons, who each commanded to be taken first, and brought him, disguised as her own pupil, to Devasmitā's house. There she bade him go inside and went away unobserved. The maid who posed as Devasmitā gave the young merchant with all due courtesies the drugged liquor to drink, and the drink (as though it were his own depravity) robbed him of his senses. Then the girls stripped him of everything he wore and robed him monastically in air.[4] Thereupon they branded the dog's-paw iron on his forehead, dragged him outside, and threw him in a cesspool. In the last hours of night he came to his senses and found himself sunk in the cesspool—the very image of the Avīcī hell[5] which his own wickedness had brought on! He got up, bathed, and, fingering the mark on his forehead, he returned naked to the nun's house.

"I won't be the only ridiculous one!" he thought, and so he told his brothers in the morning that he had been robbed on his way back. Pretending a headache from his long night and deep drinking, he kept his marked forehead wrapped in a turban's cloth.

The second merchant's son who went to Devasmitā's house that night was manhandled in the same way. He too came home naked and said that, despite leaving his jewelry at home, he had been stripped by robbers as he came back. And the next morning he too kept his head bandaged, supposedly because of a headache, to conceal the brand on his forehead. All four of them, though they dissimulated everything, were castigated, branded, plundered, and put to shame in the same fashion. Without disclosing to the nun

---

3. A narcotic plant.   4. The Digaṃbaras ("clad in air"), a major sect of Jaina monks, wander naked.   5. One of the many hells described in Hindu and Buddhist mythology.

how they had been maltreated ("Let the same thing happen to her!"), they departed.

The next day the nun, who thought that her plan had succeeded, went with her pupil to Devasmitā's house. With a show of gratitude Devasmitā courteously poured them drinks with Datura, and when the nun and her pupil had passed out, the chaste wife cut off their noses and ears[6] and tossed them outside in a sewage pit.

But then Devasmitā began to worry. "Might those merchant's sons now kill my husband in revenge?" She went to her mother-in-law and told her everything that had happened.

"Daughter," said her mother-in-law, "you have done well. But something bad may now happen to my son."

"Then I shall save him as Śaktimatī once saved her husband with her presence of mind!"

"And how did she save her husband?" asked her mother-in-law. "Tell me, my daughter."

"In my country," Devasmitā began, "we have a great Yakṣa[7] who is famous under the name of Maṇibhadra. He is very powerful, and our ancestors have built him a temple in our town. My countrymen come to this temple, each with his own presents, to offer them to Maṇibhadra in order to gain whatever it is they wish. There is a custom that any man who is found in this temple at night with another man's wife is kept with the woman in the sanctum of Maṇibhadra for the rest of the night, and the next morning they are brought to court, where they will confess to their behavior and be thrown in jail.

"One night a merchant named Samudradatta was caught in the act with another man's wife by one of the temple guards. The guard led the merchant away with the woman and threw them into the sanctum of the temple where they were securely chained. After a while the merchant's faithful wife, Śaktimatī, who was very ingenious, got to know what had happened. Immediately she took an offering for pūjā worship[8] and, disguised, went out into the night to the temple, full of self-confidence and chaperoned by her confidantes. When she came to the temple, the pūjā priest, greedy for the stipend she offered him, opened the gates for her, after informing the captain of the guard. Inside the temple she found her husband who was caught with the woman. She dressed the woman up to pass for herself and told her to get out. The woman went out into the night in her disguise, and Śaktimatī herself stayed in the sanctum with her husband. When in the morning the king's magistrates came to examine them, they all saw that the merchant had only his wife with him. The king, on learning the fact, punished the captain of the guard and released the merchant from the temple as from the yawning mouth of death.

"So did Śaktimatī save her husband that time with her wits," concluded Devasmitā, and the virtuous wife added in confidence to her mother-in-law, "I shall go and save my husband with a trick, as she did."

Then Devasmitā and her maids disguised themselves as merchants,[9]

---

6. In Hindu law a punishment for women who commit adultery.　7. A type of demigod common to Hindu, Buddhist, and Jaina mythologies.　8. The rite of worshiping holy or noble persons, guests, and images of gods and goddesses.　9. The motif of a woman disguising herself as a man, especially to perform some daring feat, is a common one in folk literature. Devasmitā bears a striking resemblance to more than one of Shakespeare's heroines.

boarded a ship on the pretext of business, and departed for Cathay where her husband was staying. And on her arrival she saw her husband Guhasena—reassurance incarnate!—in the midst of traders. Guhasena saw her too, from a distance, and drank deep of the male image of his beloved wife. He wondered what such a delicate person could have to do with the merchant's profession.

Devasmitā went to the local king and announced: "I have a message. Assemble all your people." Curious, the king summoned all citizens and asked Devasmitā, who still wore her merchant's disguise, "What is your message?"

"Among these people here," said Devasmitā, "are four runaway slaves of mine. May it please Your Majesty to surrender them."

"All the people of this town are assembled here," replied the king. "Look them over, and when you recognize your slaves, take them back."

Thereupon she arrested on their own threshold the four merchant's sons, whom she had manhandled before. They still wore her mark on their foreheads.

"But these are the sons of a caravan trader," protested the merchants who were present. "How can they be your slaves?"

"If you do not believe me," she retorted, "have a look at their foreheads. I have branded them with a dog's paw."

"So we shall," they said. They unwound the turbans of the four men, and they all saw the dog's paw on their foreheads. The merchants' guild was ashamed, and the king surprised.

"What is behind this?" the king asked, questioning Devasmitā in person, and she told the story, and they all burst out laughing.

"By rights they are your slaves, my lady," said the king, whereupon the other merchants paid the king a fine and the virtuous woman a large ransom to free the four from bondage. Honored by all upright people, Devasmitā, with the ransom she had received and the husband she had rejoined, returned to their city Tāmraliptī and never again was she separated from the husband she loved.

T'ang China
ca. 650

0   200   400   600 km
0   100   200   300   400 miles

Manchu
homeland

Frontier commands
(lost after 755)

Yellow

GREAT WALL

Peking
(Beijing)

Fen

Yellow

Yellow
Sea

Wei

Lo-yang

GRAND CANAL

Han

Huai

Yang-chou

Ch'eng-tu

Nanking
(Nanjing)

K'uei-chou

Yangtse

Hang-chou

Yangtse

P'eng-tse

Hsiang

Kuang-chou

South China

Sea

CHAZAUD

China's "Middle Period"

The "middle" in our Western concept of the Middle Ages signifies an "in between," the centuries between the collapse of the Roman empire and the Renaissance. And though many cultural and literary historians have sought to correct the common image of these centuries as a period of intellectual and cultural stagnation, they remain a problematic phase in the story of Western civilization and its literature. In the case of China the situation is quite the reverse. If we use Western period terms, the *middle* of a Chinese "Middle Age" would mean "central." It is a period when Chinese thought and literature reached what many regard as their highest forms. And it is a period that later ages of Chinese history looked back to with awe. In the eleventh century Su Shih expressed a sense of intimidation by the past that was to continue through later centuries.

> Those with knowledge first fashion a thing; those with ability carry it through to fullness. It is not accomplished by one person alone. The superior man in his studies and all the various artisans in their skills reached a state of completion in the passage from the Three Dynasties of antiquity through the Han to the T'ang. When poetry reached Tu Fu, when prose reached Han Yü, when calligraphy reached Yen Chen-ch'ing, and when painting reached Wu Tao-tzu, all the variations of past and present and all the possibilities in the world were over.

Tu Fu, Han Yü, Yen Chen-ch'ing, and Wu Tao-tzu all lived during the T'ang Dynasty (618–907). Su Shih's own dynasty, the Sung (960–1279), might equally claim to have brought thought (and despite Su Shih's partiality for Wu Tao-tzu, painting as well) to a height that became a standard of achievement for the centuries that followed. Neither claim is true, of course. Chinese culture and literature continued to evolve after this splendid "Middle Age." They did not merely repeat the past any more than the European Renaissance merely recapitulated classical antiquity. Nevertheless, the great medieval dynasties of T'ang and Sung have loomed large in the national imagination.

In the second century the Han empire was crumbling. Great families dominated the central government, regional warlords were carving out their own domains, and peasant uprisings weakened the central government's authority. In the face of a collapsing social order, writers and intellectuals began to show widespread disenchantment with the Confucian values of public service. By the turn of the third century, China had become divided into three regional states, known as the Three Kingdoms: Shu in the west; Wu in the south; and in the heartland in the state of the warlord Ts'ao Ts'ao, who used the last puppet emperor of the Han empire to give him legitimacy.

After Ts'ao Ts'ao's death in A.D. 220, his successor declared the Han empire ended and established a new dynasty, the Wei. This survived only a few generations before it was overthrown by another dynasty, the Chin, which managed briefly to reunify the old empire. The Chin Dynasty fell in 316 to non-Chinese invaders from the north, and many of the great families of the north fled south of the Yangtse River, where a new Chin government had been set up by a prince of the royal house. Thus began a period of division known as the northern and southern dynasties. The north was divided among various states, each with a non-Chinese ruling and military class. The south was ruled by a succession of short-lived Chinese dynasties.

During this period Confucianism ebbed dramatically. Taoist sects, concentrating on medical, alchemical, and magical arts, flourished and founded great temples in the south. Buddhism, which had been making minor inroads for many centuries, became a major force. Buddhist missionaries from India and central Asia came to China in increasing numbers, and, working together with Chinese monks, they began the immense task of translating the important Buddhist scriptures into Chinese. Both Taoism and Buddhism promised, each in its own way, the means for personal salvation, which lay outside the purely social and ethical interests of Confucianism.

Hence the private life of the individual apart from social role became an important concern in literature after the Han empire. Writers were fascinated by the figure of the "recluse," whether a true hermit or simply someone who decided, like T'ao Ch'ien, to live at home and not serve in government. This interest was greatly encouraged by political instability and court factionalism, which led to the execution of more than a few writers. But the concern for the individual was deeper than a simple desire to escape the hazards of public life. Those who did serve in the government often cultivated and approved a stylish self-conscious eccentricity that was the very opposite of the self-effacing norms of behavior enjoined by the Confucian tradition. Nature, rather than the polity, held their attention, whether *nature* meant that of the individual or the magnificent and solitary landscapes of south China.

Owing to the loss of north China to non-Chinese overlords, most literature of the period comes from the southern dynasties, where the people saw themselves as the inheritors of traditional Chinese culture. In an important moment for the history of Chinese civilization, cultural legitimacy came to be defined not as occupation of a place (the north China plain, the ancient heartland) but as a portable tradition. Most of our knowledge of early China reaches us through the filter of the southern dynasties—their libraries, their literary histories, their criticism, and their anthologies. Although the north tried desperately to assert itself as the legitimate heir of the Chinese past, it too felt the power of the southern dynasties' appropriation of "tradition."

In the long run it was a northern dynasty, the Sui, that reunified China, to be quickly supplanted by another northern dynasty, the T'ang. Drawn by the cultural legacy of the south, the two dynasties slowly forged a new culture that combined northern and southern traditions. The T'ang Dynasty was an age of cultural confidence and, initially at least, of expansion, with T'ang armies pushing at the frontiers on all sides. Particularly important was the expansion to the northwest and control of the trade routes to the west. The upper class was attracted by the exotic goods, music, and ideas that came in along the caravan routes. Taoism and Buddhism continued to be powerful, supported by the common people and the imperial government alike; and Confucianism, the basis of state organization, enjoyed a resurgence.

Even today, a reader's first association with the T'ang period is likely to be its poetry. The composition of poetry came to be used in the examination by which intellectuals entered government service. It became an integral part of social life, a medium of basic social exchange. Perhaps nowhere else in the world has lyric poetry ever occupied such a central position, and from this context emerged a number of major poets whose work made them familiar personalities throughout the rest of Chinese history. A great poem might deal with large philosophical issues but just as easily with meeting an old friend. Poetry was seen as a way to record both individual personality and the historical moment. Through the poem the poet became alive for future readers, and in that person the philosophical idea or the moment became alive.

In the 750s, the confidence of the dynasty was broken by a major rebellion of the northeastern armies. The capital at Ch'ang-an was taken and the emperor was forced to flee. Although the rebellion was soon put down, the dynasty never quite regained its former authority. In 907 the T'ang Dynasty finally fell, and after a half-century interregnum of warring kingdoms, it was replaced in 960 by a new dynasty, the Sung.

The Sung Dynasty saw major social and intellectual changes. The old aristocratic families that dominated the T'ang Dynasty had lost their power, and the government was opened up to social groups that had previously been largely excluded from political participation. The lower Yangtse River region became a major population center, and southeasterners increasingly dominated Chinese intellectual life, as they would in later ages. In 1127 the Chin, a sinicized but non-Chinese state on the northeastern frontier, conquered north China, and the Sung Dynasty was reestablished in the south, with its capital in Hang-chou.

Although printing existed earlier, the eleventh century saw the rapid development of commercial printing, allowing literary works and scholarship a far wider audience than ever before. As in Europe, the dissemination of learning through the printed book had a significant impact on the civilization. A reexamination of the Confucian classics gave rise to a movement known as neo-Confucianism, which came to dominate intellectual life. Meanwhile Sung Dynasty classical literature continued the forms of the T'ang period, but with a difference of tone—a less intense, more reflective manner that for later ages seemed to embody the personality of the dynasty. In the urban centers of the south in the twelfth and thirteenth centuries there also developed a new vernacular literature, re-creating in writing the ambience of professional storytelling. Thus began a vernacular literary tradition that would evolve alongside classical literature up to the present.

FURTHER READING

A general study of Chinese poetry from the Han Dynasty through the T'ang can be found in Burton Watson, *Chinese Lyricism* (1971). For a general introduction to the forms of Chinese poetry there is James J. Y. Liu, *The Art of Chinese Poetry* (1962). A somewhat different approach can be found in Stephen Owen, *Traditional Chinese Poetry and Poetics: Omen of the World* (1985). A general study of poetry before the T'ang is Kang-i Sun Chang, *Six Dynasties Poetry* (1986); the eighth century is covered in Stephen Owen, *The Great Age of Chinese Poetry: The High T'ang* (1980). The Sung period is studied in Burton Watson's translation of Yoshikawa Kojiro, *An Introduction to Sung Poetry* (1967).

PRONOUNCING GLOSSARY

The following list uses common English syllables to provide rough equivalents of selected words whose pronunciation may be unfamiliar to the general reader.

Ch'ang-an: *chahng–ahn* Tao Ch'ien: *tau chyen*

Hang-chou: *hahng–joe* Wei: *way*

Sui: *sway* Wu Tao-tzu: *woo dau–dzuh*

Su Shih: *soo shir* Yen Chen-ch'ing: *yen juhn–ching*

TIME LINE

TEXTS	CONTEXTS
	220–280 The Three Kingdoms period, when China is divided into three regional states
	280 China is briefly reunified under the Chin Dynasty
	316 North China falls into the hands of non-Chinese invaders and the court moves to the south; the following period is known as the northern and southern dynasties
365–427 T'ao Ch'ien, poet and farmer	350–550 Flourishing of Buddhism and translation of Buddhist scriptures
400–450 The flourishing of landscape poetry	
500–550 Development of literary criticism, literary history, and anthology making in the south	
	589 A northern dynasty, the Sui, reunifies China
	618 The T'ang Dynasty supplants the Sui
	629 The journey of the Buddhist monk Tripitaka, the hero of *Monkey*
ca. 690 Composition of poetry included as part of the *chin-shih* examination, which young men take to qualify for the best posts in the government	
ca. 699–761 Wang Wei, poet	
701–762 Li Po, poet	
712–770 Tu Fu, poet	713–755 The "High T'ang" and the reign of Hsüan-tsung; the capital, Ch'ang-an, is a cosmopolitan center
	755 The rebellion of the north-eastern armies under their general An Lu-shan drives the emperor from the capital

Boldface titles indicate works in the anthology.

TIME LINE

TEXTS	CONTEXTS
768–824 Han Yü, poet and prose writer, advocate of "old-style" prose	
772–846 Po Chü-i, poet	
779–831 Yüan Chen, poet and author of *The Story of Ying-ying*	
791–817 Li Ho, poet	
803–852 Tu Mu, poet	**800** Revival of Confucianism under Han Yu
813–858 Li Shang-yin, poet	
	907 Final collapse of the T'ang into numerous regional kingdoms
	960 Founding of the Sung Dynasty and the reunification of China
981 Completion of the *T'ai-p'ing kuang-chi*, a vast compendium in which is preserved almost all the prose fiction from the T'ang and earlier	
1000–1100 Rise in popularity of song lyrics or *tz'u*, sung at parties and by courtesans from the Entertainment Quarters • Rapid expansion of commercial and state-supported printing	**1000–1100** Development of Neo-Confucianism, which used the Confucian classics as a ground for philosophical reflection on human nature
1084–ca. 1151 Li Ch'ing-chao, lyricist and author of Afterword to *Records on Metal and Stone*	
1127–1279 Rise of drama and professional storytelling in vernacular Chinese, especially in Hang-chou, the capital of the Southern Sung	**1127** North China falls to non-Chinese invaders from the northeast; the dynasty is reestablished south of the Yangtse River. This period, lasting until the Mongol conquest, is known as the Southern Sung
	1279 Mongols conquer south China
	1299 Marco Polo's account of his visit to China

T'AO CH'IEN
365–427

In the second decade of the fourth century, non-Chinese invaders from the north conquered north China and took the reigning Chin emperor captive. In the ensuing turmoil many of the great families and their retainers emigrated to the region south of the Yangtse River, where one of the Chin imperial princes had established his own branch of the dynasty. This was an unprecedented situation, in which "China" became a purely cultural tradition, no longer tied to the traditional heartland.

The great families from the north considered themselves an aristocracy, as compared with the local population. Buddhism established itself as a major force and received lavish patronage from the court and aristocracy. Monasteries supported schools and housed non-Chinese monks, who joined their Chinese counterparts in translating the Buddhist scriptures into Chinese. The Taoist "church" (an organized religion to be distinguished from the philosophical Taoism of early China) grew in importance and attracted distinguished followers. While society since the Han empire had always offered many alternatives to a Confucian dedication to political life, in the southern dynasties such alternatives became more and more prominent.

Individualism and eccentricity were much admired in this period, both within the aristocracy and by those who scorned social life altogether and went to live as recluses among the beautiful mountain regions south of the Yangtse. T'ao Ch'ien, who finally came to be seen as the outstanding writer of the age, was very much an individualist, and his courage of conviction was undoubtedly strengthened by the intellectual currents of the time. Despite a claim to at least one illustrious ancestor, T'ao's immediate family consisted of poor provincial gentry. He prided himself on bumbling naïveté rather than aristocratic sophistication, and instead of opulent leisure, he saw pleasure in the simple life of a rural community, offering contentment in the rhythms of farm labor.

An old strain in the Chinese tradition idealized and even sentimentalized the peasant farmer. T'ao Ch'ien stands out from earlier writers by choosing such a life as his own and finding contentment in it. Celebration of this decision and his subsequent life can be found throughout his poetry. T'ao Ch'ien's family background made him a good candidate for minor provincial posts or a place in the entourage of one of the powerful aristocrats who had usurped the political power of the eastern Chin ruler, and he did indeed serve in both capacities. Each time, however, something happened that led him to resign his post: sometimes a death in the family, sometimes sheer dissatisfaction with a career whose formalities and burdens he loathed. His final post was as magistrate of P'eng-tse, a county seat not far from his hometown. After only a little more than two months in office, he quit his post and went home, where he quietly spent the last twenty-two years of his life. It was on this occasion that he wrote his long poem *The Return*, in which he states the problem eloquently: "Whenever I have been involved in official life I was mortgaging myself to my mouth and belly."

In his own distinctive way, T'ao Ch'ien shared with other Chin intellectuals a fascination with freedom and the idea of leading a natural life. It was thought that what individuals felt was "natural" and was distinct from their will and bodily desires. Thus T'ao could will himself to serve, even wish to serve, and could satisfy his "mouth and belly," yet still be going against his nature. A joke of the same period clarifies the issue. A poor scholar once visited the house of a wealthy aristocrat. He had to use the toilet and came to a room so lavishly decorated that he thought he had stumbled into the women's quarters by mistake. He made a hasty retreat and apologized to the aristocrat, who told him that it had, indeed, been the toilet. So informed, he returned, but on trying to use the room as it was intended, he found that he could not relieve himself. He returned, said good-bye, and as the anecdote ends, "went to somebody else's toilet." Beneath the joke lies a recognition that we each have a nature in which we feel at ease; that nature can be compelled neither by will (the intention to use the opulent toilet) nor by the body's demands (which sent the scholar to the toilet in the first place). Happiness is possible only in circumstances in which one's nature is not violated.

Throughout his work T'ao returns again and again to defining what is natural to him as an individual, discovering how to live so that his nature will be content, and observing how few needs he actually has. When a fire burns down his house, he looks around and concludes that he still has enough, though the danger of hunger and want is always there, threatening to drive him forth into the world, as it does on several occasions.

The good society, then, is the small world of the farming community, supplying human needs adequately but without excess. The unpleasant alternative is the empire and its government, with its false hierarchies and continual threat of violence. His most famous image of the happy life is based on a legend then current about Peach Blossom Spring, a farming community hidden deep in the mountains, whose inhabitants were the descendants of people who had fled the Chinese heartland during wars some five centuries earlier. A fisherman, following a trail of peach blossoms in the water, stumbles on this village and gives the curious villagers a summary of the war-torn preceding half millennium of Chinese history. On leaving to go home, he pays careful attention to the route, but no one is ever able to find the place again.

In many ways the fisherman is the emblem of T'ao Ch'ien's poetry and prose. He moves from the public world to an enclosed private world, safely cut off from the outside. For the sake of the story he must go back to the public world to tell about Peach Blossom Spring, even though no one will ever be able to get there. In the same way T'ao Ch'ien's poetry and prose writings are sent out from his village to the larger world, to be read by the literate officials who serve in the imperial government. These poems tell them of a possibility of contentment that eludes them and will be hard to find even if they go looking for it.

There are two complete English translations of T'ao Ch'ien's poetry (and much of his prose), *The Poetry of T'ao Ch'ien* (1970), by James Robert Hightower, and *T'ao Yüan-ming* (1984), by A. R. Davis.

PRONOUNCING GLOSSARY

The following list uses common English syllables to provide rough equivalents of selected words whose pronunciation may be unfamiliar to the general reader.

Ch'ien-lou: *chyen–loh*

Han Hsin: *hahn shin*

Huan T'ui: *hwahn tway*

Ko-t'ien: *guh–tyen*

Kuo: *gwoh*

Liu Pang: *lyoh bahng*

Liu Tzu-chi: *lyoh dzuh–jee*

P'eng-tse: *puhng–dzuh*

T'ai-yüan: *tay–yooan*

T'ao Ch'ien: *tau chyen*

ting-mao: *ding–mau*

Yang Wang-sun: *yahng wahng–swun*

[SELECTED PROSE AND POETRY]

The Peach Blossom Spring[1]

During the T'ai-yüan period[2] of the Chin dynasty a fisherman of Wu-ling once rowed upstream unmindful of the distance he had gone, when he suddenly came to a grove of peach trees in bloom. For several hundred paces on both banks of the stream there was no other kind of tree. The wild flowers growing under them were fresh and lovely, and fallen petals covered the ground—it made a great impression on the fisherman. He went on for a way with the idea of finding out how far the grove extended. It came to an end at the foot of a mountain whence issued the spring that supplied the stream. There was a small opening in the mountain and it seemed as though light was coming through it. The fisherman left his boat and entered the cave, which at first was extremely narrow, barely admitting his body; after a few dozen steps it suddenly opened out onto a broad and level plain where well-built houses were surrounded by rich fields and pretty ponds. Mulberry, bamboo and other trees and plants grew there, and criss-cross paths skirted the fields. The sounds of cocks crowing and dogs barking could be heard from one courtyard to the next. Men and women were coming and going about their work in the fields. The clothes they wore were like those of ordinary people. Old men and boys were carefree and happy.

When they caught sight of the fisherman, they asked in surprise how he had got there. The fisherman told the whole story, and was invited to go to their house, where he was served wine while they killed a chicken for a feast. When the other villagers heard about the fisherman's arrival they all came to pay him a visit. They told him that their ancestors had fled the disorders of Ch'in times[3] and, having taken refuge here with wives and children and neighbors, had never ventured out again; consequently they had lost all contact with the outside world. They asked what the present ruling dynasty was, for they had never heard of the Han, let alone the Wei and the Chin. They sighed unhappily as the fisherman enumerated the dynasties one by one and recounted the vicissitudes of each. The visitors all asked him to come to their houses in turn, and at every house he had wine and food. He stayed several days. As he was about to go away, the people said, 'There's no need to mention our existence to outsiders.'

After the fisherman had gone out and recovered his boat, he carefully marked the route. On reaching the city, he reported what he had found to the magistrate, who at once sent a man to follow him back to the place. They proceeded according to the marks he had made, but went astray and were unable to find the cave again.

A high-minded gentleman of Nan-yang named Liu Tzu-chi heard the story and happily made preparations to go there, but before he could leave he fell sick and died. Since then there has been no one interested in trying to find such a place.

---

1. All selections translated by James Robert Hightower except *Biography of Master Five Willows,* translated by Stephen Owen.   2. From 376 to 396.   3. From 221 to 207 B.C.

The Return

I was poor, and what I got from farming was not enough to support my family. The house was full of children, the rice-jar was empty, and I could not see any way to supply the necessities of life. Friends and relatives kept urging me to become a magistrate, and I had at last come to think I should do it, but there was no way for me to get such a position. At the time I happened to have business abroad and made a good impression on the grandees as a conciliatory and humane sort of person. Because of my poverty an uncle offered me a job in a small town, but the region was still unquiet and I trembled at the thought of going away from home. However, P'eng-tse was only thirty miles from my native place, and the yield of the fields assigned the magistrate was sufficient to keep me in wine, so I applied for the office. Before many days had passed, I longed to give it up and go back home. Why, you may ask. Because my instinct is all for freedom, and will not brook discipline or restraint. Hunger and cold may be sharp, but this going against myself really sickens me. Whenever I have been involved in official life I was mortgaging myself to my mouth and belly, and the realization of this greatly upset me. I was deeply ashamed that I had so compromised my principles, but I was still going to wait out the year, after which I might pack up my clothes and slip away at night. Then my sister who had married into the Ch'eng family died in Wu-ch'ang, and my only desire was to go there as quickly as possible. I gave up my office and left of my own accord. From mid-autumn to winter I was altogether some eighty days in office, when events made it possible for me to do what I wished. I have entitled my piece 'The Return'; my preface is dated the eleventh moon of the year *i-ssu*.[1]

To get out of this and go back home!
My fields and garden will be overgrown with weeds—I must go back.
It was my own doing that made my mind my body's slave
Why should I go on in melancholy and lonely grief?
I realize that there's no remedying the past   5
But I know that there's hope in the future.
After all I have not gone far on the wrong road
And I am aware that what I do today is right, yesterday wrong.
My boat rocks in the gentle breeze
Flap, flap, the wind blows my gown;   10
I ask a passerby about the road ahead,
Grudging the dimness of the light at dawn.
Then I catch sight of my cottage—
　　Filled with joy I run.
The servant boy comes to welcome me   15
　　My little son waits at the door.
The three paths are almost obliterated
　　But pines and chrysanthemums are still here.
Leading the children by the hand I enter my house
　　Where there is a bottle filled with wine.   20
I draw the bottle to me and pour myself a cup;

---

1. A cyclical date name. China used a lunar calendar in which the first month began in late January or early February. The eleventh moon or month was probably December.

Seeing the trees in the courtyard brings joy to my face.
I lean on the south window and let my pride expand,
I consider how easy it is to be content with a little space.
Every day I stroll in the garden for pleasure,   25
There is a gate there, but it is always shut.
Cane in hand I walk and rest
Occasionally raising my head to gaze into the distance.
The clouds aimlessly rise from the peaks,
The birds, weary of flying, know it is time to come home.   30
As the sun's rays grow dim and disappear from view
I walk around a lonely pine tree, stroking it.

Back home again!
May my friendships be broken off and my wanderings come to an end.
The world and I shall have nothing more to do with one another.   35
If I were again to go abroad, what should I seek?
Here I enjoy honest conversation with my family
And take pleasure in books and zither to dispel my worries.
The farmers tell me that now spring is here
There will be work to do in the west fields.   40
Sometimes I call for a covered cart
Sometimes I row a lonely boat
Following a deep gully through the still water
Or crossing the hill on a rugged path.
The trees put forth luxuriant foliage,   45
The spring begins to flow in a trickle.
I admire the seasonableness of nature
And am moved to think that my life will come to its close.
    It is all over—
So little time are we granted human form in the world!   50
Let us then follow the inclinations of the heart:
Where would we go that we are so agitated?
I have no desire for riches
And no expectation of Heaven.
Rather on some fine morning to walk alone   55
Now planting my staff to take up a hoe,
Or climbing the east hill and whistling long
Or composing verses beside the clear stream:
So I manage to accept my lot until the ultimate homecoming.
Rejoicing in Heaven's command, what is there to doubt?   60

Biography of Master Five Willows[1]

We don't know what age the master lived in, and we aren't certain about his
real name. Beside his cottage were five willow trees, so he took his name
from them. He lived in perfect peace, a man of few words, with no desire for
glory or gain. He liked to read but didn't try too hard to understand. Yet
whenever there was something that caught his fancy, he would be so happy

---

1. Master Five Willows is T'ao Ch'ien's image of himself.

he would forget to eat. He had a wine-loving nature, but his household was so poor he couldn't always obtain wine. His friends, knowing how he was, would invite him to drink. And whenever he drank, he finished what he had right away, hoping to get very drunk. When drunk, he would withdraw, not really caring whether he went or stayed. His dwelling was a shambles, providing no protection against wind and sun. His coarse clothes were full of holes and patches; his plate and pitcher always empty; he was at peace. He forgot all about gain and loss and in this way lived out his life.

Ch'ien-lou's[2] wife once said, "Feel no anxiety about loss or low station; don't be too eager for wealth and honor." When we reflect on her words, we suspect that Five Willows may have been such a man—swigging wine and writing poems to satisfy his inclinations. Was he a person of the age of Lord No-Cares? Was he a person of the age of Ko-t'ien?[3]

Substance, Shadow, and Spirit

Noble or base, wise or stupid, none but cling tenaciously to life. This is a great delusion. I have put in the strongest terms the complaints of Substance and Shadow and then, to resolve the matter, have made Spirit the spokesman for naturalness. Those who share my tastes will all get what I am driving at.

I
Substance to Shadow

Earth and heaven endure forever,
Streams and mountains never change.
Plants observe a constant rhythm,
Withered by frost, by dew restored.
But man, most sentient being of all,   5
In this is not their equal.
He is present here in the world today,
Then leaves abruptly, to return no more.
No one marks there's one man less—
Not even friends and family think of him;   10
The things that he once used are all that's left
To catch their eye and move them to grief.
I have no way to transcend change,
That it must be, I no longer doubt.
I hope you will take my advice: 15
When wine is offered, don't refuse.

II
Shadow to Substance

No use discussing immortality
When just to keep alive is hard enough.
Of course I want to roam in paradise,

---

2. A figure of antiquity who preferred a life of poverty to serving in office.   3. Both are mythical emperors of earliest antiquity, before there were troubles in the world.

But it's a long way there and the road is lost.
In all the time since I met up with you   5
We never differed in our grief and joy.
In shade we may have parted for a time,
But sunshine always brings us close again.
Still this union cannot last forever—
Together we will vanish into darkness.   10
The body goes; that fame should also end
Is a thought that makes me burn inside.
Do good, and your love will outlive you;
Surely this is worth your every effort.
While it is true, wine may dissolve care   15
That is not so good a way as this.

III
Spirit's Solution

The Great Potter[1] cannot intervene—
All creation thrives of itself.
That Man ranks with Earth and Heaven
Is it not because of me?
Though we belong to different orders,   5
Being alive, I am joined to you.
Bound together for good or ill
I cannot refuse to tell you what I know:
The Three August Ones[2] were great saints
But where are they living today?   10
Though P'eng-tsu lasted a long time[3]
He still had to go before he was ready.
Die old or die young, the death is the same,
Wise or stupid, there is no difference.
Drunk every day you may forget,   15
But won't it shorten your life span?
Doing good is always a joyous thing
But no one has to praise you for it.
Too much thinking harms my life;
Just surrender to the cycle of things,   20
Give yourself to the waves of the Great Change
Neither happy nor yet afraid.
And when it is time to go, then simply go
Without any unnecessary fuss.

Returning to the Farm to Dwell

I
From early days I have been at odds with the world;
My instinctive love is hills and mountains.
By mischance I fell into the dusty net
And was thirteen years away from home.

---

1. The personified force of creation and change.   2. Sage kings of early antiquity who were supposed to have lived remarkably long lives.   3. He was supposed to have lived eight hundred years.

The migrant bird longs for its native grove.   5
The fish in the pond recalls the former depths.
Now I have cleared some land to the south of town,
Simplicity intact, I have returned to farm.
The land I own amounts to a couple of acres
The thatched-roof house has four or five rooms.   10
Elms and willows shade the eaves in back,
Peach and plum stretch out before the hall.
Distant villages are lost in haze,
Above the houses smoke hangs in the air.
A dog is barking somewhere in a hidden lane,   15
A cock crows from the top of a mulberry tree.
My home remains unsoiled by worldly dust
Within bare rooms I have my peace of mind.
For long I was a prisoner in a cage
And now I have my freedom back again.   20

II

Here in the country human contacts are few
On this narrow lane carriages seldom come.
In broad daylight I keep my rustic gate closed,
From the bare rooms all dusty thoughts are banned.
From time to time through the tall grass   5
Like me, village farmers come and go;
When we meet we talk of nothing else
Than how the hemp and mulberry are growing.
Hemp and mulberry grow longer every day
Every day the fields I have plowed are wider;   10
My constant worry is that frost may come
And my crops will wither with the weeds.

Begging for Food

Hunger came and drove me out
To go I had no notion where.
I walked until I reached this town,
Knocked at a door and fumbled for words
The owner guessed what I was after   5
And gave it, but not just the gift alone.
We talked together all day long,
And drained our cups as the bottle passed.
Happy in our new acquaintance
We sang old songs and wrote new poems.   10
You are as kind as the washerwoman,
But to my shame I lack Han's talent.
I have no way to show my thanks[1]
And must repay you from the grave.[2]

1. When Han Hsin was a young man, he found himself in hard straits; a washerwoman pitied him and fed him. Later he became a general of Liu Pang, the founder of the Han Dynasty, and was made a nobleman, able to repay the kindness he had received long before.   2. This echoes a story of a ghost who, out of gratitude, tripped the enemy of Lord Huan of Wei at a crucial moment.

On Moving House

I

For long I yearned to live in Southtown—
Not that a diviner told me to—
Where many simple-hearted people live
With whom I would rejoice to pass my days.
This I have had in mind for several years   5
And now at last have carried out my plan.
A modest cottage does not need be large
To give us shelter where we sit and sleep.
From time to time my neighbors come
And we discuss affairs of long ago.   10
A good poem excites our admiration
Together we expound the doubtful points.

II

In spring and fall are many perfect days
For climbing high to write new poetry.
As we pass the doors, we hail each other,
And anyone with wine will pour us some.
When the farm work is done, we all go home   5
And then have time to think of one another—
So thinking, we at once throw on a coat
And visit, never tired of talk and jokes.
There is no better way of life than this,
No need to be in a hurry to go away.   10
Since food and clothing have to be provided,
If I do the plowing, it will not cheat me.

From A Reply to Secretary Kuo

I

The trees before the house grow thick, thick
In midsummer they store refreshing shade.
The gentle southern breeze arrives on time,
It soothes my heart as it blows and whirls my gown.
I have renounced the world to have my leisure   5
And occupy myself with lute and books.
The garden produce is more than plentiful—
Of last year's grain some is left today.
What one can do oneself has its limits;
More than enough is not what I desire.   10
I crush the grain to brew a first-rate wine
And when it is ripe I pour myself a cup.
My little son, who is playing by my side,
Has begun to talk, but cannot yet pronounce.
Here is truly something to rejoice in   15
It helps me to forget the badge of rank.

The white clouds I watch are ever so far away—
How deep my yearning is for ages past.

In the Sixth Month of 408, Fire

I built my thatched hut in a narrow lane,
Glad to renounce the carriages of the great.
In midsummer, while the wind blew long and sharp,
Of a sudden grove and house caught fire and burned.
In all the place not a roof was left to us   5
And we took shelter in the boat by the gate.

Space is vast this early autumn evening,
The moon, nearly full, rides high above.
The vegetables begin to grow again
But the frightened birds still have not returned.   10
Tonight I stand a long time lost in thought;
A glance encompasses the Nine Heavens.[1]
Since youth I've held my solitary course
Until all at once forty years have passed.
My outward form follows the way of change   15
But my heart remains untrammelled still.
Firm and true, it keeps its constant nature,
No jadestone is as strong, adamantine.
I think back to the time when East-Gate[2] ruled
When there was grain left out in the fields   20
And people, free of care, drummed full bellies,
Rising mornings and coming home to sleep.
Since I was not born in such a time,
Let me just go on watering my garden.

From Twenty Poems After Drinking Wine

Preface

Living in retirement here I have few pleasures, and now the nights are growing longer; so, as I happen to have some excellent wine, not an evening passes
without a drink. All alone with my shadow I empty a bottle until suddenly I
find myself drunk. And once I am drunk I write a few verses for my own
amusement. In the course of time the pages have multiplied, but there is no
particular sequence in what I have written. I have had a friend make a copy,
with no more in mind than to provide a diversion.

V

I built my hut beside a traveled road
Yet here no noise of passing carts and horses.
You would like to know how it is done?

---

1. Heaven was described as having nine levels; here, simply the whole sky.   2. One of the mythical
rulers of high antiquity when there was such plenty that no one bothered to steal.

With the mind detached, one's place becomes remote.
Picking chrysanthemums by the eastern hedge   5
I catch sight of the distant southern hills:
The mountain air is lovely as the sun sets
And flocks of flying birds return together.
In these things is a fundamental truth
I would like to tell, but lack the words.   10

IX

I heard a knock this morning at my door
In haste I pulled my gown on wrongside out
And went to ask the caller, Who is there?
It was a well-intentioned farmer, come
With a jug of wine to pay a distant call.   5
Suspecting me to be at odds with the times:
'Dressed in rags beneath a roof of thatch
Is not the way a gentleman should live.
All the world agrees on what to do—
I hope that you will join the muddy game.'   10
'My sincere thanks for your advice, old man.
It's my nature keeps me out of tune.
Though one can learn of course to pull the reins,
To go against oneself is a real mistake.
So let's just have a drink of this together—   15
There's no turning back my carriage now.'[1]

X

Once I made a distant trip
Right to the shore of the Eastern Sea
The road I went was long and far,
The way beset by wind and waves.
Who was it made me take this trip?   5
It seems that I was forced by hunger.
I gave my all to eat my fill
When just a bit was more than enough.
Since this was not a famous plan
I stopped my cart and came back home.   10

From On Reading the *Seas and Mountains Classic*[2]

I

In early summer when the grasses grow
And trees surround my house with greenery,
The birds rejoice to have a refuge there
And I too love my home.
The fields are plowed and the new seed planted   5
And now is time again to read my books.

1. That is, from following the course of life he has chosen.   2. A fabulous geography of the countries
surrounding China, inhabited by strange creatures and oddly shaped human beings.

This out-of-the-way lane has no deep-worn ruts
And tends to turn my friends' carts away.
With happy face I pour the spring-brewed wine
And in the garden pick some greens to cook.   10
A gentle shower approaches from the east
Accompanied by a temperate breeze.
I skim through the *Story of King Mu*³
And view the pictures in the *Seas and Mountains Classic*.
A glance encompasses the ends of the universe—   15
Where is there any joy, if not in these?

Elegy

The year is *ting-mao* of the cycle, the season that of the tone *wu-i*,¹ when days are cold and the nights long, when the wind blows mournfully as the wild fowl migrate, and leaves turn yellow and fall. Master T'ao is about to depart from this lodging house to return for all time to his own home. Old friends are grieved and mourn for him: this evening they give him a farewell banquet, offering a sacrificial food, pouring libations of clear wine. They look, and his face is dim; listening, they no longer hear the sound of his voice.

Alas, alas, this vast clod, earth, that illimitable high firmament, together produce all things, even me who am a man. But from the time I attained human estate, my lot has been poverty. Rice-bin and wine-gourd have often been empty, and I have faced winters in thin clothes. Still I have gone happily to draw water from the brook and have sung as I walked under a load of firewood, going about my daily affairs in the obscurity of my cottage. As springs gave way to autumn, I have busied myself in my garden, hoeing, cultivating, planting or tending. I have rejoiced in my books and have been soothed by my zither. Winters I have warmed myself in the sun, summers I have bathed in the brook. There was little enough reward for my labor, but my mind enjoyed a constant leisure. Content with Heaven and accepting my lot, I have lived out the years of my life.

Men fear to waste their lives, concerned that they may fail to succeed. They cling to the days and lament passing time. During their life they are honored by the world, and after their death they still are mourned. But I have gone my own way, which is not their way. I take no glory in their esteem, nor do I feel defamed by their slander. I have lived alone in my poor house, drinking wine and writing poetry.

Aware of my destined end, of which one cannot be ignorant, I find no cause for regret in this present transformation. I have lived out my lifespan, and all my life I have desired quiet retirement. Now that I am dying, an old man, what have I left to wish for?

Hot and cold hasten on, one after the other.² The dead have nothing in common with the survivors. Relatives come in the morning, friends arrive in the evening, to bury me in the meadow and give comfort to my soul. Dark is

---

3. This is a travel narrative of the Chou king Mu's visits to fantastic places beyond China. **1.** Winter. *Ting-mao*: a cyclical date name, corresponding to the year 427. **2.** Refers to the passage of the seasons.

my journey, desolate the grave. It is shameful to be buried extravagantly as was Huan T'ui (whose stone coffin was three years a-making), and ridiculous to be parsimonious like Yang Wang-sun (who was buried naked), for after death there is nothing. Raise me no mound, plant me no grove; time will pass with the revolving sun and moon. I never cared for praise in my lifetime, and it matters not at all what eulogies are sung after my death. Man's life is hard enough in truth; and death is not to be avoided.

T'ANG POETRY

Lyric poetry has generally been considered China's most important traditional literary form, and in the two millennia during which classical poetry played a powerful role in the culture, no period ever quite seemed to equal the T'ang Dynasty (618–907). The role of lyric poetry in traditional China was very different from that of lyric poetry in the West. By the T'ang Dynasty lyric poems had come to be used in a wide range of situations in both private and social life—in letters to friends, as contributions to a party, or as commemorations of visits to famous places. An educated person visiting the home of a friend might leave a poem if the host was not at home. On returning the host might reply by sending a poem to express regret at having missed the visit. Officials traveling on imperial business would write poems about their journeys on the white plaster walls of government post houses, sometimes responding to other poems on the wall left by previous visitors. In addition to the wide range of social situations that called for or invited the composition of poetry, poems were also written for the more private occasions that are familiar subjects of Western poetry: finding words for the difficult moments of life, communicating love, and simply evoking imaginary scenes and old legends.

In such a world few people defined themselves exclusively as "poets." To write poetry with grace (or at least technical competence) was expected of an educated person. During much of the T'ang period, poetic composition made part of the *chin-shih* examination, by which a candidate qualified for a government appointment. Thus poetic skill touched career, social life, and private life. Although in later centuries women's circles engaged widely in poetic composition, in the T'ang period composition of poetry by women was most common at the top and on the margins of the social order. In certain periods women of the imperial court actively participated in poetry competitions and court occasions for composition. But poetry played an even larger role in the demimonde, as part of the commerce between courtesans, often trained in music and song, and their clients.

On one level, poetry was a craft that taught people how to pay attention to significant moments in their lives—to find something lovely in a scene, to express feelings about some painful or joyous event, and to find words for what would otherwise be awkward or impossible to say. Among a much smaller group, that shared social craft achieved the status of great art. Of some fifty thousand T'ang poems that survive today, by more than twenty-two hundred individuals, the works of thirty or forty truly talented poets constitute about half. Yet there are a remarkable number of memorable poems by otherwise undistinguished writers, who, by some gift of circumstance and their shared poetic training, rose briefly to compose poems that would be read and memorized for the next thousand years.

Most Chinese poems of this period have lines of either five or seven syllables. Because Chinese words are of either one or two syllables, these rhythms came as easily as iambic pentameter comes to English. The couplet was the basic unit of verse, and the last syllable of the couplet rhymed with the last syllable of other couplets.

There were many forms; the most common were the two-couplet quatrain (*chüeh-chü*) and the four-couplet regulated verse (*lü-shih*). Longer poems and stanzaic ballads were also common. Poems that had no metrical requirements other than line length and rhyme were called old-style verse. Poems requiring a balance of tones (Chinese being a tonal* language) and parallelism within the couplet were said to be in the recent style.

Parallelism, which involved matching words of similar categories in corresponding positions in the lines of a couplet, was not only a structuring device but also a way of looking at the world and seeing significant pattern in it. Hence a brilliant parallel couplet held the kind of aesthetic interest that a good metaphor has in English poetry. The following couplet is by Po Chü-i:

Or to paraphrase: "the path is glossy and slick, so that the moss sticks to the bottom of my shoes; where the stream deepens into a pool, the pole, by which the boat is pushed along, sinks under the water." The reader first notices the visual similarity between the shiny wet surface of the mossy path and the surface of the stream (the "pool" here is a deep and wide section of a river or stream). The word *hua* ("slippery" or "glossy") suggests the danger of losing one's footing. The couplet encourages us to imagine legs walking on this shiny, slippery surface, a foot sinking down into the moss, meeting solid ground, and coming up with moss stuck to the shoe. The second line shifts to a parallel motion, punting down a stream instead of walking down a path, with the boat pole taking the place of the walking legs. Coming to a deep pool, the pilot pushes the pole into the water but instead of hitting bottom, the pole unexpectedly sinks under the surface. With wit and a beautiful play of visual pattern, Po Chü-i says something about peril and pitfalls, both anticipated and unexpected.

The Chinese poetic language differs strongly from English or European poetic languages. Although in context a couplet like the one above would be only slightly more ambiguous than an English couplet, much depends on the reader's trained expectations. A situation established in the title will let a reader know that such a couplet is to be read with a first person subject and in the present tense, even though pronouns and tense markers are missing in the text. Furthermore, what seems impersonal and general in English glosses can be personal and even idiosyncratic in Chinese.

Because poetry was a sociable art exchanged among friends, readers who would never meet the poets whose work they read came to think of them as familiar characters. Even today T'ang period poets are often spoken of as acquaintances, each with a distinct, sometimes quirky personality. The best way to approach such poetry is as a cultural drama with a vivid cast of characters. Their real lives, mostly spent passing through the vagaries of government service, are finally less important than the personalities they created for themselves in their poetry.

READING T'ANG POETRY

The root meaning of *poetry* is "something made"; the Chinese word *shih*, translated as "poetry," is etymologically explained as "speaking what is intensely on the mind." Between those two ideas—*poetry* and *shih*—there is a subtle but profound difference. *Poetry*, in the sense used in the European tradition, is neither true nor false; it is a

---

*All languages are "tonal," but in most languages, including English, the tones are associated with sentence patterns. Chinese differs in having the tones attached to individual words.

"fiction" (from the Latin translation of the Greek *poetry*); a *shih*, by contrast, is always true, even if the writer tries to lie or put the best face on things. The reader of *shih* is supposed to be like a close friend; he or she knows when the writer is evasive, uneasy, or directly blurting out "what is intensely on the mind."

Reading *shih* (which I will now call "Chinese poetry") is a different kind of skill than one learns in reading Western poetry. Reading Chinese poetry can be very easy and natural, but it is an easy and natural attention to language that we learn to forget when we learn to read "literature" in the European tradition. And, like all simple things we forget, it takes a moment to relearn.

There are different kinds of T'ang poetry, but the descriptive poems are often the most perplexing, seeming to be only a pleasing sequence of images. If, however, we assume that those images come through the mind of a person with concerns and shifting attention, then those images can take on a different kind of significance. Consider Wang Wei's *Written Crossing the Yellow River to Ch'ing-ho* on page 1375. The poet is traveling; and when we think about the nature of travel, the images begin to make sense.

> The boat set sail upon the great river
> whose swollen waters stretched to sky's edge.

The Yellow River is so broad that when leaving the shore he cannot see the other side. There is some anxiety in facing such vast waters, and at this moment he looks for the far shore, his destination.

> Sky and waves split suddenly apart—
> the thousands of homes of a district capital.

The poet does not say that the boat is gradually crossing the river. His attention is focused entirely on his destination, which suddenly appears and expands on the horizon. Motion is implied in the changes of what is seen by the person moving.

> Moving on, I can see the city market
> and vaguely make out mulberry and hemp.

Now, somewhat relieved that his destination is in sight, he becomes self-conscious about moving closer, elements of the town and its surroundings becoming ever clearer as he draws closer. Travel, however, is defined by two points. Although his attention has been directed entirely to his destination, given his anxiety about the crossing and eagerness to reach the security of land on the far side, the moment he feels the security of Ch'ing-ho, as he gets closer, he turns to look back.

> I turn to gaze back toward my homeland:
> only vast floods that stretch to the clouds.

The scene looking back is the mirror image of the scene setting off; reaching his destination also means being cut off from a secure land route to his home. His absorption in the attainment of one goal, reaching Ch'ing-ho, has kept him from thinking about what he has left behind; now that the goal is almost attained, his attention is suddenly turned back toward home, and all he can see is the river and the clouds. He says very little about traveling and nothing explicit about his state of mind, but through a sequence of scenes he tells a compact story about the subjective experience of travel and the nature of reaching desired goals.

A general survey of the poetry of the eighth century can be found in Stephen Owen, *The Great Age of Chinese Poetry: The High T'ang* (1980). A more general introduction to Chinese poetry can be found in James Liu, *The Art of Chinese Poetry* (1962), and in Stephen Owen, *Traditional Chinese Poetry and Poetics: An Omen of the World* (1985).

PRONOUNCING GLOSSARY

The following list uses common English syllables to provide rough equivalents of selected words whose pronunciation may be unfamiliar to the general reader.

chin-shih: *jin–sherr*   lü-shih: *loo–shir*

chüeh-chü: *jooeh–joo*   Po Chü-i: *bwoh joo-ee*

hua: *hwa*

WANG WEI
ca. 699–761

Wang Wei, the child of an aristocratic family, was a favorite as a youth in the courts of the T'ang princes. Like other court poets, he could produce gracefully ornate verse on public occasions. But he also had an austere side; and on other, less ceremonious, occasions he wrote a poetry that combined simplicity with deliberate craft. There is often a strangeness of vision in what seem to be very simple lines. Only Wang Wei could have written "The setting sun goes down beside a bird," in which a small creature that never stays long in one place becomes the stable reference point defining the motion of the huge and regular sun.

Wang Wei served in various posts in the imperial government, both in the capital and in the provinces, but his real love was his estate at Wang Stream, in the mountains south of the capital. He celebrated this both in poetry and in monochrome landscape painting. Wang Wei was one of the founders of Chinese landscape painting, and copies of his work survive. Most critics have seen in Wang Wei's poetry something of the painter's eye. This is true in a far deeper sense than is involved in describing picturesque landscapes; Wang Wei's poetry shows his continuing interest in the organization of space and how it changes with a moving viewer.

In his later years Wang grew increasingly attracted to Buddhism and eventually took vows as a Buddhist layman. Other poets celebrated the landscape as it appears to the senses, but Wang Wei's representations often show an insubstantiality that corresponds to the Buddhist notion of the "emptiness" of things, that all we perceive is illusion. One of his most famous couplets first describes an open expanse, then suddenly turns to a massive mountain—or what seems to be a mountain—as an uncertain darkening of color in dense mist:

> The river flows out beyond Heaven and Earth;
> the mountain's color, in between presence and absence.

There are two useful studies of Wang Wei, including translations: Pauline Yu, *The Poetry of Wang Wei* (1980), and Marsha Wagner, *Wang Wei* (1981).

PRONOUNCING GLOSSARY

The following list uses common English syllables to provide rough equivalents of selected words whose pronunciation may be unfamiliar to the general reader.

Chieh Yü: *jyeh yoo*   P'ei Ti: *pay dee*

Ch'ing-ho: *ching–heh*   Wang-ch'uan: *wahng–chooahn*

Chung-nan: *joong–nahn*   Wang Wei: *wahng way*

Huang-fu Yüeh: *hwahng–foo yooeh*

Villa on Chung-nan Mountain[1]

In my middle years I came to love the Way[2]
and made my home late by South Mountain's edge.

When the mood came upon me, I went off alone,
and had moments of splendor all to myself.

I would walk to the point where a stream ends,   5
and sitting, would watch when the clouds rise.

By chance I would meet old men in the woods;
we would laugh and chat, no fixed time to turn home.

When Living Quietly at Wang-ch'uan I Gave This to P'ei Ti

Cold mountains grow ever more azure-grey,
fall's floods churn more loudly each passing day.

And I rest on my staff outside this rough gate;
breeze on my face, I listen to twilight cicadas.

The ford holds the remnants of setting sun;   5
from a hamlet rises a lone column of smoke.

Now once again I meet Chieh Yü, the drunk,[3]
that reckless singer before the five willows.[4]

Answering Magistrate Chang

Now late in life I love only stillness,
all the world's troubles touch not my heart.

I look within and find there no great plans,
know only to return to the woods of my home.

There wind through pines blows my sash untied,   5
moon of the hills shines on playing a harp.

You ask the pattern of failure and success?—
the fisherman's song reaches deep over the shore.

1. All selections translated by Stephen Owen.   2. Buddhism.   3. A famous virtuous madman of antiquity. By referring to his friend P'ei Ti as Chieh Yü, Wang Wei is complimenting his genuineness and unconventionality.   4. The willows traditionally suggest the dwelling of a recluse.

Various Topics on Huang-fu Yüeh's Cloudy Valley

The Torrent Where the Birds Sang

Into the mortal world a cassia flower falls,[5]
the night is still, spring mountains are deserted.
The moon comes out, alarming the mountain birds
that sing out now and then in the spring torrent.

Cormorant[6] Dike

All at once it dives down through red lotus,
coming out again, flies to cool shores.
It stands alone, its feathers puffed out,
fish in its beak, upon an old log.

From Wang Stream Collection

Deer Fence

I see no one in the deserted hills,
hear only the echo of men's speech.
Sunlight cast back[7] comes deep in the woods
and shines once again upon the green moss.

Lodge in the Bamboo

I sit alone in bamboo that hides me,
plucking the harp and whistling long.
It is deep in the woods and no one knows—
the bright moon comes to shine on me.

Written Crossing the Yellow River to Ch'ing-ho

The boat set sail upon the great river
whose swollen waters stretched to sky's edge.

Sky and waves split suddenly apart—
the thousands of homes of a district capital.

Moving on, I can see the city market   5
and vaguely make out mulberry and hemp.

I turn to gaze back toward my homeland:
only vast floods that stretch to the clouds.

---

5. The dark pattern in the moon was, in Chinese myth, a cassia tree. The fall of an ordinary cassia flower hints at the coming moonrise.   6. Cormorants were often used by fishermen for catching fish, although this one is obviously wild.   7. Refers to the late afternoon sunlight that, being low in the sky, comes in under overhead obstructions and seems to cast its rays back toward the east.

Parting

I get off my horse, drink wine with you
and ask you where you are going.

You say things have not turned out as you wished,
you go home to rest by South Mountain's edge.

Then go off, and I will ask no more—   5
the white clouds that never end.

HAN-SHAN
ca. 600–800

The Buddhist monk Han-shan may or may not have been a real person. The biography included in the preface to his collected poems is more a sketch of a typical eccentric than the story of a real person. Han-shan, Cold Mountain, was indeed the real name of a mountain (of many mountains, in fact) and the site of a famous temple. It seems likely that the name—perhaps the name of a real monk who wrote some poems— was a name around which a corpus of Buddhist poems gradually accumulated throughout the T'ang period. The Han-shan poems were admired in Japan and more recently in the United States; they were not much appreciated in China until modern times.

The three-hundred-odd poems that make up the Han-shan corpus are of very uneven quality. The best are among the finest expressions of Ch'an (Zen) Buddhism. Cold Mountain, whether person or place, is a state of mind. The voice in the poems addresses outsiders, telling them about enlightenment. But enlightenment cannot be put into words. The speaker can only point toward it in a series of figures; it is a landscape of the mind.

Burton Watson, *Cold Mountain* (1962), contains lively translations of a selection of Han-shan's poetry. Excellent literary translations have been done by Gary Snyder, *Riprap and Cold Mountain Poems* (1965), and by Red Pine, *The Collected Songs of Cold Mountain* (1983). The latter is a complete translation. There is also a complete annotated translation by Robert Henricks, *The Poetry of Han-shan* (1990), with an extensive introduction.

PRONOUNCING GLOSSARY

The following list uses common English syllables to provide rough equivalents of selected words whose pronunciation may be unfamiliar to the general reader.

Ch'an: *chahn*   Han-shan: *hahn–shahn*

40[1]

I climb the road to Cold Mountain,
The road to Cold Mountain that never ends.
The valleys are long and strewn with stones;
The streams broad and banked with thick grass.
The moss is slippery, though no rain has fallen; 5
Pines sigh, but it is not the wind.
Who can break from the snares of the world
And sit with me among the white clouds?

45

Cold Mountain is full of weird sights;
People who try to climb it always get scared.
When the moon shines, the water glints and sparkles;
When the wind blows, the grasses rustle and sigh.
Snowflakes make blossoms for the bare plum, 5
Clouds in place of leaves for the naked trees.
At a touch of rain, the whole mountain shimmers—
But only in good weather can you make the climb.

48

Wonderful, this road to Cold Mountain—
Yet there's no sign of horse or carriage.
In winding valleys too tortuous to trace,
On crags piled who knows how high,
A thousand different grasses weep with dew 5
And pines hum together in the wind.
Now it is that, straying from the path,
You ask your shadow, "What way from here?"

57

When people see the man of Cold Mountain
They all say, "There's a crackpot!
Hardly a face to make one look twice,
His body wrapped in nothing but rags . . ."
The things I say they don't understand; 5
The things they say I would not utter.
A word to those of you passing by—
Try coming to Cold Mountain sometime!

1. All selections translated by Burton Watson.

62

High, high from the summit of the peak,
Whatever way I look, no limit in sight!
No one knows I am sitting here alone.
A solitary moon shines in the cold spring.
Here in the spring—this is not the moon.   5
The moon is where it always is—in the sky above.
And though I sing this one little song,
In the song there is no Zen.

80

Man, living in the dust,
Is like a bug trapped in a bowl.
All day he scrabbles round and round,
But never escapes from the bowl that holds him.
The immortals are beyond his reach,   5
His cravings have no end,
While months and years flow by like a river
Until, in an instant, he has grown old.

82

People ask the way to Cold Mountain.
Cold Mountain? There is no road that goes through.
Even in summer the ice doesn't melt;
Though the sun comes out, the fog is blinding.
How can you hope to get there by aping me?   5
Your heart and mine are not alike.
If your heart were the same as mine,
Then you could journey to the very center!

96

Have I a body or have I none?
Am I who I am or am I not?
Pondering these questions,
I sit leaning against the cliff while the years go by,
Till the green grass grows between my feet   5
And the red dust settles on my head,
And the men of the world, thinking me dead,
Come with offerings of wine and fruit to lay by my corpse.

99

So Han-shan writes you these words,
These words which no one will believe.
Honey is sweet; men love the taste.
Medicine is bitter and hard to swallow.
What soothes the feelings brings contentment,   5
What opposes the will calls forth anger.
Yet I ask you to look at the wooden puppets,
Worn out by their moment of play on the stage!

LI PO
701–762

Li Po was from western China, and some have suspected that his family was of Turkish origin. In an age that valued family background, he was a nobody. To make a place for himself in upper-class society, he had to "invent" himself as an eccentric personality and as poet, a task he undertook with gusto. Social success in T'ang period China depended either on family connections or on the civil service examination (the training for which depended in some measure on family). Li Po had neither. But the dynasty also patronized Taoist "wizards," and through his connection with one eminent wizard, Li Po gained entrance to the Han-lin Academy, an imperial establishment for entertainers, intellectuals who did not advance through the normal channels, and interesting eccentrics.

In the Han-lin Academy Li Po seems to have been something of a cross between court poet and jester. As legend has it, his much-admired eccentricity, aided by alcohol, passed over the delicate boundary into rudeness; he offended powerful figures in the court and was dismissed. He dignified this dismissal as an exile brought on by the slander of his enemies and a failure to recognize his exceptional worth. The emperor may have been no longer amused, but Li Po retained the admiration of many intellectuals, who saw his rare talent.

Li Po's sometimes extravagant brashness contrasts sharply with Wang Wei's austere control. Much T'ang poetry tended to treat the world at hand; Li Po gave it an additional dimension of poetic fantasy, describing the worlds of the Taoist heavens, evoking moments of history and legend, and even transforming more everyday occasions into something wondrous and strange. For such flair and capacity to see the world with fresh eyes, his contemporaries called him the "banished immortal," one of those ethereal beings who dwell in the heavens and who, for some extravagant misdemeanor, have been exiled to live out a lifetime in the world of mortals.

Arthur Waley, *The Genius of Li Po* (1950), is an excellent biography. There is a long chapter on Li Po's poetry in Stephen Owen, *The Great Age of Chinese Poetry: The High T'ang* (1980).

PRONOUNCING GLOSSARY

The following list uses common English syllables to provide rough equivalents of selected words whose pronunciation may be unfamiliar to the general reader.

Ch'ang-an: *chahng–ahn*   P'ing-lo: *ping–luh*
Ching-t'ing: *jing–ting*   Tan-ch'iu: *dahn–chyoh*
Hsi-ho: *shee–huh*   Ts'ao Chih: *tsau jerr*
Jo-yeh: *rwoh–ye*   Ts'en: *tsuhn*
Li Po: *lee bwoh*   Wang Wei: *wahng way*
Lu-yang: *loo–yahng*   Yüeh: *yooeh*

The Sun Rises and Sets[1]

The sun comes up from its nook in the east,
Seems to rise from beneath the earth,
Passes on through Heaven,
    sets once again in the western sea,
And where, oh, where, can its team of six dragons   5
    ever find any rest?
Its daily beginnings and endings,
    since ancient times never resting.
And man is not made of its Primal Stuff—
    how can he linger beside it long?   10
Plants feel no thanks for their flowering in spring's wind,
Nor do trees hate losing their leaves
    under autumn skies:
Who wields the whip that drives along
    four seasons of changes—   15
The rise and the ending of all things
    is just the way things are.

Hsi-ho![2] Hsi-ho!
Why must you always drown yourself
    in those wild and reckless waves?   20
What power had Lu-yang[3]
That he halted your course by shaking his spear?
This perverts the Path of things,
    errs from Heaven's will—
So many lies and deceits!   25
I'll wrap this Mighty Mudball of a world
    all up in a bag
And be wild and free like Chaos itself!

Bring in the Wine

Look there!
The waters of the Yellow River,
coming down from Heaven,

---

1. All selections translated by Stephen Owen.   2. Goddess who drove the sun's carriage.   3. Reference to the legend that the lord of Lu-yang, engaged in combat, made the sun stop in its course so that the fight could continue.

rush in their flow to the sea,
   never turn back again   5
Look there!
   Bright in the mirrors of mighty halls
   a grieving for white hair,
   this morning blue-black strands of silk,
   now turned to snow with evening.   10
For satisfaction in this life
   taste pleasure to the limit,
And never let a goblet of gold
   face the bright moon empty.
Heaven bred in me talents,   15
   and they must be put to use.
I toss away a thousand in gold,
   it comes right back to me.
So boil a sheep,
   butcher an ox,   20
      make merry for a while,
And when you sit yourself to drink, always
   down three hundred cups.
   Hey, Master Ts'en,
   Ho, Tan-ch'iu,[1]   25
   Bring in the wine!
   Keep the cups coming!
And I, I'll sing you a song,
You bend me your ears and listen—
The bells and the drums, the tastiest morsels,   30
   it's not these that I love—
All I want is to stay dead drunk
   and never sober up.
The sages and worthies of ancient days
   now lie silent forever,   35
And only the greatest drinkers
   have a fame that lingers on!
Once long ago
   the prince of Ch'en[2]
      held a party at P'ing-lo Lodge.[3]   40
A gallon of wine cost ten thousand cash,
   all the joy and laughter they pleased.
      So you, my host,
How can you tell me you're short on cash?
Go right out!   45
   Buy us some wine!
      And I'll do the pouring for you!
Then take my dappled horse,
   Take my furs worth a fortune,
Just call the boy to get them,   50
   and trade them for lovely wine,
And here together we'll melt the sorrows
   of all eternity!

---

1. Master Ts'en and Tan-ch'iu are Li Po's friends.   2. The poet Ts'ao Chih (192–232).   3. Reference to a party described in one of Ts'ao Chih's poems.

Yearning

Endless yearning
Here in Ch'ang-an,[4]
Where the cricket spinners cry autumn
   by the rail of the golden well,
Where flecks of frost blow chill,   5
   and the bedmat's color, cold.
No light from the lonely lantern,
   the longing almost broken—
Then roll up the curtain, gaze on the moon,
   heave the sigh that does no good.   10
A lady lovely like the flowers,
   beyond that wall of clouds,
And above, the blue dark of heavens high,
And below, the waves of pale waters.
Endless the sky, far the journey,   15
   the fleet soul suffers in flight,
And in its dreams can't touch its goal
   through the fastness of barrier mountains—
Then endless yearning
Crushes a man's heart.   20

Ballad of Youth

A young man of Five Barrows suburb
   east of the Golden Market,[1]
Silver saddle and white horse
   cross through wind of spring.
When fallen flowers are trampled all under,   5
   where is it he will roam?
With a laugh he enters the tavern
   of a lovely Turkish wench.

The Girls of Yüeh

A girl picking lotus on Jo-yeh Creek[2]
Sees the boatman return, singing a rowing song.
With a giggle she hides in the lotus flowers
And, pretending shyness, won't come out.

---

4. The T'ang Dynasty's capital.   1. In Ch'ang-an.   2. In southeastern China in a region famous for
its beautiful women.

Dialogue in the Mountains

You ask me why I lodge in these emerald hills;
I laugh, don't answer—my heart is at peace.
Peach blossoms and flowing waters
   go off to mysterious dark,
And there is another world,[3]   5
   not of mortal men.

Summer Day in the Mountains

Lazily waving a fan of white feathers,
Stripped naked here in the green woods,
I take off my headband, hang it on a cliff,
My bare head splattered by wind through pines.

My Feelings

Facing my wine, unaware of darkness growing,
Falling flowers cover my robes.
Drunk I rise, step on the moon in the creek—
Birds are turning back now,
   men too are growing fewer.   5

Drinking Alone by Moonlight

Here among flowers a single jug of wine,
No close friends here, I pour alone
And lift cup to bright moon, ask it to join me,
Then face my shadow and we become three.
The moon never has known how to drink,   5
All my shadow does is follow my body,
But with moon and shadow as companions a while,
This joy I find must catch spring while it's here.
I sing, the moon just lingers on,
I dance, and my shadow scatters wildly.   10
When still sober we share friendship and pleasure,
Then entirely drunk each goes his own way—
Let us join in travels beyond human feelings
And plan to meet far in the river of stars.

---

3. The image suggests the Peach Blossom Spring described by T'ao Ch'ien, a place removed from the troubles of this world.

Sitting Alone by Ching-t'ing Mountain

The flocks of birds have flown high and away,
A solitary cloud goes off calmly alone.
We look at each other and never get bored—
Just me and Ching-t'ing Mountain.

TU FU
712–770

If Li Po was associated with Taoism and the free, uncaring immortals, Tu Fu has always been strongly associated with Confucian virtues, embodied in his political commitment, his social concerns, and his love of family. A consensus of readers considers Tu Fu to be China's greatest poet, with each successive age finding in Tu Fu's work its own sense of what constitutes greatness. That very ability to satisfy changing values is a tribute to the diversity of his work. Yet he was esteemed in every age of Chinese poetry but his own.

During his lifetime Tu Fu was eminently unsuccessful, both as political figure and as poet. The grandson of one of the most famous court poets of the early eighth century, the young Tu Fu sought political office with no success. When the great rebellion of 755 took the capital by surprise and the emperor fled west, Tu Fu was trapped behind enemy lines. Some of his finest early poems were written at this period, as he heard of the defeat of one imperial army after another. Eventually he slipped through the lines and made his way to the court of the new emperor, who was directing military operations against the rebels. There he briefly held one of those court posts he had so much desired, but following the recapture of the capital, he was exiled to a minor provincial post, a job he came to detest. He quit this post in disgust and took up a life of wandering, first to the northwest, then west to Ch'eng-tu, the capital of Szechwan, then down the Yangtse River, coming in his last year to the lakes region in central China. It was during these last years of his life that Tu Fu wrote most of his poetry.

Because Chinese poetry treats both the minor details and the major crises of a person's life, a poet's work as a whole can be seen as autobiography or even diary. The culture valued poetry as a key to the historical person. One reason for Tu Fu's appeal may be the way he documents his life, from the smallest details to the largest dimensions of social context. Traditional critics often refer to him as the poet historian, in whose work incidents from that important moment in Chinese history come alive. He was also a meticulous craftsman, constantly revising his poems. In that process, like Li Po, he created the personality later readers so admire. But unlike Li Po, he presents himself as a character who has suffered, endured much, and changed.

Particularly recommended is David Hawkes, *A Little Primer of Tu Fu* (1967), which gives the Chinese text and a word-by-word explanation of a small group of Tu Fu's poems. Another study is A. R. Davis, *Tu Fu* (1971).

PRONOUNCING GLOSSARY

The following list uses common English syllables to provide rough equivalents of selected words whose pronunciation may be unfamiliar to the general reader.

An Lu-shan: *ahn loo–shahn*

Ch'ang-an: *chahng–ahn*

Ch'eng-tu: *chuhng–doo*

Chiang: *jyahng*

Fu-chou: *foo–joe*

Lu-tzu: *loo–dzuh*

P'eng-ya: *puhng–yah*

Sun Tsai: *swun dzai*

T'ung-chia: *toohng–jyah*

Song of P'eng-ya[1]

I remember when first we fled the rebellion,[2]
Hurrying north, we passed through hardship and danger.
The night was deep on the P'eng-ya Road,
And the moon was shining on Whitewater Mountain.
The whole family had been traveling long on foot—   5
Most whom we met seemed to have no shame.
Here and there birds of the valley sang,
We saw no travelers going the other way.
My baby girl gnawed at me in her hunger,
And I feared wild beasts would hear her cries: 10
I held her to my chest, covered her mouth,
But she twisted and turned crying louder in rage.
My little son did his best to take care of things,
With purpose went off and got sour plums to eat.
It had thundered and rained half the past week,   15
We clung together, pulling through mud and mire,
And having made no provision against the rain,
The paths were slippery, our clothes were cold.
At times we went through great agony
Making only a few miles in an entire day.   20
Fruits of the wilds served as our provisions,
Low-hanging branches became our roof.
Then early in mornings we went through the runoff,
To spend the evening at homestead smoke on horizon.
We stayed a while in T'ung-chia Swamp   25
And were about to go out Lu-tzu Pass,
When an old friend of mine, Sun Tsai by name—
His great goodness reached the tiers of cloud—
Welcomed us as night's blackness was falling,
Hung out lanterns, opened his many gates,   30
With warm water had us wash our feet,
Cut paper flags to summon our souls,
Then afterward brought in his wife and children,
Whose eyes, seeing us, streamed with tears.
As if unconscious, my brood was sleeping;   35
He woke them kindly and gave them plates of food.

---

1. All selections translated by Stephen Owen. 2. That is, the time Tu Fu took his family out of the path of An Lu-shan's rebel army.

And I make this vow to you,
That forever I will be your brother, your kin.
Then he emptied the hall where we sat,
I rested peacefully—he offered what gave me joy.   40
Who else would be willing in times of such trouble
To show his good heart so openly?
Since we have parted, a year has run its course,
And still the barbarian weaves his calamities.
When shall I ever have the wings   45
To fly off and alight before your eyes?

Moonlit Night[1]

The moon tonight in Fu-chou
She[2] watches alone from her chamber,
While faraway I think lovingly on daughters and sons,
Who do not yet know how to remember Ch'ang-an.[3]
In scented fog, her cloudlike hairdo moist,   5
In its clear beams, her jade-white arms are cold.
When shall we lean in the empty window,
Moonlit together, its light drying traces of tears.

Chiang Village[1]

From west of the towering ochre clouds
the sun's rays descend to the level earth.

Birds raise a racket in the brushwood gate
as the traveler comes home from a thousand miles.

Wife and children are amazed I survived,   5
when surprise settles, they wipe away tears.

I was swept along in the turmoil of the times,
by chance I managed to make it back alive.

Our neighbors are filling the wall,[2]
so deeply moved they're sobbing too.   10

Toward night's end I take another candle,
and face you, as if it still is a dream.

---

1. Tu Fu is trapped behind rebel lines in the capital Ch'ang-an.   2. His wife.   3. That is, the person in the capital, Tu Fu himself.   1. Written after Tu Fu finally rejoined his wife after escaping through rebel lines.   2. In other words, all the neighbors are gathering to witness the reunion. Even modest houses had low walls around the yard.

Thousand League Pool

The blue creek fuses dark mystery within,
A holy creature, sometimes appearing, sometimes concealed—
A dragon resting in massed waters coiled,
His lair sunken under a thousand leagues.
Pace each step with care, pass over cliff rim,   5
Bent for balance go down into mist and haze,
Look out over a stretch of mighty waves,
Then stand back on a greatness of gray stone.
The mountain is steep, the one path here now ends
Where sheer banks form two facing walls: 10
Thus were they hewn, rooted in nothingness,
Their inverted reflections hung in shaking waters.
The black tells of the vortex's bottom,
The clear parts display a shattered sparkling.
Deep within it a lone cloud comes,   15
And the birds in flight are not outside.
High-hung vines for its battle tents,
The winter trees rank its legions' standards.
Streams from afar twist their flows to reach here,
Caves give subterranean vent to swift scouring.   20
I have come to a place hidden, a realm without men,
The response it stirs is all our own.
Now, asking my leave, unwillingness hangs strongly on,
As old age approaches, this visit, the finest.

Hiding himself away, he sleeps in long scales;   25
The mighty stone blocks his going and his coming—
Oh, when shall the blazing skies of summer pass,
That his will may exult in the meeting of wind and rain.

My Thatched Roof Is Ruined by the Autumn Wind

In the high autumn skies of September
   the wind cried out in rage,
Tearing off in whirls from my rooftop
   three plies of thatch.
The thatch flew across the river,   5
   was strewn on the floodplain,
The high stalks tangled in tips
   of tall forest trees,
The low ones swirled in gusts across ground
   and sank into mud puddles.   10
The children from the village to the south
   made a fool of me, impotent with age,
Without compunction plundered what was mine
   before my very eyes,
Brazenly took armfuls of thatch,   15
   ran off into the bamboo,

And I screamed lips dry and throat raw,
  but no use.
Then I made my way home, learning on staff,
  sighing to myself.   20
A moment later the wind calmed down,
  clouds turned dark as ink,
The autumn sky rolling and overcast,
  blacker towards sunset,
And our cotton quilts were years old   25
  and cold as iron,
My little boy slept poorly,
  kicked rips in them.
Above the bed the roof leaked,
  no place was dry,   30
And the raindrops ran down like strings,
  without a break.
I have lived through upheavals and ruin
  and have seldom slept very well,
But have no idea how I shall pass   35
  this night of soaking.
Oh, to own a mighty mansion
  of a hundred thousand rooms,
A great roof for the poorest gentlemen
  of all this world,   40
  a place to make them smile,
A building unshaken by wind or rain,
  as solid as a mountain,
Oh, when shall I see before my eyes
  a towering roof such as this?   45
Then I'd accept the ruin of my own little hut
  and death by freezing.

A Guest Comes

North of my cottage, south of my cottage,
  spring waters everywhere,
And all that I see are the flocks of gulls
  coming here day after day,
My path through the flowers has never yet   5
  been swept for a visitor,
But today this wicker gate of mine
  stands open just for you.
The market is far, so for dinner
  there'll be no wide range of tastes,   10
Our home is poor, and for wine
  we have only an older vintage.
Are you willing to sit here and drink
  with the old man who lives next door?
I'll call to him over the hedge,   15
  and we'll finish the last of the cups.

Spending the Night in a Tower by the River

A visible darkness grows up mountain paths,
I lodge by river gate high in a study,
Frail cloud on cliff edge passing the night,
The lonely moon topples amid the waves.
Steady, one after another, a line of cranes in flight;   5
Howling over the kill, wild dogs and wolves.
No sleep for me. I worry over battles.
I have no strength to right the universe.

Writing of My Feelings Traveling by Night

Slender grasses, breeze faint on the shore;
here, the looming mast, the lonely night boat.

Stars hang down on the breadth of the plain,
the moon gushes in the great river's current.

My name shall not be known from my writing,   5
sick, growing old, I must yield up my post.

Wind-tossed, fluttering—what is my likeness?
in Heaven and Earth, a single gull of the sands.

LI HO
791–817

Li Ho descended from a minor and impoverished branch of the T'ang Dynasty royal house. A brilliant graduate of the provincial examinations, he caught the attention of the influential Han Yü, who recommended him to take the capital examination. His political hopes were thwarted because of a technical violation of the taboo against having the same name as one's father (part of his father's name was homophonous with the *chin* of *chin-shih*, the title he would have held if he'd passed the examination). His father's rank, however, did entitle him to a minor position in the government. Eventually, he gave up hopes for a political career and returned to his home, where he died in his mid-twenties.

The playful fantasy of Li Po's work becomes demonic in Li Ho. His obsession with death and the supernatural, combined with a passion for dense, daring lines, produced a small body of poetry that is unique in the tradition. Li Ho saw unseen worlds more vividly than the world close at hand. An object of this world, such as an arrowhead from an ancient battlefield, becomes less an object in its own right than a means to gain access to the spirit world. Yet because of his brilliant images and the intensity of his poetic voice, Western readers have often found his work more easily accessible than that of any other T'ang poet.

The translations of A. C. Graham in *Poems of the Late T'ang* (1965) remain unsurpassed. There is also a complete translation by J. D. Frodsham, *The Poems of Li Ho* (1970), and a study by Tu Kuo-ch'ing, *Li Ho* (1979).

PRONOUNCING GLOSSARY

The following list uses common English syllables to provide rough equivalents of selected words whose pronunciation may be unfamiliar to the general reader.

Ch'ang-an: *chahng–ahn*

Ch'ang-p'ing: *chahng–ping*

Chao: *jau*

Ch'in: *chin*

chin-shih: *jin–sherr*

Chung-nan: *joong–nahn*

Han Yü: *hahn yoo*

Li Ho: *lee huh*

Su: *soo*

Tung-t'ing: *doong–ting*

Magic Strings[1]

The witch pours the libation, clouds fill the sky,
In the flaming coals of the jade brazier the fumes of incense throb.
The God of the Sea and the Hill Nymph take their places,
Votive papers rustle in the howling whirlwind.
On her inlaid lute of passion-wood a goldleaf phoenix dances: 5
With knitted brow at each muttered phrase she plucks the strings once.
She calls to the stars and summons the demons to taste of her dish
    and cup:
Mankind shudders when the mountain goblins feed.
The glow of the sun behind Chung-nan[2] hangs low in a trough of
    the hills:
The gods are here, for ever present between somewhere and nowhere!   10
The gods scold, the gods are pleased, in spasms on the medium's face.
—Then the gods with a myriad outriders go back to the blue mountains.

Song of an Arrowhead from the Battlefield of Ch'ang-p'ing[1]

Char of lacquer, powder of bone,
    pebble of cinnabar:
In the chill gloom ancient blood
    blooms flowers in the bronze.
The white feathers and gilt shaft   5
    have gone in the rains,
And all that remains is this
    three-spined, broken wolf's fang.

---

1. All selections translated by A. C. Graham except *Song of an Arrowhead*, translated by Stephen Owen.
2. A mountain south of the T'ang capital of Ch'ang-an.   1. The site of a battle in 260 B.C. in which the army of the Ch'in completely destroyed a huge army from the state of Chao.

I went searching over that level plain,
   driving my two-horse team,   10
Through the stony fields east of the station
   by the foot of a weed-grown slope;
Daylight shortened, the wind was steady,
   stars hung in its moaning,
Black banners of cloud were draped soaking   15
   in the empty night sky.
To my right and left their phantoms
   cried out, starving, lean:
I poured a jug of cream in libation,
   took a lamb to roast.   20
Insects settled, the geese flew sick,
   the sprouts of reeds turned red,
And spiraling gusts sent the traveler on his way,
   blowing their shadowy fires.

Seeker of the past, tears streaming,   25
   I reaped this snapped barb,
Whose broken point and red-brown cracks
   once cut through flesh.
On a southern lane in the capital's eastern ward
   a boy on horseback   30
Tried to get me to trade the metal
   for an offering basket.

The King of Ch'in Drinks Wine

The King of Ch'in rides out on his tiger and roams to the Eight
   Bounds,[1]
The flash of his sword lights up the sky against the resisting blue:
He is Hsi-ho[2] flogging the sun forward with the sound of ringing glass.
The ashes of the kalpas[3] have flown away, rebellion has never been.
Dragon's heads spout wine and the Wine Star is his guest,   5
Gold-grooved mandolins twang in the night;
The feet of the rain on Lake Tung-t'ing come blown on a gust from
   the pan-pipes,
Heated by the wine his shout makes the moon run backward!

Under combed layers of silvered cloud the jasper hall brightens,
A messenger from the palace gate reports the first watch.   10
The jade phoenix of the painted tower has a sweet and fierce voice,
Mermaid silks patterned in crimson have a faint and cool scent.
The yellow swans trip over in the dance. A thousand years in the cup!

Beneath the immortal's tree of candles, where the wax lightly smokes,
The tears flood Blue Zither's[4] drunken eyes.   15

1. The ends of the cosmos. The king of Ch'in here is a fantastic transformation of the first emperor, who unified China in 221 B.C.   2. Charioteer of the sun.   3. Buddhist term for eons; at the completion of each, fires burn over the earth, and life starts anew.   4. An immortal woman.

The Grave of Little Su

I ride a coach with lacquered sides,
My love rides a dark piebald horse.
Where shall we bind our hearts as one?
On West Mound,[5] beneath the pines and cypresses.
  (Ballad ascribed to the singing girl Little Su,
            ca. A.D. 500)

Dew on the secret orchid
Like crying eyes.
No thing to bind the heart to.
Misted flowers I cannot bear to cut.
Grass like a cushion,   5
The pine like a parasol:
The wind is a skirt,
The waters are tinkling pendants.
A coach with lacquered sides
Waits for someone in the evening.   10
Cold blue candle-flames
Strain to shine bright.
Beneath West Mound
The wind puffs the rain.

The Northern Cold

The sky glows one side black, three sides purple.
The Yellow River's ice closes, fish and dragons die.
Bark three inches thick cracks across the grain,
Carts a hundred piculs[1] heavy mount the river's water.
Flowers of frost on the grass are as big as coins,   5
Brandished swords will not pierce the foggy sky,
Crashing ice flies in the swirling seas,
And cascades hang noiseless in the mountains, rainbows of jade.

A Dream of Heaven

The old hare and the chilled frog[2] weep the sky's sheen,
Through a door ajar in a mansion of cloud the rays slant white on
  the wall.
The white-jade wheel[3] shivers the dew into wet globes of light;
Chariot bells[4] meet girdle pendants on cassia-scented[5] paths.

---

5. A funeral mound. 1. Three tons; a picul is equal to approximately sixty pounds. 2. The hare and
the frog are on the moon. 3. The moon. 4. Men out driving meet girls walking with jade pendants
tinkling at their waists [Translator's note]. 5. The cassia tree is on the moon.

Yellow dust and clear water beneath the Fairy Mountains   5
Change places once in a thousand years which pass like galloping horses.
When you peer at far-off China, nine puffs of smoke:[6]
And the single pool of the ocean has drained into a cup.

6. Generally identified with the nine ancient provinces of China, surely indistinguishable at this altitude. But according to Tsou Yen (ca. 300 B.C.) China is itself one of nine continents each separated from the rest by impassible seas. Probably the immortal who tries to make out China sees all nine inside the tiny cupful of ocean [Translator's note].

PO CHÜ-I
772–846

Po Chü-i was the most prolific of all T'ang Dynasty poets, with more than twenty-eight hundred poems to his credit. A group of his poems, known as the "New Ballads," were verse narratives dramatizing what he saw as social abuses in the period. In writing these, Po saw himself as fulfilling the true vocation of the Confucian poet, using his talents to stir the hearts of those in power to remedy these evils.

The larger and finally more influential part of Po Chü-i's poetry celebrates the small events of his life with a genial wit. He wrote on such topics as eating fresh bamboo shoots, gardening, and his grandchildren. More than any other T'ang poet Po Chü-i developed Tu Fu's use of poetry as a kind of autobiography, tracing the poet's inner life as well as outer experiences. This set the model for many later poets who came to use poetry both as celebration and as documentation of everyday life.

No less than other T'ang poets, Po also created a poetic persona for himself. A successful official, he was compelled in his public life to obey all the polite constraints and formalities of that world. In compensation he created for his private identity an easygoing eccentric, one who cared nothing for the opinion of others. Beneath his protestations of spontaneity, however, he remained an intensely self-reflective writer, attempting through his poetry to live up to an impossible ideal of the "natural man."

Arthur Waley, *The Life and Times of Po Chü-i* (1949), is recommended not only as the best biography of Po but as one of the best introductions to the context of Chinese poetry.

PRONOUNCING GLOSSARY

The following list uses common English syllables to provide rough equivalents of selected words whose pronunciation may be unfamiliar to the general reader.

Ch'ang-an: *chahng–ahn*

Chuang Tzu: *jooahng dzuh*

Chung-nan: *joong–nahn*

Hsi K'ang: *shee kahng*

Hsün-yang: *shun–yahng*

Po Chü-i: *bwoh joo–ee*

T'ien-mên: *tyen–mehn*

Yen Hui: *yen hway*

Yüan Chen: *yooahn juhn*

Watching the Reapers[1]

(A.D. 806)

Tillers of the earth have few idle months;
In the fifth month[2] their toil is double-fold.
A south wind visits the fields at night;
Suddenly the ridges are covered with yellow corn.
Wives and daughters shoulder baskets of rice,   5
Youths and boys carry flasks of wine,
In a long train, to feed the workers in the field—
The strong reapers toiling on the southern hill,
Whose feet are burned by the hot earth they tread,
Whose backs are scorched by the flames of the shining sky.   10
Tired they toil, caring nothing for the heat,
Grudging the shortness of the long summer day.
A poor woman with a young child at her side
Follows behind, to glean the unwanted grain.
In her right hand she holds the fallen ears,   15
On her left arm a broken basket hangs.
Listening to what they said as they worked together
I heard something that made me very sad:
They lost in grain-tax[3] the whole of their own crop;
What they glean here is all they will have to eat.   20

And I today—in virtue of what desert
Have I never once tended field or tree?
My government-pay is three hundred 'stones';[4]
At the year's end I have still grain in hand.
Thinking of this, secretly I grew ashamed   25
And all day the thought lingered in my head.

Passing T'ien-mên Street in Ch'ang-an and Seeing a Distant View of Chung-nan Mountains

The snow has gone from Chung-nan;[1] spring is almost come.
Lovely in the distance its blue colours, against the brown of the streets.
A thousand coaches, ten thousand horsemen pass down the Nine Roads;[2]
Turns his head and looks at the mountains—not one man!

The Flower Market

In the Royal City spring is almost over;
Tinkle, tinkle—the coaches and horsemen pass.
We tell each other 'This is the peony season';
And follow with the crowd that goes to the Flower Market.

---

1. All selections translated by Arthur Waley.   2. Midsummer.   3. Chinese peasants paid taxes in kind.
4. Measures of grain in which an official's pay was counted.   1. A mountain south of Ch'ang-an.
2. The major avenues of the capital.

"Cheap and dear—no uniform price;   5
The cost of the plant depends on the number of blossoms.
The flaming reds, a hundred on one stalk;
The humble white with only five flowers.
Above is spread an awning to protect them;
Around is woven a wattle-fence to screen them.   10
If you sprinkle water and cover the roots with mud,
When they are transplanted, they will not lose their beauty."
Each household thoughtlessly follows the custom,
Man by man, no one realizing.
There happened to be an old farm labourer   15
        Who came by chance that way.
He bowed his head and sighed a deep sigh;
But this sigh nobody understood.
He was thinking, "A cluster of deep-red flowers
Would pay the taxes of ten poor houses."   20

Golden Bells

When I was almost forty
I had a daughter whose name was Golden Bells.
Now it is just a year since she was born;
She is learning to sit and cannot yet talk.
Ashamed—to find that I have not a sage's heart;   5
I cannot resist vulgar thoughts and feelings.
Hencefoward I am tied to things outside myself;
My only reward—the pleasure I am getting now.
If I am spared the grief of her dying young,
Then I shall have the trouble of getting her married.   10
My plan for retiring and going back to the hills
Must now be postponed for fifteen years!

Lazy Man's Song

(A.D. 811)

I could have a job, but am too lazy to choose it;
I have got land, but am too lazy to farm it.
My house leaks; I am too lazy to mend it.
My clothes are torn; I am too lazy to darn them.
I have got wine, but I am too lazy to drink;   5
So it's just the same as if my cup were empty.
I have got a lute, but am too lazy to play;
So it's just the same as if it had no strings.
My family tells me there is no more steamed rice;
I want to cook, but am too lazy to grind.   10
My friends and relatives write me long letters;
I should like to read them, but they're such a bother to open.
I have always been told that Hsi Shu-yeh[1]

---

1. Hsi K'ang (223–262), an eccentric alchemist, musician, and poet.

Passed his whole life in absolute idleness.
But he played his lute and sometimes worked at his forge;   15
So even *he* was not so lazy as I.

Winter Night

Written during his confinement in 812

My house is poor; those that I love have left me.
My body is sick; I cannot join the feast.
There is not a living soul before my eyes
As I lie alone locked in my cottage room.
My broken lamp burns with a feeble flame;   5
My tattered curtains are crooked and do not meet.
"Tsek, tsek" on the door-step and window-sill
Again I hear the new snow fall.
As I grow older, gradually I sleep less;
I wake at midnight and sit up straight in bed.   10
If I had not learned the "art of sitting and forgetting,"[2]
How could I bear this utter loneliness?
Stiff and stark my body cleaves to the earth;
Unimpeded my soul yields to Change.[3]
So has it been for four tedious years,   15
Through one thousand and three hundred nights!

Remembering Golden Bells

Ruined and ill—a man of two score;
Pretty and guileless—a girl of three.
Not a boy—but still better than nothing:
To soothe one's feeling—from time to time a kiss!
There came a day—they suddenly took her from me;   5
Her soul's shadow wandered I know not where.
And when I remember how just at the time she died
She lisped strange sounds, beginning to learn to talk,
Then I know that the ties of flesh and blood
Only bind us to a load of grief and sorrow.   10
At last, by thinking of the time before she was born,
By thought and reason I drove the pain away.
Since my heart forgot her, many days have passed
And three times winter has changed to spring.
This morning, for a little, the old grief came back,   15
Because, in the road, I met her foster-nurse.

2. Yen Hui told Confucius that he had acquired the "art of sitting and forgetting." Asking what that meant, Yen Hui replied: "I have learnt to discard my body and obliterate my intelligence; to abandon matter and be impervious to sense-perception. By this method I become one with the All-pervading."—*Chuang Tzŭ*, chap. vi [Translator's note].   3. The principle of endless mutation which governs the Universe [Translator's note].

On Board Ship:
Reading Yüan Chên's Poems

I take your poems in my hand and read them beside the candle;
The poems are finished, the candle is low, dawn not yet come.
My eyes smart; I put out the lamp and go on sitting in the dark,
Listening to waves that, driven by the wind, strike the prow of the ship.

Madly Singing in the Mountains

There is no one among men that has not a special failing;
And my failing consists in writing verses.
I have broken away from the thousand ties of life;
But this infirmity still remains behind.
Each time that I look at a fine landscape,   5
Each time that I meet a loved friend,
I raise my voice and recite a stanza of poetry
And marvel as though a God had crossed my path.
Ever since the day I was banished to Hsün-yang
Half my time I have lived among the hills.   10
And often, when I have finished a new poem,
Alone I climb the road to the Eastern Rock.
I lean my body on the banks of white Stone;
I pull down with my hands a green cassia branch.
My mad singing startles the valleys and hills;   15
The apes and birds all come to peep.
Fearing to become a laughing-stock to the world,
I choose a place that is unfrequented by men.

The Cranes

The western wind has blown but a few days;
Yet the first leaf already flies from the bough.
On the drying paths I walk in my thin shoes;
In the first cold I have donned my quilted coat.
Through shallow ditches the floods are clearing away;   5
Through sparse bamboos trickles a slanting light.
In the early dusk, down an alley of green moss,
The garden-boy is leading the cranes home.

Pruning Trees

(A.D. 830)

Trees growing—right in front of my window;
The trees are high and the leaves grow thick.

Sad alas! the distant mountain view,
Obscured by this, dimly shows between.
One morning I took knife and axe;   5
With my own hand I lopped the branches off.
Ten thousand leaves fell about my head;
A thousand hills came before my eyes.
Suddenly, as when clouds or mists break
And straight through, the blue sky appears.   10
Again, like the face of a friend one has loved
Seen at last after an age of parting.
First there came a gentle wind blowing;
One by one the birds flew back to the tree.
To ease my mind I gazed to the South-East;   15
As my eyes wandered, my thoughts went far away.
Of men there is none that has not some preference;
Of things there is none but mixes good with ill.
It was not that I did not love the tender branches;
But better still—to see the green hills!   20

Last Poem

They have put my bed beside the unpainted screen;
They have shifted my stove in front of the blue curtain.
I listen to my grandchildren reading me a book;
I watch the servants, heating up my soup.
With rapid pencil I answer the poems of friends,   5
I feel in my pockets and pull out medicine-money.
When this superintendence of trifling affairs is done,
I lie back on my pillows and sleep with my face to the South.

YÜAN CHEN
779–831

Long fiction was a relatively late development in China. Some elements of a tradition of historical saga survive from the ancient period, but early Chinese literature showed its considerable narrative genius primarily in the anecdote and parable. During the early middle period, between the third and seventh centuries, the anecdotal tradition was further developed in accounts of eccentric or exemplary behavior and witty dialogues. At the same time we begin to find collections of short tales about ghosts, fox spirits, and assorted demons, a genre that remained very popular up to the present century. During the T'ang period (618–907), writers began to expand on the skeletal narrative style of the earlier period.

There are two distinct groups of T'ang stories: one written in classical Chinese and the other in early vernacular Chinese. The vernacular narratives, elaborating known stories from the Buddhist tradition and Chinese history, were discovered early in the twentieth century in a sealed Buddhist repository at Tun-huang, an outpost of the caravan route in northwest China. Most of the tales in classical Chinese, a far larger corpus, were printed in a large collection in 981 and have been known throughout the tradition. The classical tales, known as *ch'uan-ch'i* ("accounts of remarkable things"), are still comparatively short by Western standards, but they show a true delight in the craft of telling—in atmosphere, characterization, and detail. Unlike the vernacular stories, these classical tales are all "original" material (even though most claim to have heard the story from someone else). Supernatural stories, particularly of erotic encounters between mortal men and supernatural women, are the most common; but the *ch'uan-ch'i* also incorporate tales of heroism and love.

T'ang love stories, whether between mortals or between mortals and supernatural beings, often turn on the question of faith kept or broken. The love was usually in some way illicit, and by the end of the eighth century we can see a fully developed idea of romantic love, which offers interesting comparisons with images of romantic love in the Western tradition. *The Story of Ying-ying* is the most famous but in many ways the most anomalous work in this tradition of love stories. The usual literary love affair involves a talented young scholar and a courtesan or a supernatural being in the guise of a mortal woman. *The Story of Ying-ying* describes an illicit affair between a young man and his distant cousin, a situation in which marriage is not only acceptable but the obvious solution. Yet the lovers, each in his or her own way, thwart the possibility of legitimate marriage to create a conventional tale of broken love. In a tradition of fiction so consistently concerned with the extraordinary, the treatment of the ordinary becomes itself extraordinary. So unexpected is this story in the context of T'ang tales of romantic love that Chinese critics have wished to see it as a thinly disguised account of the personal experiences of the author, the famous poet Yüan Chen. If it is indeed autobiographical, the author is portraying himself in a most unflattering way.

The plot of *The Story of Ying-ying* could not be more straightforward: a young man has an affair with his cousin, leaves her to go to the capital to take the civil service examination, loses interest in her, and breaks off the relationship. But within this simple plot *The Story of Ying-ying* mocks the T'ang love narrative. Both of the lovers are acting roles that never quite fit them. The young man, like any hero of a T'ang love story, at first disdains the usual erotic adventures of his peers, looking for the perfect woman; and as a lover should, he falls helplessly in love with Ying-ying at their first meeting. When he falls out of love and it serves his interests, he changes his role and condemns Ying-ying with platitudes of conventional public morality. Yet this pose of rectitude does not keep him from wanting to see her again, after she is married, when he happens to be in the neighborhood.

Ying-ying herself is no less an actor. By a display of bad temper to her mother she blocks the first stage of an easy route to a socially acceptable marriage. Then she plays the role of the conventionally virtuous young woman, offended by the young man's advances. Next she is the romantic heroine, overcome with passion. Finally she plays the lover who keeps faith, cruelly abandoned by a heartless young man. Yet despite her vows of undying love and faith unto death, she soon marries someone else. Everywhere the story calls attention to the difference between real people and the roles they play, both literary and social. In the context of the narrative, even poetry is exposed as a glittering lie: Yüan Chen's poem transforms the rather mundane affair into one between a mortal and a goddess, and poetic convention transforms his desertion into the inevitable separation of the goddess and her mortal lover.

The context makes Ying-ying's letter to her lover Chang, written in the most florid and formal prose, an ambiguous piece of T'ang eloquence. It may be read either as a genuine expression of a young woman's pain or as a manipulative attempt to work on his sympathies and regain control of the situation. Irony, whether intentional or not, pervades the story. At the close of the letter she warns him, "Be circumspect [in what you say] and careful, and do not think too often of my unworthy person." The very next sentence is: "Chang showed her letter to his friends, and in this way word of the affair got around." Both Ying-ying and Chang try to make claims on the reader's sympathy and approval, but in the end it is hard to give full approval to either. None of the cherished values of T'ang society survive unquestioned—whether pious public values or the private values of passionate and faithful love. By the end of the story these all seem merely the convenient excuses of the fallible human beings who use them. Almost unique among contemporary works, the story is finally ambivalent; each of the main characters tries to assert that his or her viewpoint is correct, and neither succeeds.

Yüan Chen was a well-known poet and close friend of Po Chü-i. Passing through the usual phases of exile and reinstatement in party politics, he eventually rose to a high position in the T'ang government. *The Story of Ying-ying* is his only tale.

The story became a popular one, and in the process of its popularization it went through some drastic transformations. The final and most famous version was the thirteenth-century play *Romance of the Western Chamber.* Here all the troubling aspects of the work are ironed smooth. The remarkably willful and tempestuous Ying-ying is transformed into an ordinary, docile heroine, and the lovers are at last reunited to live happily ever after.

PRONOUNCING GLOSSARY

The following list uses common English syllables to provide rough equivalents of selected words whose pronunciation may be unfamiliar to the general reader.

Chen-yüan: *juhn–yooahn*

Cho Wen-chün: *jwoh wuhn–joon*

ch'uan-ch'i: *chwahn–chee*

Hsiao shih: *shyao shir*

Hsieh K'un: *shyeh kwun*

Hsi wang-mu: *shee wahng–moo*

Huan-lang: *hwahn–lahng*

Hung-niang: *huhng–nyahng*

Li Kung-ch'ui: *lee guhng–chway*

Pao-ssu: *bao–suh*

Po Chü-i: *bwoh joo–ee*

P'u: *poo*

Ssu-ma Hsiang-ju: *szih–mah shyahng–roo*

Teng-tu tzu: *duhng–too dzuh*

Ting Wen-ya: *ding wun–yah*

Ts'ui: *tsway*

Tu Ch'üeh: *doo chooeh*

Tun-huang: *dwuhn–hwahng*

Yu: *yoh*

Yü: *yoo*

Yüan Chen: *yooahn juhn*

The Story of Ying-ying[1]

During the Chen-yüan period[2] there lived a young man named Chang. He was agreeable and refined, and good looking, but firm and self-contained, and capable of no improper act. When his companions included him in one of their parties, the others could all be brawling as though they would never get enough, but Chang would just watch tolerantly without ever taking part. In this way he had gotten to be twenty-three years old without ever having had relations with a woman. When asked by his friends, he explained, "Teng-t'u tzu[3] was no lover, but a lecher. I am the true lover—I just never happened to meet the right girl. How do I know that? It's because things of outstanding

---

1. Translated by James Robert Hightower. 2. From 785 to 804. 3. An archetypal lecher.

beauty never fail to make a permanent impression on me. That shows I am not without feelings." His friends took note of what he said.

Not long afterward Chang was traveling in P'u,[4] where he lodged some ten li^5 east of the city in a monastery called the Temple of Universal Salvation. It happened that a widowed Mrs. Ts'ui had also stopped there on her way back to Ch'ang-an. She had been born a Cheng; Chang's mother had been a Cheng, and when they worked out their common ancestry, this Mrs. Ts'ui turned out to be a rather distant cousin once removed on his mother's side.

This year Hun Chen[6] died in P'u, and the eunuch Ting Wen-ya proved unpopular with the troops, who took advantage of the mourning period to mutiny. They plundered the citizens of P'u, and Mrs. Ts'ui, in a strange place with all her wealth and servants, was terrified, having no one to turn to. Before the mutiny Chang had made friends with some of the officers in P'u, and now he requested a detachment of soldiers to protect the Ts'ui family. As a result all escaped harm. In about ten days the imperial commissioner of inquiry, Tu Ch'üeh, came with full power from the throne and restored order among the troops.

Out of gratitude to Chang for the favor he had done them, Mrs. Ts'ui invited him to a banquet in the central hall. She addressed him: "Your widowed aunt with her helpless children would never have been able to escape alive from these rioting soldiers. It is no ordinary favor you have done us; it is rather as though you had given my son and daughter their lives, and I want to introduce them to you as their elder brother so that they can express their thanks." She summoned her son Huan-lang, a very attractive child of ten or so. Then she called her daughter: "Come out and pay your respects to your brother, who saved your life." There was a delay; then word was brought that she was indisposed and asked to be excused. Her mother exclaimed in anger, "Your brother Chang saved your life. You would have been abducted if it were not for him—how can you give yourself airs?"

After a while she appeared, wearing an everyday dress and no makeup on her smooth face, except for a remaining spot of rouge. Her hair coils straggled down to touch her eyebrows. Her beauty was extraordinary, so radiant it took the breath away. Startled, Chang made her a deep bow as she sat down beside her mother. Because she had been forced to come out against her will, she looked angrily straight ahead, as though unable to endure the company. Chang asked her age. Mrs. Ts'ui said, "From the seventh month of the fifth year of the reigning emperor to the present twenty-first year, it is just seventeen years."

Chang tried to make conversation with her, but she would not respond, and he had to leave after the meal was over. From this time on Chang was infatuated but had no way to make his feelings known to her. She had a maid named Hung-niang with whom Chang had managed to exchange greetings several times, and finally he took the occasion to tell her how he felt. Not surprisingly, the maid was alarmed and fled in embarrassment. Chang was sorry he had said anything, and when she returned the next day he made shamefaced apologies without repeating his request. The maid said, "Sir, what you said is something I would not dare repeat to my mistress or let

---

4. A province northeast of Ch'ang-an.   5. A unit of measure equal to one-quarter of a mile.   6. The regional commander of Chiang-chow died in P'u-chou in 799 [Translator's note].

anyone else know about. But you know very well who Miss Ts'ui's relatives are; why don't you ask for her hand in marriage, as you are entitled to do because of the favor you did them?"

"From my earliest years I have never been one to make any improper connections," Chang said. "Whenever I have found myself in the company of young women, I would not even look at them, and it never occurred to me that I would be trapped in any such way. But the other day at the dinner I was hardly able to control myself, and in the days since, I walk without knowing where I am going and eat without hunger—I am afraid I cannot last another day. If I were to go through a regular matchmaker, taking three months and more for the exchange of betrothal presents and names and birthdates[7]—you might just as well look for me among the dried fish in the shop.[8] Can't you tell me what to do?"

"Miss Ts'ui is so very strict that not even her elders could suggest anything improper to her," the maid replied. "It would be hard for someone in my position to say such a thing. But I have noticed she writes a lot. She is always reciting poetry to herself and is moved by it for a long time after. You might see if you can seduce her with a love poem. That is the only way I can think of."

Chang was delighted and on the spot composed two stanzas of spring verses which he handed over to her. That evening Hung-niang came back with a note on colored paper for him, saying, "By Miss Ts'ui's instructions."

The title of her poem was "Bright Moon on the Night of the Fifteenth":

> I await the moon in the western chamber
> Where the breeze comes through the half-opened door.
> Sweeping the wall the flower shadows move:
> I imagine it is my lover who comes.

Chang understood the message: that day was the fourteenth of the second month, and an apricot tree was next to the wall east of the Ts'uis' courtyard. It would be possible to climb it.

On the night of the fifteenth Chang used the tree as a ladder to get over the wall. When he came to the western chamber, the door was ajar. Inside, Hung-niang was asleep on a bed. He awakened her, and she asked, frightened, "How did you get here?"

"Miss Ts'ui's letter told me to come," he said, not quite accurately. "You go tell her I am here."

In a minute Hung-niang was back. "She's coming! She's coming!"

Chang was both happy and nervous, convinced that success was his. Then Miss Ts'ui appeared in formal dress, with a serious face, and began to upbraid him: "You did us a great kindness when you saved our lives, and that is why my mother entrusted my young brother and myself to you. Why then did you get my silly maid to bring me that filthy poem? You began by doing a good deed in preserving me from the hands of ravishers, and you end by seeking to ravish me. You substitute seduction for rape—is there any great difference? My first impulse was to keep quiet about it, but that would have been to condone your wrongdoing, and not right. If I told my mother, it would

---

7. To determine an astrologically suitable date for a wedding [Translator's note].   8. An allusion to the parable of help that comes too late in chapter 9 of pre-Ch'in philosophical work *Chuang-tzu* [Translator's note].

amount to ingratitude, and the consequences would be unfortunate. I thought of having a servant convey my disapproval, but feared she would not get it right. Then I thought of writing a short message to state my case, but was afraid it would only put you on your guard. So finally I composed those vulgar lines to make sure you would come here. It was an improper thing to do, and of course I feel ashamed. But I hope that you will keep within the bounds of decency and commit no outrage."

As she finished speaking, she turned on her heel and left him. For some time Chang stood, dumbfounded. Then he went back over the wall to his quarters, all hope gone.

A few nights later Chang was sleeping alone by the veranda when someone shook him awake. Startled, he rose up, to see Hung-niang standing there, a coverlet and pillow in her arms. She patted him and said, "She is coming! She is coming! Why are you sleeping?" And she spread the quilt and put the pillow beside his. As she left, Chang sat up straight and rubbed his eyes. For some time it seemed as though he were still dreaming, but nonetheless he waited dutifully. Then there was Hung-niang again, with Miss Ts'ui leaning on her arm. She was shy and yielding, and appeared almost not to have the strength to move her limbs. The contrast with her stiff formality at their last encounter was complete.

This evening was the night of the eighteenth, and the slanting rays of the moon cast a soft light over half the bed. Chang felt a kind of floating lightness and wondered whether this was an immortal who visited him, not someone from the world of men. After a while the temple bell sounded. Daybreak was near. As Hung-niang urged her to leave, she wept softly and clung to him. Hung-niang helped her up, and they left. The whole time she had not spoken a single word. With the first light of dawn Chang got up, wondering, was it a dream? But the perfume still lingered, and as it got lighter he could see on his arm traces of her makeup and the teardrops sparkling still on the mat.

For some ten days afterward there was no word from her. Chang composed a poem of sixty lines on "An Encounter with an Immortal" which he had not yet completed when Hung-niang happened by, and he gave it to her for her mistress. After that she let him see her again, and for nearly a month he would join her in what her poem called the "western chamber," slipping out at dawn and returning stealthily at night. Chang once asked what her mother thought about the situation. She said, "She knows there is nothing she can do about it, and so she hopes you will regularize things."

Before long Chang was about to go to Ch'ang-an, and he let her know his intentions in a poem. Miss Ts'ui made no objections at all, but the look of pain on her face was very touching. On the eve of his departure he was unable to see her again. Then Chang went off to the west. A few months later he again made a trip to P'u and stayed several months with Miss Ts'ui.

She was a very good calligrapher and wrote poetry, but for all that he kept begging to see her work, she would never show it. Chang wrote poems for her, challenging her to match them, but she paid them little attention. The thing that made her unusual was that, while she excelled in the arts, she always acted as though she were ignorant, and although she was quick and clever in speaking, she would seldom indulge in repartee. She loved Chang very much, but would never say so in words. At the time she was subject to moods of profound melancholy, but she never let on. She seldom showed on her face the emotions she felt. On one occasion she was playing her zither alone at night. She did not know Chang was listening, and the music was full of sadness. As soon as he spoke, she stopped and would play no more. This made him all the more infatuated with her.

Some time later Chang had to go west again for the scheduled examinations. It was the eve of his departure, and though he had said nothing about what it involved, he sat sighing unhappily at her side. Miss Ts'ui had guessed that he was going to leave for good. Her manner was respectful, but she spoke deliberately and in a low voice. "To seduce someone and then abandon her is perfectly natural, and it would be presumptuous of me to resent it. It would be an act of charity on your part if, having first seduced me, you were to go through with it and fulfill your oath of lifelong devotion. But in either case, what is there to be so upset about in this trip? However, I see you are not happy and I have no way to cheer you up. You have praised my zither playing, and in the past I have been embarrassed to play for you. Now that you are going away, I shall do what you so often requested."

She had them prepare her zither and started to play the prelude to the "Rainbow Robe and Feather Skirt." After a few notes, her playing grew wild with grief until the piece was no longer recognizable. Everyone was reduced to tears, and Miss Ts'ui abruptly stopped playing, put down the zither, and ran back to her mother's room with tears streaming down her face. She did not come back.

The next morning Chang went away. The following year he stayed on in the capital, having failed the examinations. He wrote a letter to Miss Ts'ui to reassure her, and her reply read roughly as follows:

> I have read your letter with its message of consolation, and it filled my childish heart with mingled grief and joy. In addition you sent me a box of ornaments to adorn my hair and a stick of pomade to make my lips smooth. It was most kind of you; but for whom am I to make myself attractive? As I look at these presents my breast is filled with sorrow.
>
> Your letter said that you will stay on in the capital to pursue your studies, and of course you need quiet and the facilities there to make progress. Still it is hard on the person left alone in this far-off place. But such is my fate, and I should not complain. Since last fall I have been listless and without hope. In company I can force myself to talk and smile, but come evening I always shed tears in the solitude of my own room. Even in my sleep I often sob, yearning for the absent one. Or I am in your arms for a moment as it used to be, but before the secret meeting is done I am awake and heartbroken. The bed seems still warm beside me, but the one I love is far away.
>
> Since you said good-bye the new year has come. Ch'ang-an is a city of pleasure with chances for love everywhere. I am truly fortunate that you have not forgotten me and that your affection is not worn out. Loving you as I do, I have no way of repaying you, except to be true to our vow of lifelong fidelity.
>
> Our first meeting was at the banquet, as cousins. Then you persuaded my maid to inform me of your love; and I was unable to keep my childish

heart firm. You made advances, like that other poet, Ssuma Hsiang-ju.[9] I failed to repulse them as the girl did who threw her shuttle.[1] When I offered myself in your bed, you treated me with the greatest kindness, and I supposed, in my innocence, that I could always depend on you. How could I have foreseen that our encounter could not possibly lead to something definite, that having disgraced myself by coming to you, there was no further chance of serving you openly as a wife? To the end of my days this will be a lasting regret—I must hide my sighs and be silent. If you, out of kindness, would condescend to fulfill my selfish wish, though it came on my dying day it would seem to be a new lease on life. But if, as a man of the world, you curtail your feelings, sacrificing the lesser to the more important, and look on this connection as shameful, so that your solemn vow can be dispensed with, still my true love will not vanish though my bones decay and my frame dissolve; in wind and dew it will seek out the ground you walk on. My love in life and death is told in this. I weep as I write, for feelings I cannot express. Take care of yourself; a thousand times over, take care of your dear self.

This bracelet of jade is something I wore as a child; I send it to serve as a gentleman's belt pendant. Like jade may you be invariably firm and tender; like a bracelet may there be no break between what came before and what is to follow. Here are also a skein of multicolored thread and a tea roller of mottled bamboo. These things have no intrinsic value, but they are to signify that I want you to be true as jade, and your love to endure unbroken as a bracelet. The spots on the bamboo are like the marks of my tears,[2] and my unhappy thoughts are as tangled as the thread: these objects are symbols of my feelings and tokens for all time of my love. Our hearts are close, though our bodies are far apart and there is no time I can expect to see you. But where the hidden desires are strong enough, there will be a meeting of spirits. Take care of yourself, a thousand times over. The springtime wind is often chill; eat well for your health's sake. Be circumspect and careful, and do not think too often of my unworthy person.

Chang showed her letter to his friends, and in this way word of the affair got around. One of them, Yang Chü-yüan, a skillful poet, wrote a quatrain on "Young Miss Ts'ui":

> For clear purity jade cannot equal his complexion;
> On the iris in the inner court snow begins to melt.
> A romantic young man filled with thoughts of love.
> A letter from the Hsiao girl,[3] brokenhearted.

Yüan Chen[4] of Ho-nan wrote a continuation of Chang's poem "Encounter with an Immortal," also in thirty couplets:

---

9. An allusion to the story of the Han poet, Ssu-ma Hsiang-ju (179–117 B.C.), who enticed the young widow Cho Wen-chün to elope by his zither playing [Translator's note]. 1. A neighboring girl, named Kao, repulsed Hsieh K'un's (280–322) advances by throwing her shuttle in his face. He lost two teeth [Translator's note]. 2. Alluding to the legend of the two wives of the sage ruler Shun, who stained the bamboo with their tears [Translator's note]. 3. In T'ang times the term "Hsiao-niang" referred to young women in general. Here it means Ying-ying [Translator's note]. 4. Yüan Chen (775–831) was a key literary figure in the middle of the T'ang period [Translator's note].

Faint moonbeams pierce the curtained window;
Fireflies glimmer across the blue sky.
The far horizon begins now to pale;
Dwarf trees gradually turn darker green.
A dragon song crosses the court bamboo;   5
A phoenix air brushes the wellside tree.
The silken robe trails through the thin mist;
The pendant circles tinkle in the light breeze.
The accredited envoy accompanies Hsi wang-mu;[5]
From the cloud's center comes Jade Boy.[6]   10
Late at night everyone is quiet;
At daybreak the rain drizzles.
Pearl radiance shines on her decorated sandals;
Flower glow shows off the embroidered skirt.
Jasper hairpin: a walking colored phoenix;   15
Gauze shawl: embracing vermilion rainbow.
She says she comes from Jasper Flower Bank
And is going to pay court at Green Jade Palace.
On an outing north of Lo-yang's[7] wall,
By chance he came to the house east of Sung Yü's.[8]   20
His dalliance she rejects a bit at first,
But her yielding love already is disclosed.
Lowered locks put in motion cicada shadows;[9]
Returning steps raise jade dust.
Her face turns to let flow flower snow   25
As she climbs into bed, silk covers in her arms.
Love birds in a neck-entwining dance;
Kingfishers in a conjugal cage.
Eyebrows, out of shyness, contracted;
Lip rouge, from the warmth, melted.   30
Her breath is pure: fragrance of orchid buds;
Her skin is smooth: richness of jade flesh.
No strength, too limp to lift a wrist;
Many charms, she likes to draw herself together.
Sweat runs: pearls drop by drop;   35
Hair in disorder: black luxuriance.
Just as they rejoice in the meeting of a lifetime
They suddenly hear the night is over.
There is no time for lingering;
It is hard to give up the wish to embrace.   40
Her comely face shows the sorrow she feels;
With fragrant words they swear eternal love.
She gives him a bracelet to plight their troth;
He ties a lovers' knot as sign their hearts are one.
Tear-borne powder runs before the clear mirror;   45

---

5. Hsi wang-mu, the Queen Mother of the West, is a mythological figure supposedly dwelling in the K'un-lun Mountains in China's far west. In early accounts she is sometimes described as part human and part beast, but since early post-Han times she has usually been described as a beautiful immortal. Her huge palace is inhabited by other immortals. Within its precincts grow the magic peach trees which bear the fruits of immortality once every three thousand years. This might be an allusion to Ying-ying's mother [Translator's note].   **6.** The Jade Boy might allude to Ying-ying's brother [Translator's note].   **7.** Possibly a reference to the goddess of the Lo River [Translator's note].   **8.** In "The Lechery of Master Teng-t'u," Sung Yü tells about the beautiful girl next door to the east who climbed up on the wall to flirt with him [Translator's note].   **9.** Referring to her hairdo in the cicada style [Translator's note].

Around the flickering lamp are nighttime insects.
Moonlight is still softly shining
As the rising sun gradually dawns.
Riding on a wild goose she returns to the Lo River.
Blowing a flute he ascends Mount Sung.[1]   50
His clothes are fragrant still with musk perfume;
The pillow is slippery yet with red traces.
Thick, thick, the grass grows on the dyke;
Floating, floating, the tumbleweed yearns for the isle.
Her plain zither plays the "Resentful Crane Song";   55
In the clear Milky Way she looks for the returning wild goose.[2]
The sea is broad and truly hard to cross;
The sky is high and not easy to traverse.
The moving cloud is nowhere to be found—
Hsiao Shih[3] *stays in his chamber.*   60

All of Chang's friends who heard of the affair marveled at it, but Chang had determined on his own course of action. Yüan Chen was especially close to him and so was in a position to ask him for an explanation. Chang said, "It is a general rule that those women endowed by Heaven with great beauty invariably either destroy themselves or destroy someone else. If this Ts'ui woman were to meet someone with wealth and position, she would use the favor her charms gain her to be cloud and rain or dragon or monster—I can't imagine what she might turn into. Of old, King Hsin of the Shang and King Yu of the Chou[4] were brought low by women, in spite of the size of their kingdoms and the extent of their power; their armies were scattered, their persons butchered, and down to the present day their names are objects of ridicule. I have no inner strength to withstand this evil influence. That is why I have resolutely suppressed my love."

At this statement everyone present sighed deeply.

Over a year later Ts'ui was married, and Chang for his part had taken a wife. Happening to pass through the town where she was living, he asked permission of her husband to see her, as a cousin. The husband spoke to her, but Ts'ui refused to appear. Chang's feelings of hurt showed on his face, and she was told about it. She secretly sent him a poem:

> *Emaciated, I have lost my looks,*
> *Tossing and turning, too weary to leave my bed.*
> *It's not because of others I am ashamed to rise;*
> *For you I am haggard and before you ashamed.*

She never did appear. Some days later when Chang was about to leave, she sent another poem of farewell:

> *Cast off and abandoned, what can I say now,*
> *Whom you loved so briefly long ago?*

---

1. This is also known as the Central Mountain. . . . Here the one ascending the mountain may refer to Chang [Translator's note].   2. Which might be carrying a message [Translator's note].   3. Hsiao Shih was a well-known flute-playing immortal of the Spring and Autumn period [Translator's note].   4. Hsin (Chou) was the familiar last ruler of the Shang Dynasty, whose misrule and fall are attributed to the influence of his favorite Ta-chi. King Yu (ruled 781–771 B.C.), last ruler of the Western Chou, was misled by his consort Pao-ssu. The behavior of both rulers is traditionally attributed to their infatuation with the wicked women they loved [Translator's note].

Any love you had then for me
Will do for the one you have now.

After this he never heard any more about her. His contemporaries for the most part conceded that Chang had done well to rectify his mistake. I have often mentioned this among friends so that, forewarned, they might avoid doing such a thing, or if they did, that they might not be led astray by it. In the ninth month of a year in the Chen-yüan period, when an official, Li Kung-ch'ui, was passing the night in my house at the Pacification Quarter, the conversation touched on the subject. He found it most extraordinary and composed a "Song of Ying-ying" to commemorate the affair. Ts'ui's child-name was Ying-ying, and Kung-ch'ui used it for his poem.

LI CH'ING-CHAO
1084–ca. 1151

There is no better introduction to Li Ch'ing-chao's life than her *Afterword* to her husband's study of early inscriptions, the *Records on Metal and Stone*. Prefaces and afterwords were usually stylized, scholarly, and relatively impersonal; but in Li Ch'ing-chao's hands the form became the means to show the relation between a work of scholarship and a pair of lives. The *Afterword* tells first of the idyllic early years of marriage while her husband Chao Te-fu was a student in the Imperial Academy and of their shared passion for books and learning. Their fate as a couple was somehow mirrored in the fate of their collection of books and antiques: begun for their joint pleasure, it increasingly grew into an obsession that dominated her husband's life, until at last both the collection and her husband's scholarly work came to reveal only the differences between them.

The fate of both the marriage and the collection are set within the larger context of the fate of the Sung Dynasty, which in 1126 and 1127 lost its capital, its emperor, and north China to the invading Chin Tartars. The captured Sung emperor, whose extravagance and inattention to political matters were blamed for the loss of the north, happened himself to be an obsessive connoisseur of artworks. As Li Ch'ing-chao hastily fled south, the huge collection was gradually scattered and lost. Soon after they escaped the north, her husband died. Thereafter the residue of the collection represented many things to Li Ch'ing-chao. At one point it seemed to be the means to purchase her husband's posthumous honor after he was falsely accused of treason; the books were also her companions in her constant flight from place to place, and the few pieces that finally remained became cherished mementos of her former life. Throughout this short work Li Ch'ing-chao returns again and again to the relation between people and their possessions, to their role in human relationships, and to the way in which such objects gain value and meaning.

Li Ch'ing-chao is considered one of the finest writers of traditional song lyric. There was a long and complex relation between poetry and song in traditional China. The works of poets were often set to music and were sometimes modified to answer musical needs. During the T'ang period, however, an entirely new kind of music became popular, stanzaic melodies with musical lines of unequal length. In a language where the pitch of a word (or "tone") is essential to understanding its meaning, Chinese song lyrics had to pay careful attention to the requirements of a particular melody to be comprehensible: the pitch of the word had to match the pitch of the music. T'ang poets began the practice of composing new lyrics for these popular irregular melodies, and this new poetic form came to be known as *tz'u*, best translated as "song lyrics." These often concerned love and were performed in the entertainment quarters of the great cities and at parties. By the early Sung Dynasty (960–1279) the song lyric had evolved into a verse form with a very different character from that of classical poetry. It was primarily associated with delicate sensibility, and it sought to evoke the mood of moments.

The relatively few of Li Ch'ing-chao's song lyrics that survive are among the finest examples of the form. In the lyrics to the melody *Note After Note* she takes up the essential concerns of the form and one of the oldest questions in the Chinese tradition, which is the capacity of language to express adequately what occurs in the mind and heart. The lyric attempts to evoke the mood of the moment and closes by comparing the emotion she has evoked to the simple word *sorrow*, which is true, yet too broad to convey what she feels. Li Ch'ing-chao had a genius for scenes that could evoke feeling, as in the lyrics to *Southern Song*, in which she changes from her light summer clothes to a warmer autumn dress, decorated with scenes of a lotus pond. But the dress is old and its gilt lotus leaves are flaking off, making it look like the dying vegetation of a real lotus pond, which becomes both the physical evidence and the symbol of her own aging. It is at such moments that she solves in her own way the ancient problem of how words can express the feeling of the moment.

A discussion of the *Afterword* can be found in Stephen Owen, *Remembrances: The Experience of the Past in Classical Chinese Literature* (1986). For a discussion of the development of the song lyric, see Kang-i (Sun) Chang, *The Evolution of Chinese Tz'u Poetry: From Late T'ang to Northern Sung* (1980). For a complete and very free translation of Li Ch'ing-chao's song lyrics, see Kenneth Rexroth and Ling Chung, *Li Ch'ing-chao: Complete Poems* (1979).

PRONOUNCING GLOSSARY

The following list uses common English syllables to provide rough equivalents of selected words whose pronunciation may be unfamiliar to the general reader.

ch'ai-hu: *chai–hoo*

Chang Fei-ch'ing: *jahng fay–ching*

Chao Te-fu: *jau duh–foo*

Chiang-tu: *jyahng–doo*

Chien-chung: *jyen–juhng*

Ch'ih-yang: *chur–yahng*

Ch'ing-chou: *ching–joh*

chüan: *jooan*

Ch'u-chou: *choo–joh*

Chung Fu-hao: *juhng foo–hau*

Ch'ung-ning: *chuhng–ning*

Hsiang-kuo: *shyahng–gwoh*

Hsiao Yi: *shyau ee*

Hsü Hsi: *shoo shee*

Ko-t'ien: *guh–tyen*

Lai-chou: *lai–joh*

Li Ch'ing-chao: *lee ching–jau*

Liu Tsung-yüan: *lyoh dzuhng–yooan*

P'eng: *puhng*

Shao-hsing: *shau–shing*

Sui: *sway*

Tse-ch'uan: *dzuh–chooahn*

Tso-chuan: *dzwoh–jooahn*

tz'u: *tsuh*

Yüan Tsai: *yooan dzai*

Yüeh-chou: *yooeh–joh*

From Records on Metal and Stone[1]

Afterword

What are the preceding chapters of *Records on Metal and Stone?*—the work of the governor, Chao Te-fu. In it he took inscriptions on bells, tripods, steamers, kettles, washbasins, ladles, goblets, and bowls from the Three Dynasties of high antiquity all the way down to the Five Dynasties (immediately preceding our Sung); here also he took the surviving traces of acts by eminent men and obscure scholars inscribed on large steles and stone disks. In all there were two thousand sections of what appeared on metal and stone. Through all these inscriptions, one might be able to correct historical errors, make historical judgements, and mete out praise and blame. It contains things which, on the highest level, correspond to the Way of the Sages, and on a lower level, supplement the omissions of historians. It is a great amount indeed. Yet catastrophe fell on Wang Ya and Yüan Tsai alike: what did it matter that the one hoarded books and paintings while the other merely hoarded pepper? Ch'ang-yu and Yüan-k'ai both had a disease—it made no difference that the disease of one was a passion for money, and of the other, a passion for transmission of knowledge and commentary. Although their reputations differed, they were the same in being deluded.

In 1101, in the first year of the Chien-chung Reign, I came as a bride to the Chao household. At that time my father was a division head in the Ministry of Rites, and my father-in-law, later Grand Councilor, was an executive in the Ministry of Personnel. My husband was then twenty-one and a student in the Imperial Academy. In those days both families, the Chaos and the Lis, were not well-to-do and were always frugal. On the first and fifteenth day of every month, my husband would get a short vacation from the Academy: he would "pawn some clothes"[2] for five hundred cash and go to the market at Hsiang-kuo Temple, where he would buy fruit and rubbings of inscriptions. When he brought these home, we would sit facing one another, rolling them out before us, examining and munching. And we thought ourselves persons of the age of Ko-t'ien.[3]

When, two years later, he went to take up a post, we lived on rice and vegetables, dressed in common cloth; but he would search out the most remote spots and out-of-the-way places to fulfill his interest in the world's most ancient writings and unusual characters. When his father, the Grand Councilor, was in office, various friends and relations held positions in the Imperial Libraries; there one might find many ancient poems omitted from the *Book of Songs,* unofficial histories, and writings never before seen, works hidden in walls and recovered from tombs. He would work hard at copying such things, drawing ever more pleasure from the activity, until he was unable to stop himself. Later, if he happened to see a work of painting or calligraphy by some person of ancient or modern times, or unusual vessels of the Three Dynasties of high antiquity, he would still pawn our clothes to buy them. I recall that in the Ch'ung-ning Reign[4] a man came with a painting

---

1. All selections translated by Stephen Owen.   2. Refers to the allowance for students at the Imperial Academy.   3. A mythical emperor of earliest antiquity, when all the world was at peace.   4. From 1102 to 1106.

of peonies by Hsü Hsi and asked twenty thousand cash for it. In those days twenty thousand cash was a hard sum to raise, even for children of nobility. We kept it with us a few days, and having thought of no plan by which we could purchase it, we returned it. For several days afterward husband and wife faced one another in deep depression.

Later we lived privately at home for ten years, gathering what we could here and there to have enough for food and clothing. Afterward, my husband governed two provinces in succession, and he used up all his salary on "lead and wooden tablets" [for scholarly work]. Whenever he got a book, we would collate it with other editions and make corrections together, repair it, and label it with the correct title. When he got hold of a piece of calligraphy, a painting, a goblet, or a tripod, we would go over it at our leisure, pointing out faults and flaws, setting for our nightly limit the time it took one candle to burn down. Thus our collection came to surpass all others in fineness of paper and the perfection of the characters.

I happen to have an excellent memory, and every evening after we finished eating, we would sit in the hall called "Return Home" and make tea. Pointing to the heaps of books and histories, we would guess on which line of which page in which chapter of which book a certain passage could be found. Success in guessing determined who got to drink his or her tea first. Whenever I got it right, I would raise the teacup, laughing so hard that the tea would spill in my lap, and I would get up, not having been able to drink anything at all. I would have been glad to grow old in such a world. Thus, even though we were living in anxiety, hardship, and poverty, our wills were not broken.

When the book collection was complete, we set up a library in "Return Home" hall, with huge bookcases where the books were catalogued in sequence. There we put the books. Whenever I wanted to read, I would ask for the key, make a note in the ledger, then take out the books. If one of them was a bit damaged or soiled, it would be our responsibility to repair the spot and copy it out in a neat hand. There was no longer the same ease and casualness as before. This was an attempt to gain convenience which led instead to nervousness and anxiety. I couldn't bear it. And I began to plan how to do away with more than one meat in our meals, how to do away with all finery in my dress; for my hair there were no ornaments of bright pearls or kingfisher feathers; the household had no implements for gilding or embroidery. Whenever we would come upon a history or the work of a major writer, if there was nothing wrong with the printing and no errors in the edition, we would buy it on the spot to have as a second copy. His family had always specialized in *The Book of Changes*[5] and the *Tso chuan*,[6] so the collection of works in those two traditions was most perfect and complete. Books lay ranged on tables and desks, scattered on top of one another on pillows and bedding. This was what took our fancy and what occupied our minds, what drew our eyes and what our spirits inclined to; and our joy was greater than the pleasure others had in dancing girls, dogs, and horses.

In 1126, the first year of the Ching-k'ang Reign, my husband was governing Tse-ch'uan when we heard that the Chin Tartars were moving against

---

5. One of the Confucian classics teaching divination.   6. Another Confucian classic treating early history.

the capital. He was in a daze, realizing that all those full trunks and over-flowing chests, which he regarded so lovingly and mournfully, would surely soon be his possessions no longer. In the third month of spring in 1127, the first year of the Chien-yen Reign, we hurried south for the funeral of his mother. Since we could not take the overabundance of our possessions with us, we first gave up the bulky printed volumes, the albums of paintings, and the most cumbersome of the vessels. Thus we reduced the size of the col-lection several times, and still we had fifteen cartloads of books. When we reached Tung-hai, it took a string of boats to ferry them all across the Huai, and again across the Yangtse to Chien-k'ang. In our old mansion in Ch'ing-chou we still had more than ten rooms of books and various items locked away, and we planned to have them all brought by boat the next year. But in the twelfth month Chin forces sacked Ch'ing-chou, and those ten or so rooms I spoke of were all reduced to ashes.

The next autumn, the ninth month of 1128, my husband took charge of Chien-k'ang Prefecture but relinquished the position in the spring of the following year. Again we put everything in boats and went up to Wu-hu and Ku-shu, intending to take up lodging on the River Kan. That summer in the fifth month we had reached Ch'ih-yang. At that point an imperial decree arrived, ordering my husband to take charge of Hu-chou, and before he assumed that office, to proceed to an audience with the Emperor. Therefore he had the household stop at Ch'ih-yang from which he would go off alone to answer the summons. On the thirteenth day of the sixth month he set off to carry out his duty. He had the boats pulled up onto the shore, and he sat there on the bank, in summer clothes with his headband set high on his forehead, his spirit like a tiger's, his eyes gleaming as though they would shoot into a person, while he gazed toward the boats and took his leave. I was in a terrible state of mind. I shouted to him, "If I hear the city is in danger, what should I do?" He answered from afar, his hands on his hips: "Follow the crowd. If you can't do otherwise, abandon the household goods first, then the clothes, then the books and scrolls, then the old bronzes—but carry the sacrificial vessels for the ancestral temple yourself; live or die with them; don't give *them* up." With this he galloped off on his horse.

As he was hurrying on his journey, he suffered sunstroke from the intense heat, and by the time he reached imperial headquarters, he had contracted a malarial fever. At the end of the seventh month I received a letter that he was lying sick. I was much alarmed, considering my husband's excitable nature and how nothing had been able to prevent the illness deteriorating into fever; his temperature might rise even higher, and in that case he would have to take chilled medicines; then the sickness would really be something to be worried about. Thereupon I set out by boat and in one day and night traveled three hundred leagues. At the point when I arrived he was taking large doses of ch'ai-hu and yellow ch'in;[7] he had a recurring fever with dys-entery, and the illness appeared terminal. I was weeping, and in such a desperate situation I could not bring myself to ask him what was to be done after his death. On the eighteenth day of the eighth month he could no longer get up; he took his brush and wrote a poem; when he finished, he passed away, with no thought at all for the future provision of his family.

7. Knowledge of herbal lore was expected of wives.

When the funeral was over I had nowhere to go. His Majesty had already sent the palace ladies elsewhere, and I heard that crossings of the Yangtse were to be prohibited. At the time I still had twenty thousand *chüan* of books, two thousand copies of inscriptions on metal and stone with colophons,[8] table service and mats enough to entertain a hundred guests, along with other possessions equaling those already mentioned. I also grew very sick, to the point that my only vital sign was a rasping breath. The situation was getting more serious every day. I thought of my husband's brother-in-law, an executive in the Ministry of War on garrison duty in Hung-chou, and I dispatched two former employees of my husband to go ahead to my brother-in-law, taking the baggage. That winter in the twelfth month Chin invaders sacked Hung-chou and all was lost. Those books which, as I said, took a string of boats to ferry across the Yangtse were scattered into clouds of smoke. What remained were a few light scrolls and calligraphy pieces; manuscript copies of the collections of Li Po, Tu Fu, Han Yü, and Liu Tsung-yüan;[9] a copy of *A New Account of Tales of the World*; a copy of *Discourses on Salt and Iron*; a few dozen rubbings of stone inscriptions from the Han and T'ang; ten or so ancient tripods and cauldrons; a few boxes of Southern T'ang manuscript editions—all of which I happened to have had removed to my chambers to pass the time during my illness—now a solitary pile of leftovers.

Since I could no longer go upriver, and since the movements of the invaders were unfathomable, I went to stay with my younger brother Li Hang, a reviser of edicts. By the time I reached T'ai-chou, the governor of the place had already fled. Proceeding on to Shan through Mu-chou, we left the clothing and linen behind. Hurrying to Yellow Cliff, we hired a boat to take us toward the sea, following the fleeing court. The court halted a while in Chang-an, then we followed the imperial barge on the sea route to Wen-chou and Yüeh-chou.[1] In the twelfth month of the fourth year of the Chien-yen Reign, early in 1131, all the officials of the government were released from their posts. We went to Ch'ü-chou, and then in the third month of spring, now the first year of the Shao-hsing Reign (1131), we returned to Yüeh-chou, and in 1132, back again to Hang-chou.

When my husband had been gravely ill, a certain academician, Chang Fei-ch'ing, had visited him with a jade pot—actually it wasn't really jade but *min*, a stone like jade. I have no idea who started the story, but there was a false rumor that they had been discussing presenting it to the Chin as a tribute gift. I also learned that someone had made formal charges in the matter. I was terrified and dared say nothing, but I took all the bronze vessels and such things in the household and was about to turn them over to the imperial court. But by the time I reached Yüeh-chou, the court had already gone on to Ssu-ming. I didn't dare keep these things in the household any longer, so I sent them along with the manuscript books to Shan. Later, when the imperial army was rounding up defeated enemy troops, I heard that these had all been taken into the household of General Li. That "solitary pile of leftovers"

---

8. Short prose works giving the essential scholarly information on the inscriptions. These were Chao Te-fu's copies and rubbings of early inscriptions. *Chüan*: like a chapter and the measure used to count the size of a library.   9. T'ang poets and prose writers.   1. This itinerary follows the general flight the northerner took to the southeast toward the sea, escaping the threat of an invasion of south China by the Chin Tartars.

of which I spoke had now been reduced by about fifty or sixty percent. All that remained were six or so baskets of books, painting, ink, and inkstones that I hadn't been able to part with. I always kept these under my bed and opened them only with my own hands.

At K'uai-chi I chose lodging in a cottage belonging to a local named Chung. Suddenly one night someone made off with five of the baskets through a hole in the wall. I was terribly upset and offered a substantial reward to get them back. Two days later Chung Fu-hao next door produced eighteen of the scrolls and asked for a reward. By that I knew the thief was not far away.[2] I tried every means I could, but I still couldn't get hold of the rest. I have now found out that they were all purchased at a low price by the Circuit Fiscal Supervisor, Wu Yüeh. Now seventy or eighty percent of that "solitary pile of leftovers" is gone. I still have a few volumes from three or so sets, none complete, and some very ordinary pieces of calligraphy, but I still treasure them as if I were protecting my own head—how foolish I am!

Nowadays, when I chance to look over these books, it's like meeting old friends. And I recall when my husband was in the hall called "Calm Governance" in Lai-chou: he had first finished binding the volumes, making title slips of rue leaves to keep out insects and tie-ribbons of pale blue silk, binding ten *chüan* into one volume. Every day in the evening when the office clerks would go home, he would do editorial collations on two *chüan* and write a colophon for one inscription. Of those two thousand items, colophons were written on five hundred and two. It is so sad—today the ink of his writing seems still fresh, yet the trees by his grave have grown to an armspan in girth.

Long ago when the city of Chiang-ling fell, Hsiao Yi, Emperor Yüan of the Liang, did not regret the fall of his kingdom, yet destroyed his books and printings [unwilling to see them fall into the hands of his conquerors]. When his capital Chiang-tu was sacked, Yang Kuang, Emperor Yang of the Sui, wasn't concerned with his own death, only with recovering his books [his spirit overturning the boat in which they were being transported so that he could have his library in the land of the dead]. It must be that the passions of human nature cannot be forgotten, even standing between life and death. Or maybe it is Heaven's will that beings as insignificant as ourselves are not fit to enjoy these superb things. Or it might be that the dead too have consciousness, and they still treasure such things, give them their devoted attention, unwilling to leave them in the world of the living. How hard they are to obtain and how easy to lose!

From the time I was eighteen until now at the age of fifty-two—a span of thirty years—how much calamity, how much gain and loss I have witnessed! When there is possession, there must be lack of possession; when there is a gathering together, there must be a dissolution—that is the constant principle of things. Someone loses a bow; someone else happens to find a bow—what's worth noticing in that? The reason why I have so minutely recorded this story from beginning to end is to serve as a warning for scholars and collectors in later generations.

Written this second year of the Shao-hsing Reign (1132), the eighth month, first day.

Li Ch'ing-chao

---

2. This suggests that her landlord, Chung Fu-hao, was involved in the theft.

[Song Lyrics]

To "Southern Song"

Up in heaven the star-river turns,
    in man's world below
        curtains are drawn.
A chill comes to pallet and pillow,
    damp with tracks of tears.   5
I rise to take off my gossamer dress
and just happen to ask, "How late is it now?"

The tiny lotus pods,
    kingfisher feathers sewn on;
as the gilt flecks away   10
    the lotus leaves grow few.
Same weather as in times before,
    the same old dress—
only the feelings in the heart
are not as they were before.   15

To "Free-Spirited Fisherman"

Billowing clouds touch sky and reach
    the early morning fog,
the river of stars is ready to set,
    a thousand sails dance.
My dreaming soul moves in a daze   5
    to where the high god dwells—
I hear Heaven speak,
asking me with urgent concern
    where I am going now.

And I reply that my road is long,   10
    and, alas, twilight draws on;
I worked at my poems and for nothing have
    bold lines that cause surprise.
Into strong winds ninety thousand miles
    upward the P'eng[1] now flies.   15
Let that wind never stop,
let it blow this tiny boat away
    to the Three Immortal Isles.[2]

---

1. The P'eng was a huge mythical bird described in the *Chuang Tzu.* When it was ready to fly from the northern ocean to the southern ocean, it would rise up ninety thousand miles in a whirlwind. Here it is used as a figure whose greatness smaller creatures cannot comprehend.   **2.** In the eastern sea, believed to be inhabited by immortals.

To "Like a Dream"

I will always recall that day at dusk,
    the pavilion by the creek,
and I was so drunk I couldn't tell
    the way home. My mood left me,
it was late when I turned back in my boat   5
and I strayed deep among lotuses—
how to get through?
how to get through?
and I startled to flight a whole shoal
    of egrets and gulls.   10

To "Drunk in the Shadow of Flowering Trees"

Pale fog, then dense clouds—
    gloomy all day long;
in the animal-shaped censer
    incense burns away.
Once again it is that autumn holiday: 5
to my jade pillow behind the gauze screen
at midnight the cold first comes.

By the eastern hedge I took wine in hand
    after twilight fell.
A fragrance filled my sleeves unseen.   10
Don't tell me this does not break your heart—
the west wind blowing up the curtains
and the person,
    as gaunt as the chrysanthemums.

To "Spring in Wu-ling"

The wind dies down, the fragrance in dirt,
    the flowers now are gone;
late afternoon, too weary to comb my hair.
Everything in the world is right; I am wrong;
    all that will happen is done;   5
before I can say it, tears come.

Yet I've heard it said that at Double Creek
    the spring is lovely still,
and I think I'll go boating there.
But then I fear   10
    those little boats of Double Creek
won't budge if they are made to bear
    this much melancholy.

To "Note After Note"

Searching and searching, seeking and seeking,
so chill, so clear,
dreary,
 and dismal,
  and forlorn.   5
That time of year
 when it's suddenly warm,
  then cold again,
now it's hardest of all to take care.
Two or three cups of weak wine—   10
how can they resist the biting wind
 that comes with evening?
The wild geese pass by—
that's what hurts the most—
and yet they're old acquaintances.   15

In piles chrysanthemums fill the ground,
looking all wasted, damaged—
who could pick them, as they are now?
I stay by the window,
how can I wait alone until blackness comes? 20
The beech tree,
 on top of that
  the fine rain,
on until dusk,
the dripping drop after drop.   25
In a situation like this
how can that one word "sorrow" grasp it?

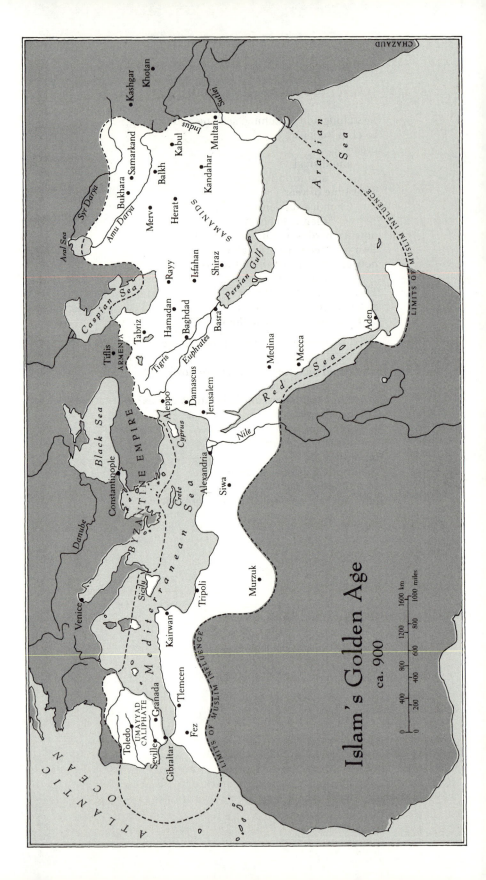

Islam's Golden Age

ca. 900

CHAZAUD

Khotan
Kashgar

Samarkand
Bukhara
Syr Darya
Amu Darya
Aral Sea

Balkh
Merv
Herat
SAMANIDS

Kabul
Kandahar
Multan
Sutlej
Indus

Arabian Sea

LIMITS OF MUSLIM INFLUENCE

Rayy
Isfahan
Shiraz
Persian Gulf

Caspian Sea

Tabriz
Hamadan
Baghdad
Basra
Euphrates
Tigris

Aden

Tiflis
ARMENIA

Black Sea

Constantinople

BYZANTINE EMPIRE

Damascus
Aleppo
Jerusalem
Cyprus

Medina
Mecca

Red Sea

Venice

Danube

Crete
Sicily

Mediterranean Sea

Alexandria
Siwa
Nile

Murzuk

Tripoli
Kairwan

Toledo
Seville
Granada
Gibraltar
Fez
Tlemcen

UMAYYAD
CALIPHATE

LIMITS OF MUSLIM INFLUENCE

ATLANTIC OCEAN

0   200   400   600   800   1000 miles
0   400   800   1200   1600 km

The Rise of Islam and Islamic Literature

In the early seventh century the prophet Muhammad received revelations in the Arabic language that his followers gathered together after his death into a book known as the Koran. That book, together with his teachings, became the basis of a new religion and community that we know as Islam. Under Muhammad's leadership, the Muslim community quickly expanded until it included the whole of Arabia, uniting all its many tribes for the first time in their history. After Muhammad's death, these tribes, now united and inspired by the faith of Islam, swept out of Arabia to conquer the Persian and Byzantine empires to the east and west of them. In so doing they radically altered the history of the world.

Charles Martel defeated a Muslim invading force at Tours in 732, an event celebrated in *The Song of Roland,* and so checked the Muslim advance into western Europe; Byzantium also halted the invading armies in central Anatolia, but elsewhere the forces of Islam advanced with miraculous invincibility. Within a century the new empire stretched from southern Spain to northern India and from the Caucasus to the Indian Ocean. Iberia, North Africa, Arabia, Syria, eastern Anatolia and the Caucasus, Mesopotamia, Iran, central Asia and the Indus Valley were all governed by Muslims. This vast empire was ruled by a succession of caliphs (vicars) drawn from the prophet's family. They continued his political and religious leadership of the Islamic community but not his prophetic office. Factional strife, regional loyalties, and personal ambition combined to fragment and weaken the political integrity of the Islamic empire at times, but the primacy of the Islamic religion throughout the region remained constant, and the caliph retained great spiritual authority even when his political authority was challenged. The Islamic civilization that grew up in the wake of the great conquests was a synthesis of the religion and culture of Arabia with the great imperial traditions of the eastern Mediterranean and the Persian empire of the Sassanians. This synthesis molded the politics, science, literature, and arts of the diverse peoples who adopted Islam and, as the dominant culture of the region, had a shaping influence on such non-Islamic peoples as the Armenians and the Jews. In almost every arena of human endeavor, Islamic norms prevailed.

Although the Koran explicitly prohibits forcible conversion to Islam, the spread of the Islamic faith was inevitably linked to the expansion of Islamic rule. Muslim rulers were tolerant of those religions whose faith was based on revelation, such as Judaism and Christianity, but strictly forbade them to increase their numbers by conversion. Islam checked the growth of these religions throughout its empire and within two centuries had virtually eliminated Zoroastrianism as a significant presence in Iran. After the period of the great conquests, the borders of Islam were extended into sub-Saharan Africa, southern India and Ceylon, and throughout Southeast Asia as far as the Philippine Islands. This further expansion was not the result of a single concerted effort but carried out over several centuries by merchants and traders as much as by military conquest.

The history of Islam in its early centuries was both turbulent and violent. The earliest dynasty of caliphs, the Umayyads, was overthrown in a long and bloody revolution from which they retained only their hold over the western-most province of Islam, al-Andalus (Spain). Their successors, the Abbasids, ruled Islam for five centuries (750–1258) and presided over its fortunes at their height. They founded Islam's great imperial city, Baghdad, in the mid-eighth century, and it became the center of a rich, cosmopolitan culture that was nourished by the ablest minds and greatest talents of every community within the empire. But after the first two centuries of their rule, the Abbasid caliphate's hold on the empire became increasingly tenuous as nominally subordinate dynasties in both the east and the west came to exercise virtually independent rule.

Religious factionalism also threatened the caliphate itself in the tenth century. Muhammad had not designated a successor before his death, and the Muslim community quickly divided between those who believed that the caliphate should remain in the prophet's bloodlines (shi'ites) and those who insisted only that it remain within his clan, the Quraysh (sunnis). Shi'ites were instrumental in the overthrow of the Umayyads, but the Abbasids betrayed their shi'ite followers almost at once, and they became an enduring opposition. In the tenth century, a shi'ite dynasty (the Fatimids) conquered Egypt and established their own caliph there, and a second shi'ite dynasty, the Buyids, gained control of the orthodox sunni caliph in Baghdad. In the eleventh century, the Saljuqs, a Turkoman tribal federation that had only recently been converted to Islam, defeated the established rulers of central Asia and Iran and established themselves as the effective rulers of the lands between Damascus and Bukhara. Despite this turbulence, throughout the Abbasid caliphate Islam enjoyed a long period of relative prosperity and surprising cultural growth.

This long, sunny day of the Islamic empire was shattered in the east by an invasion from outside. In 1219–1220 the Mongol Chinghis Khan's armies, which had already subjugated all of China, swept through central Asia, northern Iran, and Iraq, leveling cities and annihilating whole populations as they advanced. This first incursion was essentially a long, punitive raid, and the Mongols did not establish effective rule over the region in the wake of their devastating conquest. In 1253 they began a new campaign under the leadership of Hulegu Khan, with the intention of adding the Middle East to their empire. They retook the cities of central Asia and northern Iran and extended their conquests into Iraq and Syria. No Muslim army could halt them until the Mamluk rulers of Egypt defeated the Mongols at Ayn Jalut in Palestine in 1260 and ended the myth of their invincibility. However, Hulegu had already dealt the Islamic empire a blow from which it never fully recovered. In 1258 he defeated the caliphal army defending Baghdad, abandoned the city to seven days of looting and burning, and had the caliph al-Musta'sim trampled to death. Hundreds of thousands were killed in the Mongol attack on Baghdad; libraries were burned and the riches that had accumulated there during five centuries of Abbasid rule were looted or destroyed. Successors to the Abbasid caliphate of Baghdad were established in Cairo by the Mamluks, who ruled in Egypt and Syria until 1517, and later in Istanbul, by the Ottomans who dominated the whole Mediterranean region from the fifteenth century to modern times. But these caliphs never became the independent political force that the original dynasty had been, and their spiritual leadership was diminished as well. Nor did Baghdad ever regain its eminence as the chief city of Islam.

The Mongol dynasties that succeeded to rule in the eastern Islamic world converted to Islam, and within a generation they accommodated themselves to Islamic norms of rule. In the fourteenth century Tamerlane (*Timur Lang*; 1336–1405), who claimed the descent from the Mongol great khans, emulated their example and led his armies from his capital at Samarkand in central Asia in successive campaigns of conquest into Iran, Turkey, and Russia. He died as he was planning further campaigns into China. The dynasty Tamerlane founded ruled in central Asia, Iran, and Iraq until the late fifteenth century, but his successors, happily, are remembered now principally for their patronage of the arts, letters, and architecture and for the promotion of Turkish as a literary language. The Timurids were the last powerful dynasty to originate in the steppes. After them, the world of Islam came to be divided between the Ottomans in the west, the Safavids in Iran, and the Moghuls in India. The Ottomans launched the last great movement of conquest, begun in the fourteenth century, when they expanded across the Bosphorus into the Balkans, eventually threatening Vienna itself (1683). The Ottomans and the Moghuls, who came to power as the impact of Columbus's discoveries was beginning to be felt, were also the first dynasties to confront the imperial ambitions of European colonial powers.

ISLAMIC LITERATURE

Before the advent of Islam, Arabia was a small state on the margin of the "civilized" world, and Arabic was the vehicle for a great but little known poetry. Islam established Arabic as the dominant language of religion, trade, and learning throughout a vast empire. The third Abbasid caliph, al-Ma'mun (died 813), established a center of translation in Baghdad in the early ninth century, and Greek science and philosophy, Indian mathematics, Chinese medicine, and Persian literature and natural history were all translated into Arabic, vastly enriching the language. By the latter half of the eighth century Arabic had ceased to be the exclusive property of the Arabs and had become instead the lingua franca of all the many communities that made up Islam, and Arabic literature had extended its horizons beyond tribal Arabia to reflect the international, cosmopolitan culture that Islam had become. Prose, which had next to no role in the pre-Islamic literature of Arabia, came to enjoy exceptional currency because it was a better vehicle than poetry both for the religious learning that was being generated by Islamic religious scholars and for the new secular and humanistic learning that was flooding into Islam from all sides. The literary aesthetic that developed in this period—a synthesis, again, of the language and poetics of pre-Islamic Arabian poetry—provided the foundation for all the literary languages of Islam that developed in subsequent centuries.

Pre-Islamic Arabic poetry was orally composed and performed. Its two principal forms were the short poem, or "fragment" (*qit'a*), on a single theme—the description and celebration of a raid, a hunt, or a romantic adventure; lament for the departure of a friend; or elegy—and the long poem, or *qasida*, that linked a number of these themes together. The themes were prescribed by convention, and the language was rhetorically complex, metaphorically dense, and enriched by the close and acute observation of nature. The dominant style of this poetry was heroic, emphasizing the virtues of bravery, loyalty, and generosity. The poetry of pre-Islamic Arabia set standards for manly behavior and for correct use of the language throughout the first two centuries of Islam.

In Baghdad, the poets of the new empire became impatient with the limits of the older poetry and created an urban, cosmopolitan style that reflected the new world of Islam. The only poetry in pre-Islamic Arabia was a highly democratic form, since the best poetry was available to anyone who understood Arabic and was able to memorize a few lines. But as the scope of imaginative writing expanded beyond poetry in Abbasid Baghdad, a new term, *adab*, was used to describe it. *Adab* means "polite learning" and implies wealth and leisure enough to devote years of one's life to the formal study of written literature. *Adab* included not only an extensive knowledge of poetry, both classical and modern, but a familiarity with important writing on virtually every subject from theology to agronomy. The *adab* style, emphasizing elegance, decorum, and wide learning, was aristocratic and antidemocratic, a fortress that set difficult meters and learned allusions as "gatemen to keep the rabble out," as one poet put it. The natural home of such a tradition was, of course, the court, and royal or aristocratic patronage was the chief prop and support of poets as well as scholars.

Though poetry enjoyed precedence over prose in the classical period, as it continued to do in all the languages of Islamic literature until virtually the present day, prose was the accepted vehicle for narrative. Given the Koranic intolerance of fiction, which it categorized as "lying," prose narratives were strongly didactic or informative—moralistic beast fables like those of Aesop (known as Luqman in Arabic), essays on natural history, collections of curious and wonderful information. Works of popular entertainment such as *The Thousand and One Nights* were not welcomed into the classical canon.

The landscape of Islamic literature lacked certain features that are commonplace in other traditions. What we would call imaginative literature was excluded from religion and religious worship. In orthodox Islam there is no equivalent to hymn singing or dramatic performance (e.g., stations of the cross, ritual processions, and morality plays in Christianity). It was only with the rise of mysticism and mystical brotherhoods in the ninth and tenth centuries that poetry became a vehicle for spirituality in Islam. Drama and the theater were also given no place in the learned literary tradition, although there is some evidence of the survival of popular theater and dramatic performance and there are elements of drama in the ritual of the pilgrimage.

While Islamic literature began in Arabic, and Arabic remained the exclusive literary language of Islam for several centuries, some time in the early ninth century Islamic poetry and prose began to be written in Persian as well, and by the beginning of the eleventh century Persian had established itself as a second language of the Islamic literary tradition. Persian poetry adopted both the Arabic poetic style and the Arabic genres, but it also invented, or radically expanded, the use of new forms—the quatrain (*ruba'i*), the erotic lyric (*ghazal*), and the long narrative poem (*masnavi*). Persian poets drew on the vast repertory of pre-Islamic Iranian stories from its national epic tradition and long tradition of court and popular poetry to create an extremely rich and varied literature in the eleventh through thirteenth centuries—generally regarded as its golden age. In the course of this golden age Persian poetry became increasingly infused with sufi mysticism, and by the end of the period the sufi brotherhood provided a new and attractive focus for poetry to set in opposition to that of the court. Persian continued to be a significant vehicle for literary production down to the fifteenth century, after which it endured a long period of decline until the rise of modernism in the late nineteenth century.

Other languages followed Persian, and over these Persian exerted an influence as great as or greater than Arabic, passing on to them the forms of the *ruba'i*, the *ghazal*, and the *masnavi*; a vast repertory of themes and stories; and a deep devotion to sufism. The origins of Islamic literature in Turkish can be traced to the eleventh century, but only with the establishment of the Ottoman state in the thirteenth century did Turkish literature begin to gain parity with Persian and Arabic. Eventually, it emerged as the third major vehicle of Islamic literature. Islamic poetry began to be written in the regional languages of India—Kashmiri, Sindhi, Panjabi—from roughly the fourteenth century on. Of these, Urdu, which began to be used for poetry in about the sixteenth century, achieved exceptional preeminence at the courts of Delhi and Lahore. A number of the other languages of the far-flung Islamic communities of Africa, eastern Europe, and Asia also added themselves to the list of languages, and at present the number of languages that should be included under the rubric of Islamic literature roughly equals the number of communities included within Islam itself.

The Islamic cultural tradition made no effort to accept any of the pre-Islamic literary or cultural traditions as essential preliminaries to its own. The literary and cultural achievements of Greece, Mesopotamia, greater Syria and Palestine, and the Nile Valley are, officially, closed books. Much pre-Islamic material has been incorporated, especially in Iran; and much of pre-Islamic culture was absorbed into the Islamic by informal and indirect means, but there was no conscious attempt to imitate, and no reverence for, the great masterpieces of the Middle Eastern civilizations that had waxed and waned before the emergence of Islam. In large part this is because that literature had been lost before the rise of Islam. That is, knowledge of the hieroglyphic and cuneiform writing systems was lost in antiquity, and only rediscovered by European scholars in the nineteenth century.

FURTHER READING

The best brief introduction to Arabic literature is still H. A. R. Gibb, *Arabic Literature* (1926). The articles "Arabic Poetics and Arabic Poetry" and "Arabic Prosody" by Roger M. A. Allen and David Semah, respectively, in *The New Princeton Encyclopedia of Poetry and Poetics* (1993) provide brief introductions to these topics as well as extensive bibliographies. For the Persian tradition, see Ehsan Yarshater, ed., *Persian Literature* (1988), and Julie Scott Meisami, *Medieval Persian Court Poetry* (1987). There are few good introductory studies of Ottoman poetry, but Walter G. Andrews, *An Introduction to Ottoman Poetry* (1976), is by far the best of these, and his study of the Ottoman lyric poetry, *Poetry's Voice, Society's Song* (1985), gives clear and illuminating insight into the relation of poetic production to the larger dynamics of an Islamic society. Marshall G. S. Hodgson, *The Venture of Islam: Volumes One to Three* (1974), is the best general history of the Islamic world and contains sections on the literary tradition. There are a number of anthologies of Arabic poetry. Charles Greville Tuetey, *Classical Arabic Poetry: 162 Poems from Imrulkais to Ma'arri* (1985), has the advantage of being comprehensive and highly readable. Tuetey also provides good historical and critical introductions to each poem.

PRONOUNCING GLOSSARY

The following list uses common English syllables and stress accents to provide rough equivalents of selected words whose pronunciation may be unfamiliar to the general reader.

Abbasids: *uh-bah'-sids*

al-Andalus: *al–an'-duh-loos*

al-Ma'mun: *al–ma-moon'*

al-Musta'sim: *al–moos-ta'-sim*

Ayn Jalut: *ayn juh-loot'*

Buyids: *boo'-yids*

Chinghis Khan: *ching'-iz kahn'*

Fatimids: *fat'-i-midz*

ghazal: *guh-zal'*

Hulegu Khan: *hoo'-luh-goo kahn'*

Kashmiri: *cash-mee'-ree*

Lahore: *luh-hore'*

Luqman: *luk-mahn'*

Mamluk: *mam-luke'*

Muhammad: *mu-ham'-mad*

Panjabi: *pun-jaw'-bee*

qit'a: *kit'-uh*

Quraysh: *koo-raysh'*

ruba'i: *roo-bah-ee'*

Safavids: *sa'-fuh-vids*

Saljuqs: *sal'-jooks*

Sassanians: *suh-say'-nee-unz*

shi'ite: *she'-ite*

Sindhi: *sin'-dee*

Timur Lang: *ti-moor' lang'*

Turkoman: *tur'-koh-man*

Umayyad: *oo-my'-yad*

Urdu: *oor'-due*

TIME LINE

TEXTS	CONTEXTS
510–622 The great age of Arabic oral heroic poetry	
6th century The Sassanian court encourages the collection of heroic and legendary tales about Iran's kings and heroes	570? Birth of Muhammad into the Quraysh tribe of Mecca
	610–632 The period of Muhammad's prophesy from first revelation, through the growth of his following, his flight (*hijra*) to Medina, and his final pilgrimage to Mecca
622–750 Invention of the love lyric (*ghazal*)	
653? The third caliph, 'Uthman, authorizes the collection and establishment of the official text of the *Koran*	633–656 Muslim armies conquer as far as India to the east and as far as Morocco to the west
	711–720 Extension of Muslim conquests into al-Andalus (Spain), northwest India, and central Asia
750–1055 The Golden Age of Arabic letters	
750 Ibn Ishaq composes *The Biography of the Prophet,* the definitive biography of Muhammad	
	778 Defeat of Charlemagne in northern Spain by Muslim armies and the fall of Roland at Roncesvalles
	786–809 Caliphate of Haroun al-Rashid, who together with his vizier, Ja'far the Barmakid, appears in stories of *The Thousand and One Nights*
810–850 Heyday of Al-Jahiz, the greatest master of Arabic prose literature	
813–833 Caliphate of al-Ma'mun, who promotes the translation of Greek philosophy and science into Arabic • The tales of *The Thousand and One Nights* may have entered Arabic at about this time	
819–1005 The Samanid court encourages poets and writers in Persian and sponsors a new version of the *Shâhnâme*	819–1005 The Samanids, the first Persian Muslim dynasty, become hereditary governors of eastern Iran and central Asia
912–961 The golden age of Islamic culture in Spain, which includes the	

Boldface titles indicate works in the anthology.

TIME LINE

TEXTS	CONTEXTS
establishment of the first major centers of learning in medieval Europe	**950** The Turkish tribes of central Asia begin conversion to Islam
	998 Mahmud of Ghazna extends his rule over central Asia and northern India and establishes a dynasty that endures until shortly before the Mongol conquests
1010 Ferdowsi completes his poetic version of the *Shâhnâme*	
	1036–1055 The Seljuqs conquer as far as the Mediterranean and give new impetus to art, literature, and science
	1096–1290 The European crusades to regain Christian control of the Holy Lands (little noted in the East)
1177 Attar completes *The Conference of the Birds.*	**1171–1193** Saladin (Salâh al-Din), who expels the crusaders and denies European traders access to India through the Red Sea route
1218? Jalâloddin Rumi composes both his great lyric works and the *Spiritual Couplets* (1283)	**1219–1260** The Mongols establish themselves as rulers of central Asia, Iran, Iraq, eastern Turkey, and parts of Syria and the Caucasus
	1236 In Spain, Muslim Cordoba capitulates to the Christian ruler, Ferdinand III
	1250–1517 The Turkish slave (*mamluk*) soldiers who served Saladin and his successors in Egypt found their own dynasty, known as the Mamluks
1257–1258 Sa'di composes the *Bustan* and *Golestan*	**1256–1353** The Il-Khanids rule over the lands conquered by Hülegü
	1281–1924 In post-Mongol Turkey, the Ottoman rulers gradually establish the last great Islamic dynasty to rule in the Middle East. They dominate the region until World War II
1370–1405 Persian poetry enters a period of gradual transformation and renewal	**1370–1405** Timur the Lame, or Tamerlane, claiming descent from Chinghis Khan, retakes most of the lands ruled by the Il-Khanids • Timur and his successors are generous patrons of poetry and painting and construct remarkable buildings

THE KORAN
610–632

For Muslims the Koran is something greater than prophetic revelation. It is an earthly duplicate of a divine Koran that exists in paradise engraved in figures of gold on tablets of marble. Like God, it was not created but exists for all eternity—a complete and sufficient guide to our conduct on earth. It is God's final revelation to humanity and was sent by Him to complete and correct all prior revelations. In its divinity it is greater than any prophet or any prophecy. It stands to Muslims as Christ does to Christians. To the glory of Muhammad's community, God chose to make this, His final revelation, in Arabic and through an Arab prophet. Because the Koran is, literally, God's word and is, like Him, miraculous and eternal, it cannot be translated. Interpretive renderings into other languages have been made and used for teaching purposes since the earliest period of Islam, but Muslims do not accept them as the Koran in the sense that Christians accept the Bible in English, or any of the other languages into which it has been translated, as still the Bible.

The Koran's revelations were received by Muhammad, known to Muslims as the Prophet of God, during the last two decades of his life—from roughly 610, when the angel Gabriel first appeared to him, to his death on June 8, 632. During his lifetime these revelations were recorded by various of his followers, but they were only gathered together into a comprehensive volume after his death. The title given this collection is the Koran (al-qur'ân), or the Recitation, and, as its title suggests, the Koran is a work to be heard and recited, an oral work with a music and rhythm of its own that does not appear to best advantage on the printed page. The text itself is far more dialogic than narrative. God speaks with Muhammad, or instructs him to give his community a particular message, or to "Recite!" Muhammad and other earlier prophets carry on frustrated dialogues with their doubting communities on the one hand and, on the other, with a demanding God. Only rarely does narrative replace the intermingling of voices in dialogue.

The revelations came to Muhammad in verses (âya) of varying length and number. These were gathered into larger divisions (Suras) that were organized roughly by subject. These gatherings often appear arbitrary, and there are abrupt transitions from subject in the longer Suras. Only the shortest are thematically unified and only Sura 12, Yusuf, tells a complete narrative. The Suras were then arranged by length, with the longer Suras preceding the shorter. Each Sura was given a name taken from some striking image or theme that appears in it. They are also identified as having been received in either Mecca or Medina, the two communities in which Muhammad lived. It is an article of faith with Muslims that the Koran we now have is a complete and accurate record of God's revelations to Muhammad and an exact copy of the divine Koran that exists in the seventh heaven.

Although the Koran was revealed over a relatively brief period, its style varies enormously. The earliest and shortest Suras sound like charms or incantations, evoking the wonder and glory of God:

> In the Name of God, the Compassionate, the Merciful
>   Say: "I seek refuge in the Lord of men, the King of men, the God of men, from the mischief of the slinking prompter who whispers in the hearts of men; from jinn and men" (Men [entire] 114.1–6).

The later and longer ones are filled with legal prescriptions:

> Do not give the feeble-minded the property with which God has entrusted you for their support; but maintain and clothe them with its proceeds, and give them good advice (Women 4.6).

And many, perhaps most, of the Suras have the quality of sermons delivered in a highly charged and poetic language, often enriched by parables and brief narratives that exhort us to remember God and live pious lives. The earlier and longer Suras, like sermons, are mixtures of various styles—exhortation, evocation, legal prescription, and sage counsel.

The style of the individual Suras reflects in general terms the moments in Muhammad's life when they were revealed. In the early Meccan period of his mission, his concerns were those of an embattled prophet exhorting his community to believe in God and fear Him and defending himself against the hostility and skepticism of those who doubted both him and his God. The Suras from this period are filled with fierce and eloquent exhortations promising paradise to those who believe in God and eternal damnation to those who deny Him. These Suras are also marked by calls for social justice, expressed principally in concern for the plight of widows and orphans. It was in Mecca, too, that the accounts of earlier prophets from Noah (Nuh) to Jesus (Isâ)— who, like Muhammad, had to defend themselves against a hostile and unbelieving community—were revealed to him.

Eventually, Muhammad's success in creating a community of believers made him so unwelcome in his home that the Meccans forced him and his followers to emigrate to the nearby oasis of Medina. There he established his community among the tribes already settled around the oasis. While Muhammad continued to be the Prophet of Islam, the legal and political demands of his community now occupied most of his attention. He also had to cope with the growing number of believers who flocked to him and, eventually, to manage a war with the Meccans. The Suras revealed in Medina reflect these concerns in setting forth an extensive and detailed legal code that addresses the demands of the day-to-day life of the community as well as its spiritual needs.

These stylistic differences point out an obvious distinction between the Koran and the Bible. The essence of the Koran is admonition and guidance. No narrative thread runs through it, nor is it embedded in the history of a single people. The Koran's coherence is a product of the themes that are reiterated throughout its many Suras. For all the importance it gives to one language, Arabic, its message is a more general one. The many allusions to Moses (Musa), for example, stress that God may choose even an ordinary, flawed man to be His prophet and say nothing of Moses' role as the leader of his people. The meaning of the Koran, as it often asserts, is for all humanity.

The Exordium, the opening Sura of the Koran, has an exceptional resonance in the life of Muslims. They recite it at the beginning of every formal address and inscribe it at the head of every written document from works of scholarship to the stones that mark a grave. It begins every prayer.

Joseph (Sura 12) is, of course, not a prophet in Judaism or Christianity, but he is in Islam. He is also the only one whose tale is told continuously, and the only one to be mentioned exclusively in a single Sura. The Koranic version of this story includes most of the key events of Genesis 36–38 but excludes virtually everything that links Joseph to the Hebrews. In Genesis, Joseph is a divinely guided young man who is first tested severely and then becomes the leader of his people, guiding them to prosperity in Egypt. In the Koran he is a divinely guided young man but not the leader of any nation. Although God tests Joseph, it is to prove that only those who follow divine guidance prosper. In the most famous scene, the temptation by his master's wife, he is not more righteous than she, but God gives him a sign that he should not succumb. Islam does not believe in original sin, and is more accepting of human error than Genesis. Joseph's innocence in this encounter is also explicitly established in Sura 12, while in Genesis only we and God see that Joseph is blameless. His master's wife, identified as Zuleikha in the commentaries, is also treated in a more tolerant fashion than Potiphar's wife. In a remarkable scene she shows the women of the city that they, too, would have been seduced by Joseph's angelic beauty. In the Koran, in short, the story of Joseph has nothing of the epic dimensions it has in Genesis but focuses instead on the more general theme of the importance of trusting in divine guidance.

Sura 19 contains the only allusion to Mary in the Koran, although Jesus appears repeatedly. The miracles surrounding the birth of Jesus do occur here but in a very different form from that in the New Testament. Islam does not accept that Jesus was the son of God. For Muslims such a mixture of divine and human attributes is unthinkable. Jesus they account a great prophet but no more, and, again, one who has no allegiance to a particular community. There is also nothing of the story of his conflicts with the Jews or his execution by the Romans. Muslims do not accept the martyrdom of Jesus but believe that at the crucial moment God placed a substitute in Jesus' place.

In the Koran, Noah (Sura 71) is the first of the major prophets, a step well above his position in the Bible. He establishes the pattern for the role of the prophet in his community. It is a disheartening one and probably reflects Muhammad's view of his relations with his fellow Meccans. The emphasis is on his prophetic role rather than on the details of the ark and the salvation of the animals. Like Muhammad, he is a warner who comes to call his people to submit to God and to threaten them with torment if they do not. His people revile and reject him for years. At last, when it is abundantly clear that their hearts are so hardened that they will never heed him, he calls down God's wrath on his tormentors. His story is alluded to in a great many Suras. One detail found only in the Koran (11.42–46) points out God's concern to give faith priority over blood. Noah has a son who refuses to enter the ark, effectively denying his father's prophecy. The rising waters kill him along with the rest of humanity. When Noah asks God why He has done this, because He promised that Noah's family would be spared, God replies, "Noah, he was no kinsman of yours: he had acted unjustly." That is, shared belief replaces blood as the strongest bond uniting people.

The most informative general introduction to the Koran is the revised edition of *Bell's Introduction to the Qur'ân* (1970). Michael Cook, *Muhammad* (1983), is an excellent brief biography of the Prophet of Islam. Fazlur Rahman, *Major Themes of the Qur'ân* (1980), is a lucid presentation by a Muslim scholar who has taught in the United States for many years of the principal beliefs of Islam as they appear in the Koran. Marilyn R. Waldman, "New Approaches to 'Biblical' Materials in the Qur'ân," *The Muslim World* 75, no. 1 (January 1985), 1–16, gives a good comparison of Joseph in the Koran and the Bible.

PRONOUNCING GLOSSARY

The following list uses common English syllables and stress accents to provide rough equivalents of selected words whose pronunciation may be unfamiliar to the general reader.

al-qur'ân: *al-ko-ran'*

âya: *eye'-yuh*

bahirah: *buh-hee'-ruh*

Idris: *ee-drees'*

Isâ: *ee'-suh*

Ka'ba: *ka'-buh*

Nuh: *nooh*

Potiphar: *poe'-tee-far*

saibah: *saw'-ee-buh*

Suwâ: *soo-wah'*

wasilah: *wuh-see'-luh*

Ya'uq: *yah-ook'*

Yaghuth: *yah-gooth'*

Yusuf: *you'-suff*

Zuleikha: *zoo-lay'-kuh*

FROM THE KORAN[1]

1. The Exordium

[MECCA]

In the Name of God the Compassionate the Merciful[2]

Praise be to God, Lord of the Creation,
The Compassionate, the Merciful,
King of the Last Judgement!
You alone we worship, and to You alone
we pray for help.
Guide us to the straight path,
The path of those whom You have favoured,
Not of those who have incurred Your wrath,
Nor of those who have gone astray.

From 4. Women

[MEDINA]

In the Name of God, the Compassionate, the Merciful

Men, have fear of your Lord, who created you from a single soul. From that soul He created its mate, and through them He bestrewed the earth with countless men and women.

Fear God, in whose name you plead with one another, and honour the mothers who bore you. God is ever watching over you.

Give orphans[3] the property which belongs to them. Do not exchange their valuables for worthless things or cheat them of their possessions; for this would surely be a great sin. If you fear that you cannot treat orphans with fairness, then you may marry other women who seem good to you: two, three, or four of them. But if you fear that you cannot maintain equality among them, marry one only or any slavegirls you may own. This will make it easier for you to avoid injustice.

Give women their dowry as a free gift; but if they choose to make over to you a part of it, you may regard it as lawfully yours.

Do not give the feeble-minded the property with which God has entrusted you for their support; but maintain and clothe them with its proceeds, and give them good advice.

Put orphans to the test until they reach a marriageable age. If you find them capable of sound judgement, hand over to them their property, and do not deprive them of it by squandering it before they come of age.

Let not the rich guardian touch the property of his orphan ward; and let him who is poor use no more than a fair portion of it for his own advantage.

When you hand over to them their property, call in some witnesses; sufficient is God's accounting of your actions.

---

1. Translated by N. J. Dawood.　2. According to Islamic law, this phrase, spoken or written, must precede all written work; it is also used by Muslims at the beginning of most formal tasks.　3. Orphan girls.

Men shall have a share in what their parents and kinsmen leave; and women shall have a share in what their parents and kinsmen leave: whether it be little or much, they shall be legally entitled to their share.

If relatives, orphans, or needy men are present at the division of an inheritance, give them, too, a share of it, and speak to them kind words.

Let those who are solicitous about the welfare of their young children after their own death take care not to wrong orphans. Let them fear God and speak for justice.

Those that devour the property of orphans unjustly, swallow fire into their bellies; they shall burn in a mighty conflagration.

God has thus enjoined you concerning your children:

A male shall inherit twice as much as a female. If there be more than two girls, they shall have two-thirds of the inheritance; but if there be one only, she shall inherit the half. Parents shall inherit a sixth each, if the deceased have a child; but if he leave no child and his parents be his heirs, his mother shall have a third. If he have brothers, his mother shall have a sixth after payment of any legacy he may have bequeathed or any debt he may have owed.

You may wonder whether your parents or your children are more beneficial to you. But this is the law of God; God is all-knowing and wise.

You shall inherit the half of your wives' estate if they die childless. If they leave children, a quarter of their estate shall be yours after payment of any legacies they may have bequeathed or any debt they may have owed.

Your wives shall inherit one quarter of your estate if you die childless. If you leave children, they shall inherit one-eighth, after payment of any legacies you may have bequeathed or any debts you may have owed.

If a man or a woman leave neither children nor parents and have a brother or a sister, they shall each inherit one-sixth. If there be more, they shall equally share the third of the estate, after payment of any legacy that he may have bequeathed or any debt he may have owed, without prejudice to the rights of the heirs. That is a commandment from God. God is all-knowing and gracious.

Such are the bounds set by God. He that obeys God and His apostle shall dwell for ever in gardens watered by running streams. That is the supreme triumph. But he that defies God and His apostle and transgresses His bounds, shall be cast into a fire wherein he will abide for ever. A shameful punishment awaits him.

If any of your women commit fornication, call in four witnesses from among yourselves against them; if they testify to their guilt confine them to their houses till death overtakes them or till God finds another way for them.

If two men among you commit indecency punish them both. If they repent and mend their ways, let them be. God is forgiving and merciful.

God forgives those who commit evil in ignorance and then quickly turn to Him in repentance. God will pardon them. God is wise and all-knowing. But He will not forgive those who do evil and, when death comes to them, say: 'Now we repent!' Nor those who die unbelievers: for them We have prepared a woeful scourge.

Believers, it is unlawful for you to inherit the women of your deceased kinsmen against their will, or to bar them from re-marrying, in order that you may force them to give up a part of what you have given them, unless they be guilty of a proven crime. Treat them with kindness; for even if you dislike them, it may well be that you may dislike a thing which God has meant for your own abundant good.

If you wish to (replace a wife with) another, do not take from her the dowry you have given her even if it be a talent of gold. That would be improper and grossly unjust; for how can you take it back when you have lain with each other and entered into a firm contract?

You shall not marry the women whom your fathers married. That was an evil practice, indecent and abominable.

Forbidden to you are your mothers, your daughters, your sisters, your paternal and maternal aunts, the daughters of your brothers and sisters, your foster-mothers, your foster sisters, the mothers of your wives, your step-daughters who are in your charge, born of the wives with whom you have lain (it is no offence for you to marry your step-daughters if you have not consummated your marriage with their mothers), and the wives of your own begotten sons. You are also forbidden to take in marriage two sisters at one and the same time: all previous such marriages excepted. God is forgiving and merciful.

Also married women, except those whom you own as slaves. Such is the decree of God. All women other than these are lawful to you, provided you seek them with your wealth in modest conduct, not in fornication. Give them their dowry for the enjoyment you have had of them as a duty; but it shall be no offence for you to make any other agreement among yourselves after you have fulfilled your duty. God is all-knowing and wise.

If any one of you cannot afford to marry a free believing woman, let him marry a slave-girl who is a believer (God best knows your faith: you are born one of another). Marry them with the permission of their masters and give them their dowry in all justice, provided they are honourable and chaste and have not entertained other men. If after marriage they commit adultery, they shall suffer half the penalty inflicted upon free adulteresses. Such is the law for those of you who fear to commit sin: but if you abstain, it will be better for you. God is forgiving and merciful.

God desires to make this known to you and to guide you along the paths of those who have gone before you, and to turn to you in mercy. God is all-knowing and wise.

God wishes to forgive you, but those who follow their own appetites wish to see you far astray. God wishes to lighten your burdens, for man was created weak.

Believers, do not consume your wealth among yourselves in vanity, but rather trade with it by mutual consent.

Do not destroy yourselves. God is merciful to you, but he that does that through wickedness and injustice shall be burned in fire. That is easy enough for God.

If you avoid the enormities you are forbidden, We shall pardon your misdeeds and usher you in with all honour. Do not covet the favours by which God has exalted some of you above others. Men shall be rewarded according to their deeds, and women shall be rewarded according to their deeds. Rather implore God to bestow on you His gifts. God has knowledge of all things.

To every parent and kinsman We have appointed heirs who will inherit from him. As for those with whom you have entered into agreements, let them, too, have their due. God bears witness to all things.

Men have authority over women because God has made the one superior to the other, and because they spend their wealth to maintain them. Good women are obedient. They guard their unseen parts because God has guarded them. As for those from whom you fear disobedience, admonish them and send them to beds apart and beat them. Then if they obey you, take no further action against them. God is high, supreme.

If you fear a breach between a man and his wife, appoint an arbiter from his people and another from hers. If they wish to be reconciled God will bring them together again. God is all-knowing and wise.

Serve God and associate none with Him. Show kindness to your parents and your kindred, to orphans and to the helpless, to near and distant neighbours, to those that keep company with you, to the traveller in need, and to the slaves whom you own. God does not love arrogant and boastful men, who are themselves niggardly and enjoin others to be niggardly; who conceal the riches which God of His bounty has bestowed upon them (We have prepared a shameful punishment for the unbelievers); and who spend their wealth for the sake of ostentation, believing neither in God nor in the Last Day. He that chooses Satan for his friend, an evil friend has he.

∗   ∗   ∗

5. The Table

[MEDINA]

In the Name of God, the Compassionate, the Merciful

Believers, be true to your obligations. It is lawful for you to eat the flesh of all beasts other than that which is hereby announced to you. Game is forbidden while you are on pilgrimage. God decrees what He will.

Believers, do not violate the rites of God, or the sacred month, or the offerings or their ornaments, or those that repair to the Sacred House seeking God's grace and pleasure. Once your pilgrimage is ended, you shall be free to go hunting.

Do not allow your hatred for those who would debar you from the Holy Mosque to lead you into sin. Help one another in what is good and pious, not in what is wicked and sinful. Have fear of God, for He is stern in retribution.

You are forbidden carrion, blood, and the flesh of swine; also any flesh dedicated to any other than God. You are forbidden the flesh of strangled animals and of those beaten or gored to death; of those killed by a fall or mangled by beasts of prey (unless you make it clean by giving the death-stroke yourselves); also of animals sacrificed to idols.

You are forbidden to settle disputes by consulting the Arrows.[4] That is a pernicious practice.

The unbelievers have this day abandoned all hope of vanquishing your religion. Have no fear of them: fear Me.

This day I have perfected your religion for you and completed My favour to you. I have chosen Islam to be your faith.

---

4. A form of casting lots.

He that is constrained by hunger to eat of what is forbidden, not intending to commit sin, will find God forgiving and merciful.

They ask you what is lawful to them. Say: "All good things are lawful to you, as well as that which you have taught the birds and beasts of prey to catch, training them as God has taught you. Eat of what they catch for you, pronouncing upon it the name of God. And have fear of God: swift is God's reckoning."

All good things have this day been made lawful to you. The food of those to whom the Book was given[5] is lawful to you, and yours to them.

Lawful to you are the believing women and the free women from among those who were given the Book before you, provided that you give them their dowries and live in honour with them, neither committing fornication nor taking them as mistresses.

He that denies the Faith shall gain nothing from his labours. In the world to come he shall have much to lose.

Believers, when you rise to pray wash your faces and your hands as far as the elbow, and wipe your heads and your feet to the ankle. If you are polluted cleanse yourselves. But if you are sick or travelling the road; or if, when you have just relieved yourselves or had intercourse with women, you can find no water, take some clean sand and rub your hands and faces with it. God does not wish to burden you; He seeks only to purify you and to perfect His favour to you, so that you may give thanks.

Remember God's favour to you, and the covenant with which He bound you when you said: "We hear and obey." Have fear of God. God knows the innermost thoughts of men.

Believers, fulfil your duties to God and bear true witness. Do not allow your hatred for other men to turn you away from justice. Deal justly; that is nearer to true piety. Have fear of God; God is cognizant of all your actions.

God has promised those that have faith and do good works forgiveness and a rich reward. As for those who disbelieve and deny Our revelations, they are the heirs of Hell.

Believers, remember the favour which God bestowed upon you when He restrained the hands of those who sought to harm you. Have fear of God. In God let the faithful put their trust.

God made a covenant with the Israelites and raised among them twelve chieftains. God said: "I shall be with you. If you attend to your prayers and render the alms levy; if you believe in My apostles and assist them and give God a generous loan, I shall forgive you your sins and admit you to gardens watered by running streams. But he that hereafter denies Me shall stray from the right path."

But because they broke their covenant We laid on them Our curse and hardened their hearts. They have tampered with words out of their context and forgotten much of what they were enjoined. You will ever find them deceitful, except for a few of them. But pardon them and bear with them. God loves those who do good.

With those who said they were Christians We made a covenant also, but they too have forgotten much of what they were enjoined. Therefore We

5. The Jews.

stirred among them enmity and hatred, which shall endure till the Day of Resurrection, when God will declare to them all that they have done.

People of the Book![6] Our apostle has come to reveal to you much of what you have hidden of the Scriptures, and to forgive you much. A light has come to you from God and a glorious Book, with which God will guide to the paths of peace those that seek to please Him; He will lead them by His will from darkness to the light; He will guide them to a straight path.

Unbelievers are those who declare: "God is the Messiah, the son of Mary." Say: "Who could prevent God, if He so willed, from destroying the Messiah, the son of Mary, his mother, and all the people of the earth? God has sovereignty over the heavens and the earth and all that lies between them. He creates what He will and God has power over all things."

The Jews and the Christians say: "We are the children of God and His loved ones." Say: "Why then does He punish you for your sins? Surely you are mortals of His own creation. He forgives whom He will and punishes whom He pleases. God has sovereignty over the heavens and the earth and all that lies between them. All shall return to Him."

People of the Book! Our apostle has come to you with revelations after an interval during which there were no apostles, lest you say: "No one has come to give us good news or to warn us." Now someone has come to give you good news and to warn you. God has power over all things.

Bear in mind the words of Moses to his people. He said: "Remember, my people, the favours which God has bestowed upon you. He has raised up prophets among you, made you kings, and given you that which He has given to no other nation. Enter, my people, the holy land which God has assigned for you. Do not turn back, or you shall be ruined."

"Moses," they replied, "a race of giants dwells in this land. We will not set foot in it till they are gone. As soon as they are gone we will enter."

Thereupon two God-fearing men whom God had favoured, said: "Go in to them through the gates, and when you have entered you shall surely be victorious. In God put your trust, if you are true believers."

But they replied: "Moses, we will not go in so long as *they* are in it. Go, you and your Lord, and fight. Here we will stay."

"Lord," cried Moses, "I have none but myself and my brother. Do not confound us with these wicked people."

He replied: "They shall be forbidden this land for forty years, during which time they shall wander homeless on the earth. Do not grieve for these wicked people."

Recount to them in all truth the story of Adam's two sons: how they each made an offering, and how the offering of the one was accepted while that of the other was not. One said: "I will surely kill you." The other replied: "God accepts offerings only from the righteous. If you stretch your hand to kill me, I shall not lift mine to slay you; for I fear God, Lord of the Universe. I would rather you should add your sin against me to your other sins and thus become an inmate of the Fire. Such is the reward of the wicked."

His soul prompted him to slay his brother; he slew him and thus became one of the lost. Then God sent down a raven, which dug the earth to show

6. Here, Jews and Christians.

him how to bury the naked corpse of his brother. "Alas!" he cried. "Have I not strength enough to do as this raven has done and so bury my brother's naked corpse?" And he repented.

That was why We laid it down for the Israelites that whoever killed a human being, except as a punishment for murder or other villainy in the land, shall be looked upon as though he had killed all mankind; and that whoever saved a human life should be regarded as though he had saved all mankind.

Our apostles brought them veritable proofs: yet it was not long before many of them committed great evils in the land.

Those that make war against God and His apostle and spread disorder in the land shall be put to death or crucified or have their hands and feet cut off on alternate sides, or be banished from the country. They shall be held up to shame in this world and sternly punished in the hereafter: except those that repent before you reduce them. For you must know that God is forgiving and merciful.

Believers, have fear of God and seek the right path to Him. Fight valiantly for His cause, so that you may triumph.

As for the unbelievers, if they offered all that the earth contains and as much besides to redeem themselves from the torment of the Day of Resurrection, it shall not be accepted from them. Theirs shall be a woeful punishment.

They will strive to get out of Hell, but they shall not: theirs shall be a lasting punishment.

As for the man or woman who is guilty of theft, cut off their hands to punish them for their crimes. That is the punishment enjoined by God. God is mighty and wise. But whoever repents after committing evil, and mends his ways, shall be pardoned by God. God is forgiving and merciful.

Do you not know that God has sovereignty over the heavens and the earth? He punishes whom He will and forgives whom He pleases. God has power over all things.

Apostle, do not grieve for those who plunge headlong into unbelief; those who say with their tongues: "We believe," but have no faith in their hearts, and those Jews who listen to the lies of others and pay no heed to you. They tamper with the words out of their context and say: "If this be given you, accept it; if not, then beware!"

You cannot help a man if God seeks to confound him. Those whose hearts He does not please to purify shall be rewarded with disgrace in this world and a grievous punishment in the hereafter.

They listen to falsehoods and practise what is unlawful. If they come to you, give them your judgement or avoid them. If you avoid them they can in no way harm you; but if you do act as their judge, judge them with fairness. God loves those that deal justly.

But how will they come to you for judgement, when they already have the Torah which enshrines God's own judgement? Soon after, they will turn their backs: they are no true believers.

We have revealed the Torah, in which there is guidance and light. By it the prophets who surrendered themselves judged the Jews, and so did the rabbis and the divines, according to God's Book which had been committed to their keeping and to which they themselves were witnesses.

Have no fear of man; fear Me, and do not sell My revelations for a paltry end. Unbelievers are those who do not judge according to God's revelations.

We decreed for them a life for a life, an eye for an eye, a nose for a nose, an ear for an ear, a tooth for a tooth, and a wound for a wound. But if a man charitably forbears from retaliation, his remission shall atone for him. Transgressors are those that do not judge according to God's revelations.

After them We sent forth Jesus, the son of Mary, confirming the Torah already revealed, and gave him the Gospel, in which there is guidance and light, corroborating what was revealed before it in the Torah, a guide and an admonition to the righteous. Therefore let the followers of the Gospel judge according to what God has revealed therein. Evil-doers are those that do not base their judgements on God's revelations.

And to you We have revealed the Book with the truth. It confirms the Scriptures which came before it and stands as a guardian over them. Therefore give judgement among men according to God's revelations and do not yield to their fancies or swerve from the truth made known to you.

We have ordained a law and assigned a path for each of you. Had God pleased, He could have made you one nation: but it is His wish to prove you by that which He has bestowed upon you. Vie with each other in good works, for to God you shall all return and He will resolve for you your differences.

Pronounce judgement among them according to God's revelations and do not be led by their desires. Take heed lest they should turn you away from a part of that which God has revealed to you. If they reject your judgement, know that it is God's wish to scourge them for their sins. A great many of mankind are evil-doers.

Is it pagan laws that they wish to be judged by? Who is a better judge than God for men whose faith is firm?

Believers, take neither Jews nor Christians for your friends. They are friends with one another. Whoever of you seeks their friendship shall become one of their number. God does not guide the wrongdoers.

You see the faint-hearted hastening to woo them. They say: "We fear lest a change of fortune should befall us." But when God grants you victory or makes known His will, they shall regret their secret plans. Then will the faithful say: "Are these the men who solemnly swore by God that they would stand with you?" Their works will come to nothing and they will lose all.

Believers, if any of you renounce the faith, God will replace them by others who love Him and are loved by Him, who are humble towards the faithful and stern towards the unbelievers, zealous for God's cause and fearless of man's censure. Such is the grace of God: He bestows it on whom He will. God is munificent and all-knowing.

Your only protectors are God, His apostle, and the faithful: those who attend to their prayers, render the alms levy, and kneel down in worship. Those who seek the protection of God, His apostle, and the faithful must know that God's followers are sure to triumph.

Believers, do not seek the friendship of the infidels and those who were given the Book before you, who have made of your religion a jest and a pastime. Have fear of God, if you are true believers. When you call them to pray, they treat their prayers as a jest and a pastime. This is because they are devoid of understanding.

Say: "People of the Book, is it not that you hate us only because we believe in God and in what has been revealed to us and to others before us, and that most of you are evil-doers?"

Say: "Shall I tell you who will receive the worse reward from God? Those whom God has cursed and with whom He has been angry, transforming them into apes and swine, and those who serve the devil. Worse is the plight of these, and they have strayed farther from the right path."

When they came to you they said: "We are believers." Indeed, infidels they came and infidels they departed. God knew best what they concealed.

You see many among them vie with one another in sin and wickedness and practice what is unlawful. Evil is what they do.

Why do their rabbis and divines not forbid them to blaspheme or to practise what is unlawful? Evil indeed are their doings.

The Jews say: "God's hand is chained." May their own hands be chained! May they be cursed for what they say! By no means. His hands are both outstretched: He bestows as He will.

That which is revealed to you from your Lord will surely increase the wickedness and unbelief of many of them. We have stirred among them enmity and hatred, which will endure till the Day of Resurrection. Whenever they kindle the fire of war, God puts it out. They spread evil in the land, but God does not love the evil-doers.

If the People of the Book accept the true faith and keep from evil, We will pardon them their sins and admit them to the gardens of delight. If they observe the Torah and the Gospel and what is revealed to them from their Lord, they shall enjoy abundance from above and from beneath.

There are some among them who are righteous men; but many among them who do nothing but evil.

Apostle, proclaim what is revealed to you from your Lord; if you do not, you will surely fail to convey His message. God will protect you from all men. He does not guide the unbelievers.

Say: "People of the Book, you will attain nothing until you observe the Torah and the Gospel and that which is revealed to you from your Lord."

That which is revealed to you from your Lord will surely increase the wickedness and unbelief of many of them. But do not grieve for the unbelievers.

Believers, Jews, Sabaeans, or Christians—whoever believes in God and the Last Day and does what is right—shall have nothing to fear or to regret.

We made a covenant with the Israelites and sent forth apostles among them. But whenever an apostle came to them with a message that did not suit their fancies, some they accused of lying and some they put to death. They thought no harm would come to them: they were blind and deaf. God turned to them in mercy, but many of them again became blind and deaf. God is ever watching over their actions.

Unbelievers are those that say: "God is the Messiah, the son of Mary." For the Messiah himself said: "Children of Israel, serve God, my Lord and your Lord." He that worships other gods besides God, God will deny him Paradise and Hell shall be his home. None shall help the evil-doers.

Unbelievers are those that say: "God is one of three." There is but one

God. If they do not desist from so saying, those of them that disbelieve shall be sternly punished.

Will they not turn to God in repentance and seek forgiveness of Him? He is forgiving and merciful.

The Messiah, the son of Mary, was no more than an apostle: other apostles passed away before him. His mother was a saintly woman. They both ate earthly food.

See how We make plain to them Our revelations. See how they ignore the truth.

Say: "Will you serve instead of God that which can neither harm nor help you? God hears all and knows all."

Say: "People of the Book! Do not transgress the bounds of truth in your religion. Do not yield to the desires of those who have erred before; who have led many astray and have themselves strayed from the even path."

Those of the Israelites who disbelieved were cursed by David and Jesus, the son of Mary: they cursed them because they rebelled and committed evil. Nor did they censure themselves for any wrong they did. Evil were their deeds.

You see many of them making friends with unbelievers. Evil is that to which their souls prompt them. They have incurred the wrath of God and shall endure eternal torment. Had they believed in God and the Prophet and that which is revealed to him, they would not have befriended them. But many of them are evil-doers.

You will find that the most implacable of men in their enmity to the faithful are the Jews and the pagans, and that the nearest in affection to them are those who say: "We are Christians." That is because there are priests and monks among them; and because they are free from pride.

When they listen to that which was revealed to the Apostle, you will see their eyes fill with tears as they recognize its truth. They say: "Lord, we believe. Count us among Your witnesses. Why should we not believe in God and in the truth that has come down to us? Why should we not hope our Lord will admit us among the righteous?" And for their words God has rewarded them with gardens watered by running streams, where they shall dwell for ever. Such is the recompense of the righteous. But those that disbelieve and deny Our revelations shall be the inmates of Hell.

Believers, do not forbid the wholesome things which God has made lawful to you. Do not transgress; God does not love the transgressors. Eat of the lawful and wholesome things which God has given you. Have fear of God, in whom you believe.

God will not punish you for that which is inadvertent in your oaths. But He will take you to task for the oaths which you solemnly swear. The penalty for a broken oath is the feeding of ten needy men with such food as you normally offer to your own people; or the clothing of ten needy men; or the freeing of one slave. He that cannot afford any of these must fast three days. In this way you shall expiate your broken oaths. Therefore be true to that which you have sworn. Thus God makes plain to you His revelations, so that you may give thanks.

Believers, wine and games of chance, idols and divining arrows, are abominations devised by Satan. Avoid them, so that you may prosper. Satan seeks to stir up enmity and hatred among you by means of wine and gambling, and to keep you from the remembrance of God and from your prayers. Will you not abstain from them?

Obey God, and obey the Apostle. Beware; if you give no heed, know that Our apostle's duty is only to give plain warning.

No blame shall be attached to those that have embraced the faith and done good works in regard to any food they may have eaten, so long as they fear God and believe in Him and do good works; so long as they fear God and believe in Him; so long as they fear God and do good works. God loves the charitable.

Believers, God will put you to the proof by means of the game which you can catch with your hands or with your spears, so that He may know those who fear Him in their hearts. He that transgresses hereafter shall be sternly punished.

Believers, kill no game whilst on pilgrimage. He that kills game by design, shall present, as an offering to the Ka'ba, an animal equivalent to that which he has killed, to be determined by two just men among you; or he shall, in expiation, either feed the poor or fast, so that he may taste the evil consequences of his deed. God has forgiven what is past; but if any one relapses into wrongdoing He will avenge Himself on him: He is mighty and capable of revenge.

Lawful to you is what you catch from the sea and the sustenance it provides; a wholesome food for you and for the seafarer. But you are forbidden the game of the land while you are on pilgrimage. Have fear of God, before whom you shall all be assembled.

God has made the Ka'ba, the Sacred House, the sacred month, and the sacrificial offerings with their ornaments, eternal values for mankind; so that you may know that God has knowledge of all that the heavens and the earth contain; that God has knowledge of all things.

Know that God is stern in retribution, and that God is forgiving and merciful.

The duty of the Apostle is only to give warning. God knows all that you hide and all that you reveal.

Say: "Good and evil are not alike, even though the abundance of evil may tempt you. Have fear of God, you men of understanding, so that you may triumph."

Believers, do not ask questions about things which, if made known to you, would only pain you; but if you ask them when the Koran is being revealed, they shall be made plain to you. God will pardon you for this; God is forgiving and gracious. Other men inquired about them before you, only to disbelieve them afterwards.

God demands neither a *bahirah*, nor a *saibah*, nor a *wasilah*, nor a *hami*.[7] The unbelievers invent falsehoods about God. Most of them are lacking in judgement.

When it is said to them: "Come to that which God has revealed, and to the Apostle," they reply: "Sufficient for us is the faith we have inherited from our fathers," even though their fathers knew nothing and were not rightly guided.

Believers, you are accountable for none but yourselves; he that goes astray

---

7. Names given by pagan Arabs to sacred animals offered at the Ka'ba.

cannot harm you if you are on the right path. To God you shall all return, and He will declare to you what you have done.

Believers, when death approaches you, let two just men from among you act as witnesses when you make your testaments; or two men from another tribe if the calamity of death overtakes you while you are travelling the land. Detain them after prayers, and if you doubt their honesty ask them to swear by God: "We will not sell our testimony for any price even to a kinsman. We will not hide the testimony of God; for we should then be evil-doers." If both prove dishonest, replace them by another pair from among those immediately concerned, and let them both swear by God, saying: "Our testimony is truer than theirs. We have told no lies, for we should then be wrongdoers." Thus they will be more likely to bear true witness or to fear that the oaths of others may contradict theirs. Have fear of God and be obedient. God does not guide the evil-doers.

One day God will gather all the apostles and ask them: "How were you received?" They will reply: "We have no knowledge. You alone know what is hidden." God will say: "Jesus, son of Mary, remember the favour I have bestowed on you and on your mother: how I strengthened you with the Holy Spirit, so that you preached to men in your cradle and in the prime of manhood; how I instructed you in the Book and in wisdom, in the Torah and in the Gospel; how by My leave you fashioned from clay the likeness of a bird and breathed into it so that, by My leave, it became a living bird; how, by My leave, you healed the blind man and the leper, and by My leave restored the dead to life; how I protected you from the Israelites when you had come to them with clear signs: when those of them who disbelieved declared: 'This is but plain sorcery'; how when I enjoined the disciples to believe in Me and in My apostle they replied: 'We believe; bear witness that we submit.' "

"Jesus, son of Mary," said the disciples, "can your Lord send down to us from heaven a table spread with food?"

He replied: "Have fear of God, if you are true believers."

"We wish to eat of it," they said, "so that we may reassure our hearts and know that what you said to us is true, and that we may be witnesses of it."

"Lord," said Jesus, the son of Mary, "send to us from heaven a table spread with food, that it may mark a feast for us and for those that will come after us: a sign from You. Give us our sustenance; You are the best Giver."

God replied: "I am sending one to you. But whoever of you disbelieves hereafter shall be punished as no man has ever been punished."

Then God will say: "Jesus, son of Mary, did you ever say to mankind: 'Worship me and my mother as gods beside God?' "

"Glory to You," he will answer, "how could I ever say that to which I have no right? If I had ever said so, You would have surely known it. You know what is in my mind, but I know not what is in Yours. You alone know what is hidden. I told them only what You bade me. I said: 'Serve God, my Lord and your Lord.' I watched over them while living in their midst, and ever since You took me to Yourself, You have been watching over them. You are the witness of all things. If You punish them, they surely are Your servants; and if You forgive them, surely You are mighty and wise."

God will say: "This is the day when their truthfulness will benefit the truthful. They shall for ever dwell in gardens watered by running streams. God is pleased with them and they are pleased with Him. That is the supreme triumph."

God has sovereignty over the heavens and the earth and all that they contain. He has power over all things.

10. Jonah

[MECCA]

In the Name of God, the Compassionate, the Merciful

Alif lām rā.[8] These are the verses of the Wise Book: Does it seem strange to mankind that We revealed Our will to a mortal from among themselves, saying: "Give warning to mankind, and tell the faithful their endeavours shall be rewarded by their Lord?"

The unbelievers say: "This man[9] is a skilled enchanter." Yet your Lord is God, who in six days created the heavens and the earth and then ascended His throne, ordaining all things. None has power to intercede for you except him who has received His sanction. Such is God, your Lord: therefore serve Him. Will you not take heed?

To Him you shall all return: God's promise shall be fulfilled. He gives being to all His creatures, and in the end He will bring them back to life, so that He may justly reward those who have believed in Him and done good works. As for the unbelievers, they shall drink scalding water and be sternly punished for their unbelief.

It was He that gave the sun his brightness and the moon her light, ordaining her phases that you may learn to compute the seasons and the years. God created them only to manifest the truth. He makes plain His revelations to men of understanding.

In the alternation of night and day, and in all that God has created in the heavens and the earth, there are signs for righteous men.

Those who entertain no hope of meeting Us, being pleased and contented with the life of this world, and those who give no heed to Our revelations, shall have the Fire as their home in requital for their deeds.

As for those that believe and do good works, God will guide them through their faith. Rivers will run at their feet in the Gardens of Delight. Their prayer will be: "Glory to You, Lord!" and their greeting: "Peace!" "Praise be to God, Lord of the Universe," will be the burthen of their plea.

Had God hastened the punishment of men as they would hasten their reward, their fate would have been sealed. Therefore We let those who entertain no hope of meeting Us blunder about in their wrongdoing.

When misfortune befalls man, he prays to Us lying on his side, standing, or sitting down. But as soon as We relieve his affliction he pursues his former ways, as though he never prayed for Our help. Thus their foul deeds seem fair to the transgressors.

We destroyed generations before your time on account of the wrongs they did; their apostles came to them with veritable signs, but they would not believe. Thus shall the guilty be rewarded. Then We made you their successors in the land, so that We might observe how you would conduct yourselves.

---

8. A number of Suras begin with several letters of the Arabic alphabet, the meaning of which is unclear.
9. Muhammad.

When Our clear revelations are recited to them, those who entertain no hope of meeting Us say to you: "Give us a different Koran, or make some changes in it."

Say:[1] "It is not for me to change it. I follow only what is revealed to me. I cannot disobey my Lord, for I fear the punishment of a fateful day."

Say: "Had God pleased, I would never have recited it to you, nor would He have given you any knowledge of it. A whole life-time I dwelt amongst you before it was revealed. Will you not understand?"

Who is more wicked than the man who invents a falsehood about God or denies His revelations? Truly, the evil-doers shall not triumph.

They worship idols that can neither harm nor help them, and say: "These will intercede for us with God."

Say: "Do you presume to tell God of what He knows to be neither in the heavens nor in the earth? Glory to Him! Exalted be He above the gods they serve beside Him!"

There was a time when men followed but one religion. Then they disagreed among themselves: and but for a word from your Lord, long since decreed, their differences would have been firmly resolved.

And they ask: "Why has no sign been given him by his Lord?"

Say: "God alone has knowledge of what is hidden. Wait if you will: I too am waiting!"

No sooner do We show mercy to a people after some misfortune has afflicted them than they begin to scheme against Our revelations. Say: "More swift is God's scheming. Our angels are recording your intrigues."

It is He who guides them by land and sea. They embark: and as the ships set sail, rejoicing in a favouring wind, a raging tempest overtakes them. Billows surge upon them from every side and they fear that they are encompassed by death. They pray to God with all fervour, saying: "Deliver us from this peril and we will be truly thankful."

Yet when He does deliver them, they commit evil in the land and act unjustly.

Men, it is your own souls that you are corrupting. Take your enjoyment in this life: to Us you shall in the end return, and We will declare to you all that you have done.

This present life is like the rich garment with which the earth adorns itself when watered by the rain We send down from the sky. Crops, sustaining man and beast, grow luxuriantly: but as its hopeful tenants prepare themselves for the rich harvest, down comes Our scourge upon it, by night or in broad day, laying it waste, even though it did not blossom but yesterday. Thus do We make plain Our revelations to thoughtful men.

God invites you to the Home of Peace. He guides whom He will to a straight path. Those that do good works shall have a good reward and more besides. Neither blackness nor misery shall overcast their faces. They are the heirs of Paradise: in it they shall abide for ever.

As for those that have earned evil, evil shall be rewarded with like evil. Misery will oppress them (they shall have none to defend them from God), as though patches of the night's own darkness veiled their faces. They are the heirs of Hell: in it they shall abide for ever.

On the day when We assemble them all together, We shall say to the

---

1. God's instruction to Muhammad.

idolaters: "Keep to your places, you and your idols!" We will separate them one from another, and then their idols will say to them: "It was not us that you worshipped, God is our all-sufficient witness. Nor were we aware of your worship."

Thereupon each soul will know what it has done. They shall be sent back to God, their true Lord, and the idols they invented will forsake them.

Say: "Who provides for you from heaven and earth? Who has endowed you with sight and hearing? Who brings forth the living from the dead, and the dead from the living? Who ordains all things?"

They will reply: "God."

Say: "Will you not take heed, then? Such is God, your true Lord. That which is not true must needs be false. How then can you turn away from Him?"

Thus is the word of your Lord made good. The evil-doers have no faith.

Say: "Can any of your idols conceive Creation, then renew it? God conceives Creation, then renews it. How is it that you are so misled?"

Say: "Can any of your idols guide you to the truth? God can guide you to the truth. Who is more worthy to be followed: He that can guide to the truth or he that cannot and is himself in need of guidance? What has come over you that you so judge?"

Most of them follow nothing but mere conjecture. But conjecture is in no way a substitute for Truth. God is cognizant of all their actions.

This Koran could not have been devised by any but God. It confirms what was revealed before it and fully explains the Scriptures. It is beyond doubt from the Lord of the Universe.

If they say: "He invented it himself," say: "Bring me one chapter like it. Call on whom you may besides God to help you, if what you say be true!"

Indeed, they disbelieve what they cannot grasp, for they have not yet seen its prophecy fulfilled. Likewise did those who passed before them disbelieve. But see what was the end of the wrong-doers.

Some believe in it, while others do not. But your Lord best knows the evil-doers.

If they disbelieve you, say: "My deeds are mine and your deeds are yours. You are not accountable for my actions, nor am I accountable for what you do."

Some of them listen to you. But can you make the deaf hear you, incapable as they are of understanding?

Some of them look upon you. But can you show the way to the blind, bereft as they are of sight?

Indeed, in no way does God wrong mankind, but men wrong themselves.

The day will come when He will gather them all together, as though they had sojourned in this world but for an hour. They will acquaint themselves with each other. Lost shall be those that disbelieved in meeting and did not follow the right path.

Whether We let you glimpse in some measure the scourge with which We threaten them, or cause you to die before we smite them, to Us they shall return. God is searching over all their actions.

An apostle is sent to every nation. When their apostle comes, justice is done among them; they are not wronged.

They ask: "When will this promise be fulfilled, if what you say be true?"

Say: "I have no control over any harm or benefit to myself, except by the will of God. A space of time is fixed for every nation; when their hour is come, not for one hour shall they delay: nor can they go before it."

Say: "Do but consider. Should His scourge fall upon you by night or by the light of day, what punishment would the guilty hasten? Will you believe in it when it does overtake you, although it was your wish to hurry it on?"

Then it shall be said to the wrongdoers: "Feel the everlasting torment! Shall you not be rewarded according to your deeds?"

They ask you if it is true. Say: "Yes, by the Lord, it is true! And you shall not be immune."

To redeem himself then, each sinner would gladly give all that the earth contains if he possessed it. When they behold the scourge, they will repent in secret. But judgement shall be fairly passed upon them; they shall not be wronged.

To God belongs all that the heavens and the earth contain. The promise of God is true, though most of them may not know it. It is He who ordains life and death, and to Him you shall all return.

Men, an admonition has come to you from your Lord, a cure for the mind, a guide and a blessing to true believers.

Say: "In the grace and mercy of God let them rejoice, for these are better than the worldly riches they amass."

Say: "Do but consider the things that God has given you. Some you pronounced unlawful and others lawful." Say: "Was it God who gave you His leave, or do you invent falsehoods about God?"

What will they think, those who invent falsehoods about God, on the Day of Resurrection? God is bountiful to men: yet most of them do not give thanks.

You shall engage in no affair, you shall recite no verse from the Koran, you shall commit no act, but We will witness it. Not an atom's weight in earth or heaven escapes your Lord, nor is there any object smaller or greater, but is recorded in a glorious book.

The servants of God have nothing to fear or to regret. Those that have faith and keep from evil shall rejoice both in this world and in the hereafter: the word of God shall never change. That is the supreme triumph.

Let their words not grieve you. All glory belongs to God. He alone hears all and knows all.

To God belong all who dwell on earth and in heaven. Those that worship gods beside God follow nothing but idle fancies and preach nothing but falsehoods.

He it is who has ordained the night for your rest and given the day its light. Surely in this there are signs for prudent men.

They say: "God has begotten a son." God forbid! Self-sufficient is He. His is all that the heavens and the earth contain. Surely for this you have no sanction. Would you say of God what you do not know?

Say: "Those that invent falsehoods about God shall not prosper. They may take their ease in this life, but to Us they shall in the end return, and We shall make them taste a grievous torment for their unbelief."

Recount to them the tale of Noah. He said to his people: "If it offends you that I should dwell in your midst and preach to you God's revelations (for in Him I have put my trust), muster all your idols and decide your course of action. Do not intrigue in secret. Execute your judgement and give me no respite. If you turn away from me, remember I demand of you no recompense. Only God will reward me. I am commanded to be one of those who shall submit to Him."

But they disbelieved him. Therefore We saved Noah and those who were with him in the Ark, so that they survived, and drowned the others who denied Our revelations. Consider the fate of those who were forewarned.

After that we sent apostles to their descendants. They showed them veritable signs, but they persisted in their unbelief. Thus do We seal up the hearts of the transgressors.

Then We sent forth Moses and Aaron with Our signs to Pharaoh and his nobles. But they rejected them with scorn, for they were wicked men. When the truth had come to them from Us, they declared: "This is but plain sorcery."

Moses replied: "Is this what you say of the Truth when it has come to you? Is this sorcery? Sorcerers shall never prosper."

They said: "Have you come to turn us away from the faith of our fathers, so that you two may lord it over the land? We will never believe in you."

Then Pharaoh said: "Bring every learned sorcerer to my presence."

And when the sorcerers attended Moses said to them: "Cast down what you wish to cast." And when they had thrown, he said: "The sorcery that you have wrought God will surely bring to nothing. He does not bless the work of those who do evil. By His words He vindicates the truth, much as the guilty may dislike it."

Few of his[2] people believed in Moses, for they feared the persecution of Pharaoh and his nobles. Pharaoh was a tyrant in the land, an evildoer.

Moses said: "If you believe in God, my people, and have surrendered yourselves to Him, in Him alone then put your trust."

They replied: "In God we have put our trust. Lord, do not let us suffer at the hands of wicked men. Deliver us, through Your mercy, from the unbelievers."

We revealed Our will to Moses and his brother, saying: "Build houses in Egypt for your people and make your homes places of worship. Conduct prayers and give good news to the faithful."

"Lord," said Moses. "You have bestowed on Pharaoh and his princes splendour and riches in this life, so that they might stray from your path. Lord, destroy their riches and harden their hearts, so that they shall persist in unbelief until they face the woeful scourge."

God replied: "Your prayer shall be answered. Follow the right path and do not walk in the footsteps of ignorant men."

We led the Israelites across the sea, and Pharaoh and his legions pursued them with wickedness and hate. But as he was drowning, Pharaoh cried: "Now I believe no god exists except the God in whom the Israelites believe. To Him I give up myself."

"Only now! But before this you were a rebel and a wrongdoer. We shall save your body this day, so that you may become a sign to all posterity: for a great many of mankind do not heed Our signs."

2. Pharaoh's.

We settled the Israelites in a blessed land and provided them with good things. Nor did they disagree among themselves until knowledge was given them. Your Lord will judge their differences on the Day of Resurrection.

If you doubt what We have revealed to you, ask those who have read the Scriptures before you. The truth has come to you from your Lord: therefore do not doubt it. Nor shall you deny the revelations of God, for then you shall be lost.

Those for whom the word of your Lord shall be fulfilled will not have faith, even if they be given every sign, until they face the woeful scourge. Were it otherwise, every nation, had it believed, would have profited from its faith. But it was so only with Jonah's people. When they believed, We spared them the penalty of disgrace in this life and gave them comfort for a while. Had your Lord pleased, all the people of the earth would have believed in Him, one and all. Would you then force people to have faith?

None can have faith except by the will of God. He will visit His scourge upon the senseless.

Say: "Behold what the heavens and the earth contain!" But neither signs nor warnings will avail the unbelievers.

What can they wait for but the fate of those who have gone before them? Say: "Wait if you will; I too am waiting."

We shall save Our apostles and the true believers. It is but just that We should save the faithful.

Say: "Men! Doubt my religion if you will, but never will I worship those that you worship besides God. I worship God, to whom you shall all return: for I am commanded to be one of the faithful, I was bidden: 'Dedicate yourself to the Faith in all uprightness and serve none besides God. You shall not pray to idols which can neither help nor harm you, for if you do, you will become a wrongdoer. If God afflicts you with a misfortune none can remove it but He; and if He bestows on you a favour, none can withhold His bounty. He is bountiful to whom He will. He is the Forgiving One, the Merciful.' "

Say: "Men! The truth has come to you from your Lord. He that follows the right path follows it to his own good, and he that goes astray does so at his own peril. I am not your keeper."

Observe what is revealed to you, and have patience till God makes known his judgement. He is the best of judges.

12. Joseph

[MECCA]

In the Name of God, the Compassionate, the Merciful

Alif lām rā. These are the verses of the Glorious Book. We have revealed the Koran in the Arabic tongue so that you may grow in understanding.

In revealing this Koran We will recount to you the best of narratives, though before it you were heedless.

Joseph said to his father: "Father, I dreamt of eleven stars and the sun and the moon; I saw them prostrate themselves before me."

"My son," he replied, "say nothing of this dream to your brothers, lest they plot evil against you: Satan is the sworn enemy of man. You shall be chosen by your Lord. He will teach you to interpret visions, and will perfect His favour to you and to the house of Jacob, as He perfected it to your forefathers Abraham and Isaac before you. Your Lord is wise and all-knowing."

Surely in Joseph and his brothers there are signs for doubting men.

They said to each other: "Joseph and his brother are dearer to our father than ourselves, though we are many. Truly, our father is much mistaken. Let us slay Joseph, or cast him away in some far-off land, so that we may have no rivals in our father's love, and after that be honourable men."

One of them said: "Do not slay Joseph; but if you must, rather cast him into a dark pit. Some caravan will take him up."

They said to their father: "Why do you not trust us with Joseph? Surely we wish him well. Send him with us tomorrow, that he may play and enjoy himself. We will take good care of him."

He replied: "It would much grieve me to let him go with you; for I fear lest the wolf should eat him when you are off your guard."

They said: "If the wolf could eat him despite our numbers, then we should surely be lost!"

And when they took Joseph with them, they decided to cast him into a dark pit. We revealed to him, saying: "You shall tell them of all this when they will not know you."

At nightfall they returned weeping to their father. They said: "We went off to compete together and left Joseph with our packs. The wolf devoured him. But you will not believe us, though we speak the truth." And they showed him their brother's shirt, stained with false blood.

"No!" he cried. "Your souls have tempted you to evil. Sweet patience! God alone can help me bear the loss you speak of."

And a caravan passed by, who sent their water-bearer to the pit. And when he had let down his pail, he cried: "Rejoice! A boy!"

They concealed him as part of their merchandise. But God knew what they did. They sold him for a trifling price, for a few pieces of silver. They cared nothing for him.

The Egyptian who bought him said to his wife:[3] "Be kind to him. He may prove useful to us, or we may adopt him as our son."

Thus We established Joseph in the land, and taught him to interpret dreams. God has power over all things, though most men may not know it. And when he reached maturity We bestowed on him wisdom and knowledge. Thus We reward the righteous.

His master's wife sought to seduce him. She bolted the doors and said: "Come!"

"God forbid!" he replied. "My lord has treated me with kindness. Wrongdoers never prosper."

She made for him, and he himself would have succumbed to her had he not been shown a sign from his Lord. Thus did We shield him from wantonness, for he was one of Our faithful servants.

They both rushed to the door. She tore his shirt from behind. And at the door they met her husband.

She cried: "Shall not the man who wished to violate your wife be thrown into prison or sternly punished?"

Joseph said: "It was she who attempted to seduce me."

---

3. Traditionally given the name Zuleikha.

"If his shirt is torn from the front," said one of her people, "she is speaking the truth and he is lying. If it is torn from behind, then he is speaking the truth and she is lying."

And when her husband saw Joseph's shirt rent from behind, he said to her: "This is but one of your tricks. Your cunning is great indeed! Joseph, say no more about this. Woman, ask pardon for your sin. You have done wrong."

In the city women were saying: "The Prince's wife has sought to seduce her servant. She has conceived a passion for him. It is clear that she has gone astray."

When she heard of their intrigues, she invited them to a banquet at her house. To each she gave a knife, and ordered Joseph to present himself before them. When they saw him, they were amazed at him and cut their hands, exclaiming: "God preserve us! This is no mortal, but a gracious angel."

"This is the man," she said, "on whose account you blamed me. I sought to seduce him, but he was unyielding. If he declines to do my bidding, he shall be thrown into prison and shall be held in scorn."

"Lord," said Joseph, "sooner would I go to prison than give in to their advances. Shield me from their cunning, or I shall yield to them and lapse into folly."

His Lord heard his prayer and warded off their wiles from him. He hears all and knows all.

Yet for all the evidence they had seen, they thought it right to jail him for a time.

Two young men entered the prison with him. One of them said: "I dreamt that I was pressing grapes." And the other said: "I dreamt that I was carrying a loaf upon my head, and that the birds came and ate of it. Tell us the meaning of these dreams, for we can see you are a virtuous man."

Joseph replied: "I can interpret them long before they are fulfilled. Whatever food you are provided with, I can divine for you its meaning, even before it reaches you. This knowledge my Lord has given me, for I have left the faith of those that disbelieve in God and deny the life to come. I follow the faith of my forefathers, Abraham, Isaac, and Jacob. We will serve no idols besides God. Such is the grace which God has bestowed on us and on all mankind. Yet most men do not give thanks.

"Fellow-prisoners! Are sundry gods better than God, the One, the One who conquers all? Those you serve besides Him are nothing but names which you and your fathers have devised and for which God has revealed no sanction. Judgement rests only with God. He has commanded you to worship none but Him. That is the true faith: yet most men do not know it.

"Fellow-prisoners, one of you will serve his lord with wine. The other will be crucified, and the birds will peck at his head. This is the answer to your question."

And Joseph said to the prisoner who he knew would be freed: "Remember me in the presence of your lord."

But Satan made him forget to mention Joseph to his lord, so that he stayed in prison for several years.

The king said: "I saw seven fatted cows which seven lean ones devoured; also seven green ears of corn and seven others dry. Tell me the meaning of this vision, my nobles, if you can interpret visions."

They replied: "It is but a medley of dream; nor are we skilled in the interpretation of dreams."

Thereupon the man who had been freed remembered Joseph after all that time. He said: "I shall tell you what it means. Give me leave to go."

He said to Joseph: "Tell us, man of truth, of the seven fatted cows which seven lean ones devoured; also of the seven green ears of corn and the other seven which were dry: so that I may go back to my masters and inform them."

He replied: "You shall sow for seven consecutive years. Leave in the ear the corn you reap, except a little which you may eat. Then there shall follow seven hungry years which will consume all but little of what you have stored. Then there will come a year of abundant rain, in which the people will press the grape."

The king said: "Bring this man before me."

But when the envoy came to him, Joseph said: "Go back to your master and ask him about the women who cut their hands. My master knows their cunning."

The king questioned the women, saying: "What made you attempt to seduce Joseph?"

"God forbid!" they replied. "We know no evil of him."

"Now the truth must come to light," said the Prince's wife. "It was I who sought to seduce him. He has told the truth."

"From this," said Joseph, "my lord will know that I did not betray him in his absence, and that God does not guide the work of the treacherous. Not that I am free from sin: man's soul is prone to evil, except his to whom God has shown mercy. My Lord is forgiving and merciful."

The king said: "Bring him before me. I will choose him for my own."

And when he had spoken with him, the king said: "You shall henceforth dwell with us, honoured and trusted."

Joseph said: "Give me charge of the granaries of the realm. I shall husband them wisely."

Thus did We establish Joseph in the land, and he dwelt there as he pleased. We bestow Our mercy on whom We will, and never deny the righteous their reward. Better is the reward of the life to come for those who believe in God and keep from evil.

Joseph's brothers arrived and presented themselves before him. He recognized them, but they knew him not. And when he had given them their provisions, he said: "Bring me your other brother from your father. Do you not see that I give just measure and am the best of hosts? If you do not bring him, you shall have no corn, nor shall you come near me again."

They replied: "We will endeavour to fetch him from his father. This we will surely do."

Joseph said to his servants: "Put their money into their packs, so that they may find it when they return to their people. Perchance they will come back."

When they returned to their father, they said: "Father, corn is henceforth denied us. Send our brother with us and we shall have our measure. We will take good care of him."

He replied: "Am I to trust you with him as I once trusted you with his brother? But God is the best of guardians: and of all those that show mercy He is the most merciful."

When they opened their packs, they discovered that their money had been returned to them. "Father," they said, "what more can we desire? Here is our money paid back to us. We will buy provisions for our people and take good care of our brother. We shall receive an extra camel-load; a camel-load should be easy enough."

He replied: "I will not let him go with you until you promise in God's name to bring him back to me, unless the worst befall you."

And when they had given him their pledge, he said: "God is the witness of your oath. My sons, enter the town by different gates. If you do wrong, I cannot ward off from you the wrath of God: judgement is His alone. In Him I have put my trust. In Him alone let the faithful put their trust."

And when they entered as their father had bade them, his counsel availed them nothing against the decree of God. It was but a wish in Jacob's soul which he had thus fulfilled. He was possessed of knowledge which We had given him, though most men have no knowledge.

When they went in to Joseph, he embraced his brother, and said: "I am your brother. Do not grieve at what they did."

And when he had given them their provisions, he hid a drinking-cup in his brother's pack.

Then a crier called out after them: "Travellers, you are thieves!"

They turned back and asked: "What have you lost?"

"We miss the king's drinking-cup," he replied. "He that brings it shall have a camel-load of corn. I pledge my word for it."

"In God's name," they cried, "you know we did not come to do evil in this land. We are no thieves."

The Egyptians said: "What penalty shall be his who stole it, if you prove to be lying?"

They replied: "He in whose pack the cup is found shall be your bondsman. Thus we punish the wrongdoers."

Joseph searched their bags before his brother's, and then took out the cup from his brother's bag.

Thus We directed Joseph. By the king's law he had no right to seize his brother: but God willed otherwise. We exalt in knowledge whom We will: but above those that have knowledge there is One more knowing.

They said: "If he has stolen—know then that a brother of his has committed theft before him."[4]

But Joseph kept his secret and revealed nothing to them. He said: "Your deed was worse. God best knows the things you speak of."

They said: "Noble prince, this boy has an aged father. Take one of us, instead of him. We can see you are a generous man."

He replied: "God forbid that we should take any but the man with whom our property was found: for then we should be unjust."

When they despaired of him, they went aside to confer in private. The eldest said: "Have you forgotten that your father took from you a pledge in God's name, and that long ago you did your worst with Joseph. I will not stir from this land until my father gives me leave or God makes known to me His judgement: He is the best of judges. Return to your father and say to him: 'Father, your son has committed a theft. We testify only to what we

---

4. Commentators say that Joseph had stolen an idol of his maternal grandfather's and broken it, so that he might not worship it.

know. How could we guard against the unforeseen? Inquire at the city where we lodged, and from the caravan with which we travelled. We speak the truth.' "

"No!" cried their father. "Your souls have tempted you to evil. But I will have sweet patience. God may bring them all to me. He alone is all-knowing and wise." And he turned away from them, crying: "Alas for Joseph!" His eyes went white with grief and he was oppressed with silent sorrow.

His sons exclaimed: "In God's name, will you not cease to think of Joseph until you ruin your health and die?"

He replied: "I complain to God of my sorrow and sadness. He has made known to me things that you know not. Go, my sons, and seek news of Joseph and his brother. Do not despair of God's spirit; none but unbelievers despair of God's spirit."

And when they went in to him, they said: "Noble prince, we and our people are scourged with famine. We have brought but little money. Give us some corn, and be charitable to us: God rewards the charitable."

"Do you know," he replied, "what you did to Joseph and his brother? You are surely unaware."

They cried: "Can you indeed be Joseph?"

"I am Joseph," he answered, "and this is my brother. God has been gracious to us. Those that keep from evil and endure with fortitude, God will not deny them their reward."

"By the Lord," they said, "God has exalted you above us all. We have indeed been guilty."

He replied: "None shall reproach you this day. May God forgive you: Of all those who show mercy, He is the most merciful. Take this shirt of mine and throw it over my father's face: he will recover his sight. Then return to me with all your people."

When the caravan departed their father said: "I feel the breath of Joseph, though you will not believe me."

"In God's name," said those who heard him, "it is but your old illusion."

And when the bearer of good news arrived, he threw Joseph's shirt over the old man's face, and he regained his sight. He said: "Did I not tell you that God has made known to me what you know not?"

His sons said: "Father, implore forgiveness for our sins. We have indeed done wrong."

He replied: "I shall implore my Lord to forgive you. He is forgiving and merciful."

And when they went in to Joseph, he embraced his parents and said: "Welcome to Egypt, safe, if God wills!"

He helped his parents to a couch, and they all fell on their knees and prostrated themselves before him.

"This," said Joseph to his father, "is the meaning of my old vision: my Lord has fulfilled it. He has been gracious to me. He has released me from prison and brought you out of the desert after Satan had stirred up strife between me and my brothers. My lord is gracious to whom He will. He alone is all-knowing and wise.

"Lord, You have given me authority and taught me to interpret dreams. Creator of the heavens and the earth, my Guardian in this world and in the hereafter. Allow me to die in submission, and admit me among the righteous."

That which We have now revealed to you[5] is a tale of the unknown. You were not present when Joseph's brothers conceived their plans and schemed against him. Yet strive as you may, most men will not believe.

You shall demand of them no recompense for this. It is an admonition to all mankind.

Many are the marvels of the heavens and the earth; yet they pass them by and pay no heed to them. The greater part of them believe in God only if they can worship other gods besides Him.

Are they confident that God's scourge will not fall upon them, or that the Hour of Doom will not overtake them unawares, without warning?

Say: "This is my path. With sure knowledge I call on you to have faith in God, I and all my followers. Glory be to God! I am no idolater."

Nor were the apostles whom We sent before you other than mortals inspired by Our will and chosen from among their people.

Have they not travelled in the land and seen what was the end of those who disbelieved before them? Better is the world to come for those that keep from evil. Can you not understand?

And when at length Our apostles despaired and thought they were denied, Our help came down to them, delivering whom We pleased. The evil-doers could not be saved from Our scourge. Their annals point to a moral to men of understanding.

This[6] is no invented tale, but a confirmation of previous scriptures, an explanation of all things, a guide and a blessing to true believers.

19. Mary

[MECCA]

In the Name of God, the Compassionate, the Merciful

Kaf hā' yā' 'ain sād. An account of your Lord's goodness to His servant Zacharias:

He invoked Him in secret, saying: "My bones are enfeebled, and my head grows silver with age. Yet never, Lord, have I prayed to You in vain. I now fear my kinsmen who will succeed me, for my wife is barren. Grant me a son who will be my heir and an heir to the house of Jacob, and who will find grace in Your sight."

"Rejoice, Zacharias," came the answer. "You shall be given a son, and he shall be called John; a name no man has borne before him."

"How shall I have a son, Lord," asked Zacharias, "when my wife is barren and I am well-advanced in years?"

He replied: "Such is the will of your Lord. It shall be no difficult task for Me, for I brought you into being when you were nothing before."

"Lord," said Zacharias, "give me a sign."

"Your sign is that for three days and three nights," He replied, "you shall be bereft of speech, though otherwise sound in body."

5. Muhammad.　6. The Koran.

Then Zacharias came out from the Shrine and exhorted his people to give glory to their Lord morning and evening.

To John We said: "Observe the Scriptures with a firm resolve." We bestowed on him wisdom, grace, and purity while yet a child, and he grew up a righteous man; honouring his father and mother, and neither arrogant nor rebellious. Blessed was he on the day he was born and the day of his death; and may peace be on him when he is raised to life.

And you shall recount in the Book the story of Mary: how she left her people and betook herself to a solitary place to the east.

We sent to her Our spirit in the semblance of a full-grown man. And when she saw him she said: "May the Merciful defend me from you! If you fear the Lord, leave me and go your way."

"I am the messenger of your Lord," he replied, "and have come to give you a holy son."

"How shall I bear a child," she answered, "when I am a virgin, untouched by man?"

"Such is the will of your Lord," he replied. "That is no difficult thing for Him. 'He shall be a sign to mankind,' says the Lord, 'and a blessing from Ourself. This is Our decree.' "

Thereupon she conceived him, and retired to a far-off place. And when she felt the throes of childbirth she lay down by the trunk of a palm-tree crying: "Oh, would that I had died and passed into oblivion!"

But a voice from below cried out to her: "Do not despair. Your Lord has provided a brook that runs at your feet, and if you shake the trunk of this palm-tree it will drop fresh ripe dates in your lap. Therefore eat and drink and rejoice; and should you meet any mortal say to him: 'I have vowed a fast to the Merciful and will not speak with any man today.' "

Carrying the child, she came to her people, who said to her: "This is indeed a strange thing! Sister of Aaron,[7] your father was never a whore-monger, nor was your mother a harlot."

She made a sign to them, pointing to the child. But they replied: "How can we speak with a babe in the cradle?"

Whereupon he spoke and said: "I am the servant of God. He has given me the Book and ordained me a prophet. His blessing is upon me wherever I go, and He has commanded me to be steadfast in prayer and to give alms to the poor as long as I shall live. He has exhorted me to honour my mother and has purged me of vanity and wickedness. I was blessed on the day I was born, and blessed I shall be on the day of my death; and may peace be upon me on the day when I shall be raised to life."

Such was Jesus, the son of Mary. That is the whole truth, which they still doubt. God forbid that He Himself should beget a son! When He decrees a thing He need only say: "Be," and it is.

God is my Lord and your Lord: therefore serve Him. That is the right path.

Yet the Sects are divided concerning Jesus. But when the fateful day arrives, woe to the unbelievers! Their sight and being shall be sharpened on the day when they appear before Us. Truly, the unbelievers are in the grossest error.

Forewarn them of that woeful day, when Our decrees shall be fulfilled

---

7. Muslim commentators deny the charge that there is confusion here between Miriam, Aaron's sister, and Maryam (Mary), mother of Jesus. *Sister of Aaron*, they argue, simply means "virtuous woman" in this context.

whilst they heedlessly persist in unbelief. For We shall inherit the earth and all who dwell upon it. To Us they shall return.

You shall also recount in the Book the story of Abraham:

He was a saintly man and a prophet. He said to his father: "How can you serve a worthless idol, a thing that can neither see nor hear?

"Father, things you know nothing of have come to my knowledge: therefore follow me, that I may guide you along an even path.

"Father, do not worship Satan; for he has rebelled against the Lord of Mercy.

"Father, I fear that a scourge will fall upon you from the Merciful, and you will become one of Satan's minions."

He replied: "Do you dare renounce my gods, Abraham? Desist from this folly or I shall stone you. Begone from my house this instant!"

"Peace be with you," said Abraham. "I shall implore my Lord to forgive you: for to me He has been gracious. But I will not live with you or with your idols. I will call on my Lord, and trust that my prayers will not be ignored."

And when Abraham had cast off his people and the idols which they worshipped, We gave him Isaac and Jacob. Each of them We made a prophet, and We bestowed on them gracious gifts and high renown.

In the Book tell also of Moses, who was a chosen man, an apostle, and a prophet.

We called out to him from the right side of the Mountain, and when he came near We communed with him in secret. We gave him, of Our mercy, his brother Aaron, himself a prophet.

And in the Book you shall tell of Ishmael: he, too, was a man of his word, an apostle, and a prophet.

He enjoined prayer and almsgiving on his people, and his Lord was pleased with him.

And of Idris:[8] he, too, was a saint and a prophet, whom We honoured and exalted.

These are the men to whom God has been gracious: the prophets from among the descendants of Adam and of those whom We carried in the Ark with Noah; the descendants of Abraham, of Israel, and of those whom We have guided and chosen. For when the revelations of the Merciful were recited to them they fell down on their knees in tears and adoration.

But the generations who succeeded them neglected their prayers and succumbed to their desires. These shall assuredly be lost. But those that repent and embrace the Faith and do what is right shall be admitted to Paradise and shall in no way be wronged. They shall enter the gardens of Eden, which the Merciful has promised His servants in reward for their faith. His promise shall be fulfilled.

There they shall hear no idle talk, but only the voice of peace. And their sustenance shall be given them morning and evening. Such is the Paradise which We shall give the righteous to inherit.

We do not descend from Heaven save at the bidding of your Lord.[9] To Him belongs what is before us and behind us, and all that lies between.

Your Lord does not forget. He is the Lord of the heavens and the earth

---

8. Enoch.   9. Commentators say that these are the words of the angel Gabriel, in reply to Muhammad's complaint of long intervals elapsing between periods of revelation.

and all that is between them. Worship Him, then, and be patient in His service; for do you know any other worthy of His name?

"What!" says man. "When I am once dead, shall I be raised to life?"

Does man forget that We created him out of the void? By the Lord, We will call them to account in company with all the devils and set them on their knees around the fire of Hell: from every sect We will carry off its stoutest rebels against the Lord of Mercy. We know best who deserves most to be burnt therein.

There is not one of you who shall not pass through it: such is the absolute decree of your Lord. We will deliver those who fear Us, but the wrongdoers shall be left there on their knees.

When Our clear revelations are recited to them the unbelievers say to the faithful: "Which of us two will have a finer dwelling and better companions?"

How many generations have We destroyed before them, far greater in riches and in splendour!

Say: "The Merciful will bear long with those in error, until they witness the fulfilment of His threats: be it a worldly scourge or the Hour of Doom. Then shall they know whose is the worse plight and whose the smaller following."

God will add guidance to those that are rightly guided. Deeds of lasting merit shall earn you a better reward in His sight and a more auspicious end.

Mark the words of him who denies Our signs and who yet boasts: "I shall surely be given wealth and children!" he boasts.

Has the future been revealed to him? Or has the Merciful made him such a promise?

By no means! We will record his words and make his punishment long and terrible. All he speaks of he shall leave behind and come before Us all alone.

They have chosen other gods to help them. But in the end they will renounce their worship and turn against them.

Know that We send down to the unbelievers devils who incite them to evil. Therefore have patience: their days are numbered. The day will surely come when We will gather the righteous in multitudes before the Lord of Mercy, and drive the sinful in great hordes into Hell. None has power to intercede for them save him who has received the sanction of the Merciful.

Those who say: "The Lord of Mercy has begotten a son," preach a monstrous falsehood, at which the very heavens might crack, the earth break asunder, and the mountains crumble to dust. That they should ascribe a son to the Merciful, when it does not become the Lord of Mercy to beget one!

There is none in the heavens or the earth but shall return to the Merciful in utter submission. He has kept strict count of all His creatures, and one by one they shall approach Him on the Day of Resurrection. He will cherish those who accepted the true faith and were charitable in their lifetime.

We have revealed to you the Koran in your own tongue that you may thereby proclaim good tidings to the upright and give warning to a contentious nation.

How many generations have We destroyed before them! Can you find one of them still alive, or hear so much as a whisper from them?

55. The Merciful[1]

[MECCA]

In the Name of God, the Compassionate, the Merciful

It is the Merciful who has taught the Koran.

He created man and taught him articulate speech. The sun and the moon pursue their ordered course. The plants and the trees bow down in adoration.

He raised the heaven on high and set the balance of all things, that you might not transgress that balance. Give just weight and full measure.

He laid the earth for His creatures, with all its fruits and blossom-bearing palm, chaff-covered grain and scented herbs. Which of your Lord's blessings would you deny?

He created man from potter's clay and the jinn[2] from smokeless fire. Which of your Lord's blessings would you deny?

The Lord of the two easts[3] is He, and the Lord of the two wests. Which of your Lord's blessings would you deny?

He has let loose the two oceans:[4] they meet one another. Yet between them stands a barrier which they cannot overrun. Which of your Lord's blessings would you deny?

Pearls and corals come from both. Which of your Lord's blessings would you deny?

His are the ships that sail like mountains upon the ocean. Which of your Lord's blessings would you deny?

All that lives on earth is doomed to die. But the face of your Lord will abide for ever, in all its majesty and glory. Which of your Lord's blessings would you deny?

All who dwell in heaven and earth entreat Him. Each day some mighty task engages Him. Which of your Lord's blessings would you deny?

Mankind and jinn, We shall surely find the time to judge you! Which of your Lord's blessings would you deny?

Mankind and jinn, if you have power to penetrate the confines of heaven and earth, then penetrate them! But this you shall not do except with Our own authority. Which of your Lord's blessings would you deny?

Flames of fire shall be lashed at you, and molten brass. There shall be none to help you. Which of your Lord's blessings would you deny?

When the sky splits asunder and reddens like a rose or stainéd leather (which of your Lord's blessings would you deny?), on that day neither man nor jinnee shall be asked about his sins. Which of your Lord's blessings would you deny?

The wrongdoers shall be known by their looks; they shall be seized by their forelocks and their feet. Which of your Lord's blessings would you deny?

That is the Hell which the sinners deny. They shall wander between fire and water fiercely seething. Which of your Lord's blessings would you deny?

But for those that fear the majesty of their Lord there are two gardens

---

1. Compare this Sura with Psalm 136.   2. A separate order of creation from humans. The question that follows is addressed to both beings.   3. The points at which the sun rises in summer and winter. 4. Saltwater and freshwater; more specifically, a reference to freshwater springs in the ocean floor.

(which of your Lord's blessings would you deny?) planted with shady trees. Which of your Lord's blessings would you deny?

Each is watered by a flowing spring. Which of your Lord's blessings would you deny?

Each bears every kind of fruit in pairs. Which of your Lord's blessings would you deny?

They shall recline on couches lined with thick brocade, and within their reach will hang the fruits of both gardens. Which of your Lord's blessings would you deny?

They shall dwell with bashful virgins whom neither man nor jinnee will have touched before. Which of your Lord's blessings would you deny?

Virgins as fair as corals and rubies. Which of your Lord's blessings would you deny?

Shall the reward of goodness be anything but good? Which of your Lord's blessings would you deny?

And beside these there shall be two other gardens (which of your Lord's blessings would you deny?) of darkest green. Which of your Lord's blessings would you deny?

A gushing fountain shall flow in each. Which of your Lord's blessings would you deny?

Each planted with fruit-trees, the palm and the pomegranate. Which of your Lord's blessings would you deny?

In each there shall be virgins chaste and fair. Which of your Lord's blessings would you deny?

Dark-eyed virgins sheltered in their tents (which of your Lord's blessings would you deny?) whom neither man nor jinnee will have touched before. Which of your Lord's blessings would you deny?

They shall recline on green cushions and rich carpets. Which of your Lord's blessings would you deny?

Blessed be the name of your Lord, the lord of majesty and glory!

62. Friday, or the Day of Congregation

[MEDINA]

In the Name of God, the Compassionate, the Merciful

All that is in heaven and earth gives glory to God, the Sovereign Lord, the Holy One, the Almighty, the Wise One.

It is He that has sent forth among the gentiles an apostle of their own to recite to them His revelations, to purify them, and to instruct them in the Book and in wisdom though they have hitherto been in gross error, together with others of their own kin who have not yet followed them. He is the Mighty, the Wise One.

Such is the grace of God: He bestows it on whom He will. His grace is infinite.

Those to whom the burden of the Torah was entrusted and yet refused to bear it are like a donkey laden with books. Wretched is the example of those who deny God's revelations. God does not guide the wrongdoers.

Say to the Jews: "If your claim be true that of all men you alone are God's friends, then you should wish for death, if what you say be true!" But, because of what their hands have done, they will never wish for death. God knows the wrongdoers.

Say: "The death from which you shrink is sure to overtake you. Then you shall be sent back to Him who knows the unknown and the manifest, and He will declare to you all that you have done."

Believers, when you are summoned to Friday prayers hasten to the remembrance of God and cease your trading. That would be best for you, if you but knew it. Then, when the prayers are ended, disperse and go in quest of God's bounty. Remember God always, so that you may prosper.

Yet no sooner do they see some commerce or merriment than they flock to it eagerly, leaving you standing all alone.

Say: "That which God has in store is far better than any commerce or merriment. God is the Most Munificent Giver."

71. Noah

[MECCA]

In the Name of God, the Compassionate, the Merciful

We sent forth Noah to his people, saying: "Give warning to your people before a woeful scourge overtakes them."

He said: "My people, I come to warn you plainly. Serve God and fear Him, and obey me. He will forgive you your sins and give you respite for an appointed time. When God's time arrives, none shall put it back. Would that you understood this!"

"Lord," said Noah, "day and night I have pleaded with my people, but my pleas have only added to their aversion. Each time I call on them to seek Your pardon, they thrust their fingers in their ears and draw their cloaks over their heads, persisting in sin and bearing themselves with insolent pride. I called out loud to them, and appealed to them in public and in private. 'Seek forgiveness of your Lord,' I said. 'He is ever ready to forgive you. He sends down for you abundant rain from heaven and bestows upon you wealth and children. He has provided you with gardens and with running brooks. Why do you deny the greatness of God when He has made you in gradual stages? Can you not see how He created the seven heavens one above the other, placing in them the moon for a light and the sun for a lantern? God has brought you forth from the earth like a plant, and to the earth He will restore you. Then He will bring you back afresh. He has made the earth a vast expanse for you, so that you may roam in spacious paths.' "

And Noah said: "Lord, my people disobey me and follow those whose wealth and offspring will only hasten their perdition. They have devised an outrageous plot, and said to each other: 'Do not renounce your gods. Do not forsake Wadd or Suwā' or Yaghuth or Ya'uq or Nasr.'⁵ They have led numerous men astray. You surely drive the wrongdoers to further error."

And because of their sins they were overwhelmed by the Flood and cast into the Fire. They found none besides God to help them.

---

5. Names of idols that were worshiped in Mecca before Muhammad had them destroyed.

And Noah said: "Lord, do not leave a single unbeliever in the land. If you spare them they will mislead Your servants and beget none but sinners and unbelievers. Forgive me, Lord, and forgive my parents and every true believer who seeks refuge in my house. Forgive all the faithful, men and women, and hasten the destruction of the wrongdoers."

76. Man

[MECCA]

In the Name of God, the Compassionate, the Merciful

Does there not pass over man a space of time when his life is a blank?[6]

We have created man from the union of the two sexes so that We may put him to the proof. We have endowed him with hearing and sight and, be he thankful or oblivious of Our favours, We have shown him the right path.

For the unbelievers We have prepared fetters and chains, and a blazing Fire. But the righteous shall drink of a cup tempered at the Camphor Fountain, a gushing spring at which the servants of God will refresh themselves: they who keep their vows and dread the far-spread terrors of Judgement-day; who, though they hold it dear, give sustenance to the poor man, the orphan, and the captive, saying: "We feed you for God's sake only; we seek of you neither recompense nor thanks: for we fear from God a day of anguish and of woe."

God will deliver them from the evil of that day and make their faces shine with joy. He will reward them for their steadfastness with robes of silk and the delights of Paradise. Reclining there upon soft couches, they shall feel neither the scorching heat nor the biting cold. Trees will spread their shade around them, and fruits will hang in clusters over them.

They shall be served with silver dishes, and beakers as large as goblets; silver goblets which they themselves shall measure: and cups brim-full with ginger-flavoured water from the Fount of Salsabīl. They shall be attended by boys graced with eternal youth, who to the beholder's eyes will seem like sprinkled pearls. When you gaze upon that scene you will behold a kingdom blissful and glorious.

They shall be arrayed in garments of fine green silk and rich brocade, and adorned with bracelets of silver. Their Lord will give them pure nectar to drink.

Thus you shall be rewarded; your high endeavours are gratifying to God.

We have made known to you the Koran by gradual revelation; therefore wait with patience the judgement of your Lord and do not yield to the wicked and the unbelieving. Remember the name of your Lord morning and evening; in the nighttime worship Him: praise Him all night long.

The unbelievers love this fleeting life too well, and thus prepare for themselves a heavy day of doom. We created them, and endowed their limbs and joints with strength; but if We please We can replace them by other men.

This is indeed an admonition. Let him that will, take the right path to his Lord. Yet you cannot will, except by the will of God. God is wise and all-knowing.

---

6. In the womb.

He is merciful to whom He will: but for the wrongdoers He has prepared a woeful punishment.

IBN ISHAQ
704–767

Roughly a century after the death of Muhammad, ibn Ishaq, the grandson of a slave who was freed on his conversion to Islam, wrote a life of the prophet that is still the principal means by which Muslims learn about the man whom God favored with His final revelation. It begins by tracing Muhammad's descent from Adam and carries the story of his life through to the ceremonies that marked his burial. It provides us with a far richer and more circumstantial account of Muhammad's life and community than we have for any other figure of comparable importance. Although its similarities with the Four Gospels are the most obvious, in its richness and variety it is like Boswell's *Life of Johnson*.

At his death Muhammad was the most famous and powerful man in Arabia. He was the head of a community founded on a new religion of which he was himself the prophet. And in his lifetime the community of Muslims had grown from nothing to encompass the whole of Arabia. He was also the source of that community's divine scripture—the Koran—because it was only through him that God's words were revealed. For many in this new community Muhammad the man was the focus of their loyalty more than Islam itself. At his death most of the tribes of Arabia, for whom conversion to Islam was a matter of submitting to Muhammad personally, abandoned their faith and had to be won back to the fold all over again. Muhammad's death left a void that could not be filled by any individual. The leaders of the community did, of course, choose a new leader, Abu Bakr, and he assumed the political and, in some measure, the spiritual leadership of the Muslim community as well. But he and all who followed him in this office explicitly acknowledged that they could not replace Muhammad in his prophetic office by calling themselves the Vicar of the Prophet of God (*khalifatu rasulillâh*). This title was eventually shortened to *khalîfah*, or caliph. Because Muhammad was the last of the prophets—the seal of the prophets—the Muslim community's direct access to divine guidance died with him as well. (Shi'ite Muslims insist that a line of Muhammad's direct descendants through his daughter, Fatimah, and his son-in-law, Ali, continued to receive guidance for the next twelve generations, though not in the form of revelations.)

During his lifetime, accounts of the prophet and his community were circulated orally among his fellow believers. The Koran was the only written record of Islam's history, and it was, for all its virtues, a document that revealed little about either the texture of Muhammad's life or the social context in which he had founded and developed his community. With his death the events of his life acquired a tremendous significance for his followers. Every event, every word or gesture of his became a possible source for guidance and understanding. The memories of all who had known him or his family were collected and passed on by professional traditionists. Along with an understandable eagerness to recover every possible fact of his life went a scrupulous concern to record only what was verifiably true. The names of those who were the source of each narrative as well as the names of those who had transmitted it were included and passed on with the tradition itself. Many of these were, of course, men and women who had played important roles in this history, who had been close to Muhammad during the crucial final decades of his life.

Traditionists collected these stories and passed them on, sometimes orally, sometimes in writing. A little over a century after Muhammad's death, Muhammad ibn Ishaq, the son and nephew of two well-known traditionists, gathered all the accounts known to him into a book that he called *The Biography of God's Prophet*. The *Biography (sira)* itself has been lost, but the bulk of it has survived in a recension made of it by ibn Hisham three-quarters of a century later. Extensive quotations from ibn Ishaq also survive in other historical works. The *Biography* is the principal source of all subsequent biographies of Muhammad, and in truth it seems to modern readers more a collection of source materials than the smooth, continuous narrative we have come to expect from the form. The traditions vary greatly in length and character. Many are long and detailed narratives, often in the form of glosses on particular verses from the Koran. Others are poems composed to commemorate a victory, ridicule an opponent, or mourn the death of a friend. Still others consist almost wholly of the names of those who supported or opposed Muhammad at some moment in his life.

The *Biography* begins with an account of Muhammad's genealogy, tracing his descent in a direct line back to Adam. It ends with a description of the preparations made for his burial, including the elegies recited at his grave. The selections printed here are all, except for the last, taken from early in Muhammad's life to give a greater sense of coherence and continuity.

Salman the Persian, also called Salman the Pure, was the first non-Arab convert to Islam. The story (*How Salman Became a Muslim*) of the long and arduous journey that led him at last to Muhammad, a journey in which he endured slavery and other privations, is still recounted with admiration. On a symbolic level, Salman's complete ignorance of the world before he begins his search for spiritual guidance makes his choice of Islam a demonstration of the Koranic assertion that all of us are Muslims in our hearts. At a more worldly level, the Arabs, who had long lived in the shadow of the great Persian empire, were thrilled that Salman, the scion of a noble Persian family, preferred Islam to Zoroastrianism and Christianity. Salman was adopted into the prophet's family and was for a time the governor of the Sassanian capital city of Ctesiphon near Baghdad after the Arab conquest of that region.

Muhammad had for many years been in the habit of retiring to a secluded place outside of Mecca to meditate, often for several days at a time. It was during one of these retreats that he had a vision in which, as he later understood it, an angel appeared to him and told him to recite the word of God. This was the beginning of the revelation of the Koran. There is no general agreement as to which were the first verses revealed to the prophet.

Muhammad's first and, during her lifetime, only wife was Khadija, a woman of intelligence and independent spirit. She was a widow with considerable experience and standing as an independent merchant when she first employed and then married Muhammad. Khadija was somewhat older than her husband, and he respected her judgment as friend and counselor as well as his wife.

Although Muslims describe the Koran as a complete and sufficient guide, it is often obscure and allusive. Believers had to turn to the traditions, as in *The Prescription of Prayer,* for guidance on so essential and routine a practice as prayer.

Muhammad's sons died before him. His line survived solely through the marriage of his daughter, Fatimah, to Ali, whom the prophet had raised virtually as his own son. Ali became the fourth caliph in succession after the death of Muhammad, but his sons did not succeed him. A large group within the community felt that by reason of his early adherence to Islam, his marriage to Fatimah, and the explicit preference of Muhammad, he ought to have been the first caliph and his sons should have succeeded him. This group was known as the *shi'a* ("party") of Ali. Hence the modern terms *shi'ite* and *shi'ism.*

The Apostle's Public Preaching and the Response begins with an anecdote that recalls the miracle of the loaves and fishes in the New Testament of the Bible (Matthew 14.15–21, Mark 6.35–44). Muhammad's preaching appears to have been essentially the recitation of his revelations with, perhaps, some additional commentary and explanation. His message was highly offensive to his community (*How the Prophet Was Treated by His Own People*), since he preached against the many gods and goddesses that were given space in the Ka'ba ("cube"), the sacred stone building in Mecca. He also said that their tribal ancestors, who had not believed, were suffering the torments of hell. Reverence for one's ancestors was an essential element of Arab belief at this time. He also elevated ties of faith above those of blood and criticized the leaders of the Quraysh, his tribe, for their materialism and their neglect of the weakest and poorest members of their clans—orphans, widows, and the elderly. Such preaching would have been offensive from whatever source, and Muhammad's was doubly offensive coming from an upstart, an orphan, who was not one of the acknowledged leaders of the city.

In *Al-Walid ibn Al-Mughira* it is noted that Muhammad was something completely new to his people. They had had no prophets before him, and so they likened him to those he most resembled—poets, soothsayers (*kahin*), and those men (perhaps epileptics) who were thought to be possessed by demons. Muhammad's language was, in fact, powerfully eloquent, and the Koran is now believed by Arab Muslims to be inimitable in the beauty of its language.

Muhammad's earliest followers were drawn from the young and disenfranchised men and women of the city—those, in short, who had little to lose and much to gain by casting their lot with a new faith. Only when established leaders of the Quraysh like Hamza and Umar (the second caliph), accepted the new faith (told in *Hamza Accepts Islam*) were the Muslims able to pray at the Ka'ba.

The ultimate source for the account of Muhammad's burial is Aisha, the favorite daughter of Abu Bakr, and the youngest and favorite of the wives Muhammad took after Khadija's death. She was the only wife in whose presence he received revelations, and it is in her room that he died. Muhammad was disdainful of poets, both because he was often accused of being one and because many mocked him. The Koran is equally harsh to them. However, they occupied a position of importance in the Arab society of that time, and Islam had need of their services as much as any other tribe. Hassan ibn Thabit, a Medinan, was the most prominent of several poets with established reputations who converted to Islam and put their talents at its service. He is remembered now as Islam's first poet laureate. His final words give eloquent voice to the sense of bereavement that overwhelmed Muhammad's community at his death.

The canonical biography of Muhammad, and the source of these passages, is ibn Ishaq, *Sirat Rasul Allah*, as transmitted by ibn Hisham. The English translation by A. Guillaume, *The Life of Muhammad* (1955), contains a useful introduction and notes. Michael Cook, *Muhammad* (1983), is an excellent brief biography of the Prophet of Islam. W. M. Watt, *Muhammad: Prophet and Statesman* (1961), gives more detailed attention to the social context of early Islam.

PRONOUNCING GLOSSARY

The following list uses common English syllables and stress accents to provide rough equivalents of selected words whose pronunciation may be unfamiliar to the general reader.

Abdullah ibn Abu Najih: *ab'-du-luh i'-bun a'-boo na'-jih*

Abdul-Muttalib: *ab'-dool—moo-ta'-lib*

Abdul-Qays: *ab'-dool—kays*

Abu Bakr Atiq ibn Abu Quhafa: *a'-bu bakr' a-teek' i'-bun a'-boo koo-ha'-fuh*

Abu Ja'far Muhammad ibn Ali ibn al-Husayn: *a'-bu ja'-far mu-ham'-mad i'-bun a'-lee i'-bun al—hu-sayn'*

Abu Talib: *a'-boo tah'-lib*

Aisha: *ai'-shuh*

al-sîra: *as—see'-ruh*

Ammuriya: *am'-moo-ree'-uh*

Asim ibn Umar ibn Qatada al-Ansari: *a'-sim i'-bun o'-mar i'-bun ku-tah'-duh al–an-sah'-ree*

Baqi'u-l-Gharqad: *ba-ki'–ool–gar'-qad*

Chosroes: *kos'-rows*

Ctesiphon: *te'-si-fawn*

Hamza ibn Abdul-Muttalib: *ham'-zuh i'-bun ab'-dool–moo-ta'-lib*

Hassân ibn Thabit: *ha-sahn' i'-bun tha'-bit*

ibn Ishaq: *i'-bun is-haq'*

Ismail ibn Iyas ibn Afif: *is'-ma-eel i'-bun i-yahs' i'-bun a-feef'*

Jayy: *jai*

Ka'ba: *ka'-buh*

Khadija: *ka-dee'-juh*

khalîfah: *ka-lee'-fuh*

Muhammad ibn Ishaq ibn Yasâr: *mo-ham'-mad i'-bun is-haq' i'-bun yuh-sar'*

Mujahid ibn Abul-Hajjaj: *moo-ja'-hid i'-bun a'-boo–haj-jahj'*

Nasibin: *na-si-been'*

qasab: *ka'-sab*

Quba: *koo'-ba*

Quraysh: *koo-raysh'*

Sad ibn Abu Waqqas: *sad i'-bun a'-boo wak-kas'*

shi'ite: *she'-ite*

Uhud: *oo-hood'*

Umar ibn al-Khattab: *u'-mar i'-bun al-kat-tahb'*

Umm Kulthum: *oom' kul-thoom'*

Urwa ibn al-Zubayr: *oor'-wa i'-bun az–zoo-bayr'*

Wadi-l-Qura: *wa'-dil–ku'-ruh*

Yazid ibn Abu Habib: *yuh-zeed' i'-bun a'-boo ha-beeb'*

Yunus ibn Bukayr: *yoo'-nus i'-bun boo-kayr'*

From The Biography of the Prophet[1]

How Salman[2] Became a Muslim

Asim ibn Umar ibn Qatada al-Ansari told me, on the authority of Mahmud ibn Labid from Abdullah ibn Abbas as follows:[3] Salman said while I listened to his words: "I am a Persian from Ispahan[4] from a village called Jayy. My father was the principal landowner in his village and I was dearer to him than the whole world. His love for me went to such lengths that he shut me in his house as though I were a slave girl. I was such a zealous Magian[5] that I became keeper of the sacred fire, replenishing it and not letting it go out for a moment. Now my father owned a large farm, and one day when he could not attend to his farm he told me to go to it and learn about it, giving me certain instructions. 'Do not let yourself be detained,' he said, 'because you are more important to me than my farm and worrying about you will prevent me going about my business.' So I started out for the farm, and when I passed by a Christian church I heard the voices of the men praying. I knew nothing about them because my father kept me shut up in his house. When I heard their voices I went to see what they were doing; their prayers pleased me and I felt drawn to their worship and thought that it was better than our religion, and I decided that I would not leave them until sunset. So I did not

1. Translated by Alfred Guillaume.   2. The first Persian convert to Islam and a major figure in the early history of the religion.   3. By including the names of all those who had passed a story down to him, the author both asserts and demonstrates the truth of the account.   4. A large city in central Iran.   5. That is, Zoroastrian, a follower of Zoroastrianism, the principal religion of pre-Islamic Iran.

go to the farm. When I asked them where their religion originated, they said 'Syria.' I returned to my father who had sent after me because anxiety on my account had interrupted all his work. He asked me where I had been and reproached me for not obeying his instructions. I told him that I had passed by some men who were praying in their church and was so pleased with what I saw of their religion that I stayed with them until sunset. He said, 'My son, there is no good in that religion; the religion of your fathers is better than that.' 'No,' I said, 'It is better than our religion.' My father was afraid of what I would do, so he bound me in fetters and imprisoned me in his house.

"I sent to the Christians and asked them if they would tell me when a caravan of Christian merchants came from Syria. They told me, and I said to them: 'When they have finished their business and want to go back to their own country, ask them if they will take me.' They did so and I cast off the fetters from my feet and went with them to Syria. Arrived there I asked for the most learned person in their religion and they directed me to the bishop. I went to him and told him that I liked his religion and should like to be with him and serve him in his church, to learn from him and to pray with him. He invited me to come in and I did so. Now he was a bad man who used to command people to give alms and induced them to do so and when they brought him money he put it in his own coffers and did not give it to the poor, until he had collected seven jars of gold and silver. I conceived a violent hatred for the man when I saw what he was doing. Sometime later when he died and the Christians came together to bury him I told them that he was a bad man who exhorted them and persuaded them to give alms, and when they brought money put it in his coffers and gave nothing to the poor. They asked how I could possibly know this, so I led them to his treasure and when I showed them the place they brought out seven jars full of gold and silver. As soon as they saw them they said, 'By God, we will never bury the fellow,' so they crucified him and stoned him and appointed another in his place.

"I have never seen any non-Muslim whom I consider more virtuous, more ascetic, more devoted to the next life, and more consistent night and day than he.[6] I loved him as I had never loved anyone before. I stayed with him a long time until when he was about to die I told him how I loved him and asked him to whom he would confide me and what orders he would give me now that he was about to die. He said, 'My dear son, I do not know anyone who is as I am. Men have died and have either altered or abandoned most of their true religion, except a man in Mausil;[7] he follows my faith, so join yourself to him.' So when he died and was buried, I attached myself to the bishop of Mausil telling him that so-and-so had confided me to him when he died and told me that he followed the same path. I stayed with him and found him just as he had been described, but it was not long before he died and I asked him to do for me what his predecessor had done. He replied that he knew of only one man, in Nasibin,[8] who followed the same path and he recommended me to go to him.[9]

"I stayed with this good man in Nasibin for some time and when he died

---

6. The new bishop.   7. A city in northern Iraq.   8. A town in upper Mesopotamia, now part of Turkey.
9. I have abbreviated the repetitive style of the narrative, which is that of popular stories all the world over. The same words, and the same details, occur in each paragraph with the change of names: Mausil, Nasibin, 'Ammuriya, leading up to the obvious climax, Muhammad [Translator's note].

he recommended me to go to a colleague in Ammuriya.[1] I stayed with him for some time and labored until I possessed some cows and a small flock of sheep; then when he was about to die I asked him to recommend me to someone else. He told me that he knew of no one who followed his way of life, but that a prophet was about to arise who would be sent with the religion of Abraham; he would come forth in Arabia and would migrate to a country between two lava belts, between which were palms. He has unmistakable marks. He will eat what is given to him but not things given as alms. Between his shoulders is the seal of prophecy. 'If you are able to go to that country, do so.' Then he died and was buried and I stayed in Ammuriya as long as God willed. Then a party of Kalbite[2] merchants passed by and I asked them to take me to Arabia and I would give them those cows and sheep of mine. They accepted the offer and took me with them until we reached Wadil-Qura,[3] when they sold me to a Jew as a slave. I saw the palm-trees and I hoped that this would be the town which my master had described to me, for I was not certain. Then a cousin of his from Bani Qurayza[4] of Medina came and bought me and carried me away to Medina, and, by God, as soon as I saw it I recognized it from my master's description. I dwelt there and the apostle of God[5] was sent and lived in Mecca; but I did not hear him mentioned because I was fully occupied as a slave. Then he migrated to Medina and as I was in the top of a palm-tree belonging to my master, carrying out my work while my master sat below, suddenly a cousin of his came up to him and said: 'God smite the Bani Qayla![6] They are gathering at this moment in Quba[7] round a man who has come to them from Mecca today asserting that he is a prophet.'

"When I heard this I was seized with trembling, so that I thought I should fall on my master; so I came down from the palm and began to say to his cousin, 'What did you say? What did you say?' My master was angered and gave me a smart blow, saying, 'What do you mean by this? Get back to your work.' I said, 'Never mind, I only wanted to find out the truth of his report.' Now I had a little food which I had gathered, and I took it that evening to the apostle of God who was in Quba and said, 'I have heard that you are an honest man and that your companions are strangers in want; here is something for alms, for I think that you have more right to it than others.' So I gave it to him. The apostle said to his companions, 'Eat!' but he did not hold out his own hand and did not eat. I said to myself, 'That is one'; then I left him and collected some food and the apostle went to Medina. Then I brought it to him and said, 'I see that you do not eat food given as alms, here is a present which I freely give you.' The apostle ate it and gave his companions some. I said, 'That's two'; then I came to the apostle when he was in Baqiu-l-Gharqad[8] where he had followed the bier of one of his companions. Now I had two cloaks, and as he was sitting with his companions, I saluted him and went round to look at his back so that I could see whether the seal which my master had described to me was there. When the apostle saw me looking at his back he knew that I was trying to find out the truth of what had been described to me, so he threw off his cloak laying bare his back and I looked at the seal and recognized it. Then I bent over him kissing him and weeping.

1. A region in southwestern Turkey, ancient Amorium.   2. From the Bani Kalb, an Arab tribe.   3. A village in northwestern Arabia.   4. A Jewish tribe.   5. Muhammad.   6. A tribe.   7. Near Medina.   8. Medina's cemetery, outside the town.

The apostle said, 'Come here'; so I came and sat before him and told him my story as I have told you, O ibn Abbas.[9] The apostle wanted his companions to hear my story." Then servitude occupied Salman so that he could not be at Badr and Uhud[1] with the apostle.

Salman continued: "Then the apostle said to me, 'Write an agreement'; so I wrote to my master agreeing to plant three hundred palm-trees for him, digging out the base, and to pay forty okes[2] of gold. The apostle called on his companions to help me, which they did; one with thirty little palms, another with twenty, another with fifteen, and another with ten, each helping as much as he could until the three hundred were complete. The apostle told me to go and dig the holes for them, saying that when I had done so he would put them in with his own hand. Helped by my companions I dug the holes and came and told him; so we all went out together, and as we brought him the palm shoots he planted them with his own hand; and by God, not one of them died. Thus I had delivered the palm-trees, but the money was still owing. Now the apostle had been given a piece of gold as large as a hen's egg from one of the mines and he summoned me and told me to take it and pay my debt with it. 'How far will this relieve me of my debt, O Apostle of God?' I said. 'Take it,' he replied, 'for God will pay your debt with it.' So I took it and weighed it out to them, and by God, it weighed forty okes, and so I paid my debt with it and Salman was free. I took part with the Apostle in the battle of the Ditch as a free man and thereafter I was at every other battle."

Yazid ibn Abu Habib from a man of Abdul-Qays from Salman told me[3] that the latter said: "When I said, 'How far will this relieve me of my debt?' the apostle took it and turned it over upon his tongue, then he said, 'Take it and pay them in full'; so I paid them in full, forty okes."

Asim ibn Umar ibn Qatada on the authority of a trustworthy informant from Umar ibn Abdul-Aziz ibn Marwan said that he was told that Salman the Persian told the apostle that his master in Ammuriya told him to go to a certain place in Syria where there was a man who lived between two thickets. "Every year as he used to go from one to the other, the sick used to stand in his way and everyone he prayed for was healed. He said, 'Ask him about this religion which you seek, for he can tell you of it.' So I went on until I came to the place I had been told of, and I found that people had gathered there with their sick until he came out to them that night passing from one thicket to the other. The people came to him with their sick and everyone he prayed for was healed. They prevented me from getting to him so that I could not approach him until he entered the thicket he was making for, but I took hold of his shoulder. He asked me who I was as he turned to me and I said, 'God have mercy on you, tell me about the Hanifiya,[4] the religion of Abraham.' He replied, 'You are asking about something men do not inquire of today; the time has come near when a prophet will be sent with this religion from the people of the *haram*.[5] Go to him, for he will bring you to it.'" Then he

---

9. The last person in the chain of transmission before ibn Ishaq. 1. Sites of two famous battles between Muhammad's followers and the people of Mecca. 2. A measurement of weight; one *olce* is roughly equivalent to one ounce. 3. In other words, ibn Ishaq heard this third hand. 4. The name by which Islam was first known: "those who follow the original true [monotheistic] religion." 5. The sacred shrine in Mecca.

went into the thicket. The apostle said to Salman, "If you have told me the truth, you met Jesus the son of Mary."

* * *

The Beginning of the Sending Down of the Quran

The apostle began to receive revelations in the month of Ramadan.[6] In the words of God, "The month of Ramadan in which the Quran was brought down as a guidance to men, and proofs of guidance and a decisive criterion." And again, "Verily we have sent it down on the night of destiny, and what has shown you what the night of destiny is? The night of destiny is better than a thousand months. In it the angels and the spirit descend by their Lord's permission with every matter. It is peace until the rise of dawn." Again, "by the perspicuous book, verily we have sent it down in a blessed night. Verily, we were warning. In it every wise matter is decided as a command from us. Verily we sent it down." And again, "Had you believed in God and what we sent down to Our servant on the day of decision, the day on which the two parties met," i.e. the meeting of the apostle with the polytheists in Badr. Abu Jafar Muhammad ibn Ali ibn al-Husayn told me that the apostle of God met the polytheists in Badr on the morning of Friday, the 17th of Ramadan.

Then revelation came fully to the apostle while he was believing in Him and in the truth of His message. He received it willingly, and took upon himself what it entailed whether of man's goodwill or anger. Prophecy is a troublesome burden—only strong, resolute messengers can bear it by God's help and grace, because of the opposition which they meet from men in conveying God's message. The apostle carried out God's orders in spite of the opposition and ill treatment which he met with.

Khadija,[7] Daughter of Khuwaylid, Accepts Islam

Khadija believed in him and accepted as true what he brought from God, and helped him in his work. She was the first to believe in God and His apostle, and in the truth of his message. By her God lightened the burden of His prophet. He never met with contradiction and charges of falsehood, which saddened him, but God comforted him by her when he went home. She strengthened him, lightened his burden, proclaimed his truth, and belittled men's opposition. May God Almighty have mercy upon her!

Hisham ibn Urwa told me on the authority of his father Urwa ibn al-Zubayr from Abdullah ibn Jafar ibn Abu Talib that the apostle said, "I was commanded to give Khadija the good news of a house of qasab[8] wherein would be no clamour and no toil."

Then revelations stopped for a time so that the apostle of God was distressed and grieved. Then Gabriel brought him the Sura of the Morning, in which his Lord, who had so honoured him, swore that He had not forsaken him, and did not hate him. God said, "By the morning and the night when it is still, thy Lord hath not forsaken nor hated thee," meaning that He has

---

6. The month of obligatory fasting.   7. Muhammad's first wife.   8. Hollowed pearl.

not left you and forsaken you, nor hated you after having loved you. "And verily, the latter end is better for you than the beginning," i.e. What I have for you when you return to Me is better than the honour which I have given you in the world. "And your Lord will give you and will satisfy you," i.e. of victory in this world and reward in the next. "Did he not find you an orphan and give you refuge, going astray and guided you, found you poor and made you rich?" God thus told him of how He had begun to honour him in his earthly life, and of His kindness to him as an orphan poor and wandering astray, and of His delivering him from all that by His compassion.

"Do not oppress the orphan and do not repel the beggar." That is, do not be a tyrant or proud or harsh or mean towards the weakest of God's creatures.

"Speak of the kindness of thy Lord," i.e. tell about the kindness of God in giving you prophecy, mention it and call men to it.

So the apostle began to mention secretly God's kindness to him and to his servants in the matter of prophecy to everyone among his people whom he could trust.

From *The Prescription of Prayer*

The apostle was ordered to pray and so he prayed. Salih ibn Kaisan from Urwa ibn al-Zubayr from Aisha[9] told me that she said, "When prayer was first laid on the apostle it was with two prostrations for every prayer: then God raised it to four prostrations at home while on a journey the former ordinance of two prostrations held."

A learned person told me that when prayer was laid on the apostle Gabriel came to him while he was on the heights of Mecca and dug a hole for him with his heel in the side of the valley from which a fountain gushed forth, and Gabriel performed the ritual ablution as the apostle watched him. This was in order to show him how to purify himself before prayer. Then the apostle performed the ritual ablution as he had seen Gabriel do it. Then Gabriel said a prayer with him while the apostle prayed with his prayer. Then Gabriel left him. The apostle came to Khadija and performed the ritual for her as Gabriel had done for him, and she copied him. Then he prayed with her as Gabriel had prayed with him, and she prayed his prayer.

Utba ibn Muslim freedman of Bani Taym from Nafi ibn Jubayr ibn Mutim (who was prolific in relating tradition) from Ibn Abbas[1] told me: "When prayer was laid upon the apostle Gabriel came to him and prayed the noon prayer when the sun declined. Then he prayed the evening prayer when his shadow equaled his own length. Then he prayed the sunset prayer when the sun set. Then he prayed the last night prayer when the twilight had disappeared. Then he prayed with him the morning prayer when the dawn rose. Then he came to him and prayed the noon prayer on the morrow when his shadow equaled his height. Then he prayed the evening prayer when his shadow equaled the height of both of them. Then he prayed the sunset prayer when the sun set at the time it had the day before. Then he prayed with him the last night prayer when the first third of the night had passed. Then he prayed the dawn prayer when it was clear but the sun was not shining. Then

9. The favorite of the women Muhammad married after Khadija's death and the only in whose home he received revelations.　1. Muhammad's cousin and a relator of many traditions.

he said, 'O Muhammad, prayer is in what is between your prayer today and your prayer yesterday.' " Yunus ibn Bukayr said that Muhammad ibn Ishaq told him that Yahya ibn Abul-Ashath al-Kindi of the people of Kufa[2] said that Ismail ibn Iyas ibin Afif from his father from his grandfather said, "When I was a merchant I came to al-Abbas during the days of pilgrimage; and while we were together a man came out to pray and stood facing the Ka'ba;[3] then a woman came out and stood praying with him; then a young man came out and stood praying with him. I said to Abbas, 'What is their religion? It is some thing new to me.' He said, 'This is Muhammad ibn Abdullah who alleges that God has sent him with it and that the treasures of Chosroes[4] and Caesar will be opened to him. The woman is his wife Khadija who believes in him, and this young man is his nephew Ali who believes in him.' Afif said, 'Would that I could have believed that day and been a third!' "

*　　*　　*

From *Ali ibn Abu Talib*,[5] *the First Male to Accept Islam*

Ali was the first male to believe in the apostle of God, to pray with him and to believe in his divine message, when he was a boy of ten. God favored him in that he was brought up in the care of the apostle before Islam began.

Abdullah ibn Abu Najih on the authority of Mujahid ibn Jabr Abul-Hajjaj told me that God showed His favor and goodwill towards him when a grievous famine overtook Quraysh.[6] Now Abu Talib had a large family, and the prophet approached his uncle, Al-Abbas, who was one of the richest of Bani Hashim,[7] suggesting that in view of his large family and the famine which affected everyone, they should go together and offer to relieve him of the burden of some of his family. Al-Abbas agreed, and so they went to Abu Talib offering to relieve him from his responsibility of two boys until conditions improved. Abu Talib said, "Do what you like so long as you leave me Aqil." So the apostle took Ali and kept him with him and Al-Abbas took Jafar. Ali continued to be with the apostle until God sent him forth as a prophet. Ali followed him, believed him, and declared his truth, while Jafar remained with Al-Abbas until he became a Muslim and was independent of him.

A traditionist mentioned that when the time of prayer came the apostle used to go out to the glens of Mecca accompanied by Ali, who went unbeknown to his father, and his uncles and the rest of his people. There they used to pray the ritual prayers, and return at nightfall. This went on as long as God intended that it should, until one day Abu Talib came upon them while they were praying, and said to the apostle, "O nephew, what is this religion which I see you practicing?" He replied, "O uncle, this is the religion of God, His angels, His apostles, and the religion of our father Abraham." Or, as he said, "God has sent me as an apostle to mankind, and you, my uncle, most deserve that I should teach you the truth and call you to guidance, and you are the most worthy to respond and help me," or words to that effect. His uncle replied, "I cannot give up the religion of my fathers which they followed, but by God you shall never meet with anything to distress you

---

2. A garrison city in southern Iraq.　3. A focus of annual pilgrimage well before Muhammad's time. 4. Emperor of Persia.　5. "Ali the son of the father of Talib." Muslims are often known as the father, or mother, of their first child, esp. a son.　6. Muhammad's tribe, from which all caliphs must come. 7. A tribe.

so long as I live." They mention that he said to Ali, "My boy, what is this religion of yours?" He answered, "I believe in God and in the apostle of God, and I declare that what he has brought is true, and I pray to God with him and follow him." They allege that he said, "He would not call you to anything but what is good so stick to him."

Zayd, the freedman of the apostle, was the first male to accept Islam after Ali. The Abu Bahr ibn Abu Quhafa,[8] whose name was Atiq, became a Muslim. . . . When he became a Muslim, he showed his faith openly and called others to God and his apostle. He was a man whose society was desired, well liked and of easy manners. He knew more about the genealogy of Quraysh than anyone else and of their faults and merits. He was a merchant of high character and kindliness. His people used to come to him to discuss many matters with him because of his wide knowledge, his experience in commerce, and his sociable nature. He began to call to God and to Islam all whom he trusted of those who came to him and sat with him.

✻   ✻   ✻

From *The Apostle's Public Preaching and the Response*

People began to accept Islam, both men and women, in large numbers until the fame of it was spread throughout Mecca, and it began to be talked about. Then God commanded His apostle to declare the truth of what he had received and to make known His commands to men and to call them to Him. Three years elapsed from the time that the apostle concealed his state until God commanded him to publish his religion, according to information which has reached me. Then God said, "Proclaim what you have been ordered and turn aside from the polytheists." And again, "Warn thy family, thy nearest relations, and lower thy wing to the followers who follow thee." And "Say, I am the one who warns plainly." Ibn Hamid . . . from Abdullah ibn Abbas from Ali ibn Abu Talib said: When these words "Warn thy family, thy nearest relations" came down to the apostle he called me and said, "God has ordered me to warn my family, my nearest relations and the task is beyond my strength. I know that when I made this message known to them I should meet with great unpleasantness so I kept silence until Gabriel came to me and told me that if I did not do as I was ordered my Lord would punish me. So get some food ready with a leg of mutton and fill a cup with milk and then get together the sons of Abdul-Muttalib[9] so that I can address them and tell them what I have been ordered to say." I did what he ordered and summoned them. There were at that time forty men more or less, including his uncles Abu Talib, Hamza, al-Abbas, and Abu Lahab.[1] When they were assembled he told me to bring in the food which I had prepared for them, and when I produced it the apostle took a bit of the meat and split it in his teeth and threw it into the dish. Then he said, "Take it in the name of God." The men ate till they could eat no more, and all I could see (in the dish) was the place where their hands had been. And as sure as I live if there had been only one man he could have eaten what I put before the lot of them. Then

---

8. A leader of the Quraysh who became the first caliph.   9. Grandfather and protector of Muhammad and father of Muhammad's uncles.   1. Muhammad's implacable foe. Abu Talib was the father of Ali and guardian of Muhammad. Hamza was a staunch supporter of Muhammad. Al-Abbas was the celebrated companion of Muhammad; his descendants founded a dynasty of caliphs (the Abbasids) that ruled from 746 to 1258.

he said, "Give the people to drink," so I brought them the cup and they drank until they were all satisfied, and as sure as I live if there had been only one man he could have drunk that amount. When the apostle wanted to address them Abu Lahab got in first and said, "Your host has bewitched you"; so they dispersed before the apostle could address them. On the morrow he said to me, "This man spoke before I could, and the people dispersed before I could address them, so do exactly as you did yesterday." Everything went as before and then the apostle said, "O Sons of Abdul-Muttalib, I know of no Arab who has come to his people with a nobler message than mine. I have brought you the best of this world and the next. God has ordered me to call you to Him. So which of you will co-operate with me in this matter, my brother, my executor, and my successor being among you?" The men remained silent and I, though the youngest, most rheumy-eyed, fattest in body and thinnest in legs, said: "O prophet of God, I will be your helper in this matter." He laid his hand on the back of my neck and said, "This is my brother, my executor, and my successor among you. Hearken to him and obey him." The men got up laughing and saying to Abu Talib, "He has ordered you to listen to your son and obey him!"

*   *   *

When the apostle's companions prayed they went to the glens so that their people could not see them praying, and while Sa'd ibn Abu Waqqas was with a number of the prophet's companions in one of the glens of Mecca, a band of polytheists came upon them while they were praying and rudely interrupted them. They blamed them for what they were doing until they came to blows, and it was on that occasion that Sad smote a polytheist with the jawbone of a camel and wounded him. This was the first blood to be shed in Islam.

When the apostle openly displayed Islam as God ordered him his people did not withdraw or turn against him, so far as I have heard, until he spoke disparagingly of their gods. When he did that they took great offence and resolved unanimously to treat him as an enemy, except those whom God had protected by Islam from such evil, but they were a despised minority. Abu Talib his uncle treated the apostle kindly and protected him, the latter continuing to obey God's commands, nothing turning him back. When Quraysh saw that he would not yield to them and withdrew from them and insulted their gods and that his uncle treated him kindly and stood up in his defence and would not give him up to them, some of their leading men went to Abu Talib. . . . They said, "O Abu Talib, your nephew has cursed our gods, insulted our religion, mocked our way of life and accused our forefathers of error; either you must stop him or you must let us get at him, for you yourself are in the same position as we are in opposition to him and we will rid you of him." He gave them a conciliatory reply and a soft answer and they went away.

The apostle continued on his way, publishing God's religion and calling men thereto. In consequence his relations with Quraysh deteriorated and men withdrew from him in enmity. They were always talking about him and inciting one another against him. Then they went to Abu Talib a second time and said, "You have a high and lofty position among us, and we have asked you to put a stop to your nephew's activities but you have not done so. By

God, we cannot endure that our fathers should be reviled, our customs mocked and our gods insulted. Until you rid us of him we will fight the pair of you until one side perishes," or words to that effect. Thus saying, they went off. Abu Talib was deeply distressed at the breach with his people and their enmity but he could not desert the apostle and give him up to them.

Yaqub ibn Utba . . . told me that he was told that after hearing these words from the Quraysh Abu Talib sent for his nephew and told him what his people had said. "Spare me and yourself," he said. "Do not put on me a burden greater than I can bear." The apostle thought that his uncle had the idea of abandoning and betraying him, and that he was going to lose his help and support. He answered, "O my uncle, by God, if they put the sun in my right hand and the moon in my left on condition that I abandoned this course, until God has made it victorious, or I perish therein, I would not abandon it." Then the apostle broke into tears, and got up. As he turned away his uncle called him and said, "Come back, my nephew," and when he came back, he said, "Go and say what you please, for by God I will never give you up on any account."

When the Quraysh perceived that Abu Talib had refused to give up the apostle, and that he was resolved to part company with them, they went to him with Umara ibn al-Walid ibn al-Mughira[2] and said, according to my information, "O Abu Talib, this is Umara, the strongest and most handsome young man among Quraysh, so take him and you will have the benefit of his intelligence and support; adopt him as a son and give up to us this nephew of yours, who has opposed your religion and the religion of your fathers, severed the unity of your people, and mocked our way of life, so that we may kill him. This will be man for man." He answered, "By God, this is an evil thing that you would put upon me, would you give me your son that I should feed him for you, and should I give you my son that you should kill him? By God, this shall never be." Al-Mutim ibn Adiy said, "Your people have treated you fairly and have taken pains to avoid what you dislike. I do not think that you are willing to accept anything from them." Abu Talib replied, "They have not treated me fairly, by God, but you have agreed to betray me and help the people against me, so do what you like," or words to that effect. So the situation worsened, the quarrel became heated and people were sharply divided, and openly showed their animosity to their opponents. Abu Talib wrote the following verses, indirectly attacking Mutim, and including those who had abandoned him from the Abdu Manaf,[3] and his enemies among the tribes of Quraysh. He mentions therein what they had asked of him and his estrangement from them.

> Say to Amr and al-Walid and Mutim
> Rather than your protection give me a young camel,
> Weak, grumbling and murmuring,
> Sprinkling its flanks with its urine
> Lagging behind the herd, and not keeping up.   5
> When it goes up the desert ridges, you would call it a weasel.
> I see our two brothers, sons of our mother and father,
> When they are asked for help, say "It is not our business."
> Nay, it is their affair, but they have fallen away.

2. The son of one of Muhammad's strongest opponents.   3. A tribe.

As a rock falls from the top of Dhu Alaq.[4]   10
I mean especially Abdu Shams and Naufal,
Who have flung us aside like a burning coal.
They have slandered their brothers among the people;
Their hands are emptied of them.
They shared their fame with men of low birth,   15
With men whose fathers were whispered about;
And Taym, and Makhzum, and Zuhra,[5] are of them
Who had been friends of ours when help was sought;
By God, there will always be enmity between us
As long as one of our descendants lives.   20
Their minds and thoughts were foolish,
They were entirely without judgment.

Then the Quraysh incited people against the companions of the apostle who had become Muslims. Every tribe fell upon the Muslims among them, beating them and seducing them from their religion. God protected His apostle from them through his uncle, who, when he saw what Quraysh were doing, called upon Bani Hashim and Bani al-Muttalib to stand with him in protecting the apostle. This they agreed to do, with the exception of Abu Lahab, the accursed enemy of God.

Abu Talib was delighted at the response of his tribe and their kindness, and began to praise them and to bring to men's memory their past. He mentioned the superiority of the apostle among them and his position so that he might strengthen their resolve and that they might extend their kindness to him. He said:

If one day Quraysh gathered together to boast,
Abdu Manaf would be their heart and soul;
And if the nobles of Abdu Manaf were reckoned,
Amongst Hashim would be their noblest and chief;
If they boast one day, then Muhammad   5
Would be the chosen noble and honorable one.
Quraysh summoned everyone against us;
They were not successful and they were beside themselves.
Of old we have never tolerated injustice;
When people turned away their faces in pride we made them face us.   10
We protected their sanctuary whenever danger threatened
And drove the assailant from its buildings.
Through us the dry wood becomes green,
Under our protection its roots expand and grow.

From *Al-Walid ibn Al-Mughira*

When the fair was due, a number of the Quraysh came to al-Walid ibn al-Mughira, who was a man of some standing, and he addressed them in these words: "The time of the fair has come round again and representatives of the Arabs will come to you and they will have heard about this fellow of yours, so agree upon one opinion without dispute so that none will give the lie to the other." They replied, "You give us your opinion about him." He said, "No,

4. A mountain.   5. Names of tribes.

you speak and I will listen." They said, "He is a kahin."[6] He said, "By God, he is not that, for he has not the unintelligent murmuring and rhymed speech of the kahin." "Then he is possessed," they said. "No, he is not that," he said, "we have seen possessed ones, and here is no choking, spasmodic movements and whispering." "Then he is a poet," they said. "No, he is no poet, for we know poetry in all its forms and metres." "Then he is a sorcerer." "No, we have seen sorcerers and their sorcery, and here is no spitting and no knots."[7] "Then what are we to say, O Abu Abdu Shams?" they asked. He replied, "By God, his speech is sweet, his root is a palm-tree whose branches are fruitful, and everything you have said would be known to be false. The nearest thing to the truth is your saying that he is a sorcerer, who has brought a message by which he separates a man from his father, or from his brother, or from his wife, or from his family."

*　　*　　*

How the Apostle Was Treated by His Own People

When the Quraysh became distressed by the trouble caused by the enmity between them and the apostle and those of their people who accepted his teaching, they stirred up against him foolish men who called him a liar, insulted him, and accused him of being a poet, a sorcerer, a diviner, and of being possessed. However, the apostle continued to proclaim what God had ordered him to proclaim, concealing nothing, and exciting their dislike by condemning their religion, forsaking their idols, and leaving them to their unbelief.

Yahya ibn Urwa ibn al-Zubayr on the authority of his father from Abdullah ibn Amr ibn al-As told me that the latter was asked what was the worst way in which Quraysh showed their enmity to the apostle. He replied: "I was with them one day when the notables had gathered in the Hijr[8] and the apostle was mentioned. They said that they had never known anything like the trouble they had endured from this fellow; he had declared their mode of life foolish, insulted their forefathers, reviled their religion, divided the community, and cursed their gods. What they had borne was past all bearing, or words to that effect.

"While they were thus discussing him the apostle came towards them and kissed the black stone,[9] then he passed them as he walked round the temple. As he passed they said some injurious things about him. This I could see from his expression. He went on and as he passed them the second time they attacked him similarly. This I could see from his expression. Then he passed the third time, and they did the same. He stopped and said, 'Will you listen to me O Quraysh? By him who holds my life in His hand I bring you slaughter.' This word so struck the people that not one of them but stood silent and still; even one who had hitherto been most violent spoke to him in the kindest way possible, saying, 'Depart, O Abul-Qasim, for by God you are not violent.' So the apostle went away, and on the morrow they assembled in the Hijr, I being there too, and they asked one another if they remembered what had taken place between them and the apostle so that when he openly said something unpleasant they let him alone. While they were talking thus

---

6. A soothsayer.　　7. A device used by sorcerers in their charms (see the Koran 113).　　8. The room in the Ka'ba where the idols were kept.　　9. The meteorite mounted in the Ka'ba wall.

the apostle appeared, and they leaped upon him as one man and encircled him, saying, 'Are you the one who said so-and-so against our gods and our religion?' The apostle said, 'Yes, I am the one who said that.' And I saw one of them seize his robe. Then Abu Bakr interposed himself weeping and saying, 'Would you kill a man for saying Allah is my Lord?' Then they left him. This is the worst that I ever saw Quraysh do to him."

One of the family of Umm Kulthum, Abu Bakr's daughter, told me that she said, "Abu Bakr returned that day with the hair of his head torn. He was a very hairy man and they had dragged him along by his beard."

[Hamza Accepts Islam]

A man of Aslum, who had a good memory, told me that Abu Jahl passed by the apostle at al-Safa,[1] insulted him and behaved most offensively, speaking spitefully of his religion and trying to bring him into disrepute. The apostle did not speak to him. Now a freedwoman, belonging to Abdullah ibn Judan . . . was in her house listening to what went on. When he went away he betook himself to the assembly of Quraysh at the Ka'ba and sat there. Within a little while Hamza ibn Abdul-Muttalib arrived with his bow hanging from his shoulder, returning from the chase, for he was fond of hunting and used to go out shooting. When he came back from a hunt he never went home until he had circumambulated the Ka'ba, and that done when he passed by an assembly of the Quraysh he stopped and saluted and talked with them. He was the strongest man of Quraysh, and the most unyielding. The apostle had gone back to his house when he passed by this woman, who asked him if he had heard of what Abul-Hakam ibn Hisham had done just recently to his nephew, Muhammad; how he had found him sitting quietly there, and insulted him, and cursed him, and treated him badly, and that Muhammad had answered not a word. Hamza was filled with rage, for God purposed to honor him, so he went out at a run and did not stop to greet anyone, meaning to punish Abu Jahl when he met him. When he got to the mosque he saw him sitting among the people, and went up to him until he stood over him, when he lifted up his bow and struck him a violent blow with it, saying, "Will you insult him when I follow his religion, and say what he says? Hit me back if you can!" Some of Bani Makhzum got up to go to Abu Jahl's help, but he said, "Let Abu Umara[2] alone for, by God, I insulted his nephew deeply." Hamza's Islam was complete, and he followed the apostle's commands. When he became a Muslim the Quraysh recognized that the apostle had become strong, and had found a protector in Hamza, and so they abandoned some of their ways of harassing him.

*   *   *

[The Burial Preparations]

On the same authority I was told that the last injunction the apostle gave was in his words "Let not two religions be left in the Arabian peninsula." The apostle died on the 12th Rabiu-l-awwal on the very day that he came to Medina as an emigrant, having completed exactly twelve years in his migra-

---

1. In Mecca. Abu Jahl was an implacable adversary of Muhammad; he was killed at Badr.   2. Hamza.

tion. When the apostle was dead the Muslims were sore stricken. I have heard that Aisha used to say, "When the apostle died the Arabs apostatized and Christianity and Judaism raised their heads and disaffection appeared. The Muslims became as sheep exposed to rain on a winter's night through the loss of their prophet until God united them under Abu Bakr."
Hassan said mourning the apostle:

> Tell the poor that plenty has left them
> With the prophet who departed from them this morning.
> Who was it who has a saddle and a camel for me,
> My family's sustenance when rain fails?
> Or with whom can we argue without anxiety   5
> When the tongue runs away with a man?
> He was the light and the brilliance we followed.
> He was sight and hearing second only to God.
> The day they laid him in the grave
> And cast the earth upon him   10
> Would that God had not left one of us
> And neither man nor woman had survived him!

*   *   *

Hassan also said:

> I swear that no man is more careful than I
> In swearing an oath true and without falsehood.
> By God, no woman has conceived and given birth
> To one like the apostle the prophet and guide of his people;
> Nor has God created among his creatures   5
> One more faithful to his sojourner or his promise
> Than he who was the source of our light,
> Blessed in his deeds, just, and upright.
> Your wives stripped the tents in mourning
> And did not strike the pegs behind the curtains.   10
> Like nuns they put on garments of hair
> Certain of misery after happiness.
> O best of men, I was as it were in a river
> Without which I have become lonely in my thirst.

ABOLQASEM FERDOWSI
932–1025

From wild horses on the plain to fish within
The sea, all creatures recognize their young.
It's only man, whose arrogance and pride
Will make his son his deadly enemy.

THE STORY OF SOHRÁB

No story in the Iranian *Book of Kings*, the *Shâhnâme*, has more engaged the interest and sympathy of audiences in the West than that of the tragic encounter between Sohráb and his father, Rostám. It was translated into English and the languages of

Europe repeatedly in the nineteenth century and Matthew Arnold gave it a place in English literature by his brilliant recasting of it (*The Story of Sohráb and Rustúm*, 1853). It is easy to understand why it was so successful. The action is fast-paced and engrossing. It includes a brief but wonderful romantic interlude and several compelling battles. Besides the principal characters there are dreadful villains and a woman warrior who is both courageous and seductive—and this in a work in which there are relatively few major roles for women. Finally, it has a death scene that would make a stone weep. Yet the story's most compelling attraction is surely the central event itself, the death of Sohráb at the unwitting hands of his father, Rostám.

The theme of filicide is a powerful and compelling one, especially when both father and son are figures of great appeal. Rostám is the noblest hero of the *Shâhnâme*, the exemplar of heroism and loyalty, and Sohráb is clearly the son who was meant to succeed Rostám, as Rostám has succeeded Zal and Sam and Narimán. Why should he, of all people, be obliged to kill him? Sohráb in turn is a young man who is devoted to his father and whose principal ambition is to find him. His death seems a ghastly reward for filial piety. Worst of all, those who benefit most by the death of Sohráb, Kay Kavús, and Afrasiyáb, hardly seem to deserve such a reward. Kay Kavús is a dreadful ruler, and Afrasiyáb, the shah of Turán, is Iran's greatest enemy. The death of Sohráb at his father's hands also violates what we accept as the normal order of things—sons replace fathers as youth triumphs over age. The story of Sohráb fascinates us in part because it violates this natural order and adds a nightmarish element to a confrontation that is already freighted with meaning.

This sense of horror and outrage at the death of Sohráb is not something we impose on the text. The story concludes with the famous lines: "It is a tale that's filled with tears and grief. / The tender heart will rage against Rostám." Rostám himself recognizes the horror of his deed the moment after he has committed it, and laments the death of his son in some of the most beautiful and moving passages in the poem. *Sohráb*, in short, raises two compelling questions for us: why must Sohráb die, and why must Rostám be responsible for his death? The first answer is the easier to supply and leads to the second. As modern readers we are inclined to see Sohráb's desire to overthrow Afrasiyáb and Kay Kavús and replace them with the worthier figure of Rostám as commendable, as a proto-modern anticipation of meritocratic rule. Yet in the world of the *Shâhnâme* only God has the authority to choose a monarch. His choice in this matter is as unchallengeable as it is unfathomable. What is more important, the underlying belief of the text is that Iran will endure only for so long as it is ruled by a line of divinely appointed shahs. To overthrow, or attempt to overthrow, one of God's chosen shahs, however great the provocation, is a crime against both God and the state. That God would choose so inept a ruler for Iran as Kay Kavús is indeed puzzling. But one has no right to question or dispute His choice. By his bold decision to overthrow Kay Kavús and put his father on the throne, Sohráb ensures his own destruction. In the same way, Rostám's harsh and arrogant rejection of the shah's authority (When I'm enraged, who then is Shah Kavús? / Who's there to humble me? Who is this Tus?), however justified, provides the dramatic justification for his bearing the tragic responsibility of killing his own son. His lapse in loyalty and obedience is brief and the breach is soon healed, but the memory lingers. Kay Kavús later alludes to it in explaining his refusal to send Rostám the royal remedy that would save Sohráb:

> ". . . [Sohráb will] make his father yet more powerful.
> Rostám will slay me then, I have no doubt. . . .
> You heard him, how he said, 'Who is Kavús?
> If he's the shah, then who is Tus?' And with
> That chest and neck, that mighty arm and fist,
> In this wide world, who's there to equal him?

Will he stand humbly by my royal seat,
Or march beneath my banner's eagle wings?"

Rostám is in part to blame for Sohráb's assault on the Iranian shah. He was as casual as a god in siring his son and left him to grow up without the guidance that would have made him a loyal subject. However, Tahminé is equally to blame because she hides the true nature of her son's heroic abilities from his father, fearing to lose him. But behind both of them stands the implacable and malignant fate that so often intrudes upon the story to ensure that father and son will not recognize each other.

In the larger context of the *Shâhnâme*, the story of Sohráb underscores the primacy of the monarch and marks a transition from stories in which the conflict between hero and shah dominates to ones in which the conflict is between princely heir and royal father. Much of the tragedy of Sohráb turns on Rostám's crucial failure to raise his own son. In the story of Siyavash, which immediately follows that of Sohráb, Rostám takes the infant Siyavash, the son of Kay Kavús, to his castle in Sistan and raises him there as virtually his own child. By this act he allows his own heroic heritage to join that of the royal line. Rostám's role in the epic diminishes from this point on. He remains an important but essentially offstage presence until, centuries later, he reappears to fight the last great battle of his life. It is as though the evolution of the *Shâhnâme* requires a shift in emphasis at this point from the conflict of shah and hero to that of shah and prince, and the sacrifice of Sohráb is the means whereby the energy of the Sistanian heroes is diverted into the royal line.

THE SHÂHNÂME

Nothing in Western literature quite prepares us for the *Shâhnâme* of Abolqasem Ferdowsi. We call it an epic because it is a long poem—some fifty thousand couplets—and is filled with heroic tales that are drawn from Iran's history and mythology. *Epic* is the only descriptive term we have that seems to fit such a work. Yet for us *epic* really means Homer and the Homeric tradition—all those poems from Virgil's *Aeneid* to Milton's *Paradise Lost* that were written in conscious imitation of the *Odyssey* and the *Iliad*, or which, like *The Song of Roland* or *Beowulf*, were written to celebrate a particular historic moment or a "heroic" way of life. The *Shâhnâme* is a very different poem from any of these, and it developed independently from the Homeric tradition. It does not begin "in the midst of things," as does the *Iliad*, but with the creation of the world and the appearance of the first shah. It lacks the elaborate celestial machinery of gods and goddesses that one finds in other epic traditions, from the *Odyssey* and the *Iliad* to *Gilgamesh* in the ancient Near East and to the *Mahābhārata* and the *Rāmāyaṇa* in India. It is a monotheistic epic like *Paradise Lost*, but its focus on the life of the royal court makes it seem closer to the tales of King Arthur and the knights of the round table than to Milton's great poem. It contains not one story but many, not a single climactic event but a multitude of them, and not one hero but a long sequence of heroes and heroic princes. Rostám, who is the last and greatest of a family of heroes from the Iranian province of Sistan and who dominates several of its finest stories, is no more than an offstage presence in other tales. He also dies when the poem is only two-thirds finished. The events in *Gilgamesh*, Homer, and the European epics are tailored to the limits of a single human life, but the events of the *Shâhnâme* stretch across millennia and a single hero may live for centuries.

Some of the stories that make up the *Shâhnâme* can be traced back well before the coming of Islam to at least the time of Cyrus and Darius some twenty-five hundred years ago. Other stories from later times were added to these, and all were gathered together into comprehensive collections from time to time. Late in the reign of the Sassanians (third to seventh centuries), the last pre-Islamic Iranian dynasty to rule in Iran, a chronicle was compiled at the court and called the *Khudáy Nâmág* (Book of Kings). The original of this work has been lost, but Arabic translations of portions of it survive in the work of early Arab historians. During the first two centuries of the Islamic period, Iran's rulers were Arab and interested only in Arabic culture. When an Iranian Muslim dynasty, the Samanids (819–1005), returned to power in central Asia, interest in the national epic of Iran revived as well. Once more the court ordered that the old stories be gathered into a single chronicle, in prose. When it was complete, they sought a poet to turn this prose into verse. The first likely candidate, Daqiqi, was killed by one of his slaves after he had completed only two thousand verses (later incorporated into the finished work), and so the way was opened for Abolqasem Ferdowsi.

Ferdowsi deliberately set about making his poetic version a vehicle for preserving Iran's pre-Islamic heritage. He ends his tale by saying that he has given new life to stories that had begun to be forgotten. He also assumed that in giving poetic life to these tales he was ensuring the survival of his own name as well.

> And when this famous book shall reach its end,
> Throughout the land my praises will be heard.
> From this day on I shall not die, but live,
> For I'll have sown my words both far and wide.

In this he was successful beyond his wildest dreams. Since Ferdowsi completed the *Shâhnâme* it has remained a work of central importance in the Iranian cultural tradition.

The events narrated in the first two-thirds of the *Shâhnâme* consist of heroic and romantic tales that belong to a mythical or legendary time. In the last third the tales are peopled with figures from historical times. One portion draws heavily on a fictional biography of Alexander the Great, who conquered all of present-day Iran and parts of central Asia and north India in the fourth century B.C. The last sequence of stories is a similarly fictionalized account of the history of the Parthian and Sassanian dynasties (247 B.C.–A.D. 651), who ruled in Iran between the time of Alexander's death and the rise of Islam. The style of presentation does not change, however, and historical figures and events are presented as the stuff of myth and legend.

In the world of the *Shâhnâme*, humankind seems to have existed before the first shah, but as an undifferentiated species. The formation of human society required the shaping presence of a divinely appointed ruler. Other shahs, most notably the wise and just Jamshid, provided human society with those gifts—fire, tools, agriculture, and the various crafts—that raise men and women above the level of beasts. In other traditions these gifts that distinguish and sustain human society are gifts from the gods. In the *Shâhnâme* it is Iran's shahs who provide them, or, rather, it is through them that Yazdán, the sole God of pre-Islamic Iranian religious belief, gives them to humanity. Indeed, while there are a number of recurrent themes in the *Shâhnâme*, such as the immortality of noble deeds, the malignancy and inevitability of fate, and the persistent hostility and envy of Iran's neighbors, the theme that underlies all of these is that God prefers Iran to other nations and sustains it through the institution of the shah. So long as His chosen shah rules, Iran will endure. When Shah Yazdegerd III is slain in 652, the Iran of the *Shâhnâme* comes to an end. Other epics provide dramatic unity with a single dominant hero (like Odysseus, Aeneas, or Roland) or a single climactic event such as the destruction of Troy, the founding of Rome, or the defeat of the Saracens. In the *Shâhnâme* it is the enduring institution of monarchy that stitches all its stories together.

Although divine support for Iranian monarchy is a central constant of the *Shâhnâme*, its ideology is not a naïve and enthusiastic monarchism. Ferdowsi was not a panegyrist who presented idealizations of the ruler for the admiration of the royal sponsors and their followers. He was as realistic about the limitations of individual monarchs as was Shakespeare about England's kings. Many of the greatest tales in the epic are as much concerned with the dilemmas of the monarchical state as with its inevitability. *Sohráb* illustrates this by showing how God favors a foolish shah, Kay

Kavús, who repeatedly and recklessly endangers himself and his people over a noble hero, Rostám, who as repeatedly rescues the nation from the shah's folly. The religion of the *Shâhnâme* is Zoroastrianism, but a Zoroastrianism that has been stripped of its fire temples, rituals, and prayers. Ferdowsi was a Muslim—as were his patron, Soltan Mahmud of Ghazna (died 1030), and the members of the court. As a consequence, either he or his sources passed the stories of the *Shâhnâme* through a filter, eliminating what would have been most offensive to Muslim beliefs. What remains is a vague but persistent dualism in which the powers of good, Ahura Mazda, and evil, Ahriman, are in perpetual conflict. Rostám and Kay Kavús pray to the supreme god, Izád, or Yazdán (Creator and Keeper of the World), who presides over this conflict. Ultimately, Yazdán will give victory to good, but in the course of the *Shâhnâme* it is Ahriman's power that increases. The shahs who rule become progressively less worthy, and "hunchbacked fate" spreads ruin and destruction where he will. The poem also ends with the conquest of the Arabs and Islam, a crushing defeat for Zoroastrian Iran.

THE PERSIAN LANGUAGE

Persian belongs to the Indo-European family of languages and has strong similarities to the major languages of Europe—the words for "father," "mother," and "brother," for instance, are *pedar, mâdar,* and *barâdar.* Old Persian, one of the court languages of Cyrus and Darius, was a contemporary of Sanskrit, which it closely resembled. Middle Persian was an Iranian language of central Asia and the Iranian plateau that had wide currency from the time of Alexander to the rise of Islam. Modern Persian, which evolved in the Islamic period, is a further development of Middle Persian grammar and syntax that contains a large vocabulary of Arabic. The language of the *Shâhnâme* is a slightly archaized form of this language. That is, it is largely free of Arabic loan words and retains some Middle Persian vocabulary. Since the ninth century modern Persian has been written in a modified form of the Arabic alphabet.

Persian and its literature first came to the West as a result of the European conquest of India. For centuries central Asian Muslims whose literary and administrative language was Persian ruled in India. When European merchants and adventurers first became interested in India in the seventeenth century, they learned Persian so they could engage in trade and successfully rule. Then as now, the principal texts for teaching the language were literary, and many of those who learned Persian for practical reasons came to value it as a source of pleasure and a focus of scholarship. One of the principal fruits of this scholarship was the "discovery" of the *Shâhnâme* and its translation into the major languages of Europe. In the nineteenth century, British rulers replaced Persian with English as the language of education and administration, but Persian continued as a major language until well into the twentieth century.

The only complete translation of the *Shâhnâme* into English verse is that of Arthur George and Edmond Warner, *The Shâhnâma of Firdausi* (1905–1925). Unfortunately, it is available only in large research libraries. Besides the translation of *Sohráb* printed here, the only modern poetic versions of the stories from the *Shâhnâme* are Dick Davis's fine verse translation, *The Legend of Seyavash* (1992) and Jerome W. Clinton's *In the Dragon's Claws: The Story of Rostam and Esfandiyar* (1999). Davis has also written the best study of the *Shâhnâme* in English, *Epic and Sedition: The Case of the Shâhnâme* (1992). And he has completed two volumes of a projected three-volume illustrated translation of the entire *Shâhnâme* into prose interspersed with poetry—I: *The Lion and the Throne* (1998); II: *Fathers and Sons* (2000). Every literary history of Iran contains a chapter or so on Ferdowsi and the *Shâhnâme*, most recently, *Persian Literature* (1988), edited by Ehsan Yarshater.

PRONOUNCING GLOSSARY

The following list uses common English syllables and stress accents to provide rough equivalents of selected words whose pronunciation may be unfamiliar to the general reader.

Abolqasem Ferdowsi: *a'-bowl qah'-sem fair-doe-see'*

Afrasiyáb: *af-raw'-see-ahb'*

Ahriman: *ah-ree-man'*

Ahura Mazda: *ah-hoo'-ruh maz'-duh*

Banu Gashasp: *bah-nu' ga-shashp'*

Daqiqi: *da-kee-kee'*

Gordafaríd: *gor-dah'-fa-reed'*

Gudárz: *goo-darz'*

Humán: *hoo-mahn'*

Jamshid: *jam-sheed'*

Kay Kavús: *kay kah-voos'*

Kay Qobád: *kay qo-bahd'*

Khudáy Nâmág: *koo-dai' nah-mag'*

nushdarú: *noosh-dah-roo'*

piltán: *peel-tan'*

Rostám: *ros-tam'*

Rudabé: *roo-dah-bay'*

Shâhnâme: *shah-nah-may'*

Siyavash: *see-uh-vash'*

Sohráb: *soh-rahb'*

Tahminé: *tah-mee-nay'*

Yazdán: *yaz-dahn'*

Yazdegerd: *yaz-duh-gerd'*

Zavaré: *za-vah-ray'*

Zhende Razm: *zhén-day razm'*

From Shâhnâme[1]

The Tragedy of Sohráb and Rostám

Prologue

A wind springs up quite suddenly, and knocks
An unripe apple from a bough. Is this
An act of justice or of tyranny?
What should we think? How weigh what's right and wrong?
If death is just, how can this not be so?   5
And if it's just, then why lament and cry?
Your soul knows nothing of this mystery.
You cannot see what lies beyond this veil.
Though all descend to face that greedy door,
For none has it revealed its secrets twice.   10
Perhaps he'll like the place he goes to better,
Within that other house he may find peace.
Death's breath is like a fiercely raging fire
That has no fear of either young or old.
Here in this place of passing, not repose,   15
Should death cinch tight the saddle on its steed,
Know this, that it is just, and not unjust.
There's no disputing justice when it comes.
Destruction knows both youth and age as one,
For nothing that exists will long endure.   20
If you can fill your heart with faith's pure light,

1. Translated by Jerome W. Clinton.

Silence befits you best, since you're His slave.
You do not understand God's mysteries,
Unless your soul is partners with some demon.
Strive here within the world as you pass through,   25
And in the end bear virtue in your heart.
Now I'll relate the battle of Sohráb—
First how his father's enmity began.

The Beginning

*   *   *

The *dehqâns* have a tale in their old books,
That I have versified from ancient prose.
The *mobads*[2] say the tale begins like this—
Rostám one day just as the sun rose up,
Was sad at heart, and so prepared to hunt.   5
He armed himself, put arrows in his quiver,
Then like a fearsome lion on the chase,
He galloped toward the borders of Turán.[3]
As he approached the Turkish borderlands,
He saw the plain was filled with onagers.[4]   10
The Giver of the Crown[5] glowed like a rose.
He laughed aloud and spurred Rakhsh[6] from his place.
With bow and arrow, and with mace and rope,
He brought down many onagers upon
The plain. Then from dead branches, brush, and thorns,   15
Rostám built up a fiercely blazing fire.
And when the fire had spread, he wrenched a tree
Out of the ground to serve him as a spit.
He placed a heavy stallion on that tree,
That was a feather in his palm, no more.   20
When it was done he tore it limb from limb
And wolfed it down, the marrow bones and all.
Rostám slept then and rested from the hunt.
Nearby Rakhsh wandered, grazing in a meadow.
Turkish horsemen, some seven or eight, passed by   25
That plain and hunting ground, and as they did
They spied a horse's tracks and turned aside
To follow them along the river's bank.
When they at last saw Rakhsh upon the plain,
They raced ahead to snare him with their ropes.   30
Once he was caught, they bore him galloping
Toward the town; each eager for his share.
Rostám, when he awoke from his sweet sleep,
Had need of his well-trained and ready steed,

2. The terms *dehqân* and *mobad* refer to the Iranian nobility of central Asia and Zoroastrian clerics, respectively. These are the two classes who are identified in the *Shâhnâme* as the principal repositories of the pre-Islamic Iranian culture of which they are a part.   3. The land of the Turks, the traditional enemy of Iran.   4. A species of wild ass native to the Iranian Plateau.   5. Rostám; he brought Kay Qobád (the first shah of the Kaianian dynasty) to the throne. Kay Kavús was Kay Qobád's successor. 6. Rostám's steed, who is hugely proportioned (as is Rostám) and the only horse able to bear his weight. He is Rostám's companion in all his adventures, sometimes taking an active role.

And was distressed to see that Rakhsh was gone.   35
Turning toward Semengán, he said, "Without
My horse I'll have to travel there on foot.
Where shall I flee from this soul-blackening shame?
What will the heroes say? 'While Rostám slept
They stole his horse, and so he lost his life.'   40
Now I must travel on in wretched state,
Abandoning my heart and soul to grief.
Now I must carry arms and armor both.
Perhaps I'll find his tracks along the way."
So Rostám journeyed on with aching heart,   45
His body bent with weariness and shame.

✳   ✳   ✳

In Semengán

As he drew near to Semengán,[7] the shah
And nobles heard, "The Giver of the Crown
Approaches now on foot. While they were on
A hunt, the shining Rakhsh fled from his hand."
The shah and all his nobles greeted him,   5
All those who wore a crown upon their heads.
The shah of Semengán inquired of him,
"What can this mean? Who's dared to challenge you?
Within this city we are all your friends.
We stand beside your path, alert to serve.   10
You may command our persons as our wealth.
The worthy heads and hearts of all are yours."
Rostám considered well his words and saw
That he'd small cause for his distrust and doubt.
He answered him and said, "While in the field,   15
Rakhsh fled from me, with neither bit nor reins.
His tracks lead to the city's edge; and on
The other side, there's only reeds and swamp.
Find him and you will have my thanks. In my
Reward I'll show you all my gratitude.   20
But if you don't, and he is lost to me,
Then many noble lords will lose their heads."
The shah replied to him, "Oh worthy man!
No one would dare to treat with you this way.
Don't act in haste, but be my welcome guest.   25
This matter will conclude as you desire.
Tonight let us rejoice our hearts with wine,
And keep them free of evil thoughts as well.
The tracks of shining Rakhsh, a steed who is
Well known to all, will not stay hidden long."   30
    Brave Tahamtán[8] rejoiced to hear his words.
His soul was freed of all uneasiness.
It now seemed right to him to visit in
His home. This happy news made him his guest.

---

7. A city within the borders of Turán.   8. Rostám; it means "huge-bodied."

The ruler then gave him a place within   35
His castle keep, and waited by his side.
He summoned all the city's great, those who
Were worthy to be seated at the feast.
The bearer of the wine, the harper too,
And dark-eyed, rose-cheeked idols of Taráz,[9]   40
All joined with the musicians gathered there,
To see that great Rostám should not be sad.
When he grew drunk, and sleep came to his eyes,
He wished to leave the feast and seek his rest.
They led him to a place fit for a prince,   45
A quiet chamber sweet with scent and musk.

Tahminé[1]

And when one watch had passed on that dark night,
And Sirius rose high on heaven's wheel.
The sound of secret voices could be heard.
The chamber door was opened quietly.
A single slave, a scented candle in   5
Her hand, approached and stood by Rostám's pillow.
Behind the slave, a moon-faced[2] maid appeared,
Adorned and scented like the shining sun.
Her eyebrows bows, her tresses lassos coiled,
In stature like a slender cypress tree.   10
Her soul was wisdom and her body seemed
Of spirit pure, as though not made of earth.
Amazed, Rostám the fearless lion-heart,
Cried out in wonder to the Maker of
The World, then asked the maid, "What is your name?   15
Why have you come here in the dead of night?"
She answered him, "My name is Tahminé.
It seems my heart's been torn in two by grief.
My father is the shah of Semengán,
From lions and from tigers comes my seed.   20
In all the world no beauty is my match.
Few are my like beneath the azure wheel.[3]
Outside these walls, there's none who's looked on me.
Nor has my voice been heard by any ear.
From everyone have I heard tales of you—   25
So wonderful they seemed to me like myths.
They say you fear no leopard and no demon.
No crocodile or lion is so fierce.
At night alone, you journey to Turán,
And wander freely there, and even sleep.   30
You spit an onager with just one hand,
And with your sword you cause the air to weep.
When you approach them with your mace in hand,

---

9. A city in central Asia famous for the beauty of its women.   1. Sohráb's mother and princess of
Semengán.   2. In Persian poetry the round face and pale skin of the moon are the models of feminine
beauty.   3. The sky.

The leopard rends his claws, the lion his heart.
The eagle, when he sees your naked blade,   35
Will not take wing and fly off to the hunt.
The tiger's skin is branded by your rope.
The clouds weep blood in fear of your sharp lance.
As I would listen to these tales of you,
I'd bite my lip in wonder, yearning so   40
To look upon those shoulders and that chest.
And then Izád[4] sent you to Semengán.
I'm yours now should you want me, and, if not,
None but the fish and birds will see my face.
It's first because I do so long for you,   45
That I've slain reason for my passion's sake.
And next, perhaps the Maker of the World
Will place a son from you within my womb.
Perhaps he'll be like you in manliness
And strength, a child of Saturn and the Sun.   50
And third, so I may bring your horse to you,
I'll search throughout the whole of Semengán."
   Rostám, when he looked on her angel face,
He saw in her a share of every grace.
What's more, she'd given him some news of Rakhsh,   55
He saw no end to this that was not good.
So with good will and joy, as she had wished,
Rostám sealed firm his bond with her that night.
When she had secretly become his mate,
The night that followed lasted late and long.   60
But then at last, from high above the world,
The radiant sun cast down his shining rope.
On Rostám's arm there was a jeweled seal
That all the world would recognize as his.
He gave this jewel to her and said, "Keep this.   65
And if the times should bring a girl to you,
Then take this gem and plait it in her hair—
A world-illumining omen of good luck.
But if the star of fate should send a son,
Then bind this father's token to his arm.   70
He'll be as tall as Sam or Narimán,[5]
In strength and manliness a noble youth.
He'll bring the eagle from the clouds above.
The sun will not look harshly on this boy."
Rostám spent all that night with his new moon,   75
And spoke with her of all he'd seen and known.
   The radiant sun at last rose to the heights
And shed his glorious light upon the earth.
The worthy shah approached the chamber then
To ask Rostám if he had rested well.   80
And this once said, he gave him news of Rakhsh.

---

4. One of the names of God.   5. Rostám's ancestors. His line included heroes famed for generations.
The likeness of Sohráb to his great-grandfather Sam is remarked on repeatedly in the course of the poem.

The Giver of the Crown rejoiced at this.
He went and stroked his steed and saddled him,
Then thanked the shah, well pleased at his return.

The Birth of Sohráb

When nine months passed for Tahminé, she bore
A healthy boy whose face shone like the moon.
It seemed he was the pahlaván[6] Rostám,
Or that he was the lion Sam, or Narimán.
Because he laughed and had a cheerful face,   5
His mother called him by the name Sohráb.[7]
In just a single month he'd grown a year.
His chest was like Rostám's, the son of Zal.
At three he learned the game of polo, and
At five he mastered bow and javelin.   10
When he was ten, in all of Semengán
Not one would dare to meet him in the field.
Sohráb went to his mother, Tahminé,
To question her, "Tell me the truth," he said.
"I'm taller than the boys who nursed with me.   15
It seems my head can touch the sky itself.
Whose son am I, what is his family?
When asked, 'Who is your father?' What shall I say?
If you should keep this answer from me now,
I will not leave you in this world alive."   20
His mother answered him, "Don't be so harsh,
But hear my words and be rejoiced by them.
Your father is the pahlaván Rostám.
Your ancestors are Sam and Narimán.
And so it is your head can touch the sky.   25
You are descended from that famous line.
Since first the World Creator made the earth,
There's been no other horseman like Rostám.
Nor one like Sam the son of Narimán.
The turning sphere does not dare brush his head."   30
She brought a letter from the pahlaván,
Rostám, and showed it secretly to him.
Enclosed with it Rostám had sent as well,
Three shining emeralds in three golden seals.
"Afrasiyáb,[8] must never know of this,"   35
She said, "he must not hear a single word.
And if your father learns that you've become
A brave and noble warrior like this,
He'll call you to his side, I know.
And then your mother's heart will break."   40
The bold Sohráb replied, "In all the world
No man could keep a secret such as this.
From ancient times till now, those great in war

6. Hero, warrior.   7. "Rosy-hued," because his face flushed red when he laughed. In Persia red is the color of health and good cheer; yellow is the color of fear and ill health.   8. Shah of Turán.

Recite for all the tales of brave Rostám.
When I have such a warlike lineage,   45
For me to keep it hidden can't be right.
Now from among the warlike Turks I will
Amass an army boundless as the sea
I'll drive Kavús from off his throne,
And from Irán I'll scour all trace of Tus.[9]   50
To brave Rostám I'll give throne, mace, and crown,
And seat him in the place of Shah Kavús.
Then from Irán will I attack Turán,
And here confront the shah, Afrasiyáb.
I'll rout his army and I'll seize his throne.   55
I'll thrust my lance's tip above the sun.
When Rostám is the father, I the son,
None else in all the world should wear a crown.
When sun and moon illuminate the sky,
What need is there for stars to flaunt their crowns?"   60
From every side an army flocked to him,
Who all were noble men, brave swordsmen too.

The Campaign Begins

This news was brought to Shah Afrasiyáb,
"Sohráb has launched his boat upon the stream.
The smell of milk still lingers on his mouth,
And yet he thinks of weapons and of war.
Since he would scour the whole earth with his blade,   5
He now would fight a war with Shah Kavús.
A teeming army's gathered to his side,
And he gives little thought to other men.
But why should speech be thus drawn out so long?
His prowess far exceeds that of his birth."   10
When Shah Afrasiyáb had heard these words,
He was well pleased. He laughed and showed his joy.
Then from among the army's valiant chiefs,
Those with the strength to wield a heavy mace,
He chose twelve thousand heroes like Humán,   15
These he entrusted to Barmán to lead.
Afrasiyáb advised his generals,
"This secret must not ever come to light.
When these two face each other on the field,
The bold Rostám will surely try some ruse.   20
His father must not recognize the boy,
Or else his love will bind his heart to him.
Rather, that brave and ancient pahlaván
Must lose his life to this young lion-heart.
Then later on destroy the fierce Sohráb.   25
Bind him one night forever in his dreams."
    Alertly both the warriors went off
To meet the bright, high-spirited Sohráb.

---

9. Rostám's rival, a hero resident at the Iranian court.

They took with them the gift of Turán's shah;
Twelve thousand horses, camels, and their gear;   30
A throne of turquoise with four silver legs;
A ruby crown whose crest was all of gold.
They brought as well a letter filled with praise,
That he had written to that worthy youth.
If you can seize the throne of all Irán,   35
You'll ease the disputations of our times.
The road that lies between us is not long.
Irán, Turán, and Semengán are one.
You sit upon the throne and wear the crown.
I'll send whatever troops you may require.   40
For bravery and generalship, Turán
Has none to match Humán and fierce Barmán.
I've sent them now, to be at your command.
Let them remain there for a time as guests.
If you seek war, they'll fight for you, and make   45
The world too narrow for your enemies.
A letter such as this, and royal robes,
They took with them, and gear for many knights.
    Word of Humán, Barmán, and all their troops
Soon reached Sohráb from lookouts on the road.   50
He and his grandsire[1] went to greet this host.
He saw so vast an army and his heart rejoiced.
Humán, when he first saw his shoulders and
His massive chest, was speechless with surprise.
He gave Sohráb the royal letter and   55
The horses, camels, and their precious loads.
When that ambitious youth had read the letter,
He quickly led his army from their camp.
For none could stand against him in a fight,
Not even if a lion should attack.   60
    There was a fortress which they called the White;
The hopes of all Irán were placed in it.
The battle-tried Hojír,[2] a man of strength
And bravery, was keeper of the fort.
For in that time, Gostáhm[3] was still a youth,   65
Although a youth of bold, heroic mien.
He had a warlike sister too, who was
Well known for her ferocity and strength.
The army of Sohráb approached the fort.
Hojír the brave looked down and saw it there.   70
Swift as the wind he mounted on his steed,
And galloped out to battle from the fort.
When bold Sohráb observed Hojír's approach,
He flushed in rage and drew his vengeful sword,
And like a lion raced onto the field.   75
As he drew near the battle-tried Hojír,
Sohráb the valiant called out to him,

---

1. The shah of Semengán.   2. Commander of the garrison at the White Fortress.   3. An Iranian hero, whose adventures come in later stories.

"Oh foolish man, to fight with me alone!
What is your name, and which your family?
Who is the mother that must weep for you?"   80
Hojír replied to him, "In all Turán
There can be few or none to equal me.
I am Hojír the brave, the army's chief.
I mean to tear your head from off your trunk
And send it to the world's shah, Kay Kavús.   85
Your body will I hide beneath the earth."
When he had heard this boast, Sohráb just laughed
And galloped forward to attack Hojír.
So swiftly did they hurl their weapons that
The eye could not distinguish lance from lance.   90
One lance Hojír thrust at Sohráb, the point
Of which slid off his waist and did not stick.
Sohráb reversed his lance, and with its butt,
He struck his chest a fierce and telling blow
That lifted him right off his horse's back   95
And stretched him stunned and gasping on the ground.
Sohráb sprang down and sat upon his chest,
Then drew his sword to sever head from trunk.
Hojír beneath him twisted to his right,
And begged Sohráb for mercy in his fear.   100
The youth released his grip and spared his life.
Pleased with himself, he gave him much advice.
Sohráb then quickly bound his hands with rope,
And sent him as a captive to Humán.
Within the fort, when all had heard the news,   105
"Hojír's been taken captive by the Turks,"
A cry rose up, and men and women wept,
Because Hojír had now been lost to them.

Gordafaríd[4]

The daughter of Gazhdáhm,[5] when she had heard
The leader of their company'd been captured;
(She was a woman who just like a knight,
Had gained renown in war, and who was called
Gordafaríd—for in her time there was   5
No mother who had borne her like), she found
The conduct of Hojír so shameful that
The tulips in her cheeks turned black as pitch.
She wasted not a moment, but bound on
The coat of mail a horseman wears to fight.   10
She hid her hair beneath that coat of mail,
And knotted on her head a Roman casque.
Then lionlike she raced down from the fort,
Girded for battle, and seated on the wind.
She faced the army like a warrior,   15

---

4. The only woman hero in the *Shâhnâme*; her name means "created a warrior." She is Gostáhm's sister.
5. Gordafaríd's father.

And roared a challenge like a thunderbolt,
"Who are your heroes, who your pahlaváns,
And who your brave and battle-tested chiefs?"
Seeing her, Sohráb the lion-killer laughed,
And in amazement bit his lip. He said,   20
"Another onager has rushed into
The trap set by the lord of mace and blade."
Swift as the wind he donned his armored shirt,
And bound a Chinese helmet on his head,
Then galloped out to meet Gordafaríd.   25
When that rope-hurling maid saw him approach,
She strung her heavy bow and drew a breath.
No bird escaped her arrows with its life.
She rained her darts upon Sohráb, and as
She rode, she dodged and feinted right and left.   30
Sohráb observed her charge and felt ashamed,
Then flushed with rage and galloped to the fray.
He lifted up his shield and charged his foe,
The blood of battle coursing in his veins.
Gordafaríd, when she could see Sohráb   35
Was racing toward her like a raging flame,
She drew the bow she'd strung upon her arm;
Her yellow horse reared up to paw the clouds.
She turned her lance's point toward Sohráb,
And then reined in her steed to face her foe.   40
Sohráb, as fierce as any leopard, had
Just like his foe, prepared himself to fight.
He seized the reins and brought his horse around,
Then set upon her like the God of Fire.
He snatched away her polished lance's point,   45
And closed upon her like a cloud of smoke.
He struck Gordafaríd upon the waist,
And one by one he split her armor's links.
Then like a mallet when it strikes the ball,
He drove her from her saddle with one blow.   50
Gordafaríd, as she was turning in
Her saddle, drew a sharp blade from her waist,
Struck at his lance, and parted it in two.
She fell back in her seat, and dust rose up.
    She saw she was no match for him in war,   55
Quickly, she turned away from him, and fled.
Sohráb then gave his dragon steed its head.
His anger robbed the world of all its light.
As he approached her roaring in his wrath,
She turned and snatched the helmet from her head,   60
Her hair was freed then of its armored cloak;
Her face shone forth as radiant as the sun.
Sohráb now saw a maiden seated there,
Whose face was worthy of a royal crown.
He spoke in awe, "That from the army of   65
Irán a maid like this should come, and fight
With mounted warriors in the field of war,

And raise the dust of battle to the sky!"
He loosed his twisted lasso from its loop,
And threw it, catching her around the waist.   70
He cautioned her, and said, "Don't seek to flee.
Oh beauteous moon, why do you wish to fight?
I've never caught an onager like you.
You won't escape my grip. Don't even try."
Gordafaríd knew she was caught at last.   75
She could not free herself save by some trick.
She turned her face to him and said, "Oh, brave
And peerless youth, so like a lion when
You face your foe, two armies watch our fight,
Our combat here of heavy mace and blade.   80
Should I reveal to them my face and hair,
Your army will be filled with murmuring.
'Sohráb in battle with a maiden foe,
Raised dust in clouds that rose up to the sky.'
To parley here in secret would be best.   85
A noble man must use his head as well.
Do not bring shame upon yourself before
These two ranked armies here because of me.
You now command the garrison and fort.
Why then should you make war instead of peace?   90
Once you accept the treaty that we'll make,
The fort, its chief and treasure will be yours."
She turned her face and smiled upon Sohráb,
And showed him pearly teeth and ruby lips.
She seemed a garden fair as paradise.   95
No gardener's seen so tall a cypress tree.
Her eyes were like a deer's, her eyebrows bows.
She seemed a flower in the height of bloom.
    These words of hers perplexed Sohráb at heart.
His cheeks grew flaming hot, his thoughts confused. 100
He said to her, "Do not betray your word—
You've faced me on the field of battle once—
Nor fix your hopes on these high fortress walls.
They are not higher than the clouds above.
My mace's blows will bring them to the ground,   105
And there's no lance will ever pierce my chest."
Gordafaríd pulled at her horse's reins,
And turned her golden steed toward the fort.
She rode along; Sohráb was at her side,
And Gazhdahám watched from the battlements.   110
    Gordafaríd swung wide the fortress gate,
And drew her bound and weary body through.
They sadly closed the gate behind her then.
Their hearts were filled with grief, their eyes with tears.
Her grievous wounds and those of brave Hojír,   115
Had saddened all within, both young and old.
"Oh brave and lion-hearted maid," they said,
"The hearts of all are mournful at your state.
You have fought well, and tried deceit and guile.

Your deeds have brought no shame upon your line." 120
Gordafaríd laughed loud and long, then climbed
The fortress wall to look upon their foes.
She saw Sohráb still seated on his mount,
And called, "Oh shah who leads the Chinese Turks,
Why strive so hard? Turn back from this attack, 125
And from all combat on the field of war."
She laughed aloud and said in mockery,
"The Turks will find no brides within Irán;
That's how it is, you had no luck with me.
But don't distress yourself too much at this. 130
You're surely not descended from these Turks.
You must be born of some more noble race.
For with your strength of arm, your chest and neck,
None of these pahlaváns can equal you.
However when Shah Kay Kavús learns that 135
Some warrior's led an army from Turán,
He'll tell Rostám to arm himself for war,
And he's a hero you can never match.
Of all your host he won't leave one alive.
And I can't guess what evil you'll endure. 140
I'm saddened that a chest and neck like yours
Should disappear within some leopard's maw.
It's better if you heed my warning now,
And turn your noble face back to Turán.
Don't trust your arm alone. The foolish bull 145
Will only feed, and think not of the knife."
    Sohráb felt shame at what he heard. The fort
Had come so easily into his grasp.
Around the citadel there lay a settlement,
A town and fields, in which the fortress stood. 150
He razed the town and burned the fields,
Abandoning himself to evil deeds.
Sohráb then said, "The day's come to an end;
Our hands are stayed from battle now by night.
At dawn tomorrow I'll pull down these walls; 155
They too shall look upon defeat in war."

Gazhdahám's Letter to Kay Kavús

When once Sohráb had gone, old Gazhdahám
Sent for a scribe and sat him by his side.
He wrote a letter to the shah, preparing
To send a courier swiftly on his way.
At first he praised the Maker of the World, 5
And next recounted what he'd heard and seen.
A mighty host is camped before our walls,
An army filled with fierce and warlike men.
Their leader is a youthful pahlaván
Whose years cannot be more than twelve. 10
His stature far exceeds a cypress tree's;

His countenance is like the burning sun's.
His chest is like an elephant's, and I
Have never seen a fist and mace like his.
When he begins to wield his Indian sword,   15
To fight with sea and mountains shames his skill.
The morning thunder cannot match his voice.
The cutting sword cannot withstand his arm.
The brave Hojír prepared himself for war,
And mounted on a swift-paced steed, he went   20
To fight Sohráb, for that's this hero's name.
I did not see him on his horse for longer
Than it takes a warrior to knit his brows,
Or for a scent to move from nose to brain.
Sohráb unhorsed him with a single blow,   25
His chest astonished by that fearful arm.
He's still alive, although his prisoner.
Our souls are filled with anguish at his state.
Many a Turkish horseman have I known;
I've never seen or heard of one like this   30
God grant no warrior of ours should ever
Fight with him before two armies' ranks.
Should he assault a mountain in his wrath,
The earth itself would pity stone and flint.
No one has seen a cavalier like him;   35
You'd think he was the horseman Sam, no less.
His height, take it as reaching to the sky.
And take our heroes' luck as slumbering.
Should we ourselves delay now for a while,
And neither do nor say what must be done;   40
Or if the shahanshah should pause to breathe;
And neither sends an army nor prepares
To fight, he'll seize both fort and barricade.
He has the strength. No one can stay his hand.
This fortress wall cannot withstand his might.   45
The lion's charge seems slow before his speed.
When he had sealed the letter late that night,
He called a messenger and spoke to him,
Advising him to take the swiftest route.
Once that was done, Gazhdahám rose up and left.   50
The rider seized his bag, put down his head,
And disappeared along untraveled ways.
The others, too, set off toward Irán,
Abandoning the fortress to Sohráb.
When dawn appeared above the mountain peaks,   55
The Turkish forces armed themselves for war.
Sohráb, the marshal, lance in hand,
And seated on a heavy-shouldered steed,
Approached the fortress walls and looked inside,
But there were few within to meet his gaze.   60
As he advanced they swung the portal wide,
Within the fort he saw not one to fight.

Those left behind approached at his command,
Each thinking how he might escape his wrath.

* * *

Kay Kavús

When this report was brought to Kay Kavús,
The words of Gazhdahám dismayed his heart.
He called the army's leaders to his side,
And spoke at length of this report with them.
The army's chiefs, both great and small, men like   5
Gudárz of Keshvad's house, like Tus and Giv,
Like Bahram and Gorgín, and like Farhád,
Sat down to take their counsel with the shah.
He read the letter for them all, and spoke
Of his distress and grave perplexity.   10
Privately he said to all his chiefs,
"I fear this matter won't be settled soon.
Gazhdáhm's report of how this matter stands
Has overwhelmed my heart with grief.
What can we do, where is the remedy?   15
In all Irán what warrior's his match?"
They all agreed that Giv should leave at once
To seek the martial chieftain of Zaból.[6]
    The shah sent for his minister at once;
This was a matter of great urgency.   20
When they'd conferred he ordered him to write
A letter to the world-renowned Rostám.
He praised the Maker of the World at first,
He who created all, and shapes our Fate.
And then he praised the noble pahlaván.   25
Be vigilant of heart and of bright soul.
You are the spine and heart of all our chiefs—
A lion in ferocity and strength.
You freed the captives of Hamavarán,
You seized the region of Mazandarán.[7]   30
The sun itself weeps at your heavy mace.
Your bright blade singes Nahid's[8] *brow.*
No indigo's so dark as Rakhsh's dust.
No elephant's so fierce as you in war.
Your lasso binds the lion on the plain;   35
Your spear uproots the mountain from the earth.
You are the refuge of Irán from every ill.
You are the diadem in all our crowns.
An urgent, fearful threat confronts us now,
The very thought of which has pierced my heart.   40
The heroes of Irán have counseled me,
As we read Gazhdahám's account, and we've

---

6. Capital city of Zabolestán, a province in southeastern Iran of which Rostám's family are the hereditary rulers.   7. Kavús flatters Rostám by alluding to the famous occasions when Rostám single-handedly rescued him and his army from defeat and captivity by the rebellious monarch of Hamavarán and by the demon army of Mazandarán.   8. Venus, both the planet and the goddess.

Concluded thus, in all the world there's none
Save you who triumphs over every foe.
Since that's the case, our noble chieftains saw   45
That worthy Giv should hasten to your court.
When you have read these words, whether it be day
Or night, don't part your lips to speak of it,
Unless to raise the battle cry and lead
Your horsemen galloping from Zabol's gates.   50
As Gazhdahám describes Sohráb, you are
His only equal on the battlefield.
The shah then ordered Giv, "Now you must grasp
Your horse's reins and gallop swift as smoke.
Proceed at once to brave Rostám, but in   55
Zaból don't pause to rest or think of sleep.
If you arrive by night, return at dawn.
Tell him the battle presses at our door."
He took the letter from his hand and rode
Swift as a stream, and neither paused nor slept.   60
As Giv approached Zabolestán, the cries
Of Zal's patrols brought word of this to him.[9]
    Rostám rode out to greet him with his troops,
The leaders dressed in crowns and robes of state.
They all dismounted from their steeds as one,   65
The nobles great and small, and Giv as well.
Rostám approached on foot, and asked him for
His news of both Irán and Shah Kavús.
They left the road to seek the royal court,
And rested there a while, and drew their breath.   70
Giv told him what he'd heard, spoke of Sohráb,
And gave Rostám the letter from the shah.
When he had heard and read these words with care,
He frowned, then laughed aloud in disbelief.
"A noble warrior has now appeared   75
Who is the equal of the hero Sam.
Were he Iranian this might be so.
Among the Turks it cannot be believed.
I have a son by princess Tahminé
Of Semengán, but he is still a child.   80
That much loved infant's not yet learned a man
Must fight to keep his name and honor pure.
I sent a message to his mother once
From here, and many jewels, and gold as well.
She answered me, 'This precious boy is still   85
A child, although he'll soon be tall and strong.
He drinks his wine with lips that smell of milk,
Though doubtless he'll grow fierce and warlike soon.'
Let's stay one day, and so refresh ourselves.
Our lips are dry, let's moisten them with wine.   90
And after that, we'll hasten to the shah,
And lead the heroes of Irán to war.

9. Rostám's father; also called Dastán.

It may be that our shining fortune sleeps.
If so, such matters are not difficult.
For when the ocean rises up in waves,   95
The fiercest flame cannot resist it long.
My banner, when he spies it from afar,
Will turn his victory feast into a wake.
I doubt that he'll be eager then to fight.
This is no threat to trouble hearts like ours."   100
    They called for wine, first toasted Kay Kavús
And then Dastán, then drank the whole day through,
The next day just at dawn, Rostám appeared,
Still dazed with drink, and called again for wine.
They drank away that second day as well,   105
Nor did they give a thought to their return.
And on the third, when they brought wine at dawn,
No thought of Kay Kavús came to their minds.
But on the fourth, the noble Giv prepared
Himself to leave and counseled Táhamtan,   110
"Kavús is quick of temper and not shrewd,
And this affair's a burden on his mind.
It's vexed his soul and sorely pained his heart.
He neither eats nor sleeps nor takes his ease.
Should we delay here longer in Zaból,   115
We'll draw this strife and turmoil to Irán."
Rostám replied, "Be easy in your mind.
There's none who dares to turn his wrath on me."
He had them saddle Rakhsh with greatest speed,
And ordered them to sound the brazen horns.   120
The horsemen of Zaból heard this alarm,
And swiftly left their homes with shields and arms.

Rostám at Court

They galloped to the court of Shah Kavús,
They came with loyal thoughts and open hearts
But when they entered and bowed low to him,
Kavús grew angry and he answered not
A word. At first he shouted once, at Giv,   5
Then washed his eyes quite free of shame.
"Who is Rostám to turn his back to me,
And give so little heed to my command?
Seize him, take him from here, and hang him high!
Then speak no more of brave Rostám to me!"   10
Giv's heart was rent asunder by these words.
"Will you indeed mistreat Rostám like this?"
When he grew angry with Piltán¹ and Giv,
Those gathered in the court were thunderstruck.
The shah commanded Tus as he stood there.   15
"Go now and hang the both of them alive!"
The shah himself then rose up from his throne,

---

1. Rostám; it means "elephant body."

His anger flaring up like flames from reeds,
As Tus approached Rostám and seized his arm
The warriors there could scarce believe their eyes.   20
Did he intend to march him from the court?
Or did his brusqueness mask a shrewd deceit?
   Rostám in turn grew angry with the shah.
"Don't nurse so hot a fire within your breast.
Each thing you do shames that already done.   25
You are unworthy of both throne and rule.
You go and hang the brave Sohráb alive!
You humble this rebellious foe yourself!"
Rostám struck Tus's hand a single blow,
But like that of a raging elephant,   30
And sent that worthy sprawling on the ground.
Rostám passed by him then with rapid strides,
Went out the door and mounted Rakhsh. "I am,"
He said, "the lion-heart who gave this crown.
When I'm enraged, who then is Shah Kavús?   35
Who's there to humble me? Who is this Tus?
The earth's my servant and my throne is Rakhsh;
This mace my signet ring, this helm my crown.
My sword illuminates the darkest night,
And scatters heads upon the battlefield.   40
My comrades are this spear and shining blade;
My heart and these two arms my only shah.
How dare he order me! I'm not his slave.
I serve the World Creator, only Him.
If this Sohráb should now invade Irán,   45
There's none who will be spared, not great or small.
You all must seek some way to save your souls.
You all must bend your wisdom to that task.
You'll see Rostám no more within Irán.
You have the land, I fly on vultures' wings."[2]   50
   The hearts of all the notables were sad.
Their shepherd was Rostám, and they the flock.
They sought Gudárz, "This is a task for you.
What's broken will be mended in your hand.
The *sepahbód*[3] will hear no speech but yours,   55
Nor will our fortune slumber at your words.
Approach this crazed and foolish shah at once,
And speak with him again of what's just passed.
If you speak shrewdly and at length, you may
Regain the smiling fortune we have lost."   60
The army's chief, Gudárz, Keshvád's brave son,
Rode swiftly off to court, and to the shah.
He asked Kavús, "What can Rostám have done
That you would cast Irán into the dust?
When he is gone, an army will attack,   65
Led by that wolflike pahlaván, Sohráb.

---

2. That is, "I will leave here as swiftly as I can and not return."   **3.** Leader of the army; may be applied to chiefs such as Rostám and Tus as well as to Shah Kay Kavús.

Who's there to equal him upon the field?
Who's there to heap dark dust upon his head?
Your warriors, both great and small, are known
To Gazhdahám, he's seen and heard them all.   70
He says, 'I pray the day may never come
That one of us must challenge him.'
Whoever has a champion like Rostám,
And drives him from the court, has little sense."
When Kay Kavús had heard the counsel of   75
Gudárz, he realized he spoke the truth.
He was ashamed of everything he'd said.
His wits had been confused by fear and wrath.
"Your speech is to the point," he told Gudárz.
"Advice sits well upon an old man's lips.   80
A padisháh should be more wise of speech,
For anger and quick words bring no reward.
You must now hasten to the brave Rostám
And speak with him at length and counsel him.
Make him forget this hastiness of mine.   85
Recall to him the thoughts of better times."
    Gudárz rose up and left the royal court,
Then galloped swiftly off toward Rostám.
The army's leaders joined him on the road,
And followed in the tracks of Tahamtán.   90
When they could see the dust that hero raised,
The lords and notables all gathered to
His side. They praised the pahlaván and said,
"Be of bright soul and live forever young.
May all the world be ever at your feet,   95
And may you sit forever on a throne.
You know Kavús, he has no brains at all.
He speaks too hastily, and that's not good.
He'll boil up in a flash, then be ashamed,
And meekly seek to mend his bonds anew.   100
If Tahamtán is angry with the shah,
The people of Irán have done no wrong.
The shah himself regrets his words and bites
The knuckles of his hand in rage and shame."
    Rostám replied to them indignantly,   105
"I have no need of Kay Kavús, not I.
This saddle is my throne, this helm my crown.
Chainmail's my robe; my heart is set on death.
Why should I fear the anger of Kavús?
The shah's no more to me than is this dirt.   110
My head's grown weary, and my heart is full.
Besides Yazdán⁴ the Pure, whom should I fear?"
When they had had their fill of his reply,
Gudárz spoke bluntly with Piltán and said,
"The shah, the nobles, and the army all   115
Will see your actions in another light.

4. One of the names of God.

Our noble lord grew fearful of this Turk,
And so departed secretly from here.
Since Gazhdahám has warned us of Sohráb,
We must abandon all Irán at once.   120
When brave Rostám flees from the battlefield,
It's not for you and me to stay and fight.
I've heard some comment on Kavús's rage
At court, and on his hasty words and deeds,
But all there speak with wonder of Sohráb.   125
Don't turn your back upon our royal shah.
Your name has grown renowned throughout the world,
Don't bring it low by turning now to flight.
What's more, the enemy is at our gate.
Do not endanger more this crown and throne."   130
Gudárz said all of this to Tahamtán,
Who heard him with astonishment and shame.
He said, "If fear afflicts my heart, then I've
No use for it. I'll tear it from my chest."
    He turned aside from shame, took to the road,   135
And galloped swiftly back toward the shah.
And when he strode into the court, Kavús
Stood up and asked forgiveness of Rostám.
"I am by nature rash in speech and act,
And one must be as God created him.   140
This unexpected foe oppressed my heart
Till like the moon, it grew both pale and weak.
To find some remedy I sent for you.
When you were slow to come, I grew enraged.
But when you were distressed, Piltán, I felt   145
Remorse, and shame has filled my mouth with dust."
Rostám replied, "Oh, shah, the world is yours.
We are your subjects. Yours is sovereignty.
I've come to court to be at your command.
May the wisdom of your soul be never less."   150
Kavús replied, "Tomorrow we'll make war.
Today let's choose instead to celebrate."
A place was then prepared, fit for a shah;
The palace was adorned like verdant spring.
And there they drank their wine while pale-   155
Cheeked beauties waited on the shah, and to
The sound of silken strings and plaintive reeds,
The sweet-voiced minstrels filled the night with song.

The Iranians Make War

Next day at dawn he ordered Giv and Tus
To bind the war drums on the elephants.
He opened wide his treasury's doors, gave out
Supplies, and loaded up the baggage train.
A hundred thousand men, all bearing shields   5
And wearing mail, assembled for the march.
Then from the court, an army rode to war

Whose dust rose up and blotted out the sun.
When camped, it spread its tents and canopies
For miles, and carpeted the earth with hooves.   10
The hills were dark as ebony, the air
Like indigo. The river boiled with drumbeats,
And as the troops proceeded stage by stage,
The world turned dark and night obscured the day.
The flash of spears and lances through the dust   15
Were like bright flames seen through a deep blue haze.
There were so many flags and shining spears,
So many golden shields and gilded boots,
It seemed a cloud as dark as ebony
Had formed, and rained down drops of yellow pitch.   20
In all the world there was no day or night;
The heavens and the Pleiades both were gone.
Thus they proceeded to the fortress gates.
The army hid the earth and stones from view.
    The shouts of lookouts on the fortress walls,   25
Informed Sohráb the army had arrived.
And when he heard the lookout's cry, Sohráb
Stood on the fortress walls to view his foe.
He showed Humán this vast and fearsome host,
The margins of whose camp could not be seen.   30
And when Humán looked down upon the foe,
His heart was filled with terror and he groaned.
But so the brave Sohráb encouraged him,
"Relieve your heart of all these fearful thoughts.
In all this endless army you won't see   35
One warrior, one wielder of the heavy mace,
Who dares approach me on the field of war,
Not even with the aid of sun and moon.
Arms there are in rich array, and many proud
And noble men, all quite unknown to me.   40
But now, thanks to the great Afrasiyáb,
I'll fill this plain with rivers of their blood."
Sohráb descended lightly from the wall,
His heart untroubled by the thought of war.
While on that side, before the fortress walls,   45
They pitched the royal tents upon the plain.
So many tents and men were gathered there,
No inch of plain or mountain could be seen.

Rostám in the Turkish Camp

When from the earth the sun withdrew its light,
Dark night arrayed its troops upon the field.
Rostám approached the seat of Kay Kavús,
Prepared for war and eager for revenge.
"Now let my monarch's orders be that I   5
Set out from here with neither sword nor helmet,
To spy upon this youthful conqueror,
See who his marshal is, and who his chiefs."

Kavús replied, "This is a task for you.
But be alert and guard your safety well."   10
Rostám put on a costume like the Turks',
And hastened swiftly to the fortress walls.
As Tahamtán approached their camp he heard
The revels of the Turkish troops within.
Then like a lion stalking wild gazelle,   15
The brave Rostám crept through the fortress gate.
He saw Sohráb, enthroned amid the feast,
At his right hand the noble Zhende Razm,[5]
And at his left so brave a horseman as
Humán, and lionlike Barmán as well.   20
And yet it seemed Sohráb filled up the throne.
His legs and trunk were like a cypress tree's;
His arms were like two camels' thighs,
His chest, an elephant's; his visage flushed
With health. A hundred Turkish youths were ranged   25
Around him there, male lions in their pride.
Some fifty servants waited on this high
And happy throne, their wrists adorned with gold.
Each one invoked God's blessing on his sword,
His lofty stature and his signet ring.   30
While from afar Rostám observed them all—
These Turkish heroes at their victory feast.
    Zhende Razm went out upon some task, and saw
A warrior there, tall as a cypress tree.
Among his troops he knew of none like this.   35
He moved toward Rostám and challenged him.
"Whose man are you?" he asked. "Tell me your name.
Come here, into the light, and show your face!"
Rostám struck Zhende Razm's neck a blow
That freed his spirit from his body's weight.   40
He lay upon the ground, now stilled by death.
Brave Zhende Razm returned no more to feast.
And when some time had passed, and Zhende Razm
Remained still absent from his side, Sohráb
Inquired about his lion-hearted friend,   45
"Where did he go? His place is empty here."
They went outside and saw him lying there,
Released from feasting and from strife and war.
They all returned lamenting in their pain,
Both anxious and perplexed by Zhende's death.   50
They told Sohráb, "Brave Zhende Razm is gone,
His days of feasting and of war are done."
Sohráb leapt up when he had heard the words,
And swift as smoke he flew to where he lay.
With servants, candles, minstrels in his train,   55
He went and looked upon this heavy death.
He was amazed, and stood in silent thought,
Then called his brave and gallant pahlaváns,

---

5. A Turanian hero.

"We must not sleep or rest," he said, "but arm
Ourselves and keep our weapons by our sides.   60
A wolf has crept within the fold tonight,
Despite the shepherd and his watchful dogs.
But if the World Creator gives me aid
When next my golden steed tears up the earth,
I'll loose my lasso from its place, and make   65
Iranians pay the cost of Zhende's death."
Then Sohráb took his seat at court once more,
And calling for his notables, he said,
"Though Zhende Razm's place is empty here,
My soul's not wearied yet of reveling."   70
    When bold Rostám returned to seek the shah,
The guard on watch before their camp was Giv.
He saw a man approach who filled the sky.
He grasped his heavy mace and drew it forth.
Then like a maddened elephant he shouted   75
Once, held up his shield, and challenged him.
Rostám, who knew the guardian of
Irán's security that night was Giv,
Laughed once aloud, and then returned a shout.
When he had heard the voice of Tahamtán,   80
Giv rushed to meet him as he neared the lines.
"Oh, noble chief," he said as he approached,
"Where have you been on foot, and in the dark
Of night?" Rostám prepared himself to speak,
And told Giv where he'd been and what he'd done,   85
And that he'd slain a lion-hearted foe.
From there he went to see the shah, and told
Him of the Turkish army and their camp,
And of Sohráb's stout arms and mighty chest,
His massive stature and his noble bearing.   90
"No man like him's appeared among the Turks
Before; his stature's like a cypress tree's.
He has no equal here, nor in their camp.
He is the image of the horseman Sam."
He told him how he'd struck brave Zhende Razm,   95
Who'd go no more to battle or to feast.
They spoke awhile, then called for wine and harp.
And all that night the army stood on watch.

Sohráb Seeks His Father

At dawn, when the sun had cast its lasso high,
And tongues of flame shot through the highest sphere,
Sohráb put on his chainmail kaftan lined
With silk, and sat upon his silver grey.
He wore a royal helmet on his head,   5
And in his fist he had an Indian blade.
He fixed his rope in sixty loops upon
The saddle bow, and anger creased his brow.
He chose a tower on the wall from which

He might observe the enemy below.   10
He ordered that Hojír be brought to him,
And cautioned him, "Try no deceits with me.
A crooked arrow has but little use.
Unless it's straight no arrow strikes its mark.
In every task you undertake, pursue   15
The truth unless you wish to suffer loss.
Whatever I may ask, speak only truth;
Don't deviate at all from right,
And I'll reward you with great wealth.
I'll give you precious goods and splendid robes.   20
But if instead you choose the crooked way,
You'll spend your life in prison and in chains."
Hojír replied, "However he should question me
About the army of Irán, I'll tell
The shah whatever I may know. Why should   25
I speak dishonestly? You'll see I know
No trade but truth, and never think to lie."
Sohráb then said, "Describe the leaders of
That land to me, its bravest warriors,
Its notables like Tus, Bahrám, Gudárz,   30
Like Shah Kavús and like far-famed Rostám.
Identify each one I ask of you.
I see a seven-hued pavilion there
Enclosing tents of leopard skin; before
It are a hundred tethered elephants,   35
A turquoise throne, as dark as indigo;
A banner blazoned with the sun—its case
Is purple and a golden moon surmounts
The staff. There, in the army's heart, whose place
Is that, which hero of Irán is he?"   40
"That is Kavús the shah," Hojír replied,
"His court holds elephants, and lions, too."
    Sohráb then asked, 'There, on the right,
I see many horsemen, elephants, and gear,
A black pavilion stretching far, with ranks   45
I cannot count of soldiers on all sides.
Around it tents, behind it elephants,
In front are steeds of war. Before them waves
A banner figured with an elephant;
And golden-booted horsemen guard its gate."   50
"That's Tus, the son of Shah Nowzár," he said.
"That hero's emblem is the elephant."
    And then he asked, "That red pavilion, whose
Is that, with horsemen all about, and on
Its banner there, a lion worked in gold,   55
Whose center holds a single, shining jewel?"
"That is Gudárz of Keshvad's camp," he said,
"The glory of Irán's nobility."
    Sohráb then said, "I see a green pavilion,
In front of which an army stands on guard.   60
A splendid throne is set there at its heart;

Before it stands the banner of Kavé[6]
Who's seated there is taller by two hands
Than any noble standing by his side.
Before him there's a horse—a lasso hangs   65
Below its knees—that stands as tall as he.
From time to time he whinnies to his lord,
And stirs beneath his saddle like the sea.
Mailed elephants of war are near to hand,
And he himself sits restless in his place.   70
There's no one in Irán who is so tall
Nor do I see a horse to equal his.
His standard's blazoned with a dragon's form,
And from its tip a golden lion roars."
He answered him, "He is a Chinese lord   75
Who's journeyed from his home to aid the shah."[7]
"What is his name?" he asked the fortunate
Hojír. "I do not know his name," he answered him,
"For I was stationed at this fort when he
First came from China to the royal court."   80
Sohráb despaired at heart. In all that camp,
No trace of Tahamtán had yet appeared.
His mother had described his father's signs.
He'd seen them all, but did not trust his eyes.
He pressed Hojír once more about Rostám,   85
And hoped his words would satisfy his heart,
His fate was written otherwise, alas,
And that command may not be changed by man.
    He asked, "Who are the other nobles there,
Who've pitched their camp far on the army's flank,   90
With horsemen and with elephants drawn up?
I hear the sound of trumpets from their camp.
A banner with the figure of a wolf
Projects its tip above their golden tent."
"That's Giv, Gudárz's son," Hojír replied,   95
"He whom the other heroes call The Bold.
The eldest and the best of all his sons.
They think him twice a noble[8] in Irán."
    Sohráb then asked, "Beneath the morning sun
I see a white pavilion made of Greek   100
Brocade; before it stands a regiment
Of cavaliers more than a thousand strong.
A corps of infantry's assembled there
In endless ranks, all armed with shields and spears.
Their general's seated on an ivory throne,   105
On which they've placed a chair of polished teak.
Brocades of silk hang from his howdah's[9] frame,
And rank on rank of slaves stand by his side.

---

6. The blacksmith who led the Iranians in revolt against the Arab tyrant Zahhak. His banner was his blacksmith's apron fixed to the point of his spear.   7. This is, of course, Rostám.   8. That is, on his father's side Giv is a member of the noble house of Keshvad and through his marriage to Rostám's daughter, Banu Gashasp, he is allied with the nobel line of Rostám.   9. A canopied seat that is cinched on an elephant's back like a saddle.

Above a tent beside this splendid camp,
A banner shows the figure of the moon."   110
"He is the one whom we call Faribórz,
The son of Kay Kavús and heroes' crown."
    Sohráb then asked, "That red pavilion there,
Whose vestibule contains some guards on foot,
Around it banners yellow, red, and blue   115
Are spread upon the wind; behind them is
A lofty staff, tipped with a golden moon,
Whose standard bears the figure of a boar."
"His name," he said, "is Gorazé, who rides
Full tilt when lions are his prey. He's of   120
The clan of Giv, both vigilant and brave,
Undaunted by the pain and strain of war."
    One sought his father's camp. One hid the truth,
And would not speak the words he longed to hear.
What can one do? This world's already made.   125
There is no task that He has left undone.
The writ of fate was otherwise, alas.
What it commands will finish as it must.
    Once more he asked about that notable.
Once more he sought the one he longed to see: 130
That green pavilion and that giant man,
That massive horse, that twisted lariat.
Hojír, who'd led the garrison, replied,
"Why should I hide the truth from you? If I
Withhold this Chinese prince's name from you,   135
It is because it is unknown to me."
"I know this can't be true," Sohráb exclaimed,
"When you have made no mention of Rostám.
The one who's pahlaván of all the world,
Could not be hidden here within this camp.   140
Did you not say he was the army's chief,
The one who keeps your border regions safe?"
Hojír responded to his questions, saying,
"That lion-slaying hero may perhaps
Have left the court to visit in Zabol.   145
It's spring, the time of wine and festival."
"Be still," Sohráb replied. "Don't waste such words
On me. Kavús has marched into the field.
Were he to sit with minstrels now and drink,
Both young and old would laugh Rostám to shame.   150
The pact we've made today's a simple one.
I'll speak it once, and in the fewest words.
If you identify Rostám to me,
You will be honored by your fellow men.
I'll open wide my treasury to you,   155
And give you wealth beyond your every need.
But if you hide this truth from me, and by
Your lying words conceal what is well known,
Your body will not keep its head for long.
Consider well. Which choice seems best to you?   160

A *mobad*[1] once advised his monarch thus,
When he'd revealed a secret of great price,
'A word unspoken's like a gem,' he said,
'But rough, unpolished, trapped within the stone.
Yet once it's freed of fetters and of bonds,   165
It then becomes a shining, priceless jewel.' "
   Hojír replied to him, "The shah, when he's
Grown weary of his crown and throne and seal,
Should seek to battle here that pahlaván
Who puts the elephant in fear of death.   170
Although his head should touch the sky, whoever
Battles with Rostám will taste the earth.
His strength is greater than a hundred men's
His head outtops the tallest tree by far.
When he grows angry on the day of war,   175
No man or lion dares to face his wrath."
   Sohráb replied, "Among the heroes of
Irán, alas, how black Gudárz's fate!
When he's possessed of wisdom, strength, and skill,
Why must he call a wretch like you his son?   180
I doubt you've looked a warrior in the face,
Or ever heard the sound of horses' hooves.
Yet now your speech is only of Rostám,
And every word you speak is lofty praise.
Perhaps, Hojír, you hold the fire in awe   185
Because the river's calm and smiling yet.
But when those emerald waters come to flood,
The hottest flame cannot withstand them long.
And when the sun draws forth its shining sword,
The night lays down its head in dark defeat."   190
   The wise Hojír thought to himself, "Should I
Now show to him the lion-slayer's tent,
This fearsome Turk, who has such mighty arms
And sits so royally upon his mount,
Will choose Rostám to fight from all this host,   195
And spur his massive steed into the field.
And with his strength, his neck and chest, I fear
Rostám will perish in his grip. And then,
In all Irán who's there to seek revenge?
Sohráb will seize the throne of Shah Kavús.   200
The *mobáds* say, "Better to die with honor,
Than to live a life that's pleasing to one's foes.
If he should slay me now, the day will not
Turn black, nor will the rivers run with blood.
The day Gudárz and all his seventy sons,   205
All worthy pahlaváns, should vanish from
Irán, then may I also cease to be.
The *mobáds* say that once the cypress tree
Has been uprooted from the plain, the scent
Of other plants won't keep the pheasants there."   210

1. Zoroastrian cleric; in the *Shâhnâme* usually a wise man or royal counselor.

Hojír replied, "Where does this anger come from?
It's you whose speech is only of Rostám.
Don't fight with him, or on the battlefield
He'll swiftly stretch you in the dust.
You won't defeat Rostám, don't even try.   215
Nor can you hope to capture him with ease."

The Challenge

When he had heard Hojír's reply, Sohráb
First turned his back to him and hid his face,
Then spun around and struck Hojír a blow
That felled him there, and then he sought his tent.
There like the wind, he donned his coat of mail   5
And placed his Chinese casque upon his head.
His rage had made the blood boil in his veins.
He seized his lance, mounted his swift-paced horse,
Then roaring in his fury like a maddened
Elephant, he rushed onto the field.   10
There was no famous hero of Irán
Who even dared to look upon Sohráb—
That sturdy foot and thigh, that hand and rein,
Those mighty arms, that finely polished lance.
The stalwarts of Irán assembled there—   15
"This surely is the pahlaván Rostám,"
They said, "one almost fears to look on him.
Who here will dare to challenge him to fight?"
And then Sohráb the hero roared once more,
And poured his curses on Kavús the Shah.   20
The noble youth, Sohráb, addressed him thus,
"What business do you have upon this field?
Why do you call yourself Kavús the Shah,
When in a fight you've neither strength nor pluck?
I'll spit your body on this lance of mine,   25
And set the stars to weeping with one blow.
The night they slew brave Zhende Razm, I swore
A solemn oath to seek revenge in war.
I'll spare no one in all Irán who bears
A lance, and Shah Kavús I'll crucify.   30
Among Irán's swift-handed pahlaváns,
Do you have one to face me here and fight?"
As Sohráb spoke, his words boiled up with rage,
But from Irán none rose to answer him.
He roared aloud and set upon their camp;   35
A tethered horse he drove off with his lance,
Then bending low, he used its sharpened tip
To pluck some seventy pegs out of the earth.
Kavús's palace tent came crashing down,
And from all sides the buglers blew retreat.   40
The army of Irán fled from Sohráb
Like onagers who flee the lion's claws.
In his distress Kavús cried out,

"Choose one among the well-born notables
And send him to Rostám with news of this.   45
Tell him that fear has struck our heroes dumb.
I've not one horseman who's the equal of
This dreadful Turk, not one to challenge him."
   Tus rushed to tell Rostám the shah's command,
Reciting for him what Kavús had said.   50
Rostám replied, "The other shahs who've called
On me when they'd some pressing need, sometimes
Invited me to battle, sometimes to feast.
Kavús has shown me but the pain of war."
He ordered that they saddle Rakhsh and that   55
His horsemen now set frowns upon their brows.
Then from his tent Rostám looked out and saw
The noble Giv was galloping toward
The battlefield. He put his saddle on
The shining Rakhsh. Gorgín urged him to haste.   60
Rohám made tight the cinch while noble Tus
Was swiftly buckling on the coat of mail.
And each one urged the other to be quick.
Within his tent, Rostám could hear the din.
"This is the work of Ahrimán,"[2] he thought,   65
"This turmoil's not the work of just one man."
He seized his famous tiger-skin cuirass,
And tied the royal belt around his waist,
Then mounted Rakhsh and rode to war. The host
He left his brother, Zavaré, to guard.   70
They bore his banner at his side, and as
He rode along, rage mounted in his heart.
   When he could see Sohráb, his neck and arms,
His chest as broad as that of warlike Sam,
He called to him, "Let's move a little way   75
Apart, and face each other on the field."
Sohráb just rubbed his hands together and
Moved off to wait before the battle lines.
He told Rostám, "I've shown my readiness
For war. It's you who now must choose to fight.   80
Don't look to any in Irán for help.
It is enough when you and I are here.
You don't belong upon the battlefield.
You can't withstand a single blow of mine.
Although you're tall in stature and you have   85
A mighty chest, your wings now droop with age."
Rostám looked on that noble mien, that fist
And neck, that massive leg, and said with warmth,
"Oh, savage youth. Your speech is full of heat.
Alas, the earth is dry and cold. In my   90
Long years I've looked on many battlefields,
And many foes I've stretched upon the ground.
Not few the demons I have slain in war,

2. The god of darkness.

And nowhere have I ever known defeat.
Look on me now. When you have fought with me,   95
And lived, you need not fear the crocodile.
The mountains and the sea know what I've done
To all the bravest heroes of Turán.
The stars bear witness too. In manliness
And bravery the world is at my feet.   100
Sohráb replied, "I have a single question,
But you must answer it with truth. I think
That you must be Rostám, or that you are
The seed of Narimán. Is this not so?"
Rostám replied to him, "I am not he,   105
Nor descended from great Sam or Narimán.
Rostám's a pahlaván, I'm less than he.
I have no throne, no palace, and no crown."
From hope Sohráb was cast into despair.
The day's bright face turned to the darkest night.   110

The First Battle

He rode onto the battlefield, armed with
His lance and wondering at his mother's words.
Upon the field of war they chose a space
In which to meet and fought with shortened lance.
When neither points nor bindings held,   5
They reined their horses in and turned aside,
And then with Indian swords renewed their fight,
Sparks pouring from their iron blades like rain.
With blows they shattered both their polished swords.
Such blows as these will fall on Judgment Day.   10
And then each hero seized his heavy mace.
The battle had now wearied both their arms.
Although their mounts were panting and both heroes
Were in pain, they bent them with their might.
The armor flew from their two steeds; the links   15
That held their coats of mail burst wide apart.
Both mounts stood still; nor could their masters move.
Neither could lift a hand or arm to fight.
Their bodies ran with sweat, dirt filled their mouths,
And heat and thirst had split their tongues. Once more   20
They faced each other on that plain—the son
Exhausted and the father weak with pain.
Oh, world! How strange your workings are! From you
Comes both what's broken and what's whole as well.
Of these two men, not one was stirred by love.   25
Wisdom was far off, the face of love not seen.
From wild horses on the plain to fish within
The sea, all beasts can recognize their young.
It's only man, whose arrogance and pride
Will make his son his deadly enemy.   30
    Rostám said to himself, "I've never seen
A warlike crocodile that fought like this.

My battle with the Div Sepíd[3] seems nothing now.
Today my heart despaired of my own strength.
While these two armies watched us here,   35
A youth who's seen but little of the world,
And who is neither noble nor well known,
Has made me weary of my destiny."
When both their steeds had rested, and they had
Recovered from the pain and shame of war,   40
These mighty warriors, one ancient and
The other still a youth, both strung their bows.
But since each wore a breast plate or cuirass
Of tiger skin, their arrows could not wound.
Although each now despaired before his foe,   45
They closed and seized each other round the waist.
Rostám, who in the heat of battle could wrench
Stones from the flinty earth with his bare hands,
Now grasped Sohráb around the waist,
And sought with all his strength to wrest him from   50
His horse's back. The youth budged not at all.
The hero's mighty grip left him unmoved.
These lion-slayers both grew weary then.
They paused to rest and ease their wounds awhile.
And then once more Sohráb drew out his mace,   55
And pressed his thighs into his horse's flanks.
He struck Rostám upon the shoulder once,
A fearful blow that made him wince with pain.
Sohráb just laughed at him, "Oh, pahlaván!
It seems you cannot bear a warrior's blow.   60
This horse of yours in battle is an ass.
Or is it that his master's hands grow weak?
Although you're tall as any cypress tree,
An ancient who would play the youth's a fool."
        But each was wearied by the other now.   65
The earth seemed strait to them, the end unsure.
They turned their steeds aside and left the field,
Abandoning their hearts and souls to grief.
Great Tahamtán attacked the Turkish host
Like some fierce leopard when he spies his prey.   70
And when that wolf appeared within their ranks,
The army of Turán all turned and fled.
Sohráb had turned his horse toward Irán,
And fell upon their camp in swift assault.
He launched himself into their very midst.   75
And slaughtered many heroes with his mace.
Rostám grew anxious when he learned of this.
He thought that he would surely harm Kavús—
This wondrous Turk who had so suddenly
Appeared with chest and arms adorned for war.   80
He galloped swiftly to his army's camp,
So greatly was Rostám distressed.

---

3. The White Demon of the kingdom of Mazandarán (see n. 7 p. 1494).

Within the army's heart he saw Sohráb,
The earth beneath him ran with blood like wine.
His spear was drenched in gore, his breast and arms   85
Blood red. He seemed a hunter drunk with sport.
Rostám grew sick at heart as he looked on,
And lionlike he roared his rage.
"You cruel bloodthirsty Turk! Which of the men
Assembled here has challenged you to fight?   90
Why did you raise your hand in war to them?
Why slaughter them, a wolf among the flock?"
Sohráb replied, "The army of Turán
Was blameless in this fight as well. You first
Attacked, though none was keen to challenge you."   95
"The day's grown dark," Rostám replied, "but when
Once more the world-illuming sun's bright blade
Appears, there'll be a gibbet and a throne
Set side by side upon this plain of war.
The whole bright world now lies beneath the sword.   100
Although your blade has grown familiar with
The smell of milk, live long and never die.
Let us return at dawn with our keen swords.
Go now; await the World Creator's wish."

The Interval

They left and then the sky turned black. The circling
Sphere looked down and wondered at Sohráb.
It seemed that he'd been formed for war and strife.
He rested not a moment from attack.
The steed he rode was made of steel, his soul   5
A wonder, and his body hardened brass.
Sohráb came to his camp as night approached,
His body scoured with wounds. He asked Humán,
"Today the rising sun filled all the world
With weapons and the sounds of war. Tell me,   10
What damage did he wreak upon our host,
That horseman with a hero's neck and lion's charge?"
Humán replied, "The shah's command to me
Was that the army should not stir from here.
We were quite unprepared. We had not looked   15
To fight at all today. When suddenly
A fierce and warlike man approached our camp,
And turned to face this broad-ranged company,
It seemed he'd just returned from drinking or
From battling singlehanded with some foe."   20
Sohráb replied, "And yet he did not slay
A single man from all this numerous host,
While I slew many heroes from Irán,
And made that campground muddy with their blood.
But now it's time to spread the board and feast.   25
Come, let's ease our hearts with ruby wine."
While on the other side, Rostám reviewed

His troops and spoke a while with Giv. "How did
The battle-tried Sohráb fare here today?
Did he attack the camp? How did he fight?"   30
Heroic Giv replied to Tahamtán,
"I've never seen a hero quite like him.
He galloped to the army's very heart.
And there within that host made straight for Tus,
For he was armed and mounted, lance in hand.   35
And while Gorgín dismounted, he sat firm.
He came and when he saw him with his lance,
He galloped toward him like a raging lion.
He bent his heavy mace upon his chest.
Its force unloosed his helmet from his head.   40
Tus saw that he must fail, and turned and fled.
Then many other warriors challenged him,
But none among those heroes had his strength.
Only Piltán's the equal of this youth.
And yet we still held fast our ancient rule,   45
And stood the army in a single rank.
No horseman went to fight with him alone.
While he paraded on the field of war."
Rostám was grieved at this report. He turned
His face toward the camp of Shah Kavús.   50
    When Kay Kavús saw him approach his tent,
He sat the pahlaván close by his throne.
Rostám described Sohráb to him, and spoke
At length of his great stature and his strength.
"None in this world has ever seen a child   55
Half grown who is so brave, so lionlike.
His head brushes against the stars above,
The earth below bends at his body's weight.
His arms and thighs are like a camel's limbs,
And yet to me they seemed more massive still.   60
We fought at length with heavy mace and sword,
With bow and arrow, and with lasso too.
No feint or weapon did we leave untried.
And finally I said, 'Before this time
I've lifted many heroes from their seats,'   65
And seized him round the waist and grasped his belt.
I thought to pluck him from his horse's back
And hurl him like the others to the ground.
The hurricane that shakes a granite peak
Would not disturb that worthy in his seat.   70
Tomorrow when he rides into the field,
My only hope's to fight him hand to hand.
And though I'll strive, I don't know who will win.
Nor do I know what choice Yazdán will make.
Strength, victory, and fame all come from Him   75
Who has created both the sun and moon."
Kavús replied, "Then may the Pure Lord split
In two the hearts of all who wish you ill!
Tonight before the Maker of the World

I'll press my brow and cheeks against the earth.   80
For strength and greatness come from Him alone.
By His command the moon sends down its light.
Once more may He renew your hopes, and raise
Your name aloft in triumph to the sun."
Rostám then said, "By the glory of the shah,   85
May the hopes of those who wish him well be heard."
    Then Tahamtán returned to camp, his soul
Distressed, his mind prepared for war.
His brother, Zavaré approached him with
An anxious heart. "How did you fare today?"   90
Rostám first called for food, and ate his fill,
Then purged his heart of all his grief and fear.
He spoke to Zavaré, advising him,
"Be vigilant of heart, do nothing rash.
Tomorrow, just at dawn, when I must meet   95
That warlike Turk in battle once again,
You bring the army and my standard to
The field, my throne and golden boots as well.
Be standing at the door of my pavilion
When first the shining sun begins to rise.   100
If in this fight I gain the victory,
I will not linger on the battlefield.
But should the matter turn out otherwise,
Don't weep for me, and do not seek revenge.
Neither enter the field to fight alone,   105
Nor yet prepare yourself for general war.
Return together to Zabolestán,
Once you are there, seek out my father, Zal.
Then you must try to ease my mother's heart.
This fate, alas, Yazdán decreed for me.   110
Tell her she should not mourn for me too long,
For she will do herself no good by that.
No one has lived for all eternity.
I've no complaint against the circling sphere.
In battle have I strangled many demons,   115
And lions, crocodiles, and leopards too.
I've leveled forts and towers to the ground,
And there's no man who's ever vanquished me.
The man who mounts a horse and gallops to
The battlefield is knocking on death's door.   120
If you should live a thousand years, or more,
At last, the end of all will be the same.
When she's content, then tell Dastán, 'Don't turn
Your back upon the monarch of the world.
Should he make war, don't slacken your support,   125
Obey his word in everything he asks.
We all are mortal, young and old alike.
There's none who lives for all eternity.' "
For half that night their words were of Sohráb.
The other half they spent in restful sleep.   130
    And on that side Sohráb with all his friends

Had passed the night with wine and minstrelsy.
Thus to Humán he said, "This lion who
Engages me so fiercely on the field,
Is not one whit less tall than I, and when   135
Engaged in single combat has no fear.
His shoulders, chest, and neck are so like mine,
It seems some craftsman marked them with a rule.
My heart is drawn to him. What's more, I see
In him the signs my mother told me of.   140
I think that he must be Rostám, for in
This world few pahlaváns can equal him.
I must not in confusion rush to meet
My father here in combat face to face."
Humán replied, "I've met Rostám in war,   145
And seen him battle many times. I've heard
How that brave hero used his heavy mace
When he was fighting in Mazandarán.
This horse of his is very like Rostám's,
But he has not the hoof or rump of Rakhsh."   150

The Second Day

The shining sun spread wide its radiance,
The raven tucked its head beneath its wings,
Rostám put on his tiger-skin cuirass,
And sat astride his huge, fierce elephant.
To his seat he bound his rope in sixty coils,   5
And in his hand he grasped an Indian sword.
He galloped to the field, the place where they
Would fight, and there put on his iron helmet.
All bitterness is born of precedence,
Alas when it is yoked to greedy pride!   10
     Sohráb stood up and armed himself. His head
Was filled with war, his heart with revelry.
Shouting his cry he rode into the field,
Within his hand, he held his bullhide mace.
He greeted him, a smile upon his lips,   15
As though they'd spent the night in company.
"How did you sleep? How do you feel today?
And how have you prepared yourself to fight?
Let's put aside this mace and sword of war.
Cast strife and wrong down to the ground.   20
Let us dismount and sit together now,
And smooth our brows with wine. And let us make
A pact before the World Preserving Lord,
That we'll repent of all our warlike plans.
Until another comes who's keen to fight,   25
Make peace with me and let us celebrate.
My heart is ever moved by love for you,
And wets my face with tears of modesty.
I'm sure you're from a noble line, come then,
Recite for me the line of your descent.   30

Aren't you the son of brave Dastán, the son
Of Sam? Aren't you the pahlaván Rostám?"
Rostám replied, "Oh, shrewd ambitious youth,
Before this hour we never spoke like this.
Last night our words were of the coming fray.   35
Your tricks won't work with me; don't try again.
Though you are but a youth, I am no child,
And I'm prepared to fight you hand to hand.
So let's begin our strife. Its end will be
As the Keeper of the World commands it should.   40
I've traveled long through hills and valleys too.
And I'm no man for guile, deceits, and lies."
Sohráb replied, "Such words do not befit
A warrior who's so advanced in years.
I wished that you might die upon your bed,   45
And that your soul would leave in its own time;
That those you leave behind could keep your bones,
Immure your flesh, but let your spirit fly.[4]
But if your life is in my grasp, then as
Yazdán commands, let us lock hands and fight."   50
    They both dismounted from their battle steeds.
In casque and tunic they approached with care,
And to a stone they tied their steeds of war.
Then they advanced, their hearts as cold as earth.
Each seized the other and they grappled till   55
Their bodies ran with sweat and blood. Sohráb
Was like a maddened elephant; he struck
Rostám a blow that felled him to the earth.
Then like a lion in the hunt whose claws
Have thrown a mighty stallion to the ground,   60
Sohráb sat firmly on the chest of huge
Rostám, fist, face, and mouth all smeared with dirt,
And from his belt he drew his polished blade.
As he bent down to sever head from trunk,
Rostám looked up and said, "Oh, lion-slayer,   65
And master of the sword and mace and rope!
The custom of our nation is not thus.
Our faith commands us to another way.
Whoever in a wrestling match first throws
His noble adversary to the ground,   70
And pins him to the earth, may not cut off
His head, not even if he seeks revenge.
But if he fells him twice, he's earned that right,
And all will call him Lion if he does."
By that deceit he shrewdly sought to free   75
Himself from this fierce dragon's mortal grip.
    The brave youth bowed his head and yielded to
The old man's words, accepting what he'd said.
He loosed his grip and rushed off to the plain,

---

4. A reference to the Zoroastrian practice of leaving the dead exposed in walled enclosures until their skeletons have been picked clean by vultures. The bones are then collected and placed in an ossuary. In this way neither earth, air, fire, nor water is defiled by the dead.

A lion who has seen a deer race by.   80
He hunted eagerly and gave no thought
To him with whom he'd fought so recently.
When it grew late, Humán came swiftly to
The field and asked him how the fight had gone.
Sohráb informed Humán of what he'd done,   85
And what Rostám had said to him. The brave
Humán just heaved a sigh and said, "Dear youth,
I see that you've grown weary of your life.
I fear for this stout neck and arms and chest,
This hero's waist and royal legs and feet.   90
You caught a tiger firm within your trap,
Then spoiled your work by letting him escape.
You'll see what consequence this foolish act
Of yours will have when next you meet to fight."
He spoke, despairing of his life. He sat   95
There for a while, still wondering at his deed.
    Then he returned toward his army's camp,
Perplexed at heart and vexed by what he'd done.
A shah once spoke a proverb on this point.
He said, "Despise no foe, however mean."   100
Rostám, when he'd escaped from his foe's hand,
Sprang up just like a blade of steel, and rushed
Off to a flowing stream that was nearby,
For he was like a man who'd been reborn.
He drank his fill, and washed his face and limbs.   105
Then he bowed low before his Lord in prayer.
He asked for strength and victory; he did
Not know what sun and moon might hold in store,
Or if the heavens as they wheeled above
Would wish to snatch the crown from off his head.   110
    Then pale of face and with an anxious heart,
He left the stream to meet his foe once more.
While like a maddened elephant, Sohráb
With bow and lasso galloped on the plain.
He wheeled and shouted as he chased his prey;   115
His golden steed leaped high and tore the earth.
Rostám could not but stand in awe of him;
He sought to take his measure for the fight.
And when the lion-slayer saw him there,
The arrogance of youth boiled up in him.   120
"Hail him who fled the lion's claws in fear,
And kept himself apart from his fierce blows."

The Death of Sohráb

Again they firmly hitched their steeds, as ill-
Intentioned fate revolved above their heads.
Once more they grappled hand to hand. Each seized
The other's belt and sought to throw him down.
Whenever evil fortune shows its wrath,   5
It makes a block of granite soft as wax.

Sohráb had mighty arms, and yet it seemed
The skies above had bound them fast. He paused
In fear; Rostám stretched out his hands and seized
That warlike leopard by his chest and arms.　　　　　10
He bent that strong and youthful back, and with
A lion's speed, he threw him to the ground.
Sohráb had not the strength; his time had come.
Rostám knew he would not stay down for long.
He swiftly drew a dagger from his belt　　　　　15
And tore the breast of that stout-hearted youth.
He writhed upon the ground; groaned once aloud,
Then thought no more of good and ill. He told
Rostám, "This was the fate allotted me.
The heavens gave my key into your hand.　　　　　20
It's not your fault. It was this hunchback fate,
Who raised me up then quickly cast me down.
While boys my age still spent their time in games,
My neck and shoulders stretched up to the clouds.
My mother told me who my father was.　　　　　25
My love for him has ended in my death.
Whenever you should thirst for someone's blood,
And stain your silver dagger with his gore,
Then Fate may thirst for yours as well, and make
Each hair upon your trunk a sharpened blade.　　　　　30
Now should you, fishlike, plunge into the sea,
Or cloak yourself in darkness like the night,
Or like a star take refuge in the sky,
And sever from the earth your shining light,
Still when he learns that earth's my pillow now,　　　　　35
My father will avenge my death on you.
A hero from among this noble band
Will take this seal and show it to Rostám.
'Sohráb's been slain, and humbled to the earth,'
He'll say, 'This happened while he searched for you.' "　　　　　40
　　When he heard this, Rostám was near to fainting.
The world around grew dark before his eyes.
And when Rostám regained his wits once more,
He asked Sohráb with sighs of grief and pain,
"What sign have you from him—Rostám? Oh, may　　　　　45
His name be lost to proud and noble men!"
"If you're Rostám," he said, "you slew me while
Some evil humor had confused your mind.
I tried in every way to draw you forth,
But not an atom of your love was stirred.　　　　　50
When first they beat the war drums at my door,
My mother came to me with bloody cheeks.[5]
Her soul was racked by grief to see me go.
She bound a seal upon my arm, and said,
'This is your father's gift, preserve it well.　　　　　55
A day will come when it will be of use.'

5. In Persian poetry intense grief is indicated by bloody tears.

Alas, its day has come when mine has passed.
The son's cast down before his father's eyes.
My mother with great wisdom thought to send
With me a worthy pahlaván as guide.   60
The noble warrior's name was Zhende Razm,
A man both wise in action and in speech.
He was to point my father out to me,
And ask for him among all groups of men.
But Zhende Razm, that worthy man, was slain.   65
And at his death my star declined as well.
Now loosen the binding of my coat of mail,
And look upon my naked, shining flesh."
When he unloosed his armor's ties and saw
That seal, he tore his clothes and wept.   70
"Oh, brave and noble youth, and praised among
All men, whom I have slain with my own hand!"
He wept a bloody stream and tore his hair;
His brow was dark with dust, tears filled his eyes.
Sohráb then said, "But this is even worse.   75
You must not fill your eyes with tears. For now
It does no good to slay yourself with grief.
What's happened here is what was meant to be."
    When the radiant sun had left the sky,
And Tahamtán had not returned to camp,   80
Some twenty cavaliers rode off to see
How matters stood upon the field of war.
They saw two horses standing on the plain,
Both caked with dirt. Rostám was somewhere else.
Because they did not see his massive form   85
Upon the battlefield and mounted on
His Rakhsh, the heroes thought that he'd been slain.
The nobles all grew fearful and perplexed.
They sent a message swiftly to the shah,
"The throne of majesty has lost Rostám."   90
From end to end the army cried aloud,
And suddenly confusion filled the air.
Kavús commanded that the horns and drums
Be sounded, and his marshal, Tus, approached.
Kavús told him, "Be quick, and send a scout   95
From here to view the battlefield
And see how matters stand with bold Sohráb.
Must we lament the passing of Irán?
If by his hand the brave Rostám's been slain,
Who from Irán will dare approach this foe?   100
We now must strike a wide and general blow;
We dare not tarry long upon this field."
    And while a tumult rose within their camp,
Sohráb was speaking thus with Tahamtán,
"The situation of the Turks has changed   105
In every way, now that my days are done.
Be kind to them, and do not let the shah
Pursue this war or urge his army on.

It was for me the Turkish troops rose up,
And mounted this campaign against Irán.   110
It was I who promised victory, and I
Who strove in every way to give them hope.
They should not suffer now as they retreat.
Be generous with them, and let them go."
    Rostám then mounted Rakhsh, as swift as dust.   115
His eyes bled tears, his lips were chilled with sighs.
He wept as he approached the army's camp,
His heart was filled with pain at what he'd done.
When they first spied his face, the army of Irán
Fell prostrate to the earth in gratitude,   120
And loudly praised the Maker of the World,
That he'd returned alive and well from war.
But when they saw him with his chest and clothes
All torn, his body heavy and his face
Begrimed by dust, they asked him all at once,   125
"What does this mean? Why are you sad at heart?"
He told them of his strange and baffling deed,
Of how he'd slain the one he held most dear.
They all began to weep and mourn with him,
And filled the earth and sky with cries of grief.   130
At last he told the nobles gathered there,
"It seems my heart is gone, my body too.
Do not pursue this battle with the Turks.
The evil I have done is quite enough."
And when he left that place, the pahlaván   135
Returned with weary heart to where he lay.
The noble lords accompanied their chief,
Men like Gudárz and Tus and Gostahám.
The army all together loosed their tongues,
And gave advice and counsel to Rostám,   140
"Yazdán alone can remedy this wound;
He yet may ease this burden's weight for you."
He grasped a dagger in his hand, and made
To cut his worthless head from his own neck.
The nobles hung upon his arm and hand, and tears   145
Of blood poured from the lashes of their eyes.
Gudárz said to Rostám, "What gain is there
If by your death you set the world in flames?[6]
Were you to give yourself a hundred wounds,
How would that ease the pain of brave Sohráb?   150
If some time yet remains for him on earth,
He'll live, and you'll remain with him, at peace.
But if this youth is destined to depart,
Look on the world, who's there that does not die?
The head that wears a helmet and the head   155
That wears a crown, to death we all are prey."

---

6. That is, warfare and chaos would result from Rostám's death, because there would be no one to defend the shah.

Rostám Asks Kay Kavús for the Nushdarú[7]

Rostám called wise Gudárz and said to him,
"Depart from here upon your swiftest horse,
And take a message to Kavús the shah.
Tell him what has befallen me. With my
Own dagger I have torn the breast of my   5
Brave son—oh, may Rostám not live for long!
If you've some recollection of my deeds,
Then share with me a portion of my grief,
And from your store send me the *nushdarú,*
That medicine that heals whatever wound.   10
It would be well if you sent it to me
With no delay, and in a cup of wine.
By your good grace, my son may yet be cured,
And like his father stand before your throne."
The *sepahbód* Gudárz rode like the wind,   15
And gave Kavús the message from Rostám.
    Kavús replied, "If such an elephant
Should stay alive and join our royal court,
He'll make his father yet more powerful.
Rostám will slay me then, I have no doubt.   20
When I may suffer evil at his hands,
What gift but evil should I make him now?
You heard him, how he said, 'Who is Kavús?
If he's the shah, then who is Tus?' And with
That chest and neck, that mighty arm and fist,   25
In this wide world, who's there to equal him?
Will he stand humbly by my royal seat,
Or march beneath my banner's eagle wings?"
    Gudárz heard his reply, then turned and rode
Back to Rostám as swift as wind-borne smoke.   30
"The evil nature of the shah is like
The tree of war, perpetually in fruit.
You must depart at once and go to him.
Perhaps you can enlighten his dark soul."

Rostám Mourns Sohráb

Rostám commanded that a servant bring
A robe and spread it by the river's bank.
He gently laid Sohráb upon the robe,
Then mounted Rakhsh and rode toward the shah.
But as he rode, his face toward the court,   5
They overtook him swiftly with sad news,
"Sohráb has passed from this wide world; he'll need
A coffin from you now, and not a crown.
'Father!' he cried, then sighed an icy wind,
Then wept aloud and closed his eyes at last."   10
    Rostám dismounted from his steed at once.

7. A panacea that only the shah can give.

Dark dust replaced the helmet on his head.
He wept and cried aloud, "Oh, noble youth,
And proud, courageous seed of pahlaváns!
The sun and moon won't see your like again,   15
No more will shield or mail, nor throne or crown.
Who else has been afflicted as I've been?
That I should slay a youth in my old age
Who is the grandson of world-conquering Sam,
Whose mother's seed's from famous men as well.   20
It would be right to sever these two hands.
No seat be mine henceforth save darkest earth.
What father's ever done a deed like this?
Cold words and scorn are what I now deserve.
Who else in all this world has slain his son,   25
His wise, courageous, youthful son?
How Zal the golden will rebuke me now,
He and the virtuous Rudabé as well.
What can I offer them as my excuse?
What plea of mine will satisfy their hearts?   30
What will the heroes and the warriors say
When word of this is carried to their ears?
And when his mother learns, what shall I say?
How can I send a messenger to her?
What can I say? Why did I slay him when   35
He'd done no wrong? Why blacken all his days?
How will her father, that worthy pahlaván,
Report this to his pure and youthful child?
He'll call this seed of Sam a godless wretch,
And heap his curses on my ancient head.   40
Alas, who could have known this precious child
Would quickly grow to cypress height, or that
He'd raise this host and think of arms and war,
Or that he'd turn my shining day to night."
     Rostám commanded that the body of   45
His son be covered with a royal robe.
He'd longed to sit upon the throne and rule;
His portion was a coffin's narrow walls.
The coffin of Sohráb was carried from
The field. Rostám returned to his own tent.   50
They set aflame Sohráb's pavilion while
His army cast dark dust upon their heads.
They threw his tents of many colored silk,
His precious throne and leopard saddle cloth
Into the flames, and tumult filled the air.   55
     He cried aloud, "Oh, youthful conqueror!
Alas, that stature and that noble face!
Alas, that wisdom and that manliness!
Alas, what sorrow and heart-rending loss—
No mother near, heart pierced by father's blade!"   60
His eyes wept bloody tears, he tore the earth,
And rent the kingly garments on his back.
     Then all the pahlaváns and Shah Kavús

Sat with him in the dust beside the road.
They spoke to him with counsel and advice—   65
In grief Rostám was like one driven mad—
"This is the way of fortune's wheel. It holds
A lasso in this hand, a crown in that.
As one sits happily upon his throne,
A loop of rope will snatch him from his place.   70
Why is it we should hold the world so dear?
We and our fellows must depart this road.
The longer we have thought about our wealth,
The sooner we must face that earthy door.
If heaven's wheel knows anything of this,   75
Or if its mind is empty of our fate,
The turning of the wheel it cannot know,
Nor can it understand the reason why.
One must lament that he should leave this world,
Yet what this means at last, I do not know."   80
    Then Kay Kavús spoke to Rostám at length,
"From Mount Alborz down to the frailest reed,
The turning heavens carry all away.
You must not fix your heart upon this world.
One sets off quickly on the road, and one   85
Will take more time, but all pass on to death.
Content your heart with his departure, and
Give careful heed to what I tell you now.
If you should bring the heavens down to earth,
Or set the world aflame from end to end,   90
You won't recall from death the one who's gone.
His soul's grown ancient in that other mansion.
Once from afar I saw his arms and neck,
His lofty stature and his massive chest.
The times impelled him and his martial host   95
To come here now and perish by your hand.
What can you do? What remedy is there
For death? How long can you bewail his loss?"
    Rostám replied, "Though he himself is gone,
Humán still sits upon this ample plain,   100
His Turkish and his Chinese chiefs as well.
Retain no hint of enmity toward them,
But strengthened by Yazdán and your command,
Let Zavaré guide all their army home."
    "Oh, famous pahlaván," said Shah Kavús,   105
"This war has caused you suffering and loss.
Though they have done me many grievous wrongs,
And though Turán has set Irán aflame,
Because my heart can feel your heavy pain,
I'll think no more of them and let them go."   110

Rostám Conveys His Son to Zabolestán

Kavús, whose radiance outshone the sun,
Commanded that his brother stay as guide.

Then Zavaré approached the royal throng,
The clothes upon his body torn to shreds.
He sent a message to Humán which said,   5
The sword of vengeance stays within its sheath.
You are commander of this army now,
Observe their conduct well, and do not sleep.
The shah departed from the field and led
His army to Irán, Rostám remained   10
To wait until brave Zavaré returned,
And brought him news of how that army fared.
When Zavaré returned at break of day,
With him was Giv, Gudárz the swordsman's son.
Rostám then led his troops toward Zaból.   15
     When news of their arrival reached Dastán,
All in Sistán went forth to meet Rostám;
They came to him prostrate with pain and grief.
When first he looked upon that wooden bier,
Dastán dismounted from his golden seat.   20
Rostám came forward then, on foot, his clothes
Were torn to shreds, his heart was pierced by grief.
The heroes one and all let fall their arms,
And bowed down to the earth before his bier.
Zal spoke, "This was a strange event indeed.   25
Sohráb could lift the heavy mace; of this
The greatest in the land would speak with awe.
No mother in the world will bear his like."
And Zal spoke on; his eyes were filled with tears,
His tongue with words of praise for bold Sohráb.   30
     When Tahamtán had reached his palace gate,
He cried aloud and set the coffin down.
He wrenched the nails out, threw the lid aside,
And drew the shroud off as his father watched.
He showed his body to those noble men.   35
It was as if the heavens burned with grief.
Those famous heroes tore their clothes and wept;
Like dust their cries ascended to the clouds.
From end to end the palace seemed a tomb,
In which a lion had been laid to rest.   40
It seemed as though great Sam were lying there.
The battle had wearied him, and now he slept.
He covered him again with gold brocade,
And firmly closed the coffin's narrow lid.
"If now I build Sohráb a golden tomb   45
And strew it round with fragrant sable musk,
When I am gone, it won't remain for long.
If that's not so, yet so it seems to me."
With horses' hooves they built a warrior's tomb,
And all the world went blind with weeping there.   50
     Thus spoke Bahrám the wise and eloquent,
"Don't bind yourself too closely to the dead,
For you yourself will not remain here long.
Prepare yourself to leave, and don't be slow.

One day your sire gave you a turn at life.   55
The turn is now your son's, that's only right.
That's how it is, the reason why's unknown.
The door is locked; nor will the key be found.
You won't discover it, why even try?
And if you do, you'll spend your life in vain."[8]   60
It is a tale that's filled with tears and grief.
The tender heart will rage against Rostám.

8. These conventional sentiments seem woefully irrelevant here when a father has killed his son.

FARIDODDIN ATTAR
1145–1221

Sheikh Faridoddin Attar was born in Nishapur in northeastern Iran near present-day Meshed. We know very little about his life, but that is true for most medieval writers. His name, Attar, tells us that he was a pharmacist, a profession that was like that of a physician in his time, and he refers in his poetry to attending to many patients in his shop. He seems to have lived a relatively quiet life and was not especially well known as a poet to his contemporaries. He is generally believed to have died in 1221, almost certainly a victim of the Mongol army that leveled Nishapur and slaughtered its entire population in that year.

Attar's fame has grown with the passing years, and he is widely known and respected now as a poet, a sufi (mystic), a theorist of mysticism, and a biographer of sufi saints. He produced a number of mystical narratives, the most famous of which is the *Manteq al-Tayr* (The Conference of the Birds). Other poets, most notably Sana'i (died ca. 1135), had composed versified collections of sufi tales before him. In these earlier works, such as Sana'i's *The Garden of Truth,* the tales and parables are united only by such formal features as rhyme, meter, and recurrent themes. Attar's poem was a new departure in that it offered a comprehensive narrative in which the other narratives are embedded. The story is that of pilgrims, the birds of the title, who come together to seek their king, the Simorgh, a remote and awesome figure whom they know only by name. Attar's choice of birds to be the characters of his poem reflects a long tradition in the Middle East of using animals and birds in works with a strong ethical and didactic purpose, such as Aesop's fables (known in Islam as the fables of Luqman). His choice of birds in particular reinforces the spiritual purpose of his work. The bird is a common metaphor for the soul—and was so understood by Attar and his audience. The remote and unknown king they seek can only be God. They elect the hoopoe as their guide, because the hoopoe was Solomon's messenger and so is more experienced in these matters than they. The hoopoe's task is to strengthen their resolve and prepare them for their coming journey.

In the first and more substantial portion of the poem the metaphor of a dialogue between master and disciples most accurately reflects what takes place than that of a journey. The first problem the hoopoe must address is that of the birds' reluctance to begin the journey toward God. Each bird embodies one of the many attachments to the world that holds him back, and each in turn justifies his resistance in a brief statement. To this the hoopoe responds first with an argument that shows the falseness of the birds' reasoning and then with a story that makes the same point by example. The owl—who is known in Islam as a bird of ill omen and a haunter of ruins—says, for example, that he prefers solitude and the presence of the treasure that lies beneath ruins to this search for a king, and concludes,

"Love for the Simorgh is a childish story;
My love is solely for gold's buried glory."

The hoopoe chastises him for his short sightedness,

"Besotted fool,
Suppose you get this gold for which you drool,
What could you do but guard it night and day
While life itself—unnoticed—slips away?"

He then recounts the story of a miser who dies and is reborn as a mouse that scurries around his burrow, frantic with his worry about his gold.

"Learn from my state;
Whoever worships gold, this is his fate—
To haunt the hidden cache for evermore."

Attar does not develop the personalities of individual birds in these exchanges. His focus is on the tales and their teachings. The birds are simply embodiments of qualities that keep us from undertaking a spiritual journey.

At last the birds decide to commit themselves to the quest and ask the hoopoe what their first step should be. They must abandon their egos (here called the Self) he says, transcend the claims of the body, and give up all attachments—even to faith. He warns them that their way will pass through pain, poverty, and humiliation, and they must be ready to confront these challenges with unquestioning submission. He then tells the story of Sheikh Sam'an as a powerful illustration of the depths to which this submission may take them.

The story of Sheikh Sam'an (or San'an, both forms of the name are used) is by far the longest of the hundred or so tales and parables in the collection, and its message is the most complex. Sheikh Sam'an (sheikh is an honorific title meaning "wise" or "learned") is the most pious of Muslims. He has passed the whole of his life in Mecca, the most sacred spot in Islam, and has performed the pilgrimage virtually every year of his life. He is a master of Islamic law and theology, and has gathered about him a vast army of disciples (four hundred, the proverbial forty times ten). He continually breathes the air of asceticism and piety and would seem to be secure against any temptation. Then he has a dream in which he sees his world turned upside down. Rome—really Constantinople, the capital of the Eastern Roman empire and the Byzantine Church—has replaced Mecca; he has become a Christian, dwells in a church, and worships idols. The vision terrifies him, yet he reads it as a sign from God that he must journey to Byzantium to meet his fate. Once there he sees a young Christian woman whose beauty is more radiant than the sun's, and he falls completely in love with her. So intense is his passion that it consumes him utterly and overwhelms his faith. At first he senses his loss and laments the darkness into which he has been cast. His disciples, who have accompanied him, see this and try to persuade him to repent. But love for the Christian girl has now transformed him so completely that what he valued before he now despises, and he is unmoved by their efforts. The Christian girl at first does not notice him. When she does she is more inclined to mock him than to take his passion seriously. At last she agrees to return his love if he will do four things that will separate him from his faith and seal him in her own: burn the Koran, drink wine, close his eyes to the true faith (Islam), and worship idols. To these she later adds the indignity of tending swine. These are all shocking acts. To Muslims the Koran is more than revelation, it is the uncreated word of God, and apostasy is a mortal sin (see the headnote "The Koran," pp. 1426–28). Worshiping idols and drinking wine are both expressly forbidden in the Koran: one of Muhammad's first acts on entering Mecca as its conqueror was to destroy the pagan idols that filled the Ka'ba, and the Koran discourages wine drinking as leading to impiety. The sheikh at first is reluctant, but eventually he yields to all her demands. His disciples, unable either to dissuade him or to bear the sight of his disgrace, return to Mecca. There a close friend of the sheikh sees them, hears their story, and upbraids them for abandoning their guide and teacher. At his insistence they return to Rome (Constantinople) to pray for the sheikh's deliverance. An agent of God appears to their leader in a dream and grants their prayer. The sheikh's fall from faith passes as though it were a dream, and he sets out with his disciples for Mecca. At that moment the Christian maid suddenly realizes the error of her ways, repents her sins against Sheikh Sam'an and sets out across the desert to join him. He is guided back to her just as she is on the point of death. He instructs her in the elements of Islam, and she dies in ecstasy.

The story assumes a strong and continuing sense of rivalry between Muslims and Christians, but it is unlikely that Attar had any direct knowledge of either Christians or Christianity. The Christian communities nearest to him were a thousand miles away, in Georgia and Armenia, and there is no evidence that he ever visited them. His characterization of Christianity is sketchy and sensational. It seems to be limited to those Christian practices that are most offensive and shocking to Muslims, as they would also be to Jews. Like virtually all Muslims, Attar does not understand the symbolism of the Eucharist and so assumes that Christians drink wine as part of their holy services. Similarly, the crucifix and other images that fill a church are idols to him. And the eating of pork, the most unclean of animals, is repugnant. Finally, that Christians allow women to go about unveiled is shocking to him. Attar uses conversion to Christianity to represent the worst possible fate that might befall a pious Muslim and so gives vivid life to his admonition to the pilgrims of the pain and danger they face, but he also gives them hope. The sheikh's unwilled passage through apostasy and defilement ends happily and strengthens him and his disciples in their faith. The seductive Christian is also converted and dies a believer in the true faith.

Once the birds have been persuaded to make the journey, they must confront the qualities within themselves that will impede their progress—cowardice, sinfulness, indecision, pride, miserliness, love of ostentation, earthly passion, fear of death, fear of misfortune, and so on. Again, the poem advances by means of an extended dialogue between the hoopoe and the other birds that frames both arguments and stories. These stories are drawn from many sources. To show the difficulty of knowing oneself, for example, Attar includes an account of the death of Socrates, about which he probably read in one of the many translations from Greek philosophy into Arabic. A pupil of the great philosopher asks him where they should bury his corpse once "we've washed the man we knew." Socrates replies,

> "If you can find me when I've died,
> Then bury me wherever you decide—
> I never found myself; I cannot see
> How when I'm dead you could discover me.
> Throughout my life not one small particle
> Had any knowledge of itself at all."

The hoopoe provides the birds with further instruction on the perils of the journey, liberally illustrating his lessons with anecdotes and tales. Then they begin their journey, and Attar describes the seven stages they traverse—Quest, Love, Insight and Mystery, Detachment, Unity, Bewilderment, and Poverty and Nothingness—vividly but succinctly. The journey exacts a fearful toll, and only thirty birds of the original company survive to reach the Simorgh's court. When they are admitted, they find not a presence, but a mirror in which they see themselves. The final revelation is that they have become the God they seek. Through the extraordinary labors of the journey they have stripped away all the worldly elements in their being, revealing the divine within. The use of a pun underscores this, the name they give to their king, *Simorgh*, can also mean "thirty" (si) "birds" (morgh). This device seems quaint to us now, but it underscores the essence of sufi belief, that divinity is found within, and the most demanding journey we can undertake is an inward one.

Islamic mysticism, or sufism, provides the themes that shape both the larger metaphors of the Conference and the many stories within it. Sufism, like the mysticism of other religious traditions, yearns for direct experience of God. Sufis often describe this experience as a vision or a dream in which the divinity addresses them directly, though usually by means of some mediating guise—an angel, a wise figure, a bright light, a voice from the clouds. The sufi, like other mystics, may also experience oneness with the divinity as a moment in which he or she transcends time and place to glimpse all eternity in a single continuum. The English mystic poet Henry Vaughan (1622–1695) describes this moment of divine consciousness in this way:

> I saw eternity the other night,
> Like a pale ring of endless light,
> All calm as it was bright.

Two sufi themes underlie the larger shape of the Conference: the first is the pain the soul feels when absent from God, usually referred to in poetry as "the Friend." The pain is intense—the newly converted Christian girl dies of it—and accounts for the soul's desire to undertake the perilous journey toward the divine. The second is that progress toward God consists principally of stripping away worldly distractions of body and ego to reach the essential divinity that lies within all of us. In eternity all souls are united in God, but God requires individual souls to separate from this immortal community, take on a cloak of flesh, and make a passage through the world. The soul remembers its origins, however, and longs to return to God. This journey through mortality to immortality is the subject of the greatest of mystical narratives: Jalâloddin Rumi's Spiritual Couplets.

Attar's poem is composed in rhyming couplets very like English heroic couplets. The translation printed here by Afkham Darbandi and Dick Davis captures the wit and charm of the original with dazzling fidelity. No English translation of Persian gives a better sense of what that poetry is like.

There are no book-length studies and few journal articles on Attar and his works in English. A thoughtful discussion of the frame narrative can be found in Dick Davis, "The Journey as Paradigm: Literal and Metaphorical Travel in Attar's Mantiq al-Tayr," in Edebiyat n.s. 4 (1993). See also Jerome W. Clinton, "The Downward Path to Wisdom: Gender and Archetype in the Story of Sheikh Sam'an," in A Pearl in Wine, ed. Z. Khan (2001). There is an abundance of useful information in articles about Attar by Benedikt Reinert in Encyclopedia Iranica (1982) and by Helmut Ritter in Encyclopedia of Islam (1950+). Beyond that there are the standard histories of Persian or Iranian literature: E. G. Browne, A Literary History of Persia, vol. 2 (1906); A. J. Arberry, Classical Persian Literature (1958); Jan Rypka et al., History of Iranian Literature (1968); and Ehsan Yarshater et al., Persian Literature (1989).

PRONOUNCING GLOSSARY

The following list uses common English syllables and stress accents to provide rough equivalents of selected words whose pronunciation may be unfamiliar to the general reader.

Faridoddin Attar: fu-reed'-ud-deen' ah-tar'

Luqman: luk-mahn'

Manteq al-Tayr: man-tek' ot–tayr'

Nishapur: nee-sha-poor'

Sana'i: sa-naw-ee'

Simorgh: see-morg'

From The Conference of the Birds[1]

Love thrives on inextinguishable pain,
Which tears the soul, then knits the threads again.
A mote of love exceeds all bounds; it gives
The vital essence to whatever lives.
But where love thrives, there pain is always found;   5
Angels alone escape this weary round—
They love without that savage agony
Which is reserved for vexed humanity.
Islam and blasphemy have both been passed
By those who set out on love's path at last;   10
Love will direct you to Dame Poverty,
And she will show the way to Blasphemy.
When neither Blasphemy nor Faith remain,
The body and the Self have both been slain;
Then the fierce fortitude the Way will ask   15
Is yours, and you are worthy of our task.
Begin the journey without fear; be calm;
Forget what is and what is not Islam;
Put childish dread aside—like heroes meet
The hundred problems which you must defeat.   20

The Story of Sheikh Sam'an

Sam'an was once the first man of his time.
Whatever praise can be expressed in rhyme
Belonged to him: for fifty years this sheikh
Kept Mecca's holy place, and for his sake
Four hundred pupils entered learning's way.   5
He mortified his body night and day,
Knew theory, practice, mysteries of great age,
And fifty times had made the Pilgrimage.[2]
He fasted, prayed, observed all sacred laws—
Astonished saints and clerics thronged his doors.   10
He split religious hairs in argument;
His breath revived the sick and impotent.
He knew the people's hearts in joy and grief
And was their living symbol of Belief.
Though conscious of his credit in their sight,   15
A strange dream troubled him, night after night;
Mecca was left behind; he lived in Rome,[3]
The temple where he worshipped was his home,
And to an idol he bowed down his head.
"Alas!" he cried, when he awoke in dread,   20
"Like Joseph I am in a well of need
And have no notion when I shall be freed.

---

1. Translated by Afkham Darbandi and Dick Davis. 2. To Mecca; one of the five fundamental obligations of Islam. To make the pilgrimage even once is remarkable. 3. Constantinople, the capital of the
Eastern Roman empire.

But every man meets problems on the Way,
And I shall conquer if I watch and pray.
If I can shift this rock my path is clear;   25
If not, then I must wait and suffer here."
Then suddenly he burst out: "It would seem
That Rome could show the meaning of this dream;
There I must go!" And off the old man strode;
Four hundred followed him along the road.   30
They left the Ka'ba[4] for Rome's boundaries,
A gentle landscape of low hills and trees,
Where, infinitely lovelier than the view,
There sat a girl, a Christian girl who knew
The secrets of her faith's theology.   35
A fairer child no man could hope to see—
In beauty's mansion she was like a sun
That never set—indeed the spoils she won
Were headed by the sun himself, whose face
Was pale with jealousy and sour disgrace.   40
The man about whose heart her ringlets curled
Became a Christian and renounced the world;
The man who saw her lips and knew defeat
Embraced the earth before her bonny feet;
And as the breeze passed through her musky hair   45
The men of Rome watched wondering in despair.
Her eyes spoke promises to those in love,
Their fine brows arched coquettishly above—
Those brows sent glancing messages that seemed
To offer everything her lovers dreamed.   50
The pupils of her eyes grew wide and smiled,
And countless souls were glad to be beguiled;
The face beneath her curls glowed like soft fire;
Her honeyed lips provoked the world's desire;
But those who thought to feast there found her eyes   55
Held pointed daggers to protect the prize,
And since she kept her counsel no one knew—
Despite the claims of some—what she would do.
Her mouth was tiny as a needle's eye,
Her breath as quickening as Jesus' sigh;   60
Her chin was dimpled with a silver well
In which a thousand drowning Josephs fell;
A glistering jewel secured her hair in place,
Which like a veil obscured her lovely face.
The Christian turned, the dark veil was removed,   65
A fire flashed through the old man's joints—he loved!
One hair converted hundreds; how could he
Resist that idol's face shown openly?
He did not know himself; in sudden fire
He knelt abjectly as the flames beat higher;   70
In that sad instant all he had been fled

4. A gray stone building at the center of the great mosque in Mecca that is circumambulated by every pilgrim seven times.

And passion's smoke obscured his heart and head.
Love sacked his heart; the girl's bewitching hair
Twined round his faith impiety's smooth snare.
The sheikh exchanged religion's wealth for shame,   75
A hopeless heart submitted to love's fame.
"I have no faith," he cried. "The heart I gave
Is useless now; I am the Christian's slave."
When his disciples saw him weeping there.
And understood the truth of the affair,   80
They stared, confounded by his frantic grief,
And strove to call him back to his belief.
Their remonstrations fell on deafened ears;
Advice has no effect when no one hears.
In turn the sheikh's disciples had their say;   85
Love has no cure, and he could not obey.
(When did a lover listen to advice?
When did a nostrum cool love's flames to ice?)
Till evening came he could not move but gazed
With stupefaction in his face, amazed.   90

When gloomy twilight spread its darkening shrouds—
Like blasphemy concealed by guilty clouds—
His ardent heart gave out the only light,
And love increased a hundredfold that night.
He put aside the Self and selfish lust;   95
In grief he smeared his locks with filth and dust
And kept his haunted vigil, watched and wept,
Lay trembling in love's grip and never slept.
"O Lord, when will this darkness end?" he cried,
"Or is it that the heavenly sun has died?   100
Those nights I passed in faith's austerities
Cannot compare with this night's agonies;
But like a candle now my flame burns high
To weep all night and in the daylight die.
Ambush and blood have been my lot this night;   105
Who knows what torments day will bring to light?
This fevered darkness and my wretched state
Were made when I was made, and are my fate;
The night continues and the hours delay—
Perhaps the world has reached its Judgement Day;   110
Perhaps the sun's extinguished with my sighs,
Or hides in shame from my belovèd's eyes.
This long, dark night is like her flowing hair—
The thought in absence comforts my despair,
But love consumes me through this endless night—   115
I yield to love, unequal to the fight.
Where is there time enough to tell my grief?
Where is the patience to regain belief?
Where is the luck to waken me, or move
Love's idol to reciprocate my love?   120
Where is the reason that could rescue me,
Or by some trick prove my auxiliary?

Where is the hand to pour dust on my head,
Or lift me from the dust where I lie dead?
Where is the foot that seeks the longed-for place? 125
Where is the eye to show me her fair face?
Where is the loved one to relieve my pain?
Where is the guide to help me turn again?
Where is the strength to utter my complaint?
Where is the mind to counsel calm restraint? 130
The loved one, reason, patience—all are gone
And I remain to suffer love alone."

At this the fond disciples gathered round,
Bewildered by his groans' pathetic sound.
"My sheikh," urged one, "forget this evil sight; 135
Rise, cleanse yourself according to our rite."
"In blood I cleanse myself," the sheikh replied;
"In blood, a hundred times, my life is dyed."
Another asked: "Where is your rosary?"
He said: "I fling the beads away from me; 140
The Christian's belt[5] is my sole sanctuary!"
One urged him to repent; he said: "I do,
Of all I was, all that belonged thereto."
One counselled prayer; he said, "Where is her face
That I may pray toward that blessèd place?"
Another cried: "Enough of this; you must
Seek solitude and in repentant dust 145
Bow down to God." "I will," replied the sheikh,
"Bow down in dust, but for my idol's sake."
And one reproached him: "Have you no regret
For Islam and those rites you would forget?"
He said: "No man repents past folly more; 150
Why is it I was not in love before?"
Another said: "A demon's poisoned dart—
Unknown to you—has pierced your trusting heart."
The sheikh said: "If a demon straight from hell
Deceives me, I rejoice and wish her well." 155
One said: "Our noble sheikh has lost his way;
Passion has led his wandering wits astray."
"True, I have lost the fame I once held dear,"
Replied their sheikh, "and fraud as well, and fear."
One said: "You break our hearts with this disgrace." 160
He laughed: "The Christian's heart will take their place."
One said: "Stay with old friends awhile, and come—
We'll seek the Ka'ba's shade and journey home."
The sheikh replied: "A Christian monastery
And not the Ka'ba's shade suffices me." 165
One said: "Return to Mecca and repent!"
He answered: "Leave me here, I am content."
One said: "You travel on hell's road." "This sigh

---

5. The *zonnar*, a belt or cord worn by Eastern Christians and Jews; thus a symbol of heresy [Translators' note].

Would shrivel seven hells" was his reply.
One said: "In hope of heaven turn again."   170
He said: "Her face is heaven; I remain."
One said: "Before our God confess your shame."
He answered: "God Himself has lit this flame."
One said: "Stop vacillating now and fight;
Defend the ways our faith proclaims as right."   175
He said: "Prepare your ears for blasphemy;
An infidel does not prate piety."
Their words could not recall him to belief,
And slowly they grew silent, sunk in grief.
They watched; each felt the heart within him fail,   180
Fearful of deeds Fate hid beneath her veil.

At last white day displayed her golden shield;
Black night declined his head, compelled to yield—
The world lay drowned in sparkling light, and dawn
Disclosed the sheikh, still wretched and forlorn,   185
Disputing with stray dogs the place before
His unattainable belovèd's door.
There in the dust he knelt, till constant prayers
Made him resemble one of her dark hairs;
A patient month he waited day and night   190
To glimpse the radiance of her beauty's light.
At last fatigue and sorrow made him ill—
Her street became his bed and he lay still.
When she perceived he would—and could—not move,
She understood the fury of his love,   195
But she pretended ignorance and said:
"What is it, sheikh? Why is our street your bed? ⎫
How can a Muslim sleep where Christians tread?" ⎭
He answered her: "I have no need to speak;
You know why I am wasted, pale and weak.   200
Restore the heart you stole, or let me see
Some glimmer in your heart of sympathy;
In all your pride find some affection for
The grey-haired, lovesick stranger at your door.
Accept my love or kill me now—your breath   205
Revives me or consigns me here to death.
Your face and curls command my life; beware
Of how the breeze displays your vagrant hair;
The sight breeds fever in me, and your deep
Hypnotic eyes induce love's restless sleep.   210
Love mists my eyes, love burns my heart—alone,⎫
Impatient and unloved, I weep and groan;   ⎬
See what a sack of sorrow I have sewn!   ⎭
I give my soul and all the world to burn,
And endless tears are all I hope to earn.   215
My eyes beheld your face, my heart despaired;
What I have seen and suffered none have shared.
My heart has turned to blood; how long must I
Subsist on misery? You need not try
To humble wretchedness, or kick the foe   220

Who in the dust submissively bows low.
It is my fortune to lament and wait—
When, if, love answers me depends on Fate.
My soul is ambushed here, and in your street
Relives each night the anguish of defeat;   225
Your threshold's dust receives my prayers—I give
As cheap as dust the soul by which I live.
How long outside your door must I complain?
Relent a moment and relieve my pain.
You are the sun and I a shadow thrown   230
By you—how then can I survive alone?
Though pain has worn me to a shadow's edge,
Like sunlight I shall leap your window's ledge;
Let me come in and I shall secretly
Bring seven heavens' happiness with me.   235
My soul is burnt to ash; my passion's fire
Destroys the world with unappeased desire.
Love binds my feet and I cannot depart;
Love holds the hand pressed hard against my heart.
My fainting soul dissolves in deathly sighs—   240
How long must you stay hidden from my eyes?"

She laughed: "You shameless fool, take my advice—
Prepare yourself for death and paradise!
Forget flirtatious games, your breath is cold;
Stop chasing love, remember you are old.   245
It is a shroud you need, not me! How could
You hope for wealth when you must beg for food?"
He answered her: "Say what you will, but I
In love's unhappy torments live and die;
To Love, both young and old are one—his dart   250
Strikes with unequalled strength in every heart."
The girl replied: "There are four things you must
Perform to show that you deserve my trust:
Burn the Koran, drink wine, seel up Faith's eye,
Bow down to images." And in reply   255
The sheikh declared: "Wine I will drink with you;
The rest are things that I could never do."
She said: "If you agree to my commands,
To start with, you must wholly wash your hands
Of Islam's faith—the love which does not care   260
To bend to love's requests is empty air."
He yielded then: "I must and will obey;
I'll do whatever you are pleased to say.
Your slave submits—lead me with ringlets twined
As chains about my neck; I am resigned!"   265
She smiled: "Come then and drink," and he allowed
Her to escort him to a hall (the crowd
Of scholars followed, weeping and afraid)
Where Christians banqueted, and there a maid
Of matchless beauty passed the cup around.   270
Love humbled our poor sheikh—without a sound

He gave his heart into the Christians' hands;
His mind had fled, he bowed to her commands,
And from those hands he took the proffered bowl;
He drank, oblivion overwhelmed his soul.   275
Wine mingled with his love—her laughter seemed
To challenge him to take the bliss he dreamed.
Passion flared up in him; again he drank
And slave-like at her feet contented sank—
This sheikh who had the whole Koran by heart   280
Felt wine spread through him and his faith depart;
Whatever he had known deserted him,
Wine conquered and his intellect grew dim;
Wine sluiced away his conscience; she alone
Lived in his heart, all other thoughts had flown.   285
Now love grew violent as an angry sea,
He watched her drink and moved instinctively—
Half-fuddled with the wine—to touch her neck.
But she drew back and held his hand in check,
Deriding him: "What do you want, old man?   290
Old hypocrite of love, who talks but can
Do nothing else? To prove your love, declare
That your religion is my rippling hair.
Love's more than childish games, if you agree—
For love—to imitate my blasphemy   295
You can embrace me here; if not, you may
Take up your stick and hobble on your way."
The abject sheikh had sunk to such a state
That he could not resist his wretched fate;
Now ignorant of shame and unafraid,   300
He heard the Christian's wishes and obeyed—
The old wine sidled through the old man's veins
And like a twisting compass turned his brains;
Old wine, young love, a lover far too old,
Her soft arms welcoming—could he be cold?   305
Beside himself with love and drink he cried:
"Command me now; whatever you decide
I will perform. I spurned idolatry
When sober, but your beauty is to me
An idol for whose sake I'll gladly burn   310
My faith's Koran." "Now you begin to learn,
Now you are mine, dear sheikh," she said. "Sleep well,
Sweet dreams; our ripening fruit begins to swell."

News spread among the Christians that this sheikh
Had chosen their religion for love's sake.   315
They took him to a nearby monastery,
Where he accepted their theology;
He burnt his dervish cloak and set his face
Against the faith and Mecca's holy place—
After so many years of true belief,   320
A young girl brought this learnèd sheikh to grief.
He said: "This dervish has been well betrayed;
The agent was mere passion for a maid.

I must obey her now—what I have done
Is worse than any crime beneath the sun."   325
(How many leave the faith through wine! It is
The mother of such evil vagaries.)
"Whatever you required is done," he said.
"What more remains? I have bowed down my head
In love's idolatry, I have drunk wine;   330
May no one pass through wretchedness like mine!
Love ruins one like me, and black disgrace
Now stares a once-loved dervish in the face.
For fifty years I walked an open road
While in my heart high seas of worship flowed;   335
Love ambushed me and at its sudden stroke
For Christian garments I gave up my cloak;
The Ka'ba has become love's secret sign,
And homeless love interprets the Divine.
Consider what, for your sake, I have done—   340
Then tell me, when shall we two be as one?
Hope for that moment justifies my pain;
Have all my troubles been endured in vain?"
The girl replied: "But you are poor, and I
Cannot be cheaply won—the price is high;   345
Bring gold, and silver too, you innocent—
Then I might pity your predicament;
But you have neither, therefore go—and take
A beggar's alms from me; be off, old sheikh!
Be on your travels like the sun—alone;   350
Be manly now and patient, do not groan!"
"A fine interpretation of your vow,"
The sheikh replied; "my love, look at me now—
I have no one but you; your cypress gait,
Your silver form, decide my wretched fate.   355
Take back your cruel commands; each moment you
Confuse me by demanding something new.
I have endured your absence, promptly done
All you have asked—what profit have I won?
I've passed beyond loss, profit, Islam, crime,   360
For how much longer must I bide my time?
Is this what we agreed? My friends have gone,
Despising me, and I am here alone.
They follow one way, you another—I
Stand witless here uncertain where to fly;   365
I know without you heaven would be hell,
Hell heaven with you; more I cannot tell."
At last his protestations moved her heart.
"You are too poor to play the bridegroom's part,"
She said, "but be my swineherd for a year   370
And then we'll stay together, never fear."
The sheikh did not refuse—a fractious way
Estranges love; he hurried to obey.
This reverend sheikh kept swine—but who does not
Keep something swinish in his nature's plot?   375

Do not imagine only he could fall;
This hidden danger lurks within us all,
Rearing its bestial head when we begin
To tread salvation's path—if you think sin
Has no place in your nature, you can stay   380
Content at home; you are excused the Way.
But if you start our journey you will find
That countless swine and idols tease the mind—
Destroy these hindrances to love or you
Must suffer that disgrace the sad sheikh knew.   385

Despair unmanned his friends; they saw his plight
And turned in helpless horror from the sight—
The dust of grief anointed each bowed head;
But one approached the hapless man and said:
"We leave for Mecca now, O weak-willed sheikh;   390
Is there some message you would have us take?
Or should we all turn Christians and embrace
This faith men call a blasphemous disgrace?
We get no pleasure from the thought of you
Left here alone—shall we be Christians too?   395
Or since we cannot bear your state should we,
Deserting you, incontinently flee;
Forget that you exist and live in prayer
Beside the Ka'ba's stone without a care?"
The sheikh replied: "What grief has filled my heart!   400
Go where you please—but quickly, now, depart;
Only the Christian keeps my soul alive,
And I shall stay with her while I survive
Though you are wise your wisdom cannot know
The wild frustrations through which lovers go.   405
If for one moment you could share my pain,
We could be old companions once again.
But now go back, dear friends; if anyone
Asks after me explain what I have done—
Say that my eyes swim blood, that parched I wait   410
Trapped in the gullet of a monstrous fate.
Say Islam's elder has outsinned the whole
Of heathen blasphemy, that self-control
Slipped from him when he saw the Christian's hair,
That faith was conquered by insane despair.   415
Should anyone reproach my actions, say
That countless others have pursued this Way,
This endless Way where no one is secure,
Where danger waits and issues are unsure."
He turned from them; a swineherd sought his swine.   420
His friends wept vehemently—their sheikh's decline
Seemed death to them. Sadly they journeyed home,
Resigning their apostate sheikh to Rome.

They skulked in corners, shameful and afraid.
A close companion of the sheikh had stayed   425
In Mecca while the group had journeyed west—

A man of wisdom, fit for any test,
Who, seeing now the vacant oratory
Where once his friend had worshipped faithfully,
Asked after their lost sheikh. In tears then they   430
Described what had occurred along the way;
How he had bound his fortunes to her hair,
And blocked the path of faith with love's despair;
How curls usurped belief and how his cloak
Had been consumed in passion's blackening smoke;   435
How he'd become a swineherd, how the four
Acts contrary to all Islamic law
Had been performed by him, how this great sheikh
Lived like a pagan for his lover's sake.
Amazement seized the friend—his face grew pale,   440
He wept and felt the heart within him fail.
"O criminals!" he cried. "O frailer than
Weak women in your faith—when does a man
Need faithful friends but in adversity?
You should be there, not prattling here to me.   445
Is this devoted love? Shame on you all,
Fair-weather friends who run when great men fall.
He put on Christian garments—so should you;
He took their faith—what else had you to do?
This was no friendship, to forsake your friend,   450
To promise your support and at the end
Abandon him—this was sheer treachery.
Friend follows friend to hell and blasphemy—
When sorrows come a man's true friends are found;
In times of joy ten thousand gather round.   455
Our sheikh is savaged by some shark—you race
To separate yourselves from his disgrace.
Love's built on readiness to share love's shame;
Such self-regarding love usurps love's name."
"Repeatedly we told him all you say,"   460
They cried. "We were companions of the Way,
Sworn to a common happiness or grief;
We should exchange the honours of belief
For odium and scorn; we should accept
The Christian cult our sheikh could not reject.   465
But he insisted that we leave—our love
Seemed pointless then; he ordered us to move.
At his express command we journeyed here
To tell his story plainly, without fear."

He answered them: "However hard the fight,   470
You should have fought for what was clearly right.
Truth struggled there with error; when you went
You only worsened his predicament.
You have abandoned him; how could you dare
To enter Mecca's uncorrupted air?"   475
They heard his speech; not one would raise his head.
And then, "There is no point in shame," he said.
"What's done is done; we must act justly now,

Bury this sin, seek out the sheikh and bow
Before him once again." They left their home   480
And made their way a second time to Rome;
They prayed a hundred thousand prayers—at times
With hope, at times disheartened by their crimes.
They neither ate nor slept but kept their gaze
Unswerving throughout forty nights and days.   485
Their wailing lamentations filled the sky,
Moving the green-robed angels ranked on high
To clothe themselves with black, and in the end
The leader of the group, the sheikh's true friend,
His heart consumed by sympathetic grief,   490
Let loose the well-aimed arrows of belief.
For forty nights he had prayed privately,
Rapt in devotion's holy ecstasy—
At dawn there came a musk-diffusing breeze,
And in his heart he knew all mysteries.   495
He saw the Prophet, lovely as the moon,
Whose face, Truth's shadow, was the sun at noon,
Whose hair in two black heavy braids was curled—
Each hair, a hundred times, outpriced the world.
As he approached with his unruffled pace,   500
A smile of haunting beauty lit his face.
The sheikh's friend rose and said: "God's Messenger,
Vouchsafe your help. Our sheikh has wandered far;
You are our Guide; guide him to Truth again."
The Prophet answered: "I have loosed the chain   505
Which bound your sheikh—your prayer is answered, go.
Thick clouds of dust have been allowed to blow
Between his sight and Truth—those clouds have gone;
I did not leave him to endure alone.
I sprinkled on the fortunes of your sheikh   510
A cleansing dew for intercession's sake—
The dust is laid; sin disappeared before   ⎱
His new-made vow. A world of sin, be sure,   ⎰
Shall with contrition's spittle be made pure.⎱
The sea of righteousness drowns in its waves   515
The sins of those sincere repentance saves."

With grateful happiness the friend cried out;
The heavens echoed his triumphant shout.
He told the good news to the group; again
They set out eagerly across the plain.   520
Weeping they ran to where the swineherd-sheikh,
Now cured of his unnatural mistake,
Had cast aside his Christian clothes, the bell,
The belt, the cap, freed from the strange faith's spell.
Seeing his friends approach his hiding-place,   525
He saw how he had forfeited God's grace;
He ripped his clothes in frenzies of distress;
He grovelled in the dust with wretchedness.
Tears flowed like rain; he longed for death; his sighs'
Great heat consumed the curtain of the skies;   530

Grief dried the blood within him when he saw
How he had lost all knowledge of God's law;
All he had once abandoned now returned
And he escaped the hell in which he'd burned.
He came back to himself, and on his knees   535
Wept bitterly for past iniquities.
When his disciples saw him weeping there,
Bathed in shame's sweat, they reeled between despair
And joy—bewildered they drew near and sighed;
From gratitude they gladly would have died.   540
They said: "The mist has fled that hid your sun;
Faith has returned and blasphemy is gone;
Truth has defeated Rome's idolatry;
Grace has surged onward like a mighty sea.
The Prophet interceded for your soul;   545
The world sends up its thanks from pole to pole.
Why should you mourn? You should thank God instead
That out of darkness you've been safely led;
God who can turn the day to darkest night
Can turn black sin to pure repentant light—   550
He kindles a repentant spark, the flame
Burns all our sins and all sin's burning shame."

I will be brief: the sheikh was purified
According to the faith; his old self died—
He put the dervish cloak on as before.   555
The group set out for Mecca's gates once more.

And then the Christian girl whom he had loved
Dreamed in her sleep; a shaft of sunlight moved
Before her eyes, and from the dazzling ray
A voice said: "Rise, follow your lost sheikh's way;   560
Accept his faith, beneath his feet be dust;
You tricked him once, be pure to him and just,
And, as he took your path without pretence,
Take his path now in truth and innocence.
Follow his lead; you once led him astray—   565
Be his companion as he points the Way;
You were a robber preying on the road
Where you should seek to share the traveller's load.
Wake now, emerge from superstition's night."
She woke, and in her heart a steady light   570
Beat like the sun, and an unwonted pain
Throbbed there, a longing she could not restrain;
Desire flared up in her; she felt her soul
Slip gently from the intellect's control.
As yet she did not know what seed was sown—   575
She had no friend and found herself alone
In an uncharted world; no tongue can tell
What then she saw—her pride and triumph fell
Like rain from her; with an unearthly shout
She tore the garments from her back, ran out   580
And heaped the dust of mourning on her head.

Her frame was weak, the heart within her bled,
But she began the journey to her sheikh,
And like a cloud that seems about to break
And shed its downpour of torrential rain   585
(The heart's rich blood) she ran across the plain.
But soon the desert's endless vacancy
Bewildered her; wild with uncertainty,
She wept and pressed her face against the sand.
"O God," she cried, "extend your saving hand   590
To one who is an outcast of the earth,
To one who tricked a saint of unmatched worth—
Do not abandon me; my evil crime
Was perpetrated in a thoughtless time;
I did not know what I know now—accept   595
The prayers of one who ignorantly slept."

The sheikh's heart spoke: "The Christian is no more;
The girl you loved knocks at religion's door—
It is our way she follows now; go back
And be the comforter her sorrows lack."   600
Like wind he ran, and his disciples cried:
"Has your repentant vow so quickly died?
Will you slip back, a shameless reprobate?"
But when the sheikh explained the girl's sad state,
Compassion moved their hearts and they agreed   605
To search for her and serve her every need.
They found her with hair draggled in the dirt,
Prone on the earth as if a corpse, her skirt
Torn from her limbs, barefoot, her face death-pale.
She saw the sheikh and felt her last strength fail;   610
She fainted at his feet, and and as she slept
The sheikh hung over her dear face and wept.

She woke, and seeing tears like rain in spring
Knew he'd kept faith with her through everything.
She knelt before him, took his hands and said   615
"The shame I brought on your respected head
Burns me with shame; how long must I remain
Behind this veil of ignorance? Make plain
The mysteries of Islam to me here,
And I shall tread its highway without fear."   620
The sheikh spelt out the faith to her; the crowd
Of gratified disciples cried aloud,
Weeping to see the lovely child embrace
The search for Truth. Then, as her comely face
Bent to his words, her heart began to feel   625
An inexpressible and troubling zeal;
Slowly she felt the pall of grief descend,
Knowing herself still absent from the Friend.
"Dear sheikh," she said, "I cannot bear such pain;
Absence undoes me and my spirits wane.   630
I go from this unhappy world; farewell

World's sheikh and mine—further I cannot tell,
Exhaustion weakens me; O sheikh, forgive . . ."
And saying this the dear child ceased to live.
The sun was hidden by a mist—her flesh   635
Yielded the sweet soul from its weakening mesh.
She was a drop returned to Truth's great sea;
She left this world, and so, like wind, must we.

Whoever knows love's path is soon aware
That stories such as this are far from rare.   640
All things are possible, and you may meet
Despair, forgiveness, certainty, deceit.
The Self ignores the secrets of the Way,
The mysteries no mortal speech can say;
Assurance whispers in the heart's dark core,   645
Not in the muddied Self—a bitter war
Must rage between these two. Turn now and mourn
That your existence is so deeply torn!

The birds set off on their journey, pause, then choose a leader

They heard the tale; the birds were all on fire   650
To quit the hindrance of the Self; desire
To gain the Simorgh had convulsed each heart.

JALÂLODDIN RUMI
1207–1283

To understand Jalâloddin Rumi and his works, one first needs some understanding of the mystical dimension—sufism—of Islamic religious belief. In place of the conventional modes of worship—prayer, public worship, alms, fasting, and pilgrimage to the holy cities of Mecca and Medina—sufism emphasizes withdrawal from the world into progressively deeper levels of meditation. It has as its goal direct union or communion with the ultimate reality of God. Sufis believe that the world we perceive through our senses is a very seductive illusion that distracts us from the true and eternal reality that lies beyond it. We cannot grasp that transcendent reality directly, but only through metaphor. Reason is a poor guide through the mystical realm, and sufis rely instead on nonrational means of knowing like intuition and the trance states induced by rhythmic movement or the chanting of verses from the Koran and other sacred phrases.

Sufis commonly use the metaphor of the journey to describe their movement toward divinity (as did Attar), but their journeying is all within themselves. For sufis, God lies within all of us, and the journey toward God begins with a stripping away of our worldly self. The purpose of sufi practices, including sufi poetry, is to strengthen and guide us in our progress on that journey. To lessen their attachment to the world, some sufis, known as dervishes, practice a radical asceticism, owning nothing and traveling from city to city as mendicant preachers. They abandon all social conventions along with other worldly concerns and express themselves with a fierce and uncompromising directness. A dervish's authority comes from his indifference to worldly rank and station, and this makes him the natural opponent of kings and princes whose authority rests on their mastery of the world. Many sufi tales, including Sa'di's, play on this opposition.

Although orthodox Muslim teachers rejected the earliest sufis as heretics and saw sufism as hostile to orthodox worship, by the eleventh century they accepted it not as an alternative to conventional forms of worship but as a complement to them. Sufi orders formed around exemplary guides and spread throughout the Islamic world, achieving great influence in many countries and at different times. Many of these orders continue to flourish today, and since early in this century, offshoots of the most prominent of these orders have taken root in Europe and the United States as well.

Jalâloddin Rumi is without question the greatest mystical poet in Persian and possibly the greatest in the Islamic tradition. In the more than seven centuries since his death, Rumi's poetry has exerted a profound influence on the spiritual life of Muslims living in the Arab world, Turkey, Iran, central Asia, and India and has also gained a wide readership in Europe and America. Rumi also founded a mystical brotherhood, the Mevlevi Order, that was influential in Turkey for many years and has survived to the present day.

Rumi was born in September 1207 in the city of Balkh in northern Afghanistan. His father, a learned theologian known as Bahâ-ye Walad, taught there and in Samarqand, until his disputes with the ruler of the region and with other theologians led him to emigrate to western Anatolia—present-day Turkey. The incursions of the Mongols almost surely contributed to his decision to move so far to the west. The family eventually settled in Konya, where they remained after the death of Bahâ-ye Walad in 1231. After his father's death, Rumi continued his education both in Islamic law, jurisprudence, and traditions as well as in Islamic mysticism, or sufism. Although he received most of his education in Konya at the hands of former students of his father, he also lived and studied in Damascus and Aleppo for several years. On the completion of his studies he became, like his father before him, a teacher in the Muslim religious college in Konya.

At this point Rumi seemed destined to follow closely in his father's footsteps as a scholar and teacher. What transformed him into a great mystical poet and sustained him in that role throughout the remainder of his life was a series of three spiritual friendships. The first and most formative of these was with Shams-e Tabrizi, a dervish who came to Konya late in 1244. We know virtually nothing about Shams, but his presence had an immediate and electrifying effect on Rumi, transforming him from an able but unexceptional teacher into a brilliant and extraordinarily fluent poet. Rumi claims never to have written a line before he encountered Shams, but by the time Rumi died in 1283 he had composed the six thousand lyrics in forty thousand double lines that make up the *Divân-e Shams-e Tabrizi,* a work that honored his teacher, and the *Masnavi-ye Ma'navi* (Spiritual Couplets), which contains more than twenty-five thousand couplets. If Rumi did indeed write all of his poetry after his meeting with Shams-e Tabrizi, he must have produced the equivalent of a sonnet virtually every day for the rest of his life, an astonishing performance considering the generally high standard of his work.

Rumi brought Shams into his own home, arranged for him to marry a young woman who was his ward, and gave him his whole and undivided attention for many months. He became so absorbed in Shams and his teaching that he neglected his own students, and they responded with a jealous intensity that eventually drove the dervish away—first for some months in 1246 and then permanently in 1247. Many modern students of Rumi's life and work believe that his students connived with Rumi's second son to murder Shams. However disturbing Rumi's love of Shams was for his students, for him it opened the wellspring of a great and unsuspected poetic talent. In response to the stimulus of Shams's presence Rumi began to compose ecstatic mystical lyrics in a continual, rushing abundance. After the disappearance of Shams, Rumi said that he had re-created him within himself and that he composed his lyrics with his voice. When these lyrics were gathered together in a single volume he called it the *Divân-e* (Collected Poems of) *Shams-e Tabrizi*.

The spring of Rumi's talent seems to have required the presence of an intimate, spiritual friend to flow freely. The second person to fill this role was Salâhoddin Zarkub, an illiterate goldsmith who had, nonetheless, pursued spiritual learning with great diligence and had been, like Rumi, a student of Borhanoddin Mohaqqeq, who had been in turn a student of Rumi's own father. Rumi's disciples were again fiercely resentful of Salâhoddin, but he was able to compel their acceptance of him. Salâhoddin remained Rumi's companion and inspiration for the rest of his life. Rumi's third spiritual friend was Chelebi Husamoddin Hasan, who lived with him for the last ten years of his life. Husamoddin inspired Rumi to begin the composition of the *Spiritual Couplets*, the long narrative, didactic poem in rhyming couplets that has an importance for sufis that is second only to the Koran. Husamoddin served as successor to Rumi as sheikh of the mystical brotherhood that took its name from Rumi's spiritual title, Mowlavi ("my master"). After Rumi's death, leadership of the order fell to his son Soltan Walad, who strove successfully during his long life (died 1312) to gain respect for the order and to extend its influence.

Rumi's poetry is divided between two quite different genres: mystical lyric (*ghazal* and *robai*) and didactic narrative (*masnavi*). In each he achieved a level of excellence that has never been surpassed and rarely equaled. In Persian, the worldly erotic lyric relies heavily on exquisite descriptions of a nature that is both sumptuous and highly conventional—a paradise of the senses. It is the same world one finds in Persian miniatures. By contrast, Rumi's references to nature in his mystical lyrics are made in the service of the soul's perception of what lies beyond it. In some an ordinary event or typical scene becomes a parable, as in the poem that begins "You miss the garden, / because you want a small fig from a random tree." In others only the context tells us that what is intended is not worldly but spiritual love.

> Come to the orchard in Spring.
> There is light and wine, and sweethearts in the pomegranate flowers.
> If you do not come, these do not matter.
> If you do come, these do not matter.

Erotic lyrics invite one to romantic love and evoke the pleasures of sensuality. Mystical lyrics, by contrast, invite one to the love of God and evoke the mixed pain and pleasure of spiritual yearning.

While the *Spiritual Couplets* retains some of Rumi's lyric fluency, it is a learned work, rich with references to the Koran and the traditions of Muhammad. It is a didactic narrative in the tradition of Sana'i and Attar. In it Rumi presents anecdotes or parables whose spiritual meaning he then explores. He wrote it at the end of his life, and in it he makes available the fruits of his long scholarly preparation and his many years as a teacher.

Rumi used three of the forms of classical Persian (and Turkish) poetry: the *robai* ("quatrain,"), *ghazal* ("short lyric"), and the *masnavi* ("couplet"). The *robai* is familiar from Edward FitzGerald's translations of Omar Khayyam and, as its name implies, contains four lines that rhyme either *aaba* or *abab*. The *masnavi* is the form used for long narrative poems like the *Masnavi-ye Ma'navi*, which may be of virtually any length but tend to be quite long. The *ghazal* uses monorhyme at the end of a long double line (*aa, xa, xa, xa, xa* . . .) and runs from five to twenty-five double lines. The monorhyme of the *ghazal* is especially hard to render into English, in which rhymes are rare. In Persian (Arabic and Turkish), in which rhymes are abundant, it is the easiest and most common of lyric forms—the sonnet of the Islamic world. Moreover, the dense allusiveness of Persian classical poetry, so similar in its texture to medieval European lyrics, demands an audience familiar with Islamic literature and learning.

Translations of Rumi are legion but few convey any sense of the poetic fabric of the original. The *Spiritual Couplets* has been translated into English only once, by R. A. Nicholson, and printed together with an edition of the texts and extended notes and commentary, *The Mathnawi of Jalaluddin Rumi* (1982). Nicholson's translation is prosaic, literal, and explanatory rather than poetic. He has also published a volume of *ghazals* with Persian text and literal Persian translation on facing pages, *The Divani Shamsi Tabrizi* (1977). A. J. Arberry has produced two collections of Rumi's *ghazals*, *The Mystical Poems of Rumi* (1968), and *The Mystical Poems of Rumi: Second Selection* (1979), that are, like Nicholson's, literal and prosaic. Recently, American poets who know no Persian—most notably Robert Bly, Coleman Barks, and W. S. Merwin—have translated Rumi into modern verse with the help of Nicholson and Arberry or some other literal rendering. The most successful of these poets is Barks. Though less literally accurate than Nicholson's or Arberry's versions, Barks's are both better poetry and truer to the spirit of Rumi. He has published extensive translations, or retranslations, from both the *Spiritual Couplets* and the *Divân-e Shams-e Tabrizi*, among them *Open Secret* (1984), *Unseen Rain* (1986), *This Longing: Forty Odes by Rumi* (1986), *Feeling the Shoulder of the Lion* (1991), *We Are Three* (1987), *Delicious Laughter* (1991), and *The Essential Rumi* (1995).

Rumi is mentioned in many studies of mysticism and mystical poetry. Annemarie Schimmel, *The Triumphal Sun* (1980), is a scholarly survey of Rumi's life and work. The best study of his lyric poetry is F. Keshavarz, *Reading Mystical Lyric: The Case of Jalal al-Din Rumi* (1998). There are also chapters on Rumi in virtually every literary history of Iran, including E. Yarshater, *Persian Literature* (1987). J. Spencer Trimingham, *The Sufi Orders of Islam* (1971), provides a comprehensive introduction to sufism as a spiritual community and social force within Islam.

PRONOUNCING GLOSSARY

The following list uses common English syllables and stress accents to provide rough equivalents of selected words whose pronunciation may be unfamiliar to the general reader.

Bahâ-ye Walad: *bu-haw'—ye wuh-lad'*

Borhanoddin Mohaqqeq: *bor-hah'-no-deen' mo-hak'-kek*

Chelebi Husamoddin Hasan: *che'-le-bee hoo-saw'-mo-deen ha'-san*

Masnavi-ye Ma'navi: *mas-na-vee'—yay ma-na-vee'*

Jalâloddin Rumi: *juh-lahl'-od-deen roo-mee*

Salâhoddin Zarkub: *su-lah'-ho-deen' zar-koob'*

Shams-e Tabrizi: *sham'—say tab-ree-zee'*

ROBAIS[1]

[Listen, if you can stand to]

Listen, if you can stand to.
Union with the Friend means not being who you've been,
being instead silence: A place: A view
where language is inside seeing.

---

1. All selections translated by Coleman Barks.

[What I most want]

What I most want
is to spring out of this personality,
then to sit apart from that leaping.
I've lived too long where I can be reached.

[Don't come to us without bringing music]

Don't come to us without bringing music.
We celebrate with drum and flute,
with wine not made from grapes,
in a place you cannot imagine.

[Sometimes visible, sometimes not, sometimes]

Sometimes visible, sometimes not, sometimes
devout Christians, sometimes staunchly Jewish.
Until our inner love fits into everyone,
all we can do is take daily these different shapes.

25

Friend, our closeness is this:
Anywhere you put your foot, feel me
in the firmness under you.

How is it with this love,
I see your world and not you?   5

82

Today, like every other day, we wake up empty
and frightened. Don't open the door to the study
and begin reading. Take down a musical instrument.

Let the beauty we love be what we do.
There are hundreds of ways to kneel and kiss the ground. 5

158

Out beyond ideas of wrongdoing and rightdoing,
there is a field. I'll meet you there.

When the soul lies down in that grass,
the world is too full to talk about.
Ideas, language, even the phrase *each other*   5
doesn't make any sense.

GHAZALS

An Empty Garlic

You miss the garden,
because you want a small fig from a random tree.
You don't meet the beautiful woman.
You're joking with an old crone.
It makes me want to cry how she detains you,   5
stinking-mouthed, with a hundred talons,
putting her head over the roofedge to call down,
tasteless fig, fold over fold, empty
as dry-rotten garlic.

She has you tight by the belt,   10
even though there's no flower and no milk
inside her body.
Death will open your eyes
to what her face is: Leather spine
of a black lizard. No more advice.   15

Let yourself be silently drawn
by the stronger pull of what you really love.

Dissolver of Sugar

Dissolver of sugar, dissolve me,
if this is the time.
Do it gently with a touch of hand, or a look.
Every morning I wait at dawn. That's when it's happened before.
Or do it suddenly like an execution. How else   5
can I get ready for death?

You breathe without a body like a spark.
You grieve, and I begin to feel lighter.
You keep me away with your arm,
but the keeping away is pulling me in.   10

FROM SPIRITUAL COUPLETS

[A chickpea leaps almost over the rim of the pot]

A chickpea leaps almost over the rim of the pot
where it's being boiled.

"Why are you doing this to me?"

The cook knocks it down with the ladle.

"Don't you try to jump out.   5
You think I'm torturing you,

I'm giving you flavor,
so you can mix with spices and rice
and be the lovely vitality of a human being.

Remember when you drank rain in the garden.   10
That was for this."

Grace first. Sexual pleasure,
then a boiling new life begins,
and the Friend has something good to eat.

Why Wine Is Forbidden

When the Prophet's ray of Intelligence
struck the dimwitted man he was with,
the man got very happy, and talkative.
Soon, he began unmannerly raving.
This is the problem with a selflessness   5
that comes quickly,
                    as with wine.
If the wine-drinker
has a deep gentleness in him,
he will show that,   10
                    when drunk.
But if he has hidden anger and arrogance,
those appear,
                    and since most people do,
wine is forbidden to everyone.   15

The Question

One dervish to another, *What was your vision of God's presence?*
I haven't seen anything.
But for the sake of conversation, I'll tell you a story.

God's presence is there in front of me, a fire on the left,
a lovely stream on the right.   5
One group walks toward the fire, *into* the fire, another
toward the sweet flowing water.
No one knows which are blessed and which not.
Whoever walks into the fire appears suddenly in the stream.
A head goes under on the water surface, that head   10
pokes out of the fire.
Most people guard against going into the fire,
and so end up in it.
Those who love the water of pleasure and make it their devotion
are cheated with this reversal.   15
The trickery goes further.
The voice of the fire tells the *truth*, saying *I am not fire.*
I am fountainhead. Come into me and don't mind the sparks.

If you are a friend of God, fire is your water.
You should wish to have a hundred thousand sets of mothwings,   20
so you could burn them away, one set a night.
The moth sees light and goes into fire. You should see fire
and go toward light. Fire is what of God is world-consuming.
Water, world-protecting.
Somehow each gives the appearance of the other. To these eyes you
    have now   25
what looks like water burns. What looks like
fire is a great relief to be inside.
You've seen a magician make a bowl of rice
seem a dish full of tiny, live worms.
Before an assembly with one breath he made the floor swarm   30
with scorpions that weren't there.
How much more amazing God's tricks.
Generation after generation lies down, defeated, they think,
but they're like a woman underneath a man, circling him.
One molecule-mote-second thinking of God's reversal of comfort and
    pain   35
is better than any attending ritual. That splinter
of intelligence is substance.
The fire and water themselves:
Accidental, done with mirrors.

FROM BIRDSONG

[Lovers in their brief delight]

Lovers in their brief delight
gamble both worlds away,
a century's worth of work
for one chance to surrender.

Many slow growth-stages build   5
to quick bursts of blossom.

A thousand half-loves
must be forsaken to take
one whole heart home.

FROM THE GLANCE

Silkworms

The hurt you embrace becomes joy.
Call it to your arms where it can

change. A silkworm eating leaves
makes a cocoon. Each of us weaves

a chamber of leaves and sticks.   5
Silkworms begin to truly exist

as they disappear inside that room.
Without legs, we fly. When I stop

speaking, this poem will close,
and open its silent wings . . .   10

SA'DI
thirteenth century

Sa'di's *Golestan* is one of the most widely read and imitated works of classical Persian literature. Sa'di's words are as often quoted in Persian as Shakespeare's are in English, and the *Golestan* has exerted a formative influence on the literary prose of every Islamic literature to take shape after its appearance. Its mixture of sound moral sense with elegant and vivid poetic expression embodies those qualities that Muslims most value in literature, and the breadth of Sa'di's insight into virtually every aspect of life give it a wide popular appeal as well. In its popularity with Muslim readers, it is second only to the Koran.

The poet Sa'di was born at the beginning of the thirteenth century in Shiraz, the principal city of the province of Pars in south central Iran. He died there roughly ninety years later. We know little about his life other than what we can infer from his books. It is clear that he received a good grounding in the humanistic learning of his day—beginning with Arabic grammar, the Koran, and the fundamentals of Islamic law and theology and going on to Arabic and Persian poetry, history, and Islamic *belles lettres.* As a young man he traveled far from Shiraz, first as a student, visiting such centers of learning as Baghdad and Damascus, later as a teacher. He almost certainly made several pilgrimages to Mecca and Medina, and while in the region it is likely that he had some contact with the crusaders as well. There are anecdotes that suggest that he may have traveled to such remote regions as Morocco and Abyssinia and even beyond the world of Islam into Byzantium and India. Such anecdotes are tempting but unreliable sources for biography. As Sa'di himself says, "One who travels widely may lie a great deal." What is clear is that in the course of his travels he acquired a deep sympathy for mendicant sufis—who are given the generic name of dervish here (see also the headnote "Jalâloddin Rumi," p. 1541). Sa'di always treats them with compassion and understanding in his writings and makes clear that he has a profound affinity with their mystical beliefs. He returned to Shiraz in his middle years and there composed the two works that ensured his fame—the *Bustan* (Garden), a work of some forty-one hundred rhymed couplets that appeared in the winter of 1257, and the *Golestan* (Rose Garden), a mixture of poetry and rhymed prose completed in the summer of 1258.

The *Bustan* and the *Golestan* both belong to the literature of advice and moral counsel, a genre that has deep roots in Iran. From the point of view of Muslim audiences both moral seriousness and stylistic felicity are essential for any literary work to succeed. Fiction, or pure fiction, is a category of literature that has no place in the canon of classical Islamic literature. Fiction as we understand the term in the West has gained respectability in the Islamic world only in the modern period. Stories that simply entertain, like those in *The Thousand and One Nights,* are, however popular, considered a degraded form of discourse—little better than outright lies. But stories, even stories that we would say are "fictional," became acceptable, even admirable, when presented in the service of moral instruction. The situation of prose in the Islamic world resembles that of medieval Europe, but in Europe prose fiction gradually came to be accepted as a literary genre, whereas in medieval Islam it never did.

The *Golestan* contains an introduction and eight chapters, called books: Book I, *On the Nature of Shahs;* II, *On the Morals of Dervishes;* III, *On the Excellence of Contentment;* IV, *On the Advantages of Silence;* V, *On Love and Youth;* VI, *On Weakness and Old Age;* VII, *On the Effects of Education;* and VIII, *On Rules for Conduct of Life.* The stories in each chapter adhere to the subject only very loosely, however, and often wander far afield. The most highly regarded chapters are the first two in which shahs and dervishes are the principal focus. Shahs and dervishes defined the two poles of Islamic society. Shahs embodied worldly authority and, at their best, humane and compassionate justice. Such enlightenment was achieved only rarely, however, and for the most part royal authority was yoked to injustice and spiritual poverty. Dervishes represented the pole of spiritual authority, a station they reached by embracing worldly poverty. Their indifference to the world freed them from the normal constraints, and one of their most attractive traits is their boldness in the presence of shahs. Their freedom from worldly responsibility licensed them to speak their minds to those in positions of authority in a way that would have been fatal to the ordinary person. Between these two clustered the viziers, princes, and courtiers who made up the court on the one hand and the craftsmen, merchants, and ordinary people on the other. The emphasis on moral instruction already mentioned deprives the anecdotes of the psychological depth and complexity of fiction. Characters and incidents never move beyond a conventional and stereotypical flatness. While the shahs and dervishes in many anecdotes are given specific, historical identities, they seem entirely interchangeable. For Sa'di's readers this conventionality did not detract from the appeal of the work, which, for them, lay principally in the familiarity of the subject matter and the elegance and beauty of the language.

For many years, the *Golestan* was universally accepted as a paradigm of Persian prose style throughout the Persian-speaking world. European students of Persian who first encountered it in India also read it and imitated it to improve their Persian. But in the present century both Persian and English have moved away from the highly poetic style of Sa'di and his imitators. Dick Davis translated the selection printed here especially for this edition and attempted to capture the essence of Sa'di in a fluent and contemporary style.

There are a number of translations of the *Golestan* (also spelled *Gulistan*), including one by Francis Gladwin, *The Gulistan or Rose Garden* (1865). Edward Rehatsek's translation, *The Gulistan or Rose Garden of Sa'di* (1888), is both reliable and readily available. The only book-length study of Sa'di in English is John D. Yohannan, *The Poet Sa'di: A Persian Humanist.* There are also chapters on Sa'di in Ehsan Yarshater, ed., *Persian Literature* (1988), and A. J. Arberry, *Classical Persian Literature* (1958).

PRONOUNCING GLOSSARY

The following list uses common English syllables and stress accents to provide rough equivalents of selected words whose pronunciation may be unfamiliar to the general reader.

Bani Tamim: *ba'-nee ta-meem'*

Bozorgmehr: *bo-zorg-mare'*

Eskandar-e Rumi: *es-kan-dar'—ay roo-me'*

Faridun: *fair-ee-doon'*

Harun al-Rashid: *haw-roon' ar—ra-sheed'*

Khosayb: *ko-sayb'*

Mahmoud-e Seboktegin: *mah-mood—ay suh-bok'-ta-geen*

Zahhak: *za-hawk'*

Zulnun-e Mesri: *zool-noon'—ay mes-ree'*

From Golestan[1]

From *Book I*

On the Nature of Shahs

THE FIRST ANECDOTE

I have heard that there was a shah who gave orders for an innocent man to be killed. The poor wretch began to curse and abuse his sovereign, since as they say,

> The man who's washed his hands of life will start
> To say whatever's hidden in his heart.

> When flight's impossible a man must stand
> And grasp his sharp sword firmly in his hand.

or as the Arabs have it

> A hopeless man will speak his mind, just as
> A cornered cat will strike out at a dog.

The shah asked, "What's he saying?"

A well-meaning courtier replied, "My Lord, he's quoting from the Koran, 'Heaven is for those who control their anger.' "[2]

The shah felt pity for the man and pardoned him. But another courtier, who was the enemy of the other, said, "It's not right for men of our calling to speak anything but truth in the presence of shahs. This man cursed the shah, and said disgusting things about him."

The shah frowned at this and replied, "I prefer his lie to your truth, since his words looked to promote peace, yours to promote oppression, and wise men have said,

> 'The lie that looks for peace is preferable to
> Remarks that stir up trouble, even if they're true.' "

> How wrong it is if one a shah relies on should
> Say any words at all but those that foster good.

On the arched entrance to Faridun's[3] castle was written,

> "The world, my brother, will not stay for anyone—
> Trust in the world's Creator rather, and have done!
> Don't lean on worldly wealth to keep and comfort you
> It's nourished many like yourself—and killed them too—
> But when the soul prepares to leave, a lowly stone
> Is just as fine a place as any throne."

THE SECOND ANECDOTE

One of the shahs of Khorasan[4] saw Sultan Mahmoud-e Seboktegin in a dream; the sultan's body had disintegrated and become dust, all but the eyes which still rolled in their sockets and looked about. Those who interpret

---

1. Translated by Dick Davis.   2. Sura 3.28.   3. Legendary shah who reestablished Iranian rule after defeating the foreign tyrant Zahhak.   4. A province in northeastern Iran.

dreams were puzzled by what this meant, but a dervish offered his services and said, "He's worried that his wealth has fallen into others' hands."

> How many lie beneath the burial mound
> Whose fame's left not a trace above the ground!
> Earth eats the corpse men thrust into the earth
> Till not a bone of it can still be found.
> But though Anushirvan's[5] been buried long
> He is, for his great justice, still renowned;
> Do good, and make the most of life—since soon
> The news that you've passed on will be passed round.

THE THIRD ANECDOTE

I've heard that there was a prince who was short and slightly built, and his brothers were all tall and good-looking. One day his father glanced at him with a show of displeasure and contempt, but the boy who had his wits about him said, "A short wise fellow's better than a lofty fool; height doesn't have to mean high value too. As the Arabs say,

> 'A sheep is lawful food although it's small and mean—
> The mighty elephant's considered as unclean;
> Mount Sinai[6] is the lowest mountain on the earth
> But since it's close to God it has the highest worth.'

> And have you heard the words a thin wise man
> Once said to an enormous silly fool?
> 'A weak and spavined Arab horse is still
> Worth more than donkeys by the stable-full!' "

His father laughed, and the courtiers were amused too, and his brothers swallowed their anger.

> Until a man has had his say, take care—
> Who knows what faults or skills lie hidden there?
> You shouldn't think that every thicket's empty—
> One might conceal a sleeping leopard's lair.

I've heard that around that time a fierce enemy appeared to oppose the shah. When the armies of each side met the first man to urge his horse forward was that same son, who said,

> "Whenever battle comes you won't see me turn tail and flee;
> If you see one whose head lies in the blood and dust that man is me.
> The blood the man who charges forward risks is all his own;
> The coward risks the army's blood—to get himself homefree."

And having said this he charged the enemy's army and dealt severely with a number of their men. When he returned to his father he kissed the ground before him in sign of submission and said,

> "I seemed to you to be contemptible,
> But don't confuse mere weight with valor now—

---

5. A shah of the pre-Islamic Sassanian dynasty; his justice was legendary. He is the subject of several anecdotes.   6. Not where Moses received the Ten Commandments but a mountain near Jerusalem where many holy men are buried.

> Since on the battlefield a thin horse is
> Of more use than a plumply nourished cow!"

News was brought that the enemy's army was huge, while their own was very small, and the men prepared to run for it. The boy bellowed out, "You call yourselves men! Fight, or wear women's clothes!" At his cry the cavalry took heart and as one man they attacked. I've heard that they gained victory over the enemy on that very day. The shah kissed his son's head and eyes and embraced him, and every day he took more notice of him until finally he made him his heir.

His brothers became jealous and put poison in his food, but his sister was watching from the balcony where the women's quarters were and slammed the shutters. The son realized something was afoot and drew his hand back from the food, saying:

> "It cannot be, if worthy men fall dead,
> That worthless men should take their place instead.
> Say that the homa[7] vanished without trace—
> No-one would seek the owl's shade in its place."

The father was told of what had happened; he called in the brothers and boxed their ears, as was only right, and then assigned to each one a separate area where he was to live until things had settled down and the quarrel was resolved—for as they say,

> A poor man makes do with a scrap of a rug,
> For a shah a whole country's too pinched and too snug.

> A godly man will dine on half a loaf of bread
> And see that with the other half the poor are fed;
> A shah will seize on seven countries'[8] wealth—and still
> He craves new countries not yet subject to his will.

THE FOURTH ANECDOTE

A group of Arab thieves had encamped on a mountain top from where they had a stranglehold on the nearby caravan route; the people of the neighboring towns were terrified of their tactics and as they'd constructed an inaccessible refuge for themselves at the summit of the mountain the sultan's army was powerless against them. The administrators of the area consulted together on how best to defend themselves against the harm done by these thieves, since if the band were allowed to continue in this way it would become impossible to oppose them.

> A sapling that has newly taken root
> Requires no more than one man's strength to lift it,
> But let it grow there for a while and soon
> Tackle and ropes and pulleys will not shift it:
> A stream's source can be blocked up with a hoe
> But elephants can't stop a river's flow.

It was decided that they would send one man to spy on them and that they would wait for an opportunity when the band had gone out on a plundering

---

7. A legendary phoenixlike bird; it also rose from its own ashes.   8. That is, the entire known world.

expedition, leaving their encampment empty. Then they dispatched a group of experienced fighters to hide in the mountain valley. That evening when the thieves returned, worn out with the journey and loaded down with plunder, they took off their armour and clothes and laid down their booty and the first enemy that attacked them was sleep.

> The sun's disk went behind its dusky veil—
> Jonah entered the belly of the whale.

As soon as one watch of the night had passed the attackers leapt out from their ambush, tied each thief's arms behind his back, and brought them at dawn to the shah's court. He gave orders that they all be killed. It so happened there was a youth among them, a young unripened fruit, a boy on whose fresh cheeks the down was just beginning to grow. One of the councilors at court kissed the shah's throne, bowed down to the ground and entreated his sovereign; "This boy has not yet eaten any fruit from life's garden, he's tasted none of youth's pleasures; I beg that for my sake my generous lord will not shed his blood."

The shah frowned at these words; he did not at all agree, and said,

> "An evil-natured man won't take
> To good men's ways, and there's no trick
> To make him learn: it's throwing nuts
> Against a dome—they just won't stick!

It's better to extirpate this rotten race, to destroy them root and branch—wise men don't put fires out and leave the ashes burning, or kill a viper and preserve its offspring:

> You won't eat fruit grown on a willow tree
> Not even if life's waters fell as rain;
> Don't spend your time in worthless company—
> You won't suck sugar from a marsh-reed cane."

The councilor heard his shah's words and willy-nilly accepted them; he praised his monarch's fine opinion and said, "That which the shah, may he live for ever, has spoken is precisely the truth, and if the boy had grown up among such wicked people he would have taken on their character and become one of them. But in my humble opinion, I hope that he will be influenced by pious company and take on the character of the wise, since he's still a child and the evil and rebellious nature of that mob has as yet no place in him. Besides the prophet[9] has said, 'Every son of man has as his birthright, before he ever speaks, an inclination to the true wisdom; but then it is his father and mother who make him a Jew or a Christian or Zoroastrian':

> When Noah's son spent time with evil men
> It ruined that prophetic family—
> The dog the Cave-Companions kept became
> A man, by keeping noble company."

When he'd said this other servants belonging to the shah joined him in asking that the boy's life be spared, until finally the shah gave up the idea of

---

9. Muhammad.

shedding his blood and said, "I grant your request, even though it does not seem advisable to me:

You know what Zal once said to Rostám,[1] that great hero?
'Don't think your enemy's a wretched little zero—
We've seen enough small streams whose waters when they swell
Can carry off a camel and its load as well.' "

To cut a long story short, the councilor brought the boy up in kindness and comfort, appointing tutors to teach him the arts of the courtier and the service of shahs; he made such progress that he was accepted by his peers at court. One day the councilor referred to his character in the shah's presence, saying that this liberal education had had a good influence on him and that the old ignorance had been expelled from his nature. The shah merely smiled and said,

"A wolf is what a wolf cub grows to finally
Although it might grow up in human company."

Two years passed, and then a group of louts living in that area got to know the boy and made a friendly agreement with him. At the first opportunity he killed the councilor and his two sons, made off with a vast quantity of wealth, took his father's place in the thieves' lair and became an outlaw. The shah bit his finger in astonishment and said,

"How can a sword be made from faulty metal?
A scoundrel cannot come to any good;
The purest rain makes tulips grow in gardens—
But, in the desert, scrub and kindling—wood.

A salty soil will not grow hyacinths,
Don't waste your bulbs and time in such a neighborhood—
To do good to such evil-minded men
Is just as bad as doing evil to the good."

*   *   *

THE SIXTH ANECDOTE

They tell a story about one of the Persian shahs, as to how he arrogantly appropriated his subjects' wealth for himself, and began to trouble them in other ways, until it reached the point that the population fled from the tricks of his oppression out into the wide world; to escape the anguish caused by his cruelty they set out for foreign lands. Since the population had decreased the income of the country declined, the treasury remained empty and the shah's enemies gained in power.

If you would hope for kindness in calamity
Be generous in the days of your prosperity;
If you don't treat him well your own slave runs from you
But kindness will make slaves of men you never knew.

One day at court they were reading in *The Shahnameh* about the fall of Zahhak during the time of Faridun.

---

1. Both Zal and Rostám are heros of the *Shâhnâme* (p. 1481).

The court minister asked the shah: "Is it possible to know how it happened that Faridun who had no treasure, tribute or tribe to his name was able to be established as a monarch?"

The shah said, "As you have heard, people gathered round him because they supported him, and so they made him strong and he gained sovereignty in this way."

The minister replied, "My lord, since people gathering round brings sovereignty why is it that you scatter your people? Don't you have a shah's head on your shoulders!

You ought to treat the army with consideration—
It's through the army that a monarch rules the nation."

The shah said, "What is it that makes an army and a people gather round?"

The minister replied, "A shah must be generous for people to gather round him, and he must be merciful for them to stay in his realm in security—and you are neither of these two things.

An evil man can't wield a monarch's sway,
The shepherd's one role that the wolf can't play;
A shah who builds his realm on tyranny
Destroys the walls of his own sovereignty."

The shah did not take at all kindly to his good councilor's advice; he frowned at his words and sent him off to prison. It wasn't long before the shah's cousins rose in rebellion; they raised an army against him and demanded their father's kingdom. The people, who had been pushed to the limit of their endurance by the shah's arrogant behavior and had scattered, now gathered round and strengthened the rebels' cause, till sovereignty deserted that shah and settled on them.

The shah who lets oppression flourish will soon see,
When trouble comes, each friend is now an enemy;
Make peace with all your people, and then fear no war—
His subjects are the just shah's troops and armory.

※　　※　　※

THE EIGHTH ANECDOTE

They asked Hormoz,[2] "What fault did you see in your father's courtiers that you had them all imprisoned?"

He said, "I found no fault in them. But I saw that though they felt boundless awe of me in their hearts they did not have complete confidence in my reign. I was afraid that out of fear for their own lives they would plot my death, so I took the advice of the wise who have said,

'Be wise—fear him who fears you, even though
You could have hundreds like him overthrown;
You know a cat will claw a leopard's eyes out
When it's defeated, cornered and alone—

---

2. A Sassanian monarch.

A snake will strike the herdsman's heel because
It fears he'll crush its head against a stone.' "

*   *   *

THE TENTH ANECDOTE

I was worshiping one day in the great mosque at Damascus, at the shrine that houses the earthly remains of the prophet John, on whom be peace, when it happened that one of the kings of the Bani Tamim[3] who had a reputation for injustice arrived on a pilgrimage; he spread his prayer mat out and set to his devotions:

> Wealthy and poor are slaves of this shrine's dust—indeed
> The wealthier they are the deeper is their need.

Then he said to me, "Since a poor dervish is a righteous and spiritual kind of person, pray along with me because I'm very worried about a particularly nasty enemy."

I answered him, "If you don't want to be harmed by a powerful enemy be kind to your powerless people."

> It's wrong for someone with a mighty arm and fist
> To break the fingers of a wretch who can't resist,
> And doesn't one who hurts the fallen fear that when
> His own foot slips there'll be no hand there to assist?
> A man who sows bad seed and hopes for splendid fruit
> Beats at his brains in vain, his mind's an empty mist:
> Unplug your ears, bring justice to the people—since,
> If you're unjust, God's Day of Justice still exists!

> Man's sons are parts of one reality
> Since all have sprung from one identity;
> If one part of a body's hurt, the rest
> Cannot remain unmoved and undistressed;
> If you're not touched by others' pain, the name
> Of "man" is one you cannot rightly claim.[4]

THE ELEVENTH ANECDOTE

A dervish whose prayers were very efficacious appeared in Baghdad. Hajaj Yusef[5] was told; he summoned him and said, "Pray a prayer that will be to my benefit."

The man said, "Oh God, take this man's soul to Yourself."

Hajaj Yusef said, "For God's sake, what kind of a prayer is this you're asking?"

The dervish replied, "This prayer would benefit you and all Moslems.

> With strong-arm tactics you oppress the poor,
> How long can all of this continue for?

3. An Arab tribe.   4. These verses are inscribed on the walls of the lobby of the United Nations building in New York.   5. An able but pitiless governor of Iraq (7th century).

The use you put your power to, it would be
Better to die than use such tyranny."

* * *

THE FIFTEENTH ANECDOTE

A shah's councilor was dismissed from court and lived among dervishes. The blessings of their conversation had such a beneficial effect on him that he achieved complete peace of mind. The shah felt kindly toward him once again and ordered him to resume his duties. He refused and said, "Being retired is better than being hired."

Those who sit in safety's private den
Have gagged the teeth of dogs, the mouths of men;
They've torn their paper up, broken their pen,
Secure from every envious citizen.

The shah said, "That's all very well but we stand in need of men of sufficient intelligence to manage the affairs of state."

He replied, "The sign of sufficient intelligence is precisely that one doesn't want to become involved with such affairs."

Of all the birds the homa's nobler than its brothers
Because it lives on bones and doesn't bother others.

There is an insect, called "the black-eared," that lives with lions; it was asked, "How is it that you attend on the lion?"

It answered, "I eat the left-overs from its kill and I live safely, protected by its ferociousness from the evil of enemies."

They said, "Since you have entered the shadow of its protection and acknowledge its magnanimity, why don't you go closer so that it admits you into the circle of its favorites and counts you as one of its dearest servants?"

He said, "Because I'm afraid it might attack me.

A hundred years a Zoroastrian might have learned
To tend his sacred fire—but one slip and he's burned."

It's happened that a shah's favorite has found gold and in so doing lost his head and so the wise have remarked, "One should beware of the capriciousness of shahs, because they can be irritated by integrity and sometimes reward rudeness with the gift of a splendid robe, and as people have said, excessive grace and wit are a necessary art for court favorites, but a fault in wise men.

Look to your dignity, be grave in everything—
Leave games and graces to the favorites of the king."

* * *

THE SEVENTEENTH ANECDOTE

I was friends with a number of men who outwardly seemed to be very pious; a lord was impressed with this group and had arranged for a regular sum to be paid to them for their maintenance. Then it happened that one of them did something unbecoming to a pious person, the lord changed his mind about them and they were in dire straits. I wanted to get my friends' allowance restored in some way and applied to see the lord. The doorkeeper wouldn't let me in and treated me very badly, which I forgave because as the knowledgeable have said,

> Without an introduction don't go near
> The doorway of a shah or an emir—
> When once a dog and doorman see a stranger
> From this his coat's, from that his neck's in danger!

When those who were intimate with this same lord heard about my plight they respectfully brought me in and assigned me a prominent place in the assembly, but I humbly sat in a more lowly place and said,

> I am the least slave here, so let me sit
> Where it is fitting for such slaves to sit.

The lord said, "Good God, good God, this is no place for such talk!" To cut a long story short I sat down and introduced various topics of conversation, until I got round to mentioning my friends' unfortunate mistake and said,

> "What evil sin has my lord seen that's made
> His slave beneath contempt in his great sight?
> To God is power and glory—Who sees sin
> And still bestows bread as a constant right."

The ruler was very pleased by this remark and ordered that the allowance be restored as before and that the arrears of the intervening period be paid. I thanked him for his generosity, kissed the ground as a sign of my submission, apologized for my impertinence, and as I was leaving said,

> "Since Mecca is the focus of the world
> Men travel there by every distant route;
> You must put up with lowly folk like us—
> No one troubles a tree that has no fruit."

THE EIGHTEENTH ANECDOTE

There was a prince who inherited a large fortune from his father. He generously opened his arms to all-comers, distributing alms and unstintingly raining down largesse on the army and his people.

> Until it's placed within the fire
> The smell of scented wood's unknown—
> And greatness means that you must give,
> A seed won't grow until it's sown.

An inconsiderate companion began to admonish him, saying "The former shahs struggled to put this wealth by and to keep it as a prudent reserve. You should stop this behavior, who knows what events may come or enemies threaten you, and God forbid that you find yourself helpless in a crisis:

> If you give treasure out to everyone like this
> One grain of rice will make up each man's measure;

> Why don't you take a grain of silver from each man
> And so each day accumulate more treasure?"

The shah frowned at this speech; he did not agree with it at all and derided the man, saying, "God made me the shah of this country so that I could enjoy and distribute its wealth, not its watchman to lock it up.

> Qarun[6] the miser who
>   had forty treasuries has died;
> The just Anushirvan
>   still lives, his name's known far and wide."

THE NINETEENTH ANECDOTE

They say that once when Anushirvan the Just was hunting they roasted one of the animals that had been killed, and there was no salt. A slave boy went to a village to get some salt. Anushirvan said, "Pay for the salt according to its price, or requisitioning will become a custom and the village will be ruined."

His attendants said, "What harm could come from such a small transaction?"

He replied, "The beginnings of oppression in the world were small, but everyone who came afterward added to it until it reached the monstrous proportions it now has."

> If once the shah should eat a peasant's apple
> His slaves will pull the tree up by its roots;
> If he should let five eggs be requisitioned
> A thousand hens will roast for his recruits.

*   *   *

THE TWENTY-FIRST ANECDOTE

They tell a story about a lout who once threw a stone at a pious man's head. The dervish had no opportunity for revenge, but he kept the stone until the shah was annoyed with this same trouble-maker and had him thrown into a well. The dervish appeared and threw the stone down on the man's head. He shouted, "Who are you, and why've you hit me with this stone?"

The dervish said, "I'm so and so, and this stone is exactly the same one you threw at my head on such and such a day."

The man said, "And where were you all this time?"

The dervish replied, "I was afraid of your position, but now I see you in this position I've seized my opportunity!"

> If one wields power for which he is unfit
> The wisest course is simply to submit,
> Since you don't have sharp claws it would be best
> To leave wild beasts alone, and not protest—
> The man who fights against an iron fist
> Will only break his own poor feeble wrist.

6. The biblical Korah.

Wait till Fate ties his hands; your friends and you
Can skin him then, just as you wanted to.

          *   *   *

THE TWENTY-SEVENTH ANECDOTE

There was a man who had become an excellent wrestler; he knew three hundred and sixty marvelous tricks and every day he demonstrated something new. A man who was learning wrestling from him had captured his heart because of his good looks, and the wrestler had taught him three hundred and fifty nine of his tricks, but one he postponed teaching him, saying he would do it later.

To cut a long story short the young man grew in strength and skill and there was no one of that time who could stand up to him; it got to the stage that he said to the shah, "My teacher's my superior because he's senior to me and has taught me, but if it weren't for that my strength is no less than his and I equal him in skill."

This remark annoyed the shah, and he gave orders that the two stage a wrestling match. They prepared a space, and the pillars of the state, the shah's courtiers and the great men of the region gathered to watch. The young man attacked like a maddened elephant, with such force that he'd have uprooted a mountain made of iron. His teacher knew the young man was stronger than he himself was, so he resorted to that one trick he'd kept back from his pupil. The young man didn't know how to counteract it, and his teacher lifted him into the air, above his head, and threw him down. A shout went up from the spectators. The shah ordered that the teacher be given a splendid robe and wealth besides, and the youth was derided and reproached for having challenged his teacher to a match and then lost.

When lowly men compete against far better men
They fall in such a way that they won't rise again.

The young man said, "O shah, he didn't defeat me through his strength, but because there was one detail of the science of wrestling left and he wouldn't pass it on to me. Today he overcame me because of that one detail."

The teacher said, "It was for just such a day that I held it back, since the canny have said, 'Don't give your friend such strength that if he becomes your enemy he'll be stronger than you.' Haven't you heard what the man whose own pupil turned on him said,

'There never was—in this world—loyalty,
Or in these days it's lost its market;
I never taught a man to use a bow
But finally I became his target.' "

THE TWENTY-EIGHTH ANECDOTE

There was a dervish who was dead to the world sitting in a corner of the desert. A shah passed by, but as such spiritual independence is in itself a kingdom of contentment the dervish did not take any notice or even move his head. Since it's the majesty of authority that constitutes royal sovereignty the shah grew annoyed and said, "This crowd of mystics who wear the dervish cloak are like animals, they've no saving graces or humanity in them."

His minister said, "Hey you, young man, the shah has just passed by you, why didn't you show him reverence and act politely?"

The dervish said, "Tell the shah to hope for reverence from those who hope for wealth from him, and besides let him know that shahs exist to protect people not people to obey shahs.

> A shah's the shepherd of his people
> Though his is all the pomp and circumstance;
> The sheep are not there for the shepherd,
> They're there to flourish through his vigilance.

> You see a man today in luxury
> And one whom sorrow's worn to skin and bone,
> But wait until the earth has swallowed them
> And all the fine thoughts from their brains have flown;
> When what Fate ordered comes, the odds is gone
> Between the servant and the royal throne;
> If someone opens up these graves, who once
> Was rich and who was poor is all unknown."

The dervish's words seemed just to the shah. He said, "Ask me for something."

The dervish said, "I ask that you not trouble me any further."

The shah said, "Give me some good advice."

The dervish answered,

> "There's one thing you must understand—
> The wealth and power within your hand
> Will be passed on, from hand to hand."

THE TWENTY-NINTH ANECDOTE

A minister went to the Egyptian sufi Zulnun-e Mesri and asked for his help; he said, "Day and night I'm busy serving the shah and I always hope for his prosperity, but I'm afraid of being punished by him."

Zulnun wept and said, "If I had feared the great God as you fear your shah I'd now be one of the truly righteous.

> The dervish would have risen to the heavens, if it
> Were not for hope of peace and fear of pain;
> And if the courtier feared his God as now he fears
> His shah, he'd also—as an angel—reign."

*   *   *

THE THIRTY-FIRST ANECDOTE

The ministers of shah Anushirvan were considering an important matter of state and each of them came up with a different proposal; the shah also put his mind to the problem. The shah's chief minister Bozorgmehr[7] approved of the shah's solution. The other ministers said to him in private,

7. Famous for his wisdom.

"How can the shah's opinion be better than that of so many wise men?"

He answered, "Because the end of this business is as yet unknown, and it's the will of God whether the others are right or wrong. So it is best to agree with the shah's opinion since, if it turns out to have been wrong, by following him we'll be safe from being blamed by him.

> To speak against the shah's words is inopportune—
> You'll find your own blood on your hands. If at high noon
> The shah says 'Night has come' then you must promptly say,
> 'Ah yes, there is Soraya,[8] and there's the moon!"

*   *   *

THE THIRTY-THIRD ANECDOTE

There was a shah's minister who was merciful to his subordinates and a peacemaker among his peers. It happened that he was imprisoned on the shah's orders. His peers tried to get him released, his jailors treated him well while he was being punished and the great men at the court repeatedly reminded the shah of his character's good qualities so that finally the shah forgave him. A pious man heard about this and said,

> "To get the good opinion of your friends
> It's right to sell the garden you've inherited;
> To heat the pot that feeds your loyal companions
> It's right to burn your household furniture, your bed;
> Even to evil minded men do good—
> Stuff the dog's mouth, and he won't bite you when he's fed."

THE THIRTY-FOURTH ANECDOTE

One of Harun al-Rashid's[9] sons came before his father in a rage saying that such and such an officer's son had made insulting remarks about his mother to him. Harun said to the state ministers, "What should such a man's punishment be?"

One advised execution, another that the man's tongue should be cut out and another a fine and banishment.

Harun said, "It would be merciful for you to forgive him, and if you can't do that then swear back at him—but not so much that you go beyond what's right by way of revenge, since then the fault will be on your side and right on his.

> Wise men don't think of manliness
> As fighting with a maddened elephant—
> A man, when all is said and done,
> Is one who when he's angry doesn't rant!

> An evil-minded person swore at one
> Who bore it calmly and, when he had done,
> Said, "Friend, I'm worse than that if you but knew—
> I know my faults more deeply than you do."

8. Pleiades, a bright constellation.   9. A caliph (9th century) who ruled in Baghdad.

THE THIRTY-FIFTH ANECDOTE

I was sitting in a boat with a group of distinguished men when a small boat following us sank and two brothers were thrown into a whirlpool. One of the company said to our boatman, "Save those two men and I'll give you fifty dinars for each one."

The boatman dived into the water and while he was saving one of them the other perished.

I said, "He wasn't fated to live any longer, that's why you delayed getting to him while you were in a hurry to save the other one."

The boatman laughed and said, "What you've said is certainly true, and besides I was more interested in saving this one because once while I was stranded in the desert he took me up on his camel, but the other one had me whipped when I was a boy."

I said, "God is most just. As the Koran says, 'He who acts justly acts to his own advantage while he who acts unjustly will suffer the effects of that injustice himself.' "[1]

> Since there are thorns enough along this road
> Try not to scratch at anyone; see you
> Help out the wretched with their heavy burdens,
> Since no doubt you have heavy burdens too.

THE THIRTY-SIXTH ANECDOTE

There were two brothers, one of whom was in the shah's service while the other lived by the strength of his arm. The rich one remarked to his poor brother, "Why don't you enter the shah's service too and so escape from the hardships you now labor under?"

He replied, "And why don't you do some work and so escape from the wretchedness of service, since as the wise have said, 'Better to sit and eat beholden to no one than to wear a gold belt and be in service'?

> Better to use your arm's strength smelting iron than
> To stand there hand-on-chest, a royal serving-man."

> I spend my precious life preoccupied
> With things like winter clothes and summer food;
> Better be doubled up with hunger, stomach
> Than that the back be bent in servitude.

THE THIRTY-SEVENTH ANECDOTE

Someone brought good news to Anushirvan the Just, saying, "I have heard that God has taken your enemy so and so." Anushirvan said, "And have you heard anything about his sparing me?"

> There is no cause for joy
>   when death destroys an enemy,
> Since our life too cannot
>   continue for eternity.

1. Sura 41.46.

THE THIRTY-EIGHTH ANECDOTE

A group of knowledgeable men at the court of Anushirvan were discussing various matters, and Bozorgmehr, who was the most distinguished person present, remained silent. They said to him, "Why don't you join in our discussion?"

He answered, "Knowledgeable men are like doctors, and a doctor only gives medicine to the sick. And so, since I see that your opinions are correct, it would be unwise of me to comment on them.

> Here all goes as it should without my interference,
> In this case my words needn't put in an appearance—
> But if I saw a blind man walking near a well
> It would be sinful to sit silent till he fell."

THE THIRTY-NINTH ANECDOTE

When the kingdom of Egypt submitted to Harun al-Rashid he said, "In contrast to that haughty fool who was so proud of ruling Egypt that he claimed to be God, I shall give this realm to the lowest of my slaves."

He had a black slave called Khosayb who was extremely ignorant, and he bestowed the kingdom of Egypt on him. They say that the level of his intelligence and learning was such that when a group of Egyptian notables complained to him that the cotton crop they had sown had been ruined by unseasonable rains he said, "You should have sown wool."

> If knowledge were the way to greatness then
> The poor would be the stupidest of men,
> But greatness can be given to such a fool
> That wise men gape in wonder at his rule.

> Good luck and princely power are not to those who know,
> They are for heaven, as it wishes, to bestow—
> How may worthy men live wretched on this earth
> How many imbeciles are seen as men of worth—
> The searcher after truth dies grieving and alone,
> The fool turns up a treasure underneath a stone.

THE FORTY-FIRST ANECDOTE

They asked Eskandar-e Rumi,[2] "How did you conquer the East and the West? Kings before you had wealth and armies greater than yours and they did not gain such easy victories."

He answered, "In every country which I conquered by the help of God I did not oppress the people there and I showed only respect to the kings.

> The wise will not consider that man great
> Who ridicules another's noble state."

---

2. Alexander the Great (356–323 B.C.), conqueror of Greece, Persia, Egypt, and northern India.

THE THOUSAND AND ONE NIGHTS
fourteenth century

The Thousand and One Nights is rich in paradoxes. An anonymous work, it is nevertheless more widely known in the Arab world than any other work of Arabic literature. It is almost as well known in Europe, and so far is the only work of Arabic letters to become a permanent part of European and, indeed, of world literature. Despite this great popularity, and despite its shaping influence on modern literature, traditional Arabic literary scholars have never recognized it as a work of serious literature, and it is still occasionally banned as immoral by Arab governments.

The history of *The Thousand and One Nights* is vague, and its shape as hard to pin down as a cloud's. The starting point of the work in Arabic was probably a collection of tales in Middle Persian called the "thousand stories" that had been translated or adapted from Sanskrit in the time of the Sassanids (226–652), the last pre-Islamic Iranian dynasty. During the ninth and tenth centuries a great deal of Persian literature, both popular and courtly, was translated into Arabic, particularly at the caliphal court in Baghdad. The tales that became the core of the *Nights* were probably among them. The Perso-Indian origins of the prologue and other tales are suggested by the Persian personal names—Shahrayar, Shahzaman, Shahrazad—and place names—Indochina, Samarkand—of the prologue. Stories set in the Baghdad of the late eighth century—those that mention the caliph Haroun al-Rashid and his vizier Ja'far the Barmakid, for instance—indicate that the original translator, or later copyists, felt free to add local tales to the originals. From Baghdad, manuscripts of this original translation circulated widely to other parts of the Islamic world, especially Syria and Egypt. The tales were also transmitted orally and adapted and translated into other languages of the region. Indeed, the initial translation into Arabic may have been an oral one—the work of a Persian storyteller who came to the great metropolis of Baghdad and adapted his wares to the language of his audience. What we know for certain is that written and oral transmissions of the tales have intermingled down to the present day. Oral versions were written down and written tales were memorized and added to oral repertories.

We can discern two quite distinct branches in the written transmission of the *Nights*. The earliest surviving manuscript, which dates from fourteenth-century Syria, belongs to the more conservative branch. Later manuscripts derived from it adhere closely to it in substance, form, and style. Others, known collectively as the Egyptian branch, depart widely from it, deleting some of the original stories and adding others from Indian, Persian, Turkish, and Egyptian sources. The story of Sindbad is one of the earliest such additions, and that of Aladdin and the magic lamp one of the latest. At times it seems that the copyists were determined to expand the number of tales to fit the fanciful "one thousand and one" of the title. The first European translator of the *Nights*, the French scholar and traveler Jean Antoine Galland (1646–1715), followed the example of the copyists in the Egyptian branch, translating whatever stories he could find. The great success of his work encouraged other European translators, notably Sir Richard Burton (1821–1890), to do likewise. Some of the tales that Galland and Burton translated from oral sources were retranslated from French or English back into Arabic for new Arabic printings of the *Nights*, and the original character of the *Nights* was distorted almost beyond recognition. The first scholarly edition of *The Thousand and One Nights*, the first, that is, to be based on the fourteenth-century Syrian manuscript, was completed only in 1984, and the selection printed here was translated from it.

From the very beginning classical Arabic literature was unable to find a place for the *Nights*. It was a work neither of history nor of useful knowledge and moral instruction. It was not composed in an elegant, poetic style but in ordinary prose that was very close to common speech. It was filled with magical and fantastic stories that were clearly untrue. While such extravagant and improbable fabrications might be tolerated in poetry, they were unacceptable in a work of prose, since prose was expected to be more serious and substantial than poetry. The qualities that exclude the *Nights* from the canon of classical Arabic are, of course, the very ones that ensure its wide popular acceptance. It is a brilliantly entertaining work, and its stories vary from lighthearted and frivolous to touchingly romantic or terrifying and painful. The themes set forth in the prologue—lust, madness, violence, justice, retribution, and heroism—are weighty ones, and they are grounded in the stuff of everyday life. But they are told with great artistry and made magical by luxurious settings, fantastic adventures, magical turns of fortune, and the timely intervention of demons and sorcerers.

THE PROLOGUE; THE STORY OF THE MERCHANT AND THE DEMON

In the Prologue, Shahrayar is a monarch driven mad by the infidelity of his wife. To ensure that another such humiliation will not occur, he has decided to marry a new young woman each night and murder her the next morning—before she has a chance to betray him. Three years pass in this way and Shahrayar has drastically depleted the number of marriageable young women in the kingdom. His chief vizier has been unable to think of a way to dissuade his monarch from this mad, self-destructive policy, but the vizier's elder daughter, Shahrazad, a young woman of exceptional learning and courage, has a plan. She will voluntarily marry Shahrayar and then use her skill as a storyteller to manipulate him into deferring her death endlessly. Her father tries, unsuccessfully, to dissuade her by telling her tales that are both irrelevant and unpersuasive, but she launches her scheme with the help of her sister, Dinarzad. Each night Shahrazad tells Shahrayar stories to while away the long hours, stopping each sunrise just before some crisis and counting on Shahrayar's eagerness to hear the end of the story to dissuade him from having her executed. In this way, she is able to hold his murderous impulses in check until the passage of time and the healing effects of the tales can do their work, and Shahrayar at last pardons her and and abandons his policy.

To Western readers, the *Nights* most resembles such other famous collections of tales as Chaucer's *Canterbury Tales,* Boccaccio's *Decameron,* and Marguerite de Navarre's *Heptameron.* Like these, its tales are set within the frame of another, larger tale. The prologue of the *Nights* does not surround or frame the tales it includes, however. There are examples of such framed collections within the *Nights,* starting with the first set that Shahrazad recites, but the *Prologue* is a frame tale with a difference. It has a single narrator, not many; and as a consequence there is none of the interplay between narrators, or between narrators and the tales they tell, that marks these other collections. That is, while there are many narrators, and tales within tales, all the stories are ultimately recounted by Shahrazad. Moreover, her motive throughout is the single and compelling one of preventing the destruction of herself and the other young women of her community. The formulaic exchange between Shahrazad, Shahrayar, and Dinarzad that is repeated each dawn and evening reminds us that Shahrazad is not telling tales simply to while away the time.

The image of Shahrazad deftly employing her skills as a narrator to buy her life a day at a time has captured the fancy of all who have read the *Nights,* but there may be more to her tales than an endlessly deferred conclusion. That is, her tales can also be read as a means of healing the wound inflicted on Shahrayar by his wife's infidelity, and of teaching him that not all women wish him ill. That she may have cure in mind as much as delay is suggested by the neat fit between the first set of tales she tells and her own plight. In the first story, for example, a demon sets a precedent for allowing Shahrazad to purchase her life with her tales by allowing three old men to pay the merchant's blood price with theirs. This story also suggests that the demon is too harsh in threatening to kill the merchant for a crime that is at worst accidental. How much more innocent of any wrongdoing are the young women of Shahrayar's realm? In each of the tales a benign but powerful woman undoes the harm caused by an ill-intentioned one. The wicked characters are punished according to their crimes, and never by death. All this suggests that Shahrazad is not simply distracting Shahrayar with her tales, she is educating him or, better, attempting to cure him of his madness. Her choice of a cure may suggest that these tales were shaped by female narrators as well as male or at least by narrators who had an understanding and appreciation of women. A more characteristically male solution to the problem that Shahrayar poses might have been to depose or destroy him.

THE FISHERMAN AND THE DEMON

Shahrazad's second series of tales falls into two parts. In the first, the fisherman and the jinn are, as the title promises, the principals. In the second, the demon vanishes from the stage entirely, and the fisherman moves into a supporting role. The focus of the first set of stories is a battle of wits between fisherman and demon. The injustice of the demon's plan to kill the blameless fisherman provides both the recurrent theme of the tales that the fisherman and the demon tell and the principal link between these stories and those of the three old men. Yet the links between them seem more tenuous, and the story of the deceitful wife actually celebrates fraud as a means of escaping just retribution. The *Tale of the Enchanted King*, however, which makes up the whole of the second narrative, draws us once more back into the world of Shahrayar and Shahrazad. The cruel sorceress queen, her deformed lover, and the innocent king immediately suggest the story that sets the *Nights* in motion. The one important change in this narrative structure is the substitution of a good man for a good woman as the agent whereby justice is done and the king and his kingdom are returned to health.

For those who wish to do more reading in the *Nights*, Husain Haddawy's *The Arabian Nights* (1990) is a complete translation of the text of Muhsin Mahdi's critical edition of the Syrian manuscript (1984), and his *Arabian Nights II: Sindbad and Other Popular Stories* (1995) is a selection of tales that were added to it by later authors. The earliest English version of the *Nights*, which was made from the French of Antoine Galland by an anonymous English translator, has been published in paperback by R. L. Mack as *Arabian Nights' Entertainments* (1995). The nineteenth-century translations by Edward William Lane (1838–42) and Richard Burton (1885–68) were made directly from Arabic but were based on late, heterogeneous manuscripts. Burton's is the better known, but Lane's is closer to the original although it bowdlerizes the erotic scenes. Muhsin Mahdi has published an introduction to his edition entitled simply *The Thousand and One Nights* (1995). Mia Gerhardt's *The Art of Storytelling: A Literary Study of the Thousand and One Nights* (1963) is virtually the only interpretive study of the whole of the *Thousand and One Nights* in English. It contains an excellent discussion of European interest in the work but is less satisfactory for individual stories. Ferial Jabouri Ghazoul, *The Arabian Nights: A Structural Analysis* (1980), focuses on several stories and groups of stories, among them the *Prologue*. She also argues the central importance of the feminine in the *Nights*. Bruno Bettelheim, *The Uses of Enchantment: The Meaning and Importance of Fairy Tales* (1976), includes a brief discussion of Shahrazad in his study of the therapeutic role of fairy tales. Jerome W. Clinton gives a more detailed discussion of this same question in "Madness and Cure in the 1001 Nights," in *Fairy Tales and Society: Illusion, Allusion, Paradigm*, edited by Ruth B. Bottigheimer (1986).

PRONOUNCING GLOSSARY

The following list uses common English syllables and stress accents to provide rough equivalents of selected words whose pronunciation may be unfamiliar to the general reader.

Dinarzad: *dee-nar-zahd'*

Haroun al-Rashid: *ha-roon' ar–ra-sheed'*

Ja'far the Barmakid: *juh-far' the bar'- muh-kid*

Sa'd al-Din Mas'ud: *sad'ad–deen mass-ood'*

Shahrazad: *shah-ruh-zahd'*

Shahrayar: *shah-ruh-yahr'*

Shahzaman: *shah-zuh-mahn'*

From The Thousand and One Nights[1]

Prologue

[*The Story of King Shahrayar and Shahrazad, His Vizier's*[2] *Daughter*]

It is related—but God knows and sees best what lies hidden in the old accounts of bygone peoples and times—that long ago, during the time of the Sasanid dynasty,[3] in the peninsulas of India and Indochina, there lived two kings who were brothers. The older brother was named Shahrayar, the younger Shahzaman. The older, Shahrayar, was a towering knight and a daring champion, invincible, energetic, and implacable. His power reached the remotest corners of the land and its people, so that the country was loyal to him, and his subjects obeyed him. Shahrayar himself lived and ruled in India and Indochina, while to his brother he gave the land of Samarkand[4] to rule as king.

Ten years went by, when one day Shahrayar felt a longing for his brother the king, summoned his vizier (who had two daughters, one called Shahrazad, the other Dinarzad) and bade him go to his brother. Having made preparations, the vizier journeyed day and night until he reached Samarkand. When Shahzaman heard of the vizier's arrival, he went out with his retainers to meet him. He dismounted, embraced him, and asked him for news from his older brother, Shahrayar. The vizier replied that he was well, and that he had sent him to request his brother to visit him. Shahzaman complied with his brother's request and proceeded to make preparations for the journey. In the meantime, he had the vizier camp on the outskirts of the city, and took care of his needs. He sent him what he required of food and fodder, slaughtered many sheep in his honor, and provided him with money and supplies, as well as many horses and camels.

For ten full days he prepared himself for the journey; then he appointed a chamberlain in his place, and left the city to spend the night in his tent, near the vizier. At midnight he returned to his palace in the city, to bid his wife good-bye. But when he entered the palace, he found his wife lying in the arms of one of the kitchen boys. When he saw them, the world turned dark before his eyes and, shaking his head, he said to himself, "I am still

---

1. All selections translated by Husain Haddawy except for *The Third Old Man's Tale*, translated by Jerome W. Clinton.   2. One who bears burdens (literal trans.); the highest state official or administrator under a caliph or shah.   3. The last pre-Islamic dynasty (226–652).   4. A city and province in central Asia, now in Uzbekistan.

here, and this is what she has done when I was barely outside the city. How will it be and what will happen behind my back when I go to visit my brother in India? No. Women are not to be trusted." He got exceedingly angry, adding, "By God, I am king and sovereign in Samarkand, yet my wife has betrayed me and has inflicted this on me." As his anger boiled, he drew his sword and struck both his wife and the cook. Then he dragged them by the heels and threw them from the top of the palace to the trench below. He then left the city and going to the vizier ordered that they depart that very hour. The drum was struck, and they set out on their journey, while Shahzaman's heart was on fire because of what his wife had done to him and how she had betrayed him with some cook, some kitchen boy. They journeyed hurriedly, day and night, through deserts and wilds, until they reached the land of King Shahrayar, who had gone out to receive them.

When Shahrayar met them, he embraced his brother, showed him favors, and treated him generously. He offered him quarters in a palace adjoining his own, for King Shahrayar had built two beautiful towering palaces in his garden, one for the guests, the other for the women and members of his household. He gave the guest house to his brother, Shahzaman, after the attendants had gone to scrub it, dry it, furnish it, and open its windows, which overlooked the garden. Thereafter, Shahzaman would spend the whole day at his brother's, return at night to sleep at the palace, then go back to his brother the next morning. But whenever he found himself alone and thought of his ordeal with his wife, he would sigh deeply, then stifle his grief, and say, "Alas, that this great misfortune should have happened to one in my position!" Then he would fret with anxiety, his spirit would sag, and he would say, "None has seen what I have seen." In his depression, he ate less and less, grew pale, and his health deteriorated. He neglected everything, wasted away, and looked ill.

When King Shahrayar looked at his brother and saw how day after day he lost weight and grew thin, pale, ashen, and sickly, he thought that this was because of his expatriation and homesickness for his country and his family, and he said to himself, "My brother is not happy here. I should prepare a goodly gift for him and send him home." For a month he gathered gifts for his brother; then he invited him to see him and said, "Brother, I would like you to know that I intend to go hunting and pursue the roaming deer, for ten days. Then I shall return to prepare you for your journey home. Would you like to go hunting with me?" Shahzaman replied, "Brother, I feel distracted and depressed. Leave me here and go with God's blessing and help." When Shahrayar heard his brother, he thought that his dejection was because of his homesickness for his country. Not wishing to coerce him, he left him behind, and set out with his retainers and men. When they entered the wilderness, he deployed his men in a circle to begin trapping and hunting.

After his brother's departure, Shahzaman stayed in the palace and, from the window overlooking the garden, watched the birds and trees as he thought of his wife and what she had done to him, and sighed in sorrow. While he agonized over his misfortune, gazing at the heavens and turning a distracted eye on the garden, the private gate of his brother's palace opened, and there emerged, strutting like a dark-eyed deer, the lady, his brother's wife, with twenty slave-girls, ten white and ten black. While Shahzaman looked at them, without being seen, they continued to walk until they stopped below his window, without looking in his direction, thinking that he had gone to the hunt with his brother. Then they sat down, took off their clothes, and suddenly there were ten slave-girls and ten black slaves dressed in the same clothes as the girls. Then the ten black slaves mounted the ten girls, while the lady called, "Mas'ud, Mas'ud!" and a black slave jumped from the tree to the ground, rushed to her, and, raising her legs, went between her thighs and made love to her. Mas'ud topped the lady, while the ten slaves topped the ten girls, and they carried on till noon. When they were done with their business, they got up and washed themselves. Then the ten slaves put on the same clothes again, mingled with the girls, and once more there appeared to be twenty slave-girls. Mas'ud himself jumped over the garden wall and disappeared, while the slave-girls and the lady sauntered to the private gate, went in and, locking the gate behind them, went their way.

All of this happened under King Shahzaman's eyes. When he saw this spectacle of the wife and the women of his brother the great king—how ten slaves put on women's clothes and slept with his brother's paramours and concubines and what Mas'ud did with his brother's wife, in his very palace—and pondered over this calamity and great misfortune, his care and sorrow left him and he said to himself, "This is our common lot. Even though my brother is king and master of the whole world, he cannot protect what is his, his wife and his concubines, and suffers misfortune in his very home. What happened to me is little by comparison. I used to think that I was the only one who has suffered, but from what I have seen, everyone suffers. By God, my misfortune is lighter than that of my brother." He kept marveling and blaming life, whose trials none can escape, and he began to find consolation in his own affliction and forget his grief. When supper came, he ate and drank with relish and zest and, feeling better, kept eating and drinking, enjoying himself and feeling happy. He thought to himself, "I am no longer alone in my misery; I am well."

For ten days, he continued to enjoy his food and drink, and when his brother, King Shahrayar, came back from the hunt, he met him happily, treated him attentively, and greeted him cheerfully. His brother, King Shahrayar, who had missed him, said, "By God, brother, I missed you on this trip and wished you were with me." Shahzaman thanked him and sat down to carouse with him, and when night fell, and food was brought before them, the two ate and drank, and again Shahzaman ate and drank with zest. As time went by, he continued to eat and drink with appetite, and became lighthearted and carefree. His face regained color and became ruddy, and his body gained weight, as his blood circulated and he regained his energy; he was himself again, or even better. King Shahrayar noticed his brother's condition, how he used to be and how he had improved, but kept it to himself until he took him aside one day and said, "My brother Shahzaman, I would like you to do something for me, to satisfy a wish, to answer a question truthfully." Shahzaman asked, "What is it, brother?" He replied, "When you first came to stay with me, I noticed that you kept losing weight, day after day, until your looks changed, your health deteriorated, and your energy sagged. As you continued like this, I thought that what ailed you was your homesickness for your family and your country, but even though I kept noticing that you were wasting away and looking ill, I refrained from questioning you and hid my feelings from you. Then I went hunting, and when I came back, I found that you had recovered and had regained your health. Now I want you to tell me everything and to explain the cause of your deterioration and the cause of your subsequent recovery, without hiding anything from me." When Shahzaman heard what King Shahrayar said, he bowed his head, then said, "As for the cause of my recovery, that I cannot tell you, and I wish that you would excuse me from telling you." The king was greatly astonished at his brother's reply and, burning with curiosity, said, "You must tell me. For now, at least, explain the first cause."

Then Shahzaman related to his brother what happened to him with his own wife, on the night of his departure, from beginning to end, and concluded, "Thus all the while I was with you, great King, whenever I thought of the event and the misfortune that had befallen me, I felt troubled, careworn, and unhappy, and my health deteriorated. This then is the cause." Then he grew silent. When King Shahrayar heard his brother's explanation, he shook his head, greatly amazed at the deceit of women, and prayed to God to protect him from their wickedness, saying, "Brother, you were fortunate in killing your wife and her lover, who gave you good reason to feel troubled, careworn, and ill. In my opinion, what happened to you has never happened to anyone else. By God, had I been in your place, I would have killed at least a hundred or even a thousand women. I would have been furious; I would have gone mad. Now praise be to God who has delivered you from sorrow and distress. But tell me what has caused you to forget your sorrow and regain your health?" Shahzaman replied, "King, I wish that for God's sake you would excuse me from telling you." Shahrayar said, "You must." Shahzaman replied, "I fear that you will feel even more troubled and careworn than I." Shahrayar asked, "How could that be, brother? I insist on hearing your explanation."

Shahzaman then told him about what he had seen from the palace window and the calamity in his very home—how ten slaves, dressed like women, were sleeping with his women and concubines, day and night. He told him everything from beginning to end (but there is no point in repeating that). Then he concluded, "When I saw your own misfortune, I felt better—and said to myself, 'My brother is king of the world, yet such a misfortune has happened to him, and in his very home.' As a result I forgot my care and sorrow, relaxed, and began to eat and drink. This is the cause of my cheer and good spirits."

When King Shahrayar heard what his brother said and found out what had happened to him, he was furious and his blood boiled. He said, "Brother, I can't believe what you say unless I see it with my own eyes." When Shahzaman saw that his brother was in a rage, he said to him, "If you do not believe me, unless you see your misfortune with your own eyes, announce that you plan to go hunting. Then you and I shall set out with your troops, and when we get outside the city, we shall leave our tents and camp with the men behind, enter the city secretly, and go together to your palace. Then the next morning you can see with your own eyes."

King Shahrayar realized that his brother had a good plan and ordered his army to prepare for the trip. He spent the night with his brother, and when God's morning broke, the two rode out of the city with their army, preceded by the camp attendants, who had gone to drive the poles and pitch the tents where the king and his army were to camp. At nightfall King Shahrayar summoned his chief chamberlain and bade him take his place. He entrusted him with the army and ordered that for three days no one was to enter the city. Then he and his brother disguised themselves and entered the city in the dark. They went directly to the palace where Shahzaman resided and slept there till the morning. When they awoke, they sat at the palace window, watching the garden and chatting, until the light broke, the day dawned, and the sun rose. As they watched, the private gate opened, and there emerged as usual the wife of King Shahrayar, walking among twenty slave-girls. They made their way under the trees until they stood below the palace window where the two kings sat. Then they took off their women's clothes, and suddenly there were ten slaves, who mounted the ten girls and made love to them. As for the lady, she called, "Mas'ud, Mas'ud," and a black slave jumped from the tree to the ground, came to her, and said, "What do you want, you slut? Here is Sa'ad al-Din Mas'ud." She laughed and fell on her back, while the slave mounted her and like the others did his business with her. Then the black slaves got up, washed themselves, and, putting on the same clothes, mingled with the girls. Then they walked away, entered the palace, and locked the gate behind them. As for Mas'ud, he jumped over the fence to the road and went on his way.

When King Shahrayar saw the spectacle of his wife and the slave-girls, he went out of his mind, and when he and his brother came down from upstairs, he said, "No one is safe in this world. Such doings are going on in my kingdom, and in my very palace. Perish the world and perish life! This is a great calamity, indeed." Then he turned to his brother and asked, "Would you like to follow me in what I shall do?" Shahzaman answered, "Yes. I will." Shahrayar said, "Let us leave our royal state and roam the world for the love of the Supreme Lord. If we should find one whose misfortune is greater than ours, we shall return. Otherwise, we shall continue to journey through the land, without need for the trappings of royalty." Shahzaman replied, "This is an excellent idea. I shall follow you."

Then they left by the private gate, took a side road, and departed, journeying till nightfall. They slept over their sorrows, and in the morning resumed their day journey until they came to a meadow by the seashore. While they sat in the meadow amid the thick plants and trees, discussing their misfortunes and the recent events, they suddenly heard a shout and a great cry coming from the middle of the sea. They trembled with fear, thinking that the sky had fallen on the earth. Then the sea parted, and there emerged a black pillar that, as it swayed forward, got taller and taller, until it touched the clouds. Shahrayar and Shahzaman were petrified; then they ran in terror and, climbing a very tall tree, sat hiding in its foliage. When they looked again, they saw that the black pillar was cleaving the sea, wading in the water toward the green meadow, until it touched the shore. When they looked again, they saw that it was a black demon, carrying on his head a large glass chest with four steel locks. He came out, walked into the meadow, and where should he stop but under the very tree where the two kings were hiding. The demon sat down and placed the glass chest on the ground. He took out four keys and, opening the locks of the chest, pulled out a full-grown woman. She had a beautiful figure, and a face like the full moon, and a lovely smile. He took her out, laid her under the tree, and looked at her, saying, "Mistress of all noble women, you whom I carried away on your wedding night, I would like to sleep a little." Then he placed his head on the young woman's lap, stretched his legs to the sea, sank into sleep, and began to snore.

Meanwhile, the woman looked up at the tree and, turning her head by chance, saw King Shahrayar and King Shahzaman. She lifted the demon's head from her lap and placed it on the ground. Then she came and stood under the tree and motioned to them with her hand, as if to say, "Come down slowly to me." When they realized that she had seen them, they were frightened, and they begged her and implored her, in the name of the Creator of the heavens, to excuse them from climbing down. She replied, "You must come down to me." They motioned to her, saying, "This sleeping demon is the enemy of mankind. For God's sake, leave us alone." She replied, "You must come down, and if you don't, I shall wake the demon and have him kill you." She kept gesturing and pressing, until they climbed down very slowly and stood before her. Then she lay on her back, raised her legs, and said, "Make love to me and satisfy my need, or else I shall wake the demon, and he will kill you." They replied, "For God's sake, mistress, don't do this to us, for at this moment we feel nothing but dismay and fear of this demon. Please, excuse us." She replied, "You must," and insisted, swearing, "By God who created the heavens, if you don't do it, I shall wake my husband the demon and ask him to kill you and throw you into the sea." As she persisted, they could no longer resist and they made love to her, first the older brother, then the younger. When they were done and withdrew from her, she said to them, "Give me your rings," and, pulling out from the folds of her dress a small purse, opened it, and shook out ninety-eight rings of different fashions and colors. Then she asked them, "Do you know what these rings are?" They answered, "No." She said, "All the owners of these rings slept with me, for whenever one of them made love to me, I took a ring from him. Since you two have slept with me, give me your rings, so that I may add them to the rest, and make a full hundred. A hundred men have known me under the very horns of this filthy, monstrous cuckold, who has imprisoned me in this chest, locked it with four locks, and kept me in the middle of this raging, roaring sea. He has guarded me and tried to keep me pure and chaste, not realizing that nothing can prevent or alter what is predestined and that when a woman desires something, no one can stop her." When Shahrayar and Shahzaman heard what the young woman said, they were greatly amazed, danced with joy, and said, "O God, O God! There is no power and no strength, save in God the Almighty, the Magnificent. Great is women's cunning." Then each of them took off his ring and handed it to her. She took them and put them with the rest in the purse. Then sitting again by the demon, she lifted his head, placed it back on her lap, and motioned to them, "Go on your way, or else I shall wake him."

They turned their backs and took to the road. Then Shahrayar turned to his brother and said, "My brother Shahzaman, look at this sorry plight. By God, it is worse than ours. This is no less than a demon who has carried a young woman away on her wedding night, imprisoned her in a glass chest, locked her up with four locks, and kept her in the middle of the sea, thinking that he could guard her from what God had foreordained, and you saw how she has managed to sleep with ninety-eight men, and added the two of us to make a hundred. Brother, let us go back to our kingdoms and our cities, never to marry a woman again. As for myself, I shall show you what I will do."

Then the two brothers headed home and journeyed till nightfall. On the morning of the third day, they reached their camp and men, entered their tent, and sat on their thrones. The chamberlains, deputies, princes, and viziers came to attend King Shahrayar, while he gave orders and bestowed robes of honor, as well as other gifts. Then at his command everyone returned to the city, and he went to his own palace and ordered his chief vizier, the father of the two girls Shahrazad and Dinarzad, who will be mentioned below, and said to him, "Take that wife of mine and put her to death." Then Shahrayar went to her himself, bound her, and handed her over to the vizier, who took her out and put her to death. Then King Shahrayar grabbed his sword, brandished it and, entering the palace chambers, killed every one of his slave-girls and replaced them with others. He then swore to marry for one night only and kill the woman the next morning, in order to save himself from the wickedness and cunning of women, saying, "There is not a single chaste woman anywhere on the entire face of the earth." Shortly thereafter he provided his brother Shahzaman with supplies for his journey and sent him back to his own country with gifts, rarities, and money. The brother bade him good-bye and set out for home.

Shahrayar sat on his throne and ordered his vizier, the father of the two girls, to find him a wife from among the princes' daughters. The vizier found him one, and he slept with her and was done with her, and the next morning he ordered the vizier to put her to death. That very night he took one of his army officers' daughters, slept with her, and the next morning ordered the vizier to put her to death. The vizier, who could not disobey him, put her to death. The third night he took one of the merchants' daughters, slept with her till the morning, then ordered his vizier to put her to death, and the vizier did so. It became King Shahrayar's custom to take every night the daughter of a merchant or a commoner, spend the night with her, then have her put to death the next morning. He continued to do this until all the girls perished, their mothers mourned, and there arose a clamor among the fathers and mothers, who called the plague upon his head, complained to the Creator of the heavens, and called for help on Him who hears and answers prayers.

Now, as mentioned earlier, the vizier, who put the girls to death, had an older daughter called Shahrazad and a younger one called Dinarzad. The older daughter, Shahrazad, had read the books of literature, philosophy, and medicine. She knew poetry by heart, had studied historical reports, and was acquainted with the sayings of men and the maxims of sages and kings. She was intelligent, knowledgeable, wise, and refined. She had read and learned. One day she said to her father, "Father, I will tell you what is in my mind." He asked, "What is it?" She answered, "I would like you to marry me to King Shahrayar, so that I may either succeed in saving the people or perish and die like the rest." When the vizier heard what his daughter Shahrazad said, he got angry and said to her, "Foolish one, don't you know that King Shahrayar has sworn to spend but one night with a girl and have her put to death the next morning? If I give you to him, he will sleep with you for one night and will ask me to put you to death the next morning, and I shall have to do it, since I cannot disobey him." She said, "Father, you must give me to him, even if he kills me." He asked, "What has possessed you that you wish to imperil yourself?" She replied, "Father, you must give me to him. This is absolute and final." Her father the vizier became furious and said to her, "Daughter, 'He who misbehaves, ends up in trouble,' and 'He who considers not the end, the world is not his friend.' As the popular saying goes, 'I would be sitting pretty, but for my curiosity.' I am afraid that what happened to the donkey and the ox with the merchant will happen to you." She asked, "Father, what happened to the donkey, the ox, and the merchant?" He said:

[The Tale of the Ox and the Donkey]

There was a prosperous and wealthy merchant who lived in the countryside and labored on a farm. He owned many camels and herds of cattle and employed many men, and he had a wife and many grown-up as well as little children. This merchant was taught the language of the beasts, on condition that if he revealed his secret to anyone, he would die; therefore, even though he knew the language of every kind of animal, he did not let anyone know, for fear of death. One day, as he sat, with his wife beside him and his children playing before him, he glanced at an ox and a donkey he kept at the farmhouse, tied to adjacent troughs, and heard the ox say to the donkey, "Watchful one, I hope that you are enjoying the comfort and the service you are getting. Your ground is swept and watered, and they serve you, feed you sifted barley, and offer you clear, cool water to drink. I, on the contrary, am taken out to plow in the middle of the night. They clamp on my neck something they call yoke and plow, push me all day under the whip to plow the field, and drive me beyond my endurance until my sides are lacerated, and my neck is flayed. They work me from nighttime to nighttime, take me back in the dark, offer me beans soiled with mud and hay mixed with chaff, and let me spend the night lying in urine and dung. Meanwhile you rest on well-swept, watered, and smoothed ground, with a clean trough full of hay. You stand in comfort, save for the rare occasion when our master the merchant rides you to do a brief errand and returns. You are comfortable, while I am weary; you sleep, while I keep awake."

When the ox finished, the donkey turned to him and said, "Greenhorn, they were right in calling you ox, for you ox harbor no deceit, malice, or meanness. Being sincere, you exert and exhaust yourself to comfort others. Have you not heard the saying 'Out of bad luck, they hastened on the road'? You go into the field from early morning to endure your torture at the plow to the point of exhaustion. When the plowman takes you back and ties you to the trough, you go on butting and beating with your horns, kicking with your hoofs, and bellowing for the beans, until they toss them to you; then you begin to eat. Next time, when they bring them to you, don't eat or even touch them, but smell them, then draw back and lie down on the hay and straw. If you do this, life will be better and kinder to you, and you will find relief."

As the ox listened, he was sure that the donkey had given him good advice. He thanked him, commended him to God, and invoked His blessing on him, and said, "May you stay safe from harm, watchful one." All of this conversation took place, daughter, while the merchant listened and understood. On the following day, the plowman came to the merchant's house and, taking the ox, placed the yoke upon his neck and worked him at the plow, but the ox lagged behind. The plowman hit him, but following the donkey's advice, the ox, dissembling, fell on his belly, and the plowman hit him again. Thus the ox kept getting up and falling until nightfall, when the plowman took him home and tied him to the trough. But this time the ox did not bellow or kick the ground with his hoofs. Instead, he withdrew, away from the trough. Astonished, the plowman brought him his beans and fodder, but the ox only smelled the fodder and pulled back and lay down at a distance with the hay and straw, complaining till the morning. When the plowman arrived, he found the trough as he had left it, full of beans and fodder, and saw the ox lying on his back, hardly breathing, his belly puffed, and his legs raised in the air. The plowman felt sorry for him and said to himself, "By God, he did seem weak and unable to work." Then he went to the merchant and said, "Master, last night, the ox refused to eat or touch his fodder."

The merchant, who knew what was going on, said to the plowman, "Go to the wily donkey, put him to the plow, and work him hard until he finishes the ox's task." The plowman left, took the donkey, and placed the yoke upon his neck. Then he took him out to the field and drove him with blows until he finished the ox's work, all the while driving him with blows and beating him until his sides were lacerated and his neck was flayed. At nightfall he took him home, barely able to drag his legs under his tired body and his drooping ears. Meanwhile the ox spent his day resting. He ate all his food, drank his water, and lay quietly, chewing his cud in comfort. All day long he kept praising the donkey's advice and invoking God's blessing on him. When the donkey came back at night, the ox stood up to greet him saying, "Good evening, watchful one! You have done me a favor beyond description, for I have been sitting in comfort. God bless you for my sake." Seething with anger, the donkey did not reply, but said to himself, "All this happened to me because of my miscalculation. 'I would be sitting pretty, but for my curiosity.' If I don't find a way to return this ox to his former situation, I will perish." Then he went to his trough and lay down, while the ox continued to chew his cud and invoke God's blessing on him.

"You, my daughter, will likewise perish because of your miscalculation. Desist, sit quietly, and don't expose yourself to peril. I advise you out of compassion for you." She replied, "Father, I must go to the king, and you must give me to him." He said, "Don't do it." She insisted, "I must." He replied, "If you don't desist, I will do to you what the merchant did to his wife." She asked, "Father, what did the merchant do to his wife?" He said:

[The Tale of the Merchant and His Wife]

After what had happened to the donkey and the ox, the merchant and his wife went out in the moonlight to the stable, and he heard the donkey ask the ox in his own language, "Listen, ox, what are you going to do tomorrow morning, and what will you do when the plowman brings you your fodder?" The ox replied, "What shall I do but follow your advice and stick to it? If he brings me my fodder, I will pretend to be ill, lie down, and puff my belly." The donkey shook his head, and said, "Don't do it. Do you know what I heard our master the merchant say to the plowman?" The ox asked, "What?" The donkey replied, "He said that if the ox failed to get up and eat his fodder, he would call the butcher to slaughter him and skin him and would distribute the meat for alms and use the skin for a mat. I am afraid for you, but good advice is a matter of faith; therefore, if he brings you your fodder, eat it and look alert lest they cut your throat and skin you." The ox farted and bellowed.

The merchant got up and laughed loudly at the conversation between the donkey and the ox, and his wife asked him, "What are you laughing at? Are you making fun of me?" He said, "No." She said, "Tell me what made you laugh." He replied, "I cannot tell you. I am afraid to disclose the secret conversation of the animals." She asked, "And what prevents you from telling me?" He answered, "The fear of death." His wife said, "By God, you are lying. This is nothing but an excuse. I swear by God, the Lord of heaven, that if you don't tell me and explain the cause of your laughter, I will leave you. You must tell me." Then she went back to the house crying, and she continued to cry till the morning. The merchant said, "Damn it! Tell me why you are crying. Ask for God's forgiveness, and stop questioning and leave me in peace." She said, "I insist and will not desist." Amazed at her, he replied, "You insist! If I tell you what the donkey said to the ox, which made me laugh, I shall die." She said, "Yes, I insist, even if you have to die." He replied, "Then call your family," and she called their two daughters, her parents and relatives, and some neighbors. The merchant told them that he was about to die, and everyone, young and old, his children, the farmhands, and the servants began to cry until the house became a place of mourning. Then he summoned legal witnesses, wrote a will, leaving his wife and children their due portions, freed his slave-girls, and bid his family good-bye, while everybody, even the witnesses, wept. Then the wife's parents approached her and said, "Desist, for if your husband had not known for certain that he would die if he revealed his secret, he wouldn't have gone through all this." She replied, "I will not change my mind," and everybody cried and prepared to mourn his death.

Well, my daughter Shahrazad, it happened that the farmer kept fifty hens and a rooster at home, and while he felt sad to depart this world and leave his children and relatives behind, pondering and about to reveal and utter his secret, he overheard a dog of his say something in dog language to the rooster, who, beating and clapping his wings, had jumped on a hen and, finishing with her, jumped down and jumped on another. The merchant heard and understood what the dog said in his own language to the rooster, "Shameless, no-good rooster. Aren't you ashamed to do such a thing on a day like this?" The rooster asked, "What is special about this day?" The dog replied, "Don't you know that our master and friend is in mourning today? His wife is demanding that he disclose his secret, and when he discloses it, he will surely die. He is in this predicament, about to interpret to her the language of the animals, and all of us are mourning for him, while you clap your wings and get off one hen and jump on another. Aren't you ashamed?" The merchant heard the rooster reply, "You fool, you lunatic! Our master and friend claims to be wise, but he is foolish, for he has only one wife, yet he does not know how to manage her." The dog asked, "What should he do with her?"

The rooster replied, "He should take an oak branch, push her into a room, lock the door, and fall on her with the stick, beating her mercilessly until he breaks her arms and legs and she cries out, 'I no longer want you to tell me or explain anything.' He should go on beating her until he cures her for life, and she will never oppose him in anything. If he does this, he will live, and live in peace, and there will be no more grief, but he does not know how to manage." Well, my daughter Shahrazad, when the merchant heard the conversation between the dog and the rooster, he jumped up and, taking an oak branch, pushed his wife into a room, got in with her, and locked the door. Then he began to beat her mercilessly on her chest and shoulders and kept beating her until she cried for mercy, screaming, "No, no, I don't want to know anything. Leave me alone, leave me alone. I don't want to know anything," until he got tired of hitting her and opened the door. The wife emerged penitent, the husband learned good management, and everybody was happy, and the mourning turned into a celebration.

"If you don't relent, I shall do to you what the merchant did to his wife." She said, "Such tales don't deter me from my request. If you wish, I can tell you many such tales. In the end, if you don't take me to King Shahrayar, I shall go to him by myself behind your back and tell him that you have refused to give me to one like him and that you have begrudged your master one like me." The vizier asked, "Must you really do this?" She replied, "Yes, I must."

Tired and exhausted, the vizier went to King Shahrayar and, kissing the ground before him, told him about his daughter, adding that he would give her to him that very night. The king was astonished and said to him, "Vizier, how is it that you have found it possible to give me your daughter, knowing that I will, by God, the Creator of heaven, ask you to put her to death the next morning and that if you refuse, I will have you put to death too?" He replied, "My King and Lord, I have told her everything and explained all this to her, but she refuses and insists on being with you tonight." The king was delighted and said, "Go to her, prepare her, and bring her to me early in the evening."

The vizier went down, repeated the king's message to his daughter, and said, "May God not deprive me of you." She was very happy and, after preparing herself and packing what she needed, went to her younger sister, Dinarzad, and said, "Sister, listen well to what I am telling you. When I go to the king, I will send for you, and when you come and see that the king has finished with me, say, 'Sister, if you are not sleepy, tell us a story.' Then I will begin to tell a story, and it will cause the king to stop his practice, save myself, and deliver the people." Dinarzad replied, "Very well."

At nightfall the vizier took Shahrazad and went with her to the great King Shahrayar. But when Shahrayar took her to bed and began to fondle her, she wept, and when he asked her, "Why are you crying?" she replied, "I have a sister, and I wish to bid her good-bye before daybreak." Then the king sent for the sister, who came and went to sleep under the bed. When the night wore on, she woke up and waited until the king had satisfied himself with her sister Shahrazad and they were by now all fully awake. Then Dinarzad cleared her throat and said, "Sister, if you are not sleepy, tell us one of your lovely little tales to while away the night, before I bid you good-bye at daybreak, for I don't know what will happen to you tomorrow." Shahrazad turned to King Shahrayar and said, "May I have your permission to tell a story?" He replied, "Yes," and Shahrazad was very happy and said, "Listen":

[The Story of the Merchant and the Demon]

THE FIRST NIGHT

It is said, O wise and happy King, that once there was a prosperous merchant who had abundant wealth and investments and commitments in every country. He had many women and children and kept many servants and slaves. One day, having resolved to visit another country, he took provisions, filling his saddlebag with loaves of bread and with dates, mounted his horse, and set out on his journey. For many days and nights, he journeyed under God's care until he reached his destination. When he finished his business, he turned back to his home and family. He journeyed for three days, and on the fourth day, chancing to come to an orchard, went in to avoid the heat and shade himself from the sun of the open country. He came to a spring under a walnut tree and, tying his horse, sat by the spring, pulled out from the saddlebag some loaves of bread and a handful of dates, and began to eat, throwing the date pits right and left until he had had enough. Then he got up, performed his ablutions, and performed his prayers.

But hardly had he finished when he saw an old demon, with sword in hand, standing with his feet on the ground and his head in the clouds. The demon approached until he stood before him and screamed, saying, "Get up, so that I may kill you with this sword, just as you have killed my son." When the merchant saw and heard the demon, he was terrified and awestricken. He asked, "Master, for what crime do you wish to kill me?" The demon replied, "I wish to kill you because you have killed my son." The merchant asked, "Who has killed your son?" The demon replied, "You have killed my son." The merchant said, "By God, I did not kill your son. When and how could that have been?" The demon said, "Didn't you sit down, take out some dates from your saddlebag, and eat, throwing the pits right and left?" The merchant replied, "Yes, I did." The demon said, "You killed my son, for as you were throwing the stones right and left, my son happened to be walking by and was struck and killed by one of them, and I must now kill you." The merchant said, "O my lord, please don't kill me." The demon replied, "I must kill you as you killed him—blood for blood." The merchant said, "To God we belong and to God we turn. There is no power or strength, save in God the Almighty, the Magnificent. If I killed him, I did it by mistake. Please forgive me." The demon replied, "By God, I must kill you, as you killed my son." Then he seized him, and throwing him to the ground, raised the sword to strike him. The merchant began to weep and mourn his family and his wife and children. Again, the demon raised his sword to strike, while the merchant cried until he was drenched with tears, saying, "There is no power or strength, save in God the Almighty, the Magnificent." Then he began to recite the following verses:

> Life has two days: one peace, one wariness,
> And has two sides: worry and happiness.
> Ask him who taunts us with adversity,
> "Does fate, save those worthy of note, oppress?
> Don't you see that the blowing, raging storms
> Only the tallest of the trees beset,
> And of earth's many green and barren lots,

5

Only the ones with fruits with stones are hit,
And of the countless stars in heaven's vault
None is eclipsed except the moon and sun?   10
You thought well of the days, when they were good,
Oblivious to the ills destined for one.
You were deluded by the peaceful nights,
Yet in the peace of night does sorrow stun."

When the merchant finished and stopped weeping, the demon said, "By God, I must kill you, as you killed my son, even if you weep blood." The merchant asked, "Must you?" The demon replied, "I must," and raised his sword to strike.

But morning overtook Shahrazad, and she lapsed into silence, leaving King Shahrayar burning with curiosity to hear the rest of the story. Then Dinarzad said to her sister Shahrazad, "What a strange and lovely story!" Shahrazad replied, "What is this compared with what I shall tell you tomorrow night if the king spares me and lets me live? It will be even better and more entertaining." The king thought to himself, "I will spare her until I hear the rest of the story; then I will have her put to death the next day." When morning broke, the day dawned, and the sun rose; the king left to attend to the affairs of the kingdom, and the vizier, Shahrazad's father, was amazed and delighted. King Shahrayar governed all day and returned home at night to his quarters and got into bed with Shahrazad. Then Dinarzad said to her sister Shahrazad, "Please, sister, if you are not sleepy, tell us one of your lovely little tales to while away the night." The king added, "Let it be the conclusion of the story of the demon and the merchant, for I would like to hear it." Shahrazad replied, "With the greatest pleasure, dear, happy King":

THE SECOND NIGHT

It is related, O wise and happy King, that when the demon raised his sword, the merchant asked the demon again, "Must you kill me?" and the demon replied, "Yes." Then the merchant said, "Please give me time to say good-bye to my family and my wife and children, divide my property among them, and appoint guardians. Then I shall come back, so that you may kill me." The demon replied, "I am afraid that if I release you and grant you time, you will go and do what you wish, but will not come back." The merchant said, "I swear to keep my pledge to come back, as the God of Heaven and earth is my witness." The demon asked, "How much time do you need?" The merchant replied, "One year, so that I may see enough of my children, bid my wife good-bye, discharge my obligations to people, and come back on New Year's Day." The demon asked, "Do you swear to God that if I let you go, you will come back on New Year's Day?" The merchant replied, "Yes, I swear to God."

After the merchant swore, the demon released him, and he mounted his horse sadly and went on his way. He journeyed until he reached his home and came to his wife and children. When he saw them, he wept bitterly, and when his family saw his sorrow and grief, they began to reproach him for his behavior, and his wife said, "Husband, what is the matter with you? Why do you mourn, when we are happy, celebrating your return?" He replied, "Why not mourn when I have only one year to live?" Then he told her of his encounter with the demon and informed her that he had sworn to return on New Year's Day, so that the demon might kill him.

When they heard what he said, everyone began to cry. His wife struck her face in lamentation and cut her hair, his daughters wailed, and his little children cried. It was a day of mourning, as all the children gathered around their father to weep and exchange good-byes. The next day he wrote his will, dividing his property, discharged his obligations to people, left bequests and gifts, distributed alms, and engaged reciters to read portions of the Quran in his house. Then he summoned legal witnesses and in their presence freed his slaves and slave-girls, divided among his elder children their shares of the property, appointed guardians for his little ones, and gave his wife her share, according to her marriage contract. He spent the rest of the time with his family, and when the year came to an end, save for the time needed for the journey, he performed his ablutions, performed his prayers, and, carrying his burial shroud, began to bid his family good-bye. His sons hung around his neck, his daughters wept, and his wife wailed. Their mourning scared him, and he began to weep, as he embraced and kissed his children good-bye. He said to them, "Children, this is God's will and decree, for man was created to die." Then he turned away and, mounting his horse, journeyed day and night until he reached the orchard on New Year's Day.

He sat at the place where he had eaten the dates, waiting for the demon, with a heavy heart and tearful eyes. As he waited, an old man, leading a deer on a leash, approached and greeted him, and he returned the greeting. The old man inquired, "Friend, why do you sit here in this place of demons and devils? For in this haunted orchard none come to good." The merchant replied by telling him what had happened to him and the demon, from beginning to end. The old man was amazed at the merchant's fidelity and said, "Yours is a magnificent pledge," adding, "By God, I shall not leave until I see what will happen to you with the demon." Then he sat down beside him and chatted with him. As they talked . . .

But morning overtook Shahrazad, and she lapsed into silence. As the day dawned, and it was light, her sister Dinarzad said, "What a strange and wonderful story!" Shahrazad replied, "Tomorrow night I shall tell something even stranger and more wonderful than this."

THE THIRD NIGHT

When it was night and Shahrazad was in bed with the king, Dinarzad said to her sister Shahrazad, "Please, if you are not sleepy, tell us one of your lovely little tales to while away the night." The king added, "Let it be the conclusion of the merchant's story." Shahrazad replied, "As you wish":

I heard, O happy King, that as the merchant and the man with the deer sat talking, another old man approached, with two black hounds, and when he reached them, he greeted them, and they returned his greeting. Then he asked them about themselves, and the man with the deer told him the story of the merchant and the demon, how the merchant had sworn to return on New Year's Day, and how the demon was waiting to kill him. He added that when he himself heard the story, he swore never to leave until he saw what would happen between the merchant and the demon. When the man with the two dogs heard the story, he was amazed, and he too swore never to leave them until he saw what would happen between them. Then he questioned the merchant, and the merchant repeated to him what had happened to him with the demon.

While they were engaged in conversation, a third old man approached and greeted them, and they returned his greeting. He asked, "Why do I see the two of you sitting here, with this merchant between you, looking abject, sad, and dejected?" They told him the merchant's story and explained that they were sitting and waiting to see what would happen to him with the demon. When he heard the story, he sat down with them, saying, "By God, I too like you will not leave, until I see what happens to this man with the demon." As they sat, conversing with one another, they suddenly saw the dust rising from the open country, and when it cleared, they saw the demon approaching, with a drawn steel sword in his hand. He stood before them without greeting them, yanked the merchant with his left hand, and, holding him fast before him, said, "Get ready to die." The merchant and the three old men began to weep and wail.

But dawn broke and morning overtook Shahrazad, and she lapsed into silence. Then Dinarzad said, "Sister, what a lovely story!" Shahrazad replied, "What is this compared with what I shall tell you tomorrow night? It will be even better; it will be more wonderful, delightful, entertaining, and delectable if the king spares me and lets me live." The king was all curiosity to hear the rest of the story and said to himself, "By God, I will not have her put to death until I hear the rest of the story and find out what happened to the merchant with the demon. Then I will have her put to death the next morning, as I did with the others." Then he went out to attend to the affairs of his kingdom, and when he saw Shahrazad's father, he treated him kindly and showed him favors, and the vizier was amazed. When night came, the king went home, and when he was in bed with Shahrazad, Dinarzad said, "Sister, if you are not sleepy, tell us one of your lovely little tales to while away the night." Shahrazad replied, "With the greatest pleasure":

THE FOURTH NIGHT

It is related, O happy King, that the first old man with the deer approached the demon and, kissing his hands and feet, said, "Fiend and King of the demon kings, if I tell you what happened to me and that deer, and you find it strange and amazing, indeed stranger and more amazing than what happened to you and the merchant, will you grant me a third of your claim on him for his crime and guilt?" The demon replied, "I will." The old man said:

[The First Old Man's Tale]

Demon, this deer is my cousin, my flesh and blood. I married her when I was very young, and she a girl of twelve, who reached womanhood only afterward. For thirty years we lived together, but I was not blessed with children, for she bore neither boy nor girl. Yet I continued to be kind to her, to care for her, and to treat her generously. Then I took a mistress, and she bore me a son, who grew up to look like a slice of the moon.⁵ Meanwhile, my wife grew jealous of my mistress and my son. One day, when he was ten, I had to go on a journey. I entrusted my wife, this one here, with my mistress and son, bade her take good care of them, and was gone for a whole year. In my absence my wife, this cousin of mine, learned soothsaying and magic and cast a spell on my son and turned him into a young bull. Then she summoned my shepherd, gave my son to him, and said, "Tend this bull with the rest of the cattle." The shepherd took him and tended him for a while. Then she cast a spell on the mother, turning her into a cow, and gave her also to the shepherd.

When I came back, after all this was done, and inquired about my mistress and my son, she answered, "Your mistress died, and your son ran away two months ago, and I have had no news from him ever since." When I heard her, I grieved for my mistress, and with an anguished heart I mourned for my son for nearly a year. When the Great Feast of the Immolation⁶ drew near, I summoned the shepherd and ordered him to bring me a fat cow for the sacrifice. The cow he brought me was in reality my enchanted mistress. When I bound her and pressed against her to cut her throat, she wept and cried, as if saying, "My son, my son," and her tears coursed down her cheeks. Astonished and seized with pity, I turned away and asked the shepherd to bring me a different cow. But my wife shouted, "Go on. Butcher her, for he has none better or fatter. Let us enjoy her meat at feast time." I approached the cow to cut her throat, and again she cried, as if saying, "My son, my son." Then I turned away from her and said to the shepherd, "Butcher her for me." The shepherd butchered her, and when he skinned her, he found neither meat nor fat but only skin and bone. I regretted having her butchered and said to the shepherd, "Take her all for yourself, or give her as alms to whomever you wish, and find me a fat young bull from among the flock." The shepherd took her away and disappeared, and I never knew what he did with her.

Then he brought me my son, my heartblood, in the guise of a fat young bull. Then my son saw me, he shook his head loose from the rope, ran toward me, and, throwing himself at my feet, kept rubbing his head against me. I was astonished and touched with sympathy, pity, and mercy, for the blood hearkened to the blood and the divine bond, and my heart throbbed within me when I saw the tears coursing over the cheeks of my son the young bull, as he dug the earth with his hoofs. I turned away and said to the shepherd, "Let him go with the rest of the flock, and be kind to him, for I have decided to spare him. Bring me another one instead of him." My wife, this very deer, shouted, "You shall sacrifice none but this bull." I got angry and replied, "I listened to you and butchered the cow uselessly. I will not listen to you and kill this bull, for I have decided to spare him." But she pressed me, saying, "You must butcher this bull," and I bound him and took the knife . . .

But dawn broke, and morning overtook Shahrazad, and she lapsed into silence, leaving the king all curiosity for the rest of the story. Then her sister

---

5. The moon is a symbol of beauty for men and women.   6. Celebrates the pilgrimage to Mecca; it lasts four days, during which sheep and cattle are sacrificed to God.

Dinarzad said, "What an entertaining story!" Shahrazad replied, "Tomorrow night I shall tell you something even stranger, more wonderful, and more entertaining if the king spares me and lets me live."

THE FIFTH NIGHT

The following night, Dinarzad said to her sister Shahrazad, "Please, sister, if you are not sleepy, tell us one of your little tales." Shahrazad replied, "With the greatest pleasure":

I heard, dear King, that the old man with the deer said to the demon and to his companions:

I took the knife and as I turned to slaughter my son, he wept, bellowed, rolled at my feet, and motioned toward me with his tongue. I suspected something, began to waver with trepidation and pity, and finally released him, saying to my wife, "I have decided to spare him, and I commit him to your care." Then I tried to appease and please my wife, this very deer, by slaughtering another bull, promising her to slaughter this one next season. We slept that night, and when God's dawn broke, the shepherd came to me without letting my wife know, and said, "Give me credit for bringing you good news." I replied, "Tell me, and the credit is yours." He said, "Master, I have a daughter who is fond of soothsaying and magic and who is adept at the art of oaths and spells. Yesterday I took home with me the bull you had spared, to let him graze with the cattle, and when my daughter saw him, she laughed and cried at the same time. When I asked her why she laughed and cried, she answered that she laughed because the bull was in reality the son of our master the cattle owner, put under a spell by his step-mother, and that she cried because his father had slaughtered the son's mother. I could hardly wait till daybreak to bring you the good news about your son."

Demon, when I heard that, I uttered a cry and fainted, and when I came to myself, I accompanied the shepherd to his home, went to my son, and threw myself at him, kissing him and crying. He turned his head toward me, his tears coursing over his cheeks, and dangled his tongue, as if to say, "Look at my plight." Then I turned to the shepherd's daughter and asked, "Can you release him from the spell? If you do, I will give you all my cattle and all my possessions." She smiled and replied, "Master, I have no desire for your wealth, cattle, or possessions. I will deliver him, but on two conditions: first, that you let me marry him; second, that you let me cast a spell on her who had cast a spell on him, in order to control her and guard against her evil power." I replied, "Do whatever you wish and more. My possessions are for you and my son. As for my wife, who has done this to my son and made me slaughter his mother, her life is forfeit to you." She said, "No, but I will let her taste what she has inflicted on others." Then the shepherd's daughter filled a bowl of water, uttered an incantation and an oath, and said to my son, "Bull, if you have been created in this image by the All-Conquering, Almighty Lord, stay as you are, but if you have been treacherously put under a spell, change back to your human form, by the will of God, Creator of the wide world." Then she sprinkled him with the water, and he shook himself and changed from a bull back to his human form.

As I rushed to him, I fainted, and when I came to myself, he told me what my wife, this very deer, had done to him and to his mother. I said to him, "Son, God has sent us someone who will pay her back for what you and your mother and I have suffered at her hands." Then, O demon, I gave my son in marriage to the shepherd's daughter, who turned my wife into this very deer, saying to me, "To me this is a pretty form, for she will be with us day and night, and it is better to turn her into a pretty deer than to suffer her sinister looks." Thus she stayed with us, while the days and nights followed one another, and the months and years went by. Then one day the shepherd's daughter died, and my son went to the country of this very man with whom you have had your encounter. Some time later I took my wife, this very deer, with me, set out to find out what had happened to my son, and chanced to stop here. This is my story, my strange and amazing story.

The demon assented, saying, "I grant you one-third of this man's life."

Then, O King Shahrayar, the second old man with the two black dogs approached the demon and said, "I too shall tell you what happened to me and to these two dogs, and if I tell it to you and you find it stranger and more amazing than this man's story will you grant me one-third of this man's life?" The demon replied, "I will." Then the old man began to tell his story, saying . . .

But dawn broke, and morning overtook Shahrazad, and she lapsed into silence. Then Dinarzad said, "This is an amazing story," and Shahrazad replied, "What is this compared with what I shall tell you tomorrow night if the king spares me and lets me live!" The king said to himself, "By God, I will not have her put to death until I find out what happened to the man with the two black dogs. Then I will have her put to death, God the Almighty willing."

THE SIXTH NIGHT

When the following night arrived and Shahrazad was in bed with King Shahrayar, her sister Dinarzad said, "Sister, if you are not sleepy, tell us a little tale. Finish the one you started." Shahrazad replied, "With the greatest pleasure":

I heard, O happy King, that the second old man with the two dogs said:

[*The Second Old Man's Tale*]

Demon, as for my story, these are the details. These two dogs are my brothers. When our father died, he left behind three sons, and left us three thousand dinars,[7] with which each of us opened a shop and became a shopkeeper. Soon my older brother, one of these very dogs, went and sold the contents of his shop for a thousand dinars, bought trading goods, and, having prepared himself for his trading trip, left us. A full year went by, when one day, as I sat in my shop, a beggar stopped by to beg. When I refused him, he tearfully asked, "Don't you recognize me?" and when I looked at him closely, I recognized my brother. I embraced him and took him into the shop, and when I asked him about his plight, he replied, "The money is gone, and

---

7. Gold coins; the basic Muslim money units [Translator's note].

the situation is bad." Then I took him to the public bath, clothed him in one of my robes, and took him home with me. Then I examined my books and checked my balance, and found out that I had made a thousand dinars and that my net worth was two thousand dinars. I divided the amount between my brother and myself, and said to him, "Think as if you have never been away." He gladly took the money and opened another shop.

Soon afterward my second brother, this other dog, went and sold his merchandise and collected his money, intending to go on a trading trip. We tried to dissuade him, but he did not listen. Instead, he bought merchandise and trading goods, joined a group of travelers, and was gone for a full year. Then he came back, just like his older brother. I said to him, "Brother, didn't I advise you not to go?" He replied tearfully, "Brother, it was foreordained. Now I am poor and penniless, without even a shirt on my back." Demon, I took him to the public bath, clothed him in one of my new robes, and took him back to the shop. After we had something to eat, I said to him, "Brother, I shall do my business accounts, calculate my net worth for the year, and after subtracting the capital, whatever the profit happens to be, I shall divide it equally between you and myself. When I examined my books and subtracted the capital, I found out that my profit was two thousand dinars, and I thanked God and felt very happy. Then I divided the money, giving him a thousand dinars and keeping a thousand for myself. With that money he opened another shop, and the three of us stayed together for a while. Then my two brothers asked me to go on a trading journey with them, but I refused, saying, "What did you gain from your ventures that I can gain?"

They dropped the matter, and for six years we worked in our stores, buying and selling. Yet every year they asked me to go on a trading journey with them, but I refused, until I finally gave in. I said, "Brothers, I am ready to go with you. How much money do you have?" I found out that they had eaten and drunk and squandered everything they had, but I said nothing to them and did not reproach them. Then I took inventory, gathered all I had together, and sold everything. I was pleased to discover that the sale netted six thousand dinars. Then I divided the money into two parts, and said to my brothers, "The sum of three thousand dinars is for you and myself to use on our trading journey. The other three thousand I shall bury in the ground, in case what happened to you happens to me, so that when we return, we will find three thousand dinars to reopen our shops." They replied, "This is an excellent idea." Then, demon, I divided my money and buried three thousand dinars. Of the remaining three I gave each of my brothers a thousand and kept a thousand for myself. After I closed my shop, we bought merchandise and trading goods, rented a large seafaring boat, and after loading it with our goods and provisions, sailed day and night, for a month.

But morning overtook Shahrazad, and she lapsed into silence. Then her sister Dinarzad said, "Sister, what a lovely story!" Shahrazad replied, "Tomorrow night I shall tell you something even lovelier, stranger, and more wonderful if I live, the Almighty God willing."

THE SEVENTH NIGHT

The following night Dinarzad said to her sister Shahrazad, "For God's sake, sister, if you are not sleepy, tell us a little tale." The king added, "Let it be the completion of the story of the merchant and the demon." Shahrazad replied, "With the greatest pleasure":

I heard, O happy King, that the second old man said to the demon:

For a month my brothers, these very dogs, and I sailed the salty sea, until we came to a port city. We entered the city and sold our goods, earning ten dinars for every dinar. Then we bought other goods, and when we got to the seashore to embark, I met a girl who was dressed in tatters. She kissed my hands and said, "O my lord, be charitable and do me a favor, and I believe that I shall be able to reward you for it." I replied, "I am willing to do you a favor regardless of any reward." She said, "O my lord, marry me, clothe me, and take me home with you on this boat, as your wife, for I wish to give myself to you. I, in turn, will reward you for your kindness and charity, the Almighty God willing. Don't be misled by my poverty and present condition." When I heard her words, I felt pity for her, and guided by what God the Most High had intended for me, I consented. I clothed her with an expensive dress and married her. Then I took her to the boat, spread the bed for her, and consummated our marriage. We sailed many days and nights, and I, feeling love for her, stayed with her day and night, neglecting my brothers. In the meantime they, these very dogs, grew jealous of me, envied me for my increasing merchandise and wealth, and coveted all our possessions. At last they decided to betray me and, tempted by the Devil, plotted to kill me. One night they waited until I was asleep beside my wife; then they carried the two of us and threw us into the sea.

When we awoke, my wife turned into a she-demon and carried me out of the sea to an island. When it was morning, she said, "Husband, I have rewarded you by saving you from drowning, for I am one of the demons who believe in God.[8] When I saw you by the seashore, I felt love for you and came to you in the guise in which you saw me, and when I expressed my love for you, you accepted me. Now I must kill your brothers." When I heard what she said, I was amazed and I thanked her and said, "As for destroying my brothers, this I do not wish, for I will not behave like them." Then I related to her what had happened to me and them, from beginning to end. When she heard my story, she got very angry at them, and said, "I shall fly to them now, drown their boat, and let them all perish." I entreated her, saying, "For God's sake, don't. The proverb advises 'Be kind to those who hurt you.' No matter what, they are my brothers after all." In this manner, I entreated her and pacified her. Afterward, she took me and flew away with me until she brought me home and put me down on the roof of my house. I climbed down, threw the doors open, and dug up the money I had buried. Then I went out and, greeting the people in the market, reopened my shop. When I came home in the evening, I found these two dogs tied up, and when they saw me, they came to me, wept, and rubbed themselves against me. I

---

8. According to the Koran God created both humans and demons (jinns), some of whom accepted Islam.

started, when I suddenly heard my wife say, "O my lord, these are your brothers." I asked, "Who has done this to them?" She replied, "I sent to my sister and asked her to do it. They will stay in this condition for ten years, after which they may be delivered." Then she told me where to find her and departed. The ten years have passed, and I was with my brothers on my way to her to have the spell lifted, when I met this man, together with this old man with the deer. When I asked him about himself, he told me about his encounter with you, and I resolved not to leave until I found out what would happen between you and him. This is my story. Isn't it amazing?

The demon replied, "By God, it is strange and amazing. I grant you one-third of my claim on him for his crime."

Then the third old man said, "Demon, don't disappoint me. If I told you a story that is stranger and more amazing than the first two would you grant me one-third of your claim on him for his crime?" The demon replied, "I will." Then the old man said, "Demon, listen":

But morning overtook Shahrazad, and she lapsed into silence. Then her sister said, "What an amazing story!" Shahrazad replied, "The rest is even more amazing." The king said to himself, "I will not have her put to death until I hear what happened to the old man and the demon; then I will have her put to death, as is my custom with the others."

THE EIGHTH NIGHT

The following night Dinarzad said to her sister Shahrazad, "For God's sake, sister, if you are not sleepy, tell us one of your lovely little tales to while away the night." Shahrazad replied, "With the greatest pleasure":

[The Third Old Man's Tale][9]

The demon said, "This is a wonderful story, and I grant you a third of my claim on the merchant's life."

The third sheikh approached and said to the demon, "I will tell you a story more wonderful than these two if you will grant me a third of your claim on his life, O demon!"

To which the demon agreed.

So the sheikh began:

O sultan and chief of the demons, this mule was my wife. I had gone off on a journey and was absent from her for a whole year. At last I came to the end of my journey and returned home late one night. When I entered the house I saw a black slave lying in bed with her. They were chatting and dallying and laughing and kissing and quarreling together. When she saw me my wife leaped out of bed, ran to the water jug, recited a spell over it, then splashed me with some of the water and said, "Leave this form for the form of a dog."

Immediately I became a dog and she chased me out of the house. I ran out of the gate and didn't stop running until I reached a butcher's shop. I

---

9. Because the earliest manuscript does not include a story for the third sheikh, later narrators supplied one. This brief anecdote comes from a manuscript found in the library of the Royal Academy in Madrid.

entered it and fell to eating the bones lying about. When the owner of the shop saw me, he grabbed me and carried me into his house. When his daughter saw me, she hid her face and said, "Why are you bringing this strange man in with you?"

"What man?" her father asked.

"This dog is a man whose wife has put a spell on him," she said, "but I can set him free again." She took a jug of water, recited a spell over it, then splashed a little water from it on me, and said, "Leave this shape for your original one."

And I became myself again. I kissed her hand and said, "I want to cast a spell on my wife as she did on me. Please give me a little of that water."

"Gladly," she said, "if you find her asleep, sprinkle a few drops on her and she will become whatever you wish."

Well, I did find her asleep, and I sprinkled some water on her and said, "Leave this shape for the shape of a she mule." She at once became the very mule you see here, oh sultan and chief of the demons."

The demon then turned to him and asked, "Is this really true?"

"Yes," he answered, nodding his head vigorously, "it's all true."

When the sheikh had finished his story, the demon shook with laughter and granted him a third of his claim on the merchant's blood.

Then the demon released the merchant and departed. The merchant turned to the three old men and thanked them, and they congratulated him on his deliverance and bade him good-bye. Then they separated, and each of them went on his way. The merchant himself went back home to his family, his wife, and his children, and he lived with them until the day he died. But this story is not as strange or as amazing as the story of the fisherman.

Dinarzad asked, "Please, sister, what is the story of the fisherman?" Shahrazad said: . . .

[The Story of the Fisherman and the Demon]

It is related that there was a very old fisherman who had a wife and three daughters and who was so poor that they did not have even enough food for the day. It was this fisherman's custom to cast his net four times a day. One day, while the moon was still up, he went out with his net at the call for the early morning prayer. He reached the outskirts of the city and came to the seashore. Then he set down his basket, rolled up his shirt, and waded to his waist in the water. He cast his net and waited for it to sink; then he gathered the rope and started to pull. As he pulled little by little, he felt that the net was getting heavier until he was unable to pull any further. He climbed ashore, drove a stake into the ground, and tied the end of the rope to the stake. Then he took off his clothes, dove into the water, and went around the net, shaking it and tugging at it until he managed to pull it ashore. Feeling extremely happy, he put on his clothes and went back to the net. But when he opened it, he found inside a dead donkey, which had torn it apart. The fisherman felt sad and depressed and said to himself, "There is no power and no strength save in God, the Almighty, the Magnificent," adding, "Indeed, this is a strange catch!" Then he began to recite the following verses:

O you who brave the danger in the dark,
Reduce your toil, for gain is not in work.
Look at the fisherman who labors at his trade,
As the stars in the night their orbits make,
And deeply wades into the raging sea,   5
Steadily gazing at the swelling net,
Till he returns, pleased with his nightly catch,
A fish whose mouth the hook of death has cut,
And sells it to a man who sleeps the night,
Safe from the cold and blessed with every wish.   10
Praised be the Lord who blesses and withholds:
This casts the net, but that one eats the fish.

*But morning overtook Shahrazad, and she lapsed into silence. Then her sister
Dinarzad said, "Sister, what a lovely story!" Shahrazad replied, "Tomorrow
night I shall tell you the rest, which is stranger and more wonderful, if the king
spares me and lets me live!"*

THE NINTH NIGHT

*The following night Dinarzad said to her sister Shahrazad, "Sister, if you are
not sleepy, finish the fisherman's story." Shahrazad replied, "With the greatest
pleasure":*

I heard, O happy King, that when the fisherman finished reciting his
verses, he pushed the donkey out of the net and sat down to mend it. When
he was done, he wrung it out and spread it to dry. Then he waded into the
water and, invoking the Almighty God, cast the net and waited for it to sink.
Then he pulled the rope little by little, but this time the net was even more
firmly snagged. Thinking that it was heavy with fish, he was extremely happy.
He took off his clothes and, diving into the water, freed the net and struggled
with it until he reached the shore, but inside the net he found a large jar full
of nothing but mud and sand. When he saw this, he felt sad and, with tears
in his eyes, said to himself, "This is a strange day! God's we are and to God
we turn," and he began to recite the following verses:

O my tormenting fate, forbear,
Or if you can't, at least be fair.
I went to seek my daily bread,
But they said to me it was dead.
And neither luck nor industry   5
Brought back my daily bread to me.
The Pleiads[1] many fools attain,
While sages sit in dark disdain.

Then the fisherman threw the jar away, washed his net, and, wringing it
out, spread it to dry. Then he begged the Almighty God for forgiveness and
went back to the water. For the third time, he cast the net and waited for it
to sink. But when he pulled it up, he found nothing inside but broken pots

---

1. Cluster of stars in the constellation of Taurus.

and bottles, stones, bones, refuse, and the like. He wept at this great injustice and ill luck and began to recite the following verses:

Your livelihood is not in your own hands;
Neither by writing nor by the pen you thrive.
Your luck and your wages are by lot;
Some lands are waste, and some are fertile lands.
The wheel of fortune lowers the man of worth,   5
Raising the base man who deserves to fall.
Come then, O death, and end this worthless life,
Where the ducks soar, while the falcons are bound to earth.
No wonder that you see the good man poor,
While the vicious exalts in his estate.   10
Our wages are alloted; 'tis our fate
To search like birds for gleanings everywhere.
One bird searches the earth from east to west,
Another gets the tidbits while at rest.

Then the fisherman raised his eyes to the heavens and, seeing that the sun had risen and that it was morning and full daylight, said, "O Lord, you know that I cast my net four times only. I have already cast it three times, and there is only one more try left. Lord, let the sea serve me, even as you let it serve Moses."[2] Having mended the net, he cast it into the sea, and waited for it to sink. When he pulled, he found that it was so heavy that he was unable to haul it. He shook it and found that it was caught at the bottom. Saying "There is no power or strength save in God, the Almighty, the Magnificent," he took off his clothes and dove for the net. He worked at it until he managed to free it, and as he hauled it to the shore, he felt that there was something heavy inside. He struggled with the net, until he opened it and found a large long-necked brass jar, with a lead stopper bearing the mark of a seal ring.[3] When the fisherman saw the jar, he was happy and said to himself, "I will sell it in the copper market, for it must be worth at least two measures of wheat." He tried to move the jar, but it was so full and so heavy that he was unable to budge it. Looking at the lead stopper, he said to himself, "I will open the jar, shake out the contents, then roll it before me until I reach the copper market." Then he took out a knife from his belt and began to scrape and struggle with the lead stopper until he pried it loose. He held the stopper in his mouth, tilted the jar to the ground, and shook it, trying to pour out its contents, but when nothing came out, he was extremely surprised.

After a while, there began to emerge from the jar a great column of smoke, which rose and spread over the face of the earth, increasing so much that it covered the sea and rising so high that it reached the clouds and hid the daylight. For a long time, the smoke kept rising from the jar; then it gathered and took shape, and suddenly it shook and there stood a demon, with his feet on the ground and his head in the clouds. He had a head like a tomb, fangs like pincers, a mouth like a cave, teeth like stones, nostrils like trumpets, ears like shields, a throat like an alley, and eyes like lanterns. In short,

2. Moses is a prophet in Islam, as well.   3. A ring that houses a precious or semiprecious stone (usually agate) engraved with the name of a person and used to imprint a signature, or in other instances engraved with talismanic words and used as a charm.

all one can say is that he was a hideous monster. When the fisherman saw him, he shook with terror, his jaws locked together, and his mouth went dry. The demon cried, "O Solomon,[4] prophet of God, forgive me, forgive me. Never again will I disobey you or defy your command."

But morning overtook Shahrazad, and she lapsed into silence. Then Dinarzad said, "Sister, what a strange and amazing story!" Shahrazad replied, "Tomorrow night I shall tell you something stranger and more amazing if I stay alive."

THE TENTH NIGHT

The following night, when Shahrazad was in bed with King Shahrayar, her sister Dinarzad said, "Please, sister, finish the story of the fisherman." Shahrazad replied, "With the greatest pleasure":

I heard, O happy King, that when the fisherman heard what the demon said, he asked, "Demon, what are you saying? It has been more than one thousand and eight hundred years since the prophet Solomon died, and we are now ages later. What is your story, and why were you in this jar?" When the demon heard the fisherman, he said, "Be glad!" The fisherman cried, "O happy day!" The demon added, "Be glad that you will soon be put to death." The fisherman said, "You deserve to be put to shame for such tidings. Why do you wish to kill me, I who have released you and delivered you from the bottom of the sea and brought you back to this world?" The demon replied, "Make a wish!" The fisherman was happy and asked, "What shall I wish of you?" The demon replied, "Tell me how you wish to die, and what manner of death you wish me to choose." The fisherman asked, "What is my crime? Is this my reward from you for having delivered you?" The demon replied, "Fisherman, listen to my story." The fisherman said, "Make it short, for I am at my rope's end."

The demon said, "You should know that I am one of the renegade, rebellious demons. I, together with the giant Sakhr, rebelled against the prophet Solomon, the son of David, who sent against me Asif ibn-Barkhiya, who took me by force and bade me be led in defeat and humiliation before the prophet Solomon. When the prophet Solomon saw me, he invoked God to protect him from me and my looks and asked me to submit to him, but I refused. So he called for this brass jar, confined me inside, and sealed it with a lead seal on which he imprinted God's Almighty name. Then he commanded his demons to carry me and throw me into the middle of the sea. I stayed there for two hundred years, saying to myself, 'Whoever sets me free during these two hundred years, I will make him rich.' But the two hundred years went by and were followed by another two hundred, and no one set me free. Then I vowed to myself, 'Whoever sets me free, I will open for him all the treasures of the earth,' but four hundred years went by, and no one set me free. When I entered the next hundred years, I vowed to myself, 'Whoever delivers me, during these hundred years, I will make him king, make myself his servant, and fulfill every day three of his wishes,' but that hundred years too, plus all

---

4. Solomon (Suleiman) is mentioned as a prophet in the Koran.

the intervening years, went by, and no one set me free. Then I raged and raved and growled and snorted and said to myself, 'Whoever delivers me from now on, I will either put him to the worst of deaths or let him choose for himself the manner of death.' Soon you came by and set me free. Tell me how you wish to die."

When the fisherman heard what the demon said, he replied, "To God we belong and to Him we return. After all these years, with my bad luck, I had to set you free now. Forgive me, and God will grant you forgiveness. Destroy me, and God will inflict on you one who will destroy you." The demon replied, "It must be. Tell me how you wish to die." When the fisherman was certain that he was going to die, he mourned and wept, saying, "O my children, may God not deprive us of each other." Again he turned to the demon and said, "For God's sake, release me as a reward for releasing you and delivering you from this jar." The demon replied, "Your death is your reward for releasing me and letting me escape." The fisherman said, "I did you a good turn, and you are about to repay me with a bad one. How true is the sentiment of the following lines:

> Our kindness they repaid with ugly deeds,
> Upon my life, the deeds of men depraved.
> He who the undeserving aids will meet
> The fate of him who the hyena saved."

The demon said, "Be brief, for as I have said, I must kill you." Then the fisherman thought to himself, "He is only a demon, while I am a human being, whom God has endowed with reason and thereby made superior to him. He may use his demonic wiles on me, but I will use my reason to deal with him." Then he asked the demon, "Must you kill me?" When the demon replied, "I must," the fisherman said, "By the Almighty name that was engraved on the ring of Solomon the son of David, will you answer me truthfully if I ask you about something?" The demon was upset and said with a shudder, "Ask, and be brief!"

But morning overtook Shahrazad, and she lapsed into silence. Then Dinarzad said, "Sister, what an amazing and lovely story!" Shahrazad replied, "What is this compared with what I shall tell you tomorrow night if the king spares me and lets me live! It will be even more amazing."

THE ELEVENTH NIGHT

The following night Dinarzad said to her sister Shahrazad, "Sister, if you are not sleepy, finish the story of the fisherman and the demon." "Shahrazad replied, "With the greatest pleasure":

I heard, O King, that the fisherman said, "By the Almighty name, tell me whether you really were inside this jar." The demon replied, "By the Almighty name, I was imprisoned in this jar." The fisherman said, "You are lying, for this jar is not large enough, not even for your hands and feet. How can it be large enough for your whole body?" The demon replied, "By God, I was inside. Don't you believe that I was inside it?" The fisherman said, "No, I don't." Whereupon the demon shook himself and turned into smoke, which rose, stretched over the sea, spread over the land, then gathered, and, little by little, began to enter the jar. When the smoke disappeared completely, the demon shouted from within, "Fisherman, here I am in the jar. Do you believe me now?"

The fisherman at once took out the sealed lead stopper and hurriedly clamped it on the mouth of the jar. Then he cried out, "Demon, now tell me how you wish to die. For I will throw you into this sea, build a house right here, and sit here and stop any fisherman who comes to fish and warn him that there is a demon here, who will kill whoever pulls him out and who will let him choose how he wishes to die." When the demon heard what the fisherman said and found himself imprisoned, he tried to get out but could not, for he was prevented by the seal of Solomon the son of David. Realizing that the fisherman had tricked him, the demon said, "Fisherman, don't do this to me. I was only joking with you." The fisherman replied, "You are lying, you the dirtiest and meanest of demons," and began to roll the jar toward the sea. The demon shouted, "Don't, don't!" But the fisherman replied, "Yes, yes." Then in a soft and submissive voice the demon asked, "Fisherman, what do you intend to do?" The fisherman replied, "I intend to throw you into the sea. The first time you stayed there for eight hundred years. This time I will let you stay until Doomsday. Haven't I said to you, 'Spare me, and God will spare you. Destroy me, and God will destroy you'? But you refused, and persisted in your resolve to do me in and kill me. Now it is my turn to do you in." The demon said, "Fisherman, if you open the jar, I will reward you and make you rich." The fisherman replied, "You are lying, you are lying. Your situation and mine is like that of King Yunan and the sage Duban." The demon asked, "What is their story?" The fisherman said:

[The Tale of King Yunan and the Sage Duban]

Demon, there was once a king called Yunan, who reigned in one of the cities of Persia, in the province of Zuman.[5] This king was afflicted with leprosy, which had defied the physicians and the sages, who, for all the medicines they gave him to drink and all the ointments they applied, were unable to cure him. One day there came to the city of King Yunan a sage called Duban. This sage had read all sorts of books, Greek, Persian, Turkish, Arabic, Byzantine, Syriac, and Hebrew, had studied the sciences, and had learned their groundwork, as well as their principles and basic benefits. Thus he was versed in all the sciences, from philosophy to the lore of plants and herbs, the harmful as well as the beneficial. A few days after he arrived in the city of King Yunan, the sage heard about the king and his leprosy and the fact that the physicians and the sages were unable to cure him. On the following day, when God's morning dawned and His sun rose, the sage Duban put on his best clothes, went to King Yunan and, introducing himself, said, "Your Majesty, I have heard of that which has afflicted your body and heard that many physicians have treated you without finding a way to cure you. Your Majesty, I can treat you without giving you any medicine to drink or ointment to apply." When the king heard this, he said, "If you succeed, I will bestow on you riches that would be enough for you and your grandchildren. I will

5. Modern Armenia.

bestow favors on you, and I will make you my companion and friend." The king bestowed robes of honor on the sage, treated him kindly, and then asked him, "Can you really cure me from my leprosy without any medicine to drink or ointment to apply?" The sage replied, "Yes, I will cure you externally." The king was astonished, and he began to feel respect as well as great affection for the sage. He said, "Now, sage, do what you have promised." The sage replied, "I hear and obey. I will do it tomorrow morning, the Almighty God willing." Then the sage went to the city, rented a house, and there he distilled and extracted medicines and drugs. Then with his great knowledge and skill, he fashioned a mallet with a curved end, hollowed the mallet, as well as the handle, and filled the handle with his medicines and drugs. He likewise made a ball. When he had perfected and prepared everything, he went on the following day to King Yunan and kissed the ground before him.

But morning overtook Shahrazad, and she lapsed into silence. Then her sister Dinarzad said, "What a lovely story!" Shahrazad replied, "You have heard nothing yet. Tomorrow night I shall tell you something stranger and more amazing if the king spares me and lets me live!"

THE TWELFTH NIGHT

The following night Dinarzad said to her sister Shahrazad, "Please, sister, finish the rest of the story of the fisherman and the demon." Shahrazad replied, "With the greatest pleasure":

I heard, O King, that the fisherman said to the demon:

The sage Duban came to King Yunan and asked him to ride to the playground to play with the ball and mallet. The king rode out, attended by his chamberlains, princes, viziers, and lords and eminent men of the realm. When the king was seated, the sage Duban entered, offered him the mallet, and said, "O happy King, take this mallet, hold it in your hand, and as you race on the playground, hold the grip tightly in your fist, and hit the ball. Race until you perspire, and the medicine will ooze from the grip into your perspiring hand, spread to your wrist, and circulate through your entire body. After you perspire and the medicine spreads in your body, return to your royal palace, take a bath, and go to sleep. You will wake up cured, and that is all there is to it." King Yunan took the mallet from the sage Duban and mounted his horse. The attendants threw the ball before the king, who, holding the grip tightly in his fist, followed it and struggled excitedly to catch up with it and hit it. He kept galloping after the ball and hitting it until his palm and the rest of his body began to perspire, and the medicine began to ooze from the handle and flow through his entire body. When the sage Duban was certain that the medicine had oozed and spread through the king's body, he advised him to return to his palace and go immediately to the bath. The king went to the bath and washed himself thoroughly. Then he put on his clothes, left the bath, and returned to his palace.

As for the sage Duban, he spent the night at home, and early in the morning, he went to the palace and asked for permission to see the king. When he was allowed in, he entered and kissed the ground before the king; then, pointing toward him with his hand, he began to recite the following verses:

The virtues you fostered are great;
For who but you could sire them?
Yours is the face whose radiant light
Effaces the night dark and grim.
Forever beams your radiant face;   5
That of the world is still in gloom.
You rained on us with ample grace,
As the clouds rain on thirsty hills,
Expending your munificence,
Attaining your magnificence.   10

When the sage Duban finished reciting these verses, the king stood up and embraced him. Then he seated the sage beside him, and with attentiveness and smiles, engaged him in conversation. Then the king bestowed on the sage robes of honor, gave him gifts and endowments, and granted his wishes. For when the king had looked at himself the morning after the bath, he found that his body was clear of leprosy, as clear and pure as silver. He therefore felt exceedingly happy and in a very generous mood. Thus when he went in the morning to the reception hall and sat on his throne, attended by the mamluks[6] and chamberlains, in the company of the viziers and the lords of the realm, and the sage Duban presented himself, as we have mentioned, the king stood up, embraced him, and seated him beside him. He treated him attentively and drank and ate with him.

But morning overtook Shahrazad, and she lapsed into silence. Then her sister Dinarzad said, "Sister, what a lovely story!" Shahrazad replied, "The rest of the story is stranger and more amazing. If the king spares me and I am alive tomorrow night, I shall tell you something even more entertaining."

THE THIRTEENTH NIGHT

The following night Dinarzad said to her sister Shahrazad, "Sister, if you are not sleepy, tell us one of your lovely little tales to while away the night." Shahrazad replied, "With the greatest pleasure":

I heard, O happy King who is praiseworthy by the Grace of God, that King Yunan bestowed favors on the sage, gave him robes of honor, and granted his wishes. At the end of the day he gave the sage a thousand dinars and sent him home. The king, who was amazed at the skill of the sage Duban, said to himself, "This man has treated me externally, without giving me any draught to drink or ointment to apply. His is indeed a great wisdom for which he deserves to be honored and rewarded. He shall become my companion, confidant, and close friend." Then the king spent the night, happy at his recovery from his illness, at his good health, and at the soundness of his body. When morning came and it was light, the king went to the royal reception hall and sat on the throne, attended by his chief officers, while the princes, viziers, and lords of the realm sat to his right and left. Then the king called for the sage, and when the sage entered and kissed the ground before him, the king stood up to salute him, seated him beside him, and invited him to eat with him. The king treated him intimately, showed him favors, and

---

6. Literally "slaves," but here members of a military force who were originally of Caucasian slaves.

bestowed on him robes of honor and many other gifts. Then he spent the whole day conversing with him, and at the end of the day he ordered that he be given a thousand dinars. The sage went home and spent the night with his wife, feeling happy and thankful to God the Arbiter.

In the morning, the king went to the royal reception hall, and the princes and viziers came to stand in attendance. It happened that King Yunan had a vizier who was sinister, greedy, envious, and fretful, and when he saw that the sage had found favor with the king, who bestowed on him much money and many robes of honor, he feared that the king would dismiss him and appoint the sage in his place; therefore, he envied the sage and harbored ill will against him, for "nobody is free from envy." The envious vizier approached the king and, kissing the ground before him, said, "O excellent King and glorious Lord, it was by your kindness and with your blessing that I rose to prominence; therefore, if I fail to advise you on a grave matter, I am not my father's son. If the great King and noble Lord commands, I shall disclose the matter to him." The king was upset and asked, "Damn you, what advice have you got?" The vizier replied, "Your Majesty, 'He who considers not the end, fortune is not his friend.' I have seen your Majesty make a mistake, for you have bestowed favors on your enemy who has come to destroy your power and steal your wealth. Indeed, you have pampered him and shown him many favors, but I fear that he will do you harm." The king asked, "Whom do you accuse, whom do you have in mind, and at whom do you point the finger?" The vizier replied, "If you are asleep, wake up, for I point the finger at the sage Duban, who has come from Byzantium." The king replied, "Damn you, is he my enemy? To me he is the most faithful, the dearest, and the most favored of people, for this sage has treated me simply by making me hold something in my hand and has cured me from the disease that had defied the physicians and the sages and rendered them helpless. In all the world, east and west, near and far, there is no one like him, yet you accuse him of such a thing. From this day onward, I will give him every month a thousand dinars, in addition to his rations and regular salary. Even if I were to share my wealth and my kingdom with him, it would be less than he deserves. I think that you have said what you said because you envy him. This is very much like the situation in the story told by the vizier of King Sinbad[7] when the king wanted to kill his own son.

But morning overtook Shahrazad, and she lapsed into silence. Then her sister Dinarzad said, "Sister, what a lovely story!" Shahrazad replied, "What is this compared with what I shall tell you tomorrow night! It will be stranger and more amazing."

THE FOURTEENTH NIGHT

The following night, when the king got into bed and Shahrazad got in with him, her sister Dinarzad said, "Please, sister, if you are not sleepy, tell us one of your lovely little tales to while away the night." Shahrazad replied, "Very well":

I heard, O happy King, that King Yunan's vizier asked, "King of the age, I beg your pardon, but what did King Sindbad's vizier tell the king when he

---

7. Not to be confused with Sindbad the Sailor.

wished to kill his own son?" King Yunan said to the vizier, "When King Sindbad, provoked by an envious man, wanted to kill his own son, his vizier said to him, 'Don't do what you will regret afterward.' "

[The Tale of the Husband and the Parrot]

I have heard it told that there was once a very jealous man who had a wife so splendidly beautiful that she was perfection itself. The wife always refused to let her husband travel and leave her behind, until one day when he found it absolutely necessary to go on a journey. He went to the bird market, bought a parrot, and brought it home. The parrot was intelligent, knowledgeable, smart, and retentive. Then he went away on his journey, and when he finished his business and came back, he brought the parrot and inquired about his wife during his absence. The parrot gave him a day-by-day account of what his wife had done with her lover and how the two carried on in his absence. When the husband heard the account, he felt very angry, went to his wife, and gave her a sound beating. Thinking that one of her maids had informed her husband about what she did with her lover in her husband's absence, the wife interrogated her maids one by one, and they all swore that they had heard the parrot inform the husband.

When the wife heard that it was the parrot who had informed the husband, she ordered one of her maids to take the grinding stone and grind under the cage, ordered a second maid to sprinkle water over the cage, and ordered a third to carry a steel mirror and walk back and forth all night long. That night her husband stayed out, and when he came home in the morning, he brought the parrot, spoke with it, and asked about what had transpired in his absence that night. The parrot replied, "Master, forgive me, for last night, all night long, I was unable to hear or see very well because of the intense darkness, the rain, and the thunder and lightning." Seeing that it was summertime, during the month of July, the husband replied, "Woe unto you, this is no season for rain." The parrot said, "Yes, by God, all night long, I saw what I told you." The husband, concluding that the parrot had lied about his wife and had accused her falsely, got angry, and he grabbed the parrot and, taking it out of the cage, smote it on the ground and killed it. But after the parrot's death, the husband heard from his neighbors that the parrot had told the truth about his wife, and he was full of regret that he had been tricked by his wife to kill the parrot.

King Yunan concluded, "Vizier, the same will happen to me."

But morning overtook Shahrazad, and she lapsed into silence. Then her sister Dinarzad said, "What a strange and lovely story!" Shahrazad replied, "What is this compared with what I shall tell you tomorrow night! If the king spares me and lets me live, I shall tell you something more amazing." The king thought to himself, "By God, this is indeed an amazing story."

THE FIFTEENTH NIGHT

The following night Dinarzad said to her sister Shahrazad, "Please, sister, if you are not sleepy, tell us one of your lovely little tales, for they entertain and help everyone to forget his cares and banish sorrow from the heart." Shahrazad replied, "With the greatest pleasure." King Shahrayar added, "Let it be the remainder of the story of King Yunan, his vizier, and the sage Duban, and of the fisherman, the demon, and the jar." Shahrazad replied, "With the greatest pleasure":

I heard, O happy King, that King Yunan said to his envious vizier, "After the husband killed the parrot and heard from his neighbors that the parrot had told him the truth, he was filled with remorse. You too, my vizier, being envious of this wise man, would like me to kill him and regret it afterward, as did the husband after he killed the parrot." When the vizier heard what King Yunan said, he replied, "O great king, what harm has this sage done to me? Why, he has not harmed me in any way. I am telling you all this out of love and fear for you. If you don't discover my veracity, let me perish like the vizier who deceived the son of the king." King Yunan asked his vizier, "How so?" The vizier replied:

[The Tale of the King's Son and the She-Ghoul]

It is said, O happy King, that there was once a king who had a son who was fond of hunting and trapping. The prince had with him a vizier appointed by his father the king to follow him wherever he went. One day the prince went with his men into the wilderness, and when he chanced to see a wild beast, the vizier urged him to go after it. The prince pursued the beast and continued to press in pursuit until he lost its track and found himself alone in the wilderness, not knowing which way to turn or where to go, when he came upon a girl, standing on the road, in tears. When the young prince asked her, "Where do you come from?" she replied, "I am the daughter of an Indian king. I was riding in the wilderness when I dozed off and in my sleep fell off my horse and found myself alone and helpless." When the young prince heard what she said, he felt sorry for her, and he placed her behind him on his horse and rode on. As they passed by some ruins, she said, "O my lord, I wish to relieve myself here." He let her down and she went into the ruins. Then he went in after her, ignorant of what she was, and discovered that she was a she-ghoul, who was saying to her children, "I brought you a good, fat boy." They replied, "Mother, bring him to us, so that we may feed on his innards." When the young prince heard what they said, he shook with terror, and fearing for his life, ran outside. The she-ghoul followed him and asked, "Why are you afraid?" and he told her about his situation and his predicament, concluding, "I have been unfairly treated." She replied, "If you have been unfairly treated, ask the Almighty God for help, and He will protect you from harm." The young prince raised his eyes to Heaven . . .

But morning overtook Shahrazad, and she lapsed into silence. Then her sister Dinarzad said, "What a strange and lovely story!" Shahrazad replied, "What is this compared with what I shall tell you tomorrow night! It will be even stranger and more amazing."

THE SIXTEENTH NIGHT

The following night Dinarzad said, "Please, sister, if you are not sleepy, tell us one of your lovely little tales." Shahrazad replied, "I shall with pleasure":

I heard, O King, that the vizier said to King Yunan:

When the young prince said to the she-ghoul, "I have been unfairly treated," she replied, "Ask God for help, and He will protect you from harm." The young prince raised his eyes to Heaven and said, "O Lord, help me to prevail upon my enemy, for 'everything is within your power.'" When the she-ghoul heard his invocation, she gave up and departed, and he returned safely to his father and told him about the vizier and how it was he who had urged him to pursue the beast and drove him to his encounter with the she-ghoul. The king summoned the vizier and had him put to death.

The vizier added, "You too, your Majesty, if you trust, befriend, and bestow favors on this sage, he will plot to destroy you and cause your death. Your Majesty should realize that I know for certain that he is a foreign agent who has come to destroy you. Haven't you seen that he cured you externally, simply with something you held in your hand?" King Yunan, who was beginning to feel angry, replied, "You are right, vizier. The sage may well be what you say and may have come to destroy me. He who has cured me with something to hold can kill me with something to smell." Then the king asked the vizier, "My vizier and good counselor, how should I deal with him?" The vizier replied, "Send for him now and have him brought before you, and when he arrives, strike off his head. In this way, you will attain your aim and fulfill your wish." The king said, "This is good and sound advice." Then he sent for the sage Duban, who came immediately, still feeling happy at the favors, the money, and the robes the king had bestowed on him. When he entered, he pointed with his hand toward the king and began to recite the following verses:

> If I have been remiss in thanking you,
> For whom then have I made my verse and prose?
> You granted me your gifts before I asked,
> Without deferment and without excuse.
> How can I fail to praise your noble deeds,   5
> Inspired in private and in public by my muse?
> I thank you for your deeds and for your gifts,
> Which, though they bend my back, my care reduce.

The king asked, "Sage, do you know why I have had you brought before me?" The sage replied, "No, your Majesty." The king said, "I brought you here to have you killed and to destroy the breath of life within you." In astonishment Duban asked, "Why does your Majesty wish to have me put to death, and for what crime?" The king replied, "I have been told that you are a spy and that you have come to kill me. Today I will have you killed before you kill me. 'I will have you for lunch before you have me for dinner.'" Then the king called for the executioner and ordered him, saying, "Strike off the head of this sage and rid me of him! Strike!"

When the sage heard what the king said, he knew that because he had been favored by the king, someone had envied him, plotted against him, and lied to the king, in order to have him killed and get rid of him. The sage realized then that the king had little wisdom, judgment, or good sense, and he was filled with regret, when it was useless to regret. He said to himself, "There is no power and no strength, save in God the Almighty, the Magnificent. I did a good deed but was rewarded with an evil one." In the meantime, the king was shouting at the executioner, "Strike off his head." The sage implored, "Spare me, your Majesty, and God will spare you; destroy me, and God will destroy you." He repeated the statement, just as I did, O demon, but you too refused, insisting on killing me. King Yunan said to the sage, "Sage, you must die, for you have cured me with a mere handle, and I fear that you can kill me with anything." The sage replied, "This is my reward from your Majesty. You reward good with evil." The king said, "Don't stall; you must die today without delay." When the sage Duban became convinced that he was going to die, he was filled with grief and sorrow, and his eyes overflowed with tears. He blamed himself for doing a favor for one who does not deserve it and for sowing seeds in a barren soil and recited the following verses:

> Maimuna was a foolish girl,
> Though from a sage descended,
> And many with pretense to skill
> Are e'en on dry land upended.

The executioner approached the sage, bandaged his eyes, bound his hands, and raised the sword, while the sage cried, expressed regret, and implored, "For God's sake, your Majesty, spare me, and God will spare you; destroy me, and God will destroy you." Then he tearfully began to recite the following verses:

> They who deceive enjoy success,
> While I with my true counsel fail
> And am rewarded with disgrace.
> If I live, I'll nothing unveil;
> If I die, then curse all the men,   5
> The men who counsel and prevail.

Then the sage added, "Is this my reward from your Majesty? It is like the reward of the crocodile." The king asked, "What is the story of the crocodile?" The sage replied, "I am in no condition to tell you a story. For God's sake, spare me, and God will spare you. Destroy me, and God will destroy you," and he wept bitterly.

Then several noblemen approached the king and said, "We beg your Majesty to forgive him for our sake, for in our view, he has done nothing to deserve this." The king replied, "You do not know the reason why I wish to have him killed. I tell you that if I spare him, I will surely perish, for I fear that he who has cured me externally from my affliction, which had defied the Greek sages, simply by having me hold a handle, can kill me with anything I touch. I must kill him, in order to protect myself from him." The sage Duban implored again, "For God's sake, your Majesty, spare me, and God will spare you. Destroy me, and God will destroy you." The king insisted, "I must kill you."

Demon, when the sage realized that he was surely going to die, he said, "I beg your Majesty to postpone my execution until I return home, leave instructions for my burial, discharge my obligations, distribute alms, and donate my scientific and medical books to one who deserves them. I have in particular a book entitled *The Secret of Secrets*, which I should like to give you for safekeeping in your library." The king asked, "What is the secret of this book?" The sage replied, "It contains countless secrets, but the chief one is that if your Majesty has my head struck off, opens the book on the sixth leaf, reads three lines from the left page, and speaks to me, my head will speak and answer whatever you ask."

The king was greatly amazed and said, "Is it possible that if I cut off your head and, as you say, open the book, read the third line, and speak to your head, it will speak to me? This is the wonder of wonders." Then the king allowed the sage to go and sent him home under guard. The sage settled his affairs and on the following day returned to the royal palace and found assembled there the princes, viziers, chamberlains, lords of the realm, and military officers, as well as the king's retinue, servants, and many of his citizens. The sage Duban entered, carrying an old book and a kohl[8] jar containing powder. He sat down, ordered a platter, and poured out the powder and smoothed it on the platter. Then he said to the king, "Take this book, your Majesty, and don't open it until after my execution. When my head is cut off, let it be placed on the platter and order that it be pressed on the powder. Then open the book and begin to ask my head a question, for it will then answer you. There is no power and no strength save in God, the Almighty, the Magnificent. For God's sake, spare me, and God will spare you; destroy me, and God will destroy you." The king replied, "I must kill you, especially to see how your head will speak to me." Then the king took the book and ordered the executioner to strike off the sage's head. The executioner drew his sword and, with one stroke, dropped the head in the middle of the platter, and when he pressed the head on the powder, the bleeding stopped. Then the sage Duban opened his eyes and said, "Now, your Majesty, open the book." When the king opened the book, he found the pages stuck. So he put his finger in his mouth, wetted it with his saliva, and opened the first page, and he kept opening the pages with difficulty until he turned seven leaves. But when he looked in the book, he found nothing written inside, and he exclaimed, "Sage, I see nothing written in this book." The sage replied, "Open more pages." The king opened some more pages but still found nothing, and while he was doing this, the drug spread through his body—for the book had been poisoned—and he began to heave, sway, and twitch.

But morning overtook Shahrazad, and she lapsed into silence. Then her sister Dinarzad said, "Sister, what an amazing and entertaining story!" Shahrazad replied, "What is this compared with what I shall tell you tomorrow night if the king spares me and lets me live!"

THE SEVENTEENTH NIGHT

The following night Dinarzad said to her sister Shahrazad, "Please, sister, if you are not sleepy, tell us one of your lovely little tales to while away the night." The king added, "Let it be the rest of the story of the sage and the king and of the fisherman and the demon." Shahrazad replied, "Very well, with the greatest pleasure":

---

8. Cosmetic, used by Eastern, especially Muslim, women to darken the eyelids.

I heard, O King, that when the sage Duban saw that the drug had spread through the king's body and that the king was heaving and swaying, he began to recite the following verses:

> For long they ruled us arbitrarily,
> But suddenly vanished their powerful rule.
> Had they been just, they would have happily
> Lived, but they oppressed, and punishing fate
> Afflicted them with ruin deservedly,   5
> And on the morrow the world taunted them,
> " 'Tis tit for tat; blame not just destiny."

As the sage's head finished reciting the verses, the king fell dead, and at that very moment the head too succumbed to death. Demon, consider this story.

But morning overtook Shahrazad, and she lapsed into silence. Then her sister Dinarzad said, "Sister, what an entertaining story!" Shahrazad replied, "What is this compared with what I shall tell you tomorrow night if I live!"

THE EIGHTEENTH NIGHT

The following night, Dinarzad said to her sister Shahrazad, "Please, sister, if you are not sleepy, tell us one of your lovely little tales to while away the night." The king added, "Let it be the rest of the story of the fisherman and the demon." Shahrazad replied, "With the greatest pleasure":

I heard, O King, that the fisherman said to the demon, "Had the king spared the sage, God would have spared him and he would have lived, but he refused and insisted on destroying the sage, and the Almighty God destroyed him. You too, demon, had you from the beginning agreed to spare me, I would have spared you, but you refused and insisted on killing me; therefore, I shall punish you by keeping you in this jar and throwing you into the bottom of the sea." The demon cried out, "Fisherman, don't do it. Spare me and save me and don't blame me for my action and my offense against you. If I did ill, you should do good. As the saying goes, 'Be kind to him who wrongs you.' Don't do what Imama did to 'Atika." The fisherman asked, "What did Imama do to 'Atika?" The demon replied, "This is no time and this narrow prison is no place to tell a story, but I shall tell it to you after you release me." The fisherman said, "I must throw you into the sea. There is no way I would let you out and set you free, for I kept imploring you and calling on you, but you refused and insisted on killing me, without any offense or injury that merits punishment, except that I had set you free. When you treated me in this way, I realized that you were unclean from birth, that you were ill-natured, and that you were one who rewards good with ill. After I throw you into the sea, I shall build me a hut here and live in it for your sake, so that if anyone pulls you out, I shall acquaint him with what I suffered at your hands and shall advise him to throw you back into the sea and let you perish or languish there to the end of time, you the dirtiest of demons." The demon replied, "Set me free this time, and I pledge never to bother you or harm you, but to make you rich." When he heard this, the fisherman made the demon pledge and covenant that if the fisherman released him and let him out, he would not harm him but would serve him and be good to him.

After the fisherman secured the demon's pledge, by making him swear by the Almighty Name, he opened the seal of the jar, and the smoke began to rise. When the smoke was completely out of the jar, it gathered and turned again into a full-fledged demon, who kicked the jar away and sent it flying to the middle of the sea. When the fisherman saw what the demon had done, sure that he was going to meet with disaster and death, he wet himself and said, "This is a bad omen." Then he summoned his courage and cried out, "Demon, you have sworn and given me your pledge. Don't betray me. Come back, lest the Almighty God punish you for your betrayal. Demon, I repeat to you what the sage Duban said to King Yunan, 'Spare me, and God will spare you; destroy me, and God will destroy you.' " When the demon heard what the fisherman said, he laughed, and when the fisherman cried out again, "Demon, spare me," he replied, "Fisherman, follow me," and the fisherman followed him, hardly believing in his escape, until they came to a mountain outside the city. They climbed over to the other side and came to a vast wilderness, in the middle of which stood a lake surrounded by four hills.

The demon halted by the lake and ordered the fisherman to cast his net and fish. The fisherman looked at the lake and marveled as he saw fish in many colors, white, red, blue, and yellow. He cast his net, and when he pulled, he found four fish inside, one red, one white, one blue, and one yellow. When he saw them, he was full of admiration and delight. The demon said to him, "Take them to the king of your city and offer them to him, and he will give you enough to make you rich. Please excuse me, for I know no other way to make you rich. But don't fish here more than once a day." Then, saying, "I shall miss you," the demon kicked the ground with his foot, and it opened and swallowed him. The fisherman, O King, returned to the city, still marveling at his encounter with the demon and at the colored fish. He entered the royal palace, and when he offered the fish to the king, the king looked at them . . .

But morning overtook Shahrazad, and she lapsed into silence. Then Dinar-zad said, "Sister, what an amazing and entertaining story!" Shahrazad replied, "What is this compared with what I shall tell you tomorrow night if the king spares me and lets me live!"

THE NINETEENTH NIGHT

The following night Dinarzad said to her sister Shahrazad, "Sister tell us the rest of the story and what happened to the fisherman." Shahrazad replied, "With the greatest pleasure":

I heard, O King, that when the fisherman presented the fish to the king, and the king looked at them and saw that they were colored, he took one of them in his hand and looked at it with great amazement. Then he said to his vizier, "Take them to the cook whom the emperor of Byzantium has given us as a present." The vizier took the fish and brought them to the girl and said to her, "Girl, as the saying goes, 'I save my tears for the time of trial.' The king has been presented these four fish, and he bids you fry them well." Then the vizier went back to report to the king, and the king ordered him to give the fisherman four hundred dirhams.[9] The vizier gave the money to the fisherman, who, receiving it, gathered it in the folds of his robe and went away, running, and as he ran, he stumbled and kept falling and getting up, thinking that he was in a dream. Then he stopped and bought some provisions for his family.

So far for the fisherman, O King. In the meantime the girl scaled the fish, cleaned them, and cut them into pieces. Then she placed the frying pan on the fire and poured in the sesame oil, and when it began to boil, she placed the fish in the frying pan. When the pieces were done on one side, she turned them over, but no sooner had she done this than the kitchen wall split open and there emerged a maiden with a beautiful figure, smooth cheeks, perfect features, and dark eyes. She wore a short-sleeved silk shirt in the Egyptian style, embroidered all around with lace and gold spangles. In her ears she wore dangling earrings; on her wrists she wore bracelets; and in her hand she held a bamboo wand. She thrust the wand into the frying pan and said in clear Arabic, "O fish, O fish, have you kept the pledge?" When the cook saw what had happened, she fainted. Then the maiden repeated what she had said, and the fish raised their heads from the frying pan and replied in clear Arabic, "Yes, yes. If you return, we shall return; if you keep your vow, we shall keep ours; and if you forsake us, we shall be even." At that moment the maiden overturned the frying pan and disappeared as she had come, and the kitchen wall closed behind her.

When the cook came to herself, she found the four fish charred, and she felt sorry for herself and afraid of the king, saying to herself, " 'He broke his lance on his very first raid.' " While she remonstrated with herself, the vizier suddenly stood before her, saying, "Give me the fish, for we have set the table before the king, and he is waiting for them." The girl wept and told the vizier what she had seen and witnessed and what had happened to the fish. The vizier was astonished and said, "This is very strange." Then he sent an officer after the fisherman, and he returned a while later with the fisherman. The vizier shouted at him, saying, "Bring us at once four more fish like the ones you brought us before, for we have had an accident with them." When he followed with threats, the fisherman went home and, taking his fishing gear, went outside the city, climbed the mountain, and descended to the wilderness on the other side. When he came to the lake, he cast his net, and when he pulled up, he found inside four fish, as he had done the first time. Then he brought them back to the vizier, who took them to the girl and said, "Fry them in front of me, so that I can see for myself." The girl prepared the fish at once, placed the frying pan over the fire, and threw them in. When the fish were done, the wall split open, and the maiden appeared in her elegant clothes, wearing necklaces and other jewelry and holding in her hand the bamboo wand. Again she thrust the wand into the frying pan and said in clear Arabic, "O fish, have you kept the pledge?" and again the fish raised their heads and replied, "Yes, yes. If you return, we shall return; if you keep your vow, we shall keep ours; and if you forsake us, we shall be even."

9. Small silver coins.

But morning overtook Shahrazad, and she lapsed into silence. Then Dinarzad said, "What an entertaining story!" Shahrazad replied, "What is this compared with what I shall tell you tomorrow night if I live, the Almighty God willing!"

THE TWENTIETH NIGHT

The following night Dinarzad said to her sister Shahrazad, "Please, sister, if you are not sleepy, tell us one of your lovely little tales to while away the night." Shahrazad replied, "With the greatest pleasure":

I heard, O happy King, that after the fish spoke, the maiden overturned the frying pan with the wand and disappeared into the opening from which she had emerged, and the wall closed behind her. The vizier said to himself, "I can no longer hide this affair from the king," and he went to him and told him what had happened to the fish before his very eyes.

The king was exceedingly amazed and said, "I wish to see this with my own eyes." Then he sent for the fisherman, who came after a little while, and the king said to him, "I want you to bring me at once four more fish like the ones you brought before. Hurry!" Then he assigned three officers to guard the fisherman and sent him away. The fisherman disappeared for a while and returned with four fish, one red, one white, one blue, and one yellow. The king commanded, "Give him four hundred dirhams," and the fisherman, receiving the money, gathered it in the folds of his robe and went away. Then the king said to the vizier, "Fry the fish here in my presence." The vizier replied, "I hear and obey," and he called for a stove and a frying pan and sat to clean the fish. Then he lit the fire and, pouring the sesame oil, placed the fish in the frying pan.

When they were almost done, the palace wall split open, and the king and vizier began to tremble, and when they looked up, they saw a black slave who stood like a towering mountain or a giant descendant of the tribe of 'Ad.[1] He was as tall as a reed, as wide as a stone bench, and he held a green palm leaf in his hand. Then in clear but unpleasant language, he said, "O fish, O fish, have you kept the pledge?" and the fish raised their heads from the frying pan and said, "Yes, yes. If you return, we shall return; if you keep your vow, we shall keep ours; and if you forsake us, we shall be even." At that moment, the black slave overturned the frying pan, in the middle of the hall, and the fish turned into charcoal. Then the black slave departed as he had come, and the wall closed behind him. When the black slave disappeared, the king said, "I cannot sleep over this affair, for there is no doubt a mystery behind these fish." Then he bade the fisherman be brought before him again.

When the fisherman arrived, the king said to him, "Damn you, where do you catch these fish?" The fisherman replied, "My lord, I catch them in a lake that lies among four hills, on the other side of the mountain." The king turned to the vizier and asked, "Do you know this lake?" The vizier replied, "No, by God, your Majesty. For sixty years, I have hunted, traveled, and roamed far and wide, sometimes for a day or two, sometimes for a month or two, but I have never seen or known that such a lake existed on the other

---

1. Tribe supposedly destroyed by God's wrath (Koran 41.15).

side of the mountain." Then the king turned to the fisherman and asked him, "How far is this lake from here?" The fisherman replied, "King of the age, it is one hour from here." The king was astonished, and he ordered his soldiers to be ready. Then he rode out with his troops, behind the fisherman, who led the way under guard, muttering curses on the demon as he went.

They rode until they were outside the city. Then they climbed the mountain, and when they descended to the other side, they saw a vast wilderness that they had never seen in all their lives, as well as the four hills and the lake in whose clear water they saw the fish in four colors, red, white, blue, and yellow. The king stood marveling; then he turned to the vizier, princes, chamberlains, and deputies and asked, "Have any of you ever seen this lake before?" They replied, "Never." He asked, "And none of you knew where it was?" They kissed the ground before him and replied, "By God, your Majesty, till now we have never in our lives seen this lake or known about it, even though it is close to our city." The king said, "There is a mystery behind this. By God, I shall not return to the city until I find the answer to the mystery behind this lake and these fish in four colors." Then he ordered his men to halt and pitch the tents, and he dismounted and waited.

When it was dark, he summoned the vizier, who was an experienced and wise man of the world. The vizier came to the king, without being seen by the soldiers, and when he arrived, the king said, "I wish to reveal to you what I intend to do. At this very hour, I shall go all by myself to look for an answer to the mystery of this lake and these fish. Early tomorrow morning you shall sit at the entrance of my tent and tell the princes that the king is indisposed and that he has given you orders not to let anyone be admitted to his presence. You must not let anyone know about my departure and absence, and you must wait for me for three days." The vizier, unable to disobey him, abided by the order, saying, "I hear and obey."

Then the king packed, prepared himself, and girded himself with the royal sword. Then he climbed one of the four hills, and when he reached the top, he journeyed on for the rest of the night. In the morning, when the sun rose and steeped the mountaintop with light, the king looked and sighted a dark mass in the distance. When he saw it, he was glad, and he headed in its direction, saying to himself, "There may be someone there to give me information." He journeyed on, and when he arrived, he found a palace, built under a lucky star, with black stones and completely overlaid with iron plates. It had double doors, one open, one shut. Pleased, the king knocked gently at the door and waited patiently for a while without hearing any reply. He knocked again, this time more loudly than before, but again waited without hearing any reply or seeing anyone. He knocked for the third time and kept knocking repeatedly but once more waited without hearing any reply or seeing anyone. Then he said to himself, "There is no doubt that there is no one inside, or perhaps the palace is deserted." Summoning his courage, he entered and shouted from the hallway, "O inhabitants of the palace, I am a stranger and a hungry traveler. Have you any food? Our Lord will requite you and reward you for it." He shouted a second and a third time but heard no reply. Feeling bold and determined, he advanced from the hallway into the center of the palace and looked around, but saw no one.

But morning overtook Shahrazad, and she lapsed into silence. Then Dinarzad said, "Sister, what an amazing and entertaining story!" Shahrazad replied,

"What is this compared with what I shall tell you tomorrow night if I live, the Almighty God willing!"

THE TWENTY-FIRST NIGHT

The following night Dinarzad said to her sister Shahrazad, "For God's sake, sister, if you are not sleepy, tell us one of your lovely little tales to while away the night." Shahrazad replied, "With the greatest pleasure":

I heard, O King, that the king walked to the center of the palace and looked around, but saw no one. The palace was furnished with silk carpets and leather mats and hung with drapes. There were also settees, benches, and seats with cushions, as well as cupboards. In the middle there stood a spacious courtyard, surrounded by four adjoining recessed courts facing each other. In the center stood a fountain, on top of which crouched four lions in red gold, spouting water from their mouths in droplets that looked like gems and pearls, and about the fountain singing birds fluttered under a high net to prevent them from flying away. When the king saw all this, without seeing anyone, he was astonished and regretted that he found none to give him any information. He sat pensively by one of the recessed courts, when he heard sad moans and lamentations and the following plaintive verses:

> My soul is torn between peril and toil;
> O life, dispatch me with one mighty blow.
> Lover, neither a bankrupt nor a noble man
> Humbled by love's law do you pity show.
> Ev'n from the breeze I jealously used to guard you, 5
> But at the blow of fate the eyes blind go.
> When, as he pulls to shoot, the bowstring breaks
> What can the bowman facing his foes do?
> And when the foes begin to congregate
> How can he then escape his cruel fate? 10

When the king heard the lamentation and the verses, he rose and moved toward the source of the voice until he came to a doorway behind a curtain, and when he lifted the curtain, he saw at the upper end of the room a young man sitting on a chair that rose about twenty inches above the floor. He was a handsome young man, with a full figure, clear voice, radiant brow, bright face, downy beard, and ruddy cheeks, graced with a mole like a speck of amber, just as the poet describes it:

> Here is a slender youth whose hair and face
> All mortals envelope with light or gloom.
> Mark on his cheek the mark of charm and grace,
> A dark spot on a red anemone.

The king greeted the seated young man, pleased to see him. The young man wore a long-sleeved robe of Egyptian silk with gold embroidery, and on his head he wore an Egyptian conical head covering, but his face showed signs of grief and sorrow. When the king greeted him, the young man greeted him back courteously and said, "Pardon me, sir, for not rising, for you deserve even a greater honor." The king replied, "Young man, you are pardoned. I myself am your guest, having come to you on a serious mission. Pray tell me the story behind the lake and the colored fish, as well as this palace and the fact that you sit alone and mourn with no one to console you." When the young man heard this, his tears began to flow over his cheeks until they drenched his breast. Then he sang the following *Mawwaliya* verses:[2]

> Say to the man whom life with arrows shot,
> "How many men have felt the blows of fate!"
> If you did sleep, the eyes of God have not;
> Who can say time is fair and life in constant state?

Then he wept bitterly. The king was astonished and asked, "Young man, why do you cry?" The young man replied, "Sir, how can I refrain from crying in my present condition?" Then he lifted the skirt of his robe, and the king saw that while one half of the young man, from the navel to the head, was human flesh, the other half, from the navel to the feet, was black stone.

But morning overcame Shahrazad, and she lapsed into silence. Then King Shahrayar thought to himself, "This is an amazing story. I am willing to postpone her execution even for a month, before having her put to death." While the king was thinking to himself, Dinarzad said to her sister Shahrazad, "Sister, what an entertaining story!" Shahrazad replied, "What is this compared with what I shall tell you tomorrow night if I live, the Almighty God willing!"

THE TWENTY-SECOND NIGHT

The following night Shahrazad said:

I heard, O King, that when the king saw the young man in this condition, he felt very sad and sorry for him, and said with a sigh, "Young man, you have added one more worry to my worries. I came to look for an answer to the mystery of the fish, in order to save them, but ended up looking for an answer to your case, as well as the fish. There is no power and no strength save in God, the Almighty, the Magnificent. Hurry up, young man, and tell me your story." The young man replied, "Lend me your ears, your eyes, and your mind." The king replied, "My ears, my eyes, and my mind are ready." The young man said:

[The Tale of the Enchanted King]

My story, and the story of the fish, is a strange and amazing one, which, if it could be engraved with needles at the corner of the eye,[3] would be a lesson to those who would consider. My lord, my father was the king of this city, and his name was King Mahmud of the Black Islands. For these four hills were islands. He ruled for seventy years, and when he died, I succeeded him and married my cousin. She loved me very much, so much so that if I was away from her even for a single day, she would refuse to eat and drink until I returned to her. In this way, we lived together for five years until one day she went to the bath and I ordered the cook to grill meat and prepare a sumptuous supper for her. Then I entered this palace, lay down in this very

---

2. Poems in colloquial language, often sung to the accompaniment of a reed pipe.   3. I.e., if a master calligrapher could by a miracle of his art write the entire story at the corner of an eye, it would then be read as a double miracle, one for the extraordinary events, one for the extraordinary art.

spot where you are sitting now, and ordered two maids to sit down, one at my head and one at my feet, to fan me. But I felt uneasy and could not go to sleep. While I lay with my eyes closed, breathing heavily, I heard the girl at my head say to the one at my feet, "O Mas'uda, what a pity for our poor master with our damned mistress, and him so young!" The other one replied, "What can one say? May God damn all treacherous, adulterous women. Alas, it is not right that such a young man like our master lives with this bitch who spends every night out." Mas'uda added, "Is our master stupid? When he wakes up at night, doesn't he find that she is not by his side?" The other replied, "Alas, may God trip the bitch our mistress. Does she leave our master with his wits about him? No. She places a sleeping potion in the last drink he takes, offers him the cup, and when he drinks it, he sleeps like a dead man. Then she leaves him and stays out till dawn. When she returns, she burns incense under his nose, and when he inhales it, he wakes up. What a pity!"

My lord, when I heard the conversation between the two maids, I was extremely angry and I could hardly wait for the night to come. When my wife returned from the bath, we had the meal served but ate very little. Then we retired to my bed and I pretended to drink the contents of the cup, which I poured out, and went to sleep. No sooner had I fallen on my side than my wife said, "Go to sleep, and may you never rise again. By God, your sight disgusts me and your company bores me." Then she put on her clothes, perfumed herself with burning incense and, taking my sword, girded herself with it. Then she opened the door and walked out. My lord, I got up . . .

But morning overtook Shahrazad, and she lapsed into silence. Then Dinarzad said, "O my lady, what an amazing and entertaining story!" Shahrazad replied, "What is this compared with what I shall tell you tomorrow night!"

THE TWENTY-THIRD NIGHT

The following night Dinarzad said to her sister Shahrazad, "Please, sister, if you are not sleepy, tell us one of your lovely little tales." Shahrazad replied, "With the greatest pleasure":

It is related, O King, that the enchanted young man said to the king:

Then I followed her, as she left the palace and traversed my city until she stood at the city gate. There she uttered words I could not understand, and the locks fell off and the gate opened by itself. She went out, and I followed her until she slipped through the trash mounds and came to a hut built with palm leaves, leading to a domed structure built with sun-dried bricks. After she entered, I climbed to the top of the dome, and when I looked inside, I saw my wife standing before a decrepit black man sitting on reed shavings and dressed in tatters. She kissed the ground before him and he raised his head and said, "Damn you, why are you late? My black cousins were here. They played with the bat and ball, sang, and drank brewed liquor. They had a good time, each with his own girlfriend, except for myself, for I refused even to drink with them because you were absent."

My wife replied, "O my lord and lover, don't you know that I am married to my cousin, who finds me most loathsome and detests me more than anyone else? Were it not for your sake, I would not have let the sun rise before reducing his city to rubble, a dwelling place for the bears and the foxes, where the owl hoots and the crow crows, and would have hurled its stones beyond Mount Qaf."[4] He replied, "Damn you, you are lying. I swear in the name of black chivalry that as of tonight, if our cousins visit me and you fail to be present, I will never befriend you, lie down with you, or let my body touch yours. You cursed woman, you have been playing with me like a piece of marble, and I am subject to your whims, you cursed, rotten woman." My lord, when I heard their conversation, the world started to turn black before my eyes, and I lost my senses. Then I heard my wife crying and imploring, "O my lover and my heart's desire, if you remain angry at me, whom else have I got, and if you turn me out, who will take me in, O my lord, my lover, and light of my eye?" She kept crying and begging until he was appeased. Then, feeling happy, she took off her outer garments, and asked, "My lord, have you anything for your little girl to eat?" The black man replied, "Open the copper basin," and when she lifted the lid, she found some leftover fried rat bones. After she ate them, he said to her, "There is some brewed liquor left in that jug. You may drink it." She drank the liquor and washed her hands and lay beside the black man on the reed shavings. Then she undressed and slipped under his tatters. I climbed down from the top of the dome and, entering through the door, grabbed the sword that my wife had brought with her, and drew it, intending to kill both of them. I first struck the black man on the neck and thought that I had killed him.

But morning overtook Shahrazad, and she lapsed into silence. Then Dinarzad said, "Sister, what an entertaining story!" Shahrazad replied, "Tomorrow night I shall tell you something more entertaining if I live!"

THE TWENTY-FOURTH NIGHT

The following night Dinarzad said to her sister Shahrazad, "For God's sake, sister, if you are not sleepy, tell us one of your lovely little tales." Shahrazad replied, "With the greatest pleasure":

I heard, O King, that the enchanted young man said to the king:

My lord, I struck the black man on the neck, but failed to cut the two arteries. Instead I only cut into the skin and flesh of the throat and thought that I had killed him. He began to snort violently, and my wife pulled away from him. I retreated, put the sword back in its place, and went back to the city. I entered the palace and went to sleep in my bed till morning. When my wife arrived and I looked at her, I saw that she had cut her hair and put on a mourning dress. She said, "Husband, don't reproach me for what I am doing, for I have received news that my mother has died, that my father was killed in the holy war, and that my two brothers have also lost their lives, one in battle, the other bitten by a snake. I have every reason to weep and

---

4. Legendary mountain cited for its remoteness.

mourn." When I heard what she said, I did not reply, except to say, "I don't reproach you. Do as you wish."

She mourned for an entire year, weeping and wailing. When the year ended, she said to me, "I want you to let me build inside the palace a mausoleum for me to use as a special place of mourning and to call it the house of sorrows." I replied, "Go ahead." Then she gave the order, and a house of mourning was erected for her, with a domed mausoleum and a tomb inside. Then, my lord, she moved the wounded black man to the mausoleum and placed him in the tomb. But, although he was still alive, from the day I cut his throat, he never spoke a word or was able to do her any good, except to drink liquids. She visited him in the mausoleum every day, morning and evening, bringing with her beverages and broth, and she kept at it for an entire year, while I held my patience and left her to her own devices. One day, while she was unaware, I entered the mausoleum and found her crying and lamenting:

> When I see your distress,
> It pains me, as you see.
> And when I see you not,
> It pains me, as you see.
> O speak to me, my life,   5
> My master, talk to me.

Then she sang:

> The day I have you is the day I crave;
> The day you leave me is the day I die.
> Were I to live in fear of promised death,
> I'd rather be with you than my life save.

Then she recited the following verses:

> If I had every blessing in the world
> And all the kingdom of the Persian king,
> If I see not your person with my eyes,
> All this will not be worth an insect's wing.

When she stopped crying, I said to her, "Wife, you have mourned and wept enough and further tears are useless." She replied, "Husband, do not interfere with my mourning. If you interfere again, I will kill myself." I kept quiet and left her alone, while she mourned, wept, and lamented for another year. One day, after the third year, feeling the strain of this drawn-out, heavy burden, something happened to trigger my anger, and when I returned, I found my wife in the mausoleum, beside the tomb, saying, "My lord, I have not had any word from you. For three years I have had no reply." Then she recited the following verses:

> O tomb, O tomb, has he his beauties lost,
> Or have you lost yourself that radiant look?
> O tomb, neither a garden nor a star,
> The sun and moon at once how can you host?

These verses added anger to my anger, and I said to myself, "Oh, how much longer shall I endure?" Then I burst out with the following verses:

> O tomb, O tomb, has he his blackness lost,
> Or have you lost yourself that filthy look?
> O tomb, neither a toilet nor a heap of dirt,
> Charcoal and mud at once how can you host?

When my wife heard me, she sprang up and said, "Damn you, dirty dog. It was you who did this to me, wounded my beloved, and tormented me by depriving me of his youth, while he has been lying here for three years, neither alive nor dead." I said to her, "You, dirtiest of whores and filthiest of all venal women who ever desired and copulated with black slaves, yes it was I who did this to him." Then I grabbed my sword and drew it to strike her. But when she heard me and realized that I was determined to kill her, she laughed and said, "Get away, you dog. Alas, alas, what is done cannot be undone; nor will the dead come back to life, but God has delivered into my hand the one who did this to me and set my heart ablaze with the fire of revenge." Then she stood up, uttered words I could not understand, and cried, "With my magic and cunning, be half man, half stone." Sir, from that instant, I have been as you now see me, dejected and sad, helpless and sleepless, neither living with the living nor dead among the dead.

But morning overtook Shahrazad, and she lapsed into silence. Then Dinarzad said, "Sister, what an amazing and entertaining story!" Shahrazad replied, "Tomorrow night I shall tell you something more entertaining if the king spares me and lets me live!"

THE TWENTY-FIFTH NIGHT

The following night Dinarzad said to her sister Shahrazad, "Sister, if you are not sleepy, tell us one of your lovely little tales to while away the night." Shahrazad replied, "With the greatest pleasure":

It is related, O King, that the enchanted young man said to the king:

"After my wife turned me into this condition, she cast a spell on the city, with all its gardens, fields, and markets, the very place where your troops are camping now. My wife turned the inhabitants of my city, who belonged to four sects, Muslims, Magians,[5] Christians, and Jews, into fish, the Muslims white, the Magians red, the Christians blue, and the Jews yellow. Likewise, she turned the islands into four hills surrounding the lake. As if what she has done to me and the city is not enough, she strips me naked every day and gives me a hundred lashes with the whip until my back is lacerated and begins to bleed. Then she clothes my upper half with a hairshirt like a coarse rug and covers it with these luxurious garments." Then the young man burst into tears and recited the following verses:

> O Lord, I bear with patience your decree,
> And so that I may please you, I endure,
> That for their tyranny and unfair use
> Our recompense your Paradise may be.

---

5. Zoroastrian priests. Zoroastrianism is the religion of ancient Persia, based on the recognition of the dual principle of good and evil or light and darkness.

You never let the tyrant go, my Lord;   5
Pluck me out of the fire, Almighty God.

The king said to the young man, "Young man, you have lifted one anxiety
but added another worry to my worries. But where is your wife, and where
is the mausoleum with the wounded black man?" The young man replied,
"O King, the black slave is lying in the tomb inside the mausoleum, which
is in the adjoining room. My wife comes to visit him at dawn every day, and
when she comes, she strips me naked and gives me a hundred lashes with
the whip, while I cry and scream without being able to stand up and defend
myself, since I am half stone, half flesh and blood. After she punishes me,
she goes to the black slave to give him beverages and broth to drink. Tomorrow at dawn she will come as usual." The king replied, "By God, young man,
I shall do something for you that will go down in history and commemorate
my name." Then the king sat to converse with the young man until night fell
and they went to sleep.

The king got up before dawn, took off his clothes, and, drawing his sword,
entered the room with the domed mausoleum and found it lit with candles
and lamps and scented with incense, perfume, saffron, and ointments. He
went straight to the black man and killed him. Then he carried him out and
threw him in a well inside the palace. When he came back, he put on the
clothes of the black man, covered himself, and lay hiding at the bottom of
the tomb, with the drawn sword hidden under his clothes.

A while later, the cursed witch arrived, and the first thing she did was to
strip her husband naked, take a whip, and whip him again and again, while
he cried, "Ah wife, have pity on me; help me; I have had enough punishment
and pain; have pity on me." She replied, "You should have had pity on me
and spared my lover."

*But morning overtook Shahrazad, and she lapsed into silence. Then Dinar-
zad said, "Sister, what an amazing and entertaining story!" Shahrazad replied,
"What is this compared with what I shall tell you tomorrow night if I live!"
King Shahrayar, with a mixture of amazement, pain, and sorrow for the
enchanted youth, said to himself, "By God, I shall postpone her execution for
tonight and many more nights, even for two months, until I hear the rest of
the story and find out what happened to the enchanted young man. Then I
shall have her put to death, as I did the others." So he said to himself.*

THE TWENTY-SIXTH NIGHT

*The following night Dinarzad said to Shahrazad, "Sister, if you are not
sleepy, tell us one of your lovely little tales to while away the night." Shahrazad
replied, "With the greatest pleasure":*

I heard, O King, that after the witch punished her husband by whipping
him until his sides and shoulders were bleeding and she satisfied her thirst
for revenge, she dressed him with the coarse hairshirt and covered it with
the outer garments. Then she headed to the black man, with the usual cup
of drink and the broth. She entered the mausoleum, reached the tomb, and
began to cry, wail, and lament, saying, "Lover, denying me yourself is not
your custom. Do not be stingy, for my foes gloat over our separation. Be

generous with your love, for forsaking is not your custom. Visit me, for my life is in your visit. O my lord, speak to me; O my lord, entertain me." Then she sang the following verses of the *Mufrad*[6] variety:

> For how long is this cruel disdain,
> Have I not paid with enough tears?
> O lover, talk to me,
> O lover, speak to me,
> O lover, answer me.   5

The king lowered his voice, stammered, and, simulating the accent of black people, said, "Ah, ah, ah! There is no power and no strength save in God the Almighty, the Magnificent." When she heard him speak, she screamed with joy and fainted, and when she came to herself, she cried, "Is it true that you spoke to me?" The king replied, "Damn you, you don't deserve that anyone should speak to you or answer you." She asked, "What is the cause?" He replied, "All day long you punish your husband, while he screams for help. From sunset till dawn he cries, implores, and invokes God against you and me, with his deafening and enervating cries that deprive me of sleep. If it had not been for this, I would have recovered a long time ago, and this is why I have not spoken to you or answered you." She said, "My lord, if you allow me, I shall deliver him from his present condition." He replied, "Deliver him and rid us of his noise."

She went out of the mausoleum, took a bowl, and, filling it with water, uttered a spell over it, and the water began to boil and bubble as in a caldron over fire. Then she sprinkled the young man with the water and said, "By the power of my spell, if the Creator has created you in this form, or if he has turned you into this form out of anger at you, stay as you are, but if you have been transformed by my magic and cunning, turn back to your normal form, by the will of God, Creator of the world." The young man shook himself at once and stood up, erect and sound, and he rejoiced and thanked God for his deliverance. Then his wife said to him, "Get out of my sight and don't ever come back, for if you do and I see you here, I shall kill you." She yelled at him, and he went away.

Then she returned to the mausoleum and, descending to the tomb, called out, "My sweet lord, come out and let me see your handsome face." The king replied in a muffled voice, "You have rid me of the limb, but failed to rid us of the body." She asked, "My sweet lord, what do you mean by the body?" He replied, "Damn you, cursed woman, it is the inhabitants of this city and its four islands, for every night at midnight, the fish raise their heads from the lake to implore and invoke God against me, and this is why I do not recover. Go to them and deliver them at once; then come back to hold my hand and help me rise, for I am beginning to feel better already." When she heard him, she rejoiced and replied joyfully, "Yes, my lord, yes, with God's help, my sweetheart." Then she rose, went to the lake, and took a little of its water.

But morning overtook Shahrazad, and she lapsed into silence. Then Dinarzad said, "What an amazing and entertaining story!" Shahrazad replied, "What

---

6. Literally "single," a verse form.

is this compared with what I shall tell you tomorrow night if the king spares me and I live!"

THE TWENTY-SEVENTH NIGHT

The following night Dinarzad said to her sister Shahrazad, "If you are not sleepy, tell us one of your lovely little tales to while away the night." Shahrazad replied, "With the greatest pleasure":

It is related, O King, that the wife uttered some words over the lake, and the fish began to dance, and at that instant the spell was lifted, and the townspeople resumed their usual activities and returned to their buying and selling. Then she went back to the palace, entered the mausoleum, and said, "My lord, give me your gracious hand and rise." The king replied in a muffled voice, "Come closer to me." She moved closer, while he urged her "Come closer still," and she moved until her body touched his. Then he pushed her back and with one stroke of the sword sliced her in half, and she fell in two to the ground.

Then the king went out and, finding the enchanted young man waiting for him, congratulated him on his deliverance, and the young man kissed his hand, thanked him, and invoked God's blessing on him. Then the king asked him, "Do you wish to stay here or come with me to my city?" The young man replied, "King of the age, and Lord of the world, do you know the distance between your city and mine?" The king replied, "It is a half-day journey." The young man said, "O King, you are dreaming, for between your city and mine it is a full year's journey. You reached us in half a day because the city was enchanted." The king asked, "Still, do you wish to stay here in your city or come with me?" The young man replied, "O King, I shall not part from you, even for one moment." The king was happy and said, "Thank God who has given you to me. You shall be a son to me, for I have never had one." They embraced, holding each other closely, and felt happy. Then they walked together back to the palace, and when they entered the palace, the enchanted young king announced to the eminent men of his kingdom and to his retinue that he was going on a journey.

He spent ten days in preparation, packing what he needed, together with the gifts that the princes and merchants of the city had given him for his journey. Then he set out with the king, with his heart on fire to be leaving his city for a whole year. He left, with fifty Mamluks and many guides and servants, bearing one hundred loads of gifts, rarities, and treasures, as well as money. They journeyed on, evening and morning, night and day, for a whole year until God granted them safe passage and they reached their destination. Then the king sent someone to inform the vizier of his safe return, and the vizier came out with all the troops and most of the townspeople to meet him. Having given him up for lost, they were exceedingly happy, and the city was decorated and its streets were spread with silk carpets. The vizier and the soldiers dismounted and, kissing the ground before the king, congratulated him on his safety and invoked God's blessing on him.

Then they entered the city, and the king sat on his throne and, meeting with the vizier, explained to him why he had been absent for an entire year. He told him the story of the young man and how he, the king, had dealt with the young man's wife and saved him and the city, and the vizier turned to the young man and congratulated him on his deliverance. Then the princes, viziers, chamberlains, and deputies took their places, and the king bestowed on them robes of honor, gifts, and other favors. Then he sent for the fisherman, who was the cause of saving the young man and the city, and when the fisherman stood before the king, the king bestowed on him robes of honor, and then asked him, "Do you have any children?" The fisherman replied that he had one boy and two girls. The king had them brought before him, and he himself married one of the girls, while he married the other to the enchanted young man. Moreover, the king took the fisherman's son into his service and made him one of his attendants. Then he conferred authority on the vizier, appointing him king of the city of the Black Islands, supplied him with provisions and fodder for the journey, and ordered the fifty Mamluks, who had come with them, as well as a host of other people, to go with him. He also sent with him many robes of honor and many fine gifts for all the princes and prominent men there. The vizier took his leave, kissed the king's hand, and departed. The king, the enchanted young man, and the fisherman lived peacefully thereafter, and the fisherman became one of the richest men of his time, with daughters married to kings.

But morning overtook Shahrazad, and she lapsed into silence. Then Dinarzad said, "What an amazing and entertaining story!" Shahrazad replied, "What is this compared with what I shall tell you tomorrow night if the king spares me and lets me live!"

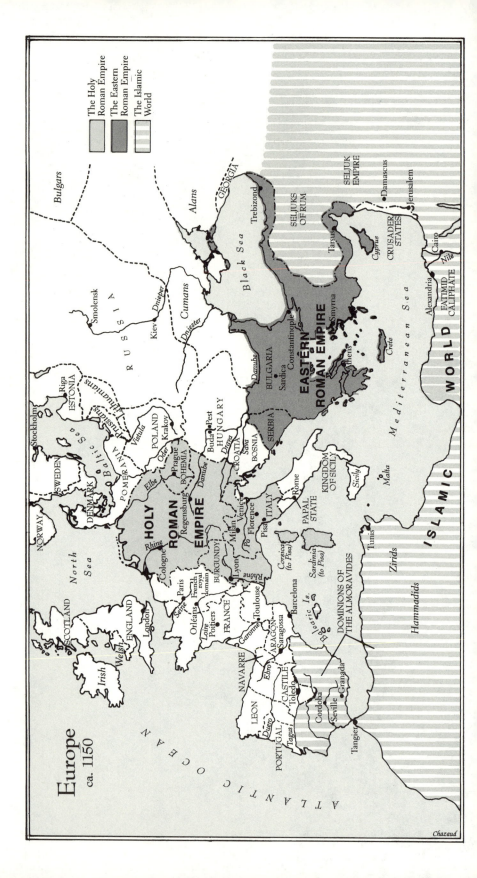

Europe
ca. 1150

The Holy
Roman Empire

The Eastern
Roman Empire

The Islamic
World

Bulgars

Alans

GEORGIA

Trebizond

SELJUKS
OF RUM

SELJUK
EMPIRE

Damascus

Jerusalem

Smolensk

Black Sea

R U S S I A

Kiev

Dnieper

Cumans

Dniester

Tarsus

Smyrna

Cyprus

CRUSADER
STATES

Cairo

Nile

Alexandria

FATIMID
CALIPHATE

Constantinople

EASTERN
ROMAN EMPIRE

Athens

Crete

Mediterranean Sea

Riga

ESTONIA

Lithuanians

Stockholm

Prussians

Vistula

POLAND

Krakov

Oder

Prague

BOHEMIA

Elbe

Buda

Pest

HUNGARY

Drava

Sava

CROATIA

BOSNIA

SERBIA

Danube

BULGARIA

Sardica

W O R L D

SWEDEN

Baltic Sea

POMERANIA

DENMARK

HOLY

ROMAN

EMPIRE

Regensburg

Danube

Venice

Po

Milan

Florence

Pisa

ITALY

Rome

PAPAL
STATE

KINGDOM
OF SICILY

Sicily

Malta

I S L A M I C

NORWAY

*North
Sea*

Cologne

Rhine

BURGUNDY

Lyons

Rhône

Corsica
(to Pisa)

Sardinia
(to Pisa)

Tunis

Zirids

Paris

Seine

French
royal
domain

Orléans

Loire

Poitiers

FRANCE

Toulouse

Garonne

Barcelona

Balearic Is.

DOMINIONS OF
THE ALMORAVIDES

Hammadids

SCOTLAND

Irish

Welsh

ENGLAND

London

NAVARRE

ARAGON

Saragossa

Ebro

LEON

Duero

CASTILE

Toledo

Tagus

Cordoba

Seville

Granada

Tangier

PORTUGAL

A T L A N T I C   O C E A N

Chazaud

The Formation of a Western Literature

The Middle Ages—approximately the thousand years from 500 to 1500—saw the classical civilization of Greece and Rome transformed by contact with three very different cultures. One was the Germanic culture of the tribes who invaded and, by the fifth century, had effectively conquered the western half of the Roman empire. The second was the Christianity that began in Palestine and then quickly spread throughout the empire until almost all of Western Europe was thoroughly Christianized by the eleventh century (as early as 325 the emperor Constantine had established Christianity as virtually the official religion of the empire). The third influence—less pronounced but still important—was Islam, which arose in the Arabian peninsula in the seventh century and quickly spread throughout North Africa and into the Iberian peninsula, where it remained a powerful force until the fifteenth century. Because it was an amalgam of these vastly different cultural forces, medieval Europe displayed an unusually wide range of values, ideas, and social forms. But for all this variety there emerged at the end of the process a recognizable culture. In the year 500 "the West" could hardly be characterized either politically or culturally, but by 1500 the map of Europe looked very much as it does today, and many of the values we think of as characteristically Western—individualism, consensual government, a recognition of religious difference, even the idea of Europe itself—were emergent realities. Another central event within Western culture during this period was the emergence of vernacular literatures. The great national literatures of Europe took form during the Middle Ages, and here we find both individual literary masterpieces and traditions of writing that have continued to define what counts as literature.

Because it is the period during which the cultural identities of the European nations took shape, the Middle Ages has always generated both fascination and controversy. Take, for example, its distinctly odd name: the *middle* of what? The answer is that the period was named by the people who came immediately after it, who called their own age the Renaissance because they saw it as the time in which the cultural achievements of antiquity were being reborn. For them the immediately preceding period was a time of middleness, a space of cultural emptiness that separated them from the classical past they so admired: hence, the Middle Ages (or, in Latin, *medium aevum,* from which we get our term *medieval*). That this narrow view of cultural history is still in force today is shown by the way in which "medieval" continues to be used to mean antiquated, or quaint, or barbaric. It is also evident in the widespread notion that the Middle Ages was unusually homogeneous, a time in which all men and women thought and felt more or less the same things and behaved in much the same way. Yet in fact this period contains not one but many different kinds of people with many different cultures.

These cultures were oral and literate; Germanic and Latin; Arabic, Jewish, and Christian; secular and religious; tolerant and repressive; vernacular and learned; rural and urban; skeptical and pious; popular and aristocratic. For every example of one kind of cultural product we can find an example of another, and most significant literary works incorporated elements and values drawn from different and often conflicting traditions. *The Song of Roland,* for instance, composed in the eleventh century, promotes with unabashed enthusiasm the superiority of Christianity to Islam. Yet already in the ninth century, Islamic scholars had translated much of Greek science and philosophy into Arabic, preserving and enriching this tradition at the very time it was in decline in Western Europe. And beginning in the twelfth century, Muslim centers of learning in Spain, Sicily, and southern Italy made it possible for European scholars to regain access to these Greek originals and to study their Muslim commentators. Similarly complex is the way *The Song of Roland* struggles with internal contradictions of its own. A poem that exalts a great warrior according to Germanic traditions of military heroism, it also affirms the necessity of subordinating individual accomplishment to the needs of a unified Christian community. Another example of the clash of competing interests can be found in the work of Geoffrey Chaucer, the founding poet of English literature. For the first two-thirds of his career he was a court poet who catered almost exclusively to the narrow tastes of an aristocratic readership, and yet in *The Canterbury Tales* he recorded with remarkable sensitivity the discontents and desires of men and women from almost every social class. These complexities and contradictions are everywhere in medieval writing, and if they frustrate modern attempts to define the period in simple terms they also make reading its literature a process of continuing surprise.

The most familiar description of the Middle Ages is as "an age of faith," by which is meant the notion that medieval people shared a uniform commitment to Catholic Christianity. The Roman empire had provided political unity, law, and order, but beyond that it had pretty much left moral and spiritual issues to be handled by the individual, either singly or in voluntary or ethnic groups. As the Middle Ages developed, however, the Church gradually extended its spiritual and institutional authority across most of Europe. By 1200, with the exception of beleaguered Jewish communities, the area of the Iberian peninsula under Muslim control, and frontier lands in the Slavic east, Europe had become virtually identical with Christendom. But this acknowledgment of the primacy of Christian doctrine and the ritual practices that went with it (such as baptism, communion, and confession) meant neither that religious values were universally recognized as primary nor that one single form of Christianity was placidly accepted by all medieval people. On the contrary, as the literature of the period makes clear, many people took the central doctrines of Christianity so much for granted that their daily lives seem largely untroubled by the moral and spiritual demands of religion. In the *Lais* of Marie de France, for example, and the vernacular love lyrics, men and women lead their romantic lives without giving much if any thought to Christian standards of behavior. In a more satiric vein, the tales from Boccaccio's *Decameron* provide an often acerbic and always witty puncturing of the pretensions of individual churchmen. The lecherous priest and the greedy friar are stock characters of medieval satire, as are the wayward nun and the gluttonous monk. Another pressure point at which Christian doctrine is tested is the Germanic epic *Beowulf,* a poem written by a believer who nonetheless deeply admires the pagan past that he knows must be left behind. Even in *The Divine Comedy,* the work that seems most securely and unproblematically located within the Christian worldview, Dante is poignantly aware of the gulf that separates him from the classical past, represented in the *Inferno* and *Purgatorio* by the man he calls "my author and my father," the pagan poet Virgil. The Middle Ages *is* an age of faith, but one that at its best is alert to the complexities and dilemmas that any faith poses to its adherents.

Another familiar description of the Middle Ages is as "an age of chivalry." Medieval literature for the most part expresses the values of the most powerful members of society, the aristocracy. These people achieved their domination through military might, both by imposing their will upon their neighbors and, more benevolently, by providing them with protection from invaders like the Vikings from the north, the Magyars and Mongols from the east, and the various Islamic peoples from the south. At times, indeed, they became themselves the invaders, most notably in the various crusading expeditions that began in the eleventh century against Islam in the Iberian peninsula and the Levant and, later, against the Slavs in what is now Eastern Europe. Not surprisingly, throughout its medieval history, from the time of *Beowulf* (about the ninth century) to the late fifteenth century, the European nobility—and the writers they supported—celebrated the values that sustained these military practices. These values included unwavering valor in the face of danger, loyalty to one's leader and companions, and an intense concern with personal honor. They also came to include a more or less explicit code of chivalry that stressed gentility of demeanor, generosity of both spirit and material goods, concern for the well-being of the powerless, and—above all—a capacity for experiencing a romantic love that was at once selfless and passionate. Whether or not medieval men actually lived up to these chivalric ideals is impossible to say, but that many believed in them—and believed that they achieved them—is undeniable. Yet many other members of medieval society, especially non-nobles like churchmen, urban dwellers, and peasants, were more likely than not to think that chivalry was just a fancy name for the heavy-handed imposition of force upon those least able to resist. More important for the writing of the time is the fact that chivalric values are never entirely consistent with each other. Where does personal bravery give way to the needs of the group?—this is a question at the heart of both *Beowulf* and *The Song of Roland*. Can one be both a full-hearted lover and a loyal warrior? And can the same people perform both the deeds of war and those of civilization?—this is a question central to Western literature since the time of Homer and still challenging to us today.

The busy millennium we call, in the absence of a more precise term, the Middle Ages is thus dominated by certain leading concerns—the demands of religious faith and the appropriate use of physical force—that remain current. What continues to make its literature compelling to us is the skill with which individual writers dealt with these themes through the creation of unforgettable literary characters. For all its accomplishments in the arts of governing and the skills of commerce, in philosophy and theology, and in art and architecture, the most vivid legacy of the Middle Ages is the roster of characters it has contributed to world literature. Roland and Charlemagne, Robin Hood, Sir Gawain and Beowulf, the pilgrims of *The Canterbury Tales* and the lost souls of the *Inferno*: whether searching for the road to salvation or killing monsters, whether battling pagan enemies or hoodwinking unwary dupes, the protagonists of medieval literature continue to intrigue readers and inspire writers. In the last analysis the central concern of medieval literature is neither religious truth nor codes of conduct, important as these may be, but individual human beings working out their individual destinies.

FURTHER READING

An excellent reference work that contains articles on virtually all medieval topics, with bibliographies, is *The Dictionary of the Middle Ages*, 13 vols. (1987). Specific questions about medieval Christian doctrines can be answered by consulting Jaroslav Pelikan, *The Christian Tradition: A History of the Development of Doctrine*, vols. 1–4 (1971–84). C. W. Previté-Orton, *Shorter Cambridge Medieval History*, 2 vols. (1952), provides useful information on the relevant historical context of each literary work. An authoritative and readable introduction to social and economic conditions is M. M. Postan, *The Medieval Economy and Society* (1975). Two classic accounts well worth reading are R. W. Southern, *The Making of the Middle Ages* (1953), and J. W. Huizinga, *The Autumn of the Middle Ages* (first published in 1919, newly translated in 1996).

TIME LINE

TEXTS	CONTEXTS
	529 Foundation of Monte Cassino, the first Benedictine monastery
ninth century *Beowulf* • Latin lyrics, saints' lives, and histories	**8th–10th centuries** Invasions of Western Europe by Arabs, Norsemen, and Magyars
	800 Charlemagne crowned Holy Roman emperor
	899 Alfred the Great, king of Wessex in England, dies
11th century Hispano-Arabic and Provençal lyrics	**11th century** Consolidation of feudal social structure
	1066 Norman invasion of England
	1099 Knights of the First Crusade capture Jerusalem
12th century *The Song of Roland* • Marie de France, *Lais* • Arthurian romances • *Romance of Renard*	**12th century** Establishment of the universities of Paris, Oxford, and Bologna • Recovery of Aristotelian philosophy • Period of religious reform
	1187 Arabs recover Jerusalem permanently
13th century Fabliaux • *Romance of the Rose* • **Thorstein the Staff-Struck**	**13th century** Age of the great cathedrals and of scholastic philosophy
	1226 Francis of Assisi, founder of the first order of friars, dies
	1274 Thomas Aquinas, leading scholastic philosopher, dies
1301–1321 Dante, *The Divine Comedy*	**1337** War begins between France and England (the Hundred Years' War), ending only in 1453
	1348–1350 Bubonic plague sweeps through Europe, killing almost half the population
1353 Boccaccio, *The Decameron*	
1380? *Sir Gawain and the Green Knight*	
	1384 John Wyclif, promoter of religious views that prepare for the Reformation, dies
1390–1400 Chaucer, *The Canterbury Tales*	
	14th century Peasant risings in England, France, Flanders, and Italy

Boldface titles indicate works in the anthology.

TIME LINE

TEXTS	CONTEXTS
	15th century Growing centralization of state power throughout Europe
	1453 Fall of Constantinople to the Muslim Turks
	1455 Gutenberg prints the Bible, the first printed book
ca. 1470 Villon, *The Testament*	
	1492 Christopher Columbus's first voyage to the Western Hemisphere
1495? *Everyman*	

BEOWULF
ca. ninth century

Beowulf, composed perhaps (but not certainly) about 850 in the Anglo-Saxon language then current in England, is both a heroic poem of dark magnificence and the most vivid account left to us of the social world and life experiences of the Germanic and Scandinavian peoples who overran the Roman empire. In its bare narrative outline the poem is a fairy-tale story of how the hero, Beowulf, conquered three monsters: first a man-eating, troll-like creature named Grendel, then Grendel's vengeance-seeking mother, and finally—when Beowulf has become an old man—a fire-breathing dragon. From these unlikely events the poet has fashioned a poem that represents with great power and specificity not merely the details of the warrior life of the Germanic tribes but its meaning to the people who lived it. Although himself a Christian, the poet provides us with a unique insight into a pagan world that had passed away by the time he was writing, but one whose legends and values he knows well. Like those of the Homeric poems and *The Song of Roland,* the historical period of the action of *Beowulf* is many centuries prior to the poem's date of composition: the one event in the poem that can be dated—the death of Beowulf's lord, Hygelac, in a raid on the Franks—occurred around 520. The protagonists of the poem are not the English who were its audience but two of their forebears, the Germanic tribes of the South Danes, who lived in Denmark, and their neighbors to the east, the Geats, who lived in southern Sweden. In addition to these two groups the poem alludes to the history of other northern European peoples, especially the Swedes, the Frisians, and the Franks, and it mentions as well more obscure tribal groupings like the Heatho-Bards, the Wulfings, and the Waegmundings. In reading the poem, we enter into a pre-Christian Germanic world that is both mysterious and fascinating. And that world is also, as Beowulf himself comes to understand, doomed.

The most important fact about Germanic tribal society is its violence, which is why the poet describes that society by means of a narrative of monster-killing. Each of the various tribes is in competition with the others for land and plunder, and even within tribes there are constant struggles for power. The central bond that holds the society together is the loyalty between a lord and his warriors, or thanes. The lord is a "ring-giver," which means that he distributes to his thanes objects of value that include bracelets and necklaces ("rings"), armor and weapons, and even land and political authority. In return the thane is expected to provide unswerving loyalty on the battlefield and good counsel during times of peace. More important, this bond of loyalty establishes the community within which individuals find meaning.

In the Germanic world the worst condition into which a man can fall is to be an outlaw or wanderer, someone who has no home. This is, in fact, the situation of the monster Grendel, described in the poem as a "grim demon / haunting the marches, marauding round the heath / and the desolate fens" (102–4). The Christian poet interprets Grendel and his mother as deriving from the race of Cain, who was condemned by God to wander the earth after his murder of Abel. The poem begins with Grendel's attack upon the great hall Heorot, built as a place to celebrate community solidarity and the beneficence of the deity by Hrothgar, the old Danish king. What motivates Grendel's attack is his sense of exclusion and singularity: in this world, to be an independent individual is to be isolated and rejected. Appropriately, Grendel's slayer, Beowulf, is himself something of an individual, who, by this act, achieves inclusion within his own social world. Almost two-thirds of the way through the poem we learn that Beowulf "had been poorly regarded / for a long time" by his people, the Geats: "They firmly believed that he lacked force, / that the prince was a weakling" (2183–88). But the victory over Grendel and his mother, and the gifts he receives from the Danes and gives in turn to his own lord, Hygelac, change all that. Hygelac gives him a sword that had belonged to his own father, Hrethel, and grants him land

and lordship: "a hall and a throne." After the deaths of Hygelac and his son Heardred, the Geats then turn to Beowulf to become their king, and he rules for fifty years until his fatal battle with a dragon.

Given that martial prowess is the primary means by which a man earns the respect of his fellows—Beowulf is recognized as worthy not because he is thoughtful or self-controlled (although he is both) but because he is fierce in battle—we should not be surprised that the poet presents a tribal world constantly engulfed in violence. The monster-killing that constitutes the main action of the poem is located within a dense historical context of tribal feuding. These feuds are mentioned so allusively and indirectly that we can assume the poet's English audience was fully informed about the early history of their Germanic ancestors. But the modern reader does not know this history, and it will be helpful to outline it here. (The genealogical table will help to keep the characters straight.)

The poem tells us of five primary feuds. The most important, which we learn about only toward the end of the poem (2379–96, 2472–89, 2922–98), is between the Geats and the Swedes, and takes place in two phases. The first phase begins when the Swedes, under their king Ongentheow, defeat the Geats in a battle at Hreosnahill (or Sorrow Hill) in which great slaughter is committed by Ongentheow's sons, Ohthere and Onela. This slaughter is then avenged by the killing of Ongentheow by the Geat Eofer in the battle of Ravenswood, in which the Geatish king Haethcyn also dies. The second phase of the Swedish-Geatish feud is initiated by a civil war within the Swedish royal family. After the death of his elder brother Ohthere, Onela seizes the throne and drives out the rightful heirs, Ohthere's sons Eanmund and Eadgils. They find refuge with the Geats, then being led by Hygelac's son Heardred. Onela attacks the Geats, killing both Heardred and one of the brothers, Eanmund. (The warrior who actually kills Eanmund is named Weohstan and is the father of Wiglaf, who at the end of the poem is the only one of Beowulf's thanes to stand by him in the attack on the dragon. How Wiglaf—who like Beowulf is referred to as a Waegmunding—came to be accepted among the Geats is never explained.) Heardred's death leaves Beowulf king of the Geats, and he later supports Eadgils, who kills Onela and regains the Swedish throne. Yet despite this apparent alliance, after the death of Beowulf we are told that "this vicious feud" (3000) between the Swedes and Geats will now lead to renewed Swedish attacks on the leaderless Geats (possibly because Wiglaf, the presumptive heir to the Geatish throne, is the son of the slayer of Eadgil's brother).

The second feud mentioned in the poem is that between the Heatho-Bards and the Danes. While Beowulf is visiting Hrothgar in order to deal with the monsters, there are several cryptic references to a deadly fire that awaits the great hall Heorot. When Beowulf returns from his adventure and describes the trip to Hygelac, he explains that Hrothgar's daughter Freawaru is promised to Ingeld, the son of the murdered Heatho-Bard king Froda. Yet Beowulf predicts, in a sinister description of the way that enmity will be stirred up when a Heatho-Bard warrior sees a Dane wearing Froda's armor, that the peace will not hold: "But generally the spear / is prompt to retaliate when a prince is killed, / no matter how admirable the bride may be" (2029–31).

The third feud, predicted but not described, is within the Danish royal house. The old king Hrothgar has two young sons, Hrethric and Hrothmund, and his queen, Wealhtheow, asks Beowulf to protect them from their uncle Hrothulf after the death of Hrothgar—protection Beowulf will be unable to provide.

As to the fourth feud, Hrothgar tells Beowulf that Beowulf's father, Ecgtheow, started a feud with the Wulfings by killing a man called Heatholaf, and that the Geats exiled him in order to protect themselves from retaliation. Hrothgar, however, not only provided Ecgtheow with asylum but also settled the feud by paying compensation to the Wulfings for Heatholaf, a compensation known among the Germanic tribes as *wergild*, or "man-money."

The fifth feud is that between the Geats and three tribes to the south of them, the Frisians, the Hetware, and the Franks. This feud started when the Geatish king Hygelac raided the other tribes' territory—as mentioned, there is an independent record of this raid, which took place about 520—and was killed in the process. As he prepares to fight the dragon, Beowulf tells us that he avenged Hygelac's death: "I killed / Dayraven the Frank in front of the two armies" (2501–2). After Beowulf's death the Geats are told that they face harsh battle at the hands of the Franks.

In addition to these feuds, which occur within the historical world of the poem, one other is mentioned in detail in a song sung by a *scop*, or bard, during the celebrations after the death of Grendel. This is known as the fight at Finnsburg. A Dane named Hnaef and his entourage of warriors, while visiting the Jute Finn at the fortress of Finnsburg, are attacked by the Jutes despite the fact that Finn is married to Hnaef's sister Hildeburh (doubtless as part of an effort to patch up a previous feud). Hnaef is killed, along with the son of Finn and Hildeburh. Neither party is powerful enough to finish off the other, and they agree to a truce: they will winter together in Finnsburg, and the Danes will sail home in the spring. Not surprisingly, the coming of spring also awakens "longing . . . for vengeance" (1138–40), and the Danes slaughter Finn and the other Jutes in their hall, returning home with plunder and with the bereft Hildeburh, whose son and husband are now dead.

The poet makes clear that the awful cost of their violence is not lost on these people. The description of the future that awaits the leaderless Geats now that Beowulf is dead—delivered to the waiting people by a messenger sent from the battle with the dragon—is only one of several chilling passages that acknowledge the effect of tribal warfare:

> . . . Many a spear,
> dawn-cold to the touch will be taken down
> and waved on high; the swept harp
> won't waken warriors, but the raven winging
> darkly over the doomed will have news,
> tidings for the eagle of how he hoked and ate,
> how the wolf and he made short work of the dead. (3021–27)

Nor will things go better for the women of the tribe:

> . . . often, repeatedly, in the path of exile
> they shall walk bereft, bowed under woe,
> now that [Beowulf's] laugh is silenced. (3018–20)

Yet the poem also argues that it is only by violence that civilization can be maintained. The attacks by both Grendel and his mother are themselves a feud, in the first instance against God (hence the monsters' descent from the race of Cain), more immediately against the peaceful society that Hrothgar has established in Heorot. As Wealhtheow says of Heorot,

> "Here each comrade is true to the other,
> loyal to lord, loving in spirit.
> The thanes have one purpose, the people are ready:
> having drunk and pledged, the ranks do as I bid." (1228–31)

Grendel wants to destroy this social harmony, and his mother is an avenging spirit who seeks retaliation for the death of her offspring. Similarly, the dragon is roused to rage by the need to avenge the theft of a drinking cup from the hoard he guards: "he worked himself up / by imagining battle" (2298–99). Thus the monsters can be understood, at least in part, as embodiments of the feuding principle that is inevitably destroying Germanic society. Yet in killing them Beowulf is involved in a paradox: violence can be controlled only by violence, a circle from which no one in the poem is able to escape.

Violence is thus part and parcel of this civilization. After Grendel's mother has killed one of Hrothgar's men, Beowulf advises the Danish king, in a succinct sentence that could stand as a motto for the poem, "It is always better / to avenge dear ones than to indulge in mourning" (1384–85). The miserable condition of the man who cannot avenge the death of a kinsman is vividly described in the story Beowulf tells about Hygelac's father, Hrethel. Hrethel had three sons, Herebeald, Haethcyn, and Hygelac. In an accident, Haethcyn killed Herebeald; because it was an accident, and because the perpetrator was his own son, Hrethel could not compensate himself for his loss with either *wergild* or vengeance. As Beowulf arms himself for the battle with the dragon he tells this grim story, and he draws a parallel between Hrethel's unassuageable grief and the sorrow of the father who sees his son die on the gallows as an outlaw. The grieving father looks at his son's empty dwelling-place, the silent winehall, and he goes then to his bed, chanting grief-songs: "everything seems too large, / the steadings and the fields" (2461–62). This sense of emptiness is an effect of more than simply the technical problem of how to find satisfaction for certain kinds of injury. By having Beowulf tell this story as he prepares for what he knows will be his final battle, the poet shows us that the hero understands at some level the futility of the entire world of Germanic heroism that he himself so fully represents. Trolls and dragons can be killed, but how does one eradicate the violence that serves to constitute society itself? The monsters are, finally, instances of a social sickness that infects the culture as a whole: they may be killed, but the violence they represent will continue unabated. Perhaps Beowulf's greatest act of heroism is found not in the physical courage he displays in his battles against human and superhuman foes but in his spiritual capacity to persevere despite his dark realization of the futility of his efforts.

The poem survives in only a single manuscript written about 1000, but it was composed earlier, probably over a period of many years. Like the Homeric poems and *The Song of Roland*, *Beowulf* emerged from an oral tradition of composition (for a discussion of oral composition, see above, p. 114). It was put into its final form by a Christian, but one who is both careful to preserve the distinction between his Christian present and the pagan past and unusually tolerant of the culture of his forebears. For one thing, he avoids putting Christian sentiments in the mouths of pre-Christian characters. The terms with which the characters refer to the deity—God, the Lord, Heavenly Powers, Almighty God, Lord of Ages, Heavenly Shepherd, King of Heaven, and so forth—are, in their original Anglo-Saxon forms, the same terms as appear in explicitly non-Christian writings. We should also remember that the habit of capitalizing sacred names is a modern convention: in the manuscript they are, like all proper names, lowercase. For example, when the Geats arrive in Denmark they are described in the translation as having "thanked God" (227) that the trip was successful. But the Anglo-Saxon could just as accurately be translated "thanked a god," which has a very different implication. Another example is the way in which the translator has Hrothgar say that Beowulf was sent to the Danes by "Holy God . . . in His goodness" (381–82); again, one could just as accurately, and more consistently, translate this as "by a divine god of his kindness." Hrothgar's speech of advice to Beowulf is certainly consistent with Christianity, but it contains nothing out of character with the values of the Germanic, pagan world in which Hrothgar and Beowulf live. Perhaps most important, the poet refrains from criticizing his pagan characters for their paganism. While he makes it clear that the Danes are wrong to offer sacrifices to their heathen gods in an effort to fend off Grendels' attacks, he is more sorrowful than judgmental or moralistic (175–88). They commit this error because they do not yet know of the true, Christian God whom the poet himself worships, just as they cannot know that the monsters are of the race of Cain. They do indeed live in a world ruled over by the Christian God: as the poet says, "Past and present, God's will prevails" (1057). But while the audience knows this truth, their pagan forebears cannot. Moreover, the poet shows remarkable restraint in not criticizing pagan practices—such as cremation—that were strictly forbidden by Christian doctrine. Indeed, in its respect for the past the poem participates in its own central theme. Feuding, after all, is caused by an inability to make peace with the past, an unwillingness to put aside what has happened and move into a new future. *Beowulf* confronts this dilemma by asking, How can one celebrate one's own cultural past while admitting that it must be left behind?

The translation is by Seamus Heaney, the Nobel Prize–winning poet from Northern Ireland. Heaney has included in his translation some Northern Irish words, encouraging us to think about the relation of the violence depicted in the poem to the violence of our own time. The original Anglo-Saxon poem is written in an alliterative verse in which each line has four stresses, three of which usually alliterate, and with a strong break or caesura in the middle of the line. For instance, the fourth and fifth lines of the poem read in the original (*sc* is pronounced as *sh* in Anglo-Saxon):

> Oft Scyld Scefing   sceathena threatum
> monegum maegthum   meodsetla ofteah.

These lines can be translated word for word: "Often Scyld Scefing from troops of the enemies, / from many races, mead-benches deprived." Heaney's translation reads: "There was Shield Sheafson, scourge of many tribes / a wrecker of mead-benches, rampaging among foes." While he does not here keep to the Anglo-Saxon pattern of alliteration, he nonetheless provides us with lines that include strong alliteration and a caesura—and one that retains the sense of the original and captures the energy both of the verse and of the world it depicts.

A good introduction to the Anglo-Saxon period, and to the techniques of Anglo-Saxon poetry, can be found in the essays collected by Malcolm Godden and Michael Lapidge, eds., *The Cambridge Companion to Old English Literature* (1991). *A Beowulf Handbook* (1997), ed. Robert E. Bjork and John D. Niles, provides useful essays about the poem, its context, and its criticism. Other useful collections of essays are R. D. Fulk, ed., *Interpretations of Beowulf* (1991), and Peter S. Baker, ed., *Beowulf: Basic Readings* (1995). An excellent account of the relation of pagan to Christian in the poem is Fred C. Robinson, *Beowulf and the Appositive Style* (1985), and a good treatment of other issues is Edward B. Irving, *Rereading Beowulf* (1989).

PRONOUNCING GLOSSARY

The following list uses common English syllables and stress accents to provide rough equivalents of selected words whose pronunciation may be unfamiliar to the general reader.

Aeschere: *ash'-hair-uh*

Eadgils: *ay'ud-yils*

Eanmund: *ay'un-mund*

Ecglaf: *edge'-lahf*

Ecgtheow: *edge'-thay-oh*

Eofor: *e'o-ver*

Freawaru: *fray'a-wa-ru*

Geats: *yay'-ats*

Haethcyn: *hath'-kin*

Heardred: *hey'ard-red*

Heatho-Bards: *hay'ath-o-bards*

Heatholaf: *hay'ath-o-lahf*

Heorogar: *hay'o-ro-gahr*

Heorot: *hay'o-rot*

Herebeald: *her'uh-bay-ald*

Hildeburh: *hil'de-burhk*

Hnaef: *hnaf*

Hondscio: *hond'-shee-o*

Hreosnahill: *hray-os'-na-hill*

Hrethel: *hray'-thuhl*

Hrethric: *hreth'-rik*

Hrothgar: *hroth'-gahr*

Hrothmund: *hroth'-mund*

Hrothulf: *hroth'-ulf*

Hygd: *higd*

Hygelac: *hee'-uh-lahk*

Ohthere: *ohkt'-her-uh*

Onela: *on'-el-a*

Ongentheow: *on-gen'-thay-oh*

Waegmundings: *wey'-mun-dings*

Wealhtheow: *way'al-thay-oh*

Weohstan: *way'oh-stahn*

Wiglaf: *wee'-lahf*

TRIBES AND GENEALOGIES

1. *The Danes (Bright-, Half-, Ring-, Spear-, North-, East-, South-, West-Danes; Shield-ings, Honor-, Victor-, War-Shieldings: Ing's friends).*

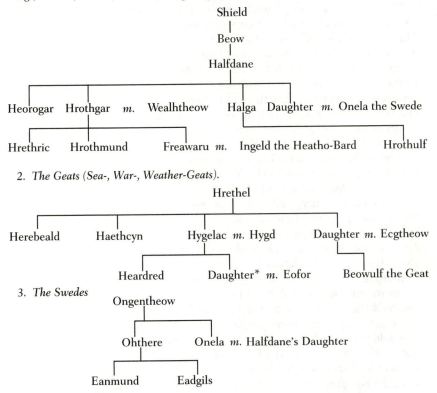

2. *The Geats (Sea-, War-, Weather-Geats).*

3. *The Swedes*

4. *Miscellaneous.*

A. The Half-Danes (also called Shieldings) involved in the fight at Finnsburg may represent a different tribe from the Danes described above. Their king Hoc had a son, Hnaef, who succeeded him, and a daughter Hildeburh, who married Finn, king of the Jutes.

B. The Jutes, or Frisians, are represented as enemies of the Danes in the fight at Finnsburg and as allies of the Franks at the time Hygelac the Geat made the attack in which he lost his life and from which Beowulf swam home. Also allied with the Franks at this time were the Hetware.

C. The Heatho-Bards (i.e., "Battle-Bards") are represented as inveterate enemies of the Danes. Their king Froda had been killed in an attack on the Danes, and Hroth-gar's attempt to make peace with them by marrying his daughter Freawaru to Froda's son Ingeld failed when the latter attacked Heorot. The attack was repulsed, although Heorot was burned.

---

*The daughter of Hygelac who was given to Eofor may have been born to him by a former wife, older than Hygd.

Beowulf[1]

[PROLOGUE: THE RISE OF THE DANISH NATION]

So. The Spear-Danes in days gone by
and the kings who ruled them had courage and greatness.
We have heard of those princes' heroic campaigns.
    There was Shield Sheafson,[2] scourge of many tribes,
a wrecker of mead-benches, rampaging among foes.   5
This terror of the hall-troops had come far.
A foundling to start with, he would flourish later on
as his powers waxed and his worth was proved.
In the end each clan on the outlying coasts
beyond the whale-road had to yield to him   10
and begin to pay tribute. That was one good king.
    Afterward a boy-child was born to Shield,
a cub in the yard, a comfort sent
by God to that nation. He knew what they had tholed,[3]
the long times and troubles they'd come through   15
without a leader; so the Lord of Life,
the glorious Almighty, made this man renowned.
Shield had fathered a famous son:
Beow's name was known through the north.
And a young prince must be prudent like that,   20
giving freely while his father lives
so that afterward in age when fighting starts
steadfast companions will stand by him
and hold the line. Behavior that's admired
is the path to power among people everywhere.   25
    Shield was still thriving when his time came
and he crossed over into the Lord's keeping.
His warrior band did what he bade them
when he laid down the law among the Danes:
they shouldered him out to the sea's flood,   30
the chief they revered who had long ruled them.
A ring-whorled prow rode in the harbor,
ice-clad, outbound, a craft for a prince.
They stretched their beloved lord in his boat,
laid out by the mast, amidships,   35
the great ring-giver. Far-fetched treasures
were piled upon him, and precious gear.
I never heard before of a ship so well furbished
with battle-tackle, bladed weapons
and coats of mail. The massed treasure   40

---

1. Translated by Seamus Heaney.   2. Translates Scyld Scefing, which probably means "son of Sheaf."
Scyld's origins are mysterious.   3. An Anglo-Saxon word that means "suffered, endured" and that survives
in the translator's native land of Northern Ireland. In using this word, he also maintains an alliterative
pattern similar to the original ("that . . . they . . . tholed").

was loaded on top of him: it would travel far
on out into the ocean's sway.
They decked his body no less bountifully
with offerings than those first ones did
who cast him away when he was a child   45
and launched him alone out over the waves.[4]
And they set a gold standard up
high above his head and let him drift
to wind and tide, bewailing him
and mourning their loss. No man can tell,   50
no wise man in hall or weathered veteran
knows for certain who salvaged that load.
    Then it fell to Beow to keep the forts.
He was well regarded and ruled the Danes
for a long time after his father took leave   55
of his life on earth. And then his heir,
the great Halfdane, held sway
for as long as he lived, their elder and warlord.
He was four times a father, this fighter prince:
one by one they entered the world,   60
Heorogar, Hrothgar, the good Halga,
and a daughter,[5] I have heard, who was Onela's queen,
a balm in bed to the battle-scarred Swede.
    The fortunes of war favored Hrothgar.
Friends and kinsmen flocked to his ranks,   65
young followers, a force that grew
to be a mighty army. So his mind turned
to hall-building: he handed down orders
for men to work on a great mead-hall
meant to be a wonder of the world forever;   70
it would be his throne-room and there he would dispense
his God-given goods to young and old—
but not the common land or people's lives.[6]
Far and wide through the world, I have heard,
orders for work to adorn that wallstead   75
were sent to many peoples. And soon it stood there
finished and ready, in full view,
the hall of halls. Heorot[7] was the name
he had settled on it, whose utterance was law.
Nor did he renege, but doled out rings   80
and torques[8] at the table. The hall towered,
its gables wide and high and awaiting
a barbarous burning.[9] That doom abided,

---

4. Since Shield arrived with nothing, this sentence is a litotes or understatement, a characteristic of the laconic style of old Germanic poetry.   **5.** The text is faulty here, so that the name of Halfdane's daughter has been lost. *Halfdane*: according to another source, Halfdane's mother was Swedish; hence his name.   **6.** Apparently, slaves, along with pastureland used by all, were not in the king's power to give away.   **7.** I.e., "hart," a symbol of royalty.   **8.** Golden bands worn around the neck.   **9.** The destruction by fire of Heorot occurred at a later time than that of the poem's action, when the Heatho-Bard Ingeld attacked his father-in-law, Hrothgar. For a more detailed account of this feud and of Hrothgar's hope that it could be settled by the marriage of his daughter to Ingeld, see lines 2020–69.

but in time it would come: the killer instinct
unleashed among in-laws, the blood-lust rampant.   85

[HEROT IS ATTACKED]

Then a powerful demon, a prowler through the dark,
nursed a hard grievance. It harrowed him
to hear the din of the loud banquet
every day in the hall, the harp being struck
and the clear song of a skilled poet   90
telling with mastery of man's beginnings,
how the Almighty had made the earth
a gleaming plain girdled with waters;
in His splendor He set the sun and the moon
to be earth's lamplight, lanterns for men,   95
and filled the broad lap of the world
with branches and leaves; and quickened life
in every other thing that moved.
   So times were pleasant for the people there
until finally one, a fiend out of hell,   100
began to work his evil in the world.
Grendel was the name of this grim demon
haunting the marches, marauding round the heath
and the desolate fens; he had dwelt for a time
in misery among the banished monsters,   105
Cain's clan, whom the Creator had outlawed
and condemned as outcasts.[1] For the killing of Abel
the Eternal Lord had exacted a price:
Cain got no good from committing that murder
because the Almighty made him anathema   110
and out of the curse of his exile there sprang
ogres and elves and evil phantoms
and the giants too who strove with God
time and again until He gave them their reward.[2]
   So, after nightfall, Grendel set out   115
for the lofty house, to see how the Ring-Danes
were settling into it after their drink,
and there he came upon them, a company of the best
asleep from their feasting, insensible to pain
and human sorrow. Suddenly then   120
the God-cursed brute was creating havoc:
greedy and grim, he grabbed thirty men
from their resting places and rushed to his lair,
flushed up and inflamed from the raid,
blundering back with the butchered corpses.   125
   Then as dawn brightened and the day broke,
Grendel's powers of destruction were plain:

---

1. Genesis 4.9–12.   2. The poet is thinking here of Genesis 6.2–8, where the Latin Bible in use at the time refers to giants mating with women who were understood to be the descendents of Cain, and thus creating the wicked race that God destroyed with the flood.

their wassail was over, they wept to heaven
and mourned under morning. Their mighty prince,
the storied leader, sat stricken and helpless, 130
humiliated by the loss of his guard,
bewildered and stunned, staring aghast
at the demon's trail, in deep distress.
He was numb with grief, but got no respite
for one night later merciless Grendel 135
struck again with more gruesome murders.
Malignant by nature, he never showed remorse.
It was easy then to meet with a man
shifting himself to a safer distance
to bed in the bothies,[3] for who could be blind 140
to the evidence of his eyes, the obviousness
of the hall-watcher's hate? Whoever escaped
kept a weather-eye open and moved away.
    So Grendel ruled in defiance of right,
one against all, until the greatest house 145
in the world stood empty, a deserted wallstead.
For twelve winters, seasons of woe,
the lord of the Shieldings[4] suffered under
his load of sorrow; and so, before long,
the news was known over the whole world. 150
Sad lays were sung about the beset king,
the vicious raids and ravages of Grendel,
his long and unrelenting feud,
nothing but war; how he would never
parley or make peace with any Dane 155
nor stop his death-dealing nor pay the death-price.[5]
No counselor could ever expect
fair reparation from those rabid hands.
All were endangered; young and old
were hunted down by that dark death-shadow 160
who lurked and swooped in the long nights
on the misty moors; nobody knows
where these reavers from hell roam on their errands.
    So Grendel waged his lonely war,
inflicting constant cruelties on the people, 165
atrocious hurt. He took over Heorot,
haunted the glittering hall after dark,
but the throne itself, the treasure-seat,
he was kept from approaching; he was the Lord's outcast.
    These were hard times, heartbreaking 170
for the prince of the Shieldings; powerful counselors,
the highest in the land, would lend advice,
plotting how best the bold defenders
might resist and beat off sudden attacks.

3. Outlying buildings; the word is current in Northern Ireland.   4. I.e., Hrothgar; as descendents of
Shield, the Danes are called Shieldings.   5. According to Germanic law, a slayer could achieve peace
with his victim's kinsmen only by paying them *wergild* ("man-price") as compensation for the slain man.

Sometimes at pagan shrines they vowed   175
offerings to idols, swore oaths
that the killer of souls might come to their aid
and save the people.[6] That was their way,
their heathenish hope; deep in their hearts
they remembered hell. The Almighty Judge   180
of good deeds and bad, the Lord God,
Head of the Heavens and High King of the World,
was unknown to them. Oh, cursed is he
who in time of trouble has to thrust his soul
in the fire's embrace, forfeiting help;   185
he has nowhere to turn. But blessed is he
who after death can approach the Lord
and find friendship in the Father's embrace.

[THE HERO COMES TO HEOROT]

So that troubled time continued, woe
that never stopped, steady affliction   190
for Halfdane's son, too hard an ordeal.
There was panic after dark, people endured
raids in the night, riven by the terror.
  When he heard about Grendel, Hygelac's thane
was on home ground, over in Geatland.   195
There was no one else like him alive.
In his day, he was the mightiest man on earth,
highborn and powerful. He ordered a boat
that would ply the waves. He announced his plan:
to sail the swan's road[7] and seek out that king, 200
the famous prince who needed defenders.
Nobody tried to keep him from going,
no elder denied him, dear as he was to them.
Instead, they inspected omens and spurred
his ambition to go, whilst he moved about   205
like the leader he was, enlisting men,
the best he could find; with fourteen others
the warrior boarded the boat as captain,
a canny pilot along coast and currents.
  Time went by, the boat was on water,   210
in close under the cliffs.
Men climbed eagerly up the gangplank,
sand churned in surf, warriors loaded
a cargo of weapons, shining war-gear
in the vessel's hold, then heaved out,   215
away with a will in their wood-wreathed ship.

---

6. The poet interprets the heathen gods to whom the Danes make offerings as different incarnations of Satan. Naturally, the pagan Danes do not think of their gods in these biblical terms, but as the poet makes clear in the following lines, they have no other recourse. 7. I.e., the sea. This is an example of a "kenning," a metaphoric phrase that is used to describe a common object. These kennings are very common throughout Anglo-Saxon poetry. See, for one other instance, line 258, where the poet describes a man's capacity for speech as his "word-hoard."

Over the waves, with the wind behind her
and foam at her neck, she flew like a bird
until her curved prow had covered the distance,
and on the following day, at the due hour,   220
those seafarers sighted land,
sunlit cliffs, sheer crags
and looming headlands, the landfall they sought.
It was the end of their voyage and the Geats vaulted
over the side, out on to the sand,   225
and moored their ship. There was a clash of mail
and a thresh of gear. They thanked God
for that easy crossing on a calm sea.
   When the watchman on the wall, the Shieldings' lookout
whose job it was to guard the sea-cliffs,   230
saw shields glittering on the gangplank
and battle-equipment being unloaded
he had to find out who and what
the arrivals were. So he rode to the shore,
this horseman of Hrothgar's, and challenged them   235
in formal terms, flourishing his spear:
"What kind of men are you who arrive
rigged out for combat in your coats of mail,
sailing here over the sea-lanes
in your steep-hulled boat? I have been stationed   240
as lookout on this coast for a long time.
My job is to watch the waves for raiders,
any danger to the Danish shore.
Never before has a force under arms
disembarked so openly—not bothering to ask   245
if the sentries allowed them safe passage
or the clan had consented. Nor have I seen
a mightier man-at-arms on this earth
than the one standing here: unless I am mistaken,
he is truly noble. This is no mere   250
hanger-on in a hero's armor.
So now, before you fare inland
as interlopers, I have to be informed
about who you are and where you hail from.
Outsiders from across the water,   255
I say it again: the sooner you tell
where you come from and why, the better."
   The leader of the troop unlocked his word-hoard;
the distinguished one delivered this answer:
"We belong by birth to the Geat people   260
and owe allegiance to Lord Hygelac.
In his day, my father was a famous man,
a noble warrior-lord named Ecgtheow.
He outlasted many a long winter
and went on his way. All over the world   265
men wise in counsel continue to remember him.

We come in good faith to find your lord
and nation's shield, the son of Halfdane.
Give us the right advice and direction.
We have arrived here on a great errand   270
to the lord of the Danes, and I believe therefore
there should be nothing hidden or withheld between us.
So tell us if what we have heard is true
about this threat, whatever it is,
this danger abroad in the dark nights,   275
this corpse-maker mongering death
in the Shieldings' country. I come to proffer
my wholehearted help and counsel.
I can show the wise Hrothgar a way
to defeat his enemy and find respite—   280
if any respite is to reach him, ever.
I can calm the turmoil and terror in his mind.
Otherwise, he must endure woes
and live with grief for as long as his hall
stands at the horizon on its high ground."   285
    Undaunted, sitting astride his horse,
the coast-guard answered: "Anyone with gumption
and a sharp mind will take the measure
of two things: what's said and what's done.
I believe what you have told me, that you are a troop   290
loyal to our king. So come ahead
with your arms and your gear, and I will guide you.
What's more, I'll order my own comrades
on their word of honor to watch your boat
down there on the strand—keep her safe   295
in her fresh tar, until the time comes
for her curved prow to preen on the waves
and bear this hero back to Geatland.
May one so valiant and venturesome
come unharmed through the clash of battle."   300
    So they went on their way. The ship rode the water,
broad-beamed, bound by its hawser
and anchored fast. Boar-shapes[8] flashed
above their cheek-guards, the brightly forged
work of goldsmiths, watching over   305
those stern-faced men. They marched in step,
hurrying on till the timbered hall
rose before them, radiant with gold.
Nobody on earth knew of another
building like it. Majesty lodged there,   310
its light shone over many lands.
So their gallant escort guided them
to that dazzling stronghold and indicated

---

8. Images of boars—a cult animal among the Germanic tribes and sacred to the god Freyr—were fixed atop helmets in the belief that they would provide protection from enemy blows.

the shortest way to it; then the noble warrior
wheeled on his horse and spoke these words: 315
"It is time for me to go. May the Almighty
Father keep you and in His kindness
watch over your exploits. I'm away to the sea,
back on alert against enemy raiders."
    It was a paved track, a path that kept them   320
in marching order. Their mail-shirts glinted,
hard and hand-linked; the high-gloss iron
of their armor rang. So they duly arrived
in their grim war-graith⁹ and gear at the hall,
and, weary from the sea, stacked wide shields   325
of the toughest hardwood against the wall,
then collapsed on the benches; battle-dress
and weapons clashed. They collected their spears
in a seafarers' stook,¹ a stand of grayish
tapering ash. And the troops themselves   330
were as good as their weapons.
                              Then a proud warrior
questioned the men concerning their origins:
"Where do you come from, carrying these
decorated shields and shirts of mail,
these cheek-hinged helmets and javelins?   335
I am Hrothgar's herald and officer.
I have never seen so impressive or large
an assembly of strangers. Stoutness of heart,
bravery not banishment, must have brought you to Hrothgar."
    The man whose name was known for courage,   340
the Geat leader, resolute in his helmet,
answered in return: "We are retainers
from Hygelac's band. Beowulf is my name.
If your lord and master, the most renowned
son of Halfdane, will hear me out   345
and graciously allow me to greet him in person,
I am ready and willing to report my errand."
    Wulfgar replied, a Wendel² chief
renowned as a warrior, well known for his wisdom
and the temper of his mind: "I will take this message,   350
in accordance with your wish, to our noble king,
our dear lord, friend of the Danes,
the giver of rings. I will go and ask him
about your coming here, then hurry back
with whatever reply it pleases him to give."   355
    With that he turned to where Hrothgar sat,
an old man among retainers;
the valiant follower stood foursquare

---

9. *Graith* is an archaic word for equipment or armor.   1. *Stook* is an archaic word for a pile or mass.
2. The *Wendels* or Vandals are another Germanic nation; it is not unusual for a person to be a member of
a nation different from the one in which he resides. Hence Beowulf himself is both a Geat and a
Waegmunding.

in front of his king: he knew the courtesies.
Wulfgar addressed his dear lord: 360
"People from Geatland have put ashore.
They have sailed far over the wide sea.
They call the chief in charge of their band
by the name of Beowulf. They beg, my lord,
an audience with you, exchange of words   365
and formal greeting. Most gracious Hrothgar,
do not refuse them, but grant them a reply.
From their arms and appointment, they appear well born
and worthy of respect, especially the one
who has led them this far: he is formidable indeed."   370
    Hrothgar, protector of Shieldings, replied:
"I used to know him when he was a young boy.
His father before him was called Ecgtheow.
Hrethel the Geat³ gave Ecgtheow
his daughter in marriage. This man is their son,   375
here to follow up an old friendship.
A crew of seamen who sailed for me once
with a gift-cargo across to Geatland
returned with marvelous tales about him:
a thane,⁴ they declared, with the strength of thirty   380
in the grip of each hand. Now Holy God
has, in His goodness, guided him here
to the West-Danes, to defend us from Grendel.
This is my hope; and for his heroism
I will recompense him with a rich treasure.   385
Go immediately, bid him and the Geats
he has in attendance to assemble and enter.
Say, moreover, when you speak to them,
they are welcome to Denmark."
                              At the door of the hall,
Wulfgar duly delivered the message: 390
"My lord, the conquering king of the Danes,
bids me announce that he knows your ancestry;
also that he welcomes you here to Heorot
and salutes your arrival from across the sea.
You are free now to move forward   395
to meet Hrothgar in helmets and armor,
but shields must stay here and spears be stacked
until the outcome of the audience is clear."
    The hero arose, surrounded closely
by his powerful thanes. A party remained   400
under orders to keep watch on the arms;
the rest proceeded, led by their prince
under Heorot's roof. And standing on the hearth
in webbed links that the smith had woven,

---

3. The leader of the Geats prior to his son Hygelac, who is the current leader. Note that Ecgtheow's marriage to Hrethel's daughter makes Beowulf part of the royal line.   4. I.e., a warrior in the service of a lord like Hrethel or Hrothgar himself.

the fine-forged mesh of his gleaming mail-shirt, 405
resolute in his helmet, Beowulf spoke:
"Greetings to Hrothgar. I am Hygelac's kinsman,
one of his hall-troop. When I was younger,
I had great triumphs. Then news of Grendel,
hard to ignore, reached me at home: 410
sailors brought stories of the plight you suffer
in this legendary hall, how it lies deserted,
empty and useless once the evening light
hides itself under heaven's dome.
So every elder and experienced councilman 415
among my people supported my resolve
to come here to you, King Hrothgar,
because all knew of my awesome strength.
They had seen me boltered[5] in the blood of enemies
when I battled and bound five beasts, 420
raided a troll-nest and in the night-sea
slaughtered sea-brutes. I have suffered extremes
and avenged the Geats (their enemies brought it
upon themselves; I devastated them).
Now I mean to be a match for Grendel, 425
settle the outcome in single combat.
And so, my request, O king of Bright-Danes,
dear prince of the Shieldings, friend of the people
and their ring of defense, my one request
is that you won't refuse me, who have come this far, 430
the privilege of purifying Heorot,
with my own men to help me, and nobody else.
I have heard moreover that the monster scorns
in his reckless way to use weapons;
therefore, to heighten Hygelac's fame 435
and gladden his heart, I hereby renounce
sword and the shelter of the broad shield,
the heavy war-board: hand-to-hand
is how it will be, a life-and-death
fight with the fiend. Whichever one death fells 440
must deem it a just judgment by God.
If Grendel wins, it will be a gruesome day;
he will glut himself on the Geats in the war-hall,
swoop without fear on that flower of manhood
as on others before. Then my face won't be there 445
to be covered in death: he will carry me away
as he goes to ground, gorged and bloodied;
he will run gloating with my raw corpse
and feed on it alone, in a cruel frenzy
fouling his moor-nest. No need then 450
to lament for long or lay out my body:
if the battle takes me, send back

5. Clotted, sticky—a Northern Irish term.

this breast-webbing that Weland[6] fashioned
and Hrethel gave me, to Lord Hygelac.
Fate goes ever as fate must."   455
   Hrothgar, the helmet of Shieldings, spoke:
"Beowulf, my friend, you have traveled here
to favor us with help and to fight for us.
There was a feud one time, begun by your father.
With his own hands he had killed Heatholaf   460
who was a Wulfing;[7] so war was looming
and his people, in fear of it, forced him to leave.
He came away then over rolling waves
to the South-Danes here, the sons of honor.
I was then in the first flush of kingship,   465
establishing my sway over the rich strongholds
of this heroic land. Heorogar,
my older brother and the better man,
also a son of Halfdane's, had died.
Finally I healed the feud by paying: 470
I shipped a treasure-trove to the Wulfings,
and Ecgtheow acknowledged me with oaths of allegiance.
   "It bothers me to have to burden anyone
with all the grief that Grendel has caused
and the havoc he has wreaked upon us in Heorot,   475
our humiliations. My household-guard
are on the wane, fate sweeps them away
into Grendel's clutches—but God can easily
halt these raids and harrowing attacks!
   "Time and again, when the goblets passed   480
and seasoned fighters got flushed with beer
they would pledge themselves to protect Heorot
and wait for Grendel with their whetted swords.
But when dawn broke and day crept in
over each empty, blood-spattered bench,   485
the floor of the mead-hall where they had feasted
would be slick with slaughter. And so they died,
faithful retainers, and my following dwindled.
Now take your place at the table, relish
the triumph of heroes to your heart's content."   490

[FEAST AT HEOROT]

   Then a bench was cleared in that banquet hall
so the Geats could have room to be together
and the party sat, proud in their bearing,
strong and stalwart. An attendant stood by
with a decorated pitcher, pouring bright   495
helpings of mead. And the minstrel sang,
filling Heorot with his head-clearing voice,

6. The blacksmith of the Norse gods.   7. The *Wulfings* are another Germanic nation.

gladdening that great rally of Geats and Danes.
From where he crouched at the king's feet,
Unferth, a son of Ecglaf's, spoke   500
contrary words.[8] Beowulf's coming,
his sea-braving, made him sick with envy:
he could not brook or abide the fact
that anyone else alive under heaven
might enjoy greater regard than he did: 505
"Are you the Beowulf who took on Breca
in a swimming match[9] on the open sea,
risking the water just to prove that you could win?
It was sheer vanity made you venture out
on the main deep. And no matter who tried,   510
friend or foe, to deflect the pair of you,
neither would back down: the sea-test obsessed you.
You waded in, embracing water,
taking its measure, mastering currents,
riding on the swell. The ocean swayed,   515
winter went wild in the waves, but you vied
for seven nights; and then he outswam you,
came ashore the stronger contender.
He was cast up safe and sound one morning
among the Heatho-Reams,[1] then made his way   520
to where he belonged in Bronding[2] country,
home again, sure of his ground
in strongroom and bawn.[3] So Breca made good
his boast upon you and was proved right.
No matter, therefore, how you may have fared   525
in every bout and battle until now,
this time you'll be worsted; no one has ever
outlasted an entire night against Grendel."
Beowulf, Ecgtheow's son, replied:
"Well, friend Unferth, you have had your say   530
about Breca and me. But it was mostly beer
that was doing the talking. The truth is this:
when the going was heavy in those high waves,
I was the strongest swimmer of all.
We'd been children together and we grew up   535
daring ourselves to outdo each other,
boasting and urging each other to risk
our lives on the sea. And so it turned out.
Each of us swam holding a sword,
a naked, hard-proofed blade for protection   540

8. Unferth is Hrothgar's *thyle*, a kind of licensed spokesman who here engages Beowulf in a traditional "flytting" or verbal combat; see the note to line 1457. Ecglaf appears in the poem only as the father of Unferth.   9. The original Anglo-Saxon describing this contest can be interpreted in such a way that Breca and Beowulf are competing not in swimming but in rowing, which is more plausible.   1. The *Heatho-Reams* are a people of southern Norway.   2. The *Brondings* are the nation to which Breca belonged, but nothing is known of their territory.   3. Fortified outwork of a court or castle. The word was used by English planters in Ulster to describe fortified dwellings they erected on lands confiscated from the Irish [Translator's note].

against the whale-beasts. But Breca could never
move out farther or faster from me
than I could manage to move from him.
Shoulder to shoulder, we struggled on
for five nights, until the long flow   545
and pitch of the waves, the perishing cold,
night falling and winds from the north
drove us apart. The deep boiled up
and its wallowing sent the sea-brutes wild.
My armor helped me to hold out;   550
my hard-ringed chain-mail, hand-forged and linked,
a fine, close-fitting filigree of gold,
kept me safe when some ocean creature
pulled me to the bottom. Pinioned fast
and swathed in its grip, I was granted one   555
final chance: my sword plunged
and the ordeal was over. Through my own hands,
the fury of battle had finished off the sea-beast.
    "Time and again, foul things attacked me,
lurking and stalking, but I lashed out,   560
gave as good as I got with my sword.
My flesh was not for feasting on,
there would be no monsters gnawing and gloating
over their banquet at the bottom of the sea.
Instead, in the morning, mangled and sleeping   565
the sleep of the sword, they slopped and floated
like the ocean's leavings. From now on
sailors would be safe, the deep-sea raids
were over for good. Light came from the east,
bright guarantee of God, and the waves   570
went quiet; I could see headlands
and buffeted cliffs. Often, for undaunted courage,
fate spares the man it has not already marked.
However it occurred, my sword had killed
nine sea-monsters. Such night dangers   575
and hard ordeals I have never heard of
nor of a man more desolate in surging waves.
But worn out as I was, I survived,
came through with my life. The ocean lifted
and laid me ashore, I landed safe   580
on the coast of Finland.
                        Now I cannot recall
any fight you entered, Unferth,
that bears comparison. I don't boast when I say
that neither you nor Breca were ever much
celebrated for swordsmanship   585
or for facing danger on the field of battle.
You killed your own kith and kin,
so for all your cleverness and quick tongue,

you will suffer damnation in the depths of hell.[4]
The fact is, Unferth, if you were truly   590
as keen or courageous as you claim to be
Grendel would never have got away with
such unchecked atrocity, attacks on your king,
havoc in Heorot and horrors everywhere.
But he knows he need never be in dread   595
of your blade making a mizzle[5] of his blood
or of vengeance arriving ever from this quarter—
from the Victory-Shieldings, the shoulderers of the spear.
He knows he can trample down you Danes
to his heart's content, humiliate and murder   600
without fear of reprisal. But he will find me different.
I will show him how Geats shape to kill
in the heat of battle. Then whoever wants to
may go bravely to mead,[6] when the morning light,
scarfed in sun-dazzle, shines forth from the south   605
and brings another daybreak to the world."
    Then the gray-haired treasure-giver was glad;
far-famed in battle, the prince of Bright-Danes
and keeper of his people counted on Beowulf,
on the warrior's steadfastness and his word.   610
So the laughter started, the din got louder
and the crowd was happy. Wealhtheow came in,
Hrothgar's queen, observing the courtesies.
Adorned in her gold, she graciously saluted
the men in the hall, then handed the cup   615
first to Hrothgar, their homeland's guardian,
urging him to drink deep and enjoy it
because he was dear to them. And he drank it down
like the warlord he was, with festive cheer.
So the Helming woman went on her rounds,   620
queenly and dignified, decked out in rings,
offering the goblet to all ranks,
treating the household and the assembled troop,
until it was Beowulf's turn to take it from her hand.
With measured words she welcomed the Geat   625
and thanked God for granting her wish
that a deliverer she could believe in would arrive
to ease their afflictions. He accepted the cup,
a daunting man, dangerous in action
and eager for it always. He addressed Wealhtheow;   630
Beowulf, son of Ecgtheow, said:
"I had a fixed purpose when I put to sea.
As I sat in the boat with my band of men,
I meant to perform to the uttermost

4. The manuscript is damaged here, and the word "hell" may well be "hall": "You will suffer condemnation in the hall" is an acceptable translation of the line.   5. I.e., drizzle.   6. *Mead* is an alcoholic drink made by fermenting honey and adding water.

what your people wanted or perish in the attempt,   635
in the fiend's clutches. And I shall fulfill that purpose,
prove myself with a proud deed
or meet my death here in the mead-hall."
This formal boast by Beowulf the Geat
pleased the lady well and she went to sit   640
by Hrothgar, regal and arrayed with gold.
    Then it was like old times in the echoing hall,
proud talk and the people happy,
loud and excited; until soon enough
Halfdane's heir had to be away   645
to his night's rest. He realized
that the demon was going to descend on the hall,
that he had plotted all day, from dawn-light
until darkness gathered again over the world
and stealthy night-shapes came stealing forth   650
under the cloud-murk. The company stood
as the two leaders took leave of each other:
Hrothgar wished Beowulf health and good luck,
named him hall-warden and announced as follows:
"Never, since my hand could hold a shield   655
have I entrusted or given control
of the Danes' hall to anyone but you.
Ward and guard it, for it is the greatest of houses.
Be on your mettle now, keep in mind your fame,
beware of the enemy. There's nothing you wish for   660
that won't be yours if you win through alive."

[THE FIGHT WITH GRENDEL]

    Hrothgar departed then with his house-guard.
The lord of the Shieldings, their shelter in war,
left the mead-hall to lie with Wealhtheow,
his queen and bedmate. The King of Glory   665
(as people learned) had posted a lookout
who was a match for Grendel, a guard against monsters,
special protection to the Danish prince.
And the Geat placed complete trust
in his strength of limb and the Lord's favor.   670
    He began to remove his iron breast-mail,
took off the helmet and handed his attendant
the patterned sword, a smith's masterpiece,
ordering him to keep the equipment guarded.
And before he bedded down, Beowulf,   675
that prince of goodness, proudly asserted:
"When it comes to fighting, I count myself
as dangerous any day as Grendel.
So it won't be a cutting edge I'll wield
to mow him down, easily as I might.   680
He has no idea of the arts of war,

of shield or sword-play, although he does possess
a wild strength. No weapons, therefore,
for either this night: unarmed he shall face me
if face me he dares. And may the Divine Lord   685
in His wisdom grant the glory of victory
to whichever side He sees fit."
    Then down the brave man lay with his bolster
under his head and his whole company
of sea-rovers at rest beside him.   690
None of them expected he would ever see
his homeland again or get back
to his native place and the people who reared him.
They knew too well the way it was before,
how often the Danes had fallen prey   695
to death in the mead-hall. But the Lord was weaving
a victory on His war-loom for the Weather-Geats.
Through the strength of one they all prevailed;
they would crush their enemy and come through
in triumph and gladness. The truth is clear: 700
Almighty God rules over mankind
and always has.
                    Then out of the night
came the shadow-stalker, stealthy and swift.
The hall-guards were slack, asleep at their posts,
all except one; it was widely understood   705
that as long as God disallowed it,
the fiend could not bear them to his shadow-bourne.
One man, however, was in fighting mood,
awake and on edge, spoiling for action.
    In off the moors, down through the mist-bands   710
God-cursed Grendel came greedily loping.
The bane of the race of men roamed forth,
hunting for a prey in the high hall.
Under the cloud-murk he moved toward it
until it shone above him, a sheer keep   715
of fortified gold. Nor was that the first time
he had scouted the grounds of Hrothgar's dwelling—
although never in his life, before or since,
did he find harder fortune or hall-defenders.
Spurned and joyless, he journeyed on ahead   720
and arrived at the bawn. The iron-braced door
turned on its hinge when his hands touched it.
Then his rage boiled over, he ripped open
the mouth of the building, maddening for blood,
pacing the length of the patterned floor   725
with his loathsome tread, while a baleful light,
flame more than light, flared from his eyes.
He saw many men in the mansion, sleeping,
a ranked company of kinsmen and warriors
quartered together. And his glee was demonic,   730

picturing the mayhem: before morning
he would rip life from limb and devour them,
feed on their flesh; but his fate that night
was due to change, his days of ravening
had come to an end.
      Mighty and canny,   735
Hygelac's kinsman was keenly watching
for the first move the monster would make.
Nor did the creature keep him waiting
but struck suddenly and started in;
he grabbed and mauled a man on his bench,   740
bit into his bone-lappings,[7] bolted down his blood
and gorged on him in lumps, leaving the body
utterly lifeless, eaten up
hand and foot. Venturing closer,
his talon was raised to attack Beowulf   745
where he lay on the bed, he was bearing in
with open claw when the alert hero's
comeback and armlock forestalled him utterly.
The captain of evil discovered himself
in a handgrip harder than anything   750
he had ever encountered in any man
on the face of the earth. Every bone in his body
quailed and recoiled, but he could not escape.
He was desperate to flee to his den and hide
with the devil's litter, for in all his days   755
he had never been clamped or cornered like this.
Then Hygelac's trusty retainer recalled
his bedtime speech, sprang to his feet
and got a firm hold. Fingers were bursting,
the monster back-tracking, the man overpowering.   760
The dread of the land was desperate to escape,
to take a roundabout road and flee
to his lair in the fens. The latching power
in his fingers weakened; it was the worst trip
the terror-monger had taken to Heorot.   765
And now the timbers trembled and sang,
a hall-session[8] that harrowed every Dane
inside the stockade: stumbling in fury,
the two contenders crashed through the building.
The hall clattered and hammered, but somehow   770
survived the onslaught and kept standing:
it was handsomely structured, a sturdy frame
braced with the best of blacksmith's work
inside and out. The story goes
that as the pair struggled, mead-benches were smashed   775
and sprung off the floor, gold fittings and all.

---

7. I.e., joints. 8. In Hiberno-English the word "session" (*seissiún* in Irish) can mean a gathering where musicians and singers perform for their own enjoyment [Translator's note]. In other words, the poet is making a laconic joke, since the main function of the hall is celebration and singing.

Before then, no Shielding elder would believe
there was any power or person upon earth
capable of wrecking their horn-rigged hall
unless the burning embrace of a fire   780
engulf it in flame. Then an extraordinary
wail arose, and bewildering fear
came over the Danes. Everyone felt it
who heard that cry as it echoed off the wall,
a God-cursed scream and strain of catastrophe,   785
the howl of the loser, the lament of the hell-serf
keening his wound. He was overwhelmed,
manacled tight by the man who of all men
was foremost and strongest in the days of this life.
    But the earl-troop's leader was not inclined   790
to allow his caller to depart alive:
he did not consider that life of much account
to anyone anywhere. Time and again,
Beowulf's warriors worked to defend
their lord's life, laying about them   795
as best they could, with their ancestral blades.
Stalwart in action, they kept striking out
on every side, seeking to cut
straight to the soul. When they joined the struggle
there was something they could not have known at the time,   800
that no blade on earth, no blacksmith's art
could ever damage their demon opponent.
He had conjured the harm from the cutting edge
of every weapon.[9] But his going away
out of this world and the days of his life   805
would be agony to him, and his alien spirit
would travel far into fiends' keeping.
    Then he who had harrowed the hearts of men
with pain and affliction in former times
and had given offense also to God   810
found that his bodily powers failed him.
Hygelac's kinsman kept him helplessly
locked in a handgrip. As long as either lived,
he was hateful to the other. The monster's whole
body was in pain; a tremendous wound   815
appeared on his shoulder. Sinews split
and the bone-lappings burst. Beowulf was granted
the glory of winning; Grendel was driven
under the fen-banks, fatally hurt,
to his desolate lair. His days were numbered,   820
the end of his life was coming over him,
he knew it for certain; and one bloody clash
had fulfilled the dearest wishes of the Danes.
The man who had lately landed among them,

9. Grendel is magically protected from weapons.

proud and sure, had purged the hall,   825
kept it from harm; he was happy with his nightwork
and the courage he had shown. The Geat captain
had boldly fulfilled his boast to the Danes:
he had healed and relieved a huge distress,
unremitting humiliations,   830
the hard fate they'd been forced to undergo,
no small affliction. Clear proof of this
could be seen in the hand the hero displayed
high up near the roof: the whole of Grendel's
shoulder and arm, his awesome grasp.   835

[CELEBRATION AT HEOROT]

   Then morning came and many a warrior
gathered, as I've heard, around the gift-hall,
clan-chiefs flocking from far and near
down wide-ranging roads, wondering greatly
at the monster's footprints. His fatal departure   840
was regretted by no one who witnessed his trail,
the ignominious marks of his flight
where he'd skulked away, exhausted in spirit
and beaten in battle, bloodying the path,
hauling his doom to the demons' mere.[1]   845
The bloodshot water wallowed and surged,
there were loathsome upthrows and overturnings
of waves and gore and wound-slurry.
With his death upon him, he had dived deep
into his marsh-den, drowned out his life   850
and his heathen soul: hell claimed him there.
   Then away they rode, the old retainers
with many a young man following after,
a troop on horseback, in high spirits
on their bay steeds. Beowulf's doings   855
were praised over and over again.
Nowhere, they said, north or south
between the two seas or under the tall sky
on the broad earth was there anyone better
to raise a shield or to rule a kingdom.   860
Yet there was no laying of blame on their lord,
the noble Hrothgar; he was a good king.
   At times the war-band broke into a gallop,
letting their chestnut horses race
wherever they found the going good   865
on those well-known tracks. Meanwhile, a thane
of the king's household, a carrier of tales,
a traditional singer deeply schooled
in the lore of the past, linked a new theme
to a strict meter.[2] The man started   870

1. A lake or pool.   2. The singer or *scop* composes extemporaneously in alliterative verse.

to recite with skill, rehearsing Beowulf's
triumphs and feats in well-fashioned lines,
entwining his words.　　　He told what he'd heard
repeated in songs about Sigemund's exploits,[3]
all of those many feats and marvels,　　　　　　　　　　　875
the struggles and wanderings of Waels's son,
things unknown to anyone
except to Fitela, feuds and foul doings
confided by uncle to nephew when he felt
the urge to speak of them: always they had been　　　　880
partners in the fight, friends in need.
They killed giants, their conquering swords
had brought them down.　　　After his death
Sigemund's glory　　grew and grew
because of his courage　　when he killed the dragon,　　885
the guardian of the hoard.　　Under gray stone
he had dared to enter　　all by himself
to face the worst　　without Fitela.
But it came to pass　　that his sword plunged
right through　　those radiant scales　　　　　　　　　　890
and drove into the wall.　　The dragon died of it.
His daring had given him　　total possession
of the treasure-hoard,　　his to dispose of
however he liked.　　He loaded a boat:
Waels's son　　weighted her hold　　　　　　　　　　895
with dazzling spoils.　　The hot dragon melted.
　　Sigemund's name　　was known everywhere.
He was utterly valiant　　and venturesome,
a fence round his fighters　　and flourished therefore
after King Heremod's　　prowess declined　　　　　　900
and his campaigns slowed down.　　The king was betrayed,
ambushed in Jutland,　　overpowered
and done away with.　　The waves of his grief
had beaten him down,　　made him a burden,
a source of anxiety　　to his own nobles:　　　　　　905
that expedition　　was often condemned
in those earlier times　　by experienced men,
men who relied　　on his lordship for redress,
who presumed that the part　　of a prince was to thrive
on his father's throne　　and defend the nation,　　　　910
the Shielding land　　where they lived and belonged,
its holdings and strongholds.　　Such was Beowulf

---

3. According to Norse legend, Sigemund, the son of Waels (or Volsung, as he is known in Norse), slept
with his sister Sigurth, who bore a son named Fitela; Fitela was thus also Sigemund's nephew, as he is
described here. The singer here contrasts Sigemund's bravery in killing a dragon with the defeat of the
Danish king Heremod, who could not protect his people. For more on Heremod as a bad king, see lines
1709–22.

in the affection of his friends   and of everyone alive.
But evil entered   into Heremod.
    Meanwhile, the Danes kept racing their mounts   915
down sandy lanes. The light of day
broke and kept brightening. Bands of retainers
galloped in excitement to the gabled hall
to see the marvel; and the king himself,
guardian of the ring-hoard, goodness in person,   920
walked in majesty from the women's quarters
with a numerous train, attended by his queen
and her crowd of maidens, across to the mead-hall.
    When Hrothgar arrived at the hall, he spoke,
standing on the steps, under the steep eaves,   925
gazing toward the roofwork and Grendel's talon:
"First and foremost, let the Almighty Father
be thanked for this sight. I suffered a long
harrowing by Grendel. But the Heavenly Shepherd
can work His wonders always and everywhere.   930
Not long since, it seemed I would never
be granted the slightest solace or relief
from any of my burdens: the best of houses
glittered and reeked and ran with blood.
This one worry outweighed all others—   935
a constant distress to counselors entrusted
with defending the people's forts from assault
by monsters and demons. But now a man,
with the Lord's assistance, has accomplished something
none of us could manage before now   940
for all our efforts. Whoever she was
who brought forth this flower of manhood,
if she is still alive, that woman can say
that in her labor the Lord of Ages
bestowed a grace on her. So now, Beowulf,   945
I adopt you in my heart as a dear son.
Nourish and maintain this new connection,
you noblest of men; there'll be nothing you'll want for,
no worldly goods that won't be yours.
I have often honored smaller achievements,   950
recognized warriors not nearly as worthy,
lavished rewards on the less deserving.
But you have made yourself immortal
by your glorious action. May the God of Ages
continue to keep and requite you well."   955
    Beowulf, son of Ecgtheow, spoke:
"We have gone through with a glorious endeavor
and been much favored in this fight we dared
against the unknown. Nevertheless,
if you could have seen the monster himself   960
where he lay beaten, I would have been better pleased.
My plan was to pounce, pin him down

in a tight grip and grapple him to death—
have him panting for life, powerless and clasped
in my bare hands, his body in thrall.   965
But I couldn't stop him from slipping my hold.
The Lord allowed it, my lock on him
wasn't strong enough; he struggled fiercely
and broke and ran. Yet he bought his freedom
at a high price, for he left his hand   970
and arm and shoulder to show he had been here,
a cold comfort for having come among us.
And now he won't be long for this world.
He has done his worst but the wound will end him.
He is hasped and hooped and hirpling[4] with pain,   975
limping and looped in it. Like a man outlawed
for wickedness, he must await
the mighty judgment of God in majesty."
    There was less tampering and big talk then
from Unferth the boaster, less of his blather   980
as the hall-thanes eyed the awful proof
of the hero's prowess, the splayed hand
up under the eaves. Every nail,
claw-scale and spur, every spike
and welt on the hand of that heathen brute   985
was like barbed steel. Everybody said
there was no honed iron hard enough
to pierce him through, no time-proofed blade
that could cut his brutal, blood-caked claw.
    Then the order was given for all hands   990
to help to refurbish Heorot immediately:
men and women thronging the wine-hall,
getting it ready. Gold thread shone
in the wall-hangings, woven scenes
that attracted and held the eye's attention.   995
But iron-braced as the inside of it had been,
that bright room lay in ruins now.
The very doors had been dragged from their hinges.
Only the roof remained unscathed
by the time the guilt-fouled fiend turned tail   1000
in despair of his life. But death is not easily
escaped from by anyone:
all of us with souls, earth-dwellers
and children of men, must make our way
to a destination already ordained   1005
where the body, after the banqueting,
sleeps on its deathbed.
                    Then the due time arrived
for Halfdane's son to proceed to the hall.
The king himself would sit down to feast.

4. I.e., limping.

No group ever gathered in greater numbers   1010
or better order around their ring-giver.
The benches filled with famous men
who fell to with relish; round upon round
of mead was passed; those powerful kinsmen,
Hrothgar and Hrothulf, were in high spirits   1015
in the raftered hall. Inside Heorot
there was nothing but friendship. The Shielding nation
was not yet familiar with feud and betrayal.[5]
    Then Halfdane's son presented Beowulf
with a gold standard as a victory gift,   1020
an embroidered banner; also breast-mail
and a helmet; and a sword carried high,
that was both precious object and token of honor.
So Beowulf drank his drink, at ease;
it was hardly a shame to be showered with such gifts   1025
in front of the hall-troops. There haven't been many
moments, I am sure, when men exchanged
four such treasures at so friendly a sitting.
An embossed ridge, a band lapped with wire
arched over the helmet: head-protection   1030
to keep the keen-ground cutting edge
from damaging it when danger threatened
and the man was battling behind his shield.
Next the king ordered eight horses
with gold bridles to be brought through the yard   1035
into the hall. The harness of one
included a saddle of sumptuous design,
the battle-seat where the son of Halfdane
rode when he wished to join the sword-play:
wherever the killing and carnage were the worst,   1040
he would be to the fore, fighting hard.
Then the Danish prince, descendant of Ing,[6]
handed over both the arms and the horses,
urging Beowulf to use them well.
And so their leader, the lord and guard   1045
of coffer and strongroom, with customary grace
bestowed upon Beowulf both sets of gifts.
A fair witness can see how well each one behaved.
    The chieftain went on to reward the others:
each man on the bench who had sailed with Beowulf   1050
and risked the voyage received a bounty,
some treasured possession. And compensation,
a price in gold, was settled for the Geat
Grendel had cruelly killed earlier—
as he would have killed more, had not mindful God   1055
and one man's daring prevented that doom.

---

5. The poet here refers to the later history of the Danes, when after Hrothgar's death his nephew Hrothulf drove his son Hrethric from the throne. For Wealhtheow's fear that this betrayal will indeed come to pass, see lines 1168–90.   6. *Ing* is a Germanic deity and the protector of the Danes.

Past and present, God's will prevails.
Hence, understanding is always best
and a prudent mind. Whoever remains
for long here in this earthly life   1060
will enjoy and endure more than enough.
   They sang then and played to please the hero,
words and music for their warrior prince,
harp tunes and tales of adventure:
there were high times on the hall benches,   1065
and the king's poet performed his part
with the saga of Finn and his sons, unfolding
the tale of the fierce attack in Friesland
where Hnaef, king of the Danes, met death.[7]

Hildeburh
                        had little cause   1070
to credit the Jutes:
                        son and brother,
she lost them both
                        on the battlefield.
She, bereft
                        and blameless, they
foredoomed, cut down
                        and spear-gored. She,
the woman in shock,
                        waylaid by grief,   1075
Hoc's daughter—
                        how could she not
lament her fate
                        when morning came
and the light broke
                        on her murdered dears?
And so farewell
                        delight on earth,
war carried away
                        Finn's troop of thanes   1080
all but a few.
                        How then could Finn
hold the line
                        or fight on
to the end with Hengest,
                        how save
the rump of his force
                        from that enemy chief?

---

7. This song recounts the fight at Finnsburg, described in the headnote, between the Dane Hengest and
the Jute (or Frisian) Finn. The poet begins with the bereft Hildeburh, daughter of the Danish king Hoc
and wife of the Jute Finn, whose unnamed son and brother Hnaef have already been killed in the first
battle with Finn. He then tells how Hengest, the new leader of the Danes, is offered a truce by the weakened
Finn, how together they cremate their dead, and then how Hengest and the remaining Danes spend the
winter with Finn and the Jutes. But with the coming of spring, the feud breaks out again and Finn and the
Jutes are slaughtered by Hengest with the help of two other Danes, Guthlaf and Oslaf.

So a truce was offered
               as follows: first   1085
separate quarters
               to be cleared for the Danes,
hall and throne
               to be shared with the Frisians.
Then, second:
               every day
at the dole-out of gifts
               Finn, son of Focwald,
should honor the Danes,
               bestow with an even   1090
hand to Hengest
               and Hengest's men
the wrought-gold rings,
               bounty to match
the measure he gave
               his own Frisians—
to keep morale
               in the beer-hall high.
Both sides then
               sealed their agreement.   1095
With oaths to Hengest
               Finn swore
openly, solemnly,
               that the battle survivors
would be guaranteed
               honor and status.
No infringement
               by word or deed,
no provocation
               would be permitted.   1100
Their own ring-giver
               after all
was dead and gone,
               they were leaderless,
in forced allegiance
               to his murderer.
So if any Frisian
               stirred up bad blood
with insinuations
               or taunts about this,   1105
the blade of the sword
               would arbitrate it.
A funeral pyre
               was then prepared,
effulgent gold
               brought out from the hoard.
The pride and prince
               of the Shieldings lay

awaiting the flame.
> Everywhere   1110
there were blood-plastered
> coats of mail.
The pyre was heaped
> with boar-shaped helmets
forged in gold,
> with the gashed corpses
of wellborn Danes—
> many had fallen.
Then Hildeburh
> ordered her own   1115
son's body
> be burnt with Hnaef's
the flesh on his bones
> to sputter and blaze
beside his uncle's.
> The woman wailed
and sang keens,
> the warrior went up.[8]
Carcass flame
> swirled and fumed,   1120
they stood round the burial
> mound and howled
as heads melted,
> crusted gashes
spattered and ran
> bloody matter.
The glutton element
> flamed and consumed
the dead of both sides.
> Their great days were gone.   1125
Warriors scattered
> to homes and forts
all over Friesland,
> fewer now, feeling
loss of friends.
> Hengest stayed,
lived out that whole
> resentful, blood-sullen
winter with Finn,
> homesick and helpless.   1130
No ring-whorled prow
> could up then
and away on the sea.
> Wind and water
raged with storms,

---

8. *Keens* is an Irish word for funeral laments; the warrior (Hildeburh's son) either goes up on the pyre or
up in smoke.

          wave and shingle
were shackled in ice
          until another year
appeared in the yard
          as it does to this day,   1135
the seasons constant,
          the wonder of light
coming over us.
          Then winter was gone,
earth's lap grew lovely,
          longing woke
in the cooped-up exile
          for a voyage home—
but more for vengeance,
          some way of bringing   1140
things to a head:
          his sword arm hankered
to greet the Jutes.
          So he did not balk
once Hunlafing[9]
          placed on his lap
Dazzle-the-Duel,
          the best sword of all,
whose edges Jutes
          knew only too well.   1145
Thus blood was spilled,
          the gallant Finn
slain in his home
          after Guthlaf and Oslaf[1]
back from their voyage
          made old accusation:
the brutal ambush,
          the fate they had suffered,
all blamed on Finn.
          The wildness in them   1150
had to brim over.
          The hall ran red
with blood of enemies.
          Finn was cut down,
the queen brought away
          and everything
the Shieldings could find
          inside Finn's walls—
the Frisian king's
          gold collars and gemstones—   1155
swept off to the ship.
          Over sea-lanes then
back to Daneland

---

9. A Danish follower of Hengest.   1. Danes who seem to have gone home in order to bring reinforcements to Hengest. But it is possible that these two have been with Hengest all along and that "their voyage" is an unrelated journey.

the warrior troop
bore that lady home.

The poem was over,
the poet had performed, a pleasant murmur
started on the benches, stewards did the rounds   1160
with wine in splendid jugs, and Wealhtheow came to sit
in her gold crown between two good men,
uncle and nephew, each one of whom
still trusted the other; and the forthright Unferth,[2]
admired by all for his mind and courage   1165
although under a cloud for killing his brothers,
reclined near the king.   The queen spoke:
"Enjoy this drink, my most generous lord;
raise up your goblet, entertain the Geats
duly and gently, discourse with them,   1170
be open-handed, happy and fond.
Relish their company, but recollect as well
all of the boons that have been bestowed on you.
The bright court of Heorot has been cleansed
and now the word is that you want to adopt   1175
this warrior as a son. So, while you may,
bask in your fortune, and then bequeath
kingdom and nation to your kith and kin,
before your decease. I am certain of Hrothulf.
He is noble and will use the young ones well.   1180
He will not let you down. Should you die before him,
he will treat our children truly and fairly.
He will honor, I am sure, our two sons,
repay them in kind, when he recollects
all the good things we gave him once,   1185
the favor and respect he found in his childhood."
She turned then to the bench where her boys sat,
Hrethric and Hrothmund, with other nobles' sons,
all the youth together; and that good man,
Beowulf the Geat, sat between the brothers.   1190
      The cup was carried to him, kind words
spoken in welcome and a wealth of wrought gold
graciously bestowed: two arm bangles,
a mail-shirt and rings, and the most resplendent
torque of gold I ever heard tell of   1195
anywhere on earth or under heaven.
There was no hoard like it since Hama snatched
the Brosings' neck-chain and bore it away
with its gems and settings to his shining fort,
away from Eormenric's wiles and hatred,   1200
and thereby ensured his eternal reward.[3]

---

2. See note 5 to lines 1017–18.   3. The legend alluded to here seems to be that Hama stole the golden necklace of the Brosings from Eormenric (a historical figure, the king of the Ostrogoths, who died c. 375), and then gave it to the goddess Freya.

Hygelac the Geat, grandson of Swerting,
wore this neck-ring on his last raid;[4]
at bay under his banner, he defended the booty,
treasure he had won. Fate swept him away   1205
because of his proud need to provoke
a feud with the Frisians. He fell beneath his shield,
in the same gem-crusted, kingly gear
he had worn when he crossed the frothing wave-vat.
So the dead king fell into Frankish hands.   1210
They took his breast-mail, also his neck-torque,
and punier warriors plundered the slain
when the carnage ended; Geat corpses
covered the field.
                    Applause filled the hall.
Then Wealhtheow pronounced in the presence of the company: 1215
"Take delight in this torque, dear Beowulf,
wear it for luck and wear also this mail
from our people's armory: may you prosper in them!
Be acclaimed for strength, for kindly guidance
to these two boys, and your bounty will be sure.   1220
You have won renown: you are known to all men
far and near, now and forever.
Your sway is wide as the wind's home,
as the sea around cliffs. And so, my prince,
I wish you a lifetime's luck and blessings   1225
to enjoy this treasure. Treat my sons
with tender care, be strong and kind.
Here each comrade is true to the other,
loyal to lord, loving in spirit.
The thanes have one purpose, the people are ready: 1230
having drunk and pledged, the ranks do as I bid."
     She moved then to her place. Men were drinking wine
at that rare feast; how could they know fate,
the grim shape of things to come,
the threat looming over many thanes   1235
as night approached and King Hrothgar prepared
to retire to his quarters? Retainers in great numbers
were posted on guard as so often in the past.
Benches were pushed back, bedding gear and bolsters
spread across the floor, and one man   1240
lay down to his rest, already marked for death.
At their heads they placed their polished timber
battle-shields; and on the bench above them,
each man's kit was kept to hand:
a towering war-helmet, webbed mail-shirt   1245
and great-shafted spear. It was their habit
always and everywhere to be ready for action,

---

4. The poet here refers to the death of Hygelac while raiding the Frisian territory of the Franks. This raid
and Hygelac's death are recorded by the historian Gregory of Tours (d. 594) as having taken place about
520.

at home or in the camp, in whatever case
and at whatever time the need arose
to rally round their lord. They were a right people.   1250

[ANOTHER ATTACK]

    They went to sleep. And one paid dearly
for his night's ease, as had happened to them often,
ever since Grendel occupied the gold-hall,
committing evil until the end came,
death after his crimes. Then it became clear,   1255
obvious to everyone once the fight was over,
that an avenger lurked and was still alive,
grimly biding time. Grendel's mother,
monstrous hell-bride, brooded on her wrongs.
She had been forced down into fearful waters,   1260
the cold depths, after Cain had killed
his father's son, felled his own
brother with a sword. Branded an outlaw,
marked by having murdered, he moved into the wilds,
shunned company and joy. And from Cain there sprang   1265
misbegotten spirits, among them Grendel,
the banished and accursed, due to come to grips
with that watcher in Heorot waiting to do battle.
The monster wrenched and wrestled with him,
but Beowulf was mindful of his mighty strength,   1270
the wondrous gifts God had showered on him:
he relied for help on the Lord of All,
on His care and favor. So he overcame the foe,
brought down the hell-brute. Broken and bowed,
outcast from all sweetness, the enemy of mankind   1275
made for his death-den. But now his mother
had sallied forth on a savage journey,
grief-racked and ravenous, desperate for revenge.
    She came to Heorot. There, inside the hall,
Danes lay asleep, earls who would soon endure   1280
a great reversal, once Grendel's mother
attacked and entered. Her onslaught was less
only by as much as an amazon warrior's
strength is less than an armed man's
when the hefted sword, its hammered edge   1285
and gleaming blade slathered in blood,
razes the sturdy boar-ridge off a helmet.
Then in the hall, hard-honed swords
were grabbed from the bench, many a broad shield
lifted and braced; there was little thought of helmets   1290
or woven mail when they woke in terror.
    The hell-dam was in panic, desperate to get out,
in mortal terror the moment she was found.
She had pounced and taken one of the retainers

in a tight hold, then headed for the fen.   1295
To Hrothgar, this man was the most beloved
of the friends he trusted between the two seas.
She had done away with a great warrior,
ambushed him at rest.
      Beowulf was elsewhere.
Earlier, after the award of the treasure,   1300
the Geat had been given another lodging.
  There was uproar in Heorot. She had snatched their trophy,
Grendel's bloodied hand. It was a fresh blow
to the afflicted bawn. The bargain was hard,
both parties having to pay   1305
with the lives of friends. And the old lord,
the gray-haired warrior, was heartsore and weary
when he heard the news: his highest-placed adviser,
his dearest companion, was dead and gone.
  Beowulf was quickly brought to the chamber: 1310
the winner of fights, the arch-warrior,
came first-footing in with his fellow troops
to where the king in his wisdom waited,
still wondering whether Almighty God
would ever turn the tide of his misfortunes.   1315
So Beowulf entered with his band in attendance
and the wooden floorboards banged and rang
as he advanced, hurrying to address
the prince of the Ingwins,[5] asking if he'd rested
since the urgent summons had come as a surprise.   1320
  Then Hrothgar, the Shieldings' helmet, spoke:
"Rest? What is rest? Sorrow has returned.
Alas for the Danes! Aeschere is dead.
He was Yrmenlaf's elder brother
and a soul-mate to me, a true mentor,   1325
my right-hand man when the ranks clashed
and our boar-crests had to take a battering
in the line of action. Aeschere was everything
the world admires in a wise man and a friend.
Then this roaming killer came in a fury   1330
and slaughtered him in Heorot. Where she is hiding,
glutting on the corpse and glorying in her escape,
I cannot tell; she has taken up the feud
because of last night, when you killed Grendel,
wrestled and racked him in ruinous combat   1335
since for too long he had terrorized us
with his depredations. He died in battle,
paid with his life; and now this powerful
other one arrives, this force for evil
driven to avenge her kinsman's death.   1340
Or so it seems to thanes in their grief,

---

5. The *Ingwins* are the friends of the god Ing—i.e., the Danes. See n. 6 to line 1042, above.

in the anguish every thane endures
at the loss of a ring-giver, now that the hand
that bestowed so richly has been stilled in death.
  "I have heard it said by my people in hall,   1345
counselors who live in the upland country,
that they have seen two such creatures
prowling the moors, huge marauders
from some other world. One of these things,
as far as anyone ever can discern,   1350
looks like a woman; the other, warped
in the shape of a man, moves beyond the pale
bigger than any man, an unnatural birth
called Grendel by the country people
in former days. They are fatherless creatures,   1355
and their whole ancestry is hidden in a past
of demons and ghosts.[6] They dwell apart
among wolves on the hills, on windswept crags
and treacherous keshes, where cold streams
pour down the mountain and disappear   1360
under mist and moorland.
                          A few miles from here
a frost-stiffened wood waits and keeps watch
above a mere; the overhanging bank
is a maze of tree-roots mirrored in its surface.
At night there, something uncanny happens: 1365
the water burns. And the mere bottom
has never been sounded by the sons of men.
On its bank, the heather-stepper halts:
the hart in flight from pursuing hounds
will turn to face them with firm-set horns   1370
and die in the wood rather than dive
beneath its surface. That is no good place.
When wind blows up and stormy weather
makes clouds scud and the skies weep,
out of its depths a dirty surge   1375
is pitched toward the heavens. Now help depends
again on you and on you alone.
The gap of danger where the demon waits
is still unknown to you. Seek it if you dare.
I will compensate you for settling the feud   1380
as I did the last time with lavish wealth,
coffers of coiled gold, if you come back."

[BEOWULF FIGHTS GRENDEL'S MOTHER]

Beowulf, son of Ecgtheow, spoke:
"Wise sir, do not grieve. It is always better
to avenge dear ones than to indulge in mourning.   1385

---

6. Note that Hrothgar doesn't know of the biblical genealogy of Grendel and his mother that the poet has
given us in lines 102–14.

For every one of us, living in this world
means waiting for our end. Let whoever can
win glory before death. When a warrior is gone,
that will be his best and only bulwark.
So arise, my lord, and let us immediately   1390
set forth on the trail of this troll-dam.
I guarantee you: she will not get away,
not to dens under ground nor upland groves
nor the ocean floor. She'll have nowhere to flee to.
Endure your troubles today. Bear up   1395
and be the man I expect you to be."
     With that the old lord sprang to his feet
and praised God for Beowulf's pledge.
Then a bit and halter were brought for his horse
with the plaited mane. The wise king mounted   1400
the royal saddle and rode out in style
with a force of shield-bearers. The forest paths
were marked all over with the monster's tracks,
her trail on the ground wherever she had gone
across the dark moors, dragging away   1405
the body of that thane, Hrothgar's best
counselor and overseer of the country.
So the noble prince proceeded undismayed
up fells and screes, along narrow footpaths
and ways where they were forced into single file,   1410
ledges on cliffs above lairs of water-monsters.
He went in front with a few men,
good judges of the lie of the land,
and suddenly discovered the dismal wood,
mountain trees growing out at an angle   1415
above gray stones: the bloodshot water
surged underneath. It was a sore blow
to all of the Danes, friends of the Shieldings,
a hurt to each and every one
of that noble company when they came upon   1420
Aeschere's head at the foot of the cliff.
     Everybody gazed as the hot gore
kept wallowing up and an urgent war-horn
repeated its notes: the whole party
sat down to watch. The water was infested   1425
with all kinds of reptiles. There were writhing sea-dragons
and monsters slouching on slopes by the cliff,
serpents and wild things such as those that often
surface at dawn to roam the sail-road
and doom the voyage. Down they plunged,   1430
lashing in anger at the loud call
of the battle-bugle. An arrow from the bow
of the Geat chief got one of them
as he surged to the surface: the seasoned shaft
stuck deep in his flank and his freedom in the water   1435

got less and less. It was his last swim.
He was swiftly overwhelmed in the shallows,
prodded by barbed boar-spears,
cornered, beaten, pulled up on the bank,
a strange lake-birth, a loathsome catch 1440
men gazed at in awe.
              Beowulf got ready,
donned his war-gear, indifferent to death;
his mighty, hand-forged, fine-webbed mail
would soon meet with the menace underwater.
It would keep the bone-cage of his body safe: 1445
no enemy's clasp could crush him in it,
no vicious armlock choke his life out.
To guard his head he had a glittering helmet
that was due to be muddied on the mere bottom
and blurred in the upswirl. It was of beaten gold, 1450
princely headgear hooped and hasped
by a weapon-smith who had worked wonders
in days gone by and adorned it with boar-shapes;
since then it had resisted every sword.
And another item lent by Unferth 1455
at that moment of need was of no small importance:
the brehon[7] handed him a hilted weapon,
a rare and ancient sword named Hrunting.
The iron blade with its ill-boding patterns
had been tempered in blood. It had never failed 1460
the hand of anyone who hefted it in battle,
anyone who had fought and faced the worst
in the gap of danger. This was not the first time
it had been called to perform heroic feats.
    When he lent that blade to the better swordsman, 1465
Unferth, the strong-built son of Ecglaf,
could hardly have remembered the ranting speech
he had made in his cups. He was not man enough
to face the turmoil of a fight under water
and the risk to his life. So there he lost 1470
fame and repute. It was different for the other
rigged out in his gear, ready to do battle.
    Beowulf, son of Ecgtheow, spoke:
"Wisest of kings, now that I have come
to the point of action, I ask you to recall 1475
what we said earlier: that you, son of Halfdane
and gold-friend to retainers, that you, if I should fall
and suffer death while serving your cause,
would act like a father to me afterward.
If this combat kills me, take care 1480
of my young company, my comrades in arms.

---

7. One of an ancient class of lawyers in Ireland [Translator's note]. The word is used to translate the Anglo-Saxon *thyle*.

And be sure also, my beloved Hrothgar,
to send Hygelac the treasures I received.
Let the lord of the Geats gaze on that gold,
let Hrethel's son take note of it and see   1485
that I found a ring-giver of rare magnificence
and enjoyed the good of his generosity.
And Unferth is to have what I inherited:
to that far-famed man I bequeath my own
sharp-honed, wave-sheened wonder-blade.   1490
With Hrunting I shall gain glory or die."
    After these words, the prince of the Weather-Geats
was impatient to be away and plunged suddenly:
without more ado, he dived into the heaving
depths of the lake. It was the best part of a day   1495
before he could see the solid bottom.
    Quickly the one who haunted those waters,
who had scavenged and gone her gluttonous rounds
for a hundred seasons, sensed a human
observing her outlandish lair from above.   1500
So she lunged and clutched and managed to catch him
in her brutal grip; but his body, for all that,
remained unscathed: the mesh of the chain-mail
saved him on the outside. Her savage talons
failed to rip the web of his war-shirt.   1505
Then once she touched bottom, that wolfish swimmer
carried the ring-mailed prince to her court
so that for all his courage he could never use
the weapons he carried; and a bewildering horde
came at him from the depths, droves of sea-beasts   1510
who attacked with tusks and tore at his chain-mail
in a ghastly onslaught. The gallant man
could see he had entered some hellish turn-hole
and yet the water there did not work against him
because the hall-roofing held off   1515
the force of the current; then he saw firelight,
a gleam and flare-up, a glimmer of brightness.
    The hero observed that swamp-thing from hell,
the tarn-hag[8] in all her terrible strength,
then heaved his war-sword and swung his arm: 1520
the decorated blade came down ringing
and singing on her head. But he soon found
his battle-torch extinguished; the shining blade
refused to bite. It spared her and failed
the man in his need. It had gone through many   1525
hand-to-hand fight, had hewed the armor
and helmets of the doomed, but here at last
the fabulous powers of that heirloom failed.
    Hygelac's kinsman kept thinking about

8. A *tarn* is a small lake.

his name and fame: he never lost heart.   1530
Then, in a fury, he flung his sword away.
The keen, inlaid, worm-loop-patterned steel
was hurled to the ground: he would have to rely
on the might of his arm. So must a man do
who intends to gain enduring glory   1535
in a combat. Life doesn't cost him a thought.
Then the prince of War-Geats, warming to this fight
with Grendel's mother, gripped her shoulder
and laid about him in a battle frenzy:
he pitched his killer opponent to the floor   1540
but she rose quickly and retaliated,
grappled him tightly in her grim embrace.
The sure-footed fighter felt daunted,
the strongest of warriors stumbled and fell.
So she pounced upon him and pulled out   1545
a broad, whetted knife: now she would avenge
her only child. But the mesh of chain-mail
on Beowulf's shoulder shielded his life,
turned the edge and tip of the blade.
The son of Ecgtheow would have surely perished   1550
and the Geats lost their warrior under the wide earth
had the strong links and locks of his war-gear
not helped to save him: holy God
decided the victory. It was easy for the Lord,
the Ruler of Heaven, to redress the balance   1555
once Beowulf got back up on his feet.
    Then he saw a blade that boded well,
a sword in her armory, an ancient heirloom
from the days of the giants, an ideal weapon,
one that any warrior would envy,   1560
but so huge and heavy of itself
only Beowulf could wield it in a battle.
So the Shieldings' hero hard-pressed and enraged,
took a firm hold of the hilt and swung
the blade in an arc, a resolute blow   1565
that bit deep into her neck-bone
and severed it entirely, toppling the doomed
house of her flesh; she fell to the floor.
The sword dripped blood, the swordsman was elated.
    A light appeared and the place brightened   1570
the way the sky does when heaven's candle
is shining clearly. He inspected the vault:
with sword held high, its hilt raised
to guard and threaten, Hygelac's thane
scouted by the wall in Grendel's wake.   1575
Now the weapon was to prove its worth.
The warrior determined to take revenge
for every gross act Grendel had committed—
and not only for that one occasion

when he'd come to slaughter the sleeping troops,   1580
fifteen of Hrothgar's house-guards
surprised on their benches and ruthlessly devoured,
and as many again carried away,
a brutal plunder. Beowulf in his fury
now settled that score: he saw the monster   1585
in his resting place, war-weary and wrecked,
a lifeless corpse, a casualty
of the battle in Heorot. The body gaped
at the stroke dealt to it after death:
Beowulf cut the corpse's head off.   1590
    Immediately the counselors keeping a lookout
with Hrothgar, watching the lake water,
saw a heave-up and surge of waves
and blood in the backwash. They bowed gray heads,
spoke in their sage, experienced way   1595
about the good warrior, how they never again
expected to see that prince returning
in triumph to their king. It was clear to many
that the wolf of the deep had destroyed him forever.
    The ninth hour of the day arrived.   1600
The brave Shieldings abandoned the cliff-top
and the king went home; but sick at heart,
staring at the mere, the strangers held on.
They wished, without hope, to behold their lord,
Beowulf himself.
          Meanwhile, the sword   1605
began to wilt into gory icicles
to slather and thaw. It was a wonderful thing,
the way it all melted as ice melts
when the Father eases the fetters off the frost
and unravels the water-ropes, He who wields power   1610
over time and tide: He is the true Lord.
    The Geat captain saw treasure in abundance
but carried no spoils from those quarters
except for the head and the inlaid hilt
embossed with jewels; its blade had melted   1615
and the scrollwork on it burned, so scalding was the blood
of the poisonous fiend who had perished there.
Then away he swam, the one who had survived
the fall of his enemies, flailing to the surface.
The wide water, the waves and pools,   1620
were no longer infested once the wandering fiend
let go of her life and this unreliable world.
    The seafarers' leader made for land,
resolutely swimming, delighted with his prize,
the mighty load he was lugging to the surface.   1625
His thanes advanced in a troop to meet him,
thanking God and taking great delight
in seeing their prince back safe and sound.

Quickly the hero's helmet and mail-shirt
were loosed and unlaced. The lake settled,   1630
clouds darkened above the bloodshot depths.
    With high hearts they headed away
along footpaths and trails through the fields,
roads that they knew, each of them wrestling
with the head they were carrying from the lakeside cliff,   1635
men kingly in their courage and capable
of difficult work. It was a task for four
to hoist Grendel's head on a spear
and bear it under strain to the bright hall.
But soon enough they neared the place,   1640
fourteen Geats in fine fettle,
striding across the outlying ground
in a delighted throng around their leader.
    In he came then, the thanes' commander,
the arch-warrior, to address Hrothgar: 1645
his courage was proven, his glory was secure.
Grendel's head was hauled by the hair,
dragged across the floor where the people were drinking,
a horror for both queen and company to behold.
They stared in awe. It was an astonishing sight.   1650

                [ANOTHER CELEBRATION AT HEOROT]

    Beowulf, son of Ecgtheow, spoke:
"So, son of Halfdane, prince of the Shieldings,
we are glad to bring this booty from the lake.
It is a token of triumph and we tender it to you.
I barely survived the battle under water.   1655
It was hard-fought, a desperate affair
that could have gone badly; if God had not helped me,
the outcome would have been quick and fatal.
Although Hrunting is hard-edged,
I could never bring it to bear in battle.   1660
But the Lord of Men allowed me to behold—
for He often helps the unbefriended—
an ancient sword shining on the wall,
a weapon made for giants, there for the wielding.
Then my moment came in the combat and I struck   1665
the dwellers in that den. Next thing the damascened[9]
sword blade melted; it bloated and it burned
in their rushing blood. I have wrested the hilt
from the enemies' hand, avenged the evil
done to the Danes; it is what was due.   1670
And this I pledge, O prince of the Shieldings:
you can sleep secure with your company of troops
in Heorot Hall. Never need you fear

---

9. Ornamented with inlaid designs.

for a single thane of your sept¹ or nation,
young warriors or old, that laying waste of life   1675
that you and your people endured of yore."
    Then the gold hilt was handed over
to the old lord, a relic from long ago
for the venerable ruler. That rare smithwork
was passed on to the prince of the Danes   1680
when those devils perished; once death removed
that murdering, guilt-steeped, God-cursed fiend,
eliminating his unholy life
and his mother's as well, it was willed to that king
who of all the lavish gift-lords of the north   1685
was the best regarded between the two seas.
    Hrothgar spoke; he examined the hilt,
that relic of old times. It was engraved all over
and showed how war first came into the world
and the flood destroyed the tribe of giants.   1690
They suffered a terrible severance from the Lord;
the Almighty made the waters rise,
drowned them in the deluge for retribution.
In pure gold inlay on the sword-guards
there were rune-markings correctly incised,   1695
stating and recording for whom the sword
had been first made and ornamented
with its scrollworked hilt. Then everyone hushed
as the son of Halfdane spoke this wisdom:
"A protector of his people, pledged to uphold   1700
truth and justice and to respect tradition,
is entitled to affirm that this man
was born to distinction. Beowulf, my friend,
your fame has gone far and wide,
you are known everywhere. In all things you are even-tempered,   1705
prudent and resolute. So I stand firm by the promise of friendship
we exchanged before. Forever you will be
your people's mainstay and your own warriors'
helping hand.
                    Heremod was different,
the way he behaved to Ecgwela's sons.²   1710
His rise in the world brought little joy
to the Danish people, only death and destruction.
He vented his rage on men he caroused with,
killed his own comrades, a pariah king
who cut himself off from his own kind,   1715
even though Almighty God had made him
eminent and powerful and marked him from the start
for a happy life. But a change happened,
he grew bloodthirsty, gave no more rings
to honor the Danes. He suffered in the end   1720

1. An Irish term meaning a clan or division of a tribe.   2. *Ecgwela's sons* are the Danes. He was evidently
a former king of the Danes.

for having plagued his people for so long:
his life lost happiness.
             So learn from this
and understand true values. I who tell you
have wintered into wisdom.
               It is a great wonder
how Almighty God in His magnificence   1725
favors our race with rank and scope
and the gift of wisdom; His sway is wide.
Sometimes He allows the mind of a man
of distinguished birth to follow its bent,
grants him fulfillment and felicity on earth   1730
and forts to command in his own country.
He permits him to lord it in many lands
until the man in his unthinkingness
forgets that it will ever end for him.
He indulges his desires; illness and old age   1735
mean nothing to him; his mind is untroubled
by envy or malice or the thought of enemies
with their hate-honed swords. The whole world
conforms to his will, he is kept from the worst
until an element of overweening   1740
enters him and takes hold
while the soul's guard, its sentry, drowses,
grown too distracted. A killer stalks him,
an archer who draws a deadly bow.
And then the man is hit in the heart,   1745
the arrow flies beneath his defenses,
the devious promptings of the demon start.
His old possessions seem paltry to him now.
He covets and resents; dishonors custom
and bestows no gold; and because of good things   1750
that the Heavenly Powers gave him in the past
he ignores the shape of things to come.
Then finally the end arrives
when the body he was lent collapses and falls
prey to its death; ancestral possessions   1755
and the goods he hoarded are inherited by another
who lets them go with a liberal hand.
   "O flower of warriors, beware of that trap.
Choose, dear Beowulf, the better part,
eternal rewards. Do not give way to pride.   1760
For a brief while your strength is in bloom
but it fades quickly; and soon there will follow
illness or the sword to lay you low,
or a sudden fire or surge of water
or jabbing blade or javelin from the air   1765
or repellent age. Your piercing eye
will dim and darken; and death will arrive,
dear warrior, to sweep you away.

"Just so I ruled the Ring-Danes' country
for fifty years, defended them in wartime   1770
with spear and sword against constant assaults
by many tribes: I came to believe
my enemies had faded from the face of the earth.
Still, what happened was a hard reversal
from bliss to grief. Grendel struck   1775
after lying in wait. He laid waste to the land
and from that moment my mind was in dread
of his depredations. So I praise God
in His heavenly glory that I lived to behold
this head dripping blood and that after such harrowing   1780
I can look upon it in triumph at last.
Take your place, then, with pride and pleasure,
and move to the feast. Tomorrow morning
our treasure will be shared and showered upon you."
    The Geat was elated and gladly obeyed   1785
the old man's bidding; he sat on the bench.
And soon all was restored, the same as before.
Happiness came back, the hall was thronged,
and a banquet set forth; black night fell
and covered them in darkness.
                            Then the company rose   1790
for the old campaigner: the gray-haired prince
was ready for bed. And a need for rest
came over the brave shield-bearing Geat.
He was a weary seafarer, far from home,
so immediately a house-guard guided him out,   1795
one whose office entailed looking after
whatever a thane on the road in those days
might need or require. It was noble courtesy.

[BEOWULF RETURNS HOME]

    That great heart rested. The hall towered,
gold-shingled and gabled, and the guest slept in it   1800
until the black raven with raucous glee
announced heaven's joy, and a hurry of brightness
overran the shadows. Warriors rose quickly,
impatient to be off: their own country
was beckoning the nobles; and the bold voyager   1805
longed to be aboard his distant boat.
Then that stalwart fighter ordered Hrunting
to be brought to Unferth, and bade Unferth
take the sword and thanked him for lending it.
He said he had found it a friend in battle   1810
and a powerful help; he put no blame
on the blade's cutting edge. He was a considerate man.
    And there the warriors stood in their war-gear,
eager to go, while their honored lord

approached the platform where the other sat.   1815
The undaunted hero addressed Hrothgar.
Beowulf, son of Ecgtheow, spoke:
"Now we who crossed the wide sea
have to inform you that we feel a desire
to return to Hygelac. Here we have been welcomed   1820
and thoroughly entertained. You have treated us well.
If there is any favor on earth I can perform
beyond deeds of arms I have done already,
anything that would merit your affections more,
I shall act, my lord, with alacrity.   1825
If ever I hear from across the ocean
that people on your borders are threatening battle
as attackers have done from time to time,
I shall land with a thousand thanes at my back
to help your cause. Hygelac may be young   1830
to rule a nation, but this much I know
about the king of the Geats: he will come to my aid
and want to support me by word and action
in your hour of need, when honor dictates
that I raise a hedge of spears around you.   1835
Then if Hrethric should think about traveling
as a king's son to the court of the Geats,
he will find many friends. Foreign places
yield more to one who is himself worth meeting."
    Hrothgar spoke and answered him: 1840
"The Lord in his wisdom sent you those words
and they came from the heart. I have never heard
so young a man make truer observations.
You are strong in body and mature in mind,
impressive in speech. If it should come to pass   1845
that Hrethel's descendant dies beneath a spear,
if deadly battle or the sword blade or disease
fells the prince who guards your people
and you are still alive, then I firmly believe
the seafaring Geats won't find a man   1850
worthier of acclaim as their king and defender
than you, if only you would undertake
the lordship of your homeland. My liking for you
deepens with time, dear Beowulf.
What you have done is to draw two peoples,   1855
the Geat nation and us neighboring Danes,
into shared peace and a pact of friendship
in spite of hatreds we have harbored in the past.
For as long as I rule this far-flung land
treasures will change hands and each side will treat   1860
the other with gifts; across the gannet's bath,
over the broad sea, whorled prows will bring
presents and tokens. I know your people
are beyond reproach in every respect,

steadfast in the old way with friend or foe."   1865
    Then the earls' defender furnished the hero
with twelve treasures and told him to set out,
sail with those gifts safely home
to the people he loved, but to return promptly.
And so the good and gray-haired Dane,   1870
that highborn king, kissed Beowulf
and embraced his neck, then broke down
in sudden tears. Two forebodings
disturbed him in his wisdom, but one was stronger:[3]
nevermore would they meet each other   1875
face to face. And such was his affection
that he could not help being overcome:
his fondness for the man was so deep-founded,
it warmed his heart and wound the heartstrings
tight in his breast.
                    The embrace ended   1880
and Beowulf, glorious in his gold regalia,
stepped the green earth. Straining at anchor
and ready for boarding, his boat awaited him.
So they went on their journey, and Hrothgar's generosity
was praised repeatedly. He was a peerless king   1885
until old age sapped his strength and did him
mortal harm, as it has done so many.
    Down to the waves then, dressed in the web
of their chain-mail and war-shirts the young men marched
in high spirits. The coast-guard spied them,   1890
thanes setting forth, the same as before.
His salute this time from the top of the cliff
was far from unmannerly; he galloped to meet them
and as they took ship in their shining gear,
he said how welcome they would be in Geatland.   1895
Then the broad hull was beached on the sand
to be cargoed with treasure, horses and war-gear.
The curved prow motioned; the mast stood high
above Hrothgar's riches in the loaded hold.
    The guard who had watched the boat was given   1900
a sword with gold fittings, and in future days
that present would make him a respected man
at his place on the mead-bench.
                    Then the keel plunged
and shook in the sea; and they sailed from Denmark.
    Right away the mast was rigged with its sea-shawl;   1905
sail-ropes were tightened, timbers drummed
and stiff winds kept the wave-crosser
skimming ahead; as she heaved forward,
her foamy neck was fleet and buoyant,

---

3. We are not told what the other foreboding is, but it is probably the old man's awareness of the imminence of his own death.

a lapped prow loping over currents, 1910
until finally the Geats caught sight of coastline
and familiar cliffs. The keel reared up,
wind lifted it home, it hit on the land.
    The harbor guard came hurrying out
to the rolling water: he had watched the offing 1915
long and hard, on the lookout for those friends.
With the anchor cables, he moored their craft
right where it had beached, in case a backwash
might catch the hull and carry it away.
Then he ordered the prince's treasure-trove 1920
to be carried ashore. It was a short step
from there to where Hrethel's son and heir,
Hygelac the gold-giver, makes his home
on a secure cliff, in the company of retainers.
    The building was magnificent, the king majestic, 1925
ensconced in his hall; and although Hygd, his queen,
was young, a few short years at court,
her mind was thoughtful and her manners sure.
Haereth's daughter[4] behaved generously
and stinted nothing when she distributed 1930
bounty to the Geats.
                    Great Queen Modthryth
perpetrated terrible wrongs.[5]
If any retainer ever made bold
to look her in the face, if an eye not her lord's[6]
stared at her directly during daylight, 1935
the outcome was sealed: he was kept bound,
in hand-tightened shackles, racked, tortured
until doom was pronounced—death by the sword,
slash of blade, blood-gush, and death-qualms
in an evil display. Even a queen 1940
outstanding in beauty must not overstep like that.
A queen should weave peace, not punish the innocent
with loss of life for imagined insults.
But Hemming's kinsman put a halt to her ways
and drinkers round the table had another tale: 1945
she was less of a bane to people's lives,
less cruel-minded, after she was married
to the brave Offa,[7] a bride arrayed
in her gold finery, given away
by a caring father, ferried to her young prince 1950
over dim seas. In days to come
she would grace the throne and grow famous
for her good deeds and conduct of life,
her high devotion to the hero king

---

4. I.e., Hygd.   5. A Danish queen whose wickedness is being used as a foil to Hygd.   6. Probably her father, although the Anglo-Saxon word can also refer to a husband.   7. *Offa* was a legendary king of the Angles, one of the Germanic peoples who invaded England and established a kingdom named Mercia in the north of the country prior to the composition of *Beowulf*. Hemming is evidently a forebear of the Angles.

who was the best king, it has been said,   1955
between the two seas or anywhere else
on the face of the earth. Offa was honored
far and wide for his generous ways,
his fighting spirit and his farseeing
defense of his homeland; from him there sprang Eomer,   1960
Garmund's grandson, kinsman of Hemming,[8]
his warriors' mainstay and master of the field.
    Heroic Beowulf and his band of men
crossed the wide strand, striding along
the sandy foreshore; the sun shone,   1965
the world's candle warmed them from the south
as they hastened to where, as they had heard,
the young king, Ongentheow's killer[9]
and his people's protector, was dispensing rings
inside his bawn. Beowulf's return   1970
was reported to Hygelac as soon as possible,
news that the captain was now in the enclosure,
his battle-brother back from the fray
alive and well, walking to the hall.
Room was quickly made, on the king's orders,   1975
and the troops filed across the cleared floor.
    After Hygelac had offered greetings
to his loyal thane in a lofty speech,
he and his kinsman, that hale survivor,
sat face to face. Haereth's daughter[1]   1980
moved about with the mead-jug in her hand,
taking care of the company, filling the cups
that warriors held out. Then Hygelac began
to put courteous questions to his old comrade
in the high hall. He hankered to know   1985
every tale the Sea-Geats had to tell:
"How did you fare on your foreign voyage,
dear Beowulf, when you abruptly decided
to sail away across the salt water
and fight at Heorot? Did you help Hrothgar   1990
much in the end? Could you ease the prince
of his well-known troubles? Your undertaking
cast my spirits down, I dreaded the outcome
of your expedition and pleaded with you
long and hard to leave the killer be,   1995
let the South-Danes settle their own
blood-feud with Grendel. So God be thanked
I am granted this sight of you, safe and sound."
    Beowulf, son of Ecgtheow, spoke:
"What happened, Lord Hygelac, is hardly a secret   2000

8. *Garmund* is Offa's father, *Eomer* his son.   9. *Ongentheow's killer* is Hygelac, king of the Geats; he led the attack against the Swedes, although a Geat named Eofor actually killed Ongentheow. This is the first reference to the feud between the Geats and the Swedes (or Shylfings) detailed in the headnote (see below, lines 2379–96, 2468–89, 2922–98).   1. I.e., Hygd.

any more among men in this world—
myself and Grendel coming to grips
on the very spot where he visited destruction
on the Victory-Shieldings and violated
life and limb, losses I avenged   2005
so no earthly offspring of Grendel's
need ever boast of that bout before dawn,
no matter how long the last of his evil
family survives.
          When I first landed
I hastened to the ring-hall and saluted Hrothgar.   2010
Once he discovered why I had come,
the son of Halfdane sent me immediately
to sit with his own sons on the bench.
It was a happy gathering. In my whole life
I have never seen mead enjoyed more   2015
in any hall on earth. Sometimes the queen
herself appeared, peace-pledge between nations,[2]
to hearten the young ones and hand out
a torque to a warrior, then take her place.
Sometimes Hrothgar's daughter distributed   2020
ale to older ranks, in order on the benches:
I heard the company call her Freawaru
as she made her rounds, presenting men
with the gem-studded bowl, young bride-to-be
to the gracious Ingeld,[3] in her gold-trimmed attire.   2025
The friend of the Shieldings favors her betrothal:
the guardian of the kingdom sees good in it
and hopes this woman will heal old wounds
and grievous feuds.
          But generally the spear
is prompt to retaliate when a prince is killed,   2030
no matter how admirable the bride may be.
  "Think how the Heatho-Bards are bound to feel,
their lord, Ingeld, and his loyal thanes,
when he walks in with that woman to the feast:
Danes are at the table, being entertained,   2035
honored guests in glittering regalia,
burnished ring-mail that was their hosts' birthright,
looted when the Heatho-Bards could no longer wield
their weapons in the shield-clash, when they went down
with their beloved comrades and forfeited their lives.   2040
Then an old spearman will speak while they are drinking,
having glimpsed some heirloom that brings alive
memories of the massacre; his mood will darken

---

2. Wealhtheow, Hrothgar's queen, is called a "peace-pledge between nations" because kings attempted to
end feuds by marrying their daughters to the sons of the kings of enemy nations. But as we have already
seen in the case of the marriage of the Dane Hildeburh to the Jute Finn, and as we shall shortly learn
again, such a strategy seems rarely to have worked. 3. *Ingeld* is the king of the Heatho-Bards, whose
father, Froda, was killed by the Danes.

and heart-stricken, in the stress of his emotion,
he will begin to test a young man's temper   2045
and stir up trouble, starting like this:
'Now, my friend, don't you recognize
your father's sword, his favorite weapon,
the one he wore when he went out in his war-mask
to face the Danes on that final day?   2050
After Withergeld[4] died and his men were doomed,
the Shieldings quickly claimed the field;
and now here's a son of one or other
of those same killers coming through our hall
overbearing us, mouthing boasts,   2055
and rigged in armor that by right is yours.'
And so he keeps on, recalling and accusing,
working things up with bitter words
until one of the lady's retainers lies
spattered in blood, split open   2060
on his father's account.[5] The killer knows
the lie of the land and escapes with his life.
Then on both sides the oath-bound lords
will break the peace, a passionate hate
will build up in Ingeld, and love for his bride   2065
will falter in him as the feud rankles.
I therefore suspect the good faith of the Heatho-Bards,
the truth of their friendship and the trustworthiness
of their alliance with the Danes.
                    But now, my lord,
I shall carry on with my account of Grendel,   2070
the whole story of everything that happened
in the hand-to-hand fight.
                    After heaven's gem
had gone mildly to earth, that maddened spirit,
the terror of those twilights, came to attack us
where we stood guard, still safe inside the hall.   2075
There deadly violence came down on Hondscio[6]
and he fell as fate ordained, the first to perish,
rigged out for the combat. A comrade from our ranks
had come to grief in Grendel's maw:
he ate up the entire body.   2080
There was blood on his teeth, he was bloated and dangerous,
all roused up, yet still unready
to leave the hall empty-handed;
renowned for his might, he matched himself against me,
wildly reaching. He had this roomy pouch,[7]   2085
a strange accoutrement, intricately strung
and hung at the ready, a rare patchwork

---

4. A Heatho-Bard warrior. 5. A Danish attendant to Freawaru, whose father killed a Heatho-Bard in
the original battle; this action is envisioned as taking place at Ingeld's court after the marriage. 6. A
Geat who was accompanying Beowulf; his name means "glove." 7. The Anglo-Saxon word translated as
"pouch" literally means "glove."

of devilishly fitted dragon-skins.
I had done him no wrong, yet the raging demon
wanted to cram me and many another   2090
into this bag—but it was not to be
once I got to my feet in a blind fury.
It would take too long to tell how I repaid
the terror of the land for every life he took
and so won credit for you, my king,   2095
and for all your people. And although he got away
to enjoy life's sweetness for a while longer,
his right hand stayed behind him in Heorot,
evidence of his miserable overthrow
as he dived into murk on the mere bottom.   2100
    "I got lavish rewards from the lord of the Danes
for my part in the battle, beaten gold
and much else, once morning came
and we took our places at the banquet table.
There was singing and excitement: an old reciter,   2105
a carrier of stories, recalled the early days.
At times some hero made the timbered harp
tremble with sweetness, or related true
and tragic happenings; at times the king
gave the proper turn to some fantastic tale,   2110
or a battle-scarred veteran, bowed with age,
would begin to remember the martial deeds
of his youth and prime and be overcome
as the past welled up in his wintry heart.
    "We were happy there the whole day long   2115
and enjoyed our time until another night
descended upon us. Then suddenly
the vehement mother avenged her son
and wreaked destruction. Death had robbed her,
Geats had slain Grendel, so his ghastly dam   2120
struck back and with bare-faced defiance
laid a man low. Thus life departed
from the sage Aeschere, an elder wise in counsel.
But afterward, on the morning following,
the Danes could not burn the dead body   2125
nor lay the remains of the man they loved
on his funeral pyre. She had fled with the corpse
and taken refuge beneath torrents on the mountain.
It was a hard blow for Hrothgar to bear,
harder than any he had undergone before.   2130
And so the heartsore king beseeched me
in your royal name to take my chances
underwater, to win glory
and prove my worth. He promised me rewards.
Hence, as is well known, I went to my encounter   2135
with the terror-monger at the bottom of the tarn.
For a while it was hand-to-hand between us,

then blood went curling along the currents
and I beheaded Grendel's mother in the hall
with a mighty sword. I barely managed   2140
to escape with my life; my time had not yet come.
But Halfdane's heir, the shelter of those earls,
again endowed me with gifts in abundance.
    "Thus the king acted with due custom.
I was paid and recompensed completely,   2145
given full measure and the freedom to choose
from Hrothgar's treasures by Hrothgar himself.
These, King Hygelac, I am happy to present
to you as gifts. It is still upon your grace
that all favor depends. I have few kinsmen   2150
who are close, my king, except for your kind self."
Then he ordered the boar-framed standard to be brought,
the battle-topping helmet, the mail-shirt gray as hoar-frost,
and the precious war-sword; and proceeded with his speech:
"When Hrothgar presented this war-gear to me   2155
he instructed me, my lord, to give you some account
of why it signifies his special favor.
He said it had belonged to his older brother,
King Heorogar, who had long kept it,
but that Heorogar had never bequeathed it   2160
to his son Heoroward, that worthy scion,
loyal as he was.
                    Enjoy it well."
    I heard four horses were handed over next.
Beowulf bestowed four bay steeds
to go with the armor, swift gallopers,   2165
all alike. So ought a kinsman act,
instead of plotting and planning in secret
to bring people to grief, or conspiring to arrange
the death of comrades. The warrior king
was uncle to Beowulf and honored by his nephew: 2170
each was concerned for the other's good.
    I heard he presented Hygd with a gorget,
the priceless torque that the prince's daughter,
Wealhtheow, had given him; and three horses,
supple creatures brilliantly saddled.   2175
The bright necklace would be luminous on Hygd's breast.
    Thus Beowulf bore himself with valor;
he was formidable in battle yet behaved with honor
and took no advantage; never cut down
a comrade who was drunk, kept his temper   2180
and, warrior that he was, watched and controlled
his God-sent strength and his outstanding
natural powers. He had been poorly regarded
for a long time, was taken by the Geats
for less than he was worth: and their lord too   2185
had never much esteemed him in the mead-hall.

They firmly believed that he lacked force,
that the prince was a weakling; but presently
every affront to his deserving was reversed.
The battle-famed king, bulwark of his earls,   2190
ordered a gold-chased heirloom of Hrethel's[8]
to be brought in; it was the best example
of a gem-studded sword in the Geat treasury.
This he laid on Beowulf's lap
and then rewarded him with land as well,   2195
seven thousand hides;[9] and a hall and a throne.
Both owned land by birth in that country,
ancestral grounds; but the greater right
and sway were inherited by the higher born.

[THE DRAGON WAKES]

A lot was to happen in later days   2200
in the fury of battle. Hygelac fell
and the shelter of Heardred's shield proved useless
against the fierce aggression of the Shylfings:[1]
ruthless swordsmen, seasoned campaigners,
they came against him and his conquering nation,   2205
and with cruel force cut him down
so that afterwards
            the wide kingdom
reverted to Beowulf. He ruled it well
for fifty winters, grew old and wise
as warden of the land
            until one began   2210
to dominate the dark, a dragon on the prowl
from the steep vaults of a stone-roofed barrow[2]
where he guarded a hoard; there was a hidden passage,
unknown to men, but someone managed[3]
to enter by it and interfere   2215
with the heathen trove. He had handled and removed
a gem-studded goblet; it gained him nothing,
though with a thief's wiles he had outwitted
the sleeping dragon. That drove him into rage,
as the people of that country would soon discover.   2220
    The intruder who broached the dragon's treasure
and moved him to wrath had never meant to.
It was desperation on the part of a slave
fleeing the heavy hand of some master,
guilt-ridden and on the run,   2225
going to ground. But he soon began
to shake with terror; . . . . . . in shock

8. Hygelac's father and, through his daughter, Beowulf's grandfather.   9. A *hide* varied in size, but was considered to be sufficient land to support a peasant and his family.   1. Hygelac died in the raid against the Franks (see note 4 to lines 1202–3); Heardred died in the long feud against the Swedes or Shylfings described in the headnote.   2. A *barrow* is a burial mound.   3. In the single manuscript of *Beowulf*, the page containing lines 2215–31 is badly damaged, and the translation is therefore conjectural. The ellipses of lines 2227–30 indicate lines that cannot be reconstructed at all.

the wretch . . . .
. . . . panicked and ran
away with the precious   2230
metalwork. There were many other
heirlooms heaped inside the earth-house,
because long ago, with deliberate care,
somebody now forgotten
had buried the riches of a highborn race   2235
in this ancient cache. Death had come
and taken them all in times gone by
and the only one left to tell their tale,
the last of their line, could look forward to nothing
but the same fate for himself: he foresaw that his joy   2240
in the treasure would be brief.
                              A newly constructed
barrow stood waiting, on a wide headland
close to the waves, its entryway secured.
Into it the keeper of the hoard had carried
all the goods and golden ware   2245
worth preserving. His words were few:
"Now, earth, hold what earls once held
and heroes can no more; it was mined from you first
by honorable men. My own people
have been ruined in war; one by one   2250
they went down to death, looked their last
on sweet life in the hall. I am left with nobody
to bear a sword or to burnish plated goblets,
put a sheen on the cup. The companies have departed.
The hard helmet, hasped with gold,   2255
will be stripped of its hoops; and the helmet-shiner
who should polish the metal of the war-mask sleeps;
the coat of mail that came through all fights,
through shield-collapse and cut of sword,
decays with the warrior. Nor may webbed mail   2260
range far and wide on the warlord's back
beside his mustered troops. No trembling harp,
no tuned timber, no tumbling hawk
swerving through the hall, no swift horse
pawing the courtyard. Pillage and slaughter   2265
have emptied the earth of entire peoples."
And so he mourned as he moved about the world,
deserted and alone, lamenting his unhappiness
day and night, until death's flood
brimmed up in his heart.
                              Then an old harrower of the dark   2270
happened to find the hoard open,
the burning one who hunts out barrows,
the slick-skinned dragon, threatening the night sky
with streamers of fire. People on the farms
are in dread of him. He is driven to hunt out   2275

hoards under ground, to guard heathen gold
through age-long vigils, though to little avail.
For three centuries, this scourge of the people
had stood guard on that stoutly protected
underground treasury, until the intruder   2280
unleashed its fury; he hurried to his lord
with the gold-plated cup and made his plea
to be reinstated. Then the vault was rifled,
the ring-hoard robbed, and the wretched man
had his request granted. His master gazed   2285
on that find from the past for the first time.
    When the dragon awoke, trouble flared again.
He rippled down the rock, writhing with anger
when he saw the footprints of the prowler who had stolen
too close to his dreaming head.   2290
So may a man not marked by fate
easily escape exile and woe
by the grace of God.
                    The hoard-guardian
scorched the ground as he scoured and hunted
for the trespasser who had troubled his sleep.   2295
Hot and savage, he kept circling and circling
the outside of the mound. No man appeared
in that desert waste, but he worked himself up
by imagining battle; then back in he'd go
in search of the cup, only to discover   2300
signs that someone had stumbled upon
the golden treasures. So the guardian of the mound,
the hoard-watcher, waited for the gloaming
with fierce impatience; his pent-up fury
at the loss of the vessel made him long to hit back   2305
and lash out in flames. Then, to his delight,
the day waned and he could wait no longer
behind the wall, but hurtled forth
in a fiery blaze. The first to suffer
were the people on the land, but before long   2310
it was their treasure-giver who would come to grief.
    The dragon began to belch out flames
and burn bright homesteads; there was a hot glow
that scared everyone, for the vile sky-winger
would leave nothing alive in his wake.   2315
Everywhere the havoc he wrought was in evidence.
Far and near, the Geat nation
bore the brunt of his brutal assaults
and virulent hate. Then back to the hoard
he would dart before daybreak, to hide in his den.   2320
He had swinged⁴ the land, swathed it in flame,
in fire and burning, and now he felt secure

_____

4. I.e., singed, scorched.

in the vaults of his barrow; but his trust was unavailing.
   Then Beowulf was given bad news,
the hard truth: his own home,   2325
the best of buildings, had been burned to a cinder,
the throne-room of the Geats. It threw the hero
into deep anguish and darkened his mood:
the wise man thought he must have thwarted
ancient ordinance of the eternal Lord,   2330
broken His commandment. His mind was in turmoil,
unaccustomed anxiety and gloom
confused his brain; the fire-dragon
had razed the coastal region and reduced
forts and earthworks to dust and ashes,   2335
so the war-king planned and plotted his revenge.
The warriors' protector, prince of the hall-troop,
ordered a marvelous all-iron shield
from his smithy works. He well knew
that linden boards would let him down   2340
and timber burn. After many trials,
he was destined to face the end of his days,
in this mortal world, as was the dragon,
for all his long leasehold on the treasure.
   Yet the prince of the rings was too proud   2345
to line up with a large army
against the sky-plague. He had scant regard
for the dragon as a threat, no dread at all
of its courage or strength, for he had kept going
often in the past, through perils and ordeals   2350
of every sort, after he had purged
Hrothgar's hall, triumphed in Heorot
and beaten Grendel. He outgrappled the monster
and his evil kin.
             One of his cruelest
hand-to-hand encounters had happened   2355
when Hygelac, king of the Geats, was killed
in Friesland: the people's friend and lord,
Hrethel's son, slaked a sword blade's
thirst for blood. But Beowulf's prodigious
gifts as a swimmer guaranteed his safety: 2360
he arrived at the shore, shouldering thirty
battle-dresses, the booty he had won.
There was little for the Hetware[5] to be happy about
as they shielded their faces and fighting on the ground
began in earnest. With Beowulf against them,   2365
few could hope to return home.
   Across the wide sea, desolate and alone,
the son of Ecgtheow swam back to his people.
There Hygd offered him throne and authority

---

5. The *Hetware* are a Frankish tribe.

as lord of the ring-hoard: with Hygelac dead,   2370
she had no belief in her son's ability
to defend their homeland against foreign invaders.
Yet there was no way the weakened nation
could get Beowulf to give in and agree
to be elevated over Heardred as his lord   2375
or to undertake the office of kingship.
But he did provide support for the prince,
honored and minded him until he matured
as the ruler of Geatland.
                    Then over sea-roads
exiles arrived, sons of Ohthere.[6]   2380
They had rebelled against the best of all
the sea-kings in Sweden, the one who held sway
in the Shylfing nation, their renowned prince,
lord of the mead-hall. That marked the end
for Hygelac's son: his hospitality   2385
was mortally rewarded with wounds from a sword.
Heardred lay slaughtered and Onela returned
to the land of Sweden, leaving Beowulf
to ascend the throne, to sit in majesty
and rule over the Geats. He was a good king.   2390
    In days to come, he contrived to avenge
the fall of his prince; he befriended Eadgils
when Eadgils was friendless, aiding his cause
with weapons and warriors over the wide sea,
sending him men. The feud was settled   2395
on a comfortless campaign when he killed Onela.
    And so the son of Ecgtheow had survived
every extreme, excelling himself
in daring and in danger, until the day arrived
when he had to come face to face with the dragon.   2400
The lord of the Geats took eleven comrades
and went in a rage to reconnoiter.
By then he had discovered the cause of the affliction
being visited on the people. The precious cup
had come to him from the hand of the finder,   2405
the one who had started all this strife
and was now added as a thirteenth to their number.
They press-ganged and compelled this poor creature
to be their guide. Against his will
he led them to the earth-vault he alone knew,   2410
an underground barrow near the sea-billows
and heaving waves, heaped inside
with exquisite metalwork. The one who stood guard
was dangerous and watchful, warden of the trove

---

6. *Ohthere* was king of the Swedes or Shylfings, but after his death his sons, Eanmund and Eadgils, were driven out by their uncle Onela. They were taken in by Heardred, Hygelac's son, who was then king of the Geats, who was then in turn attacked and killed (along with Eanmund) by Onela. At this point Beowulf became king of the Geats and supported Eadgils in his successful attack on Onela.

buried under earth: no easy bargain   2415
would be made in that place by any man.
  The veteran king sat down on the cliff-top.
He wished good luck to the Geats who had shared
his hearth and his gold. He was sad at heart,
unsettled yet ready, sensing his death.   2420
His fate hovered near, unknowable but certain:
it would soon claim his coffered soul,
part life from limb. Before long
the prince's spirit would spin free from his body.
  Beowulf, son of Ecgtheow, spoke: 2425
"Many a skirmish I survived when I was young
and many times of war: I remember them well.
At seven, I was fostered out by my father,
left in the charge of my people's lord.
King Hrethel kept me and took care of me,   2430
was openhanded, behaved like a kinsman.
While I was his ward, he treated me no worse
as a wean⁷ about the place than one of his own boys,
Herebeald and Haethcyn, or my own Hygelac.
For the eldest, Herebeald, an unexpected   2435
deathbed was laid out, through a brother's doing,
when Haethcyn bent his horn-tipped bow
and loosed the arrow that destroyed his life.
He shot wide and buried a shaft
in the flesh and blood of his own brother.   2440
That offense was beyond redress, a wrongfooting
of the heart's affections; for who could avenge
the prince's life or pay his death-price?
It was like the misery felt by an old man
who has lived to see his son's body   2445
swing on the gallows. He begins to keen
and weep for his boy, watching the raven
gloat where he hangs: he can be of no help.
The wisdom of age is worthless to him.
Morning after morning, he wakes to remember   2450
that his child is gone; he has no interest
in living on until another heir
is born in the hall, now that his first-born
has entered death's dominion forever.
He gazes sorrowfully at his son's dwelling,   2455
the banquet hall bereft of all delight,
the windswept hearthstone; the horsemen are sleeping,
the warriors under ground; what was is no more.
No tunes from the harp, no cheer raised in the yard.
Alone with his longing, he lies down on his bed   2460
and sings a lament; everything seems too large,
the steadings and the fields.

7. A young child [Translator's note]; a Northern Irish word.

Such was the feeling
of loss endured by the lord of the Geats
after Herebeald's death. He was helplessly placed
to set to rights the wrong committed,   2465
could not punish the killer in accordance with the law
of the blood-feud, although he felt no love for him.
Heartsore, wearied, he turned away
from life's joys, chose God's light
and departed, leaving buildings and lands   2470
to his sons, as a man of substance will.
  "Then over the wide sea Swedes and Geats
battled and feuded and fought without quarter.
Hostilities broke out when Hrethel died.
Ongentheow's sons[8] were unrelenting,   2475
refusing to make peace, campaigning violently
from coast to coast, constantly setting up
terrible ambushes around Hreosnahill.[9]
My own kith and kin avenged
these evil events, as everybody knows,   2480
but the price was high: one of them paid
with his life. Haethcyn, lord of the Geats,
met his fate there and fell in the battle.
Then, as I have heard, Hygelac's sword
was raised in the morning against Ongentheow,   2485
his brother's killer. When Eofor cleft
the old Swede's helmet, halved it open,
he fell, death-pale: his feud-calloused hand
could not stave off the fatal stroke.
  "The treasures that Hygelac lavished on me   2490
I paid for when I fought, as fortune allowed me,
with my glittering sword. He gave me land
and the security land brings, so he had no call
to go looking for some lesser champion,
some mercenary from among the Gifthas[1]   2495
or the Spear-Danes or the men of Sweden.
I marched ahead of him, always there
at the front of the line; and I shall fight like that
for as long as I live, as long as this sword
shall last, which has stood me in good stead   2500
late and soon, ever since I killed
Dayraven the Frank in front of the two armies.
He brought back no looted breastplate
to the Frisian king but fell in battle,
their standard-bearer, highborn and brave.   2505
No sword blade sent him to his death:

8. *Ongentheow's sons* are Ohthere and Onela, who attacked the Geats and killed Haethcyn; Haethcyn was
then avenged by his brother Hygelac, whose attack on the Swedes resulted in the death of Ongentheow at
the hands of the Geat Eofor (described below in lines 2922–98). These events took place before those of
lines 2379–96, which describe the Geats' role in the struggle between Onela and Ohthere's two sons after
Ongentheow's death.   9. The place of the battle can be translated as Sorrow Hill.   1. A tribe related
to the Goths.

my bare hands stilled his heartbeats
and wrecked the bone-house. Now blade and hand,
sword and sword-stroke, will assay the hoard."

[BEOWULF ATTACKS THE DRAGON]

Beowulf spoke, made a formal boast   2510
for the last time: "I risked my life
often when I was young. Now I am old,
but as king of the people I shall pursue this fight
for the glory of winning, if the evil one will only
abandon his earth-fort and face me in the open."   2515
    Then he addressed each dear companion
one final time, those fighters in their helmets,
resolute and highborn: "I would rather not
use a weapon if I knew another way
to grapple with the dragon and make good my boast   2520
as I did against Grendel in days gone by.
But I shall be meeting molten venom
in the fire he breathes, so I go forth
in mail-shirt and shield. I won't shift a foot
when I meet the cave-guard: what occurs on the wall   2525
between the two of us will turn out as fate,
overseer of men, decides. I am resolved.
I scorn further words against this sky-borne foe.
    "Men-at-arms, remain here on the barrow,
safe in your armor, to see which one of us   2530
is better in the end at bearing wounds
in a deadly fray. This fight is not yours,
nor is it up to any man except me
to measure his strength against the monster
or to prove his worth. I shall win the gold   2535
by my courage, or else mortal combat,
doom of battle, will bear your lord away."
    Then he drew himself up beside his shield.
The fabled warrior in his war-shirt and helmet
trusted in his own strength entirely   2540
and went under the crag. No coward path.
    Hard by the rock-face that hale veteran,
a good man who had gone repeatedly
into combat and danger and come through,
saw a stone arch and a gushing stream   2545
that burst from the barrow, blazing and wafting
a deadly heat. It would be hard to survive
unscathed near the hoard, to hold firm
against the dragon in those flaming depths.
Then he gave a shout. The lord of the Geats   2550
unburdened his breast and broke out
in a storm of anger. Under gray stone
his voice challenged and resounded clearly.

Hate was ignited. The hoard-guard recognized
a human voice, the time was over   2555
for peace and parleying. Pouring forth
in a hot battle-fume, the breath of the monster
burst from the rock. There was a rumble under ground.
Down there in the barrow, Beowulf the warrior
lifted his shield: the outlandish thing   2560
writhed and convulsed and viciously
turned on the king, whose keen-edged sword,
an heirloom inherited by ancient right,
was already in his hand. Roused to a fury,
each antagonist struck terror in the other.   2565
Unyielding, the lord of his people loomed
by his tall shield, sure of his ground,
while the serpent looped and unleashed itself.
Swaddled in flames, it came gliding and flexing
and racing toward its fate. Yet his shield defended   2570
the renowned leader's life and limb
for a shorter time than he meant it to:
that final day was the first time
when Beowulf fought and fate denied him
glory in battle. So the king of the Geats   2575
raised his hand and struck hard
at the enameled scales, but scarcely cut through:
the blade flashed and slashed yet the blow
was far less powerful than the hard-pressed king
had need of at that moment. The mound-keeper   2580
went into a spasm and spouted deadly flames:
when he felt the stroke, battle-fire
billowed and spewed. Beowulf was foiled
of a glorious victory. The glittering sword,
infallible before that day,   2585
failed when he unsheathed it, as it never should have.
For the son of Ecgtheow, it was no easy thing
to have to give ground like that and go
unwillingly to inhabit another home
in a place beyond; so every man must yield   2590
the leasehold of his days.
                         Before long
the fierce contenders clashed again.
The hoard-guard took heart, inhaled and swelled up
and got a new wind; he who had once ruled
was furled in fire and had to face the worst.   2595
No help or backing was to be had then
from his highborn comrades; that hand-picked troop
broke ranks and ran for their lives
to the safety of the wood. But within one heart
sorrow welled up: in a man of worth   2600
the claims of kinship cannot be denied.
    His name was Wiglaf, a son of Weohstan's,

a well-regarded Shylfing warrior
related to Aelfhere.[2] When he saw his lord
tormented by the heat of his scalding helmet,   2605
he remembered the bountiful gifts bestowed on him,
how well he lived among the Waegmundings,
the freehold he inherited from his father[3] before him.
He could not hold back: one hand brandished
the yellow-timbered shield, the other drew his sword—   2610
an ancient blade that was said to have belonged
to Eanmund, the son of Ohthere, the one
Weohstan had slain when he was an exile without friends.
He carried the arms to the victim's kinfolk,
the burnished helmet, the webbed chain-mail   2615
and that relic of the giants. But Onela returned
the weapons to him, rewarded Weohstan
with Eanmund's war-gear. He ignored the blood-feud,
the fact that Eanmund was his brother's son.[4]
Weohstan kept that war-gear for a lifetime,   2620
the sword and the mail-shirt, until it was the son's turn
to follow his father and perform his part.
Then, in old age, at the end of his days
among the Weather-Geats, he bequeathed to Wiglaf
innumerable weapons.
                And now the youth   2625
was to enter the line of battle with his lord,
his first time to be tested as a fighter.
His spirit did not break and the ancestral blade
would keep its edge, as the dragon discovered
as soon as they came together in the combat.   2630
    Sad at heart, addressing his companions,
Wiglaf spoke wise and fluent words:
"I remember that time when mead was flowing,
how we pledged loyalty to our lord in the hall,
promised our ring-giver we would be worth our price,   2635
make good the gift of the war-gear,
those swords and helmets, as and when
his need required it. He picked us out
from the army deliberately, honored us and judged us
fit for this action, made me these lavish gifts—   2640
and all because he considered us the best
of his arms-bearing thanes. And now, although
he wanted this challenge to be one he'd face
by himself alone—the shepherd of our land,
a man unequaled in the quest for glory   2645

2. *Wiglaf* is, like Beowulf, a member of the clan of the Waegmundings (see lines 2813–14), although both consider themselves Geats as well. See note 2 to line 347. Nothing is known of Aelfhere.   **3.** Wiglaf's father is Weohstan, who, as we learn shortly, was the man who killed Eanmund, Ohthere's son, when he had taken refuge among the Geats (2379–84). How Wiglaf then became a Geat is not clear, although it may have been when Beowulf helped Eanmund's brother Eadgils avenge himself on Onela, who had usurped the throne of the Swedes; Eadgils then became king.   **4.** That is, Onela ignored the fact that Weohstan had killed his nephew Eanmund since he in fact wanted Eanmund dead.

and a name for daring—now the day has come
when this lord we serve needs sound men
to give him their support. Let us go to him,
help our leader through the hot flame
and dread of the fire. As God is my witness,   2650
I would rather my body were robed in the same
burning blaze as my gold-giver's body
than go back home bearing arms.
That is unthinkable, unless we have first
slain the foe and defended the life   2655
of the prince of the Weather-Geats. I well know
the things he has done for us deserve better.
Should he alone be left exposed
to fall in battle? We must bond together,
shield and helmet, mail-shirt and sword."   2660
Then he waded the dangerous reek and went
under arms to his lord, saying only:
"Go on, dear Beowulf, do everything
you said you would when you were still young
and vowed you would never let your name and fame   2665
be dimmed while you lived. Your deeds are famous,
so stay resolute, my lord, defend your life now
with the whole of your strength. I shall stand by you."
    After those words, a wildness rose
in the dragon again and drove it to attack,   2670
heaving up fire, hunting for enemies,
the humans it loathed. Flames lapped the shield,
charred it to the boss, and the body armor
on the young warrior was useless to him.
But Wiglaf did well under the wide rim   2675
Beowulf shared with him once his own had shattered
in sparks and ashes.
                        Inspired again
by the thought of glory, the war-king threw
his whole strength behind a sword stroke
and connected with the skull. And Naegling snapped.   2680
Beowulf's ancient iron-gray sword
let him down in the fight. It was never his fortune
to be helped in combat by the cutting edge
of weapons made of iron. When he wielded a sword,
no matter how blooded and hard-edged the blade,   2685
his hand was too strong, the stroke he dealt
(I have heard) would ruin it. He could reap no advantage.
    Then the bane of that people, the fire-breathing dragon,
was mad to attack for a third time.
When a chance came, he caught the hero   2690
in a rush of flame and clamped sharp fangs
into his neck. Beowulf's body
ran wet with his life-blood: it came welling out.
    Next thing, they say, the noble son of Weohstan

saw the king in danger at his side   2695
and displayed his inborn bravery and strength.
He left the head alone,[5] but his fighting hand
was burned when he came to his kinsman's aid.
He lunged at the enemy lower down
so that his decorated sword sank into its belly   2700
and the flames grew weaker.
                  Once again the king
gathered his strength and drew a stabbing knife
he carried on his belt, sharpened for battle.
He stuck it deep in the dragon's flank.
Beowulf dealt it a deadly wound.   2705
They had killed the enemy, courage quelled his life;
that pair of kinsmen, partners in nobility,
had destroyed the foe. So every man should act,
be at hand when needed; but now, for the king,
this would be the last of his many labors   2710
and triumphs in the world.
                  Then the wound
dealt by the ground-burner earlier began
to scald and swell; Beowulf discovered
deadly poison suppurating inside him,
surges of nausea, and so, in his wisdom,   2715
the prince realized his state and struggled
toward a seat on the rampart. He steadied his gaze
on those gigantic stones, saw how the earthwork
was braced with arches built over columns.
And now that thane unequaled for goodness   2720
with his own hands washed his lord's wounds,
swabbed the weary prince with water,
bathed him clean, unbuckled his helmet.
    Beowulf spoke: in spite of his wounds,
mortal wounds, he still spoke   2725
for he well knew his days in the world
had been lived out to the end—his allotted time
was drawing to a close, death was very near.
    "Now is the time when I would have wanted
to bestow this armor on my own son,   2730
had it been my fortune to have fathered an heir
and live on in his flesh. For fifty years
I ruled this nation. No king
of any neighboring clan would dare
face me with troops, none had the power   2735
to intimidate me. I took what came,
cared for and stood by things in my keeping,
never fomented quarrels, never
swore to a lie. All this consoles me,
doomed as I am and sickening for death;   2740

5. I.e., the dragon's flame-breathing head.

because of my right ways, the Ruler of mankind
need never blame me when the breath leaves my body
for murder of kinsmen. Go now quickly,
dearest Wiglaf, under the gray stone
where the dragon is laid out, lost to his treasure;   2745
hurry to feast your eyes on the hoard.
Away you go: I want to examine
that ancient gold, gaze my fill
on those garnered jewels; my going will be easier
for having seen the treasure, a less troubled letting-go   2750
of the life and lordship I have long maintained."
    And so, I have heard, the son of Weohstan
quickly obeyed the command of his languishing
war-weary lord; he went in his chain-mail
under the rock-piled roof of the barrow,   2755
exulting in his triumph, and saw beyond the seat
a treasure-trove of astonishing richness,
wall-hangings that were a wonder to behold,
glittering gold spread across the ground,
the old dawn-scorching serpent's den   2760
packed with goblets and vessels from the past,
tarnished and corroding. Rusty helmets
all eaten away. Armbands everywhere,
artfully wrought. How easily treasure
buried in the ground, gold hidden   2765
however skillfully, can escape from any man!
    And he saw too a standard, entirely of gold,
hanging high over the hoard,
a masterpiece of filigree; it glowed with light
so he could make out the ground at his feet   2770
and inspect the valuables. Of the dragon there was no
remaining sign: the sword had dispatched him.
Then, the story goes, a certain man[6]
plundered the hoard in that immemorial howe,[7]
filled his arms with flagons and plates,   2775
anything he wanted; and took the standard also,
most brilliant of banners.
                                    Already the blade
of the old king's sharp killing-sword
had done its worst: the one who had for long
minded the hoard, hovering over gold,   2780
unleashing fire, surging forth
midnight after midnight, had been mown down.
    Wiglaf went quickly, keen to get back,
excited by the treasure. Anxiety weighed
on his brave heart—he was hoping he would find   2785
the leader of the Geats alive where he had left him
helpless, earlier, on the open ground.

6. I.e., Wiglaf.   7. *Howe* is an Irish word for dwelling.

So he came to the place, carrying the treasure
and found his lord bleeding profusely,
his life at an end; again he began   2790
to swab his body. The beginnings of an utterance
broke out from the king's breast-cage.
The old lord gazed sadly at the gold.
    "To the everlasting Lord of all,
to the King of Glory, I give thanks   2795
that I behold this treasure here in front of me,
that I have been allowed to leave my people
so well endowed on the day I die.
Now that I have bartered my last breath
to own this fortune, it is up to you   2800
to look after their needs. I can hold out no longer.
Order my troop to construct a barrow
on a headland on the coast, after my pyre has cooled.
It will loom on the horizon at Hronesness[8]
and be a reminder among my people—   2805
so that in coming times crews under sail
will call it Beowulf's Barrow, as they steer
ships across the wide and shrouded waters."
    Then the king in his great-heartedness unclasped
the collar of gold from his neck and gave it   2810
to the young thane, telling him to use
it and the war-shirt and gilded helmet well.
"You are the last of us, the only one left
of the Waegmundings. Fate swept us away,
sent my whole brave highborn clan   2815
to their final doom. Now I must follow them."
    That was the warrior's last word.
He had no more to confide. The furious heat
of the pyre would assail him. His soul fled from his breast
to its destined place among the steadfast ones.   2820

[BEOWULF'S FUNERAL]

    It was hard then on the young hero,
having to watch the one he held so dear
there on the ground, going through
his death agony. The dragon from underearth,
his nightmarish destroyer, lay destroyed as well,   2825
utterly without life. No longer would his snakefolds
ply themselves to safeguard hidden gold.
Hard-edged blades, hammered out
and keenly filed, had finished him
so that the sky-roamer lay there rigid,   2830
brought low beside the treasure-lodge.
    Never again would he glitter and glide

---

8. The name means "Whaleness."

and show himself off in midnight air,
exulting in his riches: he fell to earth
through the battle-strength in Beowulf's arm.   2835
There were few, indeed, as far as I have heard,
big and brave as they may have been,
few who would have held out if they had had to face
the outpourings of that poison-breather
or gone foraging on the ring-hall floor   2840
and found the deep barrow-dweller
on guard and awake.
           The treasure had been won,
bought and paid for by Beowulf's death.
Both had reached the end of the road
through the life they had been lent.
                Before long   2845
the battle-dodgers abandoned the wood,
the ones who had let down their lord earlier,
the tail-turners, ten of them together.
When he needed them most, they had made off.
Now they were ashamed and came behind shields,   2850
in their battle-outfits, to where the old man lay.
They watched Wiglaf, sitting worn out,
a comrade shoulder to shoulder with his lord,
trying in vain to bring him round with water.
Much as he wanted to, there was no way   2855
he could preserve his lord's life on earth
or alter in the least the Almighty's will.
What God judged right would rule what happened
to every man, as it does to this day.
   Then a stern rebuke was bound to come   2860
from the young warrior to the ones who had been cowards.
Wiglaf, son of Weohstan, spoke
disdainfully and in disappointment:
"Anyone ready to admit the truth
will surely realize that the lord of men   2865
who showered you with gifts and gave you the armor
you are standing in—when he would distribute
helmets and mail-shirts to men on the mead-benches,
a prince treating his thanes in hall
to the best he could find, far or near—   2870
was throwing weapons uselessly away.
It would be a sad waste when the war broke out.
Beowulf had little cause to brag
about his armed guard; yet God who ordains
who wins or loses allowed him to strike   2875
with his own blade when bravery was needed.
There was little I could do to protect his life
in the heat of the fray, but I found new strength
welling up when I went to help him.
Then my sword connected and the deadly assaults   2880

of our foe grew weaker, the fire coursed
less strongly from his head. But when the worst happened
too few rallied around the prince.
   "So it is good-bye now to all you know and love
on your home ground, the open-handedness,   2885
the giving of war-swords. Every one of you
with freeholds of land, our whole nation,
will be dispossessed, once princes from beyond
get tidings of how you turned and fled
and disgraced yourselves. A warrior will sooner   2890
die than live a life of shame."
   Then he ordered the outcome of the fight to be reported
to those camped on the ridge, that crowd of retainers
who had sat all morning, sad at heart,
shield-bearers wondering about   2895
the man they loved: would this day be his last
or would he return? He told the truth
and did not balk, the rider who bore
news to the cliff-top. He addressed them all:
"Now the people's pride and love,   2900
the lord of the Geats, is laid on his deathbed,
brought down by the dragon's attack.
Beside him lies the bane of his life,
dead from knife-wounds. There was no way
Beowulf could manage to get the better   2905
of the monster with his sword. Wiglaf sits
at Beowulf's side, the son of Weohstan,
the living warrior watching by the dead,
keeping weary vigil, holding a wake
for the loved and the loathed.
                 Now war is looming   2910
over our nation, soon it will be known
to Franks and Frisians, far and wide,
that the king is gone. Hostility has been great
among the Franks since Hygelac sailed forth
at the head of a war-fleet into Friesland: 2915
there the Hetware harried and attacked
and overwhelmed him with great odds.
The leader in his war-gear was laid low,
fell among followers: that lord did not favor
his company with spoils. The Merovingian king   2920
has been an enemy to us ever since.
   "Nor do I expect peace or pact-keeping
of any sort from the Swedes. Remember:
at Ravenswood, Ongentheow
slaughtered Haethcyn, Hrethel's son,   2925
when the Geat people in their arrogance
first attacked the fierce Shylfings.
The return blow was quickly struck

by Ohthere's father.[9] Old and terrible,
he felled the sea-king and saved his own   2930
aged wife, the mother of Onela
and of Ohthere, bereft of her gold rings.
Then he kept hard on the heels of the foe
and drove them, leaderless, lucky to get away
in a desperate rout into Ravenswood.   2935
His army surrounded the weary remnant
where they nursed their wounds; all through the night
he howled threats at those huddled survivors,
promised to axe their bodies open
when dawn broke, dangle them from gallows   2940
to feed the birds. But at first light
when their spirits were lowest, relief arrived.
They heard the sound of Hygelac's horn,
his trumpet calling as he came to find them,
the hero in pursuit, at hand with troops.   2945
    "The bloody swathe that Swedes and Geats
cut through each other was everywhere.
No one could miss their murderous feuding.
Then the old man made his move,
pulled back, barred his people in: 2950
Ongentheow withdrew to higher ground.
Hygelac's pride and prowess as a fighter
were known to the earl; he had no confidence
that he could hold out against that horde of seamen,
defend his wife and the ones he loved   2955
from the shock of the attack. He retreated for shelter
behind the earthwall. Then Hygelac swooped
on the Swedes at bay, his banners swarmed
into their refuge, his Geat forces
drove forward to destroy the camp.   2960
There in his gray hairs, Ongentheow
was cornered, ringed around with swords.
And it came to pass that the king's fate
was in Eofor's hands,[1] and in his alone.
Wulf, son of Wonred, went for him in anger,   2965
split him open so that blood came spurting
from under his hair. The old hero
still did not flinch, but parried fast,
hit back with a harder stroke:
the king turned and took him on.   2970
Then Wonred's son, the brave Wulf,
could land no blow against the aged lord.
Ongentheow divided his helmet
so that he buckled and bowed his bloodied head

9. Ongentheow.   1. The killing of Ongentheow by Eofor has been previously described in lines 2486–
89.

and dropped to the ground. But his doom held off. 2975
Though he was cut deep, he recovered again.
    "With his brother down, the undaunted Eofor,
Hygelac's thane, hefted his sword
and smashed murderously at the massive helmet
past the lifted shield. And the king collapsed, 2980
the shepherd of people was sheared of life.
Many then hurried to help Wulf,
bandaged and lifted him, now that they were left
masters of the blood-soaked battle-ground.
One warrior stripped the other, 2985
looted Ongentheow's iron mail-coat,
his hard sword-hilt, his helmet too,
and carried the graith² to King Hygelac,
he accepted the prize, promised fairly
that reward would come, and kept his word. 2990
For their bravery in action, when they arrived home,
Eofor and Wulf were overloaded
by Hrethel's son, Hygelac the Geat,
with gifts of land and linked rings
that were worth a fortune. They had won glory, 2995
so there was no gainsaying his generosity.
And he gave Eofor his only daughter
to bide at home with him, an honor and a bond.
    "So this bad blood between us and the Swedes,
this vicious feud, I am convinced, 3000
is bound to revive; they will cross our borders
and attack in force when they find out
that Beowulf is dead. In days gone by
when our warriors fell and we were undefended,
he kept our coffers and our kingdom safe. 3005
He worked for the people, but as well as that
he behaved like a hero.
                                We must hurry now
to take a last look at the king
and launch him, lord and lavisher of rings,
on the funeral road. His royal pyre 3010
will melt no small amount of gold:
heaped there in a hoard, it was bought at heavy cost,
and that pile of rings he paid for at the end
with his own life will go up with the flame,
be furled in fire: treasure no follower 3015
will wear in his memory, nor lovely woman
link and attach as a torque around her neck—
but often, repeatedly, in the path of exile
they shall walk bereft, bowed under woe,
now that their leader's laugh is silenced, 3020
high spirits quenched. Many a spear

2. Armor.

dawn-cold to the touch will be taken down
and waved on high; the swept harp
won't waken warriors, but the raven winging
darkly over the doomed will have news,   3025
tidings for the eagle of how he hoked[3] and ate,
how the wolf and he made short work of the dead."
    Such was the drift of the dire report
that gallant man delivered. He got little wrong
in what he told and predicted.
                        The whole troop   3030
rose in tears, then took their way
to the uncanny scene under Earnaness.[4]
There, on the sand, where his soul had left him,
they found him at rest, their ring-giver
from days gone by. The great man   3035
had breathed his last. Beowulf the king
had indeed met with a marvelous death.
    But what they saw first was far stranger:
the serpent on the ground, gruesome and vile,
lying facing him. The fire-dragon   3040
was scaresomely burned, scorched all colors.
From head to tail, his entire length
was fifty feet. He had shimmered forth
on the night air once, then winged back
down to his den; but death owned him now,   3045
he would never enter his earth-gallery again.
Beside him stood pitchers and piled-up dishes,
silent flagons, precious swords
eaten through with rust, ranged as they had been
while they waited their thousand winters under ground.   3050
That huge cache, gold inherited
from an ancient race, was under a spell—
which meant no one was ever permitted
to enter the ring-hall unless God Himself,
mankind's Keeper, True King of Triumphs,   3055
allowed some person pleasing to Him—
and in His eyes worthy—to open the hoard.
    What came about brought to nothing
the hopes of the one who had wrongly hidden
riches under the rock-face. First the dragon slew   3060
that man among men, who in turn made fierce amends
and settled the feud. Famous for his deeds
a warrior may be, but it remains a mystery
where his life will end, when he may no longer
dwell in the mead-hall among his own.   3065
So it was with Beowulf, when he faced the cruelty
and cunning of the mound-guard. He himself was ignorant

---

3. *Hoked*: rooted about, a Northern Irish word [adapted from Translator's note].   4. The place where
Beowulf fought the dragon; it means "Eagleness."

of how his departure from the world would happen.
The highborn chiefs who had buried the treasure
declared it until doomsday so accursed   3070
that whoever robbed it would be guilty of wrong
and grimly punished for their transgression,
hasped in hell-bonds in heathen shrines.
Yet Beowulf's gaze at the gold treasure
when he first saw it had not been selfish.   3075
   Wiglaf, son of Weohstan, spoke:
"Often when one man follows his own will
many are hurt. This happened to us.
Nothing we advised could ever convince
the prince we loved, our land's guardian,   3080
not to vex the custodian of the gold,
let him lie where he was long accustomed,
lurk there under earth until the end of the world.
He held to his high destiny. The hoard is laid bare,
but at a grave cost; it was too cruel a fate   3085
that forced the king to that encounter.
I have been inside and seen everything
amassed in the vault. I managed to enter
although no great welcome awaited me
under the earthwall. I quickly gathered up   3090
a huge pile of the priceless treasures
handpicked from the hoard and carried them here
where the king could see them. He was still himself,
alive, aware, and in spite of his weakness
he had many requests. He wanted me to greet you   3095
and order the building of a barrow that would crown
the site of his pyre, serve as his memorial,
in a commanding position, since of all men
to have lived and thrived and lorded it on earth
his worth and due as a warrior were the greatest.   3100
Now let us again go quickly
and feast our eyes on that amazing fortune
heaped under the wall. I will show the way
and take you close to those coffers packed with rings
and bars of gold. Let a bier be made   3105
and got ready quickly when we come out
and then let us bring the body of our lord,
the man we loved, to where he will lodge
for a long time in the care of the Almighty."
   Then Weohstan's son, stalwart to the end,   3110
had orders given to owners of dwellings,
many people of importance in the land,
to fetch wood from far and wide
for the good man's pyre:
                       "Now shall flame consume
our leader in battle, the blaze darken   3115
round him who stood his ground in the steel-hail,

when the arrow-storm shot from bowstrings
pelted the shield-wall. The shaft hit home.
Feather-fledged, it finned the barb in flight."
    Next the wise son of Weohstan   3120
called from among the king's thanes
a group of seven: he selected the best
and entered with them, the eighth of their number,
under the God-cursed roof; one raised
a lighted torch and led the way.   3125
No lots were cast for who should loot the hoard
for it was obvious to them that every bit of it
lay unprotected within the vault,
there for the taking. It was no trouble
to hurry to work and haul out   3130
the priceless store. They pitched the dragon
over the cliff-top, let tide's flow
and backwash take the treasure-minder.
Then coiled gold was loaded on a cart
in great abundance, and the gray-haired leader,   3135
the prince on his bier, borne to Hronesness.
    The Geat people built a pyre for Beowulf,
stacked and decked it until it stood foursquare,
hung with helmets, heavy war-shields
and shining armor, just as he had ordered.   3140
Then his warriors laid him in the middle of it,
mourning a lord far-famed and beloved.
On a height they kindled the hugest of all
funeral fires; fumes of woodsmoke
billowed darkly up, the blaze roared   3145
and drowned out their weeping, wind died down
and flames wrought havoc in the hot bone-house,
burning it to the core. They were disconsolate
and wailed aloud for their lord's decease.
A Geat woman too sang out in grief;   3150
with hair bound up, she unburdened herself
of her worst fears, a wild litany
of nightmare and lament: her nation invaded,
enemies on the rampage, bodies in piles,
slavery and abasement. Heaven swallowed the smoke.   3155
    Then the Geat people began to construct
a mound on a headland, high and imposing,
a marker that sailors could see from far away,
and in ten days they had done the work.
It was their hero's memorial; what remained from the fire   3160
they housed inside it, behind a wall
as worthy of him as their workmanship could make it.
And they buried torques in the barrow, and jewels
and a trove of such things as trespassing men
had once dared to drag from the hoard.   3165
They let the ground keep that ancestral treasure,

gold under gravel, gone to earth,
as useless to men now as it ever was.
Then twelve warriors rode around the tomb,
chieftains' sons, champions in battle,   3170
all of them distraught, chanting in dirges,
mourning his loss as a man and a king.
They extolled his heroic nature and exploits
and gave thanks for his greatness; which was the proper thing,
for a man should praise a prince whom he holds dear   3175
and cherish his memory when that moment comes
when he has to be convoyed from his bodily home.
So the Geat people, his hearth-companions,
sorrowed for the lord who had been laid low.
They said that of all the kings upon earth   3180
he was the man most gracious and fair-minded,
kindest to his people and keenest to win fame.

THE SONG OF ROLAND
ca. 1100

The Song of Roland is the foundational text of the French literary tradition. One of
the earliest poems written in French, it describes the process by which France left
behind its Germanic past as a loose confederation of powerful families and accepted
its future as a Christian nation united by loyalties to king and country. This story is
told as a clash of powerful personalities who are together engaged in a holy war against
the Muslims in Spain. The central protagonist is the great warrior Roland, who
embodies in an especially pure form the spirit of feudal loyalty to one's overlord. The
emperor Charlemagne is the object of this loyalty, but his commitments are split: he
owes to Roland a reciprocal loyalty, but he is also the head of the Holy Roman empire,
the institutional heir to classical Rome that is endowed with the mission not merely
to defend but to expand Christendom. Opposed to Roland is his stepfather Ganelon,
a member of Charlemagne's Frankish nobility who believes he can settle a feud with
Roland without compromising his loyalty to the king. And surrounding these three
main characters are men who provide further perspectives on the central issue of
what kind of loyalty is valid. Oliver, Roland's closest companion in arms, criticizes
Roland's narrow conception of his duty; Turpin, a warrior archbishop, provides jus-
tifications for Roland's actions that may be merely rationalizations; Pinabel, one of
Ganelon's kinsmen, comes to his defense when he is charged with treason for his
part in Roland's death; and Tierri, a warrior, challenges Pinabel not merely to defend
Roland or even Charlemagne but to promote national and supranational loyalties that
transcend Ganelon's tribal conception.

Many modern readers have been tempted to read the poem as a kind of medieval
Iliad, with the heroic yet arrogantly intransigent Roland as a French Achilles. Yet in
the manuscript the poem is untitled, Roland dies less than two-thirds of the way
through, and the beginning and ending of the poem focus on "Charles the King, our
Emperor, the Great." The poem could with equal justice be entitled—as indeed it
was in some of its medieval translations—The Song of Charlemagne. In fact, the
relation of Roland's story to Charles's—the relation, that is, of the heroic acts of one

man to the historically transcendent mission of establishing a universal Christian empire—is the poem's overriding theme. Roland embodies the unswerving and reciprocal allegiance that bound together lord and vassal into a stable unit, a relationship that made possible the establishment of the feudal system that, from the tenth through twelfth centuries, came to dominate Europe. From his first appearance in the poem, at the council scene in which the Franks debate whether to accept the offer of the Saracen leader Marsilion to submit to Charles if the Franks will leave Spain, Roland both promotes and himself displays this fidelity. He argues against accepting the offer for three reasons, all of them having to do with loyalty. First, Marsilion has already been proven untrustworthy in fulfilling his sworn oath; second, Basan and Basile, the ambassadors whom Marsilion killed during the previous negotiations, must be avenged (they were, Roland reminds Charles, "*your* men"); and third, Charles must also be true to his commitment to conquer Spain ("Fight the war you came to fight!"), an obligation he owes to God, who has sanctioned this Holy War. Again, the poem's climactic scene, in which the members of the rear guard are ambushed and Roland refuses to blow his horn to call back the army to help them, has often been read as expressing Roland's intemperate and unjustified reliance upon his own prowess. Yet another interpretation, centered on loyalty, is also possible. As the leader of the rear guard, Roland has sworn to protect the army: to call it back now, in the face of overwhelming enemy forces, would be to place it in danger and to betray his commitment. Indeed, when he accepted this dangerous assignment— dangerous because everyone, including Roland, suspected that Ganelon had conspired with the Saracens to set a trap—he promised Charles not victory over any Saracen attack but rather that he would not lose any part of his baggage train "that has not first been bought and paid for with swords." In other words, Roland swore an oath to fight to the utmost to protect the army, and this he must now do. At this point in the poem he explicitly describes the values that guide his life:

> We know our duty: to stand here for our King.
> A man must bear some hardships for his lord,
> stand everything, the great heat, the great cold,
> lose the hide and hair on him for his good lord.
> Now let each man make sure to strike hard here:
> let them not sing a bad song about us!

Certainly Roland is concerned with personal honor, but this depends above all not on valor but on loyalty: he fights not for himself but "for his good lord." Surprisingly, however, when it is clear that the Saracens have been defeated at the cost of the whole of the rear guard, Roland does blow the horn. Is this an admission that he was wrong before, as his companion Oliver implies? Perhaps; yet Turpin says that Roland should blow the horn to summon Charles so that he may, as is required of a good lord, avenge the deaths of the men who died for him. Moreover, it is this final act of feudal loyalty, and not the wounds inflicted by the Saracens, that kills Roland: the force of the horn blast bursts his temples. As the battle nears its end the poet describes Roland as "a brave man keeping faith," and the religious imagery with which his passing is surrounded makes it clear that, whatever the modern reader may think, the poet wants his audience to approve of Roland's choices. Yet we also cannot forget that Roland has said that his companions died "for me," which could mean simply that they performed their feudal duty to him but could also mean that they died "because of him."

If loyalty is the theme of the poem, it is analyzed rather than simply celebrated. The poem provides three other perspectives from which to make an assessment. One is provided by Oliver. In a famous line, we are told that "Roland is good [*proz*], and Oliver is wise [*sages*]." It is not easy to know exactly what the poet means by these terms. Is Roland primarily a fighter, a man of prowess, while Oliver is a strategist, a man of thought? While the poem is unwilling to criticize Roland's decisions about the horn, it also presents Oliver as capable of a larger, more pragmatic view than his companion. As Oliver urges him to look at the surrounding pagan hordes, Roland gazes instead at his sword, Durendal; as Oliver argues for Charles's need for the twelve peers and the warriors of the rear guard, Roland focuses only on the immediate challenge posed by the Saracen ambush. Roland's intensity and narrow commitment may be necessary for the functioning of the feudal system, but the poet also wants us to know that it is bought at a fearful price, that there are other ways of understanding one's duty.

The same could be said of Ganelon. He is no petty traitor: as the poet says of him at his trial, he would have been "a great man, had he been loyal." His behavior as an ambassador at Marsilion's camp is both shrewd and courageous. In order to accomplish Roland's downfall he must first provoke the now peacefully inclined Marsilion to wrath and then turn his anger against Roland. To this end he takes a calculated risk for the sake of a calculated—but far from guaranteed—result. Insulting Marsilion deliberately, in the name of the emperor, he makes himself the first target of the Saracen king's fury and certainly endangers his own life. Luckily for him, the king's hand is stayed, and the Saracens applaud Ganelon's magnificent courage. We are never told, however, why this otherwise admirable man so loathes Roland that he betrays both his companions and his lord—and himself—in order to bring about his death. Ganelon is Roland's stepfather, and the poet may have known of the legend that made Roland the offspring of an incestuous relationship between Charlemagne and his sister and thus (as with Arthur and Mordred) both his uncle and his father. But nothing is made of these family relationships, and we are probably on firmer ground to think that Ganelon simply cannot bear Roland's utter self-confidence in his own virtue and prowess. The story—perhaps true, perhaps not—that he tells the Saracen Blancandrin of Roland's plundering expedition, and of his haughty offer to Charles of a bright red apple as a sign that he can deliver to him "the crowns of all earth's kings," is a more reliable indicator of Ganelon's abhorrence than of Roland's character. At his trial Ganelon claims that his betrayal of the rear guard was justified by his formal defiance of Roland: this was a private matter, a feud, and no business of Charles's. But we get no sense that this argument carries much weight with either the Franks or the poet. The reluctance of Charles's council to punish Ganelon comes not from sympathy with his self-justification but from fear of his champion Pinabel. The danger Ganelon presents, then, is that he will return the Franks to a world of private vengeance where might makes right and where the larger interests of the community can be sacrificed to the impulses of its individual members. If Oliver sees the largest view, Ganelon sees the narrowest.

The final perspective we are offered is Charles's. He is in some ways the most complex character in the poem. On the one hand, he is the great Christian emperor, the agent of God in bringing about the unification of the world under the cross. As Roland lies dying, he recites a list of the lands he has brought under Charles's rule—a list that includes not just France but most of Europe, exceeding the boundaries of even the huge empire ruled over by the historical Charlemagne (742–814). This idea of a single Christendom under a divinely authorized emperor was one of the persistent dreams of medieval Christians. It was part of the justification for the crusades, and we will meet it again in Dante's *Divine Comedy*. It also contributed to the incapacity of most medieval Christians to recognize cultural differences as anything other than either threatening or contemptible, an affront to the cultural unity that God desired. In this poem Islamic religion and culture are presented in a degrading travesty: the Saracens are shown as idolaters and worshipers of Muhammad and Apollo, when in fact Islam rejects religious images, regards Muhammad as a prophet, not a god, and is monotheistic. (This ill-informed picture was produced, ironically, at the very time that Christian scholars were beginning to benefit from contact with their far more sophisticated Arab contemporaries, who had direct access to Greek texts, especially those of Aristotle, that were lost to the Latin West.) In any case, the fullest expression of Charles's role as God's agent in spreading Christian rule comes in the battle against Marsilion's overlord Baligant. Omitted in this selection, this battle is presented as an apocalyptic confrontation between good and evil, and Charles's victory is capped by the conversion of Marsilion's queen Bramimonde and her renaming as Juliana.

Yet Charles is also a human being, in some ways the most human in the poem. He is the only character whose inner life is made visible to us, partly in his dreams, partly in the single, sad line he speaks when informed by the angel Gabriel that further campaigns await him: " 'God!' said the King, 'the pains, the labors of my life!' " Charles embodies the weariness that made the Franks vulnerable to Marsilion's and Ganelon's deceptions at the outset, and that led them to want to avoid confronting Ganelon and Pinabel at the end. This is a weariness that is utterly foreign to Roland, that he seems not even to notice much less sympathize with. That the poet allows it so much room in his poem, while acknowledging that it must not be allowed to prevail, is testimony to the breadth of his own sympathies.

The Song of Roland derives ultimately from a historical event. In the year 778 the thirty-six-year-old Charles, then king of the Franks (he did not become the emperor Charlemagne until 800), entered Spain at the request of an Arabic ruler in revolt against his overlord. But Charles's self-interested intervention in this Muslim civil war went awry, and by the end of July he had decided to return to France. On August 15, as the army made its way through the narrow valleys of the Pyrenees, the rear guard protecting its retreat was annihilated in an ambush set by the native Basques. Among those killed was one Hruodlandus, governor of the marches (or borders) of Brittany. About 350 years later, between 1125 and 1150, someone wrote out the manuscript that contains the poem that we now call *The Song of Roland*. This manuscript was written in the French spoken at the time in England, a dialect known as Anglo-Norman, but the poem itself was composed in continental French around the year 1100. This date fits well with two contemporary conditions. One is the struggle then under way between the French king Philip I and the powerful barons who were technically subordinate to him but controlled much of what now constitutes France—a struggle that finds a parallel in the poem in the confrontation between Charles and Ganelon. The other is the growing interest in crusading. Throughout the eleventh century French knights fought against the Arab rulers of Spain, and in 1095 Pope Urban urged the nobility of Europe, and especially of France, to direct their martial energies away from their internal wrangling and toward the Holy Land, at the time governed by Muslim "infidels" (although governed in fact in a spirit of religious tolerance). The result was the First Crusade, which succeeded in capturing Jerusalem in 1099, in massacring most of the non-Christian population, and in establishing the French-controlled Kingdom of Jerusalem. *The Song of Roland* is steeped in this crusading spirit: as Roland says, and as the poem continually insists, "Pagans are wrong and Christians are right!"

Although there have been a number of theories, no one really knows how—or why—the story of the ill-fated Hruodlandus survived. It was a traditional story by at least the eleventh century: one later medieval chronicler even tells us that a minstrel called Taillefer sang about Roland to the Norman army of William the Conqueror before the battle of Hastings in 1066. The poem shows unmistakable signs of having emerged from a period of oral composition. As in the Homeric poems and *Beowulf,* many of its phrases are metrical formulas originally combined by an oral poet into complete lines and then larger passages as he re-created the poem anew at each performance (for a fuller account of oral composition, see above, p. 114). As testimony to its oral prehistory, the vocabulary of the whole of *The Song of Roland* comprises only some eighteen hundred words. In its written form the poem is comprised of 291 stanzas, or *laisses* (from the Latin *lectio,* or "reading"); the number of lines in each *laisse* varies widely, but it averages about fourteen. Each line contains ten or eleven syllables, with a strong caesura, or break, in the middle; the lines are then linked by assonance, which means that their final stressed vowels are identical (the final words of lines 1240–42, for example, are *vil*, *guarit*, and *murir*, the *i* being pronounced the same in each case). Even when written, the poem was almost certainly presented orally by a minstrel, or *jongleur* (like Taillefer), who would accompany himself with a simple stringed instrument. Like *Beowulf*, the poem would be chanted rather than sung, producing an effect of cadenced, ritualistic ceremony. This effect was doubtless enhanced by the so-called *laisses similaires*, groups of *laisses* that repeat, with variations, an especially significant scene or act (see, for example, lines 1049–92). These groups of *laisses* endow such moments with an unavoidable sense of solemnity and consequence.

A scholarly edition, with translation and commentary, is Gerald S. Brault, *The Song of Roland: An Analytical Edition*, 2 vols. (1978). Useful critical discussions are Eugene Vance, *Reading the Song of Roland* (1970), and Robert Francis Cook, *The Sense of the Song of Roland* (1987).

PRONOUNCING GLOSSARY

The following list uses common English syllables to provide rough equivalents of selected words whose pronunciation may be unfamiliar to the general reader.

Aquitaine: *ah-kee-ten*

Blancandrin: *blanh-cahn-drinh*

Durendal: *dur-ahn-dahl*

Geret: *zhehr-ay*

Gerin: *zhehr-inh*

Halteclere: *ahlt-clehr*

Haltille: *ahl-tee*

Malduit: *mahl-dwee*

Marsilion: *mah-seel-yonh*

Munjoie: *munh-zhwah*

Ogier: *oh-zhyay*

Rencesvals: *rahnc-vahl*

Roland: *roh-lanh*

Rousillon: *roo-see-yonh*

Veillantif: *ve-yanh-teef*

From The Song of Roland[1]

1

Charles the King, our Emperor, the Great,
has been in Spain for seven full years,
has conquered the high land down to the sea.
There is no castle that stands against him now,
no wall, no citadel left to break down—   5
except Saragossa, high on a mountain.[2]
King Marsilion holds it, who does not love God,
who serves Mahumet and prays to Apollin.[3]
He cannot save himself: his ruin will find him there. AOI.[4]

2

King Marsilion was in Saragossa.   10
He has gone forth into a grove, beneath its shade,

---

1. Translated by Frederick Goldin. Many of Goldin's notes have been adapted for use here.   2. Saragossa, in northeastern Spain, is not actually on a mountaintop. The poet's geography is not always accurate.   3. The Greek god Apollo; but the poet is mistaken, for these people worship only one god, Allah. *Mahumet*: Muhammad, founder of the Islamic religion.   4. These three mysterious letters appear at certain moments throughout the text, 180 times in all. No one has ever adequately explained them, though every reader feels their effect.

and he lies down on a block of blue marble,
twenty thousand men, and more, all around him.
He calls aloud to his dukes and his counts:
"Listen, my lords, to the troubles we have.   15
The Emperor Charles of the sweet land of France
has come into this country to destroy us.
I have no army able to give him battle,
I do not have the force to break his force.
Now act like my wise men: give me counsel,   20
save me, save me from death, save me from shame!"
No pagan there has one word to say to him
except Blancandrin, of the castle of Valfunde.

3

One of the wisest pagans was Blancandrin,
brave and loyal, a great mounted warrior,   25
a useful man, the man to aid his lord;
said to the King: "Do not give way to panic.
Do this: send Charles, that wild, terrible man,
tokens of loyal service and great friendship:
you will give him bears and lions and dogs,   30
seven hundred camels, a thousand molted hawks,
four hundred mules weighed down with gold and silver,
and fifty carts, to cart it all away:
he'll have good wages for his men who fight for pay.
Say he's made war long enough in this land: 35
let him go home, to France, to Aix, at last—
come Michaelmas⁵ you will follow him there,
say you will take their faith, become a Christian,
and be his man with honor, with all you have.
If he wants hostages, why, you'll send them,   40
ten, or twenty, to give him security.
Let us send him the sons our wives have borne.
I'll send my son with all the others named to die.
It is better that they should lose their heads⁶
than that we, Lord, should lose our dignity   45
and our honors—and be turned into beggars!" AOI.

4

Said Blancandrin: "By this right hand of mine
and by this beard that flutters on my chest,
you will soon see the French army disband,
the Franks will go to their own land, to France.   50
When each of them is in his dearest home,
King Charles will be in Aix, in his chapel.
At Michaelmas he will hold a great feast—
that day will come, and then our time runs out,
he'll hear no news, he'll get no word from us.   55

---

5. The feast of St. Michael, September 29. *Aix*: Aix-la-Chapelle, or Aachen, was the capital of Charlemagne's empire.   6. The speaker expects that the hostages will be killed by the French when the deception becomes clear. Sometime before, hostages sent by the French had been similarly slain (see lines 207–9).

This King is wild, the heart in him is cruel:
he'll take the heads of the hostages we gave.
It is better, Lord, that they lose their heads
than that we lose our bright, our beautiful Spain—
and nothing more for us but misery and pain!"   60
The pagans say: "It may be as he says."

5

King Marsilion brought his counsel to end,
then he summoned Clarin of Balaguét,
Estramarin and Eudropin, his peer,
And Priamun, Guarlan, that bearded one,   65
and Machiner and his uncle Maheu,
and Joüner, Malbien from over-sea,
and Blancandrin, to tell what was proposed.
From the worst of criminals he called these ten.
"Barons, my lords, you're to go to Charlemagne;   70
he's at the siege of Cordres,⁷ the citadel.
Olive branches are to be in your hands—
that signifies peace and humility.
If you've the skill to get me an agreement,
I will give you a mass of gold and silver   75
and lands and fiefs, as much as you could want."
Say the pagans: "We'll benefit from this!" AOI.

6

Marsilion brought his council to an end,
said to his men: "Lords, you will go on now,
and remember: olive branches in your hands;   80
and in my name tell Charlemagne the King
for his god's sake to have pity on me—
he will not see a month from this day pass
before I come with a thousand faithful;
say I will take that Christian religion   85
and be his man in love and loyalty.
If he wants hostages, why, he'll have them."
Said Blancandrin: "Now you will get good terms." AOI.

7

King Marsilion had ten white mules led out,
sent to him once by the King of Suatilie,⁸   90
with golden bits and saddles wrought with silver.
The men are mounted, the men who brought the message,
and in their hands they carry olive branches.
They came to Charles, who has France in his keeping.
He cannot prevent it: they will fool him. AOI.   95

8

The Emperor is secure and jubilant:

7. Córdoba, in southern Spain, at that time part of the Muslim empire.   8. A subordinate king, owing
allegiance to Marsilion.

he has taken Cordres, broken the walls,
knocked down the towers with his catapults.
And what tremendous spoils his knights have won—
gold and silver, precious arms, equipment.   100
In the city not one pagan remained
who is not killed or turned into a Christian.
The Emperor is in an ample grove,
Roland and Oliver are with him there,
Samson the Duke and Ansëis the fierce,   105
Geoffrey d'Anjou, the King's own standard-bearer;
and Gerin and Gerer, these two together always,
and the others, the simple knights, in force:
fifteen thousand from the sweet land of France.
The warriors sit on bright brocaded silk;   110
they are playing at tables to pass the time,
the old and the wisest men sitting at chess,
the young light-footed men fencing with swords.
Beneath a pine, beside a wild sweet-briar,
there was a throne, every inch of pure gold.   115
There sits the King, who rules over sweet France.
His beard is white, his hair flowering white.
That lordly body! the proud fierce look of him!—
If someone should come here asking for him,
      there'd be no need to point out the King of France.
The messengers dismounted, and on their feet   120
they greeted him in all love and good faith.

9

Blancandrin spoke, he was the first to speak,
said to the King: "Greetings, and God save you,
that glorious God whom we all must adore.
Here is the word of the great king Marsilion: 125
he has looked into this law of salvation,
wants to give you a great part of his wealth,
bears and lions and hunting dogs on chains,
seven hundred camels, a thousand molted hawks,
four hundred mules packed tight with gold and silver,   130
and fifty carts, to cart it all away;
and there will be so many fine gold bezants,[9]
you'll have good wages for the men in your pay.
You have stayed long—long enough!—in this land,
it is time to go home, to France, to Aix.   135
My master swears he will follow you there."
The Emperor holds out his hands toward God,
bows down his head, begins to meditate. AOI.

10

The Emperor held his head bowed down;
never was he too hasty with his words: 140
his custom is to speak in his good time.

9. Gold coins; the name is derived from Byzantium.

When his head rises, how fierce the look of him;
he said to them: "You have spoken quite well.
King Marsilion is my great enemy.
Now all these words that you have spoken here—   145
how far can I trust them? How can I be sure?"
The Saracen: "He wants to give you hostages.
How many will you want? ten? fifteen? twenty?
I'll put my son with the others named to die.[1]
You will get some, I think, still better born.   150
When you are at home in your high royal palace,
at the great feast of Saint Michael-in-Peril,[2]
the lord who nurtures me will follow you,
and in those baths[3]—the baths God made for you—
my lord will come and want to be made Christian."   155
King Charles replies: "He may yet save his soul." AOI.

11

Late in the day it was fair, the sun was bright.
Charles has them put the ten mules into stables.
The King commands a tent pitched in the broad grove,
and there he has the ten messengers lodged;   160
twelve serving men took splendid care of them.
There they remained that night till the bright day.
The Emperor rose early in the morning,
the King of France, and heard the mass and matins.
And then the King went forth beneath a pine,   165
calls for his barons to complete his council:
he will proceed only with the men of France. AOI.

12

The Emperor goes forth beneath a pine,
calls for his barons to complete his council:
Ogier the Duke, and Archbishop Turpin,   170
Richard the Old, and his nephew Henri;
from Gascony, the brave Count Acelin,
Thibaut of Reims, and his cousin Milun;
and Gerer and Gerin, they were both there,
and there was Count Roland, he came with them,   175
and Oliver, the valiant and well-born;
a thousand Franks of France, and more, were there.
Ganelon came, who committed the treason.
Now here begins the council that went wrong.[4] AOI.

13

"Barons, my lords," said Charles the Emperor,   180
"King Marsilion has sent me messengers,
wants to give me a great mass of his wealth,

---

1. I.e., if the promise is broken. *Saracen:* the usual term for the enemy.   2. The epithet *in peril of the sea* was applied to the famous sanctuary Mont-St.-Michel off the Normandy coast because it could be reached on foot only at low tide, and pilgrims were endangered by the incoming tide. Eventually, the phrase was applied to the saint himself.   3. Famous healing springs at Aix-la-Chapelle.   4. The poet anticipates that the plan adopted at the council will prove to be a mistake and that Ganelon will commit treason.

bears and lions and hunting dogs on chains,
seven hundred camels, a thousand molting hawks,
four hundred mules packed with gold of Araby,   185
and with all that, more than fifty great carts;
but also asks that I go back to France:
he'll follow me to Aix, my residence,
and take our faith, the one redeeming faith,
become a Christian, hold his march[5] lands from me.   190
But what lies in his heart? I do not know."
And the French say: "We must be on our guard!" AOI.

14

The Emperor has told them what was proposed.
Roland the Count will never assent to that,
gets to his feet, comes forth to speak against it;   195
says to the King: "Trust Marsilion—and suffer!
We came to Spain seven long years ago,
I won Noples for you, I won Commibles,
I took Valterne and all the land of Pine,
and Balaguer and Tudela and Seville.   200
And then this king, Marsilion, played the traitor:
he sent you men, fifteen of his pagans—
and sure enough, each held an olive branch;
and they recited just these same words to you.
You took counsel with all your men of France;   205
they counseled you to a bit of madness:
you sent two Counts across to the Pagans,
one was Basan, the other was Basile.
On the hills below Haltille, he took their heads.
They were your men. Fight the war you came to fight!   210
Lead the army you summoned on to Saragossa!
Lay siege to it all the rest of your life!
Avenge the men that this criminal murdered!" AOI.

15

The Emperor held his head bowed down with this,
and stroked his beard, and smoothed his mustache down,   215
and speaks no word, good or bad, to his nephew.
The French keep still, all except Ganelon:
he gets to his feet and, come before King Charles,
how fierce he is as he begins his speech;
said to the King: "Believe a fool—me or   220
another—and suffer! Protect your interest!
When Marsilion the King sends you his word
that he will join his hands[6] and be your man,
and hold all Spain as a gift from your hands
and then receive the faith that we uphold—   225
whoever urges that we refuse this peace,
that man does not care, Lord, what death we die.

---

5. A frontier province or territory.   **6.** Part of the gesture of homage; the lord enclosed the joined hands
of his vassal with his own.

That wild man's counsel must not win the day here—
let us leave fools, let us hold with wise men!" AOI.

16

And after that there came Naimon the Duke—   230
no greater vassal in that court than Naimon—
said to the King: "You've heard it clearly now,
Count Ganelon has given you your answer:
let it be heeded, there is wisdom in it.
King Marsilion is beaten in this war,   235
you have taken every one of his castles,
broken his walls with your catapults,
burnt his cities and defeated his men.
Now when he sends to ask you to have mercy,
it would be a sin to do still more to him.   240
Since he'll give you hostages as guarantee,
this great war must not go on, it is not right."
And the French say: "The Duke has spoken well." AOI.

17

"Barons, my lords, whom shall we send down there,
to Saragossa, to King Marsilion?"   245
Naimon replies, "I'll go, if you grant it!
At once, my lord! give me the glove and the staff."[7]
The King replies: "You're a man of great wisdom:
now by my beard, now by this mustache of mine,
you will not go so far from me this year; or ever.   250
Go take your seat when no one calls on you."

18

"Barons, my lords, whom can we send down there,
to this Saracen who holds Saragossa?"
Roland replies: "I can go there! No trouble!"
"No, no, not you!" said Oliver the Count,   255
"that heart in you is wild, spoils for a fight,
how I would worry—you'd fight with them, I know.
Now I myself could go, if the King wishes."
The King replies: "Be still, the two of you!
Not you, not he—neither will set foot there.   260
Now by this beard, as sure as you see white,
let no man here name one of the Twelve Peers!"
The French keep still, see how he silenced them.

19

Turpin of Reims has come forth from the ranks,
said to the King: "Let your Franks have a rest.   265
You have been in this land for seven years,
the many pains, the struggles they've endured!

---

7. Symbols of his commission from the Emperor Charles.

I'm the one, Lord, give me the glove and the staff,
and I'll go down to this Saracen of Spain
and then I'll see what kind of man we have."   270
The Emperor replies to him in anger:
"Now you go back and sit on that white silk
and say no more unless I command it!" AOI.

20

"My noble knights," said the Emperor Charles,
"choose me one man: a baron from my march,[8]   275
to bring my message to King Marsilion."
And Roland said: "Ganelon, my stepfather."
The French respond: "Why, that's the very man!
pass this man by and you won't send a wiser."
And hearing this Count Ganelon began to choke,   280
pulls from his neck the great furs of marten
and stands there now, in his silken tunic,
eyes full of lights, the look on him of fury,
he has the body, the great chest of a lord;
stood there so fair, all his peers gazed on him;   285
said to Roland: "Madman, what makes you rave?
Every man knows I am your stepfather,
yet you named me to go to Marsilion.
Now if God grants that I come back from there,
you will have trouble: I'll start a feud with you,   290
it will go on till the end of your life."
Roland replies: "What wild words—all that blustering!
Every man knows that threats don't worry me.
But we need a wise man to bring the message:
if the King wills, I'll gladly go in your place."   295

21

Ganelon answers: "You will not go for me. AOI.
You're not my man, and I am not your lord.
Charles commands me to perform this service:
I'll go to Marsilion in Saragossa.
And I tell you, I'll play a few wild tricks   300
before I cool the anger in me now."
When he heard that, Roland began to laugh. AOI.

22

Ganelon sees: *Roland laughing at him!*
and feels such pain he almost bursts with rage,
needs little more to go out of his mind;   305
says to the Count: "I have no love for you,
you *made* this choice fall on me, and that was wrong.
Just Emperor, here I am, before you.
I have one will: to fulfill your command."

---

8. Charlemagne wants them to choose a baron from an outlying region and not one of the Twelve Peers,
the circle of his dearest men.

23

"I know now I must go to Saragossa. AOI.   310
Any man who goes there cannot return.
And there is this: I am your sister's husband,
have a son by her, the finest boy there can be,
Baldewin," says he, "who will be a good man.
To him I leave my honors, fiefs, and lands.   315
Protect my son: these eyes will never see him."
Charles answers him: "That tender heart of yours!
You have to go, I have commanded it."

24

And the King said: "Ganelon, come forward, AOI.
come and receive the staff and the glove.   320
You have heard it: the Franks have chosen you."
Said Ganelon: "Lord, it's Roland who did this.
In all my days I'll have no love for him,
or Oliver, because he's his companion,
or the Twelve Peers, because they love him so.   325
I defy them, here in your presence, Lord."
And the King said: "What hate there is in you!
You will go there, for I command you to."
"I can go there, but I'll have no protector. AOI.
Basile had none, nor did Basan his brother."   330

25

The Emperor offers him his right glove.
But Ganelon would have liked not to be there.
When he had to take it, it fell to the ground.
"God!" say the French, "What's that going to mean?
What disaster will this message bring us!"   335
Said Ganelon: "Lords, you'll be hearing news."

26

Said Ganelon: "Lord, give me leave to go,
since go I must, there's no reason to linger."
And the King said: "In Jesus' name and mine,"
absolved him and blessed him with his right hand.   340
Then he gave him the letter and the staff.

27

Count Ganelon goes away to his camp.
He chooses, with great care, his battle-gear,
picks the most precious arms that he can find.
The spurs he fastened on were golden spurs;   345
he girds his sword, Murgleis, upon his side;
he has mounted Tachebrun, his battle horse,
his uncle, Guinemer, held the stirrup.
And there you would have seen brave men in tears,
his men, who say: "Baron, what bad luck for you!   350
All your long years in the court of the King,
always proclaimed a great and noble vassal!

Whoever it was doomed you to go down there—
Charlemagne himself will not protect that man.
Roland the Count should not have thought of this—   355
and you the living issue of a mighty line!"
And then they say: "Lord, take us there with you!"
Ganelon answers: "May the Lord God forbid!
It is better that I alone should die
     than so many good men and noble knights.
You will be going back, Lords, to sweet France: 360
go to my wife and greet her in my name,
and Pinabel, my dear friend and peer,
and Baldewin, my son, whom you all know:
give him your aid, and hold him as your lord."
And he starts down the road; he is on his way. AOI.   365

28

Ganelon rides to a tall olive tree,
there he has joined the pagan messengers.
And here is Blancandrin, who slows down for him:
and what great art they speak to one another.
Said Blancandrin: "An amazing man, Charles!   370
conquered Apulia, conquered all of Calabria,
crossed the salt sea on his way into England,
won its tribute,[9] got Peter's pence[1] for Rome:
what does he want from us here in our march?"
Ganelon answers: "That is the heart in him.   375
There'll never be a man the like of him." AOI.

29

Said Blancandrin: "The Franks are a great people.
Now what great harm all those dukes and counts do
to their own lord when they give him such counsel:
they torment him, they'll destroy him, and others."   380
Ganelon answers: "Well, now, I know no such man
except Roland, who'll suffer for it yet.
One day the Emperor was sitting in the shade:
his nephew came, still wearing his hauberk,
he had gone plundering near Carcassonne;   385
and in his hand he held a bright red apple:
'Dear Lord, here, take,' said Roland to his uncle;
'I offer you the crowns of all earth's kings.'
Yes, Lord, that pride of his will destroy him,
for every day he goes riding at death.   390
And *should* someone kill him, we would have peace." AOI.

30

Said Blancandrin: "A wild man, this Roland!
wants to make every nation beg for his mercy
and claims a right to every land on earth!

---

9. Although begun perhaps as early as the eighth century, the tribute was not the result of any effort of Charlemagne, who did not in fact visit England.   1. A tribute of one penny per house "for the use of Saint Peter," i.e., for the pope in Rome.

But what men support him, if that is his aim?"   395
Ganelon answers: "Why, Lord, the men of France.
They love him so, they will never fail him.
He gives them gifts, masses of gold and silver,
mules, battle horses, brocaded silks, supplies.
And it is all as the Emperor desires: 400
he'll win the lands from here to the Orient." AOI.

31

Ganelon and Blancandrin rode on until
each pledged his faith to the other and swore
they'd find a way to have Count Roland killed.
They rode along the paths and ways until,   405
in Saragossa, they dismount beneath a yew.
There was a throne in the shade of a pine,
covered with silk from Alexandria.
There sat the king who held the land of Spain,
and around him twenty thousand Saracens.   410
There is no man who speaks or breathes a word,
poised for the news that all would like to hear.
Now here they are: Ganelon and Blancandrin.

32

Blancandrin came before Marsilion,
his hand around the fist of Ganelon,   415
said to the King: "May Mahumet save you,
and Apollin, whose sacred laws we keep!
We delivered your message to Charlemagne:
when we finished, he raised up both his hands
and praised his god. He made no other answer.   420
Here he sends you one of his noble barons,
a man of France, and very powerful.
You'll learn from him whether or not you'll have peace."
"Let him speak, we shall hear him," Marsilion answers. AOI.

33

But Ganelon had it all well thought out.   425
With what great art he commences his speech,
a man who knows his way about these things;
said to the King: "May the Lord God save you,
that glorious God, whom we must all adore.
Here is the word of Charlemagne the King: 430
you are to take the holy Christian faith;
he will give you one half of Spain in fief.
If you refuse, if you reject this peace,
you will be taken by force, put into chains,
and then led forth to the King's seat at Aix;   435
you will be tried; you will be put to death:
you will die there, in shame, vilely, degraded."
King Marsilion, hearing this, was much shaken.
In his hand was a spear, with golden feathers.
He would have struck, had they not held him back. AOI.   440

34

Marsilion the King—his color changed!
He shook his spear, waved the shaft to and fro.
When he saw that, Ganelon laid hand to sword,
he drew it out two fingers from its sheath;
and spoke to it: "How beautiful and bright!   445
How long did I bear you in the King's court
before I died! The Emperor will not say
I died alone in that foreign country:
they'll buy you first, with the best men they have!"
The pagans say: "Let us break up this quarrel!"   450

35

The pagan chiefs pleaded with Marsilion
till he sat down once again on his throne.
The Caliph² spoke: "You did us harm just now,
served us badly, trying to strike this Frenchman.
You should have listened, you should have heard him out."   455
Said Ganelon: "Lord, I must endure it.
I shall not fail, for all the gold God made,
for all the wealth there may be in this land,
to tell him, as long as I have breath, all
that Charlemagne—that great and mighty King!—   460
has sent through me to his mortal enemy."
He is buckled in a great cloak of sable,
covered with silk from Alexandria:
he throws it down. Blancandrin picks it up.
But his great sword he will never throw down!   465
In his right fist he grasps its golden pommel.
Say the pagans: "That's a great man! A noble!" AOI.

36

Now Ganelon drew closer to the King
and said to him: "You are wrong to get angry,
for Charles, who rules all France, sends you this word: 470
you are to take the Christian people's faith;
he will give you one half of Spain in fief,
the other half goes to his nephew: Roland—
quite a partner you will be getting there!
If you refuse, if you reject this peace,   475
he will come and lay siege to Saragossa;
you will be taken by force, put into chains,
and brought straight on to Aix, the capital.
No saddle horse, no war horse for you then,
no he-mule, no she-mule for you to ride: 480
you will be thrown on some miserable dray;
you will be tried, and you will lose your head.
Our Emperor sends you this letter."
He put the letter in the pagan's right fist.

---

2. A high official of King Marsilion.

37

Marsilion turned white; he was enraged;   485
he breaks the seal, he's knocked away the wax,
runs through the letter, sees what is written there:
"Charles sends me word, this king who rules in France:
I'm to think of his anger and his grief—
he means Basan and his brother Basile,   490
I took their heads in the hills below Haltille;
if I want to redeem the life of my body,
I must send him my uncle: the Algalife.[3]
And otherwise he'll have no love for me."
Then his son came and spoke to Marsilion,   495
said to the King: "Ganelon has spoken madness.
He crossed the line, he has no right to live.
Give him to me, I will do justice on him."
When he heard that, Ganelon brandished his sword;
he runs to the pine, set his back against the trunk.   500

38

King Marsilion went forth into the orchard,
he takes with him the greatest of his men;
Blancandrin came, that gray-haired counselor,
and Jurfaleu, Marsilion's son and heir,
the Algalife, uncle and faithful friend.   505
Said Blancandrin: "Lord, call the Frenchman back.
He swore to me to keep faith with our cause."
And the King said: "Go, bring him back here, then."
He took Ganelon's right hand by the fingers,
leads him into the orchard before the King.   510
And there they plotted that criminal treason. AOI.

39

Said Marsilion: "My dear Lord Ganelon,
that was foolish, what I just did to you,
I showed my anger, even tried to strike you.
Here's a pledge of good faith, these sable furs,   515
the gold alone worth over five hundred pounds:
I'll make it all up before tomorrow night."
Ganelon answers: "I will not refuse it.
May it please God to reward you for it." AOI.

40

Said Marsilion: "I tell you, Ganelon,   520
I have a great desire to love you dearly.
I want to hear you speak of Charlemagne.
He is so old, he's used up all his time—
from what I hear, he is past two hundred!
He has pushed his old body through so many lands,   525
taken so many blows on his buckled shield,

---

3. The Caliph.

made beggars of so many mighty kings:
when will he lose the heart for making war?"
Ganelon answers: "Charles is not one to lose heart.
No man sees him, no man learns to know him   530
who does not say: the Emperor is great.
I do not know how to praise him so highly
that his great merit would not surpass my praise.
Who could recount his glory and his valor?
God put the light in him of such lordliness,   535
he would choose death before he failed his barons."

41

Said the pagan: "I have reason to marvel
at Charlemagne, a man so old and gray—
he's two hundred years old, I hear, and more;
he has tortured his body through so many lands,   540
and borne so many blows from lance and spear,
made beggars of so many mighty kings:
when will he lose the heart for making war?"
"Never," said Ganelon, "while his nephew lives,
he's a fighter, there's no vassal like him
    under the vault of heaven. And he has friends.   545
There's Oliver, a good man, his companion.
And the Twelve Peers, whom Charles holds very dear,
form the vanguard, with twenty thousand knights.
Charles is secure, he fears no man on earth." AOI.

42

Said the pagan: "Truly, how I must marvel   550
at Charlemagne, who is so gray and white—
over two hundred years, from what I hear;
gone through so many lands a conqueror,
and borne so many blows from strong sharp spears,
killed and conquered so many mighty kings: 555
when will he lose the heart for making war?"
"Never," said Ganelon, "while one man lives: Roland!
no man like him from here to the Orient!
There's his companion, Oliver, a brave man.
And the Twelve Peers, whom Charles holds very dear,   560
form the vanguard, with twenty thousand Franks.
Charles is secure, he fears no man alive." AOI.

43

"Dear Lord Ganelon," said Marsilion the King,
"I have my army, you won't find one more handsome:
I can muster four hundred thousand knights!   565
With this host, now, can I fight Charles and the French?"
Ganelon answers: "No, no, don't try that now,
you'd take a loss: thousands of your pagans!
Forget such foolishness, listen to wisdom:
send the Emperor so many gifts   570

there'll be no Frenchman there who does not marvel.
For twenty hostages—those you'll be sending—
he will go home: home again to sweet France!
And he will leave his rear-guard behind him.
There will be Roland, I do believe, his nephew,   575
and Oliver, brave man, born to the court.
These Counts are dead, if anyone trusts me.
Then Charles will see that great pride of his go down,
he'll have no heart to make war on you again." AOI.

44

"Dear Lord Ganelon," said Marsilion the King,   580
"What must I do to kill Roland the Count?"
Ganelon answers: "Now I can tell you that.
The King will be at Cize,[4] in the great passes,
he will have placed his rear-guard at his back:
there'll be his nephew, Count Roland, that great man,   585
and Oliver, in whom he puts such faith,
and twenty thousand Franks in their company.
Now send one hundred thousand of your pagans
against the French—let them give the first battle.
The French army will be hit hard and shaken.   590
I must tell you: your men will be martyred.
Give them a second battle, then, like the first.
One will get him, Roland will not escape.
Then you'll have done a deed, a noble deed,
and no more war for the rest of your life!" AOI.   595

45

"If someone can bring about the death of Roland,
then Charles would lose the right arm of his body,
that marvelous army would disappear—
never again could Charles gather such forces.
Then peace at last for the Land of Fathers!"[5]   600
When Marsilion heard that, he kissed his neck.
Then he begins to open up his treasures. AOI.

46

Marsilion said, "Why talk. . . .
No plan has any worth which one. . . . [6]
Now swear to me that you will betray Roland."   605
Ganelon answers: "Let it be as you wish."
On the relics in his great sword Murgleis
he swore treason and became a criminal. AOI.

47

There stood a throne made all of ivory.
Marsilion commands them bring forth a book: 610
it was the law of Mahum and Tervagant.[7]

---

4. The pass through the Pyrenees.   5. *Tere Major,* in the original; it can mean either "the great land"
or "the land of fathers, ancestors." It always refers to France.   6. Parts of lines 603–4 are unintelligible
in the manuscript.   7. A fictitious deity whom the poet mistakenly says the Saracens worshiped.

This is the vow sworn by the Saracen of Spain:
if he shall find Roland in the rear-guard,
he shall fight him, all his men shall fight him,
and once he finds Roland, Roland will die.   615
Says Ganelon: "May it be as you will." AOI.

48

And now there came a pagan, Valdabrun,
he was the man who raised Marsilion.
And, all bright smiles, he said to Ganelon:
"You take my sword, there's no man has one better: 620
a thousand coins, and more, are in the hilt.
It is a gift, dear lord, made in friendship,
only help us to Roland, that great baron,
let us find him standing in the rear-guard."
"It shall be done," replies Count Ganelon.   625
And then they kissed, on the face, on the chin.

49

And there came then a pagan, Climborin,
and, all bright smiles, he said to Ganelon:
"You take my helmet, I never saw one better,
only help us to Roland, lord of the march,   630
show us the way to put Roland to shame."
"It shall be done," replied Count Ganelon.
And then they kissed, on the face, on the mouth. AOI.

50

And then there came the Queen, Bramimunde;
said to the Count: "Lord, I love you well,   635
for my lord and all his men esteem you so.
I wish to send your wife two necklaces,
they are all gold, jacinths, and amethysts,
they are worth more than all the wealth of Rome.
Your Emperor has never seen their like."   640
He has taken them, thrusts them into his boot. AOI.

51

The King calls for Malduit, his treasurer:
"The gifts for Charles—is everything prepared?"
And he replies: "Yes, Lord, and well prepared:
seven hundred camels, packed with gold and silver,   645
and twenty hostages, the noblest under heaven." AOI.

52

Marsilion took Ganelon by the shoulder
and said to him: "You're a brave man, a wise man.
Now by that faith you think will save your soul,
take care you do not turn your heart from us.   650
I will give you a great mass of my wealth,
ten mules weighed down with fine Arabian gold;
and come each year, I'll do the same again.

Now you take these, the keys to this vast city:
present King Charles with all of its great treasure;   655
then get me Roland picked for the rear-guard.
Let me find him in some defile or pass,
I will fight him, a battle to the death."
Ganelon answers: "It's high time that I go."
Now he is mounted, and he is on his way. AOI.   660

53

The Emperor moves homeward, he's drawing near.
Now he has reached the city of Valterne:
Roland had stormed it, destroyed it, and it stood
from that day forth a hundred years laid waste.
Charles is waiting for news of Ganelon   665
and the tribute from Spain, from that great land.
In the morning, at dawn, with the first light,
Count Ganelon came to the Christian camp. AOI.

54

The Emperor rose early in the morning,
the King of France, and has heard mass and matins.   670
On the green grass he stood before his tent.
Roland was there, and Oliver, brave man,
Naimon the Duke, and many other knights.
Ganelon came, the traitor, the foresworn.
With what great cunning he commences his speech;   675
said to the King: "May the Lord God save you!
Here I bring you the keys to Saragossa.
And I bring you great treasure from that city,
and twenty hostages, have them well guarded.
And good King Marsilion sends you this word: 680
Do not blame him concerning the Algalife:
I saw it all myself, with my own eyes:
     four hundred thousand men, and all in arms,
their hauberks on, some with their helms laced on,
swords on their belts, the hilts enameled gold,
who went with him to the edge of the sea.   685
They are in flight: it is the Christian faith—
they do not want it, they will not keep its law.
They had not sailed four full leagues out to sea
when a high wind, a tempest swept them up.
They were all drowned; you will never see them;   690
if he were still alive, I'd have brought him.
As for the pagan King, Lord, believe this:
before you see one month from this day pass,
he'll follow you to the Kingdom of France
and take the faith—he will take your faith, Lord,   695
and join his hands and become your vassal.
He will hold Spain as a fief from your hand."
Then the King said: "May God be thanked for this.
You have done well, you will be well rewarded."
Throughout the host they sound a thousand trumpets.   700

The French break camp, strap their gear on their pack-horses.
They take the road to the sweet land of France. AOI.

55

King Charlemagne laid waste the land of Spain,
stormed its castles, ravaged its citadels.
The King declares his war is at an end.   705
The Emperor rides toward the land of sweet France.
Roland the Count affixed the gonfanon,[8]
raised it toward heaven on the height of a hill;
the men of France make camp across that country.
Pagans are riding up through these great valleys,   710
their hauberks on, their tunics of double mail,
their helms laced on, their swords fixed on their belts,
shields on their necks, lances trimmed with their banners.
In a forest high in the hills they gathered:
four hundred thousand men waiting for dawn.   715
God, the pity of it! the French do not know! AOI.

56

The day goes by; now the darkness of night.
Charlemagne sleeps, the mighty Emperor.
He dreamt he was at Cize, in the great passes,
and in his fists held his great ashen lance.   720
Count Ganelon tore it away from him
and brandished it, shook it with such fury
the splinters of the shaft fly up toward heaven.
Charlemagne sleeps, his dream does not wake him.

57

And after that he dreamed another vision: 725
he was in France, in his chapel at Aix,
a cruel wild boar was biting his right arm;
saw coming at him—from the Ardennes—a leopard,
it attacked him, fell wildly on his body.
And a swift hound running down from the hall   730
came galloping, bounding over to Charles,
tore the right ear off that first beast, the boar,
turns, in fury, to fight against the leopard.
And the French say: It is a mighty battle,
but cannot tell which one of them will win.   735
Charlemagne sleeps, his dream does not wake him. AOI.

58

The day goes by, and the bright dawn arises.
Throughout that host. . . .[9]
The Emperor rides forth with such fierce pride.
"Barons, my lords," said the Emperor Charles,   740
"look at those passes, at those narrow defiles—

---

8. Pennant.   9. The rest of the line is unintelligible in the manuscript.

pick me a man to command the rear-guard."
Ganelon answers: "Roland, here, my stepson.
You have no baron as great and brave as Roland."
When he hears that, the King stares at him in fury; 745
and said to him: "You are the living devil,
a mad dog—the murderous rage in you!
And who will precede me, in the vanguard?"
Ganelon answers, "Why, Ogier of Denmark,
you have no baron who could lead it so well." 750

59

Roland the Count, when he heard himself named,
knew what to say, and spoke as a knight must speak:
"Lord Stepfather, I have to cherish you!
You have had the rear-guard assigned to me.
Charles will not lose, this great King who rules France, 755
I swear it now, one palfrey, one war horse—
while I'm alive and know what's happening—
one he-mule, one she-mule that he might ride,
Charles will not lose one sumpter, not one pack horse
that has not first been bought and paid for with swords."
Ganelon answers: "You speak the truth, I know." AOI. 760

60

When Roland hears he will lead the rear-guard,
he spoke in great fury to his stepfather:
"Hah! you nobody, you base-born little fellow,
and did you think the glove would fall from my hands
as the staff fell¹ from yours before King Charles?" AOI. 765

61

"Just Emperor," said Roland, that great man,
"give me the bow that you hold in your hand.
And no man here, I think, will say in reproach
I let it drop, as Ganelon let the staff drop²
from his right hand, when he should have taken it." 770
The Emperor bowed down his head with this,
he pulled his beard, he twisted his mustache,
cannot hold back, tears fill his eyes, he weeps.

62

And after that there came Naimon the Duke,
no greater vassal in the court than Naimon, 775
said to the King: "You've heard it clearly now:
it is Count Roland. How furious he is.
He is the one to whom the rear-guard falls,
no baron here can ever change that now.
Give him the bow that you have stretched and bent, 780

---

1. Ganelon had let fall a glove, not a staff (line 333). For this and other less objective reasons, some editors have questioned the authenticity of this *laisse*. 2. In this *laisse* a reviser tried to make the text more consistent by adding the reference to the staff.

and then find him good men to stand with him."
The King gives him the bow; Roland has it now.

63

The Emperor calls forth Roland the Count:
"My lord, my dear nephew, of course you know
I will give you half my men, they are yours.   785
Let them serve you, it is your salvation."
"None of that!" said the Count. "May God strike me
if I discredit the history of my line.
I'll keep twenty thousand Franks—they are good men.
Go your way through the passes, you will be safe.   790
You must not fear any man while I live."

64

Roland the Count mounted his battle horse. AOI.
Oliver came to him, his companion.
And Gerin came, and the brave Count Gerer,
and Aton came, and there came Berenger,   795
and Astor came, and Anseïs, fierce and proud,
and the old man Gerard of Roussillon,
and Gaifier, that great and mighty duke.
Said the Archbishop: "I'm going, by my head!"
"And I with you," said Gautier the Count,   800
"I am Count Roland's man and must not fail him."
And together they choose twenty thousand men. AOI.

65

Roland the Count summons Gautier de l'Hum:
"Now take a thousand Franks from our land, France,
and occupy those passes and the heights there.   805
The Emperor must not lose a single man." AOI.
Gautier replies: "Lord, I'll fight well for you."
And with a thousand French of France, their land,
Gautier rides out to the hills and defiles;
will not come down, for all the bad news, again,   810
till seven hundred swords have been drawn out.
King Almaris of the Kingdom of Belferne
gave them battle that day, and it was bitter.

66

High are the hills, the valleys tenebrous,
the cliffs are dark, the defiles mysterious.   815
That day, and with much pain, the French passed through.
For fifteen leagues around one heard their clamor.
When they reach Tere Majur, the Land of Fathers,
they beheld Gascony, their lord's domain.
Then they remembered: their fiefs, their realms, their honors,   820
remembered their young girls, their gentle wives:
not one who does not weep for what he feels.
Beyond these others King Charles is in bad straits:

his nephew left in the defiles of Spain!
feels the pity of it; tears break through. AOI.   825

67

And the Twelve Peers are left behind in Spain,
and twenty thousand Franks are left with them.
They have no fear, they have no dread of death.
The Emperor is going home to France.
Beneath his cloak, his face shows all he feels.   830
Naimon the Duke is riding beside him;
and he said to the King: "What is this grief?"
And Charles replies: "Whoever asks me, wrongs me.
I feel such pain, I cannot keep from wailing.
France will be destroyed by Ganelon.   835
Last night I saw a vision brought by angels:
the one who named my nephew for the rear-guard
shattered the lance between my fists to pieces.
I have left him in a march among strangers.
If I lose him, God! I won't find his like." AOI.   840

68

King Charles the Great cannot keep from weeping.
A hundred thousand Franks feel pity for him;
and for Roland, an amazing fear.
Ganelon the criminal has betrayed him;
got gifts for it from the pagan king,   845
gold and silver, cloths of silk, gold brocade,
mules and horses and camels and lions.
Marsilion sends for the barons of Spain,
counts and viscounts and dukes and almaçurs,
and the emirs,³ and the sons of great lords: 850
four hundred thousand assembled in three days.
In Saragossa he has them beat the drums,
they raise Mahumet upon the highest tower:
no pagan now who does not worship him
and adore him. Then they ride, racing each other,   855
search through the land, the valleys, the mountains;
and then they saw the banners of the French.
The rear-guard of the Twelve Companions
will not fail now, they'll give the pagans battle.

69

Marsilion's nephew has come forward   860
riding a mule that he goads with a stick;
said—a warrior's laugh on him—to his uncle:
"Dear Lord and King, how long I have served you,
and all the troubles, the pains I have endured,
so many battles fought and won on the field   865
Give me a fief, the first blow at Roland.
I will kill him, here's the spear I'll do it with.

3. All lords of high rank.

If Mahumet will only stand by me,
I will set free every strip of land in Spain,
from the passes of Aspre to Durestant.   870
Charles will be weary, his Franks will give it up:
and no more war for the rest of your life!"
King Marsilion gave him his glove, as sign. AOI.

70

The King's nephew holds the glove in his fist,
speaks these proud words to Marsilion his uncle: 875
"You've given me, dear Lord, King, a great gift!
Choose me twelve men, twelve of your noble barons,
and I will fight against the Twelve Companions."
And Falsaron was the first to respond—
he was the brother of King Marsilion: 880
"Dear Lord, Nephew, it's you and I together!
We'll fight, that's sure! We'll battle the rear-guard
of Charlemagne's grand army! We are the ones!
We have been chosen. We'll kill them all! It is fated." AOI.

71

And now again: there comes King Corsablis,   885
a Berber, a bad man, a man of cunning;
and now he spoke as a brave vassal speaks:
for all God's gold he would not be a coward.
Now rushing up: Malprimis de Brigal,
faster on his two feet than any horse;   890
and cries great-voiced before Marsilion:
"I'm on my way to Rencesvals to fight!
Let me find Roland, I won't stop till I kill him!"

[Lines 894–993 continue the roll call of volunteers.]

79

They arm themselves in Saracen hauberks,
all but a few are lined with triple mail;   995
they lace on their good helms of Saragossa,
gird on their swords, the steel forged in Vienne;
they have rich shields, spears of Valencia,
and gonfanons of white and blue and red.
They leave the mules and riding horses now,   1000
mount their war horses and ride in close array.
The day was fair, the sun was shining bright,
all their armor was aflame with the light;
a thousand trumpets blow: that was to make it finer.
That made a great noise, and the men of France heard.   1005
Said Oliver: "Companion, I believe
we may yet have a battle with the pagans."
Roland replies: "Now may God grant us that.
We know our duty: to stand here for our King.
A man must bear some hardships for his lord,   1010
stand everything, the great heat, the great cold,

lose the hide and hair on him for his good lord.
Now let each man make sure to strike hard here:
let them not sing a bad song about us!
Pagans are wrong and Christians are right!   1015
They'll make no bad example of me this day!" AOI.

80

Oliver climbs to the top of a hill,
looks to his right, across a grassy vale,
sees the pagan army on its way there;
and called down to Roland, his companion: 1020
"That way, toward Spain: the uproar I see coming!
All their hauberks, all blazing, helmets like flames!
It will be a bitter thing for our French.
Ganelon knew, that criminal, that traitor,
when he marked us out before the Emperor."   1025
"Be still, Oliver," Roland the Count replies.
"He is my stepfather—my stepfather.
        I won't have you speak one word against him."

81

Oliver has gone up upon a hill,
sees clearly now: the kingdom of Spain,
and the Saracens assembled in such numbers: 1030
helmets blazing, bedecked with gems in gold,
those shields of theirs, those hauberks sewn with brass,
and all their spears, the gonfanons affixed;
cannot begin to count their battle corps,
there are too many, he cannot take their number.   1035
And he is deeply troubled by what he sees.
He made his way quickly down from the hill,
came to the French, told them all he had seen.

82

Said Oliver: "I saw the Saracens,
no man on earth ever saw more of them—   1040
one hundred thousand, with their shields, up in front,
helmets laced on, hauberks blazing on them,
the shafts straight up, the iron heads like flames—
you'll get a battle, nothing like it before.
My lords, my French, may God give you the strength.   1045
Hold your ground now! Let them not defeat us!"
And the French say: "God hate the man who runs!
We may die here, but no man will fail you." AOI.

83

Said Oliver: "The pagan force is great;
from what I see, our French here are too few.   1050
Roland, my companion, sound your horn then,
Charles will hear it, the army will come back."
Roland replies: "I'd be a fool to do it.
I would lose my good name all through sweet France.

I will strike now, I'll strike with Durendal,   1055
the blade will be bloody to the gold from striking!
These pagan traitors came to these passes doomed!
I promise you, they are marked men, they'll die." AOI.

84

"Roland, Companion, now sound the olifant,[4]
Charles will hear it, he will bring the army,   1060
the King will come with all his barons to help us."
Roland replies: "May it never please God
that my kin should be shamed because of me,
or that sweet France should fall into disgrace.
Never! Never! I'll strike with Durendal,   1065
I'll strike with this good sword strapped to my side,
you'll see this blade running its whole length with blood.
These pagan traitors have gathered here to die.
I promise you, they are all bound for death." AOI.

85

"Roland, Companion, sound your olifant now,   1070
Charles will hear it, marching through those passes.
I promise you, the Franks will come at once."
Roland replies: "May it never please God
that any man alive should come to say
that pagans—pagans!—once made me sound this horn: 1075
no kin of mine will ever bear that shame.
Once I enter this great battle coming
and strike my thousand seven hundred blows,
you'll see the bloody steel of Durendal.
These French are good—they will strike like brave men.   1080
Nothing can save the men of Spain from death."

86

Said Oliver: "I see no blame in it—
I watched the Saracens coming from Spain,
the valleys and mountains covered with them,
every hillside and every plain all covered,   1085
hosts and hosts everywhere of those strange men—
and here we have a little company."
Roland replies: "That whets my appetite.
May it not please God and his angels and saints
to let France lose its glory because of me—   1090
let me not end in shame, let me die first.
The Emperor loves us when we fight well."

87

Roland is good, and Oliver is wise,
both these vassals men of amazing courage:
once they are armed and mounted on their horses,   1095

---

4. A form of *elephant*, which means "ivory" or "a horn made of ivory." It is used specifically, almost as a
proper name, to denote Roland's horn, made of an elephant's tusk and adorned with gold and jewels about
the rim.

they will not run, though they die for it, from battle.
Good men, these Counts, and their words full of spirit.
Traitor pagans are riding up in fury.
Said Oliver: "Roland, look—the first ones,
on top of us—and Charles is far away.   1100
You did not think it right to sound your olifant:
if the King were here, we'd come out without losses.
Now look up there, toward the passes of Aspre—
you can see the rear-guard: it will suffer.
No man in that detail will be in another."   1105
Roland replies: "Don't speak such foolishness—
shame on the heart gone coward in the chest.
We'll hold our ground, we'll stand firm—we're the ones!
We'll fight with spears, we'll fight them hand to hand!" AOI.

88

When Roland sees that there will be a battle,   1110
it makes him fiercer than a lion or leopard;
shouts to the French, calls out to Oliver:
"Lord, companion: friend, do not say such things.
The Emperor, who left us these good French,
had set apart these twenty thousand men: 1115
he knew there was no coward in their ranks.
A man must meet great troubles for his lord,
stand up to the great heat and the great cold,
give up some flesh and blood—it is his duty.
Strike with the lance, I'll strike with Durendal—   1120
it was the King who gave me this good sword!
If I die here, the man who gets it can say:
it was a noble's, a vassal's, a good man's sword."

89

And now there comes the Archbishop Turpin.
He spurs his horse, goes up into a mountain,   1125
summons the French; and he preached them a sermon:
"Barons, my lords, Charles left us in this place.
We know our duty: to die like good men for our King.
Fight to defend the holy Christian faith.
Now you will have a battle, you know it now,   1130
you see the Saracens with your own eyes.
Confess your sins, pray to the Lord for mercy.
I will absolve you all, to save your souls.
If you die here, you will stand up holy martyrs,
you will have seats in highest Paradise."   1135
The French dismount, cast themselves on the ground;
the Archbishop blesses them in God's name.
He commands them to do one penance: strike.

90

The French arise, stand on their feet again;
they are absolved, released from all their sins: 1140
the Archbishop has blessed them in God's name.

Now they are mounted on their swift battle horses,
bearing their arms like faithful warriors;
and every man stands ready for the battle.
Roland the Count calls out to Oliver: 1145
"Lord, Companion, you knew it, you were right,
Ganelon watched for his chance to betray us,
got gold for it, got goods for it, and money.
The Emperor will have to avenge us now.
King Marsilion made a bargain for our lives,   1150
but still must pay, and that must be with swords." AOI.

91

Roland went forth into the Spanish passes
on Veillantif, his good swift-running horse.
He bears his arms—how they become this man!—
grips his lance now, hefting it, working it,   1155
now swings the iron point up toward the sky,
the gonfanon all white laced on above—
the golden streamers beat down upon his hands:
a noble's body, the face aglow and smiling.
Close behind him his good companion follows;   1160
the men of France hail him: their protector!
He looks wildly toward the Saracens,
and humbly and gently to the men of France;
and spoke a word to them, in all courtesy:
"Barons, my lords, easy now, keep at a walk.   1165
These pagans are searching for martyrdom.
We'll get good spoils before this day is over,
no king of France ever got such treasure!"
And with these words, the hosts are at each other. AOI.

92

Said Oliver: "I will waste no more words.   1170
You did not think it right to sound your olifant,
there'll be no Charles coming to your aid now.
He knows nothing, brave man, he's done no wrong;
those men down there—they have no blame in this.
Well, then, ride now, and ride with all your might!   1175
Lords, you brave men, stand your ground, hold the field!
Make up your minds, I beg you in God's name,
to strike some blows, take them and give them back!
Here we must not forget Charlemagne's war cry."
And with that word the men of France cried out.   1180
A man who heard that shout: Munjoie! Munjoie![5]
would always remember what manhood is.
Then they ride, God! Look at their pride and spirit!
and they spur hard, to ride with all their speed,
come on to strike—what else would these men do?   1185
The Saracens kept coming, never fearing them.
Franks and pagans, here they are, at each other.

---

5. For the poet's derivation of this war cry, see *laisse* 183, below.

93

Marsilion's nephew is named Aëlroth.
He rides in front, at the head of the army,
comes on shouting insults against our French: 1190
"French criminals, today you fight our men.
One man should have saved you: he betrayed you.
A fool, your King, to leave you in these passes.
This is the day sweet France will lose its name,
and Charlemagne the right arm of his body." 1195
When he hears that—God!—Roland is outraged!
He spurs his horse, gives Veillantif its head.
The Count comes on to strike with all his might,
smashes his shield, breaks his hauberk apart,
and drives: rips through his chest, shatters the bones, 1200
knocks the whole backbone out of his back,
casts out the soul of Aëlroth with his lance;
which he thrusts deep, makes the whole body shake,
throws him down dead, lance straight out,[6] from his horse;
he has broken his neck; broken it in two. 1205
There is something, he says, he must tell him:
"Clown! Nobody! Now you know Charles is no fool,
he never was the man to love treason.
It took his valor to leave us in these passes!
France will not lose its name, sweet France! today. 1210
Brave men of France, strike hard! The first blow is ours!
We're in the right, and these swine in the wrong!" AOI.

94

A duke is there whose name is Falsaron,
he was the brother of King Marsilion,
held the wild land of Dathan and Abiram;[7] 1215
under heaven, no criminal more vile;
a tremendous forehead between his eyes—
a good half-foot long, if you had measured it.
His pain is bitter to see his nephew dead;
rides out alone, baits the foe with his body, 1220
and riding shouts the war cry of the pagans,
full of hate and insults against the French:
"This is the day sweet France will lose its honor!"
Oliver hears, and it fills him with fury,
digs with his golden spurs into his horse, 1225
comes on to strike the blow a baron strikes,
smashes his shield, breaks his hauberk apart,
thrusts into him the long streamers of his gonfalon,
knocks him down, dead, lance straight out, from the saddle;
looks to the ground and sees the swine stretched out, 1230
and spoke these words—proud words, terrible words:
"You nobody, what are your threats to me!

---

6. The lance is held, not thrown, and used to knock the enemy from his horse. To throw one's weapons is savage and ignoble. See *laisses* 154 and 160 and the outlandish names of the things the pagans throw at Roland, Gautier, and Turpin.   7. See Numbers 16.1–35.

Men of France, strike! Strike and we will beat them!"
Munjoie! he shouts—the war cry of King Charles. AOI.

95

A king is there whose name is Corsablis,   1235
a Berber, come from that far country.
He spoke these words to all his Saracens:
"Now here's one battle we'll have no trouble with,
look at that little troop of Frenchmen there,
a few odd men—they're not worth noticing!   1240
King Charles won't save a single one of them.
Their day has come, they must all die today."
And Archbishop Turpin heard every word:
no man on earth he wants so much to hate!
digs with spurs of fine gold into his horse,   1245
comes on to strike with all his awful might;
smashed through his shield, burst the rings of his hauberk,
sent his great lance into the body's center,
drove it in deep, he made the dead man shake,
knocked him down, dead, lance straight out, on the road;   1250
looks to the ground and sees the swine stretched out;
there is something, he says, he must tell him:
"You pagan! You nobody! You told lies there:
King Charles my lord is our safeguard forever!
Our men of France have no heart for running.   1255
As for your companions—we'll nail them to the ground;
and then you must all die the second death.[8]
At them, you French! No man forget what he is!
Thanks be to God, now the first blow is ours";
and shouts Munjoie! Munjoie! to hold the field.   1260

[Lines 1261–1319 narrate a series of single combats, many of them quite similar.]

104

The battle is fearful and wonderful   1320
and everywhere. Roland never spares himself,
strikes with his lance as long as the wood lasts:
the fifteenth blow he struck, it broke, was lost.
Then he draws Durendal, his good sword, bare,
and spurs his horse, comes on to strike Chernuble,   1325
smashes his helmet, carbuncles shed their light,
cuts through the coif, through the hair on his head,
cut through his eyes, through his face, through that look,
the bright, shining hauberk with its fine rings,
down through the trunk to the fork of his legs,   1330
through the saddle, adorned with beaten gold,
into the horse; and the sword came to rest:
cut through the spine, never felt for the joint;
knocks him down, dead, on the rich grass of the meadow;
then said to him: "You were doomed when you started,   1335

8. The death of the soul, eternal damnation (see Revelation 20.14 and 21.8).

Clown! Nobody! Let Mahum help you now.
No pagan swine will win this field today."

105

Roland the Count comes riding through the field,
holds Durendal, that sword! it carves its way!
and brings terrible slaughter down on the pagans.   1340
To have seen him cast one man dead on another,
the bright red blood pouring out on the ground,
his hauberk, his two arms, running with blood,
his good horse—neck and shoulders running with blood!
And Oliver does not linger, he strikes!   1345
and the Twelve Peers, no man could reproach them;
and the brave French, they fight with lance and sword.
The pagans die, some simply faint away!
Said the Archbishop: "Bless our band of brave men!"
Munjoie! he shouts—the war cry of King Charles. AOI.   1350

106

Oliver rides into that battle-storm,
his lance is broken, he holds only the stump;
comes on to strike a pagan, Malsarun;
and he smashes his shield, all flowers and gold,
sends his two eyes flying out of his head,   1355
and his brains come pouring down to his feet;
casts him down, dead, with seven hundred others.
Now he has killed Turgis and Esturguz,
and the shaft bursts, shivers down to his fists.
Count Roland said: "Companion, what are you doing?   1360
Why bother with a stick in such a battle?
Iron and steel will do much better work!
Where is your sword, your Halteclere—that name!
Where is that crystal hilt, that golden guard?"
"Haven't had any time to draw it out,   1365
been so busy fighting," said Oliver. AOI.

107

Lord Oliver has drawn out his good sword—
that sword his companion had longed to see—
and showed him how a good man uses it:
strikes a pagan, Justin of Val Ferrée,   1370
and comes down through his head, cuts through the center,
through his body, his hauberk sewn with brass,
the good saddle beset with gems in gold,
into the horse, the backbone cut in two;
knocks him down, dead, before him on the meadow.   1375
Count Roland said: "Now I know it's you, Brother.
The Emperor loves us for blows like that."
Munjoie! that cry! goes up on every side. AOI.

108

Gerin the Count sits on his bay Sorél
and Gerer his companion on Passe-Cerf;   1380

and they ride, spurring hard, let loose their reins,
come on to strike a pagan, Timozel,
one on his shield, the other on his hauberk.
They broke their two lances in his body;
turn him over, dead, in a fallow field.   1385
I do not know and have never heard tell
which of these two was swifter, though both were swift.
Esperveris: he was the son of Borel
and now struck dead by Engeler of Bordeaux.
Turpin the Archbishop killed Siglorel,   1390
the enchanter, who had been in Hell before:
Jupiter brought him there, with that strange magic.
Then Turpin said: "That swine owed us his life!
Roland replies: "And now the scoundrel's dead.
Oliver, Brother, those were blows! I approve!"   1395

109

In the meantime, the fighting grew bitter.
Franks and pagans, the fearful blows they strike—
those who attack, those who defend themselves;
so many lances broken, running with blood,
the gonfanons in shreds, the ensigns torn,   1400
so many good French fallen, their young lives lost:
they will not see their mothers or wives again,
or the men of France who wait for them at the passes. AOI.
Charlemagne waits and weeps and wails for them.
What does that matter? They'll get no help from him.   1405
Ganelon served him ill that day he sold,
in Saragossa, the barons of his house.
He lost his life and limbs for what he did:
was doomed to hang in the great trial at Aix,
and thirty of his kin were doomed with him,   1410
who never expected to die that death. AOI.

110

The battle is fearful and full of grief.
Oliver and Roland strike like good men,
the Archbishop, more than a thousand blows,
and the Twelve Peers do not hang back, they strike!   1415
the French fight side by side, all as one man.
The pagans die by hundreds, by thousands:
whoever does not flee finds no refuge from death,
like it or not, there he ends all his days.
And there the men of France lose their greatest arms;   1420
they will not see their fathers, their kin again,
or Charlemagne, who looks for them in the passes.
Tremendous torment now comes forth in France,
a mighty whirlwind, tempests of wind and thunder,
rains and hailstones, great and immeasurable,   1425
bolts of lightning hurtling and hurtling down:
it is, in truth, a trembling of the earth.
From Saint Michael-in-Peril to the Saints,
from Besançon to the port of Wissant,

there is no house whose veil of walls does not crumble.   1430
A great darkness at noon falls on the land,
there is no light but when the heavens crack.
No man sees this who is not terrified,
and many say: "The Last Day! Judgment Day!
The end! The end of the world is upon us!"   1435
They do not know, they do not speak the truth:
it is the worldwide grief for the death of Roland.

111

The French have fought with all their hearts and strength,
pagans are dead by the thousands, in droves:
of one hundred thousand, not two are saved.   1440
Said the Archbishop: "Our men! What valiant fighters!
No king under heaven could have better.
It is written in the Gesta Francorum:[9]
our Emperor's vassals were all good men."
They walk over the field to seek their dead,   1445
they weep, tears fill their eyes, in grief and pity
for their kindred, with love, with all their hearts.
Marsilion the King, with all his men
        in that great host, rises up before them. AOI.

112

King Marsilion comes along a valley
with all his men, the great host he assembled: 1450
twenty divisions, formed and numbered by the King,
helmets ablaze with gems beset in gold,
and those bright shields, those hauberks sewn with brass.
Seven thousand clarions sound the pursuit,
and the great noise resounds across that country.   1455
Said Roland then: "Oliver, Companion, Brother,
that traitor Ganelon has sworn our deaths:
it is treason, it cannot stay hidden,
the Emperor will take his terrible revenge.
We have this battle now, it will be bitter,   1460
no man has ever seen the like of it.
I will fight here with Durendal, this sword,
and you, my companion, with Halteclere—
we've fought with them before, in many lands!
how many battles have we won with these two!   1465
Let no one sing a bad song of our swords." AOI.

113

When the French see the pagans so numerous,
the fields swarming with them on every side,
they call the names of Oliver, and Roland,
and the Twelve Peers: protect them, be their warranter.   1470
The Archbishop told them how he saw things:

---

9. The Deeds of the French (Latin), title of an account of these events that has not survived.

"Barons, my lords, do not think shameful thoughts,
do not, I beg you all in God's name, run.
Let no brave man sing shameful songs of us:
let us all die here fighting: that is far better.   1475
We are promised: we shall soon find our deaths,
after today we won't be living here.
But here's one thing, and I am your witness:
Holy Paradise lies open to you,
you will take seats among the Innocents."[1]   1480
And with these words the Franks are filled with joy,
there is no man who does not shout Munjoie! AOI.

114

A Saracen was there of Saragossa,
half that city was in this pagan's keeping,
this Climborin, who fled before no man,   1485
who took the word of Ganelon the Count,
kissed in friendship the mouth that spoke that word,
gave him a gift: his helmet and its carbuncle.
Now he will shame, says he, the Land of Fathers,
he will tear off the crown of the Emperor;   1490
sits on the horse that he calls Barbamusche,
swifter than the sparrowhawk, than the swallow;
digs in his spurs, gives that war horse its head,
comes on to strike Engeler of Gascony,
whose shield and fine hauberk cannot save him;   1495
gets the head of his spear into his body,
drives it in deep, gets all the iron through,
throws him back, dead, lance straight out, on the field.
And then he cries: "It's good to kill these swine!
At them, Pagans! At them and break their ranks!"   1500
"God!" say the French, "the loss of that good man!" AOI.

115

Roland the Count calls out to Oliver:
"Lord, Companion, there is Engeler dead,
we never had a braver man on horse."
The Count replies: "God let me avenge him";   1505
and digs with golden spurs into his horse,
grips—the steel running with blood—Halteclere,
comes on to strike with all his mighty power:
the blow comes flashing down; the pagan falls.
Devils take away the soul of Climborin.   1510
And then he killed Alphaïen the duke,
cut off the head of Escababi,
struck from their horses seven great Arrabites:
they'll be no use for fighting any more!
And Roland said: "My companion is enraged!   1515
Why, he compares with me! he earns his praise!

1. The infants slain by King Herod (see Matthew 2.16).

Fighting like that makes us dearer to Charles";
lifts up his voice and shouts: "Strike! you are warriors!" AOI.

[Lines 1519–1627 narrate another series of single combats.]

125

Marsilion sees his people's martyrdom.
He commands them: sound his horns and trumpets;
and he rides now with the great host he has gathered.   1630
At their head rides the Saracen Abisme:
no worse criminal rides in that company,
stained with the marks of his crimes and great treasons,
lacking the faith in God, Saint Mary's son.
And he is black, as black as melted pitch,   1635
a man who loves murder and treason more
than all the gold of rich Galicia,
no living man ever saw him play or laugh;
a great fighter, a wild man, mad with pride,
and therefore dear to that criminal king;   1640
holds high his dragon,[2] where all his people gather.
The Archbishop will never love that man,
no sooner saw than wanted to strike him;
considered quietly, said to himself:
"That Saracen—a heretic, I'll wager.   1645
Now let me die if I do not kill him—
I never loved cowards or cowards' ways." AOI.

126

Turpin the Archbishop begins the battle.
He rides the horse that he took from Grossaille,
who was a king this priest once killed in Denmark.   1650
Now this war horse is quick and spirited,
his hooves high-arched, the quick legs long and flat,
short in the thigh, wide in the rump, long in the flanks,
and the backbone so high, a battle horse!
and that white tail, the yellow mane on him,   1655
the little ears on him, the tawny head!
No beast on earth could ever run with him.
The Archbishop—that valiant man!—spurs hard,
he will attack Abisme, he will not falter,
strikes on his shield, a miraculous blow: 1660
a shield of stones, of amethysts, topazes,
esterminals,[3] carbuncles all on fire—
a gift from a devil, in Val Metas,
sent on to him by the Amiral Galafre.
There Turpin strikes, he does not treat it gently—   1665
after that blow, I'd not give one cent for it;
cut through his body, from one side to the other,
and casts him down dead in a barren place.

---

2. Banner.   3. Precious ornaments.

And the French say: "A fighter, that Archbishop!
Look at him there, saving souls with that crozier!"   1670

127

Roland the Count calls out to Oliver:
"Lord, Companion, now you have to agree
the Archbishop is a good man on horse,
there's none better on earth or under heaven,
he knows his way with a lance and a spear."   1675
The Count replies: "Right! Let us help him then."
And with these words the Franks began anew,
the blows strike hard, and the fighting is bitter;
there is a painful loss of Christian men.
To have seen them, Roland and Oliver,   1680
these fighting men, striking down with their swords,
the Archbishop with them, striking with his lance!
One can recount the number these three killed:
it is written—in charters, in documents;
the Geste tells it: it was more than four thousand.   1685
Through four assaults all went well with our men;
then comes the fifth, and that one crushes them.
They are all killed, all these warriors of France,
all but sixty, whom the Lord God has spared:
they will die too, but first sell themselves dear. AOI.   1690

128

Count Roland sees the great loss of his men,
calls on his companion, on Oliver:
"Lord, Companion, in God's name, what would you do?
All these good men you see stretched on the ground.
We can mourn for sweet France, fair land of France!   1695
a desert now, stripped of such great vassals.
Oh King, and friend, if only you were here!
Oliver, Brother, how shall we manage it?
What shall we do to get word to the King?"
Said Oliver: "I don't see any way.   1700
I would rather die now than hear us shamed." AOI.

129

And Roland said: "I'll sound the olifant,
Charles will hear it, drawing through the passes,
I promise you, the Franks will return at once."
Said Oliver: "That would be a great disgrace,   1705
a dishonor and reproach to all your kin,
the shame of it would last them all their lives.
When I urged it, you would not hear of it;
you will not do it now with my consent.
It is not acting bravely to sound it now—   1710
look at your arms, they are covered with blood."
The Count replies: "I've fought here like a lord."[4] AOI.

4. Some have found lines 1710–12 difficult. Oliver means, "We have fought this far—look at the enemy's blood on your arms: It is too late, it would be a disgrace to summon help when there is no longer any chance of being saved." But Roland thinks that that is the one time when it is not a disgrace.

130

And Roland says: "We are in a rough battle.
I'll sound the olifant, Charles will hear it."
Said Oliver: "No good vassal would do it.   1715
When I urged it, friend, you did not think it right.
If Charles were here, we'd come out with no losses.
Those men down there—no blame can fall on them."
Oliver said: "Now by this beard of mine,
If I can see my noble sister, Aude,   1720
once more, you will never lie in her arms!"[5] AOI.

131

And Roland said: "Why are you angry at me?"
Oliver answers: "Companion, it is your doing.
I will tell you what makes a vassal good:
    it is judgment, it is never madness;
restraint is worth more than the raw nerve of a fool.   1725
Frenchmen are dead because of your wildness.
And what service will Charles ever have from us?
If you had trusted me, my lord would be here,
we would have fought this battle through to the end,
Marsilion would be dead, or our prisoner.   1730
Roland, your prowess—had we never seen it!
    And now, dear friend, we've seen the last of it.
No more aid from us now for Charlemagne,
a man without equal till Judgment Day,
you will die here, and your death will shame France.
We kept faith, you and I, we were companions;
    and everything we were will end today.   1735
We part before evening, and it will be hard." AOI.

132

Turpin the Archbishop hears their bitter words,
digs hard into his horse with golden spurs
and rides to them; begins to set them right:
"You, Lord Roland, and you, Lord Oliver,   1740
I beg you in God's name do not quarrel.
To sound the horn could not help us now, true,
but still it is far better that you do it:
let the King come, he can avenge us then—
these men of Spain must not go home exulting!   1745
Our French will come, they'll get down on their feet,
and find us here—we'll be dead, cut to pieces.
They will lift us into coffins on the backs of mules,
and weep for us, in rage and pain and grief,
and bury us in the courts of churches;   1750
and we will not be eaten by wolves or pigs or dogs."
Roland replies, "Lord, you have spoken well." AOI.

---

5. Aude had been betrothed to Roland.

133

Roland has put the olifant to his mouth,
he sets it well, sounds it with all his strength.
The hills are high, and that voice ranges far,   1755
they heard it echo thirty great leagues away.
King Charles heard it, and all his faithful men.
And the King says: "Our men are in a battle."
And Ganelon disputed him and said:
"Had someone else said that, I'd call him liar!" AOI.   1760

134

And now the mighty effort of Roland the Count:
he sounds his olifant; his pain is great,
and from his mouth the bright blood comes leaping out,
and the temple bursts in his forehead.
That horn, in Roland's hands, has a mighty voice: 1765
King Charles hears it drawing through the passes.
Naimon heard it, the Franks listen to it.
And the King said: "I hear Count Roland's horn;
he'd never sound it unless he had a battle."
Says Ganelon: "Now no more talk of battles!   1770
You are old now, your hair is white as snow,
the things you say make you sound like a child.
You know Roland and that wild pride of his—
what a wonder God has suffered it so long!
Remember? he took Noples without your command: 1775
the Saracens rode out, to break the siege;
they fought with him, the great vassal Roland.
Afterwards he used the streams to wash the blood
from the meadows: so that nothing would show.
He blasts his horn all day to catch a rabbit,   1780
he's strutting now before his peers and bragging—
who under heaven would dare meet him on the field?
So now: ride on! Why do you keep on stopping?
The Land of Fathers lies far ahead of us." AOI.

135

The blood leaping from Count Roland's mouth,   1785
the temple broken with effort in his forehead,
he sounds his horn in great travail and pain.
King Charles heard it, and his French listen hard.
And the King said: "That horn has a long breath!"
Naimon answers: "It is a baron's breath.   1790
There is a battle there, I know there is.
He betrayed him! and now asks you to fail him!
Put on your armor! Lord, shout your battle cry,
and save the noble barons of your house!
You hear Roland's call. He is in trouble."   1795

136

The Emperor commanded the horns to sound,
the French dismount, and they put on their armor:
their hauberks, their helmets, their gold-dressed swords,
their handsome shields; and take up their great lances,
the gonfalons of white and red and blue.   1800
The barons of that host mount their war horses
and spur them hard the whole length of the pass;
and every man of them says to the other:
"If only we find Roland before he's killed,
we'll stand with him, and then we'll do some fighting!"   1805
What does it matter what they say? They are too late.

137

It is the end of day, and full of light,
arms and armor are ablaze in the sun,
and fire flashes from hauberks and helmets,
and from those shields, painted fair with flowers,   1810
and from those lances, those gold-dressed gonfanons.
The Emperor rides on in rage and sorrow,
the men of France indignant and full of grief.
There is no man of them who does not weep,
they are in fear for the life of Roland.   1815
The King commands: seize Ganelon the Count!
and gave him over to the cooks of his house;
summons the master cook, their chief, Besgun:
"Guard him for me like the traitor he is:
he has betrayed the barons of my house."   1820
Besgun takes him, sets his kitchen comrades,
a hundred men, the best, the worst, on him;
and they tear out his beard and his mustache,
each one strikes him four good blows with his fist;
and they lay into him with cudgels and sticks,   1825
put an iron collar around his neck
and chain him up, as they would chain a bear;
dumped him, in dishonor, on a packhorse,
and guard him well till they give him back to Charles.

138

High are the hills, and tenebrous, and vast, AOI.   1830
the valleys deep, the raging waters swift;
to the rear, to the front, the trumpets sound:
they answer the lone voice of the olifant.
The Emperor rides on, rides on in fury,
the men of France in grief and indignation.   1835
There is no man who does not weep and wail,
and they pray God: protect the life of Roland
till they come, one great host, into the field
and fight at Roland's side like true men all.
What does it matter what they pray? It does no good.   1840
They are too late, they cannot come in time. AOI.

139

King Charles the Great rides on, a man in wrath,
his great white beard spread out upon his hauberk.[6]
All the barons of France ride spurring hard,
there is no man who does not wail, furious   1845
not to be with Roland, the captain count,
who stands and fights the Saracens of Spain,
so set upon, I cannot think his soul abides.
God! those sixty men who stand with him, what men!
No king, no captain ever stood with better. AOI.   1850

140

Roland looks up on the mountains and slopes,
sees the French dead, so many good men fallen,
and weeps for them, as a great warrior weeps:
"Barons, my lords, may God give you his grace,
may he grant Paradise to all your souls,   1855
make them lie down among the holy flowers.
I never saw better vassals than you.
All the years you've served me, and all the times,
the mighty lands you conquered for Charles our King!
The Emperor raised you for this terrible hour!   1860
Land of France, how sweet you are, native land,
laid waste this day, ravaged, made a desert.
Barons of France, I see you die for me,
and I, your lord—I cannot protect you.
May *God* come to your aid, that God who never failed.   1865
Oliver, brother, now I will not fail *you*.
I will die here—of grief, if no man kills me.
Lord, Companion, let us return and fight."

141

Roland returned to his place on the field,
strikes—a brave man keeping faith—with Durendal,   1870
struck through Faldrun de Pui, cut him to pieces,
and twenty-four of the men they valued most;
no man will ever want his vengeance more!
As when the deer turns tail before the dogs,
so the pagans flee before Roland the Count.   1875
Said the Archbishop: "You! Roland! What a fighter!
Now that's what every knight must have in him
who carries arms and rides on a fine horse:
he must be strong, a savage, when he's in battle;
for otherwise, what's he worth? Not four cents!   1880
Let that four-cent man be a monk in some minster,
and he can pray all day long for our sins."
Roland replies: "Attack, do not spare them!"
And with that word the Franks began again.
There was a heavy loss of Christian men.   1885

---

6. A gesture of defiance toward the enemy.

142

When a man knows there'll be no prisoners,
what will that man not do to defend himself!
And so the Franks fight with the fury of lions.
Now Marsilion, the image of a baron,
mounted on that war horse he calls Gaignun,   1890
digs in his spurs, comes on to strike Bevon,
who was the lord of Beaune and of Dijon;
smashes his shield, rips apart his hauberk,
knocks him down, dead, no need to wound him more.
And then he killed Yvorie and Yvon,   1895
and more: he killed Gerard of Rousillon.
Roland the Count is not far away now,
said to the pagan: "The Lord God's curse on you!
You kill my companions, how you wrong me!
You'll feel the pain of it before we part,   1900
you will learn my sword's name by heart today";
comes on to strike—the image of a baron.
He has cut off Marsilion's right fist;
now takes the head of Jurfaleu the blond—
the head of Jurfaleu! Marsilion's son.   1905
The pagans cry: "Help, Mahumet! Help us!
Vengeance, our gods, on Charles! the man who set
these criminals on us in our own land,
they will not quit the field, they'll stand and die!"
And one said to the other: "Let *us* run then."   1910
And with that word, some hundred thousand flee.
Now try to call them back: they won't return. AOI.

143

What does it matter? If Marsilion has fled,
his uncle has remained: the Algalife,[7]
who holds Carthage, Alfrere, and Garmalie,   1915
and Ethiopia: a land accursed;
holds its immense black race under his power,
the huge noses, the enormous ears on them;
and they number more than fifty thousand.
These are the men who come riding in fury,   1920
and now they shout that pagan battle cry.
And Roland said: "Here comes our martyrdom;
I see it now: we have not long to live.
But let the world call any man a traitor
    who does not make them pay before he dies!
My lords, attack! Use those bright shining swords!   1925
Fight a good fight for your deaths and your lives,
let no shame touch sweet France because of us!
When Charles my lord comes to this battlefield
and sees how well we punished these Saracens,
finds fifteen of their dead for one of ours,   1930
I'll tell you what he will do: he will bless us." AOI.

---

7. The Caliph, Marsilion's uncle, whom Ganelon lied about to Charlemagne (see lines 680–91).

144

When Roland sees that unbelieving race,
those hordes and hordes blacker than blackest ink—
no shred of white on them except their teeth—
then said the Count: "I see it clearly now,   1935
we die today: it is there before us.
Men of France, strike! I will start it once more."
Said Oliver: "God curse the slowest man."
And with that word, the French strike into battle.

145

The Saracens, when they saw these few French,   1940
looked at each other, took courage, and presumed,
telling themselves: "The Emperor is wrong!"
The Algalife rides a great sorrel horse,
digs into it with his spurs of fine gold,
strikes Oliver, from behind, in the back,   1945
shattered the white hauberk upon his flesh,
drove his spear through the middle of his chest;
and speaks to him: "Now you feel you've been struck!
Your great Charles doomed you when he left you in this pass.
That man wronged us, he must not boast of it.   1950
I've avenged all our dead in you alone!"

146

Oliver feels: he has been struck to death;
grips Halteclere, that steel blade shining, strikes
on the gold-dressed pointed helm of the Algalife,
sends jewels and flowers crackling down to the earth,   1955
into the head, into the little teeth;
draws up his flashing sword, casts him down, dead,
and then he says: "Pagan, a curse on you!
If only I could say Charles has lost nothing—
but no woman, no lady you ever knew   1960
will hear you boast, in the land you came from,
that you could take one thing worth a cent from me,
or do me harm, or do any man harm";
then cries out to Roland to come to his aid. AOI.

147

Oliver feels he is wounded to death,   1965
will never have his fill of vengeance, strikes,
as a baron strikes, where they are thickest,
cuts through their lances, cuts through those buckled shields,
through feet, through fists, through saddles, and through flanks.
Had you seen him, cutting the pagans limb   1970
from limb, casting one corpse down on another,
you would remember a brave man keeping faith.
Never would he forget Charles' battle-cry,
Munjoie! he shouts, that mighty voice ringing;
calls to Roland, to his friend and his peer: 1975

"Lord, Companion, come stand beside me now.
We must part from each other in pain today." AOI.

148

Roland looks hard into Oliver's face,
it is ashen, all its color is gone,
the bright red blood streams down upon his body,   1980
Oliver's blood spattering on the earth.
"God!" said the Count, "I don't know what to do,
Lord, Companion, your fight is finished now.
There'll never be a man the like of you.
Sweet land of France, today you will be stripped   1985
of good vassals, laid low, a fallen land!
The Emperor will suffer the great loss";
faints with that word, mounted upon his horse. AOI.

149

Here is Roland, lords, fainted on his horse,
and Oliver the Count, wounded to death: 1990
he has lost so much blood, his eyes are darkened—
he cannot see, near or far, well enough
to recognize a friend or enemy:
struck when he came upon his companion,
strikes on his helm, adorned with gems in gold,   1995
cuts down straight through, from the point to the nasal,[8]
but never harmed him, he never touched his head.
Under this blow, Count Roland looked at him;
and gently, softly now, he asks of him:
"Lord, Companion, do you mean to do this?   2000
It is Roland, who always loved you greatly.
You never declared that we were enemies."
Said Oliver: "Now I hear it is you—
I don't see you, may the Lord God see you.
Was it you that I struck? Forgive me then."   2005
Roland replies: "I am not harmed, not harmed,
I forgive you, Friend, here and before God."
And with that word, each bowed to the other.
And this is the love, lords, in which they parted.

150

Oliver feels: death pressing hard on him;   2010
his two eyes turn, roll up into his head,
all hearing is lost now, all sight is gone;
gets down on foot, stretches out on the ground,
cries out now and again: *mea culpa!*[9]
his two hands joined, raised aloft toward heaven,   2015
he prays to God: grant him His Paradise;
and blesses Charles, and the sweet land of France,
his companion, Roland, above all men.

---

8. The nosepiece protruding down from the cone-shaped helmet.   9. My guilt (Latin); a formula used in the confession of one's sins.

The heart fails him, his helmet falls away,
the great body settles upon the earth.   2020
The Count is dead, he stands with us no longer.
Roland, brave man, weeps for him, mourns for him,
you will not hear a man of greater sorrow.

151

Roland the Count, when he sees his friend dead,
lying stretched out, his face against the earth,   2025
softly, gently, begins to speak the regret:[1]
"Lord, Companion, you were brave and died for it.
We have stood side by side through days and years,
you never caused me harm, I never wronged you;
when you are dead, to be alive pains me."   2030
And with that word the lord of marches faints
upon his horse, which he calls Veillantif.
He is held firm by his spurs of fine gold,
whichever way he leans, he cannot fall.

152

Before Roland could recover his senses   2035
and come out of his faint, and be aware,
a great disaster had come forth before him:
the French are dead, he has lost every man
except the Archbishop, and Gautier de l'Hum,
who has come back, down from that high mountain: 2040
he has fought well, he fought those men of Spain.
His men are dead, the pagans finished them;
flees now down to these valleys, he has no choice,
and calls on Count Roland to come to his aid:
"My noble Count, my brave lord, where are you?   2045
I never feared whenever you were there.
It is Walter: I conquered Maëlgut,
my uncle is Droün, old and gray: your Walter
and always dear to you for the way I fought;
and I have fought this time: my lance is shattered,   2050
my good shield pierced, my hauberk's meshes broken;
and I am wounded, a lance struck through my body.
I will die soon, but I sold myself dear."
And with that word, Count Roland has heard him,
he spurs his horse, rides spurring to his man. AOI.   2055

153

Roland in pain, maddened with grief and rage:
rushes where they are thickest and strikes again,
strikes twenty men of Spain, strikes twenty dead,
and Walter six, and the Archbishop five.
The pagans say: "Look at those criminals!   2060
Now take care, Lords, they don't get out alive,

---

1. What follows is a formal and customary lament for the dead.

only a traitor will not attack them now!
Only a coward will let them save their skins!"
And then they raise their hue and cry once more,
rush in on them, once more, from every side. AOI.   2065

154

Count Roland was always a noble warrior,
Gautier de l'Hum is a fine mounted man,
the Archbishop, a good man tried and proved:
not one of them will ever leave the others;
strike, where they are thickest, at the pagans.   2070
A thousand Saracens get down on foot,
and forty thousand more are on their mounts:
and I tell you, not one will dare come close,
they throw, and from afar, lances and spears,
wigars and darts, mizraks, javelins, pikes.   2075
With the first blows they killed Gautier de l'Hum
and struck Turpin of Reims, pierced through his shield,
broke the helmet on him, wounded his head;
ripped his hauberk, shattered its rings of mail,
and pierced him with four spears in his body,   2080
the war horse killed under him; and now there comes
great pain and rage when the Archbishop falls. AOI.

155

Turpin of Reims, when he feels he is unhorsed,
struck to the earth with four spears in his body,
quickly, brave man, leaps to his feet again;   2085
his eyes find Roland now, he runs to him
and says one word: "See! I'm not finished yet!
What good vassal ever gives up alive!";
and draws Almace, his sword, that shining steel!
and strikes, where they are thickest, a thousand blows, and more.   2090
Later, Charles said: Turpin had spared no one;
he found four hundred men prostrate around him,
some of them wounded, some pierced from front to back,
some with their heads hacked off. So says the Geste,
and so says one who was there, on that field,   2095
the baron Saint Gilles,[2] for whom God performs miracles,
who made the charter setting forth these great things
        in the Church of Laon. Now any man
who does not know this much understands nothing.

156

Roland the Count fights well and with great skill,
but he is hot, his body soaked with sweat;   2100
has a great wound in his head, and much pain,
his temple broken because he blew the horn.
But he must know whether King Charles will come;

---

2. St. Gilles of Provence. These lines explain how the story of Rencesvals could be told after all who had
fought there died.

draws out the olifant, sounds it, so feebly.
The Emperor drew to a halt, listened.   2105
"Seigneurs," he said, "it goes badly for us—
My nephew Roland falls from our ranks today.
I hear it in the horn's voice: he hasn't long.
Let every man who wants to be with Roland
ride fast! Sound trumpets! Every trumpet in this host!"   2110
Sixty thousand, on these words, sound, so high
the mountains sound, and the valleys resound.
The pagans hear: it is no joke to them;
cry to each other: "We're getting Charles on us!"

157

The pagans say: "The Emperor is coming, AOI.   2115
listen to their trumpets—it is the French!
If Charles comes back, it's all over for us,
if Roland lives, this war begins again
and we have lost our land, we have lost Spain."
Some four hundred, helmets laced on, assemble,   2120
some of the best, as they think, on that field.
They storm Roland, in one fierce, bitter attack.
And now Count Roland has some work on his hands. AOI.

158

Roland the Count, when he sees them coming,
how strong and fierce and alert he becomes!   2125
He will not yield to them, not while he lives.
He rides the horse they call Veillantif, spurs,
digs into it with his spurs of fine gold,
and rushes at them all where they are thickest,
the Archbishop—that Turpin!—at his side.   2130
Said one man to the other: "Go at it, friend.
The horns we heard were the horns of the French,
King Charles is coming back with all his strength."[3]

159

Roland the Count never loved a coward,
a blusterer, an evil-natured man,   2135
a man on horse who was not a good vassal.
And now he called to Archbishop Turpin:
"You are on foot, Lord, and here I am mounted,
and so, here I take my stand: for love of you.
We'll take whatever comes, the good and bad,   2140
together, Lord: no one can make me leave you.
They will learn our swords' names today in battle,
the name of Almace, the name of Durendal!"
Said the Archbishop: "Let us strike or be shamed!
Charles is returning, and he brings our revenge."   2145

---

3. The lines could be spoken either by Roland and the archbishop or by the pagans.

160

Say the pagans: "We were all born unlucky!
The evil day that dawned for us today!
We have lost our lords and peers, and now comes Charles—
that Charlemagne!—with his great host. Those trumpets!
that shrill sound on us—the trumpets of the French!   2150
And the loud roar of that Munjoie! This Roland
is a wild man, he is too great a fighter—
What man of flesh and blood can ever hope
to bring him down? Let us cast at him, and leave him there."
And so they did: arrows, wigars, darts,   2155
lances and spears, javelots dressed with feathers;
struck Roland's shield, pierced it, broke it to pieces,
ripped his hauberk, shattered its rings of mail,
but never touched his body, never his flesh.
They wounded Veillantif in thirty places,   2160
struck him dead, from afar, under the Count.
The pagans flee, they leave the field to him.
Roland the Count stood alone, on his feet. AOI.

161

The pagans flee, in bitterness and rage,
strain every nerve running headlong toward Spain,   2165
and Count Roland has no way to chase them,
he has lost Veillantif, his battle horse;
he has no choice, left alone there on foot.
He went to the aid of Archbishop Turpin,
unlaced the gold-dressed helmet, raised it from his head,   2170
lifted away his bright, light coat of mail,
cut his under tunic into some lengths,
stilled his great wounds with thrusting on the strips;
then held him in his arms, against his chest,
and laid him down, gently, on the green grass;   2175
and softly now Roland entreated him:
"My noble lord, I beg you, give me leave:
our companions, whom we have loved so dearly,
are all dead now, we must not abandon them.
I want to look for them, know them once more,   2180
and set them in ranks, side by side, before you."
Said the Archbishop: "Go then, go and come back.
The field is ours, thanks be to God, yours and mine."

162

So Roland leaves him, walks the field all alone,
seeks in the valleys, and seeks in the mountains.   2185
He found Gerin, and Gerer his companion,
and then he found Berenger and Otun,
Anseïs and Sansun, and on that field
he found Gerard the old of Roussillon;
and carried them, brave man, all, one by one,   2190
came back to the Archbishop with these French dead,
and set them down in ranks before his knees.

The Archbishop cannot keep from weeping,
raises his hand and makes his benediction;
and said: "Lords, Lords, it was your terrible hour.   2195
May the Glorious God set all your souls
among the holy flowers of Paradise!
Here is my own death, Lords, pressing on me,
I shall not see our mighty Emperor."

163

And Roland leaves, seeks in the field again;   2200
he has found Oliver, his companion,
held him tight in his arms against his chest;
came back to the Archbishop, laid Oliver
down on a shield among the other dead.
The Archbishop absolved him, signed him with the Cross.   2205
And pity now and rage and grief increase;
and Roland says: "Oliver, dear companion,
you were the son of the great duke Renier,
who held the march of the vale of Runers.
Lord, for shattering lances, for breaking shields,   2210
for making men great with presumption weak with fright,
for giving life and counsel to good men,
for striking fear in that unbelieving race,
no warrior on earth surpasses you."

164

Roland the Count, when he sees his peers dead,   2215
and Oliver, whom he had good cause to love,
felt such grief and pity, he begins to weep;
and his face lost its color with what he felt:
a pain so great he cannot keep on standing,
he has no choice, falls fainting to the ground.   2220
Said the Archbishop: "Baron, what grief for you."

165

The Archbishop, when he saw Roland faint,
felt such pain then as he had never felt;
stretched out his hand and grasped the olifant.
At Rencesvals there is a running stream: 2225
he will go there and fetch some water for Roland;
and turns that way, with small steps, staggering;
he is too weak, he cannot go ahead,
he has no strength: all the blood he has lost.
In less time than a man takes to cross a little field   2230
that great heart fails, he falls forward, falls down;
and Turpin's death comes crushing down on him.

166

Roland the Count recovers from his faint,
gets to his feet, but stands with pain and grief;
looks down the valley, looks up the mountain, sees: 2235

on the green grass, beyond his companions,
that great and noble man down on the ground,
the Archbishop, whom God sent in His name;
who confesses his sins, lifts up his eyes,
holds up his hands joined together to heaven,   2240
and prays to God: grant him that Paradise.
Turpin is dead, King Charles' good warrior.
In great battles, in beautiful sermons
he was ever a champion against the pagans.
Now God grant Turpin's soul His holy blessing. AOI.   2245

167

Roland the Count sees the Archbishop down,
sees the bowels fallen out of his body,
and the brain boiling down from his forehead.
Turpin has crossed his hands upon his chest
beneath the collarbone, those fine white hands.   2250
Roland speaks the lament, after the custom
followed in his land: aloud, with all his heart:
"My noble lord, you great and well-born warrior,
I commend you today to the God of Glory,
whom none will ever serve with a sweeter will.   2255
Since the Apostles no prophet the like of you[4]
arose to keep the faith and draw men to it.
May your soul know no suffering or want,
and behold the gate open to Paradise."

168

Now Roland feels that death is very near.   2260
His brain comes spilling out through his two ears;
prays to God for his peers: let them be called;
and for himself, to the angel Gabriel;
took the olifant: there must be no reproach!
took Durendal his sword in his other hand,   2265
and farther than a crossbow's farthest shot
he walks toward Spain, into a fallow land,
and climbs a hill: there beneath two fine trees
stand four great blocks of stone, all are of marble;
and he fell back, to earth, on the green grass,   2270
has fainted there, for death is very near.

169

High are the hills, and high, high are the trees;
there stand four blocks of stone, gleaming of marble.
Count Roland falls fainting on the green grass,
and is watched, all this time, by a Saracen: 2275
who has feigned death and lies now with the others,
has smeared blood on his face and on his body;
and quickly now gets to his feet and runs—

---

4. Cf. Deuteronomy 34.10, on the death of Moses: "And there arose not a prophet since in Israel like unto Moses, whom the Lord knew face to face."

a handsome man, strong, brave, and so crazed with pride
that he does something mad and dies for it: 2280
laid hands on Roland, and on the arms of Roland,
and cried: "Conquered! Charles's nephew conquered!
I'll carry this sword home to Arabia!"
As he draws it, the Count begins to come round.

170

Now Roland feels: *someone taking his sword!*   2285
opened his eyes, and had one word for him:
"I don't know you, you aren't one of ours";
grasps that olifant that he will never lose,
strikes on the helm beset with gems in gold,
shatters the steel, and the head, and the bones,   2290
sent his two eyes flying out of his head,
dumped him over stretched out at his feet dead;
and said: "You nobody! how could you dare
lay hands on me—rightly or wrongly: how?
Who'll hear of this and not call you a fool?   2295
Ah! the bell-mouth of the olifant is smashed,
the crystal and the gold fallen away."

171

Now Roland the Count feels: his sight is gone;
gets on his feet, draws on his final strength,
the color on his face lost now for good.   2300
Before him stands a rock; and on that dark rock
in rage and bitterness he strikes ten blows:
the steel blade grates, it will not break, it stands unmarked.
"Ah!" said the Count, "Blessed Mary, your help!
Ah Durendal, good sword, your unlucky day,   2305
for I am lost and cannot keep you in my care.
The battles I have won, fighting with you,
the mighty lands that holding you I conquered,
that Charles rules now, our King, whose beard is white!
Now you fall to another: it must not be
        a man who'd run before another man!   2310
For a long while a good vassal held you:
there'll never be the like in France's holy land."

172

Roland strikes down on that rock of Cerritania:
the steel blade grates, will not break, stands unmarked.
Now when he sees he can never break that sword,   2315
Roland speaks the lament, in his own presence:
"Ah Durendal, how beautiful and bright!
so full of light, all on fire in the sun!
King Charles was in the vales of Moriane
when God sent his angel and commanded him,   2320
from heaven, to give you to a captain count.
That great and noble King girded it on me.

And with this sword I won Anjou and Brittany,
I won Poitou, I won Le Maine for Charles,
and Normandy, that land where men are free,   2325
I won Provence and Aquitaine with this,
and Lombardy, and every field of Romagna,
I won Bavaria, and all of Flanders,
all of Poland, and Bulgaria, for Charles,
Constantinople, which pledged him loyalty,   2330
and Saxony, where he does as he wills;
and with this sword I won Scotland and Ireland,
and England, his chamber, his own domain—
the lands, the nations I conquered with this sword,
for Charles, who rules them now, whose beard is white!   2335
Now, for this sword, I am pained with grief and rage:
Let it not fall to pagans! Let me die first!
Our Father God, save France from that dishonor."

173

Roland the Count strikes down on a dark rock,
and the rock breaks, breaks more than I can tell,   2340
and the blade grates, but Durendal will not break,
the sword leaped up, rebounded toward the sky.
The Count, when he sees that sword will not be broken,
softly, in his own presence, speaks the lament:
"Ah Durendal, beautiful, and most sacred,   2345
the holy relics in this golden pommel!
Saint Peter's tooth and blood of Saint Basile,
a lock of hair of my lord Saint Denis,
and a fragment of blessed Mary's robe:
your power must not fall to the pagans,   2350
you must be served by Christian warriors.
May no coward ever come to hold you!
It was with you I conquered those great lands
that Charles has in his keeping, whose beard is white,
the Emperor's lands, that make him rich and strong."   2355

174

Now Roland feels: death coming over him,
death descending from his temples to his heart.
He came running underneath a pine tree
and there stretched out, face down, on the green grass,
lays beneath him his sword and the olifant.   2360
He turned his head toward the Saracen hosts,
and this is why: with all his heart he wants
King Charles the Great and all his men to say,
he died, that noble Count, a conqueror;
makes confession, beats his breast often, so feebly,   2365
offers his glove, for all his sins, to God. AOI.

175

Now Roland feels that his time has run out;
he lies on a steep hill, his face toward Spain;

and with one of his hands he beat his breast:
"Almighty God, *mea culpa* in thy sight,[5]   2370
forgive my sins, both the great and the small,
sins I committed from the hour I was born
until this day, in which I lie struck down."
And then he held his right glove out to God.
Angels descend from heaven and stand by him. AOI.   2375

176

Count Roland lay stretched out beneath a pine;
he turned his face toward the land of Spain,
began to remember many things now:
how many lands, brave man, he had conquered;
and he remembered: sweet France, the men of his line,   2380
remembered Charles, his lord, who fostered him:
cannot keep, remembering, from weeping, sighing;
but would not be unmindful of himself:
he confesses his sins, prays God for mercy:
"Loyal Father, you who never failed us,   2385
who resurrected Saint Lazarus from the dead,
and saved your servant Daniel from the lions:[6]
now save the soul of me from every peril
for the sins I committed while I still lived."
Then he held out his right glove to his Lord: 2390
Saint Gabriel took the glove from his hand.
He held his head bowed down upon his arm,
he is gone, his two hands joined, to his end.
Then God sent him his angel Cherubin[7]
and Saint Michael, angel of the sea's Peril;   2395
and with these two there came Saint Gabriel:
they bear Count Roland's soul to Paradise.

177

Roland is dead, God has his soul in heaven.
The Emperor rides into Rencesvals;
there is no passage there, there is no track,   2400
no empty ground, not an elle, not one foot,
that does not bear French dead or pagan dead.
King Charles cries out: "Dear Nephew, where are you?
Where is the Archbishop? Count Oliver?
Where is Gerin, his companion Gerer?   2405
Where is Otun, where is Count Berenger,
Yves and Yvoire, men I have loved so dearly?
What has become of Engeler the Gascon,
Sansun the Duke, and Anseïs, that fighter?
Where is Gerard the Old of Roussillon,   2410
and the Twelve Peers, whom I left in these passes?"
And so forth—what's the difference? No one answered.

---

5. See Psalm 51.4: "Against thee, thee only, have I sinned, and done this evil in thy sight." 6. See
Daniel 6.12–23. For the raising of Lazarus, see John 11.1–44. 7. The poet seems to have regarded this
as the name of a single angel.

"God!" said the King, "how much I must regret
I was not here when the battle began";
pulls his great beard, a man in grief and rage.   2415
His brave knights weep, their eyes are filled with tears,
twenty thousand fall fainting to the ground;
Duke Naimon feels the great pity of it.

178

There is no knight or baron on that field
who does not weep in bitterness and grief;   2420
for they all weep: for their sons, brothers, nephew,
weep for their friends, for their sworn men and lords;
the mass of them fall fainting to the ground.
Here Naimon proved a brave and useful man:
he was the first to urge the Emperor: 2425
"Look ahead there, two leagues in front of us,
you can see the dust rising on those wide roads:
the pagan host—and how many they are!
After them now! Ride! Avenge this outrage!"
"Oh! God!" said Charles, "look how far they have gotten!   2430
Lord, let me have my right, let me have honor,
they tore from me the flower of sweet France."
The King commands Gebuïn and Othon,
Thibaut of Reims and Count Milun his cousin:
"Now guard this field, the valleys, the mountains,   2435
let the dead lie, all of them, as they are,
let no lion, let no beast come near them,
let no servant, let no groom come near them,
I command you, let no man come near these dead
until God wills we come back to this field."   2440
And they reply, gently, and in great love:
"Just Emperor, dear Lord, we shall do that."
They keep with them a thousand of their knights. AOI.

179

The Emperor has his high-pitched trumpets sound,
and then he rides, brave man, with his great host.   2445
They made the men of Spain show them their heels,
and they keep after them, all as one man.
When the King sees the twilight faltering,
he gets down in a meadow on the green grass,
lies on the ground, prays to the Lord his God   2450
to make the sun stand still for him in heaven,
hold back the night, let the day linger on.
Now comes the angel[8] always sent to speak with Charles;
and the angel at once commanded him:
"Charles, ride: God knows. The light will not fail you.   2455
God knows that you have lost the flower of France.
You can take vengeance now on that criminal race."
The Emperor, on that word, mounts his horse. AOI.

---

8. Gabriel. Cf. *laisses* 185, 291, and others.

180

God made great miracles for Charlemagne,
for on that day in heaven the sun stood still.   2460
The pagans flee, the Franks keep at their heels,
catch up with them in the Vale Tenebrous,
chase them on spurring hard to Saragossa,
and always killing them, striking with fury;
cut off their paths, the widest roads away: 2465
the waters of the Ebro lie before them,
very deep, an amazing sight, and swift;
and there is no boat, no barge, no dromond, no galley.
They call on Tervagant, one of their gods.
Then they jump in, but no god is with them: 2470
those in full armor, the ones who weigh the most,
sank down, and they were many, to the bottom;
the others float downstream: the luckiest ones,
who fare best in those waters, have drunk so much,
they all drown there, struggling, it is amazing.   2475
The French cry out: "Curse the day you saw Roland!" AOI.

181

When Charlemagne sees all the pagans dead,
many struck down, the great mass of them drowned—
the immense spoils his knights win from that battle!—
the mighty King at once gets down on foot,   2480
lies on the ground, and gives thanks to the Lord.
When he stands up again, the sun has set.
Said the Emperor: "It is time to make camp.
It is late now to return to Rencesvals;
our horses are worn out, they have no strength—   2485
take off their saddles, the bridles on their heads,
let them cool down and rest in these meadows."
The Franks reply: "Yes, as you well say, Lord." AOI.

182

The Emperor commands them to make camp.
The French dismount into that wilderness;   2490
they have removed the saddles from their horses,
and the bridles, dressed in gold, from their heads,
free them to the meadows and the good grass;
and that is all the care they can give them.
Those who are weary sleep on the naked earth;   2495
and all sleep, they set no watch that night.

183

The Emperor lay down in a meadow,
puts his great spear, brave man, beside his head;
he does not wish, on this night, to disarm:
he has put on his bright, brass-sewn hauberk,   2500
laced on his helm, adorned with gems in gold,
and girded on Joiuse, there never was its like:

each day it shines with thirty different lights.
There are great things that we can say about the lance
with which Our Lord was wounded on the Cross: 2505
thanks be to God, Charles has its iron point,
he had it mounted in that sword's golden pommel.
For this honor, and for this mighty grace,
the name Joiuse was given to that sword.
Brave men of France must never forget this: 2510
from this sword's name they get their cry Munjoie!
This is why no nation can withstand them.

184

The night is clear, the moon is shining bright,
Charles lies down in grief and pain for Roland,
and for Oliver, it weighs down on him hard,   2515
for the Twelve Peers, for all the men of France
whom he left dead, covered with blood, at Rencesvals;
and cannot keep from weeping, wailing aloud,
and prays to God: lead their souls to safety.
His weariness is great, for his pain is great;   2520
he has fallen asleep, he cannot go on.
Through all the meadows now the Franks are sleeping.
There is no horse that has the strength to stand:
if one wants grass, he grazes lying down.
He has learned much who knows much suffering.   2525

185

Charlemagne sleeps, a man worn out with pain.
God sent Saint Gabriel to him that night
with this command: watch over the Emperor.
All through the night the angel stands at his head;
and in a vision he brought the King dread tidings   2530
of a great battle soon to come against him:
revealed to him its grave signification:
Charles raised his eyes and looked up to the sky,
he sees the thunder, the winds, the blasts of ice,
the hurricanes, the dreadful tempests,   2535
the fires and flames made ready in the sky.
And suddenly all things fall on his men.
Their lances burn, the wood of ash and apple,
and their shields burn down to their golden bosses,
the shafts of their sharp spears burst into pieces,   2540
then the grating of hauberks, helmets of steel.
He sees his warriors in great distress—
leopards and bears furious to devour them,
serpents, vipers, dragons, demons of hell,
swarms of griffins, thirty thousand and more,   2545
and all come swooping down upon the French;
and the French cry: "Charlemagne, come help us!"
The King is filled with rage and pain and pity,
wants to go there, but something blocks his way:
out of a wood a great lion coming at him,   2550

it is tremendous, wild, and great with pride:
seeks the King's very body, attacks the King!
and they lock arms, King and lion, to fight,
and still he cannot tell who strikes, who falls.
The Emperor sleeps, his dream does not wake him.   2555

186

And after this he was shown another vision:
he was in France, at Aix, on a stone step,
and two chains in his hands holding a bear;
from the Ardennes he saw thirty bears coming,
and each of them was speaking like a man;   2560
they said to him: "Lord, give him back to us,
you must not keep him longer, it is not right;
he is our kin, we must deliver him."
From his palace a greyhound now, running,
leaps on the greatest bear among them all,   2565
on the green grass beyond his companions,
there the King sees an amazing struggle
but cannot tell who conquers, who goes down.
These are the things God's angel showed this baron.
Charles sleeps until the morning and the bright day.   2570

[Lines 2571–3675 describe the death of Marsilion and Charlemagne's defeat of the
army of Baligant, the emir of Cairo and Marsilion's overlord.]

267

Night passes on, and the bright day appears.
Charles fortified the towers of Saragossa,
left a thousand knights there, fighting men all;
they guard the city in the Emperor's name.
Now the King mounts his horse, all his men mount,   3680
and Bramimunde, whom he leads prisoner,
though he has but one will: to do her good.
They turn toward home, in joy, in jubilation,
and pass in force, a mighty host, through Nerbone;
and Charles came to Bordeaux, that . . . city, sets[9]   3685
on the altar of the baron saint Sevrin
the olifant, filled with gold and pagan coins—
pilgrims passing can see it there today;
crosses the Gironde in great ships that lie there;
he has escorted as far as Blaye his nephew   3690
and Oliver, his noble companion,
and the Archbishop, who was so wise and brave;
and bids these lords be laid in white stone coffins:
at Saint-Romain the brave men lie there still;
the Franks leave them to the Lord and His Names.[1]   3695
And Charles rides over the valleys and the mountains,

9. The line is incomplete in the manuscript.   1. A reference to prayers containing some of the many
names (Adonai, Emmanuel, Yehovah, and so on) by which God is called in sacred writings. These prayers
were considered effective in times of danger.

would take no rest all the long way to Aix,
and rode until he dismounts at the steps.
When he is in his sovereign high palace,
he summons all his judges, sends messengers: 3700
Saxons, Bavarians, Frisians, men of Lorraine,
the Alemans, the men of Burgundy,
the Poitevins, the Normans, the Bretons,
the wisest men among the men of France.
And now begins the trial of Ganelon.   3705

268

The Emperor is home again from Spain,
and comes to Aix, best residence of France,
ascends to the palace; entered the hall.
And now comes Aude, fair maid, before the King;
and said to him: "Where is Roland the captain,   3710
who swore to me to take me for his wife?"
And Charlemagne feels the weight and grief of this,
tears fill his eyes, he weeps, pulls his white beard:
"Sweet friend, dear sister, you ask for a dead man.
I will give you a good man in his place,   3715
it is Louis, I cannot name a better—
he is my son, he will possess my marches."
And Aude replies: "How strange these words sound to me.
May it never please God or his angels or saints
that I should go on living after Roland";   3720
loses color, falls at Charlemagne's feet,
already dead, God take pity on her soul.
Brave men of France weep and lament for Aude.

269

Aude the fair maid is gone now to her end;
the King believes that she has only fainted;   3725
and he is moved, the Emperor weeps for Aude,
takes her two hands; now he has raised her up,
her head sinks down, fallen upon her shoulders;
when Charlemagne sees she is dead in his arms,
he has four countesses sent for at once,   3730
and Aude is borne to a minster of nuns;
all through the night till dawn they wake beside her,
then nobly buried her by an altar.
The King gave Aude great honors, the church great gifts. AOI.

270

The Emperor has come home again to Aix.   3735
In iron chains, the traitor Ganelon
stands before the palace, within the city.
He has been bound, and by serfs, to a stake;
they tie his hands with deerhide straps and thongs,
and beat him hard, with butcher's hooks, with clubs—   3740
for what better reward has this man earned?
There he stands, in pain and rage, awaiting his trial.

271

It is written in the ancient Geste
that Charles summons his vassals from many lands;
they are gathered in the chapel at Aix,   3745
a high day this, a very solemn feast,
the feast, some say, of the baron saint Sylvester.[2]
Now here begin the trial and the pleadings
of Ganelon, who committed treason.
The Emperor has had this man brought forth. AOI.   3750

272

"Barons, my lords," said Charlemagne the King,
"judge what is right concerning Ganelon.
He was with me, came in my army to Spain,
and took from me twenty thousand of my French,
and my nephew, whom you'll not see again,   3755
and Oliver, brave man, born to the court,
and the Twelve Peers—betrayed them all for money."
Said Ganelon: "Let me be called a traitor
    if I hide what I did. It was Roland
who cheated me of gold and goods; and so I wanted
to make him suffer and die; and found the way.   3760
But treason, no—I'll grant no treason there!"
The Franks reply: "We shall take counsel now."

273

And there Ganelon stood, before the King,
breathing power—that lordly color on his face:
the image of a great man, had he been loyal.   3765
He sees his judges, he sees the men of France,
and his kinsmen, the thirty with him there;
then he cried out, with that great ringing voice:
"Barons, hear me, hear me for the love of God!
I was in that army with the Emperor   3770
and served him well, in love and loyalty.
Then his nephew Roland began to hate me,
and he doomed me to die an outrageous death:
I was sent as messenger to King Marsilion.
I used my wits, and I came back alive.   3775
Now I had challenged Roland, that great fighter,
and Oliver, and all of their companions:
King Charles heard it, and all his noble barons.
I took *revenge,* but there's no treason there."
The Franks reply: "We shall go into council."   3780

274

When Ganelon sees that his great trial commences,
he got his thirty kinsmen all around him.
There is one man the others listen to:

---

2. The feast of Saint Sylvester: December 31.

it is Pinabel of the castle of Sorence,
a man who counsels well and judges well,   3785
a valiant fighter—no man can win his arms. AOI.
Said Ganelon: "In you, friend . . . ³
free me from death and from this accusation!"
Said Pinabel: "You will soon be out of this.
Let one Frenchman dare sentence you to hang: 3790
once the Emperor sets us down man to man,
I will give him the lie with this steel sword."
And Ganelon, the Count, falls at his feet.

275

Bavarians, Saxons have gone into council,
Poitevins and Normans and men of France,   3795
the Alemans, the Germans from the North,
men of Auvergne, the courtliest of all.
They keep their voices low, because of Pinabel;
said to each other: "Best to let it stop here—
let's leave this trial and then entreat the King   3800
to let Count Ganelon go free this time
and serve henceforth in love and loyalty.
Roland is dead: you won't see him again,
he will not come for gold or goods again:
only a fool would fight over this now."   3805
All go along, no one there disagrees
except one man, Lord Gefrei's brother: Tierri. AOI.

276

The barons now come back to Charlemagne,
say to the King: "Lord, this we beg of you:
let Ganelon go free, renounce your claim,   3810
then let him serve you in love and loyalty:
let this man live, for his family is great.
Roland is dead: we'll not see a hair of him,
    though we die for it, not a shred of his garment,
or get him back for gold or goods again."
And the King said: "You are all my traitors." AOI.   3815

277

When Charles perceives all have abandoned him,
he bowed his head with that and hid his face,
and in such pain calls himself wretched man.
But now we see: a warrior before him,
Tierri, brother of Gefrei, a duke of Anjou—   3820
the meager body on him, such a slight man!
his hair all black, and his face rather dark;
hardly a giant, but at least not too small;
said to the Emperor, as one born to the court:
"Dear Lord and King, do not lament before us.   3825

---

3. The line is incomplete in the manuscript.

You know I have served you well: I have the right,
my forebears' right! to give this judgment here:
Whatever wrong Count Roland may have done
to Ganelon, he was in your service,
    and serving you should have protected him,
Ganelon is a traitor: he betrayed Roland.   3830
It's you he wronged when he perjured himself,
and broke faith. Therefore, I sentence him
to die, to hang . . . his body cast . . . [4]
like a traitor, a man who committed treason.
If his kinsman wants to give me the lie,   3835
here is my sword, girded on: and with this sword
I am ready to make my judgment good."
The Franks reply: "Now you have spoken well."

278

Now Pinabel has come before the King:
a huge man of swift grace, a valiant man—   3840
time has run out for the poor wretch he strikes!—
said to the King: "Lord, is this not your court?
Give orders then, tell them to stop this noise.
Here I see Tierri, who has given his judgment:
I declare it is false; I shall fight with him";   3845
places his deerhide glove in Charles's fist.
Said the Emperor: "I must have good surety."
Thirty kinsmen go hostage for his loyalty.
Then the King said: "I shall release him then";
and has them guarded until justice is done. AOI.   3850

279

When Tierri sees the battle will take place
he gave to Charles his own right glove as gage.
The Emperor sets him free, for hostages;
then has four benches set round that battle ground:
there they will sit: the two men pledged to fight.   3855
The others judge they have been duly summoned,
Oger of Denmark had settled every question.
And then they call for their horses and arms.

280

Now since both men have been brought forth for battle, AOI.
they make confession and are absolved and blessed;   3860
they hear their mass, receive the Sacrament,
lay down great offerings in these minsters.
Now the two men have come back before Charles.
They have fastened their spurs upon their feet,
and they put on white hauberks, strong and light,   3865
and laced their bright helmets glowing upon their heads,
gird on their swords, the hilts of purest gold;

---

4. The line is incomplete in manuscript.

hang their great quartered shields upon their necks,
take hold of their sharp spears in their right fists;
now they are mounted upon their swift war horses.   3870
And then a hundred thousand warriors wept,
moved for love of Roland to pity Tierri.
The Lord well knows how this battle will end.

281

Down below Aix there is a broad meadow;
there the battle is joined between these barons.   3875
They are brave men, great warriors keeping faith,
and their horses are swift and spirited.
They spur them hard, reins loosened all the way,
come on to strike, the great strength that is theirs!
their two shields burst in that attack to pieces,   3880
their hauberks tear, their saddle girths rip open,
the bosses turn, the saddles fall to earth.
A hundred thousand men, who watch them, weep.

282

Now the two warriors are on the ground, AOI.
now on their feet, and with what speed! again—   3885
the grace and lightness, the strength of Pinabel!—
fall on each other, they have no horses now,
strike with their swords, the hilts of purest gold,
and strike again on these helmets of steel
tremendous blows—blows that cut through helms of steel!   3890
The knights of France are wild with grief and worry.
"Oh, God," said Charles, "make the right between
        them clear!"

283

Said Pinabel: "Tierri, now give it up!
I'll be your man, in love and loyalty,
I'll give you all I own, take what you please,   3895
only make peace with the King for Ganelon."
Tierri replies: "I cannot hear of that,
call me traitor if I consent to that!
May God do right between us two today." AOI.

284

Now Tierri spoke: "Pinabel, you are good,   3900
the great body on you formed like a lord's;
your peers know you: all that a vassal should be;
let this battle go then, let it end here,
I will make peace for you with Charlemagne.
But justice will be done on Ganelon,
        such justice will be done on his body,   3905
no day will pass that men do not speak of it."
Said Pinabel: "May the Lord God forbid!
I will stand up for all my kin, I'll fight,

no man alive will make me quit my kin
   and cry defeat and beg for his mercy,
I'd sooner die than be reproached for that."   3910
And they begin to beat down with their swords
on these helmets beset with gems in gold,
and the bright fires fly from that fight toward heaven;
and no chance now that these two can be parted:
it cannot end without one of them dead. AOI.   3915

285

Pinabel of Sorence, that valiant man,
strikes Tierri now on that helm of Provence:
the fire shoots out and sets the grass aflame;
and shows Tierri the point of that steel sword:
he brought it down. Pinabel brought it down   3920
on his forehead, and down across his face,
the whole right cheek is bloody from that blow,
his hauberk runs with blood down to his waist.
God protects him, he is not struck down dead. AOI.

286

And Tierri sees: he is struck on the face—   3925
the bright blood falling on the grass in the meadow;
strikes Pinabel on his helm of bright steel,
and shattered it, split it to the nosepiece,
struck his brain out spattering from his head;
and raised his sword; he has cast him down, dead.   3930
That was the blow, and the battle is won.
The Franks cry out: "God has made a miracle!
Now Ganelon must hang, it is right now,
and all his kin who stood for him in court." AOI.

287

Now when Tierri had won his great battle,   3935
there came to him the Emperor Charlemagne,
and forty of his barons along with him,
Naimon the Duke, and Oger of Denmark,
William of Blaye, and Gefrei of Anjou.
The King has taken Tierri into his arms,   3940
he wipes his face with his great furs of marten,
throws them aside; they clasp new furs round him.
Very gently, they disarm the warrior,
then they mount him on a mule of Araby,
and he comes home in joy among brave men.   3945
They come to Aix, it is there they dismount.
It is the time now for the executions.

288

Now Charlemagne summons his counts and dukes:
"What is your counsel regarding those I have held?
They came to court to stand for Ganelon,   3950

bound themselves hostages for Pinabel."
The Franks reply: "Not one of them must live."
The King commands his officer, Basbrun:
"Go, hang them all on the accursed tree,
and by this beard, by the white hairs in this beard,   3955
if one escapes, you are lost, a dead man."
Basbrun replies: "What should I do but hang them?";
leads them, by force, with a hundred sergeants.
They are thirty men, and thirty men are hanged.
A traitor brings death, on himself and on others. AOI.   3960

289

Bavarians and Alemans returned,
and Poitevins, and Bretons, and Normans,
and all agreed, the Franks before the others,
Ganelon must die, and in amazing pain.
Four war horses are led out and brought forward;   3965
then they attach his two feet, his two hands.
These battle horses are swift and spirited,
four sergeants come and drive them on ahead
toward a river in the midst of a field.
Ganelon is brought to terrible perdition,   3970
all his mighty sinews are pulled to pieces,
and the limbs of his body burst apart;
on the green grass flows that bright and famous blood.
Ganelon died a traitor's and recreant's death.
Now when one man betrays another,
    it is not right that he should live to boast of it.   3975

290

When the Emperor had taken his revenge,
he called to him his bishops of France,
Bavaria, Germany: "In my household
there is a noble captive, and she has heard,
for so long now, such sermons and examples,   3980
she longs for faith in God, the Christian faith.
Baptize this Queen, that God may have her soul."
And they reply: "Let her be baptized now
by godmothers, ladies of noble birth."
At the baths of Aix there is a great crowd gathered,   3985
there they baptized the noble Queen of Spain,
and they found her the name Juliana;
she is Christian, by knowledge of the Truth.

291

When the Emperor had brought his justice to pass
and peace comes now to that great wrath of his,   3990
he put the Christian faith in Bramimunde;
the day passes, the soft night has gathered,
the King lay down in his vaulted chamber.
Saint Gabriel! come in God's name to say:

"Charles, gather the great hosts of your Empire!   3995
Go to the land of Bire, with all your force,
you must relieve King Vivien at Imphe,
the citadel, pagans have besieged it:
Christians are calling you, they cry your name!"
The Emperor would have wished not to go.   4000
"God!" said the King, "the pains, the labors of my life!";
weeps from his eyes, pulls his white beard.

Here ends the song   that Turold composes, paraphrases, amplifies,[5] 4003
                       that Turold completes, relates,
Here ends the tale   that Turold declaims, recounts, narrates,
                       that Turold copies, transcribes,
Here ends the geste   for Turold grows weak, grows weary, declines,
Here ends the written history,
Here ends the source   that Turold turns into poetry.

5. The last line of the poem reads *Ci falt la geste que Turoldus declinet.* The meaning of the words *geste* and *declinet* and the syntax of *que* have never been finally settled, and no line in the poem contains so many possible meanings as the last one. Some of the interpretations that have been proposed are given here, and every one is plausible.

MARIE DE FRANCE
twelfth century

The first woman writer in French (at least so far as we know), Marie de France created her work at a crucial time in the history of literature, a history to which she made a central contribution. For it was in the twelfth century that most of the major forms and themes that have shaped Western literature emerged in the vernacular languages of Europe. Primary among them were the works we now call romances, novelistic narratives that dealt with adventure and—above all—love. The most familiar of these narratives are the stories of King Arthur and his knights, stories that in the twelfth century received the literary treatment, and enjoyed the enormous popularity, they still have today. The Arthurian legends were part of a vast mythology developed by the Celts of Western Europe, peoples who were driven from their lands by the Germanic invaders of the fourth and fifth centuries and took refuge on the Atlantic fringe of the continent in what are now Ireland, Wales, and Brittany. Yet if they were conquered as a people, the Celts triumphed through their stories. There is hardly a work of medieval literature that does not reveal the influence of Celtic mythology.

Less popular than the long Arthurian narratives but more finely crafted as works of art were the short narratives of love, adventure, and the supernatural, also of Celtic origin, known as *lais* or, in English, lays. As a form of literature, the lay first appears in a collection composed about 1165 by a woman who identifies herself only as "Marie." In another work she tells us that she is "from France," and ever since the Renaissance she has been given the designation "Marie de France." From the evidence of her writing, we know that she was a noblewoman, that she could read French, English, and Latin, and that she was familiar with a royal household, probably that of Henry II, king of England (reigned 1154–89). She may well have been a nun or even an abbess, since many noble daughters were placed in the elegant aristocratic nunneries of Europe. All of her work, including the twelve lays that survive, is written in octosyllabic verse in Anglo-Norman, a French dialect spoken by the nobility of postconquest England. The sources for her lays, she tells us, were stories that she heard, and while she provides us with several Breton terms—like the word *laüstic* for nightingale—we cannot know if she heard these stories in English, French, or Breton.

The two lays presented here deal with a topic that is central to the collection as a whole. These are stories in which love serves as an alternative—in one case successfully, in the other not—to an uncaring or unjust society. In both stories Marie combines an acute awareness of contemporary social conditions with sympathy for individuals who seek personal fulfillment. In the lay that bears his name, Lanval is a young foreigner who has come to the Arthurian court to seek his fortune. He is the son of a king, but his "inheritance"—by which Marie means his ancestral domain—is far away. The implication is that Lanval is like many noble young men in twelfth-century France and England who, as younger sons, were largely excluded from inheriting the family land under the recently established system of primogeniture, by which only the eldest son inherited. Thus when at the beginning of the story Arthur hands out lands and wives to his knights but neglects the deserving Lanval, he is dooming Lanval to a life of continued obscurity and lonely service. Rescue comes to him in the form of the fairy lover, who is not merely beautiful and loving but—as Marie is careful to stress—rich. Now that Lanval can comport himself with the confidence and liberality that befits a nobleman, he becomes attractive to the queen (presumably Guinevere, although she is not named). And in rejecting her advances he asserts not simply the superior beauty of his lady but the superiority of her handmaiden, making it clear that he is attached to a court that surpasses in its grandeur that of Arthur himself. This is why Arthur so quickly supports his queen in her false accusation, and why Lanval is accused not just of a social gaffe but of felony and treason. For as Arthur's barons say, Lanval ought to honor his lord at all times, while he is acting (rightly, as it turns out) as if he is obligated to a different sovereign entirely. Yet the power of Marie's story derives from the fact that, despite this emphasis on social and material benefits, Lanval is primarily distressed because he has lost not the fairy queen's financial support but her love. And when the two pairs of damsels appear, he remains true to her by refusing to claim either of them as warrant for his rash words to the queen. Perhaps it is because he passes this test that his lover then herself appears and takes him away with her to Avalon, a world in which the petty jealousies and unfulfilled ambitions of the Arthurian court can be forgotten. Here love seems to conquer all, but no reader can ignore that its triumph is possible only in the fantasy world of fiction.

Laüstic, on the other hand, is a story of unfulfilled love. In this case the social reality to which the story is addressed is the aristocratic custom of arranged marriages. In *Lanval* Arthur gives away wives, yet there is no indication that the women involved have any say in their marital fate. Yet at the same time as the European nobility was treating marriage as a financial and political matter, the Church was teaching that marriage was above all a matter of free consent, that what made two people husband and wife was their agreement to enter into marriage with each other. Marie's lays are filled with unhappy wives—unhappy not only because they were forced into marriages against their will but because they know they deserve better (indeed, perhaps we should understand Guinevere's misbehavior in *Lanval* as caused by such knowledge). The young wife in *Laüstic* can only dream of escape as she gazes out her confining room at her would-be lover. The nightingale that she invokes to quiet her jealous husband becomes a symbol of this yearning to escape, and when her husband brutally kills it and throws its bleeding corpse at her, we can understand that the stain it leaves on the breast of her tunic is the outward sign of a broken heart. Yet this is not the end, for the golden casket in which her lover entombs the nightingale serves to celebrate a love that may not have found earthly fulfillment but has achieved another, higher permanence. In its exquisite concision, *Laüstic* is itself a literary version of that golden casket, a verbal equivalent to the jeweled reliquaries in which medieval people encased the bodies of their saints.

A complete translation of the *Lais*, with a helpful introduction and full bibliography, can be found in Glyn S. Burgess and Keith Busby, trans., *The Lais of Marie de France* (1986). A verse translation with commentary is provided by Robert Hanning and Joan Ferrante, *The Lais of Marie de France* (1978).

Lanval[1]

Just as it happened, I shall relate to you the story of another lay, which tells of a very noble young man whose name in Breton is Lanval.

Arthur, the worthy and courtly king, was at Carlisle[2] on account of the Scots and the Picts who were ravaging the country, penetrating into the land of Logres[3] and frequently laying it waste.

The king was there during the summer, at Pentecost,[4] and he gave many rich gifts to counts and barons and to those of the Round Table: there was no such company in the whole world. He apportioned wives and lands to all, save to one who had served him: this was Lanval, whom he did not remember, and for whom no one put in a good word. Because of his valor, generosity, beauty and prowess, many were envious of him. There were those who pretended to hold him in esteem, but who would not have uttered a single regret if misfortune had befallen him. He was the son of a king of noble birth, but far from his inheritance, and although he belonged to Arthur's household he had spent all his wealth, for the king gave him nothing and Lanval asked for nothing. Now he was in a plight, very sad and forlorn. Lords, do not be surprised: a stranger bereft of advice can be very downcast in another land when he does not know where to seek help.

This knight whose tale I am telling you had served the king well. One day he mounted his horse and went to take his ease. He left the town and came alone to a meadow, dismounting by a stream; but there his horse trembled violently, so he loosened its saddlegirth and left it, allowing it to enter the meadow to roll over on its back. He folded his cloak, which he placed beneath his head, very disconsolate because of his troubles, and nothing could please him. Lying thus, he looked downriver and saw two damsels coming, more beautiful than any he had ever seen: they were richly dressed in closely fitting tunics of dark purple and their faces were very beautiful. The older one carried dishes of gold, well and finely made—I will not fail to tell you the truth—and the other carried a towel. They went straight to where the knight lay and Lanval, who was very well-mannered, stood up to meet them. They first greeted him and then delivered their message: "Sir Lanval, my damsel, who is very worthy, wise and fair, has sent us for you. Come with us, for we will conduct you safely. Look, her tent is near." The knight went with them, disregarding his horse which was grazing before him in the meadow. They led him to the tent, which was so beautiful and well-appointed that neither Queen Semiramis at the height of her wealth, power and knowledge, nor the Emperor Octavian,[5] could have afforded even the right-hand side of it. There

---

1. Translated by Glyn S. Burgess and Keith Busby. 2. City near the Scottish border. 3. The Arthurian name for England. 4. A feast day celebrated on the seventh Sunday after Easter. 5. Roman emperor Caesar Augustus (63 B.C.–A.D. 14); *Semiramis*: a legendary queen of Assyria.

was a golden eagle placed on the top, the value of which I cannot tell, nor of the ropes or the poles which supported the walls of the tent. There is no king under the sun who could afford it, however much he might give. Inside this tent was the maiden who surpassed in beauty the lily and the new rose when it appears in summer. She lay on a very beautiful bed—the coverlets cost as much as a castle—clad only in her shift. Her body was well formed and handsome, and in order to protect herself from the heat of the sun, she had cast about her a costly mantle of white ermine covered with Alexandrian purple. Her side, though, was uncovered, as well as her face, neck and breast; she was whiter than the hawthorn blossom.

The maiden called the knight, who came forward and sat before the bed. "Lanval," she said, "fair friend, for you I came from my country. I have come far in search of you and if you are worthy and courtly, no emperor, count or king will have felt as much joy or happiness as you, for I love you above all else." He looked at her and saw that she was beautiful. Love's spark pricked him so that his heart was set alight, and he replied to her in seemly manner: "Fair lady, if it were to please you to grant me the joy of wanting to love me, you could ask nothing that I would not do as best I could, be it foolish or wise. I shall do as you bid and abandon all others for you. I never want to leave you and this is what I most desire." When the girl heard these words from the man who loved her so, she granted him her love and her body. Now Lanval was on the right path! She gave him a boon, that henceforth he could wish for nothing which he would not have, and however generously he gave or spent, she would still find enough for him. Lanval was very well lodged, for the more he spent, the more gold and silver he would have. "Beloved," she said, "I admonish, order, and beg you not to reveal this secret to anyone! I shall tell you the long and the short of it: you would lose me forever if this love were to become known. You would never be able to see me or possess me." He replied that he would do what she commanded. He lay down beside her on the bed: now Lanval was well lodged. That afternoon he remained with her until evening and would have done so longer had he been able and had his love allowed him. "Beloved," she said, "arise! You can stay no longer. Go from here and I shall remain, but I shall tell you one thing: whenever you wish to speak with me, you will not be able to think of a place where a man may enjoy his love without reproach or wickedness, that I shall not be there with you to do your bidding. No man save you will see me or hear my voice." When he heard this, Lanval was well pleased and, kissing her, he arose. The damsels who had led him to the tent dressed him in rich garments, and in his new clothes there was no more handsome young man on earth. He was neither foolish nor ill-mannered. The damsels gave him water to wash his hands and a towel to dry them and then brought him food. He took his supper, which was not to be disdained, with his beloved. He was very courteously served and dined joyfully. There was one dish in abundance that pleased the knight particularly, for he often kissed his beloved and embraced her closely.

When they had risen from table, his horse was brought to him, well saddled. Lanval was richly served there. He took his leave, mounted, and went towards the city, often looking behind him, for he was greatly disturbed, thinking of his adventure and uneasy in his heart. He was at a loss to know what to think, for he could not believe it was true. When he came to his lodgings, he found his men finely dressed. That night he offered lavish hospitality but no one knew how this came to be. There was no knight in the town in sore need of shelter whom he did not summon and serve richly and well. Lanval gave costly gifts, Lanval freed prisoners, Lanval clothed the jongleurs,[6] Lanval performed many honorable acts. There was no one, stranger or friend, to whom he would not have given gifts. He experienced great joy and pleasure, for day or night he could see his beloved often and she was entirely at his command.

In the same year, I believe, after St John's day,[7] as many as thirty knights had gone to relax in a garden beneath the tower where the queen was staying. Gawain was with them and his cousin, the fair Ywain. Gawain, the noble and the worthy, who endeared himself to all, said: "In God's name, lords, we treat our companion Lanval ill, for he is so generous and courtly, and his father is a rich king, yet we have not brought him with us." So they returned, went to his lodgings and persuaded him to come with them.

The queen, in the company of three ladies, was reclining by a window cut out of the stone when she caught sight of the king's household and recognized Lanval. She called one of her ladies to summon her most elegant and beautiful damsels to relax with her in the garden where the others were. She took more than thirty with her, and they went down the steps where the knights, glad of their coming, came to meet them. They took the girls by the hand and the conversation was not uncourtly. Lanval withdrew to one side, far from the others, for he was impatient to hold his beloved, to kiss, embrace and touch her. He cared little for other people's joy when he could not have his own pleasure. When the queen saw the knight alone, she approached him straightaway. Sitting down beside him, she spoke to him and opened her heart. "Lanval, I have honored, cherished and loved you much. You may have all my love: just tell me what you desire! I grant you my love and you should be glad to have me." "Lady," he said, "leave me be! I have no desire to love you, for I have long served the king and do not want to betray my faith. Neither you nor your love will ever lead me to wrong my lord!" The queen became angry and distressed, and spoke unwisely: "Lanval," she said, "I well believe that you do not like this kind of pleasure. I have been told often enough that you have no desire for women. You have well-trained young men and enjoy yourself with them. Base coward, wicked recreant, my lord is extremely unfortunate to have suffered you near him. I think he may have lost his salvation because of it!"

When he heard her, he was distressed, but not slow to reply. He said something in spite that he was often to regret. "Lady, I am not skilled in the profession you mention, but I love and am loved by a lady who should be prized above all others I know. And I will tell you one thing: you can be sure that one of her servants, even the very poorest girl, is worth more than you, my lady the Queen, in body, face and beauty, wisdom and goodness." Thereupon the queen left and went in tears to her chamber, very distressed and angry that he had humiliated her in this way. She took to her bed ill and said that she would never again get up, unless the king saw that justice was done her in respect of her complaint.

The king had returned from the woods after an extremely happy day. He

6. Minstrels.   7. June 24.

entered the queen's apartments and when she saw him, she complained aloud, fell at his feet, cried for mercy and said that Lanval had shamed her. He had requested her love and because she had refused him, had insulted and deeply humiliated her. He had boasted of a beloved who was so well-bred, noble and proud that her chambermaid, the poorest servant she had, was worthier than the queen. The king grew very angry and swore on oath that, if Lanval could not defend himself in court, he would have him burned or hanged. The king left the room, summoned three of his barons and sent them for Lanval, who was suffering great pain. He had returned to his lodgings, well aware of having lost his beloved by revealing their love. Alone in his chamber, distraught and anguished, he called his beloved repeatedly, but to no avail. He lamented and sighed, fainting from time to time; a hundred times he cried to her to have mercy, to come and speak with her beloved. He cursed his heart and his mouth and it was a wonder he did not kill himself. His cries and moans were not loud enough nor his agitation and torment such that she would have mercy on him, or even permit him to see her. Alas, what will he do?

The king's men arrived and told Lanval to go to court without delay: the king had summoned him through them, for the queen had accused him. Lanval went sorrowfully and would have been happy for them to kill him. He came before the king, sad, subdued and silent, betraying his great sorrow. The king said to him angrily: "Vassal, you have wronged me greatly! You were extremely ill-advised to shame and vilify me, and to slander the queen. You boasted out of folly, for your beloved must be very noble for her handmaiden to be more beautiful and more worthy than the queen."

Lanval denied point by point having offended and shamed his lord, and maintained that he had not sought the queen's love, but he acknowledged the truth of his words about the love of which he had boasted. He now regretted this, for as a result he had lost her. He told them he would do whatever the court decreed in this matter, but the king was very angry and sent for all his men to tell him exactly what he should do, so that his action would not be unfavourably interpreted. Whether they liked it or not, they obeyed his command and assembled to make a judgement, deciding that a day should be fixed for the trial, but that Lanval should provide his lord with pledges that he would await his judgement and return later to his presence. Then the court would be larger, for at that moment only the king's household itself was present. The barons returned to the king and explained their reasoning. The king asked for pledges, but Lanval was alone and forlorn, having no relation or friend there. Then Gawain approached and offered to stand bail, and all his companions did likewise. The king said to them: "I entrust him to you on surety of all that you hold from me, lands and fiefs, each man separately." When this had been pledged, there was no more to be done, and Lanval returned to his lodging with the knights escorting him. They chastised him and urged him strongly not to be so sorrowful, and cursed such foolish love. They went to see him every day, as they wished to know whether he was drinking and eating properly, being very much afraid that he might harm himself.

On the appointed day the barons assembled. The king and queen were there and the guarantors brought Lanval to court. They were all very sad on his account and I think there were a hundred who would have done all in their power to have him released without a trial because he had been wrongly accused. The king demanded the verdict according to the charge and the rebuttal, and now everything lay in the hands of the barons. They considered their judgement, very troubled and concerned on account of this noble man from abroad, who was in such a plight in their midst. Some of them wanted to harm him in conformity with their lord's will. Thus spoke the count of Cornwall: "There shall be no default on our part. Like it or not, right must prevail. The king accused his vassal, whom I heard you call Lanval, of a felony and charged him with a crime, about a love he boasted of which angered my lady. Only the king is accusing him, so by the faith I owe you, there ought, to tell the truth, to be no case to answer, were it not that one should honour one's lord in all things. An oath will bind Lanval and the king will put the matter in our hands. If he can provide proof and his beloved comes forward, and if what he said to incur the queen's displeasure is true, then he will be pardoned, since he did not say it to spite her. And if he cannot furnish proof, then we must inform him that he will lose the king's service and that the king must banish him." They sent word to the knight and informed him that he should send for his beloved to defend and protect him. He told them that this was not possible and that he would receive no help from her. The messengers returned to the judges, expecting no help to be forthcoming for Lanval. The king pressed them hard because the queen was waiting for them.

When they were about to give their verdict, they saw two maidens approaching on two fine ambling palfreys. They were extremely comely and dressed only in purple taffeta, next to their bare skin; the knights were pleased to see them. Gawain and three other knights went to Lanval, told him about this, and pointed the two maidens out to him. Gawain was very glad and strongly urged Lanval to tell him if this was his beloved, but he told them that he did not know who they were, whence they came or where they were going. The maidens continued to approach, still on horseback, and then dismounted before the dais where King Arthur was seated. They were of great beauty and spoke in courtly fashion: "King, make your chambers available and hang them with silken curtains so that my lady may stay here, for she wishes to lodge with you." This he granted them willingly and summoned two knights who led them to the upper chambers. For the moment they said no more.

The king asked his barons for the judgement and the responses, and said that they had greatly angered him by the long delay. "Lord," they said, "we are deliberating, but because of the ladies we saw, we have not reached a verdict. Let us continue with the trial." So they assembled in some anxiety, and there was a good deal of commotion and contention.

While they were in this troubled state, they saw two finely accoutred maidens coming along the street, dressed in garments of Phrygian[8] silk and riding on Spanish mules. The vassals were glad of this and they said to each other that Lanval, the worthy and brave, was now saved. Ywain went up to him with his companions, and said: "Lord, rejoice! For the love of God, speak to us! Two damsels are approaching, very comely and beautiful. It is surely your beloved." Lanval quickly replied that he did not recognize them, nor did he

---

8. Phrygia is in modern Turkey, but here designates more generally the East.

know or love them. When they had arrived, they dismounted before the king and many praised them highly for their bodies, faces, and complexions. They were both more worthy than the queen had ever been. The older of the two, who was courtly and wise, delivered her message fittingly: "King, place your chambers at our disposal for the purpose of lodging my lady. She is coming here to speak with you." He ordered them to be taken to the others who had arrived earlier. They paid no heed to their mules, and, as soon as they had left the king, he summoned all his barons so that they might deliver their verdict. This had taken up too much of the day and the queen, who had been waiting for them for such a long time, was getting angry.

Just as they were about to give their verdict, a maiden on horseback entered the town. There was none more beautiful in the whole world. She was riding a white palfrey which carried her well and gently; its neck and head were well-formed and there was no finer animal on earth. The palfrey was richly equipped, for no count or king on earth could have paid for it, save by selling or pledging his lands. The lady was dressed in a white tunic and shift, laced left and right so as to reveal her sides. Her body was comely, her lips low, her neck whiter than snow on a branch; her eyes were bright and her face white, her mouth fair and her nose well-placed; her eyebrows were brown and her brow fair, and her hair curly and rather blond. A golden thread does not shine as brightly as the rays reflected in the light from her hair. Her cloak was of dark silk and she had wrapped its skirts about her. She held a sparrowhawk on her wrist and behind her there followed a dog. There was no one in the town, humble or powerful, old or young, who did not watch her arrival, and no one jested about her beauty. She approached slowly and the judges who saw her thought it was a great wonder. No one who had looked at her could have failed to be inspired with real joy. Those who loved the knight went and told him about the maiden who was coming and who, please God, would deliver him. "Lord and friend, here comes a lady whose hair is neither tawny nor brown. She is the most beautiful of all women in the world." Lanval heard this and raised his head, for he knew her well, and sighed. His blood rushed to his face and he was quick to speak: "In faith," he said, "it is my beloved! If she shows me no mercy, I hardly care if anyone should kill me, for my cure is in seeing her." The lady entered the palace, where no one so beautiful had ever before been seen. She dismounted before the king, and in the sight of all, let her cloak fall so that they could see her better. The king, who was well-mannered, rose to meet her, and all the others honored her and offered themselves as her servants. When they had looked at her and praised her beauty greatly, she spoke thus, for she had no wish to remain: "King, I have loved one of your vassals, Lanval, whom you see there. Because of what he said, he was accused in your court, and I do not wish him to come to any harm. You should know that the queen was wrong, as he never sought her love. As regards the boast he made, if he can be acquitted by me, let your barons release him!" The king granted that it should be as the judges recommended, in accordance with justice. There was not one who did not consider that Lanval had successfully defended himself, and so he was freed by their decision. The maiden, who had many servants, then left, for the king could not retain her. Outside the hall there was a large block of dark marble on to which heavily armed men climbed when they left the king's court. Lanval mounted it and when the maiden came through the door, he leapt in a single bound on to the palfrey behind her. He went with her to Avalon,[9] so the Bretons tell us, to a very beautiful island. Thither the young man was borne and no one has heard any more about him, nor can I relate any more.

Laüstic[1]

I shall relate an adventure to you from which the Bretons composed a lay. *Laüstic* is its name, I believe, and that is what the Bretons call it in their land. In French the title is *Rossignol,* and Nightingale is the correct English word.

In the region of St Malo[2] was a famous town and two knights dwelt there, each with a fortified house. Because of the fine qualities of the two men the town acquired a good reputation. One of the knights had taken a wise, courtly and elegant wife who conducted herself, as custom dictated, with admirable propriety. The other knight was a young man who was well known amongst his peers for his prowess and great valour. He performed honorable deeds gladly and attended many tournaments, spending freely and giving generously whatever he had. He loved his neighbour's wife and so persistently did he request her love, so frequent were his entreaties and so many qualities did he possess that she loved him above all things, both for the good she had heard about him and because he lived close by. They loved each other prudently and well, concealing their love carefully to ensure that they were not seen, disturbed or suspected. This they could do because their dwellings were adjoining. Their houses, halls and keeps were close by each other and there was no barrier or division, apart from a high wall of dark-hued stone. When she stood at her bedroom window, the lady could talk to her beloved in the other house and he to her, and they could toss gifts to each other. There was scarcely anything to displease them and they were both very content except for the fact that they could not meet and take their pleasure with each other, for the lady was closely guarded when her husband was in the region. But they were so resourceful that day or night they managed to speak to each other and no one could prevent their coming to the window and seeing each other there. For a long time they loved each other, until one summer when the copses and meadows were green and the gardens in full bloom. On the flower-tops the birds sang joyfully and sweetly. If love is on anyone's mind, no wonder he turns his attention towards it. I shall tell you the truth about the knight. Both he and the lady made the greatest possible effort with their words and with their eyes. At night, when the moon was shining and her husband was asleep, she often rose from beside him and put on her mantle. Knowing her beloved would be doing the same, she would go and stand at the window and stay awake most of the night. They took delight in seeing each other, since they were denied anything more. But so frequently did she stand there and so frequently leave her bed that her husband became angry and asked her repeatedly why she got up and where she went. "Lord," replied the lady, "anyone who does not hear the song of the nightingale knows none of the joys of this world. This is why I come and stand here. So sweet is the

9. The Celtic isle of the blessed.   1. Translated by Glyn S. Burgess and Keith Busby.   2. A town in Brittany.

song I hear by night that it brings me great pleasure. I take such delight in it and desire it so much that I can get no sleep at all." When the lord heard what she said, he gave a spiteful, angry laugh and devised a plan to ensnare the nightingale. Every single servant in his household constructed some trap, net or snare and then arranged them throughout the garden. There was no hazel tree or chestnut tree on which they did not place a snare or bird-lime, until they had captured and retained it. When they had taken the nightingale, it was handed over, still alive, to the lord, who was overjoyed to hold it in his hands. He entered the lady's chamber. "Lady," he said, "where are you? Come forward and speak to us. With bird-lime I have trapped the nightingale which has kept you awake so much. Now you can sleep in peace, for it will never awaken you again." When the lady heard him she was grief-stricken and distressed. She asked her husband for the bird, but he killed it out of spite, breaking its neck wickedly with his two hands. He threw the body at the lady, so that the front of her tunic was bespattered with blood, just on her breast. Thereupon he left the chamber. The lady took the tiny corpse, wept profusely and cursed those who had betrayed the nightingale by constructing the traps and snares, for they had taken so much joy from her. "Alas," she said, "misfortune is upon me. Never again can I get up at night or go to stand at the window where I used to see my beloved. I know one thing for certain. He will think I am faint-hearted, so I must take action. I shall send him the nightingale and let him know what has happened." She wrapped the little bird in a piece of samite, embroidered in gold and covered in designs. She called one of her servants, entrusted him with her message and sent him to her beloved. He went to the knight, greeted him on behalf of his lady, related the whole message to him and presented him with the nightingale. When the messenger had finished speaking, the knight, who had listened attentively, was distressed by what had happened. But he was not uncourtly or tardy. He had a small vessel prepared, not of iron or steel, but of pure gold with fine stones, very precious and valuable. On it he carefully placed a lid and put the nightingale in it. Then he had the casket sealed and carried it with him at all times.

This adventure was related and could not long be concealed. The Bretons composed a lay about it which is called *Laüstic*.

THORSTEIN THE STAFF-STRUCK
thirteenth century

Medieval Iceland produced not only a unique and highly interesting body of poetry but also some of the finest prose narratives in European literature. Some of these, like the *Saga of the Volsungs*, deal with figures of early Germanic tradition. But some thirty or forty, called sagas of Icelanders, are about men and women who lived in Iceland (and often in Norway in their youth) from the late ninth to the early eleventh centuries. Written mostly in the thirteenth century, they may remind us a bit of the historical novels of a later time. But in the historical novel, usually, the major characters are fictional, products of the author's invention, while those well known to history serve as framework or background. In the Icelandic saga the converse is true: the principal figures were actual people attested by documents and other evidence, as were also most of the events and acts attributed to them. Oral tradition bridged the interval between the tenth century and the thirteenth. Thus the author of an extant saga was free to shape characterization, motivation, mood, and tone as he saw fit. It is now believed that the milieu of thirteenth-century Iceland may have influenced features of some of these narratives. A few may have been entirely fictional, except for the use of the names of actual persons. Like the Eddic poems, the sagas are nearly always anonymous. Some of the most notable are of novel length, like the *Saga of the Laxdalers* or the Grettir saga, or the *Saga of Burnt Njal,* greatest of all.

As must be evident, the story of Thorstein the Staff-Struck is very short; in fact, it was not called a saga but a *thattr,* literally, a "thread." Nevertheless, it shows the characteristic features of a family saga. Although the action is "strong," to use a modern term—people kill and are killed—violence is not included for its own sake; instead, it interests the narrator chiefly as an expression of personality and character. The incidents of the story are conducted in such a way as to distinguish sharply nearly all of the participants; these are all members of one or the other of two families or households who live in northeast Iceland. The "fierce," now aged, but still irascible Thorarin is contrasted with his husky and confident but even-tempered son, Thorstein; only when the insolent Thord willfully insults him does Thorstein take action. In prosecuting Thorstein for manslaughter, Bjarni, Thord's employer and also the district chieftain, fulfills a more or less automatic obligation. However, when Thorstein ignores the sentence of exile, Bjarni (whose responsibility it was to attack Thorstein) takes no action. We learn that he is unwilling to deprive the infirm, nearly blind Thorarin of his son's support. Nevertheless, when Bjarni overhears the malicious gossip of Thorhall and Thorvald, he sends them out with instructions to kill Thorstein. We are not told what he expected would happen, but when he learns that Thorstein has slain the two brothers, once again he does nothing; when his wife Rannveig goads him, he remarks that "Thorstein has never killed anyone without a good reason." All the same, when she tells him of the taunts in circulation about him, he decides that he cannot avoid a confrontation with Thorstein.

Although the circumstances are different, Bjarni's motive in his (reluctant) challenge of Thorstein is the same as the latter's when he (at last) challenges Thord. Each man considers the respect of the community essential to his self-respect; hence they act as the code requires, regardless of their personal inclination or of the intrinsic merits of the case. The thirteenth-century Christian author faithfully presents this pre-Christian pattern; the ethical dilemma, unacknowledged by the protagonists, is implicit in the narration. Hence in the final encounter Bjarni and Thorstein carry out the *form* of conduct that tradition makes obligatory, while the *manner* in which they do so ensures a morally satisfactory result.

Readers will enjoy this succinct narrative best if they ask themselves such questions—among others—as: What purposes are served by the dialogue? What is Thorarin's motive for each of his acts? How does the author make use of the two female characters?

A concise general account of the family sagas is Peter Hallberg, trans. Paul Schach, *The Icelandic Saga* (1962). A critical study of structure and organization, with plot summaries, is Theodore M. Anderson, *The Icelandic Family Saga* (1967). Admirable translations of several of the principal sagas are available in the Penguin paperback series. Jesse Byock, *Feud in the Icelandic Saga* (1982), is a recent scholarly study. Jacqueline Simpson, *Icelandic Folktales and Legends* (1972), paperback printing (1979), provides a modern translation of short narratives (not sagas) collected especially from oral sources.

PRONOUNCING GLOSSARY

The following list uses common English syllables to provide rough equivalents of selected words whose pronunciation may be unfamiliar to the general reader.

Bjorni: *b-yorn'-ee*   Thorstein: *thor'-stain*

From Thorstein the Staff-Struck[1]

There was a man called Thorarin who lived at Sunnudale; he was old and nearly blind. He had been a fierce viking in his younger years, and even in his old age he was very hard to deal with. He had an only son, Thorstein, who was a tall man, powerful but even-tempered; he worked so hard on his father's farm that three other men could hardly have done any better. Thorarin had little money, but a good many weapons. He and his son owned some breeding horses and that was their main source of income, for the young colts they sold never failed in spirit or strength.

Bjarni of Hof[2] had a servant called Thord who looked after his riding horses and was considered very good at the job. Thord was an arrogant man and would never let anyone forget the fact that he was in the service of a chieftain. But this didn't make him a better man and added nothing to his popularity. Bjarni also had two brothers working for him who were called Thorhall and Thorvald, both great scandalmongers about any gossip they heard in the district.

Thorstein and Thord arranged a horse-fight for their young stallions.[3] During the fight, Thord's horse started giving way, and when Thord realized he was losing, he struck Thorstein's horse a hard blow on the jaw. Thorstein saw this and hit back with an even heavier blow at Thord's horse, forcing it to back away. This got the spectators shouting with excitement. Then Thord aimed a blow at Thornstein with his horse-goad, hitting him so hard on the eye-brow that the skin broke and the lid fell hanging down over the eye. Thorstein tore a piece off his shirt and bandaged his head. He said nothing about what had happened, apart from asking people to keep this from his father. That should have been the end of the incident, but Thorvald and Thorhall kept jeering at Thorstein and gave him the nickname Staff-Struck.

One morning that winter just before Christmas, when the women at Sunnudale were getting up for their work, Thorstein went out to feed the cattle. He soon came back and lay down on a bench. His father, old Thorarin, came into the room and asked who was lying there. Thorstein told him.

"Why are you up so early, son?" said Thorarin.

Thorstein answered, "It seems to me there aren't many men about to share the work with me."

"Have you got a head-ache, son?" said Thorarin.

"Not that I've noticed," said Thorstein.

"What can you tell me about the horse-fight last summer, son?" said Thorarin. "Weren't you beaten senseless like a dog?"

"It's no credit to me if you call it a deliberate blow, not an accident," said Thorstein.

Thorarin said, "I'd never have thought I could have a coward for a son."

"Father," said Thorstein, "Don't say anything now that you'll live to regret later."

"I'm not going to say as much as I've a mind to," said Thorarin.

---

1. Translated, with footnotes, by Hermann Pálsson. 2. Bjarni of Hof was the local chieftain, and the wealthiest and most powerful farmer in the district. 3. Horse-fights used to be a favourite sport in Iceland. Two stallions were pitted against one another, and behind each of them there was a man equipped with a goad to prod them on. At these horse fights tempers would often run high.

Thorstein got to his feet, seized his weapons and set off. He came to the stable where Thord was grooming Bjarni's horses, and when he saw Thord he said, "I'd like to know, friend Thord, whether it was accidental when you hit me in the horse-fight last summer, or deliberate. If it was deliberate, you'll be willing to pay me compensation."

"If only you were double-tongued," said Thord, "then you could easily speak with two voices and call the blow accidental with one and deliberate with the other. That's all the compensation you're getting from me."

"In that case don't expect me to make this claim a second time," said Thorstein.

With that he rushed at Thord and dealt him his death-blow. Then he went up to the house at Hof where he saw a woman standing outside the door. "Tell Bjarni that a bull has gored Thord, his horse-boy," he said to her, "and also that Thord will be waiting for him at the stable."

"Go back home, man," she said. "I'll tell Bjarni in my own good time."

Thorstein went back home, and the woman carried on with her work.

After Bjarni had got up that morning and was sitting at table, he asked where Thord could be, and was told he had gone to see to the horses.

"I'd have thought he'd be back by now, unless something has happened to him," said Bjarni.

The woman Thorstein had spoken to broke in. "It's true what we women are often told, we're not very clever. Thorstein the Staff-Struck came here this morning and he said Thord had been gored by a bull and couldn't look after himself. I didn't want to wake you, and then I forgot all about it."

Bjarni left the table, went over to the stable and found Thord lying there, dead. Bjarni had him buried, then brought a court action against Thorstein and had him sentenced to outlawry for manslaughter. But Thorstein stayed on at Sunnudale and worked for his father, and Bjarni did nothing more about it.

One day in the autumn when the men of Hof were busy singeing sheep's heads,[4] Bjarni lay down on top of the kitchen wall to listen to their talk. Now the brothers Thorhall and Thorvald started gossiping; "It never occurred to us when we came to live here with Killer-Bjarni[5] that we'd be singeing lambs' heads while his outlaw Thorstein is singeing the heads of wethers. It would have been better for Bjarni to have been more lenient with his kinsmen at Bodvarsdale and not to let his outlaw at Sunnudale act just like his own equal. But 'A wounded coward lies low,' and it's not likely that he'll ever wipe away this stain on his honour."

One of the men said, "Those words were better left unsaid, the trolls must have twisted your tongue. I think Bjarni simply isn't prepared to take the only breadwinner at Sunnudale away from Thorstein's blind father and other dependents there. I'll be more than surprised if you singe many more lambs' heads here, or tattle on much longer about the fight at Bodvarsdale."

Then they went inside to have their meal, and after that to bed. Bjarni gave no sign that he had heard anything of what had been said. But early next morning he roused Thorhall and Thorvald and told them to ride over to

---

4. In Iceland, as in some other sheep-raising countries, sheep's heads were (and still are) considered a great delicacy. The heads are singed over a fire to remove all traces of wool before they are cleaned and cooked.   5. The name Killer-Bjarni is an allusion to the fact that Bjarni fought and killed some of his own kinsmen in the battle of Bodvarsdale which is mentioned in the following sentence.

Sunnudale and bring him Thorstein's severed head before mid-morning. "I think you're more likely than anyone else to wipe away that stain from my honour, since I haven't the courage to do it for myself," he said.

The brothers realized they had said too much, but they set off and went over to Sunnudale. Thorstein was standing in the doorway, sharpening a short sword. He asked them where they were going, and they told him they were looking for some horses. Thorstein said they didn't have very far to go. "The horses are down by the fence."

"We're not sure we'll be able to find them unless you tell us more precisely," they said.

Thorstein came outside, and as they were walking together across the meadow, Thorvald raised his axe and rushed at him. But Thorstein pushed him back so hard that he fell, then ran him through with the short sword. Thorhall tried to attack Thorstein and went the same way as his brother. Thorstein tied them to their saddles, fixed the reins to the horses' manes, and drove them off.

The horses went back to Hof. Some of the servants there were out of doors and went inside to tell Bjarni that Thorvald and Thorhall had come back and their journey hadn't been wasted. Bjarni went outside and saw what had happened. He said nothing and had the two men buried. Then everything was quiet till after Christmas.

One evening after Bjarni and his wife Rannveig had gone to bed, she said to him, "What do you think everyone in the district is talking about these days?"

"I couldn't say," said Bjarni. "In my opinion most people talk a lot of rubbish."

"This is what people are mainly talking about now," she continued: "They're wondering how far Thorstein the Staff-Struck can go before you bother to take revenge. He's killed three of your servants, and your supporters are beginning to doubt whether you can protect them, seeing that you've failed to avenge this. You often take action when you shouldn't and hold back when you should."

"It's the same old story," said Bjarni, "no one seems willing to learn from another man's lesson. Thorstein has never killed anyone without a good reason—but still, I'll think about your suggestion."

With that they dropped the subject and slept through the night. In the morning Rannveig woke up as Bjarni was taking down his sword and shield. She asked him where he was going.

"The time has come for me to settle that matter of honour between Thorstein of Sunnudale and myself," he said.

"How many men are you taking with you?" she asked.

"I'm not taking a whole army to attack Thorstein," he said. "I'm going alone."

"You mustn't do that," she said, "risking your life against the weapons of that killer."

"You're a typical woman," said Bjarni, "arguing against the very thing you were urging just a few hours ago! There's a limit to my patience, I can only stand so much taunting from you and others. And once my mind's made up, there's no point in trying to hold me back."

Bjarni went over to Sunnudale. He saw Thorstein standing in the doorway, and they exchanged some words.

"You'll fight me in single combat," said Bjarni, "on that hillock over there in the home-meadow."

"I'm in no way good enough to fight you," said Thorstein. "I give you my promise to leave the country with the first ship that sails abroad. I know a generous man like you will provide my father with labour to run the farm if I go away."

"You can't talk yourself out of this now," said Bjarni.

"You'll surely let me go and see my father first," said Thorstein.

"Certainly," said Bjarni.

Thorstein went inside and told his father that Bjarni had come and challenged him to a duel.

The old man said, "Anybody who offends a more powerful man in his own district can hardly expect to wear out many more new shirts. In my opinion your offences are so serious, I can't find any excuse for you. So you'd better take your weapons and defend yourself the best you can. In my younger days I'd never have given way before someone like Bjarni, great fighting-man though he may be. I'd much rather lose you than have a coward for a son."

Thorstein went outside and walked with Bjarni up the hillock. They started fighting with determination and destroyed each other's shield. When they had been fighting for a long time, Bjarni said to Thorstein, "I'm getting very thirsty now, I'm not so used to hard work as you are."

"Go down to the stream then and drink," said Thorstein.

Bjarni did so, and laid the sword down beside him. Thorstein picked it up, examined it and said, "You can't have been using this sword at Bodvarsdale."

Bjarni said nothing, and they went back to the hillock. After they'd been fighting for a time, it became obvious to Bjarni that Thorstein was a highly skilled fighter, and the outcome seemed less certain than he'd expected.

"Everything seems to go wrong for me today," he said. "Now my shoe-thong's loose."

"Tie it up then," said Thorstein.

When Bjarni bent down to tie it, Thorstein went into the house and brought back two shields and a sword. He joined Bjarni on the hillock and said, "Here's a sword and shield my father sends you. The sword shouldn't get so easily blunted as the one you've been using. And I don't want to stand here any longer with no shield to protect me against your blows. I'd very much like us to stop this game now, for I'm afraid your good luck will prove stronger than my bad luck. Every man wants to save his life, and I would too, if I could."

"There's no point in your trying to talk yourself out of this," said Bjarni. "The fight must go on."

"I wouldn't like to be the first to strike," said Thorstein.

Then Bjarni struck at Thorstein, destroying his shield, and Thorstein hacked down Bjarni's shield in return.

"That was a blow," said Bjarni.

Thorstein replied, "Yours wasn't any lighter."

Bjarni said, "Your sword seems to be biting much better now than it was earlier."

"I want to save myself from the foulest of luck if I possibly can," said Thorstein. "It scares me to have to fight you, so I want you yourself to settle the matter between us."

It was Bjarni's turn to strike. Both men had lost their shields. Bjarni said,

"It would be a great mistake in one stroke both to throw away good fortune and do wrong. In my opinion I'd be fully paid for my three servants if you took their place and served me faithfully."

Thorstein said, "I've had plenty of opportunity today to take advantage of you, if my bad luck had been stronger than your good luck. I'll never deceive you."

"Now I can see what a remarkable man you must be," said Bjarni. "You'll allow me to go inside to see your father and tell him about this in my own words?"

"You can go if you want as far as I'm concerned," said Thorstein, "but be on your guard."

Bjarni went up to the bed-closet where Old Thorarin was lying. Thorarin asked who was there, and Bjarni told him.

"What's your news, friend Bjarni?" said Thorarin.

"The killing of Thorstein, your son," said Bjarni.

"Did he put up any defence at all?" asked Thorarin.

"I don't think there's ever been a better fighter than your son, Thorarin," said Bjarni.

"It's no wonder your opponents at Bodvarsdale found you so hard to deal with," said Thorarin, "seeing that you've overcome my son."

Bjarni said, "I want to invite you to come over to Hof and take the seat of honour there for the rest of your life. I'll be just like a son to you."

"I'm in the same position now as any other pauper," said Thorarin. "Only a fool accepts a promise gladly, and promises of chieftains like yourself aren't usually honoured for more than a month after the event, while you're trying to console us. After that we're treated as ordinary paupers, though our grief doesn't grow any the less for that. Still, anyone who shakes hands on a bargain with a man of your character should be satisfied, in spite of other men's lessons. So I'd like to shake hands with you, and you'd better come into the bed-closet to me. Come closer now, for I'm an old man and trembling on my feet because of ill-health and old age. And I must admit, the loss of my son has upset me a bit."

Bjarni went into the bed-closet and shook Thorarin by the hand. Then he realized the old man was groping for a short sword with the idea of thrusting it at him. Bjarni pulled back his hand and said, "You merciless old rascal! I can promise you now you'll get what you deserve. Your son Thorstein is alive and well, and he'll come with me over to Hof, but you'll be given slaves to run the farm for you, and never suffer any want for the rest of your life."

Thorstein went with Bjarni over to Hof, and stayed in his service for the rest of his life. He was considered a man of great courage and integrity. Bjarni kept his standing and became better-liked and more self-controlled the older he grew. He was a very trustworthy man. In the last years of his life he became a devout Christian and went to Rome on pilgrimage. He died on that journey, and is buried at a town called Sutri,[6] just north of Rome.[7]

*   *   *

---

6. The MSS have Vateri, which is probably a scribal error. The town Sutri is mentioned elsewhere in early Icelandic records.   7. The story concludes with a long account of Bjarni's descendants, extending into the thirteenth century [Editor's note].

MEDIEVAL LYRICS: A SELECTION

While in classical Greece the term *lyric* referred to poems sung to the accompaniment of the lyre, the short poems of Rome, such as those by Catullus, were composed to be read silently. The medieval period saw a return to the tradition of poetry as performance. Most medieval lyrics, including many written in Latin, were verses sung to an accompanying tune. One major reason for this return to performance was the influence of the vernacular traditions of song brought into prominence by the various cultures that reshaped Europe after the fall of Rome. All the peoples that together created the Middle Ages—the multifarious nations of the Roman empire (from the Persians in the east to the Celts in the west), the tribes (Germanic, Scandinavian, Slavic, and Eurasian) that divided the fallen Roman empire, and the inhabitants (both Arabic and non-Arabic) of the Islamic world—had traditions of song that stretched back into time immemorial. By their very nature most of these songs were ephemeral. Arabic and Anglo-Saxon songs do survive from as early as the seventh and eighth centuries, and early Latin lyrics show the influence of vernacular forms. But we lack all but a very few of the vernacular songs composed prior to about the year 1100. The reason is not just that it is less likely for a vernacular text to be preserved in an expensive manuscript than one in Latin, but that virtually all medieval lyrics were performed in public rather than read in private. Those that were written down and survived thus are only a small fraction of the lyrics that actually circulated throughout the Middle Ages.

The medieval lyrics selected here represent the most important linguistic communities and demonstrate both the range of topics treated by medieval lyricists and their extraordinary skill. While the poems are printed in chronological order, regardless of their original language of composition, readers will notice that certain topics recur with some frequency. Unsurprisingly, the most common is love. Most important here are the lyrics written beginning around 1100 in Provençal, a literary language derived from the various dialects spoken in the southern half of France and the bordering regions of Italy and Spain. Here we find expressed, if not for the first time in Western literature, then in terms that became decisive, our modern form of romantic love. Often called *courtly love*, a term coined by French scholars in the nineteenth century, it was in the Middle Ages known as *fin'amors* (Provençal), *fine amour* (French), or *minne* (German). Its central elements are that love is an overwhelming emotion that promises ecstatic bliss but also causes painful yearning; that the beloved is an embodiment of all virtue and yet often remains cool and distant, even unaware of the lover's sufferings; and that love is an ennobling emotion, in the sense both that it can be fully experienced only by gentlemen and ladies and that it causes them to behave in exalted and selfless ways. Various aspects of this emotional complex are certainly present in earlier writing. In the *Phaedrus* and the *Symposium*, for instance, Plato (429–347 B.C.) described erotic love between men as providing a means for philosophical and moral improvement, and the Roman poet Ovid (43 B.C.–A.D. 17) described passionate, unrequited love between men and women in terms that medieval poets knew and imitated. So too, as early as the Umayyad period (A.D. 650–750) Arabic poets described a love—known as ʿUdhrite love—that was ardent, chaste, and incapacitating to the point of death. Indeed, it is likely that the Provençal poets were influenced by singers and composers from the Iberian peninsula who continued to celebrate this kind of love. One of these Arabic lyrics is *The Singing Lute*, written by a poet of whom we know only his name, Ibn Arfaʿ Raʾsuh. (In the manuscripts medieval lyrics are untitled, so that all titles are supplied by the editor or translator.) The poem was composed in Spain—or al-Andalus, as it was known to its Arab rulers—in the mid-eleventh century to celebrate the poet's patron, known as al-Maʾmūn or Yahya ibn Dhī n-Nūn, the ruler of Toledo. Written according to a strict scheme of meter and rhyme, and deploying the delicate natural imagery characteristic of medieval Arabic poetry, it compares the disdain of the beautiful lady to the haughtiness of the great warrior, a comparison that implies that because he is "the terrorizer of armies" al-Ma'mūn is able to sustain a sophisticated culture that supports both poetry and love. Other love poems from al-Andalus included here are the beautiful *Summer*, written in Hebrew by Judah Halevi, perhaps the most distinguished of the many Jewish scholars and poets who flourished under Arab rule, and the compact *In Battle*, by the Arabic poet Abu-l-Hasan ibn Al-Qabturnuh, a poem that combines love and war in a surprisingly effective way.

Quite apart from its originality or sources, the influence of the Provençal celebration of *fin'amors* was enormous. Like the poets of al-Andalus, those of Provence drew connections among the virtuosity and elegance of their lyrics, the exalted delicacy of the emotion they celebrated, and the aristocratic courts in which they lived and composed. In this way the love lyric became not merely a private statement but an expression of a way of life that was elegantly mannered and knowingly sophisticated. As the French term *courtoisie*, or "courtliness," suggests, the love lyric described values that derived from noble society: intensity of feeling matched elevation of social standing. In this way the poetry combined private and public concerns, and the relation of lover to beloved is often phrased in the same terms as the feudal relation of a lord to his vassal (the beloved was, in Provençal poetry, referred to as *midons*, "my lord"). It is hardly surprising, then, that many of the poems that survive are written by noble authors. The ability to compose both lyrics and music was one that every well-bred aristocrat wanted to possess. Certainly there were professional composers and performers, but they often served as mouthpieces or instructors to their noble patrons. The oldest datable Provençal lyrics are by William IX, duke of Aquitaine (ca. 1071–1127). He is represented here by his *Spring Song*, which includes in a few stanzas a remarkable range of amorous feelings, from a rather conventional statement about love in general through an anxious lover's doubt to a rousing celebration of mutual pleasure and a scornful rejection of mere braggarts. Another noble author is Beatrice, countess of Dia—one of a significant number of women troubadours—whose witty *A Lover's Prize* begins with resentment at her lover's betrayal and ends with a boldly explicit insistence on her own rights as a lover. On the other hand, the *Love Song* by Jaufré Rudel, who was probably not an aristocrat, begins by celebrating love, but the possibility of disappointment leads him to turn away from eroticism to religion: according to tradition, Jaufré died on crusade. In *The Art of Love*, Arnaut Daniel, one of the most technically proficient of the troubadours, draws a connection between the control required for poetic virtuosity and the overwhelming ardor caused by love, a paradox that he triumphantly accepts in the poem's final lines.

Beginning in Provence around the year 1100, then, the love lyric spread throughout Europe to Sicily, Italy, France, Germany, and England. In each of these environments it took on slightly different characteristics. In Sicily and Italy there was a strong interest both in verbal and metrical virtuosity and in the way in which intense love could lead to religious truth. The great Italian poets of the late thirteenth century created what Dante called the *dolce stil nuovo*, or "sweet new manner" (see below, p. 1955). By this Dante meant that poetic virtuosity was not opposed to but rather expressed the intensity and authenticity of the lover's feelings; and above all, that the lady opened her admirer to a love that was genuinely religious. As he said in his lyric autobiography, the *Vita nuova* or *New Life*, the lady "seems to be a creature come from Heaven to earth, to manifest a miracle." Dante and the other *stilnovisti*, as they are called, were thus the direct precursors of Petrarch. The earliest of the four Italian poems selected here is by Guido Guinizzelli, a Bolognese poet much admired by Dante. This famous poem, *Love and Nobility*, argues that true nobility is a function not of ancestry but of virtue, and that virtue is in turn a function of a love that is more philosophical and religious than emotional. The next poem, *An Encounter*, is by Guido Cavalcanti, a friend of Dante and the true founder of the *dolce stil nuovo*. Avoiding philosophical speculations about love, his poem celebrates instead a dreamlike moment of amorous fulfillment. The sonnet that follows, *Love and Poetry*, is addressed by Dante to Guido Cavalcanti and another poet of their circle, Lapo Gianni. Here Dante invokes a company of poets "enchanted" by Merlin and devoted to a love that is simultaneously earthly and heavenly, a charmingly lighthearted treatment of a theme that in other places he expresses with greater seriousness. An example is the next sonnet, in which Dante provides his own version of Guinizzelli's equation of nobility, virtue, and love.

The two German love poems show how both the Provençal interest in the psychology of love and the Italian concern with its metaphysics were taken up by the poets of the north. *The Wound of Love*, by Heinrich von Morungen, one of the earliest of the *minnesingers*, combines the troubadour theme of unrequited love with an awareness that hostility often accompanies desire, a complexity of feeling intensified by the reduction of both lover and lady to two pairs of lips. Walther von der Vogelweide, generally regarded as the finest of the *minnesingers*, is represented here by *Dancing Girl*, which hides great depths beneath its apparently simple surface: vacillating between dreaming and waking, the poem ends with the poet searching for an ideal that is again more than simply amorous. Another poem that begins as a love poem but then develops into an enigmatic account of a natural creature that is more than natural is *The Fox*, by Dafydd ap Gwilym, the best-known representative of the rich poetic traditions of medieval Wales.

The two French love poems included here also show how the motifs of the Provençal lyric continued to provide poets with fresh inspiration until the very end of the Middle Ages. *Aubade* is an anonymous dawn song, a traditional poem in which lovers—in this case, the woman only—lament the coming of day because it will mean their parting. Charles d'Orleans, the author of the *Balade*, was captured at the battle of Agincourt in 1415 and spent twenty-five years as a prisoner in England. This delicate lyric, written in a traditional form, neatly combines the old feudal metaphors of the lady as lord and the lover as vassal with commercial imagery that derives from a new and very different world.

While medieval lyricists were preoccupied by love in its many manifestations, they also used the short poem to express and explore religious feelings. Many of these poems are in Latin, the language of the Church, and they are often written to serve as part of a religious service. The poems by Notker Balbulus, a monk in the great monastery at St. Gall in present-day Switzerland, and by Hildegard of Bingen, a German nun who became famous as a religious visionary, scientist, poet, musician, and reformer of Church abuses, are the words to a musical work known as a sequence, a chant sung during the Mass. Notker's *Hymn to Holy Women*, written to be sung on the feast days of holy women, is based on the traditional idea that Mary was the New Testament counterpart to Eve: where Eve had brought human beings into the grasp of Satan by her disobedience, it was through Mary that Christ came to free them. The other central idea of the poem is the harrowing of hell, when Christ, after his death on the cross, descended into hell and released the souls of the just held captive by the Devil, represented in the poem by the Ethiop and the dragon. Here the cross is symbolized both by the ladder that stretches up to heaven and by the hook that pierces the dragon's jaw, an image derived from the Book of Job. Hildegard's sequence, *A Hymn to St. Maximinus*, celebrates an early Christian saint. Using images derived from the Bible, and especially the Song of Songs, Hildegard describes a vision in which Maximinus is seen both as a priest celebrating the Mass and as a saint welcomed into heaven. He is both an embodiment of divine virtue and the means by which others can ascend to it. Other Latin poems drew upon the themes of secular poetry and turned them to religious purposes. *Song of Summer* is an anonymous work found in an anthology of various poems that were originally composed in Germany, France, and Italy and were copied together into a manuscript in eleventh-century England. By means of a catalog of birds and their songs it celebrates the fecundity, variety, and beauty of nature, invoking in its final stanza the Virgin Mary, who as the

Mother of God is simultaneously the source of this goodness, a perfect instance of it, and—paradoxically—an alternative to it (hence she is represented by the bee rather than by a bird).

By no means were all religious poems in Latin, however, and vernacular poets were adept at expressing powerful religious feelings and complex thoughts. Two English examples are *Calvary*, which encapsulates the meaning of the Crucifixion in only four lines, and the late poem *Lament of the Virgin*, which describes the sufferings of the Virgin in a voice that reaches out to all men and women. Another example of the way secular and religious languages are brought together is *Strawberry Picking*, by the mysterious poet known as Alexander the Wild (i.e., the Vagabond), a poem that oscillates delicately between secular and religious meanings, between an observant realism and a suggestive symbolism. Finally, the woman writer Hadewijch of Antwerp (or Brabant), who composed in Flemish, is represented by *The Cult of Love*, a poem that begins within the conventions of troubadour verse but transforms them into a personal experience that is both intense and enigmatic: is it an earthly lover of whom she speaks, or—as we would expect of a religious writer like Hadewijch—Christ?

The subjects treated by medieval lyrics were by no means confined to love and religion. Then as now, one of the most common lyric themes was loss, and medieval poems are often elegiac. The first poem in our selection was written by a German monk named Walahfrid Strabo in 829, when he was about twenty: in order to further his education, he had been sent from Reichenau, a monastery on an island in Lake Constance where he had grown up, to Fulda, a monastery several hundred miles away. In the poem Walahfrid connects his own loneliness to the idea that all Christians are exiles from their true homeland, heaven, a heaven of which the island monastery is an earthly image; he defines himself as the child not of earthly parents—who no doubt committed him to the monastery at an early age—but as the son of his first teacher who was his spiritual father, of the monastery that is his spiritual mother, and finally of God Himself; and in the course of the poem he comes to understand that the "wisdom" he has come to Fulda to find can also be found in "the teaching of life" that his exile has forced upon him. Some ten years later Walahfrid did in fact return to Reichenau as its abbot. Another elegy, written almost six hundred years later, in the early 1400s, is *Alone in Martyrdom*, by Christine de Pizan, a remarkable writer who composed a wide range of works including treatises on moral, political, and feminist issues. Here she laments the early death of her husband in a graceful lyric whose elegance enhances its depth of feeling. A similar elegy, but one in which loss finds compensation in the thought of God's mercy, is *A Letter from the Grave*, by the Hebrew poet Meir Halevi Abulafia, written for his sister in 1212. Conversely, a poem that functions as an elegy for an entire civilization is the Anglo-Saxon *The Ruin*. Composed probably in the ninth or tenth century, it describes the wonder with which someone from the Germanic world—in which most building was done with timber—gazes on the mighty architectural achievements of the Romans (who preceded the Anglo-Saxons as rulers of England) while implicitly acknowledging the transience of all human accomplishment. Finally, *The Sacrifice of Isaac*, by Rabbi Ephraim ben Jacob of Bonn, combines elegy with prayer. Ephraim was a Hebrew scholar who witnessed and chronicled the massacres endured by the Jews of the Rhineland in 1146 during the Second Crusade, as they had endured similarly pitiless massacres in 1096 at the time of the First Crusade. His powerful poem memorializes these dreadful events—in which rather than abandon their religion Jews chose suicide or murder, often killing their own children—by locating them in the context of the biblical story of the sacrifice of Isaac. Ephraim here adopts an ancient Jewish tradition that interpreted the biblical story to mean that Isaac was actually killed by his father, Abraham, but resurrected, transported to Eden, and then returned to his father. Yet Ephraim's poem refuses to embrace any easy consolation, and it remains an unflinching affirmation of faith in the face of injustice and terrible suffering.

Last but not least, medieval poets often wrote poems simply about themselves—

or, more accurately, about selves they pretended (or wanted) to be. A salient example is the Archpoet's *His Confession*. The Archpoet is the name given to an anonymous writer who made popular the idea of the vagabond-poet, and while his vivid picture of the riotous life of the wandering scholar has been very influential, it now seems to have been composed as much of theatrical extravagance as hard fact. Similarly theatrical are two other "autobiographical" poems. *In Praise of War*, by Bertran de Born, a minor noble and notorious troublemaker, celebrates with unrestrained enthusiasm the war-making that was so central a part of the life of the twelfth-century knight and brought misery to so many ordinary people (Bertran appears in Dante's *Inferno* among the sowers of discord [p. 1922]). And a selection from François Villon's *Testament* also moves us away from the aristocratic world of much medieval lyric to the harsher realities of economic and emotional necessity endured by the population at large. Villon, a man who knew both poverty and imprisonment, provides us with the dramatic monologue of an old woman who—like Chaucer's Wife of Bath—expresses the familiar medieval concern about mutability with a powerful sense of its personal meaning. These apparently personal poems are best read as dramatic monologues, virtually as theatrical performances. But that doesn't mean that they don't express, as do all of these lyrics, human feelings that were as real to medieval people as they are to us. Perhaps more immediate in its appeal, albeit deriving from the other end of the social scale, is *The Scorpions* by Alfonso X, thirteenth-century king of Castile and Léon, who created at his court an environment in which Christian, Jewish, and Muslim scholars and poets worked in harmony. In this poem Alfonso wistfully yearns to escape from the demands of kingship, and perhaps especially from the armed rebellions that characterized his reign, into the life of the merchant, which he romanticizes in an act of wistful imaginative freedom.

Accessible guides to the individual poets and to the development of the lyric within the various languages of medieval Europe can be found in the relevant articles in *The Dictionary of the Middle Ages*, 13 vols., ed. J. P. Strayer (1987). An excellent introduction, with commentary on a number of the poems printed here, is Peter Dronke, *The Medieval Lyric*, 3rd ed. (1996). Both these works contain suggestions for further reading. A brilliant study that locates Rabbi Ephraim's poem in the context of both Jewish tradition and the Christian massacres of Jews in the eleventh and twelfth centuries is Shalom Spiegel, *The Last Trial* (1979).

PRONOUNCING GLOSSARY

The following list uses common English syllables and stress accents to provide rough equivalents of selected words whose pronunciation may be unfamiliar to the general reader.

Abu-1-Hasan ibn Al-Qabturnuh: *a-boo-1-ha'san ibun al kwab-turn-uh*

al-Mamun: *al-ma-moon'*

Annwn: *an'-wun*

Arnaut Daniel: *ar-no'dan-yel'*

Dafydd ap Gwilem: *daff'-id ap gwil'-em*

François Villon: *frahn-swaw' vee-yonh'*

Guido Guinizzelli: *gwee'-do gween'-itz-elli*

Hadewijch: *had'-e-witch*

Ibn Arfaᶜ Raʾsuh: *i'bun ar'-fah rah'-suh*

Jaufré Rudel: *jo-fray' ru-del'*

Meir Halevi Abulafia: *mey-er hal-ay-vee a-bool-a-fia'*

Reichenau: *raik'-en-ow*

Sulayma: *sul-ay'-ma*

Walther von der Vogelweide: *val'ter von der vo'-gel-vai'-duh*

Yahya ibn Dhi n-Nun: *ya'hya ibun thee' en-noon'*

Ya'rub: *yah'-roob*

WALAHFRID STRABO
808/9–849

Elegy on Reichenau[1]

Sister Muse, lament for my pain,
speak of my sad parting,
alas, from the land of my fathers, ceaselessly
harassed as I was by shameful penury.

Wretched, I seek heart-felt wisdom,   5
and so I leave my homeland,
stricken by many kinds of hardship, I lament,
loathed and in exile.

No kindly teacher consoles me,
nor does any good master hearten me;   10
the only thing that keeps my miserable body alive
is the food I eat.

Bitter cold assails my naked flesh,
there is no warmth in my hands,
goose-pimples stand out on my feet   15
and my face flinches before the harsh winter.

Indoors I suffer the icy cold,
the sight of my frozen bed gives no pleasure,
warm neither when I get up nor where I sleep,
I snatch what rest I can.   20

If only wisdom which I esteem
could take hold in my mind
even the smallest part of it, the warmth of my wits
would make me safer.

Alas, father,[2] if only you were there—   25
you whom I have followed to the ends of the earth—
I believe that no harm would have come
to the poor little heart of your pupil.

Look, tears burst forth as I recall
how good was the peace I long ago enjoyed,   30
when happy Reichenau gave me
a modest roof over my head.

May you always be my holy and dear, dear
mother, consecrated by your throngs of saints,

---

1. Translated from the Latin by Peter Godman. Reichenau is a monastery on an island in Lake Constance, which is located on what is now the Swiss-German border.   **2.** An older monk named Grimald.

through praise-giving, the promotion of good deeds, and worship, 35
happy island.

Now too let us call that island holy
because there the mother of God is richly worshipped,
so that we joyously cry out as we should,
happy island! 40

Although you are surrounded by deep waters,
nonetheless your foundations are firm in love,
and you spread its holy teachings among all men,
happy island.

Always wishing to see you, 45
I remember you day and night,
recalling all the kindness you bring me,
happy island.

Grow now and flourish, develop and prosper
so that, following the Lord's will, 50
with your children you may be called
happy Reichenau!

Let almighty Christ grant in His mercy
that I may return and rejoice on your site,
saying: "Hail, glorious mother, 55
forever!"

Christ, king of kings, lord of the mighty,
you who are called wisdom of the Father,
deign to refresh my heart
with the teaching of life. 60

Grant, redeemer, I pray, a span of years,
so that, on returning to the bosom of my fatherland[3]
for which I have longed, I may sing
to Christ in songs of praise.

We sing in thanks to the highest father, 65
joined to His son in all-embracing love
and to the Spirit ruling with equal power
forever and ever. Amen.

3. Could refer either to Reichenau or to heaven.

NOTKER BALBULUS
ca. 840–912

A Hymn to Holy Women[1]

1. A ladder stretching up to heaven,
   circled by torments—

2. At whose foot an attentive
     dragon
   stands on guard, forever
     awake,

3. So that no one can climb even
     to the first rung and not be
     torn—

4. The ascent of the ladder barred
     by an Ethiop,[2] brandishing
   a drawn sword, threatening
     death,

5. While over the topmost rung
     leans a young man, radiant,
   a golden bough in his hand—

6. This is the ladder the love of
     Christ
   made so free for women
   that, treading down the
     dragon
   and striding past the Ethiop's
     sword,

7. By way of torments of every kind
     they can reach heaven's
     summit
   and take the golden laurel
   from the hand of the strength-
     giving king.

8. What good did it do you,
     impious serpent,
   once to have a deceived a
     woman,

9. Since a virgin brought forth
     God incarnate,
   only-begotten of the Father:

10. He who took your spoils away
    and pierces your jaw with a hook[3]

11. To make of it an open gate
    for Eve's race, whom you long to
      hold.

12. So now you can see girls
      defeating you, envious one,

13. And married women now
      bearing sons who please
      God.

14. Now you groan at the loyalty
      of widows to their dead
      husbands,

15. You who once seduced a girl
      to disloyalty towards her
      creator.

16. Now you can see women made
      captains
    in the war that is waged against
      you,

17. Women who spur on their sons
      bravely to conquer all your
      tortures.

18. Even courtesans, your vessels,
      are purified by God,

19. Transmuted into a burnished
      temple for him alone.

---

1. Translated from the Latin by Peter Dronke.   2. I.e., the Devil.   3. See Job 40.20.

20. For these graces let us now
   glorify him together,
   both the sinners and those who
      are just,

21. Him who strengthens those who
      stand
   and gives his right hand to
      the fallen,
   that at least after crimes we may
      rise.

ANONYMOUS

ca. ninth or tenth century

The Ruin[1]

Marvelous is this wall-stone—but the fates broke,
smashed this city; this work of giants is decaying.
The roofs are fallen, the towers are in ruins,
the frosty gate is despoiled, frost is on the masonry,
damaged buildings are torn, collapsed,   5
undermined by age. The grasp of the earth holds
the master builder, he's dead and gone
into the hard grasp of the ground, until a hundred generations
of people shall have passed away. Often this wall,
red-stained and gray with lichen, one reign after another,   10
has withstood storms; high and wide, now it has fallen.
The wall-stone still survives, broken down by the weather . . .
. . . .
                        . . . he put together a shrewd,
keen plan with rings, the clever man who bound
these wall braces together with wire, wonderfully!   20
Bright were the city halls, many the bath-houses,
high the crowd of gables, loud the noise of warriors,
many the mead-halls[2] full of people's joy—
until fate the powerful overturned all that.
Slaughtered men died everywhere, days of pestilence came,   25
death took away all the brave men.
Their sanctuaries became waste places,
their city decayed. The craftsmen died,
the warriors fell to the earth. So these halls decay,
and this red-curved roof of the vault splits off from   30
its tiles. The ruin fell to the ground,
broken into heaps, where once many a man,
happy of heart and bright with gold, adorned with splendor,
proud and flushed with wine, shone in his armor,
gazed on his treasure, on his silver, on jewels,   35
on wealth, on possessions, on valuable stone,
on this bright city and its broad kingdom.
Stone halls stood here, the streams gave off heat

1. Translated from the Anglo-Saxon by Lee Patterson. The poem survives in fragmentary form.   2. Mead
is an alcoholic drink made from honey.

in a great surge; the wall enclosed everything
in its bright bosom, there where the baths were.   40
hot to the core. That was elegant!
They let the hot streams gush . . .
over the gray stone . . .

. . . .
                                 . . . there the baths were . . .   46

. . . .
                                 . . . That is a kingly thing,
a house . . . . a city . . . .

ANONYMOUS

ca. eleventh century

Song of Summer[1]

The woodlands clothe the slender shoots
of boughs, laden with fruits;
from high perches wood pigeons sing
    songs to one and all.
Here the turtledove moans, here the thrush resounds,   5
here the age-old song of blackbirds rings out,
and the sparrow, not silent, with its chatter
    takes possession of the heights beneath the elms.
Here the nightingale sings, delighting in leafy boughs,
pours out a long warbling through the breeze,   10
solemnly, and with tremulous voice the kite
    causes the sky to echo.
The eagle as it soars starward sings, upon the breezes
the lark sings and produces sounds in melodies.
From above it swoops, with a different melody   15
    as it touches ground.
The swift swallow ever makes its call,
the quail sings, the jackdaw resounds:
thus birds everywhere celebrate for everyone
    the song of summer.   20
None among the birds is like the bee,
who represents the ideal of chastity,
if not she who bore Christ in her womb
    inviolate.

1. Translated from the Latin by Jan Ziolkowski.

IBN ARFAʿ RAʾSUH
eleventh century

The Singing Lute[1]

The lute trills the most wondrous melodies
And the watercourses cut through the flower beds of the gardens.
The birds sing on the branches of the *bān*,[2]
And joy enlivens the lions of the battlefield.
Every one of us is an Emir[3] and a sultan because of the wine.   5
The lute-strings speak with eloquent charm
While the birds respond to them from the myrtle branches.
Come, give me wine to drink for the garden exudes fragrance;
The Pleiads[4] have set and it is sweet to take the morning drink
Offered to me by a lovely gazelle   10
Who is like a tender branch enveloped in a cloak of eglantine,
Whose sides are covered in embroidered silks, who almost breaks
    because he is so tender.
Hold fast to the love and drink to the health of the Possessor of Dual Glory,[5]
Who supports the lands of the East and the West,
And who gives succor to believers, a descendant of Yaʾrub,[6]   15
The lofty king, who humbles sultans,
Who leads cavalcades, and is the lion of the battlefields.
He is a king whose heart is braver than the lion's,
Just as his finger is more generous than the rain clouds.
Should Time ever appear frowning or with a severe face   20
He meets it smiling like the flowers in the gardens.
His deeds are stars [shining out over] this world and religion.
The beloved refuses to return the greeting
While the heart is aflame from the excess of love.
Thus the sorrowing one sings the song of one confused by love: 25
"You go by, yet you give no greeting as though you were al-Maʾmūn,[7]
The terrorizer of armies, Yahya ibn Dhī n-Nūn."[8]

1. Translated from the Arabic by James T. Monroe. Bracketed words are the translator's interpolation.
2. The bonduc, or horse-radish tree, which has fragrant white flowers.   3. A ruler.   4. A constellation.
5. The poet's patron, who is here presented as ruling over both the Islamic east (Persia, Arabia, and Egypt) and west (Spain).   6. The mythical ancestor of the patron's tribe.   7. One of the patron's names.
8. Another of the patron's names.

WILLIAM IX, DUKE OF AQUITAINE
1071–1127

Spring Song[1]

In the sweetness of new spring
the woods grow leafy, little birds,

1. Translated from the Provençal by Peter Dronke.

each in their own language, sing,
rehearse new stanzas with new words,
and it is good that man should find   5
the joy that most enchants his mind.

I see no messenger or note
from her, my first source of delight;
my heart can neither sleep nor laugh,
I dare not make a further move,   10
till I know what the end will be—
is she what I would have her be?

Our love together goes the way
of the branch on the hawthorn-tree,
trembling in the night, a prey   15
to the hoar-frost and the showers,
till next morning, when the sun
enfolds the green leaves and the boughs.

One morning I remember still
we put an end to skirmishing,   20
and she gave me so great a gift:
her loving body, and her ring.
May God keep me alive until
my hands again move in her mantle!

For I shun that strange talk which might pull   25
my Helpmeet and myself apart;
I know that words have their own life,
and swift discourses spread about—
let others vaunt love as they will,
we have love's food, we have the knife!   30

JUDAH HALEVI
ca. 1075–1141

Summer[1]

The earth, like a girl, sipped the rains
Of winter past, and those the ministering cloud distilled
Or perhaps, like a secluded bride in winter,
Whose soul longs for the coming of love's time
She waited, and sought the season ripe for love   5
Till summer came, and calmed her anxious heart
Wearing golden tunics and white embroidered flax.

---

1. Translated from the Hebrew by William M. Davis.

Like a girl who delights in her finery and raiment,
Every day she renews the grace of her embroiderers
And provides all her neighbors with new garments.   10
Every day she changes the colors of her fields
Now with strings of pearls, now with emeralds or rubies,
Offering her meadows now white or green or gold
Or blushing like the sweetheart kissing her beloved.
Her trellises display such gorgeous flowers   15
It seems as if she stole the stars from heaven.
Here is paradise, whose sheltered buds are clustered
Among the vines, kindled with blushes that incite to love.
The grapes are cold as snow in the hand of him who plucks them.
But in his entrails, they burn as hot as fire.   20
From the whirling cask, the wine, like sun, is rising.
And we shall bring our onyx² cups to pour it.
In the love of wine we shall stroll beneath the bowers
Around the garden, and smile with tears of rain,
Bright with shining drops spilled by the clouds   25
That scatter round like strings of pearls.
She finds joy in the song of the swallow, and in the song of the vintagers,
And in cooing pigeons tamed by love.
She twitters in the branches, as the maiden sings
Behind her zither, swaying as she dances.   30
My soul is attentive to the breeze of dawn,
For it fondles the breath of my beloved.
A wanton breeze it is, that steals the scent of myrtles
To waft it off to lovers apart.
The heads of the myrtle rise and nod in turn   35
While the tremulous fronds of the palm tree
Seem to applaud the singing of the birds.

2. A semiprecious stone.

ABU-L-HASAN IBN AL-QABTURNUH
twelfth century

In Battle¹

I remembered Sulayma² when the passion
    of battle was as fierce
as the passion of my body when we parted.

I thought I saw, among the lances, the tall
    perfection of her body,   5
and when they bent toward me I embraced them.

1. Translated from the Arabic by Lysander Kemp.   2. The name of the beloved.

HILDEGARD OF BINGEN
1098–1179

A Hymn to St. Maximinus[1]

1A

The dove peered in
through the latticed window,
where before her gaze
raining, a balm rained down
from the brightness of Maximinus.[2]   5

1B

The sun's heat blazed
and streamed into the darkness
from which blossomed the gem
—in the building of the temple—
of the purest generous heart.   10

2A

He, the sublime tower
made of Lebanon's tree,[3]
made of cypress,
is decked with jacinth and sardonyx,[4]
city that no architect's skill can match.   15

2B

He, the swift hart
ran up to the fountain
of purest water
bubbling from the mightiest stone
whose moisture made the sweet perfumes flow.   20

3A

You perfumers
who live in the gentlest greenness
of the king's gardens,
you who mount into the heights
when you have consummated   25
the only sacrifice among the rams,

3B

Lucent[5] among you
is this architect, wall of the temple,
he who longed
for an eagle's wings as he kissed   30

---

1. Translated from the Latin by Peter Dronke.   2. A fourth-century saint, patron of the nuns at the Benedictine Abbey at Trier for whom Hildegard probably wrote this sequence.   3. The cypress.
4. Precious stones.   5. I.e., glowing.

his foster-mother, Wisdom,
in Ekklesia's[6] glorious fecundity!

4A

Maximinus, you are mountain and valley,
and in both you appear, a pinnacle,
where the mountain-goat walked, and the elephant,   35
and Wisdom played in her delight.

4B

You are both brave and gentle;
in the rites and in the sparkling of the altar
you mount as a smoke of fragrant spices
to the column of praise   40

5

Where you plead the cause of your people
who aspire to the mirror of light
for which there is praise on high.

6. The Church.

THE ARCHPOET
d. 1165?

His Confession[1]

Seething over inwardly
    With fierce indignation,
In my bitterness of soul,
    Hear my declaration.
I am of one element,   5
    Levity my matter,
Like enough a withered leaf
    For the winds to scatter.

Since it is the property
    Of the sapient   10
To sit firm upon a rock,
    It is evident
That I am a fool, since I
    Am a flowing river,
Never under the same sky,   15
    Transient for ever.

1. Translated from the Latin by Helen Waddell.

Hither, thither, masterless
   Ship upon the sea,
Wandering through the ways of air,
   Go the birds like me.   20
Bound am I by ne'er a bond,
   Prisoner to no key,
Questing go I for my kind,
   Find depravity.

Never yet could I endure   25
   Soberness and sadness,
Jests I love and sweeter than
   Honey find I gladness.
Whatsoever Venus bids
   Is a joy excelling,   30
Never in an evil heart
   Did she make her dwelling.

Down the broad way do I go,
   Young and unregretting,
Wrap me in my vices up,   35
   Virtue all forgetting,
Greedier for all delight
   Than heaven to enter in:
Since the soul in me is dead,
   Better save the skin.   40

Pardon, pray you, good my lord,
   Master of discretion,
But this death I die is sweet,
   Most delicious poison.
Wounded to the quick am I   45
   By a young girl's beauty:
She's beyond my touching? Well,
   Can't the mind do duty?

Hard beyond all hardness, this
   Mastering of Nature: 50
Who shall say his heart is clean,
   Near so fair a creature?
Young are we, so hard a law,
   How should we obey it?
And our bodies, they are young,   55
   Shall they have no say in't?

Sit you down amid the fire,
   Will the fire not burn you?
To Pavia[2] come, will you
   Just as chaste return you?   60
Pavia, where Beauty draws

---

2. Italian city then known for its wild life.

Youth with finger-tips,
Youth entangled in her eyes,
    Ravished with her lips.

Let you bring Hippolytus,[3]   65
    In Pavia dine him,
Never more Hippolytus
    Will the morning find him.
In Pavia not a road
    But leads to venery,   70
Nor among its crowding towers
    One to chastity.

Yet a second charge they bring:
    I'm for ever gaming.
Yea, the dice hath many a time   75
    Stripped me to my shaming.
What an if the body's cold,
    If the mind is burning,
On the anvil hammering,
    Rhymes and verses turning?   80

Look again upon your list.
    Is the tavern on it?
Yea, and never have I scorned,
    Never shall I scorn it,
Till the holy angels come,   85
    And my eyes discern them,
Singing for the dying soul,
    Requiem aeternam.[4]

For on this my heart is set:
    When the hour is nigh me,   90
Let me in the tavern die,
    With a tankard by me,
While the angels looking down
    Joyously sing o'er me,
Deus sit propitius   95
    Huic potatori.[5]

'Tis the fire that's in the cup
    Kindles the soul's torches,
'Tis the heart that drenched in wine
    Flies to heaven's porches.   100
Sweeter tastes the wine to me
    In a tavern tankard
Than the watered stuff my Lord
    Bishop hath decanted.

---

3. Legendary figure of ancient Greece, noted for his vehement opposition to the pleasures of the flesh.
4. Eternal rest (Latin), the opening words of the Catholic Mass for the dead.   5. May God be gracious to this drinker (Latin).

Let them fast and water drink,   105
    All the poets' chorus,
Fly the market and the crowd
    Racketing uproarious:
Sit in quiet spots and think,
    Shun the tavern's portal,   110
Write, and never having lived,
    Die to be immortal.

Never hath the spirit of
    Poetry descended,
Till with food and drink my lean   115
    Belly was distended,
But when Bacchus lords it in
    My cerebral story,
Comes Apollo with a rush,
    Fills me with his glory.   120

Unto every man his gift.
    Mine was not for fasting.
Never could I find a rhyme
    With my stomach wasting.
As the wine is, so the verse: 125
    'Tis a better chorus
When the landlord hath a good
    Vintage set before us.

Good my lord, the case is heard,
    I myself betray me,
And affirm myself to be   130
    All my fellows say me.
See, they in thy presence are:
    Let whoe'er hath known
His own heart and found it clean,   135
    Cast at me the stone.

JAUFRÉ RUDEL
twelfth century

Love Song[1]

When the nightingale in the leaves
Gives, seeks, and takes love,
And happily begins his song,
And gazes often at his mate,
And the streams are clear and the meadows fair,   5

1. Translated from the Provençal by George Wolf and Roy Rosenstein.

Because of the new pleasure which prevails,
A great joy settles in my heart.

I am eager for a love affair—
For I know no more worthy enjoyment—
Which I pray for and desire, and it would be good   10
If she made me a gift of love;
For she has a full body, delicate and fair,
With nothing that could be unbecoming,
And her good, pleasurable love.

I am preoccupied with this love   15
Awake and then asleep in dreams,
For there I have amazing joy,
Because I enjoy her and am joyously happy;
But her beauty is worth nothing to me,
Because no friend will inform me   20
How I might obtain this pleasure.

I am so anxious about this love
That when I go running towards her
It seems to me I'm turning
Backwards and that she's fleeing;   25
And my horse runs so slowly . . .
I do not think I shall ever get there,
Unless love makes her hold back.

Love, I leave you cheerfully,
For I seek what is best for me;   30
And I am so fortunate in this
That I am still rejoicing,
Thanks to my Good Protector
Who wants, calls, and approves me,
And has made me very hopeful.   35

And whoever stays here enjoying himself,
And does not follow God to Bethlehem,
I do not know how he will ever be worthy,
Or how he will ever reach salvation;
For I know and indeed believe   40
That whoever teaches of Jesus
Holds a good school.

RABBI EPHRAIM BEN JACOB
1132–1200

The Sacrifice of Isaac[1]

Let me recall my Fathers' (names)
  Today before Thee, examiner and knower (of hearts).
Oh grant the Fathers' merits to the sons,
  The father an old man, and the child, of his old age.[2]

You told your favorite[3] to offer up his only one,[4]   5
  On one of the mountains to enact the priest:
"Offer Me as sacrifice the soul of him you love,
  Get it for Me, for it pleases Me well."[5]

You called upon him to withstand the trial,
  As calls a king upon a seasoned warrior: 10
By this you shall be tested and prove victorious.
  The Lord trieth the righteous.[6]

The wild ass took pride in his bleeding and brayed:
  Drops of my blood I gave at the age of thirteen![7]
The beloved whispered: Oh that God would take me,   15
  Yea, let Him take all.[8]

Alert, (the father) ran to carry out a *mitsvah,*[9]
  And yearned to saddle his own ass himself,
(Bound to God) by a knot of love, that outweighed dignity.
  Behold, O Lord, Thou knowest it altogether.[1]   20

Then came the Satan, standing close by them,
  Murmuring, "Might one exchange a word with thee?"
Cried the perfect one, "I will walk in mine integrity,"
  For so the King has appointed.[2]

On the third day they arrived at Scopus,[3]   25
  Then to their Maker they looked:
The pillar of cloud shone in its splendor
  On the top of the mount, like devouring fire.[4]

The alert one piled on his son
  Faggots for the sacrifice, for the burnt offering.   30
Then the son opened his mouth to ask,
  Behold fire and wood, but where is the lamb for a burnt offering?[5]

---

1. Translated from the Hebrew by Judah Goldin; the parenthetical phrases are expansions of the original by the translator. For the biblical story of Abraham's obedience to God's command that he sacrifice his son Isaac, see Genesis 22.1–19. **2.** Genesis 44.20; the last line of each stanza is a citation from the Bible. **3.** Abraham. **4.** Isaac. **5.** Judges 14.3. **6.** Psalms 11.5. **7.** *The wild ass* refers to Ishmael, Isaac's half brother; he was circumcised at thirteen (Genesis 17.25), and according to Jewish tradition he taunted Isaac that he was the more pious because he felt the pain of circumcision, while Isaac was circumcised when only eight days old. **8.** 2 Samuel 19.30. **9.** Sacrifice. **1.** Psalms 139.4. **2.** Esther 1.8. **3.** A mountain near Jerusalem. **4.** Exodus 24.17. **5.** Genesis 22.7.

In his reply, the saint spoke the rightful thing:
  The Lord will make it known who shall be His.
My son, the Master will look to His lamb   35
  And who is holy, He will draw to Him.[6]

The Pure One showed him the altar of the ancients.
  A male without blemish you shall offer of your own free will.
Whispered the soft-spoken dove:[7] Bind me as sacrifice
  With cords to the horns of the altar.[8]   40

Bind for me my hands and my feet
  Lest I be found wanting and profane the sacrifice.
I am afraid of panic; I am concerned to honor you,
  My will is to honor you greatly.[9]

When the one whose life was bound up in the lad's   45
  Heard this, he bound him hand and foot like the perpetual
    offering.
In their right order he prepared fire and wood,
  And offered upon them the burnt offering.[1]

Then did the father and the son embrace,
  Mercy and Truth met and kissed each other.   50
Oh, my father, fill your mouth with praise,
  For He doth bless the sacrifice.[2]

I long to open my mouth to recite the Grace:
  Forever blessed be the Lord. Amen.
Gather my ashes, bring them to the city,   55
  Unto the tent, to Sarah.[3]

He made haste, he pinned him down with his knees,
  He made his two arms strong.
With steady hands he slaughtered him according to the rite,
  Full right was the slaughter.[4]   60

Down upon him fell the resurrecting dew, and he revived.
  (The father) seized him (then) to slaughter him once more.
Scripture, bear witness! Well-grounded is the fact:
  And the Lord called Abraham, even a second time from heaven.[5]

The ministering angels cried out, terrified: 65
  Even animal victims, were they ever slaughtered twice?
Instantly they made their outcry heard on high,
  Lo, Ariels cried out above the earth.[6]

We beg of Thee, have pity upon him!
  In his father's house, we were given hospitality.   70

---

6. Numbers 16.5.   **7.** Isaac.   **8.** Psalms 118.28.   **9.** Numbers 24.11.   **1.** Exodus 40.29.
2. Psalms 89.53.   **3.** Genesis 18.6. Sarah is Isaac's mother.   **4.** Genesis 43.16.   **5.** Genesis 22.15.
6. Isaiah 33.7.

He was swept by the flood of celestial tears
Into Eden, the garden of God.[7]

The pure one thought: The child is free of guilt,
Now I, whither shall I go?
Then he heard: Your son was found an acceptable sacrifice,   75
By Myself have I sworn it, saith the Lord.[8]

In a nearby thicket did the Lord prepare
A ram, meant for this *mitsvah*[9] even from Creation.
The proxy caught its leg in the skirts of his coat,
And behold, he stood by his burnt offering.[1]   80

So he offered the ram, as he desired to do,
Rather than his son, as a burnt offering.
Rejoicing, he beheld the ransom of his only one
Which God delivered into his hand.[2]

This place he called Adonai-Yireh,[3]   85
The place where light and the law are manifest.
He swore to bless it as the Temple site,
For there the Lord commanded the blessing.[4]

Thus prayed the binder and the bound,
That when their descendants commit a wrong   90
This act be recalled to save them from disaster,
From all their transgressions and sins.[5]

O Righteous One, do us this grace!
You promised our fathers mercy to Abraham.[6]
Let then their merit stand as our witness,   95
*And pardon our iniquity and our sin, and take us for Thine
inheritance.*[7]

Recall to our credit the many Akedahs,[8]
The saints, men and women, slain for Thy sake.
Remember the righteous martyrs of Judah,
Those that were bound of Jacob.[9]   100

Be Thou the shepherd of the surviving flock
Scattered and dispersed among the nations.
Break the yoke and snap the bands
Of the bound flock that yearns toward Thee[1]

O GOD! O KING. . .   105

---

7. Ezekiel 28.13.   8. Genesis 22.16.   9. Sacrifice.   1. Numbers 23.17.   2. Exodus 21.13. Isaac
returns to his father from Eden.   3. Provision of the Lord.   4. Psalms 133.3.   5. Leviticus 16.16.
6. Abraham figures here as both an individual and Israel as a whole.   7. Exodus 34.9.   8. Sacrifices.
9. Genesis 30.42.   1. Genesis 30.41.

BEATRICE, COUNTESS OF DIA
ca. 1150–1200

A Lover's Prize[1]

I have been in great distress
for a knight for whom I longed;
I want all future times to know
how I loved him to excess
    Now I see I am betrayed—   5
he claims I did not give him love—
such was the mistake I made,
    naked in bed, and dressed.

How I'd long to hold him pressed
naked in my arms one night—   10
if I could be his pillow once,
would he not know the height of bliss?
    Floris was all to Blanchefleur,[2]
yet not so much as I am his:
I am giving my heart, my love,   15
    my mind, my life, my eyes.

Fair, gentle lover, gracious knight,
if once I held you as my prize
and lay with you a single night
and gave you a love-laden kiss—   20
    my greatest longing is for you
to lie there in my husband's place,
but only if you promise this:
    to do all I'd want to do.

1. Translated from the Provençal by Peter Dronke.   2. Lovers in a well-known romance.

BERTRAN DE BORN
ca. 1140–ca. 1215

In Praise of War[1]

I love the joyful time of Easter,
that makes the leaves and flowers come forth,
and it pleases me to hear the mirth
of the birds, who make their song
resound through the woods,   5
and it pleases me to see upon the meadows
tents and pavilions planted,

1. Translated from the Provençal by Frederick Goldin.

and I feel a great joy
when I see ranged along the field
knights and horses armed for war.   10

And it pleases me when the skirmishers
make the people and their baggage run away,
and it pleases me when I see behind them coming
a great mass of armed men together,
and I have pleasure in my heart   15
when I see strong castles besieged,
the broken ramparts caving in,
and I see the host on the water's edge,
closed in all around by ditches,
with palisades, strong stakes close together   20

And I am as well pleased by a lord
when he is first in the attack,
armed, upon his horse, unafraid,
so he makes his men take heart
by his own brave lordliness.   25
And when the armies mix in battle,
each man should be poised
to follow him, smiling,
for no man is worth a thing
till he has given and gotten blow on blow.   30

Maces and swords and painted helms,
the useless shields cut through,
we shall see as the fighting starts,
and many vassals together striking,
and wandering wildly,   35
the unreined horses of the wounded and dead.
And once entered into battle
let every man proud of his birth
think only of breaking arms and heads,
for a man is worth more dead than alive and beaten.   40

I tell you there is not so much savor
in eating or drinking or sleeping,
as when I hear them scream, "There they are! Let's get them!"
on both sides, and I hear riderless
horses in the shadows, neighing,   45
and I hear them scream, "Help! Help!"
and I see them fall among the ditches,
little men and great men on the grass,
and I see fixed in the flanks of the corpses
stumps of lances with silken streamers.   50

Barons, pawn your castles,
and your villages, and your cities
before you stop making war on one another.

Papiols,[2] gladly go
fast to my Lord Yes-and-No[3]   55
and tell him he has lived in peace too long.

2. Bertran's *joglar*, or minstrel, who will sing the lyric.   3. A mocking reference to Bertran's lord at the
time, Richard the Lion-Hearted, whom he accuses of indecisiveness.

HEINRICH VON MORUNGEN
ca. 1150–1222

The Wound of Love[1]

She has wounded me
  in my innermost soul,
within the mortal core,
  when I told her
    that I was raving and anguished   5
in desire for her glorious lips.
Once I bade my own lips
  to commend me to her service,
  and to steal me
a tender kiss of hers,   10
  that I might for ever be well.

How I begin to hate
  her rose-red lips,
which I never yet forgot!
It troubles me still,   15
  that they once refused me
with such vehemence.
Thus I have grown so weak
  that I would far rather—alive—
  burn in the abyss   20
of hell than serve her still,
  not knowing to what end.

1. Translated from the German by Peter Dronke.

ARNAUT DANIEL
twelfth century

The Art of Love[1]

To this sweet and pretty air
I set words that I plane and finish;
and every word will fit well,
once I have passed the file there,
for at once Love polishes and aureates   5
my song, which proceeds from her,
ruler and guardian of merit.

Each day I am a better man and purer,
for I serve the noblest lady in the world,
and I worship her, I tell you this in the open.   10
I belong to her from my foot to the top of my head;
and let the cold wind blow,
love raining in my heart
keeps me warm when it winters most.

I hear a thousand masses and pay to have them said,   15
I burn lights of wax and oil,
so may God give me good luck with her,
for no defense against her does me any good.
When I look at her golden hair,
her soft young spirited body,   20
if someone gave me Luserna,[2] I'd still love her more.

I love her and seek her out with a heart so full,
I think I am stealing her out of my own hands by too much wanting,
if a man can lose a thing by loving it well.
For the heart of her submerges   25
mine and does not abate.
So usurious is her demand,
she gets craftsman and workshop together.

I do not want the empire of Rome,
do not make me pope of it   30
so that I could not turn back to her
for whom the heart in me burns and breaks apart.
If she does not cure me of this torment
with a kiss before new year's,
she murders me and sends herself to hell.   35

But this torment I endure
could not make me turn away from loving well,
though it holds me fast in loneliness,
for in this desert I cast my words in rhyme.
I labor in loving more than a man who works the earth,   40

---

1. Translated from the Provençal by Frederick Goldin.   2. A city, probably in Spain.

for the Lord of Moncli did not love
N'Audierna an egg's worth more.[3]

I am Arnaut, who hoards the wind,
and chases the hare on an ox,
and swims against the tide.   45

---

3. Both the Lord of Moncli and his love, N'Audierna, have not been identified.

WALTHER VON DER VOGELWEIDE
ca. 1170–ca. 1230

Dancing Girl[1]

"Lady, accept this garland"—
these were the words I spoke to a pretty girl:
"then you will grace the dance
with the lovely flowers crowning you.
If I had priceless stones,   5
they would be for your hair—
indeed you must believe me,
by my faith, I mean it truly!"

She took my offering
as a gently nurtured child would take it.   10
Her cheeks became as red
as the rose that stands beside the lilies.
Her shining eyes were lowered then in shame,
yet she curtsied graciously.
That was my reward—   15
if any more becomes mine, I'll hold it secret.

"You are so fair,
that I want to give you my chaplet now,
the very best I have.
I know of many flowers, white and red,   20
so far away, on the heath over there,
where they spring up beautiful,
and where the birds are singing—
let us pluck them together there."

I thought that never yet   25
had I known such bliss as I knew then.
From the tree the flowers
rained on us endlessly as we lay in the grass.
Yes, I was filled with laughter in sheer joy.

---

1. Translated from the German by Peter Dronke.

Just then, when I was so gloriously   30
rich in my dreaming,
then day broke, and I was forced to wake.

She has stirred me so
that this summer, with every girl I meet,
I must gaze deep in her eyes: 35
perhaps one will be mine: then all my cares are gone.
What if she were dancing here?
Ladies, be so kind,
set your hats back a little.
Oh, if only, under a garland, I could see that face!   40

MEIR HALEVI ABULAFIA
ca. 1170–1244

A Letter from the Grave[1]

He wrote this when his sister—may God delight in her—died on
the Sabbath of 10 November 1212; he wrote to his father, in the
name of his sister, to inform him and to bring him comfort.

O clouds, bear these greetings to my father from my grave, in words not
spoken but written. Tell him, with the dumb lips of my disaster, what has
become of my lips and my voice. But take care that my distress should not
overwhelm him, that my great sorrow should not oppress him. What good
would it do to oppress him with my sorrow? Would his pain spare me mine?
Would it be right to tear open his heart because of me? No, I would be
wronging my father, whose loving wings were my bed, whose compassionate
shoulders were my chariot. Once I shone like a sun in his house, but now I
have set in the abyss.

Turn away from me! How much longer will you call to me? Know that the
hand of God has touched me. Death, like a ravening lion, tore me out of the
room of my beloved. No longer can I cast my fortunes on the dear friend of
my youth; now I must commit my fortunes to the grave. They buried me,
covering my face with the very dust which only yesterday I trampled under-
foot. But I shall draw all men after me; both my loved ones and my rivals
will join me. God summons all mortals to the house of the dead. Sinner and
prophet perish alike. When He restores all souls to their bodies, then shall
I come into your presence again.

Though He has made your heart—my heart's guardian—share my grief,
though He has made a sea of tears flow over you and almost flooded you
with weeping, He will now fill my grave with His dew of sparkling light, He
will say to your welling tears: "Subside and dry!"

1. Translated from the Hebrew by T. Carmi.

HADEWIJCH OF BRABANT
thirteenth century

The Cult of Love[1]

1

The birds have long been silent
that were blithe here before:
their blitheness has departed,
they have lost their summer now;
they would swiftly sing again   5
if that summer came again,
which they have chosen above all
and for which they were born:
one hears it in their voices then.

2

I'll say no more of birds' laments: 10
their joy, their pain, is quickly gone;
I have more grievous cause to moan:
Love, to whom we should aspire,
weighs us down with her noble cares,
so we chase after false delights   15
and Love cannot enfold us then.
Ah, what has baseness done to us!
Who shall erase that faithlessness?

3

The mighty ones, whose hand is strong,
it is on them I still rely,   20
who work at all times in Love's bond,
heedless of pain, grief, tragedy;
they want to ride through all the land
that lovers loving by love have found,
so perfect is their noble heart;   25
they know what Love can teach by love,
how Love exalts lovers by love.

4

Why then should anyone refuse,
since by loving Love can be won?
Why not ride, longing, through the storm,   30
trusting in the power of Love,
aspiring to the cult of Love?
Love's peerlessness will then be seen—
there, in the brightness of Love's dawn,
where for Love's sake is shunned no pain   35
and no pain caused by Love weighs down.

1. Translated from the Flemish by Peter Dronke.

5

Often I call for help as a lost one,
but then, when you come close, my dear one,
with new solace you bear me up
and with high spirit I ride on,   40
sport with my dear so joyously
as if north and south and east
and west all lands belonged to me!
Then suddenly I am dashed down.—
Oh, what use to tell my pain?   45

ALFONSO X

1221–1284

The Scorpions[1]

I cannot find such great delight
in the song
of birds, or in their twittering,
in love or in ambition
or in arms—for I fear   5
that these indeed
are fraught with danger—
as in a good galleon
that can take me speedily
from this demonic landscape   10
where the scorpions dwell;
for within my heart
I have felt their sting!

And by the holy God I swear
I would wear   15
neither cloak nor beard,
nor would I involve myself in love
or arms, for injury
and lamentation
come from these at every season—   20
no, I'd pilot a merchant-ship
and sail across the ocean,
selling vinegar and flour,
and I would fly from the poison
of the scorpion, for I know   25
no other medicine against it.

I can take no pleasure here
in tilting,

1. Translated from the Spanish by Peter Dronke.

nor, God save the mark,
in mock-tournaments;   30
as for going armed by night
or patrolling,
I do it without any joy—
for I find more enchantment in the sea
than in being a knight: 35
long ago I was a mariner,
and henceforth I long to guard
myself against the scorpion, and return
to what I was in the beginning.

I must try to explain to you: 40
the demon
will never be able to trick me
now into speaking the language
of arms, for this is not my role—
(useless   45
for me to reason thus,
I have not even arms to try)—
rather, I long to go alone
and in a merchant's guise
to find some land   50
where they cannot strike at me:
the black scorpion, and the mottled.

GUIDO GUINIZZELLI
thirteenth century

Love and Nobility[1]

Love always repairs to the noble heart
    Like a bird winging back into its grove:
Nor was love made before the noble heart,
    Nor did nature, before the heart, make love.
For they were there as long as was the Sun,   5
    Whose splendor's ever bright;
Never did love before that shining come.
Love nestles deep inside nobility
    Exactly the way
One sees the heart within the fiery blaze.   10

Fire of love in noble heart is caught
    Like power gleaming inside a precious stone.
The value does not come down from the stars

1. Translated from the Italian by James J. Wilhelm.

Until the Sun has blenched the stone all pure.
Only after the might of the Sun   15
   Has drawn out all that's vile
Does the star bestow its noble power.
Just so a heart transformed by nature pure,
   Noble and elect,
A woman starlike with her love injects.   20

Love for this reason stays in noble heart
   Like a waving flame atop a burning brand,
Shining, its own delight, subtle and bright;
   It is so proud, it knows no other way.
Yet a nature which is still debased   25
   Greets love as water greets the fire,
With the cold hissing against the heat.
Love in noble heart will find a haven
   Like the shine
Of a diamond glinting in ore within the mine.   30

Sun beats against the mud the livelong day;
   Mud it remains; Sun does not lose its ray;
The haughty one says: "I am noble by my tribe."
   He is the mud; Sun is the noble power.
Man must never believe   35
   That nobility exists outside the heart
In the grandness of his ancestry,
For without virtue, heart has no noble worth;
   It's a ray through a wave;
The heavens retain the sparkle and splendor they gave.   40

Shines among the powers of heaven
   God the creator, more than Sun in our eye;
Each angel knows the Maker beyond its sphere,
   And turning its circle, obeys God's noble power.
And thus it follows at once: 45
   The blesséd tasks of the Master transpire.
In the same way, in all truth, the beautiful lady
Should behave, for in her eyes reflects the desire
   Of a noble man
Who will turn his every thought to her command.   50

Lady, God will ask me: "Why did you presume?"
   When my soul stands before his mighty throne.
"You passed the heavens, came all the way to me,
   And cheapened me in the light of profane love.
To me is due all the praise   55
   And to the Queen of the Royal Realm[2]
Who makes all fraudulence cease."
I'll tell him then: "She had an angel look—
   A heavenly face.
What harm occurred if my love in her was placed?"   60

2. The Virgin Mary.

GUIDO CAVALCANTI
ca. 1255–1300

An Encounter[1]

Once within a little grove a shepherdess I spied;
More than any star of sky beauteous did she prove.

Ringlets she had, blonde and curly locks,
Eyes filled with love, a face of rosy hue,
And with her staff she led her gentle flocks,   5
Barefoot, with their feet bathed by the dew.
She sang, indeed, as if she were enamored;
She had the glamour of every pleasing art.

I greeted her, and asked her then at once
If she had any company that day;   10
She answered sweetly: "For the nonce,
Alone throughout this grove I make my way."
And added: "Listen, but when the gentle bird is heard,
A friend should have my heart."

And when she told me of this state of mind,   15
Suddenly I heard birdsongs in the wood.
I said to myself: "This surely would be the time
To take from this shepherdess what joy I could."
Grace I requested—just to kiss her face—
And then embrace if she should feel like me.   20

She took my hand, seized with love's old power,
And said she'd give me her heart too;
She led me then into a fresh green bower,
And there I saw flowers of every hue.
And I was filled so full of sweetened joy   25
Love's godlike boy[2] there too I seemed to see.

1. Translated from the Italian by James J. Wilhelm.   2. Cupid.

DANTE ALIGHIERI
1265–1321

Love and Poetry[1]

Guido, I wish that you and Lapo[2] and I,
Spirited on the wings of a magic spell,

1. Translated from the Italian by James J. Wilhelm.   2. Guido Cavalcanti and Lapo Gianni were poets in Dante's literary circle.

Could drift in a ship where every rising swell
Would sweep us at our will across the skies;
Then tempest never, or any weather dire   5
Could ever make our blissful living cease;
No, but abiding in a steady, blessèd peace
Together we'd share the increase of desire.

And Lady Vanna and Lady Lagia[3] then
And she[4] who looms above the thirty best[5]   10
Would join us at the good enchanter's[6] behest;
And there we'd talk of Love without an end
To make those ladies happy in the sky—
With Lapo enchanted too, and you and I.

Sonnet[1]

Love and the gentle heart are one thing,
    even as the sage[2] affirms in his poem,
and so one can be without the other
as much as rational soul without reason.
Nature creates them when she is amorous: 5
Love as lord and the heart as his mansion,
in which, sleeping, he rests
sometimes a brief and sometimes a long season.
Beauty appears in a wise lady, then,
which so pleases the eyes that in the heart   10
is born a desire for that which pleases;
and so long it lasts sometimes therein
that it wakens the spirit of Love.
And the same to a lady does a worthy man.

3. Giovanna and Lagia were Guido and Lapo's ladies.   4. Beatrice, Dante's beloved.   5. Dante wrote
a poem naming the most beautiful ladies of Florence.   6. Merlin.   1. Translated from the Italian by
Dino Cervigni and Edward Vasta.   2. Guido Guinizzelli; see above, p. 1813.

ANONYMOUS
thirteenth century

Calvary

Now goeth sonne[1] under wood,
Me rueth, Mary, thy fair rood;[2]
Now goeth sonne under tree,
Me rueth, Mary, thy son and thee.

1. Both "sun" and "son."   2. Both "face" and "cross."

ALEXANDER THE WILD
thirteenth century

Strawberry Picking[1]

Long ago, when we were children,
in the time that spanned the years
when we ran across the meadows,
over from those, now back to these,
there, where we at times   5
found violets,
you now see cattle leap for flies.

I remember how we sat
deep in flowers, and decided
which girl was the prettiest.   10
Our young looks were radiant then
with the new garland
for the dance.
And so the time goes by.

Look, there we ran to find strawberries,   15
ran to the beech from the fir-tree,
over sticks and stones,
as long as the sun shone.
Then a forester called out
through the branches   20
"Come along, children, go home!"

All our hands were stained,
picking strawberries yesterday;
to us it was nothing but play.
Then, again and again, we heard   25
our shepherd calling
and moaning:
"Children, the forest is full of snakes!"

One child walked in the tall grass,
started, and cried aloud: 30
"Children, right here there was a snake!
He has bitten our pony—
it will never heal;
it must always
remain poisoned and unwell."   35

"Come along then, out of the forest!
If you do not now make haste
it will happen as I say:
if you are not sure to be gone
from the forest while there is day,   40

1. Translated from the German by Peter Dronke.

you will lose your way
and your joy will become a moan."

Do you know that five young women
loitered in the meadow-lands
till the king locked up his hall?   45
Great were their moans and their distress—
for the bailiffs tore
their clothes away,
so that they stood naked, without a dress.[2]

2. Probably an allusion to the parable of the five foolish virgins in the New Testament: see Matthew 25.1–13.

DAFYDD AP GWILYM

ca. 1310–1370

The Fox[1]

Yesterday was I, sure of purpose,
Under the trees (alas that the girl doesn't see it)
Standing under Ovid's[2] stems
And waiting for a pretty girl beneath the trees;
She made me weep on her way.   5
I saw when I looked there
(An ape's shape where I did not love)
A red fox (he doesn't love our hounds' place)
Sitting like a tame animal,
On his haunches near his den.   10

   I drew between my hands
A bow of yew there, it was brave,
About, like an armed man,
On the brow of the hill, a stirring of high spirits,
Weapon for coursing along a district,   15
To hit him with a long, stout bolt.
I drew for a try a shaft
Clear past the jaw.
My grief, my bow went
In three pieces, luckless disaster.   20

   I got mad (I did not dread him,
Unhappy bear) at the fox.
He's a lad who'd love a hen,
A silly bird, and bird flesh;
He doesn't follow the cry of horns,   25
Rough his voice and his carol.

1. Translated from the Welsh by Richard Morgan Loomis.   2. Roman love poet (43 B.C.–A.D. 17).

Ruddy is he in front of a talus³ slope,
Like an ape among green trees.
At both ends of a field there turns up
A dog-shape looking for a goose.   30
Crows' beacon near the brink of a hill,
Acre-strider, color of an ember,
Likeness of a lure for crows and magpies at a fair,
Portent looking like a dragon.
Lord of excitement, chewer of a fat hen,   35
Of acclaimed fleece, glowing flesh.
An awl of hollowed-out fine earth,
Fire-dish at the edge of a shuttered window.
Copper bow of light feet,
Tongs like a beak of blood.   40

    Not easy for me to follow him,
And his dwelling toward Annwn.⁴
Red roamer, he was found to be too fierce,
He'd run ahead of a course of hounds.
Sharp his rushing, gorse-strider,   45
Leopard with a dart in his rump.

3. A pile of rock fragments.   4. The otherworld of Welsh myth.

ANONYMOUS
fourteenth century

Aubade¹

Deep in an orchard, under hawthorn leaves,
the lady holds her lover in her arms,
until the watcher cries, he sees the dawn.
Dear God, the daybreak! oh how soon it comes!

"If only God let night stay without end,   5
and my beloved never left my side,
and never again the guard saw day or dawn—
dear God, the daybreak! oh how soon it comes!"

"Let us kiss, sweet beloved, you and I,
down in the meadows where the birds now sing—   10
defy my jealous husband and do all!
Dear God, the daybreak! oh how soon it comes!

"Let us create new love-sports, sweet beloved,
down in the meadows where the birds now sing—

1. Translated from the French by Peter Dronke.

until the watcher plays his pipe again.   15
Dear God, the daybreak! oh how soon it comes!

"In the sweet wind that came to me from there
I drank a ray of my beloved's breath,
my fair and joyous, gracious lover's breath—
dear God, the daybreak! oh how soon it comes!"   20

The lady is delightful, lovable,
admired by many for her beauty's sake,
and holds her heart most loyally in love.
Dear God, the daybreak! oh how soon it comes!

CHRISTINE DE PIZAN
ca. 1364–ca. 1431

Alone in Martyrdom[1]

Alone in martyrdom I have been left
In the desert of this world, that's full of sadness,
By my sweet love, who held my heart
In sorrowless joy and in perfect gladness;
But he is dead, and such deep griefs oppress   5
Me, my weary heart such sorrows gnaw,
I shall bewail his death for evermore.

What can I ever do but weep and sigh for
My departed love, what wonder is this?
For when my heart profoundly ponders how   10
I lived secure and without bitterness,
Since childhood and early youthfulness
With him—at me such sufferings gnaw
I shall bewail his death for evermore.

As the turtledove without her mate does turn   15
To dry things only, nor cares more for greenness;
As the ewe that the wolf seeks to kill
Is terrified, by her shepherd left defenseless;
So am I left in great distress
By my dear love whose loss to me is sore;   20
I shall bewail his death for evermore.

1. Translated from the French by Muriel Kittel.

ANONYMOUS
fifteenth century

Lament of the Virgin

Of all women that ever were born,
That bear children, abide and see,
How my son lies me before,
Upon my knee, taken from the tree.
Your children ye dance upon your knee.   5
With laughing, kissing and merry cheer;
Behold my child, behold now me,
For now lies dead my dear son dear.

O woman, woman, well is thee,
Thy child's cap thee dotes upon;   10
Thou picks his hair, beholds his ble,[1]
Thou wost not well when thou hast done.
But ever, alas, I make my moan
To see my son's head as it is here;
I pick out thorns by one and one,   15
For now lies dead my dear son dear.

O woman, a chaplet chosen thou has
Thy child to wear, it does thee great liking;
Thou pins it on with great solace,
And I sit with my son sore weeping.   20
His chaplet is thorns' sore pricking,
His mouth I kiss with a careful[2] cheer;
I sit weeping and thou singing,
For now lies dead my dear son dear.

O woman, look to me again,   25
That plays and kisses your children's pappis.[3]
To see my son I have great pain,
In his breast so great a gap is.
And on his body so many swappis.[4]
With bloody lips I kiss him here,   30
Alas! full hard methink me happis,[5]
For now lies dead my dear son dear.

O woman, thou takes thy child by the hand
And says, "My son, give me a strake!"[6]
My son's hands are sorely bleeding;   35
To look on him me list not lake.[7]
His hands he suffered for thy sake
Thus to be bored with nail and spear;
When thou make mirth great sorrow I make,
For now lies dead my dear son dear.   40

1. Complexion.   2. Woeful.   3. Breasts.   4. Wounds.   5. I suffer.   6. Stroke—i.e., caress.
7. Is no pleasure to me.

Behold, women, when that ye play
And have your children on knees dansand;[8]
You feel their feet, so feat[9] are they,
And to your sight well likand,[1]
But the most[2] finger of any hand,   45
Through my son's feet I may put here,
And pull it out sorely bledand,[3]
For now lies dead my dear son dear.

Therefore, women, by town and street,
Your children's hands when ye behold   50
Their breasts, their body, and their feet,
Then good it were on my son think you wolde,[4]
How care has made my heart full cold
To see my son, with nail and spear,
With scourge and thorns many-fold,   55
Wounded and dead, my dear son dear.

Thou hast thy son full whole and sound,
And mine is dead upon my knee;
Thy child is loose and mine is bound,
Thy child is alive and mine dead is he.   60
Why was this ought[5] but for thee?
For my child trespassed never here.
Me thinks ye be holden to weep with me,
For now lies dead my dear son dear.

Weep with me, both man and wife,   65
My child is yours and loves you well.
If your child had lost his life
You would weep at every mele.[6]
But for my son weep ye never a del.[7]
If you love yours, mine has no peer;   70
He sends yours both hap and hele[8]
And for you died my dear son dear.

Now all women that have your wit,[9]
And see my child on my knees dead,
Weep not for yours but weep for it,   75
And ye shall have full muchel mede.[1]
He would again for your love bleed
Rather than that ye damnéd were.
I pray you all to him take heed,
For now lies dead my dear son dear.   80

Farewell, woman, I may no more
For dread of death rehearse his pain.
Ye may laugh when ye list[2] and I weep sore,
That may ye see and ye look to me again.

8. Dancing.   9. Pretty.   1. Liking.   2. Largest.   3. Bleeding.   4. Would.   5. At   all.   6. Occasion.   7. Not   at   all.   8. Both   fortune   and   health.   9. I.e., wits.   1. A   great   reward.
2. Please.

To love my son and ye be fain,[3]   85
I will love yours with heart entere,[4]
And he shall bring your children and you, certain,
To bliss where is my dear son dear.

3. If you be willing.   4. Entire.

CHARLES D'ORLEANS
ca. 1394–1465

Balade[1]

If you wish to sell your kisses,
I will gladly buy some,
And in return you will have my heart as deposit.
To use them as inheritance,
By the dozens, hundreds, or thousands.   5
Don't sell them to me at as high a price
As you would to a total stranger
For you are receiving me as your liegeman.
    If you wish to sell your kisses,
    I will gladly buy some.   10
    And in return you will have my heart as deposit.
My complete wish and desire
Are yours in spite of all suspicion;
Allow, as a faithful and wise woman,
That for my reward and share
I may be among the first served,   15
    If you wish to sell your kisses.

1. Translated from the French by Sarah Spence.

FRANÇOIS VILLON
1431–ca. 1470

From The Testament[1]

*   *   *

Now I think I hear the laments
Of the once-beautiful Helmet-seller[2]
Wishing she were a girl again   455
And saying something like this

1. Translated from the French by Galway Kinnell.   2. A woman who sells armor.

"Ah, cruel, arrogant old age
Why have you beaten me down so soon?
What holds me back from striking myself
From killing myself with a blow?   460

"You have taken from me the high hand
That I had by right of beauty
Over clerics, merchants, men of the Church
For then there wasn't a man born
Who wouldn't have given me all he owned   465
Repent though he might later on
If I'd just have let him have
What now tramps won't take for free.

"To many a man I refused it
Which wasn't exactly good sense   470
For the love of a smooth operator
Whom I gave free play with it
And what if I did fool around
I swear I loved him truly
But he just gave me a hard time   475
And loved me for my money.

"He could wipe the floor with me
Or kick me I loved him still
And even if he's broken my back
He could just ask for a kiss   480
And I'd forget my misery
The rascal rotten right through
Would take me in his arms (a lot I got for it)
What's left? The shame and sin.

"Dead he's been these thirty years   485
And here I am old and grizzled
When I think also of the happy times
What I was, what I've become
When I look at myself naked
And see how I've changed so much   490
Poor, dried-up, lean and bony
I nearly go off my head.

"What's become of the smooth forehead
The yellow hair, the arching eyebrows
The wide-set eyes, the fair gaze   495
That took in all the cleverest men
The straight nose neither large nor small
The little flattened ears
The dimpled chin, the bright rounded cheeks
And the lips beautiful and red?   500

"The delicate little shoulders
The long arms and slender hands

The small breasts, the full buttocks
High, broad, perfectly built
For holding the jousts of love   505
The wide loins and the sweet quim
Set over thick firm thighs
In its own little garden?

"The forehead lined, the hair gray
The eyebrows all fallen out, the eyes clouded   510
Which threw those bright glances
That felled many a poor devil
The nose hooked far from beauty
The ears hairy and lopping down
The cheeks washed out, dead and pasty   515
The chin furrowed, the lips just skin.

"This is what human beauty comes to
The arms short, the hands shriveled
The shoulders all hunched up
The breasts? Shrunk in again   520
The buttocks gone the way of the tits
The quim? aagh! As for the thighs
They aren't thighs now but sticks
Speckled all over like sausages.

"This is how we lament the good old days   525
Among ourselves, poor silly crones
Dumped down on our hunkers
In little heaps like so many skeins
Around a tiny hempstalk fire
That's soon lit and soon gone out   530
And once we were so adorable
So it goes for men and women.

"Now look here pretty Glover
Who used to study under me
And you too Blanche the Shoe-fitter   535
It's time you got it straight
Take what you can right and left
Don't spare a man I beg you
For there's no run on old crones
No more than cried-down money.   540

"And you sweet Sausage-filler
Such a born dancer
And Guillemette the Tapester[3]
Don't fall out with your man
Soon you'll have to close up shop   545
When you've gotten old and flabby

___

3. Properly a maker or seller of rugs; her shop may have been headquarters for a prostitute.

And good for no one but an old priest
No more than cried-down money.

"Jeanneton the Bonnet-maker
Don't let that one lover tie you down   550
And Catherine the Purse-seller
Stop putting men out to pasture
She who's lost her looks can ask them
To come back, she can flash her smile
But ugly old age can't buy love   555
No more than cried-down money.

"Girls, stop a moment
And let it sink in why I weep and cry
I can't get back in circulation
No more than cried-down money."   560

*   *   *

DANTE ALIGHIERI
1265–1321

Called by its author a comedy, and named by later ages—in recognition of both its subject matter and its achievement—*The Divine Comedy*, Dante's poem is one of the indisputably great works of world literature. It combines into an astonishingly coherent whole a remarkable range of disparate literary elements. Both structurally and thematically it is organized with the precision and harmony of the great philosophical systems and the vast Gothic cathedrals of its time; and yet it attends with extraordinary care to the tiniest detail. It celebrates with unqualified enthusiasm and at times even a dogmatic triumphalism the central doctrines of medieval Christianity; and yet it remains persistently alert to the complex sympathies of the human heart. It is epic in its scope and its central themes; and yet it sings with an exquisite lyricism. It is a poem that declares everywhere its commitment to the culture of medieval Christendom; and yet it celebrates the achievements of the classical world and extends its admiration even to Islamic philosophy. It is one of the most deeply serious works in world literature, concerned with nothing less than the relation of the Creator to His creatures and the ultimate destiny of the human soul; and yet it has room for not just grim irony but scenes of generous good humor and even vulgar horseplay. It does not shy away from episodes that the German writer Goethe accurately called "repulsive and often disgusting"; and yet it also includes moments of sublime beauty that have been rarely matched and never surpassed. Perhaps above all, it declares that a great work of literary art can be created in the vernacular, providing the declaration of independence that made possible the various national traditions of post-medieval literature. In this sense *The Divine Comedy* is the foundational text for the European literary imagination.

Dante was born in Florence in the spring of 1265. In his early years he wrote some ninety lyrics, thirty-one of which he collected and provided with a narrative commentary in a work he called the *Vita nuova* or *New Life* (completed between 1292 and 1295). This work recounted his love for a young woman he named Beatrice ("blessed" in Italian), who died in 1290. More than a love story, it described how Beatrice led him from a merely human love to something transcendental, almost divine. Dante realized that this transformation also required a new form of poetry, and it is from the New Life that The Divine Comedy was to spring as both a fulfillment and an alternative.

Meanwhile, however, political conflicts had decisively altered Dante's life. The Florentine political class, like that of much of northern Italy, was divided into two factions. The Guelphs, generally members of the urban elite and artisans, supported Florentine independence and resisted the claims of the Holy Roman empire to sovereignty over the city or indeed any part of Italy, often by soliciting the support of the military power of the papacy. The Ghibellines, on the other hand, were drawn from the ancient feudal aristocracy and saw the empire as a means of furthering their own interests. After a series of bitter struggles, the Florentine Guelphs—of which Dante was a member—were triumphant. Around 1300, however, the Guelphs themselves broke into two parties, the Blacks and the Whites, and civil strife was renewed. The Whites, with Dante as a member, became associated with the Ghibellines in their resistance to the power of the pope. In 1301, while Dante was on a diplomatic mission for the city, the Blacks staged a coup with the help of Pope Boniface VII and his ally, the Frenchman Charles of Anjou. The next year Dante was condemned to exile, and he never returned to Florence. Dependent on the generosity of wealthy patrons throughout northern Italy, he was without a permanent home. This experience of exile is central to The Divine Comedy, which on the most literal level recounts the journey of a lost traveler back to his ultimate fatherland, Heaven. Also central is Dante's outrage at the internecine strife that tore northern Italy apart throughout his lifetime. Soon he came to believe that only the Holy Roman emperor could bring order out of chaos, and he condemned the interference of the Church, and especially the pope, in political affairs, just as he condemned the Ghibellines' misuse of the empire's prestige for their own, self-seeking purposes. Dante's politics in The Divine Comedy are also religious and prophetic: he is concerned with restoring the conditions in which Christ first came—when Caesar Augustus presided over the "Roman peace" or pax Romana—so that He can come again and usher in the Final Judgment. Thus for Dante the Roman empire is divinely ordained: it first provided the earthly unity and order appropriate to the birth of Christ, and only when it is restored will His second coming be possible.

As a sign of the availability of the divine, this unity and order are everywhere present in Dante's poem. The three parts or canticles—the Inferno, Purgatorio, and Paradiso—are of equal length. Each of the latter two has thirty-three cantos; the first, the Inferno, has thirty-four, but the first canto is a prologue to the whole. This threefold pattern serves to embody the Trinity within the very structure of the poem, as does the verse form. Dante created a verse known as terza rima, which rhymes in the Italian original according to the scheme aba bcb cdc and so on. The lines thus form groups of three (known in Italian as terzine, or tercets) interlocked by a repeated rhyme word—a verbal equivalent to the three-in-one of the Trinity. Moreover, since each line contains eleven syllables, the total number of syllables in each tercet is thirty-three, the same as the number of cantos in each canticle (again, if we take Inferno 1 as a prologue). Each canticle even ends with the same word, stelle (stars), objects that are for Dante the visible signs of God's providential oversight. Nine, the square of three, figures centrally in the interior structure of each canticle. In Hell, the lost souls are arranged in three main groups and occupy nine circles; Purgatory is divided into an Ante-Purgatory, seven terraces, and the Earthly Paradise, for a total of nine locations; and Heaven consists of nine embedded spheres beyond which lies the infinite Empyrean of the Trinity (see diagrams on pp. 1828–29).

In addition to these formal and cosmological structures, the poem is organized according to an ethical pattern. For Dante, as for medieval philosophy generally, the natural inclination of every human being is love, a movement toward something out-

STRUCTURE OF DANTE'S HELL
(SEE CANTO 11.16–111)

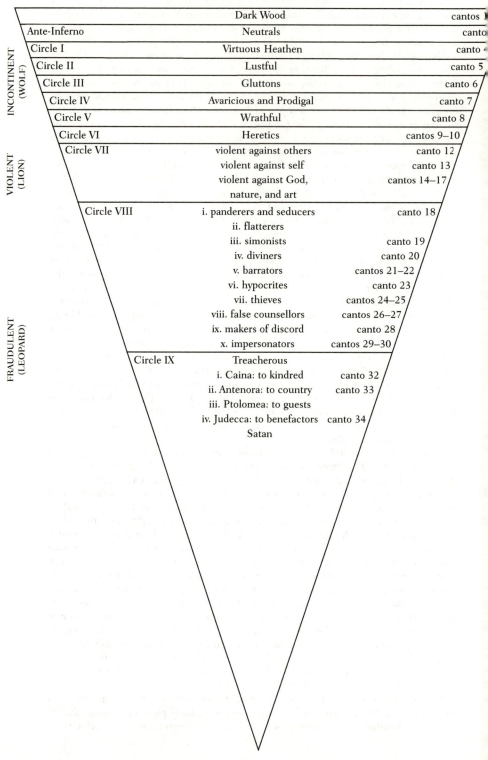

		Dark Wood	cantos 1
	Ante-Inferno	Neutrals	canto
INCONTINENT (WOLF)	Circle I	Virtuous Heathen	canto 4
	Circle II	Lustful	canto 5
	Circle III	Gluttons	canto 6
	Circle IV	Avaricious and Prodigal	canto 7
	Circle V	Wrathful	canto 8
VIOLENT (LION)	Circle VI	Heretics	cantos 9–10
	Circle VII	violent against others	canto 12
		violent against self	canto 13
		violent against God, nature, and art	cantos 14–17
FRAUDULENT (LEOPARD)	Circle VIII	i. panderers and seducers	canto 18
		ii. flatterers	
		iii. simonists	canto 19
		iv. diviners	canto 20
		v. barrators	cantos 21–22
		vi. hypocrites	canto 23
		vii. thieves	cantos 24–25
		viii. false counsellors	cantos 26–27
		ix. makers of discord	canto 28
		x. impersonators	cantos 29–30
	Circle IX	Treacherous	
		i. Caina: to kindred	canto 32
		ii. Antenora: to country	canto 33
		iii. Ptolomea: to guests	
		iv. Judecca: to benefactors	canto 34
		Satan	

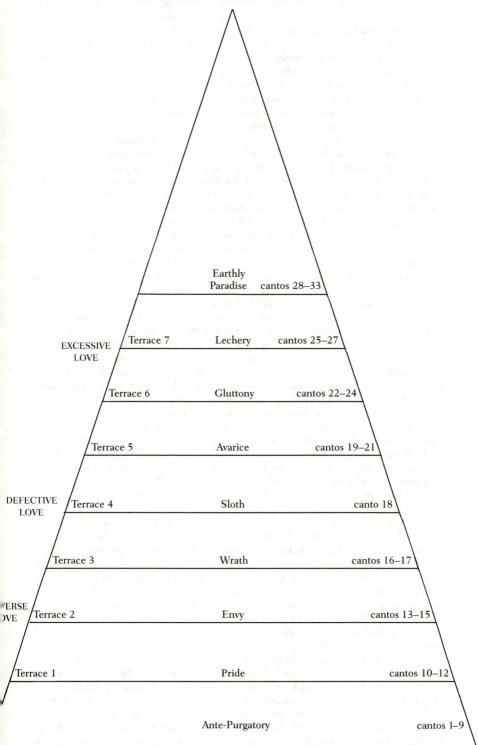

STRUCTURE OF DANTE'S PURGATORY

Earthly Paradise   cantos 28–33

EXCESSIVE LOVE   Terrace 7   Lechery   cantos 25–27

Terrace 6   Gluttony   cantos 22–24

Terrace 5   Avarice   cantos 19–21

DEFECTIVE LOVE   Terrace 4   Sloth   canto 18

Terrace 3   Wrath   cantos 16–17

ERSE VE   Terrace 2   Envy   cantos 13–15

Terrace 1   Pride   cantos 10–12

Ante-Purgatory   cantos 1–9

side the self. The natural and proper object of love is God, either directly or as medi-
ated through the created world. Sin occurs when love is immoderately directed to the
wrong object, when the creature (including the self) is loved not *for* but *instead of* the
Creator. In Hell, perverse love is represented in three forms, as incontinence, violence, and fraudulence. In Purgatory, it is also represented in three forms, as misdi-
rected (pride, envy, and wrath), as defective (sloth), and as excessive (avarice,
gluttony, and lust). In Paradise, the blessed are distinguished by the extent to which
they enjoy the vision of God, and are again divided into three categories: those whose
vision is limited by incomplete love, those who have fulfilled the four cardinal virtues
(wisdom, fortitude, justice, and temperance), and finally those—like the angels—
whose love comes nearest to perfection. Finally, Dante's geography is equally symmetrical. The globe is divided into a northern and southern hemisphere, but only the
northern is inhabited. Its central point is Jerusalem, while to the east lies the Ganges
and to the west the straits of Gibraltar. Hell is a huge funnel extending into the center
of the Earth that was created when Lucifer fell from Heaven. The earth displaced by
his fall rose into the southern hemisphere—which had previously been covered
entirely with water—and formed Mount Purgatory. This mountain, organized into its
three parts as described above, has at its top the Earthly Paradise, or Eden, the original
home of the human race. After descending into Hell, climbing up through the Earth,
and then mounting to the Earthly Paradise, Dante is transported through the nine
spheres described by medieval astronomy—those of the moon, Mercury, Venus, the
sun, Mars, Jupiter, Saturn, the fixed stars, and the *primum mobile*, or outermost
sphere, which moves the others—until he reaches the Empyrean, which exists beyond
time and space. This final vision is presented in our selection from the *Paradiso*.

There is, finally, one other organizing principle that governs the form of the poem
as a whole. When Dante is told that he is to journey through Hell, Purgatory, and
Paradise, he protests that he is not worthy by comparing himself to two previous
otherworldly travelers: "I am not Aeneas, am not Paul." Aeneas visits the underworld
in book 6 of Virgil's *Aeneid*, and Virgil plays a large role as both a literary influence
and a character in Dante's poem. The reference to Paul is to a passage in 2 Corinthians 12.2: "I knew a man in Christ above fourteen years ago, (whether in the body,
I cannot tell; whether out of the body, I cannot tell: God knoweth;) such an one
caught up to the third heaven." Medieval readers understood Paul to be talking about
himself, but their problem was to understand what he meant by the third heaven,
since there is presumably only one kingdom of God. The solution was provided by
Augustine in one of his commentaries on Genesis, in which he argued that the three
Pauline "heavens" were really metaphors for three ways in which human beings can
know. These three are, in ascending order of clarity, "corporeal vision," or knowledge
by means of the senses; "spiritual" or "imaginative vision," or knowledge through
images that have corporeal shape without corporeal substance, as in dreams; and
finally "intellectual vision," which is the direct cognition of God and other realities,
such as love, that have neither corporeal shape nor corporeal substance. God can be
known in all three ways, which Augustine illustrated by passages from the Bible. He
is known corporeally by Moses and the burning bush (Exodus 3–4); spiritually or
imaginatively in the symbolic images of the Book of Revelation; and intellectually by
Paul's vision, which he himself describes in 1 Corinthians 13.12: "For now we see
through a glass, darkly; but then face to face: now I know in part; but then shall I
know even as also I am known."

The important point for us is that the three canticles of *The Divine Comedy* are
each constructed according to one of these modes of vision. The *Purgatorio*, for example, is a place of images that have corporeal shape but not corporeal substance. In
Purgatorio 2 we have a vivid illustration of this in a scene that appears in both Homer's
and Virgil's underworlds: Dante tries three times to embrace his old friend Casella
and three times he fails. With the form of a human being but not the substance,
Casella is not merely *seen* by the imagination; he *exists* as an image rather than a

thing. He is dematerialized, which shows that he is on his way up to Paradise. For in the *Paradiso* we find that its inhabitants are neither bodies nor images but simply lights. Furthermore, Dante himself, as he ascends the paradisal ladder, becomes "enlightened" or "illuminated." But because he is still in this life rather than a pure spirit this happens to him not literally but metaphorically, as he is instructed by various people in the nature of ultimate truth. This is the reason that the *Paradiso* is so didactic, with characters talking little about themselves and instead explaining what are to us often abstruse points of theological or scholastic teaching. In the *Paradiso* Dante is "enlightened" or "illuminated" by this teaching. So what do we find in the *Inferno*? Not only are the inhabitants of Hell known corporeally but they *are* corporeal, and indeed become all the more so as Dante descends deeper into the pit. At the beginning of the journey, while Dante is in the upper levels, the characters flit about like the shades we expect them to be (as in canto 5), but very soon they become more and more substantial, so that—for example—Virgil and Dante can actually touch them, as in canto 8, where Virgil hurls Filippo Argenti back into the mud. Appropriately, the most corporeal place in Hell is the bottom circle, which is the most materialistic place in the universe. Dante calls it "the center / to which all weight is drawn," "the point / to which, from every part, all weights are drawn," because it is furthest from the pure spirituality and immateriality of Paradise (the Empyrean). At the bottom of Hell we find the heaviest thing in the universe, Satan: although originally Lucifer, the Angel of Light, he is now the being with the least amount of spirit. And with Satan we find not a wily tempter but a kind of idiot, a speechless creature from whose mouths—he has three heads, an infernal parody of the Trinity, to prove that God is present even here in the pit of Hell—flows a bloody drool, what Dante calls in Italian *bava*, a word that refers to infantile slaver.

If the least sinful people are spun round with wind, then, the worst are frozen into ice and utterly immobile. This is Dante's way of showing us that the perfect order of the universe includes the moral law that one's punishment is not merely appropriate to the crime but *is* the crime: these are the sinners who most fully denied the spirit, and so their spirit, which was created eternal by God, has come as close to pure matter as is possible. This moral law is called by one of the sinners a "counter-penalty," or *contrapasso*. It is clear from discussions by philosophers known to Dante—such as Thomas Aquinas—that the Latin term *contrapassum* meant "retribution" according to the law of retribution as defined in the Old Testament: an eye for an eye, a tooth for a tooth (see Exodus 21.23–24). But this is not really the principle that governs the distribution of punishment in Hell: this is what the sinners think, but they are oversimplifying. On the contrary, the moral economy of Hell is explained in a single sentence by another of the sinners (Capaneus): "That which I was in life, I am in death." The punishment of sin is the sin itself, as Augustine taught in the *Confessions* and as was the common understanding throughout the Middle Ages: "For [God has] ordered it, and so it is, that every disordered mind should be its own punishment." What this means is that in the *Inferno* every sinner commits his sin forever, for all of eternity: and it is this endless act of sinning that is the punishment.

Before exploring in more detail the workings of divine justice in the *Inferno*, we need to understand the role of Virgil, and of the *Aeneid*, in the poem. When Dante protests in *Inferno* 2 that he is neither Aeneas nor Paul, he is indicating that his poem will bring together, in a combination that will find its ultimate fulfillment in Milton's *Paradise Lost*, both the classical and the Christian traditions. This is a bold and largely unprecedented initiative in Western literature. In the *Confessions* Augustine struggles with and finally rejects the *Aeneid*: he describes how as a student he was seduced by the beauty of Virgil's poetry into weeping for the death of Dido while ignoring the spiritual death of his own soul. For Augustine the poem's poetic power was irresistible, but its meaning was worse than useless to the Christian; as another of the Church Fathers put it, the *Aeneid* was "a beautiful vase filled with vipers." For Virgil's poem celebrated the founding of an earthly empire and, worse, one that Jupiter prophesied would continue "without end" (book 1). In the *City of God,* written in part to defend Christians from the charge that it was their defection from Rome's traditional deities that had caused the sack of Rome by the Goths in 410, Augustine poured scorn on these words, "without end." For the Christian, nothing earthly can be eternal. For him there was only one city, the Heavenly Jerusalem, which was not a physical place at all but a condition of the soul—a vision of peace—available both in this life and in the life to come to those who have faith. The "eternal city" was not Rome but the City of God, populated by citizens faithful not to the emperor or the Roman deities but to the gospel of Jesus Christ.

But for Dante, as we have seen, Rome had a different meaning. For him, the establishment of the empire by Augustus, and the extension of Roman peace over the Western world, was the necessary precondition for the birth of Christ. It was not just one city among many but the source of an imperial order that was divinely sanctioned. For Dante, since Virgil was the prophet and celebrant of this empire, he was—although he could not know it—inspired in writing the *Aeneid* not by Jupiter but by the Christian God. This notion of Virgilian inspiration was furthered by a Christian interpretation of one of Virgil's early poems, the Fourth Eclogue. The poem begins in this way:

> Now comes the last age [prophesied] by the song of the Cumaean sybil; the great order of the ages is born anew; now the Virgin returns, now the reign of Saturn comes again; now a new child is sent down from heaven above.

It's easy enough to see how a devout reader could see in these words, and in the poem as a whole, a prophecy of the birth of Christ, although Virgil was in all likelihood actually thinking of a son born to some prominent Roman, perhaps even to Augustus. Dante believed that the second coming of Christ, and the fulfillment of history, was dependent upon the reestablishment of the imperial authority whose initial establishment Virgil had described in the *Aeneid.* This is why it is Virgil who in *Inferno* 1 prophesies the coming of the hound who will defeat the she-wolf and restore Italy by hunting her through all the cities of Italy—cities now torn by civil wars provoked by the *concupiscence* that the she-wolf represents, a sinfulness inherent in the flesh that Paul lamented (see Romans 5), and a quality that Augustine interpreted in political terms as the "the lust for domination." This hound will be the new Augustus (if Dante had anyone specific in mind it may have been either one of his patrons, Cangrande della Scala or, later, the Holy Roman emperor, Henry VII). Apart from these details, however, the important point is that for Dante, Rome and its empire played a crucial role in history.

So part of the reason Virgil is chosen as the guide is that he is a poet who was divinely inspired to make known the meaning of history, a role that Dante assumes for himself as well—hence the political prophecies scattered throughout the poem. But Virgil is also chosen because he taught Dante what in *Inferno* 1 Dante calls "the noble style." What he means by this is that reading Virgil allowed him to move beyond the lyric love poetry that had characterized the early part of his career. This poetry was, as Dante's discussion in *Purgatorio* 24 and 26 makes clear, a necessary precondition to the writing of the *Comedy.* But it was Virgil who showed him that poetry might aspire to a vision of experience that dealt with the ultimate issues of life and death, and with a vision of the meaning of history. It was Virgil, in other words, who persuaded him that poetry could be a vehicle for moral and philosophical truth, and a means of self-fulfillment, as his final ratification of Dante's spiritual growth in *Purgatorio* 30 shows.

Yet despite the fact that Virgil is Dante's "master" and "author," there are important differences between them. Indeed, a central theme in both the *Inferno* and the *Purgatorio* is the fluctuation in the relationship between Dante and Virgil. Dante is usually submissive before Virgil, but there are moments when Virgil appears baffled and even inept. One of these occurs in canto 9 of the *Inferno,* when the devils in the City of Dis refuse Virgil entrance and he has to call upon a divine messenger sent from Heaven. In that canto the Furies threaten to bring Medusa in order to turn Dante to stone; Virgil makes Dante turn around and then covers up his eyes with both Dante's and his own hands. As soon as Virgil does this, Dante speaks—in the present tense—to the reader:

> O you possessed of sturdy intellects,
> observe the teaching that is hidden here
> beneath the veil of verses so obscure.

While Virgil the non-Christian covers up, Christian readers must *un*cover: they must interpret this action and this scene as a whole in order to understand the nature of the spiritual—not literal—threat posed by the Furies and Medusa. The answer has to do with the meaning of *petrification*, which in Christian terms means turning the heart to stone, being hard-hearted or *impenitent*; and the greatest source of impenitence is *despair*, which is the belief that you have committed sins so grave that they cannot be forgiven. The Furies are, for the Middle Ages, symbols of this despair, and despair is the condition of everyone in Hell, including Virgil: they have abandoned all hope of being saved. That is why in this very canto—canto 9—Dante mentions "the first circle, one whose only punishment is crippled hope" and Virgil mentions "Judas' circle," Judas representing the New Testament type of despair: according to medieval interpreters, Judas sinned more in hanging himself than in selling Christ. As a pagan, Virgil can *experience* this condition but cannot *understand* it: the despair or absence of hope at work here is Virgil's—he doesn't think they will get into the city of Dis—not Dante's; and the heavenly messenger who arrives is "full of high disdain" not only because of the useless resistance of the inhabitants of Dis but also because of Virgil's incapacity. To appreciate something of the subtlety of Dante's poetry, we should notice that this messenger opens the gate with a touch of his wand, or *verghetta*. In the Middle Ages the power of Virgil's poetry was such that there developed a tradition that he was a magician, perhaps even a soothsayer: we meet this tradition in canto 20, where Dante will have Virgil revise his own poem so as to distance himself from this accusation. But one of the effects of this connection between Virgil and magic was that the spelling of his name was revised from Vergil—in Latin his name is *Vergilius Maro*—to Virgil by assimilation with the Latin word for a magician's wand, which is *virga*. In other words, Virgil wields a *virga*. But here Virgil's powers fail him, and it is an angel of God—the God whom Virgil did not know—who wields the *verghetta*.

There are many examples of the way in which Dante marks the difference between Virgil's pre-Christian understanding and his own confident location within the context of Christian belief. The reader might want to compare, for instance, the description in *Aeneid* 6 of the souls awaiting their trip across the river Acheron with its rewriting in *Inferno* 3, or any of the other passages—indicated in the notes—where Dante draws directly upon the *Aeneid*. In addition to this indication of cultural and (for Dante) spiritual difference, Dante's relation to Virgil is not just literary but deeply emotional. Virgil may be a figure of authority, but he is also one of pathos, and nowhere more so than in the *Purgatorio*. There, in cantos 21 and 22, he meets his disciple Statius, the author of an epic poem that was, as Statius says, inspired by the *Aeneid*. More important is that Dante, quite unhistorically, presents Statius as having converted to Christianity by reading the lines from Virgil's Fourth Eclogue cited above. Statius says to Virgil,

> You did as he who goes by night and carries
> the lamp behind him—he is of no help
> to his own self but teaches those who follow.

Dante is here, even more anachronistically, having Statius apply to Virgil a description that in one of his treatises Augustine applied to the Jews: "O Jews, you carried in your hands the lamp of the law in order to show the way to others while you remained in the darkness." The point is twofold: Virgil is a classical version of Moses, who saw the promised land but could not himself enter; and Virgil is to Statius (and to Dante) as Moses is to Christ: he is the prefiguration, and they are the fulfillment. This sense of Virgil's exclusion from the ultimate reward of the righteous life is expressed with great poignancy in *Purgatorio* 30, where Virgil disappears from the poem to be replaced by Beatrice.

A further distinction between Dante and Virgil is generic: in *Inferno* 20, Virgil refers to his poem as "my high tragedy"; in the next canto, Dante calls his poem "my Comedy" (the epithet "Divine" was not added until the sixteenth century). What are the differences between tragedy and comedy? In the Middle Ages, there are essentially four. First, *narrative structure*: a tragedy begins in happiness and ends in misery, while a comedy works in reverse, so that Dante begins in Hell and ends in Paradise. Second, *style*: tragedy is exalted in style, while comedy can indulge in a range of styles, and we see this in the *Inferno*, for example, where canto 21 provides a wonderful scene of a group of naughty devils who tease Virgil by pretending to be Roman soldiers but then, as they set off on their march, signal their departure with an obscene gesture— the leader "made a trumpet of his ass." Third, *character*: a tragedy deals with important historical figures (and for the Middle Ages the term *tragedy* indicated that the narrative was historically true), while a comedy deals with all sorts of people, the common as well as the high-born—and certainly this is true of Dante's poem. And fourth, *subject matter*: tragedy deals with events of grand historical importance while comedy deals with people's private or inward lives.

We can understand this last, most important difference in the way Dante manipulates the word "pity" (*pietà* in the Italian). This is the Italian version of the key Virgilian term *pietas*: for Virgil piety means essentially a dutiful or obedient compliance to a larger responsibility—one that in fact entails the abandonment of one's own personal or inner self. But for Dante *pietà* means pity or compassion. In Virgil *pietas* is always a moral good; but in Dante it is not. In *Inferno* 2, for instance, Virgil explains that Beatrice feels compassion or *pietà* for Dante, but that the sufferings of those in Hell, including Virgil himself, do not touch her. It would have been wrong for her to feel pity for Virgil: everyone in Hell is there as an effect not just of God's justice but of his love as well, as the inscription over the gate in canto 3 tells us. As Virgil says to Dante in one of the several times when he is misled into sympathizing with the sufferings of the damned, "Here pity only lives when it is dead." In a larger sense, one of the central concerns of the poem is precisely what the protagonist feels and the shifts of his personality—the turmoil within his inner self—throughout the course of the journey he undertakes. This is clearly not true, for example, of Aeneas, who is pretty much denied any but the most obvious emotions—and often not many of them. Indeed, Aeneas's piety is fully accomplished precisely when he has sacrificed his personality in the interest of founding Rome, whereas *The Divine Comedy* is concerned throughout with the spiritual development of its protagonist.

The Divine Comedy is concerned as well with the spiritual development of its readers. As Augustine's *Confessions* make clear, for the medieval Christian reading was itself a spiritual action with serious moral consequences. One of the greatest impediments to Augustine's conversion was his inability to understand how the Hebrew Bible—with what he thought its unsophisticated language and outlandish narratives—could compete with either the wisdom available in Greek philosophy or the beautiful style of Latin poetry, or how it could be reconciled to Christian doctrine. But he learned, with the help of Bishop Ambrose of Milan, to read the Bible not literally but, as he calls it, spiritually. He means by this what we would call an allegorical reading. For example, throughout the Middle Ages the Song of Songs in the Hebrew Bible was read not as a love poem but as an allegory about the love of God for the individual soul, or of Christ for the Church, or of the Holy Spirit for the Virgin Mary. Moses, Isaac, Noah, and the other patriarchs were seen not just as leaders of Israel but as prefigurations of Christ. And so on: virtually every passage in the Hebrew

Bible was interpreted so as to render it consistent with both the New Testament and Christian doctrine as defined by the Church. In 2 Corinthians 3.6 Paul says that "for the letter killeth, but the spirit giveth life": to read the Bible only literally, simply as a series of historical narratives, is not merely to miss its deeper significance but to place oneself in spiritual danger, to risk one's very soul. As Augustine argues, to read literally is to read carnally or corporeally, with the eye of the flesh; but to interpret is to read spiritually, with the eye of the heart.

We have already seen how at a crucial moment in the *Inferno* (canto 9) Virgil seeks to cover Dante's eyes while Dante himself urges the reader to uncover the meaning of the events being portrayed. Throughout the *Comedy*, and especially in the *Inferno*, the most corporeal of the three canticles, both Dante the pilgrim and the reader are tempted to read carnally or corporeally, to be distracted from the need for interpretation by the visually powerful scenes presented to them. An example is the account in canto 5 of Paolo and Francesca, who are located in the third circle, where the lustful are punished. These young lovers are here because they committed adultery, and the winds that blow them about are an infernal version of the gusts of desire that drove them in life. But if we stop here we will make the same mistake as does the pilgrim Dante, who feels for them exactly the wrong sort of pity. For Francesca's punishment is not to whirl about endlessly, locked in the arms of her beloved: after all, is that really a punishment? No, her punishment is to repeat throughout eternity the act of seduction that brought about her damnation; and Paolo's punishment is to watch her as she works her wiles. It is no accident that in the conversation with Dante and Virgil Paolo says not a word but only sobs; indeed, Francesca refers to him only once, with the contemptuous demonstrative pronoun *questi*, "*this one*, who never shall be parted from me." And whom does Francesca seduce? After listening to her tell her carefully crafted tale of love—one that incorporates within it lines from the kind of lyric poetry that Dante himself had written as a youth—Dante falls to the ground with pity. Indeed, his description is painfully apt: "And then I fell as a dead body falls"—an act all too appropriate for a man in Hell. Nor does Francesca's power stop at Dante, for it has worked its magic on generations of readers. The challenge of this scene is to remember its deep significance—that this woman is in Hell, that she is currently repeating the very sin that put her there—while she does everything in her power to make you forget.

The interpretive drama acted out in this scene is repeated throughout the *Inferno*. The poem is peopled with brilliantly realized personalities who engage in rhetorical subtleties that simultaneously conceal and yet reveal their moral corruption. Farinata and Cavalcanti, Pier delle Vigne, Brunetto Latini, Vanni Fucci, Ulysses, Guido da Montefeltro, Bertran de Born, Geri del Bello, Ugolino—these and more provide a human drama that is unsurpassed in Western literature. Yet we are simultaneously never allowed to forget that they are all damned by a divine justice that is, for Dante, infallible. We are simultaneously intrigued and wary, powerfully drawn toward these men and women whose personalities have here, in eternity, achieved their full and at times glorious potential and yet also on the alert for the full meaning of their words. Of all the accomplishments of this great poem, perhaps its most enduring achievement is its capacity to provide the reader with a virtually limitless sense of the deep meaningfulness that literature can provide. For Dante this meaningfulness derived from God, but whatever its source, we can still agree with those readers who thought the poem divine.

The notes to this selection have been kept to a minimum. Of the many excellent commentaries in English, one of the most complete is in the edition and translation by Charles S. Singleton (1970–75). An excellent commentary on the *Inferno* can be found in the edition and translation by Robert M. Durling and Ronald L. Martinez (1996), who are preparing similar volumes for the rest of the poem. Useful commentaries on individual cantos can also be found in Ricardo Quinones, *Dante* (1979). A rightly celebrated essay on *Inferno* 10, with important comments on the *Comedy* as a whole, is by Erich Auerbach in his *Mimesis*, and illuminating and learned essays by one of the leading English-speaking Dantists are in John Freccero, *Dante: The Poetics of Conversion* (1986). *Dante Studies* is published annually and includes an annotated bibliography.

PRONOUNCING GLOSSARY

The following list uses common English syllables to provide rough equivalents of selected words whose pronunciation may be unfamiliar to the general reader.

Abbagliato: *ah-bahl-lee-ah'-toh*

Aghinolfo: *ah-gee-nol'-foh*

Alichino: *a-lee-kee'-noh*

Bacchiglione: *bahk-eel-lee-oh'-nay*

Barbariccia: *bar-bar-eetch'-yah*

Caccia: *cah'-chyah*

Capocchio: *ka-pawk'-yoh*

Ciacco: *chyah'-koh*

Draghignazzo: *drah-gee-nyah'-zoh*

Focaccia: *foh-cah'-chyah*

Gianfigliazzi: *jyahn'-feel-yah-tzee*

Gianni Schicchi: *jyahn'-ee skee'-kee*

Hypsipyle: *hip-sip'-il-ay*

Maghinardo: *mah-ghee-nard'-oh*

Malebolge: *mahl-uh-bowl'-jay*

Malebranche: *mahl-uh-branck'-eh*

Paolo: *powl'-oh*

Peschiera: *pes-kee-ehr'-ah*

Puccio: *poo'-chyoh*

Rinier: *ree-nyay*

Romagna: *row-mah'-nyah*

Ruggieri: *roo-jyehr'-ee*

Tagliacozzo: *tah-lyah-cot'-soh*

Tegghiaio: *teh-gyai'-oh*

Thibault: *tee'-bow*

Uguiccione: *oo-gwee-chyoh'-nay*

Verrucchio: *vehr-oo'-kyoh*

FROM THE DIVINE COMEDY[1]

Inferno

CANTO I

The voyager-narrator astray by night in a dark forest. Morning and the sunlit hill. Three beasts that impede his ascent. The encounter with Virgil, who offers his guidance and an alternative path through two of the three realms the voyager must visit.

When I had journeyed half of our life's way,[2]
I found myself within a shadowed forest,
for I had lost the path that does not stray.[3]
    Ah, it is hard to speak of what it was,
that savage forest, dense and difficult,   5
which even in recall renews my fear:
    so bitter—death is hardly more severe!
But to retell the good discovered there,

---

1. Translated by Allen Mandelbaum. The notes are by Mandelbaum and Lee Patterson.   2. Born in 1265, Dante was thirty-five in 1300, the fictional date of the poem. The biblical span of human life is seventy (see Psalms 90.10 and Isaiah 38.10).   3. See Proverbs 2.13–14 and 4.18–19, and also 2 Peter 2.15.

I'll also tell the other things I saw.
    I cannot clearly say how I had entered   10
the wood; I was so full of sleep[4] just at
the point where I abandoned the true path.[5]
    But when I'd reached the bottom of a hill—
it rose along the boundary of the valley
that had harassed my heart with so much fear—   15
    I looked on high and saw its shoulders clothed
already by the rays of that same planet[6]
which serves to lead men straight along all roads.
    At this my fear was somewhat quieted;
for through the night of sorrow I had spent,   20
the lake within my heart[7] felt terror present.
    And just as he who, with exhausted breath,
having escaped from sea to shore, turns back
to watch the dangerous waters he has quit,
    so did my spirit, still a fugitive,   25
turn back to look intently at the pass
that never has let any man survive.[8]
    I let my tired body rest awhile.
Moving again, I tried the lonely slope—
my firm foot always was the one below.   30
    And almost where the hillside starts to rise—
look there!—a leopard, very quick and lithe,
a leopard covered with a spotted hide.
    He did not disappear from sight, but stayed;
indeed, he so impeded my ascent   35
that I had often to turn back again.
    The time was the beginning of the morning;
the sun was rising now in fellowship
with the same stars that had escorted it
    when Divine Love first moved those things of beauty;[9]   40
so that the hour and the gentle season
gave me good cause for hopefulness on seeing
    that beast before me with his speckled skin;
but hope was hardly able to prevent
the fear I felt when I beheld a lion.   45
    His head held high and ravenous with hunger—
even the air around him seemed to shudder—
this lion seemed to make his way against me.
    And then a she-wolf showed herself; she seemed
to carry every craving in her leanness;   50
she had already brought despair to many.
    The very sight of her so weighted me
with fearfulness that I abandoned hope

---

4. See Romans 13.11–12.   **5.** See Psalms 23.3.   **6.** The sun, which in the astronomical system of Dante's time was a planet thought to revolve around the Earth.   **7.** This phrase referred to the inner chamber of the heart, a cavity that in the physiology of Dante's time was the physical location of fear. Not coincidentally, the *Inferno* ends at the lake of Cocytus (see 32.23).   **8.** This simile of Dante as the survivor of a passage through the sea invokes the story of the escape of the Israelites from Egypt through the Red Sea, a central metaphor throughout the *Comedy* (see *Purgatorio* 24.46). See Exodus 14.   **9.** The world was believed to have been created in spring, with the sun in the constellation of Aries.

of ever climbing up that mountain slope.[1]
   Even as he who glories while he gains   55
will, when the time has come to tally loss,
lament with every thought and turn despondent,
   so was I when I faced that restless beast,
which, even as she stalked me, step by step
had thrust me back to where the sun is speechless.   60
   While I retreated down to lower ground,
before my eyes there suddenly appeared
one who seemed faint because of the long silence.[2]
   When I saw him in that vast wilderness,
"Have pity on me," were the words I cried,   65
"whatever you may be—a shade, a man."
   He answered me: "Not man; I once was man.
Both of my parents came from Lombardy,
and both claimed Mantua as native city.[3]
   And I was born, though late, *sub Julio,*   70
and lived in Rome under the good Augustus—
the season of the false and lying gods.[4]
   I was a poet, and I sang the righteous
son of Anchises[5] who had come from Troy
when flames destroyed the pride of Ilium.   75
   But why do you return to wretchedness?
Why not climb up the mountain of delight,
the origin and cause of every joy?"
   "And are you then that Virgil, you the fountain
that freely pours so rich a stream of speech?"   80
I answered him with shame upon my brow.
   "O light and honor of all other poets,
may my long study and the intense love
that made me search your volume serve me now.
   You are my master and my author, you—   85
the only one from whom my writing drew
the noble style for which I have been honored.
   You see the beast that made me turn aside;
help me, o famous sage, to stand against her,
for she has made my blood and pulses shudder."   90
   "It is another path that you must take,"
he answered when he saw my tearfulness,
"if you would leave this savage wilderness;
   the beast that is the cause of your outcry
allows no man to pass along her track,   95
but blocks him even to the point of death;
   her nature is so squalid, so malicious
that she can never state her greedy will;
when she has fed, she's hungrier than ever.
   She mates with many living souls and shall   100

1. The meaning of the leopard, lion, and she-wolf is open to a number of interpretations, the most plausible being that they represent the three major forms of sin found in Hell, respectively fraud, violence, and incontinence or immoderation (see 11.78ff.). The structure of Hell indicates that the last is the least serious morally, but its role in this canto shows that it is the most difficult to overcome psychologically.   2. The Roman poet Virgil's voice has not been heard since he died in 19 B.C.   3. Lombardy is the most northern area of Italy; Mantua is located to the east of Milan.   4. Virgil (70–19 B.C.) was born *sub Julio,* in the time of Julius Caesar (assassinated in 44 B.C.), who was regarded by Dante as the founder of the Roman empire.   5. Aeneas, the hero of Virgil's *Aeneid.*

yet mate with many more, until the Greyhound[6]
arrives, inflicting painful death on her.
  That Hound will never feed on land or pewter,
but find his fare in wisdom, love, and virtue;
his place of birth shall be between two felts.[7]   105
  He will restore low-lying Italy
for which the maid Camilla died of wounds,
and Nisus, Turnus, and Euryalus.[8]
  And he will hunt that beast through every city
until he thrusts her back again to Hell,   110
from which she was first sent above by envy.
  Therefore, I think and judge it best for you
to follow me, and I shall guide you, taking
you from this place through an eternal place,
  where you shall hear the howls of desperation   115
and see the ancient spirits in their pain,
as each of them laments his second death;[9]
  and you shall see those souls who are content
within the fire,[1] for they hope to reach—
whenever that may be—the blessed people.[2]   120
  If you would then ascend as high as these,
a soul more worthy than I am[3] will guide you;
I'll leave you in her care when I depart,
  because that Emperor who reigns above,
since I have been rebellious to His law,   125
will not allow me entry to His city.
  He governs everywhere, but rules from there;
there is His city, His high capital:
o happy those He chooses to be there!"
  And I replied: "O poet—by that God   130
whom you had never come to know—I beg you,
that I may flee this evil and worse evils,
  to lead me to the place of which you spoke,
that I may see the gateway of Saint Peter
and those whom you describe as sorrowful."   135
  Then he set out, and I moved on behind him.

CANTO II

*The following evening. Invocation to the Muses. The narrator's
questioning of his worthiness to visit the deathless world. Virgil's
comforting explanation that he has been sent to help Dante by three
Ladies of Heaven. The voyager heartened. Their setting out.*

  The day was now departing; the dark air
released the living beings of the earth
from work and weariness; and I myself
alone prepared to undergo the battle

---

6. Dante's prediction of a modern redeemer is so enigmatic that there can be no certainty of his identity.
Most commentators designate Cangrande (i.e., the great dog) della Scala of Verona, Dante's benefactor
after his exile from Florence.   7. Those who opt for Cangrande as the redeemer note that Feltre and
Montefeltro are towns that roughly mark the limits of Cangrande's domains. But other interpretations
are possible.   8. Characters in the *Aeneid* who die during Aeneas's conquest of Italy.   9. The second
death is damnation; see Revelation 21.8.   1. The souls in Purgatory.   2. The saved in Paradise.
3. Beatrice.

both of the journeying and of the pity,   5
which memory, mistaking not, shall show.
  O Muses, o high genius, help me now;
o memory that set down what I saw,
here shall your excellence reveal itself!
  I started: "Poet, you who are my guide,   10
see if the force in me is strong enough
before you let me face that rugged pass.
  You say that he who fathered Sylvius,[4]
while he was still corruptible, had journeyed
into the deathless world with his live body.   15
  For, if the Enemy of every evil
was courteous to him, considering
all he would cause and who and what he was,
  that does not seem incomprehensible,
since in the empyrean heaven he was chosen   20
to father honored Rome and her empire;
  and if the truth be told, Rome and her realm
were destined to became the sacred place,
the seat of the successor of great Peter.[5]
  And through the journey you ascribe to him,   25
he came to learn of things that were to bring
his victory and, too, the papal mantle.
  Later the Chosen Vessel[6] travelled there,
to bring us back assurance of that faith
with which the way to our salvation starts.   30
  But why should I go there? Who sanctions it?
For I am not Aeneas, am not Paul;
nor I nor others think myself so worthy.
  Therefore, if I consent to start this journey,
I fear my venture may be wild and empty.   35
You're wise; you know far more than what I say."
  And just as he who unwills what he wills
and shifts what he intends to seek new ends
so that he's drawn from what he had begun,
  so was I in the midst of that dark land,   40
because, with all my thinking, I annulled
the task I had so quickly undertaken.
  "If I have understood what you have said,"
replied the shade of that great-hearted one,
"your soul has been assailed by cowardice,   45
  which often weighs so heavily on a man—
distracting him from honorable trials—
as phantoms frighten beasts when shadows fall.
  That you may be delivered from this fear,
I'll tell you why I came and what I heard   50
when I first felt compassion for your pain.
  I was among those souls who are suspended;[7]
a lady called to me, so blessed, so lovely
that I implored to serve at her command.
  Her eyes surpassed the splendor of the star's;   55

4. Aeneas in *Aeneid* 6.   5. The apostle Peter is considered by the Catholic Church to be the first pope.
6. St. Paul; see 2 Corinthians 12.2–4.   7. In Limbo, where the souls are "neither sad nor joyous" (4.84).

and she began to speak to me—so gently
and softly—with angelic voice. She said:
    'O spirit of the courteous Mantuan,
whose fame is still a presence in the world,
and shall endure as long as the world lasts,   60
    my friend, who has not been the friend of fortune,
is hindered in his path along that lonely
hillside; he has been turned aside by terror.
    From all that I have heard of him in Heaven,
he is, I fear, already so astray   65
that I have come to help him much too late.
    Go now; with your persuasive word, with all
that is required to see that he escapes,
bring help to him, that I may be consoled.
    For I am Beatrice who send you on;   70
I come from where I most long to return;[8]
Love prompted me, that Love which makes me speak.
    When once again I stand before my Lord,
then I shall often let Him hear your praises.'
Now Beatrice was silent. I began: 75
    'O Lady of virtue, the sole reason why
the human race surpasses all that lies
beneath the heaven with the smallest sphere,[9]
    so welcome is your wish, that even if
it were already done, it would seem tardy;   80
all you need do is let me know your will.
    But tell me why you have not been more prudent—
descending to this center, moving from
that spacious place where you long to return?'
    'Because you want to fathom things so deeply,   85
I now shall tell you promptly,' she replied,
'why I am not afraid to enter here.
    One ought to be afraid of nothing other
than things possessed of power to do us harm,
but things innocuous need not be feared.   90
    God, in His graciousness, has made me so
that this, your misery, cannot touch me;
I can withstand the fires flaming here.
    In Heaven there's a gentle lady[1]—one
who weeps for the distress toward which I send you,   95
so that stern judgment up above is shattered.
    And it was she who called upon Lucia,[2]
requesting of her: "Now your faithful one
has need of you, and I commend him to you."
    Lucia, enemy of every cruelty,   100
arose and made her way to where I was,
sitting beside the venerable Rachel.[3]
    She said: "You, Beatrice, true praise of God,
why have you not helped him who loved you so
that—for your sake—he's left the vulgar crowd?   105
    Do you not hear the anguish in his cry?

8. Paradise.   9. The moon.   1. The Virgin Mary.   2. St. Lucy, a third-century martyr and the
patron saint of sight.   3. Rachel signifies the contemplative life: see Genesis 29.16–17.

Do you not see the death he wars against
upon that river ruthless as the sea?"[4]
No one within this world has ever been
so quick to seek his good or flee his harm   110
as I—when she had finished speaking thus—
to come below, down from my blessed station;
I trusted in your honest utterance,
which honors you and those who've listened to you.'
When she had finished with her words to me,   115
she turned aside her gleaming, tearful eyes,
which only made me hurry all the more.
And, just as she had wished, I came to you:
I snatched you from the path of the fierce beast
that barred the shortest way up the fair mountain.   120
What is it then? Why, why do you resist?
Why does your heart host so much cowardice?
Where are your daring and your openness
as long as there are three such blessed women
concerned for you within the court of Heaven   125
and my words promise you so great a good?"
As little flowers, which the chill of night
has bent and huddled, when the white sun strikes,
grow straight and open fully on their stems,
so did I, too, with my exhausted force;   130
and such warm daring rushed into my heart
that I—as one who has been freed—began:
"O she, compassionate, who has helped me!
And you who, courteous, obeyed so quickly
the true words that she had addressed to you!   135
You, with your words, have so disposed my heart
to longing for this journey—I return
to what I was at first prepared to do.
Now go; a single will fills both of us:
you are my guide, my governor, my master."   140
These were my words to him; when he advanced,
I entered on the steep and savage path.

CANTO III

*The inscription above the Gate of Hell. The Ante-Inferno, where the
shades of those who lived without praise and without blame now
intermingle with the neutral angels. He who made the great refusal. The
River Acheron. Charon. Dante's loss of his senses as the earth trembles.*

THROUGH ME THE WAY INTO THE SUFFERING CITY,
THROUGH ME THE WAY TO THE ETERNAL PAIN,
THROUGH ME THE WAY THAT RUNS AMONG THE LOST.
JUSTICE URGED ON MY HIGH ARTIFICER;
MY MAKER WAS DIVINE AUTHORITY,   5
THE HIGHEST WISDOM, AND THE PRIMAL LOVE.[5]
BEFORE ME NOTHING BUT ETERNAL THINGS

---

4. These are the waters of 1.22–24.   5. God as Father, Son, and Holy Ghost.

WERE MADE, AND I ENDURE ETERNALLY.
ABANDON EVERY HOPE, WHO ENTER HERE.
   These words—their aspect was obscure—I read   10
inscribed above a gateway, and I said:
"Master, their meaning is difficult for me."
   And he to me, as one who comprehends:
"Here one must leave behind all hesitation;
here every cowardice must meet its death.   15
   For we have reached the place of which I spoke,
where you will see the miserable people,
those who have lost the good of the intellect."[6]
   And when, with gladness in his face, he placed
his hand upon my own, to comfort me,   20
he drew me in among the hidden things.
   Here sighs and lamentations and loud cries
were echoing across the starless air,
so that, as soon as I set out, I wept.
   Strange utterances, horrible pronouncements,   25
accents of anger, words of suffering,
and voices shrill and faint, and beating hands—
all went to make a tumult that will whirl
forever through that turbid, timeless air,
like sand that eddies when a whirlwind swirls.   30
   And I—my head oppressed by horror—said:
"Master, what is it that I hear? Who are
those people so defeated by their pain?"
   And he to me: "This miserable way
is taken by the sorry souls of those   35
who lived without disgrace and without praise.[7]
   They now commingle with the coward angels,
the company of those who were not rebels
nor faithful to their God, but stood apart.
   The heavens, that their beauty not be lessened,   40
have cast them out, nor will deep Hell receive them—
even the wicked cannot glory in them."
   And I: "What is it, master, that oppresses
these souls, compelling them to wail so loud?"
He answered: "I shall tell you in few words.   45
   Those who are here can place no hope in death,
and their blind life is so abject that they
are envious of every other fate.
   The world will let no fame of theirs endure;
both justice and compassion must disdain them;   50
let us not talk to them, but look and pass."
   And I, looking more closely, saw a banner
that, as it wheeled about, raced on—so quick
that any respite seemed unsuited to it.
   Behind that banner trailed so long a file   55
of people—I should never have believed
that death could have unmade so many souls.

6. *The good of the intellect:* i.e., God.   7. Those who declined to choose between good and evil.

After I had identified a few,
I saw and recognized the shade of him[8]
who made, through cowardice, the great refusal.   60
    At once I understood with certainty:
this company contained the cowardly,
hateful to God and to His enemies.
    These wretched ones, who never were alive,
went naked and were stung again, again   65
by horseflies and by wasps that circled them.
    The insects streaked their faces with their blood,
which, mingled with their tears, fell at their feet,
where it was gathered up by sickening worms.
    And then, looking beyond them, I could see   70
a crowd along the bank of a great river;
at which I said: "Allow me now to know
    who are these people—master—and what law
has made them seem so eager for the crossing,
as I can see despite the feeble light."   75
    And he to me: "When we have stopped along
the melancholy shore of Acheron,[9]
then all these matters will be plain to you."
    At that, with eyes ashamed, downcast, and fearing
that what I said had given him offense,   80
I did not speak until we reached the river.
    And here, advancing toward us, in a boat,
an aged man[1]—his hair was white with years—
was shouting: "Woe to you, corrupted souls!
    Forget your hope of ever seeing Heaven: 85
I come to lead you to the other shore,
to the eternal dark, to fire and frost.
    And you approaching there, you living soul,
keep well away from these—they are the dead."
But when he saw I made no move to go,   90
    he said: "Another way and other harbors—
not here—will bring you passage to your shore:
a lighter craft will have to carry you."
    My guide then: "Charon, don't torment yourself:
our passage has been willed above, where One   95
can do what He has willed; and ask no more."
    Now silence fell upon the wooly cheeks
of Charon, pilot of the livid marsh,
whose eyes were ringed about with wheels of flame.
    But all those spirits, naked and exhausted,   100
had lost their color, and they gnashed their teeth
as soon as they heard Charon's cruel words;
    they execrated God and their own parents
and humankind, and then the place and time
of their conception's seed and of their birth.   105
    Then they forgathered, huddled in one throng,

8. Pope Celestine V, who was elected pope in July 1294 and then resigned five months later.   9. The
first of the four rivers of Hell.   1. Charon; see *Aeneid* 6.

weeping aloud along that wretched shore
which waits for all who have no fear of God.
The demon Charon, with his eyes like embers,
by signaling to them, has all embark;   110
his oar strikes anyone who stretches out.
    As, in the autumn, leaves detach themselves,[2]
first one and then the other, till the bough
sees all its fallen garments on the ground,
    similarly, the evil seed of Adam   115
descended form the shoreline one by one,
when signaled, as a falcon—called—will come.
    So do they move across the darkened waters;
even before they reach the farther shore,
new ranks already gather on this bank.   120
    "My son," the gracious master said to me,
"those who have died beneath the wrath of God,
all these assemble here from every country;
    and they are eager for the river crossing
because celestial justice spurs them on,   125
so that their fear is turned into desire.
    No good soul ever takes its passage here;
therefore, if Charon has complained of you,
by now you can be sure what his words mean."
    And after this was said, the darkened plain   130
quaked so tremendously—the memory
of terror then, bathes me in sweat again.
    A whirlwind burst out of the tear-drenched earth,[3]
a wind that crackled with a bloodred light,
a light that overcame all of my senses;   135
and like a man whom sleep has seized, I fell.

CANTO IV

*Dante's awakening to the First Circle, or Limbo, inhabited by those who
were worthy but lived before Christianity and/or without baptism. The
welcoming of Virgil and Dante by Homer, Horace, Ovid, Lucan. The
catalogue of other great-hearted spirits in the noble castle of Limbo.*

The heavy sleep within my head was smashed
by an enormous thunderclap, so that
I started up as one whom force awakens;
    I stood erect and turned my rested eyes
from side to side, and I stared steadily   5
to learn what place it was surrounding me.
    In truth I found myself upon the brink
of an abyss, the melancholy valley
containing thundering, unending wailings.
    That valley, dark and deep and filled with mist,   10
is such that, though I gazed into its pit,

---

2. This simile is a rewriting of one in *Aeneid* 6.   3. The science of Dante's time explained earthquakes
as caused by the escape of pent-up vapors; it is while he is unconscious that Dante crosses Acheron into
Hell proper.

I was unable to discern a thing.
"Let us descend into the blind world now,"
the poet, who was deathly pale, began;
"I shall go first and you will follow me."   15
But I, who'd seen the change in his complexion,
said: "How shall I go on if you are frightened,
you who have always helped dispel my doubts?"
And he to me: "The anguish of the people
whose place is here below, has touched my face   20
with the compassion you mistake for fear.
Let us go on, the way that waits is long."
So he set out, and so he had me enter
on that first circle girdling the abyss.
Here, for as much as hearing could discover,   25
there was no outcry louder than the sighs
that caused the everlasting air to tremble.
The sighs arose from sorrow without torments,
out of the crowds—the many multitudes—
of infants and of women and of men.   30
The kindly master said: "Do you not ask
who are these spirits whom you see before you?
I'd have you know, before you go ahead,
they did not sin; and yet, though they have merits,
that's not enough, because they lacked baptism,   35
the portal of the faith that you embrace.
And if they lived before Christianity,
they did not worship God in fitting ways;
and of such spirits I myself am one.
For these defects, and for no other evil,   40
we now are lost and punished just with this:
we have no hope and yet we live in longing."
Great sorrow seized my heart on hearing him,
for I had seen some estimable men
among the souls suspended in that limbo.[4]   45
"Tell me, my master, tell me, lord," I then
began because I wanted to be certain
of that belief which vanquishes all errors,
"did any ever go—by his own merit
or others'—from this place toward blessedness?"   50
And he, who understood my covert speech,
replied:[5] "I was new-entered on this state
when I beheld a Great Lord enter here;
the crown he wore, a sign of victory.
He carried off the shade of our first father,[6]   55
of his son Abel, and the shade of Noah,
of Moses, the obedient legislator,
of father Abraham, David the king
of Israel, his father, and his sons,

---

4. Limbo is the location of unbaptized infants and virtuous pagans who lived before the birth of Christ.
5. Virgil here describes the Harrowing of Hell, when after being crucified—according to the Apocryphal Gospel of Nicodemus and confirmed by the medieval Church—Christ descended into Hell and rescued the souls of the righteous of Israel; see also 12.44.   6. Adam.

and Rachel, she for whom he worked so long,   60
   and many others—and He made them blessed;
and I should have you know that, before them,
there were no human souls that had been saved."
   We did not stay our steps although he spoke;
we still continued onward through the wood—   65
the wood, I say, where many spirits thronged.
   Our path had not gone far beyond the point
where I had slept, when I beheld a fire
win out against a hemisphere of shadows.
   We still were at a little distance from it,   70
but not so far I could not see in part
that honorable men possessed that place.
   "O you who honor art and science both,
who are these souls whose dignity has kept
their way of being, separate from the rest?"   75
   And he to me: "The honor of their name,
which echoes up above within your life,
gains Heaven's grace, and that advances them."
   Meanwhile there was a voice that I could hear:
"Pay honor to the estimable poet;   80
his shadow, which had left us, now returns."
   After that voice was done, when there was silence,
I saw four giant shades approaching us;
in aspect, they were neither sad nor joyous.
   My kindly master then began by saying: 85
"Look well at him who holds that sword in hand,
who moves before the other three as lord.
   That shade is Homer, the consummate poet;
the other one is Horace, satirist;
the third is Ovid, and the last is Lucan.[7]   90
   Because each of these spirits shares with me
the name called out before by the lone voice,
they welcome me—and, doing that, do well."
   And so I saw that splendid school assembled,
led by the lord of song incomparable,   95
who like an eagle soars above the rest.
   Soon after they had talked a while together,
they turned to me, saluting cordially;
and having witnessed this, my master smiled;
   and even greater honor then was mine,   100
for they invited me to join their ranks—
I was the sixth among such intellects.
   So did we move along and toward the light,
talking of things about which silence here
is just as seemly as our speech was there.   105
   We reached the base of an exalted castle,[8]
encircled seven times by towering walls,
defended all around by a fair stream.

7. Horace, Ovid, and Lucan are famous Roman poets.   8. Commentators have suggested that this is a Castle of Fame, its seven walls symbolizing the seven liberal arts, a systemization of knowledge developed in the classical period.

We forded this as if upon hard ground;
I entered seven portals with these sages;   110
we reached a meadow of green flowering plants.[9]
The people here had eyes both grave and slow;
their features carried great authority;
they spoke infrequently, with gentle voices.
We drew aside to one part of the meadow,   115
an open place both on high and filled with light,
and we could see all those who were assembled.[1]
Facing me there, on the enameled green,
great-hearted souls were shown to me and I
still glory in my having witnessed them.   120
I saw Electra with her many comrades,
among whom I knew Hector and Aeneas,
and Caesar,[2] in his armor, falcon-eyed.
I saw Camilla and Penthesilea
and, on the other side, saw King Latinus,   125
who sat beside Lavinia, his daughter.[3]
I saw that Brutus who drove Tarquin out,
Lucretia, Julia, Marcia, and Cornelia,
and, solitary, set apart, Saladin.[4]
When I had raised my eyes a little higher,   130
I saw the master of the men who know,[5]
seated in philosophic family.
There all look up to him, all do him honor:
there I beheld both Socrates and Plato,
closest to him, in front of all the rest;   135
Democritus, who ascribes the world to chance,
Diogenes, Empedocles, and Zeno,
and Thales, Anaxagoras, Heraclitus;
I saw the good collector of medicinals,
I mean Dioscorides; and I saw Orpheus,   140
and Tully, Linus, moral Seneca;[6]
and Euclid the geometer, and Ptolemy,
Hippocrates and Galen, Avicenna,
Averroës,[7] of the great Commentary.
I cannot here describe them all in full;   145
my ample theme impels me onward so:
what's told is often less than the event.

---

9. A scene reminiscent of the classical Elysian fields (see *Aeneid* 6).   1. See *Aeneid* 6.   2. Julius
Caesar (d. 44 B.C.). *Electra:* the mother of Dardanus, the founder of Troy. *Hector:* the leading warrior of
the Trojans in the *Iliad. Aeneas:* the hero of the *Aeneid.*   3. Heiress to King Latinus who ruled the area
of Italy where Rome was later located and who married Aeneas. *Camilla:* a female warrior in the *Aeneid*,
where she is compared to Penthesilea, who fought for the Trojans against the Greeks.   4. Admired for
his chivalry in fighting against the crusaders, he was sultan of Egypt and Syria and died in 1193. *Brutus:*
not the Brutus who killed Julius Caesar, but an earlier Roman who drove out the tyrant Tarquin. All four
of the women mentioned were virtuous Roman matrons.   5. Aristotle (384–322 B.C.), Greek philosopher.
The men mentioned in lines 132–38 are Greek philosophers of the seventh through the fourth centuries
B.C.   6. Roman philosopher and dramatist (d. A.D. 65). *Dioscorides:* Greek physician (first century A.D.).
Orpheus: mythical Greek poet. *Tully:* Cicero (d. 43 B.C.), Roman orator. *Seneca:* mythical Greek poet.
7. Avicenna (d. 1037) and Averroës (d. 1198) were Islamic philosophers who wrote commentaries on
Aristotle's works that were highly influential in Christian Europe. *Euclid:* Greek mathematician (fourth
century B.C.). *Ptolemy:* Greek astronomer and geographer (first century A.D.) credited with devising the
cosomological system that was accepted until the time of Copernicus in the sixteenth century (hence the
term *Ptolomaic universe*). *Hippocrates and Galen:* Greek physicians (fourth and second centuries B.C.,
respectively).

The company of six divides in two;
my knowing guide leads me another way,
beyond the quiet, into trembling air.   150
And I have reached a part where no thing gleams.

CANTO V

The Second Circle, where the Lustful are forever buffeted by violent
storm. Minos. The catalogue of carnal sinners. Francesca da Rimini and
her brother-in-law, Paolo Malatesta. Francesca's tale of their love and
death, at which Dante faints.

So I descended from the first enclosure
down to the second circle, that which girdles
less space but grief more great, that goads to weeping.
      There dreadful Minos[8] stands, gnashing his teeth:
examining the sins of those who enter,   5
he judges and assigns as his tail twines.
      I mean that when the spirit born to evil
appears before him, it confesses all;
and he, the connoisseur of sin, can tell
the depth in Hell appropriate to it;   10
as many times as Minos wraps his tail
around himself, that marks the sinner's level.
      Always there is a crowd that stands before him:
each soul in turn advances toward that judgment;
they speak and hear, then they are cast below.   15
      Arresting his extraordinary task,
Minos, as soon as he had seen me, said:
"O you who reach this house of suffering,
      be careful how you enter, whom you trust;
the gate is wide,[9] but do not be deceived!"   20
To which my guide replied: "But why protest?
      Do not attempt to block his fated path:
our passage has been willed above, where One
can do what He has willed; and ask no more."
      Now notes of desperation have begun   25
to overtake my hearing; now I come
where mighty lamentation beats against me.
      I reached a place where every light is muted,
which bellows like the sea beneath a tempest,
when it is battered by opposing winds.   30
      The hellish hurricane, which never rests,
drives on the spirits with its violence:
wheeling and pounding, it harasses them.
      When they come up against the ruined slope,[1]
then there are cries and wailing and lament,   35
and there they curse the force of the divine.
      I learned that those who undergo this torment
are damned because they sinned within the flesh,

---

8. In *Aeneid* 6, Minos is described as judge of the underworld.   **9.** Matthew 7.13.   **1.** A reference to
the earthquake that occurred after the death of Christ (Matthew 27.51); see also 12.45.

subjecting reason to the rule of lust.
    And as, in the cold season, starlings' wings   40
bear them along in broad and crowded ranks,
so does that blast bear on the guilty spirits:
    now here, now there, now down, now up, it drives them.
There is no hope that ever comforts them—
no hope for rest and none for lesser pain.   45
    And just as cranes in flight will chant their lays,
arraying their long file across the air,
so did the shades I saw approaching, borne
    by that assailing wind, lament and moan;
so that I asked him: "Master, who are those   50
who suffer punishment in this dark air?"
    "The first of those about whose history
you want to know," my master then told me,
"once ruled as empress over many nations.
    Her vice of lust became so customary   55
that she made license licit in her laws
to free her from the scandal she had caused.
    She is Semíramis,[2] of whom we read
that she was Ninus' wife and his successor:
she held the land the Sultan now commands.   60
    That other spirit killed herself for love,
and she betrayed the ashes of Sychaeus;
the wanton Cleopatra[3] follows next.
    See Helen, for whose sake so many years
of evil had to pass; see great Achilles,[4]   65
who finally met love—in his last battle.
    See Paris, Tristan[5] . . ."—and he pointed out
and named to me more than a thousand shades
departed from our life because of love.
    No sooner had I heard my teacher name   70
the ancient ladies and the knights, than pity
seized me, and I was like a man astray.
    My first words: "Poet, I should willingly
speak with those two[6] who go together there
and seem so lightly carried by the wind."   75
    And he to me: "You'll see when they draw closer
to us, and then you may appeal to them
by that love which impels them. They will come."
    No sooner had the wind bent them toward us
than I urged on my voice: "O battered souls,   80
if One does not forbid it, speak with us."
    Even as doves when summoned by desire,
borne forward by their will, move through the air

---

2. Renowned for licentiousness, a mythical queen of Assyria. Because both the capital of Assyria and Old Cairo were known as Babylon, her land is here confused with that ruled by the sultan of Egypt.   **3.** Who killed herself after the death of her lover, Marc Antony, in 30 B.C. *That other spirit:* Dido, widow of Sychaeus, whose suicide for love of Aeneas is described in *Aeneid* 4.   **4.** The medieval version of the Troy story described Achilles as enamored of a Trojan princess, Polyxena, and killed in an ambush set by Paris when he went to meet her. Helen's seduction by Paris (see line 67 below) was the cause of the Trojan War. **5.** The lover of Iseult, wife of his lord King Mark.   **6.** Francesca da Rimini and her brother-in-law Paolo Malatesta.

with wings uplifted, still, to their sweet nest,
   those spirits left the ranks where Dido suffers,   85
approaching us through the malignant air;
so powerful had been my loving cry.
   "O living being, gracious and benign,
who through the darkened air have come to visit
our souls that stained the world with blood, if He   90
   who rules the universe were friend to us,
then we should pray to Him to give you peace,
for you have pitied our atrocious state.
   Whatever pleases you to hear and speak
will please us, too, to hear and speak with you,   95
now while the wind is silent, in this place.
   The land where I was born lies on that shore
to which the Po[7] together with the waters
that follow it descends to final rest.
   Love,[8] that can quickly seize the gentle heart,   100
took hold of him because of the fair body
taken from me—how that was done still wounds me.
   Love, that releases no beloved from loving,
took hold of me so strongly through his beauty
that, as you see, it has not left me yet.   105
   Love led the two of us unto one death.
Caïna waits for him[9] who took our life."
These words were borne across from them to us.
   When I had listened to those injured souls,
I bent my head and held it low until   110
the poet asked of me: "What are you thinking?"
   When I replied, my words began: "Alas,
how many gentle thoughts, how deep a longing,
had led them to the agonizing pass!"
   Then I addressed my speech again to them,   115
and I began: "Francesca, your afflictions
move me to tears of sorrow and of pity.
   But tell me, in the time of gentle sighs,
with what and in what way did Love allow you
to recognize your still uncertain longings?"   120
   And she to me: "There is no greater sorrow
than thinking back upon a happy time
in misery—and this your teacher knows.
   Yet if you long so much to understand
the first root of our love, then I shall tell   125
my tale to you as one who weeps and speaks.
   One day, to pass the time away, we read
of Lancelot[1]—how love had overcome him.
We were alone, and we suspected nothing.
   And time and time again that reading led   130

---

7. A river in northern Italy. *The land:* Ravenna, a city on the Adriatic coast in northeastern Italy.   8. Cf.
the next nine lines to the poems by Guido Guinizzelli and Dante included in *Medieval Lyrics: A Selection*
(pp. 1813–14 and 1815–16).   9. Gianciotto Malatesta, Francesca's husband and Paolo's brother. *Caïna:*
The circle of Cain (described in canto 32), where those who killed their kin are punished.   1. In Arthurian legend, the lover of Arthur's wife, Guinevere.

our eyes to meet, and made our faces pale,
and yet one point alone defeated us.
When we had read how the desired smile
was kissed by one who was so true a lover,
this one, who never shall be parted from me,   135
while all his body trembled, kissed my mouth.
A Gallehault² indeed, that book and he
who wrote it, too; that day we read no more."
And while one spirit said these words to me,
the other wept, so that—because of pity—   140
I fainted, as if I had met my death.
And then I fell as a dead body falls.

CANTO VI

*Dante's awakening to the Third Circle, where the Gluttonous, supine, are
flailed by cold and filthy rain and tormented by Cerberus. Ciacco and his
prophecy concerning Florence. The state of the damned after the
Resurrection.*

Upon my mind's reviving—it had closed
on hearing the lament of those two kindred,
since sorrow had confounded me completely—
    I see new sufferings, new sufferers
surrounding me on every side, wherever   5
I move or turn about or set my eyes.
    I am in the third circle, filled with cold,
unending, heavy, and accursèd rain;
its measure and its kind are never changed.
    Gross hailstones, water gray with filth, and snow 10
come streaking down across the shadowed air;
the earth, as it receives that shower, stinks.
    Over the souls of those submerged beneath
that mess, is an outlandish, vicious beast,
his three throats barking, doglike: Cerberus.³   15
    His eyes are bloodred; greasy, black, his beard;
his belly bulges, and his hands are claws;
his talons tear and flay and rend the shades.
    That downpour makes the sinners howl like dogs;
they use one of their sides to screen the other—   20
those miserable wretches turn and turn.
    When Cerberus, the great worm, noticed us,
he opened wide his mouths, showed us his fangs;
there was no part of him that did not twitch.
    My guide opened his hands to their full span,   25
plucked up some earth, and with his fists filled full
he hurled it straight into those famished jaws.
    Just as a dog that barks with greedy hunger
will then fall quiet when he gnaws his food,
intent and straining hard to cram it in,   30

2. The knight who, in the French romance being read by the lovers, acted as a go-between for Lancelot
and Guinevere.   3. For this creature as one of the guardians of Hell, see *Aeneid* 6.

so were the filthy faces of the demon
Cerberus transformed—after he'd stunned
the spirits so, they wished that they were deaf.
    We walked across the shades on whom there thuds
that heavy rain, and set our soles upon   35
their empty images that seem like persons.
    And all those spirits lay upon the ground,
except for one[4] who sat erect as soon
as he caught sight of us in front of him.
    "O you who are conducted through this Hell,"   40
he said to me, "recall me, if you can;
for you, before I was unmade, were made."[5]
    And I to him: "It is perhaps your anguish
that snatches you out of my memory,
so that it seems that I have never seen you.   45
    But tell me who you are, you who are set
in such a dismal place, such punishment—
if other pains are more, none's more disgusting."
    And he to me: "Your city—one so full
of envy that its sack has always spilled—   50
that city held me in the sunlit life.
    The name you citizens gave me was Ciacco;
and for the damning sin of gluttony,
as you can see, I languish in the rain.
    And I, a wretched soul, am not alone,   55
for all of these have this same penalty
for this same sin." And he said nothing more.
    I answered him: "Ciacco, your suffering
so weighs on me that I am forced to weep;
but tell me, if you know, what end awaits   60
the citizens of that divided city;
is any just man there? Tell me the reason
why it has been assailed by so much schism."
    And he to me:[6] "After long controversy,
they'll come to blood; the party of the woods   65
will chase the other out with much offense.
    But then, within three suns, they too must fall;
at which the other party will prevail,
using the power of one who tacks his sails.
    This party will hold high its head for long   70
and heap great weights upon its enemies,
however much they weep indignantly.
    Two men are just,[7] but no one listens to them.
Three sparks that set on fire every heart
are envy, pride, and avariciousness."   75
    With this, his words, inciting tears, were done;
and I to him: "I would learn more from you;
I ask you for a gift of further speech:

---

4. A Florentine named Ciacco, known only through his appearance here.   5. You were born before I died.   6. This enigmatic "prophecy" refers first to the triumph of the Whites, or "the party of the woods" (to which Dante was allied), in 1300 and then their defeat by the Blacks, aided by Pope Boniface ("one who tacks his sails"), in 1302, at which time Dante was exiled.   7. The identity of these two is not known.

Tegghiaio, Farinata, men so worthy,
Arrigo, Mosca, Jacopo Rusticucci,   80
and all the rest whose minds bent toward the good,
   do tell me where they are and let me meet them;
for my great longing drives me on to learn
if Heaven sweetens or Hell poisons them."8
   And he: "They are among the blackest souls;   85
a different sin has dragged them to the bottom;
if you descend so low, there you can see them.
   But when you have returned to the sweet world,
I pray, recall me to men's memory:
I say no more to you, answer no more."   90
   Then his straight gaze grew twisted and awry;
he looked at me awhile, then bent his head;
he fell as low as all his blind companions.
   And my guide said to me: "He'll rise no more
until the blast of the angelic trumpet   95
upon the coming of the hostile Judge:
   each one shall see his sorry tomb again
and once again take on his flesh and form,
and hear what shall resound eternally."9
   So did we pass across that squalid mixture   100
of shadows and of rain, our steps slowed down,
talking awhile about the life to come.
   At which I said: "And after the great sentence—
o master—will these torments grow, or else
be less, or will they be just as intense?"   105
   And he to me: "Remember now your science,
which says that when a thing has more perfection,
so much the greater is its pain or pleasure.
   Though these accursed sinners never shall
attain the true perfection, yet they can   110
expect to be more perfect then than now."1
   We took the circling way traced by that road;
we said much more than I can here recount;
we reached the point that marks the downward slope.
Here we found Plutus,2 the great enemy.   115

CANTO VII

*The demon Plutus. The Fourth Circle, where the Avaricious and the
Prodigal, in opposite directions, roll weights in semicircles. Fortune and
her ways. Descent into the Fifth Circle: the Wrathful and the Sullen, the
former besmirched by the muddy Styx, the latter immersed in it.*

"Pape Satàn, pape Satàn aleppe!"3
so Plutus, with his grating voice, began.

---

8. Dante asks about famous Florentines; he will find Farinata in canto 10, Tegghiaio and Rusticucci in
canto 16, and Mosca in canto 28. Arrigo does not appear.   9. Virgil refers to the Last Judgment, when
the dead will regain their bodies.   1. They will be more perfect because body and soul will be reunited
(a principle derived from Aristotelian science), which will increase their pain.   2. Dante combines Pluto,
the mythological god of the underworld, with Plutus, the classical god of wealth.   3. Virgil apparently
understands this mysterious outburst regarding Satan, but commentators have remained baffled.

The gentle sage, aware of everything,
   said reassuringly, "Don't let your fear
defeat you; for whatever power he has,   5
he cannot stop our climbing down this crag."
   Then he turned back to Plutus' swollen face
and said to him: "Be quiet, cursed wolf!
Let your vindictiveness feed on yourself.
   His is no random journey to the deep: 10
it has been willed on high, where Michael[4] took
revenge upon the arrogant rebellion."
   As sails inflated by the wind collapse,
entangled in a heap, when the mast cracks,
so that ferocious beast fell to the ground.   15
   Thus we made our way down to the fourth ditch,
to take in more of that despondent shore
where all the universe's ill is stored.
   Justice of God! Who has amassed as many
strange tortures and travails as I have seen?   20
Why do we let our guilt consume us so?
   Even as waves that break above Charybdis,[5]
each shattering the other when they meet,
so must the spirits here dance their round dance.
   Here, more than elsewhere, I saw multitudes   25
to every side of me; their howls were loud
while, wheeling weights, they used their chests to push.
   They struck against each other; at that point,
each turned around and, wheeling back those weights,
cried out: "Why do you hoard?" "Why do you squander?"[6]   25
   So did they move around the sorry circle
from left and right to the opposing point;
again, again they cried their chant of scorn;
   and so, when each of them had changed positions,
he circled halfway back to his next joust.   35
And I, who felt my heart almost pierced through,
   requested: "Master, show me now what shades
are these and tell me if they all were clerics—
those tonsured ones[7] who circle on our left."
   And he to me: "All these, to left and right   40
were so squint-eyed of mind in the first life—
no spending that they did was done with measure.
   Their voices bark this out with clarity
when they have reached the two points of the circle
where their opposing guilts divide their ranks.   45
   These to the left—their heads bereft of hair—
were clergymen, and popes and cardinals,
within whom avarice works its excess."
   And I to him: "Master, among this kind
I certainly might hope to recognize   50
some who have been bespattered by these crimes."

---

4. The angel Michael; see Revelation 12.7–9.   **5.** A famous whirlpool in the Straits of Messina, between Sicily and Italy; see *Aeneid* 3.   **6.** Both misers and spendthrifts are punished here.   **7.** The tonsure—a shaving of part of the head—was a mark of clerical status.

And he to me: "That thought of yours is empty:
the undiscerning life that made them filthy
now renders them unrecognizable.
For all eternity they'll come to blows: 55
these here will rise up from their sepulchers
with fists clenched tight; and these, with hair cropped close.
Ill giving and ill keeping have robbed both
of the fair world and set them to this fracas—
what that is like, my words need not embellish.   60
Now you can see, my son, how brief's the sport
of all those goods that are in Fortune's care,
for which the tribe of men contend and brawl;
for all the gold that is or ever was
beneath the moon could never offer rest   65
to even one of these exhausted spirits."
"Master," I asked of him, "now tell me too:
this Fortune whom you've touched upon just now—
what's she, who clutches so all the world's goods?"
And he to me: "O unenlightened creatures,   70
how deep—the ignorance that hampers you!
I want you to digest my words on this.[8]
Who made the heavens and who gave them guides
was He whose wisdom transcends everything;
that every part may shine unto the other,   75
He had the light apportioned equally;
similarly, for wordly splendors, He
ordained a general minister and guide
to shift, from time to time, those empty goods
from nation unto nation, clan to clan,   80
in ways that human reason can't prevent;
just so, one people rules, one languishes,
obeying the decision she has given,
which, like a serpent in the grass, is hidden.
Your knowledge cannot stand against her force;   85
for she foresees and judges and maintains
her kingdom as the other gods do theirs.
The changes that she brings are without respite:
it is necessity that makes her swift;
and for this reason, men change state so often.   90
She is the one so frequently maligned
even by those who should give praise to her—
they blame her wrongfully with words of scorn.
But she is blessed and does not hear these things;
for with the other primal beings, happy,   95
she turns her sphere and glories in her bliss.[9]
But now let us descend to greater sorrow,

---

8. Virgil now explains that each area of life is presided over by a *guide* or *intelligence*, a kind of angel, under the ultimate authority of God. The classical goddess Fortune, thought to distribute the world's goods capriciously, is here described to agree with this Christian conception.   9. Fortune was traditionally depicted as turning a wheel, but here the term *sphere* is revised to refer to her area of authority in the Christian scheme.

for every star that rose when I first moved
is setting now;[1] we cannot stay too long."
  We crossed the circle to the other shore;   100
we reached a foaming watercourse that spills
into a trench formed by its overflow.
  That stream was even darker than deep purple;
and we, together with those shadowed waves,
moved downward and along a strange pathway.   105
  When it has reached the foot of those malign
gray slopes, that melancholy stream descends,
forming a swamp that bears the name of Styx.[2]
  And I, who was intent on watching it,
could make out muddied people in that slime,   110
all naked and their faces furious.
  These struck each other not with hands alone,
but with their heads and chests and with their feet,
and tore each other piecemeal with their teeth.
  The kindly master told me: "Son, now see   115
the souls of those whom anger has defeated;
and I should also have you know for certain
  that underneath the water there are souls
who sigh and make this plain of water bubble,
as your eye, looking anywhere, can tell.   120
  Wedged in the slime, they say: 'We had been sullen
in the sweet air that's gladdened by the sun;
we bore the mist of sluggishness in us:
  now we are bitter in the blackened mud.'
This hymn they have to gurgle in their gullets,   125
because they cannot speak it in full words."
  And so, between the dry shore and the swamp,
we circled much of that disgusting pond,
our eyes upon the swallowers of slime.
  We came at last upon a tower's base.   130

CANTO VIII

Still the Fifth Circle: the Wrathful and the Sullen. The tall tower.
Phlegyas and the crossing of the Styx. Filippo Argenti and Dante's fury.
Approach to Dis, the lower part of Hell: its moat, its walls, its gate. The
demons, fallen angels, and their obstruction of the poets' entry into Dis.

  I say, continuing, that long before
we two had reached the foot of that tall tower,[3]
our eyes had risen upward, toward its summit,
  because of two small flames that flickered there,
while still another flame returned their signal,   5
so far off it was scarcely visible.
  And I turned toward the sea of all good sense;

1. The stars that were rising at the start of the journey (1.37–40) are now setting: Good Friday has passed, and the time is now the early hours of Holy Saturday.   2. The second river of Hell.   3. The watchtower that guards the entrance to lower Hell or the city of Dis, which is a name for the classical god of the underworld, Pluto, that is applied to Satan (see 11.65, 12.39, and 34.20).

I said: "What does this mean? And what reply
comes from that other fire? Who kindled it?"
    And he to me: "Above the filthy waters   10
you can already see what waits for us,
if it's not hid by vapors from the marsh."
    Bowstring has not thrust from itself an arrow
that ever rushed as swiftly through the air
as did the little bark that at that moment   15
    I saw as it skimmed toward us on the water,
a solitary boatman at its helm.
I heard him howl: "Now you are caught, foul soul!"
    "O Phlegyas, Phlegyas,[4] such a shout is useless
this time," my master said; "we're yours no longer   20
than it will take to cross the muddy sluice."
    And just as one who hears some great deception
was done to him, and then resents it, so
was Phlegyas when he had to store his anger.
    My guide preceded me into the boat.   25
Once he was in, he had me follow him;
there seemed to be no weight until I boarded.
    No sooner were my guide and I embarked
than off that ancient prow went, cutting water
more deeply than it does when bearing others.[5]   30
    And while we steered across the stagnant channel,
before me stood a sinner thick with mud,
saying: "Who are you, come before your time?"
    And I to him: "I've come, but I don't stay;
but who are you, who have become so ugly?"   35
He answered: "You can see—I'm one who weeps."
    And I to him: "In weeping and in grieving,
accursèd spirit, may you long remain;
though you're disguised by filth, I know your name."
    Then he stretched both his hands out toward the boat,   40
at which my master quickly shoved him back,
saying: "Be off there with the other dogs!"
    That done, he threw his arms around my neck
and kissed my face and said: "Indignant soul,
blessèd is she who bore you in her womb![6]   45
    When in the world, he was presumptuous;
there is no good to gild his memory,
and so his shade down here is hot with fury.
    How many up above now count themselves
great kings, who'll wallow here like pigs in slime,   50
leaving behind foul memories of their crimes!"
    And I: "O master, I am very eager
to see that spirit soused within this broth
before we've made our way across the lake."
    And he to me: "Before the other shore   55
comes into view, you shall be satisfied;

---

4. A mythological figure condemned to Hell for setting fire to the temple of Apollo in revenge for the god's seduction of his daughter; see *Aeneid* 6.   **5.** Because of the weight of the living Dante.   **6.** See Luke 11.27.

to gratify so fine a wish is right."
    Soon after I had heard these words, I saw
the muddy sinners so dismember him
that even now I praise and thank God for it.   60
    They all were shouting: "At Filippo Argenti!"[7]
At this, the Florentine, gone wild with spleen,
began to turn his teeth against himself.
    We left him there; I tell no more of him.
But in my ears so loud a wailing pounded   65
that I lean forward, all intent to see.
    The kindly master said: "My son, the city
that bears the name of Dis is drawing near,
with its grave citizens, its great battalions."
    I said: "I can already see distinctly—   70
master—the mosques that gleam within the valley,
as crimson as if they had just been drawn
out of the fire." He told me: "The eternal
flame burning there appears to make them red,
as you can see, within this lower Hell."   75
    So we arrived inside the deep-cut trenches
that are the moats of this despondent land:
the ramparts seemed to me to be of iron.
    But not before we'd ranged in a wide circuit
did we approach a place where that shrill pilot   80
shouted: "Get out; the entrance way is here."
    About the gates I saw more than a thousand[8]—
who once had rained from Heaven—and they cried
in anger: "Who is this who, without death,
can journey through the kingdom of the dead?"   85
And my wise master made a sign that said
he wanted to speak secretly to them.
    Then they suppressed—somewhat—their great disdain
and said: "You come alone; let him be gone—
for he was reckless, entering this realm.   90
    Let him return alone on his mad road—
or try to, if he can, since you, his guide
across so dark a land, you are to stay."
    Consider, reader, my dismay before
the sound of those abominable words: 95
returning here seemed so impossible.
    "O my dear guide, who more than seven times
has given back to me my confidence
and snatched me from deep danger that had menaced,
do not desert me when I'm so undone;   100
and if they will not let us pass beyond,
let us retrace our steps together, quickly."
    These were my words; the lord who'd led me there
replied: "Forget your fear, no one can hinder
our passage; One so great has granted it.   105

7. A Florentine contemporary of Dante.   8. The rebel angels, cast out of Heaven; see Luke 10.18 and Revelation 12.9.

But you wait here for me, and feed and comfort
your tired spirit with good hope, for I
will not abandon you in this low world."
    So he goes on his way; that gentle father
has left me there to wait and hesitate,   110
for *yes* and *no* contend within my head.
    I could not hear what he was telling them;
but he had not been long with them when each
ran back into the city, scrambling fast.
    And these, our adversaries, slammed the gates   115
in my lord's face; and he remained outside,
then, with slow steps, turned back again to me.
    His eyes turned to the ground, his brows deprived
of every confidence, he said with sighs:
"See who has kept me from the house of sorrow!"   120
    To me he added: "You—though I am vexed—
must not be daunted; I shall win this contest,
whoever tries—within—to block our way.
    This insolence of theirs is nothing new;
they used it once before and at a gate   125
less secret—it is still without its bolts[9]—
    the place where you made out the fatal text;
and now, already well within that gate,
across the circles—and alone—descends
the one who will unlock this realm for us."   130

CANTO IX

*The gate of Dis. Dante's fear. The three Furies, invoking Medusa. Virgil's
warning to Dante lest he look at Gorgon, Medusa's head. A heavenly
messenger. The flight of the demons. Entry into Dis, where Virgil and
Dante reach the Sixth Circle and its Arch-Heretics, entombed in red-hot
sepulchers.*

    The color cowardice displayed in me
when I saw that my guide was driven back,
made him more quickly mask his own new pallor.
    He stood alert, like an attentive listener,
because his eye could hardly journey far   5
across the black air and the heavy fog.
    "We have to win this battle," he began,
"if not . . . But one so great had offered aid.
But he seems slow in coming: I must wait."
    But I saw well enough how he had covered   10
his first words with the words that followed after—
so different from what he had said before;
    nevertheless, his speech made me afraid,
because I drew out from his broken phrase
a meaning worse—perhaps—than he'd intended.   15
    "Does anyone from the first circle, one

9. A reference to Christ's Harrowing of Hell; see 4.52, and Psalm 106.16 and Matthew 16.18.

whose only punishment is crippled hope,
ever descend so deep in this sad hollow?"[1]
   That was my question. And he answered so:
"It is quite rare for one of us to go   20
along the way that I have taken now.
   But I, in truth, have been here once before:
that savage witch Erichtho,[2] she who called
the shades back to their bodies, summoned me.
   My flesh had not been long stripped off when she   25
had me descend through all the rings of Hell,
to draw a spirit back from Judas' circle.[3]
   That is the deepest and the darkest place,
the farthest from the heaven that girds all:
so rest assured, I know the pathway well.   30
   This swamp that breeds and breathes the giant stench
surrounds the city of the sorrowing,
which now we cannot enter without anger."
   And he said more, but I cannot remember
because my eyes had wholly taken me   35
to that high tower with the glowing summit
   where, at one single point, there suddenly
stood three infernal Furies[4] flecked with blood,
who had the limbs of women and their ways
   but wore, as girdles, snakes of deepest green;   40
small serpents and horned vipers formed their hairs,
and these were used to bind their bestial temples.
   And he, who knew these handmaids well—they served
the Queen of never-ending lamentation[5]—
said: "Look at the ferocious Erinyes!   45
   That is Megaera on the left, and she
who weeps upon the right, that is Allecto;
Tisiphone's between them." He was done.
   Each Fury tore her breast with taloned nails;
each, with her palms, beat on herself and wailed   50
so loud that I, in fear, drew near the poet.
   "Just let Medusa[6] come; then we shall turn
him into stone," they all cried, looking down;
"we should have punished Theseus' assault."[7]
   "Turn round and keep your eyes shut fast, for should   55
the Gorgon show herself and you behold her,
never again would you return above,"
   my master said; and he himself turned me
around and, not content with just my hands,

---

1. I.e., has anyone from Limbo ever descended into lower Hell before?   2. A legendary sorceress. The
story of Virgil's descent into Hell is apparently Dante's own invention, although in the Middle Ages Virgil
had the reputation of being a magician.   3. Judecca, the last subdivision of the last circle of Hell, where
Judas is punished.   4. Three mythological monsters who represent the spirit of vengeance, known in
Greek as the Erinyes (see below, line 45, and lines 46–48 for their individual names); see *Aeneid* 6, 7, and
12.   5. Hecate, or Proserpina, the wife of Pluto.   6. A mythological figure known as a Gorgon (line
56), so frightful in appearance that she turned those who gazed on her into stone.   7. Theseus, a legendary Athenian hero, descended into the underworld in order to try to rescue Proserpina, whom Pluto
had abducted.

used his as well to cover up my eyes. 60
O you possessed of sturdy intellects,
observe the teaching that is hidden here
beneath the veil of verses so obscure.[8]
And now, across the turbid waves, there passed
a reboantic[9] fracas—horrid sound, 65
enough to make both of the shorelines quake:
a sound not other than a wind's when, wild
because it must contend with warmer currents,
it strikes against the forest without let,
shattering, beating down, bearing off branches, 70
as it moves proudly, clouds of dust before it,
and puts to flight both animals and shepherds.
He freed my eyes and said: "Now let your optic
nerve turn directly toward that ancient foam,
there where the mist is thickest and most acrid." 75
As frogs confronted by their enemy,
the snake, will scatter underwater till
each hunches in a heap along the bottom,
so did the thousand ruined souls I saw
take flight before a figure[1] crossing Styx 80
who walked as if on land and with dry soles.
He thrust away the thick air from his face,
waving his left hand frequently before him;
that seemed the only task that wearied him.
I knew well he was Heaven's messenger, 85
and I turned toward my master; and he made
a sign that I be still and bow before him.
How full of high disdain he seemed to me!
He came up to the gate, and with a wand,
he opened it, for there was no resistance. 90
"O you cast out of Heaven, hated crowd,"
were his first words upon that horrid threshold,
"why do you harbor this presumptuousness?
Why are you so reluctant to endure
that Will whose aim can never be cut short, 95
and which so often added to your hurts?
What good is it to thrust against the fates?
Your Cerberus, if you remember well,
for that, had both his throat and chin stripped clean."[2]
At that he turned and took the filthy road, 100
and did not speak to us, but had the look
of one who is obsessed by other cares
than those that press and gnaw at those before him;
and we moved forward, on into the city,
in safety, having heard his holy words. 105
We made our way inside without a struggle;
and I, who wanted so much to observe

---

8. Dante here reminds us of the need to interpret his poetry, although the lesson of this particular episode
is far from self-evident.   9. Reverberating.   1. An angel, here described in a way reminiscent of Mercury, the classical messenger of the gods.   2. Hercules dragged Cerberus into the daylight; see *Aeneid*
6.

the state of things that such a fortress guarded,
    as soon as I had entered, looked about.
    I saw, on every side, a spreading plain   110
of lamentation and atrocious pain.
    Just as at Arles,[3] where Rhone becomes a marsh,
    just as at Pola, near Quarnero's gulf,
    that closes Italy and bathes its borders,
    the sepulchers make all the plain uneven,   115
so they did here on every side, except
    that here the sepulchers were much more harsh;
    for flames were scattered through the tombs, and these
had kindled all of them to glowing heat;
    no artisan could ask for hotter iron.   120
    The lid of every tomb was lifted up,
and from each tomb such sorry cries arose
    as could come only from the sad and hurt.
    And I: "Master, who can these people be
who, buried in great chests of stone like these,   125
    must speak by way of sighs in agony?"
    And he to me: "Here are arch-heretics
and those who followed them, from every sect;
    those tombs are much more crowded than you think.
    Here, like has been ensepulchered with like;   130
some monuments are heated more, some less."
    And then he turned around and to his right;
    we passed between the torments and high walls.

CANTO X

Still the Sixth Circle: the Heretics. The tombs of the Epicureans.
Farinata degli Uberti. Cavalcante dei Cavalcanti. Farinata's prediction of
Dante's difficulty in returning to Florence from exile. The inability of the
damned to see the present, although they can foresee the future.

    Now, by a narrow path that ran between
those torments and the ramparts of the city,
    my master moves ahead, I following.
    "O highest virtue, you who lead me through
these circles of transgression, at your will,   5
    do speak to me, and satisfy my longings.
    Can those who lie within the sepulchers
be seen? The lids—in fact—have all been lifted;
    no guardian is watching over them."
    And he to me: "They'll all be shuttered up   10
when they return here from Jehosaphat[4]
    together with the flesh they left above.
    Within this region is the cemetery
of Epicurus[5] and his followers,
    all those who say the soul dies with the body.   15

---

3. Arles, located on the Rhône River in southern France, and Pola, located on the bay of Quarnero in what
is now Yugoslavia, were the sites of Roman cemeteries.   **4.** According to the Bible, the Last Judgment
will take place in the Valley of Jehosaphat: see Joel 3.2 and 3.12, and Matthew 25.31–32.   **5.** Greek
philosopher (d. 270 B.C.) who rejected the idea of the immortality of the soul.

And so the question you have asked of me
will soon find satisfaction while we're here,
as will the longing you have hid from me."[6]
And I: "Good guide, the only reason I
have hid my heart was that I might speak briefly,   20
and you, long since, encouraged me in this."
"O Tuscan, you who pass alive across
the fiery city with such seemly words,
be kind enough to stay your journey here.
Your accent makes it clear that you belong   25
among the natives of the noble city
I may have dealt with too vindictively."
This sound had burst so unexpectedly
out of one sepulcher that, trembling, I
then drew a little closer to my guide.   30
But he told me: "Turn round! What are you doing?
That's Farinata[7] who has risen there—
you will see all of him from the waist up."
My eyes already were intent on his;
and up he rose—his forehead and his chest—   35
as if he had tremendous scorn for Hell.
My guide—his hands encouraging and quick—
thrust me between the sepulchers toward him,
saying: "Your words must be appropriate."
When I'd drawn closer to his sepulcher,   40
he glanced at me, and as if in disdain,
he asked of me: "Who were your ancestors?"
Because I wanted so to be compliant,
I hid no thing from him: I told him all.
At this he lifted up his brows a bit,   45
then said: "They were ferocious enemies
of mine and of my parents and my party,
so that I had to scatter them twice over."[8]
"If they were driven out," I answered him,
"they still returned, both times, from every quarter;   50
but yours were never quick to learn that art."[9]
At this there rose another shade alongside,[1]
uncovered to my sight down to his chin;
I think that he had risen on his knees.
He looked around me, just as if he longed   55
to see if I had come with someone else;
but then, his expectation spent, he said
in tears: "If it is your high intellect
that lets you journey here, through this blind prison,
where is my son? Why is he not with you?"   60

6. Presumably Dante's desire to see the Florentines who inhabit this circle.   7. Farinata degli Uberti (d. 1264), a leader of the Ghibelline faction in Florence.   8. Dante's family were Guelphs, who were driven out of Florence twice, in 1248 and 1260.   9. The Ghibellines were exiled in 1280, never to return. 1. This is Cavalcante de Cavalcanti, father of Dante's friend and superb fellow poet Guido; a Guelph, Guido married the daughter of Farinata in an unsuccessful attempt to heal the feud. In June 1300—after the fictional date of this conversation—Guido was exiled to a part of Italy where he caught the malaria from which he died in August. Dante was at that time a member of the governing body that made the decision to exile Guido.

I answered: "My own powers have not brought me;
he who awaits me there, leads me through here
perhaps to one[2] your Guido did disdain."
His words, the nature of his punishment—
these had already let me read his name;   65
therefore, my answer was so fully made.
Then suddenly erect, he cried: "What's that:
He '*did* disdain'?[3] He is not still alive?
The sweet light does not strike against his eyes?"
And when he noticed how I hesitated   70
a moment in my answer, he fell back—
supine—and did not show himself again.
But that great-hearted one, the other shade
at whose request I'd stayed, did not change aspect
or turn aside his head or lean or bend;   75
and taking up his words where he'd left off,
"If they were slow," he said, "to learn that art,
that is more torment to me than this bed.
And yet the Lady[4] who is ruler here
will not have her face kindled fifty times   80
before you learn how heavy is that art.[5]
And so may you return to the sweet world,
tell me: why are those citizens so cruel
against my kin in all of their decrees?"
To which I said: "The carnage, the great bloodshed   85
that stained the waters of the Arbia[6] red
have led us to such prayers in our temple."
He sighed and shook his head, then said: "In that,
I did not act alone, but certainly
I'd not have joined the others without cause.   90
But where I was alone was *there*[7] where all
the rest would have annihilated Florence,
had I not interceded forcefully."
"Ah, as I hope your seed may yet find peace,"
I asked, "so may you help me to undo   95
the knot that here has snarled my course of thought.
It seems, if I hear right, that you can see
beforehand that which time is carrying,
but you're denied the sight of present things."
"We see, even as men who are farsighted,   100
those things," he said, "that are remote from us;
the Highest Lord allots us that much light.
But when events draw near or are, our minds
are useless; were we not informed by others,
we should know nothing of your human state.   105

---

2. The passage is ambiguous in the original Italian: as translated here, the "one" refers to Beatrice; but the word can also be translated to refer to Virgil, so that these two lines would read: "he who awaits me there leads me through here, / him whom your Guido did perhaps disdain." **3.** In lines 61–63 Dante uses a verbal form known in Italian as the remote past, which leads Cavalcante to believe, wrongly, that now, in April 1300, Guido is dead—although, ironically, in about four months he will die. **4.** Proserpina, who is also the goddess of the moon. **5.** Farinata here predicts Dante's own exile. **6.** A stream near the hill of Montaperti, where the Ghibellines defeated the Guelphs in 1260. **7.** At Montaperti, where the other Ghibellines wanted to destroy Florence.

So you can understand how our awareness
will die completely at the moment when
the portal of the future has been shut."[8]
Then, as if penitent for my omission,
I said: "Will you now tell that fallen man   110
his son is still among the living ones;[9]
and if, a while ago, I held my tongue
before his question, let him know it was
because I had in mind the doubt you've answered."
And now my master was recalling me;   115
so that, more hurriedly, I asked the spirit
to name the others who were there with him.
He said: "More than a thousand lie with me:
the second Frederick[1] is but one among them,
as is the Cardinal;[2] I name no others."   120
With that, he hid himself; and pondering
the speech that seemed to me so menacing,
I turned my steps to meet the ancient poet.
He moved ahead, and as we made our way,
he said to me: "Why are you so dismayed?"   125
I satisfied him, answering him fully.[3]
And then that sage exhorted me: "Remember
the words that have been spoken here against you.
Now pay attention," and he raised his finger;
"when you shall stand before the gentle splendor   130
of one whose gracious eyes see everything,[4]
then you shall learn—from her—your lifetime's journey."
Following that, his steps turned to the left,
leaving the wall and moving toward the middle
along a path that strikes into a valley   135
whose stench, as it rose up, disgusted us.

CANTO XI

*Still the Sixth Circle. Pope Anastasius' tomb. Virgil on the parts of Dis
they now will visit, where the modes of malice are punished: violence in
the Seventh Circle's Three Rings; "ordinary" fraud in the Eighth Circle;
and treacherous fraud in the Ninth Circle. Hell's previous circles, Two
through Five, as circles of incontinence. Usury condemned.*

Along the upper rim of a high bank
formed by a ring of massive broken boulders,
we came above a crowd more cruelly pent.
And here, because of the outrageous stench
thrown up in excess by that deep abyss,   5
we drew back till we were behind the lid
of a great tomb, on which I made out this,

---

8. The damned can see the future but not the present; after the Last Judgment, when human time is
abolished, they will know nothing.   9. See note to line 68 above.   1. Frederick II, Holy Roman
emperor from 1215 until his death in 1250; he reputedly denied life after death.   2. Ottaviano degli
Ubaldini (d. 1273), who is reputed to have said, "If I have a soul, I have lost it for the Ghibellines."
3. Dante is upset by Farinata's prediction of his exile.   4. Beatrice.

inscribed: "I hold Pope Anastasius,
enticed to leave the true path by Photinus."[5]
"It would be better to delay descent   10
so that our senses may grow somewhat used
to this foul stench; and then we can ignore it."
So said my master, and I answered him:
"Do find some compensation, lest this time
be lost." And he: "You see, I've thought of that."   15
"My son, within this ring of broken rocks,"
he then began, "there are three smaller circles;[6]
like those that you are leaving, they range down.
Those circles are all full of cursed spirits;
so that your seeing of them may suffice,   20
learn now the how and why of their confinement.
Of every malice that earns hate in Heaven,
injustice is the end; and each such end
by force or fraud brings harm to other men.
However, fraud is man's peculiar vice;   25
God finds it more displeasing—and therefore,
the fraudulent are lower, suffering more.
The violent take all of the first circle;
but since one uses force against three persons,
that circle's built of three divided rings.   30
To God and to one's self and to one's neighbor—
I mean, to them or what is theirs—one can
do violence, as you shall now hear clearly.
Violent death and painful wounds may be
inflicted on one's neighbor; his possessions   35
may suffer ruin, fire, and extortion;
thus, murderers and those who strike in malice,
as well as plunderers and robbers—these,
in separated ranks, the first ring racks.
A man can set violent hands against   40
himself or his belongings; so within
the second ring repents, though uselessly,
whoever would deny himself your world,
gambling away, wasting his patrimony,
and weeping where he should instead be happy.   45
One can be violent against the Godhead,
one's heart denying and blaspheming Him
and scorning nature and the good in her;
so, with its sign, the smallest ring has sealed
both Sodom and Cahors[7] and all of those   50
who speak in passionate contempt of God.

---

5. Pope Anastasius (d. 498) was thought, wrongly, to have accepted a heresy promoted by the fifth-century theologian Photinus that Christ was not divine but only human.   6. Virgil now describes the three remaining circles of Hell, the seventh, eighth, and ninth. The seventh is for the violent and is divided into three parts; the eighth and ninth are for the fraudulent, the eighth for those who deceive generally, the ninth for those who betray those who love them. For the scheme of Hell as a whole, see the diagram on p. 1828.   7. In the Middle Ages the names of Sodom (see Genesis 18.20–19.26) and Cahors, a city in southern France, became synonymous with sodomites and userers respectively. Usury, forbidden by the medieval Church, is charging interest on loans; the logic of this prohibition is explained in lines 97ff below.

Now fraud, that eats away at every conscience,
is practiced by a man against another
who trusts in him, or one who has no trust.
    This latter way seems only to cut off   55
the bond of love that nature forges; thus,
nestled within the second circle are:
    hypocrisy and flattery, sorcerers,
and falsifiers, simony, and theft,
and barrators and panders and like trash.   60
    But in the former way of fraud, not only
the love that nature forges is forgotten,
but added love that builds a special trust;
    thus, in the tightest circle, where there is
the universe's center, seat of Dis,[8]   65
all traitors are consumed eternally."
    "Master, your reasoning is clear indeed,"
I said; "it has made plain for me the nature
of this pit and the population in it.
    But tell me: those the dense marsh holds, or those   70
driven before the wind, or those on whom
rain falls, or those who clash with such harsh tongues,
    why are they not all punished in the city
of flaming red if God is angry with them?
And if He's not, why then are they tormented?"   75
    And then to me, "Why does your reason wander
so far from its accustomed course?" he said.
"Or of what other things are you now thinking?
    Have you forgotten, then, the words with which
your *Ethics*[9] treats of those three dispositions   80
that strike at Heaven's will: incontinence
and malice and mad bestiality?
And how the fault that is the least condemned
and least offends God is incontinence?
    If you consider carefully this judgment   85
and call to mind the souls of upper Hell,
who bear their penalties outside this city,
    you'll see why they have been set off from these
unrighteous ones, and why, when heaven's vengeance
hammers at them, it carries lesser anger."   90
    "O sun that heals all sight that is perplexed,
when I ask you, your answer so contents
that doubting pleases me as much as knowing.
    Go back a little to that point," I said,
"where you told me that usury offends   95
divine goodness; unravel now that knot."
    "Philosophy, for one who understands,
points out, and not in just one place," he said,
"how nature follows—as she takes her course—
the Divine Intellect and Divine Art;[1]   100

---

8. Dis is Satan, who is found at the bottom of Hell (see canto 34).   9. Aristotle's *Nicomachean Ethics*.
1. The laws of nature are determined by God.

and if you read your *Physics*[2] carefully,
not many pages from the start, you'll see
　　that when it can, your art would follow nature,
just as a pupil imitates his master;
so that your art is almost God's grandchild.　　　　　105
　　From these two, art and nature, it is fitting,
if you recall how *Genesis* begins,[3]
for men to make their way, to gain their living;
　　and since the usurer prefers another
pathway, he scorns both nature in herself　　　　　110
and art, her follower; his hope is elsewhere.[4]
　　But follow me, for it is time to move;
the Fishes glitter now on the horizon
and all the Wain is spread out over Caurus;[5]
　　only beyond, can one climb down the cliff."　　　　　115

CANTO XII

*The Seventh Circle, First Ring: the Violent against their Neighbors. The
Minotaur. The Centaurs, led by Chiron, who assigns Nessus to guide
Dante and Virgil across the boiling river of blood (Phlegethon). In that
river, Tyrants and Murderers, immersed, watched over by the Centaurs.*

The place that we had reached for our descent
along the bank was alpine; what reclined
　　upon that bank would, too, repel all eyes.
　　Just like the toppled mass of rock that struck—
because of earthquake or eroded props—　　　　　5
the Adige on its flank, this side of Trent,[6]
　　where from the mountain top from which it thrust
down to the plain, the rock is shattered so
that it permits a path for those above:
　　such was the passage down to that ravine.　　　　　10
And at the edge above the cracked abyss,
there lay outstretched the infamy of Crete,
　　conceived within the counterfeited cow;[7]
and, catching sight of us, he bit himself
like one whom fury devastates within.　　　　　15
　　Turning to him, my sage cried out: "Perhaps
you think this is the Duke of Athens here,[8]
who, in the world above, brought you your death.
　　Be off, you beast; this man who comes has not
been tutored by your sister;[9] all he wants　　　　　20
in coming here is to observe your torments."

2. Aristotle's *Physics*, which argues that human art should follow natural laws.　　3. In Genesis 3.17–19,
God decrees that because of the Fall people must toil, supporting themselves by the sweat of their brows.
4. The usurer makes money not from labor but from money itself, which is an unnatural and therefore
illicit art.　　5. The position of stars shows that it is now about 4 A.M. on Holy Saturday.　　6. A famous
landslide on a mountain on the Adige River near Trent, a city in northern Italy.　　7. The Minotaur, half
man and half bull, was conceived when Pasiphaë, the wife of King Minos of Crete, had a wooden cow built
within which she placed herself so as to have intercourse with a bull. The story of the Minotaur is told by
Ovid, *Metamorphoses* 8.　　8. Virgil is referring to Theseus, who killed the Minotaur in the labyrinth in
which it was imprisoned.　　9. Ariadne, daughter of Minos and Pasiphaë, who taught Theseus how to kill
the Minotaur.

Just as the bull that breaks loose from its halter
the moment it receives the fatal stroke,
and cannot run but plunges back and forth,
  so did I see the Minotaur respond;   25
and my alert guide cried: "Run toward the pass;
it's better to descend while he's berserk."
  And so we made our way across that heap
of stones, which often moved beneath my feet
because my weight was somewhat strange for them.   30
  While climbing down, I thought. He said: "You wonder,
perhaps, about that fallen mass, watched over
by the inhuman rage I have just quenched.
  Now I would have you know: the other time
that I descended into lower Hell,   35
this mass of boulders had not yet collapsed;
  but if I reason rightly, it was just
before the coming of the One who took
from Dis the highest circle's splendid spoils
  that, on all sides, the steep and filthy valley   40
had trembled so,[1] I thought the universe
felt love (by which, as some believe, the world
  has often been converted into chaos);[2]
and at that moment, here as well as elsewhere,
these ancient boulders toppled, in this way.   45
  But fix your eyes below, upon the valley,
for now we near the stream of blood, where those
who injure others violently, boil."
  O blind cupidity[3] and insane anger,
which goad us on so much in our short life,   50
then steep us in such grief eternally!
  I saw a broad ditch bent into an arc
so that it could embrace all of that plain,
precisely as my guide had said before;
  between it and the base of the embankment   55
raced files of Centaurs[4] who were armed with arrows,
as, in the world above, they used to hunt.
  On seeing us descend, they all reined in;
and, after they had chosen bows and shafts,
three of their number moved out from their ranks;   60
  and still far off, one cried: "What punishment
do you approach as you descend the slope?
But speak from there; if not, I draw my bow."
  My master told him: "We shall make reply
only to Chiron,[5] when we reach his side;   65
your hasty will has never served you well."
  Then he nudged me and said: "That one is Nessus,

---

1. Because of the earthquake that accompanied Christ's death; see also 5.34.   2. A reference to a theory
of the Greek philosopher Empedocles that the universe is held together by alternating forces of love and
hate, and that if either one predominates the result is chaos. This classical theory is not consistent with
the Christian belief that the universe is created and organized by God's love.   3. Desire for wealth.
4. Mythological creatures that are half man and half horse.   5. A centaur renowned for wisdom who
educated many legendary Greek heroes, including Achilles.

who died because of lovely Deianira
and of himself wrought vengeance for himself.[6]
And in the middle, gazing at his chest,   70
is mighty Chiron, tutor of Achilles;
the third is Pholus,[7] he who was so frenzied.
And many thousands wheel around the moat,
their arrows aimed at any soul that thrusts
above the blood more than its guilt allots."   75
By now we had drawn near those agile beasts;
Chiron drew out an arrow; with the notch,
he parted his beard back upon his jaws.
When he'd uncovered his enormous mouth,
he said to his companions: "Have you noticed   80
how he who walks behind moves what he touches?
Dead soles are not accustomed to do that."
And my good guide—now near the Centaur's chest,
the place where his two natures[8] met—replied:
"He is indeed alive, and so alone   85
it falls to me to show him the dark valley.
Necessity has brought him here, not pleasure.
For she[9] who gave me this new task was one
who had just come from singing halleluiah:
he is no robber; I am not a thief.[1]   90
But by the Power that permits my steps
to journey on so wild a path, give us
one of your band, to serve as our companion;
and let him show us where to ford the ditch,[2]
and let him bear this man upon his back,   95
for he's no spirit who can fly through air."
Then Chiron wheeled about and right and said
to Nessus: "Then, return and be their guide;
if other troops disturb you, fend them off."
Now, with our faithful escort, we advanced   100
along the bloodred, boiling ditch's banks,
beside the piercing cries of those who boiled.
I saw some who were sunk up to their brows,
and that huge Centaur said: "These are the tyrants
who plunged their hands in blood and plundering.   105
Here they lament their ruthless crimes; here are
both Alexander and the fierce Dionysius,[3]
who brought such years of grief to Sicily.
That brow with hair so black is Ezzelino;[4]
that other there, the blonde one, is Obizzo   110
of Este,[5] he who was indeed undone,

---

6. Nessus fell in love with Deianira, wife of Hercules, who killed him; while dying, Nessus poisoned with his own blood a robe that killed Hercules when he put it on.   7. Another centaur, whose rage seems typical of the race.   8. That is, of beast and man.   9. Beatrice   1. Virgil is answering the question asked in lines 61–62: we are here not because we are condemned to this circle for cupidity (see line 49). 2. The river of blood, which we later learn is named Phlegethon (see 14.116).   3. Dionysius of Syracuse in Sicily (d. 367 B.C.). *Alexander*: Alexander the Great (d. 323 B.C.).   4. Ezzolino III (d. 1259), a brutal ruler in northern Italy.   5. Obizzo II d'Este (d. 1293), another northern Italian ruler, reputedly murdered by his son.

within the world above, by his fierce son."
Then I turned to the poet, and he said:
"Now let him be your first guide, me your second."
     A little farther on, the Centaur stopped   115
above a group that seemed to rise above
the boiling blood as far up as their throats.
     He pointed out one shade,[6] alone, apart,
and said: "Within God's bosom, he impaled
the heart that still drips blood upon the Thames."   120
     Then I caught sight of some who kept their heads
and even their full chests above the tide;
among them—many whom I recognized.
     And so the blood grew always shallower
until it only scorched the feet; and here   125
we found a place where we could ford the ditch.
     "Just as you see that, on this side, the brook
continually thins," the Centaur said,
"so I should have you know the rivulet,
     along the other side, will slowly deepen   130
its bed, until it reaches once again
the depth where tyranny must make lament.
     And there divine justice torments Attila[7]
he who was such a scourge upon the earth,
and Pyrrhus, Sextus;[8] to eternity   135
     it milks the tears that boiling brook unlocks
from Rinier of Corneto, Rinier Pazzo,[9]
those two who waged such war upon the highroads."
Then he turned round and crossed the ford again.

CANTO XIII

The Seventh Circle, Second Ring: the Violent against Themselves
(Suicides) or against their Possessions (Squanderers). The dreary wood,
with the Suicides transformed into strange trees, and the Squanderers,
hounded and rent by bitches. Pier della Vigna. Lano and Jacopo da Santo
Andrea. The anonymous Florentine suicide.

Nessus had not yet reached the other bank
when we began to make our way across
a wood on which no path had left its mark.
     No green leaves in that forest, only black;
no branches straight and smooth, but knotted, gnarled;   5
no fruits were there, but briers bearing poison.
     Even those savage beasts that roam between
Cécina and Corneto,[1] beasts that hate

---

6. Guy de Montfort (d. 1298), who killed his cousin Prince Henry of Cornwall during a church service
("within God's bosom") in the Italian city of Viterbo. Nessus's image of the blood dripping from the victim's
heart indicates his focus on the fact that the murder is still unavenged.   **7.** Attila the Hun (d. 453).
8. Roman pirate (first century B.C.). Pyrrhus, Achilles' son, killed the aged Priam at the fall of Troy; see
Aeneid 2.   **9.** Both Riniers were bandits of Dante's day; they are now weeping from pain, whereas in life
they never wept for their sins.   **1.** Two towns that mark the limits of the Maremma, a desolate area in
Tuscany.

tilled lands, do not have holts so harsh and dense.
　　This is the nesting place of the foul Harpies,[2]　　10
who chased the Trojans from the Strophades
with sad foretelling of their future trials.
　　Their wings are wide, their necks and faces human;
their feet are taloned, their great bellies feathered;
they utter their laments on the strange trees.　　15
　　And my kind master then instructed me:
"Before you enter farther know that now
you are within the second ring and shall
　　be here until you reach the horrid sand;[3]
therefore look carefully; you'll see such things　　20
as would deprive my speech of all belief."
　　From every side I heard the sound of cries,
but I could not see any source for them,
so that, in my bewilderment, I stopped.
　　I think that he was thinking that I thought　　25
so many voices moaned among those trunks
from people who had been concealed from us.
　　Therefore my master said: "If you would tear
a little twig from any of these plants,
the thoughts you have will also be cut off."[4]　　30
　　Then I stretched out my hand a little way[5]
and from a great thornbush snapped off a branch,
at which its trunk cried out: "Why do you tear me?"
　　And then, when it had grown more dark with blood,
it asked again: "Why do you break me off?　　35
Are you without all sentiment of pity?
　　We once were men and now are arid stumps:
your hand might well have shown us greater mercy
had we been nothing more than souls of serpents."
　　As from a sapling log that catches fire　　40
along one of its ends, while at the other
it drips and hisses with escaping vapor,
　　so from that broken stump issued together
both words and blood; at which I let the branch
fall, and I stood like one who is afraid.　　45
　　My sage said: "Wounded soul, if, earlier,
he had been able to believe what he
had only glimpsed within my poetry,[6]
　　then he would not have set his hand against you;
but its incredibility made me　　50
urge him to do a deed that grieves me deeply.

2. Birds with the faces of women and clawed hands; in *Aeneid* 3 they drive the wandering Trojans from their refuge in the Strophades Islands and predict their future suffering.　3. The third ring of the seventh circle.　4. Your thoughts that the moans come from people concealed among the trees will be contradicted.　5. This episode derives from *Aeneid* 3, where Aeneas and his Trojan companions, stopping in their search for a new home, discover Polydorus transformed into a bush. Sent out by Priam during the war to solicit aid from the Thracians, Polydorus had been murdered by his hosts, and the javelins with which his body had been pierced had grown into the bush from which Aeneas breaks off a branch that bleeds. See also Ovid, *Metamorphoses* 2.　6. Had Dante been able to believe the story of Polydorus recounted in the *Aeneid*.

But tell him who you were, so that he may,
to make amends, refresh your fame within
the world above, where he can still return."
To which the trunk:[7] "Your sweet speech draws me so   55
that I cannot be still; and may it not
oppress you, if I linger now in talk.
   I am the one who guarded both the keys
of Frederick's heart and turned them, locking and
unlocking them with such dexterity   60
   that none but I could share his confidence;
and I was faithful to my splendid office,
so faithful that I lost both sleep and strength.
   The whore[8] who never turned her harlot's eyes
away from Caesar's dwelling,[9] she who is   65
the death of all and vice of every court,
   inflamed the minds of everyone against me;
and those inflamed, then so inflamed Augustus[1]
that my delighted honors turned to sadness.
   My mind, because of its disdainful temper,   70
believing it could flee disdain through death,
made me unjust against my own just self.[2]
   I swear to you by the peculiar roots
of this thornbush, I never broke my faith
with him who was so worthy—with my lord.   75
   If one of you returns into the world,
then let him help my memory, which still
lies prone beneath the battering of envy."
   The poet waited briefly, then he said
to me: "Since he is silent, do not lose   80
this chance, but speak and ask what you would know."
   And I: "Do you continue; ask of him
whatever you believe I should request;
I cannot, so much pity takes my heart."
   Then he began again: "Imprisoned spirit,   85
so may this man do freely what you ask,
may it please you to tell us something more
   of how the soul is bound into these knots;
and tell us, if you can, if any one
can ever find his freedom from these limbs."   90
   At this the trunk breathed violently, then
that wind became this voice: "You shall be answered
promptly. When the savage spirit quits
   the body from which it has torn itself,
then Minos sends it to the seventh maw.   95
It falls into the wood, and there's no place
   to which it is allotted, but wherever
fortune has flung that soul, that is the space
where, even as a grain of spelt,[3] it sprouts.

---

7. This is the soul of Pier della Vigna (ca. 1190–1249), who had risen to become minister to the emperor Frederick II (on whom see the note to 10.119). His name means Peter of the Vine, probably because his father had been a simple worker in a vineyard.   8. Pier blames his fall from favor on Envy.   9. The imperial court.   1. Frederick.   2. I unjustly committed suicide.   3. Wheat.

It rises as a sapling, a wild plant;   100
and then the Harpies, feeding on its leaves,
cause pain and for that pain provide a vent.
    Like other souls, we shall seek out the flesh
that we have left,[4] but none of us shall wear it;
it is not right for any man to have   105
what he himself has cast aside. We'll drag
our bodies here; they'll hang in this sad wood,
each on the stump of its vindictive shade."
    And we were still intent upon the trunk—
believing it had wanted to say more—   110
when we were overtaken by a roar,
    just as the hunter is aware of chase
and boar as they draw near his post—he hears
the beasts and then the branches as they crack.
    And there upon the left were two[5] who, scratched   115
and naked, fled so violently that
they tore away each forest bough they passed.
    The one in front: "Now come, death, quickly come!"
The other shade, who thought himself too slow,
was shouting after him: "Lano, your legs   120
    were not so nimble at the jousts of Toppo!"[6]
And then, perhaps because he'd lost his breath,
he fell into one tangle with a bush.
    Behind these two, black bitches filled the wood,
and they were just as eager and as swift   125
as greyhounds that have been let off their leash.
    They set their teeth in him where he had crouched;
and, piece by piece, those dogs dismembered him
and carried off his miserable limbs.
    Then he who was my escort took my hand;   130
he led me to the lacerated thorn
that wept in vain where it was bleeding, broken.
    "O Jacopo," it[7] said, "da Santo Andrea,
what have you gained by using me as screen?
Am I to blame for your indecent life?"   135
    When my good master stood beside that bush,
he said: "Who were you, who through many wounds
must breathe with blood your melancholy words?"
    And he to us: "O spirits who have come
to witness the outrageous laceration   140
that leaves so many of my branches torn,
    collect them at the foot of this sad thorn.
My home was in the city[8] whose first patron
gave way to John the Baptist; for this reason,
    he'll always use his art to make it sorrow;   145
and if—along the crossing of the Arno[9]—

4. At the Last Judgment.   5. Lano of Siena and Jacopo da Santo Andrea of Padua, two Italians of a
generation earlier than Dante's; both were reputed to be spendthrifts.   6. Lano was killed at a battle on
the river Toppo in 1287.   7. Nothing is known about this suicide, who hanged himself from his own
house.   8. Florence; when the Florentines converted to Christianity, John the Baptist replaced Mars as
patron of the city, and therefore Mars will forever persecute the city with civil war.   9. The river that
runs through Florence.

some effigy of Mars had not remained,
those citizens who afterward rebuilt
their city on the ashes that Attila[1]
had left to them, would have travailed in vain.   150
I made—of my own house—my gallows place."

CANTO XIV

The Seventh Circle, Third Ring: the Violent against God. The First Zone:
Blasphemers, supine on fiery sands. Capaneus. Virgil on the Old Man of
Crete, whose streaming tears form the rivers of Hell: Acheron, Phlegethon,
Styx, and Cocytus. The sight of Lethe postponed.

Love of our native city overcame me;
I gathered up the scattered boughs and gave
them back to him whose voice was spent already.
From there we reached the boundary that divides
the second from the third ring—and the sight   5
of a dread work that justice had devised.
To make these strange things clear, I must explain
that we had come upon an open plain
that banishes all green things from its bed.
The wood of sorrow is a garland round it,   10
just as that wood is ringed by a sad channel;[2]
here, at the very edge, we stayed our steps.
The ground was made of sand, dry and compact,
a sand not different in kind from that
on which the feet of Cato[3] had once tramped.   15
O vengeance of the Lord, how you should be
dreaded by everyone who now can read
whatever was made manifest to me!
I saw so many flocks of naked souls,
all weeping miserably, and it seemed   20
that they were ruled by different decrees.
Some lay upon the ground, flat on their backs;
some huddled in a crouch, and there they sat;
and others moved about incessantly.
The largest group was those who walked about,   25
the smallest, those supine in punishment;
but these had looser tongues to tell their torment.
Above that plain of sand, distended flakes
of fire showered down; their fall was slow—
as snow descends on alps when no wind blows.   30
Just like the flames that Alexander saw
in India's hot zones, when fires fell,
intact and to the ground, on his battalions,
for which—wisely—he had his soldiers tramp

---

1. According to legend, Attila the Hun destroyed Florence when he invaded Italy in the fifth century.
2. The third ring of the seventh circle is surrounded by the second ring of the woods through which Dante
has just passed and the first ring of the river of blood described in canto 12.   3. Roman general (first
century B.C.) who campaigned in Libya.

the soil to see that every fire was spent 35
before new flames were added to the old;[4]
so did the never-ending heat descend;
with this, the sand was kindled just as tinder
on meeting flint will flame—doubling the pain.
    The dance of wretched hands was never done; 40
now here, now there, they tried to beat aside
the fresh flames as they fell. And I began
    to speak: "My master, you who can defeat
all things except for those tenacious demons
who tried to block us at the entryway, 45
    who is that giant there,[5] who does not seem
to heed the singeing—he who lies and scorns
and scowls, he whom the rains can't seem to soften?"
    And he himself, on noticing that I
was querying my guide about him, cried: 50
"That which I was in life, I am in death.
    Though Jove wear out the smith[6] from whom he took,
in wrath, the keen-edged thunderbolt with which
on my last day I was to be transfixed;
    or if he tire the others, one by one, 55
in Mongibello,[7] at the sooty forge,
while bellowing: 'O help, good Vulcan, help!'—
    just as he did when there was war at Phlegra[8]—
and casts his shafts at me with all his force,
not even then would he have happy vengeance." 60
    Then did my guide speak with such vehemence
as I had never heard him use before:
"O Capaneus, for your arrogance
    that is not quenched, you're punished all the more:
no torture other than your own madness 65
could offer pain enough to match your wrath."
    But then, with gentler face he turned to me
and said: "That man was one of seven kings
besieging Thebes; he held—and still, it seems,
    holds—God in great disdain, disprizing Him; 70
but as I told him now, his maledictions
sit well as ornaments upon his chest.
    Now follow me and—take care—do not set
your feet upon the sand that's burning hot,
but always keep them back, close to the forest." 75
    In silence we had reached a place where flowed
a slender watercourse out of the wood—
a stream whose redness makes me shudder still.
    As from the Bulicame[9] pours a brook
whose waters then are shared by prostitutes, 80

---

4. Dante is here following an account by the German philosopher Albertus Magnus (d. 1280) of a legendary adventure that befell Alexander the Great in his conquest of India.   5. Capaneus, one of the seven legendary kings who beseiged Thebes as described in the *Thebaid* by Statius (d. A.D. 95). He was struck with a thunderbolt when he boasted that not even Jupiter could stop him.   6. Vulcan   7. The Sicilian name for Mt. Etna, thought to be Vulcan's furnace. *The others:* The Cyclopes, Vulcan's helpers.   8. Capaneus refers to the battle of Phlegra, where Jove defeated the rebellious Titans (see 31.43).   9. A hot sulphurous spring that supplied water to the houses of prostitutes in the region north of Viterbo.

so did this stream run down across the sand.
Its bed and both its banks were made of stone,
together with the slopes along its shores,
so that I saw our passageway lay there.
"Among all other things that I have shown you   85
since we first made our way across the gate
whose threshold is forbidden to no one,
no thing has yet been witnessed by your eyes
as notable as this red rivulet,
which quenches every flame that burns above it."   90
These words were spoken by my guide; at this,
I begged him to bestow the food for which
he had already given me the craving.
"A devastated land lies in midsea,
a land that is called Crete," he answered me.   95
"Under its king¹ the world once lived chastely.
Within that land there was a mountain blessed
with leaves and waters, and they called it Ida;
but it is withered now like some old thing.
It once was chosen as a trusted cradle   100
by Rhea for her son;² to hide him better,
when he cried out, she had her servants clamor.
Within the mountain is a huge Old Man,
who stands erect—his back turned toward Damietta³—
and looks at Rome as if it were his mirror.   105
The Old Man's head is fashioned of fine gold,
the purest silver forms his arms and chest,
but he is made of brass down to the cleft;
below that point he is of choicest iron
except for his right foot, made of baked clay;   110
and he rests more on this than on the left.⁴
Each part of him, except the gold, is cracked;
and down that fissure there are tears that drip;
when gathered, they pierce through that cavern's floor
and, crossing rocks into this valley, form   115
the Acheron and Styx and Phlegethon;
and then they make their way down this tight channel,
and at the point past which there's no descent,
they form Cocytus;⁵ since you are to see
what that pool is, I'll not describe it here."   120
And I asked him: "But if the rivulet
must follow such a course down from our world,
why can we see it only at this boundary?"⁶
And he to me: "You know this place is round;
and though the way that you have come is long,   125

---

1. Saturn, mythical king of Crete during the golden age.   2. Jupiter was hidden by his mother, Rhea,
from his father, Saturn, who tried to devour all his children to thwart a prophecy that he would be dethroned
by one of them. So that Saturn would not hear the infant's cries, Rhea had her servants cry out and beat
their shields with their swords.   3. A city in Egypt. The Old Man has been interpreted as an emblem of
degenerating humankind.   4. The four metals and the clay represent the degeneration of history: see
Daniel 2.31–35.   5. The frozen lake at the bottom of Hell: see 32.22–30 and 34.52.   6. Not entirely
consistently, Dante seems to have thought of the four rivers of Hell as ponds or pools formed by a single
river that flows from the tears of the Old Man of Crete.

and always toward the left and toward the bottom,
    you still have not completed all the circle:
so that, if something new appears to us,
it need not bring such wonder to your face."[7]
    And I again: "Master, where's Phlegethon   130
and where is Lethe? You omit the second
and say this rain of tears has formed the first."
    "I'm pleased indeed," he said, "with all your questions;
yet one of them might well have found its answer
already—when you saw the red stream boiling.[8]   135
    You shall see Lethe, but past this abyss,
there where the spirits go to cleanse themselves
when their repented guilt is set aside."[9]
    Then he declared: "The time has come to quit
this wood; see that you follow close behind me;   140
these margins form a path that does not scorch,
and over them, all flaming vapor is quenched."

CANTO XV

*Still the Seventh Circle, Third Ring: the Violent against God. Second
Zone: the Sodomites, endlessly crossing the fiery sands beneath the rain of
fire. Brunetto Latini, whom Dante treats as mentor. Priscian, Francesco
d'Accorso, and Andrea dei Mozzi, Bishop of Florence.*

    Now one of the hard borders bears us forward;
the river mist forms shadows overhead
and shields the shores and water from the fire.
    Just as between Wissant and Bruges,[1] the Flemings,
in terror of the tide that floods toward them,   5
have built a wall of dykes to daunt the sea;
    and as the Paduans, along the Brenta,[2]
build bulwarks to defend their towns and castles
before the dog days fall on Carentana;
    just so were these embankments, even though   10
they were not built so high and not so broad,
whoever was the artisan who made them.
    By now we were so distant from the wood
that I should not have made out where it was—
not even if I'd turned around to look—   15
    when we came on a company of spirits
who made their way along the bank; and each
stared steadily at us, as in the dusk,
    beneath the new moon, men look at each other.
They knit their brows and squinted at us—just   20
as an old tailor at his needle's eye.
    And when that family looked harder, I
was recognized by one, who took me by

---

7. Since Dante has not yet completed a full round of the circular pit that is Hell he should not be surprised
to see something new.   8. See note to 12.94.   9. Lethe is crossed when Dante passes into the Earthly
Paradise on the top of Mount Purgatory.   1. Cities that, for Dante, mark the two ends of the dike that
protects Flanders from the sea.   2. A river that flows through Padua, fed by the melting snows in the
mountains of the province of Carentana (modern Carinthia in Austria).

the hem and cried out: "This is marvelous!"
That spirit having stretched his arm toward me,   25
I fixed my eyes upon his baked, brown features,
so that the scorching of his face could not
    prevent my mind from recognizing him;
and lowering my face to meet his face,
I answered him: "Are you here, Ser Brunetto?"   30
And he: "My son, do not mind if Brunetto
Latino[3] lingers for a while with you
and lets the file he's with pass on ahead."
I said: "With all my strength I pray you, stay;
and if you'd have me rest awhile with you,   35
I shall, if that please him with whom I go."
"O son," he said, "whoever of this flock
stops but a moment, stays a hundred years
and cannot shield himself when fire strikes.
Therefore move on; below—but close—I'll follow;   40
and then I shall rejoin my company,
who go lamenting their eternal sorrows."
I did not dare to leave my path for his
own level; but I walked with head bent low
as does a man who goes in reverence.   45
And he began: "What destiny or chance
has led you here below before your last
day came, and who is he who shows the way?"
"There, in the sunlit life above," I answered,
"before my years were full, I went astray   50
within a valley. Only yesterday
    at dawn I turned my back upon it—but
when I was newly lost, he here appeared,
to guide me home again along this path."
And he to me: "If you pursue your star,   55
you cannot fail to reach a splendid harbor,
if in fair life, I judged you properly;
    and if I had not died too soon for this,
on seeing Heaven was so kind to you,
I should have helped sustain you in your work.   60
But that malicious, that ungrateful people
come down, in ancient times, from Fiesole[4]—
still keeping something of the rock and mountain—
    for your good deeds, will be your enemy:
and there is cause—among the sour sorbs,   65
the sweet fig is not meant to bear its fruit.[5]
The world has long since called them blind, a people
presumptuous, avaricious, envious;
be sure to cleanse yourself of their foul ways.

---

3. Brunetto Latini (ca. 1220–1294), active in Florentine politics and the author of—among other works—two books: a prose encyclopedia in French called the *Tresor*, which emphasizes the qualities needed for civic duty, and a shorter allegorical poem in Italian called the *Tesoretto*, which combines autobiography with philosophy.   4. A hill town north of Florence whose rustic inhabitants were supposed to have joined with noble Romans in the founding of Florence, creating an unstable mixture.   5. The *sour sorbs*—a sorb is a small fruit, edible only when overripe—are the Florentines descended from Fiesole; the *sweet fig* is Brunetto's term for the aristocratic Dante.

Your fortune holds in store such honor for you,   70
one party and the other will be hungry
for you—but keep the grass far from the goat.[6]
   For let the beasts of Fiesole find forage
among themselves, and leave the plant alone—
if still, among their dung, it rises up—   75
   in which there lives again the sacred seed
of those few Romans who remained in Florence
when such a nest of wickedness was built."
   "If my desire were answered totally,"
I said to Ser Brunetto, "you'd still be   80
among, not banished from, humanity.
   Within my memory is fixed—and now
moves me—your dear, your kind paternal image
when, in the world above, from time to time
you taught me how man makes himself eternal;[7]   85
and while I live, my gratitude for that
must always be apparent in my words.
   What you have told me of my course, I write;
I keep it with another text, for comment
by one who'll understand, if I may reach her.[8]   90
   One thing alone I'd have you plainly see:
so long as I am not rebuked by conscience,
I stand prepared for Fortune, come what may.
   My ears find no new pledge in that prediction;
therefore, let Fortune turn her wheel as she   95
may please, and let the peasant turn his mattock."[9]
   At this, my master turned his head around
and toward the right, and looked at me and said:
"He who takes note of this has listened well."
   But nonetheless, my talk with Ser Brunetto   100
continues, and I ask of him who are
his comrades of repute and excellence.
   And he to me: "To know of some is good;
but for the rest, silence is to be praised;
the time we have is short for so much talk.   105
   In brief, know that my company has clerics
and men of letters and of fame—and all
were stained by one same sin upon the earth.[1]
   That sorry crowd holds Priscian and Francesco
d'Accorso;[2] and among them you can see,   110
if you have any longing for such scurf,
   the one[3] the Servant of His Servants sent
from the Arno to the Bacchiglione's banks,[4]
and there he left his tendons strained by sin.

---

6. Either both parties will ask you to join them or both parties will want to devour you—but keep yourself apart.   7. In the *Tresor* Brunetto says that earthly glory gives man a second life through an enduring reputation.   8. Beatrice.   9. The traditional image of Fortune and her wheel is here compared to the rustic image of the peasant turning the soil with his hoe.   1. Sodomy, condemned in the Middle Ages as unnatural.   2. A Florentine law professor (d. 1293). *Priscian:* Greek-language grammarian (sixth century A.D.).   3. Andrea de' Mozzi, bishop of Florence (1287–95), transferred by Pope Boniface (designated here by an official title for the pope, *the Servant of His* [i.e., Christ's] *Servants*) from Florence to Vicenza.   4. The Arno runs through Florence, the Bacchiglione through Vicenza.

I would say more; but both my walk and words 115
must not be longer, for—beyond—I see
new smoke emerging from the sandy bed.
   Now people come with whom I must not be.
Let my *Tesoro,* in which I still live,
be precious to you; and I ask no more." 120
   And then he turned and seemed like one of those
who race across the fields to win the green
cloth at Verona;[5] of those runners, he
appeared to be the winner, not the loser.

CANTO XVI

Still the Seventh Circle, Third Ring, Second Zone: other Sodomites.
Three Florentines, Guido Guerra, Tegghiaio Aldobrandi, Jacopo
Rusticucci. The decadence of Florence. Phlegethon, cascading into the
next zone. The cord of Dante, used by Virgil to summon a monstrous
figure from the waters.

No sooner had I reached the place where one
could hear a murmur, like a beehive's hum,
of waters as they fell to the next circle,
   when, setting out together, three shades ran,
leaving another company that passed 5
beneath the rain of bitter punishment.
   They came toward us, and each of them cried out:
"Stop, you who by your clothing seem to be
someone who comes from our indecent country!"[6]
   Ah me, what wounds I saw upon their limbs, 10
wounds new and old, wounds that the flames seared in!
It pains me still as I remember it.
   When they cried out, my master paid attention;
he turned his face toward me and then he said:
"Now wait: to these one must show courtesy. 15
   And were it not the nature of this place
for shafts of fire to fall, I'd say that haste
was seemlier for you than for those three."[7]
   As soon as we stood still, they started up
their ancient wail again; and when they reached us, 20
they formed a wheel, all three of them together.
   As champions, naked, oiled, will always do,
each studying the grip that serves him best
before the blows and wounds begin to fall,[8]
   while wheeling so, each one made sure his face 25
was turned to me, so that their necks opposed
their feet in one uninterrupted flow.
   And, "If the squalor of this shifting sand,
together with our baked and barren features,
makes us and our requests contemptible," 30

---

5. A footrace run at Verona on the first Sunday in Lent, the prize being a piece of green cloth (the *palio*). For the race to be run by the Christian, see 1 Corinthians 9.24–25.   **6.** Florence.   **7.** To hurry was considered undignified.   **8.** The three naked Florentines form a circle and are compared to oiled wrestlers (a sport practiced in Dante's time).

one said, "then may our fame incline your mind
to tell us who you are, whose living feet
can make their way through Hell with such assurance.
    He in whose steps you see me tread, although
he now must wheel about both peeled and naked,   35
was higher in degree than you believe:
    he was a grandson of the good Gualdrada,
and Guido Guerra[9] was his name; in life
his sword and his good sense accomplished much.
    The other who, behind me, tramples sand—   40
Tegghiaio Aldobrandi,[1] one whose voice
should have been heeded in the world above.
    And I, who share this punishment with them,
was Jacopo Rusticucci;[2] certainly,
more than all else, my savage wife destroyed me."   45
    If I'd had shield and shelter from the fire,
I should have thrown myself down there among them—
I think my master would have sanctioned that;
    but since that would have left me burned and baked,
my fear won out against the good intention   50
that made me so impatient to embrace them.
    Then I began: "Your present state had fixed
not scorn but sorrow in me—and so deeply
that it will only disappear slowly—
    as soon as my lord spoke to me with words   55
that made me understand what kind of men
were coming toward us, men of worth like yours.
    For I am of your city; and with fondness,
I've always told and heard the others tell
of both your actions and your honored names.   60
    I leave the gall and go for the sweet apples[3]
that I was promised by my truthful guide;
but first I must descend into the center."
    "So may your soul long lead your limbs and may
your fame shine after you," he answered then,   65
"tell us if courtesy and valor still
    abide within our city as they did
when we were there, or have they disappeared
completely; for Guiglielmo Borsiere,[4]
    who only recently has come to share   70
our torments, and goes there with our companions,
has caused us much affliction with his words."[5]
    "Newcomers to the city and quick gains
have brought excess and arrogance to you,
o Florence, and you weep for it already!"   75
    So I cried out with face upraised; the three
looked at each other when they heard my answer
as men will stare when they have heard the truth.

---

9. A leading participant in the civil strife in Florence (d. 1272).   1. An ally of Guido (see 6.79).   2. An ally of Tegghiaio who blames his wife for his sodomy (see 6.80).   3. Leave Hell and head for Paradise.
4. An elegant member of Florentine society.   5. An account of the recent dissension within the city, to which Dante himself was soon to fall victim.

"If you can always offer a reply
so readily to others," said all three,   80
"then happy you who speak, at will, so clearly.

So, if you can escape these lands of darkness
and see the lovely stars on your return,
when you repeat with pleasure, 'I was there,'
be sure that you remember us to men."   85
At this they broke their wheel; and as they fled,
their swift legs seemed to be no less than wings.

The time it took for them to disappear—
more brief than time it takes to say "amen";
and so, my master thought it right to leave.   90
I followed him. We'd only walked a little
when roaring water grew so near to us
we hardly could have heard each other speak.

And even as the river[6] that is first
to take its own course eastward from Mount Viso,   95
along the left flank of the Apennines
(which up above is called the Acquacheta,
before it spills into its valley bed
and flows without that name beyond Forlì),
reverberates above San Benedetto   100
dell'Alpe as it cascades in one leap,
where there is space enough to house a thousand;
so did we hear that blackened water roar
as it plunged down a steep and craggy bank,
enough to deafen us in a few hours.   105
Around my waist I had a cord[7] as girdle,
and with it once I thought I should be able
to catch the leopard with the painted hide.[8]
And after I had loosened it completely,
just as my guide commanded me to do,   110
I handed it to him, knotted and coiled.

At this, he wheeled around upon his right
and cast it, at some distance from the edge,
straight down into the depth of the ravine.

"And surely something strange must here reply,"   115
I said within myself, "to this strange sign—
the sign my master follows with his eye."

Ah, how much care men ought to exercise
with those whose penetrating intellect
can see our thoughts—not just our outer act![9]   120
He said to me: "Now there will soon emerge
what I await and what your thought has conjured:
it soon must be discovered to your sight."

Faced with that truth which seems a lie, a man
should always close his lips as long as he can—   125

6. Dante compares the roar of Phlegethon to the Montone River in northern Italy, whose course he traces in the next few lines.   7. While commentators disagree, it seems likely that this cord is a reference both to Job 41.1, where God says He can draw Leviathan up with a hook and bind his tongue with a cord, and to Francis of Assisi, who wore a cord as a sign of humility and obedience. As a layman, Dante may have had a connection with the Franciscan friars, a common circumstance at the time.   8. The leopard of canto 1, representing fraud.   9. Dante now realizes that Virgil can read his thoughts.

to tell it shames him, even though he's blameless;
  but here I can't be still; and by the lines
of this my Comedy, reader, I swear—
and may my verse find favor for long years—
that through the dense and darkened air I saw   130
a figure swimming, rising up, enough
to bring amazement to the firmest heart,
  like one returning from the waves where he
went down to loose an anchor snagged upon
a reef or something else hid in the sea,   135
  who stretches upward and draws in his feet.

CANTO XVII

The monster Geryon. The Seventh Circle, Third Ring, Third Zone: the
Violent against Nature and Art (Usurers), each seated beneath the rain of
fire with a purse—bearing his family's heraldic emblem—around his neck.
Descent to the Eighth Circle on the back of Geryon.

"Behold the beast who bears the pointed tail,
who crosses mountains, shatters weapons, walls!
Behold the one whose stench fills all the world!"[1]
  So did my guide begin to speak to me,
and then he signaled him to come ashore   5
close to the end of those stone passageways.
  And he came on, that filthy effigy
of fraud, and landed with his head and torso
but did not draw his tail onto the bank.
  The face he wore was that of a just man,   10
so gracious was his features' outer semblance;
and all his trunk, the body of a serpent;
  he had two paws, with hair up to the armpits;
his back and chest as well as both his flanks
had been adorned with twining knots and circlets.   15
  No Turks or Tartars ever fashioned fabrics
more colorful in background and relief,
nor had Arachne[2] ever loomed such webs.
  As boats will sometimes lie along the shore,
with part of them on land and part in water,   20
and just as there, among the guzzling Germans,[3]
  the beaver[4] sets himself when he means war,
so did that squalid beast lie on the margin
of stone that serves as border for the sand.
  And all his tail was quivering in the void   25
while twisting upward its envenomed fork,
which had a tip just like a scorpion's.
  My guide said: "Now we'd better bend our path
a little, till we reach as far as that

1. Geryon, the embodiment of fraud. For this figure Dante drew upon classical literature, where he had
not three natures—human, reptilian, and bestial—combined into one, as here, but three bodies and three
heads.   2. A woman in classical literature famous for weaving, turned into a spider: see Ovid, *Metamor-*
phoses 6.   3. A tradition going back to the Romans accused the Germans of gluttony.   4. Which was
thought to catch fish by putting its tail into the water.

malicious beast which crouches over there."   30
Thus we descended on the right hand side
and moved ten paces on the stony brink
in order to avoid the sand and fire.
When we had reached the sprawling beast, I saw—
a little farther on, upon the sand—   35
some sinners sitting near the fissured rock.
And here my master said to me: "So that
you may experience this ring in full,
go now, and see the state in which they are.
But keep your conversation with them brief;   40
till you return, I'll parley with this beast,
to see if he can lend us his strong shoulders."
So I went on alone and even farther
along the seventh circle's outer margin,
to where the melancholy people sat.   45
Despondency was bursting from their eyes;
this side, then that, their hands kept fending off,
at times the flames, at times the burning soil:
not otherwise do dogs in summer—now
with muzzle, now with paw—when they are bitten   50
by fleas or gnats or by the sharp gadfly.
When I had set my eyes upon the faces
of some on whom that painful fire falls,
I recognized no one; but I did notice
that from the neck of each a purse was hung   55
that had a special color and an emblem,
and their eyes seemed to feast upon these pouches.[5]
Looking about—when I had come among them—
I saw a yellow purse with azure on it
that had the face and manner of a lion.   60
Then, as I let my eyes move farther on,
I saw another purse that was bloodred,
and it displayed a goose more white than butter.
And one who had an azure, pregnant sow
inscribed as emblem on his white pouch, said   65
to me: "What are you doing in this pit?
Now you be off; and since you're still alive,
remember that my neighbor Vitaliano[6]
shall yet sit here, upon my left hand side.
Among these Florentines, I'm Paduan;   70
I often hear them thunder in my ears,
shouting, 'Now let the sovereign cavalier,
the one who'll bring the purse with three goats,[7] come!' "
At this he slewed his mouth, and then he stuck
his tongue out, like an ox that licks its nose.   75
And I, afraid that any longer stay
might anger him who'd warned me to be brief,

5. These are usurers, men who lent money for interest, which was forbidden by the Church in the Middle Ages (although often practiced). Each has a coat of arms on his purse by which he can be identified; all are Italians.   6. The speaker is from Padua and here maliciously identifies another Paduan who will soon be joining him.   7. A prominent Florentine banker.

made my way back from those exhausted souls.
I found my guide, who had already climbed
upon the back of that brute animal,   80
and he told me: "Be strong and daring now,
for our descent is by this kind of stairs:
you mount in front; I want to be between,
so that the tail can't do you any harm."[8]
As one who feels the quartan fever near   85
and shivers, with his nails already blue,
the sight of shade enough to make him shudder,
so I became when I had heard these words;
but then I felt the threat of shame, which makes
a servant—in his kind lord's presence—brave.   90
I settled down on those enormous shoulders;
I wished to say (and yet my voice did not
come as I thought): "See that you hold me tight."
But he who—other times, in other dangers—
sustained me, just as soon as I had mounted,   95
clasped me within his arms and propped me up,
and said: "Now, Geryon, move on; take care
to keep your circles wide, your landing slow;
remember the new weight you're carrying."
Just like a boat that, starting from its moorings,   100
moves backward, backward, so that beast took off;
and when he felt himself completely clear,
he turned his tail to where his chest had been
and, having stretched it, moved it like an eel,
and with his paws he gathered in the air.   105
I do not think that there was greater fear
in Phaethon[9] when he let his reins go free—
for which the sky, as one still sees, was scorched—
nor in poor Icarus[1] when he could feel
his sides unwinged because the wax was melting,   110
his father shouting to him, "That way's wrong!"
than was in me when, on all sides, I saw
that I was in the air, and everything
had faded from my sight—except the beast.
Slowly, slowly, swimming, he moves on;   115
he wheels and he descends, but I feel only
the wind upon my face and the wind rising.
Already, on our right, I heard the torrent
resounding, there beneath us, horribly,
so that I stretched my neck and looked below.   120
Then I was more afraid of falling off,
for I saw fires and I heard laments,
at which I tremble, crouching, and hold fast.
And now I saw what I had missed before:
his wheeling and descent—because great torments   125

8. Virgil protects Dante from Geryon's scorpion's tail.   9. Son of Apollo, Phaethon tried to drive the chariot of the sun, but when it got out of control it scorched both Earth and the heavens, creating the Milky Way (Ovid, *Metamorphoses* 2).   1. Who, flying with wings made of wax and feathers, went too near the sun and fell (Ovid, *Metamorphoses* 8).

were drawing closer to us on all sides.
  Just as a falcon long upon the wing—
who, seeing neither lure nor bird, compels
the falconer to cry, "Ah me, you fall!"—
  descends, exhausted, in a hundred circles,   130
where he had once been swift, and sets himself,
embittered and enraged, far from his master;[2]
  such, at the bottom of the jagged rock,
was Geryon, when he had set us down.
And once our weight was lifted from his back,   135
  he vanished like an arrow from a bow.

CANTO XVIII

*The Eighth Circle, called Malebolge ("Evil-Pouches"), with its Ten
Pouches, where "ordinary" fraud is punished. The First Pouch, with
Panderers and Seducers scourged by horned demons. Venèdico
Caccianemico. Jason. The Second Pouch, with Flatterers immersed in
excrement. Alessio Interminei. Thaïs.*

There is a place in Hell called Malebolge,[3]
made all of stone the color of crude iron,
as is the wall that makes its way around it.
  Right in the middle of this evil field
is an abyss, a broad and yawning pit,[4]   5
whose structure I shall tell in its due place.
  The belt, then, that extends between the pit
and that hard, steep wall's base is circular;
its bottom has been split into ten valleys.
  Just as, where moat on moat surrounds a castle   10
in order to keep guard upon the walls,
the ground they occupy will form a pattern,
  so did the valleys here from a design;
and as such fortresses have bridges running
right from their thresholds toward the outer bank,   15
  so here, across the banks and ditches, ridges
ran from the base of that rock wall until
the pit that cuts them short and joins them all.
  This was the place in which we found ourselves
when Geryon had put us down; the poet   20
held to the left, and I walked at his back.
  Upon the right I saw new misery,
I saw new tortures and new torturers,
filling the first of Malebolge's moats.
  Along its bottom, naked sinners moved,   25
to our side of the middle, facing us;
beyond that, they moved with us, but more quickly—
  as, in the year of Jubilee,[5] the Romans,

2. Unless it sights prey or is called back with a lure by its master, a trained falcon will continue flying until exhaustion compels it to descend.   3. Evil-pouches (Italian), since the eighth circle is divided into ten *bolge*, pouches or ditches.   4. The last, or ninth, circle of Hell, described in cantos 21–34.   5. Thirteen hundred was a Jubilee Year, and Dante here describes the crowd control on the bridge that ran between the Castle of St. Angelo and St. Peter's.

confronted by great crowds, contrived a plan
that let the people pass across the bridge,   30
    for to one side went all who had their eyes
upon the Castle, heading toward St. Peter's,
and to the other, those who faced the Mount.
    Both left and right, along the somber rock,
I saw horned demons with enormous whips,   35
who lashed those spirits cruelly from behind.
    Ah, how their first strokes made those sinners lift
their heels! Indeed no sinner waited for
a second stroke to fall—or for a third.
    And as I moved ahead, my eyes met those   40
of someone else, and suddenly I said:
"I was not spared the sight of him before."
    And so I stayed my steps, to study him;
my gentle guide had stopped together with me
and gave me leave to take a few steps back.   45
    That scourged soul thought that he could hide himself
by lowering his face; it helped him little,
for I said: "You, who cast your eyes upon
    the ground, if these your features are not false,
must be Venèdico Caccianemico;[6]   50
but what brings you to sauces so piquant?"
    And he to me: "I speak unwillingly;
but your plain speech, that brings the memory
of the old world to me, is what compels me;
    For it was I who led Ghisolabella   55
to do as the Marquis would have her do—
however they retell that filthy tale.
    I'm not the only Bolognese who weeps here;
indeed, this place is so crammed full of us
that not so many tongues have learned to say   60
    sipa between the Sàvena and Reno;[7]
if you want faith and testament of that,
just call to mind our avaricious hearts."
    And as he spoke, a demon cudgeled him
with his horsewhip and cried: "Be off, you pimp,   65
there are no women here for you to trick."
    I joined my escort once again; and then
with but few steps, we came upon a place
where, from the bank, a rocky ridge ran out.
    We climbed quite easily along that height;   70
and turning right upon its jagged back,
we took our leave of those eternal circlings.
    When we had reached the point where that ridge opens
below to leave a passage for the lashed,
my guide said: "Stay, and make sure that the sight   75
    of still more ill-born spirits strikes your eyes,
for you have not yet seen their faces, since

---

6. A man from Bologna (renowned for its good food) who was reputed to have turned his sister Gisobella over to the Marquis of Este.   7. *Sipa* is a word for "yes" in the dialect spoken in the territory between the rivers Sàvena and Reno, which comprise the boundaries of Bologna.

they have been moving in our own direction."
    From the old bridge we looked down at the ranks
of those approaching from the other side;   80
they too were driven onward by the lash.
    And my good master, though I had not asked,
urged me: "Look at that mighty one who comes
and does not seem to shed a tear of pain:
    how he still keeps the image of a king!   85
That shade is Jason,[8] who with heart and head
deprived the men of Colchis of their ram.
    He made a landfall on the isle of Lemnos
after its women, bold and pitiless,
had given all their island males to death.   90
    With polished words and love signs he took in
Hypsipyle, the girl whose own deception
had earlier deceived the other women.
    And he abandoned her, alone and pregnant;
such guilt condemns him to such punishment;   95
and for Medea, too, revenge is taken.
    With him go those who cheated so: this is
enough for you to know of that first valley
and of the souls it clamps within its jaws."
    We were already where the narrow path   100
reaches and intersects the second bank
and serves as shoulder for another bridge.
    We heard the people whine in the next pouch
and heard them as they snorted with their snouts;
we heard them use their palms to beat themselves.   105
    And exhalations, rising from below,
stuck to the banks, encrusting them with mold,
and so waged war against both eyes and nose.
    The bottom is so deep, we found no spot
to see it from, except by climbing up   110
the arch until the bridge's highest point.
    This was the place we reached; the ditch beneath
held people plunged in excrement that seemed
as if it had been poured from human privies.
    And while my eyes searched that abysmal sight,   115
I saw one with a head so smeared with shit,
one could not see if he were lay or cleric.
    He howled: "Why do you stare more greedily
at me than at the others who are filthy?"
And I: "Because, if I remember right,   120
    I have seen you before, with your hair dry;
and so I eye you more than all: you are
Alessio Interminei of Lucca."[9]
    Then he continued, pounding on his pate:
"I am plunged here because of flatteries—   125

8. Jason led the Argonauts on the voyage to the island of Colchis, where they stole the golden fleece. He seduced and abandoned Hypsipyle, who had hidden her father when the other women of Lemnos were killing all the males. He also abandoned Medea. For his story, see Ovid, *Metamorphoses* 7.   **9.** A prominent citizen of Lucca, in northern Italy.

of which my tongue had such sufficiency."
At which my guide advised me: "See you thrust
your head a little farther to the front,
so that your eyes can clearly glimpse the face
of that besmirched, bedraggled harridan   130
who scratches at herself with shit-filled nails,
and now she crouches, now she stands upright.
That is Thaïs,¹ the harlot who returned
her lover's question, 'Are you very grateful
to me?' by saying, 'Yes, enormously.'   135
And now our sight has had its fill of this."

CANTO XIX

*The Eighth Circle, Third Pouch, where the Simonists are set, heads
down, into holes in the rock, with their protruding feet tormented by
flames. Pope Nicholas III. Dante's invective against simoniacal popes.*

O Simon Magus!² O his sad disciples!
Rapacious ones, who take the things of God,
that ought to be the brides of Righteousness,
and make them fornicate for gold and silver!
The time has come to let the trumpet sound   5
for you; your place is here in this third pouch.
    We had already reached the tomb beyond
and climbed onto the ridge, where its high point
hangs just above the middle of the ditch.
    O Highest Wisdom, how much art you show   10
in heaven, earth, and this sad world below,
how just your power is when it allots!³
    Along the sides and down along the bottom,
I saw that livid rock was perforated:
the openings were all one width and round.   15
    They did not seem to me less broad or more
than those that in my handsome San Giovanni⁴
were made to serve as basins for baptizing;
and one of these, not many years ago,
I broke for someone who was drowning in it: 20
and let this be my seal to set men straight.
    Out from the mouth of each hole there emerged
a sinner's feet and so much of his legs
up to the thigh; the rest remained within.
    Both soles of every sinner were on fire;   25
their joints were writhing with such violence,
they would have severed withes⁵ and ropes of grass.
    As flame on oily things will only stir
along the outer surface, so there, too,

1. A character in a play by the Roman writer Terence (186 or 185–159? B.C.)   2. Because in the Bible
Simon Magus tried to buy spiritual power from the apostles (Acts 8.9–24), the selling of any spiritual good
for material gain was known in the Middle Ages as simony. The most common form of simony was the
selling of Church offices.   3. Dante is here applauding the artfulness of infernal justice because the
simoniacs, who cared most for their purses, are here stuffed into fiery purses hewn into the rock; see line
72 below.   4. The baptistery in Florence where Dante was baptized. The subsequent personal reference
has never been satisfactorily explained.   5. Ropes made of twisted vines.

that fire made its way from heels to toes.   30
"Master," I said, "who is that shade who suffers
and quivers more than all his other comrades,
that sinner who is licked by redder flames?"
And he to me: "If you would have me lead
you down along the steepest of the banks,   35
from him you'll learn about his self and sins."
And I: "What pleases you will please me too:
you are my lord; you know I do not swerve
from what you will; you know what is unspoken."
At this we came upon the fourth embankment;   40
we turned and, keeping to the left, descended
into the narrow, perforated bottom.
My good lord did not let me leave his side
until he'd brought me to the hole that held
that sinner who lamented with his legs.   45
"Whoever you may be, dejected soul,[6]
whose head is downward, planted like a pole,"
my words began, "do speak if you are able."
I stood as does the friar who confesses
the foul assassin who, fixed fast, head down,   50
calls back the friar, and so delays his death;
    and he cried out: "Are you already standing,
already standing there, o Boniface?
The book has lied to me by several years.
Are you so quickly sated with the riches   55
for which you did not fear to take by guile
the Lovely Lady,[7] then to violate her?"
And I became like those who stand as if
they have been mocked, who cannot understand
what has been said to them and can't respond.   60
    But Virgil said: "Tell this to him at once:
'I am not he—not whom you think I am.' "
And I replied as I was told to do.
At this the spirit twisted both his feet,
and sighing and with a despairing voice,   65
he said: "What is it, then, you want of me?
If you have crossed the bank and climbed so far
to find out who I am, then know that I
was one of those who wore the mighty mantle,
and surely was a son of the she-bear,[8]   70
so eager to advance the cubs that I
pursed wealth above while here I purse myself.
Below my head there is the place of those
who took the way of simony before me;
and they are stuffed within the clefts of stone.   75
    I, too, shall yield my place and fall below
when he arrives, the one for whom I had

---

6. Pope Nicholas III (pope 1277–80). He mistakenly believes that one of his successors, Boniface VIII, has come to be squeezed into the hole (line 53). Like all damned souls, Nicholas has foreknowledge, and because Boniface did not die until 1303 Nicholas is surprised at what he thinks is his appearance in 1300.
7. The Church.   8. The arms of Nicholas's family (the Orsini) included a she-bear.

mistaken you when I was quick to question.
But I have baked my feet a longer time,
have stood like this, upon my head, than he   80
is to stand planted here with scarlet feet:
for after him, one uglier in deeds
will come, a lawless shepherd from the west,
worthy to cover him and cover me.[9]
He'll be a second Jason,[1] of whom we read   85
in *Maccabees;* and just as Jason's king
was soft to him, so shall the king of France
be soft to this one." And I do not know
if I was too rash here—I answered so:
"Then tell me now, how much gold did our Lord   90
ask that Saint Peter give to him before
he placed the keys within his care?[2] Surely
the only thing he said was: 'Follow me.'
And Peter and the others never asked
for gold or silver when they chose Matthias   95
to take the place of the transgressing soul.[3]
Stay as you are, for you are rightly punished;
and guard with care the money got by evil
that made you so audacious against Charles.[4]
And were it not that I am still prevented   100
by reverence for those exalted keys
that you had held within the happy life,
I'd utter words much heavier than these,
because your avarice afflicts the world:
it tramples on the good, lifts up the wicked.   105
You, shepherds, the Evangelist[5] had noticed
when he saw her who sits upon the waters
and realized she fornicates with kings,
she who was born with seven heads and had
the power and support of the ten horns,   110
as long as virtue was her husband's pleasure.
You've made yourselves a god of gold and silver;
how are you different from idolaters,
save that they worship one and you a hundred?
Ah, Constantine,[6] what wickedness was born—   115
and not from your conversion—from the dower
that you bestowed upon the first rich father!"
And while I sang such notes to him—whether
it was his indignation or his conscience
that bit him—he kicked hard with both his soles.   120

9. Clement V, who became pope in 1305 after agreeing with the French king to remove the papacy to Avignon in France.   1. Jason became high priest of the Jews by bribing the king: see 2 Maccabees 4.7–9. 2. See Matthew 16.18–19 and 4.18–19. The keys are the Church's power to bind (condemn) and to loose (absolve).   3. Matthias was chosen by lot to fill the place of Judas (Acts 1.23–26).   4. Nicholas was supposed to be involved in a plot against Charles of Anjou (1226–1285), ruler of Naples and Sicily. 5. John, author of Revelation: for this passage, which was originally interpreted as referring to pagan Rome but which Dante applies to the corrupt Church, see Revelation 17.1–18. The seven heads are the seven sacraments; the ten horns, the ten commandments; the husband, God.   6. Reputed author (d. 337) of a document—known as the Donation of Constantine—in which he granted temporal power and the right to acquire wealth to Pope Sylvester I, *the first rich father* of this passage. The document was proved to be a forgery in the fifteenth century.

I do indeed believe it pleased my guide:
he listened always with such satisfied
expression to the sound of those true words.
And then he gathered me in both his arms
and, when he had me fast against his chest,   125
where he climbed down before, climbed upward now;
nor did he tire of clasping me until
he brought me to the summit of the arch
that crosses from the fourth to the fifth rampart.
And here he gently set his burden down—   130
gently because the ridge was rough and steep,
and would have been a rugged pass for goats.
From there another valley lay before me.

CANTO XX

The Eighth Circle, Fourth Pouch, where Diviners, Astrologers, Magicians,
all have their heads turned backward. Amphiaraus. Tiresias. Aruns.
Manto. Virgil on the origin of Mantua, his native city. Eurypylus.
Michael Scot and other moderns adept at fraud.

I must make verses of new punishment
and offer matter now for Canto Twenty
of this first canticle—of the submerged.
I was already well prepared to stare
below, into the depth that was disclosed,   5
where tears of anguished sorrow bathed the ground;
and in the valley's circle I saw souls
advancing, mute and weeping, at the pace
that, in our world, holy processions take.
As I inclined my head still more, I saw   10
that each, amazingly, appeared contorted
between the chin and where the chest begins;
they had their faces twisted toward their haunches
and found it necessary to walk backward,
because they could not see ahead of them.   15
Perhaps the force of palsy has so fully
distorted some, but that I've yet to see,
and I do not believe that that can be.
May God so let you, reader, gather fruit
from what you read; and now think for yourself   20
how I could ever keep my own face dry
when I beheld our image so nearby
and so awry that tears, down from the eyes,
bathed the buttocks, running down the cleft.
Of course I wept, leaning against a rock   25
along that rugged ridge, so that my guide
told me: "Are you as foolish as the rest?
Here pity only lives when it is dead:
for who can be more impious than he
who links God's judgment to passivity?[7]   30

7. This is a rebuke to Dante, whose *passivity* is shown in his sympathy for the damned.

Lift, lift your head and see the one for whom
the earth was opened while the Thebans watched,
so that they all cried: 'Amphiaraus,[8]
where are you rushing? Have you quit the fight?'
Nor did he interrupt his downward plunge   35
to Minos, who lays hands on every sinner.
        See how he's made a chest out of his shoulders;
and since he wanted so to see ahead,
he looks behind and walks a backward path.
        And see Tiresias,[9] who changed his mien   40
when from a man he turned into a woman,
so totally transforming all his limbs
        that then he had to strike once more upon
the two entwining serpents with his wand
before he had his manly plumes again.   45
        And Aruns[1] is the one who backs against
the belly of Tiresias—Aruns who,
in Luni's hills, tilled by the Carrarese,
        who live below, had as his home, a cave
among white marbles, from which he could gaze   50
at stars and sea with unimpeded view.
        And she who covers up her breasts—which you
can't see—with her disheveled locks, who keeps
all of her hairy parts to the far side,
        was Manto,[2] who had searched through many lands,   55
then settled in the place where I was born;
on this, I'd have you hear me now a while.
        When Manto's father took his leave of life,
and Bacchus' city[3] found itself enslaved,
she wandered through the world for many years.   60
        High up, in lovely Italy, beneath
the Alps that shut in Germany above
Tirolo, lies a lake known as Benaco.[4]
        A thousand springs and more, I think, must flow
out of the waters of that lake to bathe   65
Pennino, Garda, Val Camonica.[5]
        And at its middle is a place where three—
the bishops of Verona, Brescia, Trento—
may bless if they should chance to come that way.
        Peschiera, strong and handsome fortress, built   70
to face the Brescians and the Bergamasques[6]
stands where the circling shore is at its lowest.
        There, all the waters that cannot be held
within the bosom of Benaco fall,

---

8. A Greek priest swallowed up by the Earth in a battle against the Thebans. For Minos, see 5.4.   9. A famous soothsayer of Thebes, he came upon two coupling serpents and, striking them with his rod, was transformed into a woman. Seven years later an identical encounter provoked the same action, and he was changed back into a man. See Ovid, *Metamorphoses* 3.   1. An Etruscan soothsayer from the city of Luni, in the area of Carrera where marble is quarried, is described by the Roman poet Lucan (d. A.D. 65) in his *Pharsalia*.   2. A famous Theban soothsayer described by Roman poets.   3. Thebes.   4. The present-day Lake Garda, located in terms of an island where the boundaries of the three dioceses of Trent, Brescia, and Verona meet. *Tirolo:* a castle on the Adige River in the Italian Alps.   5. Two towns and a valley below the lake.   6. Inhabitants of two towns to the northwest of Peschiera, which is a town on the south shore of the lake.

to form a river running through green meadows.   75
No sooner has that stream begun to flow
than it is called the Mincio, not Benaco—
until Govèrnolo,[7] where it joins the Po.
   It's not flowed far before it finds flat land;
and there it stretches out to form a fen   80
that in the summer can at times be fetid.
   And when she passed that way, the savage virgin
saw land along the middle of the swamp,
untilled and stripped of its inhabitants.
   And there, to flee all human intercourse,   85
she halted with her slaves to ply her arts;
and there she lived, there left her empty body.
   And afterward, the people of those parts
collected at that place, because the marsh—
surrounding it on all sides—made it strong.   90
   They built a city over her dead bones;
and after her who first had picked that spot,
they called it Mantua—they cast no lots.
   There once were far more people in its walls,
before the foolishness of Casalodi   95
was tricked by the deceit of Pinamonte.[8]
   Therefore, I charge you, if you ever hear
a different tale of my town's origin,
do not let any falsehood gull the truth."[9]
   And I: "O master, that which you have spoken   100
convinces me and so compels my trust
that others' words would only be spent coals.
   But tell me if among the passing souls
you see some spirits worthy of our notice,
because my mind is bent on that alone."   105
   Then he to me: "That shade who spreads his beard
down from his cheeks across his swarthy shoulders—
when Greece had been so emptied of its males
   that hardly any cradle held a son,
he was an augur; and at Aulis, he   110
and Calchas set the time to cut the cables.
   His name's Eurypylus;[1] a certain passage
of my high tragedy has sung it so;
you know that well enough, who know the whole.
   That other there, his flanks extremely spare,   115
was Michael Scot,[2] a man who certainly
knew how the game of magic fraud was played.
   See there Guido Bonatti; see Asdente,[3]
who now would wish he had attended to

---

7. A town some thirty miles south of Peschiera.   8. A reference to the internal intrigues of the rulers of Mantua in the thirteenth century.   9. Oddly enough, another account is given by Virgil in *Aeneid* 10. 1. Calchas and Eurypylus were prophets (or augurs) involved in the Trojan War; here Virgil says that they determined when the Greeks were to set out for the war from the island of Aulis, although *Aeneid* 2 gives a different account.   2. A famous scientist, philosopher, and astrologer from Scotland, he spent many years at the court of Frederick II (10.119) in Palermo and died in 1235.   3. A shoemaker famous as a soothsayer in thirteen-century Italy. *Guido Bonatti*: an astrologer at the court of Guido da Montefeltro (see canto 32).

his cord and leather, but repents too late.   120
    See those sad women who had left their needle,
shuttle, and spindle to become diviners;[4]
they cast their spells with herbs and effigies.
    But let us go; Cain with his thorns already
is at the border of both hemispheres   125
and there, below Seville, touches the sea.[5]
    Last night the moon was at its full; you should
be well aware of this, for there were times
when it did you no harm in the deep wood."
    These were his words to me; meanwhile we journeyed.   130

CANTO XXI

*The Eighth Circle, Fifth Pouch, with Barrators plunged into boiling pitch
and guarded by demons armed with prongs. A newly arrived magistrate
from Lucca. Ten demons assigned by Malacoda ("Evil-Tail"), the chief of
the Malebranche ("Evil-Claws"), to escort Dante and Virgil. The
remarkable signal for their march.*

    We came along from one bridge to another,
talking of things my Comedy is not
concerned to sing. We held fast to the summit,
    then stayed our steps to spy the other cleft
of Malebolge and other vain laments.   5
I saw that it was wonderfully dark.
    As in the arsenal of the Venetians,[6]
all winter long a stew of sticky pitch
boils up to patch their sick and tattered ships
    that cannot sail (instead of voyaging,   10
some build new keels, some tow and tar the ribs
of hulls worn out by too much journeying;
    some hammer at the prow, some at the stern,
and some make oars, and some braid ropes and cords;
one mends the jib, another, the mainsail);   15
    so, not by fire but by the art of God,
below there boiled a thick and tarry mass
that covered all the banks and clamminess.
    I saw it, but I could not see within it;
no thing was visible but boiling bubbles,   20
the swelling of the pitch; and then it settled.
    And while I watched below attentively,
my guide called out to me: "Take care! Take care!"
And then, from where I stood, he drew me near.
    I turned around as one who is keen to see   25
a sight from which it would be wise to flee,
and then is horror-stricken suddenly—
    who does not stop his flight and yet looks back.
And then—behind us there—I saw a black

---

4. Local soothsayers and potion makers.   5. Popular belief held that God placed Cain in the moon after
the murder of Abel; *Cain with his thorns* means the moon with its spots, which is now setting at the western
edge of the northern hemisphere. Overhead, in Jerusalem, it is the dawn of Holy Saturday.   6. The
Arsenal at Venice was one of the most important shipyards in Europe.

demon as he came racing up the crags.   30
    Ah, he was surely barbarous to see!
And how relentless seemed to me his acts!
His wings were open and his feet were lithe;
    across his shoulder, which was sharp and high,
he had slung a sinner, upward from the thighs;   35
in front, the demon gripped him by the ankles.
    Then from our bridge, he called: "O Malebranche,
I've got an elder of Saint Zita[7] for you!
Shove this one under—I'll go back for more—
    his city is well furnished with such stores;   40
there, everyone's a grafter but Bonturo;[8]
and there—for cash—they'll change a *no* to *yes*."
    He threw the sinner down, then wheeled along
the stony cliff: no mastiff's ever been
unleashed with so much haste to chase a thief.   45
    The sinner plunged, then surfaced, black with pitch;
but now the demons, from beneath the bridge,
shouted: "The Sacred Face[9] has no place here;
    here we swim differently than in the Serchio;[1]
if you don't want to feel our grappling hooks,   50
don't try to lift yourself above that ditch."
    They pricked him with a hundred prongs and more,
then taunted: "Here one dances under cover,
so try to grab your secret graft below."
    The demons did the same as any cook   55
who has his urchins force the meat with hooks
deep down into the pot, that it not float.
    Then my good master said to me: "Don't let
those demons see that you are here; take care
to crouch behind the cover of a crag.   60
    No matter what offense they offer me,
don't be afraid; I know how these things go—
I've had to face such fracases before."[2]
    When this was said, he moved beyond the bridgehead.
And on the sixth embankment, he had need   65
to show his imperturbability.
    With the same frenzy, with the brouhaha
of dogs, when they beset a sorry wretch
who—startled—stops dead in his tracks and begs,
    so, from beneath the bridge, the demons rushed   70
against my guide with all their prongs, but he
called out: "Can't you forget your savagery!
    Before you try to maul me, just let one
of all your troop step forward. Hear me out,
and then decide if I am to be hooked."   75
    At this they howled, "Let Malacoda[3] go!"

7. The elders of Saint Zita in Lucca (a town near Florence) were ten citizens who ran the government. Malebranche (Evil-claws [Italian]) is the generic name for the devils in this ditch, and each has a proper name as well (lines 76, 105, 118–26).   8. A current official in Lucca, Bonturo Dati was in fact known as the most corrupt of all; the devil is being ironic.   9. The Sacred Face of Lucca, a venerated icon. 1. A river near Lucca.   2. Virgil may be referring to his difficulties with the devils in 8.82–130, when he and Dante tried to enter the city of Dis.   3. Evil-tail (Italian).

And one of them moved up—the others stayed—
and as he came, he asked: "How can he win?"
"O Malacoda, do you think I've come,"
my master answered him, "already armed—   80
as you can see—against your obstacles,
without the will of God and helpful fate?
Let us move on; it is the will of Heaven
for me to show this wild way to another."
At this the pride of Malacoda fell;   85
his prong dropped to his feet. He told his fellows:
"Since that's the way things stand, let us not wound him."
My guide then spoke to me: "O you, who crouch,
bent low among the bridge's splintered rocks,
you can feel safe—and now return to me."   90
At this I moved and quickly came to him.
The devils had edged forward, all of them;
I feared that they might fail to keep their word:
just so, I saw the infantry when they
marched out, under safe conduct, from Caprona;[4]   95
they trembled when they passed their enemies.
My body huddled closer to my guide;
I did not let the demons out of sight;
the looks they cast at us were less than kind.
They bent their hooks and shouted to each other: 100
"And shall I give it to him on the rump?"
And all of them replied, "yes, let him have it!"
But Malacoda, still in conversation
with my good guide, turned quickly to his squadron
and said: "Be still, Scarmiglione, still!"   105
To us he said: "There is no use in going
much farther on this ridge, because the sixth
bridge—at the bottom there—is smashed to bits.[5]
Yet if you two still want to go ahead,
move up and walk along this rocky edge;   110
nearby, another ridge will form a path.[6]
Five hours from this hour yesterday,
one thousand and two hundred sixty-six
years passed since that roadway was shattered here.[7]
I'm sending ten of mine out there to see   115
if any sinner lifts his head for air;
go with my men—there is no malice in them."
"Step forward, Alichino and Calcabrina,"
he then began to say, "and you, Cagnazzo;
and Barbariccia, who can lead the ten.   120
Let Libicocco go, and Draghignazzo
and tusky Ciriatto and Graffiacane
and Farfarello and mad Rubicante.[8]

---

4. A battle outside Florence in 1289, in which Dante may have taken part.   5. The bridge across the fifth ditch was smashed, as Malacoda soon explains, by the earthquake that occurred at the time of the Crucifixion.   6. As the travelers discover, this is a lie.   7. This account makes the current time 7 A.M. on Holy Saturday, April 9, 1300.   8. These names—like Scarmiglione in line 105—imply raffish irreverence in general, although some do have specific if ignoble meanings: Cagnazzo = "Big Dog," Barbariccia = "Curly Beard," Graffiacane = "Dog-Scratcher."

Search all around the clammy stew of pitch;
keep these two safe and sound till the next ridge   125
that rises without break across the dens."
"Ah me! What is this, master, that I see?"
I said. "Can't we do without company?
If you know how to go, I want no escort.
If you are just as keen as usual,   130
can't you see how those demons grind their teeth?
Their brows are menacing, they promise trouble."
And he to me: "I do not want you frightened:
just let them gnash away as they may wish;
they do it for the wretches boiled in pitch."   135
They turned around along the left hand bank:
but first each pressed his tongue between his teeth
as signal for their leader, Barbariccia.
And he had made a trumpet of his ass.

CANTO XXII

*Still the Eighth Circle, Fifth Pouch: the Barrators. The Barrator from
Navarre. Fra Gomita and Michele Zanche, two Sardinians. The astuteness
of the Navarrese that leads two demons to fall into the pitch.*

Before this I've seen horsemen start to march
and open the assault and muster ranks
and seen them, too, at times beat their retreat;
    and on your land, o Aretines,[9] I've seen
rangers and raiding parties galloping,   5
the clash of tournaments, the rush of jousts,
    now done with trumpets, now with bells, and now
with drums, and now with signs from castle walls,
with native things and with imported ware;
    but never yet have I seen horsemen or   10
seen infantry or ship that sails by signal
of land or star move to so strange a bugle!
    We made our way together with ten demons:
ah, what ferocious company! And yet
"in church with saints, with rotters in the tavern."   15
    But I was all intent upon the pitch,
to seek out every feature of the pouch
and of the people who were burning in it.
    Just as the dolphins do, when with arched back,
they signal to the seamen to prepare   20
for tempest, that their vessel may be spared,
    so here from time to time, to ease his torment,
some sinner showed his back above the surface,
then hid more quickly than a lightning flash.
    And just as on the margin of a ditch   25
frogs crouch, their snouts alone above the water,
so as to hide their feet and their plump flesh,
    so here on every side these sinners crouched;

9. The people of Arezzo, a city south of Florence.

but faster than a flash, when Barbariccia
drew near, they plunged beneath the boiling pitch.   30
    I saw—my heart still shudders in recall—
one who delayed, just as at times a frog
is left behind while others dive below;
    and Graffiacane, who was closest to him,
then hooked him by his pitch-entangled locks   35
and hauled him up; he seemed to me an otter.
    By now I knew the names of all those demons—
I'd paid attention when the fiends were chosen;
I'd watched as they stepped forward one by one.
    "O Rubicante, see you set your talons   40
right into him, so you can flay his flesh!"
So did those cursed ones cry out together.
    And I: "My master, if you can, find out
what is the name of that unfortunate
who's fallen victim to his enemies."   45
    My guide, who then drew near that sinner's side,
asked him to tell his birthplace. He replied:
"My homeland was the kingdom of Navarre.
    My mother, who had had me by a wastrel,
destroyer of himself and his possessions,   50
had placed me in the service of a lord.
    Then I was in the household of the worthy
King Thibault; there I started taking graft;
with this heat I pay reckoning for that."[1]
    And Ciriatto, from whose mouth there bulged   55
to right and left two tusks like a wild hog's,
then let him feel how one of them could mangle.
    The mouse had fallen in with evil cats;
but Barbariccia clasped him in his arms
and said: "Stand off there, while I fork him fast."   60
    And turning toward my master then, he said:
"Ask on, if you would learn some more from him
before one of the others does him in."
    At which my guide: "Now tell: among the sinners
who hide beneath the pitch, are any others   65
Italian?" And he: "I have just left
one who was nearby there; and would I were
still covered by the pitch as he is hidden,
for then I'd have no fear of hook or talon."
    And Libicocco said, "We've been too patient!"   70
and, with his grapple, grabbed him by the arm
and, ripping, carried off a hunk of flesh.
    But Draghignazzo also looked as if
to grab his legs; at which, their captain wheeled
and threatened all of them with raging looks.   75
    When they'd grown somewhat less tumultuous,
without delay my guide asked of that one

---

1. The identity of this sinner is not known, but he was employed in the household of Thibaut II of Champagne, a man renowned for his honesty who was also king of Navarre, the area of Spain that is now Basque country.

who had his eyes still fixed upon his wound:
"Who was the one you left to come ashore—
unluckily—as you just said before?"　　　　　　　　　　80
He answered: "Fra Gomita of Gallura,[2]
who was a vessel fit for every fraud;
he had his master's enemies in hand,
but handled them in ways that pleased them all.
He took their gold and smoothly let them off,　　　　85
as he himself says; and in other matters,
he was a sovereign, not a petty, swindler.
His comrade there is Don Michele Zanche[3]
of Logodoro; and their tongues are never
too tired to talk of their Sardinia.　　　　　　　　　90
Ah me, see that one there who grinds his teeth!
If I were not afraid, I'd speak some more,
but he is getting set to scratch my scurf."
And their great marshal, facing Farfarello—
who was so hot to strike he rolled his eyes,　　　　　95
said: "Get away from there, you filthy bird!"
"If you perhaps would like to see or hear,"
that sinner, terrified, began again,
"Lombards or Tuscans, I can fetch you some;
but let the Malebranche stand aside　　　　　　　　100
so that my comrades need not fear their vengeance.
Remaining in this very spot, I shall,
although alone, make seven more appear
when I have whistled, as has been our custom
when one of us has managed to get out."　　　　　　105
At that, Cagnazzo lifted up his snout
and shook his head, and said: "Just listen to
that trick by which he thinks he can dive back!"
To this, he who was rich in artifice
replied: "Then I must have too many tricks,　　　　　110
if I bring greater torment to my friends."
This was too much for Alichino and,
despite the others, he cried out: "If you
dive back, I shall not gallop after you
but beat my wings above the pitch; we'll leave　　　115
this height; with the embankment as a screen,
we'll see if you—alone—can handle us."
O you who read, hear now of this new sport:
each turned his eyes upon the other shore,
he first who'd been most hesitant before.　　　　　　120
The Navarrese, in nick of time, had planted
his feet upon the ground; then in an instant
he jumped and freed himself from their commander.
At this each demon felt the prick of guilt,
and most, he who had led his band to blunder;[4]　　125
so he took off and shouted: "You are caught!"

---

2. A friar who was chancellor of the Gallura district on the island of Sardinia. He was hanged by his master, a lord of Pisa, when it was discovered that he had sold prisoners their freedom.　　3. Little is known of this sinner, except that he too was a Sardinian.　　4. Alichino.

But this could help him little; wings were not
more fast than fear; the sinner plunged right under;
the other, flying up, lifted his chest:
    not otherwise the wild duck when it plunges   130
precipitously, when the falcon nears
and then—exhausted, thwarted—flies back up.
    But Calcabrina, raging at the trick,
flew after Alichino; he was keen
to see the sinner free and have a brawl;   135
    and once the Navarrese had disappeared,
he turned his talons on his fellow demon
and tangled with him just above the ditch.
    But Alichino clawed him well—he was
indeed a full-grown kestrel;[5] and both fell   140
into the middle of the boiling pond.
    The heat was quick to disentangle them,
but still there was no way they could get out;
their wings were stuck, enmeshed in glue-like pitch.
    And Barbariccia, grieving with the rest,   145
sent four to fly out toward the other shore
with all their forks, and speedily enough
    on this side and on that they took their posts;
and toward those two—stuck fast, already cooked
beneath that crust—they stretched their grappling hooks.   150
We left them still contending with that mess.

CANTO XXIII

*Still the Eighth Circle, Fifth Pouch: the Barrators. Pursuit by the
demons, with Virgil snatching up Dante and sliding down to the Sixth
Pouch, where the Hypocrites file along slowly, clothed in caps of lead.
Two Jovial Friars of Bologna, Catalano and Loderingo. Caiaphas. Virgil's
distress at Malacoda's deceitfulness.*

    Silent, alone, no one escorting us,
we made our way—one went before, one after—
as Friars Minor[6] when they walk together.
    The present fracas made me think of Aesop—
that fable where he tells about the mouse   5
and frog; for "near" and "nigh" are not more close
    than are that fable and this incident,
if you compare with care how each begins
and then compare the endings that they share.[7]
    And even as one thought springs from another,   10
so out of that was still another born,
which made the fear I felt before redouble.
    I thought: "Because of us, they have been mocked,
and this inflicted so much hurt and scorn
that I am sure they feel deep indignation.   15

5. A kind of falcon.   6. Franciscan friars.   7. The fable that Dante seems to be referring to tells how
a frog offers to ferry a mouse across a river, then halfway over tries to drown him, only to be seized by a
kite (a hawklike bird) while the mouse escapes.

If anger's to be added to their malice,
they'll hunt us down with more ferocity
than any hound whose teeth have trapped a hare."
    I could already feel my hair curl up
from fear, and I looked back attentively,   20
while saying: "Master, if you don't conceal
    yourself and me at once—they terrify me,
those Malebranche; they are after us;
I so imagine them, I hear them now."
    And he to me: "Were I a leaded mirror,   25
I could not gather in your outer image
more quickly than I have received your inner.
    For even now your thoughts have joined my own;
in both our acts and aspects we are kin—
with both our minds I've come to one decision.   30
    If that right bank is not extremely steep,
we can descend into the other moat
and so escape from the imagined chase."
    He'd hardly finished telling me his plan
when I saw them approach with outstretched wings,   35
not too far off, and keen on taking us.
    My guide snatched me up instantly, just as
the mother who is wakened by a roar
and catches sight of blazing flames beside her,
    will lift her son and run without a stop—   40
she cares more for the child than for herself—
not pausing even to throw on a shift;
    and down the hard embankment's edge—his back
lay flat along the sloping rock that closes
one side of the adjacent moat—he slid.   45
    No water ever ran so fast along
a sluice to turn the wheels of a land mill,[8]
not even when its flow approached the paddles,
    as did my master race down that embankment
while bearing me with him upon his chest,   50
just like a son, and not like a companion.
    His feet had scarcely reached the bed that lies
along the deep below, than those ten demons
were on the edge above us; but there was
    nothing to fear; for that High Providence   55
that willed them ministers of the fifth ditch,
denies to all of them the power to leave it.
    Below that point we found a painted people,
who moved about with lagging steps, in circles,
weeping, with features tired and defeated.   60
    And they were dressed in cloaks with cowls so low
they fell before their eyes, of that same cut
that's used to make the clothes for Cluny's[9] monks.

---

8. A mill built on the land while the water of the river turns its wheel.   9. One of the largest monasteries
in Europe, located in Burgundy in France.

Outside, these cloaks were gilded and they dazzled;
but inside they were all of lead, so heavy   65
that Frederick's capes were straw compared to them.[1]
A tiring mantle for eternity!
We turned again, as always, to the left,
along with them, intent on their sad weeping;
    but with their weights that weary people paced   70
so slowly that we found ourselves among
new company each time we took a step.
    At which I told my guide: "Please try to find
someone whose name or deed I recognize;
and while we walk, be watchful with your eyes."   75
    And one who'd taken in my Tuscan speech
cried out behind us: "Stay your steps, o you
who hurry so along this darkened air!
Perhaps you'll have from me that which you seek."
    At which my guide turned to me, saying: "Wait,   80
and then continue, following his pace."
I stopped, and I saw two whose faces showed
their minds were keen to be with me; but both
their load and the tight path forced them to slow.
    When they came up, they looked askance at me   85
a long while, and they uttered not a word
until they turned to one another, saying:
    "The throbbing of his throat makes this one seem
alive; and if they're dead, what privilege
lets them appear without the heavy mantle?"   90
    Then they addressed me: "Tuscan, you who come
to this assembly of sad hypocrites,
do not disdain to tell us who you are."
    I answered: "Where the lovely Arno flows,[2]
there I was born and raised, in the great city;   95
I'm with the body I have always had.
    But who are you, upon whose cheeks I see
such tears distilled by grief? And let me know
what punishment it is that glitters so."
    And one of them replied: "The yellow cloaks   100
are of a lead so thick, their heaviness
makes us, the balances beneath them, creak.
    We both were Jovial Friars,[3] and Bolognese;
my name was Catalano, Loderingo[4]
was his, and we were chosen by your city   105
    together, for the post that's usually
one man's, to keep the peace; and what we were
is still to be observed around Gardingo."

1. Frederick II (see note to 10.119) was reported to have punished traitors by encasing them in lead and throwing them into heated cauldrons.   2. Florence.   3. A military and religious order in Bologna called the Knights of the Blessed Virgin Mary, or popularly the Jovial Friars because of the laxity of its rules. The members were meant to fight only in order to protect the weak and enforce peace.   4. Two citizens of Bologna who were involved in founding the Jovial Friars in 1261. They shared the office of governor in 1265 and 1267. Gardingo (line 108), a district in Florence, was destroyed by a civil war incited by their meddling in Florentine affairs.

I then began, "O Friars, your misdeeds . . ."
but said no more, because my eyes had caught   110
one crucified by three stakes on the ground.⁵
When he saw me, that sinner writhed all over,
and he breathed hard into his beard with sighs;
observing that, Fra Catalano said
to me: "That one impaled there, whom you see,   115
counseled the Pharisees that it was prudent
to let one man—and not one nation—suffer.
Naked, he has been stretched across the path,
as you can see, and he must feel the weight
of anyone who passes over him.   120
Like torment, in this ditch, afflicts both his
father-in-law⁶ and others in that council,
which for the Jews has seeded so much evil."
Then I saw Virgil stand amazed above
that one who lay stretched out upon a cross   125
so squalidly in his eternal exile.
And he addressed the friar in this way:
"If it does not displease you—if you may—
tell us if there's some passage on the right
that would allow the two of us to leave   130
without our having to compel black angels
to travel to this deep, to get us out."
He answered: "Closer than you hope, you'll find
a rocky ridge that stretches from the great
round wall and crosses all the savage valleys,   135
except that here it's broken—not a bridge.
But where its ruins slope along the bank
and heap up at the bottom, you can climb."
My leader stood a while with his head bent,
then said: "He who hooks sinners over there   140
gave us a false account of this affair."⁷
At which the Friar: "In Bologna, I
once heard about the devil's many vices—
they said he was a liar and father of lies."
And then my guide moved on with giant strides,   145
somewhat disturbed, with anger in his eyes;
at this I left those overburdened spirits,
while following the prints of his dear feet.

CANTO XXIV

Still the Eighth Circle, Sixth Pouch: the Hypocrites. Hard passage to the
Seventh Pouch: the Thieves. Bitten by a serpent, a thieving sinner who
turns to ashes and is then restored: Vanni Fucci. His prediction of the
defeat of the Whites—Dante's party—at Pistoia.

In that part of the young year when the sun
begins to warm its locks beneath Aquarius⁸

---

5. This is Caiaphas, the high priest under Pontius Pilate who advised that Christ be crucified (John 11.45–
52).   6. Annas; see John 18.13.   7. See 21.111.   8. January 21–February 21.

and nights grow shorter, equaling the days,
    when hoarfrost mimes the image of his white
sister[9] upon the ground—but not for long,   5
because the pen he uses is not sharp—
    the farmer who is short of fodder rises
and looks and sees the fields all white, at which
he slaps his thigh, turns back into the house,
    and here and there complains like some poor wretch   10
who doesn't know what can be done, and then
goes out again and gathers up new hope
    on seeing that the world has changed its face
in so few hours, and he takes his staff
and hurries out his flock of sheep to pasture.   15
    So did my master fill me with dismay
when I saw how his brow was deeply troubled,
yet then the plaster soothed the sore as quickly:
    for soon as we were on the broken bridge,
my guide turned back to me with that sweet manner   20
I first had seen along the mountain's base.
    And he examined carefully the ruin;
then having picked the way we would ascend,
he opened up his arms and thrust me forward.
    And just as he who ponders as he labors,   25
who's always ready for the step ahead,
so, as he lifted me up toward the summit
    of one great crag, he'd see another spur,
saying: "That is the one you will grip next,
but try it first to see if it is firm."   30
    That was no path for those with cloaks of lead,
for he and I—he, light; I, with support—
could hardly make it up from spur to spur.
    And were it not that, down from this enclosure,
the slope was shorter than the bank before,   35
I cannot speak for him, but I should surely
    have been defeated. But since Malebolge
runs right into the mouth of its last well,
the placement of each valley means it must
    have one bank high and have the other short;[1]   40
and so we reached, at length, the jutting where
the last stone of the ruined bridge breaks off.
    The breath within my lungs was so exhausted
from climbing, I could not go on; in fact,
as soon as I had reached that stone, I sat.   45
    "Now you must cast aside your laziness,"
my master said, "for he who rests on down
or under covers cannot come to fame;
    and he who spends his life without renown
leaves such a vestige of himself on earth   50
as smoke bequeaths to air or foam to water.

---

9. Snow.   **1.** Because the whole of the eighth circle is tilted downward, the downside wall of each ditch
is lower than that on the upside.

Therefore, get up; defeat your breathlessness
with spirit that can win all battles if
the body's heaviness does not deter it.
A longer ladder still is to be climbed;[2]   55
it's not enough to have left them behind;
if you have understood, now profit from it."
Then I arose and showed myself far better
equipped with breath than I had been before:
"Go on, for I am strong and confident."   60
We took our upward way upon the ridge,
with crags more jagged, narrow, difficult,
and much more steep than we had crossed before.
I spoke as we went on, not to seem weak;
at this, a voice came from the ditch beyond—   65
a voice that was not suited to form words.
I know not what he said, although I was
already at the summit of the bridge
that crosses there; and yet he seemed to move.
I had bent downward, but my living eyes   70
could not see to the bottom through that dark;
at which I said: "O master, can we reach
the other belt? Let us descend the wall,[3]
for as I hear and cannot understand,
so I see down but can distinguish nothing."   75
"The only answer that I give to you
is doing it," he said. "A just request
is to be met in silence, by the act."
We then climbed down the bridge, just at the end
where it runs right into the eighth embankment,[4]   80
and now the moat was plain enough to me;
and there within I saw a dreadful swarm
of serpents so extravagant in form—
remembering them still drains my blood from me.
Let Libya boast no more about her sands;[5]   85
for if she breeds chelydri, jaculi,
cenchres with amphisbaena, pareae,
she never showed—with all of Ethiopia
or all the land that borders the Red Sea—
so many, such malignant, pestilences.   90
Among this cruel and depressing swarm,
ran people who were naked, terrified,
with no hope of a hole or heliotrope.[6]
Their hands were tied behind by serpents; these
had thrust their head and tail right through the loins,   95
and then were knotted on the other side.
And—there!—a serpent sprang with force at one
who stood upon our shore, transfixing him

---

2. Both the climb from the pit of Hell back to Earth and the climb up Mount Purgatory.   3. Of the
seventh ditch.   4. They cross the bridge over the seventh ditch and then climb down the wall between
the seventh and eighth ditches.   5. The following list of exotic serpents derives from a description by the
Roman poet Lucan (A.D. 39–65) of the plagues of Libya.   6. A fictitious stone that was supposed to
make the bearer invisible.

just where the neck and shoulders form a knot.
No *o* or *i* has ever been transcribed 100
so quickly as that soul caught fire and burned
and, as he fell, completely turned to ashes;
   and when he lay, undone, upon the ground,
the dust of him collected by itself
and instantly returned to what it was: 105
   just so, it is asserted by great sages,
that, when it reaches its five-hundredth year,
the phoenix[7] dies and then is born again;
   lifelong it never feeds on grass or grain,
only on drops of incense and amomum; 110
its final winding sheets are nard and myrrh.
   And just as he who falls, and knows not how—
by demon's force that drags him to the ground
or by some other hindrance that binds man—
   who, when he rises, stares about him, all 115
bewildered by the heavy anguish he
has suffered, sighing as he looks around;
   so did this sinner stare when he arose.
Oh, how severe it is, the power of God
that, as its vengeance, showers down such blows! 120
   My guide then asked that sinner who he was;
to this he answered: "Not long since, I rained
from Tuscany into this savage maw.
   Mule that I was, the bestial life pleased me
and not the human; I am Vanni Fucci,[8] 125
beast; and the den that suited me—Pistoia."
   And I to Virgil: "Tell him not to slip
away, and ask what sin has thrust him here;
I knew him as a man of blood and anger."
   The sinner heard and did not try to feign 130
but turned his mind and face, intent, toward me;
and coloring with miserable shame,
   he said: "I suffer more because you've caught me
in this, the misery you see, than I
suffered when taken from the other life. 135
   I can't refuse to answer what you ask:
I am set down so far because I robbed
the sacristy of its fair ornaments,
   and someone else was falsely blamed for that.
But lest this sight give you too much delight, 140
if you can ever leave these lands of darkness,
open your ears to my announcement, hear:[9]

7. The phoenix is a mythical bird that is supposed to burn to death in its own nest every five hundred years, after which either itself or its son is reborn from the ashes; for these details, including its diet of exotic herbs and its funeral preparations (lines 110–11), see Ovid, *Metamorphoses* 15. In medieval mythography the phoenix was often taken as an image of Christ. 8. The illegitimate son (*mule*) of a noble father of Pistoia, a town just north of Florence; known as "the beast" because of the extravagance of his misbehavior. He reputedly robbed a church in Pistoia, a crime for which a similarly named man was wrongly hanged. 9. Vanni Fucci now prophesies, in the enigmatic terms appropriate to the genre, that the party of the Blacks (of which he was a member) will first be expelled from Pistoia by the Whites, but that then the Whites of Florence (Dante's party) will be defeated. The prophecy refers to events that occurred in either 1302 or 1306.

Pistoia first will strip herself of Blacks,
then Florence will renew her men and manners.
From Val di Magra, Mars will draw a vapor   145
which turbid clouds will try to wrap; the clash
between them will be fierce, impetuous,
a tempest, fought upon Campo Piceno,
until that vapor, vigorous, shall crack
the mist, and every White be struck by it.   150
And I have told you this to make you grieve."

CANTO XXV

Still the Eighth Circle, Seventh Pouch: the Thieves. Vanni Fucci and his
obscene figs against God. The Centaur Cacus. Five Florentine Thieves,
three of them humans and two of them serpents. The astounding
metamorphoses undergone by four of them.

When he had finished with his words, the thief
raised high his fists with both figs[1] cocked and cried:
"Take that, o God; I square them off for you!"
From that time on, those serpents were my friends,
for one of them coiled then around his neck,   5
as if to say, "I'll have you speak no more";
another wound about his arms and bound him
again and wrapped itself in front so firmly,
he could not even make them budge an inch.
Pistoia, ah, Pistoia, must you last: 10
why not decree your self-incineration,
since you surpass your seed[2] in wickedness?
Throughout the shadowed circles of deep Hell,
I saw no soul against God so rebel,
not even he who fell from Theban walls.[3]   15
He fled and could not say another word;
and then I saw a Centaur full of anger,
shouting: "Where is he, where's that bitter one?"
I do not think Maremma[4] has the number
of snakes that Centaur carried on his haunch   20
until the part that takes our human form.
Upon his shoulders and behind his nape
there lay a dragon with its wings outstretched;
it sets ablaze all those it intercepts.
My master said: "That Centaur there is Cacus,[5]   25
who often made a lake of blood within
a grotto underneath Mount Aventine.
He does not ride the same road as his brothers
because he stole—and most deceitfully—
from the great herd nearby; his crooked deeds   30
ended beneath the club of Hercules,

---

1. An obscene gesture made by thrusting a protruding thumb between the first and second fingers of a
closed fist.   2. Its founder Catiline, who was a traitor against the Roman Republic in the first century
B.C.   3. Capaneus (see 14.46–75).   4. A region infested with snakes; see 13.8.   5. A monster who
lived in a cave on Mount Aventine in Rome and was killed by Hercules, from whom he stole cattle; see
Aeneid 8.

who may have given him a hundred blows—
but he was not alive to feel the tenth."
　　While he was talking so, Cacus ran by
and, just beneath our ledge, three souls arrived;　　　　35
but neither I nor my guide noticed them
until they had cried out: "And who are you?"
At this the words we shared were interrupted,
and we attended only to those spirits.
　　I did not recognize them, but it happened,　　　　40
as chance will usually bring about,
that one of them called out the other's name,
exclaiming: "Where was Cianfa⁶ left behind?"
At this, so that my guide might be alert,
I held my finger up from chin to nose.　　　　45
　　If, reader, you are slow now to believe
what I shall tell, that is no cause for wonder,
for I—who saw it—hardly can accept it.
　　As I kept my eyes fixed upon those sinners,
a serpent with six feet springs out against　　　　50
one of the three, and clutches him completely.
　　It gripped his belly with its middle feet,
and with its forefeet grappled his two arms;
and then it sank its teeth in both his cheeks;
　　it stretched its rear feet out along his thighs　　　　55
and ran its tail along between the two,
then straightened it again behind his loins.
　　No ivy ever gripped a tree so fast
as when that horrifying monster clasped
and intertwined the other's limbs with its.　　　　60
　　Then—just as if their substance were warm wax—
they stuck together and they mixed their colors,
so neither seemed what he had been before;
　　just as, when paper's kindled, where it still
has not caught flame in full, its color's dark　　　　65
though not yet black, while white is dying off.
　　The other two souls stared, and each one cried:
"Ah me, Agnello,⁷ how you change! Just see,
you are already neither two nor one!"
　　Then two heads were already joined in one,　　　　70
when in one face where two had been dissolved,
two intermingled shapes appeared to us.
　　Two arms came into being from four lengths;
the thighs and legs, the belly and the chest
became such limbs as never had been seen.　　　　75
　　And every former shape was canceled there:
that perverse image seemed to share in both—
and none; and so, and slowly, it moved on.
　　Just as the lizard, when it darts from hedge
to hedge, beneath the dog days' giant lash,　　　　80
seems, if it cross one's path, a lightning flash,

6. A noble Florentine reputedly a thief.　　7. Another noble Florentine thief.

so seemed a blazing little serpent moving
against the bellies of the other two,
as black and livid as a peppercorn.
    Attacking one of them, it pierced right through   85
the part where we first take our nourishment;
and then it fell before him at full length.
    The one it had transfixed stared but said nothing;
in fact he only stood his ground and yawned
as one whom sleep or fever has undone.   90
    The serpent stared at him, he at the serpent;
one through his wound, the other through his mouth
were smoking violently; their smoke met.
    Let Lucan now be silent, where he sings
of sad Sabellus and Nasidius,[8]   95
and wait to hear what flies off from my bow.
    Let Ovid now be silent, where he tells
of Cadmus, Arethusa;[9] if his verse
has made of one a serpent, one a fountain,
    I do not envy him; he never did   100
transmute two natures, face to face, so that
both forms were ready to exchange their matter.
    These were the ways they answered to each other:
the serpent split its tail into a fork;
the wounded sinner drew his steps together.   105
    The legs and then the thighs along with them
so fastened to each other that the juncture
soon left no sign that was discernible.
    Meanwhile the cleft tail took upon itself
the form the other gradually lost;   110
its skin grew soft, the other's skin grew hard.
    I saw the arms that drew in at his armpits
and also saw the monster's two short feet
grow long for just as much as those were shortened.
    The serpent's hind feet, twisted up together,   115
became the member that man hides; just as
the wretch put out two hind paws from his member.
    And while the smoke veils each with a new color,
and now breeds hair upon the skin of one,
just as it strips the hair from off the other,   120
    the one rose up, the other fell; and yet
they never turned aside their impious eyelamps,
beneath which each of them transformed his snout:
    he who stood up drew his back toward the temples,
and from the excess matter growing there   125
came ears upon the cheeks that had been bare;
    whatever had not been pulled back but kept,
superfluous, then made his face a nose
and thickened out his lips appropriately.
    He who was lying down thrust out his snout;   130
and even as the snail hauls in its horns,

---

8. Two soldiers bitten by serpents in Lucan's *Pharsalia*.   9. See *Metamorphoses* 4.

he drew his ears straight back into his head;
his tongue, which had before been whole and fit
for speech, now cleaves; the other's tongue, which had
been forked, now closes up; and the smoke stops.   135
The soul that had become an animal,
now hissing, hurried off along the valley;
the other one, behind him, speaks and spits.
And then he turned aside his new-made shoulders
and told the third soul: "I'd have Buoso[1] run   140
on all fours down this road, as I have done."
And so I saw the seventh ballast[2] change
and rechange; may the strangeness plead for me
if there's been some confusion in my pen.
And though my eyes were somewhat blurred, my mind   145
bewildered, those three sinners did not flee
so secretly that I could not perceive
Puccio Sciancato[3] clearly, he who was
the only soul[4] who'd not been changed among
the three companions we had met at first;   150
the other one made you, Gaville, grieve.

CANTO XXVI

*Still the Eighth Circle, Seventh Pouch: the Thieves. Dante's invective
against Florence. View of the Eighth Pouch, where Fraudulent
Counselors are clothed in the flames that burn them. Ulysses and
Diomedes in one shared flame. Ulysses' tale of his final voyage.*

Be joyous, Florence, you are great indeed,
for over sea and land you beat your wings;
through every part of Hell your name extends!
Among the thieves I found five citizens[5]
of yours—and such, that shame has taken me;   5
with them, you can ascend to no high honor.
But if the dreams dreamt close to dawn are true,
then little time will pass before you feel
what Prato[6] and the others crave for you.
Were that already come, it would not be   10
too soon—and let it come, since it must be!
As I grow older, it will be more heavy.
We left that deep and, by protruding stones
that served as stairs for our descent before,
my guide climbed up again and drew me forward;   15
and as we took our solitary path
among the ridge's jagged spurs and rocks,
our feet could not make way without our hands.
It grieved me then and now grieves me again

1. The identity of this Buoso is uncertain.   2. The sinners of this ditch are here reduced to dead weight.
3. The third thief, also a noble Florentine.   4. The little serpent of line 82 above, identified as Francesco,
a Florentine nobleman who lived in Gaville (line 151), a town south of Florence. When he was murdered
by the townsmen, his kinsmen took brutal revenge.   5. Cianfa (25.43), Agnello (25.68), Francesco
(25.82, 149), Buoso (25.140), and Puccio (25.148), all Florentines.   6. A town just north of Florence,
on the way to Pistoia. The exact significance of this threat is unclear.

when I direct my mind to what I saw; 20
and more than usual, I curb my talent,
    that it not run where virtue does not guide;
so that, if my kind star or something better
has given me that gift, I not abuse it.
    As many as the fireflies the peasant 25
(while resting on a hillside in the season
when he who lights the world least hides his face),
    just when the fly gives way to the mosquito,
sees glimmering below, down in the valley,
there where perhaps he gathers grapes and tills— 30
    so many were the flames that glittered in
the eighth abyss; I made this out as soon
as I had come to where one sees the bottom.
    Even as he[7] who was avenged by bears
saw, as it left, Elijah's chariot— 35
its horses rearing, rising right to heaven—
    when he could not keep track of it except
by watching one lone flame in its ascent,
just like a little cloud that climbs on high:
    so, through the gullet of that ditch, each flame 40
must make its way; no flame displays its prey,
though every flame has carried off a sinner.
    I stood upon the bridge and leaned straight out
to see; and if I had not gripped a rock,
I should have fallen off—without a push. 45
    My guide, who noted how intent I was,
told me: "Within those fires there are souls;
each one is swathed in that which scorches him."
    "My master," I replied, "on hearing you,
I am more sure; but I'd already thought 50
that it was so, and I had meant to ask:
    Who is within the flame that comes so twinned
above that it would seem to rise out of
the pyre Eteocles shared with his brother?"[8]
    He answered me: "Within that flame, Ulysses 55
and Diomedes[9] suffer; they, who went
as one to rage, now share one punishment.
    And there, together in their flame, they grieve
over the horse's fraud that caused a breach—
the gate that let Rome's noble seed escape.[1] 60
    There they regret the guile that makes the dead
Deïdamia[2] still lament Achilles;
and there, for the Palladium, they pay."
    "If they can speak within those sparks," I said,
"I pray you and repray and, master, may 65

7. Elisha, an Old Testament prophet, was mocked by children, who were then attacked by bears. He saw the ascent to heaven of the prophet Elijah in his chariot and continued Elijah's mission: 2 Kings 2.1–25. 8. Eteocles and his brother, Polynices, were the sons of Oedipus; cursed by their father for their imprisonment of him, they engaged in a civil war over Thebes, killed each other, and were cremated on the same pyre, the flame of which divided into two as a sign of their enmity. 9. Two of the Greek leaders in the Trojan War. They devised the trick of the Trojan horse and stole the Palladium, a statue of Pallas Athena that protected the city. Their villainy is described by Aeneas in *Aeneid* 2. 1. The Trojan survivors, who founded Rome. 2. Achilles' lover, who tried to prevent him from going to the Trojan War but was thwarted by Ulysses.

my prayer be worth a thousand pleas, do not
forbid my waiting here until the flame
with horns approaches us; for you can see
how, out of my desire, I bend toward it."
And he to me: "What you have asked is worthy   70
of every praise; therefore, I favor it.
I only ask you this: refrain from talking.
Let me address them—I have understood
what you desire of them. Since they were Greek,
perhaps they'd be disdainful of your speech."[3]   75
And when my guide adjudged the flame had reached
a point where time and place were opportune,
this was the form I heard his words assume:
"You two who move as one within the flame,
if I deserved of you while I still lived,   80
if I deserved of you much or a little
when in the world I wrote my noble lines,
do not move on; let one of you retell
where, having gone astray, he found his death."
The greater horn within that ancient flame   85
began to sway and tremble, murmuring
just like a fire that struggles in the wind;
and then he waved his flame-tip back and forth
as if it were a tongue that tried to speak,
and flung toward us a voice that answered: "When   90
I sailed away from Circe,[4] who'd beguiled me
to stay more than a year there, near Gaeta—
before Aeneas gave that place a name[5]—
neither my fondness for my son nor pity
for my old father nor the love I owed   95
Penelope,[6] which would have gladdened her,
was able to defeat in me the longing
I had to gain experience of the world
and of the vices and the worth of men.
Therefore, I set out on the open sea   100
with but one ship and that small company
of those who never had deserted me.
I saw as far as Spain, far as Morocco,
along both shores; I saw Sardinia
and saw the other islands that sea bathes.   105
And I and my companions were already
old and slow, when we approached the narrows
where Hercules set up his boundary stones
that men might heed and never reach beyond:
upon my right, I had gone past Seville,   110
and on the left, already passed Ceüta.[7]
'Brothers,' I said, 'o you, who having crossed

---

3. Virgil may assume that Greeks would disdain anyone who, like Dante, did not know Greek (and was therefore a "barbarian"); or that because he derives from the classical world he is the more appropriate interlocutor.   **4.** Who in this version lives near Gaeta, on the coast of Italy north of Naples; she transforms men into beasts.   **5.** Aeneas named it after his nurse Caieta, who died there: *Aeneid* 7.   **6.** Ulysses' faithful wife.   **7.** The straits of Gibraltar, with Seville on the European side and Ceüta on the African. According to myth, Hercules separated a single mountain into two to mark the point beyond which human beings should not venture.

a hundred thousand dangers, reach the west,
to this brief waking-time that still is left
   unto your senses, you must not deny   115
experience of that which lies beyond
the sun, and of the world that is unpeopled.[8]
   Consider well the seed that gave you birth:
you were not made to live your lives as brutes,
but to be followers of worth and knowledge.'   120
   I spurred my comrades with this brief address
to meet the journey with such eagerness
that I could hardly, then, have held them back;
   and having turned our stern toward morning, we
made wings out of our oars in a wild flight   125
and always gained upon our left-hand side.
   At night I now could see the other pole
and all its stars; the stars of ours had fallen
and never rose above the plain of the ocean.[9]
   Five times the light beneath the moon had been   130
rekindled, and, as many times, was spent,
since that hard passage faced our first attempt,
   when there before us rose a mountain,[1] dark
because of distance, and it seemed to me
the highest mountain I had ever seen.   135
   And we were glad, but this soon turned to sorrow,
for out of that new land a whirlwind rose
and hammered at our ship, against her bow.
   Three times it turned her round with all the waters;
and at the fourth, it lifted up the stern   140
so that our prow plunged deep, as pleased an Other,[2]
until the sea again closed—over us."

CANTO XXVII

*Still the Eighth Circle, Eighth Pouch: the Fraudulent Counselors. Guido
da Montefeltro, for whom Dante provides a panorama of the state of
political affairs in Romagna. Guido's tale of the anticipatory—but
unavailing—absolution given him by Boniface VIII. The quarrel of a
demon and St Francis over Guido's soul.*

The flame already was erect and silent—
it had no more to say. Now it had left us
with the permission of the gentle poet,
   when, just behind it, came another flame
that drew our eyes to watch its tip because   5
of the perplexing sound that it sent forth.
   Even as the Sicilian bull[3] (that first
had bellowed with the cry—and this was just—
of him who shaped it with his instruments)

---

8. According to the geography of Dante's day, the southern hemisphere was made up entirely of water, with the only land being Mount Purgatory. To go *beyond the sun* means to follow a westward course. **9.** They had crossed the equator and could see only the stars of the southern hemisphere. **1.** Mount Purgatory. **2.** God. **3.** According to classical legend, Phalaris, the tyrant of Agrigentum in Sicily, had an artisan build a brazen bull in which he roasted his victims alive, their shrieks emerging as the sounds of a bull's bellowing. His first victim was the artisan himself, Perillus.

would always bellow with its victim's voice,   10
so that, although that bull was only brass,
it seemed as if it were pierced through by pain;
    so were the helpless words that, from the first,
had found no path or exit from the flame,
transformed into the language of the fire.   15
    But after they had found their way up toward
the tip, and given it that movement which
the tongue had given them along their passage,
    we heard: "O you to whom I turn my voice,[4]
who only now were talking Lombard,[5] saying,   20
'Now you may leave—I'll not provoke more speech,'
    though I have come perhaps a little late,
may it not trouble you to stop and speak
with me; see how I stay—and I am burning!
    If you have fallen into this blind world   25
but recently, out of the sweet Italian
country from which I carry all my guilt,
    do tell me if the Romagnoles[6] have peace
or war; I was from there—the hills between
Urbino and the ridge where Tiber springs."   30
    I still was bent, attentive, over him,
when my guide nudged me lightly at the side
and said: "You speak; he is Italian."
    And I, who had my answer set already,
without delay began to speak to him: 35
"O soul that is concealed below in flame,
    Romagna is not now and never was
quite free of war inside its tyrants' hearts;
but when I left her, none had broken out.
    Ravenna[7] stands as it has stood for years;   40
the eagle of Polenta shelters it
and also covers Cervia with his wings.
    The city[8] that already stood long trial
and made a bloody heap out of the French,
now finds itself again beneath green paws.   45
    Both mastiffs of Verrucchio,[9] old and new,
who dealt so badly with Montagna, use
their teeth to bore where they have always gnawed.
    The cities on Lamone and Santerno[1]
are led by the young lion of the white lair;   50
from summer unto winter, he shifts factions.
    That city with its side bathed by the Savio,[2]

4. The speaker is Guido da Montefeltro (d. 1298), a nobleman deeply involved in the constant warfare of thirteenth-century Italy but who became a friar two years before his death (see line 67).   5. The dialect of northern Italy. Dante believed that since Virgil came from Mantua, his spoken language would be not Latin but this dialect.   6. The people of Romagna, an area northeast of Florence and bordering the Adriatic Sea; the city of Urbino marks its southern limit, the Apennine mountains its northern. The subsequent passage describes the political conditions in the cities of Romagna.   7. The major city of Romagna, ruled at the time by the Polenta family, who also controlled the small city of Cervia.   8. Forlì, which defeated French invaders but then fell under the control of the tyrannical Ordelaffi family, which had green paws on its coat of arms.   9. The Verrucchio, Malatesta and his son Malatestino, were tyrants of Rimini who killed their enemy Montagna.   1. The cities of Faenza and Imola, on the Lamone and Santerno Rivers respectively, governed by an unreliable ruler who had a lion on a white ground on his coat of arms.   2. Cesena, located on the Savio River, was a free municipality although its politics were dominated by a single family.

just as it lies between the plain and mountain,
lives somewhere between tyranny and freedom.
 And now, I pray you, tell me who you are: 55
do not be harder than I've been with you,
that in the world your name may still endure."
 After the flame, in customary fashion,
had roared awhile, it moved its pointed tip
this side and that and then set free this breath: 60
 "If I thought my reply were meant for one
who ever could return into the world,
this flame would stir no more; and yet, since none—
if what I hear is true—ever returned
alive from this abyss, then without fear   65
of facing infamy, I answer you.
 I was a man of arms, then wore the cord,
believing that, so girt, I made amends;
and surely what I thought would have been true
 had not the Highest Priest[3]—may he be damned!—   70
made me fall back into my former sins;
and how and why, I'd have you hear from me.
 While I still had the form of bones and flesh
my mother gave to me, my deeds were not
those of the lion but those of the fox.   75
 The wiles and secret ways—I knew them all
and so employed their arts that my renown
had reached the very boundaries of earth.
 But when I saw myself come to that part
of life when it is fitting for all men   80
to lower sails and gather in their ropes,
 what once had been my joy was now dejection;
repenting and confessing, I became
a friar; and—poor me—it would have helped.
 The prince of the new Pharisees, who then   85
was waging war so near the Lateran[4]—
and not against the Jews or Saracens,
 for every enemy of his was Christian,
and none of them had gone to conquer Acre[5]
or been a trader in the Sultan's lands—   90
 took no care for the highest office or
the holy orders that were his, or for
my cord, which used to make its wearers leaner.
 But just as Constantine,[6] on Mount Soracte,
to cure his leprosy, sought out Sylvester,   95
so this one sought me out as his instructor,
 to ease the fever of his arrogance.
He asked me to give counsel. I was silent—
his words had seemed to me delirious.
 And then he said: 'Your heart must not mistrust: 100

---

3. Pope Boniface VIII.   4. Boniface was struggling to retain the papacy against the challenge of another
Roman family, the Colonnas.   5. City in the Holy Land, captured by the crusaders and then recaptured
by the Saracens.   6. According to legend, the Emperor Constantine (d. 337) was cured of his leprosy by
Pope Sylvester, who was hiding on Mount Soracte, some twenty miles north of Rome; see 19.115.

I now absolve you in advance—teach me
to batter Penestrino[7] to the ground.
　　You surely know that I posses the power
to lock and unlock Heaven; for the keys
my predecessor[8] did not prize are two.'　　　　　　　　105
　　Then his grave arguments compelled me so,
my silence seemed a worse offense than speech,
and I said: 'Since you cleanse me of the sin
　　that I must now fall into, Father, know:
long promises and very brief fulfillments　　　　　　110
will bring a victory to your high throne.'
　　Then Francis[9] came, as soon as I was dead,
for me; but one of the black cherubim
told him: 'Don't bear him off; do not cheat me.
　　He must come down among my menials;　　　　　115
the counsel that he gave was fraudulent;
since then, I've kept close track, to snatch his scalp;
　　one can't absolve a man who's not repented,
and no one can repent and will at once;
the law of contradiction won't allow it.'[1]　　　　　120
　　O miserable me, for how I started
when he took hold of me and said: 'Perhaps
you did not think that I was a logician!'[2]
　　He carried me to Minos;[3] and that monster
twisted his tail eight times around his hide　　　　125
and then, when he had bit it in great anger,
　　announced: 'This one is for the thieving fire';
for which—and where, you see—I now am lost,
and in this garb I move in bitterness."
　　And when, with this, his words were at an end,　　130
the flame departed, sorrowing and writhing
and tossing its sharp horn. We moved beyond;
　　I went together with my guide, along
the ridge until the other arch that bridges
the ditch where payment is imposed on those　　　135
　　who, since they brought such discord, bear such loads.

CANTO XXVIII

*The Eighth Circle, Ninth Pouch, where the Sowers of Scandal and
Schism, perpetually circling, are wounded and—after each healing—
wounded again by a demon with a sword. Mohammed and Alì. Warning
to Fra Dolcino. Curio. Mosca. Bertran de Born.*

Who, even with untrammeled words and many
attempts at telling, ever could recount
in full the blood and wounds that I now saw?

7. The fortress of the Colonnas.　　8. Celestine V, who resigned after five months (3.59–60). The keys
are those of damnation and absolution, given by Christ to Peter: see 19.92.　　9. Francis of Assisi (1181
or 1182–1226), founder of the order of friars joined by Guido.　　1. The contradiction is that Guido wanted
forgiveness for his sin of guile at the same time as he was committing it; in willing the sin he showed that
he was not truly repentant, the precondition for forgiveness.　　2. The devil is referring to the logical law
of noncontradiction.　　3. For Minos, see 5.4.

Each tongue that tried would certainly fall short
because the shallowness of both our speech   5
and intellect cannot contain so much.
    Were you to reassemble all the men
who once, within Apulia's fateful land,
had mourned their blood, shed at the Trojans' hands,[4]
    as well as those who fell in the long war   10
where massive mounds of rings were battle spoils—
even as Livy[5] writes, who does not err—
    and those who felt the thrust of painful blows
when they fought hard against Robert Guiscard;[6]
with all the rest whose bones are still piled up   15
at Ceperano[7]—each Apulian was
a traitor there—and, too, at Tagliacozzo,[8]
where old Alardo conquered without weapons;
    and then, were one to show his limb pierced through
and one his limb hacked off, that would not match   20
the hideousness of the ninth abyss.
    No barrel, even though it's lost a hoop
or end-piece, ever gapes as one whom I
saw ripped right from his chin to where we fart:
    his bowels hung between his legs, one saw   25
his vitals and the miserable sack
that makes of what we swallow excrement.
    While I was all intent on watching him,
he looked at me, and with his hands he spread
his chest and said: "See how I split myself!   30
    See now how maimed Mohammed[9] is! And he
who walks and weeps before me is Alì,
whose face is opened wide from chin to forelock.
    And all the others here whom you can see
were, when alive, the sowers of dissension   35
and scandal, and for this they now are split.
    Behind us here, a devil decks us out
so cruelly, re-placing every one
of this throng underneath the sword edge when
we've made our way around the road of pain,   40
because our wounds have closed again before
we have returned to meet his blade once more.
    But who are you who dawdle on this ridge,
perhaps to slow your going to the verdict
that was pronounced on your self-accusations?"   45
    "Death has not reached him yet," my master answered,
"nor is it guilt that summons him to torment;

---

4. Those killed when the Trojans conquered Latium, in the *Aeneid* 7–12. *Apulia's . . . land:* Southern Italy.
5. Roman historian (d. A.D. 17). *Long war:* the Second Punic War (218–01 B.C.) between Rome and Carthage under Hannibal. After the Battle of Cannae (216) the victorious Carthaginians displayed rings taken from fallen Romans.   **6.** Norman adventurer (1015–1085) who fought the Greeks and Saracens.
7. A town that the barons of Apulia were pledged to defend for Manfred, the natural son of Frederick II (10.119), but whom they betrayed; he was then killed at the battle of Benevento in 1266.   **8.** A town where in 1268 Manfred's nephew Conradin was defeated by the strategy rather than the brute force of Erard (or Alardo) de Valery.   **9.** Founder of Islam (570–632), regarded by some as a renegade Christian and a creator of religious disunity. Alì was his nephew and son-in-law, and his disputed claim to the rulership (or caliphate) divided Islam into Suni and Shia sects.

but that he may gain full experience,
I, who am dead, must guide him here below,
to circle after circle, throughout Hell: 50
this is as true as that I speak to you."
More than a hundred, when they heard him, stopped
within the ditch and turned to look at me,
forgetful of their torture, wondering.
    "Then you, who will perhaps soon see the sun,   55
tell Fra Dolcino[1] to provide himself
with food, if he has no desire to join me
    here quickly, lest when snow besieges him,
it bring the Novarese the victory
that otherwise they would not find too easy."   60
    When he had raised his heel, as if to go,
Mohammed said these words to me, and then
he set it on the ground and off he went.
    Another sinner, with his throat slit through
and with his nose hacked off up to his eyebrows,   65
and no more than a single ear remaining,
    had—with the others—stayed his steps in wonder;
he was the first, before the rest, to open
his windpipe—on the outside, all bloodred—
    and said: "O you whom guilt does not condemn,   70
and whom, unless too close resemblance cheats me,
I've seen above upon Italian soil,
    remember Pier da Medicina if
you ever see again the gentle plain
that from Vercelli slopes to Marcabò.[2]   75
    And let the two best men of Fano[3] know—
I mean both Messer Guido and Angiolello—
that, if the foresight we have here's not vain,
    they will be cast out of their ship and drowned,
weighed down with stones, near La Cattolica,   80
because of a foul tyrant's treachery.
    Between the isles of Cyprus and Majorca,
Neptune has never seen so cruel a crime
committed by the pirates or the Argives.[4]
    That traitor who sees only with one eye   85
and rules the land which one who's here with me
would wish his sight had never seen, will call
    Guido and Angiolello to a parley,
and then will so arrange it that they'll need
no vow or prayer to Focara's wind!"   90
    And I to him: "If you would have me carry
some news of you above, then tell and show me

---

1. In 1300 Fra Dolcino was head of a reformist order known as the Apostolic Brothers that was condemned as heretical by the pope. He and his followers escaped to the hills near the town of Novara, but starvation forced them out and many were executed.   2. The town of Medicina lies in the Po Valley between Vercelli and Marcabò. Nothing certain is known of Pier da Medicina.   3. A town on the Adriatic coast of Italy; its two leaders—named in the next line—were drowned in 1312 by the one-eyed tyrant Malatestino of Rimini (27.46) near the promontory of Focara after he had invited them to the town of La Cattolica for a parley.   4. Greeks. *Cyprus and Majorca:* islands at the western and eastern ends of the Mediterranean. *Neptune:* classical god of the sea.

who so detests the sight of Rimini."
　　And then he set his hand upon the jaw
of a companion, opening his mouth　　　　　　　　　　95
and shouting: "This is he,[5] and he speaks not.
　　A man cast out, he quenched the doubt in Caesar,
insisting that the one who is prepared
can only suffer harm if he delays."
　　Oh, how dismayed and pained he seemed to me,　　　100
his tongue slit in his gullet: Curio,
who once was so audacious in his talk!
　　And one who walked with both his hands hacked off,
while lifting up his stumps through the dark air,
so that his face was hideous with blood,　　　　　　　105
cried out: "You will remember Mosca,[6] too,
who said—alas—'What's done is at an end,'
which was the seed of evil for the Tuscans."
　　I added: "—and brought death to your own kinsmen";
then having heard me speak, grief heaped on grief,　　110
he went his way as one gone mad with sadness.
　　But I stayed there to watch that company
and saw a thing that I should be afraid
to tell with no more proof than my own self—
　　except that I am reassured by conscience,　　　　　115
that good companion, heartening a man
beneath the breastplate of its purity.
　　I surely saw, and it still seems I see,
a trunk without a head that walked just like
the others in that melancholy herd;　　　　　　　　　120
　　it carried by the hair its severed head,
which swayed within its hand just like a lantern;
and that head looked at us and said: "Ah me!"
　　Out of itself it made itself a lamp,
and they were two in one and one in two;　　　　　　125
how that can be, He knows who so decrees.
　　When it was just below the bridge, it lifted
its arm together with its head, so that
its words might be more near us, words that said:
　　"Now you can see atrocious punishment,　　　　　　130
you who, still breathing, go to view the dead:
see if there's any pain as great as this.
　　And so that you may carry news of me,
know that I am Bertran de Born,[7] the one
who gave bad counsel to the fledgling king.　　　　　135
　　I made the son and father enemies:
Achitophel with his malicious urgings
did not do worse with Absalom and David.

---

5. Caius Curio, a Roman of the first century B.C., was bribed by Julius Caesar to betray his friends; he urged Caesar to cross the Rubicon and invade the Roman republic, starting a civil war.　6. A Florentine noble, who in 1215 started the disastrous civil strife by advising a father to avenge the slight to his daughter by killing the man who had broken his engagement to her. Mosca's own family was a victim of the strife some sixty years later.　7. A Provençal nobleman and poet, who reputedly advised the son of Henry II of England to rebel against his father. For Achitophel's similar scheming between David and his son Absalom, see 2 Samuel 15–17. A poem by Bertran is included in *Medieval Lyrics: A Selection* (pp. 1805–7).

Because I severed those so joined, I carry—
alas—my brain dissevered from its source,   140
which is within my trunk. And thus, in me
one sees the law of counter-penalty."

CANTO XXIX

*Still the Eighth Circle, Ninth Pouch: the Sowers of Scandal and Schism.
Geri del Bello, an unavenged ancestor of Dante. The Tenth Pouch: the
Falsifiers. The First Group, Falsifiers of Metals (Alchemists), plagued by
scabs, lying on the earth, scratching furiously. Griffolino. Capocchio.*

So many souls and such outlandish wounds
had made my eyes inebriate—they longed
to stay and weep. But Virgil said to me:
"Why are you staring so insistently?
Why does your vision linger there below   5
among the lost and mutilated shadows?
You did not do so at the other moats.
If you would count them all, consider: twenty-
two miles[8] make up the circuit of the valley.
The moon already is beneath our feet;[9]   10
the time alloted to us now is short,
and there is more to see than you see here."
"Had you," I answered him without a pause,
"been able to consider why I looked,
you might have granted me a longer stay."   15
Meanwhile my guide had moved ahead; I went
behind him, answering as I walked on,
and adding: "In that hollow upon which,
just now, I kept my eyes intent, I think
a spirit born of my own blood laments   20
the guilt which, down below, costs one so much."
At this my master said: "Don't let your thoughts
about him interrupt you from here on:
attend to other things, let him stay there;
for I saw him below the little bridge,   25
his finger pointing at you, threatening,
and heard him called by name—Geri del Bello.[1]
But at that moment you were occupied
with him who once was lord of Hautefort;[2]
you did not notice Geri—he moved off."   30
"My guide, it was his death by violence,
for which he still is not avenged," I said,
"by anyone who shares his shame, that made
him so disdainful now; and—I suppose—
for this he left without a word to me,   35

8. The reason for this exact measurement is not known. At 30.86 we are told that the circumference of
the ninth circle is eleven miles, showing that Hell is shaped like a funnel.   9. This means that the sun
(which they cannot see) is over their heads, and the time is about 2 P.M. The journey to the center of Hell
lasts twenty-four hours, so only four hours are left.   1. First cousin to Dante's father; his death at the
hands of a member of another Florentine family initiated a feud between the two families that lasted some
fifty years.   2. Bertran de Born (see 28.134).

and this has made me pity him the more."
And so we talked until we found the first
point of the ridge that, if there were more light,
would show the other valley to the bottom.
    When we had climbed above the final cloister   40
of Malebolge, so that its lay brothers
were able to appear before our eyes,
    I felt the force of strange laments, like arrows
whose shafts are barbed with pity; and at this,
I had to place my hands across my ears.   45
    Just like the sufferings that all the sick
of Val di Chiana's hospitals, Maremma's,
Sardinia's,[3] from July until September
would muster if assembled in one ditch—
so was it here, and such a stench rose up   50
as usually comes from festering limbs.
    And keeping always to the left, we climbed
down to the final bank of the long ridge,
and then my sight could see more vividly
into the bottom, where unerring Justice,   55
the minister of the High Lord, punishes
the falsifiers she had registered.
    I do not think that there was greater grief
in seeing all Aegina's[4] people sick
(then, when the air was so infected that   60
all animals, down to the little worm,
collapsed; and afterward, as poets hold
to be the certain truth, those ancient peoples
received their health again through seed of ants)
than I felt when I saw, in that dark valley,   65
the spirits languishing in scattered heaps.
    Some lay upon their bellies, some upon
the shoulders of another spirit, some
crawled on all fours along that squalid road.
    We journeyed step by step without a word,   70
watching and listening to those sick souls,
who had not strength enough to lift themselves.
    I saw two sitting propped against each other—
as pan is propped on pan to heat them up[5]—
and each, from head to foot, spotted with scabs;   75
    and I have never seen a stableboy
whose master waits for him, or one who stays
awake reluctantly, so ply a horse
with currycomb, as they assailed themselves
with clawing nails—their itching had such force   80
and fury, and there was no other help.
    And so their nails kept scraping off the scabs,
just as a knife scrapes off the scales of carp

---

3. The river valley of Val di Chiana, the region of Maremma, and the island of Sardinia were all plagued by malaria.   4. A mythical island that was infected by Juno with a pestilence that killed all its inhabitants and was then repopulated when Jupiter turned ants into men: see Ovid, *Metamorphoses* 7.   5. The image is of pans leaned against one another on the stove.

or of another fish with scales more large.
"O you who use your nails to strip yourself,"   85
my guide began to say to one of them,
"and sometimes have to turn them into pincers,
tell us if there are some Italians
among the sinners in this moat—so may
your nails hold out, eternal, at their work."   90
"We two whom you see so disfigured here,
we are Italians," one said, in tears.
"But who are you who have inquired of us?"
My guide replied: " From circle down to circle,
together with this living man, I am   95
one who descends; I mean to show him Hell."
At this their mutual support broke off;
and, quivering, each spirit turned toward me
with others who, by chance, had heard his words.
Then my good master drew more close to me,   100
saying: "Now tell them what it is you want."
And I began to speak, just as he wished:
"So that your memory may never fade
within the first world from the minds of men,
but still live on—and under many suns—   105
do tell me who you are and from what city,
and do not let your vile and filthy torment
make you afraid to let me know your names."
One answered me: "My city was Arezzo
and Albero of Siena had me burned;[6]   110
but what I died for does not bring me here.
It's true that I had told him—jestingly—
'I'd know enough to fly through air'; and he,
with curiosity, but little sense,
wished me to show that art to him and, just   115
because I had not made him Daedalus,
had one who held him as a son burn me.
But Minos, who cannot mistake, condemned
my spirit to the final pouch of ten
for alchemy[7] I practiced in the world."   120
And then I asked the poet: "Was there ever
so vain a people as the Sienese?
Even the French can't match such vanity."
At this, the other leper,[8] who had heard me,
replied to what I'd said: "Except for Stricca,   125
for he knew how to spend most frugally;
and Niccolò, the first to make men see
that cloves can serve as luxury (such seed,
in gardens where it suits, can take fast root);
and, too, Caccia d'Asciano's company,   130

6. Griffolino of Arezzo cheated Albero of Siena by promising to teach him the art of Daedalus—flying. The bishop of Siena, father of the illegitimate Albero, had Griffolino burned as a heretic.   7. A practice that sought to turn base metals like lead into gold.   8. Capocchio, a Florentine burned in 1293 for alchemy, which he here admits was mere counterfeiting. The people he lists were rich young noblemen of Siena who joined a "Spendthrifts' Club"—the *company* of line 130—and sought to outdo each other in profligacy. For another member of this club, Lano of Siena, see 13.115.

with whom he squandered vineyards and tilled fields,
while Abbagliato showed such subtlety.
    But if you want to know who joins you so
against the Sienese, look hard at me—
that way, my face can also answer rightly—   135
and see that I'm the shade of that Capocchio
whose alchemy could counterfeit fine metals.
And you, if I correctly take your measure,
recall how apt I was at aping nature."

CANTO XXX

Still the Eighth Circle, Tenth Pouch: the Falsifiers. Gianni Schicchi and
Myrrha in the Second Group, Counterfeiters of Others' Persons. Master
Adam in the Third Group, Counterfeiters of Coins. Potiphar's wife and
Sinon the Greek in the Fourth Group, Falsifiers of Words, Liars. The
quarrel between Adam and Sinon.

    When Juno was incensed with Semele[9]
and, thus, against the Theban family
had shown her fury time and time again,
    then Athamas was driven so insane
that, seeing both his wife and their two sons,   5
as she bore one upon each arm, he cried:
    "Let's spread the nets, to take the lioness
together with her cubs along the pass";
and he stretched out his talons, pitiless,
    and snatched the son who bore the name Learchus,   10
whirled him around and dashed him on a rock;
she, with her other burden, drowned herself.
    And after fortune turned against the pride
of Troy,[1] which had dared all, so that the king
together with his kingdom, was destroyed,   15
    then Hecuba was wretched, sad, a captive;
and after she had seen Polyxena
dead and, in misery, had recognized
    her Polydorus lying on the shore,
she barked, out of her senses, like a dog—   20
her agony had so deformed her mind.
    But neither fury—Theban, Trojan—ever
was seen to be so cruel against another,
in rending beasts and even human limbs,
    as were two shades I saw, both pale and naked,   25
who, biting, ran berserk in just the way
a hog does when it's let loose from its sty.
    The one came at Capocchio and sank

9. Daughter of the king of Thebes, she was loved by Jupiter and therefore incited the wrath of Juno, who drove Semele's brother-in-law Athamas insane. While mad, Athamas thought his wife, Ino, and his two sons, Learchus and Melicertes, were a lioness and two cubs; he killed Learchus, and Ino drowned herself and Melicertes. See Ovid, *Metamorphoses* 4.   1. Parallel to the fate of Thebes is that of Troy, which is here represented by the madness into which Queen Hecuba fell when she saw her daughter Polyxena sacrificed on Achilles' tomb and the unburied body of her betrayed son Polydorus. See Ovid, *Metamorphoses* 13.

his tusks into his neck so that, by dragging,
he made the hard ground scrape against his belly.   30
    And he who stayed behind, the Aretine,[2]
trembled and said: "That phantom's Gianni Schicchi,[3]
and he goes raging, rending others so."
    And, "Oh," I said to him, "so may the other
not sink its teeth in you, please tell me who   35
it is before it hurries off from here."
    And he to me: "That is the ancient soul
of the indecent Myrrha,[4] she who loved
her father past the limits of just love.
    She came to sin with him by falsely taking   40
another's shape upon herself, just as
the other phantom who goes there had done,
    that he might gain the lady of the herd,
when he disguised himself as Buoso Donati,
making a will as if most properly."   45
    And when the pair of raging ones had passed,
those two on whom my eyes were fixed, I turned
around to see the rest of the ill-born.
    I saw one who'd be fashioned like a lute
if he had only had his groin cut off   50
from that part of his body where it forks.
    The heavy dropsy,[5] which so disproportions
the limbs with unassimilated humors
that there's no match between the face and belly,
    had made him part his lips like a consumptive,[6]   55
who will, because of thirst, let one lip drop
down to his chin and lift the other up.
    "O you exempt from every punishment
in this grim world, and I do not know why,"
he said to us, "look now and pay attention   60
to this, the misery of Master Adam:[7]
alive, I had enough of all I wanted;
alas, I now long for one drop of water.
    The rivulets that fall into the Arno
down from the green hills of the Casentino   65
with channels cool and moist, are constantly
    before me; I am racked by memory—
the image of their flow parches me more
than the disease that robs my face of flesh.
    The rigid Justice that would torment me   70
uses, as most appropriate, the place
where I had sinned, to draw swift sighs from me.
    There is Romena, there I counterfeited

2. Griffolino (see 29.110).   3. A Florentine who impersonated Buoso Donati (line 44), who had just
died, and dictated a new will that gave him Buoso's best beast (*the lady of the herd* of line 43).   4. Who
impersonated another woman in order to sleep with her father: see Ovid, *Metamorphoses* 10.   5. A disease
in which fluid (*humors* of line 53) gathers in the cells and the affected part becomes grotesqucly swollen.
6. A person with a fever.   7. A counterfeiter, burned in 1281, who made coins stamped with the image
of John the Baptist, the patron saint of Florence, that contained twenty-one rather than twenty-four carats
of gold (see line 90); he worked for a noble family of Romena (individual members are mentioned in line
77), a town in the Florentine district of Casentino.

the currency that bears the Baptist's seal;
for this I left my body, burned, above.   75
    But could I see the miserable souls
of Guido, Alessandro, or their brother,
I'd not give up the sight for Fonte Branda.[8]
    And one of them is in this moat already,
if what the angry shades report is true.   80
What use is that to me whose limbs are tied?
    Were I so light that, in a hundred years,
I could advance an inch, I should already
be well upon the road to search for him
    among the mutilated ones, although   85
this circuit measures some eleven miles
and is at least a half a mile across.
    Because of them I'm in this family;
it was those three who had incited me
to coin the florins with three carats' dross."   90
    And I to him: "Who are those two poor sinners
who give off smoke like wet hands in the winter
and lie so close to you upon the right?"
    "I found them here," he answered, "when I rained
down to this rocky slope; they've not stirred since   95
and will not move, I think, eternally.
    One is the lying woman who blamed Joseph;
the other, lying Sinon,[9] Greek from Troy:
because of raging fever they reek so."
    And one of them, who seemed to take offense,   100
perhaps at being named so squalidly,
struck with his fist at Adam's rigid belly.
    It sounded as if it had been a drum;
and Master Adam struck him in the face,
using his arm, which did not seem less hard,   105
    saying to him: "Although I cannot move
my limbs because they are too heavy, I
still have an arm that's free to serve that need."
    And he replied: "But when you went to burning,
your arm was not as quick as it was now;   110
though when you coined, it was as quick and more."
    To which the dropsied one: "Here you speak true;
but you were not so true a witness there,
when you were asked to tell the truth at Troy."
    "If I spoke false, you falsified the coin,"   115
said Sinon; "I am here for just one crime—
but you've committed more than any demon."
    "Do not forget the horse, you perjurer,"
replied the one who had the bloated belly,
"may you be plagued because the whole world knows it."   120
    The Greek: "And you be plagued by thirst that cracks
your tongue, and putrid water that has made

8. A fountain near Romena.   9. A Greek priest who persuaded the Trojans to accept the wooden horse
(*Aeneid* 2). *Lying woman*: Potiphar's wife, who falsely accused Joseph of trying to lie with her (Genesis
39.6–20).

your belly such a hedge before your eyes."
   And then the coiner: "So, as usual,
your mouth, because of racking fever, gapes;   125
for if I thirst and if my humor bloats me,
   you have both dryness and a head that aches;
few words would be sufficient invitation
to have you lick the mirror of Narcissus."[1]
   I was intent on listening to them   130
when this was what my master said: "If you
insist on looking more, I'll quarrel with you!"
   And when I heard him speak so angrily,
I turned around to him with shame so great
that it still stirs within my memory.   135
   Even as one who dreams that he is harmed
and, dreaming, wishes he were dreaming, thus
desiring that which is, as if it were not,
   so I became within my speechlessness:
I wanted to excuse myself and did   140
excuse myself, although I knew it not.
   "Less shame would wash away a greater fault
than was your fault," my master said to me;
"therefore release yourself from all remorse
   and see that I am always at your side,   145
should it so happen—once again—that fortune
brings you where men would quarrel in this fashion:
   to want to hear such bickering is base."

CANTO XXXI

Passage to the Ninth Circle. The central pit or well of Hell, where Cocytus, the last river of Hell, freezes. The Giants: Nimrod, Ephialtes, Briareus, Antaeus. Antaeus's compliance with Virgil's request to lower the two poets into the pit.

   The very tongue that first had wounded me,
sending the color up in both my cheeks,
was then to cure me with its medicine—
   as did Achilles' and his father's lance,[2]
even as I have heard, when it dispensed   5
a sad stroke first and then a healing one.
   We turned our backs upon that dismal valley
by climbing up the bank that girdles it;
we made our way across without a word.
   Here it was less than night and less than day,   10
so that my sight could only move ahead
slightly, but then I heard a bugle blast
   so strong, it would have made a thunder clap
seem faint; at this, my eyes—which doubled back
upon their path—turned fully toward one place.   15

---

1. Narcissus saw his reflection in a pool of water (Ovid, *Metamorphoses* 3).   2. Achilles' father, Peleus, gave him a lance that would heal any wound it inflicted.

Not even Roland's horn,[3] which followed on
the sad defeat when Charlemagne had lost
his holy army, was as dread as this.
    I'd only turned my head there briefly when
I seemed to make out many high towers; then   20
I asked him: "Master, tell me, what's this city?"
    And he to me: "It is because you try
to penetrate from far into these shadows
that you have formed such faulty images.
    When you have reached that place, you shall see clearly   25
how much the distance has deceived your sense;
and, therefore, let this spur you on your way."
    Then lovingly he took me by the hand
and said: "Before we have moved farther on,
so that the fact may seem less strange to you,   30
I'd have you know they are not towers, but giants,
and from the navel downward, all of them
are in the central pit, at the embankment."
    Just as, whenever mists begin to thin,
when, gradually, vision finds the form   35
that in the vapor-thickened air was hidden,
    so I pierced through the dense and darkened fog;
as I drew always nearer to the shore,
my error fled from me, my terror grew;
    for as, on its round wall, Montereggioni[4]   40
is crowned with towers, so there towered here,
above the bank that runs around the pit,
    with half their bulk, the terrifying giants,[5]
who still—whenever Jove hurls bolts from heaven—
remember how his thunder shattered them.   45
    And I could now make out the face of one,[6]
his shoulders and his chest, much of his belly,
and both his arms that hung along his sides.
    Surely when she gave up the art of making
such creatures, Nature acted well indeed,   50
depriving Mars of instruments like these.
    And if she still produces elephants
and whales, whoever sees with subtlety
holds her—for this—to be more just and prudent;
    for where the mind's acutest reasoning   55
is joined to evil will and evil power,
there human beings can't defend themselves.
    His face appeared to me as broad and long
as Rome can claim for its St. Peter's pine cone;[7]
his other bones shared in that same proportion;   60

---

3. In *The Song of Roland* (see pp. 1706ff.), Roland blows his horn to alert Charlemagne to the fact that the rear guard Roland commands has been slaughtered.   **4.** A castle surrounded by towers, built to protect Siena from attack by Florence.   **5.** According to classical mythology, Titans, giants born of the Earth, assaulted Olympus and were defeated and imprisoned by Jupiter.   **6.** Nimrod, described in Genesis as "the first on earth to be a mighty man" (10.8) and understood by medieval commentators to be a giant. He ruled over Babylon, where the tower of Babel was built (11.1–9).   **7.** This bronze pine cone, over twelve feet high, stood outside St. Peter's Cathedral in Dante's time; today it can be seen in the papal gardens in the Vatican.

so that the bank, which served him as an apron
down from his middle, showed so much of him
above, that three Frieslanders[8] would in vain
    have boasted of their reaching to his hair;
for downward from the place where one would buckle   65
a mantle, I saw thirty spans[9] of him.
    "Raphèl maì amècche zabì almi,"[1]
began to bellow that brute mouth, for which
no sweeter psalms would be appropriate.
    And my guide turned to him: "O stupid soul,   70
keep to your horn[2] and use that as an outlet
when rage or other passion touches you!
    Look at your neck, and you will find the strap
that holds it fast; and see, bewildered spirit,
how it lies straight across your massive chest."   75
    And then to me: "He is his own accuser;
for this is Nimrod, through whose wicked thought
one single language cannot serve the world.
    Leave him alone—let's not waste time in talk;
for every language is to him the same   80
as his to others—no one knows his tongue."
    So, turning to the left, we journeyed on
and, at the distance of a bow-shot, found
another giant, far more huge and fierce.
    Who was the master who had tied him so,   85
I cannot say, but his left arm was bent
behind him and his right was bent in front,
    both pinioned by a chain that held him tight
down from the neck; and round the part of him
that was exposed, it had been wound five times.   90
    "This giant in his arrogance had tested
his force against the force of highest Jove,"
my guide said, "so he merits this reward.
    His name is Ephialtes;[3] and he showed
tremendous power when the giants frightened   95
the gods; the arms he moved now move no more."
    And I to him: "If it is possible,
I'd like my eyes to have experience
of the enormous one, Briareus."[4]
    At which he answered: "You shall see Antaeus[5]   100
nearby. He is unfettered and can speak;
he'll take us to the bottom of all evil.
    The one you wish to see lies far beyond
and is bound up and just as huge as this one,
and even more ferocious in his gaze."   105
    No earthquake ever was so violent

---

8. Inhabitants of the northernmost province of what is now the Netherlands, considered the tallest men of the time.   **9.** About fifteen feet.   **1.** Appropriately for the builder of Babel, he speaks an incomprehensible language.   **2.** Nimrod has a horn because in the Bible he is described as a hunter (Genesis 10.9).   **3.** Ephialtes and his twin brother, Otus, were Titans who tried to attack Olympus by piling Mount Ossa on Mount Pelion: see Virgil, *Aeneid* 6.   **4.** Another Titan.   **5.** A Titan born too late to participate in the rebellion against Jupiter and therefore not chained; he was known for eating lions (line 118) and was defeated by Hercules in a wrestling match (line 132).

when called to shake a tower so robust,
as Ephialtes quick to shake himself.
Then I was more afraid of death than ever;
that fear would have been quite enough to kill me,   110
had I not seen how he was held by chains.
And we continued on until we reached
Antaeus, who, not reckoning his head,
stood out above the rock wall full five ells.[6]
"O you, who lived within the famous valley[7]   115
(where Scipio became the heir of glory
when Hannibal retreated with his men),
who took a thousand lions as your prey—
and had you been together with your brothers
in their high war, it seems some still believe   120
the sons of earth would have become the victors—
do set us down below, where cold shuts in
Cocytus,[8] and do not disdain that task.
Don't send us on to Tityus or Typhon;[9]
this man can give you what is longed for here;   125
therefore bend down and do not curl your lip.
He still can bring you fame within the world,
for he's alive and still expects long life,
unless grace summon him before his time."
So said my master; and in haste Antaeus   130
stretched out his hands, whose massive grip had once
been felt by Hercules, and grasped my guide.
And Virgil, when he felt himself caught up,
called out to me: "Come here, so I can hold you,"
then made one bundle of himself and me.   135
Just as the Garisenda[1] seems when seen
beneath the leaning side, when clouds run past
and it hangs down as if about to crash,
so did Antaeus seem to me as I
watched him bend over me—a moment when   140
I'd have preferred to take some other road.
But gently—on the deep that swallows up
both Lucifer and Judas[2]—he placed us;
nor did he, so bent over, stay there long,
but, like a mast above a ship, he rose.   145

CANTO XXXII

*The Ninth Circle, First Ring, called Caïna, where Traitors to their Kin
are immersed in the ice, heads bent down. Camiscione dei Pazzi. The
Second Ring, called Antenora: the Traitors to their Homeland or Party.
Bocca degli Abati's provocation of Dante. Two traitors, one gnawing at
the other's head.*

6. About fifteen feet.   7. The valley of the Bagradas River in Tunisia, where the Roman Scipio defeated
the Carthaginian Hannibal in 202 B.C.   8. The frozen lake of Cocytus is in the ninth and last circle of
Hell.   9. Two more Titans.   1. A leaning tower of Bologna; when a cloud passes over it, moving opposite to the tower's slant, it appears to be falling away from the sky.   2. Two of the inhabitants of Cocytus.

Had I the crude and scrannel rhymes to suit
the melancholy hole upon which all
the other circling crags converge and rest,
    the juice of my conception would be pressed
more fully; but because I feel their lack,   5
I bring myself to speak, yet speak in fear;
    for it is not a task to take in jest,
to show the base of all the universe—
nor for a tongue that cries out, "mama," "papa."
    But may those ladies[3] now sustain my verse   10
who helped Amphion when he walled up Thebes,
so that my tale not differ from the fact.
    O rabble, miscreated past all others,
there in the place of which it's hard to speak,
better if here you had been goats or sheep!   15
    When we were down below in the dark well,
beneath the giant's feet and lower yet,
with my eyes still upon the steep embankment,
    I heard this said to me: "Watch how you pass;
walk so that you not trample with your soles   20
the heads of your exhausted, wretched brothers."
    At this I turned and saw in front of me,
beneath my feet, a lake[4] that, frozen fast,
had lost the look of water and seemed glass.
    The Danube where it flows in Austria,   25
the Don beneath its frozen sky, have never
made for their course so thick a veil in winter
    as there was here; for had Mount Tambernic[5]
or Pietrapana's mountain crashed upon it,
not even at the edge would it have creaked.   30
    And as the croaking frog sits with its muzzle
above the water, in the season when
the peasant woman often dreams of gleaning,[6]
    so, livid in the ice, up to the place
where shame can show itself, were those sad shades,   35
whose teeth were chattering with notes like storks'.[7]
    Each kept his face bent downward steadily;
their mouths bore witness to the cold they felt,
just as their eyes proclaimed their sorry hearts.
    When I had looked around a while, my eyes   40
turned toward my feet and saw two locked so close,
the hair upon their heads had intermingled.
    "Do tell me, you whose chests are pressed so tight,"
I said, "who are you?" They bent back their necks,
and when they'd lifted up their faces toward me,   45
    their eyes, which wept upon the ground before,
shed tears down on their lips until the cold

3. The Muses who helped the legendary musician Amphion raise the walls of Thebes with the music of
his lyre.   4. The water for this lake derives from the crack in the Old Man of Crete (14.103).   5. Probably Mt. Tambura, close to Mt. Pietrapana in the Italian Alps.   6. Picking over harvested fields for bits
of grain left behind, an activity for the early summer.   7. A harsh, clacking sound. *The place . . . itself*:
the face.

held fast the tears and locked their lids still more.
No clamp has ever fastened plank to plank
so tightly; and because of this, they butted   50
each other like two rams, such was their fury.
And one from whom the cold had taken both
his ears, who kept his face bent low, then said:
"Why do you keep on staring so at us?
If you would like to know who these two are: 55
that valley where Bisenzio descends,
belonged to them and to their father Alberto.[8]
They came out of one body; and you can
search all Caïna,[9] you will never find
a shade more fit to sit within this ice—   60
not him who, at one blow, had chest and shadow
shattered by Arthur's hand; and not Focaccia;[1]
and not this sinner here who so impedes
my vision with his head, I can't see past him;
his name was Sassol Mascheroni;[2] if   65
you're Tuscan, now you know who he has been.
And lest you keep me talking any longer,
know that I was Camiscion de' Pazzi;[3]
I'm waiting for Carlino[4] to absolve me."
And after that I saw a thousand faces   70
made doglike by the cold; for which I shudder—
and always will—when I face frozen fords.
And while we were advancing toward the center
to which all weight is drawn[5]—I, shivering
in that eternally cold shadow—I   75
know not if it was will or destiny
or chance, but as I walked among the heads,
I struck my foot hard in the face of one.[6]
Weeping, he chided then: "Why trample me?
If you've not come to add to the revenge   80
of Montaperti, why do you molest me?"
And I: "My master, now wait here for me,
that I may clear up just one doubt about him;
then you can make me hurry as you will."
My guide stood fast, and I went on to ask   85
of him who still was cursing bitterly:
"Who are you that rebukes another so?"
"And who are you who go through Antenora,[7]
striking the cheeks of others," he replied,

---

8. When Count Alberto degli Alberti died (ca. 1280), his two sons killed each other over politics and their inheritance. *Bisenzio:* a river north of Florence.   **9.** Named after Cain, the first of the four subdivisions of Cocytus is where those who betrayed their kin are imprisoned.   **1.** A nobleman of Pistoia who killed his cousin. *Not him . . . hand:* Mordred, Arthur's nephew and son; when Arthur pierced him with a sword, he created a wound so large that the sun shone through, thus creating a hole in Mordred's shadow.   **2.** A Florentine nobleman who murdered a relative.   **3.** A Florentine who killed his kinsman.   **4.** A Florentine who betrayed a castle belonging to his party. When he dies he will therefore be sent to the next subdivision, Antenora, for those who committed treachery against their country, city, or party—a harsher punishment, which Camiscion says will "absolve" him.   **5.** The *base of all the universe* (line 8) is where gravity is most strong and to which all material things are drawn.   **6.** Bocca degli Abati, who betrayed his party at the battle of Montaperti in 1260.   **7.** Named after Antenor, a Trojan who betrayed the city to the Greeks.

"too roughly—even if you were alive?"   90
"I am alive, and can be precious to you
if you want fame," was my reply, "for I
can set your name among my other notes."
And he to me: "I want the contrary;
so go away and do not harass me—   95
your flattery is useless in this valley."
At that I grabbed him by the scruff[8] and said:
"You'll have to name yourself to me or else
you won't have even one hair left up here."
And he to me: "Though you should strip me bald,   100
I shall not tell you who I am or show it,
not if you pound my head a thousand times."
His hairs were wound around my hand already,
and I had plucked from him more than one tuft
while he was barking and his eyes stared down,   105
when someone else cried out: "What is it, Bocca?
Isn't the music of your jaws enough
for you without your bark? What devil's at you?"
"And now," I said, "you traitor bent on evil,
I do not need your talk, for I shall carry   110
true news of you, and that will bring you shame."
"Be off," he answered; "tell them what you like,
but don't be silent, if you make it back,
about the one whose tongue was now so quick.[9]
Here he laments the silver of the Frenchmen;   115
'I saw,' you then can say, 'him of Duera,
down there, where all the sinners are kept cool.'
And if you're asked who else was there in ice,
one of the Beccheria[1] is beside you—
he had his gullet sliced right through by Florence. 120
Gianni de' Soldanieri, I believe,
lies there with Ganelon and Tebaldello,[2]
he who unlocked Faenza while it slept."
We had already taken leave of him,
when I saw two shades frozen in one hole,   125
so that one's head served as the other's cap;
and just as he who's hungry chews his bread,
one sinner dug his teeth into the other
right at the place where brain is joined to nape:
no differently had Tydeus[3] gnawed the temples   130
of Menalippus, out of indignation,
than this one chewed the skull and other parts.
"O you who show, with such a bestial sign,
your hatred for the one on whom you feed,
tell me the cause," I said; "we can agree   135
that if your quarrel with him is justified,

---

8. The hair at the nape of the neck.   **9.** Buoso da Duera, who betrayed the ruler of Naples, Manfred, to his enemy Charles of Anjou in 1265.   **1.** A churchman executed for treason in Florence in 1258. **2.** A citizen of Faenza (a town east of Florence) who betrayed it to its enemies. *Gianni de' Soldanieri:* a Florentine nobleman who switched political parties. *Ganelon:* the betrayer of Roland in *The Song of Roland.* **3.** In the war against Thebes, Tydeus was mortally wounded by Menalippus, whom he killed and whose skull he gnawed in fury while dying.

then knowing who you are and what's his sin,
I shall repay you yet on earth above,
if that with which I speak does not dry up."

CANTO XXXIII

Still the Ninth Circle, Second Ring. Ugolino's tale of his and his sons'
death in a Pisan prison. Dante's invective against Pisa. The Third Ring,
Ptolomea, where Traitors against their Guests jut out from ice, their eyes
sealed by frozen tears. Fra Alberigo and Branca Doria, still alive on earth
but already in Hell.

That sinner[4] raised his mouth from his fierce meal,
then used the head that he had ripped apart
in back: he wiped his lips upon its hair.
    Then he began: "You want me to renew
despairing pain that presses at my heart   5
even as I think back, before I speak.
    But if my words are seed from which the fruit
is infamy for this betrayer whom
I gnaw, you'll see me speak and weep at once.
    I don't know who you are or in what way   10
you've come down here; and yet you surely seem—
from what I hear—to be a Florentine.
    You are to know I was Count Ugolino,
and this one here, Archbishop Ruggieri;
and now I'll tell you why I am his neighbor.   15
    There is no need to tell you that, because
of his malicious tricks, I first was taken
and then was killed—since I had trusted him;
    however, that which you cannot have heard—
that is, the cruel death devised for me—   20
you now shall hear and know if he has wronged me.
    A narrow window in the Eagles' Tower,[5]
which now, through me, is called the Hunger Tower,
a cage in which still others will be locked,
    had, through its opening, already showed me   25
several moons, when I dreamed that bad dream
which rent the curtain of the future for me.
    This man appeared to me as lord and master;
he hunted down the wolf and its young whelps
upon the mountain[6] that prevents the Pisans   30
    from seeing Lucca; and with lean and keen
and practiced hounds, he'd sent up front, before him,
Gualandi and Sismondi and Lanfranchi.[7]
    But after a brief course, it seemed to me
that both the father and the sons were weary;   35
I seemed to see their flanks torn by sharp fangs.
    When I awoke at daybreak, I could hear

4. Ugolino, a governor of Pisa who was betrayed by his enemy Archbishop Ruggieri in 1289. His own crime
is obliquely explained by his narrative.   5. The prison in Pisa.   6. Mt. San Giuliano lies between Pisa
and Lucca. *Wolf and . . . whelps:* Ugolino and his four sons, each of whom he names in subsequent lines.
7. Pisan families of the political party opposed to that of Ugolino.

my sons, who were together with me there,
weeping within their sleep, asking for bread.
    You would be cruel indeed if, thinking what   40
my heart foresaw, you don't already grieve;
and if you don't weep now, when would you weep?
    They were awake by now; the hour drew near
at which our food was usually brought,
and each, because of what he'd dreamed, was anxious;   45
    below, I heard them nailing up the door
of that appalling tower; without a word,
I looked into the faces of my sons.
    I did not weep; within, I turned to stone.
They wept; and my poor little Anselm said: 50
'Father, you look so . . . What is wrong with you?'
    At that I shed no tears and—all day long
and through the night that followed—did not answer
until another sun had touched the world.
    As soon as a thin ray had made its way   55
into that sorry prison, and I saw,
reflected in four faces, my own gaze,
    out of my grief, I bit at both my hands;
and they, who thought I'd done that out of hunger,
immediately rose and told me: 'Father,   60
    it would be far less painful for us if
you ate of us; for you clothed us in this
sad flesh—it is for you to strip it off.'[8]
    Then I grew calm, to keep them from more sadness;
through that day and the next, we all were silent;   65
O hard earth, why did you not open up?
    But after we had reached the fourth day, Gaddo,
throwing himself, outstretched, down at my feet,
implored me: 'Father, why do you not help me?'[9]
    And there he died; and just as you see me,   70
I saw the other three fall one by one
between the fifth day and the sixth; at which,
    now blind, I started groping over each;
and after they were dead, I called them for
two days; then fasting had more force than grief."   75
    When he had spoken this, with eyes awry,
again he gripped the sad skull in his teeth,
which, like a dog's, were strong down to the bone.
    Ah, Pisa, you the scandal of the peoples
of that fair land where *si* is heard,[1] because   80
your neighbors are so slow to punish you,
    may, then, Caprara and Gorgona[2] move
and build a hedge across the Arno's mouth,
so that it may drown every soul in you!
    For if Count Ugolino was reputed   85
to have betrayed your fortresses, there was

---

8. See Job 1.21.   **9.** See Matthew 27.46.   **1.** I.e., Italy, where *si* means "yes."   **2.** Islands belonging
to Pisa that lie close to the mouth of the Arno, which flows through Pisa.

no need to have his sons endure such torment.
O Thebes renewed,[3] their years were innocent
and young—Brigata, Uguiccione, and
the other two my song has named above!   90
We passed beyond,[4] where frozen water wraps—
a rugged covering—still other sinners,
who were not bent, but flat upon their backs.
Their very weeping there won't let them weep,
and grief that finds a barrier in their eyes   95
turns inward to increase their agony;
    because their first tears freeze into a cluster,
and, like a crystal visor, fill up all
the hollow that is underneath the eyebrow.
    And though, because of cold, my every sense   100
had left its dwelling in my face, just as
a callus has no feeling, nonetheless,
    I seemed to feel some wind now, and I said:
"My master, who has set this gust in motion?
For isn't every vapor quenched down here?"[5]   105
    And he to me: "You soon shall be where your
own eye will answer that, when you shall see
the reason why this wind blasts from above."
    And one of those sad sinners in the cold
crust, cried to us: "O souls who are so cruel   110
that this last place has been assigned to you,
    take off the hard veils from my face so that
I can release the suffering that fills
my heart before lament freezes again."
    To which I answered: "If you'd have me help you,   115
then tell me who you are; if I don't free you,
may I go to the bottom of the ice."
    He answered then: "I am Fra Alberigo,[6]
the one who tended fruits in a bad garden,
and here my figs have been repaid with dates."   120
    "But then," I said, "are you already dead?"
And he to me: "I have no knowledge of
my body's fate within the world above.
    For Ptolomea has this privilege:
quite frequently the soul falls here before   125
it has been thrust away by Atropos.[7]
    And that you may with much more willingness
scrape these glazed tears from off my face, know this:
as soon as any soul becomes a traitor,
as I was, then a demon takes its body   130

3. In classical mythology, Thebes was notorious for its intergenerational horrors, such as the story of Oedipus; his father, Laius; and his sons, Eteocles and Polynices (see 26.54).   4. They pass into the third division of Cocytus, called Ptolomea (line 124) after Ptolemy, governor of Jericho, who killed his father-in-law, Simon, and two of his sons while they were dining with him (1 Maccabees 16.11–17). In Ptolomea those who have betrayed their guests are punished.   5. Since the sun's heat was thought to cause wind, Dante wonders why he feels wind in this cold place.   6. A member of the Jovial Friars (see 23.103), he killed two of his relatives during a banquet at his house, signaling the assassins with an order to bring the fruit. In saying that his figs have been repaid with dates, he is ironically complimenting God for His generosity, since a date would be more valuable than a fig.   7. One of the mythological figures known as the Fates; she is the one who cuts the thread of life.

away—and keeps that body in his power
until its years have run their course completely.
 The soul falls headlong, down into this cistern;
and up above, perhaps, there still appears
the body of the shade that winters here   135
 behind me; you must know him, if you've just
come down; he is Ser Branca Doria;[8]
for many years he has been thus pent up."
 I said to him: "I think that you deceive me,
for Branca Doria is not yet dead;   140
he eats and drinks and sleeps and puts on clothes."
 "There in the Malebranche's ditch above,
where sticky pitch boils up, Michele Zanche
had still not come," he said to me, "when this one—
 together with a kinsman, who had done   145
the treachery together with him—left
a devil in his stead inside his body.
 But now reach out your hand; open my eyes."
And yet I did not open them for him;
and it was courtesy to show him rudeness.   150
 Ah, Genoese, a people strange to every
constraint of custom, full of all corruption,
why have you not been driven from the world?
 For with the foulest spirit of Romagna,[9]
I found one of you such that, for his acts,   155
in soul he bathes already in Cocytus
and up above appears alive, in body.

CANTO XXXIV

*The Ninth Circle, Fourth Ring, called Judecca, where Tratiors against
their Benefactors are fully covered by ice. Dis, or Lucifer, emperor of that
kingdom, his three mouths rending Judas, Brutus, and Cassius. Descent of
Virgil and Dante down Lucifer's body to the other, southern hemisphere.
Their vision of the stars.*

 "*Vexilla regis prodeunt inferni*[1]
toward us; and therefore keep your eyes ahead,"
my master said, "to see if you can spy him."
 Just as, when night falls on our hemisphere
or when a heavy fog is blowing thick,   5
a windmill seems to wheel when seen far off,
 so then I seemed to see that sort of structure.
And next, because the wind was strong, I shrank
behind my guide; there was no other shelter.
 And now—with fear I set it down in meter—   10
I was where all the shades were fully covered
but visible as wisps of straw in glass.

---

8. A nobleman of Genoa, who with a kinsman (line 145) killed his father-in-law, Michel Zanche, at a
banquet in 1275 or 1290. 9. Fra Alberigo. 1. The first three words—"the banners of the king
advance"—are the opening lines of a sixth-century Latin hymn traditionally sung during Holy Week to
celebrate Christ's Passion. Dante has added the last word, *inferni*—"the banners of the king of Hell
advance"—in order to apply the words to Satan.

There some lie flat and others stand erect,
one on his head, and one upon his soles;
and some bend face to feet, just like a bow.   15
    But after we had made our way ahead,
my master felt he now should have me see
that creature who was once a handsome presence;[2]
    he stepped aside and made me stop, and said:
"Look! Here is Dis,[3] and this the place where you   20
will have to arm yourself with fortitude."
    O reader, do not ask of me how I
grew faint and frozen then—I cannot write it:
all words would fall far short of what it was.
    I did not die, and I was not alive;   25
think for yourself, if you have any wit,
what I became, deprived of life and death.
    The emperor of the despondent kingdom
so towered—from midchest—above the ice,
that I match better with a giant's height   30
than giants match the measure of his arms;
now you can gauge the size of all of him
if it is in proportion to such limbs.
    If he was once as handsome as he now
is ugly and, despite that, raised his brows   35
against his Maker, one can understand
how every sorrow has its source in him!
    I marveled when I saw that, on his head,
he had three faces:[4] one—in front—bloodred;
and then another two that, just above   40
the midpoint of each shoulder, joined the first;
    and at the crown, all three were reattached;
the right looked somewhat yellow, somewhat white;
the left in its appearance was like those[5]
who come from where the Nile, descending, flows.   45
    Beneath each face of his, two wings spread out,
as broad as suited so immense a bird:
I've never seen a ship with sails so wide.
    They had no feathers, but were fashioned like
a bat's; and he was agitating them,   50
so that three winds made their way out from him—
and all Cocytus froze before those winds.
    He wept out of six eyes; and down three chins,
tears gushed together with a bloody froth.
    Within each mouth—he used it like a grinder—   55
with gnashing teeth he tore to bits a sinner,
so that he brought much pain to three at once.
    The forward sinner found that biting nothing
when matched against the clawing, for at times
his back was stripped completely of its hide.   60

---

2. Lucifer, the "light-bearer," was the most beautiful of angels before he rebelled and was renamed Satan.
3. A classical name for Pluto, here applied to Satan (see also 11.65 and 12.39).   4. Satan's three faces
(and much else) make him an infernal parody of the Trinity.   5. I.e., Ethiopians. The significance of
these three colors is not certain; it has been suggested that they represent hatred, impotence, and ignorance.

"That soul up there who has to suffer most,"
my master said: "Judas Iscariot—
his head inside, he jerks his legs without.
Of those two others, with their heads beneath,
the one who hangs from that black snout is Brutus[6]—   65
see how he writhes and does not say a word!
That other, who seems so robust, is Cassius.[7]
But night is come again, and it is time
for us to leave; we have seen everything."
    Just as he asked, I clasped him round the neck;   70
and he watched for the chance of time and place,
and when the wings were open wide enough,
    he took fast hold upon the shaggy flanks
and then descended, down from tuft to tuft,
between the tangled hair and icy crusts.   75
    When we had reached the point at which the thigh
revolves, just at the swelling of the hip,
my guide, with heavy strain and rugged work,
    reversed his head to where his legs had been
and grappled on the hair, as one who climbs—   80
I thought that we were going back to Hell.[8]
    "Hold tight," my master said—he panted like
a man exhausted—"it is by such stairs
that we must take our leave of so much evil."
    Then he slipped through a crevice in a rock   85
and placed me on the edge of it, to sit;
that done, he climbed toward me with steady steps.
    I raised my eyes, believing I should see
the half of Lucifer that I had left;
instead I saw him with his legs turned up;   90
    and if I then became perplexed, do let
the ignorant be judges—those who can
not understand what point I had just crossed.
    "Get up," my master said, "be on your feet:
the way is long, the path is difficult;   95
the sun's already back to middle tierce."[9]
    It was no palace hall, the place in which
we found ourselves, but with its rough-hewn floor
and scanty light, a dungeon built by nature.
    "Before I free myself from this abyss,   100
master," I said when I had stood up straight,
"tell me enough to see I don't mistake:
    Where is the ice? And how is he so placed
head downward? Tell me, too, how has the sun
in so few hours gone from night to morning?"   105

6. The murderer of Julius Caesar in 44 B.C., and thus for Dante a betrayer of the empire.   7. The other murderer of Caesar.   8. Virgil's reversal marks the point at which the two travelers pass from the Northern to the Southern Hemisphere. They began by climbing down Satan's body, but now reverse directions and climb up from the Earth's center (hence when they have passed through the center Dante sees Satan's legs sticking up [line 90]. Note that the travelers pass through the glassy ice, a passage that probably echoes 1 Corinthians 13.12: "For now we see through a glass, darkly; but then face to face."   9. About 7:30 A.M. on Holy Saturday. Dante has added twelve hours to his scheme so that the travelers will emerge from the Earth and arrive at the shore of Mount Purgatory just before sunrise on the next day, Easter Sunday.

And he to me: "You still believe you are
north of the center, where I grasped the hair
of the damned worm who pierces through the world.
And you were there as long as I descended;
but when I turned, that's when you passed the point   110
to which, from every part, all weights are drawn.
And now you stand beneath the hemisphere
opposing that which cloaks the great dry lands
and underneath whose zenith died the Man
whose birth and life were sinless in this world.[1]   115
Your feet are placed upon a little sphere
that forms the other face of the Judecca.
Here it is morning when it's evening there;[2]
and he whose hair has served us as a ladder
is still fixed, even as he was before.   120
This was the side on which he fell from Heaven;[3]
for fear of him, the land that once loomed here
made of the sea a veil and rose into
our hemisphere; and that land which appears
upon this side—perhaps to flee from him—   125
left here this hollow space and hurried upward."
There is a place below, the limit of
that cave, its farthest point from Beelzebub,[4]
a place one cannot see: it is discovered
by ear—there is a sounding stream[5] that flows   130
along the hollow of a rock eroded
by winding waters, and the slope is easy.
My guide and I came on that hidden road
to make our way back into the bright world;
and with no care for any rest, we climbed—   135
he first, I following—until I saw,
through a round opening, some of those things
of beauty Heaven bears. It was from there
that we emerged, to see—once more—the stars.

From Purgatorio

CANTO I

Proem and Invocation. The skies of the Southern Pole before dawn. The four stars. Cato of Utica, custodian of the island Mountain of Purgatory. Cato's queries and Virgil's reply. Instructions by Cato. Virgil bathing Dante's face and, on the shore, girding him with a rush.

---

1. I.e., under the Southern Hemisphere, exactly opposite Jerusalem, the center of the Northern Hemisphere (see Ezekiel 5.5), which is right over the cavity of Hell.   2. The sun is now over the Southern Hemisphere, and it is night in the Northern.   3. The land that was in the Southern Hemisphere before Satan fell fled to the Northern to avoid him, while the earth that he displaced rose up in the Southern Hemisphere to form Mount Purgatory. This geography is Dante's own poetic scheme.   4. Satan. 5. This stream must flow down from Purgatory, perhaps from Lethe.

To course across more kindly waters now
my talent's little vessel lifts her sails,
leaving behind herself a sea so cruel;[1]
and what I sing will be that second kingdom,
in which the human soul is cleansed of sin,   5
becoming worthy of ascent to Heaven.
But here, since I am yours, o holy Muses,
may this poem rise again from Hell's dead realm;
and may Calliope[2] rise somewhat here,
accompanying my singing with that music   10
whose power struck the poor Pierides
so forcefully that they despaired of pardon.[3]
The gentle hue of oriental sapphire
in which the sky's serenity was steeped[4]—
its aspect pure as far as the horizon—   15
brought back my joy in seeing just as soon
as I had left behind the air of death
that had afflicted both my sight and breast.
The lovely planet that is patroness
of love[5] made all the eastern heavens glad,   20
veiling the Pisces[6] in the train she led.
Then I turned to the right, setting my mind
upon the other pole, and saw four stars
not seen before except by the first people.[7]
Heaven appeared to revel in their flames: 25
o northern hemisphere, because you were
denied that sight, you are a widower![8]
After my eyes took leave of those four stars,
turning a little toward the other pole,
from which the Wain[9] had disappeared by now,   30
I saw a solitary patriarch[1]
near me—his aspect worthy of such reverence
that even son to father owes no more.
His beard was long and mixed with white, as were
the hairs upon his head; and his hair spread   35
down to his chest in a divided tress.
The rays of the four holy stars so framed
his face with light that in my sight he seemed
like one who is confronted by the sun.
"Who are you—who, against the hidden river,[2]   40

1. The metaphor of the poem as a ship is traditional; the *kindly waters* refer to Purgatory, while the cruel sea is Hell.   2. The Muse of epic poetry.   3. The nine daughters of Pierus—the Pierides—challenged the Muses to a singing contest and, having lost, were turned into magpies: see Ovid, *Metamorphoses* 5.   4. The time is meant to be just before sunrise on Easter Sunday, 1300.   5. Venus, the morning star, although in fact on this date Venus would have been visible only after sunrise.   6. The constellation in which Venus would be located if it had risen before the sun on this date.   7. Prior to their expulsion from Eden, Adam and Eve saw four stars above the South Pole, which is located on the summit of Mount Purgatory. These stars symbolize the four cardinal virtues: prudence, temperance, justice, and fortitude. 8. Dante is lamenting the corruption of his present time compared to the perfection of prelapsarian life. 9. The constellation Ursa Major, which never disappears from northern skies but is not visible to an observer in the Southern Hemisphere. *The other pole*: the North Pole.   1. Cato (95–46 B.C.), a Roman known for his uncompromising morality and love of liberty; rather than submit to what he saw as Julius Caesar's tyranny, he committed suicide in Utica, a city in North Africa. Dante is here influenced by Virgil's treatment of Cato in the underworld, where he is presented not as a suicide but as the lawgiver to the righteous (*Aeneid* 6).   2. Probably Lethe (see *Inferno* 34.130–32).

were able to escape the eternal prison?"
he said, moving those venerable plumes.
"Who was your guide? What served you both as lantern
when, from the deep night that will always keep
the hellish valley dark, you were set free?   45
The laws of the abyss—have they been broken?
Or has a new, a changed decree in Heaven
let you, though damned, approach my rocky slopes?"
My guide took hold of me decisively;
by way of words and hands and other signs,   50
he made my knees and brow show reverence.
Then he replied: "I do not come through my
own self. There was a lady sent from Heaven;[3]
her pleas led me to help and guide this man.
But since your will would have a far more full   55
and accurate account of our condition,
my will cannot withhold what you request.
This man had yet to see his final evening;
but, through his folly, little time was left
before he did—he was so close to it.   60
As I have told you, I was sent to him
for his deliverance; the only road
I could have taken was the road I took.
I showed him all the people of perdition;
now I intend to show to him those spirits   65
who, in your care, are bent on expiation.
To tell you how I led him would take long;
it is a power descending from above
that helps me guide him here, to see and hear you.
Now may it please you to approve his coming;   70
he goes in search of liberty—so precious,
as he who gives his life for it must know.
You know it—who, in Utica, found death
for freedom was not bitter, when you left
the garb[4] that will be bright on the great day.   75
Eternal edicts are not broken for us;
this man's alive, and I'm not bound by Minos;[5]
but I am from the circle where the chaste
eyes of your Marcia[6] are; and she still prays
to you, o holy breast, to keep her as   80
your own: for her love, then, incline to us.
Allow our journey through your seven realms.
I shall thank her for kindness you bestow—
if you would let your name be named below."
"While I was there, within the other world,   85
Marcia so pleased my eyes," he then replied,
"each kindness she required, I satisfied.
Now that she dwells beyond the evil river,

---

3. Beatrice.   4. The body, which will be glorified in its resurrection on Judgment Day.   5. See *Inferno* 5.4.   6. Cato's wife, now in Limbo (see *Inferno* 4.128); according to a story told by the Roman poet Lucan (A.D. 39–65), Cato ceded Marcia to his friend Hortensius, but on Hortensius's death Marcia's entreaty to Cato that he remarry her was granted.

she has no power to move me any longer,
such was the law decreed when I was freed.[7]   90
    But if a lady come from Heaven speeds
and helps you, as you say, there is no need
of flattery; it is enough, indeed,
    to ask me for her sake. Go then; but first
wind a smooth rush[8] around his waist and bathe   95
his face, to wash away all of Hell's stains;
    for it would not be seemly to approach
with eyes still dimmed by any mists, the first
custodian angel, one from Paradise.
    This solitary island, all around   100
its very base, there where the breakers pound,
bears rushes on its soft and muddy ground.
    There is no other plant that lives below:
no plant with leaves or plant that, as it grows,
hardens—and breaks beneath the waves' harsh blows.   105
    That done, do not return by this same pass;
the sun, which rises now, will show you how
this hillside can be climbed more easily."
    With that he vanished; and without a word,
I rose and drew in closer to my guide,   110
and it was on him that I set my eyes.
    And he began: "Son, follow in my steps;
let us go back; this is the point at which
the plain slopes down to reach its lowest bounds."
    Daybreak was vanquishing the dark's last hour,   115
which fled before it; in the distance, I
could recognize the trembling of the sea.
    We made our way across the lonely plain,
like one returning to a lost pathway,
who, till he finds it, seems to move in vain.   120
    When we had reached the point where dew contends
with sun and, under sea winds, in the shade,
wins out because it won't evaporate,
    my master gently placed both of his hands—
outspread—upon the grass; therefore, aware   125
of what his gesture and intention were,
    I reached and offered him my tear-stained cheeks;
and on my cheeks, he totally revealed
the color that Inferno had concealed.
    Then we arrived at the deserted shore,   130
which never yet had seen its waters coursed
by any man who journeyed back again.
    There, just as pleased another, he girt me.
O wonder! Where he plucked the humble plant
that he had chosen, there that plant sprang up   135
again, identical, immediately.

---

7. Cato was freed during the Harrowing of Hell (see *Inferno* 4.52) and is now unmoved by the sufferings
of those left behind. *The evil river:* Acheron.   8. The rush is a symbol of humility.

CANTO II

*Ante-Purgatory. Dawn on the shore of the island mountain. The sudden
light upon the sea. The helmsman angel and the boat full of arriving
souls. The encounter with Casella, Dante's friend. Casella's singing. Cato's
rebuke. The simile of the doves.*

By now[9] the sun was crossing the horizon
of the meridian whose highest point
covers Jerusalem; and from the Ganges,
    night, circling opposite the sun, was moving
together with the Scales that, when the length   5
of dark defeats the day, desert night's hands;
    so that, above the shore that I had reached,
the fair Aurora's white and scarlet cheeks
were, as Aurora aged, becoming orange.
    We still were by the sea, like those who think   10
about the journey they will undertake,
who go in heart but in the body stay.
    And just as Mars, when it is overcome
by the invading mists of dawn, glows red
above the waters' plain, low in the west,   15
    so there appeared to me—and may I see it
again—a light that crossed the sea: so swift,
there is no flight of bird to equal it.
    When, for a moment, I'd withdrawn my eyes
that I might ask a question of my guide,   20
I saw that light again, larger, more bright.
    Then, to each side of it, I saw a whiteness,
though I did not know what that whiteness was;
below, another whiteness slowly showed.
    My master did not say a word before   25
the whitenesses first seen appeared as wings;
but then, when he had recognized the helmsman,
    he cried: "Bend, bend your knees: behold the angel
of God, and join your hands; from this point on,
this is the kind of minister you'll meet.   30
    See how much scorn he has for human means;
he'd have no other sail than his own wings
and use no oar between such distant shores.
    See how he holds his wings, pointing to Heaven,
piercing the air with his eternal pinions,   35
which do not change as mortal plumage does."
    Then he—that bird divine—as he drew closer
and closer to us, seemed to gain in brightness,
so that my eyes could not endure his nearness,
    and I was forced to lower them; and he   40
came on to shore with boat so light, so quick

9. These opening nine lines designate the time by reference to Jerusalem (where the sun is setting), the Ganges (where it is midnight, and where the constellation Libra—the scales—is in the sky), and Mount Purgatory (where the dawn—Aurora—is gradually reddening).

that nowhere did the water swallow it.
  The helmsman sent from Heaven, at the stern,
seemed to have blessedness inscribed upon him;
more than a hundred spirits sat within.   45
  "In exitu Isräel de Aegypto,"[1]
with what is written after of that psalm,
all of those spirits sang as with one voice.
  Then over them he made the holy cross
as sign; they flung themselves down on the shore,   50
and he moved off as he had come—swiftly.
  The crowd that he had left along the beach
seemed not to know the place; they looked about
like those whose eyes try out things new to them.
  Upon all sides the sun shot forth the day;   55
and from mid-heaven its incisive arrows
already had chased Capricorn[2] away,
  when those who'd just arrived lifted their heads
toward us and said: "Do show us, if you know,
the way by which we can ascend this slope."   60
  And Virgil answered: "You may be convinced
that we are quite familiar with this shore;
but we are strangers here, just as you are;
  we came but now, a little while before you,
though by another path, so difficult   65
and dense that this ascent seems sport to us."
  The souls who, noticing my breathing, sensed
that I was still a living being, then,
out of astonishment, turned pale; and just
  as people crowd around a messenger   70
who bears an olive branch, to hear his news,
and no one hesitates to join that crush,
  so here those happy spirits—all of them—
stared hard at my face, just as if they had
forgotten to proceed to their perfection.   75
  I saw one of those spirits moving forward
in order to embrace me—his affection
so great that I was moved to mime his welcome.
  O shades—in all except appearance—empty!
Three times I clasped my hands behind him and   80
as often brought them back against my chest.[3]
  Dismay, I think, was painted on my face;
at this, that shadow smiled as he withdrew;
and I, still seeking him, again advanced.
  Gently, he said that I could now stand back;   85
then I knew who he was, and I beseeched
him to remain awhile and talk with me.
  He answered: "As I loved you when I was
within my mortal flesh, so, freed, I love you:

---

1. When Israel went out of Egypt (Latin). The initial verse of Psalms 113 (114 in Protestant Bibles), which is a song of thanksgiving for the liberation of the Israelites in Exodus.   2. This constellation has now passed beyond the horizon.   3. On the thwarted embrace of Aeneas and Anchisës, see *Aeneid* 6.

therefore I stay. But you, why do you journey?"   90
"My own Casella, to return again
to where I am, I journey thus;⁴ but why,"
I said, "were you deprived of so much time?"
And he: "No injury is done to me
if he who takes up whom—and when—he pleases   95
has kept me from this crossing many times,
for his own will derives from a just will.⁵
And yet, for three months now, he has accepted,
most tranquilly, all those who would embark.⁶
Therefore, I, who had turned then to the shore   100
at which the Tiber's waters mix with salt,⁷
was gathered in by his benevolence.
Straight to that river mouth, he set his wings:
that always is the place of gathering
for those who do not sink to Acheron."⁸   105
And I: "If there's no new law that denies
you memory or practice of the songs
of love that used to quiet all my longings,
then may it please you with those songs to solace
my soul somewhat; for—having journeyed here   110
together with my body—it is weary."
"Love that discourses to me in my mind"⁹
he then began to sing—and sang so sweetly
that I still hear that sweetness sound in me.
My master, I, and all that company   115
around the singer seemed so satisfied,
as if no other thing might touch our minds.
We all were motionless and fixed upon
the notes, when all at once the grave old man¹
cried out: "What have we here, you laggard spirits?   120
What negligence, what lingering is this?
Quick, to the mountain to cast off the slough
that will not let you see God show Himself!"
Even as doves, assembled where they feed,
quietly gathering their grain or weeds,   125
forgetful of their customary strut,
will, if some thing appears that makes them fear,
immediately leave their food behind
because they are assailed by greater care;
so did I see that new-come company—   130
they left the song behind, turned toward the slope,
like those who go and yet do not know where.
And we were no less hasty in departure.

---

4. He journeys now so that after death he may return to purgatory. Casella, a Florentine musician, was said to have set some of Dante's lyrics to music. The question that follows assumes that Casella died well before the present moment.   **5.** The angel who chooses the souls to cross in his boat is directed by God. **6.** Pope Boniface proclaimed 1300—the year of the poem's action—a Jubilee or Holy Year, when those making pilgrimage to Rome were granted release from punishments for their sins (see *Inferno* 18, 28). Dante follows popular belief in assuming that this grant applies to the souls awaiting transport to Purgatory as well as to the living.   **7.** At Ostia, where the Tiber enters the sea.   **8.** Hell.   **9.** The first line of a lyric that Dante included in his prose philosophical work, the *Convivio*, which he left incomplete, interrupted in 1307 or thereabouts.   **1.** Cato.

CANTO XXI

The Fifth Terrace: the Avaricious and the Prodigal. The appearance of Statius. Virgil's explanation of Dante's and his presence in Purgatory. Statius' explanation of the earthquake and the exultation. Statius on himself and on his love for the Aeneid. *Dante's embarrassment, then his introduction of Virgil to Statius. Statius' reverence for Virgil.*

The natural thirst that never can be quenched
except by water that gives grace—the draught
the simple woman of Samaria sought[2]—
tormented me; haste spurred me on the path
crowded with souls, behind my guide; and I   5
felt pity, though their pain was justified.
　　And here—even as Luke records for us
that Christ, new-risen from his burial cave,
appeared to two along his way[3]—a shade
　　appeared; and he advanced behind our backs   10
while we were careful not to trample on
the outstretched crowd.[4] We did not notice him
　　until he had addressed us with: "God give
you, o my brothers, peace!" We turned at once;
then, after offering suitable response,   15
　　Virgil began: "And may that just tribunal
which has consigned me to eternal exile
place you in peace within the blessed assembly!"
　　"What!" he exclaimed, as we moved forward quickly.
"If God's not deemed you worthy of ascent,   20
who's guided you so far along His stairs?"
　　"If you observe the signs the angel traced
upon this man,"[5] my teacher said, "you'll see
plainly—he's meant to reign with all the righteous;
　　but since she who spins night and day had not   25
yet spun the spool that Clotho set upon
the distaff and adjusts for everyone,[6]
　　his soul, the sister of your soul and mine,
in its ascent, could not—alone—have climbed
here, for it does not see the way we see.   30
　　Therefore, I was brought forth from Hell's broad jaws
to guide him in his going; I shall lead
him just as far as where I teach can reach.
　　But tell me, if you can, why, just before,
the mountain shook and shouted, all of it—   35
for so it seemed—down to its sea-bathed shore."
　　His question threaded so the needle's eye

2. The thirst for knowledge can be quenched only by divine revelation. In the previous canto Dante has heard a cry of exultation and felt Mount Purgatory shake; it is the meaning of these events that he wishes to know. See John 4.5–15.   3. Luke 24.13–17.   4. The avaricious are punished by being bound prone to the Earth since they worshiped earthly things in life.   5. Before Dante entered Purgatory proper, an angel traced seven *P*s upon his forehead, one for each deadly sin (*peccatum* in Latin): see *Purgatorio* 9.112–14. The marks disappear one by one as he climbs the mountain and passes through each of the seven terraces appointed for the purgation of a sin.   6. According to classical mythology, the three Fates determine the span of a person's life: Clotho holds the spool, Lachesis spins the thread, and Atropos cuts it at the predestined time.

of my desire that just the hope alone
of knowing left my thirst more satisfied.
  That other shade began: "The sanctity   40
of these slopes does not suffer anything
that's without order or uncustomary.
  This place is free from every perturbation:[7]
what heaven from itself and in itself
receives may serve as cause here—no thing else.   45
  Therefore, no rain, no hail, no snow, no dew,
no hoarfrost falls here any higher than
the stairs of entry with their three brief steps;[8]
  neither thick clouds nor thin appear, nor flash
of lightning; Thaumas' daughter,[9] who so often   50
shifts places in your world, is absent here.
  Dry vapor cannot climb up any higher
than to the top of the three steps of which
I spoke—where Peter's vicar[1] plants his feet.
  Below that point, there may be small or ample   55
tremors; but here above, I know not why,
no wind concealed in earth has ever caused
  a tremor; for it only trembles here
when some soul feels it's cleansed, so that it rises
or stirs to climb on high; and that shout follows.   60
  The will alone is proof of purity
and, fully free, surprises soul into
a change of dwelling place—effectively.
  Soul had the will to climb before, but that
will was opposed by longing to do penance   65
(as once, to sin), instilled by divine justice.
  And I, who have lain in this suffering
five hundred years and more, just now have felt
my free will for a better threshold: thus,
  you heard the earthquake and the pious spirits   70
throughout the mountain as they praised the Lord—
and may He send them speedily upward."
  So did he speak to us; and just as joy
is greater when we quench a greater thirst,
the joy he brought cannot be told in words.   75
  And my wise guide: "I now can see the net
impeding you, how one slips through, and why
it quakes here, and what makes you all rejoice.
  And now may it please you to tell me who
you were, and in your words may I find why   80
you've lain here for so many centuries."[2]
  "In that age when the worthy Titus, with
help from the Highest King, avenged the wounds

---

7. Purgatory is free from any earthly influence, and therefore any change must be caused by motion from
above.   8. To reach the gate of Purgatory proper one must climb three steps, which represent the three
stages of penance: contrition of heart, confession of mouth, and satisfaction by deeds (see *Purgatorio* 9.94–
102).   9. Iris, goddess of the rainbow.   1. The angel who guards the entrance to Purgatory and who
marked Dante's forehead.   2. The spirit reveals himself to be Statius (d. A.D. 96), a Roman poet who
composed the *Thebaid* and the unfinished *Achilleid*.

from which the blood that Judas sold had flowed,[3]
I had sufficient fame beyond," that spirit   85
replied; "I bore the name that lasts the longest
and honors most—but faith was not yet mine.[4]
    So gentle was the spirit of my verse
that Rome drew me, son of Toulouse,[5] to her,
and there my brow deserved a crown of myrtle.   90
    On earth my name is still remembered—Statius:
I sang of Thebes and then of great Achilles;
I fell along the way of that last labor.
    The sparks that warmed me, the seeds of my ardor,
were from the holy fire—the same that gave   95
more than a thousand poets light and flame.
    I speak of the Aeneid; when I wrote
verse, it was mother to me, it was nurse;
my work, without it, would not weigh an ounce.
    And to have lived on earth when Virgil lived—   100
for that I would extend by one more year
the time I owe before my exile's end."
    These words made Virgil turn to me, and as
he turned, his face, through silence, said: "Be still"
(and yet the power of will cannot do all,   105
for tears and smiles are both so faithful to
the feelings that have prompted them that true
feeling escapes the will that would subdue).
    But I smiled like a man whose eyes would signal;
at this, the shade was silent, and he stared   110
where sentiment is clearest—at my eyes—
and said: "So may your trying labor end
successfully, do tell me why—just now—
your face showed me the flashing of a smile."
    Now I am held by one side and the other: 115
one keeps me still, the other conjures me
to speak; but when, therefore, I sigh, my master
    knows why and tells me: "Do not be afraid
to speak, but speak and answer what he has
asked you to tell him with such earnestness."   120
    At this, I answered: "Ancient spirit, you
perhaps are wondering at the smile I smiled:
but I would have you feel still more surprise.
    He who is guide, who leads my eyes on high,
is that same Virgil from whom you derived   125
the power to sing of men and of the gods.
    Do not suppose my smile had any source
beyond the speech you spoke; be sure—it was
those words you said of him that were the cause."
    Now he had bent to kiss my teacher's feet,   130
but Virgil told him: "Brother, there's no need—
you are a shade, a shade is what you see."

---

3. The destruction of Jerusalem in A.D. 70 by the Roman Titus was understood by Christians to be a divine
punishment for the crucifixion of Christ.   4. He was a poet but not yet a Christian.   5. A city in
southern France; Statius actually came from Naples, but Dante is following a medieval tradition.

And, rising, he: "Now you can understand
how much love burns in me for you, when I
forget our insubstantiality,   135
treating the shades as one treats solid things."

FROM CANTO XXII

*From the Fifth to the Sixth Terrace: the Gluttonous. The angel of justice.
First part of the Fourth Beatitude. Ascent to the Sixth Terrace. Statius:
his true sin, prodigality; his conversion. Virgil on the other souls in
Limbo.*

The angel now was left behind us, he
who had directed us to the sixth terrace,
having erased one *P* that scarred my face;[6]
he had declared that those who longed for justice
are blessed, and his voice concluded that   5
message with *"sitiunt,"* without the rest.[7]
And while I climbed behind the two swift spirits,
not laboring at all, for I was lighter
than I had been along the other stairs,[8]
Virgil began: "Love that is kindled by   10
virtue, will, in another, find reply,
as long as that love's flame appears without;[9]
so, from the time when Juvenal,[1] descending
among us, in Hell's Limbo, had made plain
the fondness that you felt for me, my own   15
benevolence toward you has been much richer
than any ever given to a person
one has not seen; thus, now these stairs seem short.
But tell me (and, as friend, forgive me if
excessive candor lets my reins relax   20
and, as a friend, exchange your words with me):
how was it that you found within your breast
a place for avarice, when you possessed
the wisdom you had nurtured with such care?"
These words at first brought something of a smile   25
to Statius; then he answered: "Every word
you speak, to me is a dear sign of love.
Indeed, because true causes are concealed,
we often face deceptive reasoning
and things provoke perplexity in us.   30
Your question makes me sure that you're convinced—
perhaps because my circle was the fifth—
that, in the life I once lived, avarice

---

6. The erased *P* was for avarice, the sin cleansed on the fifth terrace.   7. The angel quotes the beginning
of the Fourth Beatitude from the Sermon on the Mount, "Blessed are they which do hunger and thirst after
righteousness: for they shall be filled" (Matthew 5.6). He mentions only "thirst" (*sitiunt* in Latin), omitting
hunger, which will appear at the end of the journey through the sixth terrace, where gluttony is purged.
8. Dante grows lighter as he is gradually relieved of the sins, symbolized by the *P*s on his forehead, that
weigh him down.   9. Virtuous love, such as Statius displayed at the end of canto 21, will elicit a similar
response.   1. A Roman poet, contemporary with Statius but who outlived him (dying about A.D. 140),
located with Virgil in Limbo, as described in *Inferno* 4.

had been my sin. Know then that I was far
from avarice—it was my lack of measure[2]   35
thousands of months have punished. And if I
    had not corrected my assessment by
my understanding what your verses meant
when you, as if enraged by human nature,
    exclaimed: 'Why cannot you, o holy hunger   40
for gold, restrain the appetite of mortals?'[3]—
I'd now, while rolling weights, know sorry jousts.[4]
    Then I became aware that hands might open
too wide, like wings, in spending; and of this,
as of my other sins, I did repent.   45
    How many are to rise again with heads
cropped close,[5] whom ignorance prevents from reaching
repentance in—and at the end of—life!
    And know that when a sin is countered by
another fault—directly opposite   50
to it—then, here, both sins see their green wither.[6]
    Thus, I join those who pay for avarice
in my purgation, though what brought me here
was prodigality—its opposite."
    "Now, when you sang the savage wars of those   55
twin sorrows of Jocasta,"[7] said the singer
of the bucolic poems,[8] "it does not seem—
    from those notes struck by you and Clio[9] there—
that you had yet turned faithful to the faith
without which righteous works do not suffice.   60
    If that is so, then what sun or what candles
drew you from darkness so that, in their wake,
you set your sails behind the fisherman?"[1]
    And he to him: "You were the first to send me
to drink within Parnassus'[2] caves and you,   65
the first who, after God, enlightened me.
    You did as he who goes by night and carries
the lamp behind him—he is of no help
to his own self but teaches those who follow—
    when you declared: 'The ages are renewed;   70
justice and man's first time on earth return;
from Heaven a new progeny descends.'[3]

---

2. Prodigality, a vice that is opposite to avarice but its counterpart as an excess in the use of money; in
Inferno 7 the avaricious and the prodigal are punished together.   3. Statius is quoting *Aeneid* 3.   4. Be
punished in the fourth circle of Hell, described in *Inferno* 7.   5. The close-cropped heads of the prodigal
are described in *Inferno* 7.57.   6. Statius uses a vegetative metaphor: sin is green when vigorous, but it
withers in Purgatory.   7. Statius's *Thebaid* deals with the history of Thebes: Jocasta's husband, Laius,
was unwittingly killed by their son, Oedipus, who then—again in ignorance—married Laius's widow, Oedipus's own mother. Their sons, Polynices and Eteocles, imprisoned their father in a dungeon and then
fought over the throne of Thebes in a war in which they killed each other. It is this fratricidal war, in which
Jocasta lost both her sons at once, to which Virgil refers.   8. Virgil is here identified not as the epic poet
of the *Aeneid* but as the pastoral or bucolic poet of the *Eclogues* and the *Georgics*.   9. The Muse of
history, whom Statius invokes in the *Thebaid*.   1. I.e., followed Peter, a fisherman who became a fisher
of men (see Mark 1.17).   2. Dante follows a tradition that takes Parnassus, a mountain in Greece, as
the home of the Muses.   3. A slightly altered citation from Virgil's *Fourth Eclogue*. A pastoral poem
written about 40 B.C., it celebrated the birth of the son of an important Roman politician but was taken by
medieval Christians as a prophecy of the birth of Christ.

Through you I was a poet and, through you,
a Christian; but that you may see more plainly,
I'll set my hand to color what I sketch. 75
Disseminated by the messengers
of the eternal kingdom,[4] the true faith
by then had penetrated all the world,
and the new preachers preached in such accord
with what you'd said (and I have just repeated), 80
that I was drawn into frequenting them.
Then they appeared to me to be so saintly
that, when Domitian[5] persecuted them,
my own laments accompanied their grief;
and while I could—as long as I had life— 85
I helped them, and their honest practices
made me disdainful of all other sects.
Before—within my poem—I'd led the Greeks
unto the streams of Thebes,[6] I was baptized;
but out of fear, I was a secret Christian 90
and, for a long time, showed myself as pagan;
for this halfheartedness, for more than four
centuries, I circled the fourth circle.[7]
And now may you, who lifted up the lid
that hid from me the good of which I speak, 95
while time is left us as we climb, tell me
where is our ancient Terence, and Caecilius
and Plautus, where is Varius,[8] if you know;
tell me if they are damned, and in what quarter."
"All these and Persius, I, and many others," 100
my guide replied, "are with that Greek to whom
the Muses gave their gifts in greatest measure.
Our place is the blind prison, its first circle;
and there we often talk about the mountain
where those who were our nurses always dwell. 105
Euripides is with us, Antiphon,
Simonides, and Agathon,[9] as well
as many other Greeks who once wore laurel
upon their brow; and there—of your own people—
one sees Antigone, Deiphyle, 110
Ismene, sad still, Argia as she was.
There one can see the woman who showed Langia,
and there, Tiresias' daughter; there is Thetis;
and, with her sister, there, Deidamia."[1]
Both poets now were silent, once again 115
intent on their surroundings—they were free
of stairs and walls; with day's first four handmaidens[2]
already left behind, and with the fifth

---

4. The apostles.   **5.** Roman emperor, A.D. 81–91; thought by early Christian historians to have persecuted Christians, but there is little evidence for this.   **6.** The *Thebaid* describes how six Greek rulers
joined with Polynices to invade Thebes and topple Eteocles from the throne.   **7.** Where sloth is purged.
8. These men and Persius (line 100) are Roman poets now in Limbo with Homer (lines 101–2).   **9.** Greek
dramatists.   **1.** Characters from Statius's *Thebaid* and *Achilleid,* which Dante considered historical epics.
2. The hours, the fifth of which is guiding the chariot of the sun: it is between 10 and 11 A.M.

guiding the chariot-pole and lifting it,
so that its horn of flame rose always higher,   120
my master said: "I think it's time that we
turn our right shoulders toward the terrace edge,
circling the mountain in the way we're used to."[3]
In this way habit served us as a banner;
and when we chose that path, our fear was less   125
because that worthy soul gave his assent.
Those two were in the lead; I walked alone,
behind them, listening to their colloquy,
which taught me much concerning poetry.[4]

FROM CANTO XXIV

Summary   Dante is still on the sixth terrace, where gluttony is purged. He meets
Bonagiunta Orbicciani, a poet of the second half of the thirteenth century who was
evidently acquainted with Dante's early lyrics. (In a literary treatise written prior to
The Divine Comedy, Dante criticized Bonagiunta's poetic language for being too specialized and therefore not contributing to the creation of an Italian literary language
that would be accessible to all educated readers.) This selection begins with Bonagiunta speaking.

*   *   *

"But tell me if the man whom I see here
is he who brought the new rhymes forth, beginning: 50
'*Ladies who have intelligence of love.*' "[5]
I answered: "I am one who, when Love breathes
in me, takes note; what he, within, dictates,
I, in that way, without, would speak and shape."
"O brother, now I see," he said, "the knot   55
that kept the Notary, Guittone, and me
short of the sweet new manner[6] that I hear.
I clearly see how your pens follow closely
behind him who dictates,[7] and certainly
that did not happen with our pens; and he   60
who sets himself to ferreting profoundly
can find no other difference between
the two styles." He fell still, contentedly.

FROM CANTO XXVI

Summary   Dante is now on the seventh and final terrace, where lust is purged
with fire. He speaks with one of the souls, who describes the rationale of the purgation
and then responds to Dante's curiosity about the identities of these souls.

---

3. Mount Purgatory is climbed by turning to the right; the travelers descended into Hell by turning to the
left.   **4.** The canto continues with a new episode, not relevant to the literary issues that have so far
occupied it.   **5.** The first line of the first lyric in Dante's *New Life,* which tells the story in poetry and
prose of his transformation by his love for Beatrice.   **6.** The *dolce still novo* that Dante saw as charac-
terizing his own poetry and that was first defined for him by Guido Guinizzelli, whom he will meet in canto
26. The Notary (Giacomo da Lentini) and Guittone d'Arezzo, like Bonagiunta, were Italian poets of the
generation before Dante's.   **7.** Love.

"But with regard to me, I'll satisfy
your wish to know: I'm Guido Guinizzelli,[8]
purged here because I grieved before my end."
As, after the sad raging of Lycurgus,
two sons, finding their mother, had embraced her,[9]   95
so I desired to do—but dared not to—
when I heard him declare his name: the father
of me and of the others—those, my betters—
who ever used sweet, gracious rhymes of love.
And without hearing, speaking, pensive I,   100
walked on, still gazing at him, a long time,
prevented by the fire from drawing closer.
When I had fed my sight on him, I offered
myself—with such a pledge that others must
believe—completely ready for his service.[1]   105
And he to me: "Because of what I hear,
you leave a trace within me—one so clear,
Lethe[2] itself can't blur or cancel it.
But if your words have now sworn truthfully,
do tell me why it is that you have shown   110
in speech and gaze that I am dear to you."
And I to him: "It's your sweet lines that, for
as long as modern usage lasts, will still
make dear their very inks." "Brother," he said,
"he there, whom I point out to you"[3]—he showed   115
us one who walked ahead—"he was a better
artisan of the mother tongue, surpassing
all those who wrote their poems of love or prose
romances—let the stupid ones contend,
who think that from Limoges there came the best.[4]   120
They credit rumor rather than the truth,
allowing their opinion to be set
before they hear what art or reason says.
So, many of our fathers once persisted,
voice after voice, in giving to Guittone[5]   125
the prize—but then, with most, the truth prevailed.
Now if you are so amply privileged
that you will be admitted to the cloister
where Christ is abbot of the college, then
pray say, for me, to Him, a Paternoster[6]—   130
that is, as much of it as those in this
place need, since we have lost the power to sin."
Then, to make place, perhaps, for those behind him,
he disappeared into the fire, just as
a fish, through water, plunges toward the bottom.   135

8. Bolognese poet (d. ca. 1276), considered the greatest Italian poet prior to Dante. A poem by him is included in *Medieval Lyrics: A Selection* (pp. 1813–14).   9. In an episode in Statius's *Thebaid*, a woman condemned to death by the warrior Lycurgus is saved at the last moment by the arrival of her twin sons. 1. Dante here swears an oath to Guinizzelli to which the reader is not given access.   2. The river of forgetfulness that the fully purged souls will pass through in order to renounce their earthly lives.   3. Guinizzelli is indicating Arnaut Daniel (d. ca. 1210), Provençal poet. A poem by him is included in *Medieval Lyrics: A Selection* (pp. 1808–9).   4. The reference is to Giraut de Borneil (d. ca. 1220), another Provençal poet.   5. See *Purgatorio* 24, 56.   6. The Lord's Prayer.

Saying that my desire was making ready
a place of welcome for his name, I moved
ahead a little, toward the one who had
been pointed out to me. And he spoke freely:[7]
"So does your courteous request please me—   140
I neither could nor would conceal myself
from you. I am Arnaut, who, going, weep
and sing; with grief, I see my former folly;
with joy, I see the hoped-for day draw near.
Now, by the Power that conducts you to   145
the summit of the stairway, I pray you:
remember, at time opportune, my pain!"
Then, in the fire that refines, he hid.

FROM CANTO XXVII

Summary   Dante, Virgil, and Statius pass through the refining fire. Dante then
sleeps.

And now, with the reflected lights that glow
before the dawn[8] and, rising, are most welcome   110
to pilgrims as, returning, they near home,
the shadows fled upon all sides; my sleep
fled with them; and at this, I woke and saw
that the great teachers had already risen.
"Today your hungerings will find their peace   115
through that sweet fruit the care of mortals seeks
among so many branches."[9] This, the speech,
the solemn words, that Virgil spoke to me;
and there were never tidings to compare,
in offering delight to me, with these.   120
My will on will to climb above was such
that at each step I took I felt the force
within my wings was growing for the flight.
When all the staircase lay beneath us and
we'd reached the highest step, then Virgil set   125
his eyes insistently on me and said:
"My son, you've seen the temporary fire
and the eternal fire;[1] you have reached
the place past which my powers cannot see.
I've brought you here through intellect and art;   130
from now on, let your pleasure be your guide;
you're past the steep and past the narrow paths.
Look at the sun that shines upon your brow;
look at the grasses, flowers, and the shrubs
born here, spontaneously, of the earth.   135
Among them, you can rest or walk until
the coming of the glad and lovely eyes—
those eyes that, weeping, sent me to your side.[2]

---

7. In the original, Arnaut speaks not in Italian but in Provençal.   8. The morning stars.   9. On this day Dante will enter the Earthly Paradise and find Beatrice, who will conduct him through Paradise. 1. Purgatory and Hell.   2. See *Inferno* 2.55–74.

Await no further word or sign from me:
your will is free, erect, and whole—to act   140
against that will would be to err: therefore
I crown and miter you over yourself."

FROM CANTO XXX

Summary   Dante has arrived at the earthly paradise on the top of Mount Purgatory and finally sees Beatrice, drawn in a chariot as the centerpiece of an elaborate pageant. These lines describe his first exchange with her.

*   *   *

I have at times seen all the eastern sky
becoming rose as day began and seen,
adorned in lovely blue, the rest of heaven;
   and seen the sun's face rise so veiled that it   25
was tempered by the mist and could permit
the eye to look at length upon it; so,
   within a cloud of flowers that were cast
by the angelic hands[3] and then rose up
and then fell back, outside and in the chariot,   30
   a woman showed herself to me; above
a white veil, she was crowned with olive boughs;
her cape was green; her dress beneath, flame-red.[4]
   Within her presence, I had once been used
to feeling—trembling—wonder, dissolution;   35
but that was long ago.[5] Still, though my soul,
   now she was veiled, could not see her directly,
by way of hidden force that she could move,
I felt the mighty power of old love.
   As soon as that deep force had struck my vision   40
(the power that, when I had not yet left
my boyhood,[6] had already transfixed me),
   I turned around and to my left—just as
a little child, afraid or in distress,
will hurry to his mother—anxiously,   45
   to say to Virgil: "I am left with less
than one drop of my blood that does not tremble:
I recognize the signs of the old flame."[7]
   But Virgil had deprived us of himself,
Virgil, the gentlest father, Virgil, he   50
to whom I gave my self for my salvation;[8]
   and even all our ancient mother[9] lost
was not enough to keep my cheeks, though washed
with dew, from darkening again with tears.
   "Dante, though Virgil's leaving you, do not   55

---

3. The chariot is accompanied by messengers of eternal life.   4. The colors of her clothing are symbolic: white signifies hope; green, faith; and red, charity.   5. Beatrice died in 1290, so it has been ten years since Dante saw her.   6. Dante was nine when he fell in love with Beatrice.   7. A quotation from Virgil's *Aeneid* 4; it is Dido's response upon first seeing Aeneas.   8. This tercet echoes Virgil's *Georgics* 4.525–27, in which Orpheus looks back and laments the loss of Eurydice.   9. Eve, who caused the loss of the Eden in which Dante is now located.

yet weep, do not weep yet; you'll need your tears
for what another sword must yet inflict."[1]
Just like an admiral who goes to stern
and prow to see the officers who guide
the other ships, encouraging their tasks;   60
so, on the left side of the chariot
(I'd turned around when I had heard my name—
which, of necessity, I transcribe here),
I saw the lady who had first appeared
to me beneath the veils of the angelic   65
flowers look at me across the stream.
Although the veil she wore—down from her head,
which was encircled by Minerva's leaves—
did not allow her to be seen distinctly,
her stance still regal and disdainful, she   70
continued, just as one who speaks but keeps
until the end the fiercest parts of speech:
"Look here! For I am Beatrice, I am!
How were you able to ascend the mountain?
Did you not know that man is happy here?"   75
My lowered eyes caught sight of the clear stream,
but when I saw myself reflected there,
such shame weighed on my brow, my eyes drew back
and toward the grass; just as a mother seems
harsh to her child, so did she seem to me—   80
how bitter is the savor of stern pity!
Her words were done.

From Paradiso

FROM CANTO XXXIII

Summary   Dante has been led by Beatrice and other guides to the highest point
of the universe, the Empyrean. The final canto of the poem begins with a prayer by
Bernard of Clairvaux (1091–1153), abbot of the monastery of Clairvaux in France
and one of the great spiritual leaders and mystical writers of the Middle Ages. Bernard
is present here both as a mystic and because of the role his writings played in developing the cult of the Virgin Mary.

"Virgin mother, daughter of your Son,
more humble and sublime than any creature,
fixed goal decreed from all eternity,
you are the one who gave to human nature
so much nobility that its Creator   5
did not disdain His being made its creature.
That love whose warmth allowed this flower[2] to bloom
within the everlasting peace—was love
rekindled in your womb; for us above,

1. The sharp words Beatrice will now speak.   2. In *Paradiso* 30 Dante saw the blessed souls arranged
in a vast rose, to which Bernard now refers.

you are the noonday torch of charity,   10
and there below, on earth, among the mortals,
you are a living spring of hope. Lady,
    you are so high, you can so intercede,
that he who would have grace but does not seek
your aid, may long to fly but has no wings.   15
    Your loving-kindness does not only answer
the one who asks, but it is often ready
to answer freely long before the asking.
    In you compassion is, in you is pity,
in you is generosity, in you   20
is every goodness found in any creature.
    This man—who from the deepest hollow in
the universe, up to this height, has seen
the lives of spirits, one by one—now pleads
    with you, through grace, to grant him so much virtue 25
that he may lift his vision higher still—
may lift it toward the ultimate salvation.
    And I, who never burned for my own vision
more than I burn for his, do offer you
all of my prayers—and pray that they may not   30
    fall short—that, with your prayers, you may disperse
all of the clouds of his mortality
so that the Highest Joy be his to see.
    This, too, o Queen, who can do what you would,
I ask of you: that after such a vision,   35
his sentiments preserve their perseverance.
    May your protection curb his mortal passions.
See Beatrice—how many saints with her!
They join my prayers! They clasp their hands to you!"
    The eyes that are revered and loved by God,   40
now fixed upon the supplicant, showed us
how welcome such devotions are to her;
    then her eyes turned to the Eternal Light—
there, do not think that any creature's eye
can find its way as clearly as her sight.   45
    And I, who now was nearing Him who is
the end of all desires, as I ought,
lifted my longing to its ardent limit.
    Bernard was signaling—he smiled—to me
to turn my eyes on high; but I, already   50
was doing what he wanted me to do,
    because my sight, becoming pure, was able
to penetrate the ray of Light more deeply—
that Light, sublime, which in Itself is true.
    From that point on, what I could see was greater   55
than speech can show: at such a sight, it fails—
and memory fails when faced with such excess.
    As one who sees within a dream, and, later,
the passion that had been imprinted stays,
but nothing of the rest returns to mind,   60
    such am I, for my vision almost fades

completely, yet it still distills within
my heart the sweetness that was born of it.
    So is the snow, beneath the sun, unsealed;[3]
and so, on the light leaves, beneath the wind,   65
the oracles the Sibyl wrote were lost.[4]
    O Highest Light, You, raised so far above
the minds of mortals, to my memory
give back something of Your epiphany,
    and make my tongue so powerful that I   70
may leave to people of the future one
gleam of the glory that is Yours, for by
    returning somewhat to my memory
and echoing awhile within these lines,
Your victory will be more understood.   75
    The living ray that I endured was so
acute that I believe I should have gone
astray had my eyes turned away from it.
    I can recall that I, because of this,
was bolder in sustaining it until   80
my vision reached the Infinite Goodness.
    O grace abounding, through which I presumed
to set my eyes on the Eternal Light
so long that I spent all my sight on it!
    In its profundity I saw—ingathered   85
and bound by love into one single volume—
what, in the universe, seems separate, scattered:
    substances, accidents, and dispositions[5]
as if conjoined—in such a way that what
I tell is only rudimentary.   90
    I think I saw the universal shape
which that knot takes; for, speaking this, I feel
a joy that is more ample. That one moment
    brings more forgetfulness to me than twenty-
five centuries have brought to the endeavor   95
that startled Neptune with the *Argo*'s shadow![6]
    So was my mind—completely rapt, intent,
steadfast, and motionless—gazing; and it
grew ever more enkindled as it watched.
    Whoever sees that Light is soon made such   100
that it would be impossible for him
to set that Light aside for other sight;
    because the good, the object of the will,
is fully gathered in that Light; outside
that Light, what there is perfect is defective.   105
    what little I recall is to be told,
from this point on, in words more weak than those
of one whose infant tongue still bathes at the breast.

---

3. Melted.   **4.** In *Aeneid* 3 Virgil describes how the Sibyl of Cumae writes down the future on leaves
that the wind then scatters.   **5.** In the philosophical tradition followed by Dante, a *substance* is that
which subsists in and of itself, an *accident* exists only as a quality or an attribute of a substance, and their
disposition is the way substances and accidents are bound together.   **6.** The voyage of Jason and the
Argonauts after the golden fleece was thought to have occurred about 1300 B.C.; see *Inferno* 18.86–87.

And not because more than one simple semblance
was in the Living Light at which I gazed—   110
for It is always what It was before—
    but through my sight, which as I gazed grew stronger,
that sole appearance, even as I altered,
seemed to be changing. In the deep and bright
    essence of that exalted Light, three circles[7]   115
appeared to me; they had three different colors,
but all of them were of the same dimension;
    one circle seemed reflected by the second,
as rainbow is by rainbow, and the third
seemed fire breathed equally by those two circles.   120
    How incomplete is speech, how weak, when set
against my thought! And this, to what I saw
is such—to call it little is too much.
    Eternal Light, You only dwell within
Yourself, and only You know You; Self-knowing,   125
Self-known, You love and smile upon Yourself!
    That circle—which, begotten so, appeared
in You as light reflected—when my eyes
had watched it with attention for some time,
    within itself and colored like itself,   130
to me seemed painted with our effigy,[8]
so that my sight was set on it completely.
    As the geometer intently seeks
to square the circle, but he cannot reach,
through thought on thought, the principle he needs,[9]   135
    so I searched that strange sight: I wished to see
the way in which our human effigy
suited the circle and found place in it—
    and my own wings were far too weak for that.
But then my mind was struck by light that flashed   140
and, with this light, received what it had asked.
    Here force failed my high fantasy;[1] but my
desire and will were moved already—like
a wheel revolving uniformly—by
    the Love that moves the sun and the other stars.[2]   145

---

7. Signifying the Trinity.   8. Dante seems to see a human image in the center of the Godhead.   9. The
problem of constructing a square equal in area to a circle is a proverbially insoluble mathematical problem.
1. By *fantasy* Dante means the capacity of the mind to form images; it is *high* because it is capable of
representing in visible form invisible truths.   2. As in the *Inferno* and the *Purgatorio*, the last word of
the *Paradiso* is *stars*, returning us to the perspective of the human gazing up at that which is beyond the
human.

GIOVANNI BOCCACCIO
1313–1375

The *Decameron* by Giovanni Boccaccio has a reputation as a ribald classic, and certainly many of its stories—including some selected here—deal with sexual misadventures. But it also gathers into its hundred stories the diversity and energy that made fourteenth-century Italy one of the great cultural resources of medieval Europe. With his predecessor Dante and his slightly older contemporary Petrarch, Boccaccio established Italy and specifically Florence as a center of literary production that influenced European writing for centuries.

Boccaccio was born in Tuscany, probably in Florence, to a merchant and banker who did not marry the child's mother until some five years later. At fourteen he was taken to Naples, where his father made him spend six years studying arithmetic and then, when it became clear that Boccaccio would not make a successful merchant, another six years preparing for a career as a lawyer. But this enterprise also failed, for Boccaccio was drawn to the sophisticated circle of writers and scholars that the ruler of southern Italy, Robert of Anjou, had assembled into a court that was the most advanced cultural center of its time. Although known to modern readers almost exclusively through the *Decameron,* Boccaccio wrote primarily either courtly tales of love in Italian verse or learned treatises on subjects such as history, classical mythology, and geography in Latin prose. Along with Petrarch, Boccaccio was one of the many medieval writers who worked to revive the literary heritage of the classical world. In a poem called the *Teseida* he produced the first vernacular version of a classical epic, initiating a tradition that was to culminate in Milton's *Paradise Lost,* and he sponsored the first translation of Homer from Greek (in this case into Latin). The humanism that was to come to fruition in the Renaissance finds one of its most important medieval inspirations in the work of Boccaccio.

The *Decameron* represents another aspect of Boccaccio's literary personality. Locating the collection, written between 1350 and 1353, in a specific historical context, Boccaccio first describes the devastating effects of the bubonic plague of 1348–50 on Florence. Indeed, while the plague killed at least one-third of the European population (as well as millions elsewhere in the world), in Florence the death rate was as high as 70 percent. For Boccaccio the effect of this unprecedented disaster was the destruction of both the social fabric of the city and the moral restraints on individual behavior. In response, he posits an alternative society by describing how seven young ladies of good family are joined by three young men and retreat from the ravaged city to a beautiful country estate, where they restore themselves with well-regulated pleasures. Among their recreations is a tale-telling game: for ten days each member of the group tells a story, creating the hundred stories that comprise the *Decameron.* But if Boccaccio presents these tales as an alternative to the social and moral collapse of plague-stricken Florence, he also insists that their goal is above all to give pleasure. In this he sets his work in opposition to that of one of his own literary heroes, Dante. Much of Boccaccio's work is heavily influenced by Dante, and near the end of his life he both wrote a treatise celebrating Dante and delivered a set of lectures commenting in detail on the first twenty-eight cantos of the *Inferno.* Yet the *Decameron* is an implicitly anti-Dantean work. Its division into one hundred tales echoes Dante's division of his *Comedy* into one hundred cantos, and Boccaccio gives his work an alternative title—"Prince Galeotto"—that refers to a crucial moment in the *Inferno.* In canto 5 of the *Inferno* Francesca explains to Dante that she and her brother-in-law Paolo fell in love while reading the story of Lancelot and Guinevere. She blames the book for their fall, calling it a Galeotto: she is referring to the knight in the Arthurian court who served as a go-between for the lovers. Dante is implying here that reading, and especially reading for pleasure, can be morally dangerous. Yet

Boccaccio insists by his subtitle, and throughout the *Decameron* as a whole, that literature can provide a pleasure that is not merely legitimate but restorative.

Many different kinds of pleasure are both described in and made available by the *Decameron*. The most obvious pleasure the characters enjoy is sexual, and the sixth story of the ninth day is a characteristic example of Boccaccio's frank celebration of the joys of sex. But the story—a version of a tale that also survives as a French fabliau, which may have been the form in which Boccaccio first heard it—is also typical in its cheerful insistence that no harm has been done, and even the duped father and husband are treated with genial warmth. The story is typical as well in its celebration of values associated with the vigorous merchant class from which Boccaccio derived and that was largely dominant in Italy. The story describes a world of bewildering fluctuation. One of the literary pleasures it provides its readers is the plotting out of movements from bed to bed that occur during the night. To do so is to see that the baby's cradle is both the narrative device that makes the amorous events of the night possible and a metaphor for the circulation of sexual favors, much as commodities circulate throughout the mercantile world. Indeed, to succeed in the world of this story, as in commerce, requires a quick wit, a flexible sense of propriety, and an alertness to one's own self-interest without a vengeful desire to harm others that might make permanent enemies. On the whole the *Decameron* celebrates just this pragmatic and relativistic value system, refusing to endow any single set of values with ultimate authority. If one story teaches one lesson, then the next will teach a contradictory one, and readers are allowed to decide for themselves where true value is to be found.

In this relativism Boccaccio's *Decameron* is very different from Dante's *Divine Comedy*. Dante is an absolutist: he insists throughout his great work that there *is* a single truth, and the multiplicitous details of the poem are controlled by the authoritative coherence of Christian doctrine. But without being in any sense unmindful of the claims of religion—Boccaccio was certainly a fully devout Christian—the *Decameron* describes a much more multifarious, much less easily judged world than does *The Divine Comedy*. The first story tells of a thoroughgoing rogue, Ser Cepperello, who provides an outrageously false deathbed confession to a credulous and self-seeking friar. But while Cepperello seems to damn himself by his impenitent mockery of the salvation offered by the Church, we are aware that he is acting out of charitable motives in trying to protect his Florentine friends. So it becomes difficult to know if the townspeople are entirely wrong in thinking he is a saint. And we are also aware that the good deed performed is itself an act of tale-telling, and a tale that is both an outrageous lie and a pleasure to read. On the other side, the story of Nastagio and the hunt of love (the eighth story of the fifth day) presents a scene straight out of the *Inferno*: a scornful lady is eternally hunted down and eviscerated by her suicidal lover. Are we to think that here divine justice is being done? The context in which the scene is placed might give us pause. Used by Nastagio to persuade his lady to accept him as a lover, this scene reveals both the emotional absolutism of the courtly lover—as does the ninth story of the fourth day, in which the noble lady commits suicide in order to remain magnificently true to her lover—but also its cruelty and violence. Finally, these complexities are brought together in the story of Griselda (the tenth story of the tenth day), which proved to be one of the most popular stories of the later Middle Ages (both Petrarch and Chaucer produced versions). Is Griselda a saint of patience who is finally rewarded for her virtue? Or is she an unreasonably passive creature who solicits her own victimization? Is Walter a monster, a tyrant both politically and domestically, and the story a psychological study of despotism? Or is he an agent of God who makes possible the revelation of Griselda's superhuman virtue, or perhaps even God himself? In this fascinating puzzle of a story, Boccaccio poses questions without providing any obvious answer, showing us that perhaps the deepest pleasure that literature can offer is the pleasure of interpretation.

Vittore Branca, *Boccaccio: The Man and His Works* (1975), is the standard biography with useful literary commentary; for guides to the *Decameron*, see Giuseppe

Mazzotta, *The World at Play in Boccaccio's Decameron* (1986), and David Wallace, *Giovanni Boccaccio: Decameron* (1991).

The following list uses common English syllables to provide rough equivalents of selected words whose pronunciation may be unfamiliar to the general reader.

Cepperello Dietaiuti: *chep-er-el-lo dee-tie-yu-tee*

Giannùcole: *gee-an-ooh'-co-lay*

Gualtieri: *gwal-tee'-e-ree*

Guido degli Anastagi: *gwee'-do day'-lee an-as-ta'-jee*

Guillaume de Cabestanh: *ghee-ohm' de cab-es-stan'*

Guillaume de Rousillon: *ghee-ohm' de roo-see-yonh*

Musciatto: *mus-chee-at'-to*

Nastagio degli Onesti: *nas-taj'-io day'-lee on-es'-tee*

Paolo Traversari: *pow'-lo tra-ver-sa'-ree*

Pinuccio: *pin-ooch'-ee-o*

The Decameron[1]

[THE FIRST STORY OF THE FIRST DAY]

Ser Cepperello deceives a holy friar with a false confession, then he dies; and although in life he was a most wicked man, in death he is reputed to be a Saint, and is called Saint Ciappelletto.

It is proper, dearest ladies,[2] that everything made by man should begin with the sacred and admirable name of Him that was maker of all things. And therefore, since I[3] am the first and must make a beginning to our story-telling, I propose to begin by telling you of one of His marvellous works, so that, when we have heard it out, our hopes will rest in Him as in something immutable, and we shall forever praise His name. It is obvious that since all temporal things are transient and mortal, so they are filled and surrounded by troubles, trials and tribulations, and fraught with infinite dangers which we, who live with them and are part of them, could without a shadow of a doubt neither endure, nor defend ourselves against, if God's special grace did not lend us strength and discernment. Nor should we suppose that His grace descends upon and within us through any merit of our own, for it is set in motion by His own loving-kindness, and is obtained by the pleas of people who like ourselves were mortal, and who, by firmly doing His pleasure whilst they were in this life, have now joined Him in eternal blessedness. To these, as to advocates made aware, through experience, of our frailty (perhaps because we have not the courage to submit our pleas personally in the presence of so great a judge) we present whatever we think is relevant to our cause. And our regard for Him, who is so compassionate and generous towards us, is all the greater when, the human eye being quite unable to penetrate the secrets of divine intelligence, common opinion

---

1. Translated by G. H. McWilliam.   2. The tale is addressed to the seven ladies of the group that has escaped the plague in Florence.   3. The speaker is Panfilo, one of the three young men in the group of ten.

deceives us and perhaps we appoint as our advocate in His majestic presence one who has been cast by Him into eternal exile. Yet He from whom nothing is hidden, paying more attention to the purity of the supplicant's motives than to his ignorance or to the banishment of the intercessor, answers those who pray to Him exactly as if the advocate were blessed in His sight. All of which can clearly be seen in the tale I propose to relate; and I say clearly because it is concerned, not with the judgement of God, but with that of men.

It is said, then, that Musciatto Franzesi,[4] having become a fine gentleman after acquiring enormous wealth and fame as a merchant in France, was obliged to come to Tuscany with the brother of the French king, the Lord Charles Lackland,[5] who had been urged and encouraged to come by Pope Boniface. But finding that his affairs, as is usually the case with merchants, were entangled here, there, and everywhere, and being unable quickly or easily to unravel them, he decided to place them in the hands of a number of different people. All this he succeeded in arranging, except that he was left with the problem of finding someone capable of recovering certain loans which he had made to various people in Burgundy.[6] The reason for his dilemma was that he had been told the Burgundians were a quarrelsome, thoroughly bad and unprincipled set of people; and he was quite unable to think of anyone he could trust, who was at the same time sufficiently villainous to match the villainy of the Burgundians. After devoting much thought to this problem, he suddenly recalled a man known as Ser Cepperello, of Prato,[7] who had been a frequent visitor to his house in Paris. This man was short in stature and used to dress very neatly, and the French, who did not know the meaning of the word Cepperello, thinking that it signified *chapel,* which in their language means "garland," and because as we have said he was a little man, used to call him, not Ciappello, but Ciappelletto: and everywhere in that part of the world, where few people knew him as Ser Cepperello, he was known as Ciappelletto.[8]

This Ciappelletto was a man of the following sort: a notary by profession, he would have taken it as a slight upon his honor if one of his legal deeds (and he drew up very few of them) were discovered to be other than false. In fact, he would have drawn up free of charge as many false documents as were requested of him, and done it more willingly than one who was highly paid for his services. He would take great delight in giving false testimony, whether asked for it or not. In those days, great reliance was placed in France upon sworn declarations, and since he had no scruples about swearing falsely, he used to win, by these nefarious means, every case in which he was required to swear upon his faith to tell the truth. He would take particular pleasure, and a great amount of trouble, in stirring up enmity, discord and bad blood between friends, relatives and anybody else; and the more calamities that ensued, the greater would be his rapture. If he were invited

---

4. Like many other characters in the *Decameron,* those appearing in this first story are based on actual people. Musciatto was a Florentine financier who made a huge fortune in France by dubious means; Cepperello Dietaiuti was one of his associates.   5. Brother of King Philip of France, who invaded Italy in 1301.   6. A region of northeastern France.   7. A city just to the north of Florence.   8. This nickname assumes that Ciappello's name derives from the Italian word *ceppo* ("log" or "tree-stump"), and the suffix *-etto* is a diminutive. Hence the name means "little stump," which may have an obscene connotation.

to witness a murder or any other criminal act, he would never refuse, but willingly go along; and he often found himself cheerfully assaulting or killing people with his own hands. He was a mighty blasphemer of God and His Saints, losing his temper on the tiniest pretext, as if he were the most hot-blooded man alive. He never went to church, and he would use foul language to pour scorn on all of her sacraments, declaring them repugnant. On the other hand, he would make a point of visiting taverns and other places of ill repute, and supplying them with his custom. Of women he was as fond as dogs are fond of a good stout stick; in their opposite, he took greater pleasure than the most depraved man on earth. He would rob and pilfer as conscientiously as if he were a saintly man making an offering. He was such a prize glutton and heavy drinker, that he would occasionally suffer for his over-indulgence in a manner that was most unseemly. He was a gambler and a card-sharper of the first order. But why do I lavish so many words upon him? He was perhaps the worst man ever born. Yet for all his villainy, he had long been protected by the power and influence of Messer Musciatto, on whose account he was many a time treated with respect, both by private individuals, whom he frequently abused, and by the courts of law, which he was forever abusing.

So that when Musciatto, who was well acquainted with his way of living, called this Ser Ciappelletto to mind, he judged him to be the very man that the perverseness of the Burgundians required. He therefore sent for him and addressed him as follows:

"Ser Ciappelletto, as you know, I am about to go away from here altogether, but I have some business to settle, amongst others with the Burgundians. These people are full of tricks, and I know of no one better fitted than yourself to recover what they owe me. And so, since you are not otherwise engaged at present, if you will attend to this matter I propose to obtain favors for you at court, and allow you a reasonable portion of the money you recover."

Ser Ciappelletto, who was out of a job at the time and ill-supplied with worldly goods, seeing that the man who had long been his prop and stay was about to depart, made up his mind without delay and said (for he really had no alternative) that he would do it willingly. So that when they had agreed on terms, Ser Ciappelletto received powers of attorney from Musciatto and letters of introduction from the King, and after Musciatto's departure he went to Burgundy, where scarcely anybody knew him. And there, in a gentle and amiable fashion that ran contrary to his nature, as though he were holding his anger in reserve as a last resort, he issued his first demands and began to do what he had gone there to do. Before long, however, while lodging in the house of two Florentine brothers who ran a money-lending business there and did him great honor out of their respect for Musciatto, he happened to fall ill; whereupon the two brothers promptly summoned doctors and servants to attend him, and provided him with everything he needed to recover his health. But all their assistance was unavailing, because the good man, who was already advanced in years and had lived a disordered existence, was reported by his doctors to be going each day from bad to worse, like one who was suffering from a fatal illness. The two brothers were filled with alarm, and one day, alongside the room in which Ser Ciappelletto was lying, they began talking together.

"What are we to do about the fellow?" said one to the other. "We've landed ourselves in a fine mess on his account, because to turn him away from our house in his present condition would arouse a lot of adverse comment and show us to be seriously lacking in common sense. What would people say if they suddenly saw us evicting a dying man after giving him hospitality in the first place, and taking so much trouble to have him nursed and waited upon, when he couldn't possibly have done anything to offend us? On the other hand, he has led such a wicked life that he will never be willing to make his confession or receive the sacraments of the Church; and if he dies unconfessed, no church will want to accept his body and he'll be flung into the moat like a dog. But even if he makes his confession, his sins are so many and so appalling that the same thing will happen, because there will be neither friar nor priest who is either willing or able to give him absolution; in which case, since he will not have been absolved, he will be flung into the moat just the same. And when the townspeople see what has happened, they'll create a commotion, not only because of our profession which they consider iniquitous and never cease to condemn, but also because they long to get their hands on our money, and they will go about shouting: 'Away with these Lombard dogs[9] that the Church refuses to accept'; and they'll come running to our lodgings and perhaps, not content with stealing our goods, they'll take away our lives into the bargain. So we shall be in a pretty fix either way, if this fellow dies."

Ser Ciappelletto, who as we have said was lying near the place where they were talking, heard everything they were saying about him, for he was sharp of hearing, as invalids invariably are. So he called them in to him, and said:

"I don't want you to worry in the slightest on my account, nor to fear that I will cause you to suffer any harm. I heard what you were saying about me and I agree entirely that what you predict will actually come to pass, if matters take the course you anticipate; but they will do nothing of the kind. I have done our good Lord so many injuries whilst I lived, that to do Him another now that I am dying will be neither here nor there. So go and bring me the holiest and ablest friar you can find, if there is such a one, and leave everything to me, for I shall set your affairs and my own neatly in order, so that all will be well and you'll have nothing to complain of."

Whilst deriving little comfort from all this, the two brothers nevertheless went off to a friary and asked for a wise and holy man to come and hear the confession of a Lombard who was lying ill in their house. They were given an ancient friar of good and holy ways who was an expert in the Scriptures and a most venerable man, towards whom all the townspeople were greatly and specially devoted, and they conducted him to their house.

On reaching the room where Ser Ciappelletto was lying, he sat down at his bedside, and first he began to comfort him with kindly words, then he asked him how long it was since he had last been to confession. Whereupon Ser Ciappelletto, who had never been to confession in his life, replied:

"Father, it has always been my custom to go to confession at least once every week, except that there are many weeks in which I go more often. But to tell the truth, since I fell ill, nearly a week ago, my illness has caused me so much discomfort that I haven't been to confession at all."

---

9. Outside Italy, Italian bankers were known as Lombards, even if they came from a different province.

"My son," said the friar, "you have done well, and you should persevere in this habit of yours. Since you go so often to confession, I can see that there will be little for me to hear or to ask."

"Master friar," said Ser Ciappelletto, "do not speak thus, for however frequently or regularly I confess, it is always my wish that I should make a general confession of all the sins I can remember committing from the day I was born till the day of my confession. I therefore beg you, good father, to question me about everything, just as closely as if I had never been confessed. Do not spare me because I happen to be ill, for I would much rather mortify this flesh of mine than that, by treating it with lenience, I should do anything that could lead to the perdition of my soul, which my Saviour redeemed with His precious blood."

These words were greatly pleasing to the holy friar, and seemed to him proof of a well-disposed mind. Having warmly commended Ser Ciappelletto for this practice of his, he began by asking him whether he had ever committed the sin of lust with any woman. To which, heaving a sigh, Ser Ciappelletto replied:

"Father, I am loath to tell you the truth on this matter, in case I should sin by way of vainglory."

To which the holy friar replied:

"Speak out freely, for no man ever sinned by telling the truth, either in confession or otherwise."

"Since you assure me that this is so," said Ser Ciappelletto, "I will tell you. I am a virgin as pure as on the day I came forth from my mother's womb."

"Oh, may God give you His blessing!" said the friar. "How nobly you have lived! And your restraint is all the more deserving of praise in that, had you wished, you would have had greater liberty to do the opposite than those who, like ourselves, are expressly forbidden by rule."

Next he asked him whether he had displeased God by committing the sin of gluttony; to which, fetching a deep sigh, Ser Ciappelletto replied that he had, and on many occasions. For although, apart from the periods of fasting normally observed in the course of the year by the devout, he was accustomed to fasting on bread and water for at least three days every week, he had drunk the water as pleasurably and avidly (especially when he had been fatigued from praying or going on a pilgrimage) as any great bibber of wine; he had often experienced a craving for those dainty little wild herb salads that women eat when they go away to the country; and sometimes the thought of food had been more attractive to him than he considered proper in one who, like himself, was fasting out of piety. Whereupon the friar said:

"My son, these sins are natural and they are very trivial, and therefore I would not have you burden your conscience with them more than necessary. No matter how holy a man may be, he will be attracted by the thought of food after a long spell of fasting, and by the thought of drink when he is fatigued."

"Oh!" said Ser Ciappelletto. "Do not tell me this to console me, father. As you are aware, I know that things done in the service of God must all be done honestly and without any grudge; and if anyone should do otherwise, he is committing a sin."

The friar, delighted, said to him:

"I am contented to see you taking such a view, and it pleases me greatly that you should have such a good and pure conscience in this matter. But tell me, have you ever been guilty of avarice, by desiring to have more than was proper, or keeping what you should not have kept?"

To which Ser Ciappelletto replied:

"Father, I would not wish you to judge me ill because I am in the house of these money-lenders. I have nothing to do with their business; indeed I had come here with the express intention of warning and reproaching them, and dissuading them from this abominable form of money-making; and I think I would have succeeded, if God had not stricken me in this manner. However, I would have you know that my father left me a wealthy man, and when he was dead, I gave the greater part of his fortune to charity. Since then, in order to support myself and enable me to assist the Christian poor, I have done a small amount of trading, in the course of which I have desired to gain, and I have always shared what I have gained with the poor, allocating one half to my own needs and giving the other half to them. And in this I have had so much help from my Creator that I have continually gone from strength to strength in the management of my affairs."

"You have done well," said the friar, "but tell me, how often have you lost your temper?"

"Oh!" said Ser Ciappelletto, "I can assure you I have done that very often. But who is there who could restrain himself, when the whole day long he sees men doing disgusting things, and failing to observe God's commandments, or to fear His terrible wrath? There have been many times in the space of a single day when I would rather have been dead than alive, looking about me and seeing young people frittering away their time, telling lies, going drinking in taverns, failing to go to church, and following the ways of the world rather than those of God."

"My son," said the friar, "this kind of anger is justified, and for my part I could not require you to do penance for it. But has it ever happened that your anger has led you to commit murder or to pour abuse on anyone or do them any other form of injury?"

To which Ser Ciappelletto replied:

"Oh, sir, however could you, that appear to be a man of God, say such a thing? If I had thought for a single moment of doing any of the things you mention, do you suppose I imagine that God would have treated me so generously? Those things are the business of cut-throats and evildoers, and whenever I have chanced upon one of their number, I have always sent him packing, and offered up a prayer for his conversion!"

"May God give you His blessing," said the friar, "but now, tell me, my son: have you ever borne false witness against any man, or spoken ill of people, or taken what belonged to others without seeking their permission?"

"Never, sir, except on one occasion," replied Ser Ciappelletto, "when I spoke ill of someone. For I once had a neighbor who, without the slightest cause, was forever beating his wife, so that on this one occasion I spoke ill of him to his wife's kinsfolk, for I felt extremely sorry for that unfortunate woman. Whenever the fellow had had too much to drink, God alone could tell you how he battered her."

Then the friar said:

"Let me see now, you tell me you were a merchant. Did you ever deceive anyone, as merchants do?"

"Faith, sir, I did," said Ser Ciappelletto. "But all I know about him is that he was a man who brought me some money that he owed me for a length of cloth I had sold him. I put the money away in a box without counting it, and a whole month passed before I discovered there were four pennies more than there should have been. I kept them for a year with the intention of giving them back, but I never saw him again, so I gave them away to a beggar."

"That was a trivial matter," said the friar, "and you did well to dispose of the money as you did."

The holy friar questioned him on many other matters, but always he answered in similar vein, and hence the friar was ready to proceed without further ado to give him absolution. But Ser Ciappelletto said:

"Sir, I still have one or two sins I have not yet told you about."

The friar asked him what they were, and he said:

"I recall that I once failed to show a proper respect for the Holy Sabbath, by making one of my servants sweep the house after nones[1] on a Saturday."

"Oh!" said the friar. "This, my son, is a trifling matter."

"No, father," said Ser Ciappelletto, "you must not call it trifling, for the Sabbath has to be greatly honored, seeing that this was the day on which our Lord rose from the dead."

Then the friar said:

"Have you done anything else?"

"Yes, sir," replied Ser Ciappelletto, "for I once, without thinking what I was doing, spat in the house of God."

The friar began to smile, and said:

"My son, this is not a thing to worry about. We members of religious orders spit there continually."

"That is very wicked of you," said Ser Ciappelletto, "for nothing should be kept more clean than the holy temple in which sacrifice is offered up to God."

In brief, he told the friar many things of this sort, and finally he began to sigh, and then to wail loudly, as he was well able to do whenever he pleased.

"My son," said the holy friar. "What is the matter?"

"Oh alas, sir," replied Ser Ciappelletto, "I have one sin left to which I have never confessed, so great is my shame in having to reveal it; and whenever I remember it, I cry as you see me doing now, and feel quite certain that God will never have mercy on me for this terrible sin."

"Come now, my son," said the holy friar, "what are you saying? If all the sins that were ever committed by the whole of mankind, together with those that men will yet commit till the end of the world, were concentrated in one single man, and he was as truly repentant and contrite as I see you to be, God is so benign and merciful that He would freely remit them on their being confessed to Him; and therefore you may safely reveal it."

Then Ser Ciappelletto said, still weeping loudly:

"Alas, father, my sin is too great, and I can scarcely believe that God will ever forgive me for it, unless you intercede with your prayers."

To which the friar replied:

"You may safely reveal it, for I promise that I will pray to God on your behalf."

---

1. A church service held about 3 P.M.

Ser Ciappelletto went on weeping, without saying anything, and the friar kept encouraging him to speak. But after Ser Ciappelletto, by weeping in this manner, had kept the friar for a very long time on tenterhooks, he heaved a great sigh, and said:

"Father, since you promise that you will pray to God for me, I will tell you. You are to know then that once, when I was a little boy, I cursed my mother." And having said this, he began to weep loudly all over again.

"There now, my son," said the friar, "does this seem so great a sin to you? Why, people curse God the whole day long, and yet He willingly forgives those who repent for having cursed Him. Why then should you suppose He will not forgive you for this? Take heart and do not weep, for even if you had been one of those who set Him on the cross, I can see that you have so much contrition that He would certainly forgive you."

"Oh alas, father," said Ser Ciappelletto, "what are you saying? My dear, sweet mother, who carried me day and night for nine months in her body, and held me more than a hundred times in her arms! It was too wicked of me to curse her, and the sin is too great; and if you do not pray to God for me, it will never be forgiven me.'

Perceiving that Ser Ciappelletto had nothing more to say, the friar absolved him and gave him his blessing. He took him for a very saintly man indeed, being fully convinced that what Ser Ciappelletto had said was true; but then, who is there who would not have been convinced, on hearing a dying man talk in this fashion? Finally, when all this was done, he said to him:

"Ser Ciappelletto, with God's help you will soon be well again. But in case it were to happen that God should summon your blessed and well-disposed soul to His presence, are you willing for your body to be buried in our convent?"

To which Ser Ciappelletto replied:

"Yes, father. In fact, I would not wish to be elsewhere, since you have promised that you will pray to God for me. Besides, I have always been especially devoted to your Order. So when you return to your convent, I beg you to see that I am sent that true body of Christ which you consecrate every morning on the altar. For although I am unworthy of it, I intend with your permission to take it, and afterwards to receive the holy Extreme Unction,[2] so that, having lived as a sinner, I shall at least die as a Christian."

The holy man said that he was greatly pleased, that the words were well spoken, and that he would see it was brought to him at once; and so it was.

The two brothers, who strongly suspected that Ser Ciappelletto was going to deceive them, had posted themselves behind a wooden partition which separated the room where Ser Ciappelletto was lying from another, and as they stood there listening they could easily follow what Ser Ciappelletto was saying to the friar. When they heard the things he confessed to having done, they were so amused that every so often they nearly exploded with mirth, and they said to each other:

"What manner of man is this, whom neither old age nor illness, nor fear of the death which he sees so close at hand, nor even the fear of God, before whose judgement he knows he must shortly appear, have managed to turn

2. The sacrament in which a dying person is anointed by a priest.

from his evil ways, or persuade to die any differently from the way he has lived?"

Seeing, however, that he had said all the right things to be received for burial in a church, they cared nothing for the rest.

Shortly thereafter Ser Ciappelletto made his communion, and, failing rapidly, he received Extreme Unction. Soon after vespers[3] on the very day that he had made his fine confession, he died. Whereupon the two brothers made all necessary arrangements, using his own money to see that he had an honorable funeral, and sending news of his death to the friars and asking them to come that evening to observe the customary vigil, and the following morning to take away the body.

On hearing that he had passed away, the holy friar who had received his confession arranged with the prior for the chapterhouse bell to be rung, and to the assembled friars he showed that Ser Ciappelletto had been a saintly man, as his confession had amply proved. He expressed the hope that through him the Lord God would work many miracles, and persuaded them that his body should be received with the utmost reverence and loving care. Credulous to a man, the prior and the other friars agreed to do so, and that evening they went to the place where Ser Ciappelletto's body lay, and celebrated a great and solemn vigil over it; and in the morning, dressed in albs and copes,[4] carrying books in their hands and bearing crosses before them, singing as they went, they all came for the body, which they then carried back to their church with tremendous pomp and ceremony, followed by nearly all the people of the town, men and women alike. And when it had been set down in the church, the holy friar who had confessed him climbed into the pulpit and began to preach marvellous things about Ser Ciappelletto's life, his fasts, his virginity, his simplicity and innocence and saintliness, relating among other things what he had tearfully confessed to him as his greatest sin, and describing how he had barely been able to convince him that God would forgive him, at which point he turned to reprimand his audience, saying:

"And yet you miserable sinners have only to catch your feet in a wisp of straw for you to curse God and the Virgin and all the Saints in heaven."

Apart from this, he said much else about his loyalty and his purity of heart. And in brief, with a torrent of words that the people of the town believed implicitly, he fixed Ser Ciappelletto so firmly in the minds and affections of all those present that when the service was over, everyone thronged round the body to kiss his feet and his hands, all the clothes were torn from his back, and those who succeeded in grabbing so much as a tiny fragment felt they were in Paradise itself. He had to be kept lying there all day, so that everyone could come and gaze upon him, and on that same night he was buried with honor in a marble tomb in one of the chapels. From the next day forth, people began to go there to light candles and pray to him, and later they began to make votive offerings and to decorate the chapel with figures made of wax, in fulfilment of promises they had given.

The fame of his saintliness, and of the veneration in which he was held, grew to such proportions that there was hardly anyone who did not pray for

---

3. A church service held at eventide.   4. Albs and copes are religious vestments worn by priests while performing a religious ritual.

his assistance in time of trouble, and they called him, and call him still, Saint Ciappelletto. Moreover it is claimed that through him God has wrought many miracles, and that He continues to work them on behalf of whoever commends himself devoutly to this particular Saint.

It was thus, then, that Ser Cepperello of Prato lived and died, becoming a Saint in the way you have heard. Nor would I wish to deny that perhaps God has blessed and admitted him to His presence. For albeit he led a wicked, sinful life, it is possible that at the eleventh hour he was so sincerely repentant that God had mercy upon him and received him into His kingdom. But since this is hidden from us, I speak only with regard to the outward appearance, and I say that the fellow should rather be in Hell, in the hands of the devil, than in Paradise. And if this is the case, we may recognize how very great is God's loving-kindness towards us, in that it takes account, not of our error, but of the purity of our faith, and grants our prayers even when we appoint as our emissary one who is His enemy, thinking him to be His friend, as though we were appealing to one who was truly holy as our intercessor for His favor. And therefore, so that we, the members of this joyful company, may be guided safely and securely by His grace through these present adversities, let us praise the name of Him with whom we began our storytelling, let us hold Him in reverence, and let us commend ourselves to Him in the hour of our need, in the certain knowledge that we shall be heard. And there the narrator fell silent.

[THE NINTH STORY OF THE FOURTH DAY][5]

Guillaume de Roussillon causes his wife to eat the heart of her lover, Guillaume de Cabestanh,[6] whom he has secretly murdered. When she finds out, she kills herself by leaping from a lofty casement to the ground below, and is subsequently buried with the man she loved.

You must know, then, that according to the Provençals, there once lived in Provence two noble knights, each of whom owned several castles and had a number of dependants. The name of the first was Guillaume de Roussillon, whilst the other was called Guillaume de Cabestanh. Since both men excelled in feats of daring, they were bosom friends and made a point of accompanying one another to jousts and tournaments and other armed contests, each bearing the same device.[7]

Although the castles in which they lived were some ten miles apart, Guillaume de Cabestanh chanced to fall hopelessly in love with the charming and very beautiful wife of Guillaume de Roussillon, and, notwithstanding the bonds of friendship and brotherhood that united the two men, he managed in various subtle ways to bring his love to the lady's notice. The lady, knowing him to be a most gallant knight, was deeply flattered, and began to regard him with so much affection that there was nothing she loved or desired more deeply. All that remained for him to do was to approach her directly, which he very soon did, and from then on they met at frequent intervals for the purpose of making passionate love to one another.

---

5. This story is told by Dioneo, one of the young men.   6. The story is based on a poetic account of the love affair between an early thirteenth-century Provençal poet of this name and the wife of his lord, Raimon de Castel-Rousillon.   7. Coat of arms.

One day, however, they were incautious enough to be espied by the lady's husband, who was so incensed by the spectacle that his great love for Cabestanh was transformed into mortal hatred. He firmly resolved to do away with him, but concealed his intentions far more successfully than the lovers had been able to conceal their love.

His mind being thus made up, Roussillon happened to hear of a great tournament that was to be held in France. He promptly sent word of it to Cabestanh and asked him whether he would care to call upon him, so that they could talk it over together and decide whether or not to go and how they were to get there. Cabestanh was delighted to hear of it, and sent back word to say that he would come and sup with him next day without fail.

On receiving Cabestanh's message, Roussillon judged this to be his opportunity for killing him. Next day, he armed himself, took horse with a few of his men, and lay in ambush about a mile away from his castle, in a wood through which Cabestanh was bound to pass. After a long wait, he saw him approaching, unarmed, and followed by two of his men, who were likewise unarmed, for he never suspected for a moment that he was running into danger. Roussillon waited until Cabestanh was at close range, then he rushed out at him with murder and destruction in his heart, brandishing a lance above his head and shouting: "Traitor, you are dead!" And before the words were out of his mouth he had driven the lance through Cabestanh's breast.

Cabestanh was powerless to defend himself, or even to utter a word, and on being run through by the lance he fell to the ground. A moment later he was dead, and his men, without stopping to see who had perpetrated the deed, turned the heads of their horses and galloped away as fast as they could in the direction of their master's castle.

Dismounting from his horse, Roussillon cut open Cabestanh's chest with a knife, tore out the heart with his own hands, and, wrapping it up in a banderole,[8] told one of his men to take it away. Having given strict orders that no one was to breathe a word about what had happened, he then remounted and rode back to his castle, by which time it was already dark.

The lady had heard that Cabestanh was to be there that evening for supper and was eagerly waiting for him to arrive. When she saw her husband arriving without him she was greatly surprised, and said to him:

"And how is it, my lord, that Cabestanh has not come?"

To which her husband replied:

"Madam, I have received word from him that he cannot be here until tomorrow."

Roussillon left her standing there, feeling somewhat perturbed, and when he had dismounted, he summoned the cook and said to him:

"You are to take this boar's heart and see to it that you prepare the finest and most succulent dish you can devise. When I am seated at table, send it in to me in a silver tureen."

The cook took the heart away, minced it, and added a goodly quantity of fine spices, employing all his skill and loving care and turning it into a dish that was too exquisite for words.

When it was time for dinner, Roussillon sat down at the table with his lady. Food was brought in, but he was unable to do more than nibble at it

---

8. A long narrow flag or streamer.

because his mind was dwelling upon the terrible deed he had committed. Then the cook sent in his special dish, which Roussillon told them to set before his lady, saying that he had no appetite that evening.

He remarked on how delicious it looked, and the lady, whose appetite was excellent, began to eat it, finding it so tasty a dish that she ate every scrap of it.

On observing that his lady had finished it down to the last morsel, the knight said:

"What did you think of that, madam?"

"In good faith, my lord," replied the lady, "I liked it very much."

"So help me God," exclaimed the knight, "I do believe you did. But I am not surprised to find that you liked it dead, because when it was alive you liked it better than anything else in the whole world."

On hearing this, the lady was silent for a while; then she said:

"How say you? What is this that you have caused me to eat?"

"That which you have eaten," replied the knight, "was in fact the heart of Guillaume de Cabestanh, with whom you, faithless woman that you are, were so infatuated. And you may rest assured that it was truly his, because I tore it from his breast myself, with these very hands, a little before I returned home."

You can all imagine the anguish suffered by the lady on hearing such tidings of Cabestanh, whom she loved more dearly than anything else in the world. But after a while, she said:

"This can only have been the work of an evil and treacherous knight, for if, of my own free will, I abused you by making him the master of my love, it was not he but I that should have paid the penalty for it. But God forbid that any other food should pass my lips now that I have partaken of such excellent fare as the heart of so gallant and courteous a knight as Guillaume de Cabestanh."

And rising to her feet, she retreated a few steps to an open window, through which without a second thought she allowed herself to fall.

The window was situated high above the ground, so that the lady was not only killed by her fall but almost completely disfigured.

The spectacle of his wife's fall threw Roussillon into a panic and made him repent the wickedness of his deed. And fearing the wrath of the local people and of the Count of Provence, he had his horses saddled and rode away.

By next morning the circumstances of the affair had become common knowledge throughout the whole of the district, and people were sent out from the castles of the lady's family and of Guillaume de Cabestanh to gather up the two bodies, which were later placed in a single tomb in the chapel of the lady's own castle amid widespread grief and mourning. And the tombstone bore an inscription, in verse, to indicate who was buried there and the manner and the cause of their deaths.

[THE EIGHTH STORY[9] OF THE FIFTH DAY]

In his love for a young lady of the Traversari family, Nastagio degli Onesti squanders his wealth without being loved in return. He is entreated by his

---

9. The teller is Filomena, one of the young ladies.

friends to leave the city, and goes away to Classe, where he sees a girl being hunted down and killed by a horseman, and devoured by a brace of hounds. He then invites his kinsfolk and the lady he loves to a banquet, where this same girl is torn to pieces before the eyes of his beloved, who, fearing a similar fate, accepts Nastagio as her husband.

In Ravenna,[1] a city of great antiquity in Romagna, there once used to live a great many nobles and men of property, among them a young man called Nastagio degli Onesti, who had inherited an incredibly large fortune on the deaths of his father and one of his uncles. Being as yet unmarried, he fell in love, as is the way with young men, with a daughter of Messer Paolo Traversari, a girl of far more noble lineage than his own, whose love he hoped to win by dint of his accomplishments. But though these were very considerable, and splendid, and laudable, far from promoting his cause they appeared to damage it, inasmuch as the girl he loved was persistently cruel, harsh and unfriendly towards him. And on account possibly of her singular beauty, or perhaps because of her exalted rank, she became so haughty and contemptuous of him that she positively loathed him and everything he stood for.

All of this was so difficult for Nastagio to bear that he was frequently seized, after much weeping and gnashing of teeth, with the longing to kill himself out of sheer despair. But, having stayed his hand, he would then decide that he must give her up altogether, or learn if possible to hate her as she hated him. All such resolutions were unavailing, however, for the more his hopes dwindled, the greater his love seemed to grow.

As the young man persisted in wooing the girl and spending money like water, certain of his friends and relatives began to feel that he was in danger of exhausting both himself and his inheritance. They therefore implored and advised him to leave Ravenna and go to live for a while in some other place, with the object of curtailing both his wooing and his spending. Nastagio rejected this advice as often as it was offered, but they eventually pressed him so hard that he could not refuse them any longer, and agreed to do as they suggested. Having mustered an enormous baggage-train, as though he were intending to go to France or Spain or some other remote part of the world, he mounted his horse, rode forth from Ravenna with several of his friends, and repaired to a place which is known as Classe, some three miles distant from the city. Having sent for a number of tents and pavilions, he told his companions that this was where he intended to stay, and that they could all go back to Ravenna. So Nastagio pitched his camp in this place, and began to live in as fine and lordly a fashion as any man ever born, from time to time inviting various groups of friends to dine or breakfast with him, as had always been his custom.

Now, it so happened that one Friday morning towards the beginning of May, the weather being very fine, Nastagio fell to thinking about his cruel mistress. Having ordered his servants to leave him to his own devices so that he could meditate at greater leisure, he sauntered off, lost in thought, and his steps led him straight into the pinewoods. The fifth hour of the day was already spent, and he had advanced at least half a mile into the woods, oblivious of food and everything else, when suddenly he seemed to hear a

1. On the west coast of Italy.

woman giving vent to dreadful wailing and ear-splitting screams. His pleasant reverie being thus interrupted, he raised his head to investigate the cause, and discovered to his surprise that he was in the pinewoods. Furthermore, on looking straight ahead he caught sight of a naked woman, young and very beautiful, who was running through a dense thicket of shrubs and briars towards the very spot where he was standing. The woman's hair was dishevelled, her flesh was all torn by the briars and brambles, and she was sobbing and screaming for mercy. Nor was this all, for a pair of big, fierce mastiffs were running at the girl's heels, one on either side, and every so often they caught up with her and savaged her. Finally, bringing up the rear he saw a swarthy-looking knight, his face contorted with anger, who was riding a jet-black steed and brandishing a rapier, and who, in terms no less abusive than terrifying, was threatening to kill her.[2]

This spectacle struck both terror and amazement into Nastagio's breast, to say nothing of compassion for the hapless woman, a sentiment that in its turn engendered the desire to rescue her from such agony and save her life, if this were possible. But on finding that he was unarmed, he hastily took up a branch of a tree to serve as a cudgel, and prepared to ward off the dogs and do battle with the knight. When the latter saw what he was doing, he shouted to him from a distance:

"Keep out of this, Nastagio! Leave me and the dogs to give this wicked sinner her deserts!"

He had no sooner spoken than the dogs seized the girl firmly by the haunches and brought her to a halt. When the knight reached the spot he dismounted from his horse, and Nastagio went up to him saying:

"I do not know who you are, or how you come to know my name; but I can tell you that it is a gross outrage for an armed knight to try and kill a naked woman, and to set dogs upon her as though she were a savage beast. I shall do all in my power to defend her, of that you may be sure."

Whereupon the knight said:

"I was a fellow citizen of yours, Nastagio, my name was Guido degli Anastagi, and you were still a little child when I fell in love with this woman. I loved her far more deeply than you love that Traversari girl of yours, but her pride and cruelty led me to such a pass that, one day, I killed myself in sheer despair with this rapier that you see in my hand, and thus I am condemned to eternal punishment. My death pleased her beyond measure, but shortly thereafter she too died, and because she had sinned by her cruelty and by gloating over my sufferings, and was quite unrepentant, being convinced that she was more of a saint than a sinner, she too was condemned to the pains of Hell. No sooner was she cast into Hell than we were both given a special punishment, which consisted in her case of fleeing before me, and in my own of pursuing her as though she were my mortal enemy rather than the woman with whom I was once so deeply in love. Every time I catch up with her, I kill her with this same rapier by which I took my own life; then I slit her back open, and (as you will now observe for yourself) I tear from her body that hard, cold heart to which neither love nor pity could ever gain access, and together with the rest of her entrails I cast it to these dogs to feed upon.

"Within a short space of time, as ordained by the power and justice of God, she springs to her feet as though she had not been dead at all, and her ago-

---

2. Cf. the account of the punishment of the spendthrifts in Dante's *Inferno*, canto 13.

nizing flight begins all over again, with the dogs and myself in pursuit. Every Friday at this hour I overtake her in this part of the woods, and slaughter her in the manner you are about to observe; but you must not imagine that we are idle for the rest of the week, because on the remaining days I hunt her down in other places where she was cruel to me in thought and deed. As you can see for yourself, I am no longer her lover but her enemy, and in this guise I am obliged to pursue her for the same number of years as the months of her cruelty towards me. Stand aside, therefore, and let me carry out the judgement of God. Do not try to oppose what you cannot prevent."

On hearing these words, Nastagio was shaken to the core, there was scarcely a single hair on his head that was not standing on end, and he stepped back to fix his gaze on the unfortunate girl, waiting in fear and trembling to see what the knight would do to her. This latter, having finished speaking, pounced like a mad dog, rapier in hand, upon the girl, who was kneeling before him, held by the two mastiffs, and screaming for mercy at the top of her voice. Applying all his strength, the knight plunged his rapier into the middle of her breast and out again at the other side, whereupon the girl fell on her face, still sobbing and screaming, whilst the knight, having laid hold of a dagger, slashed open her back, extracted her heart and everything else around it, and hurled it to the two mastiffs, who devoured it greedily on the instant. But before very long the girl rose suddenly to her feet as though none of these things had happened, and sped off in the direction of the sea, being pursued by the dogs, who kept tearing away at her flesh as she ran. Remounting his horse, and seizing his rapier, the knight too began to give chase, and within a short space of time they were so far away that Nastagio could no longer see them.

For some time after bearing witness to these events, Nastagio stood rooted to the spot out of fear and compassion, but after a while it occurred to him that since this scene was enacted every Friday, it ought to prove very useful to him. So he marked the place and returned to his servants; and when the time seemed ripe, he sent for his friends and kinsfolk, and said to them:

"For some little time you have been urging me to desist from wooing this hostile mistress of mine and place a curb on my extravagance, and I am willing to do so on condition that you obtain for me a single favor, which is this: that on Friday next you arrange for Messer Paolo Traversari and his wife and daughter and all their womenfolk, together with any other lady you care to invite, to join me in this place for breakfast. My reason for wanting this will become apparent to you on the day itself."

They thought this a very trifling commission for them to undertake, and promised him they would do it. On their return to Ravenna, they invited all the people he had specified. And although they had a hard job, when the time came, in persuading Nastagio's beloved to go, she nevertheless went there along with the others.

Nastagio saw to it that a magnificent banquet was prepared, and had the tables placed beneath the pine-trees in such a way as to surround the place where he had witnessed the massacre of the cruel lady. Moreover, in seating the ladies and gentlemen at table, he so arranged matters that the girl he loved sat directly facing the spot where the scene would be enacted.

The last course had already been served, when they all began to hear the agonized yells of the fugitive girl. Everyone was greatly astonished and wanted to know what it was, but nobody was able to say. So they all stood up to see if they could find out what was going on, and caught sight of the wailing girl, together with the knight and the dogs. And shortly thereafter they came into the very midst of the company.

Everyone began shouting and bawling at the dogs and the knight, and several people rushed forward to the girl's assistance; but the knight, by repeating to them the story he had related to Nastagio, not only caused them to retreat but filled them all with terror and amazement. And when he dealt with the girl in the same way as before, all the ladies present (many of whom, being related either to the suffering girl or to the knight, still remembered his great love and the manner of his death) wept as plaintively as though what they had witnessed had been done to themselves.

When the spectacle was at an end, and the knight and the lady had gone, they all began to talk about what they had seen. But none was stricken with so much terror as the cruel maiden loved by Nastagio, for she had heard and seen everything distinctly and realized that these matters had more to do with herself than with any of the other guests, in view of the harshness she had always displayed towards Nastagio; consequently, she already had the sensation of fleeing before her enraged suitor, with the mastiffs tearing away at her haunches.

So great was the fear engendered within her by this episode, that in order to avoid a similar fate she converted her enmity into love; and, seizing the earliest opportunity (which came to her that very evening), she privily sent a trusted maidservant to Nastagio, requesting him to be good enough to call upon her, as she was ready to do anything he desired. Nastagio was overjoyed, and told her so in his reply, but added that if she had no objection he preferred to combine his pleasure with the preservation of her good name, by making her his lawful wedded wife.

Knowing that she alone was to blame for the fact that she and Nastagio were not already married, the girl readily sent him her consent. And so, acting as her own intermediary, she announced to her father and mother, to their enormous satisfaction, that she would be pleased to become Nastagio's wife. On the following Sunday Nastagio married her, and after celebrating their nuptials they settled down to a long and happy life together.

Their marriage was by no means the only good effect to be produced by this horrible apparition, for from that day forth the ladies of Ravenna in general were so frightened by it that they became much more tractable to men's pleasures than they had ever been in the past.

[THE SIXTH STORY OF THE NINTH DAY][3]

Two young men lodge overnight at a cottage, where one of them goes and sleeps with their host's daughter, whilst his wife inadvertently sleeps with the other. The one who was with the daughter clambers into bed beside her father, mistaking him for his companion, and tells him all about it. A great furor then ensues, and the wife, realizing her mistake, gets into her daughter's bed, whence with a timely explanation she restores the peace.

Not long ago, there lived in the valley of the Mugnone[4] a worthy man who earned an honest penny by supplying food and drink to wayfarers; and

---

3. The teller is Panfilo, one of the young men.　　4. This valley runs north from Florence into the Romagna.

although he was poor, and his house was tiny, he would from time to time, in cases of urgent need, offer them a night's lodging, but only if they happened to be people he knew.

Now, this man had a most attractive wife, who had borne him two children, the first being a charming and beautiful girl of about fifteen or sixteen, as yet unmarried, whilst the second was an infant, not yet twelve months old, who was still being nursed at his mother's breast.

The daughter had caught the eye of a lively and handsome young Florentine gentleman who used to spend much of his time in the countryside, and he fell passionately in love with her. Nor was it long before the girl, being highly flattered to have won the affection of so noble a youth, which she strove hard to retain by displaying the greatest affability towards him, fell in love with him. And neither of the pair would have hesitated to consummate their love, but for the fact that Pinuccio (for such was the young man's name) was not prepared to expose the girl or himself to censure.

At length however, his ardor growing daily more intense, Pinuccio was seized with a longing to consort with her, come what may, and it occurred to him that he must find some excuse for lodging with her father overnight, since, being conversant with the layout of the premises, he had good reason to think that he and the girl could be together without anyone ever being any the wiser. And no sooner did this idea enter his head than he promptly took steps to carry it into effect.

Late one afternoon, he and a trusted companion of his called Adriano, who knew of his love for the girl, hired a couple of pack-horses, and having laden them with a pair of saddlebags, filled probably with straw, they set forth from Florence; and after riding round in a wide circle they came to the valley of the Mugnone, some time after nightfall. They then wheeled their horses round to make it look as though they were returning from Romagna, rode up to the cottage of our worthy friend, and knocked at the door. And since the man was well acquainted with both Pinuccio and his companion, he immediately came down to let them in.

"You'll have to put us up for the night," said Pinuccio. "We had intended to reach Florence before dark, but as you can see, we've made such slow progress that this is as far as we've come, and it's too late to enter the city at this hour."

"My dear Pinuccio," replied the host, "as you know, I can't exactly offer you a princely sort of lodging. But no matter: since night has fallen and you've nowhere else to go, I shall be glad to put you up as best I can."

So the two young men dismounted, and having seen that their nags were comfortably stabled, they went into the house, where, since they had brought plenty to eat with them, they made a hearty supper along with their host. Now, their host had only one bedroom, which was very tiny, and into this he had crammed three small beds, leaving so little space that it was almost impossible to move between them. Two of the beds stood alongside one of the bedroom walls, whilst the third was against the wall on the opposite side of the room; and having seen that the least uncomfortable of the three was made ready for his guests, the host invited them to sleep in that for the night. Shortly afterwards, when they appeared to be asleep, though in reality they were wide awake, he settled his daughter in one of the other two beds, whilst he and his wife got into the third; and beside the bed in which she was sleeping, his wife had placed the cradle containing her infant son.

Having made a mental note of all these arrangements, Pinuccio waited until he was sure that everyone was asleep, then quietly left his bed, stole across to the bed in which his lady-love was sleeping, and lay down beside her. Although she was somewhat alarmed, the girl received him joyously in her arms, and they then proceeded to take their fill of that sweet pleasure for which they yearned above all else.

Whilst Pinuccio and the girl were thus employed, a cat, somewhere in the house, happened to knock something over, causing the man's wife to wake up with a start. Being anxious to discover what it was, she got up and groped her way naked in the dark towards that part of the house from which the noise had come.

Meanwhile Adriano also happened to get up, not for the same reason, but in order to obey the call of nature, and as he was groping his way towards the door with this purpose in view, he came in contact with the cradle deposited there by the woman. Being unable to pass without moving it out of his way, he picked it up and set it down beside his own bed; and after doing what he had to do, he returned to his bed and forgot all about it.

Having discovered the cause of the noise and assured herself that nothing important had fallen, the woman swore at the cat, and, without bothering to light a lamp and explore the matter further, returned to the bedroom. Picking her way carefully through the darkness, she went straight to the bed where her husband was lying; but on finding no trace of the cradle, she said to herself: "How stupid I am! What a fine thing to do! Heavens above, I was just about to step into the bed where my guests are sleeping." So she walked a little further up the room, found the cradle, and got into bed beside Adriano, thinking him to be her husband.

On perceiving this, Adriano, who was still awake, gave her a most cordial reception; and without a murmur he tacked hard to windward over and over again, much to her delight and satisfaction.

This, then, was how matters stood when Pinuccio, who had gratified his longings to the full and was afraid of falling asleep in the young lady's arms, abandoned her so as to go back and sleep in his own bed. But on reaching the bed to find the cradle lying there, he moved on, thinking he had mistaken his host's bed for his own, and ended up by getting into bed with the host, who was awakened by his coming. And being under the impression that the man who lay beside him was Adriano, Pinuccio said:

"I swear to you that there was never anything so delicious as Niccolosa. By the body of God, no man ever had so much pleasure with any woman as I have been having with her. Since the time I left you, I assure you I've been to the bower of bliss half a dozen times at the very least."

The host was not exactly pleased to hear Pinuccio's tidings, and having first of all asked himself what the devil the fellow was doing in his bed, he allowed his anger to get the better of his prudence, and exclaimed:

"What villainy is this, Pinuccio? I can't think why you should have played me so scurvy a trick, but by all that's holy, I shall pay you back for it."

Now, Pinuccio was not the wisest of young men, and on perceiving his error, instead of doing all he could to remedy matters, he said:

"Pay me back? How? What could you do to me?"

Whereupon the host's wife, thinking she was with her husband, said to Adriano:

"Heavens! Just listen to the way those guests of ours are arguing with one another!"

Adriano laughed, and said:

"Let them get on with it, and to hell with them. They had far too much to drink last night."

The woman had already thought she could detect the angry tones of her husband, and on hearing Adriano's voice, she realized at once whose bed she was sharing. So being a person of some intelligence, she promptly got up without a word, seized her baby's cradle, and having picked her way across the room, which was in total darkness, she set the cradle down beside the bed in which her daughter was sleeping and scrambled in beside her. Then, pretending to have been aroused by the noise her husband was making, she called out to him and demanded to know what he was quarrelling with Pinuccio about. Whereupon her husband replied:

"Don't you hear what he says he has done to Niccolosa this night?"

"He's telling a pack of lies," said the woman. "He hasn't been anywhere near Niccolosa, for I've been lying beside her myself the whole time and I haven't managed to sleep a wink. You're a fool to take any notice of him. You men drink so much in the evening that you spend the night dreaming and wandering all over the place in your sleep, and imagine you've performed all sorts of miracles: it's a thousand pities you don't trip over and break your necks! What's Pinuccio doing there anyway? Why isn't he in his own bed?"

At which point, seeing how adroitly the woman was concealing both her own and her daughter's dishonor, Adriano came to her support by saying:

"How many times do I have to tell you, Pinuccio, not to wander about in the middle of the night? You'll land yourself in serious trouble one of these days, with this habit of walking in your sleep, and claiming to have actually done the fantastic things you dream about. Come back to bed, curse you!"

When he heard Adriano confirm what his wife had been saying, the host began to think that Pinuccio really had been dreaming after all; and seizing him by the shoulder, he shook him and yelled at him, saying:

"Wake up, Pinuccio! Go back to your own bed!"

Having taken all of this in, Pinuccio now began to thresh about as though he were dreaming again, causing his host to split his sides with laughter. But in the end, after a thorough shaking, he pretended to wake up; and calling to Adriano, he said:

"Why have you woken me up? Is it morning already?"

"Yes," said Adriano. "Come back here."

Pinuccio kept up the pretence, showing every sign of being extremely drowsy, but in the end he left his host's side and staggered back to bed with Adriano. When they got up next morning, their host began to laugh and make fun of Pinuccio and his dreams. And so, amid a constant stream of merry banter, the two young men saddled and loaded their horses, and after drinking the health of their host, they remounted and rode back to Florence, feeling no less delighted with the manner than with the outcome of the night's activities.

From then on, Pinuccio discovered other ways of consorting with Niccolosa, who meanwhile assured her mother that he had certainly been dreaming. And thus the woman, who retained a vivid memory of Adriano's embraces, was left with the firm conviction that she alone had been awake on the night in question.

[THE TENTH STORY OF THE TENTH DAY][5]

The Marquis of Saluzzo, obliged by the entreaties of his subjects to take a wife, follows his personal whims and marries the daughter of a peasant. She bears him two children, and he gives her the impression that he has put them to death. Later on, pretending that she has incurred his displeasure and that he has remarried, he arranges for his own daughter to return home and passes her off as his bride, having meanwhile turned his wife out of doors in no more than the shift she is wearing. But on finding that she endures it all with patience, he cherishes her all the more deeply, brings her back to his house, shows her their children, who have now grown up, and honors her as the Marchioness, causing others to honor her likewise.

A very long time ago, there succeeded to the marquisate of Saluzzo[6] a young man called Gualtieri, who, having neither wife nor children, spent the whole of his time hunting and hawking, and never even thought about marrying or raising a family, which says a great deal for his intelligence. His followers, however, disapproved of this, and repeatedly begged him to marry so that he should not be left without an heir nor they without a lord. Moreover, they offered to find him a wife whose parentage would be such as to strengthen their expectations and who would make him exceedingly happy.

So Gualtieri answered them as follows:

"My friends, you are pressing me to do something that I had always set my mind firmly against, seeing how difficult it is to find a person who will easily adapt to one's own way of living, how many thousands there are who will do precisely the opposite, and what a miserable life is in store for the man who stumbles upon a woman ill-suited to his own temperament. Moreover it is foolish of you to believe that you can judge the character of daughters from the ways of their fathers and mothers, hence claiming to provide me with a wife who will please me. For I cannot see how you are to know the fathers, or to discover the secrets of the mothers; and even if this were possible, daughters are very often different from either of their parents. Since, however, you are so determined to bind me in chains of this sort, I am ready to do as you ask; but so that I have only myself to blame if it should turn out badly, I must insist on marrying a wife of my own choosing. And I hereby declare that no matter who she may be, if you fail to honor her as your lady you will learn to your great cost how serious a matter it is for you to have urged me to marry against my will."

To this the gentlemen replied that if only he would bring himself to take a wife, they would be satisfied.

Now, for some little time, Gualtieri had been casting an appreciative eye on the manners of a poor girl from a neighboring village, and thinking her very beautiful, he considered that a life with her would have much to commend it. So without looking further afield, he resolved to marry the girl; and

---

5. The teller is Dioneo, the young man who tells the last story of each day.   6. A town at the foot of the Alps about thirty miles south of Turin.

having summoned her father, who was very poor indeed, he arranged with him that he should take her as his wife.

This done, Gualtieri brought together all his friends from the various parts of his domain, and said to them:

"My friends, since you still persist in wanting me to take a wife, I am prepared to do it, not because I have any desire to marry, but rather in order to gratify your wishes. You will recall the promise you gave me, that no matter whom I should choose, you would rest content and honor her as your lady. The time has now come when I want you to keep that promise, and for me to honor the promise I gave to you. I have found a girl after my own heart, in this very district, and a few days hence I intend to marry her and convey her to my house. See to it, therefore, that the wedding-feast lacks nothing in splendor, and consider how you may honorably receive her, so that all of us may call ourselves contented—I with you for keeping your promise, and you with me for keeping mine."

As of one voice, the good folk joyously gave him their blessing, and said that whoever she happened to be, they would accept her as their lady and honor her as such in all respects. Then they all prepared to celebrate the wedding in a suitably grand and sumptuous manner, and Gualtieri did the same. A rich and splendid nuptial feast was arranged, to which he invited many of his friends, his kinsfolk, great nobles and other people of the locality; moreover he caused a quantity of fine, rich robes to be tailored to fit a girl whose figure appeared to match that of the young woman he intended to marry; and lastly he laid in a number of rings and ornamental belts, along with a precious and beautiful crown, and everything else that a bride could possibly need.

Early on the morning of the day he had fixed for the nuptials, Gualtieri, his preparations now complete, mounted his horse together with all the people who had come to do him honor, and said:

"Gentlemen, it is time for us to go and fetch the bride."

He then set forth with the whole of the company in train, and eventually they came to the village and made their way to the house of the girl's father, where they met her as she was returning with water from the fountain, making great haste so that she could go with other women to see Gualtieri's bride arriving. As soon as Gualtieri caught sight of her, he called to her by her name, which was Griselda, and asked her where her father was, to which she blushingly replied:

"My lord, he is at home."

So Gualtieri dismounted, and having ordered everyone to wait for him outside, he went alone into the humble dwelling, where he found the girl's father, whose name was Giannùcole, and said to him:

"I have come to marry Griselda, but first I want to ask her certain questions in your presence." He then asked her whether, if he were to marry her, she would always try to please him and never be upset by anything he said or did, whether she would obey him, and many other questions of this sort, to all of which she answered that she would.

Whereupon Gualtieri, having taken her by the hand, led her out of the house, and in the presence of his whole company and of all the other people there he caused her to be stripped naked. Then he called for the clothes and shoes which he had had specially made, and quickly got her to put them on, after which he caused a crown to be placed upon the dishevelled hair of her head. And just as everyone was wondering what this might signify, he said:

"Gentlemen, this is the woman I intend to marry, provided she will have me as her husband." Then, turning to Griselda, who was so embarrassed that she hardly knew where to look, he said: "Griselda, will you have me as your wedded husband?"

To which she replied:

"I will, my lord."

"And I will have you as my wedded wife," said Gualtieri, and he married her then and there before all the people present. He then helped her mount a palfrey, and led her back, honorably attended, to his house, where the nuptials were as splendid and as sumptuous, and the rejoicing as unrestrained, as if he had married the King of France's daughter.

Along with her new clothes, the young bride appeared to take on a new lease of life, and she seemed a different woman entirely. She was endowed, as we have said, with a fine figure and beautiful features, and lovely as she already was, she now acquired so confident, graceful and decorous a manner that she could have been taken for the daughter, not of the shepherd Giannùcole, but of some great nobleman, and consequently everyone who had known her before her marriage was filled with astonishment. But apart from this, she was so obedient to her husband, and so compliant to his wishes, that he thought himself the happiest and most contented man on earth. At the same time she was so gracious and benign towards her husband's subjects, that each and every one of them was glad to honor her, and accorded her his unselfish devotion, praying for her happiness, prosperity, and greater glory. And whereas they had been wont to say that Gualtieri had shown some lack of discretion in taking this woman as his wife, they now regarded him as the wisest and most discerning man on earth. For no one apart from Gualtieri could ever have perceived the noble qualities that lay concealed beneath her ragged and rustic attire.

In short, she comported herself in such a manner that she quickly earned widespread acclaim for her virtuous deeds and excellent character not only in her husband's domain but also in the world at large; and those who had formerly censured Gualtieri for choosing to marry her were now compelled to reverse their opinion.

Not long after she had gone to live with Gualtieri she conceived a child, and in the fullness of time, to her husband's enormous joy, she bore him a daughter. But shortly thereafter Gualtieri was seized with the strange desire to test Griselda's patience, by subjecting her to constant provocation and making her life unbearable.

At first he lashed her with his tongue, feigning to be angry and claiming that his subjects were thoroughly disgruntled with her on account of her lowly condition, especially now that they saw her bearing children; and he said they were greatly distressed about this infant daughter of theirs, of whom they did nothing but grumble.

The lady betrayed no sign of bitterness on hearing these words, and without changing her expression she said to him:

"My lord, deal with me as you think best[7] for your own good name and

---

7. See Luke 1.38, where the Virgin Mary replies to the Angel Gabriel, "Be it unto me according to thy word."

peace of mind, for I shall rest content whatever you decide, knowing myself to be their inferior and that I was unworthy of the honor which you so generously bestowed upon me."

This reply was much to Gualtieri's liking, for it showed him that she had not been puffed with pride by any honor that he or others had paid her.

A little while later, having told his wife in general terms that his subjects could not abide the daughter she had borne him, he gave certain instructions to one of his attendants, whom he sent to Griselda. The man looked very sorrowful, and said:

"My lady, if I do not wish to die, I must do as my lord commands me. He has ordered me to take this daughter of yours, and to . . ." And his voice trailed off into silence.

On hearing these words and perceiving the man's expression, Griselda, recalling what she had been told, concluded that he had been instructed to murder her child. So she quickly picked it up from its cradle, kissed it, gave it her blessing, and albeit she felt that her heart was about to break, placed the child in the arms of the servant without any trace of emotion, saying:

"There: do exactly as your lord, who is my lord too, has instructed you. But do not leave her to be devoured by the beasts and the birds, unless that is what he has ordered you to do."

The servant took away the little girl and reported Griselda's words to Gualtieri, who, marvelling at her constancy, sent him with the child to a kinswoman of his in Bologna,[8] requesting her to rear and educate her carefully, but without ever making it known whose daughter she was.

Then it came about that his wife once more became pregnant, and in due course she gave birth to a son, which pleased Gualtieri enormously. But not being content with the mischief he had done already, he abused her more viciously than ever, and one day he glowered at her angrily and said:

"Woman, from the day you produced this infant son, the people have made my life a complete misery, so bitterly do they resent the thought of a grandson of Giannùcole succeeding me as their lord. So unless I want to be deposed, I'm afraid I shall be forced to do as I did before, and eventually to leave you and marry someone else."

His wife listened patiently, and all she replied was:

"My lord, look to your own comfort, see that you fulfil your wishes, and spare no thought for me, since nothing brings me pleasure unless it pleases you also."

Before many days had elapsed, Gualtieri sent for his son in the same way that he had sent for his daughter, and having likewise pretended to have had the child put to death, he sent him, like the little girl, to Bologna. To all of this his wife reacted no differently, either in her speech or in her looks, than she had on the previous occasion, much to the astonishment of Gualtieri, who told himself that no other woman could have remained so impassive. But for the fact that he had observed her doting upon the children for as long as he allowed her to do so, he would have assumed that she was glad to be rid of them, whereas he knew that she was too judicious to behave in any other way.

His subjects, thinking he had caused the children to be murdered, roundly condemned him and judged him a cruel tyrant, whilst his wife became the

---

8. A city in northern Italy, not far from Florence.

object of their deepest compassion. But to the women who offered her their sympathy in the loss of her children, all she ever said was that the decision of their father was good enough for her.

Many years after the birth of his daughter, Gualtieri decided that the time had come to put Griselda's patience to the final test. So he told a number of his men that in no circumstances could he put up with Griselda as his wife any longer, having now come to realize that his marriage was an aberration of his youth. He would therefore do everything in his power to obtain a dispensation from the Pope, enabling him to divorce Griselda and marry someone else. For this he was chided severely by many worthy men, but his only reply was that it had to be done.

On learning of her husband's intentions, from which it appeared she would have to return to her father's house, in order perhaps to look after the sheep as she had in the past, meanwhile seeing the man she adored being cherished by some other woman, Griselda was secretly filled with despair. But she prepared herself to endure this final blow as stoically as she had borne Fortune's earlier assaults.

Shortly thereafter, Gualtieri arranged for some counterfeit letters of his to arrive from Rome, and led his subjects to believe that in these, the Pope had granted him permission to abandon Griselda and remarry.

He accordingly sent for Griselda, and before a large number of people he said to her:

"Woman, I have had a dispensation from the Pope, allowing me to leave you and take another wife. Since my ancestors were great noblemen and rulers of these lands, whereas yours have always been peasants, I intend that you shall no longer be my wife, but return to Giannùcole's house with the dowry you brought me, after which I shall bring another lady here. I have already chosen her and she is far better suited to a man of my condition.'

On hearing these words, the lady, with an effort beyond the power of any normal woman's nature, suppressed her tears and replied:

"My lord, I have always known that my lowly condition was totally at odds with your nobility, and that it is to God and to yourself that I owe whatever standing I possess. Nor have I ever regarded this as a gift that I might keep and cherish as my own, but rather as something I have borrowed; and now that you want me to return it, I must give it back to you with good grace. Here is the ring with which you married me: take it. As to your ordering me to take away the dowry that I brought, you will require no accountant, nor will I need a purse or a pack-horse, for this to be done. For it has not escaped my memory that you took me naked as on the day I was born.[9] If you think it proper that the body in which I have borne your children should be seen by all the people, I shall go away naked. But in return for my virginity, which I brought to you and cannot retrieve, I trust you will at least allow me, in addition to my dowry, to take one shift away with me."

Gualtieri wanted above all else to burst into tears, but maintaining a stern expression he said:

"Very well, you may take a shift."

All the people present implored Gualtieri to let her have a dress, so that

---

9. See Job 1.21: "Naked came I out of my mother's womb, and naked shall I return thither: the Lord gave, and the Lord hath taken away."

she who had been his wife for thirteen years and more would not have to suffer the indignity of leaving his house in a shift, like a pauper; but their pleas were unavailing. And so Griselda, wearing a shift, barefoot, and with nothing to cover her head, having bidden them farewell, set forth from Gualtieri's house and returned to her father amid the weeping and the wailing of all who set eyes upon her.

Giannùcole, who had never thought it possible that Gualtieri would keep his daughter as his wife, and was daily expecting this to happen, had preserved the clothes she discarded on the morning Gualtieri had married her. So he brought them to her, and Griselda, having put them on, applied herself as before to the menial chores in her father's house, bravely enduring the cruel assault of hostile Fortune.

No sooner did Gualtieri drive Griselda away, than he gave his subjects to understand that he was betrothed to a daughter of one of the Counts of Panago.[1] And having ordered that grandiose preparations were to be made for the nuptials, he sent for Griselda and said to her:

"I am about to fetch home this new bride of mine, and from the moment she sets foot inside the house, I intend to accord her an honorable welcome. As you know, I have no women here who can set the rooms in order for me, or attend to many of the things that a festive occasion of this sort requires. No one knows better than you how to handle these household affairs, so I want you to make all the necessary arrangements. Invite all the ladies you need, and receive them as though you were mistress of the house. And when the nuptials are over, you can go back home to your father."

Since Griselda was unable to lay aside her love for Gualtieri as readily as she had dispensed with her good fortune, his words pierced her heart like so many knives. But she replied:

"My lord, I am ready to do as you ask."[2]

And so, in her coarse, thick, woollen garments, Griselda returned to the house she had quitted shortly before in her shift, and started to sweep and tidy the various chambers. On her instructions, the beds were draped with hangings, the benches in the halls were suitably adorned, the kitchen was made ready; and she set her hand, as though she were a petty serving wench, to every conceivable household task, never stopping to draw breath until she had everything prepared and arranged as befitted the occasion.

Having done all this, she caused invitations to be sent, in Gualtieri's name, to all the ladies living in those parts, and began to await the event. And when at last the nuptial day arrived, heedless of her beggarly attire, she bade a cheerful welcome to each of the lady guests, displaying all the warmth and courtesy of a lady of the manor.

Gualtieri's children having meanwhile been carefully reared by his kinswoman in Bologna, who had married into the family of the Counts of Panago, the girl was now twelve years old, the loveliest creature ever seen, whilst the boy had reached the age of six. Gualtieri had sent word to his kinswoman's husband, asking him to do him the kindness of bringing this daughter of his to Saluzzo along with her little brother, to see that she was nobly and honorably escorted, and to tell everyone he met that he was taking her to marry Gualtieri, without revealing who she really was to a living soul.

---

1. An area near Bologna.   2. See again Luke 1.38: "Behold the handmaid of the Lord."

In accordance with the Marquis's request, the gentleman set forth with the girl and her brother and a noble company, and a few days later, shortly before the hour of breakfast, he arrived at Saluzzo, where he found that all the folk thereabouts, and numerous others from neighboring parts, were waiting for Gualtieri's latest bride.

After being welcomed by the ladies, she made her way to the hall where the tables were set, and Griselda, just as we have described her, went cordially up to meet her, saying:

"My lady, you are welcome."

The ladies, who in vain had implored Gualtieri to see that Griselda remained in another room, or to lend her one of the dresses that had once been hers, so that she would not cut such a sorry figure in front of his guests, took their seats at table and addressed themselves to the meal. All eyes were fixed upon the girl, and everyone said that Gualtieri had made a good exchange. But Griselda praised her as warmly as anyone present, speaking no less admiringly of her little brother.

Gualtieri felt that he had now seen all he wished to see of the patience of his lady, for he perceived that no event, however singular, produced the slightest change in her demeanor, and he was certain that this was not because of her obtuseness, as he knew her to be very intelligent. He therefore considered that the time had come for him to free her from the rancor that he judged her to be hiding beneath her tranquil outward expression. And having summoned her to his table, before all the people present he smiled at her and said:

"What do you think of our new bride?"

"My lord," replied Griselda, "I think very well of her. And if, as I believe, her wisdom matches her beauty, I have no doubt whatever that your life with her will bring you greater happiness than any gentleman on earth has ever known. But with all my heart I beg you not to inflict those same wounds upon her that you imposed upon her predecessor, for I doubt whether she could withstand them, not only because she is younger, but also because she has had a refined upbringing, whereas the other had to face continual hardship from her infancy."

On observing that Griselda was firmly convinced that the young lady was to be his wife, and that even so she allowed no hint of resentment to escape her lips, Gualtieri got her to sit down beside him, and said:

"Griselda, the time has come for you to reap the reward of your unfailing patience, and for those who considered me a cruel and bestial tyrant, to know that whatever I have done was done of set purpose, for I wished to show you how to be a wife, to teach these people how to choose and keep a wife, and to guarantee my own peace and quiet for as long as we were living beneath the same roof. When I came to take a wife, I was greatly afraid that this peace would be denied me, and in order to prove otherwise I tormented and provoked you in the ways you have seen. But as I have never known you to oppose my wishes, I now intend, being persuaded that you can offer me all the happiness I desired, to restore to you in a single instant that which I took from you little by little, and delectably assuage the pains I have inflicted upon you. Receive with gladsome heart, then, this girl whom you believe to be my bride, and also her brother. These are our children, whom you and many others have long supposed that I caused to be cruelly murdered; and

I am your husband, who loves you above all else, for I think I can boast that there is no other man on earth whose contentment in his wife exceeds my own."

Having spoken these words, he embraced and kissed Griselda, who by now was weeping with joy; then they both got up from table and made their way to the place where their daughter sat listening in utter amazement to these tidings. And after they had fondly embraced the girl and her brother, the mystery was unravelled to her, as well as to many of the others who were present.

The ladies rose from table in transports of joy, and escorted Griselda to a chamber, where, with greater assurance of her future happiness, they divested her of her tattered garments and clothed her anew in one of her stately robes. And as their lady and their mistress, a rôle which even in her rags had seemed to be hers, they led her back to the hall, where she and Gualtieri rejoiced with the children in a manner marvellous to behold.

Everyone being delighted with the turn that events had taken, the feasting and the merrymaking were redoubled, and continued unabated for the next few days. Gualtieri was acknowledged to be very wise, though the trials to which he had subjected his lady were regarded as harsh and intolerable, whilst Griselda was accounted the wisest of all.

The Count of Panago returned a few days later to Bologna, and Gualtieri, having removed Giannùcole from his drudgery, set him up in a style befitting his father-in-law, so that he lived in great comfort and honor for the rest of his days. As for Gualtieri himself, having married off his daughter to a gentleman of renown, he lived long and contentedly with Griselda, never failing to honor her to the best of his ability.

What more needs to be said, except that celestial spirits may sometimes descend even into the houses of the poor, whilst there are those in royal palaces who would be better employed as swineherds than as rulers of men? Who else but Griselda could have endured so cheerfully the cruel and unheard of trials that Gualtieri imposed upon her without shedding a tear? For perhaps it would have served him right if he had chanced upon a wife, who, being driven from the house in her shift, had found some other man to shake her skin-coat for her, earning herself a fine new dress in the process.

SIR GAWAIN AND THE GREEN KNIGHT
1380?

Although concerned with King Arthur and his knights, *Sir Gawain and the Green Knight* is far from a typical Arthurian romance. It focuses with unusual intensity on a single knight, it displays a remarkable economy and elegance of narrative form, and it deals not with the usual deeds of martial prowess but with an inner moral testing. In addition, it is written not only in verse, unlike the vast majority of late medieval romances, but in a verse of such subtlety and beauty that the work stands out as a masterpiece of literary craftsmanship. *Gawain* was composed sometime between 1370 and 1390 in the northwest midlands in England, in an area near the present city of Birmingham, and its anonymous author used alliteration for his primary poetic form. Each line has four stresses, at least two and usually three of which fall on words that begin with the same sound: "King Arthur was counted most courteous of all." The only exception to this pattern is the five-line verse that ends each stanza, known as a *bob and wheel*. The translation reproduces this pattern with great skill and fidelity, one result of which is the occasional use of unusual words or ordinary words in slightly unaccustomed senses: some of these have been glossed, while the meanings of others may be surmised from the context or, if necessary, found in a dictionary. This minor difficulty also replicates the experience of reading the original, which is written not only in a provincial dialect but with a deliberately artful vocabulary. The poem is, as the poet says, "linked in measures meetly / By letters tried and true," and much of its success derives from its verbal virtuosity.

In using this alliterative line the poet was harking back to the tradition of Anglo-Saxon verse, as represented in this anthology by *Beowulf* and by the lyric poem *The Ruin*. We do not know how this tradition survived from the middle of the twelfth century, when it disappeared from view under the influence of continental forms imported by the conquering Normans, until the second half of the fourteenth, when it burst forth in an impressive number of excellent poems. But the *Gawain*-poet seems to have been aware that he was using a native tradition, for one of the themes of his work is the contrast between Bercilak, who for all his sophistication is powerfully linked to a vividly described natural world, and Gawain, the representative of an elegant court that may be a bit too civilized. The poem is constructed from two originally separate narrative motifs, "The Beheading Game" and "The Exchange of Winnings." In both cases Gawain must meet a standard of behavior that is both courtly and more than courtly. He must show himself to be honorable both in submitting to the blow of an ax that must surely prove fatal and in exchanging with his host what each man has won that day. This second test then has an added challenge: each morning the host goes out hunting, while his wife offers *herself* to her husband's guest. Much of the comedy of the poem derives from the way in which Gawain refuses this attractive offer while avoiding any hint of discourtesy. But in both of the main tests the hero's resolve is weakened by the most natural of impulses: self-preservation. When he finally does accept from the lady what she says is a magic belt that will preserve his life, he violates his agreement with his host by not offering this gift in exchange for the pelt he receives. When his deception is discovered, Gawain is deeply humiliated and berates both himself and the lady, who has, he thinks, finally seduced him into disloyalty. But Bercilak is far less disturbed: he recognizes that Gawain is, after all, only a human being, not a paragon of perfect virtue. One way the poet stresses this theme is in the contrast between the pentangle that Gawain carries on his shield—a symbol of perfect fidelity—and the green baldrick that he comes to wear as a sign of his fallibility. When upon his return to the court Arthur and his household adopt the green baldrick as a sign of honor, Gawain is suddenly placed in the unusual—and difficult—position of knowing more about human nature, both his own and others, than does his sovereign. And oddly enough, not even the reader can be certain that Gawain's acceptance of the baldrick, which he sees as his failure, did not in fact save his life.

One of the most striking aspects of the poem is the symmetry it establishes between Bercilak's three days of hunting and the three wooing scenes between Gawain and his host's wife. The precise significance of this symmetry has never been satisfactorily explained, but every reader recognizes its instinctive fittingness. As Bercilak rushes through the wintry landscape in pursuit of his prey, Gawain uses his verbal dexterity to evade the lady's none too subtle advances. Gawain may be warmly tucked up in bed, but we can well imagine that he would prefer to be testing his mettle in a more active, less cerebral way. But his fate is to be denied the opportunity to act, and perhaps the most subtle aspect of the poet's genius is his ability to get us to admire a hero who must learn to succeed by doing nothing.

An accessible edition of the original poem is by J. A. Burrow (1972). Helpful articles, and a full bibliography, are available in Derek Brewer and Jonathan Gibson, eds., *A Companion to the Gawain-Poet* (1997).

PRONOUNCING GLOSSARY

The following list uses common English syllables and stress accents to provide rough equivalents of selected words whose pronunciation may be unfamiliar to the general reader.

Bercilak: *behr-see-lak'*   Sauvage: *soh-vazh'*

Sir Gawain and the Green Knight[1]

PART I

Since the siege and the assault was ceased at Troy,
The walls breached and burnt down to brands and ashes,
The knight that had knotted the nets of deceit
Was impeached for his perfidy,[2] proven most true,
It was high-born Aeneas and his haughty race   5
That since prevailed over provinces, and proudly reigned
Over well-nigh all the wealth of the West Isles.[3]
Great Romulus[4] to Rome repairs in haste;
With boast and with bravery builds he that city
And names it with his own name, that it now bears.   10
Ticius to Tuscany,[5] and towers raises,
Langobard[6] in Lombardy lays out homes,
And far over the French Sea, Felix Brutus[7]
On many broad hills and high Britain he sets,[8]
    most fair.   15
  Where war and wrack and wonder
  By shifts have sojourned there,
  And bliss by turns with blunder
  In that land's lot had share.

And since this Britain was built by this baron great,   20
Bold boys bred there, in broils delighting,
That did in their day many a deed most dire.
More marvels have happened in this merry land
Than in any other I know, since that olden time,
But of those that here built, of British kings,   25
King Arthur was counted most courteous of all,
Wherefore an adventure I aim to unfold,
That a marvel of might some men think it,
And one unmatched among Arthur's wonders.
If you will listen to my lay but a little while,   30

---

1. Translated by Marie Borroff. Many of the notes are by E. Talbot Donaldson.   2. The treacherous knight is either Aeneas himself or Antenor, both of whom were, according to medieval tradition, traitors to their city, Troy; but Aeneas was actually tried ("impeached") by the Greeks for his refusal to hand over to them his sister Polyxena.   3. Perhaps western Europe.   4. The legendary founder of Rome is here given Trojan ancestry, like Aeneas.   5. A region north of Rome; modern Florence is located in it. *Ticius:* not otherwise known.   6. The reputed founder of Lombardy, a region in the north centered on modern Milan.   7. Great-grandson of Aeneas and legendary founder of Britain; not elsewhere given the name Felix (Latin "happy"). *French Sea:* the North Sea, including the English Channel.   8. Establishes.

As I heard it in hall, I shall hasten to tell
    anew,
    As it was fashioned featly
    In tale of derring-do,
    And linked in measures meetly[9]   35
    By letters tried and true.

This king lay at Camelot[1] at Christmastide;
Many good knights and gay his guests were there,
Arrayed of the Round Table rightful brothers,[2]
With feasting and fellowship and carefree mirth.   40
There true men contended in tournaments many,
Joined there in jousting these gentle knights,
Then came to the court for carol-dancing,
For the feast was in force full fifteen days,
With all the meat and the mirth that men could devise,   45
Such gaiety and glee, glorious to hear,
Brave din by day, dancing by night.
High were their hearts in halls and chambers,
These lords and these ladies, for life was sweet.
In peerless pleasures passed they their days,   50
The most noble knights known under Christ,
And the loveliest ladies that lived on earth ever,
And he the comeliest king, that that court holds,
For all this fair folk in their first age
    were still.   55
    Happiest of mortal kind,
    King noblest famed of will;
    You would now go far to find
    So hardy a host on hill.

While the New Year was new, but yesternight come,   60
This fair folk at feast two-fold was served,
When the king and his company were come in together,
The chanting in chapel achieved and ended.
Clerics and all the court acclaimed the glad season,
Cried Noel anew, good news to men;   65
Then gallants gather gaily, hand-gifts to make,
Called them out clearly, claimed them by hand,
Bickered long and busily about those gifts.
Ladies laughed aloud, though losers they were,
And he that won was not angered, as well you will know.[3]   70
All this mirth they made until meat was served;
When they had washed them worthily, they went to their seats,
The best seated above, as best it beseemed,
Guenevere the goodly queen gay in the midst
On a dais well-decked and duly arrayed   75

---

9. Suitably.   1. Capital of Arthur's kingdom, presumably located in southwest England or southern Wales.   2. According to legend, the Round Table was made by Merlin, the wise magician who had helped Arthur become king after a dispute broke out among Arthur's knights about precedence: it seated one hundred knights. The table described in the poem is not round.   3. The dispensing of New Year's gifts seems to have involved kissing.

With costly silk curtains, a canopy over,
Of Toulouse and Turkestan tapestries rich,
All broidered and bordered with the best gems
Ever brought into Britain, with bright pennies
                    to pay.   80
          Fair queen, without a flaw,
          She glanced with eyes of grey.
          A seemlier⁴ that once he saw,
          In truth, no man could say.

But Arthur would not eat till all were served;   85
So light was his lordly heart, and a little boyish;
His life he liked lively—the less he cared
To be lying for long, or long to sit,
So busy his young blood, his brain so wild.
And also a point of pride pricked him in heart,   90
For he nobly had willed, he would never eat
On so high a holiday, till he had heard first
Of some fair feat or fray, some far-borne tale,
Of some marvel of might, that he might trust,
By champions of chivalry achieved in arms,   95
Or some suppliant came seeking some single knight
To join with him in jousting, in jeopardy each
To lay life for life, and leave it to fortune
To afford him on field fair hap⁵ or other.
Such is the king's custom, when his court he holds   100
At each far-famed feast amid his fair host
                    so dear.
          The stout king stands in state
          Till a wonder shall appear;
          He leads, with heart elate,   105
          High mirth in the New Year.

So he stands there in state, the stout young king,
Talking before the high table⁶ of trifles fair.
There Gawain the good knight by Guenevere sits,
With Agravain à la dure main⁷ on her other side,   110
Both knights of renown, and nephews of the king.
Bishop Baldwin above begins the table,
And Yvain, son of Urien, ate with him there.
These few with the fair queen were fittingly served;
At the side-tables sat many stalwart knights.   115
Then the first course comes, with clamor of trumpets
That were bravely bedecked with bannerets bright,
With noise of new drums and the noble pipes.
Wild were the warbles that wakened that day
In strains that stirred many strong men's hearts.   120
There dainties were dealt out, dishes rare,
Choice fare to choose, on chargers so many

---

4. More suitable and pleasing (queen).   5. Good luck.   6. The high table is on a dais; the side tables (lines 115) are on the main floor and run along the walls at a right angle to the high table.   7. Of the hard hand.

That scarce was there space to set before the people
The service of silver, with sundry meats,
     on cloth.   125
    Each fair guest freely there
    Partakes, and nothing loth;[8]
    Twelve dishes before each pair;
    Good beer and bright wine both.

Of the service itself I need say no more,   130
For well you will know no tittle was wanting.
Another noise and a new was well-nigh at hand,
That the lord might have leave his life to nourish;
For scarce were the sweet strains still in the hall,
And the first course come to that company fair,   135
There hurtles in at the hall-door an unknown rider,
One the greatest on ground in growth of his frame:
From broad neck to buttocks so bulky and thick,
And his loins and his legs so long and so great,
Half a giant on earth I hold him to be,   140
But believe him no less than the largest of men,
And that the seemliest in his stature to see, as he rides,
For in back and in breast though his body was grim,
His waist in its width was worthily small,
And formed with every feature in fair accord   145
     was he.
    Great wonder grew in hall
    At his hue most strange to see,
    For man and gear and all
    Were green as green could be.   150

And in guise all of green, the gear and the man:
A coat cut close, that clung to his sides,
And a mantle to match, made with a lining
Of furs cut and fitted—the fabric was noble,
Embellished all with ermine, and his hood beside, 155
That was loosed from his locks, and laid on his shoulders.
With trim hose and tight, the same tint of green,
His great calves were girt, and gold spurs under
He bore on silk bands that embellished his heels,
And footgear well-fashioned, for riding most fit. 160
And all his vesture verily was verdant green;
Both the bosses[9] on his belt and other bright gems
That were richly ranged on his raiment noble
About himself and his saddle, set upon silk,
That to tell half the trifles would tax my wits,   165
The butterflies and birds embroidered thereon
In green of the gayest, with many a gold thread.
The pendants of the breast-band, the princely crupper,[1]
And the bars of the bit were brightly enameled;
The stout stirrups were green, that steadied his feet, 170

---

8. Not unwillingly. 9. Ornamental knobs. 1. *Breast-band . . . crupper:* parts of the horse's harness.

And the bows of the saddle and the side-panels both,
That gleamed all and glinted with green gems about.
The steed he bestrides of that same green
               so bright.
        A green horse great and thick;   175
        A headstrong steed of might;
        In broidered bridle quick,
        Mount matched man aright.

Gay was this goodly man in guise all of green,
And the hair of his head to his horse suited;   180
Fair flowing tresses enfold his shoulders;
A beard big as a bush on his breast hangs,
That with his heavy hair, that from his head falls,
Was evened all about above both his elbows,
That half his arms thereunder were hid in the fashion   185
Of a king's cap-à-dos,[2] that covers his throat.
The mane of that mighty horse much to it like,
Well curled and becombed, and cunningly knotted
With filaments of fine gold amid the fair green,
Here a strand of the hair, here one of gold;   190
His tail and his foretop twin in their hue,
And bound both with a band of a bright green
That was decked adown the dock[3] with dazzling stones
And tied tight at the top with a triple knot
Where many bells well burnished rang bright and clear.   195
Such a mount in his might, nor man on him riding,
None had seen, I dare swear, with sight in that hall
              so grand.
        As lightning quick and light
        He looked to all at hand;   200
        It seemed that no man might
        His deadly dints withstand.

Yet had he no helm, nor hauberk[4] neither,
Nor plate, nor appurtenance appending to arms,
Nor shaft pointed sharp, nor shield for defense,   205
But in his one hand he had a holly bob
That is goodliest in green when groves are bare,
And an ax in his other, a huge and immense,
A wicked piece of work in words to expound:
The head on its haft was an ell[5] long;   210
The spike of green steel, resplendent with gold;
The blade burnished bright, with a broad edge,
As well shaped to shear as a sharp razor;
Stout was the stave in the strong man's gripe,
That was wound all with iron to the weapon's end,   215
With engravings in green of goodliest work.
A lace lightly about, that led to a knot,

---

2. Or *capados*, interpreted by the translator as a garment covering its wearer "from head to back."   **3.** The solid part of the tail.   **4.** Tunic of chain mail.   **5.** Three or four feet long.

Was looped in by lengths along the fair haft,
And tassels thereto attached in a row,
With buttons of bright green, brave to behold.   220
This horseman hurtles in, and the hall enters;
Riding to the high dais, recked he no danger;
Not a greeting he gave as the guests he o'erlooked,
Nor wasted his words, but "Where is," he said,
"The captain of this crowd? Keenly I wish   225
To see that sire with sight, and to himself say
                    my say."
          He swaggered all about
          To scan the host so gay;
          He halted, as if in doubt   230
          Who in that hall held sway.

There were stares on all sides as the stranger spoke,
For much did they marvel what it might mean
That a horseman and a horse should have such a hue,
Grow green as the grass, and greener, it seemed,   235
Than green fused on gold more glorious by far.
All the onlookers eyed him, and edged nearer,
And awaited in wonder what he would do,
For many sights had they seen, but such a one never,
So that phantom and faerie the folk there deemed it,   240
Therefore chary of answer was many a champion bold,
And stunned at his strong words stone-still they sat
In a swooning silence in the stately hall.
As all were slipped into sleep, so slackened their speech
                    apace   245
          Not all, I think, for dread,
          But some of courteous grace
          Let him who was their head
          Be spokesman in that place.

Then Arthur before the high dais that entrance beholds,   250
And hailed him, as behooved, for he had no fear,
And said "Fellow, in faith you have found fair welcome;
The head of this hostelry Arthur am I;
Leap lightly down, and linger, I pray,
And the tale of your intent you shall tell us after."   255
"Nay, so help me," said the other, "He that on high sits,
To tarry here any time, 'twas not mine errand;
But as the praise of you, prince, is puffed up so high,
And your court and your company are counted the best,
Stoutest under steel-gear on steeds to ride,   260
Worthiest of their works the wide world over,
And peerless to prove in passages of arms,
And courtesy here is carried to its height,
And so at this season I have sought you out.
You may be certain by the branch that I bear in hand   265
That I pass here in peace, and would part friends,
For had I come to this court on combat bent,

I have a hauberk at home, and a helm beside,
A shield and a sharp spear, shining bright,
And other weapons to wield, I ween[6] well, to boot,   270
But as I willed no war, I wore no metal.
But if you be so bold as all men believe,
You will graciously grant the game that I ask
               by right."
          Arthur answer gave   275
          And said, "Sir courteous knight,
          If contest here you crave,
          You shall not fail to fight."

"Nay, to fight, in good faith, is far from my thought;
There are about on these benches but beardless children,   280
Were I here in full arms on a haughty steed,
For measured against mine, their might is puny.
And so I call in this court for a Christmas game,
For 'tis Yule and New Year, and many young bloods about;
If any in this house such hardihood claims,   285
Be so bold in his blood, his brain so wild,
As stoutly to strike one stroke for another,
I shall give him as my gift this gisarme[7] noble,
This ax, that is heavy enough, to handle as he likes,
And I shall bide[8] the first blow, as bare as I sit.   290
If there be one so wilful my words to assay,
Let him leap hither lightly, lay hold of this weapon;
I quitclaim it forever, keep it[9] as his own,
And I shall stand him a stroke, steady on this floor,
So you grant me the guerdon[1] to give him another,   295
               sans[2] blame.
          In a twelvemonth and a day
          He shall have of me the same;
          Now be it seen straightway
          Who dares take up the game."   300

If he astonished them at first, stiller were then
All that household in hall, the high and the low;
The stranger on his green steed stirred in the saddle,
And roisterously his red eyes he rolled all about,
Bent his bristling brows, that were bright green,   305
Wagged his beard as he watched who would arise.
When the court kept its counsel he coughed aloud,
And cleared his throat coolly, the clearer to speak:
"What, is this Arthur's house," said that horseman then,
"Whose fame is so fair in far realms and wide?   310
Where is now your arrogance and your awesome deeds,
Your valor and your victories and your vaunting words?
Now are the revel and renown of the Round Table
Overwhelmed with a word of one man's speech,
For all cower and quake, and no cut felt!"   315

6. Believe.   7. Weapon.   8. Endure.   9. I.e., let him keep it.   1. Reward.   2. Without.

With this he laughs so loud that the lord grieved;
The blood for sheer shame shot to his face,
                    and pride.
            With rage his face flushed red,
            And so did all beside.   320
            Then the king as bold man bred
            Toward the stranger took a stride.

And said "Sir, now we see you will say but folly,
Which whoso has sought, it suits that he find.
No guest here is aghast of your great words.   325
Give to me your gisarme, in God's own name,
And the boon you have begged shall straight be granted."
He leaps to him lightly, lays hold of his weapon;
The green fellow on foot fiercely alights.
Now has Arthur his ax, and the haft grips,   330
And sternly stirs it about, on striking bent.
The stranger before him stood there erect,
Higher than any in the house by a head and more;
With stern look as he stood, he stroked his beard,
And with undaunted countenance drew down his coat,   335
No more moved nor dismayed for his mighty dints
Than any bold man on bench had brought him a drink
                    of wine.
            Gawain by Guenevere
            Toward the king doth now incline: 340
            "I beseech, before all here,
            That this melee may be mine."

"Would you grant me the grace," said Gawain to the king,
"To be gone from this bench and stand by you there,
If I without discourtesy might quit this board,   345
And if my liege lady³ misliked it not,
I would come to your counsel before your court noble.
For I find it not fit, as in faith it is known,
When such a boon is begged before all these knights,
Though you be tempted thereto, to take it on yourself   350
While so bold men about upon benches sit,
That no host under heaven is hardier of will,
Nor better brothers-in-arms where battle is joined;
I am the weakest, well I know, and of wit feeblest;
And the loss of my life would be least of any;   355
That I have you for uncle is my only praise;
My body, but for your blood, is barren of worth;
And for that this folly befits not a king,
And 'tis I that have asked it, it ought to be mine,
And if my claim be not comely let all this court judge,   360
                    in sight."
            The court assays the claim,
            And in counsel all unite

___
3. Lady entitled to the knight's feudal service.

To give Gawain the game
And release the king outright.   365

Then the king called the knight to come to his side,
And he rose up readily, and reached him with speed,
Bows low to his lord, lays hold of the weapon,
And he releases it lightly, and lifts up his hand,
And gives him God's blessing, and graciously prays   370
That his heart and his hand may be hardy both.
"Keep, cousin," said the king, "what you cut with this day,
And if you rule it aright, then readily, I know,
You shall stand the stroke it will strike after."
Gawain goes to the guest with gisarme in hand,   375
And boldly he bides there, abashed not a whit.
Then hails he Sir Gawain, the horseman in green:
"Recount we our contract, ere you come further.
First I ask and adjure you, how you are called
That you tell me true, so that trust it I may."   380
"In good faith," said the good knight, "Gawain am I
Whose buffet befalls you, whate'er betide after,
And at this time twelvemonth take from you another
With what weapon you will, and with no man else

alive."   385
The other nods assent:
"Sir Gawain, as I may thrive,
I am wondrous well content
That you this dint shall drive."

"Sir Gawain," said the Green Knight, "By God, I rejoice   390
That your fist shall fetch this favor I seek,
And you have readily rehearsed, and in right terms,
Each clause of my covenant with the king your lord,
Save that you shall assure me, sir, upon oath,
That you shall seek me yourself, wheresoever you deem   395
My lodgings may lie, and look for such wages
As you have offered me here before all this host."
"What is the way there?" said Gawain, "Where do you dwell?
I heard never of your house, by Him that made me,
Nor I know you not, knight, your name nor your court.   400
But tell me truly thereof, and teach me your name,
And I shall fare forth to find you, so far as I may,
And this I say in good certain, and swear upon oath."
"That is enough in New Year, you need say no more,"
Said the knight in the green to Gawain the noble,   405
"If I tell you true, when I have taken your knock,
And if you handily have hit, you shall hear straightway
Of my house and my home and my own name;
Then follow in my footsteps by faithful accord.
And if I spend no speech, you shall speed the better: 410
You can feast with your friends, nor further trace

my tracks.
Now hold your grim tool steady

And show us how it hacks."
"Gladly, sir; all ready,"   415
Says Gawain; he strokes the ax.

The Green Knight upon ground girds him with care:
Bows a bit with his head, and bares his flesh:
His long lovely locks he laid over his crown,
Let the naked nape for the need be shown.   420
Gawain grips to his ax and gathers it aloft—
The left foot on the floor before him he set—
Brought it down deftly upon the bare neck,
That the shock of the sharp blow shivered the bones
And cut the flesh cleanly and clove it in twain,   425
That the blade of bright steel bit into the ground.
The head was hewn off and fell to the floor;
Many found it at their feet, as forth it rolled;
The blood gushed from the body, bright on the green,
Yet fell not the fellow, nor faltered a whit,   430
But stoutly he starts forth upon stiff shanks,
And as all stood staring he stretched forth his hand,
Laid hold of his head and heaved it aloft,
Then goes to the green steed, grasps the bridle,
Steps into the stirrup, bestrides his mount,   435
And his head by the hair in his hand holds,
And as steady he sits in the stately saddle
As he had met with no mishap, nor missing were
        his head.
      His bulk about he haled,[4]   440
      That fearsome body that bled;
      There were many in the court that quailed
      Before all his say was said.

For the head in his hand he holds right up;
Toward the first on the dais directs he the face,   445
And it lifted up its lids, and looked with wide eyes,
And said as much with its mouth as now you may hear:
"Sir Gawain, forget not to go as agreed,
And cease not to seek till me, sir, you find,
As you promised in the presence of these proud knights.   450
To the Green Chapel come, I charge you, to take
Such a dint as you have dealt—you have well deserved
That your neck should have a knock on New Year's morn.
The Knight of the Green Chapel I am well-known to many,
Wherefore you cannot fail to find me at last;   455
Therefore come, or be counted a recreant[5] knight."
With a roisterous rush he flings round the reins,
Hurtles out at the hall-door, his head in his hand,
That the flint-fire flew from the flashing hooves.
Which way he went, not one of them knew   460
Nor whence he was come in the wide world

---

4. Hauled. 5. Cowardly.

so fair.
The king and Gawain gay
Make game of the Green Knight there,
Yet all who saw it say   465
'Twas a wonder past compare.

Though high-born Arthur at heart had wonder,
He let no sign be seen, but said aloud
To the comely queen, with courteous speech,
"Dear dame, on this day dismay you no whit;   470
Such crafts are becoming at Christmastide,
Laughing at interludes, light songs and mirth,
Amid dancing of damsels with doughty knights.
Nevertheless of my meat now let me partake,
For I have met with a marvel, I may not deny."   475
He glanced at Sir Gawain, and gaily he said,
"Now, sir, hang up your ax, that has hewn enough,"
And over the high dais it was hung on the wall
That men in amazement might on it look,
And tell in true terms the tale of the wonder.   480
Then they turned toward the table, these two together,
The good king and Gawain, and made great feast,
With all dainties double, dishes rare,
With all manner of meat and minstrelsy both,
Such happiness wholly had they that day   485
                    in hold.
          Now take care, Sir Gawain,
          That your courage wax not cold
          When you must turn again
          To your enterprise foretold.   490

PART II

This adventure had Arthur of handsels[6] first
When young was the year, for he yearned to hear tales;
Though they wanted for words when they went to sup,
Now are fierce deeds to follow, their fists stuffed full.
Gawain was glad to begin those games in hall,   495
But if the end be harsher, hold it no wonder,
For though men are merry in mind after much drink,
A year passes apace, and proves ever new:
First things and final conform but seldom.
And so this Yule to the young year yielded place,   500
And each season ensued at its set time;
After Christmas there came the cold cheer of Lent,
When with fish and plainer fare our flesh we reprove;
But then the world's weather with winter contends:
The keen cold lessens, the low clouds lift;   505
Fresh falls the rain in fostering showers
On the face of the fields; flowers appear.

6. Gifts to mark the New Year.

The ground and the groves wear gowns of green;
Birds build their nests, and blithely sing
That solace of all sorrow with summer comes   510
                    ere long.
            And blossoms day by day
            Bloom rich and rife in throng;
            Then every grove so gay
            Of the greenwood rings with song.   515

And then the season of summer with the soft winds,
When Zephyr sighs low over seeds and shoots;
Glad is the green plant growing abroad,
When the dew at dawn drops from the leaves,
To get a gracious glance from the golden sun.   520
But harvest with harsher winds follows hard after,
Warns him to ripen well ere winter comes;
Drives forth the dust in the droughty season,
From the face of the fields to fly high in air.
Wroth winds in the welkin[7] wrestle with the sun,   525
The leaves launch from the linden and light on the ground,
And the grass turns to gray, that once grew green.
Then all ripens and rots that rose up at first,
And so the year moves on in yesterdays many,
And winter once more, by the world's law,   530
                    draws nigh.
            At Michaelmas[8] the moon
            Hangs wintry pale in sky;
            Sir Gawain girds him soon
            For travails yet to try.   535

Till All-Hallows' Day[9] with Arthur he dwells,
And he held a high feast to honor that knight
With great revels and rich, of the Round Table.
Then ladies lovely and lords debonair
With sorrow for Sir Gawain were sore at heart;   540
Yet they covered their care with countenance glad:
Many a mournful man made mirth for his sake.
So after supper soberly he speaks to his uncle
Of the hard hour at hand, and openly says,
"Now, liege lord of my life, my leave I take;   545
The terms of this task too well you know—
To count the cost over concerns me nothing.
But I am bound forth betimes[1] to bear a stroke
From the grim man in green, as God may direct."
Then the first and foremost came forth in throng: 550
Yvain and Eric and others of note,
Sir Dodinal le Sauvage, the Duke of Clarence,
Lionel and Lancelot and Lucan the good,
Sir Bors and Sir Bedivere, big men both,
And many manly knights more, with Mador de la Porte.   555

7. The heavens.   8. September 29.   9. November 1.   1. Soon.

All this courtly company comes to the king
To counsel their comrade, with care in their hearts;
There was much secret sorrow suffered that day
That one so good as Gawain must go in such wise
To bear a bitter blow, and his bright sword   560
               lay by.
        He said, "Why should I tarry?"
        And smiled with tranquil eye;
        "In destinies sad or merry,
        True men can but try."   565

He dwelt there all that day, and dressed in the morning;
Asked early for his arms, and all were brought.
First a carpet of rare cost was cast on the floor
Where much goodly gear gleamed golden bright;
He takes his place promptly and picks up the steel,   570
Attired in a tight coat of Turkestan silk
And a kingly cap-à-dos, closed at the throat,
That was lavishly lined with a lustrous fur.
Then they set the steel shoes on his sturdy feet
And clad his calves about with comely greaves,   575
And plate well-polished protected his knees,
Affixed with fastenings of the finest gold.
Fair cuisses enclosed, that were cunningly wrought,
His thick-thewed thighs, with thongs bound fast,
And massy chain-mail of many a steel ring   580
He bore on his body, above the best cloth,
With brace burnished bright upon both his arms,
Good couters[2] and gay, and gloves of plate,
And all the goodly gear to grace him well
               that tide.   585
        His surcoat[3] blazoned bold;
        Sharp spurs to prick with pride;
        And a brave silk band to hold
        The broadsword at his side.

When he had on his arms, his harness was rich,   590
The least latchet or loop laden with gold;
So armored as he was, he heard a mass,
Honored God humbly at the high altar.
Then he comes to the king and his comrades-in-arms,
Takes his leave at last of lords and ladies,   595
And they clasped and kissed him, commending him to Christ.
By then Gringolet[4] was girt with a great saddle
That was gaily agleam with fine gilt fringe,
New-furbished for the need with nail-heads bright;
The bridle and the bars bedecked all with gold;   600
The breast-plate, the saddlebow, the side-panels both,
The caparison and the crupper accorded in hue,
And all ranged on the red the resplendent studs

2. Armor for the elbows.   3. Cloth tunic worn over the armor.   4. Gawain's horse.

That glittered and glowed like the glorious sun.
His helm now he holds up and hastily kisses,   605
Well-closed with iron clinches, and cushioned within;
It was high on his head, with a hasp behind,
And a covering of cloth to encase the visor,
All bound and embroidered with the best gems
On broad bands of silk, and bordered with birds,   610
Parrots and popinjays preening their wings,
Lovebirds and love-knots as lavishly wrought
As many women had worked seven winters thereon,
                    entire.
          The diadem costlier yet   615
          That crowned that comely sire,
          With diamonds richly set,
          That flashed as if on fire.

Then they showed forth the shield, that shone all red,
With the pentangle⁵ portrayed in purest gold.   620
About his broad neck by the baldric⁶ he casts it,
That was meet for the man, and matched him well.
And why the pentangle is proper to that peerless prince
I intend now to tell, though detain me it must.
It is a sign by Solomon sagely devised   625
To be a token of truth, by its title of old,
For it is a figure formed of five points,
And each line is linked and locked with the next
For ever and ever, and hence it is called
In all England, as I hear, the endless knot.   630
And well may he wear it on his worthy arms,
For ever faithful five-fold in five-fold fashion
Was Gawain in good works, as gold unalloyed,
Devoid of all villainy, with virtues adorned
                    in sight.   635
          On shield and coat in view
          He bore that emblem bright,
          As to his word most true
          And in speech most courteous knight.

And first, he was faultless in his five senses,   640
Nor found ever to fail in his five fingers,
And all his fealty was fixed upon the five wounds
That Christ got on the cross, as the creed tells;
And wherever this man in melee took part,
His one thought was of this, past all things else,   645
That all his force was founded on the five joys⁷
That the high Queen of heaven had in her child.
And therefore, as I find, he fittingly had

---

5. A five-pointed star, formed by five lines drawn without lifting the pen, supposed to have mystical significance. The ancient concept of the five-pointed star merged in medieval thought with that of the six-pointed seal of Solomon.   6. Belt worn diagonally across the chest.   7. These were the annunciation to Mary that she was to bear the Son of God, Christ's Nativity, Resurrection, and Ascension into heaven, and the "Assumption" or bodily taking up of Mary into heaven to join Him.

On the inner part of his shield her image portrayed,
That when his look on it lighted, he never lost heart. 650
The fifth of the five fives followed by this knight
Were beneficence boundless and brotherly love
And pure mind and manners, that none might impeach,
And compassion most precious—these peerless five
Were forged and made fast in him, foremost of men. 655
Now all these five fives were confirmed in this knight,
And each linked in other, that end there was none,
And fixed to five points, whose force never failed,
Nor assembled all on a side, nor asunder either,
Nor anywhere at an end, but whole and entire 660
However the pattern proceeded or played out its course.
And so on his shining shield shaped was the knot
Royally in red gold against red gules,[8]
That is the peerless pentangle, prized of old
                              in lore. 665
               Now armed is Gawain gay,
               And bears his lance before,
               And soberly said good day,
               He thought forevermore.

He struck his steed with the spurs and sped on his way 670
So fast that the flint-fire flashed from the stones.
When they saw him set forth they were sore aggrieved,
And all sighed softly, and said to each other,
Fearing for their fellow, "Ill fortune it is
That you, man, must be marred, that most are worthy! 675
His equal on this earth can hardly be found;
To have dealt more discreetly had done less harm,
And have dubbed him a duke, with all due honor.
A great leader of lords he was like to become,
And better so to have been than battered to bits, 680
Beheaded by an elf-man,[9] for empty pride!
Who would credit that a king could be counseled so,
And caught in a cavil in a Christmas game?"
Many were the warm tears they wept from their eyes
When goodly Sir Gawain was gone from the court 685
                              that day.
               No longer he abode,
               But speedily went his way
               Over many a wandering road,
               As I heard my author say. 690

Now he rides in his array through the realm of Logres,[1]
Sir Gawain, God knows, though it gave him small joy!
All alone must he lodge through many a long night
Where the food that he fancied was far from his plate;
He had no mate but his mount, over mountain and plain, 695

8. Background (*gules* is the heraldic name for red).   9. Supernatural being, in this case obviously not small.   1. Another name for Arthur's kingdom.

Nor man to say his mind to but almighty God,
Till he had wandered well-nigh into North Wales.
All the islands of Anglesey he holds on his left,
And follows, as he fares, the fords by the coast,
Comes over at Holy Head, and enters next   700
The Wilderness of Wirral²—few were within
That had great good will toward God or man.
And earnestly he asked of each mortal he met
If he had ever heard aught of a knight all green,
Or of a Green Chapel, on ground thereabouts,   705
And all said the same, and solemnly swore
They saw no such knight all solely green
                    in hue.
          Over country wild and strange
          The knight sets off anew;   710
          Often his course must change
          Ere the Chapel comes in view.

Many a cliff must he climb in country wild;
Far off from all his friends, forlorn must he ride;
At each strand or stream where the stalwart passed   715
'Twere a marvel if he met not some monstrous foe,
And that so fierce and forbidding that fight he must.
So many were the wonders he wandered among
That to tell but the tenth part would tax my wits.
Now with serpents he wars, now with savage wolves,   720
Now with wild men of the woods, that watched from the rocks,
Both with bulls and with bears, and with boars besides,
And giants that came gibbering from the jagged steeps.
Had he not borne himself bravely, and been on God's side,
He had met with many mishaps and mortal harms.   725
And if the wars were unwelcome, the winter was worse,
When the cold clear rains rushed from the clouds
And froze before they could fall to the frosty earth.
Near slain by the sleet he sleeps in his irons
More nights than enough, among naked rocks,   730
Where clattering from the crest the cold stream ran
And hung in hard icicles high overhead.
Thus in peril and pain and predicaments dire
He rides across country till Christmas Eve,
                    our knight.   735
          And at that holy tide
          He prays with all his might
          That Mary may be his guide
          Till a dwelling comes in sight.

By a mountain next morning he makes his way   740
Into a forest fastness, fearsome and wild;
High hills on either hand, with hoar woods below,
Oaks old and huge by the hundred together.

---

2. *North Wales . . . Wirral:* Gawain went from Camelot north to the northern coast of Wales, opposite the
islands of Anglesey; there he turned east across the river Dee to the forest of Wirral, near what is now
Liverpool.

The hazel and the hawthorn were all intertwined
With rough raveled moss, that raggedly hung,   745
With many birds unblithe upon bare twigs
That peeped most piteously for pain of the cold.
The good knight on Gringolet glides thereunder
Through many a marsh and mire, a man all alone;
He feared for his default, should he fail to see   750
The service of that Sire that on that same night
Was born of a bright maid, to bring us His peace.
And therefore sighing he said, "I beseech of Thee, Lord,
And Mary, thou mildest mother so dear,
Some harborage where haply I might hear mass   755
And Thy matins tomorrow—meekly I ask it,
And thereto proffer and pray my pater and ave[3]
                                              and creed."
              He said his prayer with sighs,
              Lamenting his misdeed;   760
              He crosses himself, and cries
              On Christ in his great need.

No sooner had Sir Gawain signed himself[4] thrice
Than he was ware, in the wood, of a wondrous dwelling,
Within a moat, on a mound, bright amid boughs   765
Of many a tree great of girth that grew by the water—
A castle as comely as a knight could own,
On grounds fair and green, in a goodly park
With a palisade of palings planted about
For two miles and more, round many a fair tree.   770
The stout knight stared at that stronghold great
As it shimmered and shone amid shining leaves,
Then with helmet in hand he offers his thanks
To Jesus and Saint Julian,[5] that are gentle both,
That in courteous accord had inclined to his prayer;   775
"Now fair harbor," said he, "I humbly beseech!"
Then he pricks his proud steed with the plated spurs,
And by chance he has chosen the chief path
That brought the bold knight to the bridge's end
                                              in haste.   780
              The bridge hung high in air;
              The gates were bolted fast;
              The walls well-framed to bear
              The fury of the blast.

The man on his mount remained on the bank   785
Of the deep double moat that defended the place.
The wall went in the water wondrous deep,
And a long way aloft it loomed overhead.
It was built of stone blocks to the battlements' height,
With corbels under cornices[6] in comeliest style;   790
Watch-towers trusty protected the gate,

3. Two prayers, the Pater Noster ("Our Father," the Lord's Prayer) and Ave Maria ("Hail Mary").
4. Made the Sign of the Cross over his own chest.   5. Patron saint of hospitality.   6. Ornamental
projections supporting the top courses of stone.

With many a lean loophole, to look from within:
A better-made barbican the knight beheld never.
And behind it there hoved a great hall and fair:
Turrets rising in tiers, with tines[7] at their tops,   795
Spires set beside them, splendidly long,
With finials well-fashioned, as filigree fine.
Chalk-white chimneys over chambers high
Gleamed in gay array upon gables and roofs;
The pinnacles in panoply, pointing in air,   800
So vied there for his view that verily it seemed
A castle cut of paper for a king's feast.
The good knight on Gringolet thought it great luck
If he could but contrive to come there within
To keep the Christmas feast in that castle fair   805
        and bright.
        There answered to his call
        A porter most polite;
        From his station on the wall
        He greets the errant knight.   810

"Good sir," said Gawain, "Wouldst go to inquire
If your lord would allow me to lodge here a space?"
"Peter!"[8] said the porter, "For my part, I think
So noble a knight will not want for a welcome!"
Then he bustles off briskly, and comes back straight,   815
And many servants beside, to receive him the better.
They let down the drawbridge and duly went forth
And kneeled down on their knees on the naked earth
To welcome this warrior as best they were able.
They proffered him passage—the portals stood wide—   820
And he beckoned them to rise, and rode over the bridge.
Men steadied his saddle as he stepped to the ground,
And there stabled his steed many stalwart folk.
Now come the knights and the noble squires
To bring him with bliss into the bright hall.   825
When his high helm was off, there hied forth a throng
Of attendants to take it, and see to its care;
They bore away his brand[9] and his blazoned shield;
Then graciously he greeted those gallants each one,
And many a noble drew near, to do the knight honor.   830
All in his armor into hall he was led,
Where fire on a fair hearth fiercely blazed.
And soon the lord himself descends from his chamber
To meet with good manners the man on his floor.
He said, "To this house you are heartily welcome: 835
What is here is wholly yours, to have in your power
        and sway."
        "Many thanks," said Sir Gawain;
        "May Christ your pains repay!"

---

7. Sharp points. *Hoved:* arose.   8. I.e., "By Saint Peter!"   9. Sword.

The two embrace amain   840
As men well met that day.

Gawain gazed on the host that greeted him there,
And a lusty fellow he looked, the lord of that place:
A man of massive mold, and of middle age;
Broad, bright was his beard, of a beaver's hue,   845
Strong, steady his stance, upon stalwart shanks,
His face fierce as fire, fair-spoken withal,
And well-suited he seemed in Sir Gawain's sight
To be a master of men in a mighty keep.
They pass into a parlor, where promptly the host   850
Has a servant assigned him to see to his needs,
And there came upon his call many courteous folk
That brought him to a bower where bedding was noble,
With heavy silk hangings hemmed all in gold,
Coverlets and counterpanes curiously wrought,   855
A canopy over the couch, clad all with fur,
Curtains running on cords, caught to gold rings,
Woven rugs on the walls of eastern work,
And the floor, under foot, well-furnished with the same.
With light talk and laughter they loosed from him then   860
His war-dress of weight and his worthy clothes.
Robes richly wrought they brought him right soon,
To change there in chamber and choose what he would.
When he had found one he fancied, and flung it about,
Well-fashioned for his frame, with flowing skirts,   865
His face fair and fresh as the flowers of spring,
All the good folk agreed, that gazed on him then,
His limbs arrayed royally in radiant hues,
That so comely a mortal never Christ made
          as he.   870
          Whatever his place of birth,
          It seemed he well might be
          Without a peer on earth
          In martial rivalry.

A couch before the fire, where fresh coals burned,   875
They spread for Sir Gawain splendidly now
With quilts quaintly stitched, and cushions beside,
And then a costly cloak they cast on his shoulders
Of bright silk, embroidered on borders and hems,
With furs of the finest well-furnished within,   880
And bound about with ermine, both mantle and hood;
And he sat at that fireside in sumptuous estate
And warmed himself well, and soon he waxed merry.
Then attendants set a table upon trestles broad,
And lustrous white linen they laid thereupon,   885
A saltcellar of silver, spoons of the same.
He washed himself well and went to his place,
Men set his fare before him in fashion most fit.
There were soups of all sorts, seasoned with skill,

Double-sized servings, and sundry fish,   890
Some baked, some breaded, some broiled on the coals,
Some simmered, some in stews, steaming with spice,
And with sauces to sup that suited his taste.
He confesses it a feast with free words and fair;
They requite him as kindly with courteous jests,   895
    well-sped.
   "Tonight you fast and pray;
   Tomorrow we'll see you fed."
   The knight grows wondrous gay
   As the wine goes to his head.   900

Then at times and by turns, as at table he sat,
They questioned him quietly, with queries discreet,
And he courteously confessed that he comes from the court,
And owns him of the brotherhood of high-famed Arthur,
The right royal ruler of the Round Table,   905
And the guest by their fireside is Gawain himself,
Who has happened on their house at that holy feast.
When the name of the knight was made known to the lord,
Then loudly he laughed, so elated he was,
And the men in that household made haste with joy   910
To appear in his presence promptly that day,
That of courage ever-constant, and customs pure,
Is pattern and paragon, and praised without end:
Of all knights on earth most honored is he.
Each said solemnly aside to his brother,   915
"Now displays of deportment shall dazzle our eyes
And the polished pearls of impeccable speech;
The high art of eloquence is ours to pursue
Since the father of fine manners is found in our midst.
Great is God's grace, and goodly indeed,   920
That a guest such as Gawain he guides to us here
When men sit and sing of their Savior's birth
    in view.
   With command of manners pure
   He shall each heart imbue;   925
   Who shares his converse, sure,
   Shall learn love's language true."

When the knight had done dining and duly arose,
The dark was drawing on; the day nigh ended.
Chaplains in chapels and churches about   930
Rang the bells aright, reminding all men
Of the holy evensong of the high feast.
The lord attends alone; his fair lady sits
In a comely closet, secluded from sight.
Gawain in gay attire goes thither soon;   935
The lord catches his coat, and calls him by name,
And has him sit beside him, and says in good faith
No guest on God's earth would he gladlier greet.
For that Gawain thanked him; the two then embraced

And sat together soberly the service through.   940
Then the lady, that longed to look on the knight,
Came forth from her closet with her comely maids.
The fair hues of her flesh, her face and her hair
And her body and her bearing were beyond praise,
And excelled the queen herself, as Sir Gawain thought.   945
He goes forth to greet her with gracious intent;
Another lady led her by the left hand
That was older than she—an ancient, it seemed,
And held in high honor by all men about.
But unlike to look upon, those ladies were,   950
For if the one was fresh, the other was faded:
Bedecked in bright red was the body of one;
Flesh hung in folds on the face of the other;
On one a high headdress, hung all with pearls;
Her bright throat and bosom fair to behold,   955
Fresh as the first snow fallen upon hills;
A wimple[1] the other one wore round her throat;
Her swart chin well swaddled, swathed all in white;
Her forehead enfolded in flounces of silk
That framed a fair fillet,[2] of fashion ornate,   960
And nothing bare beneath save the black brows,
The two eyes and the nose, the naked lips,
And they unsightly to see, and sorrily bleared.
A beldame, by God, she may well be deemed,
                  of pride!   965
           She was short and thick of waist,
           Her buttocks round and wide;
           More toothsome, to his taste,
           Was the beauty by her side.

When Gawain had gazed on that gay lady,   970
With leave of her lord, he politely approached;
To the elder in homage he humbly bows;
The lovelier he salutes with a light embrace.
He claims a comely kiss, and courteously he speaks;
They welcome him warmly, and straightway he asks   975
To be received as their servant, if they so desire.
They take him between them; with talking they bring him
Beside a bright fire; bade then that spices
Be freely fetched forth, to refresh them the better,
And the good wine therewith, to warm their hearts.   980
The lord leaps about in light-hearted mood;
Contrives entertainments and timely sports;
Takes his hood from his head and hangs it on a spear,
And offers him openly the honor thereof
Who should promote the most mirth at that Christmas feast;   985
"And I shall try for it, trust me—contend with the best,
Ere I go without my headgear by grace of my friends!"
Thus with light talk and laughter the lord makes merry

1. A garment covering the neck and sides of the head.   2. Ornamental ribbon or headband.

To gladden the guest he had greeted in hall
                    that day.   990
            At the last he called for light
            The company to convey;
            Gawain says goodnight
            And retires to bed straightway.

On the morn when each man is mindful in heart   995
That God's son was sent down to suffer our death,
No household but is blithe for His blessed sake;
So was it there on that day, with many delights.
Both at larger meals and less they were lavishly served
By doughty lads on dais, with delicate fare;   1000
The old ancient lady, highest she sits;
The lord at her left hand leaned, as I hear;
Sir Gawain in the center, beside the gay lady,
Where the food was brought first to that festive board,
And thence throughout the hall, as they held most fit, 1005
To each man was offered in order of rank.
There was meat, there was mirth, there was much joy,
That to tell all the tale would tax my wits,
Though I pained me, perchance, to paint it with care;
But yet I know that our knight and the noble lady   1010
Were accorded so closely in company there,
With the seemly solace of their secret words,
With speeches well-sped, spotless and pure,
That each prince's pastime their pleasures far
                    outshone.   1015
            Sweet pipes beguile their cares,
            And the trumpet of martial tone;
            Each tends his affairs
            And those two tend their own.

That day and all the next, their disport was noble,   1020
And the third day, I think, pleased them no less;
The joys of St. John's Day[3] were justly praised,
And were the last of their like for those lords and ladies;
Then guests were to go in the gray morning,
Wherefore they whiled the night away with wine and with mirth, 1025
Moved to the measures of many a blithe carol;
At last, when it was late, took leave of each other,
Each one of those worthies, to wend his way.
Gawain bids goodbye to his goodly host
Who brings him to his chamber, the chimney beside,   1030
And detains him in talk, and tenders his thanks
And holds it an honor to him and his people
That he has harbored in his house at that holy time
And embellished his abode with his inborn grace.
"As long as I may live, my luck is the better   1035
That Gawain was my guest at God's own feast!"

3. December 27.

"Noble sir," said the knight, "I cannot but think
All the honor is your own—may heaven requite it!
And your man to command I account myself here
As I am bound and beholden, and shall be, come   1040
              what may."
          The lord with all his might
          Entreats his guest to stay;
          Brief answer makes the knight:
          Next morning he must away.   1045

Then the lord of that land politely inquired
What dire affair had forced him, at that festive time,
So far from the king's court to fare forth alone
Ere the holidays wholly had ended in hall.
"In good faith," said Gawain, "you have guessed the truth: 1050
On a high errand and urgent I hastened away,
For I am summoned by myself to seek for a place—
I would I knew whither, or where it might be!
Far rather would I find it before the New Year
Than own the land of Logres, so help me our Lord!   1055
Wherefore, sir, in friendship this favor I ask,
That you say in sober earnest, if something you know
Of the Green Chapel, on ground far or near,
Or the lone knight that lives there, of like hue of green.
A certain day was set by assent of us both   1060
To meet at that landmark, if I might last,
And from now to the New Year is nothing too long,
And I would greet the Green Knight there, would God but allow,
More gladly, by God's Son, than gain the world's wealth!
And I must set forth to search, as soon as I may;   1065
To be about the business I have but three days
And would as soon sink down dead as desist from my errand."
Then smiling said the lord, "Your search, sir, is done,
For we shall see you to that site by the set time.
Let Gawain grieve no more over the Green Chapel;   1070
You shall be in your own bed, in blissful ease,
All the forenoon, and fare forth the first of the year,
And make the goal by midmorn, to mind your affairs,
              no fear!
          Tarry till the fourth day   1075
          And ride on the first of the year.
          We shall set you on your way;
          It is not two miles from here."

Then Gawain was glad, and gleefully he laughed:
"Now I thank you for this, past all things else!   1080
Now my goal is here at hand! With a glad heart I shall
Both tarry, and undertake any task you devise."
Then the host seized his arm and seated him there;
Let the ladies be brought, to delight them the better,
And in fellowship fair by the fireside they sit;   1085
So gay waxed the good host, so giddy his words,

All waited in wonder what next he would say.
Then he stares on the stout knight, and sternly he speaks:
"You have bound yourself boldly my bidding to do—
Will you stand by that boast, and obey me this once?"   1090
"I shall do so indeed," said the doughty knight;
"While I lie in your lodging, your laws will I follow."
"As you have had," said the host, "many hardships abroad
And little sleep of late, you are lacking, I judge,
Both in nourishment needful and nightly rest;   1095
You shall lie abed late in your lofty chamber
Tomorrow until mass, and meet then to dine
When you will, with my wife, who will sit by your side
And talk with you at table, the better to cheer
                our guest.   1100
        A-hunting I will go
        While you lie late and rest."
        The knight, inclining low,
        Assents to each behest.

"And Gawain," said the good host, "agree now to this: 1105
Whatever I win in the woods I will give you at eve,
And all you have earned you must offer to me;
Swear now, sweet friend, to swap as I say,
Whether hands, in the end, be empty or better."
"By God," said Sir Gawain, "I grant it forthwith!   1110
If you find the game good, I shall gladly take part."
"Let the bright wine be brought, and our bargain is done,"
Said the lord of that land—the two laughed together.
Then they drank and they dallied and doffed all constraint,
These lords and these ladies, as late as they chose,   1115
And then with gaiety and gallantries and graceful adieux
They talked in low tones, and tarried at parting.
With compliments comely they kiss at the last;
There were brisk lads about with blazing torches
To see them safe to bed, for soft repose   1120
                long due.
        Their covenants, yet awhile,
        They repeat, and pledge anew;
        That lord could well beguile
        Men's hearts, with mirth in view.   1125

PART III

Long before daylight they left their beds;
Guests that wished to go gave word to their grooms,
And they set about briskly to bind on saddles,
Tend to their tackle, tie up trunks.
The proud lords appear, appareled to ride,   1130
Leap lightly astride, lay hold of their bridles,
Each one on his way to his worthy house.
The liege lord of the land was not the last
Arrayed there to ride, with retainers many;

He had a bite to eat when he had heard mass;   1135
With horn to the hills he hastens amain.
By the dawn of that day over the dim earth,
Master and men were mounted and ready.
Then they harnessed in couples the keen-scented hounds,
Cast wide the kennel-door and called them forth,   1140
Blew upon their bugles bold blasts three;
The dogs began to bay with a deafening din,
And they quieted them quickly and called them to heel,
A hundred brave huntsmen, as I have heard tell,
                    together.   1145
        Men at stations meet;
        From the hounds they slip the tether;
        The echoing horns repeat,
        Clear in the merry weather.

At the clamor of the quest, the quarry trembled;   1150
Deer dashed through the dale, dazed with dread;
Hastened to the high ground, only to be
Turned back by the beaters, who boldly shouted.
They harmed not the harts, with their high heads,
Let the bucks go by, with their broad antlers,   1155
For it was counted a crime, in the close[4] season,
If a man of that demesne should molest the male deer.
The hinds were headed up, with "Hey!" and "Ware!"
The does with great din were driven to the valleys.
Then you were ware, as they went, of the whistling of arrows;   1160
At each bend under boughs the bright shafts flew
That tore the tawny hide with their tapered heads.
Ah! They bray and they bleed, on banks they die,
And ever the pack pell-mell comes panting behind;
Hunters with shrill horns hot on their heels—   1165
Like the cracking of cliffs their cries resounded.
What game got away from the gallant archers
Was promptly picked off at the posts below
When they were harried on the heights and herded to the streams:
The watchers were so wary at the waiting-stations,   1170
And the greyhounds so huge, that eagerly snatched,
And finished them off as fast as folk could see
                 with sight.
        The lord, now here, now there,
        Spurs forth in sheer delight.   1175
        And drives, with pleasures rare,
        The day to the dark night.

So the lord in the linden-wood leads the hunt
And Gawain the good knight in gay bed lies,
Lingered late alone, till daylight gleamed,   1180
Under coverlet costly, curtained about.
And as he slips into slumber, slyly there comes

---

4. Or closed.

A little din at his door, and the latch lifted,
And he holds up his heavy head out of the clothes;
A corner of the curtain he caught back a little   1185
And waited there warily, to see what befell.
Lo! it was the lady, loveliest to behold,
That drew the door behind her deftly and still
And was bound for his bed—abashed was the knight,
And laid his head low again in likeness of sleep;   1190
And she stepped stealthily, and stole to his bed,
Cast aside the curtain and came within,
And set herself softly on the bedside there,
And lingered at her leisure, to look on his waking.
The fair knight lay feigning for a long while,   1195
Conning in his conscience what his case might
Mean or amount to—a marvel he thought it.
But yet he said within himself, "More seemly it were
To try her intent by talking a little."
So he started and stretched, as startled from sleep,   1200
Lifts wide his lids in likeness of wonder,
And signs himself swiftly, as safer to be,
                              with art.
                    Sweetly does she speak
                    And kindling glances dart,   1205
                    Blent white and red on cheek
                    And laughing lips apart.

"Good morning, Sir Gawain," said that gay lady,
"A slack sleeper you are, to let one slip in!
Now you are taken in a trice—a truce we must make,   1210
Or I shall bind you in your bed, of that be assured."
Thus laughing lightly that lady jested.
"Good morning, good lady," said Gawain the blithe,
"Be it with me as you will; I am well content!
For I surrender myself, and sue for your grace,   1215
And that is best, I believe, and behooves me now."
Thus jested in answer that gentle knight.
"But if, lovely lady, you misliked it not,
And were pleased to permit your prisoner to rise,
I should quit this couch and accoutre me better,   1220
And be clad in more comfort for converse here."
"Nay, not so, sweet sir," said the smiling lady;
"You shall not rise from your bed; I direct you better:
I shall hem and hold you on either hand,
And keep company awhile with my captive knight.   1225
For as certain as I sit here, Sir Gawain you are,
Whom all the world worships, whereso you ride;
Your honor, your courtesy are highest acclaimed
By lords and by ladies, by all living men;
And lo! we are alone here, and left to ourselves: 1230
My lord and his liegemen are long departed,
The household asleep, my handmaids too,

The door drawn, and held by a well-driven bolt,
And since I have in this house him whom all love,
I shall while the time away with mirthful speech   1235
                    at will.
          My body is here at hand,
          Your each wish to fulfill;
          Your servant to command
          I am, and shall be still."   1240

"In good faith," said Gawain, "my gain is the greater,
Though I am not he of whom you have heard;
To arrive at such reverence as you recount here
I am one all unworthy, and well do I know it.
By heaven, I would hold me the happiest of men   1245
If by word or by work I once might aspire
To the prize of your praise—'twere a pure joy!"
"In good faith, Sir Gawain," said that gay lady,
"The well-proven prowess that pleases all others,
Did I scant or scout⁵ it, 'twere scarce becoming.   1250
But there are ladies, believe me, that had liefer far⁶
Have thee here in their hold, as I have today,
To pass an hour in pastime with pleasant words,
Assuage all their sorrows and solace their hearts,
Than much of the goodly gems and gold they possess.   1255
But laud be to the Lord of the lofty skies,
For here in my hands all hearts' desire
                    doth lie."
          Great welcome got he there
          From the lady who sat him by;   1260
          With fitting speech and fair
          The good knight makes reply.

"Madame," said the merry man, "Mary reward you!
For in good faith, I find your beneficence noble.
And the fame of fair deeds runs far and wide,   1265
But the praise you report pertains not to me,
But comes of your courtesy and kindness of heart."
"By the high Queen of heaven" (said she) "I count it not so,
For were I worth all the women in this world alive,
And all wealth and all worship were in my hands,   1270
And I should hunt high and low, a husband to take,
For the nurture I have noted in thee, knight, here,
The comeliness and courtesies and courtly mirth—
And so I had ever heard, and now hold it true—
No other on this earth should have me for wife."   1275
"You are bound to a better man," the bold knight said,
"Yet I prize the praise you have proffered me here,
And soberly your servant, my sovereign I hold you,
And acknowledge me your knight, in the name of Christ."

5. Mock.   6. Would much rather.

So they talked of this and that until 'twas nigh noon,   1280
And ever the lady languishing in likeness of love.
With feat[7] words and fair he framed his defence,
For were she never so winsome, the warrior had
The less will to woo, for the wound that his bane
                        must be.   1285
        He must bear the blinding blow,
        For such is fate's decree;
        The lady asks leave to go;
        He grants it full and free.

Then she gaily said goodbye, and glanced at him, laughing,   1290
And as she stood, she astonished him with a stern speech:
"Now may the Giver of all good words these glad hours repay!
But our guest is not Gawain—forgot is that thought."
"How so?" said the other, and asks in some haste,
For he feared he had been at fault in the forms of his speech.   1295
But she held up her hand, and made answer thus:
"So good a knight as Gawain is given out to be,
And the model of fair demeanor and manners pure,
Had he lain so long at a lady's side,
Would have claimed a kiss, by his courtesy,   1300
Through some touch or trick of phrase at some tale's end."
Said Gawain, "Good lady, I grant it at once!
I shall kiss at your command, as becomes a knight,
And more, lest you mislike, so let be, I pray."
With that she turns toward him, takes him in her arms,   1305
Leans down her lovely head, and lo! he is kissed.
They commend each other to Christ with comely words,
He sees her forth safely, in silence they part,
And then he lies no later in his lofty bed,
But calls to his chamberlain, chooses his clothes,   1310
Goes in those garments gladly to mass,
Then takes his way to table, where attendants wait,
And made merry all day, till the moon rose
                  in view
        Was never knight beset   1315
        'Twixt worthier ladies two:
        The crone and the coquette;
        Fair pastimes they pursue.

And the lord of the land rides late and long,
Hunting the barren hind[8] over the broad heath.   1320
He had slain such a sum, when the sun sank low,
Of does and other deer, as would dizzy one's wits.
Then they trooped in together in triumph at last,
And the count of the quarry quickly they take.
The lords lent a hand with their liegemen many,   1325
Picked out the plumpest and put them together
And duly dressed the deer, as the deed requires.

---

7. Fitting.   8. Female deer that are not pregnant.

Some were assigned the assay of the fat:
Two fingers'-width fully they found on the leanest.
Then they slit the slot[9] open and searched out the paunch,   1330
Trimmed it with trencher-knives and tied it up tight.
They flayed the fair hide from the legs and trunk,
Then broke open the belly and laid bare the bowels,
Deftly detaching and drawing them forth.
And next at the neck they neatly parted   1335
The weasand[1] from the windpipe, and cast away the guts.
At the shoulders with sharp blades they showed their skill,
Boning them from beneath, lest the sides be marred;
They breached the broad breast and broke it in twain,
And again at the gullet they begin with their knives,   1340
Cleave down the carcass clear to the breach;
Two tender morsels they take from the throat,
Then round the inner ribs they rid off a layer
And carve out the kidney-fat, close to the spine,
Hewing down to the haunch, that all hung together,   1345
And held it up whole, and hacked it free,
And this they named the numbles,[2] that knew such terms
                                    of art.
                    They divide the crotch in two,
                    And straightway then they start   1350
                    To cut the backbone through
                    And cleave the trunk apart.

With hard strokes they hewed off the head and the neck,
Then swiftly from the sides they severed the chine,
And the corbie's bone[3] they cast on a branch.   1355
Then they pierced the plump sides, impaled either one
With the hock of the hind foot, and hung it aloft,
To each person his portion most proper and fit.
On a hide of a hind the hounds they fed
With the liver and the lights,[4] the leathery paunches,   1360
And bread soaked in blood well blended therewith.
High horns and shrill set hounds a-baying,
Then merrily with their meat they make their way home,
Blowing on their bugles many a brave blast.
Ere dark had descended, that doughty band   1365
Was come within the walls where Gawain waits
                                    at leisure.
                    Bliss and hearth-fire bright
                    Await the master's pleasure;
                    When the two men met that night,   1370
                    Joy surpassed all measure.

Then the host in the hall his household assembles,
With the dames of high degree and their damsels fair.
In the presence of the people, a party he sends

---

9. The hollow above the breastbone.   1. Esophagus.   2. Other internal organs.   3. A bit of gristle
for the ravens ("corbies").   4. Lungs.

To convey him his venison in view of the knight.   1375
And in high good-humor he hails him then,
Counts over the kill, the cuts on the tallies,[5]
Holds high the hewn ribs, heavy with fat.
"What think you, sir, of this? Have I thriven well?
Have I won with my woodcraft a worthy prize?"   1380
"In good earnest," said Gawain, "this game is the finest
I have seen in seven years in the season of winter."
"And I give it to you, Gawain," said the goodly host,
"For according to our covenant, you claim it as your own."
"That is so," said Sir Gawain, "the same say I: 1385
What I worthily have won within these fair walls,
Herewith I as willingly award it to you."
He embraces his broad neck with both his arms,
And confers on him a kiss in the comeliest style.
"Have here my profit, it proved no better;   1390
Ungrudging do I grant it, were it greater far."
"Such a gift," said the good host, "I gladly accept—
Yet it might be all the better, would you but say
Where you won this same award, by your wits alone."
"That was no part of the pact; press me no further,   1395
For you have had what behooves; all other claims
       forbear."
     With jest and compliment
     They conversed, and cast off care;
     To the table soon they went;   1400
     Fresh dainties wait them there.

And then by the chimney-side they chat at their ease;
The best wine was brought them, and bounteously served;
And after in their jesting they jointly accord
To do on the second day the deeds of the first: 1405
That the two men should trade, betide as it may,
What each had taken in, at eve when they met.
They seal the pact solemnly in sight of the court;
Their cups were filled afresh to confirm the jest;
Then at last they took their leave, for late was the hour,   1410
Each to his own bed hastening away.
Before the barnyard cock had crowed but thrice
The lord had leapt from his rest, his liegemen as well.
Both of mass and their meal they made short work:
By the dim light of dawn they were deep in the woods   1415
       away.
     With huntsmen and with horns
     Over plains they pass that day;
     They release, amid the thorns,
     Swift hounds that run and bay.   1420

Soon some were on a scent by the side of a marsh;
When the hounds opened cry, the head of the hunt

5. Notched sticks were used to count the animals taken in the hunt.

Rallied them with rough words, raised a great noise.
The hounds that had heard it came hurrying straight
And followed along with their fellows, forty together.　　1425
Then such a clamor and cry of coursing hounds
Arose, that the rocks resounded again.
Hunters exhorted them with horn and with voice;
Then all in a body bore off together
Between a mere[6] in the marsh and a menacing crag,　　1430
To a rise where the rock stood rugged and steep,
And boulders lay about, that blocked their approach.
Then the company in consort closed on their prey:
They surrounded the rise and the rocks both,
For well they were aware that it waited within,　　1435
The beast that the bloodhounds boldly proclaimed.
Then they beat on the bushes and bade him appear,
And he made a murderous rush in the midst of them all;
The best of all boars broke from his cover,
That had ranged long unrivaled, a renegade old,　　1440
For of tough-brawned boars he was biggest far,
Most grim when he grunted—then grieved were many,
For three at the first thrust he threw to the earth,
And dashed away at once without more damage.
With "Hi!" "Hi!" and "Hey!" "Hey!" the others followed,　　1445
Had horns at their lips, blew high and clear.
Merry was the music of men and of hounds
That were bound after this boar, his bloodthirsty heart
　　　　　　　　to quell.
　　　　　　Often he stands at bay,　　1450
　　　　　　Then scatters the pack pell-mell;
　　　　　　He hurts the hounds, and they
　　　　　　Most dolefully yowl and yell.

Men then with mighty bows moved in to shoot,
Aimed at him with their arrows and often hit,　　1455
But the points had no power to pierce through his hide,
And the barbs were brushed aside by his bristly brow;
Though the shank of the shaft shivered in pieces,
The head hopped away, wheresoever it struck.
But when their stubborn strokes had stung him at last,　　1460
Then, foaming in his frenzy, fiercely he charges,
Hies at them headlong that hindered his flight,
And many feared for their lives, and fell back a little.
But the lord on a lively horse leads the chase;
As a high-mettled huntsman his horn he blows;　　1465
He sounds the assembly and sweeps through the brush,
Pursuing this wild swine till the sunlight slanted.
All day with this deed they drive forth the time
While our lone knight so lovesome lies in his bed,
Sir Gawain safe at home, in silken bower　　1470
　　　　　　　so gay.
　　　　　The lady, with guile in heart,

6. Pool.

Came early where he lay;
She was at him with all her art
To turn his mind her way.   1475

She comes to the curtain and coyly peeps in;
Gawain thought it good to greet her at once,
And she richly repays him with her ready words,
Settles softly at his side, and suddenly she laughs,
And with a gracious glance, she begins on him thus: 1480
"Sir, if you be Gawain, it seems a great wonder—
A man so well-meaning, and mannerly disposed,
And cannot act in company as courtesy bids,
And if one takes the trouble to teach him, 'tis all in vain.
That lesson learned lately is lightly forgot,   1485
Though I painted it as plain as my poor wit allowed."
"What lesson, dear lady?" he asked all alarmed;
"I have been much to blame, if your story be true."
"Yet my counsel was of kissing," came her answer then,
"Where favor has been found, freely to claim   1490
As accords with the conduct of courteous knights."
"My dear," said the doughty man, "dismiss that thought;
Such freedom, I fear, might offend you much;
It were rude to request if the right were denied."
"But none can deny you," said the noble dame,   1495
"You are stout enough to constrain with strength, if you choose,
Were any so ungracious as to grudge you aught."
"By heaven," said he, "you have answered well,
But threats never throve among those of my land,
Nor any gift not freely given, good though it be.   1500
I am yours to command, to kiss when you please;
You may lay on as you like, and leave off at will."
              With this,
          The lady lightly bends
          And graciously gives him a kiss;   1505
          The two converse as friends
          Of true love's trials and bliss.

"I should like, by your leave," said the lovely lady,
"If it did not annoy you, to know for what cause
So brisk and so bold a young blood as you,   1510
And acclaimed for all courtesies becoming a knight—
And name what knight you will, they are noblest esteemed
For loyal faith in love, in life as in story;
For to tell the tribulations of these true hearts,
Why, 'tis the very title and text of their deeds,   1515
How bold knights for beauty have braved many a foe,
Suffered heavy sorrows out of secret love,
And then valorously avenged them on villainous churls
And made happy ever after the hearts of their ladies.
And you are the noblest knight known in your time;   1520
No household under heaven but has heard of your fame,
And here by your side I have sat for two days

Yet never has a fair phrase fallen from your lips
Of the language of love, not one little word!
And you, that with sweet vows sway women's hearts,   1525
Should show your winsome ways, and woo a young thing,
And teach by some tokens the craft of true love.
How! are you artless, whom all men praise?
Or do you deem me so dull, or deaf to such words?
                             Fie! Fie!   1530
                    In hope of pastimes new
                    I have come where none can spy;
                    Instruct me a little, do,
                    While my husband is not nearby."

"God love you, gracious lady!" said Gawain then;   1535
"It is a pleasure surpassing, and a peerless joy,
That one so worthy as you would willingly come
And take the time and trouble to talk with your knight
And content you with his company—it comforts my heart.
But to take to myself the task of telling of love,   1540
And touch upon its texts, and treat of its themes
To one that, I know well, wields more power
In that art, by a half, than a hundred such
As I am where I live, or am like to become,
It were folly, fair dame, in the first degree!   1545
In all that I am able, my aim is to please,
As in honor behooves me, and am evermore
Your servant heart and soul, so save me our Lord!"
Thus she tested his temper and tried many a time,
Whatever her true intent, to entice him to sin,   1550
But so fair was his defense that no fault appeared,
Nor evil on either hand, but only bliss
                             they knew.
                    They linger and laugh awhile;
                    She kisses the knight so true,   1555
                    Takes leave in comeliest style
                    And departs without more ado.

Then he rose from his rest and made ready for mass,
And then a meal was set and served, in sumptuous style;
He dallied at home all day with the dear ladies,   1560
But the lord lingered late at his lusty sport;
Pursued his sorry swine, that swerved as he fled,
And bit asunder the backs of the best of his hounds
When they brought him to bay, till the bowmen appeared
And soon forced him forth, though he fought for dear life,   1565
So sharp were the shafts they shot at him there.
But yet the boldest drew back from his battering head,
Till at last he was so tired he could travel no more,
But in as much haste as he might, he makes his retreat
To a rise on rocky ground, by a rushing stream.   1570
With the bank at his back he scrapes the bare earth,
The froth foams at his jaws, frightful to see.

He whets his white tusks—then weary were all
Those hunters so hardy that hoved[7] round about
Of aiming from afar, but ever they mistrust   1575
        his mood.
        He had hurt so many by then
        That none had hardihood
        To be torn by his tusks again,
        That was brainsick, and out for blood.   1580

Till the lord came at last on his lofty steed,
Beheld him there at bay before all his folk;
Lightly he leaps down, leaves his courser,
Bares his bright sword, and boldly advances;
Straight into the stream he strides towards his foe.   1585
The wild thing was wary of weapon and man;
His hackles rose high; so hotly he snorts
That many watched with alarm, lest the worst befall.
The boar makes for the man with a mighty bound
So that he and his hunter came headlong together   1590
Where the water ran wildest—the worse for the beast,
For the man, when they first met, marked him with care,
Sights well the slot, slips in the blade,
Shoves it home to the hilt, and the heart shattered,
And he falls in his fury and floats down the water,   1595
        ill-sped.
        Hounds hasten by the score
        To maul him, hide and head;
        Men drag him in to shore
        And dogs pronounce him dead.   1600

With many a brave blast they boast of their prize,
All hallooed in high glee, that had their wind;
The hounds bayed their best, as the bold men bade
That were charged with chief rank in that chase of renown.
Then one wise in woodcraft, and worthily skilled,   1605
Began to dress the boar in becoming style:
He severs the savage head and sets it aloft,
Then rends the body roughly right down the spine;
Takes the bowels from the belly, broils them on coals,
Blends them well with bread to bestow on the hounds.   1610
Then he breaks out the brawn in fair broad flitches,
And the innards to be eaten in order he takes.
The two sides, attached to each other all whole,
He suspended from a spar that was springy and tough;
And so with this swine they set out for home;   1615
The boar's head was borne before the same man
That had stabbed him in the stream with his strong arm,
        right through.
        He thought it long indeed
        Till he had the knight in view;   1620

7. Hovered.

> At his call, he comes with speed
> To claim his payment due.

The lord laughed aloud, with many a light word,
When he greeted Sir Gawain—with good cheer he speaks.
They fetch the fair dames and the folk of the house;   1625
He brings forth the brawn, and begins the tale
Of the great length and girth, the grim rage as well,
Of the battle of the boar they beset in the wood.
The other men meetly commended his deeds
And praised well the prize of his princely sport,   1630
For the brawn of that boar, the bold knight said,
And the sides of that swine surpassed all others.
Then they handled the huge head; he owns it a wonder,
And eyes it with abhorrence, to heighten his praise.
"Now, Gawain," said the good man, "this game becomes yours   1635
By those fair terms we fixed, as you know full well."
"That is true," returned the knight, "and trust me, fair friend,
All my gains, as agreed, I shall give you forthwith."
He clasps him and kisses him in courteous style,
Then serves him with the same fare a second time.   1640
"Now we are even," said he, "at this evening feast,
And clear is every claim incurred here to date,
> and debt."
> "By Saint Giles!" the host replies,
> "You're the best I ever met!   1645
> If your profits are all this size,
> We'll see you wealthy yet!"

Then attendants set tables on trestles about,
And laid them with linen; light shone forth,
Wakened along the walls in waxen torches.   1650
The service was set and the supper brought;
Royal were the revels that rose then in hall
At that feast by the fire, with many fair sports:
Amid the meal and after, melody sweet,
Carol-dances comely and Christmas songs,   1655
With all the mannerly mirth my tongue may describe.
And ever our gallant knight beside the gay lady;
So uncommonly kind and complaisant was she,
With sweet stolen glances, that stirred his stout heart,
That he was at his wits' end, and wondrous vexed;   1660
But he could not in conscience her courtship repay,
Yet took pains to please her, though the plan might
> go wrong.
> When they to heart's delight
> Had reveled there in throng,   1665
> To his chamber he calls the knight,
> And thither they go along.

And there they dallied and drank, and deemed it good sport
To enact their play anew on New Year's Eve,

But Gawain asked again to go on the morrow, 1670
For the time until his tryst was not two days.
The host hindered that, and urged him to stay,
And said, "On my honor, my oath here I take
That you shall get to the Green Chapel to begin your chores
By dawn on New Year's Day, if you so desire. 1675
Wherefore lie at your leisure in your lofty bed,
And I shall hunt hereabouts, and hold to our terms,
And we shall trade winnings when once more we meet,
For I have tested you twice, and true have I found you;
Now think this tomorrow: the third pays for all; 1680
Be we merry while we may, and mindful of joy,
For heaviness of heart can be had for the asking."
This is gravely agreed on and Gawain will stay.
They drink a last draught and with torches depart
                       to rest. 1685
          To bed Sir Gawain went;
          His sleep was of the best;
          The lord, on his craft intent,
          Was early up and dressed.

After mass, with his men, a morsel he takes; 1690
Clear and crisp the morning; he calls for his mount;
The folk that were to follow him afield that day
Were high astride their horses before the hall gates.
Wondrous fair were the fields, for the frost was light;
The sun rises red amid radiant clouds, 1695
Sails into the sky, and sends forth his beams.
They let loose the hounds by a leafy wood;
The rocks all around re-echo to their horns;
Soon some have set off in pursuit of the fox,
Cast about with craft for a clearer scent; 1700
A young dog yaps, and is yelled at in turn;
His fellows fall to sniffing, and follow his lead,
Running in a rabble on the right track,
And he scampers all before; they discover him soon,
And when they see him with sight they pursue him the faster, 1705
Railing at him rudely with a wrathful din.
Often he reverses over rough terrain,
Or loops back to listen in the lee of a hedge;
At last, by a little ditch, he leaps over the brush,
Comes into a clearing at a cautious pace, 1710
Then he thought through his wiles to have thrown off the hounds
Till he was ware, as he went, of a waiting-station
Where three athwart his path threatened him at once,
                   all gray.
          Quick as a flash he wheels 1715
          And darts off in dismay;
          With hard luck at his heels
          He is off to the wood away.

Then it was heaven on earth to hark to the hounds
When they had come on their quarry, coursing together! 1720

Such harsh cries and howls they hurled at his head
As all the cliffs with a crash had come down at once.
Here he was hailed, when huntsmen met him;
Yonder they yelled at him, yapping and snarling;
There they cried "Thief!" and threatened his life,   1725
And ever the harriers at his heels, that he had no rest.
Often he was menaced when he made for the open,
And often rushed in again, for Reynard was wily;
And so he leads them a merry chase, the lord and his men,
In this manner on the mountains, till midday or near,   1730
While our hero lies at home in wholesome sleep
Within the comely curtains on the cold morning.
But the lady, as love would allow her no rest,
And pursuing ever the purpose that pricked her heart,
Was awake with the dawn, and went to his chamber   1735
In a fair flowing mantle that fell to the earth,
All edged and embellished with ermines fine;
No hood on her head, but heavy with gems
Were her fillet and the fret[8] that confined her tresses;
Her face and her fair throat freely displayed;   1740
Her bosom all but bare, and her back as well.
She comes in at the chamber-door, and closes it with care,
Throws wide a window—then waits no longer,
But hails him thus airily with her artful words,
      with cheer: 1745
   "Ah, man, how can you sleep?
   The morning is so clear!"
   Though dreams have drowned him deep,
   He cannot choose but hear.

Deep in his dreams he darkly mutters   1750
As a man may that mourns, with many grim thoughts
Of that day when destiny shall deal him his doom
When he greets his grim host at the Green Chapel
And must bow to his buffet, bating all strife.
But when he sees her at his side he summons his wits,   1755
Breaks from the black dreams, and blithely answers.
That lovely lady comes laughing sweet,
Sinks down at his side, and salutes him with a kiss.
He accords her fair welcome in courtliest style;
He sees her so glorious, so gaily attired,   1760
So faultless her features, so fair and so bright,
His heart swelled swiftly with surging joys.
They melt into mirth with many a fond smile,
And there was bliss beyond telling between those two,
     at height.   1765
   Good were their words of greeting;
   Each joyed in other's sight;
   Great peril attends that meeting
   Should Mary forget her knight.

8. Ornamental net.

For that high-born beauty so hemmed him about,   1770
Made so plain her meaning, the man must needs
Either take her tendered love or distastefully refuse.
His courtesy concerned him, lest crass he appear,
But more his soul's mischief, should he commit sin
And belie his loyal oath to the lord of that house.   1775
"God forbid!" said the bold knight, "That shall not befall!"
With a little fond laughter he lightly let pass
All the words of special weight that were sped his way;
"I find you much at fault," the fair one said,
"Who can be cold toward a creature so close by your side,   1780
Of all women in this world most wounded in heart,
Unless you have a sweetheart, one you hold dearer,
And allegiance to that lady so loyally knit
That you will never love another, as now I believe.
And, sir, if it be so, then say it, I beg you;   1785
By all your heart holds dear, hide it no longer
                         with guile."
               "Lady, by Saint John,"
               He answers with a smile,
               "Lover have I none,   1790
               Nor will have, yet awhile."

"Those words," said the woman, "are the worst of all,
But I have had my answer, and hard do I find it!
Kiss me now kindly; I can but go hence
To lament my life long like a maid lovelorn."   1795
She inclines her head quickly and kisses the knight,
Then straightens with a sigh, and says as she stands,
"Now, dear, ere I depart, do me this pleasure:
Give me some little gift, your glove or the like,
That I may think on you, man, and mourn the less."   1800
"Now by heaven," said he, "I wish I had here
My most precious possession, to put it in your hands,
For your deeds, beyond doubt, have often deserved
A repayment far passing my power to bestow.
But a love-token, lady, were of little avail;   1805
It is not to your honor to have at this time
A glove as a guerdon from Gawain's hand,
And I am here on an errand in unknown realms
And have no bearers with baggage with becoming gifts,
Which distresses me, madame, for your dear sake.   1810
A man must keep within his compass: account it neither grief
                         nor slight."
               "Nay, noblest knight alive,"
               Said that beauty of body white,
               "Though you be loath to give,   1815
               Yet you shall take, by right."

She reached out a rich ring, wrought all of gold,
With a splendid stone displayed on the band
That flashed before his eyes like a fiery sun;

It was worth a king's wealth, you may well believe.   1820
But he waved it away with these ready words:
"Before God, good lady, I forego all gifts;
None have I to offer, nor any will I take."
And she urged it on him eagerly, and ever he refused,
And vowed in very earnest, prevail she would not.   1825
And she sad to find it so, and said to him then,
"If my ring is refused for its rich cost—
You would not be my debtor for so dear a thing—
I shall give you my girdle;⁹ you gain less thereby."
She released a knot lightly, and loosened a belt   1830
That was caught about her kirtle, the bright cloak beneath,
Of a gay green silk, with gold overwrought,
And the borders all bound with embroidery fine,
And this she presses upon him, and pleads with a smile,
Unworthy though it were, that it would not be scorned.   1835
But the man still maintains that he means to accept
Neither gold nor any gift, till by God's grace
The fate that lay before him was fully achieved.
"And be not offended, fair lady, I beg,
And give over your offer, for ever I must   1840
                            decline.
                I am grateful for favor shown
                Past all deserts of mine,
                And ever shall be your own
                True servant, rain or shine."   1845

"Now does my present displease you," she promptly inquired,
"Because it seems in your sight so simple a thing?
And belike, as it is little, it is less to praise,
But if the virtue that invests it were verily known,
It would be held, I hope, in higher esteem.   1850
For the man that possesses this piece of silk,
If he bore it on his body, belted about,
There is no hand under heaven that could hew him down,
For he could not be killed by any craft on earth."
Then the man began to muse, and mainly he thought   1855
It was a pearl for his plight, the peril to come
When he gains the Green Chapel to get his reward:
Could he escape unscathed, the scheme were noble!
Then he bore with her words and withstood them no more,
And she repeated her petition and pleaded anew,   1860
And he granted it, and gladly she gave him the belt,
And besought him for her sake to conceal it well,
Lest the noble lord should know—and the knight agrees
That not a soul save themselves shall see it thenceforth
                            with sight.   1865
                He thanked her with fervent heart,
                As often as ever he might;

9. Belt.

Three times, before they part,
She has kissed the stalwart knight.

Then the lady took her leave, and left him there,   1870
For more mirth with that man she might not have.
When she was gone, Sir Gawain got from his bed,
Arose and arrayed him in his rich attire;
Tucked away the token the temptress had left,
Laid it reliably where he looked for it after.   1875
And then with good cheer to the chapel he goes,
Approached a priest in private, and prayed to be taught
To lead a better life and lift up his mind,
Lest he be among the lost when he must leave this world.
And shamefaced at shrift[1] he showed his misdeeds   1880
From the largest to the least, and asked the Lord's mercy,
And called on his confessor to cleanse his soul,
And he absolved him of his sins as safe and as clean
As if the dread Day of Judgment should dawn on the morrow.
And then he made merry amid the fine ladies   1885
With deft-footed dances and dalliance light,
As never until now, while the afternoon wore
                          away.
            He delighted all around him,
            And all agreed, that day,   1890
            They never before had found him
            So gracious and so gay.

Now peaceful be his pasture, and love play him fair!
The host is on horseback, hunting afield;
He has finished off this fox that he followed so long: 1895
As he leapt a low hedge to look for the villain
Where he heard all the hounds in hot pursuit,
Reynard comes racing out of a rough thicket,
And all the rabble in a rush, right at his heels.
The man beholds the beast, and bides his time,   1900
And bares his bright sword, and brings it down hard,
And he blenches from the blade, and backward he starts;
A hound hurries up and hinders that move,
And before the horse's feet they fell on him at once
And ripped the rascal's throat with a wrathful din.   1905
The lord soon alighted and lifted him free,
Swiftly snatched him up from the snapping jaws,
Holds him over his head, halloos with a will,
And the dogs bayed the dirge, that had done him to death.
Hunters hastened thither with horns at their lips,   1910
Sounding the assembly till they saw him at last.
When that comely company was come in together,
All that bore bugles blew them at once,
And the others all hallooed, that had no horns.
It was the merriest medley that ever a man heard,   1915

---

1. Confession.

The racket that they raised for Sir Reynard's soul
                    that died.
         Their hounds they praised and fed,
         Fondling their heads with pride,
         And they took Reynard the Red   1920
         And stripped away his hide.

And then they headed homeward, for evening had come,
Blowing many a blast on their bugles bright.
The lord at long last alights at his house,
Finds fire on the hearth where the fair knight waits,   1925
Sir Gawain the good, that was glad in heart.
With the ladies, that loved him, he lingered at ease;
He wore a rich robe of blue, that reached to the earth
And a surcoat lined softly with sumptuous furs;
A hood of the same hue hung on his shoulders;   1930
With bands of bright ermine embellished were both.
He comes to meet the man amid all the folk,
And greets him good-humoredly, and gaily he says,
"I shall follow forthwith the form of our pledge
That we framed to good effect amid fresh-filled cups."   1935
He clasps him accordingly and kisses him thrice,
As amiably and as earnestly as ever he could.
"By heaven," said the host, "you have had some luck
Since you took up this trade, if the terms were good."
"Never trouble about the terms," he returned at once,   1940
"Since all that I owe here is openly paid."
"Marry!" said the other man, "mine is much less,
For I have hunted all day, and nought have I got
But this foul fox pelt, the fiend take the goods!
Which but poorly repays those precious things   1945
That you have cordially conferred, those kisses three
                so good."
         "Enough!" said Sir Gawain;
         "I thank you, by the rood!"[2]
         And how the fox was slain   1950
         He told him, as they stood.

With minstrelsy and mirth, with all manner of meats,
They made as much merriment as any men might
(Amid laughing of ladies and light-hearted girls,
So gay grew Sir Gawain and the goodly host)   1955
Unless they had been besotted, or brainless fools.
The knight joined in jesting with that joyous folk,
Until at last it was late; ere long they must part,
And be off to their beds, as behooved them each one.
Then politely his leave of the lord of the house   1960
Our noble knight takes, and renews his thanks:
"The courtesies countless accorded me here,
Your kindness at this Christmas, may heaven's King repay!

2. Cross.

Henceforth, if you will have me, I hold you my liege,
And so, as I have said, I must set forth tomorrow,   1965
If I may take some trusty man to teach, as you promised,
The way to the Green Chapel, that as God allows
I shall see my fate fulfilled on the first of the year."
"In good faith," said the good man, "with a good will
Every promise on my part shall be fully performed."   1970
He assigns him a servant to set him on the path,
To see him safe and sound over the snowy hills,
To follow the fastest way through forest green
                    and grove.
                Gawain thanks him again,   1975
                So kind his favors prove,
                of the ladies then
                He takes his leave, with love.

Courteously he kissed them, with care in his heart,
And often wished them well, with warmest thanks,   1980
Which they for their part were prompt to repay.
They commend him to Christ with disconsolate sighs;
And then in that hall with the household he parts—
Each man that he met, he remembered to thank
or his deeds of devotion and diligent pains,   1985
And the trouble he had taken to tend to his needs;
And each one as woeful, that watched him depart,
As he had lived with him loyally all his life long.
By lads bearing lights he was led to his chamber
And blithely brought to his bed, to be at his rest.   1990
How soundly he slept, I presume not to say,
For there were matters of moment his thoughts might well
                    pursue.
                Let him lie and wait;
                He has little more to do,   1995
                Then listen, while I relate
                How they kept their rendezvous.

PART IV

Now the New Year draws near, and the night passes,
The day dispels the dark, by the Lord's decree;
But wild weather awoke in the world without: 2000
The clouds in the cold sky cast down their snow
With great gusts from the north, grievous to bear.
Sleet showered aslant upon shivering beasts;
The wind warbled wild as it whipped from aloft,
And drove the drifts deep in the dales below.   2005
Long and well he listens, that lies in his bed;
Though he lifts not his eyelids, little he sleeps;
Each crow of the cock he counts without fail.
Readily from his rest he rose before dawn,
For a lamp had been left him, that lighted his chamber.   2010
He called to his chamberlain, who quickly appeared,

And bade him get him his gear, and gird his good steed,
And he sets about briskly to bring in his arms,
And makes ready his master in manner most fit.
First he clad him in his clothes, to keep out the cold,   2015
And then his other harness, made handsome anew,
His plate-armor of proof, polished with pains,
The rings of his rich mail rid of their rust,
And all was fresh as at first, and for this he gave thanks
                    indeed.   2020
          With pride he wears each piece,
          New-furbished for his need:
          No gayer from here to Greece;
          He bids them bring his steed.

In his richest raiment he robed himself then: 2025
His crested coat-armor, close-stitched with craft,
With stones of strange virtue on silk velvet set;
All bound with embroidery on borders and seams
And lined warmly and well with furs of the best.
Yet he left not his love-gift, the lady's girdle;   2030
Gawain, for his own good, forgot not that:
When the bright sword was belted and bound on his haunches,
Then twice with that token he twined him about.
Sweetly did he swathe him in that swatch of silk,
That girdle of green so goodly to see,   2035
That against the gay red showed gorgeous bright.
Yet he wore not for its wealth that wondrous girdle,
Nor pride in its pendants, though polished they were,
Though glittering gold gleamed at the tips,
But to keep himself safe when consent he must   2040
To endure a deadly dint, and all defense
                    denied.
          And now the bold knight came
          Into the courtyard wide;
          That folk of worthy fame   2045
          He thanks on every side.

Then was Gringolet girt, that was great and huge,
And had sojourned safe and sound, and savored his fare;
He pawed the earth in his pride, that princely steed.
The good knight draws near him and notes well his look,   2050
And says sagely to himself, and soberly swears,
"Here is a household in hall that upholds the right!
The man that maintains it, may happiness be his!
Likewise the dear lady, may love betide her!
If thus they in charity cherish a guest   2055
That are honored here on earth, may they have His reward
That reigns high in heaven—and also you all;
And were I to live in this land but a little while,
I should willingly reward you, and well, if I might."
Then he steps into the stirrup and bestrides his mount;   2060
His shield is shown forth; on his shoulder he casts it;

Strikes the side of his steed with his steel spurs,
And he starts across the stones, nor stands any longer
        to prance.
        On horseback was the swain   2065
        That bore his spear and lance;
        "May Christ this house maintain
        And guard it from mischance!"

The bridge was brought down, and the broad gates
Unbarred and carried back upon both sides;   2070
He commended him[3] to Christ, and crossed over the planks;
Praised the noble porter, who prayed on his knees
That God save Sir Gawain, and bade him good day,
And went on his way alone with the man
That was to lead him ere long to that luckless place   2075
Where the dolorous dint must be dealt him at last.
Under bare boughs they ride, where steep banks rise,
Over high cliffs they climb, where cold snow clings;
The heavens held aloof, but heavy thereunder
Mist mantled the moors, moved on the slopes.   2080
Each hill had a hat, a huge cape of cloud;
Brooks bubbled and broke over broken rocks,
Flashing in freshets that waterfalls fed.
Roundabout was the road that ran through the wood
Till the sun at that season was soon to rise,   2085
        that day.
        They were on a hilltop high;
        The white snow round them lay;
        The man that rode nearby
        Now bade his master stay.   2090

"For I have seen you here safe at the set time,
And now you are not far from that notable place
That you have sought for so long with such special pains.
But this I say for certain, since I know you, sir knight,
And have your good at heart, and hold you dear—   2095
Would you heed well my words, it were worth your while—
You are rushing into risks that you reck not of:
There is a villain in yon valley, the veriest on earth,
For he is rugged and rude, and ready with fists,
And most immense in his mold of mortals alive,   2100
And his body bigger than the best four
That are in Arthur's house, Hector[4] or any.
He gets his grim way at the Green Chapel;
None passes by that place so proud in his arms
That he does not dash him down with his deadly blows,   2105
For he is heartless wholly, and heedless of right,
For be it chaplain or churl that by the Chapel rides,
Monk or mass-priest or any man else,
He would as soon strike him dead as stand on two feet.

---

3. I.e., himself.   4. Either the Trojan hero or one of Arthur's knights.

Wherefore I say, just as certain as you sit there astride,   2110
You cannot but be killed, if his counsel holds,
For he would trounce you in a trice, had you twenty lives
            for sale.
        He has lived long in this land
        And dealt out deadly bale;   2115
        Against his heavy hand
        Your power cannot prevail.

"And so, good Sir Gawain, let the grim man be;
Go off by some other road, in God's own name!
Leave by some other land, for the love of Christ,   2120
And I shall get me home again, and give you my word
That I shall swear by God's self and the saints above,
By heaven and by my halidom[5] and other oaths more,
To conceal this day's deed, nor say to a soul
That ever you fled for fear from any that I knew."   2125
"Many thanks!" said the other man—and demurring he speaks—
"Fair fortune befall you for your friendly words!
And conceal this day's deed I doubt not you would,
But though you never told the tale, if I turned back now,
Forsook this place for fear, and fled, as you say,   2130
I were a caitiff[6] coward; I could not be excused.
But I must to the Chapel to chance my luck
And say to that same man such words as I please,
Befall what may befall through Fortune's will
           or whim.   2135
        Though he be a quarrelsome knave
        With a cudgel great and grim,
        The Lord is strong to save:
        His servants trust in Him."

"Marry," said the man, "since you tell me so much,   2140
And I see you are set to seek your own harm,
If you crave a quick death, let me keep you no longer!
Put your helm on your head, your hand on your lance,
And ride the narrow road down yon rocky slope
Till it brings you to the bottom of the broad valley.   2145
Then look a little ahead, on your left hand,
And you will soon see before you that self-same Chapel,
And the man of great might that is master there.
Now goodbye in God's name, Gawain the noble!
For all the world's wealth I would not stay here,   2150
Or go with you in this wood one footstep further!"
He tarried no more to talk, but turned his bridle,
Hit his horse with his heels as hard as he might,
Leaves the knight alone, and off like the wind
           goes leaping.   2155
        "By God," said Gawain then,

---

5. Holiness or, more likely, patron saints.   6. Despicable.

> "I shall not give way to weeping;
> God's will be done, amen!
> I commend me to His keeping."

He puts his heels to his horse, and picks up the path;　　　　2160
Goes in beside a grove where the ground is steep,
Rides down the rough slope right to the valley;
And then he looked a little about him—the landscape was wild,
And not a soul to be seen, nor sign of a dwelling,
But high banks on either hand hemmed it about,　　　　2165
With many a ragged rock and rough-hewn crag;
The skies seemed scored by the scowling peaks.
Then he halted his horse, and hoved there a space,
And sought on every side for a sight of the Chapel,
But no such place appeared, which puzzled him sore,　　　　2170
Yet he saw some way off what seemed like a mound,
A hillock high and broad, hard by the water,
Where the stream fell in foam down the face of the steep
And bubbled as if it boiled on its bed below.
The knight urges his horse, and heads for the knoll;　　　　2175
Leaps lightly to earth; loops well the rein
Of his steed to a stout branch, and stations him there.
He strides straight to the mound, and strolls all about,
Much wondering what it was, but no whit the wiser;
It had a hole at one end, and on either side,　　　　2180
And was covered with coarse grass in clumps all without,
And hollow all within, like some old cave,
Or a crevice of an old crag—he could not discern
　　　　　　　　aright.
　　　　"Can this be the Chapel Green?　　　　2185
　　　　Alack!" said the man, "Here might
　　　　The devil himself be seen
　　　　Saying matins[7] at black midnight!"

"Now by heaven," said he, "it is bleak hereabouts;
This prayer-house is hideous, half-covered with grass!　　　　2190
Well may the grim man mantled in green
Hold here his orisons, in hell's own style!
Now I feel it is the Fiend, in my five wits,
That has tempted me to this tryst, to take my life;
This is a Chapel of mischance, may the mischief take it!　　　　2195
As accursed a country church as I came upon ever!"
With his helm on his head, his lance in his hand,
He stalks toward the steep wall of that strange house.
Then he heard, on the hill, behind a hard rock,
Beyond the brook, from the bank, a most barbarous din:　　　　2200
Lord! it clattered in the cliff fit to cleave it in two,
As one upon a grindstone ground a great scythe!
Lord! it whirred like a mill-wheel whirling about!
Lord! it echoed loud and long, lamentable to hear!

---

7. Morning prayers.

Then "By heaven," said the bold knight, "That business up there 2205
Is arranged for my arrival, or else I am much
      misled.
    Let God work! Ah me!
    All hope of help has fled!
    Forfeit my life may be 2210
    But noise I do not dread."

Then he listened no longer, but loudly he called,
"Who has power in this place, high parley to hold?
For none greets Sir Gawain, or gives him good day;
If any would a word with him, let him walk forth 2215
And speak now or never, to speed his affairs."
"Abide," said one on the bank above over his head,
"And what I promised you once shall straightway be given."
Yet he stayed not his grindstone, nor stinted its noise,
But worked awhile at his whetting before he would rest, 2220
And then he comes around a crag, from a cave in the rocks,
Hurtling out of hiding with a hateful weapon,
A Danish ax devised for that day's deed,
With a broad blade and bright, bent in a curve,
Filed to a fine edge—four feet it measured 2225
By the length of the lace that was looped round the haft.
And in form as at first, the fellow all green,
His lordly face and his legs, his locks and his beard,
Save that firm upon two feet forward he strides,
Sets a hand on the ax-head, the haft to the earth; 2230
When he came to the cold stream, and cared not to wade,
He vaults over on his ax, and advances amain
On a broad bank of snow, overbearing and brisk
      of mood.
    Little did the knight incline 2235
    When face to face they stood;
    Said the other man, "Friend mine,
    It seems your word holds good!"

"God love you, Sir Gawain!" said the Green Knight then,
"And well met this morning, man, at my place! 2240
And you have followed me faithfully and found me betimes,[8]
And on the business between us we both are agreed:
Twelve months ago today you took what was yours,
And you at this New Year must yield me the same.
And we have met in these mountains, remote from all eyes: 2245
There is none here to halt us or hinder our sport;
Unhasp your high helm, and have here your wages;
Make no more demur than I did myself
When you hacked off my head with one hard blow."
"No, by God," said Sir Gawain, "that granted me life, 2250
I shall grudge not the guerdon, grim though it prove;
Bestow but one stroke, and I shall stand still,

8. In good time.

And you may lay on as you like till the last of my part
      be paid."
          He proffered, with good grace,   2255
          His bare neck to the blade,
          And feigned a cheerful face:
          He scorned to seem afraid.

Then the grim man in green gathers his strength,
Heaves high the heavy ax to hit him the blow.   2260
With all the force in his frame he fetches it aloft,
With a grimace as grim as he would grind him to bits;
Had the blow he bestowed been as big as he threatened,
A good knight and gallant had gone to his grave.
But Gawain at the great ax glanced up aside   2265
As down it descended with death-dealing force,
And his shoulders shrank a little from the sharp iron.
Abruptly the brawny man breaks off the stroke,
And then reproved with proud words that prince among knights.
"You are not Gawain the glorious," the green man said,   2270
"That never fell back on field in the face of the foe,
And now you flee for fear, and have felt no harm:
Such news of that knight I never heard yet!
I moved not a muscle when you made to strike,
Nor caviled at the cut in King Arthur's house;   2275
My head fell to my feet, yet steadfast I stood,
And you, all unharmed, are wholly dismayed—
Wherefore the better man I, by all odds,
              must be."
          Said Gawain, "Strike once more;   2280
          I shall neither flinch nor flee;
          But if my head falls to the floor
          There is no mending me!

"But go on, man, in God's name, and get to the point!
Deliver me my destiny, and do it out of hand,   2285
For I shall stand to the stroke and stir not an inch
Till your ax has hit home—on my honor I swear it!"
"Have at thee then!" said the other, and heaves it aloft,
And glares down as grimly as he had gone mad.
He made a mighty feint, but marred not his hide;   2290
Withdrew the ax adroitly before it did damage.
Gawain gave no ground, nor glanced up aside,
But stood still as a stone, or else a stout stump
That is held in hard earth by a hundred roots.
Then merrily does he mock him, the man all in green: 2295
"So now you have your nerve again, I needs must strike;
Uphold the high knighthood that Arthur bestowed,
And keep your neck-bone clear, if this cut allows!"
Then was Gawain gripped with rage, and grimly he said,
"Why, thrash away, tyrant, I tire of your threats;   2300
You make such a scene, you must frighten yourself."
Said the green fellow, "In faith, so fiercely you speak

That I shall finish this affair, nor further grace
allow."
He stands prepared to strike 2305
And scowls with both lip and brow;
No marvel if the man mislike
Who can hope no rescue now.

He gathered up the grim ax and guided it well:
Let the barb at the blade's end brush the bare throat; 2310
He hammered down hard, yet harmed him no whit
Save a scratch on one side, that severed the skin;
The end of the hooked edge entered the flesh,
And a little blood lightly leapt to the earth.
And when the man beheld his own blood bright on the snow, 2315
He sprang a spear's length with feet spread wide,
Seized his high helm, and set it on his head,
Shoved before his shoulders the shield at his back,
Bares his trusty blade, and boldly he speaks—
Not since he was a babe born of his mother 2320
Was he once in this world one-half so blithe—
"Have done with your hacking—harry me no more!
I have borne, as behooved, one blow in this place;
If you make another move I shall meet it midway
And promptly, I promise you, pay back each blow 2325
with brand.
One stroke acquits me here;
So did our covenant stand
In Arthur's court last year—
Wherefore, sir, hold your hand!" 2330

He lowers the long ax and leans on it there,
Sets his arms on the head, the haft on the earth,
And beholds the bold knight that bides there afoot,
How he faces him fearless, fierce in full arms,
And plies him with proud words—it pleases him well. 2335
Then once again gaily to Gawain he calls,
And in a loud voice and lusty, delivers these words:
"Bold fellow, on this field your anger forbear!
No man has made demands here in manner uncouth,
Nor done, save as duly determined at court. 2340
I owed you a hit and you have it; be happy therewith!
The rest of my rights here I freely resign.
Had I been a bit busier, a buffet, perhaps,
I could have dealt more directly, and done you some harm.
First I flourished with a feint, in frolicsome mood, 2345
And left your hide unhurt—and here I did well
By the fair terms we fixed on the first night;
And fully and faithfully you followed accord:
Gave over all your gains as a good man should.
A second feint, sir, I assigned for the morning 2350
You kissed my comely wife—each kiss you restored.
For both of these there behooved but two feigned blows

by right.
True men pay what they owe;
No danger then in sight.   2355
You failed at the third throw,
So take my tap, sir knight.

"For that is my belt about you, that same braided girdle,
My wife it was that wore it; I know well the tale,
And the count of your kisses and your conduct too,   2360
And the wooing of my wife—it was all my scheme!
She made trial of a man most faultless by far
Of all that ever walked over the wide earth;
As pearls to white peas, more precious and prized,
So is Gawain, in good faith, to other gay knights.   2365
Yet you lacked, sir, a little in loyalty there,
But the cause was not cunning, nor courtship either,
But that you loved your own life; the less, then, to blame."
The other stout knight in a study stood a long while,
So gripped with grim rage that his great heart shook.   2370
All the blood of his body burned in his face
As he shrank back in shame from the man's sharp speech.
The first words that fell from the fair knight's lips:
"Accursed be a cowardly and covetous heart!
In you is villainy and vice, and virtue laid low!"   2375
Then he grasps the green girdle and lets go the knot,
Hands it over in haste, and hotly he says:
"Behold there my falsehood, ill hap betide it!
Your cut taught me cowardice, care for my life,
And coveting came after, contrary both   2380
To largesse and loyalty belonging to knights.
Now am I faulty and false, that fearful was ever
Of disloyalty and lies, bad luck to them both!
              and greed.
        I confess, knight, in this place,   2385
        Most dire is my misdeed;
        Let me gain back your good grace,
        And thereafter I shall take heed."

Then the other laughed aloud, and lightly he said,
"Such harm as I have had, I hold it quite healed.   2390
You are so fully confessed, your failings made known,
And bear the plain penance of the point of my blade,
I hold you polished as a pearl, as pure and as bright
As you had lived free of fault since first you were born.
And I give you, sir, this girdle that is gold-hemmed   2395
And green as my garments, that, Gawain, you may
Be mindful of this meeting when you mingle in throng
With nobles of renown—and known by this token
How it chanced at the Green Chapel, to chivalrous knights.
And you shall in this New Year come yet again   2400
And we shall finish out our feast in my fair hall,
              with cheer."

He urged the knight to stay,
And said, "With my wife so dear
We shall see you friends this day,   2405
Whose enmity touched you near."

"Indeed," said the doughty knight, and doffed his high helm,
And held it in his hands as he offered his thanks,
"I have lingered long enough—may good luck be yours,
And He reward you well that all worship bestows!   2410
And commend me to that comely one, your courteous wife,
Both herself and that other, my honoured ladies,
That have trapped their true knight in their trammels so quaint.
But if a dullard should dote, deem it no wonder,
And through the wiles of a woman be wooed into sorrow,   2415
For so was Adam by one, when the world began,
And Solomon by many more, and Samson the mighty—
Delilah was his doom, and David thereafter
Was beguiled by Bathsheba, and bore much distress;
Now these were vexed by their devices—'twere a very joy   2420
Could one but learn to love, and believe them not.
For these were proud princes, most prosperous of old,
Past all lovers lucky, that languished under heaven,
                    bemused.
            And one and all fell prey   2425
            To women that they had used;
            If I be led astray,
            Methinks I may be excused.

"But your girdle, God love you! I gladly shall take
And be pleased to possess, not for the pure gold,   2430
Nor the bright belt itself, nor the beauteous pendants,
Nor for wealth, nor worldly state, nor workmanship fine,
But a sign of excess it shall seem oftentimes
When I ride in renown, and remember with shame
The faults and the frailty of the flesh perverse,   2435
How its tenderness entices the foul taint of sin;
And so when praise and high prowess have pleased my heart,
A look at this love-lace will lower my pride.
But one thing would I learn, if you were not loath,
Since you are lord of yonder land where I have long sojourned   2440
With honor in your house—may you have His reward
That upholds all the heavens, highest on throne!
How runs your right name?—and let the rest go."
"That shall I give you gladly," said the Green Knight then;
"Bercilak de Hautdesert this barony I hold,   2445
Through the might of Morgan le Fay,[9] that lodges at my house,
By subtleties of science and sorcerers' arts,
The mistress of Merlin, she has caught many a man,
For sweet love in secret she shared sometime

9. Arthur's half-sister, an enchantress (*Faye:* fairy) who sometimes abetted him, sometimes made trouble for him.

With that wizard, that knows well each one of your knights 2450
     and you.
    Morgan the Goddess, she,
    So styled by title true;
    None holds so high degree
    That her arts cannot subdue. 2455

"She guided me in this guise to your glorious hall,
To assay, if such it were, the surfeit of pride
That is rumored of the retinue of the Round Table.
She put this shape upon me to puzzle your wits,
To afflict the fair queen, and frighten her to death 2460
With awe of that elvish man that eerily spoke
With his head in his hand before the high table.
She was with my wife at home, that old withered lady,
Your own aunt is she,[1] Arthur's half-sister,
The Duchess' daughter of Tintagel, that dear King Uther 2465
Got Arthur on after, that honored is now.
And therefore, good friend, come feast with your aunt;
Make merry in my house; my men hold you dear,
And I wish you as well, sir, with all my heart,
As any mortal man, for your matchless faith." 2470
But the knight said him nay, that he might by no means.
They clasped then and kissed, and commended each other
To the Prince of Paradise, and parted with one
     assent.
    Gawain sets out anew; 2475
    Toward the court his course is bent;
    And the knight all green in hue,
    Wheresoever he wished, he went.

Wild ways in the world our worthy knight rides
On Gringolet, that by grace had been granted his life. 2480
He harbored often in houses, and often abroad,
And with many valiant adventures verily he met
That I shall not take time to tell in this story.
The hurt was whole that he had had in his neck,
And the bright green belt on his body he bore, 2485
Oblique, like a baldric, bound at his side,
Below his left shoulder, laced in a knot,
In betokening of the blame he had borne for his fault;
And so to court in due course he comes safe and sound.
Bliss abounded in hall when the high-born heard 2490
That good Gawain was come; glad tidings they thought it.
The king kisses the knight, and the queen as well,
And many a comrade came to clasp him in arms,
And eagerly they asked, and awesomely he told,
Confessed all his cares and discomfitures many, 2495
How it chanced at the Chapel, what cheer made the knight,

---

1. Morgan was the daughter of Igraine, duchess of Tintagel, and her husband, the duke. Igraine conceived Arthur when his father, Uther, lay with her through one of Merlin's trickeries.

The love of the lady, the green lace at last.
The nick on his neck he naked displayed
That he got in his disgrace at the Green Knight's hands,
alone. 2500
With rage in heart he speaks,
And grieves with many a groan;
The blood burns in his cheeks
For shame at what must be shown.

"Behold, sir," said he, and handles the belt, 2505
"This is the blazon of the blemish that I bear on my neck;
This is the sign of sore loss that I have suffered there
For the cowardice and coveting that I came to there;
This is the badge of false faith that I was found in there,
And I must bear it on my body till I breathe my last. 2510
For one may keep a deed dark, but undo it no whit,
For where a fault is made fast, it is fixed evermore."
The king comforts the knight, and the court all together
Agree with gay laughter and gracious intent
That the lords and the ladies belonging to the Table, 2515
Each brother of that band, a baldric should have,
A belt borne oblique, of a bright green,
To be worn with one accord for that worthy's sake.
So that was taken as a token by the Table Round,
And he honored that had it, evermore after, 2520
As the best book of knighthood bids it be known.
In the old days of Arthur this happening befell;
The books of Brutus' deeds bear witness thereto
Since Brutus, the bold knight, embarked for this land
After the siege ceased at Troy and the city fared 2525
amiss.
Many such, ere we were born,
Have befallen here, ere this.
May He that was crowned with thorn
Bring all men to His bliss! Amen.</div> 2530

GEOFFREY CHAUCER
1340?–1400

Chaucer is not only one of the earliest poets in the English literary tradition but also one of the greatest. Apart from the poetic virtuosity, psychological subtlety, and humane good humor of his writing, he is worthy of his place here because he is the poet who endowed English literature with a status equal to that of the other European vernaculars—who in effect showed that it could become a world literature. Ironically, the earliest important body of vernacular writing in the medieval period was that of Anglo-Saxon England (represented in this anthology by *Beowulf* and by the lyric poem *The Ruin*). With the Norman conquest of England in 1066 this rich tradition was soon extinguished, and cultural leadership was assumed by literature written in the languages of France—French, Provençal (the dialect of southern France), and Anglo-Norman (the dialect of Normandy and England)—and, to a lesser extent, Italy. Having undergone the break in cultural continuity caused by the Norman conquest, and hindered by the internal struggle for cultural dominance between French and English, English speakers did not develop their own national literature in their own language until the last third of the fourteenth century. This was when *Sir Gawain and the Green Knight* was written, and when other significant writers emerged, especially William Langland, the author of a brilliantly difficult long poem called *Piers Plowman*, and John Gower, who wrote in French and Latin but also composed a major English poem, the *Confessio amantis* (or *Lover's Confession*). Both Langland and Gower lived and worked in London, which was also Chaucer's home. But unlike these contemporaries, Chaucer was very much aware of the European literary traditions not just as collections of texts but as *traditions*, as ongoing cultural projects. This awareness gave to his poetry an artistic subtlety and cultural sophistication that has ensured his position in world literature. But just as important, it also allowed Chaucer to conceive of—and to accomplish—the establishment of an English literary tradition. For it was to his poetry that later English poets, including Shakespeare, Spenser, and Milton, turned to find the foundations of an English literary tradition upon which they could then build.

Chaucer was the son of a wealthy London merchant, and like many children in his position he was sent at an early age to serve as a page in a noble household, in his case that of the countess of Ulster, who was married to one of the sons of King Edward III. Although from a bourgeois background, Chaucer would there have been educated in the values of the aristocratic culture of the time, including its literary tastes, which were for the most part formed on French models. In 1359–60 Chaucer participated in one of the king's military expeditions against the French, was captured, and as was usual at the time, was ransomed by the king. By 1367 Chaucer was a squire in the king's household. This meant not that he resided with the king (although he may have), but that he was called upon to perform a number of services, primarily traveling abroad on the king's business. Chaucer undertook diplomatic journeys to Spain, to France, and—first in 1372–73, then again in 1378—to Italy. These last trips are particularly important because they suggest that Chaucer knew Italian (which he could have learned in London from dealings with the many Italian merchants and bankers who lived there). His poetry—virtually alone among his contemporaries—shows the strong influence of Dante, Petrarch, and Boccaccio, and it is in part their example that provided him with the model for a national literature. In 1374 Chaucer became the Controller of the Customs in London, and he leased a house there (he had already been married for some eight years). He kept this job until 1386, when—probably under political pressure—he resigned. By this time the king was the young Richard II, who had ascended the throne in 1377 at the age of ten. Richard was throughout his reign involved in dangerous struggles for power with the leading members of the aristocracy, and in 1386 he seemed on the verge of being deposed. Chaucer was probably a member of the king's party, and his resignation reflects the decline of Richard's power. By 1389 Richard had regained command, and Chaucer was given other posts and gifts, but ten years later Richard was first deposed and then murdered by Henry Bolingbroke, who became Henry IV. This made little financial difference to Chaucer, who had long maintained a relationship with Henry's father, John of Gaunt, and with Henry himself: his annuity was quickly renewed.

As even this brief account suggests, Chaucer lived in turbulent times. In addition to the struggles for power among the royal family, England was throughout this time at war with France and with the Scots, wars that went progressively badly. It was also during this time—in 1381—that England experienced the shock of the Peasants' Revolt, a violent rebellion that accomplished little substantively but made disturbingly clear the intense animosity that existed between the classes. Finally, this was a period of religious turmoil, when John Wyclif and his supporters were challenging the

Church in terms of both its doctrine and its immense economic power—a challenge that would finally culminate in the Protestant Reformation of the sixteenth century. Oddly enough, most of these events find only the barest mention in Chaucer's poetry. Unlike Dante, he seems not to have held strong political convictions, and his religious commitments seem both generally orthodox and lacking in any special intensity. Finally, although Chaucer was generously rewarded by the great men of his day, there is no clear evidence that these rewards were given to him because he wrote poetry. He seems to have followed a career path much like that of other men of his background, and we do not know to what extent, if any, his extraordinary talent was appreciated in his own day. Indeed, two of the characteristics that make Chaucer such an appealing writer are a tolerant inquisitiveness toward all sorts of people and opinions and a self-effacing if sometimes disingenuous modesty. While he lacks Dante's learning, for example, and his intensity, he is a far more agreeable poet: one can hardly imagine Dante appreciating either the Miller's hilarious bawdy or the witty self-promotions of the Wife of Bath.

Chaucer's career as a poet can be usefully divided into three stages. The first stage comprises the poetry he wrote primarily under the influence of the fashionable French court poetry of the time. When Chaucer was a young man the literary language of the king's household was probably French, yet Chaucer seems to have written only in English. The earliest poem we can date with any certainty is an elegy, in English, for Blanche, duchess of Lancaster and the wife of John of Gaunt, who died in 1368. But while written in English, much of this poem is derived from the work of contemporary French court poets: Chaucer here accommodates the tastes of an elegant society hypersensitive to French fashions. This interest continues in all the poetry Chaucer wrote prior to *The Canterbury Tales*, even when his work begins to show the powerful influence of the Italian poets. This second phase begins as early as the late 1370s, when in a poem called the *House of Fame* Chaucer struggles to locate himself in relation to Dante, whose work he seems to have found both intimidating and pretentious. In the 1380s he wrote *Troilus and Criseyde*, a very beautiful narrative love poem based on a poem by Boccaccio, which explores the psychological depths and the ethical questions that are now treated by the novel. The third part of Chaucer's career is called the English period and comprises *The Canterbury Tales*, a work begun about 1386 and left incomplete. The twenty-four tales that Chaucer completed in fact draw on a wide variety of sources, almost all of them Continental: Chaucer was never very interested in what native tradition of English writing there was. But *The Canterbury Tales* is still a very English work. It begins with a *General Prologue* that describes a group of about thirty pilgrims who meet by chance at an inn in a suburb of London prior to the trip to the shrine of St. Thomas à Becket at Canterbury cathedral. These pilgrims are drawn from almost every rank of fourteenth-century English society, with a decided emphasis on the middle strata, and the reader is left in no doubt that one of the purposes of the work as a whole is to provide a kind of portrait of the nation as a whole. Here Chaucer moves beyond the aristocratic circles to which all of his previous work had been addressed and writes for a larger, national audience. Whether he found such an audience in his own lifetime is very doubtful, but certainly his ambition has been amply rewarded by posterity.

The Canterbury Tales, like the *Decameron* and *The Thousand and One Nights*, is a collection of tales located within a frame. At the urging of their host, Harry Bailly, the pilgrims who have gathered at the Tabard Inn agree to tell two tales each, one while going to and one while returning from Canterbury. It seems doubtful that Chaucer himself meant to compose 120 tales, and there are clear indications that the tale-telling game is meant to end before the pilgrims reach Canterbury. Whether Chaucer decided that the twenty-four tales he did include were sufficient is not known, but he certainly did not complete all the links between the tales, and as a result the order in which many of the tales should be read is unclear. Yet this is not a serious impediment to understanding the individual tales, which together provide a brilliant anthology of virtually every medieval kind of writing. Chaucer offers us fabliaux, a mini-epic, romances, saints' lives, *exempla*, a lay, an animal fable, anecdotes, and even two prose treatises dealing with political and spiritual behavior. If he wants to show us almost every kind of person to be found in late medieval England, he also wants to survey almost the full range of medieval writing. Even the *General Prologue,* which describes with an air of casual spontaneity the pilgrims who gather at the Tabard Inn, is a recognizable kind of medieval writing. Medieval social theory held that society was divided into three *estates,* or classes: the nobility, who ruled; the clergy, who prayed; and the laborers, who worked. Much social criticism of the time was offered in the form of a critical commentary on the members of each of these estates. These works are known as *estates satires,* and the *General Prologue* fits the pattern. Chaucer begins with portraits of the knightly estate (the Knight, the Squire, and their servant, the Yeoman), then moves to the clergy (the Prioress, Monk, and Friar), and then to the largest group of all, the estate of those who work for a living. And if he doesn't keep strictly to this scheme—the Clerk, the Parson, the Summoner, and the Pardoner are all technically members of the clergy—he nonetheless includes two "ideal" portraits of each estate: the Knight and the Squire, the Clerk and the Parson, and the Yeoman and the Plowman. Yet, as is usual with Chaucer, he adopts a conventional form only in order to revise it in a new direction. The estates satire is a social form: its focus is on the ills of society and how they can be cured. But Chaucer's focus in the *General Prologue* is primarily on individuals and their psychological makeup. We are much less interested in the degree to which the Prioress fulfills her spiritual duties than we are in the needs she seeks to fulfill with her elegant dress, her love of pets, and her refined but avid dining. We know that the Friar violates his vows, but our attention is drawn to the sort of *person* he is. Striking in this regard is the fact that not until the final portraits does Chaucer pay much attention to the social effects of his characters' misbehavior: until we come to the out-and-out rogues (the Manciple, Miller, Reeve, Summoner and Pardoner—a group in which the narrator places himself!), there is remarkably little sense of anyone being seriously victimized by the pilgrims' foibles. This is not to say that Chaucer is uninterested in morality, but that the moralist's responsibility to judge seems often to conflict with the artist's desire to understand and to appreciate. This conflict corresponds to one within the *General Prologue* itself, between the duty of pilgrimage and the pleasure of tale-telling. In reading this vivid gallery of portraits, then, we do well to try to balance moral judgment with psychological analysis, and to seek to understand the many motivations and needs of these characters and the differing attitudes that the enthusiastic narrator—who is not to be identified with the historical Chaucer—takes toward them.

When the tale-telling game begins, the Knight—the highest representative of the aristocratic estate—is asked to tell the first story. He responds with a medievalized version of a classical epic: it deals with the fervent love of two knights for a fair maiden, and the inconclusive efforts of a wise ruler to bring order out of the chaos their passion creates. The Host then begins to call upon the highest representative of the clergy, the Monk, but is rudely interrupted by one of the lowest ranking members of the third estate, the Miller. The Miller says he will "pay off" the Knight, which means that he will both reward him and retaliate against him. But the social tensions of the time that for a moment burst into the tale-telling game are immediately displaced into *The Miller's Tale,* which is itself about reward and retaliation. Like the Knight, the Miller tells of two young men (Nicholas and Absalom) who desire a beautiful woman (Alison), and of an older man (John) who tries unsuccessfully to control events. But rather than the Knight's high seriousness the Miller presents ribald comedy; and rather than the courtly love the Knight celebrates the Miller presents sexual desire in much less exalted terms. *The Miller's Tale* is a fabliau— indeed, it is two fabliaux brought brilliantly together. One deals with the triangle of Nicholas, Alison, and John and ends with Nicholas's triumph and John's humiliation;

the other is the triangle of Nicholas, Absalom and Alison and ends with both men humiliated and Alison cheerfully unscathed. Both these plots are brought together with a single word—"Water!"—that creates an almost metaphysical sense of harmonious resolution. Two stories have unfolded in apparently random ways, and yet suddenly we see that they are in fact one beautifully complex story. One is tempted to say that each story "pays off"—rewards and retaliates against—the other. But does the harmony of the plot extend to the theme as well? Is there moral as well as narrative order? To answer this question the reader must realize that what is being punished is not transgression against social or religious conventions but a presumptuous desire to overcontrol. All three men want to control Alison, but she not only has a mind of her own but also knows when a joke has gone far enough. It is this combination of frank self-gratification with prudent self-restraint that the Miller seems to admire, and that the three men lack.

The Wife of Bath is also called Alison, and it is not unreasonable to see her as Chaucer's idea of how the Miller's beautiful young woman might deal with growing old. But instead of being primarily an object that men desire, this Alison is endowed with a vivid personality and a complex inner life that she herself tells us all about. In her *Prologue* she sets her female experience against the misogynist stereotypes of women, as lawless, sexually voracious, and manipulative creatures, promoted by certain traditions of medieval religious thought. Yet the reader is forced to ask if the Wife's frank celebration of her own sexuality, and her account of the torment she has inflicted on her three old husbands, does not actually confirm those stereotypes. An answer is suggested by the Wife's claim that in her *Prologue* she is only playing: indeed, at one point she speaks as if she were showing her almost exclusively male audience how she would conduct a kind of school for wives. She seems, in other words, to be putting on a performance, pretending to reveal to her fascinated audience the secrets that women share among themselves and so letting men witness the intimate life of a woman. Yet as the *Prologue* proceeds we feel that her playful dramatics give way to a more serious, more authentic self-revelation. We learn that not only have her husbands suffered in marriage but that she has too, that she is unavoidably (if cheerfully) aware of the advancing years, and that what she seems most to value is neither money nor the sex she so aggressively celebrates but the companionship and love she comes finally to share with Jankin. In the same way her *Tale* gradually reveals itself to be more than simply a nostalgic wish fulfillment for the return of youth and beauty. When the criminal knight tries to learn what women most desire he is offered a series of misogynist answers, but when forced to marry he discovers, through the moral lecture his old wife delivers, that she possesses a wisdom he himself lacks. This is why he leaves the final decision about what form she will assume up to her, and in granting her mastery he is rewarded not merely with youth and beauty but with a marriage of mutual affection. It is through this experience, then, rather than by relying on the authority of time-honored opinions, that the knight comes to learn about the true nature of women.

The Pardoner provides a performance that is very similar to that of the Wife, but his subject is not marriage but religion. His function is to raise money for a charitable institution—in this case, a hospital—by selling papal indulgences. These were documents by which the Church remitted some of the punishment that awaited sinners in purgatory by virtue of their charitable gifts. On no account, despite what this Pardoner says, did indulgences remit the guilt of sin: only Christ could do that. In his *Prologue* the Pardoner admits that he is a thorough rogue—indeed, he trumpets his viciousness, and his impenitent lack of concern for his own spiritual future, so loudly and so brazenly that we may think he protests too much. Even in the *Prologue* we get hints that the Pardoner harbors somewhere in his tortured soul the thought that he is, despite himself, doing God's work. And in fact the story he tells is one of the most brilliantly effective religious stories in all medieval literature. Generically it is an exemplum, one of those tales with which preachers would enliven their sermons.

It demonstrates with an almost mathematical efficiency that the wages of sin are death, and it also provides us with a startling insight into the Pardoner himself. For he too is seeking the spiritual death of damnation, and in the figure of the eerie old man he expresses with painful vividness the common medieval understanding of damnation as a condition of perpetual dying, a dying that never finds death. Just as the Wife of Bath is more than a stereotype, so too the Pardoner is more than an impenitent sinner. On the contrary, Chaucer allows us to see the deep suffering endured by a man who mocks religious truths while simultaneously yearning for them.

CHAUCER IN MIDDLE ENGLISH

Chaucer is presented here in a Modern English version by Theodore Morrison, which is remarkably clear, accurate, and easy to read. But, to get some idea of Chaucer's original language, we may profitably compare the first eighteen lines of the *General Prologue* in the two forms. It will be possible to point out only a few of the changes that have occurred in pronunciation, in grammatical forms, and sometimes in the use and meaning of words.

> Whan that Aprille with his shoures sote
> The droghte of Marche hath perced to the rote,
> And bathed every veyne in swich licour,
> Of which vertu engendred is the flour;
> When Zephirus eek with his swete breeth   5
> Inspired hath in every holt and heeth
> The tendre croppes, and the yonge sonne
> Hath in the Ram his halfe cours y-ronne,
> And smale fowles maken melodye,
> That slepen al the night with open yë,   10
> So priketh hem nature in hir corages:
> Than longen folk to goon on pilgrimages
> And palmers for to seken straunge strandes
> To ferne halwes, couthe in sondry landes;
> And specially, from every shires ende   15
> Of Engeland, to Caunterbury they wende,
> The holy blisful martir for to seke,
> That hem hath holpen, whan that they were seke.

In Middle English of the late fourteenth century, the letters representing the stressed vowels were pronounced about as they are in Spanish or Italian in our time. Thus the A of *Aprille* sounded like *a* in our *father;* the first *e* in *swete* (line 5) was like the *a* in modern English *late;* and the second *i* in *Inspired* (line 6) was like *i* in our *machine.* In verbs, the third person singular ended in *-th,* not *-s,* as in *hath* (line 2); and the plural ending, either *-en* or *-e,* formed a separate syllable, as in *maken* (line 9), *slepen* (line 10), and *wende* (line 16). Among the pronouns and pronominal adjectives, Chaucer's language did not have our *its, their,* or *them.* Instead, the corresponding forms were, respectively, *his* (line 1), *hir(e)* (line 11), and *hem* (line 18). Changes in the meaning or use of words may compel a substitution. Thus Chaucer's *couthe* (line 14) has become obsolete and hence is translated as *renowned* instead; so also *corages* (line 11) becomes *hearts,* and *ferne halwes* (line 14) becomes *foreign shrines.* Readers interested in hearing Chaucer's poetry read in its original language can order tapes from any good music store.

The standard edition of Chaucer's works is Larry Benson, ed., *The Riverside Chaucer,* 3rd ed. (1987), which provides a fully annotated text in Middle English with a glossary and full introductions and notes. Useful guides to *The Canterbury Tales* are provided in accessible books by Derek A. Pearsall (1985) and Winthrop Wetherbee (1989). More detailed analyses of the three tales selected here may be found in Lee Patterson, *Chaucer and the Subject of History* (1991).

The Canterbury Tales[1]

General Prologue

As soon as April pierces to the root
The drought of March, and bathes each bud and shoot
Through every vein of sap with gentle showers
From whose engendering liquor spring the flowers;
When zephyrs[2] have breathed softly all about   5
Inspiring every wood and field to sprout,
And in the zodiac the youthful sun
His journey halfway through the Ram[3] has run;
When little birds are busy with their song
Who sleep with open eyes the whole night long   10
Life stirs their hearts and tingles in them so,
Then off as pilgrims people long to go,
And palmers[4] to set out for distant strands
And foreign shrines renowned in many lands.
And specially in England people ride   15
To Canterbury from every countryside
To visit there the blessed martyred saint[5]
Who gave them strength when they were sick and faint.
   In Southwark at the Tabard[6] one spring day
It happened, as I stopped there on my way,   20
Myself a pilgrim with a heart devout
Ready for Canterbury to set out,
At night came all of twenty-nine assorted
Travelers, and to that same inn resorted,
Who by a turn of fortune chanced to fall   25
In fellowship together, and they were all
Pilgrims who had it in their minds to ride
Toward Canterbury. The stable doors were wide,
The rooms were large, and we enjoyed the best,
And shortly, when the sun had gone to rest,   30
I had so talked with each that presently
I was a member of their company
And promised to rise early the next day
To start, as I shall show, upon our way.
   But none the less, while I have time and space,   35
Before this tale has gone a further pace,
I should in reason tell you the condition
Of each of them, his rank and his position,
And also what array they all were in;
And so then, with a knight I will begin.   40
   A Knight was with us, and an excellent man,
Who from the earliest moment he began
To follow his career loved chivalry,
Truth, openhandedness, and courtesy.

1. Translated by Theodore Morrison.   2. The west wind.   3. A sign of the zodiac (Aries); the sun is in the Ram from March 12 to April 11.   4. Pilgrims, who, originally, brought back palm leaves from the Holy Land.   5. St. Thomas à Becket, slain in Canterbury cathedral in 1170.   6. An inn at Southwark, across the river Thames from London.

He was a stout man in his lord's campaigns 45
And in that cause had gripped his horse's reins
In Christian lands and pagan through the earth,
None farther, and always honored for his worth.
He was on hand at Alexandria's[7] fall.
He had often sat in precedence to all 50
The nations at the banquet board in Prussia.[8]
He had fought in Lithuania and in Russia,
No Christian knight more often; he had been
In Moorish Africa at Benmarin,
At the siege of Algeciras in Granada, 55
And sailed in many a glorious armada
In the Mediterranean, and fought as well
At Ayas and Attalia when they fell
In Armenia and on Asia Minor's coast.
Of fifteen deadly battles he could boast, 60
And in Algeria, at Tremessen,
Fought for the faith and killed three separate men
In single combat. He had done good work
Joining against another pagan Turk
With the king of Palathia.[9] And he was wise, 65
Despite his prowess, honored in men's eyes,
Meek as a girl and gentle in his ways.
He had never spoken ignobly all his days
To any man by even a rude inflection.
He was a knight in all things to perfection. 70
He rode a good horse, but his gear was plain,
For he had lately served on a campaign.
His tunic was still spattered by the rust
Left by his coat of mail, for he had just
Returned and set out on his pilgrimage. 75
   His son was with him, a young Squire, in age
Some twenty years as near as I could guess.
His hair curled as if taken from a press.
He was a lover and would become a knight.
In stature he was of a moderate height 80
But powerful and wonderfully quick.
He had been in Flanders, riding in the thick
Of forays in Artois and Picardy,[1]
And bore up well for one so young as he,
Still hoping by his exploits in such places 85
To stand the better in his lady's graces.
He wore embroidered flowers, red and white,
And blazed like a spring meadow to the sight.
He sang or played his flute the livelong day.
He was as lusty as the month of May. 90
His coat was short, its sleeves were long and wide.
He sat his horse well, and knew how to ride,
And how to make a song and use his lance,

---

7. In Egypt, captured in 1365 by King Peter of Cyprus.   8. A reference to crusades against the still-pagan Slavs.   9. An independent emirate on the southwest coast of Turkey.   1. Provinces in the north of France and in Flanders.

And he could write and draw well, too, and dance.
So hot his love that when the moon rose pale   95
He got no more sleep than a nightingale.
He was modest, and helped whomever he was able,
And carved as his father's squire at the table.
    But one more servant had the Knight beside,
Choosing thus simply for the time to ride: 100
A Yeoman, in a coat and hood of green.
His peacock-feathered arrows, bright and keen,
He carried under his belt in tidy fashion.
For well-kept gear he had a yeoman's passion,
No draggled feather might his arrows show,   105
And in his hand he held a mighty bow.
He kept his hair close-cropped, his face was brown.
He knew the lore of woodcraft up and down.
His arm was guarded from the bowstring's whip
By a bracer, gaily trimmed. He had at hip   110
A sword and buckler, and at his other side
A dagger whose fine mounting was his pride,
Sharp-pointed as a spear. His horn he bore
In a sling of green, and on his chest he wore
A silver image of St. Christopher,   115
His patron, since he was a forester.
    There was also a Nun, a Prioress,
Whose smile was gentle and full of guilelessness.
"By St. Loy!"[2] was the worst oath she would say.
She sang mass well, in a becoming way,   120
Intoning through her nose the words divine,
And she was known as Madame Eglantine.
She spoke good French, as taught at Stratford-Bow[3]
For the Parisian French she did not know.
She was schooled to eat so primly and so well   125
That from her lips no morsel ever fell.
She wet her fingers lightly in the dish
Of sauce, for courtesy was her first wish.
With every bite she did her skillful best
To see that no drop fell upon her breast.   130
She always wiped her upper lip so clean
That in her cup was never to be seen
A hint of grease when she had drunk her share.
She reached out for her meat with comely air.
She was a great delight, and always tried   135
To imitate court ways, and had her pride,
Both amiable and gracious in her dealings.
As for her charity and tender feelings,
She melted at whatever was piteous.
She would weep if she but came upon a mouse   140
Caught in a trap, if it were dead or bleeding.
Some little dogs that she took pleasure feeding

2. Perhaps St. Eligius, apparently a popular saint at this time.   3. In Middlesex, near London, where
there was a nunnery.

On roasted meat or milk or good wheat bread
She had, but how she wept to find one dead
Or yelping from a blow that made it smart,   145
And all was sympathy and loving heart.
Neat was her wimple in its every plait,
Her nose well formed, her eyes as gray as slate.
Her mouth was very small and soft and red.
She had so wide a brow I think her head   150
Was nearly a span broad, for certainly
She was not undergrown, as all could see.
She wore her cloak with dignity and charm,
And had her rosary about her arm,
The small beads coral and the larger green,   155
And from them hung a brooch of golden sheen,
On it a large A and a crown above;[4]
Beneath, "All things are subject unto love."
    A Priest accompanied her toward Canterbury,
And an attendant Nun, her secretary.   160
    There was a Monk, and nowhere was his peer,
A hunter, and a roving overseer.[5]
He was a manly man, and fully able
To be an abbot. He kept a hunting stable,
And when he rode the neighborhood could hear   165
His bridle jingling in the wind as clear
And loud as if it were a chapel bell.
Wherever he was master of a cell
The principles of good St. Benedict,[6]
For being a little old and somewhat strict,   170
Were honored in the breach, as past their prime.
He lived by the fashion of a newer time.
He would have swapped that text for a plucked hen
Which says that hunters are not holy men,
Or a monk outside his discipline and rule   175
Is too much like a fish outside his pool;
That is to say, a monk outside his cloister.
But such a text he deemed not worth an oyster.
I told him his opinion made me glad.
Why should he study always and go mad,   180
Mewed in his cell with only a book for neighbor?
Or why, as Augustine[7] commanded, labor
And sweat his hands? How shall the world be served?
To Augustine be all such toil reserved!
And so he hunted, as was only right.   185
He had greyhounds as swift as birds in flight.
His taste was all for tracking down the hare,
And what his sport might cost he did not care.
His sleeves I noticed, where they met his hand,
Trimmed with gray fur, the finest in the land.   190

4. The A stands for Amor, Latin for "love"; in the original the motto is Amor vincit omnia, "Love conquers all."   5. He is responsible for the monastery's outlying properties.   6. Monastic rules authored by St. Benedict in the sixth century.   7. St. Augustine (A.D. 354–430) argued that monks should perform manual labor.

His hood was fastened with a curious pin
Made of wrought gold and clasped beneath his chin,
A love knot at the tip. His head might pass,
Bald as it was, for a lump of shining glass,
And his face was glistening as if anointed.   195
Fat as a lord he was, and well appointed.
His eyes were large, and rolled inside his head
As if they gleamed from a furnace of hot lead.
His boots were supple, his horse superbly kept.
He was a prelate to dream of while you slept.   200
He was not pale nor peaked like a ghost.
He relished a plump swan as his favorite roast.
He rode a palfrey brown as a ripe berry.
    A Friar was with us, a gay dog and a merry,
Who begged his district with a jolly air.   205
No friar in all four orders[8] could compare
With him for gallantry; his tongue was wooing.
Many a girl was married by his doing,
And at his own cost it was often done.
He was a pillar, and a noble one,   210
To his whole order. In his neighborhood
Rich franklins[9] knew him well, who served good food,
And worthy women welcomed him to town;
For the license that his order handed down,
He said himself, conferred on him possession   215
Of more than a curate's[1] power of confession.
Sweetly the list of frailties he heard,
Assigning penance with a pleasant word.
He was an easy man for absolution
Where he looked forward to a contribution,   220
For if to a poor order a man has given
It signifies that he has been well shriven,[2]
And if a sinner let his purse be dented
The Friar would stake his oath he had repented.
For many men become so hard of heart   225
They cannot weep, though conscience makes them smart.
Instead of tears and prayers, then, let the sinner
Supply the poor friars with the price of dinner.
For pretty women he had more than shrift.[3]
His cape was stuffed with many a little gift,   230
As knives and pins and suchlike. He could sing
A merry note, and pluck a tender string,
And had no rival at all in balladry.
His neck was whiter than a fleur-de-lis,[4]
And yet he could have knocked a strong man down.   235
He knew the taverns well in every town.
The barmaids and innkeepers pleased his mind
Better than beggars and lepers and their kind.
In his position it was unbecoming

8. Most friars belonged to one of four groups, or orders.   9. Landowners or country squires, not belonging to the nobility.   1. A parish priest.   2. Confessed.   3. Confession.   4. Lily.

Among the wretched lepers to go slumming.   240
It mocks all decency, it sews no stitch
To deal with such riffraff, but with the rich,
With sellers of victuals, that's another thing.
Wherever he saw some hope of profiting,
None so polite, so humble. He was good,   245
The champion beggar of his brotherhood.
Should a woman have no shoes against the snow,
So pleasant was his *"In principio"*[5]
He would have her widow's mite before he went.
He took in far more than he paid in rent   250
For his right of begging within certain bounds.[6]
None of his brethren trespassed on his grounds!
He loved as freely as a half-grown whelp.
On arbitration-days[7] he gave great help,
For his cloak was never shiny nor threadbare   255
Like a poor cloistered scholar's. He had an air
As if he were a doctor or a pope.
It took stout wool to make his semicope[8]
That plumped out like a bell for portliness.
He lisped a little in his rakishness   260
To make his English sweeter on his tongue,
And twanging his harp to end some song he'd sung
His eyes would twinkle in his head as bright
As the stars twinkle on a frosty night.
Hubert this gallant Friar was by name.   265
    Among the rest a Merchant also came.
He wore a forked beard and a beaver hat
From Flanders. High up in the saddle he sat,
In figured cloth,[9] his boots clasped handsomely,
Delivering his opinions pompously,   270
Always on how his gains might be increased.
At all costs he desired the sea policed[1]
From Middleburg in Holland to Orwell.[2]
He knew the exchange rates, and the time to sell
French currency, and there was never yet   275
A man who could have told he was in debt
So grave he seemed and hid so well his feelings
With all his shrewd engagements and close dealings.
You'd find no better man at any turn;
But what his name was I could never learn.   280
    There was an Oxford Student too, it chanced,
Already in his logic well advanced.
He rode a mount as skinny as a rake,
And he was hardly fat. For learning's sake
He let himself look hollow and sober enough.   285
He wore an outer coat of threadbare stuff,
For he had no benefice[3] for his enjoyment

<hr>

5. In the beginning (Latin); the opening phrase of a famous passage in the New Testament of the Bible (John 1.1–16).   6. The territory in which he could beg, for which he paid a fee.   7. Days appointed for settling disputes.   8. A short cape.   9. Cloth of mixed color.   1. For protection from piracy.   2. An English port near Harwich.   3. A paid position in the Church.

And was too unworldly for some lay employment.
He much preferred to have beside his bed
His twenty volumes bound in black or red 290
All packed with Aristotle from end to middle
Than a sumptuous wardrobe or a merry fiddle.
For though he knew what learning had to offer
There was little coin to jingle in his coffer.
Whatever he got by touching up a friend 295
On books and learning he would promptly spend
And busily pray for the soul of anybody
Who furnished him the wherewithal for study.
His scholarship was what he truly heeded.
He never spoke a word more than was needed, 300
And that was said with dignity and force,
And quick and brief. He was of grave discourse
Giving new weight to virtue by his speech,
And gladly would he learn and gladly teach.

　　There was a Lawyer, cunning and discreet, 305
Who had often been to St. Paul's porch[4] to meet
His clients. He was a Sergeant of the Law,[5]
A man deserving to be held in awe,
Or so he seemed, his manner was so wise.
He had often served as Justice of Assize[6] 310
By the king's appointment, with a broad commission,
For his knowledge and his eminent position.
He had many a handsome gift by way of fee.
There was no buyer of land as shrewd as he.
All ownership to him became fee simple.[7] 315
His titles were never faulty by a pimple.
None was so busy as he with case and cause,
And yet he seemed much busier than he was.
In all cases and decisions he was schooled
That were of record since King William[8] ruled. 320
No one could pick a loophole or a flaw
In any lease or contract he might draw.
Each statute on the books he knew by rote.
He traveled in a plain, silk-belted coat.

　　A Franklin traveled in his company. 325
Whiter could never daisy petal be
Than was his beard. His ruddy face gave sign
He liked his morning sop of toast in wine.
He lived in comfort, as he would assure us,
For he was a true son of Epicurus[9] 330
Who held the opinion that the only measure
Of perfect happiness was simply pleasure.
Such hospitality did he provide,
He was St. Julian[1] to his countryside.

---

4. A meeting place for lawyers and their clients in the porch of St. Paul's Cathedral, London.　5. Sergeants of the Law were the most prestigious and powerful lawyers of the time.　6. A judge in the circuit court.　7. Owned outright without legal impediments.　8. The Conqueror (reigned 1066–1087). 9. Greek philosopher whose teaching (presented here in a somewhat debased form) is believed to make pleasure the goal of life.　1. Patron saint of hospitality.

His bread and ale were always up to scratch. 335
He had a cellar none on earth could match.
There was no lack of pasties in his house,
Both fish and flesh, and that so plenteous
That where he lived it snowed of meat and drink.
With every dish of which a man can think, 340
After the various seasons of the year,
He changed his diet for his better cheer.
He had coops of partridges as fat as cream,
He had a fishpond stocked with pike and bream.
Woe to his cook for an unready pot 345
Or a sauce that wasn't seasoned and spiced hot!
A table in his hall stood on display
Prepared and covered through the livelong day.
He presided at court sessions for his bounty
And sat in Parliament often for his county. 350
A well-wrought dagger and a purse of silk
Hung at his belt, as white as morning milk.
He had been a sheriff and county auditor.
On earth was no such rich proprietor!
    There were five Guildsmen, in the livery 355
Of one august and great fraternity,[2]
A Weaver, a Dyer, and a Carpenter,
A Tapestry-maker and a Haberdasher.
Their gear was furbished new and clean as glass.
The mountings of their knives were not of brass 360
But silver. Their pouches were well made and neat,
And each of them, it seemed, deserved a seat
On the platform at the Guildhall,[3] for each one
Was likely timber to make an alderman.
They had goods enough, and money to be spent, 365
Also their wives would willingly consent
And would have been at fault if they had not.
For to be "Madamed" is a pleasant lot,
And to march in first at feasts for being well married,
And royally to have their mantles carried. 370
    For the pilgrimage these Guildsmen brought their own
Cook to boil their chicken and marrow bone
With seasoning powder and capers and sharp spice.
In judging London ale his taste was nice.
He well knew how to roast and broil and fry, 375
To mix a stew, and bake a good meat pie,
Or capon creamed with almond, rice, and egg.
Pity he had an ulcer on his leg!
    A Skipper was with us, his home far in the west.
He came from the port of Dartmouth,[4] as I guessed. 380
He sat his carthorse pretty much at sea
In a coarse smock that joggled on his knee.
From his neck a dagger on a string hung down

2. Members of a parish fraternity, an organization centered on the parish church that served both religious and social purposes. 3. London's city hall. 4. On the southwest coast.

Under his arm. His face was burnished brown
By the summer sun. He was a true good fellow. 385
Many a time he had tapped a wine cask mellow
Sailing from Bordeaux⁵ while the owner slept.
Too nice a point of honor he never kept.
In a sea fight, if he got the upper hand,
Drowned prisoners floated home to every land. 390
But in navigation, whether reckoning tides,
Currents, or what might threaten him besides,
Harborage, pilotage, or the moon's demeanor,
None was his like from Hull to Cartagena.⁶
He knew each harbor and the anchorage there 395
From Gotland to the Cape of Finisterre⁷
And every creek in Brittany and Spain,
And he had called his ship the *Madeleine.*
    With us came also an astute Physician.
There was none like him for a disquisition 400
On the art of medicine or surgery,
For he was grounded in astrology.
He kept his patient long in observation,
Choosing the proper hour for application
Of charms and images by intuition 405
Of magic, and the planets' best position.
For he was one who understood the laws
That rule the humors, and could tell the cause
That brought on every human malady,
Whether of hot or cold, or moist or dry. 410
He was a perfect medico, for sure.
The cause once known, he would prescribe the cure
For he had his druggists ready at a motion
To provide the sick man with some pill or potion—
A game of mutual aid, with each one winning. 415
Their partnership was hardly just beginning!
He was well versed in his authorities,
Old Aesculapius, Dioscorides,
Rufus, and old Hippocrates, and Galen,
Haly, and Rhazes, and Serapion, 420
Averroës, Bernard, Johannes Damascenus,
Avicenna, Gilbert, Gaddesden, Constantinus.⁸
He urged a moderate fare on principle,
But rich in nourishment, digestible;
Of nothing in excess would he admit. 425
He gave but little heed to Holy Writ.
His clothes were lined with taffeta; their hue
Was all of blood red and of Persian blue,
Yet he was far from careless of expense.
He saved his fees from times of pestilence, 430
For gold is a cordial,⁹ as physicians hold,

---

5. On the southwest coast of France.   6. A Spanish port. *Hull:* an English port.   7. On the Spanish coast. *Gotland:* a Swedish island.   8. Eminent medical authorities from ancient Greece, ancient and medieval Arabic civilization, and England in the thirteenth and fourteenth centuries.   9. Gold was thought to be a stimulant.

And so he had a special love for gold.
  A worthy woman there was from near the city
Of Bath,[1] but somewhat deaf, and more's the pity.
For weaving she possessed so great a bent   435
She outdid the people of Ypres and of Ghent.[2]
No other woman dreamed of such a thing
As to precede her at the offering,
Or if any did, she fell in such a wrath
She dried up all the charity in Bath.   440
She wore fine kerchiefs of old-fashioned air,
And on a Sunday morning, I could swear,
She had ten pounds of linen on her head.
Her stockings were of finest scarlet-red,
Laced tightly, and her shoes were soft and new.   445
Bold was her face, and fair, and red in hue.
She had been an excellent woman all her life
Five men in turn had taken her to wife,
Omitting other youthful company—
But let that pass for now! Over the sea   450
She had traveled freely; many a distant stream
She crossed, and visited Jerusalem
Three times. She had been at Rome and at Boulogne,
At the shrine of Compostella, and at Cologne.[3]
She had wandered by the way through many a scene.   455
Her teeth were set with little gaps between.[4]
Easily on her ambling horse she sat.
She was well wimpled, and she wore a hat
As wide in circuit as a shield or targe.[5]
A skirt swathed up her hips, and they were large.   460
Upon her feet she wore sharp-roweled spurs.
She was a good fellow; a ready tongue was hers.
All remedies of love she knew by name,[6]
For she had all the tricks of that old game.
  There was a good man of the priests' vocation,   465
A poor town Parson of true consecration,
But he was rich in holy thought and work.
Learned he was, in the truest sense a clerk
Who meant Christ's gospel faithfully to preach
And truly his parishioners to teach.   470
He was a kind man, full of industry,
Many times tested by adversity
And always patient. If tithes[7] were in arrears,
He was loth to threaten any man with fears
Of excommunication; past a doubt   475
He would rather spread his offering about
To his poor flock, or spend his property.
To him a little meant sufficiency.
Wide was his parish, with houses far asunder,

---

1. A town in southwest England.   2. Towns in Flanders famous for their cloth.   3. Sites of shrines much visited by pilgrims.   4. I.e., gap-toothed; in a woman considered a sign of sexual prowess.   5. A small shield.   6. Chaucer has Ovid's *Love Cures* (*Remedia Amoris*) in mind.   7. Payments due to the priest, usually a tenth of annual income.

But he would not be kept by rain or thunder,   480
If any had suffered a sickness or a blow,
From visiting the farthest, high or low
Plodding his way on foot, his staff in hand.
He was a model his flock could understand,
For first he did and afterward he taught.   485
That precept from the Gospel he had caught,
And he added as a metaphor thereto,
"If the gold rusts, what will the iron do?"
For if a priest is foul, in whom we trust,
No wonder a layman shows a little rust.   490
A priest should take to heart the shameful scene
Of shepherds filthy while the sheep are clean.
By his own purity a priest should give
The example to his sheep, how they should live.
He did not rent his benefice for hire,[8]   495
Leaving his flock to flounder in the mire,
And run to London, happiest of goals,
To sing paid masses in St. Paul's for souls,[9]
Or as chaplain from some rich guild take his keep,
But dwelt at home and guarded well his sheep   500
So that no wolf should make his flock miscarry.
He was a shepherd, and not a mercenary.
And though himself a man of strict vocation
He was not harsh to weak souls in temptation,
Not overbearing nor haughty in his speech,   505
But wise and kind in all he tried to teach.
By good example and just words to turn
Sinners to heaven was his whole concern.
But should a man in truth prove obstinate,
Whoever he was, of rich or mean estate,   510
The Parson would give him a snub to meet the case.
I doubt there was a priest in any place
His better. He did not stand on dignity
Nor affect in conscience too much nicety,
But Christ's and his disciples' words he sought   515
To teach, and first he followed what he taught.
     There was a Plowman with him on the road,
His brother, who had forked up many a load
Of good manure. A hearty worker he,
Living in peace and perfect charity.   520
Whether his fortune made him smart or smile,
He loved God with his whole heart all the while
And his neighbor as himself. He would undertake,
For every luckless poor man, for the sake
Of Christ to thresh and ditch and dig by the hour   525
And with no wage, if it was in his power.
His tithes[1] on goods and earnings he paid fair.
He wore a coarse, rough coat and rode a mare.

8. Rent out his appointment to a substitute.   9. Many wealthy people endowed positions for priests, who would sing Masses for the souls of their patrons after their deaths.   1. A tenth part of one's goods or income given to the Church.

There also were a Manciple, a Miller,
A Reeve, a Summoner, and a Pardoner,[2]   530
And I—this makes our company complete.
 As tough a yokel as you care to meet
The Miller was. His big-beefed arms and thighs
Took many a ram put up as wrestling prize.
He was a thick, squat-shouldered lump of sins.   535
No door but he could heave it off its pins
Or break it running at it with his head.
His beard was broader than a shovel, and red
As a fat sow or fox. A wart stood clear
Atop his nose, and red as a pig's ear   540
A tuft of bristles on it. Black and wide
His nostrils were. He carried at his side
A sword and buckler.[3] His mouth would open out
Like a great furnace, and he would sing and shout
His ballads and jokes of harlotries and crimes.   545
He could steal corn and charge for it three times,
And yet was honest enough, as millers come,
For a miller, as they say, has a golden thumb.[4]
In white coat and blue hood this lusty clown,
Blowing his bagpipes, brought us out of town.   550
 The Manciple was of a lawyers' college,[5]
And other buyers might have used his knowledge
How to be shrewd provisioners, for whether
He bought on cash or credit, altogether
He managed that the end should be the same: 555
He came out more than even with the game.
Now isn't it an instance of God's grace
How a man of little knowledge can keep pace
In wit with a whole school of learned men?
He had masters to the number of three times ten   560
Who knew each twist of equity and tort;[6]
A dozen in that very Inn of Court
Were worthy to be steward of the estate
To any of England's lords, however great,
And keep him to his income well confined   565
And free from debt, unless he lost his mind,
Or let him scrimp, if he were mean in bounty;
They could have given help to a whole county
In any sort of case that might befall;
And yet this Manciple could cheat them all!   570
 The Reeve was a slender, fiery-tempered man.
He shaved as closely as a razor can.
His hair was cropped about his ears, and shorn
Above his forehead as a priest's is worn.[7]

---

2. A seller of indulgences that purported to release sinful souls from purgatory early. *Manciple:* an officer in charge of supplies. *Reeve:* farm overseer. *Summoner:* he summoned people to appear before the church court (presided over by the archdeacon) and in general acted as a kind of bailiff. 3. Shield. 4. A reference to the proverb "an honest miller has a golden thumb," i.e., there are no honest millers. 5. The Manciple manages the affairs of an Inn of Court (see line 562), an institution where young men training to be lawyers lived and worked. 6. Different kinds of legal cases. 7. His head was shaved in the form of the tonsure that indicated clerical status.

His legs were very long and very lean.   575
No calf on his lank spindles could be seen.
But he knew how to keep a barn or bin,
He could play the game with auditors and win.
He knew well how to judge by drought and rain
The harvest of his seed and of his grain.   580
His master's cattle, swine, and poultry flock,
Horses and sheep and dairy, all his stock,
Were altogether in this Reeve's control.
And by agreement, he had given the sole
Accounting since his lord reached twenty years.   585
No man could ever catch him in arrears.
There wasn't a bailiff, shepherd, or farmer working
But the Reeve knew all his tricks of cheating and shirking.
He would not let him draw an easy breath.
They feared him as they feared the very death.   590
He lived in a good house on an open space,
Well shaded by green trees, a pleasant place.
He was shrewder in acquisition than his lord.
With private riches he was amply stored.
He had learned a good trade young by work and will.   595
He was a carpenter of first-rate skill.
On a fine mount, a stallion, dappled gray.
Whose name was Scot, he rode along the way.
He wore a long blue coat hitched up and tied
As if it were a friar's, and at his side   600
A sword with rusty blade was hanging down.
He came from Norfolk, from nearby the town
That men call Bawdswell.[8] As we rode the while,
The Reeve kept always hindmost in our file.
    A Summoner in our company had his place.   605
Red as the fiery cherubim[9] his face.
He was pocked and pimpled, and his eyes were narrow.
He was lecherous and hot as a cock sparrow.
His brows were scabby and black, and thin his beard.
His was a face that little children feared.   610
Brimstone or litharge bought in any quarter,
Quicksilver, ceruse, borax, oil of tartar,
No salve nor ointment that will cleanse or bite
Could cure him of his blotches, livid white,
Or the nobs and nubbins sitting on his cheeks.[1]   615
He loved his garlic, his onions, and his leeks.
He loved to drink the strong wine down blood-red.
Then would he bellow as if he had lost his head.
And when he had drunk enough to parch his drouth,
Nothing but Latin issued from his mouth.   620
He had smattered up a few terms, two or three,
That he had gathered out of some decree—
No wonder; he heard law Latin all the day,

---

8. A town in northern Norfolk, a county northwest of London.   9. An order of angels that Chaucer seems to have thought (wrongly) were represented with red faces.   1. The Summoner seems to suffer from a form of leprosy; these remedies were recommended by medieval physicians for his condition.

And everyone knows a parrot or a jay
Can cry out "Wat" or "Poll" as well as the pope;   625
But give him a strange term, he began to grope.
His little store of learning was paid out,
So *"Questio quod juris"*[2] he would shout.
He was a goodhearted bastard and a kind one.
If there were better, it was hard to find one.   630
He would let a good fellow, for a quart of wine,
The whole year round enjoy his concubine
Scot-free from summons, hearing, fine, or bail,
And on the sly he too could flush a quail.
If he liked a scoundrel, no matter for church law.   635
He would teach him that he need not stand in awe
If the archdeacon threatened with his curse—
That is, unless his soul was in his purse,
For in his purse he would be punished well.
"The purse," he said, "is the archdeacon's hell."[3]   640
Of course I know he lied in what he said.
There is nothing a guilty man should so much dread
As the curse that damns his soul, when, without fail,
The church can save him, or send him off to jail.
He had the young men and girls in his control   645
Throughout the diocese; he knew the soul
Of youth, and heard their every last design.
A garland big enough to be the sign
Above an alehouse balanced on his head,
And he made a shield of a great round loaf of bread.   650
    There was a Pardoner of Rouncivalle
With him, of the blessed Mary's hospital,[4]
But now come straight from Rome (or so said he).
Loudly he sang, "Come hither, love, to me,"
While the Summoner's counterbass trolled out profound—   655
No trumpet blew with half so vast a sound.
This Pardoner had hair as yellow as wax,
But it hung as smoothly as a hank of flax.
His locks trailed down in bunches from his head,
And he let the ends about his shoulders spread,   660
But in thin clusters, lying one by one.
Of hood, for rakishness, he would have none,
For in his wallet he kept it safely stowed.
He traveled, as he thought, in the latest mode,
Disheveled. Save for his cap, his head was bare,   665
And in his eyes he glittered like a hare.
A Veronica[5] was stitched upon his cap
His wallet lay before him in his lap
Brimful of pardons from the very seat
In Rome. He had a voice like a goat's bleat.   670

---

2. The question is, what (part) of the law [applies] (Latin).   3. I.e., the archdeacon would punish sinners with a fine rather than send them to hell by excommunicating them, a view with which the narrator disagrees in the following lines.   4. The hospital of St. Mary of Rouncivalle was located at Charing Cross, now part of London. The money the Pardoner collects is supposed to go to the hospital.   5. A reproduction of the handkerchief bearing the miraculous impression of Christ's face, said to have been impressed on the handkerchief that St. Veronica gave Him to wipe His face with on the way to His Crucifixion.

He was beardless and would never have a beard.
His cheek was always smooth as if just sheared.
I think he was a gelding or a mare;
But in this trade, from Berwick down to Ware,[6]
No pardoner could beat him in the race,   675
For in his wallet he had a pillow case
Which he represented as Our Lady's veil;
He said he had a piece of the very sail
St. Peter, when he fished in Galilee
Before Christ caught him, used upon the sea.   680
He had a latten[7] cross embossed with stones
And in a glass he carried some pig's bones,
And with these holy relics, when he found
Some village parson grubbing his poor ground,
He would get more money in a single day   685
Than in two months would come the parson's way.
Thus with his flattery and his trumped-up stock
He made dupes of the parson and his flock.
But though his conscience was a little plastic
He was in church a noble ecclesiastic.   690
Well could he read the Scripture or saint's story,
But best of all he sang the offertory,
For he understood that when this song was sung,
Then he must preach, and sharpen up his tongue
To rake in cash, as well he knew the art,   695
And so he sang out gaily, with full heart.
   Now I have set down briefly, as it was,
Our rank, our dress, our number, and the cause
That made our sundry fellowship begin
In Southwark, at this hospitable inn   700
Known as the Tabard, nor far from the Bell.
But what we did that night I ought to tell,
And after that our journey, stage by stage,
And the whole story of our pilgrimage.
But first, in justice, do not look askance   705
I plead, nor lay it to my ignorance
If in this matter I should use plain speech
And tell you just the words and style of each,
Reporting all their language faithfully.
For it must be known to you as well as me   710
That whoever tells a story after a man
Must follow him as closely as he can.
If he takes the tale in charge, he must be true
To every word, unless he would find new
Or else invent a thing or falsify.   715
Better some breadth of language than a lie!
He may not spare the truth to save his brother.
He might as well use one word as another.
In Holy Writ Christ spoke in a broad sense

---

6. Berwick was at the northern end of the Great North Road that traversed England; Ware, at the southern.
7. An alloy of copper and tin made to resemble brass.

And surely his word is without offense. 720
Plato, if his pages you can read,
Says let the word be cousin to the deed.[8]
So I petition your indulgence for it
If I have cut the cloth just as men wore it,
Here in this tale, and shown its very weave. 725
My wits are none too sharp, you must believe.
    Our Host gave each of us a cheerful greeting
And promptly of our supper had us eating.
The victuals that he served us were his best.
The wine was potent, and we drank with zest. 730
Our Host cut such a figure, all in all,
He might have been a marshal in a hall.
He was a big man, and his eyes bulged wide.
No sturdier citizen lived in all Cheapside,[9]
Lacking no trace of manhood, bold in speech, 735
Prudent, and well versed in what life can teach,
And with all this he was a jovial man.
And so when supper ended he began
To jolly us, when all our debts were clear.
"Welcome," he said. "I have not seen this year 740
So merry a company in this tavern as now,
And I would give you pleasure if I knew how.
And just this very minute a plan has crossed
My mind that might amuse you at no cost.
    "You go to Canterbury—may the Lord 745
Speed you, and may the martyred saint reward
Your journey! And to while the time away
You mean to talk and pass the time of day,
For you would be as cheerful all alone
As riding on your journey dumb as stone. 750
Therefore, if you'll abide by what I say,
Tomorrow, when you ride off on your way,
Now, by my father's soul, and he is dead,
If you don't enjoy yourselves, cut off my head!
Hold up your hands, if you accept my speech." 755
    Our counsel did not take us long to reach.
We bade him give his orders at his will.
"Well, sirs," he said, "then do not take it ill,
But hear me in good part, and for your sport.
Each one of you, to make our journey short, 760
Shall tell two stories, as we ride, I mean,
Toward Canterbury; and coming home again
Shall tell two other tales he may have heard
Of happenings that some time have occurred.
And the one of you whose stories please us most, 765
Here in this tavern, sitting by this post
Shall sup at our expense while we make merry
When we come riding home from Canterbury.

---

8. The Platonic text to which Chaucer refers is the *Timaeus*, but he knew it indirectly through references in Latin works.   9. A London district.

And to cheer you still the more, I too will ride
With you at my own cost, and be your guide.   770
And if anyone my judgment shall gainsay
He must pay for all we spend along the way.
If you agree, no need to stand and reason.
Tell me, and I'll be stirring in good season."
    This thing was granted, and we swore our pledge   775
To take his judgment on our pilgrimage,
His verdict on our tales, and his advice.
He was to plan a supper at a price
Agreed upon; and so we all assented
To his command, and we were well contented.   780
The wine was fetched; we drank, and went to rest.
    Next morning, when the dawn was in the east,
Up spring our Host, who acted as our cock,
And gathered us together in a flock,
And off we rode, till presently our pace   785
Had brought us to St. Thomas' watering place.[1]
And there our Host began to check his horse.
"Good sirs," he said, "you know your promise, of course.
Shall I remind you what it was about?
If evensong and matins don't fall out,[2]   790
We'll soon find who shall tell us the first tale.
But as I hope to drink my wine and ale,
Whoever won't accept what I decide
Pays everything we spend along the ride.
Draw lots, before we're farther from the Inn.   795
Whoever draws the shortest shall begin.
Sir Knight," said he, "my master, choose your straw.
Come here, my lady Prioress, and draw,
And you, Sir Scholar, don't look thoughtful, man!
Pitch in now, everyone!" So all began   800
To draw the lots, and as the luck would fall
The draw went to the Knight, which pleased us all.
And when this excellent man saw how it stood,
Ready to keep his promise, he said, "Good!
Since it appears that I must start the game,   805
Why then, the draw is welcome, in God's name.
Now let's ride on, and listen, what I say."
And with that word we rode forth on our way,
And he, with his courteous manner and good cheer,
Began to tell his tale, as you shall hear.   810

The Miller's Prologue and Tale

THE PROLOGUE

When the Knight had finished,[3] no one, young or old,
In the whole company, but said he had told

---

1. A stream about a mile from London on the road to Canterbury.   2. Evening and morning church
services; the Host is asking if what was said in the evening is still acceptable in the morning.   3. *The
Knight's Tale* is the first told, immediately following the *General Prologue*.

A noble story, one that ought to be
Preserved and kept alive in memory,
Especially the gentlefolk, each one.   5
Our good Host laughed, and swore, "The game's begun,
The ball is rolling! This is going well.
Let's see who has another tale to tell.
Come, match the Knight's tale if you can, Sir Monk!"
     The Miller, who by this time was so drunk   10
He looked quite bloodless, and who hardly sat
His horse, he was never one to doff his hat
Or stand on courtesy for any man.
Like Pilate in the Church plays⁴ he began
To bellow. "Arms and blood and bones," he swore,   15
"I know a yarn that will even up the score,
A noble one, I'll pay off the Knight's tale!"
     Our Host could see that he was drunk on ale.
"Robin," he said, "hold on a minute, brother.
Some better man shall come first with another.   20
Let's do this right. You tell yours by and by."
     "God's soul," the Miller told him, "that won't I!
Either I'll speak, or go on my own way."
     "The devil with you! Say what you have to say,"
Answered our Host. "You are a fool. Your head   25
Is overpowered."
                    "Now," the Miller said,
"Everyone listen! But first I will propound
That I am drunk, I know it by my sound.
If I can't get my words out, put the blame
On Southwark ale, I ask you, in God's name!   30
For I'll tell a golden legend and a life⁵
Both of a carpenter and of his wife,
How a student put horns on the fellow's head."
     "Shut up and stop your racket," the Reeve said.
"Forget your ignorant drunken bawdiness.   35
It is a sin and a great foolishness
To injure any man by defamation
And to give women such a reputation.
Tell us of other things; you'll find no lack."
     Promptly this drunken Miller answered back: 40
"Oswald, my brother, true as babes are suckled,
The man who has no wife, he is no cuckold.
I don't say for this reason that you are.
There are plenty of faithful wives, both near and far,
Always a thousand good for every bad,   45
And you know this yourself, unless you're mad.
I see you are angry with my tale, but why?
You have a wife; no less, by God, do I.
But I wouldn't, for the oxen in my plow,
Shoulder more than I need by thinking how   50

---

4. Mystery plays represented Pilate as a braggart and loudmouth.   5. A saint's life.

I may myself, for aught I know, be one.
I'll certainly believe that I am none.
A husband mustn't be curious, for his life,
About God's secrets or about his wife.
If she gives him plenty and he's in the clover,   55
No need to worry about what's left over."
    The Miller, to make the best of it I can,
Refused to hold his tongue for any man,
But told his tale like any low-born clown.
I am sorry that I have to set it down,   60
And all you people, for God's love, I pray,
Whose taste is higher, do not think I say
A word with evil purpose; I must rehearse
Their stories one and all, both better and worse,
Or play false with my matter, that is clear.   65
Whoever, therefore, may not wish to hear,
Turn over the page and choose another tale;
For small and great, he'll find enough, no fail,
Of things from history, touching courtliness,
And virtue too, and also holiness.   70
If you choose wrong, don't lay it on my head.
You know the Miller couldn't be called well bred.
So with the Reeve, and many more as well,
And both of them had bawdy tales to tell.
Reflect a little, and don't hold me to blame.   75
There's no sense making earnest out of game.

THE TALE

There used to be a rich old oaf who made
His home at Oxford, a carpenter by trade,
And took in boarders. With him used to dwell
A student who had done his studies well,
But he was poor; for all that he had learned,   5
It was toward astrology his fancy turned.
He knew a number of figures and constructions
By which he could supply men with deductions
If they should ask him at a given hour
Whether to look for sunshine or for shower,   10
Or want to know whatever might befall,
Events of all sorts, I can't count them all.
    He was known as handy Nicholas,[6] this student.
Well versed in love, he knew how to be prudent,
Going about unnoticed, sly, and sure.   15
In looks no girl was ever more demure.
Lodged at this carpenter's, he lived alone;
He had a room there that he made his own,
Festooned with herbs, and he was sweet himself
As licorice or ginger. On a shelf   20
Above his bed's head, neatly stowed apart,

---

6. Chaucer's word is hendë, implying both *ready to hand* and *ingratiating* [Translator's note].

He kept the trappings that went with his art,
His astrolabe,[7] his books—among the rest,
Thick ones and thin ones, lay his *Almagest*[8]—
And the counters for his abacus as well.   25
Over his cupboard a red curtain fell
And up above a pretty zither lay
On which at night so sweetly would he play
That with the music the whole room would ring.
"Angelus to the Virgin" [9] he would sing   30
And then the song that's known as "The King's Note."[1]
Blessings were called down on his merry throat!
So this sweet scholar passed his time, his end
Being to eat and live upon his friend.[2]
    This carpenter had newly wed a wife   35
And loved her better than he loved his life.
He was jealous, for she was eighteen in age;
He tried to keep her close as in a cage,
For she was wild and young, and old was he
And guessed that he might smack of cuckoldry.   40
His ignorant wits had never chanced to strike
On Cato's[3] word, that man should wed his like;
Men ought to wed where their conditions point,
For youth and age are often out of joint.
But now, since he had fallen in the snare,   45
He must, like other men, endure his care.
    Fair this young woman was, her body trim
As any mink, so graceful and so slim.
She wore a striped belt that was all of silk;
A piece-work apron, white as morning milk,   50
About her loins and down her lap she wore.
White was her smock, her collar both before
And on the back embroidered all about
In coal-black silk, inside as well as out.
And like her collar, her white-laundered bonnet   55
Had ribbons of the same embroidery on it.
Wide was her silken fillet, worn up high,
And for a fact she had a willing eye.
She plucked each brow into a little bow,
And each one was as black as any sloe.[4]   60
She was a prettier sight to see by far
Than the blossoms of the early pear tree are,
And softer than the wool of an old wether.
Down from her belt there hung a purse of leather
With silken tassels and with studs of brass.   65
No man so wise, wherever people pass,
Who could imagine in this world at all
A wench like her, the pretty little doll!

---

7. An astronomical instrument for telling time.   8. A second-century treatise by Ptolemy, an astronomy
textbook.   9. A song about the Annunciation, when the angel Gabriel tells Mary she is to bear Jesus.
1. Unidentified.   2. I.e., the friend who provided him with money for his education.   3. Dionysius
Cato, the supposed author of a book of maxims employed in elementary education.   4. The sloeberry.

Far brighter was the dazzle of her hue
Than a coin struck in the Tower,[5] fresh and new.   70
As for her song, it twittered from her head
Sharp as a swallow perching on a shed.
And she could skip and sport as a young ram
Or calf will gambol, following his dam.
Her mouth was sweet as honey-ale or mead   75
Or apples in the hay, stored up for need.
She was as skittish as an untrained colt,
Slim as a mast and straighter than a bolt.
On her simple collar she wore a big brooch-pin
Wide as a shield's boss underneath her chin.   80
High up along her legs she laced her shoes.
She was a pigsney,[6] she was a primrose
For any lord to tumble in his bed
Or a good yeoman honestly to wed.
   Now sir, and again sir, this is how it was: 85
A day came round when handy Nicholas,
While her husband was at Oseney,[7] well away,
Began to fool with this young wife, and play.
These students always have a wily head.
He caught her in between the legs, and said,   90
"Sweetheart, unless I have my will with you
I'll die for stifled love, by all that's true,"
And held her by the haunches, hard. "I vow
I'll die unless you love me here and now,
Sure as my soul," he said, "is God's to save."   95
   She shied just as a colt does in the trave,[8]
And turned her head hard from him, this young wife,
And said, "I will not kiss you, on my life.
Why, stop it now," she said, "stop, Nicholas,
Or I will cry out 'Help, help,' and 'Alas!'   100
Be good enough to take your hands away."
   "Mercy," this Nicholas began to pray,
And spoke so well and poured it on so fast
She promised she would be his love at last,
And swore by Thomas à Becket, saint of Kent,   105
That she would serve him when she could invent
Or spy out some good opportunity.
"My husband is so full of jealousy
You must be watchful and take care," she said,
"Or well I know I'll be as good as dead.   110
You must go secretly about this business."
   "Don't give a thought to that," said Nicholas.
"A student has been wasting time at school
If he can't make a carpenter a fool."
And so they were agreed, these two, and swore   115
To watch their chance, as I have said before.

---

5. Minted in the Tower of London.   6. Pig's eye, probably the name of a wild flower.   7. A town near
Oxford.   8. A wooden frame confining a horse being shod.

When Nicholas had spanked her haunches neatly
And done all I have spoken of, he sweetly
Gave her a kiss, and then he took his zither
And loudly played, and sang his music with her.   120
    Now in her Christian duty, one saint's day,
To the parish church this good wife made her way,
And as she went her forehead cast a glow
As bright as noon, for she had washed it so
It glistened when she finished with her work.   125
    Serving this church there was a parish clerk
Whose name was Absolom, a ruddy man
With goose-gray eyes and curls like a great fan
That shone like gold on his neatly parted head.
His tunic was light blue and his nose red,   130
And he had patterns that had been cut through
Like the windows of St. Paul's in either shoe.[9]
He wore above his tunic, fresh and gay,
A surplice white as a blossom on a spray.
A merry devil, as true as God can save,   135
He knew how to let blood, trim hair, and shave,
Or write a deed of land in proper phrase,
And he could dance in twenty different ways
In the Oxford fashion, and sometimes he would sing
A loud falsetto to his fiddle string   140
Or his guitar. No tavern anywhere
But he had furnished entertainment there.
Yet his speech was delicate, and for his part
He was a little squeamish toward a fart.
    This Absolom, so jolly and so gay,   145
With a censer[1] went about on the saint's day
Censing the parish women one and all.
Many the doting look that he let fall,
And specially on this carpenter's young wife.
To look at her, he thought, was a good life,   150
She was so trim, so sweetly lecherous.
I dare say that if she had been a mouse
And he a cat, he would have made short work
Of catching her. This jolly parish clerk
Had such a heartful of love-hankerings   155
He would not take the women's offerings;
No, no, he said, it would not be polite.
    The moon, when darkness fell, shone full and bright
And Absolom was ready for love's sake
With his guitar to be up and awake,   160
And toward the carpenter's, brisk and amorous,
He made his way until he reached the house
A little after the cocks began to crow.
Under a casement he sang sweet and low,
"Dear lady, by your will, be kind to me,"   165

---

9. The patterns cut in his shoes resembled the windows in St. Paul's Cathedral in London.   1. A receptacle for incense with which to bless (or "cense") the wives of the parish as they made their offerings in church.

And strummed on his guitar in harmony.
This lovelorn singing woke the carpenter
Who said to his wife, "What, Alison, don't you hear
Absolom singing under our bedroom wall?"
    "Yes, God knows, John," she answered, "I hear it all."   170
    What would you like? In this way things went on
Till jolly Absolom was woebegone
For wooing her, awake all night and day.
He combed his curls and made himself look gay.
He swore to be her slave and used all means   175
To court her with his gifts and go-betweens.
He sang and quavered like a nightingale.
He sent her sweet spiced wine and seasoned ale,
Cakes that were piping hot, mead sweet with honey,
And since she was town-bred, he proffered money.   180
For some are won by wealth, and some no less
By blows, and others yet by gentleness.
    Sometimes, to keep his talents in her gaze,
He acted Herod[2] in the mystery plays
High on the stage. But what can help his case?   185
For she so loves this handy Nicholas
That Absolom is living in a bubble.
He has nothing but a laugh for all his trouble.
She leaves his earnestness for scorn to cool
And makes this Absolom her proper fool.   190
For this is a true proverb, and no lie;
"It always happens that the nigh and sly
Will let the absent suffer." So 'tis said,
And Absolom may rage or lose his head
But just because he was farther from her sight   195
This nearby Nicholas got in his light.
    Now hold your chin up, handy Nicholas,
For Absolom may wail and sing "Alas!"
One Saturday when the carpenter had gone
To Oseney, Nicholas and Alison   200
Agreed that he should use his wit and guile
This simple jealous husband to beguile.
And if it happened that the game went right
She would sleep in his arms the livelong night,
For this was his desire and hers as well.   205
At once, with no more words, this Nicholas fell
To working out his plan. He would not tarry,
But quietly to his room began to carry
Both food and drink to last him out a day,
Or more than one, and told her what to say   210
If her husband asked her about Nicholas.
She must say she had no notion where he was;
She hadn't laid eyes on him all day long;
He must be sick, or something must be wrong;
No matter how her maid had called and cried   215

2. A role traditionally played as a bully in the mystery plays.

He wouldn't answer, whatever might betide.
   This was the plan, and Nicholas kept away,
Shut in his room, for that whole Saturday.
He ate and slept or did as he thought best
Till Sunday, when the sun was going to rest,   220
This carpenter began to wonder greatly
Where Nicholas was and what might ail him lately,
"Now, by St. Thomas, I begin to dread
All isn't right with Nicholas," he said.
"He hasn't, God forbid, died suddenly!   225
The world is ticklish these days, certainly.
Today I saw a corpse to church go past,
A man that I saw working Monday last!
Go up," he told his chore-boy, "call and shout,
Knock with a stone, find what it's all about   230
And let me know."
               The boy went up and pounded
And yelled as if his wits had been confounded.
"What, how, what's doing, Master Nicholas?
How can you sleep all day?" But all his fuss
Was wasted, for he could not hear a word.   235
He noticed at the bottom of a board
A hole the cat used when she wished to creep
Into the room, and through it looked in deep
And finally of Nicholas caught sight.
This Nicholas sat gaping there upright   240
As though his wits were addled by the moon
When it was new. The boy went down, and soon
Had told his master how he had seen the man.
   The carpenter, when he heard this news, began
To cross himself. "Help us, St. Frideswide![3]   245
Little can we foresee what may betide!
The man's astronomy has turned his wit,
Or else he's in some agonizing fit.
I always knew that it would turn out so.
What God has hidden is not for men to know.   250
Aye, blessed is the ignorant man indeed,
Blessed is he that only knows his creed!
So fared another scholar of the sky,
For walking in the meadows once to spy
Upon the stars and what they might foretell,   255
Down in a clay-pit suddenly he fell!
He overlooked that! By St. Thomas, though,
I'm sorry for handy Nicholas. I'll go
And scold him roundly for his studying
If so I may, by Jesus, heaven's king!   260
Give me a staff, I'll pry up from the floor
While you, Robin, are heaving at the door.
He'll quit his books, I think."

---

3. An eighth-century English saint noted for her ability to cast out devils. She was the patron saint of Oxford.

He took his stand
Outside the room. The boy had a strong hand
And by the hasp he heaved it off at once.   265
The door fell flat. With gaping countenance
This Nicholas sat studying the air
As still as stone. He was in black despair,
The carpenter believed, and hard about
The shoulders caught and shook him, and cried out   270
Rudely, "What, how! What is it? Look down at us!
Wake up, think of Christ's passion, Nicholas!
I'll sign you with the cross to keep away
These elves and things!" And he began to say,
Facing the quarters of the house, each side,   275
And on the threshold of the door outside,
The night-spell:[4] "Jesu and St. Benedict
From every wicked thing this house protect . . ."
    Choosing his time, this handy Nicholas
Produced a dreadful sigh, and said, "Alas,   280
This world, must it be all destroyed straightway?"
    "What," asked the carpenter, "what's that you say?
Do as we do, we working men, and think
Of God."
            Nicholas answered, "Get me a drink,
And afterwards I'll tell you privately   285
Of something that concerns us, you and me.
I'll tell you only, you among all men."
    This carpenter went down and came again
With a draught of mighty ale, a generous quart.
As soon as each of them had drunk his part   290
Nicholas shut the door and made it fast
And sat down by the carpenter at last
And spoke to him. "My host," he said, "John dear,
You must swear by all that you hold sacred here
That not to any man will you betray   295
My confidence. What I'm about to say
Is Christ's own secret. If you tell a soul
You are undone, and this will be the toll:
If you betray me, you shall go stark mad."
    "Now Christ forbid it, by His holy blood,"   300
Answered this simple man. "I don't go blabbing.
If I say it myself, I have no taste for gabbing.
Speak up just as you like, I'll never tell,
Not wife nor child, by Him that harrowed hell."[5]
    "Now, John," said Nicholas, "this is no lie.   305
I have discovered through astrology,
And studying the moon that shines so bright
That Monday next, a quarter through the night,
A rain will fall, and such a mad, wild spate
That Noah's flood was never half so great.   310

---

4. A magic charm said at night to protect a house from evil spirits.   5. I.e., Christ, who descended into
hell and led away Adam, Eve, the Patriarchs, John the Baptist, and others, redeeming and releasing them.

This world," he said, "in less time than an hour
Shall drown entirely in that hideous shower.
Yes, every man shall drown and lose his life."
    "Alas," the carpenter answered, "for my wife!
Alas, my Alison! And shall she drown?"   315
For grief at this he nearly tumbled down,
And said, "But is there nothing to be done?"
    "Why, happily there is, for anyone
Who will take advice," this handy Nicholas said.
"You mustn't expect to follow your own head.   320
For what said Solomon, whose words were true?
'Proceed by counsel, and you'll never rue.'
If you will act on good advice, no fail,
I'll promise, and without a mast or sail,
To see that she's preserved, and you and I.   325
Haven't you heard how Noah was kept dry
When, warned by Christ beforehand, he discovered
That the whole earth with water should be covered?"
    "Yes," said the carpenter, "long, long ago."
    "And then again," said Nicholas, "don't you know   330
The grief they all had trying to embark
Till Noah could get his wife into the Ark?[6]
That was a time when Noah, I dare say,
Would gladly have given his best black wethers away
If she could have had a ship herself alone.   335
And therefore do you know what must be done?
This demands haste, and with a hasty thing
People can't stop for talk and tarrying.
    "Start out and get into the house right off
For each of us a tub or kneading-trough,   340
Above all making sure that they are large,
In which we'll float away as in a barge.
And put in food enough to last a day.
Beyond won't matter; the flood will fall away
Early next morning. Take care not to spill   345
A word to your boy Robin, nor to Jill
Your maid. I cannot save her, don't ask why.
I will not tell God's secrets, no, not I.
Let it be enough, unless your wits are mad,
To have as good a grace as Noah had.   350
I'll save your wife for certain, never doubt it.
Now go along, and make good time about it.
    "But when you have, for her and you and me,
Brought to the house these kneading-tubs, all three,
Then you must hang them under the roof, up high,   355
To keep our plans from any watchful eye.
When you have done exactly as I've said,
And put in snug our victuals and our bread,
Also an ax to cut the ropes apart
So when the rain comes we can make our start,   360

6. A stock comedy scene in the mystery plays.

And when you've broken a hole high in the gable
Facing the garden plot, above the stable,
To give us a free passage out, each one,
Then, soon as the great fall of rain is done,
You'll swim as merrily, I undertake,   365
As the white duck paddles along behind her drake.
Then I shall call, 'How, Alison! How, John!
Be cheerful, for the flood will soon be gone.'
And 'Master Nicholas, what ho!' you'll say.
'Good morning, I see you clearly, for it's day.'   370
Then we shall lord it for the rest of life
Over the world, like Noah and his wife.
    "But one thing I must warn you of downright.
Use every care that on that selfsame night
When we have taken ship and climbed aboard,   375
No one of us must speak a single word,
Nor call, nor cry, but pray with all his heart.
It is God's will. You must hang far apart,
You and your wife, for there must be no sin
Between you, no more in a look than in   380
The very deed. Go now, the plans are drawn.
Go, set to work, and may God spur you on!
Tomorrow night when all men are asleep
Into our kneading-troughs we three shall creep
And sit there waiting, and abide God's grace.   385
Go along now, this isn't the time or place
For me to talk at length or sermonize.
The proverb says, 'Don't waste words on the wise.'
You are so wise there is no need to teach you.
Go, save our lives—that's all that I beseech you!"   390
    This simple carpenter went on his way.
Many a time he said, "Alack the day,"
And to his wife he laid the secret bare.
She knew it better than he; she was aware
What this quaint bargain was designed to buy.   395
She carried on as if about to die,
And said, "Alas, go get this business done.
Help us escape, or we are dead, each one.
I am your true, your faithful wedded wife.
Go, my dear husband, save us, limb and life!"   400
    Great things, in all truth, can the emotions be!
A man can perish through credulity
So deep the print imagination makes.
This simple carpenter, he quails and quakes.
He really sees, according to his notion,   405
Noah's flood come wallowing like an ocean
To drown his Alison, his pet, his dear.
He weeps and wails, and gone is his good cheer,
And wretchedly he sighs. But he goes off
And gets himself a tub, a kneading-trough,   410
Another tub, and has them on the sly
Sent home, and there in secret hangs them high

Beneath the roof. He made three ladders, these
With his own hands, and stowed in bread and cheese
And a jug of good ale, plenty for a day.   415
Before all this was done, he sent away
His chore-boy Robin and his wench likewise
To London on some trumped-up enterprise,
And so on Monday, when it drew toward night,
He shut the door without a candlelight   420
And saw that all was just as it should be,
And shortly they went clambering up, all three.
They sat there still, and let a moment pass.
    "Now then, 'Our Father,' mum!" said Nicholas,
And "Mum!" said John, and "Mum!" said Alison,   425
And piously this carpenter went on
Saying his prayers. He sat there still and straining,
Trying to make out whether he heard it raining.
    The dead of sleep, for very weariness,
Fell on this carpenter, as I should guess,   430
At about curfew time, or little more.
His head was twisted, and that made him snore.
His spirit groaned in its uneasiness.
Down from his ladder slipped this Nicholas,
And Alison too, downward she softly sped   435
And without further word they went to bed
Where the carpenter himself slept other nights.
There were the revels, there were the delights!
And so this Alison and Nicholas lay
Busy about their solace and their play   440
Until the bell for lauds[7] began to ring
And in the chancel friars began to sing.
    Now on this Monday, woebegone and glum
For love, this parish clerk, this Absolom
Was with some friends at Oseney, and while there   445
Inquired after John the carpenter.
A member of the cloister drew him away
Out of the church, and told him, "I can't say.
I haven't seen him working hereabout
Since Saturday. The abbot sent him out   450
For timber, I suppose. He'll often go
And stay at the granary a day or so.
Or else he's at his own house, possibly.
I can't for certain say where he may be."
    Absolom at once felt jolly and light,   455
And thought, "Time now to be awake all night,
For certainly I haven't seen him making
A stir about his door since day was breaking.
Don't call me a man if when I hear the cock
Begin to crow I don't slip up and knock   460
On the low window by his bedroom wall.
To Alison at last I'll pour out all

---

7. The second of the seven church services celebrated each day; it took place before sunrise.

My love-pangs, for at this point I can't miss,
Whatever happens, at the least a kiss.
Some comfort, by my word, will come my way.   465
I've felt my mouth itch the whole livelong day,
And that's a sign of kissing at the least.
I dreamed all night that I was at a feast.
So now I'll go and sleep an hour or two,
And then I'll wake and play the whole night through."   470
    When the first cockcrow through the dark had come
Up rose this jolly lover Absolom
And dressed up smartly. He was not remiss
About the least point. He chewed licorice
And cardamom to smell sweet, even before   475
He combed his hair. Beneath his tongue he bore
A sprig of Paris[8] like a truelove knot.
He strolled off to the carpenter's house, and got
Beneath the window. It came so near the ground
It reached his chest. Softly, with half a sound,   480
He coughed, "My honeycomb, sweet Alison,
What are you doing, my sweet cinnamon?
Awake, my sweetheart and my pretty bird,
Awake, and give me from your lips a word!
Little enough you care for all my woe,   485
How for your love I sweat wherever I go!
No wonder I sweat and faint and cannot eat
More than a girl; as a lamb does for the teat
I pine. Yes, truly, I so long for love
I mourn as if I were a turtledove."   490
    Said she, "You jack-fool, get away from here!
So help me God, I won't sing 'Kiss me, dear!'
I love another more than you. Get on,
For Christ's sake, Absolom, or I'll throw a stone.
The devil with you! Go and let me sleep."   495
    "Ah, that true love should ever have to reap
So evil a fortune," Absolom said. "A kiss,
At least, if it can be no more than this,
Give me, for love of Jesus and of me."
    "And will you go away for that?" said she.   500
    "Yes, truly, sweetheart," answered Absolom.
    "Get ready then," she said, "for here I come,"
And softly said to Nicholas, "Keep still,
And in a minute you can laugh your fill."
This Absolom got down upon his knee   505
And said, "I am a lord of pure degree,
For after this, I hope, comes more to savor.
Sweetheart, your grace, and pretty bird, your favor!"
    She undid the window quickly. "That will do,"
She said. "Be quick about it, and get through,   510
For fear the neighbors will look out and spy."
    Absolom wiped his mouth to make it dry.

8. A cloverlike plant.

The night was pitch dark, coal-black all about.
Her rear end through the window she thrust out.
He got no better or worse, did Absolom,   515
Than to kiss her with his mouth on the bare bum
Before he had caught on, a smacking kiss.
    He jumped back, thinking something was amiss.
A woman had no beard, he was well aware,
But what he felt was rough and had long hair.   520
    "Alas," he cried, "what have you made me do?"
"Te-hee!" she said, and banged the window to.
Absolom backed away a sorry pace.
    "You've bearded him!"[9] said handy Nicholas.
"God's body, this is going fair and fit!"   525
    This luckless Absolom heard every bit,
And gnawed his mouth, so angry he became.
He said to himself, "I'll square you, all the same."
    But who now scrubs and rubs, who chafes his lips
With dust, with sand, with straw, with cloth and chips   530
If not this Absolom? "The devil," says he,
"Welcome my soul if I wouldn't rather be
Revenged than have the whole town in a sack!
Alas," he cries, "if only I'd held back!"
His hot love had become all cold and ashen.   535
He didn't have a curse to spare for passion
From the moment when he kissed her on the ass.
That was the cure to make his sickness pass!
He cried as a child does after being whipped;
He railed at love. Then quietly he slipped   540
Across the street to a smith who was forging out
Parts that the farmers needed round about.
He was busy sharpening colter[1] and plowshare
When Absolom knocked as though without a care.
    "Undo the door, Jervice, and let me come."   545
    "What? Who are you?"
                    "It is I, Absolom."
    "Absolom, is it! By Christ's precious tree,
Why are you up so early? Lord bless me,
What's ailing you? Some gay girl has the power
To bring you out, God knows, at such an hour!   550
Yes, by St. Neot,[2] you know well what I mean!"
    Absolom thought his jokes not worth a bean.
Without a word he let them all go by.
He had another kind of fish to fry
Than Jervice guessed. "Lend me this colter here   555
That's hot in the chimney, friend," he said. "Don't fear,
I'll bring it back right off when I am through.
I need it for a job I have to do."
    "Of course," said Jervice. "Why, if it were gold
Or coins in a sack, uncounted and untold,   560

---

9. "To beard" in Middle English means to trick, but Nicholas is also punning on the literal meaning of the word.   1. A turf cutter on a plow.   2. A ninth-century English saint.

As I'm a rightful smith, I wouldn't refuse it.
But, Christ's foot! how on earth do you mean to use it?"
    "Let that," said Absolom, "be as it may.
I'll let you know tomorrow or next day,"
And took the colter where the steel was cold   565
And slipped out with it safely in his hold
And softly over to the carpenter's wall.
He coughed and then he rapped the window, all
As he had done before.
                        "Who's knocking there?"
Said Alison. "It is a thief, I swear."   570
    "No, no," said he. "God knows, my sugarplum,
My bird, my darling, it's your Absolom.
I've brought a golden ring my mother gave me,
Fine and well cut, as I hope that God will save me.
It's yours, if you will let me have a kiss."   575
    Nicholas had got up to take a piss
And thought he would improve the whole affair.
This clerk, before he got away from there,
Should give *his* ass a smack; and hastily
He opened the window, and thrust out quietly,   580
Buttocks and haunches, all the way, his bum.
Up spoke this clerk, this jolly Absolom:
"Speak, for I don't know where you are, sweetheart."
    Nicholas promptly let fly with a fart
As loud as if a clap of thunder broke,   585
So great he was nearly blinded by the stroke,
And ready with his hot iron to make a pass,
Absolom caught him fairly on the ass.
    Off flew the skin, a good handbreadth of fat
Lay bare, the iron so scorched him where he sat.   590
As for the pain, he thought that he would die,
And like a madman he began to cry.
"Help! Water! Water! Help, for God's own heart!"
    At this the carpenter came to with a start.
He heard a man cry "Water!" as if mad.   595
"It's coming now," was the first thought he had.
"It's Noah's flood, alas, God be our hope!"
He sat up with his ax and chopped the rope
And down at once the whole contraption fell.
He didn't take time out to buy or sell   600
Till he hit the floor and lay there in a swoon.
    Then up jumped Nicholas and Alison
And in the street began to cry, "Help, ho!"
The neighbors all came running, high and low,
And poured into the house to see the sight.   605
The man still lay there, passed out cold and white,
For in his tumble he had broken an arm.
But he himself brought on his greatest harm,
For when he spoke he was at once outdone
By handy Nicholas and Alison   610
Who told them one and all that he was mad.

So great a fear of Noah's flood he had,
By some delusion, that in his vanity
He had bought himself these kneading-troughs, all three.
And hung them from the roof there, up above,   615
And he had pleaded with them, for God's love,
To sit there in the loft for company.
    The neighbors laughed at such a fantasy,
And round the loft began to pry and poke
And turned his whole disaster to a joke.   620
He found it was no use to say a word.
Whatever reason he offered, no one heard.
With oaths and curses people swore him down
Until he passed for mad in the whole town.
Wit, clerk, and student all stood by each other.   625
They said, "It's clear the man is crazy, brother."
Everyone had his laugh about this feud.
So Alison, the carpenter's wife, got screwed
For all the jealous watching he could try,
And Absolom, he kissed her nether eye,   630
And Nicholas got his bottom roasted well.
God save this troop! That's all I have to tell.

The Wife of Bath's Prologue and Tale

THE PROLOGUE

"Experience, though all authority
Was lacking in the world, confers on me
The right to speak of marriage, and unfold
Its woes. For, lords, since I was twelve years old[3]
—Thanks to eternal God in heaven alive—   5
I've married at church door no less than five
Husbands, provided that I can have been
So often wed,[4] and all were worthy men.
But I was told, indeed, and not long since,
That Christ went to a wedding only once   10
At Cana, in the land of Galilee.[5]
By this example he instructed me
To wed once only—that's what I have heard!
Again, consider now what a sharp word,
Beside a well, Jesus, both God and man,   15
Spoke in reproving the Samaritan:
'Five husbands thou hast had'—this certainly
He said to her—'and the man that now hath thee
Is not thy husband.'[6] True, he spoke this way,
But what he meant is more than I can say   20
Except that I would ask why the fifth man
Was not a husband to the Samaritan?
To just how many could she be a wife?

---

3. According to Church law, twelve was the earliest age at which a girl could be married; the Wife is probably bragging rather than telling the literal truth.   4. Assuming so many marriages are legitimate.
5. John 2.1–2.   6. John 4.6–19.

I've never heard this number all my life
Determined up to now. For round and round   25
Scholars may gloze,[7] interpret, and expound,
But plainly, this I know without a lie,
God told us to increase and multiply.[8]
That noble text I can well understand.
My husband—this too I have well in hand—   30
Should leave both father and mother and cleave to me.[9]
Number God never mentioned, bigamy,
No, nor even octogamy; why do men
Talk of it as a sin and scandal, then?
    "Think of that monarch, wise King Solomon.   35
It strikes me that *he* had more wives than one![1]
To be refreshed, God willing, would please me
If I got it half as many times as he!
He had a gift, and one of God's own giving,
For all his wives! There isn't a man now living   40
Who has the like. By all that I make out
On the first night this king had many a bout
With each, he was so thoroughly alive.
Blessed be God that I have married five,
And always, for the money in his chest   45
And for his nether purse, I picked the best.
In divers schools ripe scholarship is made,
And various practice in all kinds of trade
Makes perfect workmen, as the world can see.
Five husbands have had turns at schooling me.   50
Welcome the sixth, whenever I am faced
With yet another. I don't mean to be chaste
At all costs. When a spouse of mine is gone,
Some other Christian man shall take me on,
For then, says the Apostle, I'll be free   55
To wed, in God's name, where it pleases me.[2]
To marry is no sin, as we can learn
From him; better to marry than to burn,[3]
He says. Why should I care what obloquy
Men heap on Lamech and his bigamy?   60
Abraham was, by all that I can tell,
A holy man; so Jacob[4] was as well,
And each of them took more than two as brides,
And many another holy man besides.
Where, may I ask, in any period,   65
In plain words can you show Almighty God
Forbade us marriage? Point it out to me!
Or where did he command virginity?
The Apostle, when he speaks of maidenhood,
Lays down no law.[5] This I have understood   70

7. Gloss, or interpret.   8. Genesis 1.28.   9. Matthew 19.5–6.   1. 1 Kings 11.3 describes Solomon
as having seven hundred wives and three hundred concubines.   2. The Apostle is Paul, and the reference
is to 1 Corinthians 7.39; throughout her *Prologue* the Wife returns to this chapter, sometimes using (or
misusing) Paul to support her views, sometimes arguing against him.   3. 1 Corinthians 7.9.   4. See
Genesis 29.15–30. For Lamech, see Genesis 4.19–23. For Abraham, Genesis 16.1–6.   5. 1 Corinthians
7.25.

As well as you, milords, for it is plain.
Men may advise a woman to abstain
From marriage, but mere counsels aren't commands.
He left it to our judgment, where it stands.
Had God enjoined us all to maidenhood   75
Then marriage would have been condemned for good.
But truth is, if no seed were ever sown,
In what soil could virginity be grown?
Paul did not dare command a thing at best
On which his Master left us no behest.   80
    "But now the prize goes to virginity.
Seize it whoever can, and let us see
What manner of man shall run best in the race!
But not all men receive this form of grace
Except where God bestows it by his will.   85
The Apostle was a maid, I know; but still,
Although he wished all men were such as he,
It was only *counsel* toward virginity.[6]
To be a wife he gave me his permission,
And so it is no blot on my condition   90
Nor slander of bigamy upon my state
If when my husband dies I take a mate.
A man does virtuously, St. Paul has said,
To touch no woman[7]—meaning in his bed.
For fire and fat are dangerous friends at best.   95
You know what this example should suggest.
Here is the nub: he held virginity
Superior to wedded frailty,
And frailty I call it unless man
And woman both are chaste for their whole span.   100
    "I am not jealous if maidenhood outweighs
My marriages; I grant it all the praise.
It pleases, them, these virgins, flesh and soul
To be immaculate. I won't extol
My own condition. In a lord's household   105
You know that every vessel can't be gold.
Some are of wood, and serve their master still.
God calls us variously to do his will.
Each has his proper gift, of all who live,
Some this, some that, as it pleases God to give.   110
    "Virginity is a high and perfect course,
And continence is holy. But the source
Of all perfection, Jesus, never bade
Each one of us to go sell all he had
And give it to the poor; he did not say   115
That all should follow him in this one way.
He spoke to those who would live perfectly,[8]
And by your leave, lords, that is not for me!
The flower of my best years I find it suits
To spend on the acts of marriage and its fruits.   120

---

6. 1 Corinthians 7.8.   7. 1 Corinthians 7.1.   8. Matthew 9.16–22.

"Tell me this also: why at our creation
Were organs given us for generation,
And for what profit were we creatures made?
Believe me, not for nothing! Ply his trade
Of twisting texts who will, and let him urge   125
That they were only given us to purge
Our urine; say without them we should fail
To tell a female rightly from a male
And that's their only object—say you so?
It won't work, as experience will show.   130
Without offense to scholars, I say this,
That they were made for both these purposes,
That we may both be cleansed, I mean, and eased
Through intercourse, where God is not displeased.
Why else in books is this opinion met,   135
That every man should pay his wife his debt?[9]
Tell me with what a man should hope to pay
Unless he put his instrument in play?
They were supplied us, then, for our purgation,
But they were also meant for generation.   140
   "But none the less I do not mean to say
That all those who are furnished in this way
Are bound to go and practice intercourse.
The world would then grant chastity no force.
Christ was a maid, yet he was formed a man,   145
And many a saint, too, since the world began,
And yet they lived in perfect chastity.
I am not spiteful toward virginity.
Let virgins be white bread of pure wheat-seed.
Barley we wives are called, and yet I read   150
In Mark, and tell the tale in truth he can,
That Christ with barley bread cheered many a man.[1]
In the state that God assigned to each of us
I'll persevere. I'm not fastidious.
In wifehood I will use my instrument   155
As freely by my Maker it was lent.
If I hold back with it, God give me sorrow!
My husband shall enjoy it night and morrow
Whenever it pleases him to pay his debt.
A husband, though—I've not been thwarted yet—   160
Shall always be my debtor and my slave.
From tribulation he shall never save
His flesh, not for as long as I'm his wife![2]
I have the power, during all my life,
Over his very body, and not he.   165
For so the Apostle has instructed me,
Who bade men love their wives for better or worse.
It pleases me from end to end, that verse!"[3]
   The Pardoner, before she could go on,

---

9. 1 Corinthians 7.3.   1. The reference is actually found not in Mark but in John 6.9.   2. 1 Corinthians 7.28; this verse, with its reference to the "tribulation of the flesh," is central to the Wife's *Prologue*.
3. 1 Corinthians 7.4.

Jumped up and cried, "By God and by St. John, 170
Upon this topic you preach nobly, Dame!
I was about to wed, but now, for shame,
Why should my body pay a price so dear?
I'd rather not be married all this year!"
    "Hold on," she said. "I haven't yet begun. 175
You'll drink a keg of this before I'm done,
I promise you, and it won't taste like ale!
And after I have told you my whole tale
Of marriage, with its fund of tribulation—
And I'm the expert of my generation, 180
For I myself, I mean, have been the whip—
You can decide then if you want a sip
Out of the barrel that I mean to broach.
Before you come too close in your approach,
Think twice. I have examples, more than ten! 185
'The man who won't be warned by other men,
To other men a warning he shall be.'
These are the words we find in Ptolemy.
Go read them right there in his *Almagest*."[4]
    "Now, Madame, if you're willing, I suggest," 190
Answered the Pardoner, "as you began,
Continue with your tale, and spare no man.
Teach us young men your practice as our guide."
    "Gladly, if it will please you," she replied.
"But first I ask you, if I speak my mind, 195
That all this company may be well inclined,
And will not take offense at what I say.
I only mean it, after all, in play.
    "Now, sirs, I will get onward with my tale.
If ever I hope to drink good wine or ale, 200
I'm speaking truth: the husbands I have had,
Three of them have been good, and two were bad.
The three were kindly men, and rich, and old.
But they were hardly able to uphold
The statute which had made them fast to me. 205
You know well what I mean by this, I see!
So help me God, I can't help laughing yet
Thinking of how at night I made them sweat,
And I thought nothing of it, on my word!
Their land and wealth they had by then conferred 210
On me, and so I safely could neglect
Tending their love or showing them respect.
So well they loved me that by God above
I hardly set a value on their love.
A woman who is wise is never done 215
Busily winning love when she has none,
But since I had them wholly in my hand
And they had given me their wealth and land,

---

4. The *Almagest* is a second-century treatise on astronomy; this proverb appears in a preface that was later added to the work.

Why task myself to spoil them or to please
Unless for my own profit and my ease?   220
I set them working so that many a night
They sang a dirge, so grievous was their plight!
They never got the bacon, well I know,
Offered as prize to couples at Dunmow
Who live a year in peace, without repentance!⁵   225
So well I ruled them, by my law and sentence,
They gladly brought me fine things from the fair,
Happy whenever I spoke with a mild air,
For God knows I could chide outrageously.
    "Now judge if I could do it properly!   230
You wives who understand and who are wise,
This is the way to throw dust in their eyes.
There isn't on the earth so bold a man
He can swear false or lie as a woman can.
I do not urge this course in every case,   235
Just when a prudent wife is caught off base;
Then she should swear the parrot's mad who tattled
Her indiscretions, and when she's once embattled
Should call her maid as witness, by collusion.
But listen, how I threw them in confusion: 240
    " 'Sir dotard, this is how you live?' I'd say.
'How can my neighbor's wife be dressed so gay?
She carries off the honors everywhere.
I sit at home. I've nothing fit to wear.
What were you doing at my neighbor's house?   245
Is she so handsome? Are you so amorous?
What do you whisper to our maid? God bless me,
Give up your jokes, old lecher. They depress me.
When I've a harmless friend myself, you balk
And scold me like a devil if I walk   250
For innocent amusement to his house.
You drink and come home reeling like a souse
And sit down on your bench, worse luck, and preach.
Taking a wife who's poor—this is the speech
That you regale me with—costs grievously,   255
And if she's rich and of good family,
It is a constant torment, you decide,
To suffer her ill humor and her pride.
And if she's fair, you scoundrel, you destroy her
By saying that every lecher will enjoy her;   260
For she can't long keep chastity intact
Who is from every side at once attacked.
    " 'Some want us for our wealth, so you declare,
Some for our figure, some think we are fair,
Some want a woman who can dance or sing,   265
Some want kindness, and some philandering,
Some look for hands and arms well turned and small.
Thus, by your tale, the devil may take us all!

---

5. At Dunmow, in Essex, a side of bacon was given to the couple who had lived a year without quarreling.

Men cannot keep a castle or redoubt
Longer, you tell me, than it can hold out.   270
Or if a woman's plain, you say that she
Is one who covets each man she may see,
For at him like a spaniel she will fly
Until she finds some man that she can buy.
Down to the lake goes never a goose so gray   275
But it will have a mate, I've heard you say.
It's hard to fasten—this too I've been told—
A thing that no man willingly will hold.
Wise men, you tell me as you go to bed,
And those who hope for heaven should never wed.   280
I hope wild lightning and a thunderstroke
Will break your wizened neck! You say that smoke
And falling timbers and a railing wife
Drive a man from his house. Lord bless my life!
What ails an old man, so to make him chide?   285
We cover our vices till the knot is tied,
We wives, you say, and then we trot them out.
Here's a fit proverb for a doddering lout!
An ox or ass, you say, a hound or horse,
These we examine as a matter of course.   290
Basins and also bowls, before we buy them,
Spoons, spools, and such utensils, first we try them,
And so with pots and clothes, beyond denial;
But of their wives men never make a trial
Until they are married. After that, you say,   295
Old fool, we put our vices on display.
   " 'I'm in a pique if you forget your duty
And aren't forever praising me for beauty
Or aren't at all hours doting on my face
And calling me "fair dame" in every place,   300
Or fail to give a feast on my birthday
To keep my spirits fresh and make me gay,
Or if all proper courtesies aren't paid
My nurse, and equally my chambermaid,
My father's kin with all his family ties—   305
You say so, you old barrelful of lies!
   " 'Yet just because he has a head of hair
Like shining gold, and squires me everywhere,
You have a false suspicion in your heart
Of Jenkin, our apprentice. For my part   310
I wouldn't have him if you died tomorrow!
But tell me this, or go and live in sorrow:
That chest of yours, why do you hide the keys
Away from me? It's my wealth, if you please,
As much as yours. Will you make a fool of me,   315
The mistress of our house? You shall not be
Lord of my body and my wealth at once!
No, by St. James himself, you must renounce
One or the other, if it drives you mad!
What do you gain by spying? You'd be glad   320

To lock me up, I think, inside your chest.
"Enjoy yourself, and go where you think best,"
You ought to say; "I won't hear tales of malice.
I know you for a faithful wife, Dame Alice."
A woman loves no man who keeps close charge   325
Of where she goes. We want to be at large.
Blessed above all other men was he,
The wise astrologer, Don Ptolemy,
Who has this proverb in his *Almagest*:
"Of all wise men his wisdom is the best   330
Who does not care who has the world in hand."⁶
Now by this proverb you should understand,
Since you have plenty, it isn't yours to care
Or fret how richly other people fare,
For by your leave, old dotard, you for one   335
Can have all you can take when day is done.
The man's a niggard to the point of scandal
Who will not lend his lamp to light a candle;
His lamp won't lose although the candle gain.
If you've enough, you ought not to complain.   340
  " 'You say, too, if we make ourselves look smart,
Put on expensive clothes and dress the part,
We lay our virtue open to disgrace.
And then you try to reinforce your case
By saying these words in the Apostle's name: 345
"In chaste apparel, with modesty and shame,
So shall you women clothe yourselves," said he,
"And not in rich coiffure or jewelry,
Pearls or the like, or gold, or costly wear."⁷
Now both your text and rubric,⁸ I declare,   350
I will not follow as I would a gnat!
  " 'You told me once that I was like a cat,
For singe her skin and she will stay at home,
But if her skin is smooth, the cat will roam.
No dawn but finds her on the neighbors calling   355
To show her skin, and go off caterwauling.
If I am looking smart, you mean to say,
I'm off to put my finery on display.
  " 'What do you gain, old fool, by setting spies?
Though you beg Argus⁹ with his hundred eyes   360
To be my bodyguard, for all his skill
He'll keep me only by my own free will.
I know enough to blind him, as I live!
  " 'There are three things, you also say, that give
Vexation to this world both south and north.   365
You add that no one can endure the fourth.
Of these catastrophes a hateful wife—
You precious wretch, may Christ cut short your life!—
Is always reckoned, as you say, for one.

---

6. See note to line 189 above.   7. 1 Timothy 2.9.   8. The rubric was a heading to the text written in red (*ruber* in Latin).   9. Argus was a hundred-eyed creature set by Juno to watch over Io, whom Jove loved and had turned into a heifer; see Ovid, *Metamorphoses* 1.

Is this your whole stock of comparison,   370
And why from all your parables of contempt
Can luckless helpmates never be exempt?
You also liken woman's love to hell,
To barren land where water will not dwell.
I've heard you call it an unruly fire;   375
The more it burns, the hotter its desire
To burn up everything that burned will be.
You say that just as worms destroy a tree
A wife destroys her spouse, as they have found
Who get themselves in holy wedlock bound.'   380
    "By these devices, lords, as you perceive,
I got my three old husbands to believe
That in their cups they said things of this sort,
And all of it was false; but for support
Jenkin bore witness, and my niece did too.   385
These innocents, Lord, what I put them through!
God's precious pains! And they had no recourse,
For I could bite and whinny like a horse.
Though in the wrong, I kept them well annoyed,
Or oftentimes I would have been destroyed!   390
First to the mill is first to grind his grain.
I was always the first one to complain,
And so our peace was made; they gladly bid
For terms to settle things they never did!
    "For wenching I would scold them out of hand   395
When they were hardly well enough to stand.
But this would tickle a man; it would restore him
To think I had so great a fondness for him!
I'd vow when darkness came and out I stepped,
It was to see the girls with whom he slept.   400
Under this pretext I had plenty of mirth!
Such wit as this is given us at our birth.
Lies, tears, and needlework the Lord will give
In kindness to us women while we live.
And thus in one point I can take just pride: 405
I showed myself in the end the stronger side.
By sleight or strength I kept them in restraint,
And chiefly by continual complaint.
In bed they met their grief in fullest measure.
There I would scold; I would not do their pleasure.   410
Bed was a place where I would not abide
Feeling my husband's arm across my side
Till he agreed to square accounts and pay,
And after that I'd let him have his way.
To every man, therefore, I tell this tale: 415
Win where you're able, all is up for sale.
No falcon by an empty hand is lured.
For victory their cravings I endured
And even feigned a show of appetite.
And yet in old meat I have no delight;   420
It made me always rail at them and chide them,

For though the pope himself sat down beside them
I would not give them peace at their own board.
No, on my honor, I paid them word for word.
Almighty God so help me, if right now   425
I had to make my last will, I can vow
For every word they said to me, we're quits.
For I so handled the contest by my wits
That they gave up, and took it for the best,
Or otherwise we should have had no rest.   430
Like a mad lion let my husband glare,
He finally got the worst of the affair.
    "Then I would say, 'My dear, you ought to keep
In mind how gentle Wilkin looks, our sheep.
Come here, my husband, let me kiss your cheek!   435
You should be patient, too; you should be meek.
Of Job and of his patience when you prate
Your conscience ought to show a cleaner slate.
He should be patient who so well can preach.
If not, then it will fall on me to teach   440
The beauty of a peaceful wedded life.
For one of us must give in, man or wife,
And since men are more reasonable creatures
Than women are, it follows that *your* features
Ought to exhibit patience. Why do you groan?   445
You want my body yours, and yours alone?
Why, take it all! Welcome to every bit!
But curse you, Peter,[1] unless you cherish it!
Were I inclined to peddle my *belle chose,*[2]
I could walk out dressed freshly as a rose.   450
But I will keep it for your own sweet tooth.
It's your fault if we fight. By God, that's truth!'
    "This was the way I talked when I had need.
But now to my fourth husband I'll proceed.
    "This fourth I married was a roisterer.   455
He had a mistress, and my passions were,
Although I say it, strong; and altogether
Stubborn and young I was, and pert in feather.
If anyone took up his harp to play,
How I could dance! I sang as merry a lay   460
As any nightingale when of sweet wine
I'd drunk my draft. Metellius,[3] the foul swine,
Who beat his spouse until he took her life
For drinking wine, if I had been his wife,
He'd never have frightened me away from drinking!   465
But after a drink, Venus gets in my thinking,
For just as true as cold engenders hail
A thirsty mouth goes with a thirsty tail.
Drinking destroys a woman's last defense
As lechers well know by experience.   470

1. This is not the husband's name but an oath by St. Peter.   2. Pretty thing (French).   3. A virtuous
Roman husband who reputedly killed his wife for drinking wine.

"But, Lord Christ, when it all comes back to me,
Remembering my youth and jollity,
It tickles me to the roots. It does me good
Down to this very day that while I could
I took my world, my time, and had my fling.   475
But age, alas, that poisons everything
Has robbed me of my beauty and my pith.
Well, let it go! Good-by! The devil with
What cannot last! There's only this to tell:
The flour is gone, I've only chaff to sell.   480
Yet I'll contrive to keep a merry cheek!
But now of my fourth husband I will speak.
    "My heart was, I can tell you, full of spite
That in another he should find delight.
I paid him for this debt; I made it good.   485
I furnished him a cross of the same wood,
By God and by St. Joce⁴—in no foul fashion,
Not with my flesh; but I put on such passion
And rendered him so jealous, I'll engage
I made him fry in his own grease for rage!   490
On earth, God knows, I was his purgatory;
I only hope his soul is now in glory.
God knows it was a sad song that he sung
When the shoe pinched him; sorely was he wrung!
Only he knew, and God, the devious system,   495
By which outrageously I used to twist him.
He died when I came home from Jerusalem.
He's buried near the chancel,⁵ under the beam
That holds the cross. His tomb is less ornate
Than that where King Darius lies in state   500
And which the paintings of Appelles graced
With subtle work.⁶ It would have been a waste
To bury him lavishly. Farewell! God save
His soul and give him rest! He's in his grave.
    "And now of my fifth husband let me tell.   505
God never let his soul go down to hell
Though he of all five was my scourge and flail!
I feel it on my ribs, right down the scale,
And ever shall until my dying day.
And yet he was so full of life and gay   510
In bed, and could so melt me and cajole me
When on my back he had a mind to roll me,
What matter if on every bone he'd beaten me!
He'd have my love, so quickly he could sweeten me.
I loved him best, in fact; for as you see,   515
His love was a more arduous prize for me.
We women, if I'm not to tell a lie,

---

4. A seventh-century Breton saint, whose relics were at an abbey near the Tabard Inn.   5. The part of
the church used by the officiating clergy; often a cross was placed on a beam that divided it from the nave,
where the congregation sat.   6. Darius, king of the Persians, reputedly had a tomb decorated by the
famous Jewish craftsman Appelles; Chaucer derived this fictional information from a twelfth-century Latin
poem.

Are quaint in this regard. Put in our eye
A thing we cannot easily obtain,
All day we'll cry about it and complain.   520
Forbid a thing, we want it bitterly,
But urge it on us, then we turn and flee.
We're chary of what we hope that men will buy.
A throng at market makes the prices high;
Men set no value on cheap merchandise,   525
A truth all women know if they are wise.
    "My fifth, may God forgive his every sin,
I took for love, not money. He had been
An Oxford student once, but in our town
Was boarding with my good friend, Alison.   530
She knew each secret that I had to give
More than our parish priest did, as I live!
I told her my full mind, I shared it all.
For if my husband pissed against a wall
Or did a thing that might have cost his life,   535
To her, and to another neighbor's wife,
And to my niece, a girl whom I loved well,
His every thought I wouldn't blush to tell.
And often enough I told them, be it said.
God knows I made his face turn hot and red   540
For secrets he confided to his shame.
He knew he only had himself to blame.
    "And so it happened once that during Lent,
As I did often, to Alison's I went,
For I have loved my life long to be gay   545
And to walk out in April or in May
To hear the talk and seek a favorite haunt.
Jenkin the student, Alice, my confidante,
And I myself into the country went.
My husband was in London all that Lent.   550
I had the greater liberty to see
And to be seen by jolly company.
How could I tell beforehand in what place
Luck might be waiting with a stroke of grace?
And so I went to every merrymaking.   555
No pilgrimage was past my undertaking.
I was at festivals, and marriages,
Processions, preachings, and at miracle plays,
And in my scarlet clothes I made a sight.
Upon that costume neither moth nor mite   560
Nor any worm with ravening hunger fell.
And how so? It was kept in use too well.
    "Now for what happened. In the fields we walked,
The three of us, and gallantly we talked,
The student and I, until I told him he,   565
If I became a widow, should marry me.
For I can say, and not with empty pride,
I've never failed for marriage to provide
Or other things as well. Let mice be meek;

A mouse's heart I hold not worth a leek.   570
He has one hole to scurry to, just one,
And if that fails him, he is quite undone.
    "I let this student think he had bewitched me.
(My mother with this piece of guile enriched me!)
All night I dreamed of him—this too I said;   575
He was about to kill me flat in bed;
My very bed in fact was full of blood;
But still I hoped it would result in good,
For blood betokens gold, as I have heard.
It was a fiction, dream and every word,   580
But I was following my mother's lore
In all this matter, as in many more.
    "Sirs—let me see; what did I mean to say?
Aha! By God, I have it! When he lay,
My fourth, of whom I've spoken, on his bier,   585
I wept of course; I showed but little cheer,
As wives must do, since custom has its place,
And with my kerchief covered up my face.
But since I had provided for a mate,
I did not cry for long, I'll freely state.   590
And so to church my husband on the morrow
Was borne away by neighbors in their sorrow.
Jenkin, the student, was among the crowd,
And when I saw him walk, so help me God,
Behind the bier, I thought he had a pair   595
Of legs and feet so cleanly turned and fair
I put my heart completely in his hold.
He was in fact some twenty winters old
And I was forty, to confess the truth;
But all my life I've still had a colt's tooth.   600
My teeth were spaced apart; that was the seal
St. Venus printed, and became me well.
So help me God, I was a lusty one,
Pretty and young and rich, and full of fun.
And truly, as my husbands have all said,   605
I was the best thing there could be in bed.
For I belong to Venus in my feelings,
Yet have the heart of Mars in all my dealings.
From Venus come my lust and appetite,
From Mars I get my courage and my might,   610
Born under Taurus, while Mars stood therein.
Alas, alas, that ever love was sin!
I yielded to my every inclination
Through the predominance of my constellation;
This made me so I never could withhold   615
My chamber of Venus, if the truth be told,
From a good fellow; yet upon my face
Mars left his mark, and in another place.
Never, so may Christ grant me intercession,
Have I yet loved a fellow with discretion,   620
But always I have followed appetite,
Let him be long or short or dark or light.

I never cared, as long as he liked me,
What his rank was or how poor he might be.
"What should I say, but when the month ran out,   625
This jolly student, always much about,
This Jenkin married me in solemn state.
To him I gave land, titles, the whole slate
Of goods that had been given me before;
But my repentance afterward was sore!   630
He wouldn't endure the pleasures I held dear.
By God, he gave me a lick once on the ear,
When from a book of his I tore a leaf,
So hard that from the blow my ear grew deaf.
Stubborn I was as a lioness with young,   635
And by the truth I had a rattling tongue,
And I would visit, as I'd done before,
No matter what forbidding oath he swore.
Against this habit he would sit and preach me
Sermons enough, and he would try to teach me   640
Old Roman stories,[7] how for his whole life
The man Sulpicius Gallus left his wife
Only because he saw her look one day
Bareheaded down the street from his doorway.
"Another Roman he told me of by name   645
Who, since his wife was at a summer's game
Without his knowledge, thereupon forsook
The woman. In his Bible he would look
And find that proverb of the Ecclesiast[8]
Where he enjoins and makes the stricture fast   650
That men forbid their wives to rove about.
Then he would quote me this, you needn't doubt:
'Build a foundation over sands or shallows,
Or gallop a blind horse across the fallows,
Let a wife traipse to shrines that some saint hallows,   655
And you are fit to swing upon the gallows.'
Talk as he would, I didn't care two haws
About his proverbs or his stale old saws.
Set right by him I never meant to be.
I hate the man who tells my faults to me,   660
And more of us than I do, by your pleasure.
This made him mad with me beyond all measure.
Under his yoke in no case would I go.
"No, by St. Thomas, I will let you know
Why from that book of his I tore a leaf,   665
For which I got the blow that made me deaf.
"He had a book,[9] *Valerius*, he called it,
And *Theophrastus*, and he always hauled it

---

7. This and much of the following information is derived from a collection of Latin misogynist and anti-matrimonial literature popular in the Middle Ages; see note to line 667 below.   **8.** Ecclesiasticus 25.31.
9. Jenkin's book contains treatises called *Valerius* (written in the twelfth century) and *Theophrastus* (second century), Jerome's *Letter Against Jovinian* (fourth century), and works by Tertullian (d. ca. 230), Crisippus (a writer mentioned in Jerome's *Letter*), Trotula (an eleventh-century woman physician who wrote gynecological works), and Heloise (the lover of Abelard, who argued in her letters that a philosopher should never marry). The *Parables of Solomon* is a reference to the biblical book of Proverbs, ascribed to Solomon in the Middle Ages, while Ovid's *Art of Love* is a guidebook for seducers.

From where it lay to read both day and night
And laughed hard at it, such was his delight.   670
There was another scholar, too, at Rome,
A cardinal, whose name was St. Jerome;
He wrote a book against Jovinian.
The book included too Tertullian,
Chrysippus, Trotula, Abbess Héloïse   675
Who lived near Paris; it contained all these,
Bound in a single volume, and many a one
Besides; the Parables of Solomon
And Ovid's *Art of Love*. On such vacation
As he could snatch from worldly occupation   680
He dredged this book for tales of wicked wives.
He knew more stories of their wretched lives
Than those told of good women in the Bible.
No scholar ever lived who did not libel
Women, believe me; to speak well of wives   685
Is quite beyond them, unless it be in lives
Of holy saints; no woman else will do.
Who was it painted the lion, tell me who?[1]
By God, if women had only written stories
Like wits and scholars in their oratories,   690
They would have pinned on men more wickedness
Than the whole breed of Adam can redress.
Venus's children clash with Mercury's;[2]
The two work evermore by contraries.
Knowledge and wisdom are of Mercury's giving,   695
Venus loves revelry and riotous living,
And with these clashing dispositions gifted
Each of them sinks when the other is uplifted.
Thus Mercury falls, God knows, in desolation
In Pisces, which is Venus' exaltation.   700
And Venus falls when Mercury is raised.
Thus by a scholar no woman can be praised.
The scholar, when he's old and cannot do
The work of Venus more than his old shoe,
Then sits he down, and in his dotage fond   705
Writes that no woman keeps her marriage bond!
    "But now for the story that I undertook—
To tell how I was beaten for a book.
    "Jenkin, one night, who never seemed to tire
Of reading in his book, sat by the fire   710
And first he read of Eve, whose wickedness
Delivered all mankind to wretchedness
For which in his own person Christ was slain
Who with his heart's blood bought us all again.
'By this,' he said, 'expressly you may find   715
That woman was the loss of all mankind.'
    "He read me next how Samson lost his hair.

---

1. A reference to Aesop's fable in which a lion objects to a picture of a lion eating a man, arguing that if
the lion had painted the picture it would have been quite different.   2. Mercury is the planet that rules
over scholars, its "children."

Sleeping, his mistress clipped it off for fair;
Through this betrayal he lost both his eyes.
He read me then—and I'm not telling lies—   720
How Deianeira, wife of Hercules,
Caused him to set himself on fire.[3] With these
He did not overlook the sad to-do
Of Socrates with *his* wives—he had two.[4]
Xantippe emptied the pisspot on his head.   725
This good man sat as patient as if dead.
He wiped his scalp; he did not dare complain
Except to say 'With thunder must come rain.'
    "Pasiphaë,[5] who was the queen of Crete,
For wickedness he thought her story sweet.   730
Ugh! That's enough, it was a grisly thing,
About her lust and filthy hankering!
And Clytemnestra[6] in her lechery
Who took her husband's life feloniously,
He grew devout in reading of her treason.   735
And then he told me also for what reason
Unhappy Amphiaraus[7] lost his life.
My husband had the story of *his* wife,
Eriphyle, who for a clasp of gold
Went to his Grecian enemies and told   740
The secret of her husband's hiding place,
For which at Thebes he met an evil grace.
Livia and Lucilia,[8] he went through
Their tale as well; they killed their husbands, too.
One killed for love, the other killed for hate.   745
At evening Livia, when the hour was late,
Poisoned her husband, for she was his foe.
Lucilia doted on her husband so
That in her lust, hoping to make him think
Ever of her, she gave him a love-drink   750
Of such a sort he died before the morrow.
And so at all turns husbands come to sorrow!
    "He told me then how one Latumius,[9]
Complaining to a friend named Arrius,
Told him that in his garden grew a tree   755
On which his wives had hanged themselves, all three,
Merely for spite against their partnership.
'Brother,' said Arrius, 'let me have a slip
From this miraculous tree, for, begging pardon,
I want to go and plant it in my garden.'   760
    "Then about wives in recent times he read,
How some had murdered husbands lying abed
And all night long had let a paramour

---

3. Driven by jealousy, Hercules' wife, Deianeira, prepared for him a poisoned shirt that burned him to death.   4. This apocryphal story is derived from Jerome's *Letter*.   5. Pasiphaë made love with a bull and gave birth to the Minotaur.   6. She murdered her husband, Agamemnon, on his return from Troy.   7. The prophet Amphiaraus attempted to avoid joining a military expedition against Thebes that he knew to be doomed, but was betrayed by his wife.   8. Roman wives; Livia poisoned her husband at the instigation of her lover, while Lucilia poisoned hers with a love potion.   9. This unpleasant story appears in a collection of popular tales.

Enjoy them with the corpse flat on the floor;
Or driven a nail into a husband's brain   765
While he was sleeping, and thus he had been slain;
And some had given them poison in their drink.
He told more harm than anyone can think,
And seasoned his wretched stories with proverbs
Outnumbering all the blades of grass and herbs   770
On earth. 'Better a dragon for a mate,
Better,' he said, 'on a lion's whims to wait
Than on a wife whose way it is to chide.
Better,' he said, 'high in the loft to bide
Than with a railing wife down in the house.   775
They always, they are so contrarious,
Hate what their husbands like,' so he would say.
'A woman,' he said, 'throws all her shame away
When she takes off her smock.' And on he'd go:
'A pretty woman, unless she's chaste also,   780
Is like a gold ring stuck in a sow's nose.'
Who could imagine, who would half suppose
The gall my heart drank, raging at each drop?
    "And when I saw that he would never stop
Reading all night from his accursed book,   785
Suddenly, in the midst of it, I took
Three leaves and tore them out in a great pique,
And with my fist I caught him on the cheek
So hard he tumbled backward in the fire.
And up he jumped, he was as mad for ire   790
As a mad lion, and caught me on the head
With such a blow I fell down as if dead.
And seeing me on the floor, how still I lay,
He was aghast, and would have fled away,
Till I came to at length, and gave a cry.   795
'You'd kill me for my lands? Before I die,
False thief,' I said, 'I'll give you a last kiss!'
    "He came to me and knelt down close at this,
And said, 'So help me God, dear Alison,
I'll never strike you. For this thing I've done   800
You are to blame. Forgive me, I implore.'
So then I hit him on the cheek once more
And said, 'Thus far I am avenged, you thief.
I cannot speak. Now I shall die for grief.'
But finally, with much care and ado,   805
We reconciled our differences, we two.
He let me have the bridle in my hand
For management of both our house and land.
To curb his tongue he also undertook,
And on the spot I made him burn his book.   810
And when I had secured in full degree
By right of triumph the whole sovereignty,
And he had said, 'My dear, my own true wife,
Do as you will as long as you have life;

Preserve your honor and keep my estate.'[1]   815
From that day on we'd settled our debate.
I was as kind, God help me, day and dark,
As any wife from India to Denmark,
And also true, and so he was to me.
I pray the Lord who sits in majesty   820
To bless his soul for Christ's own mercy dear.
And now I'll tell my tale, if you will hear."
"Dame," laughed the Friar, "as I hope for bliss,
It was a long preamble to a tale, all this!"
"God's arms!" the Summoner said, "it is a sin,   825
Good people, how friars are always butting in!
A fly and a friar will fall in every dish
And every question, whatever people wish.
What do you know, with your talk about 'preambling'?
Amble or trot or keep still or go scrambling,   830
You interrupt our pleasure."
                                        "You think so,
Sir Summoner?" said the Friar. "Before I go,
I'll give the people here a chance or two
For laughs at summoners, I promise you."
"Curse on your face," the Summoner said, "curse me,   835
If I don't tell some stories, two or three,
On friars, before I get to Sittingborne,[2]
With which I'll twist your heart and make it mourn,
For you have lost your temper, I can see."
"Be quiet," cried our Host, "immediately,"   840
And ordered, "Let the woman tell her tale.
You act like people who've got drunk on ale.
Do, Madame, tell us. That is the best measure."
"All ready, sir," she answered, "at your pleasure,
With license from this worthy Friar here."   845
"Madame, tell on," he said. "You have my ear."

THE TALE

In the old days when King Arthur ruled the nation,
Whom Welshmen speak of with such veneration,
This realm we live in was a fairy land.
The fairy queen danced with her jolly band
On the green meadows where they held dominion.   5
This was, as I have read, the old opinion;
I speak of many hundred years ago.
But no one sees an elf now, as you know,
For in our time the charity and prayers
And all the begging of these holy friars   10
Who swarm through every nook and every stream
Thicker than motes of dust in a sunbeam,
Blessing our chambers, kitchens, halls, and bowers,

---

1. Status.   2. A town about two-thirds of the way to Canterbury.

Our cities, towns, and castles, our high towers,
Our villages, our stables, barns, and dairies,   15
They keep us all from seeing any fairies,
For where you might have come upon an elf
There now you find the holy friar himself
Working his district on industrious legs
And saying his devotions while he begs.   20
Women are safe now under every tree.
No incubus[3] is there unless it's he,
And all they have to fear from him is shame.
    It chanced that Arthur had a knight who came
Lustily riding home one day from hawking,   25
And in his path he saw a maiden walking
Before him, stark alone, right in his course.
This young knight took her maidenhead by force,
A crime at which the outcry was so keen
It would have cost his neck, but that the queen,   30
With other ladies, begged the king so long
That Arthur spared his life, for right or wrong,
And gave him to the queen, at her own will,
According to her choice, to save or kill.
    She thanked the king, and later told this knight,   35
Choosing her time, "You are still in such a plight
Your very life has no security.
I grant your life, if you can answer me
This question: what is the thing that most of all
Women desire? Think, or your neck will fall   40
Under the ax! If you cannot let me know
Immediately, I give you leave to go
A twelvemonth and a day, no more, in quest
Of such an answer as will meet the test.
But you must pledge your honor to return   45
And yield your body, whatever you may learn."
    The knight sighed; he was rueful beyond measure.
But what! He could not follow his own pleasure.
He chose at last upon his way to ride
And with such answer as God might provide   50
To come back when the year was at the close.
And so he takes his leave, and off he goes.
    He seeks out every house and every place
Where he has any hope, by luck or grace,
Of learning what thing women covet most.   55
But he could never light on any coast
Where on this point two people would agree,
For some said wealth and some said jollity,
Some said position, some said sport in bed
And often to be widowed, often wed.   60
Some said that to a woman's heart what mattered
Above all else was to be pleased and flattered.
That shaft, to tell the truth, was a close hit.

---

3. A wicked spirit that fornicates with women.

Men win us best by flattery, I admit,
And by attention. Some say our greatest ease   65
Is to be free and do just as we please,
And not to have our faults thrown in our eyes,
But always to be praised for being wise.
And true enough, there's not one of us all
Who will not kick if you rub us on a gall.   70
Whatever vices we may have within,
We won't be taxed with any fault or sin.
    Some say that women are delighted well
If it is thought that they will never tell
A secret they are trusted with, or scandal.   75
But that tale isn't worth an old rake handle!
We women, for a fact, can never hold
A secret. Will you hear a story told?
Then witness Midas![4] For it can be read
In Ovid that he had upon his head   80
Two ass's ears that he kept out of sight
Beneath his long hair with such skill and sleight
That no one else besides his wife could guess.
He loved her well, and trusted her no less.
He begged her not to make his blemish known,   85
But keep her knowledge to herself alone.
She swore that never, though to save her skin,
Would she be guilty of so mean a sin,
And yet it seemed to her she nearly died
Keeping a secret locked so long inside.   90
It swelled about her heart so hard and deep
She was afraid some word was bound to leap
Out of her mouth, and since there was no man
She dared to tell, down to a swamp she ran—
Her heart, until she got there, all agog—   95
And like a bittern[5] booming in the bog
She put her mouth close to the watery ground:
"Water, do not betray me with your sound!
I speak to you, and you alone," she said.
"Two ass's ears grow on my husband's head!   100
And now my heart is whole, now it is out.
I'd burst if I held it longer, past all doubt."
Safely, you see, awhile you may confide
In us, but it will out; we cannot hide
A secret. Look in Ovid if you care   105
To learn what followed; the whole tale is there.
    This knight, when he perceived he could not find
What women covet most, was low in mind;
But the day came when homeward he must ride,
And as he crossed a wooded countryside   110
Some four and twenty ladies there by chance
He saw, all circling in a woodland dance,

---

4. The story of Midas and his ass's ears (given to him because he preferred Pan's songs to those of Apollo) is found in Ovid, *Metamorphoses* 11.174–93. In Ovid the secret is known not to Midas's wife but to his barber.   **5.** A kind of heron.

And toward this dance he eagerly drew near
In hope of any counsel he might hear.
But the truth was, he had not reached the place   115
When dance and all, they vanished into space.
No living soul remained there to be seen
Save an old woman sitting on the green,
As ugly a witch as fancy could devise.
As he approached her she began to rise   120
And said, "Sir knight, here runs no thoroughfare.
What are you seeking with such anxious air?
Tell me! The better may your fortune be.
We old folk know a lot of things," said she.
    "Good mother," said the knight, "my life's to pay,   125
That's all too certain, if I cannot say
What women covet most. If you could tell
That secret to me, I'd requite you well."
    "Give me your hand," she answered. "Swear me true
That whatsoever I next ask of you,   130
You'll do it if it lies within your might
And I'll enlighten you before the night."
    "Granted, upon my honor," he replied.
    "Then I dare boast, and with no empty pride,
Your life is safe," she told him. "Let me die   135
If she, the queen, won't say the same as I.
Let's learn if the haughtiest of all who wear
A net or coverchief upon their hair
Will be so forward as to answer 'no'
To what I'll teach you. No more; let us go."   140
With that she whispered something in his ear,
And told him to be glad and have no fear.
    When they had reached the court, the knight declared
That he had kept his day, and was prepared
To give his answer, standing for his life.   145
Many the wise widow, many the wife,
Many the maid who rallied to the scene,
And at the head as justice sat the queen.
Then silence was enjoined; the knight was told
In open court to say what women hold   150
Precious above all else. He did not stand
Dumb like a beast, but spoke up at command
And plainly offered them his answering word
In manly voice, so that the whole court heard.
    "My liege and lady, most of all," said he,   155
"Women desire to have the sovereignty
And sit in rule and government above
Their husbands, and to have their way in love.
This is what most you want. Spare me or kill
As you may like; I stand here by your will."   160
    No widow, wife, or maid gave any token
Of contradicting what the knight had spoken.
He should not die; he should be spared instead;
He well deserved his life, the whole court said.

The old woman whom the knight met on the grass 165
Sprang up at this."My sovereign lady queen,
Before your court has risen, do me right!
I taught, myself, this answer to the knight,
For which he pledged his honor in my hand,
Solemnly, that the first thing I demand, 170
He'd do it, if it lay within his might.
Before the court I ask you, then, sir knight,
To take me," said the woman,"as your wife,
For well you know that I have saved your life.
Deny me, on your honor, if you can." 175
    "Alas," replied this miserable man,
"That was my promise, it must be confessed.
For the love of God, though, choose a new request!
Take all my wealth, and let my body be."
    "If that's your tune, then curse both you and me," 180
She said. "Though I am ugly, old, and poor,
I'll have, for all the metal and the ore
That under earth is hidden or lies above,
Nothing, except to be your wife and love."
    "My love? No, my damnation, if you can! 185
Alas," he said, "that any of my clan
Should be so miserably misallied!"
    All to no good; force overruled his pride,
And in the end he is constrained to wed,
And marries his old wife and goes to bed. 190
    Now some will charge me with an oversight
In failing to describe the day's delight,
The merriment, the food, the dress at least.
But I reply, there was no joy nor feast;
Nothing but sorrow and sharp misery. 195
He married her in private, secretly,
And all day after, such was his distress,
Hid like an owl from his wife's ugliness.
    Great was the woe this knight had in his head
When in due time they both were brought to bed. 200
He shuddered, tossed, and turned, and all the while
His old wife lay and waited with a smile.
"Is every knight so backward with a spouse?
Is it," she said, "a law in Arthur's house?
I am your love, your own, your wedded wife. 205
I am the woman who has saved your life.
I've never done you anything but right.
Why do you treat me this way the first night?
You must be mad, the way that you behave!
Tell me my fault, and as God's love can save, 210
I will amend it, truly, if I can."
    "Amend it?" answered this unhappy man.
"It never can be amended, truth to tell.
You are so loathsome and so old as well,
And your low birth besides is such a cross 215
It is no wonder that I turn and toss.

God take my woeful spirit from my breast!"
"Is this," she said, "the cause of your unrest?"
"No wonder!" said the knight."It truly is."
"Now sir," she said, "I could amend all this   220
Within three days, if it should please me to,
And if you deal with me as you should do.
    "But since you speak of that nobility
That comes from ancient wealth and pedigree,
As if *that* constituted gentlemen,   225
I hold such arrogance not worth a hen!
The man whose virtue is pre-eminent,
In public and alone, always intent
On doing every generous act he can,
Take him—he is the greatest gentleman!   230
Christ wills that we should claim nobility
From him, not from old wealth or family.
Our elders left us all that they were worth
And through their wealth and blood we claim high birth,
But never, since it was beyond their giving,   235
Could they bequeath to us their virtuous living;
Although it first conferred on them the name
Of gentlemen, they could not leave that claim!
    "Dante the Florentine on this was wise:
'Frail is the branch on which man's virtues rise'—   240
Thus runs his rhyme—'God's goodness wills that we
Should claim from him alone nobility.'⁶
Thus from our elders we can only claim
Such temporal things as men may hurt and maim.
    "It's plain enough that true nobility   245
Is not bequeathed along with property,
For many a lord's son does a deed of shame
And yet, God knows, enjoys his noble name.
But he, though scion of a noble house
And elders who were wise and virtuous,   250
Who will not follow his elders, who are dead,
But leads, himself, a shameful life instead,
He is not noble, be he duke or earl.
It is the churlish deed that makes the churl.
And therefore, my dear husband, I conclude   255
That though my ancestors were rough and rude,
Yet may Almighty God confer on me
The grace to live, as I hope, virtuously.
Call me of noble blood when I begin
To live in virtue and to cast out sin.   260
    "As for my poverty, at which you grieve,
Almighty God in whom we all believe
In willful poverty chose to lead his life,
And surely every man and maid and wife
Can understand that Jesus, heaven's king,   265
Would never choose a low or vicious thing.

6. Chaucer's sources are Dante's *Convivio* and *Purgatorio* 7.121–23.

A poor and cheerful life is nobly led;
So Seneca[7] and others have well said.
The man so poor he doesn't have a stitch
Who thinks himself repaid, I count as rich.   270
He that is covetous, he is the poor man,
Pining to have the things he never can.
It is of cheerful mind, true poverty.
Juvenal[8] says about it happily:
'The poor man as he goes along his way   275
And passes thieves is free to sing and play.'
Poverty is a good we loathe, a great
Reliever of our busy worldly state,
A great amender also of our minds
As he that patiently will bear it finds.   280
And poverty, for all it seems distressed,
Is a possession no one will contest.
Poverty, too, by bringing a man low,
Helps him the better God and self to know.
Poverty is a glass where we can see   285
Which are our true friends, as it seems to me.
So, sir, I do not wrong you on this score;
Reproach me with my poverty no more.
      "Now, sir, you tax me with my age; but, sir,
You gentlemen of breeding all aver   290
That men should not despise old age, but rather
Grant an old man respect, and call him 'father.'
      "If I am old and ugly, as you have said,
You have less fear of being cuckolded,
For ugliness and age, as all agree,   295
Are notable guardians of chastity.
But since I know in what you take delight,
I'll gratify your worldly appetite.
      "Choose now, which of two courses you will try:
To have me old and ugly till I die   300
But evermore your true and humble wife,
Never displeasing you in all my life,
Or will you have me rather young and fair
And take your chances on who may repair
Either to your house on account of me   305
Or to some other place, it well may be.
Now make your choice, whichever you prefer."
      The knight took thought, and sighed, and said to her
At last, "My love and lady, my dear wife,
In your wise government I put my life.   310
Choose for yourself which course will best agree
With pleasure and honor, both for you and me.
I do not care, choose either of the two;
I am content, whatever pleases you."
      "Then have I won from you the sovereignty,   315
Since I may choose and rule at will?" said she.

7. A Roman philosopher.   8. A Roman poet.

He answered, "That is best, I think, dear wife."
"Kiss me," she said. "Now we are done with strife,
For on my word, I will be both to you,
That is to say, fair, yes, and faithful too.   320
May I die mad unless I am as true
As ever wife was since the world was new.
Unless I am as lovely to be seen
By morning as an empress or a queen
Or any lady between east and west,   325
Do with my life or death as you think best.
Lift up the curtain, see what you may see."
    And when the knight saw what had come to be
And knew her as she was, so young, so fair,
His joy was such that it was past compare.   330
He took her in his arms and gave her kisses
A thousand times on end; he bathed in blisses.
And she obeyed him also in full measure
In everything that tended to his pleasure.
    And so they lived in full joy to the end.   335
And now to all us women may Christ send
Submissive husbands, full of youth in bed,
And grace to outlive all the men we wed.
And I pray Jesus to cut short the lives
Of those who won't be governed by their wives;   340
And old, ill-tempered niggards who hate expense,
God promptly bring them down with pestilence!

The Pardoner's Prologue and Tale

Now my fine friend," he[9] said, "you Pardoner,
Be quick, tell us a tale of mirth or fun."
    "St. Ninian!"[1] he said, "it shall be done,
But at this tavern here, before my tale,
I'll just go in and have some bread and ale."   5
    The proper pilgrims in our company
Cried quickly, "Let him speak no ribaldry!
Tell us a moral tale, one to make clear
Some lesson to us, and we'll gladly hear."
    "Just as you wish," he said. "I'll try to think   10
Of something edifying while I drink."

THE PROLOGUE

"In churches," said the Pardoner, "when I preach,
I use, milords, a lofty style of speech
And ring it out as roundly as a bell,
Knowing by rote all that I have to tell.
My text is ever the same, and ever was: 5
Radix malorum est cupiditas.[2]

---

9. The Host; the Physician has just finished his tale.   1. A Scottish saint.   2. Avarice is the root of all evil (Latin).

"First I inform them whence I come; that done,
I then display my papal bulls,[3] each one.
I show my license[4] first, my body's warrant,
Sealed by the bishop, for it would be abhorrent   10
If any man made bold, though priest or clerk,
To interrupt me in Christ's holy work.
And after that I give myself full scope.
Bulls in the name of cardinal and pope,
Of bishops and of patriarchs I show.   15
I say in Latin some few words or so
To spice my sermon; it flavors my appeal
And stirs my listeners to greater zeal.
Then I display my cases made of glass
Crammed to the top with rags and bones. They pass   20
For relics with all the people in the place.
I have a shoulder bone in a metal case,
Part of a sheep owned by a holy Jew.
'Good men,' I say, 'heed what I'm telling you:
Just let this bone be dipped in any well   25
And if cow, calf, or sheep, or ox should swell
From eating a worm, or by a worm be stung,
Take water from this well and wash its tongue
And it is healed at once. And furthermore
Of scab and ulcers and of every sore   30
Shall every sheep be cured, and that straightway,
That drinks from the same well. Heed what I say:
If the good man who owns the beasts will go,
Fasting, each week, and drink before cockcrow
Out of this well, his cattle shall be brought   35
To multiply—that holy Jew so taught
Our elders—and his property increase.
    " 'Moreover, sirs, this bone cures jealousies.
Though into a jealous madness a man fell,
Let him cook his soup in water from this well,   40
He'll never, though for truth he knew her sin,
Suspect his wife again, though she took in
A priest, or even two of them or three.
    " 'Now here's a mitten that you all can see.
Whoever puts his hand in it shall gain,   45
When he sows his land, increasing crops of grain,
Be it wheat or oats, provided that he bring
His penny or so to make his offering.
    " 'There is one word of warning I must say,
Good men and women. If any here today   50
Has done a sin so horrible to name
He daren't be shriven[5] of it for the shame,
Or if any woman, young or old, is here
Who has cuckolded her husband, be it clear
They may not make an offering in that case   55

---

3. Letters of indulgence, with the pope's seal (Latin *bulla*), which promise the purchaser release from some
of the pains of purgatory.   4. A license from the bishop was required of all those who would preach in
his diocese.   5. Confessed.

To these my relics; they have no power nor grace.
But any who is free of such dire blame,
Let him come up and offer in God's name
And I'll absolve him through the authority
That by the pope's bull has been granted me.'   60
    "By such hornswoggling I've won, year by year,
A hundred marks[6] since being a pardoner.
I stand in my pulpit like a true divine,
And when the people sit I preach my line
To ignorant souls, as you have heard before,   65
And tell skullduggeries by the hundred more.
Then I take care to stretch my neck well out
And over the people I nod and peer about
Just like a dove perching on a shed.
My hands fly and my tongue wags in my head   70
So busily that to watch me is a joy.
Avarice is the theme that I employ
In all my sermons, to make the people free
In giving pennies—especially to me.
My mind is fixed on what I stand to win   75
And not at all upon correcting sin.
I do not care, when they are in the grave,
If souls go berry-picking that I could save.
Truth is that evil purposes determine,
And many a time, the origin of a sermon: 80
Some to please people and by flattery
To gain advancement through hypocrisy,
Some for vainglory, some again for hate.
For when I daren't fight otherwise, I wait
And give him a tongue-lashing when I preach.   85
No man escapes or gets beyond the reach
Of my defaming tongue, supposing he
Has done a wrong to my brethren or to me.
For though I do not tell his proper name,
People will recognize him all the same.   90
By sign and circumstance I let them learn.
Thus I serve those who have done us an ill turn.
Thus I spit out my venom under hue
Of sanctity, and seem devout and true!
    "But to put my purpose briefly, I confess   95
I preach for nothing but for covetousness.
That's why my text is still and ever was
Radix malorum est cupiditas.
For by this text I can denounce, indeed,
The very vice I practice, which is greed.   100
But though that sin is lodged in my own heart,
I am able to make other people part
From avarice, and sorely to repent,
Though that is not my principal intent.
    "Then I bring in examples, many a one,   105

6. A very large sum; the Pardoner is almost certainly exaggerating.

And tell them many a tale of days long done.
Plain folk love tales that come down from of old.
Such things their minds can well report and hold.
Do you think that while I have the power to preach
And take in silver and gold for what I teach 110
I shall ever live in willful poverty?
No, no, that never was my thought, certainly.
I mean to preach and beg in sundry lands.
I won't do any labor with my hands,
Nor live by making baskets.[7] I don't intend 115
To beg for nothing; that is not my end.
I won't ape the apostles; I must eat,
I must have money, wool, and cheese, and wheat,
Though I took it from the meanest wretch's tillage
Or from the poorest widow in a village, 120
Yes, though her children starved for want. In fine,
I mean to drink the liquor of the vine
And have a jolly wench in every town.
But, in conclusion, lords, I will get down
To business: you would have me tell a tale. 125
Now that I've had a drink of corny ale,
By God, I hope the thing I'm going to tell
Is one that you'll have reason to like well.
For though myself a very sinful man,
I can tell a moral tale, indeed I can, 130
One that I use to bring the profits in
While preaching. Now be still, and I'll begin."

THE TALE

There was a company of young folk living
One time in Flanders, who were bent on giving
Their lives to follies and extravagances,
Brothels and taverns, where they held their dances
With lutes, harps, and guitars, diced at all hours, 5
And also ate and drank beyond their powers,
Through which they paid the devil sacrifice
In the devil's temple with their drink and dice,
Their abominable excess and dissipation.
They swore oaths that were worthy of damnation; 10
It was grisly to be listening when they swore.
The blessed body of our Lord they tore[8]—
The Jews, it seemed to them, had failed to rend
His body enough—and each laughed at his friend
And fellow in sin. To encourage their pursuits 15
Came comely dancing girls, peddlers of fruits,
Singers with harps, bawds and confectioners
Who are the very devil's officers
To kindle and blow the fire of lechery
That is the follower of gluttony. 20

---

7. A medieval tradition asserted that the apostle Paul was a basket maker. 8. They swore by the various parts of Christ's body (see line 171 for examples).

Witness the Bible, if licentiousness
Does not reside in wine and drunkenness!
Recall how drunken Lot, unnaturally,
With his two daughters lay unwittingly,
So drunk he had no notion what he did.[9]   25
    Herod, the stories tell us, God forbid,
When full of liquor at his banquet board
Right at his very table gave the word
To kill the Baptist, John, though guiltless he.[1]
    Seneca says a good word, certainly.   30
He says there is no difference he can find
Between a man who has gone out of his mind
And one who carries drinking to excess,
Only that madness outlasts drunkenness.[2]
O gluttony, first cause of mankind's fall,[3]   35
Of our damnation the cursed original
Until Christ bought[4] us with his blood again!
How dearly paid for by the race of men
Was this detestable iniquity!
This whole world was destroyed through gluttony.   40
    Adam our father and his wife also
From paradise to labor and to woe
Were driven for that selfsame vice, indeed.
As long as Adam fasted—so I read—
He was in heaven; but as soon as he   45
Devoured the fruit of that forbidden tree
Then he was driven out in sorrow and pain.
Of gluttony well ought we to complain!
Could a man know how many maladies
Follow indulgences and gluttonies   50
He would keep his diet under stricter measure
And sit at table with more temperate pleasure.
The throat is short and tender is the mouth,
And hence men toil east, west, and north, and south,
In earth, and air, and water—alas to think—   55
Fetching a glutton dainty meat and drink.
    This is a theme, O Paul, that you well treat:
"Meat unto belly, and belly unto meat,
God shall destroy them both," as Paul has said.[5]
When a man drinks the white wine and the red—   60
This is a foul word, by my soul, to say,
And fouler is the deed in every way—
He makes his throat his privy through excess.
    The Apostle says, weeping for piteousness,
"There are many of whom I told you—at a loss   65
I say it, weeping—enemies of Christ's cross,
Whose belly is their god; their end is death."[6]
O cursed belly! Sack of stinking breath
In which corruption lodges, dung abounds!

9. Genesis 19.33–35.   1. Matthew 14.1–11; Mark 6.14–28.   2. Seneca's *Epistles* 83.   3. Since the Fall was caused by eating the forbidden fruit.   4. Redeemed.   5. 1 Corinthians 6.13.   6. Philippians 3.18–19.

At either end of you come forth foul sounds.   70
Great cost it is to fill you, and great pain!
These cooks, how they must grind and pound and strain
And transform substance into accident[7]
To please your cravings, though exorbitant!
From the hard bones they knock the marrow out.   75
They'll find a use for everything, past doubt,
That down the gullet sweet and soft will glide.
The spiceries of leaf and root provide
Sauces that are concocted for delight,
To give a man a second appetite.   80
But truly, he whom gluttonies entice
Is dead, while he continues in that vice.
　　O drunken man, disfigured is your face,
Sour is your breath, foul are you to embrace!
You seem to mutter through your drunken nose   85
The sound of "Samson, Samson," yet God knows
That Samson never indulged himself in wine.[8]
Your tongue is lost, you fall like a stuck swine,
And all the self-respect that you possess
Is gone, for of man's judgment, drunkenness   90
Is the very sepulcher and annihilation.
A man whom drink has under domination
Can never keep a secret in his head.
Now steer away from both the white and red,
And most of all from that white wine keep wide   95
That comes from Lepe.[9] They sell it in Cheapside
And Fish Street.[1] It's a Spanish wine, and sly
To creep in other wines that grow nearby,
And such a vapor it has that with three drinks
It takes a man to Spain; although he thinks   100
He is home in Cheapside, he is far away
At Lepe. Then "Samson, Samson" will he say!
　　By God himself, who is omnipotent,
All the great exploits in the Old Testament
Were done in abstinence, I say, and prayer.   105
Look in the Bible, you may learn it there.
　　Attila,[2] conqueror of many a place,
Died in his sleep in shame and in disgrace
Bleeding out of his nose in drunkenness.
A captain ought to live in temperateness!   110
And more than this, I say, remember well
The injunction that was laid on Lemuel[3]—
Not Samuel, but Lemuel, I say!
Read in the Bible; in the plainest way
Wine is forbidden to judges and to kings.   115
This will suffice; no more upon these things.
　　Now that I've shown what gluttony will do,
Now I will warn you against gambling, too;

---

7. A distinction was made in philosophy between *substance*, the real nature of a thing, and *accident*, its merely sensory qualities, such as flavor.　　8. Judges 13.4.　　9. A town in Spain noted for strong wines.
1. London streets.　　2. Leader of the Hun invasion of Europe, fifth century.　　3. Proverbs 31.4–7.

Gambling, the very mother of low scheming,
Of lying and forswearing and blaspheming   120
Against Christ's name, of murder and waste as well
Alike of goods and time; and, truth to tell,
With honor and renown it cannot suit
To be held a common gambler by repute.
The higher a gambler stands in power and place,   125
The more his name is lowered in disgrace.
If a prince gambles, whatever his kingdom be,
In his whole government and policy
He is, in all the general estimation,
Considered so much less in reputation.   130
    Stilbon,[4] who was a wise ambassador,
From Lacedaemon once to Corinth bore
A mission of alliance. When he came
It happened that he found there at a game
Of hazard all the great ones of the land,   135
And so, as quickly as it could be planned,
He stole back, saying, "I will not lose my name
Nor have my reputation put to shame
Allying you with gamblers. You may send
Other wise emissaries to gain your end,   140
For by my honor, rather than ally
My countrymen to gamblers, I will die.
For you that are so gloriously renowned
Shall never with this gambling race be bound
By will of mine or treaty I prepare."   145
Thus did this wise philosopher declare.
    Remember also how the Parthians' lord
Sent King Demetrius, as the books record,
A pair of golden dice, by this proclaiming
His scorn, because that king was known for gaming,   150
And the king of Parthia therefore held his crown
Devoid of glory, value, or renown.
Lords can discover other means of play
More suitable to while the time away.
    Now about oaths I'll say a word or two,   155
Great oaths and false oaths, as the old books do.
Great swearing is a thing abominable,
And false oaths yet more reprehensible.
Almighty God forbade swearing at all,
Matthew be witness;[5] but specially I call   160
The holy Jeremiah on this head.
"Swear thine oaths truly, do not lie," he said.
"Swear under judgment, and in righteousness."[6]
But idle swearing is a great wickedness.
Consult and see, and he that understands   165
In the first table of the Lord's commands
Will find the second of his commandments this:
"Take not the Lord's name idly or amiss."[7]

---

4. Chaucer adapted this and the next story—both fictitious—from a twelfth-century work. **5.** Matthew
5.34.   **6.** Jeremiah 4.2.   **7.** Exodus 20.7.

If a man's oaths and curses are extreme,
Vengeance shall find his house, both roof and beam. 170
"By the precious heart of God," and "By his nails"—
"My chance is seven,[8] by Christ's blood at Hailes,[9]
Yours five and three." "Cheat me, and if you do,
By God's arms, with this knife I'll run you through!"—
Such fruit comes from the bones,[1] that pair of bitches: 175
Oaths broken, treachery, murder. For the riches
Of Christ's love, give up curses, without fail,
Both great and small!—Now, sirs, I'll tell my tale.
    These three young roisterers of whom I tell
Long before prime had rung from any bell 180
Were seated in a tavern at their drinking,
And as they sat, they heard a bell go clinking
Before a corpse being carried to his grave.
One of these roisterers, when he heard it, gave
An order to his boy: "Go out and try 185
To learn whose corpse is being carried by.
Get me his name, and get it right. Take heed."
    "Sir," said the boy, "there isn't any need.
I learned before you came here, by two hours.
He was, it happens, an old friend of yours, 190
And all at once, there on his bench upright
As he was sitting drunk, he was killed last night.
A sly thief, Death men call him, who deprives
All the people in this country of their lives,
Came with his spear and smiting his heart in two 195
Went on his business with no more ado.
A thousand have been slaughtered by his hand
During this plague. And, sir, before you stand
Within his presence, it should be necessary,
It seems to me, to know your adversary. 200
Be evermore prepared to meet this foe.
My mother taught me thus; that's all I know."
    "Now by St. Mary," said the innkeeper,
"This child speaks truth. Man, woman, laborer,
Servant, and child the thief has slain this year 205
In a big village a mile or more from here.
I think it is his place of habitation.
It would be wise to make some preparation
Before he brought a man into disgrace."
    "God's arms!" this roisterer said. "So that's the case! 210
Is it so dangerous with this thief to meet?
I'll look for him by every path and street,
I vow it, by God's holy bones! Hear me,
Fellows of mine, we are all one, we three.
Let each of us hold up his hand to the other 215
And each of us become his fellow's brother.
We'll slay this Death, who slaughters and betrays.
He shall be slain whose hand so many slays,

8. I.e., "My number is seven." 9. An abbey in Gloucestershire, where some of Christ's blood was
believed to be preserved. 1. Dice.

By the dignity of God, before tonight!"
   The three together set about to plight 220
Their oaths to live and die each for the other
Just as though each had been to each born brother,
And in their drunken frenzy up they get
And toward the village off at once they set
Which the innkeeper had spoken of before, 225
And many were the grisly oaths they swore.
They rent Christ's precious body limb from limb—
Death shall be dead, if they lay hands on him!
   When they had hardly gone the first half mile,
Just as they were about to cross a stile, 230
An old man, poor and humble, met them there.
The old man greeted them with a meek air
And said, "God bless you, lords, and be your guide."
   "What's this?" the proudest of the three replied.
"Old beggar, I hope you meet with evil grace! 235
Why are you all wrapped up except your face?
What are you doing alive so many a year?"
   The old man at these words began to peer
Into this gambler's face. "Because I can,
Though I should walk to India, find no man," 240
He said, "in any village or any town,
Who for my age is willing to lay down
His youth. So I must keep my old age still
For as long a time as it may be God's will.
Nor will Death take my life from me, alas! 245
Thus like a restless prisoner I pass
And on the ground, which is my mother's gate,
I walk and with my staff both early and late
I knock and say, 'Dear mother, let me in!
See how I vanish, flesh, and blood, and skin! 250
Alas, when shall my bones be laid to rest?
I would exchange with you my clothing chest,
Mother, that in my chamber long has been
For an old haircloth rag to wrap me in.'
And yet she still refuses me that grace. 255
All white, therefore, and withered is my face.
   "But, sirs, you do yourselves no courtesy
To speak to an old man so churlishly
Unless he had wronged you either in word or deed.
As you yourselves in Holy Writ may read, 260
'Before an aged man whose head is hoar
Men ought to rise.'[2] I counsel you, therefore,
No harm nor wrong here to an old man do,
No more than you would have men do to you
In your old age, if you so long abide. 265
And God be with you, whether you walk or ride!
I must go yonder where I have to go."
   "No, you old beggar, by St. John, not so,"

---

2. Leviticus 19.32.

Said another of these gamblers. "As for me,
By God, you won't get off so easily!   270
You spoke just now of that false traitor, Death,
Who in this land robs all our friends of breath.
Tell where he is, since you must be his spy,
Or you will suffer for it, so say I
By God and by the holy sacrament.   275
You are in league with him, false thief, and bent
On killing us young folk, that's clear to my mind."
    "If you are so impatient, sirs, to find
Death," he replied, "turn up this crooked way,
For in that grove I left him, truth to say,   280
Beneath a tree, and there he will abide.
No boast of yours will make him run and hide.
Do you see that oak tree? Just there you will find
This Death, and God, who bought again mankind,
Save and amend you!" So said this old man;   285
And promptly each of these three gamblers ran
Until he reached the tree, and there they found
Florins of fine gold, minted bright and round,
Nearly eight bushels of them, as they thought.
And after Death no longer then they sought.   290
Each of them was so ravished at the sight,
So fair the florins glittered and so bright,
That down they sat beside the precious hoard.
The worst of them, he uttered the first word.
    "Brothers," he told them, "listen to what I say.   295
My head is sharp, for all I joke and play.
Fortune has given us this pile of treasure
To set us up in lives of ease and pleasure.
Lightly it comes, lightly we'll make it go.
God's precious dignity! Who was to know   300
We'd ever tumble on such luck today?
If we could only carry this gold away,
Home to my house, or either one of yours—
For well you know that all this gold is ours—
We'd touch the summit of felicity.   305
But still, by daylight that can hardly be.
People would call us thieves, too bold for stealth,
And they would have us hanged for our own wealth.
It must be done by night, that's our best plan,
As prudently and slyly as we can.   310
Hence my proposal is that we should all
Draw lots, and let's see where the lot will fall,
And the one of us who draws the shortest stick
Shall run back to the town, and make it quick,
And bring us bread and wine here on the sly,   315
And two of us will keep a watchful eye
Over this gold; and if he doesn't stay
Too long in town, we'll carry this gold away
By night, wherever we all agree it's best."
    One of them held the cut out in his fist   320

And had them draw to see where it would fall,
And the cut fell on the youngest of them all.
At once he set off on his way to town,
And the very moment after he was gone
The one who urged this plan said to the other: 325
"You know that by sworn oath you are my brother.
I'll tell you something you can profit by.
Our friend has gone, that's clear to any eye,
And here is gold, abundant as can be,
That we propose to share alike, we three.   330
But if I worked it out, as I could do,
So that it could be shared between us two,
Wouldn't that be a favor, a friendly one?"
    The other answered, "How that can be done,
I don't quite see. He knows we have the gold.   335
What shall we do, or what shall he be told?"
    "Will you keep the secret tucked inside your head?
And in a few words," the first scoundrel said,
"I'll tell you how to bring this end about."
    "Granted," the other told him. "Never doubt,   340
I won't betray you, that you can believe."
    "Now," said the first, "we are two, as you perceive,
And two of us must have more strength than one.
When he sits down, get up as if in fun
And wrestle with him. While you play this game   345
I'll run him through the ribs. You do the same
With your dagger there, and then this gold shall be
Divided, dear friend, between you and me.
Then all that we desire we can fulfill,
And both of us can roll the dice at will."   350
Thus in agreement these two scoundrels fell
To slay the third, as you have heard me tell.
    The youngest, who had started off to town,
Within his heart kept rolling up and down
The beauty of those florins, new and bright.   355
"O Lord," he thought, "were there some way I might
Have all this treasure to myself alone,
There isn't a man who dwells beneath God's throne
Could live a life as merry as mine should be!"
And so at last the fiend, our enemy,   360
Put in his head that he could gain his ends
If he bought poison to kill off his friends.
Finding his life in such a sinful state,
The devil was allowed to seal his fate.
For it was altogether his intent   365
To kill his friends, and never to repent.
So off he set, no longer would he tarry,
Into the town, to an apothecary,
And begged for poison; he wanted it because
He meant to kill his rats; besides, there was   370
A polecat living in his hedge, he said,
Who killed his capons; and when he went to bed

He wanted to take vengeance, if he might,
On vermin that devoured him by night.
    The apothecary answered, "You shall have   375
A drug that as I hope the Lord will save
My soul, no living thing in all creation,
Eating or drinking of this preparation
A dose no bigger than a grain of wheat,
But promptly with his death-stroke he shall meet.   380
Die, that he will, and in a briefer while
Than you can walk the distance of a mile,
This poison is so strong and virulent."
    Taking the poison, off the scoundrel went,
Holding it in a box, and next he ran   385
To the neighboring street, and borrowed from a man
Three generous flagons. He emptied out his drug
In two of them, and kept the other jug
For his own drink; he let no poison lurk
In that! And so all night he meant to work   390
Carrying off the gold. Such was his plan,
And when he had filled them, this accursed man
Retraced his path, still following his design,
Back to his friends with his three jugs of wine.
    But why dilate upon it any more?   395
For just as they had planned his death before,
Just so they killed him, and with no delay.
When it was finished, one spoke up to say:
"Now let's sit down and drink, and we can bury
His body later on. First we'll be merry,"   400
And as he said the words, he took the jug
That, as it happened, held the poisonous drug,
And drank, and gave his friend a drink as well,
And promptly they both died. But truth to tell,
In all that Avicenna[3] ever wrote   405
He never described in chapter, rule, or note
More marvelous signs of poisoning, I suppose,
Than appeared in these two wretches at the close.
Thus they both perished for their homicide,
And thus the traitorous poisoner also died.   410
    O sin accursed above all cursedness,
O treacherous murder, O foul wickedness,
O gambling, lustfulness, and gluttony,
Traducer of Christ's name by blasphemy
And monstrous oaths, through habit and through pride!   415
Alas, mankind! Ah, how may it betide
That you to your Creator, he that wrought you
And even with his precious heart's blood bought you,
So falsely and ungratefully can live?
    And now, good men, your sins may God forgive   420
And keep you specially from avarice!
My holy pardon will avail in this,

---

3. An Arab physician.

For it can heal each one of you that brings
His pennies, silver brooches, spoons, or rings.
Come, bow your head under this holy bull!   425
You wives, come offer up your cloth or wool!
I write your names here in my roll, just so.
Into the bliss of heaven you shall go!
I will absolve you here by my high power,[4]
You that will offer, as clean as in the hour   430
When you were born.—Sirs, thus I preach. And now
Christ Jesus, our souls' healer, show you how
Within his pardon evermore to rest,
For that, I will not lie to you, is best.
    But in my tale, sirs, I forgot one thing.   435
The relics and the pardons that I bring
Here in my pouch, no man in the whole land
Has finer, given me by the pope's own hand.
If any of you devoutly wants to offer
And have my absolution, come and proffer   440
Whatever you have to give. Kneel down right here,
Humbly, and take my pardon, full and clear,
Or have a new, fresh pardon if you like
At the end of every mile of road we strike,
As long as you keep offering ever newly   445
Good coins, not counterfeit, but minted truly.
Indeed it is an honor I confer
On each of you, an authentic pardoner
Going along to absolve you as you ride.
For in the country mishaps may betide—   450
One or another of you in due course
May break his neck by falling from his horse.
Think what security it gives you all
That in this company I chanced to fall
Who can absolve you each, both low and high,   455
When the soul, alas, shall from the body fly!
By my advice, our Host here shall begin,
For he's the man enveloped most by sin.
Come, offer first, Sir Host, and once that's done,
Then you shall kiss the relics, every one,   460
Yes, for a penny! Come, undo your purse!
    "No, no," said he. "Then I should have Christ's curse!
I'll do nothing of the sort, for love or riches!
You'd make me kiss a piece of your old britches
And for a saintly relic make it pass   465
Although it had the tincture of your ass.
By the cross St. Helen[5] found in the Holy Land,
I wish I had your balls here in my hand
For relics! Cut 'em off, and I'll be bound
If I don't help you carry them around.   470

---

4. The Pardoner is overstating the effect of his indulgences, which can promise relief only from punishment of sin, not from its guilt. According to medieval doctrine, full absolution can be provided only by Christ.
5. Mother of Constantine the Great; believed to have found the True Cross.

I'll have the things enshrined in a hog's turd!"
The Pardoner did not answer; not a word,
He was so angry, could he find to say.
"Now," said our Host, "I will not try to play
With you, nor any other angry man."   475
Immediately the worthy Knight began,
When he saw that all the people laughed, "No more,
This has gone far enough. Now as before,
Sir Pardoner, be gay, look cheerfully,
And you, Sir Host, who are so dear to me,   480
Come, kiss the Pardoner, I beg of you,
And Pardoner, draw near, and let us do
As we've been doing, let us laugh and play."
And so they kissed, and rode along their way.

EVERYMAN
1495?

Although drama never attained the status of a dominant literary form in the Middle Ages, in the later centuries of the period it was popular, fairly abundant, and varied in character. It began with the impersonation or dramatization of passages from the liturgy of the Resurrection and the Nativity of Christ. Produced at first in the Latin language and inside a church, it was later moved outside and Latin was replaced with the vernacular languages of several European peoples. By the fourteenth century, if not earlier, whole "cycles" of short plays were performed on certain feast days of the Church, especially Corpus Christi. A complete sequence began with the revolt of Satan and his followers against God and ended with the Last Judgment; inside these limits, some forty "one-act" pieces presented the important events in the divine plan for human history. These plays were produced in the towns, with each of the various craft and trade guilds responsible for one of the plays. The carpenters, for example, would perform the story of Noah, while the "pinners," or nail-makers, would perform the Crucifixion. Because of their scriptural content, modern scholars sometimes called these works *miracle plays*, but the more current term is *mystery plays*, referring not to their content but to the guilds that mounted them: in Middle English a craft or trade is known as a *mystery*.

About the time when the mystery plays had reached their fullest development, another kind of dramatic composition emerged, also religious in nature and purpose. As the mystery plays dramatize biblical events, so the *morality* plays dramatize the content of a typical homily or sermon. By common consent, *Everyman* is regarded as the best of this kind of drama. We do not know the author's name, but the play belongs to the late fifteenth century; it almost certainly derives from a Dutch piece on the same theme. Whereas mystery plays were produced in a long sequence, with amateur casts, morality plays may have been acted by professional or semiprofessional companies. Nothing is actually known about the original productions of *Everyman*; it is well suited, however, to outdoor performance. Its comparative length, along with the large role of the title character, favors the possibility of some degree of professionalism in the cast.

The modern reader may find it profitable to compare *Everyman* with such different kinds of drama as Greek tragedy or Samuel Beckett's *Endgame*. In its brevity, simplicity, and concentration on a single theme and situation, it recalls especially the shorter plays of the ancient Greeks. Its topic has much in common with that of Beckett's play—facing death and coming to terms with life—but the choices involved and the consequent ending (or "ending," in Beckett's work) are different.

As in most morality plays, the characters are personifications of more abstract concepts. Everyman himself, of course, represents all humanity. But we should not assume in advance that "abstract" characters make a dull play. In the first place, dramatizing the characters gives them actuality; the actors must be flesh and blood. Then, in *Everyman*, the situations, the speech, and the behavior of the various characters are thoroughly realistic as well as representative of their generalized significance. For example, Fellowship does and says what a single boon companion would be likely to say and do under the same circumstances. Good Deeds is not a static figure: we see her first bound to the Earth (the floor of the stage) by Everyman's sins; when he scourges himself in penance, she rises joyfully to accompany him. The author's ingenuity is notable in the character Goods (Riches): Goods is offstage when Everyman calls him; the audience hears but does not see him at first as he explains that he lies there in corners, trussed and piled up, locked in chests, stuffed in bags! Surely he must have got a laugh when he did come on stage. And of course God, who instigates the action by sending Death to call Everyman to his account, is no abstraction. He was probably a voice offstage rather than an actor—but a very effective character nonetheless.

Together with the lean and rapidly moving plot, it is the rightness of its words that makes *Everyman* a success. God speaks with an unfailing simplicity and directness:

> Charity they do all clean forgeet.
> I hoped well that every man
> In my glory should make his mansion;
> And thereto I had them all elect. . . .
> They be so cumbered with worldly riches
> That needs on them I must do justice— . . .

Nor is humor absent from the play. Cousin, asked by Everyman to go with him at the summons of Death, exclaims: "No, by Our Lady! I have the cramp in my toe"; and later, Beauty replies to the same effect: "I cross out all this! Adieu, by Saint John— / I take my tape in my lap, and am gone." There is irony in Fellowship's farewell verse: "For you I will remember that parting is mourning." Best of all, perhaps, are the short speeches, scattered throughout the earlier parts of the play especially, that express Everyman's disappointment in his friends and consequent disillusion. One example must suffice. After a long colloquy with Goods, that character asks Everyman, "What! weenest thou that I am thine?" Reversal, the necessary prelude to reorientation, is condensed in Everyman's brief reply: "I had weened [believed] so."

A good collection of medieval English plays, with commentary, is David Bevington, ed., *Medieval Drama* (1975). For discussions of *Everyman*, see Robert Potter, *The English Morality Play* (1975), and the edition, with bibliography, by A. C. Cawley, ed., *Everyman and Medieval Miracle Plays*, revised by Anne Rooney (1993). Guides to drama in the Middle Ages generally are provided by Glynne Wickham, *The Medieval Theatre*, 3rd ed. (1987), and John W. Harris, *Medieval Theatre in Context* (1992).

Everyman[1]

DRAMATIS PERSONAE

MESSENGER	KNOWLEDGE
GOD	CONFESSION
DEATH	BEAUTY
EVERYMAN	STRENGTH
FELLOWSHIP	DISCRETION
KINDRED	FIVE-WITS
COUSIN	ANGEL
GOODS	DOCTOR
GOOD DEEDS	

*Here Beginneth a Treatise How the High Father of
Heaven Sendeth Death to Summon Every Creature
to Come and Give Account of Their Lives in This
World, and is in Manner of a Moral Play*

[*Enter* MESSENGER.]

MESSENGER I pray you all give your audience,
  And hear this matter with reverence,
  By figure[2] a moral play,
  The Summoning of Everyman called it is,
  That of our lives and ending shows   5
  How transitory we be all day.[3]
  The matter is wonder precious,
  But the intent of it is more gracious
  And sweet to bear away.
  The story saith: Man, in the beginning   10
  Look well, and take good heed to the ending,
  Be you never so gay.
  You think sin in the beginning full sweet,
  Which in the end causeth the soul to weep,
  When the body lieth in clay.   15
  Here shall you see how fellowship and jollity,
  Both strength, pleasure, and beauty,
  Will fade from thee as flower in May.
  For ye shall hear how our Heaven-King
  Calleth Everyman to a general reckoning.   20
  Give audience and hear what he doth say.
    [*Exit* MESSENGER.—*Enter* GOD.]

GOD I perceive, here in my majesty,
  How that all creatures be to me unkind,[4]
  Living without dread in worldly prosperity.
  Of ghostly[5] sight the people be so blind,   25
  Drowned in sin, they know me not for their God.

---

1. Modernized text by E. Talbot Donaldson, whose notes have been adapted here. 2. In form.
3. Always. 4. Thoughtless. 5. Spiritual.

In worldly riches is all their mind:
They fear not of my righteousness the sharp rod;
My law that I showed when I for them died
They forget clean, and shedding of my blood red.   30
I hanged between two,[6] it cannot be denied:
To get them life I suffered to be dead.
I healed their feet, with thorns hurt was my head.
I could do no more than I did, truly—
And now I see the people do clean forsake me.   35
They use the seven deadly sins damnable,
As pride, coveitise,[7] wrath, and lechery
Now in the world be made commendable.
And thus they leave of angels the heavenly company.
Every man liveth so after his own pleasure,   40
And yet of their life they be nothing sure.
I see the more that I them forbear,
The worse they be from year to year:
All that liveth appaireth[8] fast.
Therefore I will, in all the haste,   45
Have a reckoning of every man's person.
For, and[9] I leave the people thus alone
In their life and wicked tempests,
Verily they will become much worse than beasts;
For now one would by envy another up eat.   50
Charity do they all clean forgeet.
I hoped well that every man
In my glory should make his mansion,
And thereto I had them all elect.[1]
But now I see, like traitors deject,[2]   55
They thank me not for the pleasure that I to them meant,
Nor yet for their being that I them have lent.
I proffered the people great multitude of mercy,
And few there be that asketh it heartily.
They be so cumbered with worldly riches   60
That needs on them I must do justice—
On every man living without fear.
Where art thou, Death, thou mighty messenger?
    [*Enter* DEATH.]
DEATH   Almighty God, I am here at your will,
  Your commandment to fulfill.   65
GOD   Go thou to Everyman,
  And show him, in my name,
  A pilgrimage he must on him take,
  Which he in no wise may escape;
  And that he bring with him a sure reckoning   70
  Without delay or any tarrying.
DEATH   Lord, I will in the world go run over all,

6. The two thieves between whom Christ was crucified.   7. Avarice.   8. Degenerates.   9. If.
1. Chosen.   2. Abased.

And cruelly out-search both great and small.
   [*Exit* GOD.]
Everyman will I beset that liveth beastly
Out of God's laws, and dreadeth not folly.   75
He that loveth riches I will strike with my dart,
His sight to blind, and from heaven to depart[3]—
Except that Almsdeeds be his good friend—
In hell for to dwell, world without end.
Lo, yonder I see Everyman walking: 80
Full little he thinketh on my coming;
His mind is on fleshly lusts and his treasure,
And great pain it shall cause him to endure
Before the Lord, Heaven-King.
    [*Enter* EVERYMAN.]
Everyman, stand still! Whither art thou going   85
Thus gaily? Hast thou thy Maker forgeet?
EVERYMAN Why askest thou?
Why wouldest thou weet?[4]
DEATH Yea, sir, I will show you:
In great haste I am sent to thee   90
From God out of his majesty.
EVERYMAN What! sent to me?
DEATH Yea, certainly.
Though thou have forgot him here,
He thinketh on thee in the heavenly sphere,   95
As, ere we depart, thou shalt know.
EVERYMAN What desireth God of me?
DEATH That shall I show thee:
A reckoning he will needs have
Without any longer respite.   100
EVERYMAN To give a reckoning longer leisure I crave.
This blind[5] matter troubleth my wit.
DEATH On thee thou must take a long journay:
Therefore thy book of count with thee thou bring,
For turn again thou cannot by no way.   105
And look thou be sure of thy reckoning,
For before God thou shalt answer and shew
Thy many bad deeds and good but a few—
How thou hast spent thy life and in what wise,
Before the Chief Lord of Paradise.   110
Have ado that we were in that way,[6]
For weet thou well thou shalt make none attornay.[7]
EVERYMAN Full unready I am such reckoning to give.
I know thee not. What messenger art thou?
DEATH I am Death that no man dreadeth,[8]   115
For every man I 'rest, and no man spareth;
For it is God's commandment

---

3. Separate.   4. Know.   5. Unexpected.   6. Let's get started at once.   7. None to appear in your stead.   8. That fears nobody.

That all to me should be obedient.
EVERYMAN   O Death, thou comest when I had thee least in mind.
In thy power it lieth me to save: 120
Yet of my good will I give thee, if thou will be kind,
Yea, a thousand pound shalt thou have—
And defer this matter till another day.
DEATH   Everyman, it may not be, by no way.
I set nought by gold, silver, nor riches,   125
Nor by pope, emperor, king, duke, nor princes,
For, and I would receive gifts great,
All the world I might get.
But my custom is clean contrary:
I give thee no respite. Come hence and not tarry!   130
EVERYMAN   Alas, shall I have no longer respite?
I may say Death giveth no warning.
To think on thee it maketh my heart sick,
For all unready is my book of reckoning.
But twelve year and I might have a biding,[9]   135
My counting-book I would make so clear
That my reckoning I should not need to fear.
Wherefore, Death, I pray thee, for God's mercy,
Spare me till I be provided of remedy.
DEATH   Thee availeth not to cry, weep, and pray;   140
But haste thee lightly[1] that thou were gone that journay,
And prove thy friends, if thou can.
For weet thou well the tide abideth no man,
And in the world each living creature
For Adam's sin must die of nature.[2]   145
EVERYMAN   Death, if I should this pilgrimage take
And my reckoning surely make,
Show me, for saint[3] charity,
Should I not come again shortly?
DEATH   No, Everyman. And thou be once there,   150
Thou mayst never more come here,
Trust me verily.
EVERYMAN   O gracious God in the high seat celestial,
Have mercy on me in this most need!
Shall I have no company from this vale terrestrial   155
Of mine acquaintance that way me to lead?
DEATH   Yea, if any be so hardy
That would go with thee and bear thee company.
Hie thee that thou were gone to God's magnificence,
Thy reckoning to give before his presence.   160
What, weenest[4] thou thy life is given thee,
And thy worldly goods also?
EVERYMAN   I had weened so, verily.
DEATH   Nay, nay, it was but lent thee.
For as soon as thou art go,   165

9. If I might have a delay for just twelve years.   1. Quickly.   2. Naturally.   3. Holy.   4. Suppose.

Another a while shall have it and then go therefro,
Even as thou hast done.
Everyman, thou art mad! Thou hast thy wits[5] five,
And here on earth will not amend thy life!
For suddenly I do come.   170
EVERYMAN   O wretched caitiff! Whither shall I flee
That I might 'scape this endless sorrow?
Now, gentle Death, spare me till tomorrow,
That I may amend me
With good advisement.[6]   175
DEATH   Nay, thereto I will not consent,
Nor no man will I respite,
But to the heart suddenly I shall smite,
Without any advisement.
And now out of thy sight I will me hie: 180
See thou make thee ready shortly,
For thou mayst say this is the day
That no man living may 'scape away.
        [*Exit* DEATH.]
EVERYMAN   Alas, I may well weep with sighs deep:
Now have I no manner of company   185
To help me in my journey and me to keep.
And also my writing[7] is full unready—
How shall I do now for to excuse me?
I would to God I had never be geet![8]
To my soul a full great profit it had be.   190
For now I fear pains huge and great.
The time passeth: Lord, help, that all wrought!
For though I mourn, it availeth nought.
The day passeth and is almost ago:
I wot[9] not well what for to do.   195
To whom were I best my complaint to make?
What and I to Fellowship thereof spake,
And showed him of this sudden chance?
For in him is all mine affiance,[1]
We have in the world so many a day   200
Be good friends in sport and play.
I see him yonder, certainly.
I trust that he will bear me company.
Therefore to him will I speak to ease my sorrow.
        [*Enter* FELLOWSHIP.]
Well met, good Fellowship, and good morrow!   205
FELLOWSHIP   Everyman, good morrow, by this day!
Sir, why lookest thou so piteously?
If anything be amiss, I pray thee me say,
That I may help to remedy.
EVERYMAN   Yea, good Fellowship, yea: 210
I am in great jeopardy.

---

5. Senses.   6. Preparation.   7. Ledger.   8. Been begotten.   9. Know.   1. Trust.

FELLOWSHIP   My true friend, show to me your mind.
   I will not forsake thee to my life's end
   In the way of good company.
EVERYMAN   That was well spoken, and lovingly!   215
FELLOWSHIP   Sir, I must needs know your heaviness.
   I have pity to see you in any distress.
   If any have you wronged, ye shall revenged be,
   Though I on the ground be slain for thee,
   Though that I know before that I should die.   220
EVERYMAN   Verily, Fellowship, gramercy.[2]
FELLOWSHIP   Tush! by thy thanks I set not a stree.[3]
   Show me your grief and say no more.
EVERYMAN   If I my heart should to you break,[4]
   And then you to turn your mind fro me,   225
   And would not me comfort when ye hear me speak,
   Then should I ten times sorrier be.
FELLOWSHIP   Sir, I say as I will do, indeed.
EVERYMAN   Then be you a good friend at need.
   I have found you true herebefore.   230
FELLOWSHIP   And so ye shall evermore.
   For, in faith, and thou go to hell,
   I will not forsake thee by the way.
EVERYMAN   Ye speak like a good friend. I believe you well.
   I shall deserve[5] it, and I may.   235
FELLOWSHIP   I speak of no deserving, by this day!
   For he that will say and nothing do
   Is not worthy with good company to go.
   Therefore show me the grief of your mind,
   As to your friend most loving and kind.   240
EVERYMAN   I shall show you how it is:
   Commanded I am to go a journay,
   A long way, hard and dangerous,
   And give a strait[6] count, without delay,
   Before the high judge Adonai.[7]   245
   Wherefore I pray you bear me company,
   As ye have promised, in this journay.
FELLOWSHIP   This is matter indeed! Promise is duty—
   But, and I should take such a voyage on me,
   I know it well, it should be to my pain.   250
   Also it maketh me afeard, certain.
   But let us take counsel here, as well as we can—
   For your words would fear a strong man.
EVERYMAN   Why, ye said if I had need,
   Ye would me never forsake, quick ne dead,   255
   Though it were to hell, truly.
FELLOWSHIP   So I said, certainly.
   But such pleasures[8] be set aside, the sooth to say.
   And also, if we took such a journay,

2. Many thanks.   3. Straw.   4. Disclose.   5. Repay.   6. Strict.   7. God.   8. Jokes.

When should we again come?   260
EVERYMAN   Nay, never again, till the day of doom.
FELLOWSHIP   In faith, then will not I come there!
Who hath you these tidings brought?
EVERYMAN   Indeed, Death was with me here.
FELLOWSHIP   Now by God that all hath bought,[9]   265
If Death were the messenger,
For no man that is living today
I will not go that loath journay—
Not for the father that begat me!
EVERYMAN   Ye promised otherwise, pardie.[1]   270
FELLOWSHIP   I wot well I said so, truly.
And yet, if thou wilt eat and drink and make good cheer,
Or haunt to women the lusty company,
I would not forsake you while the day is clear,
Trust me verily!   275
EVERYMAN   Yea, thereto ye would be ready—
To go to mirth, solace,[2] and play:
Your mind to folly will sooner apply
Than to bear me company in my long journay.
FELLOWSHIP   Now in good faith, I will not that way.   280
But, and thou will murder or any man kill,
In that I will help thee with a good will.
EVERYMAN   O that is simple[3] advice, indeed!
Gentle fellow, help me in my necessity:
We have loved long, and now I need—   285
And now, gentle Fellowship, remember me!
FELLOWSHIP   Whether ye have loved me or no,
By Saint John, I will not with thee go!
EVERYMAN   Yet I pray thee take the labor and do so much for me,
To bring me forward,[4] for saint charity,   290
And comfort me till I come without the town.
FELLOWSHIP   Nay, and thou would give me a new gown,
I will not a foot with thee go.
But, and thou had tarried, I would not have left thee so.
And as now, God speed thee in thy journay!   295
For from thee I will depart as fast as I may.
EVERYMAN   Whither away, Fellowship? Will thou forsake me?
FELLOWSHIP   Yea, by my fay! To God I betake[5] thee.
EVERYMAN   Farewell, good Fellowship! For thee my heart is sore.
Adieu forever—I shall see thee no more   300
FELLOWSHIP   In faith, Everyman, farewell now at the ending:
For you I will remember that parting is mourning.
        [*Exit* FELLOWSHIP.]
EVERYMAN   Alack, shall we thus depart[6] indeed—
Ah, Lady, help!—without any more comfort?
Lo, Fellowship forsaketh me in my most need!   305

9. Redeemed.   1. By God.   2. Pleasure.   3. Foolish.   4. Escort me.   5. Commend.   6. Part.

For help in this world whither shall I resort?
Fellowship herebefore with me would merry make,
And now little sorrow for me doth he take.
It is said, "In prosperity men friends may find
Which in adversity be full unkind."   310
Now whither for succor shall I flee,
Sith[7] that Fellowship hath forsaken me?
To my kinsmen I will, truly,
Praying them to help me in my necessity.
I believe that they will do so,   315
For kind will creep where it may not go.[8]
I will go 'say[9]—for yonder I see them—
Where[1] be ye now my friends and kinsmen.
    [*Enter* KINDRED *and* COUSIN.]
KINDRED   Here be we now at your commandment:
Cousin, I pray you show us your intent   320
In any wise, and not spare.
COUSIN   Yea, Everyman, and to us declare
If ye be disposed to go anywhither.
For, weet you well, we will live and die togither.
KINDRED   In wealth and woe we will with you hold,   325
For over his kin a man may be bold.
EVERYMAN   Gramercy, my friends and kinsmen kind.
Now shall I show you the grief of my mind.
I was commanded by a messenger
That is a high king's chief officer: 330
He bade me go a pilgrimage, to my pain—
And I know well I shall never come again.
Also I must give a reckoning strait,
For I have a great enemy that hath me in wait,[2]
Which intendeth me to hinder.   335
KINDRED   What account is that which ye must render?
That would I know.
EVERYMAN   Of all my works I must show
How I have lived and my days spent;
Also of ill deeds that I have used   340
In my time sith life was me lent,
And of all virtues that I have refused.
Therefore I pray you go thither with me
To help me make mine account, for saint charity.
COUSIN   What, to go thither? Is that the matter?   345
Nay, Everyman, I had liefer fast[3] bread and water
All this five year and more!
EVERYMAN   Alas, that ever I was bore!
For now shall I never be merry
If that you forsake me.   350
KINDRED   Ah, sir, what? Ye be a merry man:
Take good heart to you and make no moan.

---

7. Since.   8. For kinship will creep where it cannot walk (or kinsmen will suffer hardship for one
another).   9. Assay.   1. Whether.   2. Satan lies in ambush for me.   3. Rather fast on.

But one thing I warn you, by Saint Anne,
As for me, ye shall go alone.
EVERYMAN   My Cousin, will you not with me go?   355
COUSIN   No, by Our Lady! I have the cramp in my toe:
Trust not to me. For, so God me speed,
I will deceive you in your most need.
KINDRED   It availeth you not us to 'tice.[4]
Ye shall have my maid with all my heart: 360
She loveth to go to feasts, there to be nice,[5]
And to dance, and abroad to start.[6]
I will give her leave to help you in that journey,
If that you and she may agree.
EVERYMAN   Now show me the very effect of your mind: 365
Will you go with me or abide behind?
KINDRED   Abide behind? Yea, that will I and I may!
Therefore farewell till another day.
       [*Exit* KINDRED.]
EVERYMAN   How should I be merry or glad?
For fair promises men to me make,   370
But when I have most need they me forsake.
I am deceived. That maketh me sad.
COUSIN   Cousin Everyman, farewell now,
For verily I will not go with you;
Also of mine own an unready reckoning   375
I have to account—therefore I make tarrying.
Now God keep thee, for now I go.
       [*Exit* COUSIN.]
EVERYMAN   Ah, Jesus, is all come hereto?
Lo, fair words maketh fools fain:[7]
They promise and nothing will do, certain.   380
My kinsmen promised me faithfully
For to abide with me steadfastly,
And now fast away do they flee.
Even so Fellowship promised me.
What friend were best me of to provide?   385
I lose my time here longer to abide.
Yet in my mind a thing there is:
All my life I have loved riches;
If that my Goods[8] now help me might,
He would make my heart full light.   390
I will speak to him in this distress.
Where art thou, my Goods and riches?
GOODS [*Within.*]   Who calleth me? Everyman? What, hast thou haste?
I lie here in corners, trussed and piled so high,
And in chests I am locked so fast—   395
Also sacked in bags—thou mayst see with thine eye
I cannot stir, in packs low where I lie.
What would ye have? Lightly[9] me say.
EVERYMAN   Come hither, Goods, in all the haste thou may,

---

4. Entice.   **5.** Wanton.   **6.** To go gadding about.   **7.** Glad.   **8.** Goods.   **9.** Quickly.

For of counsel I must desire thee.   400
    [*Enter* GOODS.]
GOODS   Sir, and ye in the world have sorrow or adversity,
That can I help you to remedy shortly.
EVERYMAN   It is another disease[1] that grieveth me:
In this world it is not, I tell thee so.
I am sent for another way to go,   405
To give a strait count general
Before the highest Jupiter of all.
And all my life I have had joy and pleasure in thee:
Therefore I pray thee go with me,
For peradventure, thou mayst before God Almighty   410
My reckoning help to clean and purify.
For it is said ever among[2]
That money maketh all right that is wrong.
GOODS   Nay, Everyman, I sing another song:
I follow no man in such voyages.   415
For, and I went with thee,
Thou shouldest fare much the worse for me;
For because on me thou did set thy mind,
Thy reckoning I have made blotted and blind,[3]
That thine account thou cannot make truly—   420
And that hast thou for the love of me.
EVERYMAN   That would grieve me full sore,
When I should come to that fearful answer.
Up, let us go thither together.
GOODS   Nay, not so, I am too brittle, I may not endure.   425
I will follow no man one foot, be ye sure.
EVERYMAN   Alas, I have thee loved and had great pleasure
All my life-days on good and treasure.
GOODS   That is to thy damnation, without leasing,[4]
For my love is contrary to the love everlasting.   430
But if thou had me loved moderately during,
As to the poor to give part of me,
Then shouldest thou not in this dolor be,
Nor in this great sorrow and care.
EVERYMAN   Lo, now was I deceived ere I was ware,   435
And all I may wite[5] misspending of time.
GOODS   What, weenest[6] thou that I am thine?
EVERYMAN   I had weened so.
GOODS   Nay, Everyman, I say no.
As for a while I was lent thee;   440
A season thou hast had me in prosperity.
My condition is man's soul to kill;
If I save one, a thousand I do spill.
Weenest thou that I will follow thee?
Nay, from this world, not verily.   445
EVERYMAN   I had weened otherwise.

---

1. Distress.   2. Now and then.   3. Illegible.   4. Lie.   5. Blame on.   6. Suppose.

GOODS   Therefore to thy soul Goods is a thief;
   For when thou art dead, this is my guise[7]—
   Another to deceive in the same wise
   As I have done thee, and all to his soul's repreef.[8]   450
EVERYMAN   O false Goods, cursed thou be,
   Thou traitor to God, that hast deceived me
   And caught me in thy snare!
GOODS   Marry, thou brought thyself in care,[9]
   Whereof I am glad: 455
   I must needs laugh, I cannot be sad.
EVERYMAN   Ah, Goods, thou hast had long my heartly[1] love;
   I gave thee that which should be the Lord's above.
   But wilt thou not go with me, indeed?
   I pray thee truth to say.   460
GOODS   No, so God me speed!
   Therefore farewell and have good day.
      [*Exit* GOODS.]
EVERYMAN   Oh, to whom shall I make my moan
   For to go with me in that heavy journay?
   First Fellowship said he would with me gone: 465
   His words were very pleasant and gay,
   But afterward he left me alone.
   Then spake I to my kinsmen, all in despair,
   And also they gave me words fair—
   They lacked no fair speaking,   470
   But all forsake me in the ending.
   Then went I to my Goods that I loved best,
   In hope to have comfort; but there had I least,
   For my Goods sharply did me tell
   That he bringeth many into hell.   475
   Then of myself I was ashamed,
   And so I am worthy to be blamed:
   Thus may I well myself hate.
   Of whom shall I now counsel take?
   I think that I shall never speed   480
   Till that I go to my Good Deed.
   But alas, she is so weak
   That she can neither go[2] nor speak.
   Yet will I venture[3] on her now.
   My Good Deeds, where be you?   485
GOOD DEEDS [*Speaking from the ground.*]   Here I lie, cold in the ground:
   Thy sins hath me sore bound
   That I cannot stear.[4]
EVERYMAN   O Good Deeds, I stand in fear:
   I must you pray of counsel,   490
   For help now should come right well.
GOOD DEEDS   Everyman, I have understanding
   That ye be summoned, account to make,

---

7. Custom.   8. Shame.   9. Sorrow.   1. Sincere.   2. Walk.   3. Gamble.   4. Stir.

Before Messiah of Jer'salem King.
And you do by me, that journey with you will I take.   495
EVERYMAN   Therefore I come to you my moan to make.
I pray you that ye will go with me.
GOOD DEEDS   I would full fain, but I cannot stand, verily.
EVERYMAN   Why, is there anything on you fall?
GOOD DEEDS   Yea, sir, I may thank you of all: 500
If ye had perfectly cheered me,
Your book of count full ready had be.
      [GOOD DEEDS *shows him the account book.*]
Look, the books of your works and deeds eke,[5]
As how they lie under the feet,
To your soul's heaviness.   505
EVERYMAN   Our Lord Jesus help me!
For one letter here I cannot see.
GOOD DEEDS   There is a blind reckoning in time of distress!
EVERYMAN   Good Deeds, I pray you help me in this need,
Or else I am forever damned indeed.   510
Therefore help me to make reckoning
Before the Redeemer of all thing
That King is and was and ever shall.
GOOD DEEDS   Everyman, I am sorry of your fall
And fain would help you and I were able.   515
EVERYMAN   Good Deeds, your counsel I pray you give me.
GOOD DEEDS   That shall I do verily,
Though that on my feet I may not go;
I have a sister that shall with you also,
Called Knowledge, which shall with you abide   520
To help you to make that dreadful reckoning.
      [*Enter* KNOWLEDGE.]
KNOWLEDGE   Everyman, I will go with thee and be thy guide,
In thy most need to go by thy side.
EVERYMAN   In good condition I am now in everything,
And am whole content with this good thing,   525
Thanked be God my Creator.
GOOD DEEDS   And when she hath brought you there
Where thou shalt heal thee of thy smart,[6]
Then go you with your reckoning and your Good Deeds together
For to make you joyful at heart   530
Before the blessed Trinity.
EVERYMAN   My Good Deeds, gramercy!
I am well content, certainly,
With your words sweet.
KNOWLEDGE   Now go we together lovingly   535
To Confession, that cleansing river.
EVERYMAN   For joy I weep—I would we were there!
But I pray you give me cognition,
Where dwelleth that holy man Confession?

5. Also.   6. Pain.

KNOWLEDGE   In the House of Salvation: 540
  We shall find him in that place
  That shall us comfort, by God's grace.
        [KNOWLEDGE *leads* EVERYMAN *to* CONFESSION.]
  Lo, this is Confession: kneel down and ask mercy,
  For he is in good conceit[7] with God Almighty.
EVERYMAN [*Kneeling.*]   O glorious fountain that all uncleanness doth
        clarify,[8]   545
  Wash from me the spots of vice unclean,
  That on me no sin may be seen.
  I come with Knowledge for my redemption,
  Redempt with heart and full contrition,
  For I am commanded a pilgrimage to take   550
  And great accounts before God to make.
  Now I pray you, Shrift, mother of Salvation,
  Help my Good Deeds for my piteous exclamation.
CONFESSION   I know your sorrow well, Everyman:
  Because with Knowledge ye come to me,   555
  I will you comfort as well as I can,
  And a precious jewel I will give thee,
  Called Penance, voider of adversity.
  Therewith shall your body chastised be—
  With abstinence and perseverance in God's service.   560
  Here shall you receive that scourge of me,
  Which is penance strong that ye must endure,
  To remember thy Saviour was scourged for thee
  With sharp scourges, and suffered it patiently.
  So must thou ere thou 'scape that painful pilgrimage.   565
  Knowledge, keep him in this voyage,
  And by that time Good Deeds will be with thee.
  But in any wise be secure of mercy—
  For your time draweth fast—and ye will saved be.
  Ask God mercy and he will grant, truly.   570
  When with the scourge of penance man doth him bind,
  The oil of forgiveness then shall he find.
EVERYMAN   Thanked be God for his gracious work,
  For now I will my penance begin.
  This hath rejoiced and lighted my heart,   575
  Though the knots be painful and hard within.[9]
KNOWLEDGE   Everyman, look your penance that ye fulfill,
  What pain that ever it to you be;
  And Knowledge shall give you counsel at will
  How your account ye shall make clearly.   580
EVERYMAN   O eternal God, O heavenly figure,
  O way of righteousness, O goodly vision,
  Which descended down in a virgin pure
  Because he would every man redeem,
  Which Adam forfeited by his disobedience;   585

7. Esteem.   8. Purify.   9. To my senses. The knots are on the scourge (whip) of penance.

O blessed Godhead, elect and high Divine,
Forgive my grievous offense!
Here I cry thee mercy in this presence:
O ghostly Treasure, O Ransomer and Redeemer,
Of all the world Hope and Conduiter,[1]   590
Mirror of joy, Foundator of mercy,
Which enlumineth heaven and earth thereby,
Hear my clamorous complaint, though it late be;
Receive my prayers, of thy benignity.
Though I be a sinner most abominable,   595
Yet let my name be written in Moses' table.[2]
O Mary, pray to the Maker of all thing
Me for to help at my ending,
And save me from the power of my enemy,
For Death assaileth me strongly.   600
And Lady, that I may by mean of thy prayer
Of your Son's glory to be partner—
By the means of his passion I it crave.
I beseech you help my soul to save.
Knowledge, give me the scourge of penance: 605
My flesh therewith shall give acquittance.[3]
I will now begin, if God give me grace.
KNOWLEDGE   Everyman, God give you time and space![4]
Thus I bequeath you in the hands of our Saviour:
Now may you make your reckoning sure.   610
EVERYMAN   In the name of the Holy Trinity
My body sore punished shall be:
Take this, body, for the sin of the flesh!
Also[5] thou delightest to go gay and fresh,
And in the way of damnation thou did me bring,   615
Therefore suffer now strokes of punishing!
Now of penance I will wade the water clear,
To save me from purgatory, that sharp fire.
GOOD DEEDS   I thank God, now can I walk and go,
And am delivered of my sickness and woe.   620
Therefore with Everyman I will go, and not spare:
His good works I will help him to declare.
KNOWLEDGE   Now Everyman, be merry and glad:
Your Good Deeds cometh now, ye may not be sad.
Now is your Good Deeds whole and sound,   625
Going upright upon the ground.
EVERYMAN   My heart is light, and shall be evermore.
Now will I smite faster than I did before.
GOOD DEEDS   Everyman, pilgrim, my special friend,
Blessed be thou without end!   630
For thee is preparate the eternal glory.
Ye have me made whole and sound

---

1. Guide.   2. Tablet on which are recorded those who have been baptized and have done penance.
3. Satisfaction for sins.   4. Opportunity.   5. As.

Therefore I will bide by thee in every stound.[6]
EVERYMAN   Welcome, my Good Deeds! Now I hear thy voice,
  I weep for very sweetness of love.   635
KNOWLEDGE   Be no more sad, but ever rejoice:
  God seeth thy living in his throne above.
  Put on this garment to thy behove,[7]
  Which is wet with your tears—
  Or else before God you may it miss   640
  When ye to your journey's end come shall.
EVERYMAN   Gentle Knowledge, what do ye it call?
KNOWLEDGE   It is a garment of sorrow;
  From pain it will you borrow:[8]
  Contrition it is   645
  That getteth forgiveness;
  It pleaseth God passing[9] well.
GOOD DEEDS   Everyman, will you wear it for your heal?[1]
EVERYMAN   Now blessed be Jesu, Mary's son,
  For now have I on true contrition.   650
  And let us go now without tarrying.
  Good Deeds, have we clear our reckoning?
GOOD DEEDS   Yea, indeed, I have it here.
EVERYMAN   Then I trust we need not fear.
  Now friends, let us not part in twain.   655
KNOWLEDGE   Nay, Everyman, that will we not, certain.
GOOD DEEDS   Yet must thou lead with thee
  Three persons of great might.
EVERYMAN   Who should they be?
GOOD DEEDS   Discretion and Strength they hight,[2]   660
  And thy Beauty may not abide behind.
KNOWLEDGE   Also ye must call to mind
  Your Five-Wits as for your counselors.
GOOD DEEDS   You must have them ready at all hours.
EVERYMAN   How shall I get them hither?   665
KNOWLEDGE   You must call them all togither,
  And they will be here incontinent.[3]
EVERYMAN   My friends, come hither and be present,
  Discretion, Strength, my Five-Wits, and Beauty!
      [*They enter.*]
BEAUTY   Here at your will we be all ready.   670
  What will ye that we should do?
GOOD DEEDS   That ye would with Everyman go
  And help him in his pilgrimage.
  Advise you: will ye with him or not in that voyage?
STRENGTH   We will bring him all thither,   675
  To his help and comfort, ye may believe me.
DISCRETION   So will we go with him all togither.
EVERYMAN   Almighty God, loved might thou be!

---

6. Trial.   7. Advantage.   8. Redeem.   9. Surpassingly.   1. Welfare.   2. Are called.   3. At once.

I give thee laud that I have hither brought
Strength, Discretion, Beauty, and Five-Wits—lack I nought—   680
And my Good Deeds, with Knowledge clear,
All be in my company at my will here:
I desire no more to my business.
STRENGTH   And I, Strength, will by you stand in distress,
Though thou would in battle fight on the ground.   685
FIVE-WITS   And though it were through the world round,
We will not depart for sweet ne sour.
BEAUTY   No more will I, until death's hour,
Whatsoever thereof befall.
DISCRETION   Everyman, advise you first of all: 690
Go with a good advisement⁴ and deliberation.
We all give you virtuous monition⁵
That all shall be well.
EVERYMAN   My friends, hearken what I will tell;
I pray God reward you in his heaven-sphere;   695
Now hearken all that be here,
For I will make my testament,
Here before you all present:
In alms half my good I will give with my hands twain,
In the way of charity with good intent;   700
And the other half, still⁶ shall remain,
I 'queath to be returned there it ought to be.
This I do in despite of the fiend of hell,
To go quit out of his perel,⁷
Ever after and this day.   705
KNOWLEDGE   Everyman, hearken what I say:
Go to Priesthood, I you advise,
And receive of him, in any wise,
The holy sacrament and ointment⁸ togither;
Then shortly see ye turn again hither: 710
We will all abide you here.
FIVE-WITS   Yea, Everyman, hie you that ye ready were.
There is no emperor, king, duke, ne baron,
That of God hath commission
As hath the least priest in the world being: 715
For of the blessed sacraments pure and bening⁹
He beareth the keys, and thereof hath the cure¹
For man's redemption—it is ever sure—
Which God for our souls' medicine
Gave us out of his heart with great pine,²   720
Here in this transitory life for thee and me.
The blessed sacraments seven there be:
Baptism, confirmation, with priesthood³ good,
And the sacrament of God's precious flesh and blood,
Marriage, the holy extreme unction, and penance: 725

---

4. Preparation.   5. Confident prediction.   6. Which still.   7. To go free from danger from him.
8. Extreme unction.   9. Benign.   1. Care.   2. Torment.   3. Ordination.

These seven be good to have in remembrance,
Gracious sacraments of high divinity.
EVERYMAN   Fain would I receive that holy body,
And meekly to my ghostly[4] father I will go.
FIVE-WITS   Everyman, that is the best that ye can do: 730
God will you to salvation bring.
For priesthood exceedeth all other thing:
To us Holy Scripture they do teach,
And converteth man from sin, heaven to reach;
God hath to them more power given   735
Than to any angel that is in heaven.
With five words[5] he may consecrate
God's body in flesh and blood to make,
And handleth his Maker between his hands.
The priest bindeth and unbindeth all bands,[6]   740
Both in earth and in heaven.
Thou ministers[7] all the sacraments seven;
Though we kiss thy feet, thou were worthy;
Thou art surgeon that cureth sin deadly;
No remedy we find under God   745
But all only priesthood.[8]
Everyman, God gave priests that dignity
And setteth them in his stead among us to be.
Thus be they above angels in degree.
          [Exit EVERYMAN.]
KNOWLEDGE   If priests be good, it is so, surely.   750
But when Jesu hanged on the cross with great smart,[9]
There he gave out of his blessed heart
The same sacrament in great torment,
He sold them not to us, that Lord omnipotent:
Therefore Saint Peter the Apostle doth say   755
That Jesu's curse hath all they
Which God their Saviour do buy or sell,[1]
Or they for any money do take or tell.[2]
Sinful priests giveth the sinners example bad:
Their children sitteth by other men's fires, I have heard;   760
And some haunteth women's company
With unclean life, as lusts of lechery.
These be with sin made blind.
FIVE-WITS   I trust to God no such may we find.
Therefore let us priesthood honor,   765
And follow their doctrine for our souls' succor.
We be their sheep and they shepherds be
By whom we all be kept in surety.
Peace, for yonder I see Everyman come,

4. Spiritual.   5. "For this is my body," spoken by the priest when he offers the wafer at communion.
6. A reference to the power of the keys, inherited by the priesthood from St. Peter, who received it from
Christ with the promise that whatever St. Peter bound or loosed on Earth would be bound or loosed in
heaven (Matthew 16.19).   7. Administers.   8. Except from priesthood alone.   9. Pain.   1. To
give or receive money for the sacraments is simony, named after Simon, who wished to buy the gift of the
Holy Ghost and was cursed by St. Peter.   2. Or who, for any sacrament, take or count out money.

Which hath made true satisfaction. 770
GOOD DEEDS   Methink it is he indeed.
  [*Re-enter* EVERYMAN.]
EVERYMAN   Now Jesu be your alder speed![3]
  I have received the sacrament for my redemption,
  And then mine extreme unction.
  Blessed be all they that counseled me to take it! 775
  And now, friends, let us go without longer respite.
  I thank God that ye have tarried so long.
  Now set each of you on this rood[4] your hond
  And shortly follow me:
  I go before there[5] I would be. God be our guide! 780
STRENGTH   Everyman, we will not from you go
  Till ye have done this voyage long.
DISCRETION   I, Discretion, will bide by you also.
KNOWLEDGE   And though this pilgrimage be never so strong,
  I will never part you fro. 785
STRENGTH   Everyman, I will be as sure by thee
  As ever I did by Judas Maccabee.[6]
EVERYMAN   Alas, I am so faint I may not stand—
  My limbs under me doth fold!
  Friends, let us not turn again to this land, 790
  Not for all the world's gold.
  For into this cave must I creep
  And turn to earth, and there to sleep.
BEAUTY   What, into this grave, alas?
EVERYMAN   Yea, there shall ye consume, more and lass.[7] 795
BEAUTY   And what, should I smother here?
EVERYMAN   Yea, by my faith, and nevermore appear.
  In this world live no more we shall,
  But in heaven before the highest Lord of all.
BEAUTY   I cross out all this! Adieu, by Saint John— 800
  I take my tape in my lap and am gone.[8]
EVERYMAN   What, Beauty, whither will ye?
BEAUTY   Peace, I am deaf—I look not behind me,
  Not and thou wouldest give me all the gold in thy chest.
  [*Exit* BEAUTY.]
EVERYMAN   Alas, whereto may I trust? 805
  Beauty goeth fast away fro me—
  She promised with me to live and die!
STRENGTH   Everyman, I will thee also forsake and deny.
  Thy game liketh me not at all.
EVERYMAN   Why then, ye will forsake me all? 810
  Sweet Strength, tarry a little space.
STRENGTH   Nay, sir, by the rood of grace,
  I will hie me from thee fast,
  Though thou weep till thy heart tobrast.[9]

---

3. The prosperer of you all.   4. Cross.   5. Where.   6. Judas Maccabaeus was an enormously powerful warrior in the defense of Israel against the Syrians in late Old Testament times.   7. Decay, all of you.   8. I tuck my skirts in my belt and am off.   9. Break.

EVERYMAN   Ye would ever bide by me, ye said.   815
STRENGTH   Yea, I have you far enough conveyed!
   Ye be old enough, I understand,
   Your pilgrimage to take on hand:
   I repent me that I hither came.
EVERYMAN   Strength, you to displease I am to blame,   820
   Yet promise is debt, this ye well wot.¹
STRENGTH   In faith, I care not:
   Thou art but a fool to complain;
   You spend your speech and waste your brain.
   Go, thrust thee into the ground.   825
      [*Exit* STRENGTH.]
EVERYMAN   I had weened² surer I should you have found.
   He that trusteth in his Strength
   She him deceiveth at the length.
   Both Strength and Beauty forsaketh me—
   Yet they promised me fair and lovingly.   830
DISCRETION   Everyman, I will after Strength be gone:
   As for me, I will leave you alone.
EVERYMAN   Why Discretion, will ye forsake me?
DISCRETION   Yea, in faith, I will go from thee.
   For when Strength goeth before,   835
   I follow after evermore.
EVERYMAN   Yet I pray thee, for the love of the Trinity,
   Look in my grave once piteously.
DISCRETION   Nay, so nigh will I not come.
   Farewell everyone!   840
      [*Exit* DISCRETION.]
EVERYMAN   Of all thing faileth save God alone—
   Beauty, Strength, and Discretion.
   For when Death bloweth his blast
   They all run fro me full fast.
FIVE-WITS   Everyman, my leave now of thee I take.   845
   I will follow the other, for here I thee forsake.
EVERYMAN   Alas, then may I wail and weep,
   For I took you for my best friend.
FIVE-WITS   I will no longer thee keep.
   Now farewell, and there an end!   850
      [*Exit* FIVE-WITS.]
EVERYMAN   O Jesu, help, all hath forsaken me!
GOOD DEEDS   Nay, Everyman, I will bide with thee:
   I will not forsake thee indeed;
   Thou shalt find me a good friend at need.
EVERYMAN   Gramercy, Good Deeds! Now may I true friends see.   855
   They have forsaken me every one—
   I loved them better than my Good Deeds alone.
   Knowledge, will ye forsake me also?
KNOWLEDGE   Yea, Everyman, when ye to Death shall go,

1. Know.   2. Supposed.

But not yet, for no manner of danger.   860
EVERYMAN   Gramercy, Knowledge, with all my heart!
KNOWLEDGE   Nay, yet will I not from hence depart
  Till I see where ye shall become.
EVERYMAN   Methink, alas, that I must be gone
  To make my reckoning and my debts pay,   865
  For I see my time is nigh spent away.
  Take example, all ye that this do hear or see,
  How they that I best loved do forsake me,
  Except my Good Deeds that bideth truly.
GOOD DEEDS   All earthly things is but vanity.   870
  Beauty, Strength, and Discretion do man forsake,
  Foolish friends and kinsmen that fair spake—
  All fleeth save Good Deeds, and that am I.
EVERYMAN   Have mercy on me, God most mighty,
  And stand by me, thou mother and maid, holy Mary!   875
GOOD DEEDS   Fear not: I will speak for thee.
EVERYMAN   Here I cry God mercy!
GOOD DEEDS   Short our end, and 'minish our pain.³
  Let us go, and never come again.
EVERYMAN   Into thy hands, Lord, my soul I commend: 880
  Receive it, Lord, that it be not lost.
  As thou me boughtest,⁴ so me defend,
  And save me from the fiend's boast,
  That I may appear with that blessed host
  That shall be saved at the day of doom.   885
  In manus tuas, of mights most,
  Forever *commendo spiritum meum.*⁵
        [EVERYMAN *and* GOOD DEEDS *descend into the grave.*]
KNOWLEDGE   Now hath he suffered that we all shall endure,
  The Good Deeds shall make all sure.
  Now hath he made ending,   890
  Methinketh that I hear angels sing
  And make great joy and melody
  Where Everyman's soul received shall be.
ANGEL [*Within.*]   Come, excellent elect spouse to Jesu!⁶
  Here above thou shalt go   895
  Because of thy singular virtue.
  Now the soul is taken the body fro,
  Thy reckoning is crystal clear:
  Now shalt thou into the heavenly sphere—
  Unto the which all ye shall come   900
  That liveth well before the day of doom.
        [*Enter* DOCTOR.⁷]
DOCTOR   This memorial⁸ men may have in mind:
  Ye hearers, take it of worth, old and young,
  And forsake Pride, for he deceiveth you in the end.

---

3. Make our dying quick and diminish our pain.   4. Redeemed.   5. Into thy hands, O greatest of powers, I commend my spirit forever (Latin).   6. The soul is often referred to as the bride of Jesus. 7. The learned theologian who explains the meaning of the play.   8. Reminder.

And remember Beauty, Five-Wits, Strength, and Discretion, 905
They all at the last do Everyman forsake,
Save his Good Deeds there doth he take—
But beware, for and they be small,
Before God he hath no help at all—
None excuse may be there for Everyman. 910
Alas, how shall he do than?[9]
For after death amends may no man make,
For then mercy and pity doth him forsake.
If his reckoning be not clear when he doth come,
God will say, "*Ite, maledicti, in ignem eternum!*"[1] 915
And he that hath his account whole and sound,
High in heaven he shall be crowned,
Unto which place God bring us all thither,
That we may live body and soul togither.
Thereto help, the Trinity! 920
Amen, say ye, for saint charity.

9. Then.   1. Depart, ye cursed, into everlasting fire (Latin).

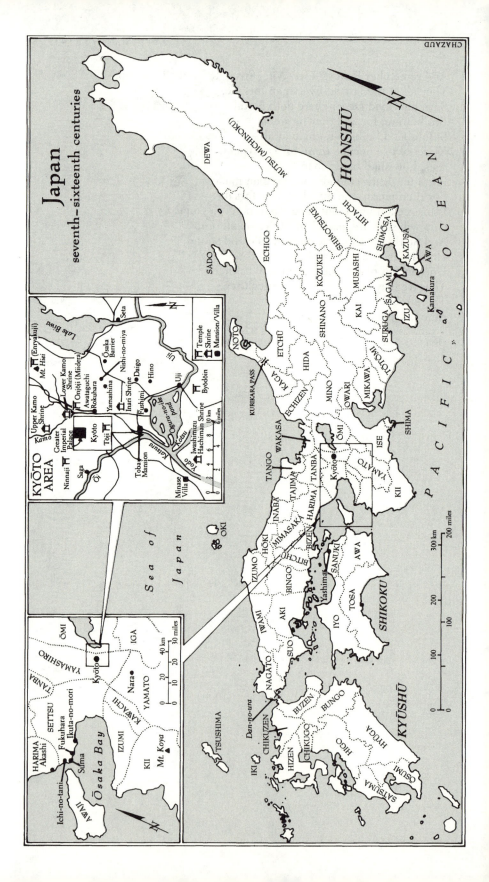

The Golden Age of Japanese Culture

Japan today looms large in the Western consciousness. Its economy, though weakened considerably in recent years, is one of the miracles of modern times. The material fortunes of Japan impinge so forcefully on our lives today, however, that they tend to crowd out all other considerations of Japan. Due in part to the barrier of language and, for much of history, a degree of geographical isolation, it is less well known that Japan has also produced one of the world's richest cultures. The first novel was written in Japan almost a thousand years ago. *The Tale of Genji* is a work that can still stand beside the finest accomplishments in fiction. One of poetry's most evocative and influential forms, *haiku*—a flash of insight expressed in a sliver of verse—is also a Japanese creation. Japanese woodblock prints had a profound influence on the French Impressionists, and the design of the traditional Japanese house, when discovered by Le Corbusier, Frank Lloyd Wright, and others in the twentieth century, helped determine the course of modern architecture.

Yet despite Japan's cultural achievements and their worldwide impact, two clichés still govern our thinking about Japan. The first is that Japan is a small country with a homogeneous population. Japan is small only in one sense. The total land mass of the Japanese archipelago, which consists of four principal islands plus some thousand smaller ones, altogether would not fill the state of California. The gross domestic product, on the other hand, is the third largest in the world, and Japan has the ninth highest population—126.5 million people—in the world. A common myth about these 126.5 million people (and a myth to which the Japanese themselves subscribe) is that they constitute a singularly homogeneous group, one "tribe" moving in lockstep. Although Japan may lack the racial and ethnic diversity of a country like the United States, by no means are its citizens all cast from the same mold. As the selections printed here will demonstrate, the Japanese speak with many voices, and the weight of their cultural output down through the centuries makes their voices anything but small.

The second stereotype is that Japan is a nation of imitators. This commonplace derives from the fact that it has been Japan's peculiar destiny to have lived at the edge of two great and contrasting traditions—Chinese civilization from the sixth century until the mid-nineteenth and Western modernity thereafter—always managing to accommodate influence while retaining the stamp of its own identity. Far from being a cultural parasite, Japan has demonstrated a genius for knowing when and what to learn from others. Furthermore, the Japanese have always been too vigorous a people to sit back and let someone else invent their culture for them. The same streak of perfectionism that defined Japanese quality control in business seems to have compelled Japan to improve perpetually on the original, whether it be Confucian theories of government or Henry Ford's assembly line. Nor should we let this agility as a cultural transformer obscure Japan's own creativity. The tea ceremony, the multicolor woodblock print, *kabuki*, *haiku*, and *sumo* all spring from native soil.

Yet in the sweep of history this is a newcomer, and twice in its existence Japan has found itself having to catch up. While the empires of Mesopotamia and ancient Egypt rose and fell and the civilizations of Greece, India, and China came to flower, the inhabitants of the Japanese islands remained hunters and gatherers. Their ancestors probably migrated to Japan in several waves, some from the Asian continent and others from the islands to the south. In the third century B.C. a new influx brought rice cultivation, and the Japanese exchanged a nomadic way of life for an agricultural one; they settled villages in the miniature plains nestled between the mountains and the sea. But the wanderers' past left its mark on Japanese civilization: an ingrained sense of the impermanence of things; an acute awareness of the changes brought by the seasons; a taste for the spare, the unrefined, the natural—even when prodigious artifice would sometimes be required to produce something "natural."

The new techniques of cultivating wet rice, one of the world's most labor-intensive crops, taught the Japanese people economy in the use of space and the advantages of cooperation. The latter, in turn, gave rise to the long-standing ideal in Japan that it is best to submit individual will to the greater needs of the group—the origin, perhaps, of the notion that the Japanese form a homogeneous and harmonious whole. This was no more true in 300 B.C. than it is today, for along with agriculture came bronze and iron; along with metallurgy came weapons; and with weapons, war. In other words, very early on another trait of Japanese culture surfaced: rule by warrior elites, precursors of the *samurai*. A class of martial aristocrats competed for power over the thickly settled countryside of the southern and central islands, until one clan succeeded in asserting its predominance, thereby establishing the imperial line.

The new governors quickly imported the superior fruits of Chinese civilization, which, by the seventh and eighth centuries, represented the most powerful, most advanced, and best administered country in the world. Having consolidated their hold over rival clans, the fledgling rulers claimed authority by absorbing Chinese theories of sovereignty and a centralized state, along with the economic and political apparatus—land surveys, districting, taxation, law codes, and bureaucratic management—to make their bold ambition work.

In many ways, the Japanese succeeded, though the political history of premodern Japan is ultimately the story of how the Chinese model proved a poor fit. It was a system that has been described by historians as a form of agricultural communism, with land divided equally among the population (and taxed uniformly) to ensure maximum returns. China's theory of government was profoundly egalitarian. The emperor reigned as an absolute sovereign, but his administrators were chosen on the basis of ability through an examination system that not only emphasized learning but fostered a true meritocracy. The emperor's bureaucrats thus provided the talent and diversity to help him rule impartially.

But the temperament and earliest traditions of the Japanese inclined them in a very different direction. Kinship ties from tribal times persisted in the emphasis of family and lineage, so that when Japan decided to adapt the Chinese model of bureaucracy, administrative positions went as a matter of course to those of good pedigree. There was no examination or open competition, because government was the right of the aristocracy. A system based on family connections rather than ability may strike us as unfair; it is also inherently unstable. Family fortunes wax and wane, and therein lies not only the formula for the political, economic, and military vicissitudes of premodern Japanese history but also the subject for much of Japan's best literature. Heroes are launched on fictional adventures when clan rivalries cost them imperial favor. The most popular tale of the classical era recounts the rise and fall of an overweening family. A kind of Japanese *Gone with the Wind* (but better as literature), *The Tale of the Heike* follows a powerful house of warrior-aristocrats through the glory days of bending even the emperor to their whims until the family's star inevitably falls, civil war comes, and a world of pride and elegant pursuits vanishes.

Life in premodern Japan, indeed the earthly realm, was seen as transitory, almost a dream. This was a central teaching of Buddhism, which Japan committed to memory during its Chinese tutelage. Buddhism had an exorbitant impact on Japanese civilization and is the best example of how much more enduring were some of the intellectual, artistic, and material influences that crossed the China Sea along with statecraft. The new religion was obviously congenial to the Japanese mind. While it is true that the native faith, Shinto, was little more than an amorphous and naïve belief in the protective or baneful effect of supernatural powers—local divinities and the mythical creators of Japan—completely lacking in creed, scripture, or a developed metaphysic, these deficiencies alone do not account for the success of Buddhism among the Japanese. In a country where earthquakes and typhoons are common occurrences and where people lived close to nature in all its changing aspects, the doctrine of universal impermanence spoke to Japanese experience. More important, Buddhism brought meaning to that discordant experience. Precisely because human existence is fleeting and illusory, life is but dissatisfaction. So long as one clings to the things of this world, one is bound to suffer. Buddhism offered hope of escape, however, because it taught that we all hold the possibility of Buddhahood within us. To realize this Buddha nature and end the painful cycle of rebirth into worlds of continued suffering, we have only to stop our grasping.

Here is the kernel of a great literature. It would sprout in Japan as luxuriantly as anywhere Buddhism ever touched: a literature that takes as its main ambition to plumb the depths of longing. If the Japanese have not been the world's metaphysicians and have proved inhospitable to the schematizing that in China elevated a taste for the symmetric almost to a national tic, they have been thinkers of another kind. Like the ancient Romans, the Japanese have always been a profoundly practical people. While they may never have distinguished themselves in abstract speculation, through art and literature rather than philosophy they have addressed, albeit more obliquely, the large questions of life: the nature of emotional attachment, the human need for affection, the clash between passion and reason, the curse of worldly ambition, the demon of the self, what courage means, what beauty is, where wisdom lies, the weight of the past, the true meaning of time.

In an astonishing series of masterpieces the Japanese developed one of their great gifts—for the play of words. That the medium employed was a foreign vessel, the Chinese writing system assimilated along with Buddhism, remains insignificant. The presence of a mentor should never obscure the accomplishments of the student.

PRONOUNCING GLOSSARY

The following list uses common English syllables to provide rough equivalents of selected words whose pronunciation may be unfamiliar to the general reader.

Genji: *gen-jee*	kabuki: *kah-boo-kee*
haiku: *hai-koo*	samurai: *sah-moo-rai*
Heike: *hay-kay*	sumo: *soo-moh*

TIME LINE

TEXTS	CONTEXTS
	4th–6th centuries Clans ally to form Yamato, precursor of Japanese state
	552 Buddhism introduced into Japan
	600 Chinese and Korean artisans settle in Japan
	645 Taika Reforms redistribute land and place imperial house in control of Japan
712 *A Record of Ancient Matters,* a mythic history legitimizing early Japanese rulers who commissioned it	**710–784** Nara period: capital established at Nara in time of first great intellectual and cultural achievement
ca. 759 *The Man'yōshū,* an anthology of over 4,500 poems	
	794–1185 Heian period: cultural life continues to flourish as capital moves to Heian (present-day Kyoto)
	800 Charlemagne crowned, inaugurating Holy Roman empire
ca. 890 *The Tale of the Bamboo Cutter,* first extant work of Japanese fiction	**9th century** Japanese syllabary is developed from Chinese characters
ca. 905 *The Kokinshū,* first imperially commissioned poetry anthology	
mid-10th century *Tales of Ise,* 125 brief lyrical episodes giving fictional context to one or more poems; influenced *The Tale of Genji*	
early 11th century *The Tale of Genji* (Murasaki Shikibu), considered world's first novel • *The Pillow Book* (Sei Shōnagon), collection of random observations on love, life at court, and human nature	**1180–1185** Gempei Wars end aristocratic monopoly of power, inspiring *The Tale of the Heike*
	1185–1333 Kamakura period: political center moves east to Kamakura with rise of warrior elite known as *samurai*

Boldface titles indicate works in the anthology.

TIME LINE

TEXTS	CONTEXTS
ca. 1206 *The New Kokinshū,* the eighth imperial anthology of poetry	
	1215 Magna Carta grants rights to "free men" of England
	1271–1295 Marco Polo journeys to China, opening trade routes and cultural ties between Europe and east Asia
13th–14th centuries **The Tale of the Heike,** an account of the Gem-pei Wars, which led to aristocracy's loss of wealth and political power	
1330s *Essays in Idleness* (Yoshida Kenkō), discursive observations revolving around aesthetic issues	1338–1573 Muromachi period: culture flourishes despite social upheaval, reflected in austere, introspective character of the arts
14th–16th centuries *Nō* drama flourishes: Zeami Motokiyo's **Atsu-mori** and **Haku Rakuten,** and **Dōjōji** by Kanze Kojirō Nobumitsu	
15th century Linked poetry, com-posed by several poets, develops from entertainment into favored literary form	15th century Rise of Zen Buddhism
1463 *Murmured Conversations* (Shinkei), a treatise on principles of linked poetry	
1488 *Three Poets at Minase,* a 100-verse sequence by Sōgi, Shōhaku, and Sōchō, epitomizes linked-poetry tradition	
	1519 Magellan circumnavigates globe, proving earth is round and revealing the Americas as a new world
	1543 Portuguese land in Japan, bringing firearms and Christianity
	1573–1600 Momoyama period: civil war leads to unification of Japan
	1597 Japanese build printing press with wooden movable type after Korean model in cast metal

THE MAN'YŌSHŪ
eighth century

The first monument of Japanese literature, and some would say its greatest, is a large collection of poetry whose range, complexity, and force still speak to us, more than one thousand years later, of the exuberance of a people experiencing literacy and cultural animation for the first time. Known as *The Man'yōshū* (The Collection of Ten Thousand Leaves), this earliest extant collection of Japanese poetry appears to have been intended as an anthology of anthologies. The compilers repeatedly refer to older anthologies, no longer existing, from which they have culled their selections. Furthermore, the "leaves" of the title refer not only to the poems but to future generations of readers, because, by tradition, the character for *leaf* also meant "age," or "generation." The anthologizers were proclaiming, then, that this "collection of ten thousand poems" (4,516 to be precise) was to serve as a "collection for ten thousand ages."

Such a claim might seem the height of audacity, given the circumstances. At the time that the last specifically dated poem in the collection was completed in 759, Japan had only recently emerged from a primitive preliterate past. A loose confederation of competing clans, who drew their wealth from the cultivation of rice and whose principal cultural accomplishment was the erection of enormous burial mounds equipped with clay statuary, had remade itself into a society with a national identity, a ruling imperial family, an elaborate government administration, a complex system of religious beliefs, a command of letters, and the other accouterments of civilization.

All this had been realized within the span of a mere century or two, as Japan worked frenetically to catch up with the world's exemplar of cultural sophistication: China. Once the Japanese comprehended the chasm separating them from this much older civilization, which by every standard—economic, political, and philosophical—threw their unseasoned situation into bold relief, national ambition and competitive pride propelled a stunning process of assimiliation. Where before there had been paddy fields and simple thatched-roof shrines intended to placate spirits residing in the rivers and mountains of the vicinity, now there were vast road networks, irrigation works, ports, and courier service and, in the capital, a hierarchy of court ranks, fine silks and brocades, and lacquered pagodas whose rooftops soared like the wings of a great bird gliding in mid-flight. These were all visible signs of the material progress Japan had accomplished as the diligent student of China.

But perhaps the most fateful decision that the Japanese made in their importation of Chinese culture was the bending of the Chinese writing system to the needs of their own very different language. The Chinese script, known as characters, had originated as a system of pictograms, evolving over time to incorporate pictographic, ideographic, and phonetic elements. Because it was designed solely to record the Chinese language and lacked the pliancy of a phonetic writing system—an alphabet or syllabary—the Chinese script required cumbersome manipulation before it could serve to record another language.

That the Japanese chose to borrow rather than invent a writing system makes them no different from most other peoples. The Greek alphabet, for example, is but a mutation of the Phoenician script, and the Roman alphabet merely the Greek slightly modified. What may set the Japanese apart, however (and would later become a cliché), is the ingenuity of their adaptation. The poems of *The Man'yōshū* were recorded using Chinese characters in three different ways: for meaning, for sound when read in Chinese, and for sound when read in Japanese. The character denoting "person," for instance, could naturally be used for its semantic value when the poet wanted to write the word *person*. But it could also be used to approximate the sound of its original Chinese pronunciation, *jen*, which Japanese phonology rendered *jin,* or *nin*. Or it could be used in an altogether different way. Because the Japanese word for "person" is *hito*, the character could represent that native sound in another word. For example, Hitomaro, the name of the first of the poets in the selections printed here, came to be written with the "person" character signifying the "Hito" element. The sheer perversity of this system (for there were thousands of Chinese characters to be mastered and the number had then to be multiplied by three) is a testament to the overwhelming desire of the Japanese people of the seventh and eighth centuries to express their new experiences through the written word.

Indeed the range of experience the early poets chronicled is one of the qualities that later generations of Japanese would prize in *The Man'yōshū*. Other qualities are its passion and sincerity, together with an innocence, vigor, and seeming artlessness that stand in marked contrast to the controlled, more self-conscious polish that would define Japanese poetry throughout the subsequent classical era. In the age of *The Man'yōshū*, the aristocratic customs of the court had yet to solidify into the weight of convention. And the cultural situation in Japan was still fluid enough that the aristocracy did not yet dominate.

In fact, one finds a surprising number of poems in *The Man'yōshū* by people completely outside court circles, whose literacy itself is surprising. The anonymous poems in the collection, nearly two thousand, far outnumber those by any of the known poets. There are rustic poems that tell of life in the wilderness of the eastern frontier, poems purportedly by fishers, poems recording local dialects, farewell poems by military conscripts, and even poems by travelers to Korea. Of course, one must allow for the possibility that aristocrats chose to romanticize rustic life, and no doubt some of the poems in a common voice are a reworking of folk elements. Nonetheless, in many cases sufficient internal evidence remains to convince scholars that a substantial number of the anonymous poems are the product of the ordinary citizen.

Authorship, however, is only one indication of the breadth of *The Man'yōshū*. Those poets who came from the privileged class and whose names we do know also ranged widely in their chosen topics. Kakinomoto Hitomaro* (flourished ca. 680–700), the undisputed master of the collection, captures the profound sadness of parting, the warrior's bravery, the shock of sudden death, the pageantry of the imperial institution, the burdens of travel, and the mysteries of the human fate. The three sets of poems included here by Hitomaro are representative of his genius. In the first he broods on the passing of time and the evanescence of worldly glory as he views the ruins of the ancient capital. In the second he laments the loneliness of parting from his wife. He depicts their union through the sensual imagery of stems of "sleek seaweed" that once "swayed toward" each other and intertwined but after too few nights have been sundered; the seaweed now grows alone "on the desolate shore."

Like so many of his best poems, it is a highly visual presentation. When the poet describes looking back through the falling leaves for a final glimpse of his wife, not only do we clearly see the sad autumn scene but we can picture the poet's wife disappearing before his (and our) eyes:

> And so I look back,
> still thinking of her . . .
> but in the storm
> of fallen scarlet leaves
> on Mount Watari,
> crossed as on
>   a great ship,
> I cannot make out the sleeves
> she waves in farewell.
> For she, alas,

*Names are given in the Japanese order, with surname first.

> is slowly hidden
> like the moon
> in its crossing
> between the clouds.

The same visual force is apparent in the third set of poems by Hitomaro, perhaps his most famous, inspired by the sight of a dead man lying amid the rocks on the forsaken shore of a distant island. Having traveled there through a storm that nearly cost him his own life, Hitomaro understandably identifies with the fate of the dead man. Through his rich use of imagistic language deployed in the lyric equivalent of narration, he makes us identify as well. In poems like these, Hitomaro perfected the techniques of the earliest Japanese poetry, still marked by the formulaic style of an oral tradition, and raised them to a poetry of high artistry.

What constituted that artistry is deceptively simple. Because the sound system of Japanese employs no stress accent, each syllable is pronounced with virtually equal emphasis, and the forms of meter based on stress that we associate with English poetry do not occur. Nor does rhyme figure in Japanese prosody. Most syllables consist of a single vowel or a consonant (or consonant cluster) followed by a vowel. With only five vowel sounds, given Japanese word structure, a poetry based on rhyme would be akin, as Robert Frost once said of free verse, to playing tennis without a net. Instead, Japanese poetry depended from its inception on the rhythm created by alternating phrases of long and short syllable counts. Japan's most archaic songs employ this pattern of alternation, which originally varied from combinations of phrases with four syllables paired with those of six to alternations of phrases of five syllables with those of three. Eventually, by the mid-seventh century the accepted pattern became an alternation of five and seven syllables, establishing a rhythm that would reign until the modern day.

The poets of *The Man'yōshū* compose in two principal forms. The *chōka*, or long poem, consists of an indeterminate number of lines of alternating five- and seven-syllable phrases, culminating in a couplet of two seven-syllable phrases. The *tanka*, or short poem, is identical in form to the last five lines of a *chōka*, that is, it is a thirty-one-syllable poem arranged in lines whose syllable counts are 5, 7, 5, 7, 7.

The long poems in *The Man'yōshū* are by far the rarest, and in fact the *chōka* disappears as a viable poetic form after *The Man'yōshū*. Approximately 4,200 of the 4,516 poems in the collection are *tanka*. Even most of the *chōka* have satellite *tanka* known as "envoys" that serve as a summing up or expand an imagistic or emotive theme from the original *chōka* to a fuller, still more lyrical realization.

Despite their numerical inferiority within the *The Man'yōshū* the longer poems by Hitomaro and others are what many readers remember best. No doubt their very scarcity makes them stand out against the subsequent history of a more confined form of poetry. At the same time, this mingling of *chōka* and *tanka* is yet another indication of the anthology's unusual range.

Among the finest *tanka* in the collection are the ironic poems in praise of wine by Ōtomo Tabito (665–731). Unlike Hitomaro, of whose extraliterary life we unfortunately know nothing, Tabito is a political figure with a well-documented government career. His affection for Chinese literature also sets him apart from Hitomaro, and his bibulous poems printed here are an excellent example of his expert handling of Chinese themes.

Like his friend Tabito, Yamanoue Okura (660–ca. 733), author of the last two sets of poems included here, was a devotee of Chinese culture. But the stances the two poets assume are completely different. If Tabito speaks as the Taoist epicure detached from the stress of life, Okura is the old Confucian gentleman, moralistic, with a strong sense of outrage at the ills of society. His poems on the impermanence of life treat a theme that had already become familiar in Japanese literature, but his poems on poverty depart radically from the norm. They become somewhat less radical, it is true, when we compare them with Chinese treatments of social injustice. Still, Okura's humble, earthy style, the vigor of his language, his genuine compassion, and the humorous, loving voice that breaks through his austere pose are all distinctive.

Owing to its amazing variety, *The Man'yōshū* has been all things to all readers. To some, it is proof that the earliest Japanese literature is derivative. For others, it is the repository of the essential Japanese identity: wholehearted, sincere, robust, and unaffected. It is important, however, to keep perspective. Susceptibility to influence does not preclude creative invention, and the Chinese example can best be viewed as a fertilizing one. Furthermore, a careful reading of *The Man'yōshū* reveals a work of considerable complexity, in which confidence in the artistic effect that language creates has overshadowed preliterate belief in the sheer incantatory power of words. Finally, it is one of the ironies of literary history that in the later generations invoked in the very title of the collection—for whom the poetic art was intended to endure—poetry was appropriated as the exclusive property of one group, the aristocracy. Compared with the later poetry of Japan's classical age, *The Man'yōshū*, in its diverse forms and multiplicity of voices, can rightly be viewed as the mirror of an entire nation.

Two good partial translations of *The Man'yōshū* exist in English: Nippon Gakujutsu Shinkōkai, *The Manyōshū* (1965), and Ian Hideo Levy, *The Ten Thousand Leaves* (1981). Both have informative introductions. Levy has also produced a detailed study of one poet, *Hitomaro and the Birth of Japanese Lyricism* (1984). The best overall study of *The Man'yōshū* is contained in Robert H. Brower and Earl Miner, *Japanese Court Poetry* (1961). For a concise history of Japan see John Whitney Hall, *Japan: From Prehistory to Modern Times* (1991), and for a short, general introduction to Japanese literature see Donald Keene, *The Pleasures of Japanese Literature* (1988).

PRONOUNCING GLOSSARY

The following list uses common English syllables to provide rough equivalents of selected words whose pronunciation may be unfamiliar to the general reader.

chōka: *choh-kah*

Dazaifu: *dah-zai-foo*

Iwami: *ee-wah-mee*

Izanagi: *ee-zah-nah-gee*

Izanami: *ee-zah-nah-mee*

Jinmu: *jeen-moo*

Kakinomoto Hitomaro: *kah-kee-noh-moh-toh hee-toh-mah-roh*

Kashiwara: *kah-shee-wah-rah*

Kyūshū: *kyoo-shoo*

Man'yōshū: *mahn-yoh-shoo*

Ōmi: *oh-mee*

Ōtomo Tabito: *oh-toh-moh tah-bee-toh*

Ōtsu: *oh-tsoo*

Samine: *sah-mee-ne*

Sanuki: *sah-noo-kee*

Sasanami: *sah-sah-nah-mee*

Shikoko: *shee-koh-ku*

tanka: *tahn-kah*

Unebi: *oo-ne-bee*

Watari: *wah-tah-ree*

Yamanoue Okura: *yah-mah-noh-oo-e oh-koo-rah*

Yamato: *yah-mah-toh*

FROM THE MAN'YŌSHŪ[1]

29–31

Poem written by Kakinomoto Hitomaro when he passed the ruined capital at Ōmi[2]

Since the reign of the Master of the Sun[3]
at Kashiwara by Unebi Mountain,
   where the maidens
      wear strands of jewels,
all gods who have been born   5
have ruled the realm under heaven,
each following each
like generations of the spruce,
   in Yamato[4]
that spreads to the sky.   10

What was in his mind
that he would leave it
and cross beyond the hills of Nara,
   beautiful in blue earth?
Though a barbarous place   15
at the far reach of the heavens,
here in the land of Ōmi
where the waters race on stone,
at the Ōtsu Palace
in Sasanami   20
   by the rippling waves,
the Emperor, divine Prince,
ruled the realm under heaven.

Though I hear
this was the great palace,   25
though they tell me
here were the mighty halls,
now it is rank with spring grasses.
Mist rises, and the spring sun is dimmed.
Gazing on the ruins of the great palace,   30
its walls once thick with wood and stone,
I am filled with sorrow.

ENVOYS

Cape Kara in Shiga
at Sasanami
   by the rippling waves,   35

---

1. All selections translated by and with notes adapted from Ian Hideo Levy.   2. Because of the ancient Japanese belief that death polluted a dwelling, when the sovereign died it was customary for his successor to take up residence in a new palace. The capital shifted from place to place among the central provinces, until an edict in 646 called for the establishment of a permanent center of government.   3. Emperor Jinmu, in legend the founding sovereign of Japan, credited with subduing rival chieftains to create the first Japanese state.   4. An archaic name for Japan, which originally referred to the area around present-day Nara.

you are as before, but I
wait for courtiers' boats in vain.

Waters, you are quiet
in deep bends of Shiga's lake
at Sasanami   40
    by the rippling waves,
but never again may I
meet the men of ancient times.

135–137

*Poem written by Kakinomoto Hitomaro when he parted from his wife in
the land of Iwami and came up to the capital*

At Cape Kara
on the Sea of Iwami,
where the vines
    crawl on the rocks,
rockweed of the deep   5
grows on the reefs
and sleek seaweed
grows on the desolate shore.
As deeply do I
think of my wife   10
who swayed toward me in sleep
    like the lithe seaweed.
Yet few were the nights
we had slept together
before we were parted   15
like crawling vines uncurled.
And so I look back,
still thinking of her
with painful heart,
this clench of inner flesh,   20
but in the storm
of fallen scarlet leaves
on Mount Watari,[1]
crossed as on
    a great ship,   25
I cannot make out the sleeves
she waves in farewell.
For she, alas,
is slowly hidden
like the moon   30
    in its crossing
        between the clouds
over Yagami Mountain
just as the evening sun

---

1. *Watari* means "crossing"; thus the leaves fall at the very spot where the poet might have caught one last
glimpse of his wife.

coursing through the heavens   35
has begun to glow,
        and even I
who thought I was a brave man
find the sleeves
of my well-woven robe   40
drenched with tears.

                    ENVOYS

The quick gallop
of my dapple-blue steed
races me to the clouds,
passing far away   45
from where my wife dwells.

O scarlet leaves
falling on the autumn mountainside:
stop, for a while, the storm
your strewing makes, that I might glimpse   50
the place where my wife dwells.

220–222

*Poem written by Kakinomoto Hitomaro upon seeing a dead man lying
among the rocks on the island of Samine in Sanuki*

The land of Sanuki,[1]
    fine in sleek seaweed:
is it for the beauty of the land
that we do not tire
    to gaze upon it?   5
Is it for its divinity
that we deem it most noble?
Eternally flourishing,
    with the heavens
        and the earth,   10
    with the sun
        and the moon,
the very face of a god—
so it has come down
        through the ages.   15

Casting off
from Naka harbor,
we came rowing.
Then tide winds

---

1. In Japan's creation myth Sanuki (part of the island now called Shikoku) was one of the first places to
be formed by the union of the gods Izanagi and Izanami.

blew through the clouds;   20
on the offing
we saw the rustled waves,
on the strand
we saw the roaring crests.
Fearing the whale-hunted seas,   25
our ship plunged through—
we bent those oars!
Many were the islands
near and far,
but we beached on Samine—   30
        beautiful its name—
and built a shelter
        on the rugged shore.

Looking around,
        we saw you   35
lying there
on a jagged bed of stones,
the beach
        for your finely woven pillow,
by the breakers' roar.   40
        If I knew your home,
I would go and tell them.
If your wife knew,
she would come and seek you out.
But she does not even know the road,   45
        straight as a jade spear.
Does she not wait for you,
        worrying and longing,
your beloved wife?

                    ENVOYS

If your wife were here,   50
she would gather and feed you
the starwort that grows
on the Sami hillsides,
but is its season not past?

Making a finely woven pillow   55
of the rocky shore
        where waves from the offing
                draw near,
you, who sleep there!

338–350

Thirteen poems in praise of wine by Lord Ōtomo Tabito, the Commander of the Dazaifu[1]

Rather than engaging
in useless worries,
it's better to down a cup
of raw wine.

Great sages of the past
gave the name of "sage"[2] to wine.
How well they spoke!

What the Seven Wise Men[3]
of ancient times
wanted, it seems,
was wine.

Rather than making pronouncements
with an air of wisdom,
it's better to down the wine
and sob drunken tears.

What is most noble,
beyond all words
and beyond all deeds,
is wine.

Rather than be half-heartedly human,
I wish I could be a jug of wine
and be soaked in it!

How ugly!
those men who,
with airs of wisdom,
refuse to drink wine.
Take a good look,
and they resemble apes.

How could even
a priceless treasure
be better than a cup
of raw wine?

---

1. Government headquarters in Kyūshū, southernmost of the four main islands of Japan, an important outpost for regulating contacts with China and Korea. In Tabito's time the flourishing city was nicknamed "the distant capital." 2. So called by those who drank it secretly during the brief time in ancient China when wine was prohibited by the emperor. 3. The Seven Sages of the Bamboo Grove of 3rd-century China, a Taoist coterie of wealthy dissidents who expressed their social and political disaffection by withdrawing into a kind of intellectual hedonism, given over to tippling, poetastering, and philosophical debate. One of the sages set the style for the group by employing an attendant who carried a wine jug in one hand to quench his master's thirst and a spade in the other to bury him if he fell dead.

How could even a gem
that glitters in the night
be as good as drinking wine
and cleansing the heart?

Here in this life,
on these roads of pleasure,
it is fun to sob drunken tears.

As long as I have fun
    in this life,
let me be an insect or a bird
    in the next.[4]

Since all who live
must finally die,
let's have fun
while we're still alive.

Smug and silent airs of wisdom
are still not as good
as downing a cup of wine
and sobbing drunken tears.

804–805[1]

Poem sorrowing on the impermanence of life in this world

PREFACE

Easy to gather and difficult to dispel are the eight great hardships.[2] Difficult to fully enjoy and easy to expend are the pleasures of life's century span.
So the ancients lamented, and so today our grief finds the same cause.
Therefore I have composed a poem, and with it hope to dispel the sorrow of
my black hair marked with white. My poem:

Our helplessness in this life
is like the streaming away
of the months and years.
Again and again
misfortune tracks us down   5
and assaults us with a hundred ills.
We cannot hold time
    in its blossoming:
        when young girls,
to be maidenly,   10
wrapped Chinese jewels
around their wrists

---

4. The poet adheres to the Buddhist belief in reincarnation, in which present deeds determine one's future
life.   1. By Yamanoue Okura.   2. In Buddhism, birth, old age, sickness, death, separation, anger,
coveting, and the so-called pain of five passions—the suffering derived from one's attachment to the five
elemental aggregates of which the body, mind, and environment are formed (perception, conception, volition, consciousness, and form).

and, hand in hand
with companions of their age,
must once have played.   15
When has frost fallen
on hair as black
as the guts of river snails?
From where do wrinkles come
to crease those crimson faces?   20
We have let time go.
        Once strong young men,
to be manly,
girt their waists
with great swords   25
and, tossing saddles
with cloth embroidered
        in Yamato patterns
on their red-maned steeds,
mounted and rode for sport—   30
how could it last forever?
Few were the nights
I pushed apart the wooden doors
that young girls creak open and shut
and, groping to their side,   35
slept arm in jewelled arm,
arm in truly jewelled arm!
But now I walk
with a cane gripped in my hand
and propped against my waist.   40
Going this way,
        I am despised.
Going that way,
        I am hated.
Such, it seems,   45
is the fate of old men.
Though I regret the passing
of my life,
        that swelled with spirit,
there is nothing I can do.   50

ENVOY

Like the unchanging cliffs,
I would remain just as I am.
But I am living in this world
and cannot hold time back.

892–893[1]

Dialog of the Destitute

"On nights when rain falls,
            mixed with wind,
on nights when snow falls,
            mixed with rain,
I am cold   5
And the cold.
        leaves me helpless:
I lick black lumps of salt
and suck up melted dregs of sake.[2]
Coughing and sniffling,   10
I smooth my uncertain wisps
            of beard.
I am proud—
        I know no man
            is better than me.   15
But I am cold.
I pull up my hempen nightclothes
and throw on every scrap
of cloth shirt that I own.
But the night is cold.   20
And I wonder how a man like you,
        even poorer than myself,
with his father and mother
starving and freezing,
with his wife and children   25
begging and begging
            through their tears,
can get through the world alive
            at times like this."

"Wide, they say,   30
            are heaven and earth—
but have they shrunk for me?
Bright, they say,
            are the sun and moon—
but do they refuse to shine for me?   35
Is it thus for all men,
            or for me alone?
Above all, I was born human,[3]
I too toil for my keep—
as much as the next man—   40
yet on my shoulders hangs
a cloth shirt
not even lined with cotton,
these tattered rags
thin as strips of seaweed.   45

---

1. By Yamanoue Okura.   2. A brewed alcoholic beverage made from fermented rice.   3. In the Buddhist doctrine of reincarnation one could not achieve enlightenment, thereby escaping the cyclical chain of rebirth, without first attaining the human level. In this, at least, he is fortunate.

In my groveling hut,
  my tilting hut,
sleeping on straw
cut and spread right on the ground,
with my father and mother   50
    huddled at my pillow
and my wife and children
    huddled at my feet,
I grieve and lament.
Not a spark rises in the stove,   55
and in the pot
a spider has drawn its web.
I have forgotten
what it is to cook rice!
As I lie here,   60
a thin cry tearing from my throat—
    a tiger thrush's moan—
then, as they say,
to slice the ends
of a thing already too short,   65
to our rough bed
comes the scream of the village headman
    with his tax collecting whip.
Is it so helpless and desperate,
the way of life in this world?"   70

ENVOY

I find this world
a hard and shameful place.
But I cannot fly away—
I am not a bird.

THE KOKINSHŪ
ca. 905

Even a fleeting acquaintance with Japanese poetry will reveal one of its most conspicuous features: extreme brevity. By the nineteenth century *haiku*, the best-known form outside Japan, had dwindled down to a scant seventeen syllables. But long before *haiku* began diminishing, Japanese poetry had already begun to shrink. In a period of less than one hundred years, from the completion of *The Man'yōshū* (in the second half of the eighth century) to the mid-ninth century, the thirty-one-syllable *tanka*, or short poem, consolidated its position as the preeminent poetic form and eclipsed forever the capacious *chōka*. Both the heroic and architectural possibilities that poets like Hitomaro had begun to explore for Japanese verse were exchanged in favor of a more constricted form.

    The nature of the language suited the short poem. In sound, Japanese has a remarkably simple structure. Almost always, vowels follow consonants, and syllables (and words) end in vowels. Because Japanese is composed of only five vowel sounds and possesses an abundance of homonyms, rhyming is too easy to be poetry. The creation of rhythmic patterns holds more interest, because Japanese is an agglutinative and polysyllabic language. It strings short semantic elements together into long, complex words. Its verbs and adjectives are highly inflected. Like a train with many cars attached, a Japanese verb will often carry a number of suffixes behind it, which qualify or soften the statement, affecting such things as the mood, probability, or duration of an action. A single verb many well require five or seven syllables—or an entire line of poetry. And the storehouse of suffixes whose nuances overlap but whose syllabic values differ combines with an assortment of emotive and exclamatory particles to create a language ripe for poetic manipulation. Japanese expresses itself in a fluid syntax, which tends to encourage indirection and subtle shadings of emotional perception over blunt and logical precision. A statement in five brief lines of five and seven syllables both takes advantage of the genius of the language and challenges the poet to stretch that language and his or her own wits beyond the confines of thirty-one syllables. At its best, the results are dazzling; at its worst, like all bad poetry, banal.

By the mid-ninth century, Japanese enjoyed another kind of fluidity. The unwieldy forcing of Chinese characters to represent Japanese sounds and words (including parts of speech that had never existed in Chinese) had been streamlined into a flexible writing system more appropriate to the needs of the native language. By abbreviating, or stylizing, certain Chinese characters to represent the sounds of their own language, the Japanese created a shorthand that could serve as a phonetic syllabary. This device gave the Japanese the best of two graphic worlds. The visually evocative quality of the Chinese characters could still be employed to represent the concepts expressed in nouns and the uninflected bases of verbs and adjectives. For example, the character representing "hand" to the Chinese was still used to write "hand" in Japanese. But now, when the Japanese needed to append suffixes to conjugate a verb or wanted to write a word that was onomatopoeic rather than conceptual, they could use the simpler phonetic script. While the Chinese characters retained their enormous prestige, any word could also be written phonetically. Reducing the number of characters one needed to command and letting the fifty elements of the syllabary fill in the gaps meant that authorship, in theory at least, fell within the purview of a wider circle.

In fact, this would prove to be only partially the case. Poetry in the new age was exclusively aristocratic. Among those at court, however, its practice was essential, and its uses were numerous. Indeed, with the exception of China, there has probably never been another society where the composition of poetry was so entwined in the fabric of everyday life. Although privilege was, of course, hereditary in the imperial court of the ninth through the twelfth centuries, the quality of a noble's existence depended to a large extent on his or her versatility as a poet. Both the large events of life and its passing pleasures were to be commemorated. The birth of a child elicited an onslaught of congratulatory verse, while to return from an outing when the cherries bloomed without having penned a suitable memento would quickly reduce one to social oblivion. A handsome, well-born man who was inarticulate was no better than a boor. His career as a bureaucrat would stagnate, and his prospects for an interesting love life were nil.

So described, classical Japanese poetry may sound precious or trivial. It could be. But the overarching demand that society placed on the educated person to be alert, sensitive, and verbally adept put a highly beneficial premium on appreciating and analyzing the nature of certain forms of human experience. The result is a lyrical, introspective poetry that tends to focus on two themes: human affairs and the emotions they engender (celebration, separation, grief, and especially love) and the affective qualities of nature (the four seasons in their changing aspects and the human response to the beauties of nature). These are restricted themes. War and battle are absent; no blood ever spills in classical poetry. Nor was anything remotely ugly or common allowed to impinge.

Nonetheless, the deceptively modest five-line poem developed into a vehicle of subtle and evocative power, capable of the most profound delineation of what it means to live, to love, to lose. The lyric themes of beauty and sadness dominate this poetry, together with an acute awareness of the implacable effects of time—which is, after all, the fundamental source of life's beauty and the ultimate cause of our sadness. In the end, one could say that the brief form this poetry assumed was itself the metaphor for its message.

But, surprisingly enough, brevity is only half the story. At the same time that Japanese poetry was fragmenting into shorter units, a countertrend was at work toward integration. This becomes clear when we examine the format in which tenth-century poets chose to "publish" their verse. Because poetry played a vital role in court society, preserving its best fruits became a major endeavor. The poets made personal collections of their own poems. The results of popular poetry contests were also recorded. And devotees often compiled private anthologies of their favorite poems, which sometimes served as source books on correct poetic usage or as textbooks for aspiring poets.

Far and away the most important form of "publishing," however, was the practice of imperially sponsored anthologizing. Perhaps inspired by the example of *The Man'yōshū*, Emperor Daigo (ruled 897–930) established a precedent that lasted through five hundred years and twenty-one anthologies when he commissioned his most literate courtiers to compile a collection that would combine the best poetry of the age with superior poems of the past. Titled *The Kokinshū* (Collection of Ancient and Modern Times), the anthology of 1,111 poems in twenty books was completed around 905 and set the pattern for all subsequent anthologies of classical Japanese verse. Two groups of books dominate the collection—the seasonal and love poems— and it is here that we can best appreciate the compilers' ingenious decision to counteract the fragmentation of Japanese poetry by integrating a series of short poems into a longer narrative sequence. In other words, the compilers of *The Kokinshū* set their sights much higher than simply assembling excellent poems.

In the case of the seasonal poems, with which the selections printed here begin, the progression is straightforward. We move from falling snow to haze and plum blossoms (both images associated with spring), and so on throughout the year, as one season gradually yields to another.

When we turn to the love poems, which constitute most of the remaining selections included here, the compilers' ability to fashion a single narrative out of poems by many different authors is even more impressive. As arranged in the collection, the poems chronicle the progress of a love affair from the first glimpse of the beloved through the various successive stages of romance: courtship, passion, marriage (or liaison), disillusion, separation, loneliness, despair. The poems printed here, it should be noted, are excerpts from the entire sequence, meant to distill the essence of the narrative progression.

Over time, the principles of association and progression invented by the compilers of *The Kokinshū* would become increasingly sophisticated. But already here in their first appearance these structural devices are evidence of the ability of one of the world's most laconic genres to transcend the limitations of its form.

Two complete translations of *The Kokinshū* are available in English: Helen Craig McCullough, *Kokin Wakashū: The First Imperial Anthology of Japanese Poetry* (1985), and Laura Rasplica Rodd and Mary Catherine Henkenius, *Kokinshū: A Collection of Poems Ancient and Modern* (1984); *A Waka Anthology*, translated, with a commentary and notes, by Edwin A. Cranston (1993–), is also recommended. McCullough's companion volume to her translation is a detailed study of the Chinese influences on the poems in the anthology, *Brocade by Night: "Kokin Wakashū" and the Court Style in Japanese Classical Poetry* (1985). Robert H. Brower and Earl Miner, *Japanese Court Poetry* (1961), is still the standard work and also the most comprehensive, covering classical poetry of all periods. For a collection of translations of classical poetry as well as poems from the age of *The Man'yōshū* and modern times, see Steven D. Carter, *Traditional Japanese Poetry: An Anthology* (1991).

The following list uses common English syllables to provide rough equivalents of selected words whose pronunciation may be unfamiliar to the general reader.

Ariwara Narihira: *ah-ree-wah-rah nah-ree-hee-rah*

chōka: *choh-kah*

Fujiwara Okikaze: *foo-jee-wah-rah oh-kee-kah-ze*

haiku: *hai-koo*

Ise: *ee-se*

Kasuga: *kah-soo-gah*

Ki no Tomonari: *kee noh toh-moh-nar-ree*

Ki no Tsurayuki: *kee noh tsoo-rah-yoo-kee*

Kokin Wakashū: *koh-keen wah-kah-shoo*

Kokinshū: *koh-keen-shoo*

Man'yōshū: *mahn-yoh-shoo*

Mibu no Tadamine: *mee-boo noh tah-dah-mee-ne*

Minemoto Muneyuki: *mee-ne-moh-toh moo-ne-yoo-kee*

Ono no Komachi: *oh-noh noh koh-mah-chee*

Ōshikōchi Mitsune: *oh-shee-koh-chee mee-tsoo-ne*

Sosei: *soh-say*

tanka: *tahn-kah*

Yoshino: *yoh-shee-noh*

FROM THE KOKINSHŪ[1]

9

When snow comes in spring—
fair season of layered haze
and burgeoning buds—
flowers fall in villages
where flowers have yet to bloom.

Ki no Tsurayuki

43

Shall I each springtime
see flowery shadows floating
on the flowing stream,
and drench my sleeve in water
that refuses to be plucked?

Lady Ise

---

1. All selections translated by and with notes adapted from Helen Craig McCullough. *The Kokinshū* opens with six books that constitute a sequence of seasonal poems, from which the first seventeen poems printed here are selected.

53

If ours were a world
where blossoming cherry trees
were not to be found,
what tranquility would bless
the human heart in springtime!

Ariwara Narihira

83

I cannot agree
that cherry blossoms scatter
uncommonly fast,
for a human heart may change
even before a wind blows.

Ki no Tsurayuki

89

In the lingering wake
of the breeze that has scattered
the cherry tree's bloom,
petal wavelets go dancing
across the waterless sky.

Ki no Tsurayuki

113

Alas! The beauty
of the flowers has faded
and come to nothing,
while I have watched the rain,
lost in melancholy thought.

Ono no Komachi

145

O cuckoo singing
amid the summer mountains:
if you have feelings,

do not harrow with your voice
one whose heart already aches.

Anonymous

153

Where does he journey—
the cuckoo whose song echoes
in the dead of night
while I sit lost in revery
listening to the summer rain?

Ki no Tomonori

166

Now that dawn has come
while the evening lingers
on this summer night,
in what cloudy hostelry
might the moon have gone to rest?

Kiyowara Fukayabu

191

With what radiance
the moon shines on an autumn night!
The eye can detect
each bird in the line of geese
flying amid snowy clouds.

Anonymous

232

Autumn has not come
for you alone, maidenflower,
nor has anyone
tired of you. Why then must you
lose your youth so very soon?

Ki no Tsurayuki

273

Did an age slip by
during those fleeting moments
when I dried my sleeves
drenched by chrysanthemum dew
on the path through the mountains?

Monk Sosei

297

Unseen by men's eyes,
the colored leaves have scattered
deep in the mountains:
truly we may say brocade
worn in the darkness of night!

Ki no Tsurayuki

305

I must pause to gaze
before crossing the river.
Though they fall like rain,
leaves dyed in autumn's colors
will not make the waters rise.

Ōshikōchi Mitsune

310

Watching the colors
in the river descending
from deep in the hills,
we feel the knowledge strike home:
this is autumn's final hour.

Fujiwara Okikaze

315

It is in winter
that a mountain hermitage
grows lonelier still,

for humans cease to visit
and grasses wither and die.

Minamoto Muneyuki

342

My heart fills with gloom
as I watch the year depart,
    for shadows descend
even on the face I see
reflected in the mirror.

Ki no Tsurayuki

349[1]

Scatter at random,
O blossoms of the cherry,
    and cloud the heavens,
that you may conceal the path
old age is said to follow.

Ariwara Narihira

460[2]

Is this hair of mine,
black as seeds of leopard-flowers,[3]
    altering its hue?
Flakes of white snow have fallen
on the head in the mirror.

Ki no Tsurayuki

471[4]

Swift indeed has been
the birth of my love for you—
    swift as the current

1. Following the seasonal poems, there are four short books in The Kokinshū devoted respectively to felicitations, parting, travel, and names of things. This poem is taken from the book of felicitations. 2. From the book of poems on names of things. In Japanese, the poem is a wordplay on the name of a river, Kamiyagawa. Embedded in the name are a homonym for "hair" (kami), plus an interrogative particle (ya), plus the stem of the verb "to alter" (gawa, the voiced variant of kawa), to which a final inflection is added, to produce "is altering." 3. Or blackberry lilies, a plant that yields seeds resembling black beads. The word (nubatama) became a standard poetic epithet whose meaning is equivalent to "pitch dark" or "jet black." 4. The next twenty-two poems are selected from the love sequence, the five books that follow the book of poems on names of things.

where waves break high over rocks
in the Yoshino River.

Ki no Tsurayuki

478

Ah! You of whom I saw
no more than of the grasses
beginning to sprout
between the patches of snow
on the plain of Kasuga!

Mibu no Tadamine

493

Others have told me
quiet pools are to be found
in the swiftest stream.
Why, then, is this love of mine
all unrelieved turbulence?

Anonymous

522

Less profitable
than writing on the waters
of a flowing stream—
such is the futility
of unrequited passion.

Anonymous

552

Did you come to me
because I dropped off to sleep
tormented by love?
If I had known I dreamed,
I would not have awakened.

Ono no Komachi

553

Since encountering
my beloved as I dozed,
I have come to feel
that it is dreams, not real life,
on which I can pin my hopes.

Ono no Komachi

625

The hours before dawn
seem saddest of all to me
since that leave-taking
when I saw in the heavens
the pale moon's indifferent face.

Mibu no Tadamine

635

Autumn nights, it seems,
are long by repute alone:
scarcely had we met
when morning's first light appeared,
leaving everything unsaid.

Ono no Komachi

647

But little better
than the vivid dream I dreamt
was our encounter
in reality's darkness,
black as leopard-flower[1] seeds.

Anonymous

656

In the waking world
you must, I suppose, take care,

1. See n. 3, p. 2167.

but how it pains me
that you should keep out of sight
even in the realm of dreams.

Ono no Komachi

657

Yielding to a love
that recognizes no bounds,
    I will go by night—
for the world will not censure
one who treads the path of dreams.

Ono no Komachi

658

Though I go to you
ceaselessly along dream paths,
    the sum of those trysts
is less than a single glimpse
granted in the waking world.

Ono no Komachi

676

Pillows know, they say,
and so we slept without one.
    Why then do rumors
like swirling pillars of dust
rise as high as the heavens?

Lady Ise

712

If this were a world
in which there were no such thing
    as false promises,
how great would be my delight
as I listened to your words!

Anonymous

741

Since your heart is not
an abandoned capital
    sinking in ruin,
why should your feeling for me
seem thus to wither away?

Lady Ise

746

This very keepsake
is now a source of misery,
    for were it not here
there might be fleeting moments
when I would not think of you.

Anonymous

747[1]

Is this not the moon?
And is this not the springtime,
    the springtime of old?
Only this body of mine
the same body as before . . .

Ariwara Narihira

756

How fitting it seems
that tears should dampen the face
    even of the moon,
whose image visits my sleeve
as I sit lost in sad thought.

Lady Ise

---

1. This is one of the most famous poems in *The Kokinshū*, where its context is explained in a headnote: "Once, quite without premeditation, Narihira began to make love to a lady who lived in the western wing of a palace belonging to the Gojō Empress. Shortly after the Tenth of the First Month, the lady moved away with no word to him. He learned where she had gone, but it was impossible to communicate with her. In the spring of the following year, when the plum blossoms were at their finest, memories of the preceding year drew him back to the western wing on a beautiful moonlit night. He lay on the floor of the bare room until the moon sank low in the sky."

770

At my dwelling place
even the paths have vanished,
    swallowed by rank growth
while I have waited in vain
for someone whose love has cooled.

Archbishop Henjō

791

Could I think myself
like a winter-wasted field,
    this fiery passion
might offer hope that springtime
would bring a new growth of love.

Lady Ise

797

So much I have learned:
the blossom that fades away,
    its color unseen,
is the flower in the heart
of one who lives in this world

Ono no Komachi

810

If it had ended
before others knew of it,
    then despite my grief
I might at least have declared,
"There was nothing between us."

Lady Ise

834[1]

I should have called it
no more than a fleeting dream,

---

1. After the love poems, *The Kokinshū* concludes with five brief books designated laments; miscellaneous poems—parts one and two; unorthodox poems; and poems from the bureau of poetry, which were sacred verse and poems of folk origin. This poem and number 861 are from the book of laments.

yet it seemed to me
to possess reality—
this world in which we exist.

Ki no Tsurayuki

861

Upon this pathway,
I have long heard others say,
   man sets forth at last—
yet I had not thought to go
so very soon as today.

Ariwara Narihira

884[2]

Must the moon vanish
in such great haste, leaving us
   still unsatisfied?
Retreat, O rim of the hills,
and refuse to let it set.

Ariwara Narihira

895

If I had but known
old age would come seeking me,
   then locking my gate
I would have answered, "Not home,"
and refused to receive him.

Anonymous

901

For sorrowing sons
who would have their parents live
   a thousand long years—
how I wish that in this world
there were no final partings.

Ariwara Narihira

2. The last five poems are selected from miscellaneous poems—parts one and two.

938

In this forlorn state
I find life dreary indeed:
    if a stream beckoned,
I would gladly cut my roots
and float away like duckweed.

Ono no Komachi

1000

I long for a way
to recapture bygone times,
    to see the palace
of which I but hear rumors
noisy as a rushing stream.

Lady Ise

MURASAKI SHIKIBU
ca. 973–1016

The Tale of Genji is the undisputed masterpiece of Japanese prose and the first great novel in the history of world literature. It was written in the early eleventh century by Murasaki Shikibu, a woman of the lower reaches of the aristocracy. Murasaki was the daughter of a provincial governor, but her service as lady-in-waiting to the empress allowed her the most intimate glimpse of the social and political doings of the imperial court. Unlike the fanciful romances that preceded it, *The Tale of Genji* (ca. 1001–13) is revered for its psychological insight, capturing a world that, however remote it might eventually become in time, has always retained the sharp authenticity of real life.

Vast in scale and peopled by hundreds of characters, this thousand-page novel has a plot of supreme simplicity. It depicts the lives and loves of a former prince and, following his death, the lives and loves of his descendants. But in a novel in which everything is finely calibrated, things are seldom really simple. To begin with, why is the hero a *former* prince? Though he is cherished by his father, the emperor, political exigencies force his removal from the imperial line. The family name *Genji* is bestowed on him, along with the sobriquet "the shining one" and generous emoluments. Nonetheless, before the first chapter is even over, the young hero has already lost the most important attribute of a man of his rank: the chance to rule someday as emperor.

Because political concerns were of little interest to the author except implicitly, she is not about to dissect the career of a favorite son as he rises through the ranks of the government. She is interested instead in how one compensates, substitutes, and replaces and in larger issues than worldly success: fate, retribution, sexual attraction, and the emotional depth of human experience.

What begins as the story of a glittering existence darkens with time. The sensitive aristocrat discovers more of life, including failure. Yet this is no ordinary story of age bringing wisdom or of the past repeating itself. As Murasaki augments her tale (which seems to have grown more by accretion than by blueprint), she questions, attenuates, and sometimes undermines the fundamental presumptions of its earlier portions.

By the time Genji dies two-thirds of the way through the book, a deep pessimism has taken over. We have entered a world diminished, not only because Genji is gone but because his survivors are somehow smaller people, flawed fragments of their forebears. Murasaki now follows the hapless lives of Genji's two descendants, but here again things are not as simple as they appear. One of the two possesses the ultimate flaw of inauthenticity. He is only passing as Genji's son, being in fact, the issue of an illicit union between Genji's wife and the son of Genji's best friend. In their different ways, the two scions represent a sad falling off. The real grandson is frivolous and inconsequential, and the putative son is so wracked by neurotic indecision that he has been dubbed world literature's first antihero.

Though the armature supporting this long story lies in the lives of three men, it is fundamentally a work of women's literature. To a degree that would have been the envy of European women writers as recently as Virginia Woolf, Murasaki thrived in a culture where women had the leisure, financial security, and intellectual freedom to become writers of significance. "A woman must have money and a room of her own if she wants to write fiction," Virginia Woolf said in 1929. She was lamenting the fact that until the late eighteenth century such favorable conditions were usually wanting and Western literature was the poorer for its slender pantheon of women writers.

The situation in Murasaki's day, courtly Japan of nearly a thousand years earlier, could not have been more different. True, women led a circumscribed existence. The role of a lady was to marry and bear children, and if she came of a suitably good family, she was apt to find herself a pawn in the marriage politics of the imperial court. The most influential family of the time, the Fujiwara, had attained its influence by marrying daughters to emperors, who produced new emperors who could be dominated by their maternal grandfathers. (Murasaki was herself a member of a subsidiary branch of the Fujiwara family.) A noblewoman's days were spent behind curtains and screens, hidden from the world (or from the male world). The verb *to see* constituted an act of possession and was synonymous with having sexual relations. Proper ladies were not seen casually. Nor did they enjoy the same mobility as men or have careers, except as ladies-in-waiting.

They did, however, have the requisite leisure that Virginia Woolf specified. And they had the income. Although at this time Japan was a polygamous society, women of the aristocracy retained a degree of independence, thanks to a system of matrilineal inheritance, so that a well-born woman was not solely dependent on her husband for financial support.

Most important of all, the women of Murasaki's circle had the intellectual attainments to produce literature. Theirs was an education by default, but it was an education all the same. As is so often the case in early Japanese literature, the issue of language becomes crucial. Despite the new native writing system (described in the headnote *"The Kokinshū,"* p. 2161) and the birth of an indigenous Japanese literature, both Chinese script and the Chinese language retained tremendous authority in eleventh-century Japan. Chinese, not Japanese, was the official language of the government, whose organization and institutions were themselves based on the model of China. The bureaucracy, the legal codes, political theory, even the calendar were of Chinese origin. To prepare for a career in the administration of the government—the only career for a male aristocrat—required a thorough education in the Chinese classics (for example, the *Classic of Poetry*, p. 812; Po Chü-i, p. 1393), which made Chinese both the language of the practical, workaday world of men and the medium of intellection, like Latin in medieval Europe.

A command of Chinese was considered irrelevant to a woman's life, and if she happened to pick it up, this "mannish" attainment was best concealed. In her diary, Murasaki tells us this:

> When my brother, Secretary at the Ministry of Ceremonial, was a young boy learning the Chinese classics, I was in the habit of listening to him and I became unusually proficient at understanding those passages which he found too difficult to grasp. Father, a most learned man, was always regretting the fact: "Just my luck!" he would say. "What a pity she was not born a man!"*

After that, Murasaki feigned ignorance and turned her attention to the native language.

Left to their own devices and with plenty of time on their hands, Murasaki and her female contemporaries explored the potential of their own language and discovered it to be a supple instrument for a literature of introspection. One of the remarkable aspects of *The Tale of Genji* and other great works by women writers of Murasaki's time is that they appeared so early in the development of the native literature. Or put another way, it is astonishing that the prestige of the Chinese classics, which permeated every official element of Japanese life, should have proved a less formidable obstacle than the Greek and Latin precedent did in Europe to the rise of a vernacular literature. All evidence suggests that this was mainly thanks to women like Murasaki, whose talent and passion for expression were indomitable.

And what was it Murasaki wanted to express in writing *The Tale of Genji*? This is a question the Japanese have spent nearly a millennium answering, not because the novel is opaque but because it is so various. Perhaps the most obvious reading of the tale is to see it as a sexual poetics, a study of the distinctive features of love—its language, forms, and conventions. This is not to suggest that *Genji* is in any way an erotic novel. In the customs of the time, men took principal wives and secondary wives, akin to concubines, as well as the occasional lover. Men moved about with a great degree of sexual freedom. Women did not; they waited. It was not only attention and affection they sat waiting for behind their screens but a definition of themselves, which depended entirely on male recognition.

The whole process was fraught with uncertainty. If a man came, would he come again? A woman's position depended more on the frequency of the man's visits than on any formal arrangements. And even marriage, that is to say as the principal wife, was no guarantee of domestic security. A man's first wife usually remained with her parents, and he visited. Secondary wives also tended to live separately from their husbands. The man, then, was often elsewhere, and the tension that this produced on the woman's part in the form of longing, loneliness, insecurity, jealousy, resentment, and other vulnerabilities was balanced on the man's part by the unhappy fate of being forever on the outside looking in (or trying to), the endless traveler, the incessant aggressor. Both sides were condemned to a world of physical separation, with all its attendant agonies. And this is what Murasaki is really interested in: the dynamics of love at the emotional and psychological level, not the physical. Courtship and seduction might seem to form the central theme of the novel, but the real theme is the longing to connect with another person.

That is why Genji's life and the lives of his successors are presented as a search for the ideal woman. Like a symphony unfolding with its themes and variations, the novel announces early on its main motif. In the second chapter, *The Broom Tree* (the first of the selections printed here), the seventeen-year-old Genji and his friends while away a rainy night in his quarters at the palace debating what makes the perfect woman. In the process, the young men trade stories of their experiences with women, which, to their credit, involve fewer conquests than failures. But they remain unde-

*Richard Bowring, *Murasaki Shikibu: Her Diary and Poetic Memoirs* (1982), p. 139.

terred to a man, and the rest of the long novel continues the quest for fulfilment in love.

Thus, in the manner of music, this early chapter anticipates episodes to follow, which in turn generate other episodes and further repercussions. The characters are unaware of it, but when Genji's best friend, Tō no Chūjō, mentions his most memorable affair, he describes the very woman with whom Genji will soon fall in love and whose death will be caused by the jealousy it inspires in a rival. These events appear in Chapter 4, *Evening Faces*. And they too have repercussions later in the novel (see *Fireflies*), when Genji, now thirty-six, pursues the daughter of this same woman. In a twist of fate emblematic of the novel's pattern, the young lady, Tamakazura, is the child of Tō no Chūjō, and the product of the affair he recounted some twenty years before when the young courtiers spent their rainy night trying to define perfect love.

Gradually, through age and experience, the once-charmed Genji begins to comprehend that there is no such thing. The tale of his life may be read as a progress from youthful idealism (involving its share of insensitivity) to disillusion and then on to the edges of insight. It may further be read, in the lives of Genji's incomplete descendants, as an ironic comment on the novel's own earlier ideals—a parable about the process of maturing and the realization that all human bonds are by nature defective.

If the lives of the heroes represent a fruitless quest for the perfect woman, Murasaki's chronicle seems also a quest, ultimately abandoned, for the perfect man. One can easily imagine Murasaki in the tedium of slow-moving days at court, or perhaps on her own long rainy night, amusing herself and her empress by conjuring up a man who would not disappoint them. In the early pages of the novel, Genji possesses every manly virtue. "He had grown into a lad of such beauty," we are told, "that he hardly seemed meant for this world—and indeed one almost feared that he might only briefly be a part of it." He is witty, artistic, amusing, sophisticated, influential, generous, and more than any of his peers, understanding of women—in short, irresistible. Even his learning takes the breath away: "When he was seven he went through the ceremonial reading of the Chinese classics, and never before had there been so fine a performance. Again a tremor of apprehension passed over the emperor—might it be that such a prodigy was not to be long for this world?"

In fact, Genji endures into his early fifties (a ripe enough age for the era), and there is ample time to see him fall short of perfection. Very quickly Murasaki forsook romance, the tale's antecedent, in favor of realism. At the start, it is a cheerful sort of realism, but it darkens as the novel progresses, and we can detect this already in *Suma* and *Akashi*. The twin chapters are numbers twelve and thirteen of the novel, relatively early in a work of fifty-four chapters. Even so, the idealization of Genji that we saw in *The Broom Tree* has been muted by now. Genji has transgressed, and he is exiled. His expansive appetite for life has finally got him into real trouble.

The proximate cause of exile is an unwise affair with the daughter of a rival family, which Genji's enemies use as a pretext to remove him from the capital. But the actual, or moral, cause is a serious misstep. Genji has also had an affair with his father's consort, Fujitsubo, and the secret liaison has produced a child. While, strictly speaking, he has not violated the taboo on sexual relations between close family members, since Fujitsubo is his stepmother, Genji has come perilously close, and he has disturbed the imperial succession. His transgression is rooted in a central theme of the novel: repetition and substitution. Things that happen once have an uncanny tendency to recur under a slightly different guise. In Buddhist belief life is a wheel; as it spins we confront situations that echo our past, or the fates of those before us. But this sense of repetition is also partly an illusion. Nothing is exactly the same, much as we sometimes want it to be. And this is Genji's problem. His desire for a mother he lost when still a child has led him to seek substitutions. His father's consort is the closest substitute of all, since the grief-stricken emperor had originally selected the woman precisely because of her resemblance to Genji's mother.

Murasaki understands not only the sheer recklessness of her protagonist but also Genji's complex psychological makeup. When Genji trifles with the incest taboo, it is not only lust that drives him. It is the lure of the forbidden, intertwined with the persistent need for a symbolic repossession of his mother and perhaps even an unconscious will to disrupt the political order. It could well be that Genji's "theft" of the emperor's wife is the subliminal revenge of a fallen prince who lost paradise too young to recall it with equanimity. In any case, Murasaki fully appreciates how seductive prohibition can be. And she continually observes in her novel the multifarious ways that obsession demands to be reincarnated.

In exile, Genji has time to ruminate on his failings, but also to seek new substitutes for the women he has left behind in the capital. The wheel of life keeps turning. Genji pursues women to replace other women. In time, he himself sees the pattern. Eventually, his own wife is unfaithful. He cannot help remembering his father and wondering if, though the emperor remained silent, he knew. Genji's youthful misdeeds have come back to haunt him. By the end of his life he comprehends what unhappiness he has caused others.

Charming and handsome, gifted and ardent, rakish but faithful in his own way (unlike other men, he never abandons any woman he has loved), Genji is a charismatic figure. Yet he is also one of the most problematic of literary characters. All the world loves a lover perhaps, but even when he brings pain and suffering to so many of his loves? Genji may intend only the best for these women—he is inherently kind and noble—but his generous intentions are clouded by an impetuous, self-centered streak that lingers long after youth might have excused it. A man of taste he may be, gregarious and totally alive; Genji is also a past master of lechery, hypocrisy, and self-deceit. His sexual connoisseurship can seem positively arrogant, though not so different from the reported behavior of some of our own heroes in the twentieth century, from rock stars to politicians. Readers may hate Genji or adore him or fall somewhere in between, but we can hardly deny that his creator has fashioned a character both larger than life and believably human.

In a certain way, one ends up feeling sorry for Genji. The eleventh-century Japanese version of machismo was as emotionally confining for a man of his delicate sentiment as court conventions were physically restricting for women. Both sexes paid the price of membership in a beautiful, exclusive little world. If the Buddhist wheel is turning, it is on a very short axis. Even the aristocrat's privileged myopia cannot obscure, finally, the ways actions have consequences—which are, if anything, magnified by the tight compass of their closed circle. Murasaki understands, as her characters do not, that narrow horizons bring their own penalties.

Loss, substitution, repetition. Transgression and retribution. In a work as oceanic as the Bible, here too the sins of the father are visited on the children. If Genji is flawed, his descendants are imperfection intensified. Time is succession, and life itself substitution. Just as youth will not return, neither will youthful assumptions. The full measure of the story's profundity is not merely its extraordinary insights into human nature, but its subversion of its own earlier suppositions. For many people *The Tale of Genji* has been a discovery. The novel's continually expanding reflection and self-scrutiny have shown them a way to look at themselves. For such readers, *Genji* is more than a book, it is an experience of life.

Nonetheless, a full appreciation of this work will elude us if we fail to comprehend some of the fundamental practical aspects and assumptions underpinning eleventh-century Japanese society. In many ways, the world of the imperial court might seem by our standards a misogynistic one. It was probably no more so, however, than European society in the Middle Ages or the Renaissance, or even the Victorian era. Its patriarchal hierarchies that denied women a formal education or a public role (except for the empress) and relegated them to a life of seclusion find their disconcerting echo in traditional Western attitudes. It is worth remembering that American women did not win the right to vote until 1919. If Buddhist doctrine held that women were inferior creatures who must first be reborn as men before attaining enlightenment or salvation, the Bible also made clear where women have customarily fit in the pecking order. Genesis asserts that the female body was created from the male and 1 Corinthians 11.3 that "the head of every man is Christ; and the head of the woman is the man."

Life for European women in the eleventh century may have been every bit as confining as it was for their Japanese sisters. Western women of the Middle Ages were also expected to live behind walls, either at home or in a convent. Even to stand by an open window was to venture too close to the outside world—the world of men— and thus risk corruption. When religious faith or family obligations made an excursion necessary, a woman was to be escorted by a servant or family member and told to keep her eyes "so low that nothing but where you put your feet matters to you."* She was instructed not to laugh, and if she must smile not to show her teeth. If she was discouraged by this world of repression, the appropriate response was not to sob or wring her hands but to suffer, predictably, in silence.

In eleventh-century Japan, however, neither laughter nor tears nor sexuality were denied women. On the contrary, the Japanese view of sex was relatively liberated. Stemming perhaps from the ancient Chinese belief that sexual intercourse was physically beneficial, the Japanese of the time attached no sense of sin to carnal relations or undue value to virginity. A woman of the upper classes was expected to be sexually alive, but this does not mean that she was licentious. In a society as stratified as the imperial court, relations between the sexes were highly regulated. Yet the underlying economic and political imperatives of a clan-based aristocracy sanctioned polygamous intermarriage, and a certain amount of premarital experimentation was deemed necessary to ensure sexual compatibility and thus progeniture. As in most polygamous societies, however, the actual number of wives kept by a Japanese aristocrat was small, usually no more than two or three—hardly harems—for the saying went that to keep many wives was to suffer many troubles.

A man's first marriage normally took place when he was, in today's view, still a boy of twelve or thirteen; women were a year or two younger. Because of the ages of the spouses and the fact that the first marriage in particular tended to be a political and economic arrangement, both husband and wife were eventually apt to seek love elsewhere. Until modern times the Japanese have not expected marriage, romance, and erotic love to weave a seamless whole. The purpose of marriage was procreation, continuation of the family line, and the striking of advantageous alliances with other families. Love had other purposes, and sexual gratification, far from being "the abomination of the flesh" that medieval Christianity condemned, was but another natural need. So long as its fulfillment did not compete with a man's responsibilities to his family, society tolerated his amours. Sometimes he found them in his other marriages. Sometimes these too were political arrangements, and the romantic type would have to seek his bliss in a discreet affair.

The possibility of forming such a liaison had much to do with the living arrangements of the time. Ordinarily a man's several wives lived in different establishments. His first wife would typically remain in her parent's house. Initially, the young husband might take up residence there or merely visit. Sometimes her parents would furnish the newlyweds with a house of their own, though this was less common when the couple married at a young age, since the maternal grandparents would then assume many of the child-rearing duties. If in time a man took a second or third wife he would usually live with his first (and main) wife and commute among the separate residences. His periodic absence obviously created a certain leeway. Thus a woman in eleventh-century Japan had greater liberty than her counterpart in medieval Europe, but it was definitely the man who moved about, while the woman stayed rooted to her spot.

*Christiane Klapisch-Zuber, ed., *A History of Women*, vol. 2 (1992), p. 95.

Among the practical ramifications of this multiple marriage system was the custom for the children of the first, or principal, wife to receive favored support from their father, although he remained a distant figure in their upbringing. Because the primary responsibility for child-rearing lay with the mother and her family and because a daughter usually inherited her parents' house (in addition sometimes to other property, including, perhaps, rights to income from provincial estates), a typical household in aristocratic Japanese society had a strong matriarchal component, despite its patriarchal clan affiliation. From the European perspective, Japanese noblewomen were surprisingly independent—economically and, to a certain extent, sexually. Yet the porous nature of marriage, which could be dissolved by the simple cessation of relations, left women emotionally vulnerable, as *The Tale of Genji* repeatedly demonstrates.

The tale also demonstrates a seemingly casual attitude toward what current Western convention would regard as incest, particularly Genji's affair with his stepmother, Fujitsubo, and his marriage to Murasaki,* whom he first treats as an adopted daughter. The young Murasaki is distressed and bewildered when Genji forces himself on her, but it is significant that none of her attendants are especially surprised, and there are those who assume that the two are already married. In the eleventh-century Japanese practice of endogamy, in this case intermarriage within one's own aristocratic clique, the only unions apparently considered incestuous were those between biological parents and children or between brothers and sisters. If the young Murasaki finds Genji's sudden advances "gross and unscrupulous," it is not because his actions amount to incest but because she is experiencing, unprepared, the disconcerting awakening of sexuality in a manner that shows Genji at his most selfish. The world of Genji will continue to startle, if not shock, us unless we remember that prohibitions governing one culture will not necessarily govern another. Just as we may be astonished by what did or did not constitute incest in Murasaki's society, Murasaki might well have been amazed to be told, for example, that in ancient Egypt and Persia marriage between the closest blood relatives was required by law.

The assumptions of societies, then, are not universal. A good example of this is the Japanese conception of time. Since 1873 Japan has followed the Gregorian calendar of the West, but the official calendar employed in Japan in the eleventh century derived from China and was divided into twelve lunations (months) of twenty-nine or thirty days. The resulting lunar year was approximately eleven days shorter than a solar year, which required the insertion of a thirteenth intercalary month every third year or thereabout to align the calendrical year with the solar. In addition, by custom the Japanese year began slightly later than the Western, so that New Year's Day fell anywhere from January 15 to February 15. The beginning of the new year also marked an increase in one's age, in contrast to the Western practice of reckoning age by birthdays. A child born in the twelfth month, for instance, would turn two with the new year.

Years were numbered serially from the year when a reigning emperor ascended the throne. In the modern period (beginning in 1868) the reign of an emperor has one name for its duration. For example, the reign of Emperor Hirohito is called the Shōwa ("enlightened peace") era, which lasted from his ascension in 1926 until his death in 1989. In addition to following the Western practice of numbering years by the Gregorian calendar, the year 1930, say, is reckoned as Shōwa 5. In the premodern period, rather than having one name throughout, an emperor's reign was usually divided into various eras, each with its own name.

In the eleventh century, both the months and the hours of the day were designated by the signs of the Chinese zodiac. The day was divided into twelve units, each equivalent to 120 minutes:

---

*The origin of the nickname court circles eventually gave Murasaki Shikibu (no doubt because the character is Genji's favorite). The second element of her name, Shikibu, refers to her father's official title.

Hour	Modern Equivalent
1 Rat	11 P.M.–1 A.M.
2 Ox	1 A.M.–3 A.M.
3 Tiger	3 A.M.–5 A.M.
4 Rabbit	5 A.M.–7 A.M.
5 Dragon	7 A.M.–9 A.M.
6 Snake	9 A.M.–11 A.M.
7 Horse	11 A.M.–1 P.M.
8 Ram	1 P.M.–3 P.M.
9 Monkey	3 P.M.–5 P.M.
10 Rooster	5 P.M.–7 P.M.
11 Dog	7 P.M.–9 P.M.
12 Boar	9 P.M.–11 P.M.

These hours were carefully measured at court with the use of a water clock to ensure that official rites, changes of the palace guard, and so forth could be observed accurately. Beyond the court, time keeping was less precise. In *The Tale of Genji*, when characters are at court, Murasaki cites the exact time, say the hour of the horse, but when they are away from court she gives only an approximation, like "the sun was high."

As you read *The Tale of Genji* you will quickly notice that poetry figures extensively in the lives of Genji and his fellow courtiers. Occasionally, they quote an existing poem. Knowledge of the canon was a necessary accomplishment for any self-respecting aristocrat. Most of the time, however, members of the nobility composed their own, original poems, peppered with traditional allusions. The thirty-one-syllable *tanka* was the verbal repository of court etiquette and cultural values. It was also the principal means of communication—the equivalent of a letter of condolence, a holiday greeting, a farewell note, a postcard, a eulogy, an invitation, a toast, a love letter. With this in mind, it is not surprising that poetry occurs so frequently in the text, although you may be surprised to see it rendered by the translator in couplets rather than in the conventional five lines of the poems in *The Kokinshū*.

There are two English translations of *The Tale of Genji*, and both have their partisans. The older translation, first published in installments between 1925 and 1933, is by Arthur Waley, *The Tale of Genji* (1960). A recent translation in a more contemporary idiom is by Edward G. Seidensticker, *The Tale of Genji* (1976). The Seidensticker translation, chosen here, is generally acknowledged to be the more faithful. Of the secondary works, the best brief introduction is Richard Bowring, *The Tale of Genji* (1988). Two excellent longer studies are Norma Field, *The Splendor of Longing in the "Tale of Genji"* (1987), and Haruo Shirane, *The Bridge of Dreams: A Poetics of "The Tale of Genji"* (1987). A collection of essays on the last part of the novel representative of recent American scholarship is Andrew Pekarik, ed., *Ukifune: Love in "The Tale of Genji"* (1982). For a glimpse into the life of the author see Richard Bowring, *Murasaki Shikibu: Her Diary and Poetic Memoirs* (1982). Ivan Morris, *The World of the Shining Prince*, with a new introduction by Barbara Ruch (1994), is a colorful account of the period during which Murasaki was writing as well as the standard introduction to the subject.

PRONOUNCING GLOSSARY

The following list uses common English syllables to provide rough equivalents of selected words whose pronunciation may be unfamiliar to the general reader.

Akashi: *ah-kah-shee*   Asagao: *ah-sah-gah-oh*

Akikonomu: *ah-kee-koh-noh-moo*   Atemiya: *ah-te-mee-yah*

Aoi: *ah-oy*   aware: *ah-wah-re*

Chūjō: *choo-joh*

Chūnagon: *choo-nah-gohn*

Fujitsubo: *foo-jee-tsoo-boh*

Fujiwara: *foo-jee-wah-rah*

Genji: *gen-jee*

Gojō: *goh-joh*

Gosechi: *goh-se-chee*

Hiei: *hee-ay*

Higekuro: *hee-ge-koo-roh*

Hirohito: *hee-roh-hee-toh*

Hitachi: *hee-tah-chee*

Hotaru: *hoh-tah-roo*

hototogisu: *hoh-toh-toh-gee-soo*

Kamo: *kah-moh*

Kaoru: *kah-oh-roo*

Kashiwagi: *kah-shee-wah-gee*

Kasugano: *kah-soo-gah-noh*

Katano: *kah-tah-noh*

Kii: *kee-ee*

Kokiden: *koh-kee-den*

Koremitsu: *koh-ray-mee-tsoo*

Kumano: *koo-mah-noh*

Kumoinokari: *koo-moy-noh-kah-ree*

Matsushima: *mah-tsoo-shee-mah*

Matsuyama: *mah-tsoo-yah-mah*

Mitake: *mee-tah-ke*

Murasaki Shikibu: *moo-rah-sah-kee shee-kee-boo*

Nakatsukasa: *nah-kah-tsoo-kah-sah*

Nijō: *nee-joh*

Niou: *nee-oh*

Oborozukiyo: *oh-boh-roh-zoo-kee-yoh*

Oe: *oh-ay*

Omyōbu: *oh-myoh-boo*

Reikeiden: *ray-kay-den*

Reizei: *ray-zay*

Rokujō: *roh-koo-joh*

Saishō: *sai-shoh*

Sanjō: *sahn-joh*

Shōnagon: *shoh-nah-gohn*

Shōwa: *shoh-wah*

Sumiyoshi: *soo-mee-yoh-shee*

Tamakazura: *tah-mah-kah-zoo-rah*

Tanabata: *tanh-ah-bah-tah*

Tatsuta: *tah-tsoo-tah*

Tō no Chūjō: *toh no choo-joh*

Uji: *oo-jee*

Ukifune: *oo-kee-foo-ne*

Ukon: *oo-kohn*

warekara: *wah-re-kah-rah*

wasuregusa: *wah-soo-re-goo-sah*

Yoshikiyo: *yoh-shee-kee-yoh*

Yūgiri: *yoo-gee-ree*

Yukihira: *yoo-kee-hee-rah*

From The Tale of Genji[1]

Summary   *The Tale of Genji* opens with the flavor of an old romance, in which the adventure is set in the distant past and the idealized characters dwell in an almost enchanted setting:

> In a certain reign there was a lady not of the first rank whom the emperor loved more than any of the others. The grand ladies with high ambitions thought her a presumptuous upstart, and lesser ladies were still more resentful. Everything she did offended someone. Probably aware of what was happening, she fell seriously ill and came to spend more time at home than at court. The emperor's pity

---

1. Translated by and with notes adapted from Edward G. Seidensticker.

and affection quite passed bounds. No longer caring what his ladies and courtiers might say, he behaved as if intent upon stirring gossip.

In time, a child is born to the woman, which makes the emperor even more devoted, but which also stirs the wrath of her rival, Kokiden, a powerful senior wife. The poor woman is persecuted, and, weakened from the strain, she dies. The emperor is devastated by her death. As solace, he takes some delight in his beautiful and brilliant son. As further solace, he installs in the palace a woman who he has heard bears a striking resemblance to his beloved. This proves true, and the new lady, Fujitsubo, wins the emperor's affections.

Meanwhile, his young son continues to dazzle almost everyone. The emperor would like to designate the boy crown prince, but he lacks political support. Furthermore, a Korean soothsayer warns that disaster will befall the country if the boy becomes emperor. Reluctantly, the emperor decides to reduce his son to the status of a mere subject, albeit a nobleman, ensuring that at least the boy will have an official career. He confers the name *Genji* on his son.

At the age of twelve, Genji undergoes the initiation into manhood. On the night of the initiation ceremonies Genji is married to Aoi, the daughter of a powerful minister of state. She is four years older than Genji, however, and they do not take a fancy to each other. Instead Genji finds himself drawn to Fujitsubo, his father's consort. "He could not remember his own mother," the narrator tells us, "and it moved him deeply to learn, from the lady who had first told the emperor of Fujitsubo, that the resemblance was striking. He wanted to be near her always."

With Genji's marriage off to a rocky start, he occupies the palace apartments that had belonged to his mother. As the handsome young man moves through the court, he becomes known as "the shining Genji."

CHAPTER 2

The Broom Tree

"The shining Genji": it was almost too grand a name. Yet he did not escape criticism for numerous little adventures. It seemed indeed that his indiscretions might give him a name for frivolity, and he did what he could to hide them. But his most secret affairs (such is the malicious work of the gossips) became common talk. If, on the other hand, he were to go through life concerned only for his name and avoid all these interesting and amusing little affairs, then he would be laughed to shame by the likes of the lieutenant of Katano.[2]

Still a guards captain, Genji spent most of his time at the palace, going infrequently to the Sanjō mansion of his father-in-law. The people there feared that he might have been stained by the lavender of Kasugano.[3] Though in fact he had an instinctive dislike for the promiscuity he saw all around him, he had a way of sometimes turning against his own better inclinations and causing unhappiness.

The summer rains came, the court was in retreat, and an even longer interval than usual had passed since his last visit to Sanjō. Though the minister and his family were much put out, they spared no effort to make him

---

2. Evidently the hero of a romance now lost. 3. Alludes to a poem from another tale: "Kasugano lavender stains my robe, / In deep disorder, like my secret loves." (Lavender suggests a romantic affinity.) Note that throughout this translation of *The Tale of Genji* Seidensticker renders the *tanka,* or classical Japanese poem, as an unrhymed couplet. However, these thirty-one-syllable compositions in metric patterns of 5, 7, 5, 7, 7 are conventionally viewed as comprising five lines and are usually so translated (see *The Kokinshū* poems, p. 2160).

feel welcome. The minister's sons were more attentive than to the emperor himself. Genji was on particularly good terms with Tō no Chūjō.[4] They enjoyed music together and more frivolous diversions as well. Tō no Chūjō was of an amorous nature and not at all comfortable in the apartments which his father-in-law, the Minister of the Right,[5] had at great expense provided for him. At Sanjō with his own family, on the other hand, he took very good care of his rooms, and when Genji came and went the two of them were always together. They were a good match for each other in study and at play. Reserve quite disappeared between them.

It had been raining all day. There were fewer courtiers than usual in the royal presence. Back in his own palace quarters, also unusually quiet, Genji pulled a lamp near and sought to while away the time with his books. He had Tō no Chūjō with him. Numerous pieces of colored paper, obviously letters, lay on a shelf. Tō no Chūjō made no attempt to hide his curiosity.

"Well," said Genji, "there are some I might let you see. But there are some I think it better not to."

"You miss the point. The ones I want to see are precisely the ones you want to hide. The ordinary ones—I'm not much of a hand at the game, you know, but even I am up to the ordinary give and take. But the ones from ladies who think you are not doing right by them, who sit alone through an evening and wait for you to come—those are the ones I want to see."

It was not likely that really delicate letters would be left scattered on a shelf, and it may be assumed that the papers treated so carelessly were the less important ones.

"You do have a variety of them," said Tō no Chūjō, reading the correspondence through piece by piece. This will be from her, and this will be from *her,* he would say. Sometimes he guessed correctly and sometimes he was far afield, to Genji's great amusement. Genji was brief with his replies and let out no secrets.

"It is I who should be asking to see *your* collection. No doubt it is huge. When I have seen it I shall be happy to throw my files open to you."

"I fear there is nothing that would interest you." Tō no Chūjō was in a contemplative mood. "It is with women as it is with everything else: the flawless ones are very few indeed. This is a sad fact which I have learned over the years. All manner of women seem presentable enough at first. Little notes, replies to this and that, they all suggest sensibility and cultivation. But when you begin sorting out the really superior ones you find that there are not many who have to be on your list. Each has her little tricks and she makes the most of them, getting in her slights at rivals, so broad sometimes that you almost have to blush. Hidden away by loving parents who build brilliant futures for them, they let word get out of this little talent and that little accomplishment and you are all in a stir. They are young and pretty and amiable and carefree, and in their boredom they begin to pick up a little from their elders, and in the natural course of things they begin to concentrate on one particular hobby and make something of it. A woman tells you

---

4. Brother of Genji's wife Aoi; he becomes Genji's closest friend.   5. One of the highest officials in the government. In rank, only the emperor, regent, chancellor, and minister of the left stood above him. The minister of the left was the legal head of government, responsible for the operation of the emperor's cabinet, known as the council of state. When he was absent, the minister of the right assumed his duties. Tō no Chūjō's father-in-law is, therefore, a powerful figure.

all about it and hides the weak points and brings out the strong ones as if they were everything, and you can't very well call her a liar. So you begin keeping company, and it is always the same. The fact is not up to the advance notices."

Tō no Chūjō sighed, a sigh clearly based on experience. Some of what he had said, though not all, accorded with Genji's own experience. "And have you come upon any," said Genji, smiling, "who would seem to have nothing at all to recommend them?"

"Who would be fool enough to notice such a woman? And in any case, I should imagine that women with no merits are as rare as women with no faults. If a woman is of good family and well taken care of, then the things she is less than proud of are hidden and she gets by well enough. When you come to the middle ranks, each woman has her own little inclinations and there are thousands of ways to separate one from another. And when you come to the lowest—well, who really pays much attention?"

He appeared to know everything. Genji was by now deeply interested.

"You speak of three ranks," he said, "but is it so easy to make the division? There are well-born ladies who fall in the world and there are people of no background who rise to the higher ranks and build themselves fine houses as if intended for them all along. How would you fit such people into your system?"

At this point two young courtiers, a guards officer and a functionary in the ministry of rites, appeared on the scene, to attend the emperor in his retreat. Both were devotees of the way of love and both were good talkers. Tō no Chūjō, as if he had been waiting for them, invited their views on the question that had just been asked. The discussion progressed, and included a number of rather unconvincing points.

"Those who have just arrived at high position," said one of the newcomers, "do not attract the same sort of notice as those who were born to it. And those who were born to the highest rank but somehow do not have the right backing—in spirit they may be as proud and noble as ever, but they cannot hide their deficiencies. And so I think that they should both be put in your middle rank.

"There are those whose families are not quite of the highest rank but who go off and work hard in the provinces. They have their place in the world, though there are all sorts of little differences among them. Some of them would belong on anyone's list. So it is these days. Myself, I would take a woman from a middling family over one who has rank and nothing else. Let us say someone whose father is almost but not quite a councillor. Someone who has a decent enough reputation and comes from a decent enough family and can live in some luxury. Such people can be very pleasant. There is nothing wrong with the household arrangements, and indeed a daughter can sometimes be set out in a way that dazzles you. I can think of several such women it would be hard to find fault with. When they go into court service, they are the ones the unexpected favors have a way of falling on. I have seen cases enough of it, I can tell you."

Genji smiled. "And so a person should limit himself to girls with money?"

"That does not sound like you," said Tō no Chūjō.

"When a woman has the highest rank and a spotless reputation," continued the other, "but something has gone wrong with her upbringing, something is wrong in the way she puts herself forward, you wonder how it can possibly have been allowed to happen. But when all the conditions are right and the girl herself is pretty enough, she is taken for granted. There is no cause for the least surprise. Such ladies are beyond the likes of me, and so I leave them where they are, the highest of the high. There are surprisingly pretty ladies wasting away behind tangles of weeds, and hardly anyone even knows of their existence. The first surprise is hard to forget. There she is, a girl with a fat, sloppy old father and boorish brothers and a house that seems common at best. Off in the women's rooms is a proud lady who has acquired bits and snatches of this and that. You get wind of them, however small the accomplishments may be, and they take hold of your imagination. She is not the equal of the one who has everything, of course, but she has her charm. She is not easy to pass by."

He looked at his companion, the young man from the ministry of rites. The latter was silent, wondering if the reference might be to his sisters, just then coming into their own as subjects for conversation. Genji, it would seem, was thinking that on the highest levels there were sadly few ladies to bestow much thought upon. He was wearing several soft white singlets with an informal court robe thrown loosely over them. As he sat in the lamplight leaning against an armrest, his companions almost wished that he were a woman. Even the "highest of the high" might seem an inadequate match for him.

They talked on, of the varieties of women.

"A man sees women, all manner of them, who seem beyond reproach," said the guards officer, "but when it comes to picking the wife who must be everything, matters are not simple. The emperor has trouble, after all, finding the minister who has all the qualifications. A man may be very wise, but no man can govern by himself. Superior is helped by subordinate, subordinate defers to superior, and so affairs proceed by agreement and concession. But when it comes to choosing the woman who is to be in charge of your house, the qualifications are altogether too many. A merit is balanced by a defect, there is this good point and that bad point, and even women who though not perfect can be made to do are not easy to find. I would not like to have you think me a profligate who has to try them all. But it is a question of the woman who must be everything, and it seems best, other things being equal, to find someone who does not require shaping and training, someone who has most of the qualifications from the start. The man who begins his search with all this in mind must be reconciled to searching for a very long time.

"He comes upon a woman not completely and in every way to his liking but he makes certain promises and finds her hard to give up. The world praises him for his honest heart and begins to note good points in the woman too; and why not? But I have seen them all, and I doubt that there are any genuinely superior specimens among them. What about you gentlemen so far above us? How is it with you when you set out to choose your ladies?

"There are those who are young enough and pretty enough and who take care of themselves as if no particle of dust were allowed to fall upon them. When they write letters they choose the most inoffensive words, and the ink is so faint a man can scarcely read them. He goes to visit, hoping for a real answer. She keeps him waiting and finally lets him have a word or two in an almost inaudible whisper. They are clever, I can tell you, at hiding their defects.

"The soft, feminine ones are likely to assume a great deal. The man seeks to please, and the result is that the woman is presently looking elsewhere. That is the first difficulty in a woman.

"In the most important matter, the matter of running his household, a man can find that his wife has too much sensibility, an elegant word and device for every occasion. But what of the too domestic sort, the wife who bustles around the house the whole day long, her hair tucked up behind her ears, no attention to her appearance, making sure that everything is in order? There are things on his mind, things he has seen and heard in his comings and goings, the private and public demeanor of his colleagues, happy things and sad things. Is he to talk of them to an outsider? Of course not. He would much prefer someone near at hand, someone who will immediately understand. A smile passes over his face, tears well up. Or some event at court has angered him, things are too much for him. What good is it to talk to such a woman? He turns his back on her, and smiles, and sighs, and murmurs something to himself. 'I beg your pardon?' she says, finally noticing. Her blank expression is hardly what he is looking for.

"When a man picks a gentle, childlike wife, he of course must see to training her and making up for her inadequacies. Even if at times she seems a bit unsteady, he may feel that his efforts have not been wasted. When she is there beside him her gentle charm makes him forget her defects. But when he is away and sends asking her to perform various services, it becomes clear, however small the service, that she has no thoughts of her own in the matter. Her uselessness can be trying.

"I wonder if a woman who is a bit chilly and unfeeling cannot at times seem preferable."

His manner said that he had known them all; and he sighed at his inability to hand down a firm decision.

"No, let us not worry too much about rank and beauty. Let us be satisfied if a woman is not too demanding and eccentric. It is best to settle on a quiet, steady girl. If she proves to have unusual talent and discrimination—well, count them an unexpected premium. Do not, on the other hand, worry too much about remedying her defects. If she seems steady and not given to tantrums, then the charms will emerge of their own accord.

"There are those who display a womanly reticence to the world, as if they had never heard of complaining. They seem utterly calm. And then when their thoughts are too much for them they leave behind the most horrendous notes, the most flamboyant poems, the sort of keepsakes certain to call up dreadful memories, and off they go into the mountains or to some remote seashore. When I was a child I would hear the women reading romantic stories, and I would join them in their sniffling and think it all very sad, all very profound and moving. Now I am afraid that it suggests certain pretenses.

"It is very stupid really, to run off and leave a perfectly kind and sympathetic man. He may have been guilty of some minor dereliction, but to run off with no understanding at all of his true feelings, with no purpose other than to attract attention and hope to upset him—it is an unpleasant sort of memory to have to live with. She gets drunk with admiration for herself and there she is, a nun. When she enters her convent she is sure that she has found enlightenment and has no regrets for the vulgar world.

"Her women come to see her. 'How very touching,' they say. 'How brave of you.'

"But she no longer feels quite as pleased with herself. The man, who has not lost his affection for her, hears of what has happened and weeps, and certain of her old attendants pass this intelligence on to her. 'He is a man of great feeling, you see. What a pity that it should have come to this.' The woman can only brush aside her newly cropped hair to reveal a face on the edge of tears. She tries to hold them back and cannot, such are her regrets for the life she has left behind; and the Buddha is not likely to think her one who has cleansed her heart of passion. Probably she is in more danger of brimstone now in this fragile vocation than if she had stayed with us in our sullied world.

"The bond between husband and wife is a strong one. Suppose the man had hunted her out and brought her back. The memory of her acts would still be there, and inevitably, sooner or later, it would be cause for rancor. When there are crises, incidents, a woman should try to overlook them, for better or for worse, and make the bond into something durable. The wounds will remain, with the woman and with the man, when there are crises such as I have described. It is very foolish for a woman to let a little dalliance upset her so much that she shows her resentment openly. He has his adventures—but if he has fond memories of their early days together, his and hers, she may be sure that she matters. A commotion means the end of everything. She should be quiet and generous, and when something comes up that quite properly arouses her resentment she should make it known by delicate hints. The man will feel guilty and with tactful guidance he will mend his ways. Too much lenience can make a woman seem charmingly docile and trusting, but it can also make her seem somewhat wanting in substance. We have had instances enough of boats abandoned to the winds and waves. Do you not agree?"

Tō no Chūjō nodded. "It may be difficult when someone you are especially fond of, someone beautiful and charming, has been guilty of an indiscretion, but magnanimity produces wonders. They may not always work, but generosity and reasonableness and patience do on the whole seem best."

His own sister was a case in point, he was thinking, and he was somewhat annoyed to note that Genji was silent because he had fallen asleep. Meanwhile the young guards officer talked on, a dedicated student of his subject. Tō no Chūjō was determined to hear him out.

"Let us make some comparisons," said the guardsman. "Let us think of the cabinetmaker. He shapes pieces as he feels like shaping them. They may be only playthings, with no real plan or pattern. They may all the same have a certain style for what they are—they may take on a certain novelty as times change and be very interesting. But when it comes to the genuine object, something of such undeniable value that a man wants to have it always with him—the perfection of the form announces that it is from the hand of a master.

"Or let us look at painting. There are any number of masters in the academy. It is not easy to separate the good from the bad among those who work on the basic sketches. But let color be added. The painter of things no one ever sees, of paradises, of fish in angry seas, raging beasts in foreign lands, devils and demons—the painter abandons himself to his fancies and paints to terrify and astonish. What does it matter if the results seem somewhat remote from real life? It is not so with the things we know, mountains, streams, houses near and like our own. The soft, unspoiled, wooded hills must be painted layer on layer, the details added gently, quietly, to give a sense of affectionate familiarity. And the foreground too, the garden inside the walls, the arrangement of the stones and grasses and waters. It is here that the master has his own power. There are details a lesser painter cannot imitate.

"Or let us look at calligraphy. A man without any great skill can stretch out this line and that in the cursive style and give an appearance of boldness and distinction. The man who has mastered the principles and writes with concentration may, on the other hand, have none of the eyecatching tricks; but when you take the trouble to compare the two the real thing is the real thing.

"So it is with trivialities like painting and calligraphy. How much more so with matters of the heart! I put no trust in the showy sort of affection that is quick to come forth when a suitable occasion presents itself. Let me tell you of something that happened to me a long time ago. You may find the story a touch wanton, but hear me through all the same."

He drew close to Genji, who awoke from his slumber. Tō no Chūjō, chin in hand, sat opposite, listening with the greatest admiration and attention. There was in the young man's manner something slightly comical, as if he were a sage expostulating upon the deepest truths of the universe, but at such times a young man is not inclined to conceal his most intimate secrets.

"It happened when I was very young, hardly more than a page. I was attracted to a woman. She was of a sort I have mentioned before, not the most beautiful in the world. In my youthful frivolity, I did not at first think of making her my wife. She was someone to visit, not someone who deserved my full attention. Other places interested me more. She was violently jealous. If only she could be a little more understanding, I thought, wanting to be away from the interminable quarreling. And on the other hand it sometimes struck me as a little sad that she should be so worried about a man of so little account as myself. In the course of time I began to mend my ways.

"For my sake, she would try to do things for which her talent and nature did not suit her, and she was determined not to seem inferior even in matters for which she had no great aptitude. She served me diligently in everything. She did not want to be guilty of the smallest thing that might go against my wishes. I had at first thought her rather strong-willed, but she proved to be docile and pliant. She thought constantly about hiding her less favorable qualities, afraid that they might put me off, and she did what she could to avoid displaying herself and causing me embarrassment. She was a model of devotion. In a word, there was nothing wrong with her—save the one thing I found so trying.

"I told myself that she was devoted to the point of fear, and that if I led her to think I might be giving her up she might be a little less suspicious and given to nagging. I had had almost all I could stand. If she really wanted to be with me and I suggested that a break was near, then she might reform. I behaved with studied coldness, and when, as always, her resentment exploded, I said to her: 'Not even the strongest bond between husband and wife can stand an unlimited amount of this sort of thing. It will eventually break, and he will not see her again. If you want to bring matters to such a pass, then go on doubting me as you have. If you would like to be with me for the years that lie ahead of us, then bear the trials as they come, difficult though they may be, and think them the way of the world. If you manage to overcome your jealousy, my affection is certain to grow. It seems likely that I will move ahead into an office of some distinction, and you will go with me and have no one you need think of as a rival.' I was very pleased with myself. I had performed brilliantly as a preceptor.

"But she only smiled. 'Oh, it won't be all that much trouble to put up with your want of consequence and wait till you are important. It will be much harder to pass the months and the years in the barely discernible hope that you will settle down and mend your fickle ways. Maybe you are right. Maybe this is the time to part.'

"I was furious, and I said so, and she answered in kind. Then, suddenly, she took my hand and bit my finger.

"I reproved her somewhat extravagantly. 'You insult me, and now you have wounded me. Do you think I can go to court like this? I am, as you say, a person of no consequence, and now, mutilated as I am, what is to help me get ahead in the world? There is nothing left for me but to become a monk.' That meeting must be our last, I said, and departed, flexing my wounded finger.

" 'I count them over, the many things between us.
One finger does not, alas, count the sum of your failures.'

"I left the verse behind, adding that now she had nothing to complain about.

"She had a verse of her own. There were tears in her eyes.

" 'I have counted them up myself, be assured, my failures.
For one bitten finger must all be bitten away?'

"I did not really mean to leave her, but my days were occupied in wanderings here and there, and I sent her no message. Then, late one evening toward the end of the year—it was an evening of rehearsals for the Kamo festival—a sleet was falling as we all started for home. Home. It came to me that I really had nowhere to go but her house. It would be no pleasure to sleep alone at the palace, and if I visited a woman of sensibility I would be kept freezing while she admired the snow. I would go look in upon *her*, and see what sort of mood she might be in. And so, brushing away the sleet, I made my way to her house. I felt just a little shy, but told myself that the sleet melting from my coat should melt her resentment. There was a dim light turned toward the wall, and a comfortable old robe of thick silk lay spread out to warm. The curtains were raised, everything suggested that she was waiting for me. I felt that I had done rather well.

"But she was nowhere in sight. She had gone that evening to stay with her parents, said the women who had been left behind. I had been feeling somewhat unhappy that she had maintained such a chilly silence, sending no amorous poems or queries. I wondered, though not very seriously, whether her shrillness and her jealousy might not have been intended for the precise purpose of disposing of me; but now I found clothes laid out with more attention to color and pattern than usual, exactly as she knew I liked them. She was seeing to my needs even now that I had apparently discarded her.

"And so, despite this strange state of affairs, I was convinced that she did not mean to do without me. I continued to send messages, and she neither protested nor gave an impression of wanting to annoy me by staying out of sight, and in her answers she was always careful not to anger or hurt me. Yet she went on saying that she could not forgive the behavior I had been guilty of in the past. If I would settle down she would be very happy to keep company with me. Sure that we would not part, I thought I would give her another lesson or two. I told her I had no intention of reforming, and made a great show of independence. She was sad, I gathered, and then without warning she died. And the game I had been playing came to seem rather inappropriate.

"She was a woman of such accomplishments that I could leave everything to her. I continue to regret what I had done. I could discuss trivial things with her and important things. For her skills in dyeing she might have been compared to Princess Tatsuta and the comparison would not have seemed ridiculous, and in sewing she could have held her own with Princess Tanabata."[6]

The young man sighed and sighed again.

Tō no Chūjō nodded. "Leaving her accomplishments as a seamstress aside, I should imagine you were looking for someone as faithful as Princess Tanabata.[7] And if she could embroider like Princess Tatsuta, well, it does not seem likely that you will come on her equal again. When the colors of a robe do not match the seasons, the flowers of spring and the autumn tints, when they are somehow vague and muddy, then the whole effort is as futile as the dew. So it is with women. It is not easy in this world to find a perfect wife. We are all pursuing the ideal and failing to find it."

The guards officer talked on. "There was another one. I was seeing her at about the same time. She was more amiable than the one I have just described to you. Everything about her told of refinement. Her poems, her handwriting when she dashed off a letter, the koto[8] she plucked a note on— everything seemed right. She was clever with her hands and clever with words. And her looks were adequate. The jealous woman's house had come to seem the place I could really call mine, and I went in secret to the other woman from time to time and became very fond of her. The jealous one died, I wondered what to do next. I was sad, of course, but a man cannot go on being sad forever. I visited the other more often. But there was something a little too aggressive, a little too sensuous about her. As I came to know her well and to think her a not very dependable sort, I called less often. And I learned that I was not her only secret visitor.

"One bright moonlit autumn night I chanced to leave court with a friend. He got in with me as I started for my father's. He was much concerned, he said, about a house where he was sure someone would be waiting. It happened to be on my way.

"Through gaps in a neglected wall I could see the moon shining on a pond. It seemed a pity not to linger a moment at a spot where the moon seemed so much at home, and so I climbed out after my friend. It would appear that this was not his first visit. He proceeded briskly to the veranda and took a seat near the gate and looked up at the moon for a time. The chrysanthe-

---

6. The goddess Tanabata was the patron of sewing and weaving. Tatsuta was the patron of autumn and, therefore, of dyeing.   7. Tanabata and her lover the Herdsman (the stars Altair and Vega) met annually on the seventh night of the Seventh Month.   8. A thirteen-stringed zither.

mums were at their best, very slightly touched by the frost, and the red leaves were beautiful in the autumn wind. He took out a flute and played a tune on it, and sang 'The Well of Asuka'[9] and several other songs. Blending nicely with the flute came the mellow tones of a Japanese koto. It had been tuned in advance, apparently, and was waiting. The *ritsu* scale[1] had a pleasant modern sound to it, right for a soft, womanly touch from behind blinds, and right for the clear moonlight too. I can assure you that the effect was not at all unpleasant.

"Delighted, my friend went up to the blinds.

" 'I see that no one has yet broken a path through your fallen leaves,' he said, somewhat sarcastically. He broke off a chrysanthemum and pushed it under the blinds.

" 'Uncommonly fine this house, for moon, for koto.
Does it bring to itself indifferent callers as well?

" 'Excuse me for asking. You must not be parsimonious with your music. You have a by no means indifferent listener.'

"He was very playful indeed. The woman's voice, when she offered a verse of her own, was suggestive and equally playful.

" 'No match the leaves for the angry winter winds.
Am I to detain the flute that joins those winds?'

"Naturally unaware of resentment so near at hand, she changed to a Chinese koto in an elegant *banjiki*.[2] Though I had to admit that she had talent, I was very annoyed. It is amusing enough, if you let things go no further, to exchange jokes from time to time with fickle and frivolous ladies; but as a place to take seriously, even for an occasional visit, matters here seemed to have gone too far. I made the events of that evening my excuse for leaving her.

"I see, as I look back on the two affairs, that young though I was the second of the two women did not seem the kind to put my trust in. I have no doubt that the wariness will grow as the years go by. The dear, uncertain ones— the dew that will fall when the *hagi*[3] branch is bent, the speck of frost that will melt when it is lifted from the bamboo leaf—no doubt they can be interesting for a time. You have seven years to go before you are my age," he said to Genji. "Just wait and you will understand. Perhaps you can take the advice of a person of no importance, and avoid the uncertain ones. They stumble sooner or later, and do a man's name no good when they do."

Tō no Chūjō nodded, as always. Genji, though he only smiled, seemed to agree.

"Neither of the tales you have given us has been a very happy one," he said.

"Let me tell you a story about a foolish woman I once knew," said Tō no Chūjō. "I was seeing her in secret, and I did not think that the affair was likely to last very long. But she was very beautiful, and as time passed I came to think that I must go on seeing her, if only infrequently. I sensed that she had come to depend on me. I expected signs of jealousy. There were none.

---

9. A folk song.   1. A pentatonic scale (that is, having five tones to an octave), resembling the Western minor without its half-steps.   2. The note B in ancient Japanese music.   3. Japanese bush clover.

She did not seem to feel the resentment a man expects from a woman he visits so seldom. She waited quietly, morning and night. My affection grew, and I let it be known that she did indeed have a man she could depend on. There was something very appealing about her (she was an orphan), letting me know that I was all she had.

"She seemed content. Untroubled, I stayed away for rather a long time. Then—I heard of it only later—my wife found a roundabout way to be objectionable. I did not know that I had become a cause of pain. I had not forgotten, but I let a long time pass without writing. The woman was desperately lonely and worried for the child she had borne. One day she sent me a letter attached to a wild carnation." His voice trembled.

"And what did it say?" Genji urged him on.

"Nothing very remarkable. I do remember her poem, though:

" 'The fence of the mountain rustic may fall to the ground.
Rest gently, O dew, upon the wild carnation.'

"I went to see her again. The talk was open and easy, as always, but she seemed pensive as she looked out at the dewy garden from the neglected house. She seemed to be weeping, joining her laments to the songs of the autumn insects. It could have been a scene from an old romance. I whispered a verse:

" 'No bloom in this wild array would I wish to slight.
But dearest of all to me is the wild carnation.'

"Her carnation had been the child. I made it clear that my own was the lady herself, the wild carnation no dust falls upon.[4]
"She answered:

" 'Dew wets the sleeve that brushes the wild carnation.
The tempest rages. Now comes autumn too.'

"She spoke quietly all the same, and she did not seem really angry. She did shed a tear from time to time, but she seemed ashamed of herself, and anxious to avoid difficult moments. I went away feeling much relieved. It was clear that she did not want to show any sign of anger at my neglect. And so once more I stayed away for rather a long time.

"And when I looked in on her again she had disappeared.

"If she is still living, it must be in very unhappy circumstances. She need not have suffered so if she had asserted herself a little more in the days when we were together. She need not have put up with my absences, and I would have seen to her needs over the years. The child was a very pretty little girl. I was fond of her, and I have not been able to find any trace of her.

"She must be listed among your reticent ones, I suppose? She let me have no hint of jealousy. Unaware of what was going on, I had no intention of giving her up. But the result was hopeless yearning, quite as if I had given her up. I am beginning to forget; and how is it with her? She must remember me sometimes, I should think, with regret, because she must remember too

---

4. Alludes to a poem in *The Kokinshū:* "Let no dust fall upon the wild carnation, / Upon the couch where lie my love and I." For the pink, or wild, carnation, she has used a word that can also mean "child." He has shifted to a synonym, the first two syllables of which mean "bed."

that it was not I who abandoned her. She was, I fear, not the sort of woman one finds it possible to keep for very long.

"Your jealous woman must be interesting enough to remember, but she must have been a bit wearying. And the other one, all her skill on the koto cannot have been much compensation for the undependability. And the one I have described to you—her very lack of jealousy might have brought a suspicion that there was another man in her life. Well, such is the way with the world—you cannot give your unqualified approval to any of them. Where are you to go for the woman who has no defects and who combines the virtues of all three? You might choose Our Lady of Felicity[5]—and find yourself married to unspeakable holiness."

The others laughed.

Tō no Chūjō turned to the young man from the ministry of rites. "You must have interesting stories too."

"Oh, please. How could the lowest of the low hope to hold your attention?"

"You must not keep us waiting."

"Let me think a minute." He seemed to be sorting out memories. "When I was still a student I knew a remarkably wise woman. She was the sort worth consulting about public affairs, and she had a good mind too for the little tangles that come into your private life. Her erudition would have put any ordinary sage to shame. In a word, I was awed into silence.

"I was studying under a learned scholar. I had heard that he had many daughters, and on some occasion or other I had made the acquaintance of this one. The father learned of the affair. Taking out wedding cups, he made reference, among other things, to a Chinese poem about the merits of an impoverished wife.[6] Although not exactly enamored of the woman, I had developed a certain fondness for her, and felt somewhat deferential toward the father. She was most attentive to my needs. I learned many estimable things from her, to add to my store of erudition and help me with my work. Her letters were lucidity itself, in the purest Chinese. None of this Japanese nonsense for her. I found it hard to think of giving her up, and under her tutelage I managed to turn out a few things in passable Chinese myself. And yet—though I would not wish to seem wanting in gratitude, it is undeniable that a man of no learning is somewhat daunted at the thought of being forever his wife's inferior. So it is in any case with an ignorant one like me; and what possible use could you gentlemen have for so formidable a wife? A stupid, senseless affair, a man tells himself, and yet he is dragged on against his will, as if there might have been a bond in some other life."

"She seems a most unusual woman." Genji and Tō no Chūjō were eager to hear more.

Quite aware that the great gentlemen were amusing themselves at his expense, he smiled somewhat impishly. "One day when I had not seen her for rather a long time I had some reason or other for calling. She was not in the room where we had been in the habit of meeting. She insisted on talking to me through a very obtrusive screen. I thought she might be sulking, and it all seemed very silly. And then again—if she was going to be so petty, I might have my excuse for leaving her. But no. She was not a person to let

---

5. A Buddhist deity who confers happiness and virtue.   6. *On Marriage*, a poem by Po Chü-i (772–846), the first of *Ten Poems Composed at Ch'ang-an.*

her jealousy show. She knew too much of the world. Her explanation of what was happening poured forth at great length, all of it very well reasoned.

" 'I have been indisposed with a malady known as coryza.[7] Discommoded to an uncommon degree, I have been imbibing of a steeped potion made from bulbaceous herbs. Because of the noisome odor, I will not find it possible to admit of greater propinquity. If you have certain random matters for my attention, perhaps you can deposit the relevant materials where you are.'

" 'Is that so?' I said. I could think of nothing else to say.

"I started to leave. Perhaps feeling a little lonely, she called after me, somewhat shrilly. "When I have disencumbered myself of this aroma, we can meet once more.'

"It seemed cruel to rush off, but the time was not right for a quiet visit. And it was as she said: her odor was rather high. Again I started out, pausing long enough to compose a verse:

" 'The spider[8] must have told you I would come.
    Then why am I asked to keep company with garlic?'

"I did not take time to accuse her of deliberately putting me off.

"She was quicker than I. She chased after me with an answer.

" 'Were we two who kept company every night,
    What would be wrong with garlic in the daytime?'[9]

"You must admit she was quick with her answers." He had quietly finished his story.

The two gentlemen, Genji and his friend, would have none of it. "A complete fabrication, from start to finish. Where could you find such a woman? Better to have a quiet evening with a witch." They thought it an outrageous story, and asked if he could come up with nothing more acceptable.

"Surely you would not wish for a more unusual sort of story?"

The guards officer took up again. "In women as in men, there is no one worse than the one who tries to display her scanty knowledge in full. It is among the least endearing of accomplishments for a woman to have delved into the Three Histories and the Five Classics;[1] and who, on the other hand, can go through life without absorbing something of public affairs and private? A reasonably alert woman does not need to be a scholar to see and hear a great many things. The very worst are the ones who scribble off Chinese characters at such a rate that they fill a good half of letters where they are most out of place, letters to other women. 'What a bore,' you say. 'If only she had mastered a few of the feminine things.' She cannot of course intend it to be so, but the words read aloud seem muscular and unyielding, and in the end hopelessly mannered. I fear that even our highest of the high are too often guilty of the fault.

"Then there is the one who fancies herself a poetess. She immerses herself in the anthologies, and brings antique references into her very first line, interesting enough in themselves but inappropriate. A man has had enough

---

7. That is, the common cold, which she would have said if she were not flaunting her superior knowledge. 8. It was believed that a busy spider foretold a visit from one's lover.   9. The word for "daytime" is homophonous with a word for numbers of strongly scented roots.   1. Ancient Chinese histories and the canonical works of early Chinese thought: *The Book of Poetry, The Book of History, The Book of Divination (I Ching), Spring and Autumn Annals,* and *The Book of Rites.*

with that first line, but he is called heartless if he does not answer, and cannot claim the honors if he does not answer in a similar vein. On the Day of the Iris he is frantic to get off to court and has no eye for irises, and there she is with subtle references to iris roots. On the Day of the Chrysanthemum,[2] his mind has no room for anything but the Chinese poem he must come up with in the course of the day, and there she is with something about the dew upon the chrysanthemum. A poem that might have been amusing and even moving on a less frantic day has been badly timed and must therefore be rejected. A woman who dashes off a poem at an unpoetic moment cannot be called a woman of taste.

"For someone who is not alive to the particular quality of each moment and each occasion, it is safer not to make a great show of taste and elegance; and from someone who is alive to it all, a man wants restraint. She should feign a certain ignorance, she should keep back a little of what she is prepared to say."

Through all the talk Genji's thoughts were on a single lady. His heart was filled with her. She answered every requirement, he thought. She had none of the defects, was guilty of none of the excesses, that had emerged from the discussion.

The talk went on and came to no conclusion, and as the rainy night gave way to dawn the stories became more and more improbable.

It appeared that the weather would be fine. Fearing that his father-in-law might resent his secluding himself in the palace, Genji set off for Sanjō. The mansion itself, his wife—every detail was admirable and in the best of taste. Nowhere did he find a trace of disorder. Here was a lady whom his friends must count among the truly dependable ones, the indispensable ones. And yet—she was too finished in her perfection, she was so cool and self-possessed that she made him uncomfortable. He turned to playful conversation with Chūnagon and Nakatsukasa and other pretty young women among her attendants. Because it was very warm, he loosened his dress, and they thought him even handsomer.

The minister came to pay his respects. Seeing Genji thus in dishabille, he made his greetings from behind a conveniently placed curtain. Though somewhat annoyed at having to receive such a distinguished visitor on such a warm day, Genji made it clear to the women that they were not to smile at his discomfort. He was a very calm, self-possessed young gentleman.

As evening approached, the women reminded him that his route from the palace had transgressed upon the domain of the Lord of the Center.[3] He must not spend the night here.

"To be sure. But my own house lies in the same direction. And I am very tired." He lay down as if he meant in spite of everything to stay the night.

"It simply will not do, my lord."

"The governor of Kii here," said one of Genji's men, pointing to another.

2. The Day of the Chrysanthemum fell on the ninth of the Ninth Month. The Day of the Iris fell on the fifth of the Fifth Month.   3. A god who changed his abode periodically and did not permit trespassers. Superstition influenced many aspects of Japanese life in the 11th century, with directional taboos among the most important. There were three main types of directional taboo. The northeast was regarded as a perpetually unlucky direction. Other directions were unfavorable during certain periods of one's life, so that at sixteen, for example, one might have to avoid the northwest. Still other directions were universally but temporarily inauspicious, caused by the transit of deities, whose descent from the heavens could close a sector to human traffic. A taboo of the third category is what affects Genji on this evening.

"He has dammed the Inner River⁴ and brought it into his garden, and the waters are very cool, very pleasant."

"An excellent idea. I really am very tired, and perhaps we can send ahead to see whether we might drive into the garden."

There were no doubt all sorts of secret places to which he could have gone to avoid the taboo. He had come to Sanjō, and after a considerable absence. The minister might suspect that he had purposely chosen a night on which he must leave early.

The governor of Kii was cordial enough with his invitation, but when he withdrew he mentioned certain misgivings to Genji's men. Ritual purification,⁵ he said, had required all the women to be away from his father's house, and unfortunately they were all crowded into his own, a cramped enough place at best. He feared that Genji would be inconvenienced.

"Nothing of the sort," said Genji, who had overheard. "It is good to have people around. There is nothing worse than a night away from home with no ladies about. Just let me have a little corner behind their curtains."

"If that is what you want," said his men, "then the governor's place should be perfect."

And so they sent runners ahead. Genji set off immediately, though in secret, thinking that no great ceremony was called for. He did not tell the minister where he was going, and took only his nearest retainers. The governor grumbled that they were in rather too much of a hurry. No one listened.

The east rooms of the main hall had been cleaned and made presentable. The waters were as they had been described, a most pleasing arrangement. A fence of wattles, of a deliberately rustic appearance, enclosed the garden, and much care had gone into the plantings. The wind was cool. Insects were humming, one scarcely knew where, fireflies drew innumerable lines of light, and all in all the time and the place could not have been more to his liking. His men were already tippling, out where they could admire a brook flowing under a gallery. The governor seemed to have "hurried off for viands."⁶ Gazing calmly about him, Genji concluded that the house would be of the young guardsman's favored in-between category. Having heard that his host's stepmother, who would be in residence, was a high-spirited lady, he listened for signs of her presence. There were signs of someone's presence immediately to the west. He heard a swishing of silk and young voices that were not at all displeasing. Young ladies seemed to be giggling self-consciously and trying to contain themselves. The shutters were raised, it seemed, but upon a word from the governor they were lowered. There was a faint light over the sliding doors. Genji went for a look, but could find no opening large enough to see through. Listening for a time, he concluded that the women had gathered in the main room, next to his.

The whispered discussion seemed to be about Genji himself.

"He is dreadfully serious, they say, and has made a fine match for himself. And still so young. Don't you imagine he might be a little lonely? But they say he finds time for a quiet little adventure now and then."

Genji was startled. There was but one lady on his mind, day after day. So

---

4. Marks the eastern limits of the capital.   5. Various purification rituals were conducted to ward off bad luck and to remove the polluting effects of sickness or a death in the family.   6. Reference to a folk song: "The jeweled flask is here. / But where is our host, what of our host? / He has hurried off for viands, / Off to the beach for viands, / To Koyurugi for seaweed."

this was what the gossips were saying; and what if, in it all, there was evidence that rumors of his real love had spread abroad? But the talk seemed harmless enough, and after a time he wearied of it. Someone misquoted a poem he had sent to his cousin Asagao,[7] attached to a morning glory. Their standards seemed not of the most rigorous. A misquoted poem for every occasion. He feared he might be disappointed when he saw the woman.

The governor had more lights set out at the eaves, and turned up those in the room. He had refreshments brought.

"And are the curtains all hung?"[8] asked Genji. "You hardly qualify as a host if they are not."

"And what will you feast upon?" rejoined the governor, somewhat stiffly. "Nothing so very elaborate, I fear."

Genji found a cool place out near the veranda and lay down. His men were quiet. Several young boys were present, all very sprucely dressed, sons of the host and of his father, the governor of Iyo.[9] There was one particularly attractive lad of perhaps twelve or thirteen. Asking who were the sons of whom, Genji learned that the boy was the younger brother of the host's stepmother, son of a guards officer no longer living. His father had had great hopes for the boy and had died while he was still very young. He had come to this house upon his sister's marriage to the governor of Iyo. He seemed to have some aptitude for the classics, said the host, and was of a quiet, pleasant disposition; but he was young and without backing, and his prospects at court were not good.

"A pity. The sister, then, is your stepmother?"

"Yes."

"A very young stepmother. My father had thought of inviting her to court. He was asking just the other day what might have happened to her. Life," he added with a solemnity rather beyond his years, "is uncertain."

"It happened almost by accident. Yes, you are right: it is a very uncertain world, and it always has been, particularly for women. They are like bits of driftwood."

"Your father is no doubt very alert to her needs. Perhaps, indeed, one has trouble knowing who is the master?"

"He quite worships her. The rest of us are not entirely happy with the arrangements he has made."

"But you cannot expect him to let you young gallants have everything. He has a name in that regard himself, you know. And where might the lady be?"

"They have all been told to spend the night in the porter's lodge, but they don't seem in a hurry to go."

The wine was having its effect, and his men were falling asleep on the veranda.

Genji lay wide awake, not pleased at the prospect of sleeping alone. He sensed that there was someone in the room to the north. It would be the lady of whom they had spoken. Holding his breath, he went to the door and listened.

"Where are you?" The pleasantly husky voice was that of the boy who had caught his eye.

---

7. The word for various morning flowers, including the morning glory.   8. Reference to a folk song: "The curtains all are hung. / Come and be my bridegroom. / And what will you feast upon? / Abalone, turbo, / And sea urchins too."   9. He is sometimes called the governor and sometimes the vice governor.

"Over here." It would be the sister. The two voices, very sleepy, resembled each other. "And where is our guest? I had thought he might be somewhere near, but he seems to have gone away."

"He's in the east room." The boy's voice was low. "I saw him. He is every bit as handsome as everyone says."

"If it were daylight I might have a look at him myself." The sister yawned, and seemed to draw the bedclothes over her face.

Genji was a little annoyed. She might have questioned her brother more energetically.

"I'll sleep out toward the veranda. But we should have more light." The boy turned up the lamp. The lady apparently lay at a diagonal remove from Genji. "And where is Chūjō? I don't like being left alone."

"She went to have a bath. She said she'd be right back." He spoke from out near the veranda.

All was quiet again. Genji slipped the latch open and tried the doors. They had not been bolted. A curtain had been set up just inside, and in the dim light he could make out Chinese chests and other furniture scattered in some disorder. He made his way through to her side. She lay by herself, a slight little figure. Though vaguely annoyed at being disturbed, she evidently took him for the woman Chūjō until he pulled back the covers.

"I heard you summoning a captain," he said, "and I thought my prayers over the months had been answered."[1]

She gave a little gasp. It was muffled by the bedclothes and no one else heard.

"You are perfectly correct if you think me unable to control myself. But I wish you to know that I have been thinking of you for a very long time. And the fact that I have finally found my opportunity and am taking advantage of it should show that my feelings are by no means shallow."

His manner was so gently persuasive that devils and demons could not have gainsaid him. The lady would have liked to announce to the world that a strange man had invaded her boudoir.

"I think you have mistaken me for someone else," she said, outraged, though the remark was under her breath.

The little figure, pathetically fragile and as if on the point of expiring from the shock, seemed to him very beautiful.

"I am driven by thoughts so powerful that a mistake is completely out of the question. It is cruel of you to pretend otherwise. I promise you that I will do nothing unseemly. I must ask you to listen to a little of what is on my mind."

She was so small that he lifted her easily. As he passed through the doors to his own room, he came upon the Chūjō who had been summoned earlier. He called out in surprise. Surprised in turn, Chūjō peered into the darkness. The perfume that came from his robes like a cloud of smoke told her who he was. She stood in confusion, unable to speak. Had he been a more ordinary intruder she might have ripped her mistress away by main force. But she would not have wished to raise an alarm all through the house.

She followed after, but Genji was quite unmoved by her pleas.

---

1. *Chūjō* means "captain," the rank Genji holds. Women's names were often derived from the titles of their fathers; hence the lady's companion is called Chūjō.

"Come for her in the morning," he said, sliding the doors closed.

The lady was bathed in perspiration and quite beside herself at the thought of what Chūjō, and the others too, would be thinking. Genji had to feel sorry for her. Yet the sweet words poured forth, the whole gamut of pretty devices for making a woman surrender.

She was not to be placated. "Can it be true? Can I be asked to believe that you are not making fun of me? Women of low estate should have husbands of low estate."

He was sorry for her and somewhat ashamed of himself, but his answer was careful and sober. "You take me for one of the young profligates you see around? I must protest. I am very young and know nothing of the estates which concern you so. You have heard of me, surely, and you must know that I do not go in for adventures. I must ask what unhappy entanglement imposes this upon me. You are making a fool of me, and nothing should surprise me, not even the tumultuous emotions that do in fact surprise me."

But now his very splendor made her resist. He might think her obstinate and insensitive, but her unfriendliness must make him dismiss her from further consideration. Naturally soft and pliant, she was suddenly firm. It was as with the young bamboo: she bent but was not to be broken. She was weeping. He had his hands full but would not for the world have missed the experience.

"Why must you so dislike me?" he asked with a sigh, unable to stop the weeping. "Don't you know that the unexpected encounters are the ones we were fated for? Really, my dear, you do seem to know altogether too little of the world."

"If I had met you before I came to this," she replied, and he had to admit the truth of it, "then I might have consoled myself with the thought—it might have been no more than self-deception, of course—that you would someday come to think fondly of me. But this is hopeless, worse than I can tell you. Well, it has happened. Say no to those who ask if you have seen me."[2]

One may imagine that he found many kind promises with which to comfort her.

The first cock was crowing and Genji's men were awake.

"Did you sleep well? I certainly did."

"Let's get the carriage ready."

Some of the women were heard asking whether people who were avoiding taboos were expected to leave again in the middle of the night.

Genji was very unhappy. He feared he could not find an excuse for another meeting. He did not see how he could visit her, and he did not see how they could write. Chūjō came out, also very unhappy. He let the lady go and then took her back again.

"How shall I write to you? Your feelings and my own—they are not shallow, and we may expect deep memories. Has anything ever been so strange?" He was in tears, which made him yet handsomer. The cocks were now crowing insistently. He was feeling somewhat harried as he composed his farewell verse:

---

2. An allusion to a poem in *The Kokinshū*: "As one small mark of your love, if such there be, / Say no to those who ask if you have seen me."

"Why must they startle with their dawn alarums
When hours are yet required to thaw the ice?"

The lady was ashamed of herself that she had caught the eye of a man so far above her. His kind words had little effect. She was thinking of her husband, whom for the most part she considered a clown and a dolt. She trembled to think that a dream might have told him of the night's happenings. This was the verse with which she replied:

"Day has broken without an end to my tears.
To my cries of sorrow are added the calls of the cocks."

It was lighter by the moment. He saw her to her door, for the house was coming to life. A barrier had fallen between them. In casual court dress, he leaned for a time against the south railing and looked out at the garden. Shutters were being raised along the west side of the house. Women seemed to be looking out at him, beyond a low screen at the veranda. He no doubt brought shivers of delight. The moon still bright in the dawn sky added to the beauty of the morning. The sky, without heart itself, can at these times be friendly or sad, as the beholder sees it. Genji was in anguish. He knew that there would be no way even to exchange notes. He cast many a glance backward as he left.

At Sanjō once more, he was unable to sleep. If the thought that they would not meet again so pained him, what must it do to the lady? She was no beauty, but she had seemed pretty and cultivated. Of the middling rank, he said to himself. The guards officer who had seen them all knew what he was talking about.

Spending most of his time now at Sanjō, he thought sadly of the unapproachable lady. At last he summoned her stepson, the governor of Kii.

"The boy I saw the other night, your foster uncle. He seemed a promising lad. I think I might have a place for him. I might even introduce him to my father."

"Your gracious words quite overpower me. Perhaps I should take the matter up with his sister."

Genji's heart leaped at the mention of the lady. "Does she have children?"

"No. She and my father have been married for two years now, but I gather that she is not happy. Her father meant to send her to court."

"How sad for her. Rumor has it that she is a beauty. Might rumor be correct?"

"Mistaken, I fear. But of course stepsons do not see a great deal of stepmothers."

Several days later he brought the boy to Genji. Examined in detail the boy was not perfect, but he had considerable charm and grace. Genji addressed him in a most friendly manner, which both confused and pleased him. Questioning him about his sister, Genji did not learn a great deal. The answers were ready enough while they were on safe ground, but the boy's self-possession was a little disconcerting. Genji hinted rather broadly at what had taken place. The boy was startled. He guessed the truth but was not old enough to pursue the matter.

Genji gave him a letter for his sister. Tears came to her eyes. How much had her brother been told? she wondered, spreading the letter to hide her flushed cheeks.

It was very long, and concluded with a poem:

> "I yearn to dream again the dream of that night.
> The nights go by in lonely wakefulness.

"There are no nights of sleep."[3]

The hand was splendid, but she could only weep at the yet stranger turn her life had taken.

The next day Genji sent for the boy.

Where was her answer? the boy asked his sister.

"Tell him you found no one to give his letter to."

"Oh, please." The boy smiled knowingly. "How can I tell him that? I have learned enough to be sure there is no mistake."

She was horrified. It was clear that Genji had told everything.

"I don't know why you must always be so clever. Perhaps it would be better if you didn't go at all."

"But he sent for me." And the boy departed.

The governor of Kii was beginning to take an interest in his pretty young stepmother, and paying insistent court. His attention turned to the brother, who became his frequent companion.

"I waited for you all day yesterday," said Genji. "Clearly I am not as much on your mind as you are on mine."

The boy flushed.

"Where is her answer?" And when the boy told him: "A fine messenger. I had hoped for something better."

There were other letters.

"But didn't you know?" he said to the boy. "I knew her before that old man she married. She thought me feeble and useless, it seems, and looked for a stouter support. Well, she may spurn me, but you needn't. You will be my son. The gentleman you are looking to for help won't be with us long."

The boy seemed to be thinking what a nuisance his sister's husband was. Genji was amused.

He treated the boy like a son, making him a constant companion, giving him clothes from his own wardrobe, taking him to court. He continued to write to the lady. She feared that with so inexperienced a messenger the secret might leak out and add suspicions of promiscuity to her other worries. These were very grand messages, but something more in keeping with her station seemed called for. Her answers were stiff and formal when she answered at all. She could not forget his extraordinary good looks and elegance, so dimly seen that night. But she belonged to another, and nothing was to be gained by trying to interest him. His longing was undiminished. He could not forget how touchingly fragile and confused she had been. With so many people around, another invasion of her boudoir was not likely to go unnoticed, and the results would be sad.

One evening after he had been at court for some days he found an excuse: his mansion again lay in a forbidden direction. Pretending to set off for Sanjō, he went instead to the house of the governor of Kii. The governor was delighted, thinking that those well-designed brooks and lakes had made an

---

3. Alludes to a classical poem, "Where shall I find comfort in my longing? / There are no dreams, for there are no nights of sleep."

impression. Genji had consulted with the boy, always in earnest attendance. The lady had been informed of the visit. She must admit that they seemed powerful, the urges that forced him to such machinations. But if she were to receive him and display herself openly, what could she expect save the anguish of the other night, a repetition of that nightmare? No, the shame would be too much.

The brother having gone off upon a summons from Genji, she called several of her women. "I think it might be in bad taste to stay too near. I am not feeling at all well, and perhaps a massage might help, somewhere far enough away that we won't disturb him."

The woman Chūjō had rooms on a secluded gallery. They would be her refuge.

It was as she had feared. Genji sent his men to bed early and dispatched his messenger. The boy could not find her. He looked everywhere and finally, at the end of his wits, came upon her in the gallery.

He was almost in tears. "But he will think me completely useless."

"And what do you propose to be doing? You are a child, and it is quite improper for you to be carrying such messages. Tell him I have not been feeling well and have kept some of my women to massage me. You should not be here. They will think it very odd."

She spoke with great firmness, but her thoughts were far from firm. How happy she might have been if she had not made this unfortunate marriage, and were still in the house filled with memories of her dead parents. Then she could have awaited his visits, however infrequent. And the coldness she must force herself to display—he must think her quite unaware of her place in the world. She had done what she thought best, and she was in anguish. Well, it all was hard fact, about which she had no choice. She must continue to play the cold and insensitive woman.

Genji lay wondering what blandishments the boy might be using. He was not sanguine, for the boy was very young. Presently he came back to report his mission a failure. What an uncommonly strong woman! Genji feared he must seem a bit feckless beside her. He heaved a deep sigh. This evidence of despondency had the boy on the point of tears.

Genji sent the lady a poem:

"I wander lost in the Sonohara moorlands,
For I did not know the deceiving ways of the broom tree.[4]

"How am I to describe my sorrow?"
She too lay sleepless. This was her answer:

"Here and not here, I lie in my shabby hut.
Would that I might like the broom tree vanish away."

The boy traveled back and forth with messages, a wish to be helpful driving sleep from his thoughts. His sister beseeched him to consider what the others might think.

Genji's men were snoring away. He lay alone with his discontent. This unique stubbornness was no broom tree. It refused to vanish away. The

4. Alludes to a poem: "O broom tree of Fuseya in Sonohara, / You seem to be there, and yet I cannot find you." The broom tree of Sonohara was said to disappear or change shape when one approached. *Fuseya* means "hut," which the lady employs in her response to Genji.

stubbornness was what interested him. But he had had enough. Let her do as she wished. And yet—not even this simple decision was easy.

"At least take me to her."

"She is shut up in a very dirty room and there are all sorts of women with her. I do not think it would be wise." The boy would have liked to be more helpful.

"Well, you at least must not abandon me." Genji pulled the boy down beside him.

The boy was delighted, such were Genji's youthful charms. Genji, for his part, or so one is informed, found the boy more attractive than his chilly sister.

Summary   Genji continues to yearn for the woman he met in the last chapter, the wife of the governor of Iyo. He pays another visit to the house where she is staying and steals into the lady's quarters. She eludes him by slipping out of the room, and, unaware of this, Genji makes love to her stepdaughter, whom she has left behind. The governor's wife will reappear in future episodes, where she is called the lady of the locust shell, a reference to the light summer singlet she discards, like a locust shedding its shell, when she avoids Genji in this chapter.

CHAPTER 4

Evening Faces

On his way from court to pay one of his calls at Rokujō,[5] Genji stopped to inquire after his old nurse, Koremitsu's[6] mother, at her house in Gojō. Gravely ill, she had become a nun. The carriage entrance was closed. He sent for Koremitsu and while he was waiting looked up and down the dirty, cluttered street. Beside the nurse's house was a new fence of plaited cypress. The four or five narrow shutters above had been raised, and new blinds, white and clean, hung in the apertures. He caught outlines of pretty foreheads beyond. He would have judged, as they moved about, that they belonged to rather tall women. What sort of women might they be? His carriage was simple and unadorned and he had no outrunners. Quite certain that he would not be recognized, he leaned out for a closer look. The hanging gate, of something like trelliswork, was propped on a pole, and he could see that the house was tiny and flimsy. He felt a little sorry for the occupants of such a place—and then asked himself who in this world had more than a temporary shelter.[7] A hut, a jeweled pavilion, they were the same. A pleasantly green vine was climbing a board wall. The white flowers, he thought, had a rather self-satisfied look about them.

" 'I needs must ask the lady far off yonder,' "[8] he said, as if to himself.

An attendant came up, bowing deeply. "The white flowers far off yonder are known as 'evening faces.' " he said. "A very human sort of name—and what a shabby place they have picked to bloom in."

---

5. The sixth ward; one of Genji's loves lives there and thus her name, the Rokujō lady. Daughter of an influential minister and widow of a crown prince, she is one of Genji's most demanding women. Although the reader does not learn much about her until chapter 9, she begins to make her presence felt here.   6. Genji's servant and confidant.   7. Alludes to a poem in *The Kokinshū*: "Where in all this world shall I call home? / A temporary shelter is my home."   8. Another allusion to *The Kokinshū*: "I needs must ask the lady far off yonder / What flower is off there that blooms so white."

It was as the man said. The neighborhood was a poor one, chiefly of small houses. Some were leaning precariously, and there were "evening faces" at the sagging eaves.

"A hapless sort of flower. Pick one off for me, would you?"

The man went inside the raised gate and broke off a flower. A pretty little girl in long, unlined yellow trousers of raw silk came out through a sliding door that seemed too good for the surroundings. Beckoning to the man, she handed him a heavily scented white fan.

"Put it on this. It isn't much of a fan, but then it isn't much of a flower either."

Koremitsu, coming out of the gate, passed it on to Genji.

"They lost the key, and I have had to keep you waiting. You aren't likely to be recognized in such a neighborhood, but it's not a very nice neighborhood to keep you waiting in."

Genji's carriage was pulled in and he dismounted. Besides Koremitsu, a son and a daughter, the former an eminent cleric, and the daughter's husband, the governor of Mikawa, were in attendance upon the old woman. They thanked him profusely for his visit.

The old woman got up to receive him. "I did not at all mind leaving the world, except for the thought that I would no longer be able to see you as I am seeing you now. My vows seem to have given me a new lease on life, and this visit makes me certain that I shall receive the radiance of Lord Amitābha[9] with a serene and tranquil heart." And she collapsed in tears.

Genji was near tears himself. "It has worried me enormously that you should be taking so long to recover, and I was very sad to learn that you have withdrawn from the world. You must live a long life and see the career I make for myself. I am sure that if you do you will be reborn upon the highest summits of the Pure Land. I am told that it is important to rid oneself of the smallest regret for this world."

Fond of the child she has reared, a nurse tends to look upon him as a paragon even if he is a half-wit. How much prouder was the old woman, who somehow gained stature, who thought of herself as eminent in her own right for having been permitted to serve him. The tears flowed on.

Her children were ashamed for her. They exchanged glances. It would not do to have these contortions taken as signs of a lingering affection for the world.

Genji was deeply touched. "The people who were fond of me left me when I was very young. Others have come along, it is true, to take care of me, but you are the only one I am really attached to. In recent years there have been restrictions upon my movements, and I have not been able to look in upon you morning and evening as I would have wished, or indeed to have a good visit with you. Yet I become very depressed when the days go by and I do not see you. 'Would that there were on this earth no final partings.' "[1] He spoke with great solemnity, and the scent of his sleeve, as he brushed away a tear, quite flooded the room.

Yes, thought the children, who had been silently reproaching their mother

9. The Buddha of Infinite Light, into whose paradise, the Pure Land, the faithful are reborn.   1. Alludes to a poem by Ariwara Narihira in *The Kokinshū*: "Would that my mother might live a thousand years. / Would there were on this earth no final partings" (see poem 901, p. 2173, for an alternate translation).

for her want of control, the fates had been kind to her. They too were now in tears.

Genji left orders that prayers and services be resumed. As he went out he asked for a torch, and in its light examined the fan on which the "evening face" had rested. It was permeated with a lady's perfume, elegant and alluring. On it was a poem in a disguised cursive hand that suggested breeding and taste. He was interested.

"I think I need not ask whose face it is,
So bright, this evening face, in the shining dew."

"Who is living in the house to the west?" he asked Koremitsu. "Have you perhaps had occasion to inquire?"

At it again, thought Koremitsu. He spoke somewhat tartly. "I must confess that these last few days I have been too busy with my mother to think about her neighbors."

"You are annoyed with me. But this fan has the appearance of something it might be interesting to look into. Make inquiries, if you will, please, of someone who knows the neighborhood."

Koremitsu went in to ask his mother's steward, and emerged with the information that the house belonged to a certain honorary vice-governor. "The husband is away in the country, and the wife seems to be a young woman of taste. Her sisters are out in service here and there. They often come visiting. I suspect the fellow is too poorly placed to know the details."

His poetess would be one of the sisters, thought Genji. A rather practiced and forward young person, and, were he to meet her, perhaps vulgar as well— but the easy familiarity of the poem had not been at all unpleasant, not something to be pushed away in disdain. His amative propensities, it will be seen, were having their way once more.

Carefully disguising his hand, he jotted down a reply on a piece of note-paper and sent it in by the attendant who had earlier been of service.

"Come a bit nearer, please. Then might you know
Whose was the evening face so dim in the twilight."

Thinking it a familiar profile, the lady had not lost the opportunity to surprise him with a letter, and when time passed and there was no answer she was left feeling somewhat embarrassed and disconsolate. Now came a poem by special messenger. Her women became quite giddy as they turned their minds to the problem of replying. Rather bored with it all, the messenger returned empty-handed. Genji made a quiet departure, lighted by very few torches. The shutters next door had been lowered. There was something sad about the light, dimmer than fireflies, that came through the cracks.

At the Rokujō house, the trees and the plantings had a quiet dignity. The lady herself was strangely cold and withdrawn. Thoughts of the "evening faces" quite left him. He overslept, and the sun was rising when he took his leave. He presented such a fine figure in the morning light that the women of the place understood well enough why he should be so universally admired. On his way he again passed those shutters, as he had no doubt done many times before. Because of that small incident he now looked at the house carefully, wondering who might be within.

"My mother is not doing at all well, and I have been with her," said Koremitsu some days later. And, coming nearer: "Because you seemed so interested, I called someone who knows about the house next door and had him questioned. His story was not completely clear. He said that in the Fifth Month or so someone came very quietly to live in the house, but that not even the domestics had been told who she might be. I have looked through the fence from time to time myself and had glimpses through blinds of several young women. Something about their dress suggests that they are in the service of someone of higher rank. Yesterday, when the evening light was coming directly through, I saw the lady herself writing a letter. She is very beautiful. She seemed lost in thought, and the women around her were weeping."

Genji had suspected something of the sort. He must find out more.

Koremitsu's view was that while Genji was undeniably someone the whole world took seriously, his youth and the fact that women found him attractive meant that to refrain from these little affairs would be less than human. It was not realistic to hold that certain people were beyond temptation.

"Looking for a chance to do a bit of exploring, I found a small pretext for writing to her. She answered immediately, in a good, practiced hand. Some of her women do not seem at all beneath contempt."

"Explore very thoroughly, if you will. I will not be satisfied until you do."

The house was what the guardsman would have described as the lowest of the low, but Genji was interested. What hidden charms might he not come upon!

He had thought the coldness of the governor's wife, the lady of "the locust shell," quite unique. Yet if she had proved amenable to his persuasions the affair would no doubt have been dropped as a sad mistake after that one encounter. As matters were, the resentment and the distinct possibility of final defeat never left his mind. The discussion that rainy night would seem to have made him curious about the several ranks. There had been a time when such a lady would not have been worth his notice. Yes, it had been broadening, that discussion! He had not found the willing and available one, the governor of Iyo's daughter, entirely uninteresting, but the thought that the stepmother must have been listening coolly to the interview was excruciating. He must await some sign of her real intentions.

The governor of Iyo returned to the city. He came immediately to Genji's mansion. Somewhat sunburned, his travel robes rumpled from the sea voyage, he was a rather heavy and displeasing sort of person. He was of good lineage, however, and, though aging, he still had good manners. As they spoke of his province, Genji wanted to ask the full count of those hot springs,[2] but he was somewhat confused to find memories chasing one another through his head. How foolish that he should be so uncomfortable before the honest old man! He remembered the guardsman's warning that such affairs are unwise, and he felt sorry for the governor. Though he resented the wife's coldness, he could see that from the husband's point of view it was admirable. He was upset to learn that the governor meant to find a suitable husband for his daughter and take his wife to the provinces. He consulted the lady's young brother upon the possibility of another meeting. It would have been difficult even with the lady's cooperation, however, and

2. The province was noted for its hot springs.

she was of the view that to receive a gentleman so far above her would be extremely unwise.

Yet she did not want him to forget her entirely. Her answers to his notes on this and that occasion were pleasant enough, and contained casual little touches that made him pause in admiration. He resented her chilliness, but she interested him. As for the stepdaughter, he was certain that she would receive him hospitably enough however formidable a husband she might acquire. Reports upon her arrangements disturbed him not at all.

Autumn came. He was kept busy and unhappy by affairs of his own making, and he visited Sanjō infrequently. There was resentment.

As for the affair at Rokujō, he had overcome the lady's resistance and had his way, and, alas, he had cooled toward her. People thought it worthy of comment that his passions should seem so much more governable than before he had made her his. She was subject to fits of despondency, more intense on sleepless nights when she awaited him in vain. She feared that if rumors were to spread the gossips would make much of the difference in their ages.

On a morning of heavy mists, insistently roused by the lady, who was determined that he be on his way, Genji emerged yawning and sighing and looking very sleepy. Chūjō, one of her women, raised a shutter and pulled a curtain aside as if urging her lady to come forward and see him off. The lady lifted her head from her pillow. He was an incomparably handsome figure as he paused to admire the profusion of flowers below the veranda. Chūjō followed him down a gallery. In an aster robe that matched the season pleasantly and a gossamer train worn with clean elegance, she was a pretty, graceful woman. Glancing back, he asked her to sit with him for a time at the corner railing. The ceremonious precision of the seated figure and the hair flowing over her robes were very fine.

He took her hand.

> "Though loath to be taxed with seeking fresher blooms,
> I feel impelled to pluck this morning glory.

"Why should it be?"

She answered with practiced alacrity, making it seem that she was speaking not for herself but for her lady:

> "In haste to plunge into the morning mists,
> You seem to have no heart for the blossoms here."

A pretty little page boy, especially decked out for the occasion, it would seem, walked out among the flowers. His trousers wet with dew, he broke off a morning glory for Genji. He made a picture that called out to be painted.

Even persons to whom Genji was nothing were drawn to him. No doubt even rough mountain men wanted to pause for a time in the shade of the flowering tree, and those who had basked even briefly in his radiance had thought, each in accordance with his rank, of a daughter who might be taken into his service, a not ill-formed sister who might perform some humble service for him. One need not be surprised, then, that people with a measure of sensibility among those who had on some occasion received a little poem from him or been treated to some little kindness found him much on their minds. No doubt it distressed them not to be always with him.

I had forgotten: Koremitsu gave a good account of the fence peeping to which he had been assigned. "I am unable to identify her. She seems determined to hide herself from the world. In their boredom her women and girls go out to the long gallery at the street, the one with the shutters, and watch for carriages. Sometimes the lady who seems to be their mistress comes quietly out to join them. I've not had a good look at her, but she seems very pretty indeed. One day a carriage with outrunners went by. The little girls shouted to a person named Ukon that she must come in a hurry. The captain[3] was going by, they said. An older woman came out and motioned to them to be quiet. How did they know? she asked, coming out toward the gallery. The passage from the main house is by a sort of makeshift bridge. She was hurrying and her skirt caught on something, and she stumbled and almost fell off. 'The sort of thing the god of Katsuragi[4] might do,' she said, and seems to have lost interest in sightseeing. They told her that the man in the carriage was wearing casual court dress and that he had a retinue. They mentioned several names, and all of them were undeniably Lord Tō no Chūjō's guards and pages."

"I wish you had made positive identification." Might she be the lady of whom Tō no Chūjō had spoken so regretfully that rainy night?

Koremitsu went on, smiling at this open curiosity. "I have as a matter of fact made the proper overtures and learned all about the place. I come and go as if I did not know that they are not all equals. They think they are hiding the truth and try to insist that there is no one there but themselves when one of the little girls makes a slip."

"Let me have a peep for myself when I call on your mother."

Even if she was only in temporary lodgings, the woman would seem to be of the lower class for which his friend had indicated such contempt that rainy evening. Yet something might come of it all. Determined not to go against his master's wishes in the smallest detail and himself driven by very considerable excitement, Koremitsu searched diligently for a chance to let Genji into the house. But the details are tiresome, and I shall not go into them.

Genji did not know who the lady was and he did not want her to know who he was. In very shabby disguise, he set out to visit her on foot. He must be taking her very seriously, thought Koremitsu, who offered his horse and himself went on foot.

"Though I do not think that our gentleman will look very good with tramps for servants."

To make quite certain that the expedition remained secret, Genji took with him only the man who had been his intermediary in the matter of the "evening faces" and a page whom no one was likely to recognize. Lest he be found out even so, he did not stop to see his nurse.

The lady had his messengers followed to see how he made his way home and tried by every means to learn where he lived; but her efforts came to nothing. For all his secretiveness, Genji had grown fond of her and felt that he must go on seeing her. They were of such different ranks, he tried to tell himself, and it was altogether too frivolous. Yet his visits were frequent. In

---

3. Tō no Chūjō.   4. Tradition held that he was very ugly and built a bridge that he used only at night. Katsuragi is south of Nara.

affairs of this sort, which can muddle the senses of the most serious and honest of men, he had always kept himself under tight control and avoided any occasion for censure. Now, to a most astonishing degree, he would be asking himself as he returned in the morning from a visit how he could wait through the day for the next. And then he would rebuke himself. It was madness, it was not an affair he should let disturb him. She was of an extraordinarily gentle and quiet nature. Though there was a certain vagueness about her, and indeed an almost childlike quality, it was clear that she knew something about men. She did not appear to be of very good family. What was there about her, he asked himself over and over again, that so drew him to her?

He took great pains to hide his rank and always wore travel dress, and he did not allow her to see his face. He came late at night when everyone was asleep. She was frightened, as if he were an apparition from an old story. She did not need to see his face to know that he was a fine gentleman. But who might he be? Her suspicions turned to Koremitsu. It was that young gallant, surely, who had brought the strange visitor. But Koremitsu pursued his own little affairs unremittingly, careful to feign indifference to and ignorance of this other affair. What could it all mean? The lady was lost in unfamiliar speculations.

Genji had his own worries. If, having lowered his guard with an appearance of complete unreserve, she were to slip away and hide, where would he seek her? This seemed to be but a temporary residence, and he could not be sure when she would choose to change it, and for what other. He hoped that he might reconcile himself to what must be and forget the affair as just another dalliance; but he was not confident.

On days when, to avoid attracting notice, he refrained from visiting her, his fretfulness came near anguish. Suppose he were to move her in secret to Nijō. If troublesome rumors were to arise, well, he could say that they had been fated from the start. He wondered what bond in a former life might have produced an infatuation such as he had not known before.

"Let's have a good talk," he said to her, "where we can be quite at our ease."

"It's all so strange. What you say is reasonable enough, but what you do is so strange. And rather frightening."

Yes, she might well be frightened. Something childlike in her fright brought a smile to his lips. "Which of us is the mischievous fox spirit?[5] I wonder. Just be quiet and give yourself up to its persuasions."

Won over by his gentle warmth, she was indeed inclined to let him have his way. She seemed such a pliant little creature, likely to submit absolutely to the most outrageous demands. He thought again of Tō no Chūjō's "wild carnation," of the equable nature his friend had described that rainy night. Fearing that it would be useless, he did not try very hard to question her. She did not seem likely to indulge in dramatics and suddenly run off and hide herself, and so the fault must have been Tō no Chūjō's. Genji himself would not be guilty of such negligence—though it did occur to him that a bit of infidelity might make her more interesting.

---

5. According to popular superstition, foxes played havoc with people by taking human form and deceiving them.

The bright full moon of the Eighth Month came flooding in through chinks in the roof. It was not the sort of dwelling he was used to, and he was fascinated. Toward dawn he was awakened by plebeian voices in the shabby houses down the street.

"Freezing, that's what it is, freezing. There's not much business this year, and when you can't get out into the country you feel like giving up. Do you hear me, neighbor?"

He could make out every word. It embarrassed the woman that, so near at hand, there should be this clamor of preparation as people set forth on their sad little enterprises. Had she been one of the stylish ladies of the world, she would have wanted to shrivel up and disappear. She was a placid sort, however, and she seemed to take nothing, painful or embarrassing or unpleasant, too seriously. Her manner elegant and yet girlish, she did not seem to know what the rather awful clamor up and down the street might mean. He much preferred this easygoing bewilderment to a show of consternation, a face scarlet with embarrassment. As if at his very pillow, there came the booming of a foot pestle, more fearsome than the stamping of the thunder god, genuinely earsplitting. He did not know what device the sound came from, but he did know that it was enough to awaken the dead. From this direction and that there came the faint thump of fulling hammers against coarse cloth; and mingled with it—these were sounds to call forth the deepest emotions—were the calls of geese flying overhead. He slid a door open and they looked out. They had been lying near the veranda. There were tasteful clumps of black bamboo just outside and the dew shone as in more familiar places. Autumn insects sang busily, as if only inches from an ear used to wall crickets at considerable distances. It was all very clamorous, and also rather wonderful. Countless details could be overlooked in the singleness of his affection for the girl. She was pretty and fragile in a soft, modest cloak of lavender and a lined white robe. She had no single feature that struck him as especially beautiful, and yet, slender and fragile, she seemed so delicately beautiful that he was almost afraid to hear her voice. He might have wished her to be a little more assertive, but he wanted only to be near her, and yet nearer.

"Let's go off somewhere and enjoy the rest of the night. This is too much."

"But how is that possible?" She spoke very quietly. "You keep taking me by surprise."

There was a newly confiding response to his offer of his services as guardian in this world and the next. She was a strange little thing. He found it hard to believe that she had had much experience of men. He no longer cared what people might think. He asked Ukon to summon his man, who got the carriage ready. The women of the house, though uneasy, sensed the depth of his feelings and were inclined to put their trust in him.

Dawn approached. No cocks were crowing. There was only the voice of an old man making deep obeisance to a Buddha, in preparation, it would seem, for a pilgrimage to Mitake. He seemed to be prostrating himself repeatedly and with much difficulty. All very sad. In a life itself like the morning dew, what could he desire so earnestly?

"Praise to the Messiah to come," intoned the voice.

"Listen," said Genji. "He is thinking of another world.

"This pious one shall lead us on our way
As we plight our troth for all the lives to come."

The vow exchanged by the Chinese emperor and Yang Kuei-fei[6] seemed to bode ill, and so he preferred to invoke Lord Maitreya, the Buddha of the Future; but such promises are rash.

"So heavy the burden I bring with me from the past,
I doubt that I should make these vows for the future."

It was a reply that suggested doubts about his "lives to come."

The moon was low over the western hills. She was reluctant to go with him. As he sought to persuade her, the moon suddenly disappeared behind clouds in a lovely dawn sky. Always in a hurry to be off before daylight exposed him, he lifted her easily into his carriage and took her to a nearby villa. Ukon was with them. Waiting for the caretaker to be summoned, Genji looked up at the rotting gate and the ferns that trailed thickly down over it. The groves beyond were still dark, and the mist and the dews were heavy. Genji's sleeve was soaking, for he had raised the blinds of the carriage.

"This is a novel adventure, and I must say that it seems like a lot of trouble.

"And did it confuse them too, the men of old,
This road through the dawn, for me so new and strange?

"How does it seem to you?"

She turned shyly away.

"And is the moon, unsure of the hills it approaches,
Foredoomed to lose its way in the empty skies?

"I am afraid."

She did seem frightened, and bewildered. She was so used to all those swarms of people, he thought with a smile.

The carriage was brought in and its traces propped against the veranda while a room was made ready in the west wing. Much excited, Ukon was thinking about earlier adventures. The furious energy with which the caretaker saw to preparations made her suspect who Genji was. It was almost daylight when they alighted from the carriage. The room was clean and pleasant, for all the haste with which it had been readied.

"There are unfortunately no women here to wait upon His Lordship." The man, who addressed him through Ukon, was a lesser steward who had served in the Sanjō mansion of Genji's father-in-law. "Shall I send for someone?"

"The last thing I want. I came here because I wanted to be in complete solitude, away from all possible visitors. You are not to tell a soul."

The man put together a hurried breakfast, but he was, as he had said, without serving women to help him.

Genji told the girl that he meant to show her a love as dependable as "the patient river of the loons."[7] He could do little else in these strange lodgings.

The sun was high when he arose. He opened the shutters. All through the badly neglected grounds not a person was to be seen. The groves were rank

6. The emperor's concubine, whose execution during a rebellion in 756 drove the heartbroken emperor to abdicate.   7. An allusion to a poem in The Man'yōshū: "The patient river of the patient loons / Will not run dry. My love will still outlast it."

and overgrown. The flowers and grasses in the foreground were a drab monotone, an autumn moor. The pond was choked with weeds, and all in all it was a forbidding place. An outbuilding seemed to be fitted with rooms for the caretaker, but it was some distance away.

"It is a forbidding place," said Genji. "But I am sure that whatever devils emerge will pass me by."

He was still in disguise. She thought it unkind of him to be so secretive, and he had to agree that their relationship had gone beyond such furtiveness.

"Because of one chance meeting by the wayside
The flower now opens in the evening dew.

"And how does it look to you?"

"The face seemed quite to shine in the evening dew,
But I was dazzled by the evening light."

Her eyes turned away. She spoke in a whisper.

To him it may have seemed an interesting poem.

As a matter of fact, she found him handsomer than her poem suggested, indeed frighteningly handsome, given the setting.

"I hid my name from you because I thought it altogether too unkind of you to be keeping your name from me. Do please tell me now. This silence makes me feel that something awful might be coming."

"Call me the fisherman's daughter."[8] Still hiding her name, she was like a little child.

"I see. I brought it all on myself? A case of *warekara?*"[9]

And so, sometimes affectionately, sometimes reproachfully, they talked the hours away.

Koremitsu had found them out and brought provisions. Feeling a little guilty about the way he had treated Ukon, he did not come near. He thought it amusing that Genji should thus be wandering the streets, and concluded that the girl must provide sufficient cause. And he could have had her himself, had he not been so generous.

Genji and the girl looked out at an evening sky of the utmost calm. Because she found the darkness in the recesses of the house frightening, he raised the blinds at the veranda and they lay side by side. As they gazed at each other in the gathering dusk, it all seemed very strange to her, unbelievably strange. Memories of past wrongs quite left her. She was more at ease with him now, and he thought her charming. Beside him all through the day, starting up in fright at each little noise, she seemed delightfully childlike. He lowered the shutters early and had lights brought.

"You seem comfortable enough with me, and yet you raise difficulties."

At court everyone would be frantic. Where would the search be directed? He thought what a strange love it was, and he thought of the turmoil the Rokujō lady was certain to be in. She had every right to be resentful, and yet her jealous ways were not pleasant. It was that sad lady to whom his thoughts first turned. Here was the girl beside him, so simple and undemanding; and

---

8. Alludes to a poem: "A fisherman's daughter, I spend my life by the waves, / The waves that tell us nothing. I have no home." 9. Alludes to a poem in The Kokinshū: "The grass the fishermen take, the *warekara*: / 'I did it myself.' I shall weep but I shall not hate you." *Warekara* is both the fishermen's catch (skeleton shrimp) and a homonym meaning "I did it myself."

the other was so impossibly forceful in her demands. How he wished he might in some measure have his freedom.

It was past midnight. He had been asleep for a time when an exceedingly beautiful woman appeared by his pillow.

"You do not even think of visiting me, when you are so much on my mind. Instead you go running off with someone who has nothing to recommend her, and raise a great stir over her. It is cruel, intolerable." She seemed about to shake the girl from her sleep. He awoke, feeling as if he were in the power of some malign being. The light had gone out. In great alarm, he pulled his sword to his pillow and awakened Ukon. She too seemed frightened.

"Go out to the gallery and wake the guard. Have him bring a light."

"It's much too dark."

He forced a smile. "You're behaving like a child."

He clapped his hands and a hollow echo answered. No one seemed to hear. The girl was trembling violently. She was bathed in sweat and as if in a trance, quite bereft of her senses.

"She is such a timid little thing," said Ukon, "frightened when there is nothing at all to be frightened of. This must be dreadful for her."

Yes, poor thing, thought Genji. She did seem so fragile, and she had spent the whole day gazing up at the sky.

"I'll go get someone. What a frightful echo. You stay here with her." He pulled Ukon to the girl's side.

The lights in the west gallery had gone out. There was a gentle wind. He had few people with him, and they were asleep. They were three in number: a young man who was one of his intimates and who was the son of the steward here, a court page, and the man who had been his intermediary in the matter of the "evening faces." He called out. Someone answered and came up to him.

"Bring a light. Wake the other, and shout and twang your bowstrings. What do you mean, going to sleep in a deserted house? I believe Lord Koremitsu was here."

"He was. But he said he had no orders and would come again at dawn."

An elite guardsman, the man was very adept at bow twanging. He went off with a shouting as of a fire watch. At court, thought Genji, the courtiers on night duty would have announced themselves, and the guard would be changing. It was not so very late.

He felt his way back inside. The girl was as before, and Ukon lay face down at her side.

"What is this? You're a fool to let yourself be so frightened. Are you worried about the fox spirits that come out and play tricks in deserted houses? But you needn't worry. They won't come near me." He pulled her to her knees.

"I'm not feeling at all well. That's why I was lying down. My poor lady must be terrified."

"She is indeed. And I can't think why."

He reached for the girl. She was not breathing. He lifted her and she was limp in his arms. There was no sign of life. She had seemed as defenseless as a child, and no doubt some evil power had taken possession of her. He could think of nothing to do. A man came with a torch. Ukon was not prepared to move, and Genji himself pulled up curtain frames to hide the girl.

"Bring the light closer."

It was a most unusual order. Not ordinarily permitted at Genji's side, the man hesitated to cross the threshold.

"Come, come, bring it here! There is a time and place for ceremony."

In the torchlight he had a fleeting glimpse of a figure by the girl's pillow. It was the woman in his dream. It faded away like an apparition in an old romance. In all the fright and horror, his confused thoughts centered upon the girl. There was no room for thoughts of himself.

He knelt over her and called out to her, but she was cold and had stopped breathing. It was too horrible. He had no confidant to whom he could turn for advice. It was the clergy one thought of first on such occasions. He had been so brave and confident, but he was young, and this was too much for him. He clung to the lifeless body.

"Come back, my dear, my dear. Don't do this awful thing to me." But she was cold and no longer seemed human.

The first paralyzing terror had left Ukon. Now she was writhing and wailing. Genji remembered a devil a certain minister had encountered in the Grand Hall.

"She can't possibly be dead." He found the strength to speak sharply. "All this noise in the middle of the night—you must try to be a little quieter." But it had been too sudden.

He turned again to the torchbearer. "There is someone here who seems to have had a very strange seizure. Tell your friend to find out where Lord Koremitsu is spending the night and have him come immediately. If the holy man is still at his mother's house, give him word, very quietly, that he is to come too. His mother and the people with her are not to hear. She does not approve of this sort of adventure."

He spoke calmly enough, but his mind was in a turmoil. Added to grief at the loss of the girl was horror, quite beyond describing, at this desolate place. It would be past midnight. The wind was higher and whistled more dolefully in the pines. There came a strange, hollow call of a bird. Might it be an owl? All was silence, terrifying solitude. He should not have chosen such a place— but it was too late now. Trembling violently, Ukon clung to him. He held her in his arms, wondering if she might be about to follow her lady. He was the only rational one present, and he could think of nothing to do. The flickering light wandered here and there. The upper parts of the screens behind them were in darkness, the lower parts fitfully in the light. There was a persistent creaking, as of someone coming up behind them. If only Koremitsu would come. But Koremitsu was a nocturnal wanderer without a fixed abode, and the man had to search for him in numerous places. The wait for dawn was like the passage of a thousand nights. Finally he heard a distant crowing. What legacy from a former life could have brought him to this mortal peril? He was being punished for a guilty love, his fault and no one else's, and his story would be remembered in infamy through all the ages to come. There were no secrets, strive though one might to have them. Soon everyone would know, from his royal father down, and the lowest court pages would be talking; and he would gain immortality as the model of the complete fool.

Finally Lord Koremitsu came. He was the perfect servant who did not go against his master's wishes in anything at any time; and Genji was angry that on this night of all nights he should have been away, and slow in answering the summons. Calling him inside even so, he could not immediately find the strength to say what must be said. Ukon burst into tears, the full horror of it all coming back to her at the sight of Koremitsu. Genji too lost control of himself. The only sane and rational one present, he had held Ukon in his arms, but now he gave himself up to his grief.

"Something very strange has happened," he said after a time. "Strange— 'unbelievable' would not be too strong a word. I wanted a priest—one does when these things happen—and asked your reverend brother to come."

"He went back up the mountain yesterday. Yes, it is very strange indeed. Had there been anything wrong with her?"

"Nothing."

He was so handsome in his grief that Koremitsu wanted to weep. An older man who has had everything happen to him and knows what to expect can be depended upon in a crisis; but they were both young, and neither had anything to suggest.

Koremitsu finally spoke. "We must not let the caretaker know. He may be dependable enough himself, but he is sure to have relatives who will talk. We must get away from this place."

"You aren't suggesting that we could find a place where we would be less likely to be seen?"

"No, I suppose not. And the women at her house will scream and wail when they hear about it, and they live in a crowded neighborhood, and all the mob around will hear, and that will be that. But mountain temples are used to this sort of thing.[1] There would not be much danger of attracting attention." He reflected on the problem for a time. "There is a woman I used to know. She has gone into a nunnery up in the eastern hills. She is very old, my father's nurse, as a matter of fact. The district seems to be rather heavily populated, but the nunnery is off by itself."

It was not yet full daylight. Koremitsu had the carriage brought up. Since Genji seemed incapable of the task, he wrapped the body in a covering and lifted it into the carriage. It was very tiny and very pretty, and not at all repellent. The wrapping was loose and the hair streamed forth, as if to darken the world before Genji's eyes.

He wanted to see the last rites through to the end, but Koremitsu would not hear of it. "Take my horse and go back to Nijō, now while the streets are still quiet."

He helped Ukon into the carriage and himself proceeded on foot, the skirts of his robe hitched up. It was a strange, bedraggled sort of funeral procession, he thought, but in the face of such anguish he was prepared to risk his life. Barely conscious, Genji made his way back to Nijō.

"Where have you been?" asked the women. "You are not looking at all well."

He did not answer. Alone in his room, he pressed a hand to his heart. Why had he not gone with the others? What would she think if she were to come back to life? She would think that he had abandoned her. Self-reproach filled his heart to breaking. He had a headache and feared he had a fever. Might he too be dying? The sun was high and still he did not emerge. Thinking it all very strange, the women pressed breakfast upon him. He could not eat.

---

1. Corpses were brought to temples for burial.

A messenger reported that the emperor had been troubled by his failure to appear the day before.

His brothers-in-law came calling.

"Come in, please, just for a moment." He received only Tō no Chūjō and kept a blind between them. "My old nurse fell seriously ill and took her vows in the Fifth Month or so. Perhaps because of them, she seemed to recover. But recently she had a relapse. Someone came to ask if I would not call on her at least once more. I thought I really must go and see an old and dear servant who was on her deathbed, and so I went. One of her servants was ailing, and quite suddenly, before he had time to leave, he died. Out of deference to me they waited until night to take the body away. All this I learned later. It would be very improper of me to go to court with all these festivities coming up,[2] I thought, and so I stayed away. I have had a headache since early this morning—perhaps I have caught cold. I must apologize."

"I see. I shall so inform your father. He sent out a search party during the concert last night, and really seemed very upset." Tō no Chūjō turned to go, and abruptly turned back. "Come now. What sort of brush did you really have? I don't believe a word of it."

Genji was startled, but managed a show of nonchalance. "You needn't go into the details. Just say that I suffered an unexpected defilement. Very unexpected, really."

Despite his cool manner, he was not up to facing people. He asked a younger brother-in-law to explain in detail his reasons for not going to court. He got off a note to Sanjō with a similar explanation.

Koremitsu came in the evening. Having announced that he had suffered a defilement, Genji had callers remain outside, and there were few people in the house. He received Koremitsu immediately.

"Are you sure she is dead?" He pressed a sleeve to his eyes.

Koremitsu too was in tears. "Yes, I fear she is most certainly dead. I could not stay shut up in a temple indefinitely, and so I have made arrangements with a venerable priest whom I happen to know rather well. Tomorrow is a good day for funerals."

"And the other woman?"

"She has seemed on the point of death herself. She does not want to be left behind by her lady. I was afraid this morning that she might throw herself over a cliff. She wanted to tell the people at Gojō, but I persuaded her to let us have a little more time."

"I am feeling rather awful myself and almost fear the worst."

"Come, now. There is nothing to be done and no point in torturing yourself. You must tell yourself that what must be must be. I shall let absolutely no one know, and I am personally taking care of everything."

"Yes, to be sure. Everything is fated. So I tell myself. But it is terrible to think that I have sent a lady to her death. You are not to tell your sister, and you must be very sure that your mother does not hear. I would not survive the scolding I would get from her."

"And the priests too: I have told them a plausible story." Koremitsu exuded confidence.

The women had caught a hint of what was going on and were more puzzled than ever. He had said that he had suffered a defilement, and he was staying away from court; but why these muffled lamentations?

Genji gave instructions for the funeral. "You must make sure that nothing goes wrong."

"Of course. No great ceremony seems called for."

Koremitsu turned to leave.

"I know you won't approve," said Genji, a fresh wave of grief sweeping over him, "but I will regret it forever if I don't see her again. I'll go on horseback."

"Very well, if you must." In fact Koremitsu thought the proposal very ill advised. "Go immediately and be back while it is still early."

Genji set out in the travel robes he had kept ready for his recent amorous excursions. He was in the bleakest despair. He was on a strange mission and the terrors of the night before made him consider turning back. Grief urged him on. If he did not see her once more, when, in another world, might he hope to see her as she had been? He had with him only Koremitsu and the attendant of that first encounter. The road seemed a long one.

The moon came out, two nights past full. They reached the river. In the dim torchlight, the darkness off towards Mount Toribe was ominous and forbidding; but Genji was too dazed with grief to be frightened. And so they reached the temple.

It was a harsh, unfriendly region at best. The board hut and chapel where the nun pursued her austerities were lonely beyond description. The light at the altar came dimly through cracks. Inside the hut a woman was weeping. In the outer chamber two or three priests were conversing and invoking the holy name in low voices. Vespers seemed to have ended in several temples nearby. Everything was quiet. There were lights and there seemed to be clusters of people in the direction of Kiyomizu. The grand tones in which the worthy monk, the son of the nun, was reading a sutra brought on what Genji thought must be the full flood tide of his tears.

He went inside. The light was turned away from the corpse. Ukon lay behind a screen. It must be very terrible for her, thought Genji. The girl's face was unchanged and very pretty.

"Won't you let me hear your voice again?" He took her hand. "What was it that made me give you all my love, for so short a time, and then made you leave me to this misery?" He was weeping uncontrollably.

The priests did not know who he was. They sensed something remarkable, however, and felt their eyes mist over.

"Come with me to Nijō," he said to Ukon.

"We have been together since I was very young. I never left her side, not for a single moment. Where am I to go now? I will have to tell the others what has happened. As if this weren't enough, I will have to put up with their accusations." She was sobbing. "I want to go with her."

"That is only natural. But it is the way of the world. Parting is always sad. Our lives must end, early or late. Try to put your trust in me." He comforted her with the usual homilies, but presently his real feelings came out. "Put your trust in me—when I fear I have not long to live myself." He did not after all seem likely to be much help.

"It will soon be light," said Koremitsu. "We must be on our way."

Looking back and looking back again, his heart near breaking, Genji went out. The way was heavy with dew and the morning mists were thick. He scarcely knew where he was. The girl was exactly as she had been that night. They had exchanged robes and she had on a red singlet of his. What might it have been in other lives that had brought them together? He managed only with great difficulty to stay in his saddle. Koremitsu was at the reins. As they came to the river Genji fell from his horse and was unable to remount.

"So I am to die by the wayside? I doubt that I can go on."

Koremitsu was in a panic. He should not have permitted this expedition, however strong Genji's wishes. Dipping his hands in the river, he turned and made supplication to Kiyomizu. Genji somehow pulled himself together. Silently invoking the holy name, he was seen back to Nijō.

The women were much upset by these untimely wanderings. "Very bad, very bad. He has been so restless lately. And why should he have gone out again when he was not feeling well?"

Now genuinely ill, he took to his bed. Two or three days passed and he was visibly thinner. The emperor heard of the illness and was much alarmed. Continuous prayers were ordered in this shrine and that temple. The varied rites, Shinto and Confucian and Buddhist, were beyond counting. Genji's good looks had been such as to arouse forebodings. All through the court it was feared that he would not live much longer. Despite his illness, he summoned Ukon to Nijō and assigned her rooms near his own. Koremitsu composed himself sufficiently to be of service to her, for he could see that she had no one else to turn to. Choosing times when he was feeling better, Genji would summon her for a talk, and she soon was accustomed to life at Nijō. Dressed in deep mourning, she was a somewhat stern and forbidding young woman, but not without her good points.

"It lasted such a very little while. I fear that I will be taken too. It must be dreadful for you, losing your only support. I had thought that as long as I lived I would see to all your needs, and it seems sad and ironical that I should be on the point of following her." He spoke softly and there were tears in his eyes. For Ukon the old grief had been hard enough to bear, and now she feared that a new grief might be added to it.

All through the Nijō mansion there was a sense of helplessness. Emissaries from court were thicker than raindrops. Not wanting to worry his father, Genji fought to control himself. His father-in-law was extremely solicitous and came to Nijō every day. Perhaps because of all the prayers and rites the crisis passed—it had lasted some twenty days—and left no ill effects. Genji's full recovery coincided with the final cleansing of the defilement. With the unhappiness he had caused his father much on his mind, he set off for his apartments at court. For a time he felt out of things, as if he had come back to a strange new world.

By the end of the Ninth Month he was his old self once more. He had lost weight, but emaciation only made him handsomer. He spent a great deal of time gazing into space, and sometimes he would weep aloud. He must be in the clutches of some malign spirit, thought the women. It was all most peculiar.

He would summon Ukon on quiet evenings. "I don't understand it at all. Why did she so insist on keeping her name from me? Even if she *was* a fisherman's daughter it was cruel of her to be so uncommunicative. It was as if she did not know how much I loved her."

"There was no reason for keeping it secret. But why should she tell you about her insignificant self? Your attitude seemed so strange from the beginning. She used to say that she hardly knew whether she was waking or dreaming. Your refusal to identify yourself, you know, helped her guess who you were. It hurt her that you should belittle her by keeping your name from her."

"An unfortunate contest of wills. I did not want anything to stand between us; but I must always be worrying about what people will say. I must refrain from things my father and all the rest of them might take me to task for. I am not permitted the smallest indiscretion. Everything is exaggerated so. The little incident of the 'evening faces' affected me strangely and I went to very great trouble to see her. There must have been a bond between us. A love doomed from the start to be fleeting—why should it have taken such complete possession of me and made me find her so precious? You must tell me everything. What point is there in keeping secrets now? I mean to make offerings every week, and I want to know in whose name I am making them."

"Yes, of course—why have secrets now? It is only that I do not want to slight what she made so much of. Her parents are dead. Her father was a guards captain. She was his special pet, but his career did not go well and his life came to an early and disappointing end. She somehow got to know Lord Tō no Chūjō—it was when he was still a lieutenant. He was very attentive for three years or so, and then about last autumn there was a rather awful threat from his father-in-law's house. She was ridiculously timid and it frightened her beyond all reason. She ran off and hid herself at her nurse's in the western part of the city. It was a wretched little hovel of a place. She wanted to go off into the hills, but the direction she had in mind has been taboo since New Year's. So she moved to the odd place where she was so upset to have you find her. She was more reserved and withdrawn than most people, and I fear that her unwillingness to show her emotions may have seemed cold."

So it was true. Affection and pity welled up yet more strongly.

"He once told me of a lost child. Was there such a one?"

"Yes, a very pretty little girl, born two years ago last spring."

"Where is she? Bring her to me without letting anyone know. It would be such a comfort. I should tell my friend Tō no Chūjō, I suppose, but why invite criticism? I doubt that anyone could reprove me for taking in the child. You must think up a way to get around the nurse."

"It would make me very happy if you were to take the child. I would hate to have her left where she is. She is there because we had no competent nurses in the house where you found us."

The evening sky was serenely beautiful. The flowers below the veranda were withered, the songs of the insects were dying too, and autumn tints were coming over the maples. Looking out upon the scene, which might have been a painting, Ukon thought what a lovely asylum she had found herself. She wanted to avert her eyes at the thought of the house of the "evening faces." A pigeon called, somewhat discordantly, from a bamboo thicket. Remembering how the same call had frightened the girl in that deserted villa, Genji could see the little figure as if an apparition were there before him.

"How old was she? She seemed so delicate, because she was not long for this world, I suppose?"

"Nineteen, perhaps? My mother, who was her nurse, died and left me behind. Her father took a fancy to me, and so we grew up together, and I never once left her side. I wonder how I can go on without her. I am almost sorry that we were so close. She seemed so weak, but I can see now that she was a source of strength."

"The weak ones do have a power over us. The clear, forceful ones I can do without. I am weak and indecisive by nature myself, and a woman who is quiet and withdrawn and follows the wishes of a man even to the point of letting herself be used has much the greater appeal. A man can shape and mold her as he wishes, and becomes fonder of her all the while."

"She was exactly what you would have wished, sir." Ukon was in tears. "That thought makes the loss seem greater."

The sky had clouded over and a chilly wind had come up. Gazing off into the distance, Genji said softly:

"One sees the clouds as smoke that rose from the pyre,
And suddenly the evening sky seems nearer."

Ukon was unable to answer. If only her lady were here! For Genji even the memory of those fulling blocks was sweet.

"In the Eighth Month, the Ninth Month, the nights are long,"[3] he whispered, and lay down.

The young page, brother of the lady of the locust shell, came to Nijō from time to time, but Genji no longer sent messages for his sister. She was sorry that he seemed angry with her and sorry to hear of his illness. The prospect of accompanying her husband to his distant province was a dreary one. She sent off a note to see whether Genji had forgotten her.

"They tell me you have not been well.

"Time goes by, you ask not why I ask not.
Think if you will how lonely a life is mine.

"I might make reference to Masuda Pond."[4]

This was a surprise; and indeed he had not forgotten her. The uncertain hand in which he set down his reply had its own beauty.

"Who, I wonder, lives the more aimless life.

"Hollow though it was, the shell of the locust
Gave me strength to face a gloomy world.

"But only precariously."

So he still remembered "the shell of the locust." She was sad and at the same time amused. It was good that they could correspond without rancor. She wished no further intimacy, and she did not want him to despise her.

As for the other, her stepdaughter, Genji heard that she had married a guards lieutenant. He thought it a strange marriage and he felt a certain pity for the lieutenant. Curious to know something of her feelings, he sent a note by his young messenger.

---

3. Alludes to the Chinese poem *The Fulling Blocks at Night,* by Po Chü-i.   4. Alludes to a poem: "Long the roots of the Masuda waters shield, / Longer still the aimless, sleepless nights."

"Did you know that thoughts of you had brought me to the point of expiring?

> "I bound them loosely, the reeds beneath the eaves,[5]
> And reprove them now for having come undone."

He attached it to a long reed.

The boy was to deliver it in secret, he said. But he thought that the lieutenant would be forgiving if he were to see it, for he would guess who the sender was. One may detect here a note of self-satisfaction.

Her husband was away. She was confused, but delighted that he should have remembered her. She sent off in reply a poem the only excuse for which was the alacrity with which it was composed:

> "The wind brings words, all softly, to the reed,
> And the under leaves are nipped again by the frost."

It might have been cleverer and in better taste not to have disguised the clumsy handwriting. He thought of the face he had seen by lamplight. He could forget neither of them, the governor's wife, seated so primly before him, or the younger woman, chattering on so contentedly, without the smallest suggestion of reserve. The stirrings of a susceptible heart suggested that he still had important lessons to learn.

Quietly, forty-ninth-day services[6] were held for the dead lady in the Lotus Hall on Mount Hiei. There was careful attention to all the details, the priestly robes and the scrolls and the altar decorations. Koremitsu's older brother was a priest of considerable renown, and his conduct of the services was beyond reproach. Genji summoned a doctor of letters with whom he was friendly and who was his tutor in Chinese poetry and asked him to prepare a final version of the memorial petition. Genji had prepared a draft. In moving language he committed the one he had loved and lost, though he did not mention her name, to the mercy of Amitābha.

"It is perfect, just as it is. Not a word needs to be changed." Noting the tears that refused to be held back, the doctor wondered who might be the subject of these prayers. That Genji should not reveal the name, and that he should be in such open grief—someone, no doubt, who had brought a very large bounty of grace from earlier lives.

Genji attached a poem to a pair of lady's trousers which were among his secret offerings:

> "I weep and weep as today I tie this cord.
> It will be untied in an unknown world to come."

He invoked the holy name with great feeling. Her spirit had wandered uncertainly these last weeks. Today it would set off down one of the ways of the future.

His heart raced each time he saw Tō no Chūjō. He longed to tell his friend that "the wild carnation" was alive and well; but there was no point in calling forth reproaches.

In the house of the "evening faces," the women were at a loss to know

---

5. The girl is traditionally called Nokiba-no-ogi, The Reeds Beneath the Eaves.   6. Held to pray for the woman's successful rebirth. Buddhist doctrine maintains that the spirit of the dead leads an indeterminate existence for forty-nine days, after which it begins a new incarnation.

what had happened to their lady. They had no way of inquiring. And Ukon too had disappeared. They whispered among themselves that they had been right about that gentleman, and they hinted at their suspicions to Koremitsu. He feigned complete ignorance, however, and continued to pursue his little affairs. For the poor women it was all like a nightmare. Perhaps the wanton son of some governor, fearing Tō no Chūjō, had spirited her off to the country? The owner of the house was her nurse's daughter. She was one of three children and related to Ukon. She could only long for her lady and lament that Ukon had not chosen to enlighten them. Ukon for her part was loath to raise a stir, and Genji did not want gossip at this late date. Ukon could not even inquire after the child. And so the days went by bringing no light on the terrible mystery.

Genji longed for a glimpse of the dead girl, if only in a dream. On the day after the services he did have a fleeting dream of the woman who had appeared that fatal night. He concluded, and the thought filled him with horror, that he had attracted the attention of an evil spirit haunting the neglected villa.

Early in the Tenth Month the governor of Iyo left for his post, taking the lady of the locust shell with him. Genji chose his farewell presents with great care. For the lady there were numerous fans, and combs of beautiful workmanship, and pieces of cloth (she could see that he had had them dyed specially) for the wayside gods. He also returned her robe, "the shell of the locust."

"A keepsake till we meet again, I had hoped,
And see, my tears have rotted the sleeves away."

There were other things too, but it would be tedious to describe them. His messenger returned empty-handed. It was through her brother that she answered his poem.

"Autumn comes, the wings of the locust are shed.
A summer robe returns, and I weep aloud."

She had remarkable singleness of purpose, whatever else she might have. It was the first day of winter. There were chilly showers, as if to mark the occasion, and the skies were dark. He spent the day lost in thought.

"The one has gone, to the other I saw farewell.
They go their unknown ways. The end of autumn."

He knew how painful a secret love can be.

I had hoped, out of deference to him, to conceal these difficult matters; but I have been accused of romancing, of pretending that because he was the son of an emperor he had no faults. Now, perhaps, I shall be accused of having revealed too much.

Summary   Nine years elapse in the chapters between *Evening Faces* and *Suma*, and many things happen. Genji meets Murasaki, a ten-year-old child, whom he grooms as his future wife, and in due course they marry. Of all the women he will know, throughout his life Genji remains supremely devoted to this one.

Although relations have been chilly with his first wife, Aoi, she bears him a son, Yūgiri, only to die soon after. It is following the period of mourning for Aoi that Genji consummates his union with Murasaki.

Despite his new love, Genji's eye continues to wander. Unwisely, he allows his obsession with Fujitsubo to run away with him. She becomes pregnant as a result, and although the emperor is delighted with the thought of an heir, Genji and Fujitsubo are greatly troubled. A son is born, a future emperor, and Fujitsubo is elevated to the rank of empress.

In the meantime, Genji has also become enamored of Oborozukiyo, the sister of his greatest enemy, his mother's old rival, Kokiden. When Kokiden discovers her sister's affair, in her fury she vows to drive Genji from the court. The death of his father abruptly alters the climate for Genji. Kokiden, with her son on the throne, is now in control. And Fujitsubo, remorseful over her actions, which have violated both her husband's trust and the sanctity of the imperial institution, renounces the world and becomes a nun. Everything has changed. It would seem that for Genji the palmy days are over.

CHAPTER 12

Suma[7]

For Genji life had become an unbroken succession of reverses and afflictions. He must consider what to do next. If he went on pretending that nothing was amiss, then even worse things might lie ahead. He thought of the Suma coast. People of worth had once lived there, he was told, but now it was deserted save for the huts of fishermen, and even they were few. The alternative was worse, to go on living this public life, so to speak, with people streaming in and out of his house. Yet he would hate to leave, and affairs at court would continue to be much on his mind if he did leave. This irresolution was making life difficult for his people.

Unsettling thoughts of the past and the future chased one another through his mind. The thought of leaving the city aroused a train of regrets, led by the image of a grieving Murasaki. It was very well to tell himself that somehow, someday, by some route they would come together again. Even when they were separated for a day or two Genji was beside himself with worry and Murasaki's gloom was beyond describing. It was not as if they would be parting for a fixed span of years; and if they had only the possibility of a reunion on some unnamed day with which to comfort themselves, well, life is uncertain, and they might be parting forever. He thought of consulting no one and taking her with him, but the inappropriateness of subjecting such a fragile lady to the rigors of life on that harsh coast, where the only callers would be the wind and the waves, was too obvious. Having her with him would only add to his worries. She guessed his thoughts and was unhappy. She let it be known that she did not want to be left behind, however forbidding the journey and life at the end of it.

Then there was the lady of the orange blossoms.[8] He did not visit her often, it is true, but he was her only support and comfort, and she would have every right to feel lonely and insecure. And there were women who, after the most fleeting affairs with him, went on nursing their various secret sorrows.

Fujitsubo, though always worried about rumors, wrote frequently. It struck him as bitterly ironical that she had not returned his affection earlier, but he told himself that a fate which they had shared from other lives must require that they know the full range of sorrows.

---

7. The village on the Inland Sea, southwest of the capital, where Genji goes into exile.   8. One of Genji's lesser loves.

He left the city late in the Third Month. He made no announcement of his departure, which was very inconspicuous, and had only seven or eight trusted retainers with him. He did write to certain people who should know of the event. I have no doubt that there were many fine passages in the letters with which he saddened the lives of his many ladies, but, grief-stricken myself, I did not listen as carefully as I might have.

Two or three days before his departure he visited his father-in-law. It was sad, indeed rather eerie, to see the care he took not to attract notice. His carriage, a humble one covered with cypress basketwork, might have been mistaken for a woman's. The apartments of his late wife wore a lonely, neglected aspect. At the arrival of this wondrous and unexpected guest, the little boy's nurse and all the other women who had not taken positions elsewhere gathered for a last look. Even the shallowest of the younger women were moved to tears at the awareness he brought of transience and mutability. Yūgiri, the little boy, was very pretty indeed, and indefatigably noisy.

"It has been so long. I am touched that he has not forgotten me." He took the boy on his knee and seemed about to weep.

The minister, his father-in-law, came in. "I know that you are shut up at home with little to occupy you, and I had been thinking I would like to call on you and have a good talk. I talk on and on when once I let myself get started. But I have told them I am ill and have been staying away from court, and I have even resigned my offices; and I know what they would say if I were to stretch my twisted old legs for my own pleasure. I hardly need to worry about such things any more, of course, but I am still capable of being upset by false accusations. When I see how things are with you, I know all too painfully what a sad day I have come on at the end of too long a life. I would have expected the world to end before this was allowed to happen, and I see not a ray of light in it all."

"Dear sir, we must accept the disabilities we bring from other lives. Everything that has happened to me is a result of my own inadequacy. I have heard that in other lands as well as our own an offense which does not, like mine, call for dismissal from office is thought to become far graver if the culprit goes on happily living his old life. And when exile is considered, as I believe it is in my case, the offense must have been thought more serious. Though I know I am innocent, I know too what insults I may look forward to if I stay, and so I think that I will forestall them by leaving."

Brushing away tears, the minister talked of old times, of Genji's father, and all he had said and thought. Genji too was weeping. The little boy scrambled and rolled about the room, now pouncing upon his father and now making demands upon his grandfather.

"I have gone on grieving for my daughter. And then I think what agony all this would have been to her, and am grateful that she lived such a short life and was spared the nightmare. So I try to tell myself, in any event. My chief sorrows and worries are for our little man here. He must grow up among us dotards, and the days and months will go by without the advantage of your company. It used to be that even people who were guilty of serious crimes escaped this sort of punishment; and I suppose we must call it fate, in our land and other lands too, that punishment should come all the same. But one does want to know what the charges are. In your case they quite defy the imagination."

Tō no Chūjō came in. They drank until very late, and Genji was induced to stay the night. He summoned Aoi's various women. Chūnagon was the one whom he had most admired, albeit in secret. He went on talking to her after everything was quiet, and it would seem to have been because of her that he was prevailed upon to spend the night. Dawn was at hand when he got up to leave. The moon in the first suggestions of daylight was very beautiful. The cherry blossoms were past their prime, and the light through the few that remained flooded the garden silver. Everything faded together into a gentle mist, sadder and more moving than on a night in autumn. He sat for a time leaning against the railing at a corner of the veranda. Chūnagon was waiting at the door as if to see him off.

"I wonder when we will be permitted to meet again." He paused, choking with tears. "Never did I dream that this would happen, and I neglected you in the days when it would have been so easy to see you."

Saishō, Yūgiri's nurse, came with a message from Princess Omiya.[9] "I would have liked to say goodbye in person, but I have waited in hope that the turmoil of my thoughts might quiet a little. And now I hear that you are leaving, and it is still so early. Everything seems changed, completely wrong. It is a pity that you cannot at least wait until our little sleepyhead is up and about."

Weeping softly, Genji whispered to himself, not precisely by way of reply:

> "There on the shore, the salt burners' fires await me.
> Will their smoke be as the smoke over Toribe Moor?

Is this the parting at dawn we are always hearing of? No doubt there are those who know.

"I have always hated the word 'farewell,' " said Saishō, whose grief seemed quite unfeigned. "And our farewells today are unlike any others."

"Over and over again," he sent back to Princess Omiya, "I have thought of all the things I would have liked to say to you; and I hope you will understand and forgive my muteness. As for our little sleepyhead, I fear that if I were to see him I would wish to stay on even in this hostile city, and so I shall collect myself and be on my way."

All the women were there to see him go. He looked more elegant and handsome than ever in the light of the setting moon, and his dejection would have reduced tigers and wolves to tears. These were women who had served him since he was very young. It was a sad day for them.

There was a poem from Princess Omiya:

> "Farther retreats the day when we bade her goodbye,
> For now you depart the skies that received the smoke."[1]

Sorrow was added to sorrow, and the tears almost seemed to invite further misfortunes.

He returned to Nijō. The women, awake the whole night through, it seemed, were gathered in sad clusters. There was no one in the guardroom. The men closest to him, reconciled to going with him, were making their own personal farewells. As for other court functionaries, there had been ominous hints of sanctions were they to come calling, and so the grounds, once crowded with horses and carriages, were empty and silent. He knew

---

9. Mother of Aoi and Tō no Chūjō.   1. Refers to Aoi's cremation.

again what a hostile world it had become. There was dust on the tables, cushions had been put away. And what would be the extremes of waste and the neglect when he was gone?

He went to Murasaki's wing of the house. She had been up all night, not even lowering the shutters. Out near the verandas little girls[2] were noisily bestirring themselves. They were so pretty in their night dress—and presently, no doubt, they would find the loneliness too much, and go their various ways. Such thoughts had not before been a part of his life.

He told Murasaki what had kept him at Sanjō. "And I suppose you are filled with the usual odd suspicions. I have wanted to be with you every moment I am still in the city, but there are things that force me to go out. Life is uncertain enough at best, and I would not want to seem cold and unfeeling."

"And what should be 'odd' now except that you are going away?"

That she should feel these sad events more cruelly than any of the others was not surprising. From her childhood she had been closer to Genji than to her own father, who now bowed to public opinion and had not offered a word of sympathy. His coldness had caused talk among her women. She was beginning to wish that they had kept him in ignorance of her whereabouts.

Someone reported what her stepmother was saying: "She had a sudden stroke of good luck, and now just as suddenly everything goes wrong. It makes a person shiver. One after another, each in his own way, they all run out on her."

This was too much. There was nothing more she wished to say to them. Henceforth she would have only Genji.

"If the years go by and I am still an outcast," he continued, "I will come for you and bring you to my 'cave among the rocks.'[3] But we must not be hasty. A man who is out of favor at court is not permitted the light of the sun and the moon, and it is thought a great crime, I am told, for him to go on being happy. The cause of it all is a great mystery to me, but I must accept it as fate. There seems to be no precedent for sharing exile with a lady, and I am sure that to suggest it would be to invite worse insanity from an insane world."

He slept until almost noon.

Tō no Chūjō and Genji's brother, Prince Hotaru, came calling. Since he was now without rank and office, he changed to informal dress of unfigured silk, more elegant, and even somehow grand, for its simplicity. As he combed his hair he could not help noticing that loss of weight had made him even handsomer.

"I am skin and bones," he said to Murasaki, who sat gazing at him, tears in her eyes. "Can I really be as emaciated as this mirror makes me? I am a little sorry for myself.

"I now must go into exile. In this mirror
An image of me will yet remain beside you."

Huddling against a pillar to hide her tears, she replied as if to herself:

---

2. Murasaki's companions in Genji's absence.   3. Alludes to a poem in *The Kokinshū*: "Where shall I go, to what cave among the rocks, / To be free of tidings of this gloomy world?"

"If when we part an image yet remains,
Then will I find some comfort in my sorrow."

Yes, she was unique—a new awareness of that fact stabbed at his heart.

Prince Hotaru kept him affectionate company through the day and left in the evening.

It was not hard to imagine the loneliness that brought frequent notes from the house of the falling orange blossoms. Fearing that he would seem unkind if he did not visit the ladies again, he resigned himself to spending yet another night away from home. It was very late before he gathered himself for the effort.

"We are honored that you should consider us worth a visit," said Lady Reikeiden—and it would be difficult to record the rest of the interview.

They lived precarious lives, completely dependent on Genji. So lonely indeed was their mansion that he could imagine the desolation awaiting it once he himself was gone; and the heavily wooded hill rising dimly beyond the wide pond in misty moonlight made him wonder whether the "cave among the rocks" at Suma would be such a place.

He went to the younger sister's room, at the west side of the house. She had been in deep despondency, almost certain that he would not find time for a visit. Then, in the soft, sad lights of the moon, his robes giving off an indescribable fragrance, he made his way in. She came to the veranda and looked up at the moon. They talked until dawn.

"What a short night it has been. I think how difficult it will be for us to meet again, and I am filled with regrets for the days I wasted. I fear I worried too much about the precedents I might be setting."

A cock was crowing busily as he talked on about the past. He made a hasty departure, fearful of attracting notice. The setting moon is always sad, and he was prompted to think its situation rather like his own. Catching the deep purple of the lady's robe, the moon itself seemed to be weeping.[4]

"Narrow these sleeves, now lodging for the moonlight.
Would they might keep a light which I do not tire of."

Sad himself, Genji sought to comfort her.

"The moon will shine upon this house once more.
Do not look at the clouds which now conceal it.

"I wish I were really sure it is so, and find the unknown future clouding my heart."

He left as dawn was coming over the sky.

His affairs were in order. He assigned all the greater and lesser affairs of the Nijō mansion to trusted retainers who had not been swept up in the currents of the times, and he selected others to go with him to Suma. He would take only the simplest essentials for a rustic life, among them a book chest, selected writings of Po Chü-i and other poets, and a seven-stringed Chinese koto. He carefully refrained from anything which in its ostentation might not become a nameless rustic.

---

4. Alludes to a poem by Lady Ise in *The Kokinshū*: "Catching the drops on my sleeves as I lay in thought, / The moonlight seemed to be shedding tears of its own" (see poem 756, p. 2171, for an alternate translation).

Assigning all the women to Murasaki's west wing, he left behind deeds to pastures and manors and the like and made provision for all his various warehouses and storerooms. Confident of Shōnagon's perspicacity he gave her careful instructions and put stewards at her disposal. He had been somewhat brisk and businesslike toward his own serving women, but they had had security—and now what was to become of them?

"I shall be back, I know, if I live long enough. Do what you can in the west wing, please, those of you who are prepared to wait."

And so they all began a new life.

To Yūgiri's nurse and maids and to the lady of the orange blossoms he sent elegant parting gifts and plain, useful everyday provisions as well.

He even wrote to Oborozukiyo. "I know that I have no right to expect a letter from you; but I am not up to describing the gloom and the bitterness of leaving this life behind.

"Snagged upon the shoals of this river of tears,
I cannot see you. Deeper waters await me.

"Remembering is the crime to which I cannot plead innocent."

He wrote nothing more, for there was a danger that his letter would be intercepted.

Though she fought to maintain her composure, there was nothing she could do about the tears that wet her sleeves.

"The foam on the river of tears will disappear
Short of the shoals of meeting that wait downstream."

There was something very fine about the hand disordered by grief.

He longed to see her again, but she had too many relatives who wished him ill. Discretion forbade further correspondence.

On the night before his departure he visited his father's grave in the northern hills. Since the moon would be coming up shortly before dawn, he went first to take leave of Fujitsubo. Receiving him in person, she spoke of her worries for the crown prince. It cannot have been, so complicated were matters between them, a less than deeply felt interview. Her dignity and beauty were as always. He would have liked to hint at old resentments; but why, at this late date, invite further unpleasantness, and risk adding to his own agitation?

He only said, and it was reasonable enough: "I can think of a single offense for which I must undergo this strange, sad punishment, and because of it I tremble before the heavens. Though I would not care in the least if my own unworthy self were to vanish away, I only hope that the crown prince's reign is without unhappy event."

She knew too well what he meant, and was unable to reply. He was almost too handsome as at last he succumbed to tears.

"I am going to pay my respects at His Majesty's grave. Do you have a message?"

She was silent for a time, seeking to control herself.

"The one whom I served is gone, the other must go.
Farewell to the world was no farewell to its sorrows."

But for both of them the sorrow was beyond words.

He replied:

"The worst of grief for him should long have passed.
And now I must leave the world where dwells the child."

The moon had risen and he set out. He was on horseback and had only
five or six attendants, all of them trusted friends. I need scarcely say that it
was a far different procession from those of old. Among his men was that
guards officer who had been his special attendant at the Kamo lustration
services.[5] The promotion he might have expected had long since passed him
by, and now his right of access to the royal presence and his offices had been
taken away. Remembering that day as they came in sight of the Lower Kamo
Shrine, he dismounted and took Genji's bridle.

"There was heartvine[6] in our caps. I led your horse.
And now at this jeweled fence I berate the gods."

Yes, the memory must be painful, for the young man had been the most
resplendent in Genji's retinue. Dismounting, Genji bowed toward the shrine
and said as if by way of farewell:

"I leave this world of gloom. I leave my name
To the offices of the god who rectifies."[7]

The guards officer, an impressionable young man, gazed at him in wonder
and admiration.

Coming to the grave, Genji almost thought he could see his father before
him. Power and position were nothing once a man was gone. He wept and
silently told his story, but there came no answer, no judgment upon it. And
all those careful instructions and admonitions had served no purpose at all?

Grasses overgrew the path to the grave, the dew seemed to gather weight
as he made his way through. The moon had gone behind a cloud and the
groves were dark and somehow terrible. It was as if he might lose his way
upon turning back. As he bowed in farewell, a chill came over him, for he
seemed to see his father as he once had been.

"And how does he look upon me? I raise my eyes,
And the moon now vanishes behind the clouds."

Back at Nijō at daybreak, he sent a last message to the crown prince. Tying
it to a cherry branch from which the blossoms had fallen, he addressed it to
Omyōbu, whom Fujitsubo had put in charge of her son's affairs. "Today I
must leave. I regret more than anything that I cannot see you again. Imagine
my feelings, if you will, and pass them on to the prince.

"When shall I, a ragged, rustic outcast,
See again the blossoms of the city?"

She explained everything to the crown prince. He gazed at her solemnly.
"How shall I answer?" Omyōbu asked.

"I am sad when he is away for a little, and he is going so far, and how—
tell him that, please."

---

5. Held to inaugurate the shrines' new high priestess. The Kamo shrines were two of the most important
Shinto shrines. In the novel, the entire imperial court turns out to observe the ceremonial procession.
During the procession the retainers of Genji's wife Aoi tangle with those of the Rokujō lady, who is humiliated.   6. A pun that suggests Genji's wife Aoi, whose name can be translated as "heartvine," or "hollyhock."   7. Tadasu no Kami, who has his abode in the Lower Kamo Shrine.

A sad little answer, thought Omyōbu.[8]

All the details of that unhappy love came back to her. The two of them should have led placid, tranquil lives, and she felt as if she and she alone had been the cause of all the troubles.

"I can think of nothing to say." It was clear to him that her answer had indeed been composed with great difficulty. "I passed your message on to the prince, and was sadder than ever to see how sad it made him.

"Quickly the blossoms fall. Though spring departs,
You will come again, I know, to a city of flowers."

There was sad talk all through the crown prince's apartments in the wake of the letter, and there were sounds of weeping. Even people who scarcely knew him were caught up in the sorrow. As for people in his regular service, even scullery maids of whose existence he can hardly have been aware were sad at the thought that they must for a time do without his presence.

So it was all through the court. Deep sorrow prevailed. He had been with his father day and night from his seventh year, and, since nothing he had said to his father had failed to have an effect, almost everyone was in his debt. A cheerful sense of gratitude should have been common in the upper ranks of the court and the ministries, and omnipresent in the lower ranks. It was there, no doubt; but the world had become a place of quick punishments. A pity, people said, silently reproving the great ones whose power was now absolute; but what was to be accomplished by playing the martyr? Not that everyone was satisfied with passive acceptance. If he had not known before, Genji knew now that the human race is not perfect.

He spent a quiet day with Murasaki and late in the night set out in rough travel dress.

"The moon is coming up. Do please come out and see me off. I know that later I will think of any number of things I wanted to say to you. My gloom strikes me as ridiculous when I am away from you for even a day or two."

He raised the blinds and urged her to come forward. Trying not to weep, she at length obeyed. She was very beautiful in the moonlight. What sort of home would this unkind, inconstant city be for her now? But she was sad enough already, and these thoughts were best kept to himself.

He said with forced lightness:

"At least for this life we might make our vows, we thought.
And so we vowed that nothing would ever part us.

How silly we were!"

This was her answer:

"I would give a life for which I have no regrets
If it might postpone for a little the time of parting."

They were not empty words, he knew; but he must be off, for he did not want the city to see him in broad daylight.

Her face was with him the whole of the journey. In great sorrow he boarded the boat that would take him to Suma. It was a long spring day and there was a tail wind, and by late afternoon he had reached the strand where he

---

8. The crown prince's answer breaks into seven-syllable lines, as if he were trying to compose a poem.

was to live. He had never before been on such a journey, however short. All the sad, exotic things along the way were new to him. The Oe station[9] was in ruins, with only a grove of pines to show where it had stood.

> "More remote, I fear, my place of exile
> Than storied ones in lands beyond the seas."

The surf came in and went out again. "I envy the waves," he whispered to himself.[1] It was a familiar poem, but it seemed new to those who heard him, and sad as never before. Looking back toward the city, he saw that the mountains were enshrouded in mist. It was as though he had indeed come "three thousand leagues."[2] The spray from the oars brought thoughts scarcely to be borne.

> "Mountain mists cut off that ancient village.
> Is the sky I see the sky that shelters it?"

Not far away Yukihira had lived in exile, "dripping brine from the sea grass."[3] Genji's new house was some distance from the coast, in mountains utterly lonely and desolate. The fences and everything within were new and strange. The grass-roofed cottages, the reed-roofed galleries—or so they seemed—were interesting enough in their way. It was a dwelling proper to a remote littoral, and different from any he had known. Having once had a taste for out-of-the-way places, he might have enjoyed this Suma had the occasion been different.

Yoshikiyo had appointed himself a sort of confidential steward. He summoned the overseers of Genji's several manors in the region and assigned them to necessary tasks. Genji watched admiringly. In very quick order he had a rather charming new house. A deep brook flowed through the garden with a pleasing murmur, new plantings were set out; and when finally he was beginning to feel a little at home he could scarcely believe that it all was real. The governor of the province, an old retainer, discreetly performed numerous services. All in all it was a brighter and livelier place than he had a right to expect, although the fact that there was no one whom he could really talk to kept him from forgetting that it was a house of exile, strange and alien. How was he to get through the months and years ahead?

The rainy season came. His thoughts traveled back to the distant city. There were people whom he longed to see, chief among them the lady at Nijō, whose forlorn figure was still before him. He thought too of the crown prince, and of little Yūgiri, running so happily, that last day, from father to grandfather and back again. He sent off letters to the city. Some of them, especially those to Murasaki and to Fujitsubo, took a great deal of time, for his eyes clouded over repeatedly.

This is what he wrote to Fujitsubo:

> "Briny our sleeves on the Suma strand; and yours
> In the fisher cots of thatch at Matsushima?[4]

---

9. In the heart of present-day Osaka; it was used by high priestesses on their way to and from the Ise Shrine.   1. Alludes to a poem by Ariwara Narihira: "Strong my yearning for what I have left behind. / I envy the waves that go back whence they came."   2. Alludes to Po Chü-i's poem *Lines Written on the Winter Solstice, in the Arbutus Hall.*   3. From a poem by Ariwara Yukihira in *The Kokinshū:* "If someone should inquire for me, reply: / 'He idles at Suma, dripping brine from the sea grass.' " Yukihira was himself exiled at Suma.   4. A very common pun makes *Matsushima* "The isle of one who waits."

"My eyes are dark as I think of what is gone and what is to come, and 'the waters rise.' "[5]

His letter to Oborozukiyo he sent as always to Chūnagon, as if it were a private matter between the two of them. "With nothing else to occupy me, I find memories of the past coming back.

"At Suma, unchastened, one longs for the deep-lying sea pine.
And she, the fisher lady burning salt?"

I shall leave the others, among them letters to his father-in-law and Yūgiri's nurse, to the reader's imagination. They reached their several destinations and gave rise to many sad and troubled thoughts.

Murasaki had taken to her bed. Her women, doing everything they could think of to comfort her, feared that in her grief and longing she might fall into a fatal decline. Brooding over the familiar things he had left behind, the koto, the perfumed robes, she almost seemed on the point of departing the world. Her women were beside themselves. Shōnagon sent asking that the bishop, her uncle, pray for her. He did so, and to double purpose, that she be relieved of her present sorrows and that she one day be permitted a tranquil life with Genji.

She sent bedding and other supplies to Suma. The robes and trousers of stiff, unfigured white silk brought new pangs of sorrow, for they were unlike anything he had worn before. She kept always with her the mirror to which he had addressed his farewell poem, though it was not acquitting itself of the duty he had assigned to it. The door through which he had come and gone, the cypress pillar at his favorite seat—everything brought sad memories. So it is even for people hardened and seasoned by trials, and how much more for her, to whom he had been father and mother! "Grasses of forgetfulness"[6] might have sprung up had he quite vanished from the earth; but he was at Suma, not so very far away, she had heard. She could not know when he would return.

For Fujitsubo, sorrow was added to uncertainty about her son. And how, at the thought of the fate that had joined them, could her feelings for Genji be of a bland and ordinary kind? Fearful of gossips, she had coldly turned away each small show of affection, she had become more and more cautious and secretive, and she had given him little sign that she sensed the depth of his affection. He had been uncommonly careful himself. Gossips are cruelly attentive people (it was a fact she knew too well), but they seemed to have caught no suspicion of the affair. He had kept himself under tight control and preserved the most careful appearances. How then could she not, in this extremity, have fond thoughts for him?

Her reply was more affectionate than usual.

"The nun of Matsushima burns the brine
And fuels the fires with the logs of her lamenting,

now more than ever."

Enclosed with Chūnagon's letter was a brief reply from Oborozukiyo:

---

5. Another poetic allusion: "The sorrow of parting brings such flood of tears / That the waters of this river must surely rise."   6. The literal translation of *wasuregusa*, "day lilies."

"The fisherwife burns salt and hides her fires
And strangles, for the smoke has no escape.

"I shall not write of things which at this late date need no saying."
Chūnagon wrote in detail of her lady's sorrows. There were tears in his
eyes as he read her letter.

And Murasaki's reply was of course deeply moving. There was this poem:

"Taking brine on that strand, let him compare
His dripping sleeves with these night sleeves of mine."

The robes that came with it were beautifully dyed and tailored. She did
everything so well. At Suma there were no silly and frivolous distractions,
and it seemed a pity that they could not enjoy the quiet life together.
Thoughts of her, day and night, became next to unbearable. Should he send
for her in secret? But no: his task in this gloomy situation must be to make
amends for past misdoings. He began a fast and spent his days in prayer and
meditation.

There were also messages about his little boy, Yūgiri. They of course filled
him with longing; but he would see the boy again one day, and in the meantime he was in good hands. Yet a father must, however he tries, "wander lost
in thoughts upon his child."[7]

In the confusion I had forgotten: he had sent off a message to the Rokujō
lady, and she on her own initiative had sent a messenger to seek out his place
of exile. Her letter was replete with statements of the deepest affection. The
style and the calligraphy, superior to those of anyone else he knew, showed
unique breeding and cultivation.

"Having been told of the unthinkable place in which you find yourself, I
feel as if I were wandering in an endless nightmare. I should imagine that
you will be returning to the city before long, but it will be a very long time
before I, so lost in sin, will be permitted to see you.

"Imagine, at Suma of the dripping brine,
The woman of Ise,[8] gathering briny sea grass.

"And what is to become of one, in a world where everything conspires to
bring new sorrow?" It was a long letter.

"The tide recedes along the coast of Ise.
No hope, no promise in the empty shells."

Laying down her brush as emotion overcame her and then beginning
again, she finally sent off some four or five sheets of white Chinese paper.
The gradations of ink were marvelous. He had been fond of her, and it had
been wrong to make so much of that one incident.[9] She had turned against
him and presently left him. It all seemed such a waste. The letter itself and
the occasion for it so moved him that he even felt a certain affection for the
messenger, an intelligent young man in her daughter's service. Detaining
him for several days, he heard about life at Ise. The house being rather small,

7. Alludes to a poem: "The heart of a parent is not darkness, and yet / He wanders lost in thoughts upon
his child."   8. She has gone to Ise, where her daughter serves as high priestess.   9. It was the Rokujō
lady's jealousy, in the form of a vengeful spirit, that killed the lady in chapter 4.

the messenger was able to observe Genji at close range. He was moved to tears of admiration by what he saw.

The reader may be left to imagine Genji's reply. He said among other things: "Had I known I was destined to leave the city, it would have been better, I tell myself in the tedium and loneliness here, to go off with you to Ise.

"With the lady of Ise I might have ridden small boats
That row the waves, and avoided dark sea tangles.[1]

"How long, dripping brine on driftwood logs,
On logs of lament, must I gaze at this Suma coast?

"I cannot know when I will see you again."
But at least his letters brought the comfort of knowing that he was well.

There came letters, sad and yet comforting, from the lady of the orange blossoms and her sister.

"Ferns of remembrance weigh our eaves ever more,
And heavily falls the dew upon our sleeves."

There was no one, he feared, whom they might now ask to clear away the rank growth. Hearing that the long rains had damaged their garden walls, he sent off orders to the city that people from nearby manors see to repairs.

Oborozukiyo had delighted the scandalmongers, and she was now in very deep gloom. Her father, the minister, for she was his favorite daughter, sought to intercede on her behalf with the emperor and Kokiden. The emperor was moved to forgive her. She had been severely punished, it was true, for her grave offense, but not as severely as if she had been one of the companions of the royal bedchamber. In the Seventh Month she was permitted to return to court. She continued to long for Genji. Much of the emperor's old love remained, and he chose to ignore criticism and keep her near him, now berating her and now making impassioned vows. He was a handsome man and he groomed himself well, and it was something of an affront that old memories should be so much with her.

"Things do not seem right now that he is gone," he said one evening when they were at music together. "I am sure that there are many who feel the loss even more strongly than I do. I cannot put away the fear that I have gone against Father's last wishes and that it is a dereliction for which I must one day suffer." There were tears in his eyes and she too was weeping. "I have awakened to the stupidity of the world and I do not feel that I wish to remain in it much longer. And how would you feel if I were to die? I hate to think that you would grieve less for me gone forever than for him gone so briefly such a short distance away. The poet[2] who said that we love while we live did not know a great deal about love." Tears were streaming from Oborozukiyo's eyes. "And whom might you be weeping for? It is sad that we have no children. I would like to follow Father's instructions and adopt the crown prince, but people will raise innumerable objections. It all seems very sad."

There were some whose ideas of government did not accord with his own,

1. From the folk song "Men of Ise": "Oh, the men of Ise are strange ones. / How so? How are they strange? / They ride small boats that row the waves, / That row the waves, they do." 2. Unidentified.

but he was too young to impose his will. He passed his days in helpless anger and sorrow.

At Suma, melancholy autumn winds were blowing. Genji's house was some distance from the sea, but at night the wind that blew over the barriers, now as in Yukihira's day, seemed to bring the surf to his bedside. Autumn was hushed and lonely at a place of exile. He had few companions. One night when they were all asleep he raised his head from his pillow and listened to the roar of the wind and of the waves, as if at his ears. Though he was unaware that he wept, his tears were enough to set his pillow afloat. He plucked a few notes on his koto, but the sound only made him sadder.

"The waves on the strand, like moans of helpless longing.
The winds—like messengers from those who grieve?"

He had awakened the others. They sat up, and one by one they were in tears.

This would not do. Because of him they had been swept into exile, leaving families from whom they had never before been parted. It must be very difficult for them, and his own gloom could scarcely be making things easier. So he set about cheering them. During the day he would invent games and make jokes, and set down this and that poem on multicolored patchwork, and paint pictures on fine specimens of figured Chinese silk. Some of his larger paintings were masterpieces. He had long ago been told of this Suma coast and these hills and had formed a picture of them in his mind, and he found now that his imagination had fallen short of the actuality. What a pity, said his men, that they could not summon Tsunenori and Chieda and other famous painters of the day to add colors to Genji's monochromes. This resolute cheerfulness had the proper effect. His men, four or five of whom were always with him, would not have dreamed of leaving him.

There was a profusion of flowers in the garden. Genji came out, when the evening colors were at their best, to a gallery from which he had a good view of the coast. His men felt chills of apprehension as they watched him, for the loneliness of the setting made him seem like a visitor from another world. In a dark robe tied loosely over singlets of figured white and aster-colored trousers, he announced himself as "a disciple of the Buddha" and slowly intoned a sutra, and his men thought that they had never heard a finer voice. From offshore came the voices of fishermen raised in song. The barely visible boats were like little seafowl on an utterly lonely sea, and as he brushed away a tear induced by the splashing of oars and the calls of wild geese overhead, the white of his hand against the jet black of his rosary was enough to bring comfort to men who had left their families behind.

"Might they be companions of those I long for?
Their cries ring sadly through the sky of their journey."

This was Yoshikiyo's reply:

"I know not why they bring these thoughts of old,
These wandering geese. They were not then my comrades."

And Koremitsu's:

"No colleagues of mine, these geese beyond the clouds.
They chose to leave their homes, and I did not."

And that of the guards officer who had cut such a proud figure on the day of the Kamo lustration:

"Sad are their cries as they wing their way from home.
They still find solace, for they still have comrades.

It is cruel to lose one's comrades."

His father had been posted to Hitachi, but he himself had come with Genji. He contrived, for all that must have been on his mind, to seem cheerful.

A radiant moon had come out. They were reminded that it was the harvest full moon. Genji could not take his eyes from it. On other such nights there had been concerts at court, and perhaps they of whom he was thinking would be gazing at this same moon and thinking of him.

"My thoughts are of you, old friend," he sang, "two thousand leagues away."[3] His men were in tears.

His longing was intense at the memory of Fujitsubo's farewell poem, and as other memories came back, one after another, he had to turn away to hide his tears. It was very late, said his men, but still he did not come inside.

"So long as I look upon it I find comfort,
The moon which comes again to the distant city."

He thought of the emperor and how much he had resembled their father, that last night when they had talked so fondly of old times. "I still have with me the robe which my lord gave me,"[4] he whispered, going inside. He did in fact have a robe that was a gift from the emperor, and he kept it always beside him.

"Not bitter thoughts alone does this singlet bring.
Its sleeves are damp with tears of affection too."

The assistant viceroy of Kyushu was returning to the capital. He had a large family and was especially well provided with daughters, and since progress by land would have been difficult he had sent his wife and the daughters by boat. They proceeded by easy stages, putting in here and there along the coast. The scenery at Suma was especially pleasing, and the news that Genji was in residence produced blushes and sighs far out at sea. The Gosechi dancer[5] would have liked to cut the tow rope and drift ashore. The sound of a koto came faint from the distance, the sadness of it joined to a sad setting and sad memories. The more sensitive members of the party were in tears.

The assistant viceroy sent a message. "I had hoped to call on you immediately upon returning to the city from my distant post, and when, to my surprise, I found myself passing your house, I was filled with the most intense feelings of sorrow and regret. Various acquaintances who might have been expected to come from the city have done so, and our party has become so numerous that it would be out of the question to call on you. I shall hope to do so soon."

His son, the governor of Chikuzen, brought the message. Genji had taken

---

3. From Po Chü-i's poem *On the Evening of the Full Moon of the Eighth Month.*   4. From a poem by Sugawara Michizane (9th century), scholar, poet, and bureaucrat; he was in exile.   5. Gosechi dances were part of a festival held in the Eleventh Month, usually performed by the young daughters of noble families. The appearance of the Gosechi dancer here is abrupt and puzzling. See n. 2, p. 2260.

notice of the youth and obtained an appointment for him in the imperial
secretariat. He was sad to see his patron in such straits, but people were
watching and had a way of talking, and he stayed only briefly.

"It was kind of you to come," said Genji. "I do not often see old friends
these days."

His reply to the assistant viceroy was in a similar vein. Everyone in the
Kyushu party and in the party newly arrived from the city as well was deeply
moved by the governor's description of what he had seen. The tears of sympathy almost seemed to invite worse misfortunes.

The Gosechi dancer contrived to send him a note.

> "Now taut, now slack, like my unruly heart,
> The tow rope is suddenly still at the sound of a koto.

"Scolding will not improve me."[6]

He smiled, so handsome a smile that his men felt rather inadequate.

> "Why, if indeed your heart is like the tow rope,
> Unheeding must you pass this strand of Suma?

"I had not expected to leave you for these wilds."[7]

There once was a man who, passing Akashi on his way into exile,[8] brought
pleasure into an innkeeper's life with an impromptu Chinese poem. For the
Gosechi dancer the pleasure was such that she would have liked to make
Suma her home.

As time passed, the people back in the city, and even the emperor himself,
found that Genji was more and more in their thoughts. The crown prince
was the saddest of all. His nurse and Omyōbu would find him weeping in a
corner and search helplessly for ways to comfort him. Once so fearful of
rumors and their possible effect on this child of hers and Genji's, Fujitsubo
now grieved that Genji must be away.

In the early days of his exile he corresponded with his brothers and with
important friends at court. Some of his Chinese poems were widely praised.
Kokiden flew into a rage. "A man out of favor with His Majesty is expected
to have trouble feeding himself. And here he is living in a fine stylish house
and saying awful things about all of us. No doubt the grovelers around him
are assuring him that a deer is a horse."[9]

And so writing to Genji came to be rather too much to ask of people, and
letters stopped coming.

The months went by, and Murasaki was never really happy. All the women
from the other wings of the house were now in her service. They had been
of the view that she was beneath their notice, but as they came to observe
her gentleness, her magnanimity in household matters, her thoughtfulness,
they changed their minds, and not one of them departed her service. Among
them were women of good family. A glimpse of her was enough to make
them admit that she deserved Genji's altogether remarkable affection.

And as time went by at Suma, Genji began to feel that he could bear to

---

6. Alludes to a poem in *The Kokinshū:* "My heart is like a ship upon the seas. / I am easily moved. Scolding
will not improve me."   7. An allusion to *The Kokinshū:* "I had not expected to leave you for these wilds.
/ A fisherman's net is mine, an angler's line."   8. Sugawara Michizane.   9. It is recorded in the *Shih
chi* (Historical Records) of ancient China that a eunuch planning a rebellion showed the high courtiers a
deer and required them to call it a horse, ensuring that they feared him.

be away from her no longer. But he dismissed the thought of sending for her: this cruel punishment was for himself alone. He was seeing a little of plebeian life, and he thought it very odd and, he must say, rather dirty. The smoke near at hand would, he supposed, be the smoke of the salt burners' fires. In fact, someone was trying to light wet kindling just behind the house.

"Over and over the rural ones light fires.
Not so unflagging the urban ones with their visits."

It was winter, and the snowy skies were wild. He beguiled the tedium with music, playing the koto himself and setting Koremitsu to the flute, with Yoshikiyo to sing for them. When he lost himself in a particularly moving strain the others would fall silent, tears in their eyes.

He thought of the lady the Chinese emperor sent off to the Huns.[1] How must the emperor have felt, how would Genji himself feel, in so disposing of a beautiful lady? He shuddered, as if some such task might be approaching, "at the end of a frosty night's dream."[2]

A bright moon flooded in, lighting the shallow-eaved cottage to the farthest corners. He was able to imitate the poet's feat of looking up at the night sky without going to the veranda.[3] There was a weird sadness in the setting moon. "The moon goes always to the west,"[4] he whispered.

"All aimless is my journey through the clouds.
It shames me that the unswerving moon should see me."

He recited it silently to himself. Sleepless as always, he heard the sad calls of the plovers in the dawn and (the others were not yet awake) repeated several times to himself:

"Cries of plovers in the dawn bring comfort
To one who awakens in a lonely bed."

His practice of going through his prayers and ablutions in the deep of night seemed strange and wonderful to his men. Far from being tempted to leave him, they did not return even for brief visits to their families.

The Akashi coast was a very short distance away. Yoshikiyo remembered the daughter of the former governor, now a monk, and wrote to her. She did not answer.

"I would like to see you for a few moments sometime at your convenience," came a note from her father. "There is something I want to ask you."

Yoshikiyo was not encouraged. He would look very silly if he went to Akashi only to be turned away. He did not go.

The former governor was an extremely proud and intractable man. The incumbent governor was all-powerful in the province, but the eccentric old man had no wish to marry his daughter to such an upstart. He learned of Genji's presence at Suma.

"I hear that the shining Genji is out of favor," he said to his wife, "and that he has come to Suma. What a rare stroke of luck—the chance we have been waiting for. We must offer our girl."

---

1. Wang Chao-chün was dispatched to the Huns from the harem of the Han emperor Yüan-ti because she had failed to bribe the artists who did portraits of court ladies, and the emperor therefore thought her ill-favored. 2. From a poem about the unlucky Wang Chao-chün. 3. Alludes to a poem written in Chinese, in which the poet describes a view of the night sky from within a ruined palace. 4. From *To the Moon*, a poem by Sugawara Michizane.

"Completely out of the question. People from the city tell me that he has any number of fine ladies of his own and that he has reached out for one of the emperor's. That is why the scandal. What interest can he possibly take in a country lump like her?"

"You don't understand the first thing about it. My own views couldn't be more different. We must make our plans. We must watch for a chance to bring him here." His mind was quite made up, and he had the look of someone whose plans were not easily changed. The finery which he had lavished upon house and daughter quite dazzled the eye.

"He may be ever so grand a grand gentleman," persisted the mother, "but it hardly seems the right and sensible thing to choose of all people a man who has been sent into exile for a serious crime. It might just possibly be different if he were likely to look at her—but no. You must be joking."

"A serious crime! Why in China too exactly this sort of thing happens to every single person who has remarkable talents and stands out from the crowd. And who do you think he is? His late mother was the daughter of my uncle, the Lord Inspector. She had talent and made a name for herself, and when there wasn't enough of the royal love to go around, the others were jealous, and finally they killed her. But she left behind a son who was a royal joy and comfort. Ladies should have pride and high ambitions. I may be a bumpkin myself, but I doubt that he will think her entirely beneath contempt."

Though the girl was no great beauty, she was intelligent and sensitive and had a gentle grace of which someone of far higher rank would have been proud. She was reconciled to her sad lot. No one among the great persons of the land was likely to think her worth a glance. The prospect of marrying someone nearer her station in life revolted her. If she was left behind by those on whom she depended, she would become a nun, or perhaps throw herself into the sea.

Her father had done everything for her. He sent her twice a year to the Sumiyoshi Shrine, hoping that the god might be persuaded to notice her.

The New Year came to Suma, the days were longer, and time went by slowly. The sapling cherry Genji had planted the year before sent out a scattering of blossoms, the air was soft and warm, and memories flooded back, bringing him often to tears. He thought longingly of the ladies for whom he had wept when, toward the end of the Second Month the year before, he had prepared to depart the city. The cherries would now be in bloom before the Grand Hall. He thought of that memorable cherry-blossom festival, and his father, and the extraordinarily handsome figure his brother, now the emperor, had presented, and he remembered how his brother had favored him by reciting his Chinese poem.

A Japanese poem[5] formed in his mind:

> "Fond thoughts I have of the noble ones on high,
> And the day of the flowered caps has come again."

Tō no Chūjō was now a councillor. He was a man of such fine character that everyone wished him well, but he was not happy. Everything made him think of Genji. Finally he decided that he did not care what rumors might

---

5. The poem he remembers was written in Chinese. The poem he composes is in Japanese.

arise and what misdeeds he might be accused of and hurried off to Suma. The sight of Genji brought tears of joy and sadness. Genji's house seemed very strange and exotic. The surroundings were such that he would have liked to paint them. The fence was of plaited bamboo and the pillars were of pine and the stairs of stone.[6] It was a rustic, provincial sort of dwelling, and very interesting.

Genji's dress too was somewhat rustic. Over a singlet dyed lightly in a yellowish color denoting no rank or office he wore a hunting robe and trousers of greenish gray. It was plain garb and intentionally countrified, but it so became the wearer as to bring an immediate smile of pleasure to his friend's lips. Genji's personal utensils and accessories were of a makeshift nature, and his room was open to anyone who wished to look in. The gaming boards and stones were also of rustic make. The religious objects that lay about told of earnest devotion. The food was very palatable and very much in the local taste. For his friend's amusement, Genji had fishermen bring fish and shells. Tō no Chūjō had them questioned about their maritime life, and learned of perils and tribulations. Their speech was as incomprehensible as the chirping of birds, but no doubt their feelings were like his own. He brightened their lives with clothes and other gifts. The stables being nearby, fodder was brought from a granary or something of the sort beyond, and the feeding process was as novel and interesting as everything else. Tō no Chūjō hummed the passage from "The Well of Asuka"[7] about the well-fed horses.

Weeping and laughing, they talked of all that had happened over the months.

"Yūgiri quite rips the house to pieces, and Father worries and worries about him."

Genji was of course sorry to hear it; but since I am not capable of recording the whole of the long conversation, I should perhaps refrain from recording any part of it. They composed Chinese poetry all through the night. Tō no Chūjō had come in defiance of the gossips and slanderers, but they intimidated him all the same. His stay was a brief one.

Wine was brought in, and their toast was from Po Chü-i:

"Sad topers we. Our springtime cups flow with tears."

The tears were general, for it had been too brief a meeting.
A line of geese flew over in the dawn sky.

"In what spring tide will I see again my old village?
I envy the geese, returning whence they came."

Sorrier than ever that he must go, Tō no Chūjō replied:

"Sad are the geese to leave their winter's lodging.
Dark my way of return to the flowery city."

He had brought gifts from the city, both elegant and practical. Genji gave him in return a black pony, a proper gift for a traveler.

"Considering its origins, you may fear that it will bring bad luck; but you will find that it neighs into the northern winds."[8]

6. Giving the house a Chinese aspect.   7. A folk song popular with the nobility.   8. Alludes to a Chinese poem: "The Tartar pony faces towards the north. / The Annamese bird nests on the southern branch."

It was a fine beast.

"To remember me by," said Tō no Chūjō, giving in return what was recognized to be a very fine flute. The situation demanded a certain reticence in the giving of gifts.

The sun was high, and Tō no Chūjō's men were becoming restive. He looked back and looked back, and Genji almost felt that no visit at all would have been better than such a brief one.

"And when will we meet again? It is impossible to believe that you will be here forever."

> "Look down upon me, cranes who skim the clouds,
> And see me unsullied as this cloudless day.

"Yes, I do hope to go back, someday. But when I think how difficult it has been for even the most remarkable men to pick up their old lives, I am no longer sure that I want to see the city again."

> "Lonely the voice of the crane among the clouds.
> Gone the comrade that once flew at its side.

"I have been closer to you than ever I have deserved. My regrets for what has happened are bitter."

They scarcely felt that they had had time to renew their friendship. For Genji the loneliness was unrelieved after his friend's departure.

It was the day of the serpent, the first such day in the Third Month.

"The day when a man who has worries goes down and washes them away," said one of his men, admirably informed, it would seem, in all the annual observances.

Wishing to have a look at the seashore, Genji set forth. Plain, rough curtains were strung up among the trees, and a soothsayer who was doing the circuit of the province was summoned to perform the lustration.

Genji thought he could see something of himself in the rather large doll being cast off to sea, bearing away sins and tribulations.

> "Cast away to drift on an alien vastness,
> I grieve for more than a doll cast out to sea."

The bright, open seashore showed him to wonderful advantage. The sea stretched placid into measureless distances. He thought of all that had happened to him, and all that was still to come.

> "You eight hundred myriad gods must surely help me,
> For well you know that blameless I stand before you."

Suddenly a wind came up and even before the services were finished the sky was black. Genji's men rushed about in confusion. Rain came pouring down, completely without warning. Though the obvious course would have been to return straightway to the house, there had been no time to send for umbrellas. The wind was now a howling tempest, everything that had not been tied down was scuttling off across the beach. The surf was biting at their feet. The sea was white, as if spread over with white linen. Fearful every moment of being struck down, they finally made their way back to the house.

"I've never seen anything like it," said one of the men. "Winds do come up from time to time, but not without warning. It is all very strange and very terrible."

The lightning and thunder seemed to announce the end of the world, and the rain to beat its way into the ground; and Genji sat calmly reading a sutra. The thunder subsided in the evening, but the wind went on through the night.

"Our prayers seem to have been answered. A little more and we would have been carried off. I've heard that tidal waves do carry people off before they know what is happening to them, but I've not seen anything like this."

Towards dawn sleep was at length possible. A man whom he did not recognize came to Genji in a dream.

"The court summons you." He seemed to be reaching for Genji. "Why do you not go?"

It would be the king of the sea, who was known to have a partiality for handsome men. Genji decided that he could stay no longer at Suma.

CHAPTER 13

Akashi[9]

The days went by and the thunder and rain continued. What was Genji to do? People would laugh if, in this extremity, out of favor at court, he were to return to the city. Should he then seek a mountain retreat? But if it were to be noised about that a storm had driven him away, then he would cut a ridiculous figure in history.

His dreams were haunted by that same apparition. Messages from the city almost entirely ceased coming as the days went by without a break in the storms. Might he end his days at Suma? No one was likely to come calling in these tempests.

A messenger did come from Murasaki, a sad, sodden creature. Had they passed in the street, Genji would scarcely have known whether he was man or beast, and of course would not have thought of inviting him to come near. Now the man brought a surge of pleasure and affection—though Genji could not help asking himself whether the storm had weakened his moorings.

Murasaki's letter, long and melancholy, said in part: "The terrifying deluge goes on without a break, day after day. Even the skies are closed off, and I am denied the comfort of gazing in your direction.

"What do they work, the sea winds down at Suma?
At home, my sleeves are assaulted by wave after wave."

Tears so darkened his eyes that it was as if they were inviting the waters to rise higher.

The man said that the storms had been fierce in the city too, and that a special reading of the Prajñāpāramitā Sutra[1] had been ordered. "The streets are all closed and the great gentlemen can't get to court, and everything has closed down."

The man spoke clumsily and haltingly, but he did bring news. Genji summoned him near and had him questioned.

"It's not the way it usually is. You don't usually have rain going on for days without a break and the wind howling on and on. Everyone is terrified. But

---

9. A coastal village on the Inland Sea, approximately six miles west of Suma.   1. "The Wisdom Sutra," which sets forth the Buddhist doctrine of Śūnyātā ("void" or "nothingness" or "relativity"): there is no such thing as static existence, since life is flux, causal factors change by the moment and all phenomena are relative and interdependent.

it's worse here. They haven't had this hail beating right through the ground and thunder going on and on and not letting a body think." The terror written so plainly on his face did nothing to improve the spirits of the people at Suma.

Might it be the end of the world? From dawn the next day the wind was so fierce and the tide so high and the surf so loud that it was as if the crags and the mountains must fall. The horror of the thunder and lightning was beyond description. Panic spread at each new flash. For what sins, Genji's men asked, were they being punished? Were they to perish without another glimpse of their mothers and fathers, their dear wives and children?

Genji tried to tell himself that he had been guilty of no misdeed for which he must perish here on the seashore. Such were the panic and confusion around him, however, that he bolstered his confidence with special offerings to the god of Sumiyoshi.[2]

"O you of Sumiyoshi who protect the lands about: if indeed you are an avatar of the Blessed One, then you must save us."

His men were of course fearful for their lives; but the thought that so fine a gentleman (and in these deplorable circumstances) might be swept beneath the waters seemed altogether too tragic. The less distraught among them prayed in loud voices to this and that favored deity, Buddhist and Shinto, that their own lives be taken if it meant that his might be spared.

They faced Sumiyoshi and prayed and made vows: "Our lord was reared deep in the fastnesses of the palace, and all blessings were his. You who, in the abundance of your mercy, have brought strength through these lands to all who have sunk beneath the weight of their troubles: in punishment for what crimes do you call forth these howling waves? Judge his case if you will, you gods of heaven and earth. Guiltless, he is accused of a crime, stripped of his offices, driven from his house and city, left as you see him with no relief from the torture and the lamentation. And now these horrors, and even his life seems threatened. Why? we must ask. Because of sins in some other life, because of crimes in this one? If your vision is clear, O you gods, then take all this away."

Genji offered prayers to the king of the sea and countless other gods as well. The thunder was increasingly more terrible, and finally the gallery adjoining his rooms was struck by lightning. Flames sprang up and the gallery was destroyed. The confusion was immense; the whole world seemed to have gone mad. Genji was moved to a building out in back, a kitchen or something of the sort it seemed to be. It was crowded with people of every station and rank. The clamor was almost enough to drown out the lightning and thunder. Night descended over a sky already as black as ink.

Presently the wind and rain subsided and stars began to come out. The kitchen being altogether too mean a place, a move back to the main hall was suggested. The charred remains of the gallery were an ugly sight, however, and the hall had been badly muddied and all the blinds and curtains blown away. Perhaps, Genji's men suggested somewhat tentatively, it might be better to wait until dawn. Genji sought to concentrate upon the holy name, but his agitation continued to be very great.

2. Deity venerated at a Shinto shrine in the Sumiyoshi ward of Osaka, a kind of patron saint of mariners and fishermen.

He opened a wattled door and looked out. The moon had come up. The line left by the waves was white and dangerously near, and the surf was still high. There was no one here whom he could turn to, no student of the deeper truths who could discourse upon past and present and perhaps explain these wild events. All the fisherfolk had gathered at what they had heard was the house of a great gentleman from the city. They were as noisy and impossible to communicate with as a flock of birds, but no one thought of telling them to leave.

"If the wind had kept up just a little longer," someone said, "absolutely everything would have been swept under. The gods did well by us."

There are no words—"lonely" and "forlorn" seem much too weak—to describe his feelings.

"Without the staying hand of the king of the sea
The roar of the eight hundred waves would have taken us under."

Genji was as exhausted as if all the buffets and fires of the tempest had been aimed at him personally. He dozed off, his head against some nondescript piece of furniture.

The old emperor came to him, quite as when he had lived. "And why are you in this wretched place?" He took Genji's hand and pulled him to his feet. "You must do as the god of Sumiyoshi tells you. You must put out to sea immediately. You must leave this shore behind."

"Since I last saw you, sir," said Genji, overjoyed, "I have suffered an unbroken series of misfortunes. I had thought of throwing myself into the sea."

"That you must not do. You are undergoing brief punishment for certain sins. I myself did not commit any conscious crimes while I reigned, but a person is guilty of transgressions and oversights without his being aware of them. I am doing penance and have no time to look back towards this world. But an echo of your troubles came to me and I could not stand idle. I fought my way through the sea and up to this shore and I am very tired; but now that I am here I must see to a matter in the city." And he disappeared.

Genji called after him, begging to be taken along. He looked around him. There was only the bright face of the moon. His father's presence had been too real for a dream, so real that he must still be here. Clouds traced sad lines across the sky. It had been clear and palpable, the figure he had so longed to see even in a dream, so clear that he could almost catch an afterimage. His father had come through the skies to help him in what had seemed the last extremity of his sufferings. He was deeply grateful, even to the tempests; and in the aftermath of the dream he was happy.

Quite different emotions now ruffled his serenity. He forgot his immediate troubles and only regretted that his father had not stayed longer. Perhaps he would come again. Genji would have liked to go back to sleep, but he lay wakeful until daylight.

A little boat had pulled in at the shore and two or three men came up.

"The revered monk who was once governor of Harima has come from Akashi. If the former Minamoto councillor, Lord Yoshikiyo, is here, we wonder if we might trouble him to come down and hear the details of our mission."

Yoshikiyo pretended to be surprised and puzzled. "He was once among my closer acquaintances here in Harima, but we had a falling out and it has been some time since we last exchanged letters. What can have brought him through such seas in that little boat?"

Genji's dream had given intimations. He sent Yoshikiyo down to the boat immediately. Yoshikiyo marveled that it could even have been launched upon such a sea.

These were the details of the mission, from the mouth of the old governor: "Early this month a strange figure came to me in a dream. I listened, though somewhat incredulously, and was told that on the thirteenth there would be a clear and present sign. I was to ready a boat and make for this shore when the waves subsided. I did ready a boat, and then came this savage wind and lightning. I thought of numerous foreign sovereigns who have received instructions in dreams on how to save their lands, and I concluded that even at the risk of incurring his ridicule I must on the day appointed inform your lord of the import of the dream. And so I did indeed put out to sea. A strange jet blew all the way and brought us to this shore. I cannot think of it except as divine intervention. And might I ask whether there have been corresponding manifestations here? I do hate to trouble you, but might I ask you to communicate all of this to your lord?"

Yoshikiyo quietly relayed the message, which brought new considerations. There had been these various unsettling signs conveyed to Genji dreaming and waking. The possibility of being laughed at for having departed these shores under threat now seemed the lesser risk. To turn his back on what might be a real offer of help from the gods would be to ask for still worse misfortunes. It was not easy to reject ordinary advice, and personal reservations counted for little when the advice came from great eminences. "Defer to them; they will cause you no reproaches," a wise man of old once said. He could scarcely face worse misfortunes by deferring than by not deferring, and he did not seem likely to gain great merit and profit by hesitating out of concern for his brave name. Had not his own father come to him? What room was there for doubts?

He sent back his answer: "I have been through a great deal in this strange place, and I hear nothing at all from the city. I but gaze upon a sun and moon going I know not where as comrades from my old home; and now comes this angler's boat, happy tidings on an angry wind.[3] Might there be a place along your Akashi coast where I can hide myself?"

The old man was delighted. Genji's men pressed him to set out even before sunrise. Taking along only four or five of his closest attendants, he boarded the boat. That strange wind came up again and they were at Akashi as if they had flown. It was very near, within crawling distance, so to speak; but still the workings of the wind were strange and marvelous.

The Akashi coast was every bit as beautiful as he had been told it was. He would have preferred fewer people, but on the whole he was pleased. Along the coast and in the hills the old monk had put up numerous buildings with which to take advantage of the four seasons: a reed-roofed beach cottage with fine seasonal vistas; beside a mountain stream a chapel of some grandeur and dignity, suitable for rites and meditation and invocation of the holy name; and rows of storehouses where the harvest was put away and a boun-

---

3. Alludes to a poem by Ki no Tsurayuki: "An angler's boat upon the waves that pound us, / Happy tidings on an angry wind."

tiful life assured for the years that remained. Fearful of the high tides, the old monk had sent his daughter and her women off to the hills. The house on the beach was at Genji's disposal.

The sun was rising as Genji left the boat and got into a carriage. This first look by daylight at his new guest brought a happy smile to the old man's lips. He felt as if the accumulated years were falling away and as if new years had been granted him. He gave silent thanks to the god of Sumiyoshi. He might have seemed ridiculous as he bustled around seeing to Genji's needs, as if the radiance of the sun and the moon had become his private property; but no one laughed at him.

I need not describe the beauty of the Akashi coast. The careful attention that had gone into the house and the rocks and plantings of the garden, the graceful line of the coast—it was infinitely pleasanter than Suma, and one would not have wished to ask a less than profoundly sensitive painter to paint it. The house was in quiet good taste. The old man's way of life was as Genji had heard it described, hardly more rustic than that of the grandees at court. In sheer luxury, indeed, he rather outdid them.

When Genji had rested for a time he got off messages to the city. He summoned Murasaki's messenger, who was still at Suma recovering from the horrors of his journey. Loaded with rewards for his services, he now set out again for the city. It would seem that Genji sent off a description of his perils to priests and others of whose services he regularly made use, but he told only Fujitsubo how narrow his escape had in fact been. He repeatedly laid down his brush as he sought to answer that very affectionate letter from Murasaki.

"I feel that I have run the whole gamut of horrors and then run it again, and more than ever I would like to renounce the world; but though everything else has fled away, the image which you entrusted to the mirror has not for an instant left me. I think that I might not see you again.

"Yet farther away, upon the beach at Akashi,
    My thoughts of a distant city, and of you.

"I am still half dazed, which fact will I fear be too apparent in the confusion and disorder of this letter."

Though it was true that his letter was somewhat disordered, his men thought it splendid. How very fond he must be of their lady! It would seem that they sent off descriptions of their own perils.

The apparently interminable rains had at last stopped and the sky was bright far into the distance. The fishermen radiated good spirits. Suma had been a lonely place with only a few huts scattered among the rocks. It was true that the crowds here at Akashi were not entirely to Genji's liking, but it was a pleasant spot with much to interest him and take his mind from his troubles.

The old man's devotion to the religious life was rather wonderful. Only one matter interfered with it: worry about his daughter. He told Genji a little of his concern for the girl. Genji was sympathetic. He had heard that she was very handsome and wondered if there might not be some bond between them,[4] that he should have come upon her in this strange place. But no;

___

4. Essentially a Buddhist conception, that their fates might be linked from former lives.

here he was in the remote provinces, and he must think of nothing but his own prayers. He would be unable to face Murasaki if he were to depart from the promises he had made her. Yet he continued to be interested in the girl. Everything suggested that her nature and appearance were very far from ordinary.

Reluctant to intrude himself, the old man had moved to an outbuilding. He was restless and unhappy when away from Genji, however, and he prayed more fervently than ever to the gods and Buddhas that his unlikely hope might be realized. Though in his sixties he had taken good care of himself and was young for his age. The religious life and the fact that he was of proud lineage may have had something to do with the matter. He was stubborn and intractable, as old people often are, but he was well versed in antiquities and not without a certain subtlety. His stories of old times did a great deal to dispel Genji's boredom. Genji had been too busy himself for the sort of erudition, the lore about customs and precedents, which he now had in bits and installments, and he told himself that it would have been a great loss if he had not known Akashi and its venerable master.

In a sense they were friends, but Genji rather overawed the old man. Though he had seemed so confident when he told his wife of his hopes, he hesitated, unable to broach the matter, now that the time for action had come, and seemed capable only of bemoaning his weakness and inadequacy. As for the daughter, she rarely saw a passable man here in the country among people of her own rank; and now she had had a glimpse of a man the like of whom she had not suspected to exist. She was a shy, modest girl, and she thought him quite beyond her reach. She had had hints of her father's ambitions and thought them wildly inappropriate, and her discomfort was greater for having Genji near.

It was the Fourth Month. The old man had all the curtains and fixtures of Genji's rooms changed for fresh summery ones. Genji was touched and a little embarrassed, feeling that the old man's attentions were perhaps a bit overdone; but he would not have wished for the world to offend so proud a nature.

A great many messages now came from the city inquiring after his safety. On a quiet moonlit night when the sea stretched off into the distance under a cloudless sky, he almost felt that he was looking at the familiar waters of his own garden. Overcome with longing, he was like a solitary, nameless wanderer. "Awaji, distant foam,"[5] he whispered to himself.

"Awaji: in your name is all my sadness,
And clear you stand in the light of the moon tonight."

He took out the seven-stringed koto, long neglected, which he had brought from the city and spread a train of sad thoughts through the house as he plucked out a few tentative notes. He exhausted all his skills on "The Wide Barrow,"[6] and the sound reached the house in the hills on a sighing of wind and waves. Sensitive young ladies heard it and were moved. Lowly rustics,

5. Alludes to a poem: "Awaji in the moonlight, like distant foam: / From these cloudy sovereign heights it seems so near." The place name *Awaji* contains the word *awa*, "foam," and also suggests the Japanese word *aware*, an exclamation of vague and undefined sadness.   **6.** A Chinese composition, apparently, which does not survive.

though they could not have identified the music, were lured out into the sea winds, there to catch cold.

The old man could not sit still. Casting aside his beads, he came running over to the main house.

"I feel as if a world I had thrown away were coming back," he said, breathless and tearful. "It is a night such as to make one feel that the blessed world for which one longs must be even so."

Genji played on in a reverie, a flood of memories of concerts over the years, of this gentleman and that lady on flute and koto, of voices raised in song, of times when he and they had been the center of attention, recipients of praise and favors from the emperor himself. Sending to the house on the hill for a lute and a thirteen-stringed koto, the old man now seemed to change roles and become one of these priestly mendicants who make their living by the lute. He played a most interesting and affecting strain. Genji played a few notes on the thirteen-stringed koto which the old man pressed on him and was thought an uncommonly impressive performer on both sorts of koto. Even the most ordinary music can seem remarkable if the time and place are right; and here on the wide seacoast, open far into the distance, the groves seemed to come alive in colors richer than the bloom of spring or the change of autumn, and the calls of the water rails were as if they were pounding on the door and demanding to be admitted.

The old man had a delicate style to which the instruments were beautifully suited and which delighted Genji. "One likes to see a gentle lady quite at her ease with a koto," said Genji, as if with nothing specific in mind.

The old man smiled. "And where, sir, is one likely to find a gentler, more refined musician than yourself? On the koto I am in the third generation from the emperor Daigo. I have left the great world for the rustic surroundings in which you have found me, and sometimes when I have been more gloomy than usual I have taken out a koto and picked away at it; and, curiously, there has been someone who has imitated me. Her playing has come quite naturally to resemble my master's. Or perhaps it has only seemed so to the degenerate ear of the mountain monk who has only the pine winds for company. I wonder if it might be possible to let you hear a strain, in the greatest secrecy of course." He brushed away a tear.

"I have been rash and impertinent. My playing must have sounded like no playing at all." Genji turned away from the koto. "I do not know why, but it has always been the case that ladies have taken especially well to the koto. One hears that with her father to teach her the fifth daughter of the emperor Saga was a great master of the instrument, but it would seem that she had no successors. The people who set themselves up as masters these days are quite ordinary performers with no real grounding at all. How fascinating that someone who still holds to the grand style should be hidden away on this coast. Do let me hear her."

"No difficulty at all, if that is what you wish. If you really wish it, I can summon her. There was once a poet,[7] you will remember, who was much pleased at the lute of a tradesman's wife. While we are on the subject of lutes, there were not many even in the old days who could bring out the best

7. Po Chü-i's *The Lutist*.

in the instrument. Yet it would seem that the person of whom I speak plays with a certain sureness and manages to affect a rather pleasing delicacy. I have no idea where she might have acquired these skills. It seems wrong that she should be asked to compete with the wild waves, but sometimes in my gloom I do have her strike up a tune."

He spoke with such spirit that Genji, much interested, pushed the lute toward him.

He did indeed play beautifully, adding decorations that have gone out of fashion. There was a Chinese elegance in his touch, and he was able to induce a particularly solemn tremolo from the instrument. Though it might have been argued that the setting was wrong, an adept among his retainers was persuaded to sing for them about the clean shore of Ise.[8] Tapping out the rhythm, Genji would join in from time to time, and the old man would pause to offer a word of praise. Refreshments were brought in, very prettily arranged. The old man was most assiduous in seeing that the cups were kept full, and it became the sort of evening when troubles are forgotten.

Late in the night the sea breezes were cool and the moon seemed brighter and clearer as it sank towards the west. All was quiet. In pieces and fragments the old man told about himself, from his feelings upon taking up residence on this Akashi coast to his hopes for the future life and the prospects which his devotions seemed to be opening. He added, unsolicited, an account of his daughter. Genji listened with interest and sympathy.

"It is not easy for me to say it, sir, but the fact that you are here even briefly in what must be for you strange and quite unexpected surroundings, and the fact that you are being asked to undergo trials new to your experience—I wonder if it might not be that the powers to whom an aged monk has so fervently prayed for so many years have taken pity on him. It is now eighteen years since I first prayed and made vows to the god of Sumiyoshi. I have had certain hopes for my daughter since she was very young, and every spring and autumn I have taken her to Sumiyoshi. At each of my six daily services, three of them in the daytime and three at night, I have put aside my own wishes for salvation and ventured a suggestion that my hopes for the girl be noticed. I have sunk to this provincial obscurity because I brought an unhappy destiny with me into this life. My father was a minister, and you see what I have become. If my family is to follow the same road in the future, I ask myself, then where will it end? But I have had high hopes for her since she was born. I have been determined that she go to some noble gentleman in the city. I have been accused of arrogance and unworthy ambitions and subjected to some rather unpleasant treatment. I have not let it worry me. I have said to her that while I live I will do what I can for her, limited though my resources may be; and that if I die before my hopes are realized she is to throw herself into the sea." He was weeping. It had taken great resolve for him to speak so openly.

Genji wept easily these days. "I had been feeling put upon, bundled off to this strange place because of crimes I was not aware of having committed. Your story makes me feel that there is a bond between us. Why did you not tell me earlier? Nothing has seemed quite real since I came here, and I have

8. Refers to the folk song *The Sea of Ise*: "On the clean shore of Ise, / Let us gather shells in the tide. / Let us gather shells and jewels."

given myself up to prayers to the exclusion of everything else, and so I fear that I will have struck you as spiritless. Though reports had reached me of the lady of whom you have spoken, I had feared that she would want to have nothing to do with an outcast like myself. You will be my guide and intermediary? May I look forward to company these lonely evenings?"

The old man was thoroughly delighted.

"Do you too know the sadness of the nights
On the shore of Akashi with only thoughts for companions?"

"Imagine, if you will, how it has been for us through the long months and years." He faltered, though with no loss of dignity, and his voice was trembling.

"But you, sir, are used to this seacoast.

"The traveler passes fretful nights at Akashi.
The grass which he reaps for his pillow reaps no dreams."

His openness delighted the old man, who talked on and on—and became rather tiresome, I fear. In my impatience I may have allowed inaccuracies to creep in, and exaggerated his eccentricities.

In any event, he felt a clean happiness sweep over him. A beginning had been made.

At about noon the next day Genji got off a note to the house on the hill. A real treasure might lie buried in this unlikely spot. He took a great deal of trouble with his note, which was on a fine saffron-colored Korean paper.

"Do I catch, as I gaze into unresponsive skies,
A glimpse of a grove of which I have had certain tidings?

"My resolve has been quite dissipated."[9]

And was that all? one wonders.

The old man had been waiting. Genji's messenger came staggering back down the hill, for he had been hospitably received.

But the girl was taking time with her reply. The old man rushed to her rooms and urged haste, but to no avail. She thought her hand quite unequal to the task, and awareness of the difference in their stations dismayed her. She was not feeling well, she said, and lay down.

Though he would certainly have wished it otherwise, the old man finally answered in her place. "Her rustic sleeves are too narrow to encompass such awesome tidings, it would seem, and indeed she seems to have found herself incapable of even reading your letter.

"She gazes into the skies into which you gaze.
May they bring your thoughts and hers into some accord.

"But I fear that I will seem impertinent and forward."

It was in a most uncompromisingly old-fashioned hand, on sturdy Michinoku paper; but there was something spruce and dashing about it too. Yes, "forward" was the proper word. Indeed, Genji was rather startled. He gave

---

9. Alludes to a poem in *The Kokinshū*: "Resolve that I would keep them to myself, / These thoughts of you, has been quite dissipated."

the messenger a "bejeweled apron," an appropriate gift, he thought, from a beach cottage.[1]

He got off another message the next day, beautifully written on soft, delicate paper. "I am not accustomed to receiving letters from ladies' secretaries.

> "Unwillingly reticent about my sorrows
> I still must be—for no one makes inquiry.

"Though it is difficult to say just what I mean."

There would have been something unnatural about a girl who refused to be interested in such a letter. She thought it splendid, but she also thought it impossibly out of her reach. Notice from such supreme heights had the perverse effect of reducing her to tears and inaction.

She was finally badgered into setting something down. She chose delicately perfumed lavender paper and took great care with the gradations of her ink.

> "Unwillingly reticent—how can it be so?
> How can you sorrow for someone you have not met?"

The diction and the handwriting would have done credit to any of the fine ladies at court. He fell into a deep reverie, for he was reminded of days back in the city. But he did not want to attract attention, and presently shook it off.

Every other day or so, choosing times when he was not likely to be noticed, and when he imagined that her thoughts might be similar to his—a quiet, uneventful evening, a lonely dawn—he would get off a note to her. There was a proud reserve in her answers which made him want more than ever to meet her. But there was Yoshikiyo to think of. He had spoken of the lady as if he thought her his property, and Genji did not wish to contravene these long-standing claims. If her parents persisted in offering her to him, he would make that fact his excuse, and seek to pursue the affair as quietly as possible. Not that she was making things easy for him. She seemed prouder and more aloof than the proudest lady at court; and so the days went by in a contest of wills.

The city was more than ever on his mind now that he had moved beyond the Suma barrier. He feared that not even in jest[2] could he do without Murasaki. Again he was asking himself if he might not bring her quietly to Akashi, and he was on the point of doing just that. But he did not expect to be here very much longer, and nothing was to be gained by inviting criticism at this late date.

In the city it had been a year of omens and disturbances. On the thirteenth day of the Third Month, as the thunder and winds mounted to new fury, the emperor had a dream. His father stood glowering at the stairs to the royal bedchamber and had a great deal to say, all of it, apparently, about Genji. Deeply troubled, the emperor described the dream to his mother.

"On stormy nights a person has a way of dreaming about the things that are on his mind," she said. "If I were you I would not give it a second thought."

---

1. There is a pun on *tamamo*, "jeweled apron" (an elegant word for "apron") and a kind of seaweed.
2. Alludes to a poem in *The Kokinshū*: "I wondered if even in jest I could do without you. / I gave it a try, to which I proved unequal."

Perhaps because his eyes had met the angry eyes of his father, he came down with a very painful eye ailment. Retreat and fasting were ordered for the whole court, even Kokiden's household. Then the minister, her father, died. He was of such years that his death need have surprised no one, but Kokiden too was unwell, and worse as the days went by; and the emperor had a great deal to worry about. So long as an innocent Genji was off in the wilderness, he feared, he must suffer. He ventured from time to time a suggestion that Genji be restored to his old rank and offices.

His mother sternly advised against it. "People will tax you with shallowness and indecision. Can you really think of having a man go into exile and then bringing him back before the minimum three years have gone by?"

And so he hesitated, and he and his mother were in increasingly poor health.

At Akashi it was the season when cold winds blow from the sea to make a lonely bed even lonelier.

Genji sometimes spoke to the old man. "If you were perhaps to bring her here when no one is looking?"

He thought that he could hardly be expected to visit her. She had her own ideas. She knew that rustic maidens should come running at a word from a city gentleman who happened to be briefly in the vicinity. No, she did not belong to his world, and she would only be inviting grief if she pretended that she did. Her parents had impossible hopes, it seemed, and were asking the unthinkable and building a future on nothing. What they were really doing was inviting endless trouble. It was good fortune enough to exchange notes with him for so long as he stayed on this shore. Her own prayers had been modest: that she be permitted a glimpse of the gentleman of whom she had heard so much. She had had her glimpse, from a distance, to be sure, and, brought in on the wind, she had also caught hints of his unmatched skill (of this too she had heard) on the koto. She had learned rather a great deal about him these past days, and she was satisfied. Indeed a nameless woman lost among the fishermen's huts had no right to expect even this. She was acutely embarrassed at any suggestion that he be invited nearer.

Her father too was uneasy. Now that his prayers were being answered he began to have thoughts of failure. It would be very sad for the girl, offered heedlessly to Genji, to learn that he did not want her. Rejection was painful at the hands of the finest gentleman. His unquestioning faith in all the invisible gods had perhaps led him to overlook human inclinations and probabilities.

"How pleasant," Genji kept saying, "if I could hear that koto to the singing of the waves. It is the season for such things. We should not let it pass."

Dismissing his wife's reservations and saying nothing to his disciples, the old man selected an auspicious day. He bustled around making preparations, the results of which were dazzling. The moon was near full. He sent off a note which said only: "This night that should not be wasted."[3] It seemed a bit arch, but Genji changed to informal court dress and set forth late in the night. He had a carriage decked out most resplendently, and then, deciding that it might seem ostentatious, went on horseback instead. The lady's house

---

3. Alludes to a poem: "If only I could show them to someone who knows, / This moon, these flowers, this night that should not be wasted."

was some distance back in the hills. The coast lay in full view below, the bay silver in the moonlight. He would have liked to show it to Murasaki. The temptation was strong to turn his horse's head and gallop on to the city.

"Race on through the moonlit sky, O roan-colored horse,
And let me be briefly with her for whom I long."[4]

The house was a fine one, set in a grove of trees. Careful attention had gone into all the details. In contrast to the solid dignity of the house on the beach, this house in the hills had a certain fragility about it, and he could imagine the melancholy thoughts that must come to one who lived here. There was sadness in the sound of the temple bells borne in on pine breezes from a hall of meditation nearby. Even the pines seemed to be asking for something as they sent their roots out over the crags. All manner of autumn insects were singing in the garden. He looked about him and saw a pavilion finer than the others. The cypress door upon which the moonlight seemed to focus was slightly open.

He hesitated and then spoke. There was no answer. She had resolved to admit him no nearer. All very aristocratic, thought Genji. Even ladies so wellborn that they were sheltered from sudden visitors usually tried to make conversation when the visitor was Genji. Perhaps she was letting him know that he was under a cloud. He was annoyed and thought of leaving. It would run against the mood of things to force himself upon her, and on the other hand he would look rather silly if it were to seem that she had bested him at this contest of wills. One would indeed have wished to show him, the picture of dejection, "to someone who knows."[5]

A curtain string brushed against a koto, to tell him that she had been passing a quiet evening at her music.

"And will you not play for me on the koto of which I have heard so much?

"Would there were someone with whom I might share my thoughts
And so dispel some part of these sad dreams."

"You speak to one for whom the night has no end.
How can she tell the dreaming from the waking?"

The almost inaudible whisper reminded him strongly of the Rokujō lady.

This lady had not been prepared for an incursion and could not cope with it. She fled to an inner room. How she could have contrived to bar it he could not tell, but it was very firmly barred indeed. Though he did not exactly force his way through, it is not to be imagined that he left matters as they were. Delicate, slender—she was almost too beautiful. Pleasure was mingled with pity at the thought that he was imposing himself upon her. She was even more pleasing than reports from afar had had her. The autumn night, usually so long, was over in a trice. Not wishing to be seen, he hurried out, leaving affectionate assurances behind.

He got off an unobtrusive note later in the morning. Perhaps he was feeling twinges of conscience. The old monk was equally intent upon secrecy, and sorry that he was impelled to treat the messenger rather coolly.

Genji called in secret from time to time. The two houses being some distance apart, he feared being seen by fishermen, who were known to relish a

4. A play on words gives a roan horse a special affinity with moonlight.   5. See n. 3, p. 2253.

good rumor, and sometimes several days would elapse between his visits. Exactly as she had expected, thought the girl. Her father, forgetting that enlightenment was his goal, quite gave his prayers over to silent queries as to when Genji might be expected to come again; and so (and it seems a pity) a tranquillity very laboriously attained was disturbed at a very late date.

Genji dreaded having Murasaki learn of the affair. He still loved her more than anyone, and he did not want her to make even joking reference to it. She was a quiet, docile lady, but she had more than once been unhappy with him. Why, for the sake of brief pleasure, had he caused her pain? He wished it were all his to do over again. The sight of the Akashi lady only brought new longing for the other lady.

He got off a more earnest and affectionate letter than usual, at the end of which he said: "I am in anguish at the thought that, because of foolish occurrences for which I have been responsible but have had little heart, might appear in a guise distasteful to you. There has been a strange, fleeting encounter. That I should volunteer this story will make you see, I hope, how little I wish to have secrets from you. Let the gods be my judges.

> "It was but the fisherman's brush with the salty sea pine
> Followed by a tide of tears of longing."

Her reply was gentle and unreproachful, and at the end of it she said: "That you should have deigned to tell me a dreamlike story which you could not keep to yourself calls to mind numbers of earlier instances.

> "Naïve of me, perhaps; yet we did make our vows.
> And now see the waves that wash the Mountain of Waiting!"[6]

It was the one note of reproach in a quiet, undemanding letter. He found it hard to put down, and for some nights he stayed away from the house in the hills.

The Akashi lady was convinced once more that her fears had become actuality. Now seemed the time to throw herself into the sea. She had only her parents to turn to and they were very old. She had had no ambitions for herself, no thought of making a respectable marriage. Yet the years had gone by happily enough, without storms or tears. Now she saw that the world can be very cruel. She managed to conceal her worries, however, and to do nothing that might annoy Genji. He was more and more pleased with her as time went by.

But there was the other, the lady in the city, waiting and waiting for his return. He did not want to do anything that would make her unhappy, and he spent his nights alone. He sent sketchbooks off to her, adding poems calculated to provoke replies. No doubt her women were delighted with them; and when the sorrow was too much for her (and as if by thought transference) she too would make sketches and set down notes which came to resemble a journal.

And what did the future have in store for the two of them?

The New Year came, the emperor was ill, and a pall settled over court life. There was a son, by Lady Shōkyōden, daughter of the Minister of the Right,

---

6. Alludes to a poem in *The Kokinshū*: "On the day that I am unfaithful to my vows, / May the waves break over the Mountain of Waiting of Sué." A very common pun makes *Matsuyama*, "Mount of Pines," also "Mountain of Waiting."

but the child was only two, far too young for the throne. The obvious course was to abdicate in favor of the crown prince. As the emperor turned over in his mind the problem of advice and counsel for his successor, he thought it more than ever a pity that Genji should be off in the provinces. Finally he went against Kokiden's injunctions and issued an amnesty. Kokiden had been ill from the previous year, the victim of a malign spirit, it seemed, and numerous other dire omens had disturbed the court. Though the emperor's eye ailment had for a time improved, perhaps because of strict fasting, it was worse again. Late in the Seventh Month, in deep despondency, he issued a second order, summoning Genji back to the city.

Genji had been sure that a pardon would presently come, but he also knew that life is uncertain. That it should come so soon was of course pleasing. At the same time the thought of leaving this Akashi coast filled him with regret. The old monk, though granting that it was most proper and just, was upset at the news. He managed all the same to tell himself that Genji's prosperity was in his own best interest. Genji visited the lady every night and sought to console her. From about the Sixth Month she had shown symptoms such as to make their relations more complex. A sad, ironical affair seemed at the same time to come to a climax and to disintegrate. He wondered at the perverseness of fates that seemed always to be bringing new surprises. The lady, and one could scarcely have blamed her, was sunk in the deepest gloom. Genji had set forth on a strange, dark journey with a comforting certainty that he would one day return to the city; and he now lamented that he would not see this Akashi again.

His men, in their several ways, were delighted. An escort came from the city, there was a joyous stir of preparation, and the master of the house was lost in tears. So the month came to an end. It was a season for sadness in any case, and sad thoughts accosted Genji. Why, now and long ago, had he abandoned himself, heedlessly but of his own accord, to random, profitless affairs of the heart?

"What a great deal of trouble he does cause," said those who knew the secret. "The same thing all over again. For almost a year he didn't tell anyone and he didn't seem to care the first thing about her. And now just when he ought to be letting well enough alone he makes things worse."

Yoshikiyo was the uncomfortable one. He knew what his fellows were saying: that he had talked too much and started it all.

Two days before his departure Genji visited his lady, setting out earlier than usual. This first really careful look at her revealed an astonishingly proud beauty. He comforted her with promises that he would choose an opportune time to bring her to the city. I shall not comment again upon his own good looks. He was thinner from fasting, and emaciation seemed to add the final touches to the picture. He made tearful vows. The lady replied in her heart that this small measure of affection was all she wanted and deserved, and that his radiance only emphasized her own dullness. The waves moaned in the autumn winds, and smoke from the salt burners' fires drew faint lines across the sky, and all the symbols of loneliness seemed to gather together.

"Even though we now must part for a time,
The smoke from these briny fires will follow me."

"Smoldering thoughts like the sea grass burned on these shores.
And what good now to ask for anything more?"

She fell silent, weeping softly, and a rather conventional poem seemed to say a great deal.

She had not, through it all, played for him on the koto of which he had heard so much.

"Do let me hear it. Let it be a memento."

Sending for the seven-stringed koto he had brought from the city, he played an unusual strain, quiet but wonderfully clear on the midnight air. Unable to restrain himself, the old man pushed a thirteen-stringed koto toward his daughter. She was apparently in a mood for music. Softly she tuned the instrument, and her touch suggested very great polish and elegance. He had thought Fujitsubo's playing quite incomparable. It was in the modern style, and enough to bring cries of wonder from anyone who knew a little about music. For him it was like Fujitsubo herself, the essence of all her delicate awareness. The koto of the lady before him was quiet and calm, and so rich in overtones as almost to arouse envy. She left off playing just as the connoisseur who was her listener had passed the first stages of surprise and become eager attention. Disappointment and regret succeeded pleasure. He had been here for nearly a year. Why had he not insisted that she play for him, time after time? All he could do now was repeat the old vows.

"Take this koto," he said, "to remember me by. Someday we will play together."

Her reply was soft and almost casual:

"One heedless word, one koto, to set me at rest.
In the sound of it the sound of my weeping, forever."

He could not let it pass.

"Do not change the middle string[7] of this koto.
Unchanging I shall be till we meet again.

"And we will meet again before it has slipped out of tune."

Yet it was not unnatural that the parting should seem more real than the reunion.

On the last morning Genji was up and ready before daybreak. Though he had little time to himself in all the stir, he contrived to write to her:

"Sad the retreating waves at leaving this shore.
Sad I am for you, remaining after."

"You leave, my reed-roofed hut will fall to ruin.
Would that I might go out with these waves."

It was an honest poem, and in spite of himself he was weeping. One could, after all, become fond of a hostile place, said those who did not know the secret. Those who did, Yoshikiyo and others, were a little jealous, concluding that it must have been a rather successful affair.

There were tears, for all the joy; but I shall not dwell upon them.

The old man had arranged the grandest of farewell ceremonies. He had

---

7. There are various theories about what this expression means. The most plausible is that the middle string remains unaltered during tuning, although the translator does not follow this interpretation.

splendid travel robes for everyone, even the lowliest footmen. One marveled that he had found time to collect them all. The gifts for Genji himself were of course the finest, chests and chests of them, borne by a retinue which he attached to Genji's. Some of them would make very suitable gifts in the city. He had overlooked nothing.

The lady had pinned a poem to a travel robe:

> "I made it for you, but the surging brine has wet it.
> And might you find it unpleasant and cast it off?"

Despite the confusion, he sent one of his own robes in return, and with it a note:

"It was very thoughtful of you.

> "Take it, this middle robe, let it be the symbol
> Of days uncounted but few between now and then."

Something else, no doubt, to put in her chest of memories. It was a fine robe and it bore a most remarkable fragrance. How could it fail to move her?

The old monk, his face like one of the twisted shells on the beach, was meanwhile making some of the younger people smile. "I have quite renounced the world," he said, "but the thought that I may not see you back to the city—

> "Though weary of life, seasoned by salty winds,
> I am not able to leave this shore behind,

and I wander lost in thoughts upon my child.[8] Do let me see you at least as far as the border. It may seem forward of me, but if something should from time to time call up thoughts of her, do please let her hear from you."

"It is an impossibility, sir, for very particular reasons, that I can ever forget her. You will very quickly be made to see my real intentions. If I seem dispirited, it is only because I am sad to leave all this behind.

> "I wept upon leaving the city in the spring.
> I weep in the autumn on leaving this home by the sea.

"What else can I do?" And he brushed away a tear.

The old man seemed on the point of expiring.

The lady did not want anyone to guess the intensity of her grief, but it was there, and with it sorrow at the lowly rank (she knew that she could not complain) that had made this parting inevitable. His image remained before her, and she seemed capable only of weeping.

Her mother tried everything to console her. "What could we have been thinking of? You have such odd ideas," she said to her husband, "and I should have been more careful."

"Enough, enough. There are reasons why he cannot abandon her. I have no doubt that he has already made his plans. Stop worrying, mix yourself a dose of something or other. This wailing will do no good." But he was sitting disconsolate in a corner.

The women of the house, the mother and the nurse and the rest, went on

8. See n. 7, p. 2234.

charging him with unreasonable methods. "We had hoped and prayed over the years that she might have the sort of life any girl wants, and things finally seemed to be going well—and now see what has happened."

It was true. Old age suddenly advanced and subdued him, and he spent his days in bed. But when night came he was up and alert.

"What can have happened to my beads?"

Unable to find them, he brought empty hands together in supplication. His disciples giggled. They giggled again when he set forth on a moonlight peregrination and managed to fall into the brook and bruise his hip on one of the garden stones he had chosen so carefully. For a time pain drove away, or at least obscured, his worries.

Genji went through lustration ceremonies at Naniwa and sent a messenger to Sumiyoshi with thanks that he had come thus far and a promise to visit at a later date in fulfillment of his vows. His retinue had grown to an army and did not permit side excursions. He made his way directly back to the city. At Nijō the reunion was like a dream. Tears of joy flowed so freely as almost to seem inauspicious. Murasaki, for whom life had come to seem of as little value as her farewell poem had suggested it to be, shared in the joy. She had matured and was more beautiful than ever. Her hair had been almost too rich and thick. Worry and sorrow had thinned it somewhat and thereby improved it. And now, thought Genji, a deep peace coming over him, they would be together. And in that instant there came to him the image of the one whom he had not been ready to leave. It seemed that his life must go on being complicated.

He told Murasaki about the other lady. A pensive, dreamy look passed over his face, and she whispered, as if to dismiss the matter: "For myself I do not worry."[9]

He smiled. It was a charmingly gentle reproof. Unable to take his eyes from her now that he had her before him, he could not think how he had survived so many months and years without her. All the old bitterness came back. He was restored to his former rank and made a supernumerary councillor. All his followers were similarly rehabilitated. It was as if spring had come to a withered tree.

The emperor summoned him and as they made their formal greetings thought how exile had improved him. Courtiers looked on with curiosity, wondering what the years in the provinces would have done to him. For the elderly women who had been in service since the reign of his late father, regret gave way to noisy rejoicing. The emperor had felt rather shy at the prospect of receiving Genji and had taken great pains with his dress. He seemed pale and sickly, though he had felt somewhat better these last few days. They talked fondly of this and that, and presently it was night. A full moon flooded the tranquil scene. There were tears in the emperor's eyes.

"We have not had music here of late," he said, "and it has been a very long time since I last heard any of the old songs."

Genji replied:

9. Alludes to a poem, "For myself, who am forgotten, I do not worry, / But for him who vowed fidelity while he lived."

"Cast out upon the sea, I passed the years
As useless as the leech child of the gods."[1]

The emperor was touched and embarrassed.

"The leech child's parents met beyond the pillar.
We meet again to forget the spring of parting."

He was a man of delicate grace and charm.

Genji's first task was to commission a grand reading of the Lotus Sutra in his father's memory. He called on the crown prince, who had grown in his absence, and was touched that the boy should be so pleased to see him. He had done so well with his studies that there need be no misgivings about his competence to rule. It would seem that Genji also called on Fujitsubo, and managed to control himself sufficiently for a quiet and affectionate conversation.

I had forgotten: he sent a note with the retinue which, like a returning wave, returned to Akashi. Very tender, it had been composed when no one was watching.

"And how is it with you these nights when the waves roll in?

"I wonder, do the morning mists yet rise,
There at Akashi of the lonely nights?"

The Kyushu Gosechi dancer[2] had had fond thoughts of the exiled Genji, and she was vaguely disappointed to learn that he was back in the city and once more in the emperor's good graces. She sent a note, with instructions that the messenger was to say nothing of its origin:

"There once came tidings from a boat at Suma,
From one who now might show you sodden sleeves."

Her hand had improved, though not enough to keep him from guessing whose it was.

"It is I, not you, from whom the complaints should come.
My sleeves have refused to dry since last you wrote."

He had not seen enough of her, and her letter brought fond memories. But he was not going to embark upon new adventures.

To the lady of the orange blossoms he sent only a note, cause more for disappointment than for pleasure.

Summary   Eight years pass in the novel before we come to Chapter 25, *Fireflies*. When Genji returns to the capital, he is quickly restored to his former glory. And when his son by Fujitsubo assumes the throne as Emperor Reizei (although neither the emperor himself nor the world at large knows his true parentage), Genji's position could hardly be more secure. Genji is promoted to minister, his father-in-law is made prime minister, and his supporters reign supreme.

In his personal life, things are as eventful as ever. The Akashi lady gives birth to a baby girl. Though jealous at first, Murasaki is persuaded by Genji to adopt the child,

---

1. Refers to the native creation myth, in which the leech child, among the Sun Goddess's siblings, lives approximately the period of Genji's exile before being cast out to sea. It is at a pillar (see the emperor's answering poem) that both the leech and the Sun Goddess are conceived.   2. See n. 5, p. 2237. The translator asserts that this is not the dancer mentioned in chapter 12, but the "charming girl, the daughter of the assistant viceroy of Kyushu" (mentioned in an earlier chapter), with whom Genji had a dalliance.

an act to which the Akashi lady accedes in the interests of her daughter's future. Now in his early thirties, however, Genji loses a woman on whom he had always been fixated and with whom he shares a terrible secret. After a grave illness, Fujitsubo succumbs, and Genji is plunged into mourning.

Even worse, once the funeral observances end, a meddling priest informs the emperor who his real father is. Shocked and feeling somehow guilty himself, Emperor Reizei considers abdicating, though Genji argues against it.

In the meantime, Genji's other son, by Aoi, is rising nicely in the world. Yūgiri completes his education and is named chamberlain, a prestigious post, if not in the very upper reaches of administration.

In his mid-thirties, Genji turns his attention to constructing a proper mansion for his various ladies—a kind of surrogate palace for the man who will never be emperor and the women who will never be his imperial consorts. It is a splendid building, particularly the gardens, which are organized in seasonal progression. Pride of place, the spring compound, naturally goes to Murasaki.

But in the summer wing Genji establishes a newcomer, Tamakazura, the twenty-year-old daughter of the woman he once loved briefly (told in Chapter 4). Genji has just discovered her, and with parental interest that quickly raises the suspicions of both Tamakazura and Murasaki, he installs her in his new palace. She is so much like her mother that Genji cannot bear it. When he confesses his feelings, however, Tamakazura rebuffs him, and for once, Genji appears abashed. "He knew that this impetuous behavior did not become his age and eminence. Collecting himself, he withdrew before the lateness of the hour brought her women to mistaken conclusions." Many a courtier would like to woo the lovely Tamakazura, but Genji, who still nurses his own unrequited affection, will allow only three contenders: Kashiwagi, the son of his old friend Tō no Chūjō; a nobleman named Higekuro; and his own brother, Prince Hotaru, whose name—literally Fireflies—makes up the title of the next chapter.

CHAPTER 25

Fireflies

Genji was famous and life was secure and peaceful. His ladies had in their several ways made their own lives and were happy. There was an exception, Tamakazura, who faced a new crisis and was wondering what to do next. She was not as genuinely frightened of him, of course, as she had been of the Higo man;[3] but since few people could possibly know what had happened, she must keep her disquiet to herself, and her growing sense of isolation. Old enough to know a little of the world, she saw more than ever what a handicap it was not to have a mother.

Genji had made his confession. The result was that his longing increased. Fearful of being overheard, however, he found the subject a difficult one to approach, even gingerly. His visits were very frequent. Choosing times when she was likely to have few people with her, he would hint at his feelings, and she would be in an agony of embarrassment. Since she was not in a position to turn him away, she could only pretend that she did not know what was happening.

She was of a cheerful, affectionate disposition. Though she was also of a

---

3. An uncouth suitor of the past. After her mother's death (in chapter 4) Tamakazura is taken by her nurse to the distant southern province of Higo, where the nurse's husband has been appointed an official. She grows up there, and in due course a rustic official (*the Higo man*) pursues her. He is powerful and persistent, but a little crude. Finally, under cover of darkness, Tamakazura and her nurse flee, setting sail for the capital.

cautious and conservative nature, the chief impression she gave was of a delicate, winsome girlishness.

Prince Hotaru continued to pay energetic court. His labors had not yet gone on for very long when he had the early-summer rains to be resentful of.

"Admit me a little nearer, please," he wrote. "I will feel better if I can unburden myself of even part of what is in my heart."

Genji saw the letter. "Princes," he said, "should be listened to. Aloofness is not permitted. You must let him have an occasional answer." He even told her what to say.

But he only made things worse. She said that she was not feeling well and did not answer.

There were few really highborn women in her household. She did have a cousin called Saishō, daughter of a maternal uncle who had held a seat on the council. Genji had heard that she had been having a difficult time since her father's death, and had put her in Tamakazura's service. She wrote a passable hand and seemed generally capable and well informed. He assigned her the task of composing replies to gentlemen who deserved them. It was she whom he summoned today. One may imagine that he was curious to see all of his brother's letters. Tamakazura herself had been reading them with more interest since that shocking evening. It must not be thought that she had fallen in love with Hotaru, but he did seem to offer a way of evading Genji. She was learning rapidly.

Unaware that Genji himself was eagerly awaiting him, Hotaru was delighted at what seemed a positive invitation and quietly came calling. A seat was put out for him near the corner doors, where she received him with only a curtain between them. Genji had given close attention to the incense, which was mysterious and seductive—rather more attention, indeed, than a guardian might have felt that his duty demanded. One had to admire the results, whatever the motive. Saishō was at a loss to reply to Hotaru's overtures. Genji pinched her gently to remind her that her mistress must not behave like an unfeeling lump, and only added to her discomfiture. The dark nights of the new moon were over and there was a bland quarter-moon in the cloudy sky. Calm and dignified, the prince was very handsome indeed. Genji's own very special perfume mixed with the incense that drifted through the room as people moved about. More interesting than he would have expected, thought the prince. In calm control of himself all the while (and in pleasant contrast to certain other people), he made his avowals.

Tamakazura withdrew to the east penthouse and lay down. Genji followed Saishō as she brought a new message from the prince.

"You are not being kind," he said to Tamakazura. "A person should behave as the occasion demands. You are unnecessarily coy. You should not be sending a messenger back and forth over such distances. If you do not wish him to hear your voice, very well, but at least you should move a little nearer."

She was in despair. She suspected that his real motive was to impose himself upon her, and each course open to her seemed worse than all the others. She slipped away and lay down at a curtain between the penthouse and the main hall.

She was sunk in thought, unable to answer the prince's outpourings. Genji came up beside her and lifted the curtain back over its frame. There was a

flash of light. She looked up startled. Had someone lighted a torch? No—
Genji had earlier in the evening put a large number of fireflies in a cloth
bag. Now, letting no one guess what he was about, he released them. Tamakazura brought a fan to her face. Her profile was very beautiful.

Genji had worked everything out very carefully. Prince Hotaru[4] was certain
to look in her direction. He was making a show of passion, Genji suspected,
because he thought her Genji's daughter, and not because he had guessed
what a beauty she was. Now he would see, and be genuinely excited. Genji
would not have gone to such trouble if she had in fact been his daughter. It
all seems rather perverse of him.

He slipped out through another door and returned to his part of the house.

The prince had guessed where the lady would be. Now he sensed that she
was perhaps a little nearer. His heart racing, he looked through an opening
in the rich gossamer curtains. Suddenly, some six or seven feet away, there
was a flash of light—and such beauty as was revealed in it! Darkness was
quickly restored, but for the brief glimpse he had had was the sort of thing
that makes for romance. The figure at the curtains may have been indistinct
but it most certainly was slim and tall and graceful. Genji would not have
been disappointed at the interest it had inspired.

"You put out this silent fire to no avail.
Can you extinguish the fire in the human heart?

"I hope I make myself understood."
Speed was the important thing in answering such a poem.

"The firefly but burns and makes no comment.
Silence sometimes tells of deeper thoughts."

It was a brisk sort of reply, and having made it, she was gone. His lament
about this chilly treatment was rather wordy, but he would not have wished
to overdo it by staying the night. It was late when he braved the dripping
eaves (and tears as well) and went out. I have no doubt that a cuckoo sent
him on his way,[5] but did not trouble myself to learn all the details.

So handsome, so poised, said the women—so very much like Genji. Not
knowing their lady's secret, they were filled with gratitude for Genji's attentions. Why, not even her mother could have done more for her.

Unwelcome attentions, the lady was thinking. If she had been recognized
by her father and her situation were nearer the ordinary, then they need not
be entirely unwelcome. She had had wretched luck, and she lived in dread
of rumors.

Genji too was determined to avoid rumors. Yet he continued to have his
ways. Can one really be sure, for instance, that he no longer had designs
upon Akikonomu?[6] There was something different about his manner when
he was with her, something especially charming and seductive. But she was
beyond the reach of direct overtures. Tamakazura was a modern sort of girl,
and approachable. Sometimes dangerously near losing control of himself, he

4. It is from this episode that the prince obtains his name, Hotaru (Firefly). 5. The narrator slips into
the mode of pathetic fallacy, attributing feelings of sympathy for Hotaru to the cuckoo (*hototogisu*), a bird
whose poetic overtones are lost in translation; nightingale would be closer to the mood. 6. Like Tamakazura, the daughter of a former love (the Rokujō lady). Genji has also posed as her father and been erotically
attracted. She is now married to the current emperor, Genji's illegitimate son with Fujitsubo, and is thus
empress.

would do things which, had they been noticed, might have aroused suspicions. It was a difficult and complicated relationship indeed, and he must be given credit for the fact that he held back from the final line.

On the fifth day of the Fifth Month, the Day of the Iris, he stopped by her apartments on his way to the equestrian grounds.

"What happened? Did he stay late? You must be careful with him. He is not to be trusted—not that there are very many men these days a girl really can trust."

He praised his brother and blamed him. He seemed very young and was very handsome as he offered this word of caution. As for his clothes, the singlets and the robe thrown casually over them glowed in such rich and pleasing colors that they seemed to brim over and seek more space. One wondered whether a supernatural hand might not have had some part in the dyeing. The colors themselves were familiar enough, but the woven patterns were as if everything had pointed to this day of flowers.[7] The lady was sure she would have been quite intoxicated with the perfumes burned into them had she not had these worries.

A letter came from Prince Hotaru, on white tissue paper in a fine, aristocratic hand. At first sight the contents seemed very interesting, but somehow they became ordinary upon repeating.

> "Even today the iris is neglected.
> Its roots, my cries, are lost among the waters."[8]

It was attached to an iris root certain to be much talked of.

"You must get off an answer," said Genji, preparing to leave.

Her women argued that she had no choice.

Whatever she may have meant to suggest by it, this was her answer, a simple one set down in a faint, delicate hand:

> "It might have flourished better in concealment,
> The iris root washed purposelessly away.

"Exposure seems rather unwise."

A connoisseur, the prince thought that the hand could just possibly be improved.

Gifts of medicinal herbs[9] in decorative packets came from this and that well-wisher. The festive brightness did much to make her forget earlier unhappiness and hope that she might come uninjured through this new trial.

Genji also called on the lady of the orange blossoms, in the east wing of the same northeast quarter.

"Yūgiri is to bring some friends around after the archery meet. I should imagine it will still be daylight. I have never understood why our efforts to avoid attention always end in failure. The princes and the rest of them hear that something is up and come around to see, and so we have a much noisier party than we had planned on. We must in any event be ready."

The equestrian stands were very near the galleries of the northeast quarter.

"Come, girls," he said. "Open all the doors and enjoy yourselves. Have a

---

7. *Ayame* means both "iris" and "patterns." The pun is repeated several times in the following passage, as for instance in Hotaru's poem, in which *ayame* suggests something like "discernment."   8. There is a pun on *ne,* which means both "root" and "cry" or "sob."   9. Conventional on the Day of the Iris.

look at all the handsome officers. The ones in the Left Guards are especially handsome, several cuts above the common run at court."

They had a delightful time. Tamakazura joined them. There were fresh green blinds all along the galleries, and new curtains too, the rich colors at the hems fading, as is the fashion these days, to white above. Women and little girls clustered at all the doors. The girls in green robes and trains of purple gossamer seemed to be from Tamakazura's wing. There were four of them, all very pretty and well behaved. Her women too were in festive dress, trains blending from lavender at the waist down to deeper purple and formal jackets the color of carnation shoots.

The lady of the orange blossoms had her little girls in very dignified dress, singlets of deep pink and trains of red lined with green. It was very amusing to see all the women striking new poses as they draped their finery about them. The young courtiers noticed and seemed to be striking poses of their own.

Genji went out to the stands toward midafternoon. All the princes were there, as he had predicted. The equestrian archery was freer and more varied than at the palace. The officers of the guard joined in, and everyone sat entranced through the afternoon. The women may not have understood all the finer points, but the uniforms of even the common guardsmen were magnificent and the horsemanship was complicated and exciting. The grounds were very wide, fronting also on Murasaki's southeast quarter, where young women were watching. There was music and dancing, Chinese polo music and the Korean dragon dance. As night came on, the triumphal music rang out high and wild. The guardsmen were richly rewarded according to their several ranks. It was very late when the assembly dispersed.

Genji spent the night with the lady of the orange blossoms.

"Prince Hotaru is a man of parts," he said. "He may not be the handsomest man in the world, but everything about him tells of breeding and cultivation, and he is excellent company. Did you chance to catch a glimpse of him? He has many good points, as I have said, but it may be that in the final analysis there is something just a bit lacking in him."

"He is younger than you but I thought he looked older. I have heard that he never misses a chance to come calling. I saw him once long ago at court and had not really seen him again until today. He has improved. Prince Sochi[1] is a very fine gentleman too, but somehow he does not quite look like royalty."

Genji smiled. Her judgment was quick and sure. But he kept his own counsel. This sort of open appraisal of people still living was not to his taste. He could not understand why the world had such a high opinion of Higekuro and would not have been pleased to receive him into the family, but these views too he kept to himself.

They were good friends, he and she, and no more, and they went to separate beds. Genji wondered when they had begun to drift apart. She never let fall the tiniest hint of jealousy. It had been the usual thing over the years for reports of such festivities to come to her through others. The events of the day seemed to bring new recognition to her and her household.

She said softly:

---

1. One of Genji's brothers.

"You honor the iris on the bank to which
No pony comes to taste of withered grasses?"[2]

One could scarcely have called it a masterpiece, but he was touched:

"This pony, like the love grebe, wants a comrade.
Shall it forget the iris on the bank?"

Nor was his a very exciting poem.

"I do not see as much of you as I would wish, but I do enjoy you." There was a certain irony in the words, from his bed to hers, but also affection. She was a dear, gentle lady. She had let him have her bed and spread quilts for herself outside the curtains. She had in the course of time come to accept such arrangements as proper, and he did not suggest changing them.

The rains of early summer continued without a break, even gloomier than in most years. The ladies at Rokujō amused themselves with illustrated romances. The Akashi lady, a talented painter, sent pictures to her daughter. Tamakazura was the most avid reader of all. She quite lost herself in pictures and stories and would spend whole days with them. Several of her young women were well informed in literary matters. She came upon all sorts of interesting and shocking incidents (she could not be sure whether they were true or not), but she found little that resembled her own unfortunate career. There was *The Tale of Sumiyoshi*,[3] popular in its day, of course, and still well thought of. She compared the plight of the heroine, within a hairbreadth of being taken by the chief accountant, with her own escape from the Higo person.

Genji could not help noticing the clutter of pictures and manuscripts. "What a nuisance this all is," he said one day. "Women seem to have been born to be cheerfully deceived. They know perfectly well that in all these old stories there is scarcely a shred of truth, and yet they are captured and made sport of by the whole range of trivialities and go on scribbling them down, quite unaware that in these warm rains their hair is all dank and knotted."

He smiled. "What would we do if there were not these old romances to relieve our boredom? But amid all the fabrication I must admit that I do find real emotions and plausible chains of events. We can be quite aware of the frivolity and the idleness and still be moved. We have to feel a little sorry for a charming princess in the depths of gloom. Sometimes a series of absurd and grotesque incidents which we know to be quite improbable holds our interest, and afterwards we must blush that it was so. Yet even then we can see what it was that held us. Sometimes I stand and listen to the stories they read to my daughter, and I think to myself that there certainly are good talkers in the world. I think that these yarns must come from people much practiced in lying. But perhaps that is not the whole of the story?"

She pushed away her inkstone. "I can see that that would be the view of someone much given to lying himself. For my part, I am convinced of their truthfulness."

He laughed. "I have been rude and unfair to your romances, haven't I.

2. Alludes to a poem in *The Kokinshū*: "Withered is the grass of Oaraki, / No pony comes for it, no harvester." 3. Does not survive except in a 13th-century revision, which is a Japanese equivalent of the Cinderella story. If the revision is faithful to the original tale, Tamakazura might well have identified with the heroine, whose stepmother plots to have her kidnapped by a man not at all to her liking, and so she runs away with her nurse (as Tamakazura fled Higo) to hide in Sumiyoshi, now part of Osaka.

They have set down and preserved happenings from the age of the gods to our own. *The Chronicles of Japan*[4] and the rest are a mere fragment of the whole truth. It is your romances that fill in the details.

"We are not told of things that happened to specific people exactly as they happened; but the beginning is when there are good things and bad things, things that happen in this life which one never tires of seeing and hearing about, things which one cannot bear not to tell of and must pass on for all generations. If the storyteller wishes to speak well, then he chooses the good things; and if he wishes to hold the reader's attention he chooses bad things, extraordinarily bad things. Good things and bad things alike, they are things of this world and no other.

"Writers in other countries approach the matter differently. Old stories in our own are different from new. There are differences in the degree of seriousness. But to dismiss them as lies is itself to depart from the truth. Even in the writ which the Buddha drew from his noble heart are parables, devices for pointing obliquely at the truth. To the ignorant they may seem to operate at cross purposes. The Greater Vehicle[5] is full of them, but the general burden is always the same. The difference between enlightenment and confusion is of about the same order as the difference between the good and the bad in a romance. If one takes the generous view, then nothing is empty and useless."

He now seemed bent on establishing the uses of fiction.

"But tell me: is there in any of your old stories a proper, upright fool like myself?" He came closer. "I doubt that even among the most unworldly of your heroines there is one who manages to be as distant and unnoticing as you are. Suppose the two of us set down our story and give the world a really interesting one."

"I think it very likely that the world will take notice of our curious story even if we do not go to the trouble." She hid her face in her sleeves.

"Our curious story? Yes, incomparably curious, I should think." Smiling and playful, he pressed nearer.

"Beside myself, I search through all the books,
And come upon no daughter so unfilial.

"You are breaking one of the commandments."

He stroked her hair as he spoke, but she refused to look up. Presently, however, she managed a reply:

"So too it is with me. I too have searched,
And found no cases quite so unparental."

Somewhat chastened, he pursued the matter no further. Yet one worried. What was to become of her?

Murasaki too had become addicted to romances. Her excuse was that Genji's little daughter[6] insisted on being read to.

"Just see what a fine one this is," she said, showing Genji an illustration for *The Tale of Kumano*.[7] The young girl in tranquil and confident slumber made her think of her own younger self. "How precocious even very little

4. One of the early histories.   5. Mahayana Buddhism, the later form of the religion that prevailed in Tibet, China, and Japan.   6. Genji's daughter by the Akashi lady, whom Murasaki has been raising.   7. Or *The Tale of Komano*. It does not survive.

children seem to have been. I suppose I might have set myself up as a specimen of the slow, plodding variety. I would have won that competition easily."

Genji might have been the hero of some rather more eccentric stories.

"You must not read love stories to her. I doubt that clandestine affairs would arouse her unduly, but we would not want her to think them commonplace."

What would Tamakazura have made of the difference between his remarks to her and these remarks to Murasaki?

"I would not of course offer the wanton ones as a model," replied Murasaki, "but I would have doubts too about the other sort. Lady Atemiya in *The Tale of the Hollow Tree*,[8] for instance. She is always very brisk and efficient and in control of things, and she never makes mistakes; but there is something unwomanly about her cool manner and clipped speech."

"I should imagine that it is in real life as in fiction. We are all human and we all have our ways. It is not easy to be unerringly right. Proper, well-educated parents go to great trouble over a daughter's education and tell themselves that they have done well if something quiet and demure emerges. It seems a pity when defects come to light one after another and people start asking what her good parents can possibly have been up to. Yet the rewards are very great when a girl's manner and behavior seem just right for her station. Even then empty praise is not satisfying. One knows that the girl is not perfect and looks at her more critically than before. I would not wish my own daughter to be praised by people who have no standards."

He was genuinely concerned that she acquit herself well in the tests that lay before her.

Wicked stepmothers are of course standard fare for the romancers, and he did not want them poisoning relations between Murasaki and the child. He spent a great deal of time selecting romances he thought suitable, and ordered them copied and illustrated.

He kept Yūgiri from Murasaki but encouraged him to be friends with the girl. While he himself was alive it might not matter a great deal one way or the other, but if they were good friends now their affection was likely to deepen after he was dead. He permitted Yūgiri inside the front room, though the inner rooms were forbidden. Having so few children, he had ample time for Yūgiri, who was a sober lad and seemed completely dependable. The girl was still devoted to her dolls. They made Yūgiri think of his own childhood games with Kumoinokari.[9] Sometimes as he waited in earnest attendance upon a doll princess, tears would come to his eyes. He sometimes joked with ladies of a certain standing, but he was careful not to lead them too far. Even those who might have expected more had to make do with a joke. The thing that really concerned him and never left his mind was getting back at the nurse who had sneered at his blue sleeves. He was fairly sure that he could better Tō no Chūjō at a contest of wills, but sometimes the old anger and chagrin came back and he wanted more.[1] He wanted to make Tō no Chūjō genuinely regretful for what he had done. He revealed these feelings only to Kumoinokari. Before everyone else he was a model of cool composure.

---

8. A late 10th-century work of fiction. The tale describes, among other things, the efforts of several suitors to win the hand of the beautiful Atemiya, their disappointment when she marries the crown prince, and the ensuing power struggle over imperial succession.   9. Tō no Chūjō's daughter; she is Yūgiri's childhood playmate and eventually his wife.   1. Tō no Chūjō has so far thwarted Yūgiri's desire to wed Kumoinokari.

Her brothers sometimes thought him rather conceited. Kashiwagi, the oldest, was greatly interested these days in Tamakazura. Lacking a better intermediary, he came sighing to Yūgiri. The friendship of the first generation was being repeated in the second.

"One does not undertake to plead another's case," replied Yūgiri quietly.

Tō no Chūjō was a very important man, and his many sons were embarked upon promising careers, as became their several pedigrees and inclinations. He had only two daughters. The one who had gone to court had been a disappointment. The prospect of having the other do poorly did not of course please him. He had not forgotten the lady of the evening faces. He often spoke of her, and he went on wondering what had happened to the child. The lady had put him off guard with her gentleness and appearance of helplessness, and so he had lost a daughter. A man must not under any circumstances let a woman out of his sight. Suppose the girl were to turn up now in some outlandish guise and stridently announce herself as his daughter—well, he would take her in.

"Do not dismiss anyone who says she is my daughter," he told his sons. "In my younger days I did many things I ought not to have done. There was a lady of not entirely contemptible birth who lost patience with me over some triviality or other, and so I lost a daughter, and I have so few."

There had been a time when he had almost forgotten the lady. Then he began to see what great things his friends were doing for their daughters, and to feel resentful that he had been granted so few.

One night he had a dream. He called in a famous seer and asked for an interpretation.

"Might it be that you will hear of a long-lost child who has been taken in by someone else?"

This was very puzzling. He could think of no daughters whom he had put out for adoption. He began to wonder about Tamakazura.

Summary   Twenty-nine chapters follow Chapter 25. Eventually Tamakazura marries Higekuro, and Genji, for political reasons, agrees to marry the favorite daughter of a retired emperor. Murasaki worries that Genji's new wife will supplant her in Genji's affections, but what happens is something else altogether. The new wife is unfaithful. After a liaison with Tō no Chūjō's son, she gives birth to the boy Kaoru. Genji learns the truth and remains indifferent to mother and child. The incident reminds Genji of his own transgression. He has no choice but to suffer in silence, mindful of the wrong he did his father.

In the meantime, Murasaki becomes ill. Before long she dies, and Genji is inconsolable. His grief is made worse when he realizes how his recent marriage had distressed Murasaki. Late in life, once again Genji confronts the unhappiness he has caused others. Sensing that his own end is near, the fifty-two-year-old Genji begins to put his affairs in order. And then, suddenly, we are told that he is dead:

The shining Genji was dead, and there was no one quite like him. . . . Niou [his grandson], the third son of the present emperor, and Kaoru, the young son of Genji's [wife, the] Third Princess, had grown up in the same house and were both thought by the world to be uncommonly handsome, but somehow they did not shine with the same radiance. They were but sensitive, cultivated young men, and the fact that they were rather more loudly acclaimed than Genji had been at their age was very probably because they had been so close to him.

They will never equal him, however, and the rest of the novel, the account of their rivalry for the affections of three sisters, is the story of their failure to do so. Niou is a brash, carefree sort, inclined to take his pleasure where he finds it. One cannot avoid the conclusion that he is a coarser version of his grandfather. Kaoru, while not in fact descended from Genji, seems to represent the extreme form of one of Genji's most admirable traits: sensitivity gone pathological. Both men are exaggerations of qualities that in Genji were "shining," like two halves—Kaoru's deference and Niou's impetuousness—that, if fused, might approximate the whole of Genji.

Instead we have their misadventures, which take place for the most part in a world removed from the capital, a forsaken spot called Uji. The very name means gloom or melancholy, and this is the tone for the balance of the tale. In search of love off the beaten path, the two men pursue an ideal first articulated at the beginning of the novel (Chapter 2): the affair of the heart unsullied by court intrigue. Unfortunately, intrigue and discontent are what Niou and Kaoru bring to the three women in the hinterlands. One dies of anxiousness, the second languishes in an unhappy marriage to Niou, and the third tries to kill herself; when she fails, she vows to have nothing more to do with men.

Not knowing whether she is dead or alive, Kaoru keeps searching for the third sister. The novel ends enigmatically, when he thinks he may have located her. His messenger is rebuffed, however, and the last, inconclusive lines of *The Tale of Genji* leave our antihero wondering, his life more unresolved than ever:

> It would seem that, as he examined the several possibilities, a suspicion crossed his mind: the memory of how he himself had behaved in earlier days made him ask whether someone might be hiding her from the world.

SEI SHŌNAGON
ca. 966–1017

The gifted coterie of women writers who served as ladies-in-waiting to the Japanese empresses of the late tenth and early eleventh centuries produced a number of superlative literary works in addition to *The Tale of Genji*. Of these, *The Pillow Book* (ca. 1002) by Sei Shōnagon is *Genji*'s foremost rival. In design, form, and purpose, the two books are polar opposites. *The Tale of Genji* is a long, intricate, sustained work of fiction. *The Pillow Book* is a slender catchall of personal observation: informal, unstructured, and highly opinionated.

The title apparently derives from the author's explanation of how she came to write her work (see *It Is Getting So Dark*, p. 2299). Paper was at this time a scarce commodity. When a surplus was provided to the empress, she inquired of her ladies how they should use it. The author responded that it would make just the right thing for a pillow. What precisely she meant by this, readers have speculated for generations, but it seems clear, both from the passage and from the nature of the entire work, that she intended to use the paper as a notebook for recording stray thoughts and observations. And this notebook was to be kept at the ready, beside her pillow, or in some other private place, so that she could jot down her fugitive impressions—those thoughts about the day and flashes of inspiration that come before one drifts off to sleep. Another theory has it that the author was alluding to a poem by Po Chü-i (p. 1393), in which the Chinese poet described himself napping on an autumn afternoon, his book for a pillow.

The second interpretation is possible. Sei Shōnagon is known to have been well versed in the Chinese classics, to the point of irritating her contemporaries. In the eyes of Murasaki, her fellow author was a know-it-all, "dreadfully conceited." Murasaki writes in her diary:

> She thought herself so clever, and littered her writings with Chinese characters, but if you examined them closely, they left a great deal to be desired. Those who think of themselves as being superior to everyone else in this way will inevitably suffer and come to a bad end, and people who have become so precious that they go out of their way to be sensitive in the most unpromising situations, trying to capture every moment of interest, however slight, are bound to look ridiculous and superficial. How can the future turn out well for them?*

While Murasaki's criticism may tell us more about Murasaki than Sei Shōnagon, it is relevant. With a work as idiosyncratic as *The Pillow Book,* the author's personality necessarily becomes an issue. As she emerges in her miscellaneous observations on court life—dictating why some kinds of carriages should move faster than others, why priests should be handsome, or how a lover should make his good-byes—Sei Shōnagon presents an impatient and imperious figure. She is every inch the aristocrat, whose fastidious standards brook no slipshod behavior. So deft is she at homing in on human foibles and skewering the offender in her sharp sallies that the effect can be shattering. We chuckle at her delicious wit, but we also get a quick tingle and we are glad we are not the objects of scrutiny. There is an asperity in the intelligence of this woman that is formidable.

If some of her cutting observations make Sei Shōnagon sound like an unpleasant snob, the charge is partly irrefutable. To deplore the sight of snow on the houses of commoners suggests she is no democrat. "Unpleasant," on the other hand, is more dubious. She is far too vivacious, too amused by life to be thus stereotyped. Her fondness for anecdote and comic detail preserve on the page some of the qualities that must have made her a scintillating companion. She is a presence. She is also ruthlessly honest, and this too is part of her appeal. When she makes fun of her own looks or concedes that she is abrasive or shows us the frivolous side of her character, her candor disarms us. We accept her hypercritical nature, seduced by this spontaneous, irrepressible, magnetic voice.

There are other failings that Sei Shōnagon has been accused of, not least the disorder of her book. Even if we grant its charm, what are we to make of its structural confusion? The text is what scholars call "corrupt," by which they mean it may not preserve exactly what she wrote in the order in which she wrote it. The original manuscript soon disappeared, but not before spawning numerous variants. At some point, probably several centuries later, copyists may have reordered the material. In one textual tradition, entries are classified according to theme, bringing together into one section, for example, all Sei Shōnagon's remarks on nature, or people. This organization has struck other authorities (including Ivan Morris, the translator of the selections printed here) as far too methodical for Sei Shōnagon, and they have adhered to a miscellaneous structure. Perhaps this format, too, is a reworking of the author's original intention, though intuitively it seems closer to Sei Shōnagon's persona. If some readers still criticize the random structure as stylistic weakness, a majority delight precisely in what the translator calls the book's "bizarre, haphazard arrangement," which captures so well the spasmodic rhythms of real life.

In any case, the apparently spontaneous form that the work took inspired a new literary genre. Known as *zuihitsu,* "following the brush," these subsequent occasional writings had great staying power, influencing even modern fiction. Twentieth-century writers have often appraised the unmediated recounting of experience or perception, however random, as more truthful than artificially plotted narratives. The term *zuihitsu* embraces a certain variety of content, but here too *The Pillow Book* serves as the norm: a grab bag of lists and classifications ("flowering trees," "wind instruments,"

---

*Richard Bowring, *Murasaki Shikibu: Her Diary and Poetic Memoirs* (1982), pp. 131–33.

"things that give an unclean feeling," and so forth), together with eyewitness accounts of actual events, anecdotes, perceptions gleaned from personal experience, and even occasional flights of fancy in which the author moves directly into the realm of imagination—the budding novelist, as it were, without the discipline.

Virtually every category in this compendium is marked by one of two qualities. Some entries display an acute realism; others, the evocative power of lyrical language. Any writer in modern Japan who claims to be a realist is descended from Sei Shōnagon. (Tanizaki and Kawabata are only two examples.) The everyday enters Sei Shōnagon's prose to a degree that would be unthinkable in *The Tale of Genji*. Murasaki may allow fireflies and locusts into her tale, but *The Pillow Book* permits fleas dancing under ladies' skirts and houseflies alighting with their "clammy feet." Were *The Pillow Book* a lesser accomplishment, one might still recommend it as an antidote to *Genji*.

At the same time, Sei Shōnagon holds her own with Murasaki as a lyrical writer. The great translator Arthur Waley, who was the first to render the works of both women into English, considered Sei Shōnagon the finer stylist:

> As a writer she is incomparably the best poet of her time. . . . Passages such as that about the stormy lake or the few lines about crossing a moonlit river show a beauty of phrasing that Murasaki, a much more deliberate writer, certainly never surpassed.*

In good Japanese fashion, Sei Shōnagon is ready to let her brush follow where the mood leads, as in this, Waley's favorite passage: "When crossing a river in bright moonlight, I love to see the water scatter in showers of crystal under the oxen's feet."

Clearly, Sei Shōnagon belonged to a society in which the enjoyment of beauty was a primal experience. Does this in some way reduce her achievement, make it too precious or bloodless? In an age like our own, less preoccupied with style—violent, populist, often impervious to graces of any kind whether in manners or speech—perhaps the ready answer is yes. But before responding, we should ask of *The Pillow Book* what we ask of all literature: what does it mean? If *The Pillow Book* deserves its reputation as a work of enduring worth, there ought to be various answers.

One answer would surely be that Sei Shōnagon is defining a sensibility. Like all writers, she was the product of her age, and she lived in a time when judgments of quality and standards of taste were the approximate equivalent of a moral code. A cult of beauty and style can be made to sound frivolous if we describe it as a finicky aesthetic. When we acknowledge the discipline involved, it becomes more impressive. The principles of refinement that Sei Shōnagon delineates in *The Pillow Book* have only a peripheral relation with luxury, or passion, or any kind of unbridled indulgence. They prescribe a restrained cultivation of feeling—a responsiveness to the emotional environment—along with physical grace and a genuine appreciation of shape, proportion, color, and tone, an appreciation that includes the power to make subtle distinctions. These standards may elude us or they may repel us. They may also liberate us into wider worlds than we usually inhabit.

The selections printed here are taken from a complete two-volume translation by Ivan Morris, *The Pillow Book of Sei Shōnagon* (1967). The second volume contains useful notes and appendices explaining cultural matters. Morris, *The World of the Shining Prince: Court Life in Ancient Japan* (1967), is a colorful account of the times of Sei Shōnagon, which will be helpful to readers of both *The Pillow Book* and *The Tale of Genji*. The reader interested in further exploring the works of this period will find a representative sampling in Helen Craig McCullough, *Classical Japanese Prose, an Anthology* (1990).

---

*Arthur Waley, *The Pillow-Book of Sei Shōnagon* (1949), p. 150.

PRONOUNCING GLOSSARY

The following list uses common English syllables to provide rough equivalents of selected words whose pronunciation may be unfamiliar to the general reader.

Fujiwara no Korechika: *foo-jee-wah-rah noh koh-ray-chee-kah*

hototogisu: *hoh-toh-toh-gee-soo*

Murasaki: *moo-rah-sah-kee*

Naniwazu: *nah-nee-wah-zoo*

Sei Shōnagon: *say shoh-nah-gohn*

zuihitsu: *zoo-ee-hee-tsoo*

FROM THE PILLOW BOOK[1]

In Spring It Is the Dawn

In spring it is the dawn that is most beautiful. As the light creeps over the hills, their outlines are dyed a faint red and wisps of purplish cloud trail over them.

In summer the nights. Not only when the moon shines, but on dark nights too, as the fireflies flit to and fro, and even when it rains, how beautiful it is!

In autumn the evenings, when the flittering sun sinks close to the edge of the hills and the crows fly back to their nests in threes and fours and twos; more charming still is a file of wild geese, like specks in the distant sky. When the sun has set, one's heart is moved by the sound of the wind and the hum of the insects.

In winter the early mornings. It is beautiful indeed when snow has fallen during the night, but splendid too when the ground is white with frost; or even when there is no snow or frost, but it is simply very cold and the attendants hurry from room to room stirring up the fires and bringing charcoal, how well this fits the season's mood! But as noon approaches and the cold wears off, no one bothers to keep the braziers alight, and soon nothing remains but piles of white ashes.

Especially Delightful Is the First Day

Especially delightful is the first day of the First Month, when the mists so often shroud the sky. Everyone pays great attention to his appearance and dresses with the utmost care. What a pleasure it is to see them all offer their congratulations to the Emperor and celebrate their own new year!

I also enjoy the seventh day, when people pluck the young herbs that have sprouted fresh and green beneath the snow.[2] It is amusing to see their excite-

1. Translated by and with notes adapted from Ivan Morris. 2. Note that the Japanese lunar calendar in use at this time differed from the Julian calendar employed in the West. On average, the Japanese calendar was ahead by about one month. For more information, see headnote "Murasaki Shikibu," p. 2147. The seventh day of the First Month was the Festival of Young Herbs, one of the seven national festivals. The various herbs were plucked and made into a gruel that was supposed to ward off evil spirits and to protect one's health throughout the year.

ment when they find such plants growing near the Palace, by no means a spot where one might expect them.[3]

This is the day when members of the nobility who live outside the Palace arrive in their magnificently decorated carriages to admire the blue horses.[4] As the carriages are drawn over the ground-beam of the Central Gate, there is always a tremendous bump, and the heads of the women passengers are knocked together; the combs fall out of their hair, and may be smashed to pieces if the owners are not careful. I enjoy the way everyone laughs when this happens.

I remember one occasion when I visited the Palace to see the procession of blue horses. Several senior courtiers were standing outside the guard-house of the Left Division; they had borrowed bows from the escorts, and, with much laughter, were twanging them to make the blue horses prance. Looking through one of the gates of the Palace enclosure, I could dimly make out a garden fence, near which a number of ladies, several of them from the Office of Grounds, went to and fro. What lucky women, I thought, who could walk about the Nine-Fold Enclosure as though they had lived there all their lives! Just then the escorts passed close to my carriage—remarkably close, in fact, considering the vastness of the Palace grounds—and I could actually see the texture of their faces. Some of them were not properly powdered; here and there their skin showed through unpleasantly like the dark patches of earth in a garden where the snow has begun to melt. When the horses in the procession reared wildly, I shrank into the back of my carriage and could no longer see what was happening.

On the eighth day[5] there is a great excitement in the Palace as people hurry to express their gratitude, and the clatter of carriages is louder than ever—all very fascinating.

The fifteenth day is the festival of the full-moon gruel, when a bowl of gruel is presented to His Majesty. On this day all the women of the house carry gruel-sticks, which they hide carefully from each other. It is most amusing to see them walking about, as they await an opportunity to hit their companions.[6] Each one is careful not to be struck herself and is constantly looking over her shoulder to make sure that no one is stealing up on her. Yet the precautions are useless, for before long one of the women manages to score a hit. She is extremely pleased with herself and laughs merrily. Everyone finds this delightful—except, of course, the victim, who looks very put out.

In a certain household, a young gentleman had been married during the previous year to one of the girls in the family. Having spent the night with her, he was now, on the morning of the fifteenth, about to set off for the Palace. There was a woman in the house who was in the habit of lording it over everyone. On this occasion she was standing in the back of the room, impatiently awaiting an opportunity to hit the man with her gruel-stick as he left. One of the other women realized what she had in mind and burst out laughing. The woman with the stick signalled excitedly that she should

---

3. Normally the palace grounds were kept clear of wild plants, but at this time of year it was possible to find *young herbs*, because they were hidden beneath the snow.   4. The Festival of the Blue Horses was an annual ceremony in which twenty-one horses were paraded in the palace courtyard. Originally the horses were steel gray (hence "blue"), later replaced with white horses, which were not as rare.   5. When presents of silk and brocade were given to the imperial princesses and many of the women at court were promoted in rank.   6. It was believed that if a woman were struck on the loins with the stick, she would soon give birth to a son.

be quiet. Fortunately the young man did not notice what was afoot and he stood there unconcernedly.

"I have to pick up something over there," said the woman with the stick, approaching the man. Suddenly she darted forward, gave him a great whack, and made her escape. Everyone in the room burst out laughing; even the young man smiled pleasantly, not in the least annoyed. He was not too startled; but he did blush a little, which was charming.

Sometimes when the women are hitting each other the men also join in the fun. The strange thing is that, when a woman is hit, she often gets angry and bursts into tears; then she will upbraid her assailant and say the most awful things about him—most amusing. Even in the Palace, where the atmosphere is usually so solemn, everything is in confusion on this day, and no one stands on ceremony.

It is fascinating to see what happens during the period of appointments. However snowy and icy it may be, candidates of the Fourth and Fifth Ranks come to the Palace with their official requests. Those who are still young and merry seem full of confidence. For the candidates who are old and white-haired things do not go so smoothly. Such men have to apply for help from the people with influence at Court; some of them even visit ladies-in-waiting in their quarters and go to great lengths in pointing out their own merits. If young women happen to be present, they are greatly amused. As soon as the candidates have left, they mimic and deride them—something that the old men cannot possibly suspect as they scurry from one part of the Palace to another, begging everyone, "Please present my petition favourably to the Emperor" and "Pray inform Her Majesty about me." It is not so bad if they finally succeed, but it really is rather pathetic when all their efforts prove in vain.

*   *   *

The Sliding Screen in the Back of the Hall

The sliding screen in the back of the hall in the north-east corner of Seiryō Palace[1] is decorated with paintings of the stormy sea and of the terrifying creatures with long arms and long legs that live there. When the doors of the Empress's room were open, we could always see this screen. One day we were sitting in the room, laughing at the paintings and remarking how unpleasant they were. By the balustrade of the veranda stood a large celadon vase, full of magnificent cherry branches; some of them were as much as five foot long, and their blossoms overflowed to the very foot of the railing. Towards noon the Major Counsellor, Fujiwara no Korechika, arrived. He was dressed in a cherry-coloured Court cloak, sufficiently worn to have lost its stiffness, a white under-robe, and loose trousers of dark purple; from beneath the cloak shone the pattern of another robe of dark red damask. Since His Majesty was present, Korechika knelt on the narrow wooden platform before the door and reported to him on official matters.

A group of ladies-in-waiting was seated behind the bamboo blinds. Their

---

1. The emperor's private residence within the palace compound.

cherry-coloured Chinese jackets hung loosely over their shoulders with the collars pulled back; they wore robes of wistaria, golden yellow, and other colours, many of which showed beneath the blind covering the half-shutter. Presently the noise of the attendants' feet told us that dinner was about to be served in the Daytime Chamber, and we heard cries of "Make way. Make way."

The bright, serene day delighted me. When the Chamberlains had brought all the dishes into the Chamber, they came to announce that dinner was ready, and His Majesty left by the middle door. After accompanying the Emperor, Korechika returned to his previous place on the veranda beside the cherry blossoms. The Empress pushed aside her curtain of state and came forward as far as the threshold. We were overwhelmed by the whole delightful scene. It was then that Korechika slowly intoned the words of the old poem,

> The days and the months flow by,
> But Mount Mimoro lasts forever.[2]

Deeply impressed, I wished that all this might indeed continue for a thousand years.

As soon as the ladies serving in the Daytime Chamber had called for the gentlemen-in-waiting to remove the trays, His Majesty returned to the Empress's room. Then he told me to rub some ink on the inkstone.[3] Dazzled, I felt that I should never be able to take my eyes off his radiant countenance. Next he folded a piece of white paper. "I should like each of you," he said, "to copy down on this paper the first ancient poem that comes into your head."

"How am I going to manage this?" I asked Korechika, who was still out on the veranda.

"Write your poem quickly," he said, "and show it to His Majesty. We men must not interfere in this." Ordering an attendant to take the Emperor's inkstone to each of the women in the room, he told us to make haste. "Write down any poem you happen to remember," he said. "The Naniwazu[4] or whatever else you can think of."

For some reason I was overcome with timidity; I flushed and had no idea what to do. Some of the other women managed to put down poems about the spring, the blossoms, and such suitable subjects; then they handed me the paper and said, "Now it's your turn." Picking up the brush, I wrote the poem that goes,

> The years have passed
> And age has come my way.
> Yet I need only look at this fair flower
> For all my cares to melt away.

---

2. Taken from *The Man'yōshū*, but with a few minor changes. Mount Mimoro, site of an ancient Shinto shrine, is associated with the eternal power that the Shinto deities were thought to have bestowed on the imperial line.   3. Ink came in a stick made of a dried compound of soot from burned wood or oil mixed with fishbone or hide glue. To produce liquid ink the stick was rubbed against an inkstone, a rectangular slab indented at one end to hold water, which blackened as the inkstone was rubbed. The result was a thick, dark, viscous fluid akin to India ink. This traditional method of making ink is still employed in Japanese calligraphy.   4. Said to be the first poem composed by an emperor. Children of aristocrats in the 11th century were taught the poem for writing practice. It was so elementary that, in setting it as the standard here, the emperor does not seem to be asking much.

I altered the third line, however, to read, "Yet I need only look upon my lord."[5]

When he had finished reading, the Emperor said, "I asked you to write these poems because I wanted to find out how quick you really were.

"A few years ago," he continued, "Emperor Enyū ordered all his courtiers to write poems in a notebook. Some excused themselves on the grounds that their handwriting was poor; but the Emperor insisted, saying that he did not care in the slightest about their handwriting or even whether their poems were suitable for the season. So they all had to swallow their embarrassment and produce something for the occasion. Among them was His Excellency, our present Chancellor, who was then Middle Captain of the Third Rank. He wrote down the old poem,

> Like the sea that beats
> Upon the shores of Izumo
> As the tide sweeps in,
> Deeper it grows and deeper—
> The love I bear for you.[6]

But he changed the last line to read, 'The love I bear my lord!' and the Emperor was full of praise."

When I heard His Majesty tell this story, I was so overcome that I felt myself perspiring. It occurred to me that no younger woman[7] would have been able to use my poem and I felt very lucky. This sort of test can be a terrible ordeal: it often happens that people who usually write fluently are so overawed that they actually make mistakes in their characters.

Next the Empress placed a notebook of *Kokin Shū*[8] poems before her and started reading out the first three lines of each one, asking us to supply the remainder. Among them were several famous poems that we had in our minds day and night; yet for some strange reason we were often unable to fill in the missing lines. Lady Saishō, for example, could manage only ten, which hardly qualified her as knowing her *Kokin Shū*. Some of the other women, even less successful, could remember only about half a dozen poems. They would have done better to tell the Empress quite simply that they had forgotten the lines; instead they came out with great lamentations like "Oh dear, how could we have done so badly in answering the questions that Your Majesty was pleased to put to us?"—all of which I found rather absurd.

When no one could complete a particular poem, the Empress continued reading to the end. This produced further wails from the women: "Oh, we all knew that one! How could we be so stupid?"

"Those of you," said the Empress, "who had taken the trouble to copy out the *Kokin Shū* several times would have been able to complete every single poem I have read. In the reign of Emperor Murakami there was a woman at Court known as the Imperial Lady of Senyō Palace.[9] She was the daughter of the Minister of the Left who lived in the Smaller Palace of the First Ward, and of course you have all heard of her. When she was still a young girl, her

---

5. The original poem is from *The Kokinshū*. Her alteration makes the poem now refer to the emperor. Note that the rhyme scheme chosen by Morris does not reflect the original, which, like all *tanka* (classical Japanese poems), was an unrhymed, five-line verse.   6. Origin unknown.   7. Sei Shōnagon was about thirty and would, therefore, have been considered well into middle age.   8. Usually, *Kokinshū*.   9. One of the buildings in the women's quarters of the palace compound.

father gave her this advice: 'First you must study penmanship. Next you must learn to play the seven-string zither better than anyone else. And also you must memorize all the poems in the twenty volumes of the *Kokin Shū*.'

"Emperor Murakami," continued Her Majesty, "had heard this story and remembered it years later when the girl had grown up and become an Imperial Concubine. Once, on a day of abstinence,[1] he came into her room, hiding a notebook of *Kokin Shū* poems in the folds of his robe. He surprised her by seating himself behind a curtain of state; then, opening the book, he asked 'Tell me the verse written by such-and-such a poet, in such-and-such a year and on such-and-such an occasion.' The lady understood what was afoot and that it was all in fun, yet the possibility of making a mistake or forgetting one of the poems must have worried her greatly. Before beginning the test, the Emperor had summoned a couple of ladies-in-waiting who were particularly adept in poetry and told them to mark each incorrect reply by a *go*[2] stone. What a splendid scene it must have been! You know, I really envy anyone who attended that Emperor even as a lady-in-waiting.

"Well," Her Majesty went on, "he then began questioning her. She answered without any hesitation, just giving a few words or phrases to show that she knew each poem. And never once did she make a mistake. After a time the Emperor began to resent the lady's flawless memory and decided to stop as soon as he detected any error or vagueness in her replies. Yet, after he had gone through ten books of the *Kokin Shū*, he had still not caught her out. At this stage he declared that it would be useless to continue. Marking where he had left off, he went to bed. What a triumph for the lady!

"He slept for some time. On waking, he decided that he must have a final verdict and that if he waited until the following day to examine her on the other ten volumes, she might use the time to refresh her memory. So he would have to settle the matter that very night. Ordering his attendants to bring up the bedroom lamp, he resumed his questions. By the time he had finished all twenty volumes, the night was well advanced; and still the lady had not made a mistake.

"During all this time His Excellency, the lady's father, was in a state of great agitation. As soon as he was informed that the Emperor was testing his daughter, he sent his attendants to various temples to arrange for special recitations of the Scriptures. Then he turned in the direction of the Imperial Palace and spent a long time in prayer. Such enthusiasm for poetry is really rather moving."

The Emperor, who had been listening to the whole story, was much impressed. "How can he possibly have read so many poems?" he remarked when Her Majesty had finished. "I doubt whether I could get through three or four volumes. But of course things have changed. In the old days even people of humble station had a taste for the arts and were interested in elegant pastimes. Such a story would hardly be possible nowadays, would it?"

1. One of the frequent inauspicious days when, according to current superstition, it was necessary to stay indoors and, as much as possible, to abstain from all activities, including eating, sexual intercourse, and even such seemingly innocuous acts as reading a letter. Particularly strict rules applied to what the emperor could and could not do on these days.   2. A complex game, sometimes erroneously called Japanese chess, originating in China and employing black and white stones, alternately placed on a board with 361 intersections. The object is to capture the opponent's stones and to secure control over open spaces on the board. Here, the court ladies simply use the *go* stones as counters.

The ladies in attendance on Her Majesty and the Emperor's own ladies-in-waiting who had been admitted into Her Majesty's presence began chatting eagerly, and as I listened I felt that my cares had really "melted away."

When I Make Myself Imagine

When I make myself imagine what it is like to be one of those women who live at home, faithfully serving their husbands—women who have not a single exciting prospect in life yet who believe that they are perfectly happy—I am filled with scorn. Often they are of quite good birth, yet have had no opportunity to find out what the world is like. I wish they could live for a while in our society, even if it should mean taking service as Attendants,[1] so that they might come to know the delights it has to offer.

I cannot bear men who believe that women serving in the Palace are bound to be frivolous and wicked. Yet I suppose their prejudice is understandable. After all, women at Court do not spend their time hiding modestly behind fans and screens, but walk about, looking openly at people they chance to meet. Yes, they see everyone face to face, not only ladies-in-waiting like themselves, but even Their Imperial Majesties (whose august names I hardly dare mention), High Court Nobles, senior courtiers, and other gentlemen of high rank. In the presence of such exalted personages the women in the Palace are all equally brazen, whether they be the maids of ladies-in-waiting, or the relations of Court ladies who have come to visit them, or housekeepers, or latrine-cleaners, or women who are of no more value than a roof-tile or a pebble. Small wonder that the young men regard them as immodest! Yet are the gentlemen themselves any less so? They are not exactly bashful when it comes to looking at the great people in the Palace. No, everyone at Court is much the same in this respect.

Women who have served in the Palace, but who later get married and live at home, are called Madam and receive the most respectful treatment. To be sure, people often consider that these women, who have displayed their faces to all and sundry during their years at Court, are lacking in feminine grace. How proud they must be, nevertheless, when they are styled Assistant Attendants, or summoned to the Palace for occasional duty, or ordered to serve as Imperial envoys during the Kamo Festival![2] Even those who stay at home lose nothing by having served at Court. In fact they make very good wives. For example, if they are married to a provincial governor and their daughter is chosen to take part in the Gosechi dances,[3] they do not have to disgrace themselves by acting like provincials and asking other people about procedure. They themselves are well versed in the formalities, which is just as it should be.

---

1. Female attendants to the personal needs of the emperor. There were two chief attendants, a handful of assistants, and a staff of one hundred female servants.   2. The main Shinto celebration of the year, in the middle of the Fourth Month.   3. Court dances performed in the Eleventh Month by young girls of good families. Of the four girls who participated in the dances, three were daughters of high court nobles and one was the daughter of a provincial governor.

Depressing Things

A dog howling in the daytime. A wickerwork fish-net[1] in spring. A red plum-blossom dress[2] in the Third or Fourth Months. A lying-in room when the baby has died. A cold, empty brazier. An ox-driver who hates oxen. A scholar whose wife has one girl child after another.[3]

One has gone to a friend's house to avoid an unlucky direction,[4] but nothing is done to entertain one; if this should happen at the time of a Seasonal Change,[5] it is still more depressing.

A letter arrives from the provinces, but no gift accompanies it. It would be bad enough if such a letter reached one in the provinces from someone in the capital; but then at least it would have interesting news about goings-on in society, and that would be a consolation.

One has written a letter, taking pains to make it as attractive as possible, and now one impatiently awaits the reply. "Surely the messenger should be back by now," one thinks. Just then he returns; but in his hand he carries, not a reply, but one's own letter, still twisted or knotted[6] as it was sent, but now so dirty and crumpled that even the ink-mark on the outside has disappeared. "Not at home," announces the messenger, or else, "They said they were observing a day of abstinence and would not accept it." Oh, how depressing!

Again, one has sent one's carriage to fetch someone who had said he would definitely pay one a visit on that day. Finally it returns with a great clatter, and the servants hurry out with cries of "Here they come!" But next one hears the carriage being pulled into the coach-house, and the unfastened shafts clatter to the ground. "What does this mean?" one asks. "The person was not at home," replies the driver, "and will not be coming." So saying, he leads the ox back to its stall, leaving the carriage in the coach-house.

With much bustle and excitement a young man has moved into the house of a certain family as the daughter's husband. One day he fails to come home, and it turns out that some high-ranking Court lady has taken him as her lover. How depressing! "Will he eventually tire of the woman and come back to us?" his wife's family wonder ruefully.

The nurse who is looking after a baby leaves the house, saying that she will be back presently. Soon the child starts crying for her. One tries to comfort it by games and other diversions, and even sends a message to the nurse telling her to return immediately. Then comes her reply: "I am afraid that I cannot be back this evening." This is not only depressing; it is no less than hateful. Yet how much more distressed must be the young man who has sent a messenger to fetch a lady friend and who awaits her arrival in vain!

It is quite late at night and a woman has been expecting a visitor. Hearing

---

1. Designed for catching whitebait during the winter; in spring they were useless.   2. Dresses of this color could be worn only during the Eleventh and Twelfth months.   3. Scholarship was not considered suitable for women.   4. Japan of the 11th century was rife with superstition, including the belief that at certain times a specific direction was to be avoided. There were three main types of directional taboo. The northeast was regarded as a perpetually unlucky direction. Other directions were unfavorable during certain periods of one's life, so that at sixteen, e.g., one might have to avoid the northwest. Still other directions were universally but temporally inauspicious, caused by the transit of deities, whose descent from the heavens could close a sector to human traffic.   5. There were observances to mark the spring and autumn equinoxes and the summer and winter solstices. Unlucky directions were a particular problem at these times of year, because an especially large number of malevolent spirits were thought to be abroad.   6. A letter was folded into a narrow strip of paper and knotted, either in the middle or at one end, or twisted at both ends. A few lines of ink were drawn over the knot or fold to make a kind of seal.

finally a stealthy tapping, she sends her maid to open the gate and lies waiting excitedly. But the name announced by the maid is that of someone with whom she has absolutely no connection. Of all the depressing things this is by far the worst.

With a look of complete self-confidence on his face an exorcist prepares to expel an evil spirit from his patient. Handing his mace, rosary, and other paraphernalia to the medium who is assisting him, he begins to recite his spells in the special shrill tone that he forces from his throat on such occasions. For all the exorcist's efforts, the spirit gives no sign of leaving, and the Guardian Demon fails to take possession of the medium. The relations and friends of the patient, who are gathered in the room praying, find this rather unfortunate. After he has recited his incantations for the length of an entire watch,[7] the exorcist is worn out. "The Guardian Demon is completely inactive," he tells his medium. "You may leave." Then, as he takes back his rosary, he adds, "Well, well, it hasn't worked!" He passes his hand over his forehead, then yawns deeply (he of all people!) and leans back against a pillar for a nap.

Most depressing is the household of some hopeful candidate who fails to receive a post during the period of official appointments.[8] Hearing that the gentleman was bound to be successful, several people have gathered in his house for the occasion; among them are a number of retainers who served him in the past but who since then have either been engaged elsewhere or moved to some remote province. Now they are all eager to accompany their former master on his visit to the shrines and temples, and their carriages pass to and fro in the courtyard. Indoors there is a great commotion as the hangers-on help themselves to food and drink. Yet the dawn of the last day of the appointments arrives and still no one has knocked at the gate. The people in the house are nervous and prick up their ears.

Presently they hear the shouts of fore-runners and realize that the high dignitaries are leaving the Palace. Some of the servants were sent to the Palace on the previous evening to hear the news and have been waiting all night, trembling with cold; now they come trudging back listlessly. The attendants who have remained faithfully in the gentleman's service year after year cannot bring themselves to ask what has happened. His former retainers, however, are not so diffident. "Tell us," they say, "what appointment did His Excellency receive?" "Indeed," murmur the servants, "His Excellency was Governor of such-and-such a province." Everyone was counting on his receiving a new appointment,[9] and is desolated by this failure. On the following day the people who had crowded into the house begin to slink away in twos and threes. The old attendants, however, cannot leave so easily. They walk restlessly about the house, counting on their fingers the provincial appointments that will become available in the following year. Pathetic and depressing in the extreme!

One has sent a friend a verse that turned out fairly well. How depressing when there is no reply-poem! Even in the case of love poems, people should at least answer that they were moved at receiving the message, or something of the sort; otherwise they will cause the keenest disappointment.

Someone who lives in a bustling, fashionable household receives a mes-

---

7. Equivalent to two hours.   8. That is, to provincial governorships.   9. The messengers cannot bring themselves to announce in so many words that their master has failed to obtain an appointment. Instead, they answer by giving his existing title, which he had hoped to shed in favor of a new one.

sage from an elderly person who is behind the times and has very little to do; the poem, of course, is old-fashioned and dull. How depressing!

One needs a particularly beautiful fan for some special occasion and instructs an artist, in whose talents one has full confidence, to decorate one with an appropriate painting. When the day comes and the fan is delivered, one is shocked to see how badly it has been painted. Oh, the dreariness of it!

A messenger arrives with a present at a house where a child has been born or where someone is about to leave on a journey. How depressing for him if he gets no reward! People should always reward a messenger, though he may bring only herbal balls or hare-sticks.[1] If he expects nothing, he will be particularly pleased to be rewarded. On the other hand, what a terrible letdown if he arrives with a self-important look on his face, his heart pounding in anticipation of a generous reward, only to have his hopes dashed!

A man has moved in as a son-in-law; yet even now, after some five years of marriage, the lying-in room has remained as quiet as on the day of his arrival.

An elderly couple who have several grown-up children, and who may even have some grandchildren crawling about the house, are taking a nap in the daytime.[2] The children who see them in this state are overcome by a forlorn feeling, and for other people it is all very depressing.

To take a hot bath when one has just woken is not only depressing; it actually puts one in a bad humour.

Persistent rain on the last day of the year.[3]

One has been observing a period of fast, but neglects it for just one day—most depressing.

A white under-robe in the Eighth Month.[4]

A wet-nurse who has run out of milk.

Hateful Things

One is in a hurry to leave, but one's visitor keeps chattering away. If it is someone of no importance, one can get rid of him by saying, "You must tell me all about it next time"; but, should it be the sort of visitor whose presence commands one's best behaviour, the situation is hateful indeed.

One finds that a hair has got caught in the stone on which one is rubbing one's inkstick,[1] or again that gravel is lodged in the inkstick, making a nasty, grating sound.

Someone has suddenly fallen ill and one summons the exorcist. Since he is not at home, one has to send messengers to look for him. After one has had a long fretful wait, the exorcist finally arrives, and with a sigh of relief

1. Short sticks with long, colored tassels presented at New Year to keep away evil spirits. They were hung on pillars in the palace and in the houses of the nobility on the fourth day of the month, which corresponds to the first day of the Hare in the Chinese zodiac. *Herbal balls:* during the Festival of the Iris of the Fifth Month various kinds of herbs were bound into balls and put into round bags of cotton or silk, which were decorated with irises and other plants. They were hung on pillars and curtains to ward off illness and other misfortunes.   2. There was a strong prejudice against taking naps in the daytime, thought particularly undignified for the elderly.   3. Because it interfered with the many New Year's celebrations.   4. This garment was normally worn only in the summer months.   1. See n. 3, p. 2276.

one asks him to start his incantations. But perhaps he has been exorcizing too many evil spirits recently; for hardly has he installed himself and begun praying when his voice becomes drowsy. Oh, how hateful!

A man who has nothing in particular to recommend him discusses all sorts of subjects at random as though he knew everything.

An elderly person warms the palms of his hands over a brazier and stretches out the wrinkles. No young man would dream of behaving in such a fashion; old people can really be quite shameless. I have seen some dreary old creatures actually resting their feet on the brazier and rubbing them against the edge while they speak. These are the kind of people who in visiting someone's house first use their fans to wipe away the dust from the mat and, when they finally sit on it, cannot stay still but are forever spreading out the front of their hunting costume or even tucking it up under their knees. One might suppose that such behaviour was restricted to people of humble station; but I have observed it in quite well-bred people, including a Senior Secretary of the Fifth Rank[2] in the Ministry of Ceremonial and a former Governor of Suruga.

I hate the sight of men in their cups who shout, poke their fingers in their mouths, stroke their beards, and pass on the wine to their neighbours with great cries of "Have some more! Drink up!" They tremble, shake their heads, twist their faces, and gesticulate like children who are singing, "We're off to see the Governor." I have seen really well-bred people behave like this and I find it most distasteful.

To envy others and to complain about one's own lot; to speak badly about people; to be inquisitive about the most trivial matters and to resent and abuse people for not telling one, or, if one does manage to worm out some facts, to inform everyone in the most detailed fashion as if one had known all from the beginning—oh, how hateful!

One is just about to be told some interesting piece of news when a baby starts crying.

A flight of crows circle about with loud caws.

An admirer has come on a clandestine visit, but a dog catches sight of him and starts barking. One feels like killing the beast.

One has been foolish enough to invite a man to spend the night in an unsuitable place—and then he starts snoring.

A gentleman has visited one secretly. Though he is wearing a tall, lacquered hat,[3] he nevertheless wants no one to see him. He is so flurried, in fact, that upon leaving he bangs into something with his hat. Most hateful! It is annoying too when he lifts up the Iyo blind[4] that hangs at the entrance of the room, then lets it fall with a great rattle. If it is a head-blind,[5] things are still worse, for being more solid it makes a terrible noise when it is

2. A codified system of court ranks designated various levels of preferment in descending order from Senior First Rank to Junior Eighth Rank, Lower Grade. The real cutoff point came after the Fifth Rank, because, in most cases, those of the first five ranks were the only ones eligible to be named *tenjōbito*, or "hall men." Their names were inscribed on a special roster, and they enjoyed the privilege of entering the Courtiers' Hall of the emperor's private quarters within the palace compound. The cream of society, numbering anywhere from twenty-five to one hundred, hall men were the courtiers who came into constant contact with the emperor and his entourage, including ladies-in-waiting like Sei Shōnagon and Murasaki Shikibu. These women, the chroniclers of court life, wrote about the men they saw every day: hall men of the Fifth Rank or above.   3. Worn by noblemen; a bit too conspicuous for a clandestine visit.   4. A rough type of reed blind made in the province of Iyo.   5. An elegant type of blind whose top and edges were decorated with silk strips; it had thin strips of bamboo along the edges and thus was heavier than ordinary blinds.

dropped. There is a no excuse for such carelessness. Even a head-blind does not make any noise if one lifts it up gently on entering and leaving the room; the same applies to sliding-doors. If one's movements are rough, even a paper door will bend and resonate when opened; but, if one lifts the door a little while pushing it, there need be no sound.

One has gone to bed and is about to doze off when a mosquito appears, announcing himself in a reedy voice. One can actually feel the wind made by his wings and, slight though it is, one finds it hateful in the extreme.

A carriage passes with a nasty, creaking noise. Annoying to think that the passengers may not even be aware of this! If I am travelling in someone's carriage and I hear it creaking, I dislike not only the noise but also the owner of the carriage.

One is in the middle of a story when someone butts in and tries to show that he is the only clever person in the room. Such a person is hateful, and so, indeed, is anyone, child or adult, who tries to push himself forward.

One is telling a story about old times when someone breaks in with a little detail that he happens to know, implying that one's own version is inaccurate—disgusting behaviour!

Very hateful is a mouse that scurries all over the place.

Some children have called at one's house. One makes a great fuss of them and gives them toys to play with. The children become accustomed to this treatment and start to come regularly, forcing their way into one's inner rooms and scattering one's furnishings and possessions. Hateful!

A certain gentleman whom one does not want to see visits one at home or in the Palace, and one pretends to be asleep. But a maid comes to tell one and shakes one awake, with a look on her face that says, "What a sleepyhead!" Very hateful.

A newcomer pushes ahead of the other members in a group; with a knowing look, this person starts laying down the law and forcing advice upon everyone—most hateful.

A man with whom one is having an affair keeps singing the praises of some woman he used to know. Even if it is a thing of the past, this can be very annoying. How much more so if he is still seeing the woman! (Yet sometimes I find that it is not as unpleasant as all that.)

A person who recites a spell himself after sneezing.[6] In fact I detest anyone who sneezes, except the master of the house.

Fleas, too, are very hateful. When they dance about under someone's clothes, they really seem to be lifting them up.

The sound of dogs when they bark for a long time in chorus is ominous and hateful.

I cannot stand people who leave without closing the panel[7] behind them.

How I detest the husbands of nurse-maids! It is not so bad if the child in the maid's charge is a girl, because then the man will keep his distance. But, if it is a boy, he will behave as though he were the father. Never letting the boy out of his sight, he insists on managing everything. He regards the other attendants in the house as less than human, and, if anyone tries to scold the child, he slanders him to the master. Despite this disgraceful behaviour, no

---

6. Sneezing, a bad omen, was counteracted by reciting an auspicious formula, such as wishing long life to the person who had sneezed.   7. A sliding door.

one dare accuse the husband; so he strides about the house with a proud, self-important look, giving all the orders.

I hate people whose letters show that they lack respect for worldly civilities, whether by discourtesy in the phrasing or by extreme politeness to someone who does not deserve it. This sort of thing is, of course, most odious if the letter is for oneself, but it is bad enough even if it is addressed to someone else.

As a matter of fact, most people are too casual, not only in their letters but in their direct conversation. Sometimes I am quite disgusted at noting how little decorum people observe when talking to each other. It is particularly unpleasant to hear some foolish man or woman omit the proper marks of respect when addressing a person of quality; and, when servants fail to use honorific forms of speech in referring to their masters, it is very bad indeed. No less odious, however, are those masters who, in addressing their servants, use such phrases as "When you were good enough to do such-and-such" or "As you so kindly remarked." No doubt there are some masters who, in describing their own actions to a servant, say, "I presumed to do so-and-so!"[8]

Sometimes a person who is utterly devoid of charm will try to create a good impression by using very elegant language; yet he only succeeds in being ridiculous. No doubt he believes this refined language is to be just what the occasion demands, but, when it goes so far that everyone bursts out laughing, surely something must be wrong.

It is most improper to address high-ranking courtiers, Imperial Advisers, and the like simply by using their names without any titles or marks of respect; but such mistakes are fortunately rare.

If one refers to the maid who is in attendance on some lady-in-waiting as "Madam" or "that lady," she will be surprised, delighted, and lavish in her praise.

When speaking to young noblemen and courtiers of high rank, one should always (unless Their Majesties are present) refer to them by their official post. Incidentally, I have been very shocked to hear important people use the word "I" while conversing in Their Majesties' presence.[9] Such a breach of etiquette is really distressing, and I fail to see why people cannot avoid it.

A man who has nothing in particular to recommend him but who speaks in an affected tone and poses as being elegant.

An inkstone with such a hard, smooth surface that the stick glides over it without leaving any deposit of ink.

Ladies-in-waiting who want to know everything that is going on.

Sometimes one greatly dislikes a person for no particular reason—and then that person goes and does something hateful.

A gentleman who travels alone in his carriage to see a procession or some other spectacle. What sort of a man is he? Even though he may not be a person of the greatest quality, surely he should have taken along a few of the many young men who are anxious to see the sights. But no, there he sits by himself (one can see his silhouette through the blinds), with a proud look on his face, keeping all his impressions to himself.

8. Shaky command of the various levels of honorific language was an anathema in this hierarchic society.
9. Court etiquette demanded that in the presence of the emperor or empress one referred to oneself by one's name rather than by the first-person singular.

A lover who is leaving at dawn announces that he has to find his fan and his paper.[1] "I know I put them somewhere last night," he says. Since it is pitch dark, he gropes about the room, bumping into the furniture and muttering, "Strange! Where on earth can they be?" Finally he discovers the objects. He thrusts the paper into the breast of his robe with a great rustling sound; then he snaps open his fan and busily fans away with it. Only now is he ready to take his leave. What charmless behaviour! "Hateful" is an understatement.

Equally disagreeable is the man who, when leaving in the middle of the night, takes care to fasten the cord of his headdress. This is quite unnecessary; he could perfectly well put it gently on his head without tying the cord. And why must he spend time adjusting his cloak or hunting costume? Does he really think someone may see him at this time of night and criticize him for not being impeccably dressed?

A good lover will behave as elegantly at dawn as at any other time. He drags himself out of bed with a look of dismay on his face. The lady urges him on: "Come, my friend, it's getting light. You don't want anyone to find you here." He gives a deep sigh, as if to say that the night has not been nearly long enough and that it is agony to leave. Once up, he does not instantly pull on his trousers. Instead he comes close to the lady and whispers whatever was left unsaid during the night. Even when he is dressed, he still lingers, vaguely pretending to be fastening his sash.

Presently he raises the lattice, and the two lovers stand together by the side door while he tells her how he dreads the coming day, which will keep them apart; then he slips away. The lady watches him go, and this moment of parting will remain among her most charming memories.

Indeed, one's attachment to a man depends largely on the elegance of his leave-taking. When he jumps out of bed, scurries about the room, tightly fastens his trouser-sash, rolls up the sleeves of his Court cloak, over-robe, or hunting costume, stuffs his belongings into the breast of his robe and then briskly secures the outer sash—one really begins to hate him.

*   *   *

Oxen Should Have Very Small Foreheads

Oxen should have very small foreheads with white hair; their underbellies, the ends of their legs, and the tips of their tails should also be white.

I like horses to be chestnut, piebald, dapple-grey, or black roan, with white patches near their shoulders and feet; I also like horses with light chestnut coats and extremely white manes and tails—so white, indeed, that their hair looks like mulberry threads.

I like a cat whose back is black and all the rest white.

*   *   *

A Preacher Ought to Be Good-Looking

A preacher[2] ought to be good-looking. For, if we are properly to understand his worthy sentiments, we must keep our eyes on him while he speaks; should

---

1. Paper squares (often colored) that courtiers carried in the folds of their clothes; they were used to write notes or poems and also as a kind of elegant tissue. 2. A Buddhist priest.

we look away, we may forget to listen. Accordingly an ugly preacher may well be the source of sin. . . .

But I really must stop writing this kind of thing. If I were still young enough, I might risk the consequence of putting down such impieties, but at my present stage of life I should be less flippant.

Some people, on hearing that a priest is particularly venerable and pious, rush off to the temple where he is preaching, determined to arrive before anyone else. They, too, are liable to bring a load of sin on themselves and would do better to stay away.

In earlier times men who had retired from the post of Chamberlain did not ride at the head of Imperial processions; in fact, during the year of their retirement they hardly ever appeared outside their houses, and did not dream of showing themselves in the precincts of the Palace. Things seem to have changed. Nowadays they are known as "Fifth Rank Chamberlains"[2] and given all sorts of official jobs.

Even so, time often hangs heavily on their hands, especially when they recall their busy days in active service. Though these Fifth Rank Chamberlains keep the fact to themselves, they know they have a good deal of leisure. Men like this frequently repair to temples and listen to the popular priests, such visits eventually becoming a habit. One will find them there even on hot summer days, decked out in bright linen robes, with loose trousers of light violet or bluish grey spread about them. Sometimes they will have taboo tags[3] attached to their black lacquered headdresses. Far from preferring to stay at home on such inauspicious days, they apparently believe that no harm can come to anyone bent on so worthy an errand. They arrive hastily, converse with the priest, look inside the carriages[4] that are being lined up outside the temple, and take an interest in everything.

Now a couple of gentlemen who have not met for some time run into each other in the temple, and are greatly surprised. They sit down together and chat away, nodding their heads, exchanging funny stories, and opening their fans wide to hold before their faces so as to laugh more freely. Toying with their elegantly decorated rosaries, they glance about, criticizing some defect they have noticed in one of the carriages or praising the elegance of another. They discuss various services that they have recently attended and compare the skill of different priests in performing the Eight Lessons or the Dedication of Sutras.[5] Meanwhile, of course, they pay not the slightest attention to the service actually in progress. To be sure, it would not interest them very much; for they have heard it all so often that the priest's words could no longer make any impression.

After the priest has been on his dais for some time, a carriage stops outside the temple. The outriders clear the way in a somewhat perfunctory fashion, and the passengers get out. They are slender young gentlemen, clad either in hunting costumes or in Court cloaks that look lighter than a cicada's

3. See n. 2, p. 2283.   4. Signs made of willow wood and hung outside one's house on days of abstinence to warn possible visitors. If obliged to venture out on one of these days men wore a taboo tag on their hats, and women wore one on their sleeves.   5. Probably women's carriages. Ladies remained in their carriages during the service, and the retired chamberlains are not too pious to have a good look. Another interpretation is that the chamberlains are looking at their own carriages, to make sure that they have been placed in a better position than those of other visitors. In any case, their minds are far from religion.   6. The practice of ordering copies of the sutra to be made and dedicated to some person or institution. After the copy was completed, the sutra would be recited in a special dedicatory service. Eight Lessons: a series of eight services in which two priests, one asking questions and the other responding, would comment on each of the eight volumes of the Lotus Sutra, among the most revered statements of Buddhist doctrine.

wings, loose trousers, and unlined robes of raw silk. As they enter the temple, accompanied by an equal number of attendants, the worshippers, including those who have been there since the beginning of the service, move back to make room for them; the young men install themselves at the foot of a pillar near the dais. As one would expect from such people, they now make a great show of rubbing their rosaries and prostrating themselves in prayer. The priest, convinced by the sight of the newcomers that this is a grand occasion, launches out on an impressive sermon that he presumes will make his name in society. But no sooner have the young men settled down and finished touching their heads on the floor than they begin to think about leaving at the first opportunity. Two of them steal glances at the women's carriages outside, and it is easy to imagine what they are saying to each other. They recognize one of the women and admire her elegance; then, catching sight of a stranger, they discuss who she can be. I find it fascinating to see such goings-on in a temple.

Often one hears exchanges like this: "There was a service at such-and-such a temple where they did the Eight Lessons." "Was Lady So-and-So present?" "Of course. How could she possibly have missed it?" It is really too bad that they should always answer like this.

One would imagine that it would be all right for ladies of quality to visit temples and take a discreet look at the preacher's dais. After all, even women of humble station may listen devoutly to religious sermons. Yet in the old days ladies almost never walked to temples to attend sermons; on the rare visits that they did undertake they had to wear elegant travelling costume, as when making proper pilgrimages to shrines and temples. If people of those times had lived long enough to see the recent conduct in the temples, how they would have criticized the women of our day!

*   *   *

Flowering Trees

Plum blossoms, whether light or dark, and in particular red plum blossoms, fill me with happiness. I also like a slender branch of cherry blossoms, with large petals and dark red leaves. How graceful is the wistaria as its branches bend down covered with whorls of delicately coloured petals!

The *u no hana* is a more modest plant and deserves no special praise; yet it flowers at a pleasant time of the year, and I enjoy thinking that a *hototogisu*[1] may be hiding in its shade. When passing through the plain of Murasaki[2] on one's way back from the Festival, it is lovely to see the white of the *u no hana* blossoms in the shaggy hedges near the cottages. They look like thin, white robes worn over a costume of yellowish green.

At the end of the Fourth Month and the beginning of the Fifth the orange trees have dark green leaves and are covered with brilliant white flowers. In the early morning, when they have been sprinkled with rain, one feels that nothing in the world can match their charm; and, if one is fortunate enough to see the fruit itself, standing out like golden spheres among the flowers, it

---

1. Sometimes translated as the cuckoo, but a far more poetic bird. *U no hana:* deutzia, a shrub of the saxifrage family that has white flowers. It blooms in the Fourth Month, around the time of the Kamo Festival. 2. North of the capital (present-day Kyoto), famous for its gromwell (*murasaki*), a plant with white or yellow flowers.

looks as beautiful as that most magnificent of sights, the cherry blossoms damp with morning dew. But I need say no more; so much has been written about the beauty of the orange trees in the many poems that link them with the *hototogisu*.[3]

The blossom of the pear tree is the most prosaic, vulgar thing in the world. The less one sees this particular blossom the better, and it should not be attached to even the most trivial message.[4] The pear blossom can be compared to the face of a plain woman; for its colouring lacks all charm. Or so, at least, I used to think. Knowing that the Chinese admire the pear blossom greatly and praise it in their poems, I wondered what they could see in it and made a point of examining the flower. Then I was surprised to find that its petals were prettily edged with a pink tinge, so faint that I could not be sure whether it was there or not. It was to the pear blossoms, I recalled, that the poet likened the face of Yang Kuei-fei[5] when she came forth in tears to meet the Emperor's messenger—"a spray of pear blossom in spring, covered with drops of rain"—and I realized that this was no idle figure of speech and that it really is a magnificent flower.

The purple blossoms of the paulownia are also delightful. I confess that I do not like the appearance of its wide leaves when they open up. . . . But I cannot speak of the paulownia as I do of the other trees; for this is where that grandiose and famous bird[6] of China makes its nest, and the idea fills me with awe. Besides, it is this tree that provides the wood for the zithers from which come so many beautiful sounds. How can I have used such a commonplace word as "delightful?" The paulownia is not delightful; it is magnificent.

The melia tree[7] is ugly, but I find its flowers very pretty indeed. One always sees them on the fifth day of the Fifth Month, and there is something charming about these dried-up, oddly shaped little flowers.

✻   ✻   ✻

Elegant Things

A white coat worn over a violet waistcoat.
Duck eggs.
Shaved ice mixed with liana[8] syrup and put in a new silver bowl.
A rosary of rock crystal.
Wistaria blossoms. Plum blossoms covered with snow.
A pretty child eating strawberries.

---

3. In the Japanese poetic tradition, certain birds had affinities with particular plants, for example, the *hototogisu* with the orange tree and the bush warbler with the plum tree.   4. It was customary to attach flowers or leaves to one's letters; the choice depended not only on the season but on the mood of the letter, the imagery of the poem it contained, and the color of the paper.   5. The most famous imperial concubine in Chinese history. The more knowledgeable of Sei Shōnagon's fellow ladies-in-waiting may well have been amused by this passage. She was known for her learning and notorious for not wearing it lightly, and she is quite incorrect here. The poet she cites, Po Chü-i, likens Yang Kuei-fei's beauty to that of jade and invokes the pear blossom only to suggest her pallor. Perhaps Sei Shōnagon had confused the poet's description with a popular account of how Yang Kuei-fei met her death: hanged from a pear tree by mutinous troops during a rebellion in 756.   6. The phoenix, whose appearance would presage the advent of a virtuous emperor.   7. *Melia japonica*, an ash, has small violet flowers.   8. A vine whose stems and leaves were used for sweetening.

Insects

The bell insect and the pine cricket; the grasshopper and the common cricket; the butterfly and the shrimp insect; the mayfly and the firefly.

I feel very sorry for the basket worm. He was begotten by a demon, and his mother, fearing that he would grow up with his father's frightening nature, abandoned the unsuspecting child, having first wrapped him in a dirty piece of clothing. "Wait for me," she said as she left. "I shall return to you as soon as the autumn winds flow." So, when autumn comes and the wind starts blowing, the wretched child hears it and desperately cries, "Milk! Milk!"[1]

The clear-toned cicada.

The snap-beetle also impresses me. They say that the reason it bows while crawling along the ground is that the faith of Buddha has sprung up in its insect heart. Sometimes one suddenly hears the snap-beetle tapping away in a dark place, and this is rather pleasant.

The fly should have been included in my list of hateful things; for such an odious creature does not belong with ordinary insects. It settles on everything, and even alights on one's face with its clammy feet. I am sorry that anyone should have been named after it.[2]

The tiger moth is very pretty and delightful. When one sits close to a lamp reading a story, a tiger moth will often flutter prettily in front of one's book.

The ant is an ugly insect; but it is light on its feet and I enjoy watching as it skims quickly over the surface of the water.

* * *

Unsuitable Things

A woman with ugly hair wearing a robe of white damask.

Hollyhock worn in frizzled hair.

Ugly handwriting on red paper.

Snow on the houses of common people. This is especially regrettable when the moonlight shines down on it.[1]

A plain wagon[2] on a moonlit night; or a light auburn ox harnessed to such a wagon.

A woman who, though well past her youth, is pregnant and walks along panting. It is unpleasant to see a woman of a certain age with a young husband; and it is most unsuitable when she becomes jealous of him because he has gone to visit someone else.

An elderly man who has overslept and who wakes up with a start; or a greybeard munching some acorns that he has plucked. An old woman who eats a plum and, finding it sour, puckers her toothless mouth.

A woman of the lower classes dressed in a scarlet trouser-skirt. The sight is all too common these days.

A handsome man with an ugly wife.

---

1. A pun difficult to translate. Chi-chi is the characteristic sound of the basket worm as well as the word for "breast," or "milk."   2. In ancient Japan people were often named after animals. Haemaro (in which hae means "fly") was probably given to members of the lower classes because of its unpleasant associations.
1. Because such beauty is wasted on mere commoners.   2. A carriage used to convey goods, not people.

An elderly man with a black beard and a disagreeable expression playing with a little child who has just learnt to talk.

It is most unseemly for an Assistant Captain of the Quiver Bearers[3] to make his night patrol in a hunting costume. And, if he wanders outside the woman's quarters, ostentatiously clad in his terrifying red cloak, people will be sure to look down on him. They disapprove of his behaviour and taunt him with remarks like "Are you searching for someone suspicious?"

A Lieutenant in the Imperial Police who serves as a Chamberlain of the Sixth Rank, and therefore has access to the Senior Courtiers' Chamber,[4] is regarded as being splendid beyond words. Country folk and people of the lower orders believe that he cannot be a creature of this world: in his presence they tremble with fear and dare not meet his eyes. It is very unsuitable that such a man should slink along the narrow corridors of some Palace building in order to steal into a woman's room.

A man's trouser-skirt hanging over a curtain of state that has been discreetly perfumed with incense.[5] The material of the trouser-skirt is disagreeably heavy; and, even though it may be shining whitely in the lamp-light, there is something unsuitable about it.

An officer who thinks he is very fashionable in his open overrobe and who folds it thinly as a rat's tail before hanging it over the curtain of state—well, such a man is simply unfit for night patrol. Officers on duty should abstain from visiting the women's quarters; the same applies to Chamberlains of the Fifth Rank.

*   *   *

Small Children and Babies

Small children and babies ought to be plump. So ought provincial governors and others who have gone ahead in the world; for, if they are lean and desiccated, one suspects them of being ill-tempered.

*   *   *

Things That Cannot Be Compared

Summer and winter. Night and day. Rain and sunshine. Youth and age. A person's laughter and his anger. Black and white. Love and hatred. The little indigo plant and the great philodendron. Rain and mist.

When one has stopped loving somebody, one feels that he has become someone else, even though he is still the same person.

In a garden full of evergreens the crows are all asleep. Then, towards the middle of the night, the crows in one of the trees suddenly wake up in a great flurry and start flapping about. Their unrest spreads to the other trees, and soon all the birds have been startled from their sleep and are cawing in alarm. How different from the same crows in daytime!

---

3. The outer palace guards, one of the three guard regiments stationed at the imperial palace.　　4. Sei Shōnagon resented these parvenu police officers who, despite their low rank, were allowed to swagger about the palace buildings without proper regard for decorum and who even had affairs with court ladies of much higher rank than themselves. See also n. 2, p. 2283.　　5. Incense was used to perfume the blinds, screens, and other furnishings in upper-class houses as well as the courtier's robes. Indiscreet as it may seem, it was normal for male visitors to hang their trouser-skirts over the curtain belonging to the lady they were visiting.

To Meet One's Lover

To meet one's lover summer is indeed the right season. True, the nights are very short, and dawn creeps up before one has had a wink of sleep. Since all the lattices have been left open, one can lie and look out at the garden in the cool morning air. There are still a few endearments to exchange before the man takes his leave, and the lovers are murmuring to each other when suddenly there is a loud noise. For a moment they are certain that they have been discovered; but it is only the caw of a crow flying past in the garden.

In the winter, when it is very cold and one lies buried under the bedclothes listening to one's lover's endearments, it is delightful to hear the booming of a temple gong, which seems to come from the bottom of a deep well. The first cry of the birds, whose beaks are still tucked under their wings, is also strange and muffled. Then one bird after another takes up the call. How pleasant it is to lie there listening as the sound becomes clearer and clearer!

* * *

Rare Things

A son-in-law who is praised by his adoptive father; a young bride who is loved by her mother-in-law.

A silver tweezer that is good at plucking out the hair.

A servant who does not speak badly about his master.

A person who is in no way eccentric or imperfect, who is superior in both mind and body, and who remains flawless all his life.

People who live together and still manage to behave with reserve towards each other. However much these people may try to hide their weaknesses, they usually fail.

To avoid getting ink stains on the notebook into which one is copying stories, poems, or the like. If it is a very fine notebook, one takes the greatest care not to make a blot; yet somehow one never seems to succeed.

When people, whether they be men or women or priests, have promised each other eternal friendship, it is rare for them to stay on good terms until the end.

A servant who is pleasant to his master.

One has given some silk to the fuller and, when he sends it back, it is so beautiful that one cries out in admiration.

* * *

Embarrassing Things

While entertaining a visitor, one hears some servants chatting without any restraint in one of the back rooms. It is embarrassing to know that one's visitor can overhear. But how to stop them?

A man whom one loves gets drunk and keeps repeating himself.

To have spoken about someone not knowing that he could overhear. This is embarrassing even if it be a servant or some other completely insignificant person.

To hear one's servants making merry. This is equally annoying if one is on a journey and staying in cramped quarters or at home and hears the servants in a neighbouring room.

Parents, convinced that their ugly child is adorable, pet him and repeat the things he has said, imitating his voice.

An ignoramus who in the presence of some learned person puts on a knowing air and converses about men of old.

A man recites his own poems (not especially good ones) and tells one about the praise they have received—most embarrassing.

Lying awake at night, one says something to one's companion, who simply goes on sleeping.

In the presence of a skilled musician, someone plays a zither just for his own pleasure and without tuning it.

A son-in-law who has long since stopped visiting his wife runs into his father-in-law in a public place.

      *   *   *

During the Long Rains in the Fifth Month

During the long rains in the Fifth Month, there is something very moving about a place with a pond. Between the dense irises, water-oats, and other plants one can see the green of the water; and the entire garden seems to be the same green colour. One stays there all day long, gazing in contemplation at the clouded sky—oh, how moving it is!

I am always moved and delighted by places that have ponds—not only in the winter (when I love waking up to find that the water has frozen over) but at every time of the year. The ponds I like best are not those in which everything is carefully laid out; I much prefer one that has been left to itself so that it is wild and covered with weeds. At night in the green spaces of water one can see nothing but the pale glow of the moonlight. At any time and in any place I find moonlight very moving.

      *   *   *

Things That Give a Hot Feeling

The hunting costume of the head of a Guards escort.
A patchwork surplice.
The Captain[1] in attendance at the Imperial Games.
An extremely fat person with a lot of hair.
A zither bag.
A Holy Teacher performing a rite of incantation at noon in the Sixth or Seventh Month. Or at the same time of the year a copper-smith working in his foundry.

Shameful Things

A thief has crept into a house and is now hiding in some well-chosen nook where he can secretly observe what is going on. Someone else comes into

---

1. The officer presiding over archery and wrestling contests held on the palace grounds wore his full uniform, despite the summer heat.

the dark room and, taking an object that lies there, slips it into his sleeve. It must be amusing for the thief to see a person who shares his own nature.

Priests on night duty[2] are often confronted with shameful things, especially if they are light sleepers. For they are liable to overhear groups of young women joking about other people, abusing them, and venting their spite on them; all this is bound to arouse a sense of shame in the priest who lies next door, hearing everything they say. Some of the Emperor's elderly ladies-in-waiting angrily tell the girls not to be so noisy; but they pay no attention and continue gossiping until finally they doze off without the slightest regard for decorum. Even after they are asleep, the priest still feels it is shameful.

A man's heart is a shameful thing. When he is with a woman whom he finds tiresome and distasteful, he does not show that he dislikes her, but makes her believe she can count on him. Still worse, a man who has the reputation of being kind and loving treats a a woman in such a way that she cannot imagine his feelings are anything but sincere. Yet he is untrue to her not only in his thoughts but in his words; for he speaks badly about her to other women just as he speaks badly about those women to her. The woman, of course, has no idea that she is being maligned; and, hearing his criticisms of the others, she fondly believes he loves her best. The man for his part is well aware that this is what she thinks. How shameful!

When a woman runs into a lover with whom (alas!) she has broken for good, there is no reason for her to be ashamed if he regards her as heartless. But if the lover shows that he has not been even slightly upset by their parting, which to her was so sad and painful and difficult, she is bound to be amazed by the man and to wonder what sort of a heart he can have. Oblivious of his own callous attitude, her abandoned lover carried on a glib conversation in which he criticizes the behaviour of other men.

How shameful when a man seduces some helpless Court lady and, having made her pregnant, abandons her without caring in the slightest about her future!

Things That Have Lost Their Power

A large boat which is high and dry in a creek at ebb-tide.

A woman who has taken off her false locks to comb the short hair that remains.

A large tree that has been blown down in a gale and lies on its side with its roots in the air.

The retreating figure of a *sumō*[1] wrestler who has been defeated in a match.

A man of no importance reprimanding an attendant.

An old man who removes his hat, uncovering his scanty topknot.

A woman, who is angry with her husband about some trifling matter, leaves home and goes somewhere to hide. She is certain that he will rush about looking for her; but he does nothing of the kind and shows the most infuri-

---

2. In case of an illness or other emergency. 1. A form of wrestling said to be two thousand years old and considered today as the national sport of Japan. Two large wrestlers clad only in elaborate loincloths face each other in a small ring about fourteen feet in diameter. With a great deal of ritual stamping, squatting, puffing, and glowering, the wrestler tries to topple his opponent or to force him out of the ring.

ating indifference. Since she cannot stay away for ever, she swallows her pride and returns.

Awkward Things

One has gone to a house and asked to see someone; but the wrong person appears, thinking that it is he who is wanted; this is especially awkward if one has brought a present.

One has allowed oneself to speak badly about someone without really intending to do so; a young child who has overheard it all goes and repeats what one has said in front of the person in question.

Someone sobs out a pathetic story. One is deeply moved; but it so happens that not a single tear comes to one's eyes—most awkward. Though one makes one's face look as if one is going to cry, it is no use: not a single tear will come. Yet there are times when, having heard something happy, one feels the tears streaming out.

* * *

I Remember a Clear Morning

I remember a clear morning in the Ninth Month when it had been raining all night. Despite the bright sun, dew was still dripping from the chrysanthemums in the garden. On the bamboo fences and criss-cross hedges I saw tatters of spider webs; and where the threads were broken the raindrops hung on them like strings of white pearls. I was greatly moved and delighted.

As it became sunnier, the dew gradually vanished from the clover and the other plants where it had lain so heavily; the branches began to stir, then suddenly sprang up of their own accord. Later I described to people how beautiful it all was. What most impressed me was that they were not at all impressed.

* * *

Things That Give a Clean Feeling

An earthen cup. A new metal bowl.
A rush mat.
The play of the light on water as one pours it into a vessel.
A new wooden chest.

Things That Give an Unclean Feeling

A rat's nest.
Someone who is late in washing his hands in the morning.
White snivel, and children who sniffle as they walk.
The containers used for oil.

Little sparrows.[1]
A person who does not bathe for a long time even though weather is hot.[2]
All faded clothes give me an unclean feeling, especially those that have glossy colours.

* * *

Wind Instruments

I love the sound of the flute: it is beautiful when one hears it gradually approaching from the distance, and also when it is played near by and then moves far away until it becomes very faint.

There is nothing so charming as a man who always carries a flute when he goes out on horseback or on foot. Though he keeps the flute tucked in his robe and one cannot actually see it, one enjoys knowing it is there.

I particularly like hearing familiar tunes played on a flute. It is also very pleasant at dawn to find that a flute had been left next to one's pillow by a gentleman who has been visiting one; presently he sends a messenger to fetch the instrument and, when one gives it to him carefully wrapped up, it looks like an elegant next-morning letter.

A thirteen-pipe flute is delightful when one hears it in a carriage on a bright, moonlit night. True, it is bulky and rather awkward to play—and what a face people make when they blow it! But they can look ungraceful with ordinary flutes also.

The flageolet is a very shrill instrument, the autumn insect it most resembles being the long cricket. It makes a terrible noise, especially when it is played badly, and it is not something one wants to hear near by. I remember one of the Special Festivals at Kamo,[1] when the musicians had not yet come into His Majesty's presence. One could hear the sound of their flutes from behind the trees, and I was just thinking how delightful it was when suddenly the flageolets joined in. They became shriller and shriller, until all the ladies, even those who were most beautifully groomed, felt their hair standing on end. Then the procession came before the Emperor with all the string and wind instruments playing in splendid unison.

* * *

When Crossing a River

When crossing a river in bright moonlight, I love to see the water scatter in showers of crystal under the oxen's feet.

Things That Should Be Large

Priests. Fruit. Houses. Provision bags. Inksticks for inkstones.
Men's eyes: when they are too narrow, they look feminine.[2] On the other

---

1. Before they are properly fledged.   2. The present custom of a daily bath did not become current until much later. Documents suggest that aristocrats bathed about once every five days, one reason for the practice of perfuming the house with incense.   1. Shinto festivals held annually in the Eleventh Month at the Kamo shrines north of the capital. They were called "special" to distinguish them from the Kamo Festival in the Fourth Month.   2. A deviation from conventional standards of male beauty, which prescribed narrow eyes for men as well as for women.

hand, if they were as large as metal bowls, I should find them rather frightening.

Round braziers. Winter cherries.[3] Pine trees. The petals of yellow roses. Horses as well as oxen should be large.

Things That Should Be Short

A piece of thread when one wants to sew something in a hurry.
A lamp stand.
The hair of a woman of the lower classes should be neat and short.
The speech of a young girl.

*   *   *

Men Really Have Strange Emotions

Men really have strange emotions and behave in the most bizarre ways. Sometimes a man will leave a very pretty woman to marry an ugly one. Surely a gentleman who frequents the Palace should choose as his love the prettiest girl of good family he can find. Though she may be of such high standing that he cannot hope to make her his wife, he should, if he is really impressed by the girl, languish for her unto death.

Sometimes, too, a man will become so fascinated by a girl of whom he has heard favourable reports that he will do everything in his power to marry her even though they have never even met.

I do not understand how a man can possibly love a girl whom other people, even those of her own sex, find ugly.

I remember a certain woman who was both attractive and good-natured and who furthermore had excellent hand-writing. Yet when she sent a beautifully written poem to the man of her choice, he replied with some pretentious jottings and did not even bother to visit her. She wept endearingly, but he was indifferent and went to see another woman instead. Everyone, even people who were not directly concerned, felt indignant about this callous behavior, and the woman's family was much grieved. The man himself, however, showed not the slightest pity.

*   *   *

It Is Absurd of People to Get Angry

It is absurd of people to get angry because one has gossiped about them. How can anyone be so simple as to believe that he is free to find fault with others while his own foibles are passed over in silence? Yet when someone hears that he has been discussed unfavourably he is always outraged, and this I find most unattractive.

If I am really close to someone, I realize that it would be hurting to speak badly about him and when the opportunity for gossip arises I hold my peace. In all other cases, however, I freely speak my mind and make everyone laugh.

3. Large winter cherries were used as toys or dolls.

Features That I Particularly Like

Features that I particularly like in someone's face continue to give a thrill of delight however often I see the person. With pictures it is different. If I look at them too often, they cease to attract me; indeed, I never so much as glance at the beautiful paintings on the screen that stands near my usual seat.

There is something really fascinating about beautiful faces. Though an object such as a vase or a fan may be ugly in general, there is always one particular part that one can gaze at with pleasure. One would expect this to apply to faces also; but, alas, there is nothing to recommend an ugly face.

Pleasing Things

Finding a large number of tales that one has not read before. Or acquiring the second volume of a tale whose first volume one has enjoyed. But often it is a disappointment.

Someone has torn up a letter and thrown it away. Picking up the pieces, one finds that many of them can be fitted together.

One has had an upsetting dream and wonders what it can mean. In great anxiety one consults a dream-interpreter, who informs one that it has no special significance.

A person of quality is holding forth about something in the past or about a recent event that is being widely discussed. Several people are gathered round him, but it is oneself that he keeps looking at as he talks.

A person who is very dear to one has fallen ill. One is miserably worried about him even if he lives in the capital and far more so if he is in some remote part of the country. What a pleasure to be told that he has recovered!

I am most pleased when I hear someone I love being praised or being mentioned approvingly by an important person.

A poem that someone has composed for a special occasion or written to another person in reply is widely praised and copied by people in their note-books. Though this is something that has never yet happened to me, I can imagine how pleasing it must be.

A person with whom one is not especially intimate refers to an old poem or story that is unfamiliar. Then one hears it being mentioned by someone else and one has the pleasure of recognizing it. Still later, when one comes across it in a book, one thinks, "Ah, this is it!" and feels delighted with the person who first brought it up.

I feel very pleased when I have acquired some Michinoku paper,[1] or some white, decorated paper, or even plain paper if it is nice and white.

A person in whose company one feels awkward asks one to supply the opening or closing line of a poem. If one happens to recall it, one is very pleased. Yet often on such occasions one completely forgets something that one would normally know.

I look for an object that I need at once, and I find it. Or again, there is a

---

1. A thick, white paper of first-rate quality named for the province where it was manufactured and used for writing letters and poetry.

book that I must see immediately; I turn everything upside down, and there it is. What a joy!

When one is competing in an object match[2] (it does not matter what kind), how can one help being pleased at winning?

I greatly enjoy taking in someone who is pleased with himself and who has a self-confident look, especially if he is a man. It is amusing to observe him as he alertly waits for my next repartee; but it is also interesting if he tries to put me off my guard by adopting an air of calm indifference as if there were not a thought in his head.

I realize that it is very sinful of me, but I cannot help being pleased when someone I dislike has a bad experience.

It is a great pleasure when the ornamental comb that one has ordered turns out to be pretty.

I am more pleased when something nice happens to a person I love than when it happens to myself.

Entering the Empress's room and finding that ladies-in-waiting are crowded round her in a tight group, I go next to a pillar which is some distance from where she is sitting. What a delight it is when Her Majesty summons me to her side so that all the others have to make way!

*   *   *

It Is Getting So Dark

It is getting so dark that I can scarcely go on writing; and my brush is all worn out. Yet I should like to add a few things before I end.

I wrote these notes at home, when I had a good deal of time to myself and thought no one would notice what I was doing. Everything that I have seen and felt is included. Since much of it might appear malicious and even harmful to other people, I was careful to keep my book hidden. But now it has become public, which is the last thing I expected.

One day Lord Korechika, the Minister of the Centre,[1] brought the Empress a bundle of notebooks. "What shall we do with them?" Her Majesty asked me. "The Emperor has already made arrangements for copying the 'Records of the Historian.' "[2]

"Let me make them into a pillow," I said.[3]

"Very well," said Her Majesty. "You may have them."

I now had a vast quantity of paper at my disposal, and I set about filling the notebooks with odd facts, stories from the past, and all sorts of other things, often including the most trivial material. On the whole I concentrated on things and people that I found charming and splendid; my notes are also full of poems and observations on trees and plants, birds and insects. I was sure that when people saw my book they would say, "It's even worse than I

2. Literally "comparison of objects" (*monoawase*), such as flowers, roots, seashells, birds, insects, fans, and paintings. Courtiers divided into two teams and vied to see which could present the finest specimens. These matches had specially appointed judges and became festive social occasions.   1. Among the most important ministers of state, who served in the emperor's cabinet and thus near the apex of the court administration. The office ranked directly below minister of the right (the fourth highest official in the government). Korechika (like the fictional Genji) was a typical holder of the post, which became a sinecure for ambitious scions of the well connected.   2. That is, the *Shih chi*, written by the great Chinese historian Ssu-ma Ch'ien (died ca. 85 B.C.).   3. Thought to be the origin of the work's title (see headnote "Sei Shōnagon," p. 2270).

expected. Now one can really tell what she is like." After all, it is written entirely for my own amusement and I put things down exactly as they came to me. How could my casual jottings possibly bear comparison with the many impressive books that exist in our time? Readers have declared, however, that I can be proud of my work. This has surprised me greatly; yet I suppose it is not so strange that people should like it, for, as will be gathered from these notes of mine, I am the sort of person who approves of what others abhor and detests the things they like.

Whatever people may think of my book, I still regret that it ever came to light.

THE TALE OF THE HEIKE
1371

No other work in Japanese literature can match *The Tale of the Heike* in its appeal to the popular imagination. Besides helping to create the *samurai* ideal, it has offered the Japanese reader practically everything: heroic spirit, dramatic energy, vivid description, musical language, humor, and pathos. The tale re-creates events of the late twelfth century, which brought a vast change to Japanese political life with the eclipse of the aristocracy and the rise and fall of great military houses. The tale's pitch-perfect rendering of the theme of evanescence—that all who flourish are destined to fail and humankind is but dust before the wind—touches a chord that resonates deep in the Japanese psyche. As a result, *The Tale of the Heike* has influenced more writers in more subsequent genres, from medieval *nō* plays to television dramas, than any other single work in Japanese literature.

By the beginning of the twelfth century the power of the court nobility was slowly withering, as the central bureaucracy and its local branches atrophied. A power vacuum began to form in the provinces, and the governors and their agents who had been deputized to maintain law and order gradually emerged as a warrior class. When things fell apart in the capital, the military clans moved in to fill the breach. By the middle of the century the court administration was in paralysis. Ex-emperors ruled behind the throne or tried to, the Fujiwara clan still clung to a shred of authority, and the bureaucracy—menaced even by the Buddhist clergy—had reduced itself to ineptitude.

The explosion that eventually ignited civil war was a dispute over imperial succession in 1156. The winner enlisted the support of the two most powerful military clans, but in so doing set in motion their rise as independent political forces within the capital. In a predictable sequence of events, the two clans quarreled, and the defeated house withdrew to the eastern provinces. This was the Minamoto clan (whose alternate Sino-Japanese designation was *Genji*). The ascendant clan, the house of Taira (or *Heike* in Sino-Japanese) remained in the capital, where it enjoyed twenty years of arrogant splendor before the Minamoto/Genji finally took revenge. Fighting began in 1180 and raged on for five years. When it was over, the Heike had been annihilated, and the Genji established a military dictatorship that would rule Japan for two centuries.

The tale of these events divides into three parts. The first depicts the brief heyday of the Heike, dominated by the figure of Kiyomori, a leader so ruthless and evil that at his death (in the first selection printed here) no water will cool the fires of hatred consuming him. The tale opens with a celebrated passage:

The sound of Gion Shōja bells echoes the impermanence of all things; the color of the śāla flowers reveals the truth that the prosperous must decline. The proud do not endure, they are like a dream on a spring night; the mighty fall at last, they are as dust before the wind.

With its theme economically established, the tale proceeds to record Kiyomori's inevitable fall, culminating in death.

The Heike are now reeling from the loss of their leader, and the second and third parts of the tale are dominated by the Genji side. The central figures are the brutish Yoshinaka and, following his death, the brilliant, youthful Yoshitsune, who deals a crippling blow to the Heike in the surprise attack at Ichi-no-tani (Chapter 9) and masterminds their final rout—the naval battle at Dan-no-ura (Chapter 11), where the emperor (a Heike offspring), Kiyomori's widow, and virtually all the men of the clan are sent to their deaths at sea. The tale ends with an epilogue that takes us far from the scene of battle—to the mountains, where the mother of the emperor goes to mourn (*The Initiates' Chapter*). In her cloister she will pray for the repose of her son's soul, as indeed the entire tale, to medieval ears, sounded an offering meant to soothe the restless spirits of the departed Heike.

Authorship of the tale has long been subject to conjecture. Most likely, it originated as a story told by itinerant performers, who traveled the countryside reciting the daring feats and tender passions of the famous warriors and accompanied themselves by playing the lute, not unlike the scop or minstrel who entertained in the Anglo-Saxon mead hall with the story of Beowulf. These chanters were blind men who re-created their tale with every performance. They relied on oral formulas rather than a written text, and the performance origins of the tale account for some of its most striking features: formulaic language, imagery, and characterization; the use of cadence and repetition; structural contrast; stress on action; exaggeration; and enumeration and other types of deliberate digression to lend authenticity or an air of antiquity to the narrative.

At some point, probably in the early thirteenth century, a court noble or a Buddhist monk (or a noble, a monk, and a chanter together) wrote down a version of the oral tale. After this, two traditions developed in tandem. One was a succession of texts intended to be read privately; the other, of scripts for oral presentation. Eventually more than a hundred variants came into being, but the one that is standard is a version perfected over a thirty-year period and set down in 1371 by a chanter named Akashi Kakuichi, who shaped the disparate materials into a unified work of literary merit.

In modern times the Japanese have tended to emphasize the epic traits of *The Tale of the Heike*. Its depiction of heroic warriors, grandeur of scale, narrative length, ceremonious style, and links with history are important epic qualities. Even its bardic origins among the allegedly blind are intriguingly "right."

Still, there are major differences. The epic form is poetry; *The Tale of the Heike* is prose. It contains, moreover, a high proportion of nonheroic material. Romantic interludes, lyrical celebrations of nature, and a continuing stress on the bittersweet brevity of all things loom large, as does the cultivation of the courtly arts of poetry and music. In its battles there is carnage but relatively little brutality.

In short, patrician standards somehow persist. Even the Heike's decline is implicitly attributed to a degeneration of martial discipline when the clan stayed too long in the capital. Whereas the true epic focuses on the military class, *The Tale of the Heike* experiences a fissure. Warriors are the subject of the tale, yet the point of view is closer to the aristocrat's. It was as though, despite the collapse of the aristocracy's political and economic viability, this was the only group considered capable of appreciating the sad implications of the tale. As the loser in history's upheaval, it could be counted on to identify with the fate of the Heike. But something else must also have happened. Courtly values were becoming common currency. Earlier, the thought that life's glory is as brief as a spring night's dream could only have been expressed in court poetry or the prose of a noblewoman. Now it was a message for the masses.

Of various translations available, Helen Craig McCullough, *The Tale of the Heike* (1988), is recommended; it also contains informative supplementary material, including a chronology of events and historical background. Paul Varley offers a useful discussion of social issues in "Warriors as Courtiers: The Taira in Heike Monogatari," in Amy Vladek Heinrich, ed., *Currents in Japanese Culture* (1997).

PRONOUNCING GLOSSARY

The following list uses common English syllables to provide rough equivalents of selected words whose pronunciation may be unfamiliar to the general reader.

Akashi Kakuichi: *ah-kah-shee kah-koo-ee-chee*

Antoku: *ahn-toh-koo*

Atsumori: *ah-tsoo-moh-ree*

Dan-no-ura: *dahn–noh–oo-rah*

Fukuhara: *foo-koo-hah-rah*

Gion Shōja: *gee-ohn shoh-jah*

Go-Shirakawa: *goh–shee-rah-kah-wah*

Heiji: *hay-jee*

Heike: *hay-kay*

Hiei: *hee-ay*

Hiyodorigoe: *hee-yoh-doh-ree-goh-e*

Ichi-no-tani: *ee-chee–noh–tah-nee*

Jakkōin: *jahk-koh-een*

Kamakura: *kah-mah-koo-rah*

Kenreimon'in: *ken-ray-mohn-een*

Kiyomori: *kee-yoh-moh-ree*

Koremori: *koh-re-moh-ree*

Kumagae no Jirō Naozane: *koo-mah-gai noh jee-roh nah-oh-zah-ne*

Kumano: *koo-mah-noh*

Motofusa: *moh-toh-foo-sah*

Munemori: *moo-ne-moh-ree*

Norimori: *noh-ree-moh-ree*

Ohara: *oh-hah-rah*

Reizei: *ray-zay*

Rokuhara: *roh-koo-hah-rah*

Shigemori: *shee-ge-moh-ree*

Shimonoseki: *shee-moh-noh-se-kee*

Tsunemori: *tsoo-ne-moh-ree*

Yorimori: *yoh-ree-moh-ree*

Yoritomo: *yoh-ree-toh-moh*

Yoshinaka: *yoh-shee-nah-kah*

Yoshitsune: *yoh-shee-tsoo-ne*

From The Tale of the Heike[1]

Summary   The selection from Chapter 6, our first excerpt, takes us halfway into the tale, which has so far been, in the main, an account of the Heike (or Taira) clan's ascendancy. The clan controls half the provinces in Japan and enjoys sufficient military might to impose its will on the capital. As head of the clan, Kiyomori has attained the pinnacle of worldly success, been named Chancellor of the Realm, and appointed to the most exalted of court ranks. His sons have also fared handsomely; they hold some of the highest titles in the imperial government. The whole family has shared in Kiyomori's prosperity. Sixteen members of the clan rank as senior nobles; more than thirty win official courtier status; and over sixty hold appointments as provincial governors, guards officers, and members of the central bureaucracy. Kiyomori's eight

---

1. Translated by and with notes adapted from Helen Craig McCullough. Bracketed words throughout the translation are McCullough's explanations.

daughters have all made advantageous marriages. One is wed to the emperor and becomes the mother of a future emperor.

The material fortunes of the Heike are described, therefore, as "flowering":

> The clan possessed innumerable private estates and agricultural fields. Their halls, thronged with damasks and gauzes, resembled flower gardens; their gates, congested with carriages and horses, were veritable marketplaces. They lacked none of the Seven Treasures or myriad precious things—Yangzhou gold, Jingzhou pearls, Wujun damask, Shujiang brocade. And as for the halls and pavilions where they danced and sang, and the trinkets with which they entertained themselves, it seemed there was no greater splendor to be found even in the palaces of the reigning sovereign and the Retired Emperor.

"It was as though there were no other people in the world," the narrator tells us—a judgment with which the Heike unfortunately concur. "All who do not belong to this clan," boasts Kiyomori's brother-in-law, "must rank as lesser men."

But this pride is part of their undoing. One famous episode in the tale will suggest how distended the Heike ego has become and how out of touch with political reality. Returning from an excursion one winter evening, Kiyomori's thirteen-year-old grandson encounters the retinue of the imperial regent and refuses to give way. Incensed at his contemptuous behavior (and unaware that they are dealing with Kiyomori's spoiled grandson), the regent's guards force the young man and his companions to dismount. The haughty youth returns home whining and Kiyomori flies into a rage. He gets his revenge several days later, when he sends three hundred horsemen to ambush the regent's procession within the very heart of the capital. The regent's escorts are dragged from their horses, beaten, and humiliated, and the regent himself is threatened when one of Kiyomori's thugs thrusts a sword inside his carriage. "Words cannot describe the wretchedness of the state in which [the regent] Lord Motofusa returned, trying to hold back his tears with the sleeve of his court robe. Never had such an experience befallen any Imperial Regent in all the generations. . . . That was the first of the Taira clan's evil deeds."

Thus does Kiyomori undermine the good will of the emperor and the entire capital, which his father had so assiduously cultivated as the keystone of Heike dominion. What the clan needs at this juncture is an astute and farsighted politician, but Kiyomori is a man of other parts: mercurial, vindictive, and megalomaniacal. He seems almost to possess a split personality. One moment he is the cunning warrior and the next, the lovesick courtier. At first, this may have kept people off guard, but eventually the brutal half—capricious and utterly immoderate—repulses even Kiyomori's own son.

Shigemori, the hope of the future, finally confronts his father, urging restraint, but Kiyomori is only temporarily chastened. His spies fan out through the capital. His rivals are tortured and viciously executed. He deals with the powerful Buddhist clergy high-handedly and treats even the emperor with contempt. "A devil controls Kiyomori's mind," people say. "Nothing can appease his wrath." Everyone trembles in fear.

Shigemori, as virtuous as his father is unsavory, makes a pilgrimage to pray for a solution to the impasse Kiyomori seems bent on creating. "The conduct of my father exhibits a distressing lack of propriety," he says to the Buddhist deities:

> This is my prayer: if my descendants are to enjoy continuous prosperity, and if they are to remain in court service, then soften my father's sinful heart and bring peace to the land. But if the glory of our house is to end with my father's generation, and if his successors are to suffer ignominy, then shorten my life and deliver me from the Wheel of Suffering in the existence to come. With all my heart, I beseech you to grant one or the other of these two petitions.

No sooner does he utter this prayer than a "radiance like a lantern" shines forth from Shigemori's body and disappears as though snuffed out. Shigemori understands that, one way or another, his petition has been answered. Within a few days he falls ill, and soon he is dead. The Heike know what they have lost.

Shigemori's untimely death is only one way that the gods seem to show their displeasure. The country is wracked with a series of natural disasters. Fires, tornadoes, and earthquakes are all interpreted as portents that Kiyomori is steering Japan down a path toward some horrendous calamity. One seer states it baldly: "There will be a succession of military disturbances."

And indeed the remainder of Kiyomori's allotted time is beset with plot and counterplot, treachery and betrayal. He has lost the support of the powerful retired emperor and the bulk of the imperial family. The aristocracy, who once saw Kiyomori as a protector, now revile him. The Buddhist temples stop their squabbling and unite their private armies against the hated despot. And worst of all, Kiyomori's depredations have driven each of these former allies into the arms of his most serious rival, the potent warrior house of the Minamoto, or Genji.

Yoritomo, head of the Genji clan, cuts a deal with the retired emperor. Go-Shirakawa agrees to pardon him for past offenses; in return, Yoritomo will lead his men against the Heike. Battle is joined in 1180. The war between the Heike and the Genji has begun, and rages inconclusively for a full year before the onset of Kiyomori's final illness.

FROM CHAPTER 6

The Death of Kiyomori

Thereafter, all the warriors in Shikoku declared allegiance to Kōno no Shirō Michinobu.[2] It was rumored that the Kumano[3] Superintendent Tanzō had also gone over to the Genji, despite his deep obligation to the Heike.

The east and the north were in revolt; the south and the west were as has been described. Tidings of barbarian rebellions shocked the ear; portents of war were reported in rapid succession. "The barbarians in the four directions have risen overnight; the regime is doomed," lamented all who possessed powers of discernment, whether they belonged to the Taira clan or not.

At a council of senior nobles on the Twenty-Third of the Second Month, Munemori[4] proposed his own appointment as Commander-in-Chief of a new expedition against the east, since the previous one had produced no noteworthy results. The suggestion was received with effusive praise. Retired Emperor Go-Shirakawa[5] issued a directive: Munemori was to command a campaign against the eastern and northern rebels,[6] and the army was to include courtiers and senior nobles who held military posts or were experienced in the martial arts.

---

2. A Genji supporter. His father has just been killed by a Heike partisan, and Michinobu's revenge rallies the warriors of Shikoku (one of the four main islands of Japan) to the side of the Genji. This is a serious setback for the Heike, because Shikoku lies in the southwestern portion of the country, where the clan has enjoyed its traditional strength. Furthermore, the defection of the Shikoku warriors follows immediately on a Heike rout in the various provinces of Kyūshū (the neighboring and southernmost of the four main islands), where the *samurai* all turn against the Heike and cast their lot with the Genji.   3. One of the most important shrines in Japan, in an area that had long been under the sway of the Heike. 4. Kiyomori's son, successor to Shigemori.   5. One of the slipperiest figures in Japanese history. Following the convention of the period, he was, if anything, even more influential after his abdication—and, in fact, abdicated so as to gain more room to maneuver. For thirty-four years he had a considerably greater say in the government than the series of reigning emperors who succeeded him. Yoritomo, head of the Genji, called Go-Shirakawa "the number one scoundrel in Japan," and he was equally disliked by Kiyomori, precisely because he did what they did: always checking to see which way the wind blew, he played one faction against another and used impressive guile to protect his own interests. At this point in the tale, Go-Shirakawa is nominally allied with the Heike, but only because Kiyomori holds him virtual hostage. On the surface, then, he does the Heike's bidding, when in fact he is in league with the Genji. The retired emperor is so duplicitous that, in the sweeping turbulence of events, it is hard at any given moment to tell whose side he is really on.   6. That is, the Genji.

On the Twenty-Seventh, Munemori postponed the eastward march of the punitive force, which had been imminent, because his father had fallen ill. From the Twenty-Eighth on, it became known that the Chancellor-Novice's condition was critical. "Ah! His deeds have come home to roost," people whispered in the city and at Rokuhara.[7]

Kiyomori could swallow nothing, not even a sip of water, after the disease took hold. His body was fiery hot; people could hardly bear to remain within twenty-five or thirty feet of the bed. His only words were, "Hot! Hot!" It seemed no ordinary ailment.

The mansion's people filled a stone tub with water drawn from the Thousand-Armed Well on Mount Hiei,[8] but the water boiled up and turned to steam as soon as Kiyomori got in to cool off. Desperate to bring him some relief, they directed a stream of water onto his body from a bamboo pipe, but the liquid spattered away without reaching him, as though from red-hot stone or iron. The few drops that struck him burst into flame, so that black smoke filled the hall and tongues of fire swirled toward the ceiling. Now, for the first time, the onlookers understood what Bishop Hōzō must have experienced when he asked about the place of his mother's rebirth while he was visiting King Enma's[9] court at the King's invitation: the compassionate King sent him to the Tapana Hot Hell[1] with an escort of torturer-guards, and inside the iron gate he beheld flames like shooting stars, which ascended into the heavens for hundreds of yojanas.[2]

Kiyomori's wife, the Nun of Second Rank,[3] had a frightful dream. A flaming carriage was brought inside the gate, attended at the front and rear by horse-faced and ox-faced creatures, and bearing on its head an iron tablet inscribed with the single graph *mu* [without].

"Where has that carriage come from?" the Nun asked in the dream.

"From Enma's tribunal; it is here to fetch the Taira Chancellor-Novice," a voice answered.

"What is the meaning of the tablet?"

"It has been decided at the tribunal that the Chancellor-Novice will fall to the bottom of [the Hell of Punishment] Without Intermission [Mugen] for the crime of burning the one-hundred-sixty-foot gilt bronze Vairocana in the world of men.[4] Enma has written the *mu* of Mugen, but he has not put in the *gen* [intermission] yet."

The Nun started awake, bathed in perspiration, and the hair of all whom she told about it stood on end. The family showered wonder-working shrines and temples with gold, silver, and the Seven Treasures; they even sent off

7. An eastern district of the capital, where the Heike had their headquarters.   8. The well was a source of holy water offerings for a nearby image of Thousand-Armed Kannon, a Buddhist deity known for compassion. Because the name of the well was sometimes written with characters meaning "thousand years," it was probably selected in the hope of prolonging Kiyomori's life through magic.   9. King of the netherworld in the Buddhist cosmology, judging human beings at the time of their death.   1. The hottest of the eight hells, reserved for punishing particularly egregious offenses, including murder, theft, lust, cruelty, and deceit.   2. Unit of distance (Sanskrit), said to be the equivalent of, variously, 96, 72, or 38 miles. 3. It was not unusual for members of the aristocratic and military classes to retire into religious life. Renunciation of emotional attachments and worldly ambitions, however, was often half-hearted. Kiyomori took Buddhist vows in 1168, with no discernible difference in his conduct; and his wife, now a nun, has obviously not forsaken her husband.   4. The Buddhist monasteries had already earned Kiyomori's ire for siding with the Genji. When the monks then mocked him in effigy, trampling a big wooden ball dubbed "Kiyomori's head" and accusing him of incompetence, Kiyomori dispatched his troops. By the time the fighting was over, the two great temples of Nara, Kōfukuji and Tōdaiji, had been burned to the ground and an immense fifty-three-foot bronze statue of the Buddha, known in Sanskrit as Vairocana and prized since its erection in the eighth century, had been completely incinerated. *The Tale of the Heike* describes Kiyomori as delighted with the results, but others at court are aghast at the level of destruction. It is clear now, as Kiyomori lies dying, that his impious actions have brought down the wrath of the gods.

horses, saddles, armor, helmets, bows, arrows, swords, and daggers—but there was no indication of divine response. The sons and daughters gathered at the head and foot of their father's bed, grieving and racking their brains for something to do, but there seemed little likelihood that matters would turn out as they wished.

On the Second of the intercalary Second Month, the Nun of Second Rank braved the intolerable heat to approach her husband's pillow. "As I watch you, I cannot help feeling that things seem more hopeless every day," she said in tears. "If there is anything in this world you crave, tell me when your mind is clear."

The man who had been so formidable a figure spoke in a painful whisper. "Since Hōgen and Heiji,[5] I have subdued court enemies more than once; I have received rewards beyond my deserts; I have become an Emperor's grandfather and a Chancellor; I have seen my prosperity extend to my offspring. There is nothing left for me to desire in this life. My sole concern is that I have not seen the severed head of the Izu Exile Yoritomo. Build no halls or pagodas after I die; dedicate no pious works. Dispatch the punitive force immediately, decapitate Yoritomo, and hang the head in front of my grave. That will be all the dedication I require." Those were deeply sinful words indeed.

On the Fourth, they tried to alleviate Kiyomori's suffering by laying him on a water-soaked board, but it did no good. Writhing in agony, he fell to the floor unconscious and died in convulsions. The second of horses and carriages galloping in every direction was enough to set the heavens echoing and the earth trembling: it seemed there could have been no greater agitation if death had claimed the imperial master of all the realm, the Lord of a Myriad Chariots.[6]

Kiyomori had turned sixty-four that year. It was not an age at which death was necessarily to have been expected, but karma had decreed that he should live no longer: the large rituals and the secret rituals lacked efficacy, the powers of the gods and the Buddhas vanished, the heavenly spirits offered no protection. What could mere mortals do? There were tens of thousands of loyal warriors seated in rows high and low at the hall, each ready to exchange his life for his lord's, but none of them could hold off the unseen, invincible messenger from the land of the dead for even an instant. Kiyomori must have been quite alone when he set out on his journey through the nether regions, over the Shide Mountains from which no man returns, and past the River of Three Crossings.[7] Most sadly, his only escorts must have been the evil deeds he had committed so often, come to greet him in the form of horse-headed and ox-headed torturers.

Since matters could not go on like that forever, they cremated the body at

---

5. The Heiji Disturbance (1160) was a clash between the two military clans, when Go-Shirakawa, Retired Emperor, encountered a second challenge, this time from a faction that included the Genji. Under Kiyomori's command the Heike defeated the Genji, but Kiyomori made the tactical mistake of sparing the life of his enemy's fourteen-year-old son, Yoritomo, around whom the Genji would later rally. The Hōgen Disturbance (1156) was a succession dispute in which the Heike and the Genji joined forces to support the then reigning emperor, Go-Shirakawa.   6. The emperor.   7. This river had to be forded by human spirits on the seventh day after death. The worst sinners were required to cross at the deepest, most difficult ford. The Shide Mountains were a range crossed by spirits of the dead on their way to Enma's court of judgment (see n. 9, p. 2305).

Otagi on the Seventh. Dharma Eye Enjitsu[8] hung the bones around his neck, took them down to Settsu Province, and buried them at Kyōno-shima Island. Kiyomori's fame and power had extended the length and breadth of Japan, yet his flesh rose into the skies over the capital as a transitory plume of smoke, and his bones survived only briefly before becoming one with the earth, indistinguishable from the sands of the beach.

Summary   With Kiyomori dead (1181), the Heike must depend for leadership on his feckless son Munemori. But cowardice and poor judgment are Munemori's most notable qualities, and the Heike position rapidly deteriorates. In the two years between the death of Kiyomori and the events of Chapter 9, the Heike troops fall back before the Genji on both northern and eastern fronts. Plagued by short supplies, long transport lines, and hostile terrain, the Heike are no match for the bold Genji offense. Then famine rages through Japan, and the war comes to a standstill for an entire year (1182). The capital and western provinces, both under Heike control, are especially hard hit.

By the time fighting resumes (1183), the Genji have raised fresh troops and rallied new supporters. The Heike, the court, and the capital, in contrast, are demoralized. When Heike troops attempt a last stand in the mountains of the north, Genji strategy surprises them and sends the confused troops into a disastrous, headlong rout. With the northern Heike forces thus defeated, the Genji make an easy sweep toward the capital, where a desperate Munemori and his frantic captains prepare to flee. Retired Emperor Go-Shirakawa, still very much the power behind the throne, openly defects to the Genji, and the Heike, torching their headquarters, scurry west with the child emperor.

FROM CHAPTER 7

The Flight of the Heike from the Capital

After burning his Ike Mansion and setting out with the others, the Ike Major Counselor Yorimori[9] pulled up his horse at the south gate of the Toba Palace. "I have forgotten something," he said. Then he tore off his red badge[1] and turned back toward the capital, leading a force of three hundred riders.

The Heike samurai Etchū no Jirōbyōe Moritsugi galloped to Munemori. "Look at that! See how those worthless samurai flocked to Yorimori when he decided to stay behind! I would not presume to attack Yorimori himself, but I would like to send an arrow after the samurai."

"We had better ignore men who are not honorable enough to see us to the end in spite of all the favors they have received over the years," Munemori said. There was nothing for Moritsugi to do but obey.

"What about Shigemori's[2] sons?" Munemori said.

"None of them has appeared yet."

Tears streamed down the New Middle Counselor Tomomori's[3] face. "Not one day has passed since our departure from the capital, yet people are already utterly callous about switching sides. I thought all along that the

---

8. A Buddhist priest. *Dharma Eye:* the literal translation of a term that designated the second of the three most distinguished priestly ranks established by the Japanese court. Dharma is the truth about Buddhism; thus Dharma eye means the awakened, or one initiated into the teachings of Buddhism.   9. Brother of Kiyomori, uncle of Munemori.   1. A red cloth affixed to the sleeve of his armor identifying him as a member of the Heike.   2. Kiyomori's more able son, whose death in 1179 made Munemori chieftain of the Heike.   3. Munemori's younger brother.

problem would only get worse as time went on; that was why I said we ought to make our last stand in the city." He gave Munemori a reproachful look.

If we ask why Yorimori stayed behind, this was the way of it. Yoritomo had made repeated demonstrations of goodwill toward the Major Counselor. "I could never feel anything but the highest regard for you. To me, you are Lady Ike. May the Great Bodhisattva Hachiman[4] be my witness!" he had pledged in many letters. And whenever he had sent forces to attack the Heike, he had shown his solicitude by telling them, "On no account are you to use your bows against Yorimori's samurai." That is why Yorimori returned to the city. "The Heike have lost their luck and fled the capital," he thought. "Now is the time when I must look to Yoritomo for help."

Yorimori took refuge in the Ninnaji Tokiwa Mansion, the residence of the Hachijō Imperial Lady, because he was married to Saishō, the Imperial Lady's foster sister. "Please help me if worst comes to worst," he said.

The Imperial Lady's reply was not reassuring. "It would be different if these were normal times . . ."

There was no way of predicting the attitudes of the other Genji, however well disposed Yoritomo might be. Isolated from his kinsmen by his rashness, Yorimori felt that he had nowhere to turn.

Meanwhile, Shigemori's sons—Middle Captain Koremori and his five brothers—overtook the imperial party at Yodo Mutsudagawara with a thousand riders. Munemori brightened up when they arrived. "What kept you so long?" he said.

"I am late because I was trying to find some way of comforting the children; they were very upset about my going," Koremori said.

"Why did you have to be so hard-hearted? Couldn't you have brought Rokudai[5] along?"

"The future was too uncertain." Koremori wept pitifully, moved to fresh grief by the question.

Who were the Heike who fled?

> The Former Palace minister Munemori
> The Taira Major Counselor Tokitada
> The Taira Middle Counselor Norimori
> The New Middle Counselor Tomomori
> The Master of the Palace Repairs Office Tsunemori
> The Commander of the Gate Guards of the Right Kiyomune
> The Komatsu Middle Captain of Third Rank Koremori
> The Senior Middle Captain of Third Rank Shigehira
> The New Middle Captain of Third Rank Sukemori
> The Echizen Governor of Third Rank Michimori
> Courtiers:
> The Director of the Palace Storehouse Bureau Nobumoto
> The Sanuki Middle Captain Tokizane
> The Middle Captain of the Left Kiyotsune

4. A Shinto deity worshiped as a war god, as a bodhisattva (a person who has attained enlightenment but postpones nirvana to help others attain enlightenment), and as a reincarnation of Emperor Ojin (ruled 270–310). He was especially revered by the Genji. Lady Ike is Yorimori's mother and Kiyomori's stepmother. She had persuaded Kiyomori to spare Yoritomo's life after the Heiji Disturbance (see n. 5, p. 2306). She takes her name from her residence, the Ike Mansion, which she shared with Yorimori. 5. Koremori's son.

The Komatsu Lesser Captain Arimori
The Tango Gentleman-in-Waiting Tadafusa
The Assistant Master of the Empress's Household Office Tsunemasa
The Director of the Stables of the Left Yukimori
The Satsuma Governor Tadanori
The Noto Governor Noritsune
The Musashi Governor Tomoakira
The Bitchū Governor Moromori
The Awaji Governor Kiyofusa
The Owari Governor Kiyosada
The Wakasa Governor Tsunetoshi
The Fifth-Rank Chamberlain Narimori
The Fifth-Rank Courtier Atsumori
Monks:
The Nii Bishop Senshin
The Hosshōji Administrator Nōen
The Middle Counselor Master of Discipline Chūkai
The Kyōjubō Holy Teacher Yūen
Samurai:
160 provincial officials, Police and Guards officers, and functionaries
in miscellaneous central offices

The total numbered barely seven thousand horsemen, all who were left after the losses in the northern and eastern campaigns of the past two or three years.

At the Yamazaki Barrier Cloister, they set down the Emperor's palanquin and paid homage to Otokoyama.[6] Most pathetically, Major Counselor Tokitada prayed, "Hail! I touch my head to the ground in obeisance to the Great Bodhisattva Hachiman. Vouchsafe that His Majesty and all the rest of us may return to the capital."

Only a lonely smoke haze was visible when they looked back. Norimori[7] composed a poem:

> Fleeting, indeed!
> Only the smoke plumes ascend
> where all has vanished
> now that the masters depart
> to journey beyond the clouds.

Tsunemori:[8]

> Having turned to see
> our former home a blackened
> wilderness of plains,
> we shall journey over sea paths
> where the mists hover like smoke.

It is sad to imagine what was in their hearts as they prepared to set out toward the distant cloud paths, their homes in ashes behind them.

The Higo Governor Sadayoshi had gone off to Kawajiri with five hundred

---

6. Site of a shrine dedicated to Hachiman.   7. Kiyomori's brother.   8. Kiyomori's brother.

riders, bent on disposing of a contingent of Genji who were said to be biding their time there. The report had proved false, and he was on his way back to the capital when he encountered the imperial procession near Udono. Springing from his horse, he presented himself respectfully before Munemori, bow under arm. "What is the destination of this flight from the capital? If you go west, you will be treated as fugitives, scattered in every direction, and subjected to dishonor. That is a terrible prospect. Won't you please make a last stand in the capital?" he said.

"Can it be that you don't know?" Munemori said. "Kiso no Yoshinaka[9] is attacking the city from the north with fifty thousand riders; they say his men are swarming everywhere at the eastern base of Mount Hiei. The Retired Emperor disappeared around midnight last night.[1] We men could take our chances if it were just a matter of ourselves, but I could not bear to let Kenreimon'in and the Nun of Second Rank[2] suffer a tragic fate before my very eyes. It seems best to take His Majesty and the women away for the time being."

"In that case, I will ask leave to go and fight it out in the capital." Sadayoshi gave Shigemori's sons his five hundred men and headed for the capital with a mere thirty riders.

To his great alarm, Yorimori heard a rumor that Sadayoshi was coming back to kill any Heike who had stayed in the city. "I must be the one he has in mind," he thought.

Sadayoshi put up curtains at the burnt-over site of the Nishihachijō Mansion[3] and waited throughout the night, but not a single Heike lord returned. It may be that discouragement overcame him, despite his valor. Determined that Shigemori's remains should not be trampled under Genji hoofs, he ordered his men to open the late Minister's grave. Then he faced the bones and spoke, weeping. "Alas! Look at your clan! It has been written since ancient times, 'All that lives perishes, happiness ends and sorrow comes,' but never have we witnessed anything like this. You must have asked the gods and the Buddhas to shorten your life because you knew what lay ahead. That was a splendid act! I ought to have performed my final service to you at that hour, but I let my worthless life continue, and so I have encountered this grief. When I die, please lead me to the Buddha-land where you dwell."

After thus tearfully unburdening himself to his master's distant spirit, he dispatched the bones to Mount Kōya[4] and ordered the dirt from around the grave to be thrown into the Kamo River. Then, perhaps because he saw no hope for the future, he fled toward the east, the opposite direction to the one taken by his masters. He sought assistance from Utsunomiya, a man he had made his friend by treating him with kindness as his custodian, and Utsunomiya gave him a cordial reception.

---

9. Yoritomo's treacherous cousin, who is about to seize the capital, and thereby turn the Heike-Genji war into a triangular conflict. With the Heike fleeing west and the Genji garrisoned in the east, Yoshinaka's high-handed hold on the capital lets loose shocking plunder. Meanwhile, Yoshinaka simultaneously pursues the Heike and plots against Yoritomo. Retired Emperor Go-Shirakawa alerts Yoritomo, who dispatches his brothers, Yoshitsune and Noriyori. Yoshinaka flees, but Yoshitsune and Noriyori converge on their cousin and eventually destroy him.   1. He has now gone over to the Genji.   2. Kiyomori's widow. Kenreimon'in is Kiyomori's daughter and mother of the infant emperor Antoku.   3. A huge complex that had been used as a secondary residence by Kiyomori, located in the western part of the capital.   4. Headquarters of one of the principal Buddhist sects.

The Flight from Fukuhara

Although Munemori and the other Heike nobles except Koremori had brought their wives and children with them, there was a limit to the number of people who could be taken along, and the lesser ranks had had to leave their families behind, with no idea of when they might be reunited. A period of separation seems long enough when the day and hour of the traveler's return are fixed, but theirs had been final goodbyes, eternal farewells; and both those who went and those who stayed had wept until their sleeves were drenched.

For the hereditary Taira retainers, obligated by years of unforgettable kindnesses, it was impossible not to follow their lords, but old and young cast constant glances backward and were quite incapable of progressing as they should have. There were those who slept on the waves near rocky strands and spent their days on the boundless sea paths; there were those who crossed vast plains and endured the perils of rugged mountains. Each fled as he thought best, some raising whips to horses and others working poles on boats.

Upon reaching Fukuhara, Munemori summoned his principal samurai of various ages, several hundred in all. "The prosperity of accumulated merit has come to an end; the calamity of accumulated evil has fallen upon us," he said. "Repudiated by the gods and abandoned by the retired sovereign, we have left the capital to lead wanderers' lives. There seems nowhere for us to turn. But a powerful karma tie from a previous existence binds those who merely take shelter under the same tree; a firm link from another world connects those who merely scoop water from the same stream. What must be the nature of the bond uniting us? You did not declare allegiance to our house yesterday for some temporary advantage; you are hereditary retainers, serving as your fathers served before you. Some of you share our blood; others have received our favors for generations. You lived by our bounty while we prospered. Can it be that you ought not to honor your obligations now? And can it be that you would not want to travel to the end of any plain or to the innermost recesses of any mountains in attendance on His Majesty the Emperor, who bears with him the Regalia?"[5]

All the old and young samurai made identical replies, their faces bathed in tears. "Even the humble birds and beasts know how to requite favors and repay kindnesses: how could men be ignorant of their duty? It was solely because of your beneficence that we were able to support our families and look after our retainers for more than twenty years. Disloyalty is a warrior's shame. We will accompany His Majesty until we die, whether the destination be inside or outside of Japan—whether it be Silla, Paekche, Koguryŏ, Bohai,[6] the farthest reaches of the clouds, or the farthest reaches of the sea." The Taira nobles seemed reassured.

5. Three objects that were viewed as symbols of the emperor's legitimacy and authority: a strand of jewels, a mirror, and a sword. In the Japanese creation myth, the sun goddess is said to have conferred the three regalia on her grandson as he was about to descend to the Japanese islands, establishing the imperial line. Here, the young emperor carries with him as a sign of his (and the Heike's) legitimacy two of the three regalia, the sword and the jewels. The mirror is at Ise, the Shinto shrine honoring the ancestral gods of the imperial family (where it is said to remain to this day). 6. Various parts of the Korean peninsula.

They spent a night at the old Fukuhara capital.[7] It was late in the first autumn month, the time of the crescent moon. As the lonely, quiet night deepened, dew and tears mingled on the travelers' grass pillows, and every aspect of the surroundings became a source of misery. Feeling that they might never return, they gazed at the buildings Kiyomori had erected. Everything had fallen into decay within the space of three years—the Hill Palace for spring blossom-viewing, the Beach Palace for autumn moon-viewing, the Bubbling Spring Hall, the Pine Shade Hall, the Race Track Hall, the two-storied Viewing-Stand Hall, the Snow-Viewing Palace, the Reed-Thatched Palace, the noble residences, the Temporary Imperial Palace built on command by the Gojō Major Counselor Kunitsuna,[8] the roof tiles shaped like mandarin ducks, the fine stone pavements. Thick moss covered the roads; autumn grasses obstructed the gates. Ferns sprouted from the roof tiles; ivy overran fences. Only the pine wind visited the sagging, mossy halls; only the moonlight entered the exposed bedchambers with their tattered blinds.

The next morning, they set fire to the Fukuhara Imperial Palace, and the Emperor and all the others boarded vessels. That was another painful farewell, even though the grief was not as sharp as when they had left the capital. Smoke plumes at dusk where fisherfolk boiled seaweed, a deer's cry toward dawn on a mountaintop, waves murmuring toward beaches, moonbeams reflected in wet sleeves, cricket choruses in grasses—no sight but called forth sorrow, no sound but pierced the fugitives' hearts. Yesterday, they were a hundred thousand riders aligning their bits at the foot of the eastern barrier; today, they were but seven thousand men untying their mooring lines on the waves of the western sea. The sky was clouded, the water was calm, the day was already drawing to its close. Evening mist shrouded lonely isles; the moon's reflection floated on the sea.

Cleaving the waves of the distant horizon, drawn onward by the tides, the boats seemed to climb ever higher into the cloudy sky. Already the passing days had interposed mountains and rivers between the travelers and the capital, which now lay far behind the clouds. They seemed to have reached the limits of the earth, the point at which all had ended save their endless tears. A flock of white birds on the waves evoked pathetic thoughts. "Those must be capital-birds, the nostalgically named waterfowl Narihira questioned at the Sumida River."[9]

7. In the present city of Kōbe. It served briefly as a capital during late 1180, when Kiyomori, who had an estate there, insisted on removing the government from Kyoto. The move met with strong opposition, including some members of his own clan, and this, combined with the aggression of the Genji in the east, forced Kiyomori to return the capital to its traditional location.   8. Fujiwara Kunitsuna, a close supporter of the Taira whose son Kiyokuni was adopted by Kiyomori. Gojō ("fifth avenue") refers to the location of Kunitsuna's residence. His post, major counselor, which made him a member of the emperor's cabinet, or the council of state, ranked just below the three ministers of state.   9. Reference to a poem in *The Kokinshū* by Ariwara Narihira, which became an icon of the courtier's nostalgia for the capital. The poem is accompanied by the following headnote: "When they reached the bank of the Sumida River, which flows between the provinces of Musashi and Shimōsa, they were miserably homesick for the capital. They dismounted and stood for a time on the bank, thinking, 'How very far we have come!' The ferryman interrupted their laments. 'Come aboard quickly; it's getting late.' They got into the boat and prepared to cross, all in wretched spirits, for there was not one among them who had not left someone dear to him in the city. A white bird with a red bill and red legs chanced to be frolicking near the river. Since it was a species unknown in the capital, none of them could identify it. 'What kind of bird is that?' they asked the ferryman. 'A capital-bird, of course,' he replied with an air of surprise. Then Narihira recited this poem. "If you are in truth / what your name seems to make you, / I will put to you, / capital-bird, this question: / do things go well with my love?"

It was on the Twenty-Fifth Day of the Seventh Month in the second year of Juei[1] that the Heike withdrew completely from the capital.

Summary   It is now 1184, seven months after the flight from Fukuhara. Heike forces have splintered, some making for nearby islands in the Inland Sea, some heading for distant provinces in Kyūshū (southernmost of the four main Japanese islands), and some returning to the vicinity of Fukuhara, where they establish strongholds. The Heike are not without their successes—they win some eight battles—and it appears as though the momentum may no longer be entirely with the Genji, who are hampered by internecine strife that will plague the clan off and on until well after the war is over. Yoshinaka, commander of the Genji troops in the capital, has one eye cocked on defeating the Heike and the other on attacking his cousin Yoritomo. The outcome of divided attention is predictable: he loses spectacularly on both counts. Stymied by the Heike in the west, Yoshinaka delays a new offensive to stave off an assault by his cousin. But Genji forces catch up with him, and Yoshinaka's most desperate efforts—breaking down bridges to keep the punitive expedition from advancing—fail to protect him. He is felled before he can commit suicide, the honorable death for a Japanese warrior, and his head is put on display in the capital.

Yet Yoshinaka's disloyalty has served his clan. Erstwhile rivals, the brothers Yoritomo and Yoshitsune have united, the bond holds (despite Yoritomo's fears that his dashing younger brother will somehow overshadow him), and they are ready to prosecute their campaign against the Heike with renewed vigor.

The stage is now set for the third act. In the capital, a new emperor has acceded to the throne to replace the child sovereign Antoku, spirited away by the Heike. And Yoritomo, for his part, has gained both increased power and a certain legitimacy; Retired Emperor Go-Shirakawa has conferred on him the title of shogun, "barbarian-subduing commander."

Meanwhile, the Heike have regrouped along the Inland Sea, flush with confidence to be back in an area they have controlled for a century. With the panic of the retreat behind them, they throw up defenses along the coast, secure control of the entrances to the Inland Sea, recruit supporters, and prepare to retake the capital.

Before they can move, however, Yoshitsune surprises them. After a number of Heike fall in preliminary skirmishes, the Genji divide into two detachments and prepare to launch the main assault. In a pincer movement, Noriyori leads one unit on a frontal attack from the east. Yoshitsune, the brilliant strategist, slips around to the west, where he perches his men on a precipice so sheer that, in the dark of early morning down below, the Heike must have felt all but invincible.

At the top of the cliff, Yoshitsune's troops experience trepidation:

"The Hiyodorigoe area is notorious for its perils," the warriors all said. "We are ready to be killed in battle, but we have no wish to fall to our deaths. Surely there must be someone who knows these mountains."

To reassure them, Yoshitsune consults a local hunter, but what he hears would discourage a lesser man:

"I want to descend from here to the Heike stronghold at Ichi-no-tani. Is that possible?"

"Not by any manner of means. There is no way for a man to get down the three-hundred-foot gorge and the hundred-and-fifty-foot rock face. It would be inconceivable on horseback."

"Do deer go through?"

1. The era name, indicating the reign of Emperor Antoku (1183). See also headnote "Murasaki Shikibu," p. 2180.

"Yes. When the weather turns warm, the Harima deer cross into Tanba to lie in the deep grass, and, when it turns cold, the Tanba deer go to Inamino in Harima to feed where the snow is shallow."

"Why, it sounds like a regular racetrack! A horse can certainly go where a deer goes. Very well, you shall be our guide."

Under duress the old hunter substitutes his son, who leads the pack down the precipice. By the time they descend, the Genji charge from the east has engaged the enemy at the main front and pushed the Heike back into Yoshitsune's clutches.

FROM CHAPTER 9

The Assault from the Cliff

After those encounters, other eastern warriors moved forward—the Chichibu, the Ashikaga, the Miura, the Kamakura, and, among the leagues, the Inomata, the Kodama, the Noiyo, the Yokoyama, the Nishitō, the Tsuzukitō, and the Shinotō. The massed Genji and Heike armies met in mingled combat, the riders charging by turns and vying to announce their names. Their shouts and yells awoke echoes in the mountains; the hoofbeats of their galloping horses reverberated like thunder; the arrows they exchanged resembled falling rain. Some men retired to the rear, carrying the wounded on their shoulders; some sustained light injuries and fought on; some suffered mortal blows and perished. There were those who rode alongside enemies, grappled with them, fell, and died in dagger fights; there were those who seized others, held them down, and cut off their heads; there were those who had their heads cut off. Neither side revealed a weakness for the other to exploit, and the main Genji force seemed unlikely to prevail without help, despite its valor.

Now Kurō Onzōshi Yoshitsune, who had circled around to the rear, had climbed to the Hiyodorigoe track behind Ichi-no-tani toward dawn on the Seventh. As he was preparing for the descent, two stags and a doe ran down to the Heike fortifications, frightened perhaps by his forces. The warriors in the stronghold were much agitated when they saw them. "Even the nearby deer ought to be fleeing deep into the mountains to get away from us," they said. "It is strange, indeed, that these animals should have come down into the middle of so great an army. The Genji must be going to descend from the mountains above."

Takechi no Mushadokoro Kiyonori, a resident of Iyo Province, stepped forward. "Be that as it may, we cannot spare anything that comes from a hostile direction." He shot the two stags and let the doe pass.

Etchū no Zenji Moritoshi cautioned Kiyonori. "Shooting the deer was an imprudent act. You could have held off ten enemies with one of those arrows. You wasted precious arrows in order to commit a sin."[2]

Yoshitsune surveyed the distant stronghold. "Let's try chasing some horses down." They chased some saddled horses down. Some of the animals broke their legs and fell; others descended in safety. Three of them reached the roof of Moritoshi's quarters and stood there trembling.

"The horses will not get hurt if the riders are careful," Yoshitsune said. "All right, take them down! Do as I do!" He galloped forward at the head of

---

2. According to Buddhist doctrine, it is a sin to take a life.

thirty horsemen, and all the others followed, descending a slope so steep that the rear riders' stirrup edges touched the front riders' armor and helmets. After slipping and sliding swiftly for seven hundred feet through sand mixed with pebbles, they pulled up on a ledge, below which they could see a huge mossy crag, a vertical drop of a hundred and forty or fifty feet. They sat aghast. "This is the end!"

Sawara no Jūrō Yoshitsura came forward. "In Miura, we gallop over such places morning and night, even if we're only chasing birds. This is a Miura racetrack!" He dashed ahead, and all the warriors followed.

The tense riders went down with their eyes closed, encouraging the horses in muffled voices. "Ei! Ei!" The feat they were accomplishing seemed beyond mortal capacity, a fit undertaking for demons.

Even before all the men had reached the bottom, they raised a great battle cry. They were only three thousand strong,[3] but the echoes made them seem a host of a hundred thousand.

Murakami no Hangandai Yasukuni's men put all the Heike sleeping quarters and camps to the torch. As luck would have it, a violent wind chanced to be blowing. Clouds of black smoke billowed forth, and great numbers of panic-stricken Heike warriors galloped into the sea to save themselves.

Many vessels had been left in readiness at the water's edge, but what good could come of it when four or five hundred armored men, and even a thousand, tried to crowd into a single craft? Three great ships sank before the beholders' eyes, after having progressed a mere three hundred and sixty yards from the shore. Thereafter, it was decreed that although men of quality might board, those of inferior status were to be kept off: instructions were issued to slash at them with swords and spears. Well aware of what to expect, the lesser orders seized and clung to the vessels from which they were barred. Some lost whole arms and others forearms, and they ended as rows of corpses, reddening the water's edge at Ichi-no-tani.

Although the Noto Governor Noritsune was a man who had fought time and again without suffering defeat, he fled westward on his charger Usuguro [Dusky Black]. (It is hard to say what was in his mind.) He boarded a ship at Akashi Shore in Harima and crossed to Yashima in Sanuki.[4]

* * *

The Death of Atsumori

Kumagae no Jirō Naozane walked his horse toward the beach after the defeat of the Heike. "The Taira nobles will be fleeing to the water's edge in the hope of boarding rescue vessels," he thought. "Ah, how I would like to grapple with a high-ranking Commander-in-Chief!" Just then, he saw a lone rider splash into the sea, headed toward a vessel in the offing. The other was attired in a crane-embroidered *nerinuki* silk *hitatare*,[5] a suit of armor with shaded green lacing, and a horned helmet. At his waist, he wore a sword with gilt bronze fittings; on his back, there rode a quiver containing arrows fledged with black-banded white eagle feathers. He grasped a rattan-wrapped

---

3. A good example of how the tale exaggerates for dramatic effect. Historical evidence suggests that Yoshitsune had approximately one hundred men with him.   4. On the island of Shikoku, across the Inland Sea from Ichi-no-tani.   5. A two-piece costume worn by warriors. *Nerinuki* refers to a specific kind of weave.

bow and bestrode a white-dappled reddish horse with a gold-edged saddle. When his mount had swum out about a hundred and fifty or two hundred feet, Naozane beckoned him with his fan.

"I see that you are a Commander-in-Chief. It is dishonorable to show your back to an enemy. Return!"

The warrior came back. As he was leaving the water, Naozane rode up alongside him, gripped him with all his strength, crashed with him to the ground, held him motionless, and pushed aside his helmet to cut off his head. He was sixteen or seventeen years old, with a lightly powdered face and blackened teeth[6]—a boy just the age of Naozane's own son Kojirō Naoie, and so handsome that Naozane could not find a place to strike.

"Who are you? Announce your name. I will spare you," Naozane said.

"Who are you?" the youth asked.

"Nobody of any importance: Kumagae no Jirō Naozane, a resident of Musashi Province."

"Then it is unnecessary to give you my name. I am a desirable opponent for you. Ask about me after you take my head. Someone will recognize me, even if I don't tell you."

"Indeed, he must be a Commander-in-Chief," Naozane thought. "Killing this one person will not change defeat into victory, nor will sparing him change victory into defeat. When I think of how I grieved when Kojirō suffered a minor wound, it is easy to imagine the sorrow of this young lord's father if he were to hear that the boy had been slain. Ah, I would like to spare him!" Casting a swift glance to the rear, he discovered Sanehira and Kagetoki coming along behind him with fifty riders.

"I would like to spare you," he said, restraining his tears, "but there are Genji warriors everywhere. You cannot possibly escape. It will be better if I kill you than if someone else does it, because I will offer prayers on your behalf."

"Just take my head and be quick about it."

Overwhelmed by compassion, Naozane could not find a place to strike. His senses reeled, his wits forsook him, and he was scarcely conscious of his surroundings. But matters could not go on like that forever: in tears, he took the head.

"Alas! No lot is as hard as a warrior's. I would never have suffered such a dreadful experience if I had not been born into a military house. How cruel I was to kill him!" He pressed his sleeve to his face and shed floods of tears.

Presently, since matters could not go on like that forever, he started to remove the youth's armor *hitatare* so that he might wrap it around the head. A brocade bag containing a flute was tucked in at the waist. "Ah, how pitiful! He must have been one of the people I heard making music inside the stronghold just before dawn. There are tens of thousands of riders in our eastern armies, but I am sure none of them has brought a flute to the battlefield. Those court nobles are refined men!"

When Naozane's trophies were presented for Yoshitsune's inspection, they drew tears from the eyes of all the beholders. It was learned later that the slain youth was Tayū Atsumori, aged seventeen, a son of Tsunemori, the Master of the Palace Repairs Office.

After that, Naozane thought increasingly of becoming a monk.

6. The trappings of a noble.

The flute in question is said to have been given by Retired Emperor Toba to Atsumori's grandfather Tadamori, who was a skilled musician. I believe I have heard that Tsunemori, who inherited it, turned it over to Atsumori because of his son's proficiency as a flautist. Saeda [Little Branch] was its name. It is deeply moving that music, a profane entertainment, should have led a warrior to the religious life.

Summary   Defeat at Ichi-no-tani is the beginning of the end for the Heike:

> The fighting at the east and west entrances continued for an hour, claiming the lives of countless Genji and Heike. Piles of dead horses and men rose like clustered hills in front of the archery platforms and under the branch barricades; the green of the bamboo-grass in the Ichi-no-tani meadows turned pale red. Quite apart from those who perished of arrow and sword wounds at Ichi-no-tani and Ikuta-no-mori [the front line to the east of Ichi-no-tani], or in the mountains and on the beaches, more than two thousand Heike heads were taken for exposure by the Genji.

Sapped of their morale, the defeated Heike escape by ship with the infant emperor. Some sail up the Inland Sea to safer coasts; others hover in the offing, too disoriented to settle on a destination.

> Thus drawn by the tides and blown by the winds, the fugitives drifted toward many different shores and islands, each group ignorant of the fate of all the others. They had held high hopes for the future . . . but now Ichi-no-tani had fallen, and every heart despaired.

Among the dead are many prominent Heike besides young Atsumori. Both his brothers perish, along with several of his cousins, his uncle Tadanori (Kiyomori's brother and commander of the western division at Ichi-no-tani), and also more than half of the clan's star *samurai*. In the ultimate infamy, the heads of the slain Heike— once the most powerful men in the land and, as elite senior nobles, among the most distinguished—are paraded through the capital like common criminals, then hung in the trees outside the prison grounds. Pathetically, Heike survivors who had been left behind in the city disguise themselves in plebeian garb and venture out for a glimpse of the death's-head parade. Only by watching will they know whether a husband or son is among the decapitated.

Kiyomori's son Shigehira, deputy commander at the front line of the recent battle, is brought back to the capital alive, surrounded by armed guards, and marched through the streets in an exposed carriage—a humiliating spectacle that no other member of the Heike has been subjected to. Retired Emperor Go-Shirakawa and the Genji hold Shigehira hostage for the return of the imperial regalia, the sacred symbols of legitimacy. This puts the Heike in a difficult position, and even Kiyomori's widow (grandmother of the child emperor Antoku) argues for returning the regalia. In practical terms, compliance is impossible. Forfeiture of the ultimate symbols of authority would not only embarrass the Heike in front of Yoritomo; it would acknowledge that the young sovereign, whom they have in tow, is indeed the *former* emperor, and would invalidate their entire cause, reducing them to the status of rebels who deserve destruction. The Heike have no choice but to defy the edict and continue their retreat, even if it means, as they announce in their response to Go-Shirakawa, fleeing finally to Korea, or China, or India.

In fact, the bulk of the Heike have gone no farther than several miles across the Inland Sea, to the island of Shikoku. But even this poses a problem for the Genji. Their traditional power base is in the land-locked eastern provinces. Unlike the Heike, who had originally flourished in these western coastal regions, the Genji are not at home on the sea. Hostilities lapse for half a year, while the Genji reconnoiter.

Then Yoshitsune strikes, and once again takes the Heike by surprise. With a mere hundred men in a few small boats and a storm brewing windward, the tactical genius braves the gale on a calculated risk that it will carry them across before the enemy notices. This is an inspired move, for the Heike expect an attack in fair weather. And the foul weather allows the Genji to make record time; the normal three-day crossing is over in six hours. Yoshitsune and his men hit land on the eastern side of the island. The enemy camp is above them, to the north. The small force rides through the night, again in record time, and surprises the Heike at daybreak. Yoshitsune lights fires to suggest a much larger expedition. Seeing the hills ablaze to their rear and the enemy approaching, the Heike, awaiting a frontal attack from the sea, assume they are outnumbered, and, discombobulated, rush to their ships and abandon the island. Offshore, the Heike put up faint resistance before they flee two hundred miles to the west, down through the Inland Sea and toward Japan's furthest reaches. On board the ships are Kiyomori's hapless son, Munemori; Kiyomori's widow, the Nun of Second Rank; their daughter, Kenreimon'in; and their grandson, Antoku, a frail, unlucky hostage of fate.

Once he acquires the necessary fleet, Yoshitsune pursues the Heike. He joins forces with Noriyori, his brother and co-captain at the Battle of Ichi-no-tani, and the two men lead the Genji against the Heike. Perhaps the Heike believe they still have a chance, because they are the more experienced seafarers. They sail out boldly to meet the Genji, into the treacherous Strait of Shimonoseki, where the tidal currents are as changeable as the fortunes of war. The battle is joined at noon in the third month of 1185 off the coast near Dan-no-ura, on the waters separating the Inland Sea from the Pacific Ocean.

One can only assume that the Heike intended to strike while the tides were in their favor. Yoshitsune knows, however, that if he wages a defensive battle until midafternoon, the current will reverse itself—rushing out toward the open sea—and he can bear down on the Heike as they are trapped in the riptide. The tides change at two thirty. The Heike are buffeted and thrown into confusion. Several ships strike their flags and defect to the enemy. The Genji breast the waves with relative ease, and by four o'clock the war is over. The Heike ships have sunk to the bottom of the sea, and both Kiyomori's widow and the young emperor have perished. The once proud clan passes into history.

FROM CHAPTER 11

The Drowning of the Former Emperor

The Genji warriors had already boarded the Heike boats, which were veering out of control because the sailors and helmsmen were lying in the bilge, slain by arrows and swords. The New Middle Counselor Tomomori went in a small craft to the Emperor's ship. "We seem to have reached the final extremity," he said. "Jettison everything that might offend the eye." He ran about from stem to stern tidying the ship with his own hands, sweeping, mopping, and dusting.

"How is the battle going, Lord Middle Counselor? How are things going?" the ladies asked.

Tomomori uttered a sarcastic laugh. "You will be getting acquainted with some remarkable eastern warriors."

"How can you joke at a time like this?" They all began to shriek and scream.

The Nun of Second Rank, who had long ago decided on a course of action, draped her two dark-gray underrobes over her head, hitched up her divided skirt of glossed silk, tucked the Bead Strand under her arm and the Sword[7]

---

7. That is, the imperial regalia that they possess (see n. 5, p. 2311).

into her belt, and took the Emperor in her arms. "Although I am only a woman, I will not fall into enemy hands. I will go where His Majesty goes. Follow swiftly, you whose hearts are loyal to him." She walked to the side of the ship.

The Emperor had turned eight that year, but seemed very grown up for his age. His face was radiantly beautiful, and his abundant black hair reached below his waist. "Where are you taking me, Grandmother?" he asked, with a puzzled look.

She turned her face to the young sovereign, holding back her tears. "Don't you understand? You became an Emperor because you obeyed the Ten Good Precepts[8] in your last life, but now an evil karma holds you fast in its toils. Your good fortune has come to an end. Turn to the east and say goodbye to the Grand Shrine of Ise,[9] then turn to the west and repeat the sacred name of Amida Buddha,[1] so that he and his host may come to escort you to the Pure Land. This country is a land of sorrow; I am taking you to a happy realm called Paradise."

His Majesty was wearing an olive-gray robe, and his hair was done up in a boy's loops at the sides. With tears swimming in his eyes, he joined his tiny hands, knelt toward the east, and bade farewell to the Grand Shrine. Then he turned toward the west and recited the sacred name of Amida. The Nun snatched him up, said in a comforting voice, "There is a capital under the waves, too," and entered the boundless depths. Ah, how sad that the spring breeze of impermanence should have scattered the august blossoms in an instant! Ah, how heartless that the wild waves of transmigration should have engulfed the jewel person! We are told of an imperial hall, Longevity by name, that was designed to be a long-standing imperial residence, and of a gate, Eternal Youth, through which old age was powerless to enter—yet now a sovereign less than ten years old had become debris at the bottom of the sea. Words cannot express the wretchedness of such a karma! A dragon above the clouds had descended to become a fish in the ocean depths. In the past, he had held sway over kin by blood and by marriage, with State Ministers and senior nobles on every side, dwelling as it were on the heights of Bonten's lofty palace and within Taishaku's[2] Joyful-to-See City; now, alas, he went from shipboard life to instant death beneath the waves.

Summary   Several ferocious Heike distinguish themselves in a last burst of bravery. One fierce warrior squeezes an enemy under each arm and bounds overboard. Others, grabbing anchors to weigh them down, dive into the sea. Those who hesitate are pushed into the water, lest their cowardice in the final extremity tarnish the virile repute of the clan. When the Genji ships depart—returning prisoners and imperial regalia to the capital—the sea is littered with the discarded red pennants of the Heike and the waves are pink from all the blood.

The march of the prisoners through the capital is a sad reminder of the evanescence of worldly glory.

---

8. The ten commandments of Buddhism, which forbid killing, stealing, adultery, lying, immoral language, slander, equivocation, coveting, anger, and the holding of false views. The reward for adhering to these precepts is, depending on the degree of fidelity, rebirth in one of the Buddhist heavens or, failing that, rebirth in the human realm.   **9.** Where the ancestral gods of the imperial family are enshrined.   **1.** The Buddha most deeply revered by the court nobles and the ruler of the Pure Land, or Western Paradise, into which those who believe in him and recite his name are reborn.   **2.** A Buddhist deity who dwells on a lofty peak towering at the center of every world and battles pugnacious demons living by the sea. Bonten is a Hindu god, ruler of heaven.

The onlookers had not forgotten the former splendor of the Heike lords in the short time since their departure from the capital, a mere year and parts of two others. They scarcely knew whether they were awake or dreaming when they beheld the present state of the men who had once inspired such fear and trembling. All of them wept until their sleeves were drenched—even coarse humble men and women devoid of sensibility. . . .

Retired Emperor Go-Shirakawa viewed the procession from a carriage near the intersection of Rokujō and Higashi-no-tōin avenues, where the carriages of senior nobles and courtiers were also drawn up in rows. The former sovereign was moved to involuntary sorrow and compassion at the sight of the men who had once been among his closest attendants, and the members of his entourage felt as though in a dream. High and low shed tears. "Back in the days when everyone was desperate for a glance or a word from one of those men, who could have thought they would come to this?" people said.

Most of the remaining chapters of the tale catalog the execution or banishment of the surviving Heike. Leaders like Munemori, Kiyomori's unworthy successor, are beheaded, though, in Munemori's case, not before we are subjected to fresh accounts of unheroic conduct. (He should have gone down with his ship.) The fortunate few, like Kenreimon'in, Kiyomori's daughter, are allowed to go on living, but even the children of the Heike are hunted and cruelly destroyed.

As the massive tale draws to a close, the narrator displays no particular love for the victors. Yoshitsune is portrayed as a kind and sensitive man, but he is locked in a deadly rivalry with Yoritomo, the power-hungry head of the Genji. War may be over, but treachery and sordid intrigue seem eternal. So does the folly of the retired emperor. Go-Shirakawa careens from one Genji faction to the other. "Change in the morning, change in the evening," the narrator throws up his hands: "a pitifully indecisive government!" But change, we should remember, is the theme of the tale. In a few pages, Go-Shirakawa is dead, then Yoritomo. And in a few more pages we take leave of the two bellicose clans, of the bloodshed and political gyrations, in an oddly subdued epilogue, a grace note after the carnage.

FROM THE INITIATES' CHAPTER

The Imperial Lady Becomes a Nun

The Imperial Lady Kenreimon'in had gone to stay in the Yoshida district, at the foot of the eastern hills. Her residence was a long-abandoned cloister that had belonged to a Nara monk, the Middle Counselor Dharma Seal[3] Kyōe. Rank grasses grew in the courtyards, ferns clustered on the eaves, and the blinds hung in tatters, leaving the exposed bedchambers unprotected from the winds and rains. Although flowers of many hues blossomed, there was no master to enjoy them; although moonbeams streamed in at night, there was no owner to watch until dawn. It is sad to imagine the feelings of the lady who had once spent her time surrounded by brocade curtains in jade mansions, and now found herself in that shockingly dilapidated abode, separated from all her kinsmen.[4] She resembled a fish on land or a bird torn from the nest—nostalgic, in her misery, even for the cheerless shipboard life at sea. Her thoughts dwelt on the distant clouds of the western ocean beyond the boundless blue waves; her tears fell as the moon illumined the courtyard

---

3. The third of three ranks conferred by the court on outstanding Buddhist monks, below Dharma Bridge and Dharma Eye (see n. 8, p. 2307).   4. That is, her father, Kiyomori; her husband, Takakura; and her son, Antoku.

of the mossy, rush-thatched dwelling in the eastern hills. No words could describe her melancholy.

On the First Day of the Fifth Month in the first year of Bunji,[5] the Imperial Lady became a nun. Inzei, the holy man of the Chōrakuji Ashōbō Cloister, was the monk who administered the precepts. The lady presented one of Emperor Antoku's informal robes as an offering. The Former Emperor had worn the garment until the hour of his death, and it still bore the scent of his body. She had brought it all the way from the western provinces to the capital with the intention of keeping it as a memento—of never letting it leave her side. But now, for lack of another suitable offering, she produced it in tears, telling herself that the deed might also help the Former Emperor attain enlightenment. The monk received it, unable to respond, and took his leave with tears drenching his black sleeves. People say it was made into a banner to be hung in front of the Buddha at the Chōrakuji.

The Imperial Lady had been designated a Junior Consort at the age of fifteen, and an Empress at sixteen. In constant attendance on the sovereign, she had urged him to preside over the dawn levees and had shared his love with none at night. At twenty-two, she had given birth to a son who had become Crown Prince; and after the Prince's accession she had received the palace name Kenreimon'in. She had enjoyed the very greatest respect as both the daughter of Kiyomori and the mother of the Emperor. In this present year, she had turned twenty-nine. Her peach-blossom beauty was still unmarred, her lotus-blossom freshness had not faded, but there was no fur-ther reason to preserve her kingfisher-black tresses, and so at last she had become a nun. Yet her grief knew no end, even though she had rejected the transitory world for the true path. Never in all the lives to come could she forget her despairing kinsmen as they cast themselves into the sea; never could she forget the faces of the Former Emperor and the Nun of Second Rank. Why had her own dewlike existence dragged on to give birth to such sorrows? She brooded constantly, her eyes never dry. The nights are short in the Fifth Month, but she found the dawns slow to arrive; she could not even recapture the past in dreams, because she did not so much as doze off. "Dim was the waning light of the lamp by the wall, lonely the nightlong beat of the dismal rain against the window."[6] It seemed that not even the Lady of Shangyang could have been more wretched when she was imprisoned in the Shangyang Palace.[7] The wind carried with it the nostalgic perfume of a flow-ering orange near the eaves—transplanted, perhaps, because the former occupant had longed for a reminder of the past[8]—and a cuckoo sang two or three times. The Imperial Lady remembered an old poem, which she scrib-bled onto the lid of her inkstone case:

> That you raise your voice,
> cuckoo, seeking the fragrance
> of the flowering orange—
> is it from nostalgia
> for that "someone long ago"?

5. That is, 1185; the events of Kenreimon'in's last years, which constitute the epilogue, overlap with those of the preceding chapters.　**6.** A paraphrase from Po Chü-i's poem *The White-Haired Lady of Shangyang*. **7.** Potential rivals of the emperor's favorite consort were consigned there.　**8.** Alludes to a poem in *The Kokinshū*: "Scenting the fragrance / of orange blossoms that await / the Fifth Month's coming, / I recall a perfumed sleeve / worn by someone long ago."

Less resolute than the Nun of Second Rank and Michimori's wife Koza-ishō,[9] the other Heike ladies had not drowned themselves in the sea, but had been captured by rough warriors and returned to the capital. Young and old alike had become nuns, donned rude attire, and gone to eke out miserable existences in hitherto undreamt-of valley depths and rocky wilds. Their old homes had all vanished in smoke, leaving only gutted sites that were fast becoming overgrown fields, no longer visited by those who had frequented them. It is moving to think of how closely the ladies' emotions must have resembled those of the men who met their own seventh-generation descendants when they returned from the immortal's dwelling.[1]

Meanwhile, the great earthquake[2] on the Ninth of the Seventh Month had crumbled the tile-capped earthen walls and tilted the dilapidated structures at the Imperial Lady's house, rendering it even less habitable than before. There was not so much as a green-robed guard at the gate.[3] Already, depressing insect plaints made officious announcement of autumn's coming in the ruined brushwood fences, which were even dewier than the lush fields. The gradually lengthening nights seemed more interminable than ever to the wakeful lady. It was too much that the melancholy of autumn should be added to her ceaseless sorrow! In the transitory world where all had changed, none remained of the old connections who would once have felt bound to show her compassion; nobody seemed left who might come to her assistance.

The Imperial Lady Goes to Ōhara

Although the Imperial Lady's plight was thus, her younger sisters, the wives of the Reizei Major Counselor Takafusa and the Shichijō Master of the Palace Repairs Office Nobutaka, found discreet ways of expressing their sympathy. "In the old days, it never occurred to me that I might have to depend on those two for a livelihood," she said, with tears streaming down her face. The ladies in attendance all drenched their sleeves.

Her present abode was close to the capital, near a road where there were many inquisitive passersby. She longed to move to some place in the innermost recesses of the deep mountains—a refuge too remote for distressing news to reach her ears, where she might remain while the dew of her life awaited the wind—but no suitable opportunity arose. Then a certain lady caller said, "The Jakkōin, far back in the mountains to Ōhara, is a very quiet place," and she resolved to go there. "It is true enough that a mountain hermitage is lonely, yet life is far better there than in the vexatious world," she said.[4] I believe I have heard that Takafusa's wife made the arrangements for the palanquin and other necessities.

The Imperial Lady proceeded to the Jakkōin late in the Ninth Month of the first year of Bunji. Perhaps because the road led through mountains, the twilight shadows began to gather as she journeyed, her eyes lingering on the

9. She commits suicide after hearing of her husband's death. Michimori is Kiyomori's nephew.
1. Refers to a legendary traveler who spends half a year in the enchanted cottage of a mountain nymph. When he returns home, his sons are dead and six generations have passed. 2. About six months after the Heike are defeated, a great earthquake ravages the country. Since spirits of the dead were held capable of returning to wreak havoc on the living, it is widely assumed, given the timing and the magnitude, that the earthquake is the Heike's revenge. 3. Kenreimon'in is thus worse off than the Lady of Shangyang, whose "palace gates were secured by green-robed guards." 4. With a slight alteration, she quotes a poem in The Kokinshū: "It is true enough / that a mountain hermitage / offers small comfort, / yet life is far better there / than in the vexatious world."

colored foliage of the surrounding trees. A lonely sunset bell boomed from a temple in the fields, the thick dew on the wayside plants added fresh moisture to her tear-dampened sleeves, a violent wind sent leaves scurrying in every direction, and a sudden shower descended from the cloud-blackened sky, accompanied by the faint belling of a deer and the almost inaudible plaints of insect voices. The melancholy effect of so many depressing sights and sounds was quite beyond comparison. "Even when we were going from bay to bay and island to island, nothing was as bad as this," she thought piteously.

With its mossy rocks and its atmosphere of tranquil antiquity, the Jakkōin seemed a place where she could settle down willingly. Might she have thought of her own self when she saw the frost-stricken clumps of dewy bush clover in the courtyard, or gazed at the withering, fading chrysanthemums by the rough-woven fence? She went before the Buddha to pray: "May the Son of Heaven's holy spirit achieve perfect wisdom; may prompt enlightenment be assured." The face of the Former Emperor was before her as she spoke. Would she ever forget it in all the lives to come?[5]

Next to the Jakkōin she built a ten-foot-square hermitage, with one bay as a bedroom and the other as a chapel, and there she spent the days in diligent performance of the six diurnal services and the perpetual Buddha-recitations.

Toward evening on the Fifteenth of the Tenth Month, the Imperial Lady heard footsteps in the scattered oak leaves blanketing the courtyard. "Who can have come to this recluse's dwelling? Look and see. If it is someone from whom I should hide, I will hurry and hide."

The intruder proved to be a passing stag. When the lady asked, "Well?" Dainagon-no-suke[6] replied in verse, suppressing her tears:

> Who might be coming,
> treading on rocks, to call here?
> The visitor whose step
> rustles through fallen oak leaves
> is but a passing stag.

With a full heart, the lady wrote the poem on the small sliding door near her window.

Despite all its hardships, the Imperial Lady's tedious existence suggested many interesting comparisons: she likened the rows of native trees at her eaves to the seven tree circles surrounding the Pure Land, and she thought of the water collecting between the rocks as the Waters of Eight Virtues.[7]

The ephemerality of worldly things is like springtime blossoms scattering in the breeze; the brevity of man's existence is like the autumn moon disappearing behind a cloud. On mornings when the lady had enjoyed blossoms at the Chengyang Hall, the wind had come and scattered their beauty; on evenings when she had composed poems about the moon at the Zhangqiu

---

5. These two paragraphs offer a virtual digest of the conventional autumn imagery in classical Japanese poetry.   6. One of Emperor Antoku's nurses and a lady-in-waiting to Kenreimon'in.   7. According to one of the Buddhist sutras a pond in the Pure Land has waters that possess eight virtues: purity, coolness, sweetness, softness, luster, peace, healing, and growth. The sutra also notes that paradise, or the *Pure Land*, is ringed with seven rows of trees having gold roots, copper-gilt trunks, white-gold branches, agate twigs, coral leaves, moonstone blossoms, and pearl fruit.

Palace, clouds had covered the moon's face and hidden its radiance.[8] Once she had dwelt in a magnificent abode with jeweled towers, golden halls, and brocade cushions; now her brushwood hermitage drew tears even from the eyes of strangers.

Summary   After Kenreimon'in has lived in her hermitage for approximately half a year, Retired Emperor Go-Shirakawa decides to visit her. Journey to the mountain recesses of the little temple known as Jakkōin proves arduous. The royal entourage, modestly limited to about a dozen nobles, makes its way through the thick summer wilderness. When they come on the humble cottage, where the only visitors have been monkeys swinging in the trees, the retired emperor is astonished, and when Kenreimon'in descends from the mountain, where she has gone to pick wildflowers, Go-Shirakawa at first does not even recognize her. Tearfully, they reminisce, as the thoughts of better days rush in upon them. And then, in an incredible passage of just a few paragraphs, Kenreimon'in relives all the horrid experiences of her clan, which the tale has spent hundreds of pages chronicling. Neither Kenreimon'in nor the retired emperor can quite believe how the world has changed, how the fortunate have fallen. When she finishes, it is time for the ex-emperor to leave.

The Death of the Imperial Lady

Presently, the boom of the Jakkōin bell announced nightfall, and the evening sun sank in the west. Hard though it was to say goodbye, the Retired Emperor set out for home, restraining his tears. The Imperial Lady flooded her sleeve with irrepressible tears, her memories more poignant than ever. After watching the procession recede gradually into the distance, the lady faced the sacred image. "May the holy spirit of the Son of Heaven and the dead spirits of the Heike clan achieve perfect wisdom and prompt enlightenment," she prayed, weeping. In the past, she had faced eastward and said, "May the Grand Shrine of Ise and the Bodhisattva Hachiman grant the Son of Heaven a thousand autumns and a myriad years of life"; now, most pathetically, she faced westward and prayed with joined hands, "May the holy spirit of the dead be reborn in Amida's Pure Land." She wrote two poems on the sliding door in her bedroom:

> How has it happened
> that suddenly of late
>   my heart grows heavy
> with nostalgia for those
> who serve the imperial court?
>
>   Since the past has become
> only a fleeting dream,
>   surely this sojourn
> behind a woven-wood door
> will prove no more permanent.

---

8. The Chinese names of two residences where the emperor's consorts lived during the Han Dynasty (206 B.C.–A.D. 220) are used to impart a faded grandeur, and the characters with which the names are written buttress the poetic feel of the sentence, so that Kenreimon'in remembers enjoying briefly the blossoms at the Brilliant Sun Pavilion (*Chengyang Hall*) and watching the moon cloud over from the Palace of Long Autumn [Nights] (*Zhangqiu Palace*).

I believe I have heard that this poem was inscribed on one of the hermitage pillars by the Tokudaiji Minister of the Left Sanesada, who was a member of the Retired Emperor's entourage:

This is the Empress
whom we compared to the moon
in earlier days,
but no radiance brightens
the lonely mountain dwelling.

A hill cuckoo flew by, singing, just at a time when the Imperial Lady happened to be choked with tears, her mind full of the past and the future. She composed this verse:

If we are to meet,
cuckoo, in this way—come, then,
let us compare tears,
for I, also, like yourself,
cry constantly in this cruel world.

The men captured at Dan-no-ura had either been paraded through the avenues and beheaded or else sent into distant exile, far from their wives and children. With the exception of the Ike Major Counselor Yorimori,[9] not one had been allowed to remain alive in the capital. The forty or more women, to whom no punishments had been meted out, had turned to relatives for assistance or gone to stay with other connections. But there was no house free of disquieting winds, even inside jade blinds; there was no dwelling where the dust never rose, even beyond brushwood doors. Husbands and wives who had slept on adjoining pillows were as remote from one another as the sky; nurturing parents and their children were set apart, neither knowing the whereabouts of the other. Tormented by ceaseless longing, they managed somehow to struggle through the melancholy days. It was all the fault of the Chancellor-Novice Kiyomori, the man who had held the whole country in the palm of his hand and executed and banished as he pleased, unawed by the Emperor above and heedless of the myriad folk below, with no concern either for society or for individuals. There seemed no room for doubt that the evil deeds of a father must be visited on his offspring.

With the passing of time, the Imperial Lady fell ill. She recited Buddha-invocations, clasping the five-colored cord attached to the hand of the central image.[1] "Hail, Amitābha Tathāgata,[2] Teaching Lord of the Western Paradise! Please admit me to the Pure Land." On her left and right, Dainagon-no-suke and Awa-no-naishi wailed and shrieked at the top of their lungs, overcome with sorrow as the end approached. After her chanting voice had gradually weakened, a purple cloud trailed in the west, a marvelous fragrance permeated the chamber, and the sound of music was heard in the heavens. Man's time on earth is finite, and thus the lady's life drew to a close at last, midway through the Second Month in the second year of Kenkyū.[3] The

9. Yorimori has not only survived, by abandoning his clan, but has prospered. He is richly rewarded by the Genji, both for his defection at the time the Heike fled the capital and because his mother was the one who persuaded the Heike to spare Yoritomo's life. As major counselor, he is a member of the emperor's cabinet.   1. That is, of Amida Buddha. At the hour of death, the cord would lead the faithful to the Pure Land.   2. "Hail, Amida Buddha, you who have gone to the world of truth."   3. It is 1191.

parting brought agonies of inconsolable grief to the two attendants who had never left her side since her days as Empress. They had nowhere to turn for help, the grasses of old ties having long withered; nonetheless, they contrived most touchingly to perform the periodic memorial services. People said both of them attained the Nāga Girl's wisdom, emulated King Bimbisāra's wife,[4] and achieved their goal of rebirth in the Pure Land.

4. The wife of an Indian king who embraced Buddhism. She is said to have entered the Pure Land after listening to the preachings of Prince Siddhārtha, the founder of Buddhism. The *Nāga Girl* was the daughter of the Nāga king, a Buddhist deity in dragon form and protector of the faith. The girl grasped the Buddhist doctrines and attained enlightenment at the remarkable age of seven.

YOSHIDA KENKŌ
ca. 1283–1352

Essays in Idleness is a work of reflection written in a time that was not hospitable to such pursuits. Emperors vied against shoguns, and conflicting allegiances pitted one family member against another. In the turmoil, a Buddhist monk with court ties chose seclusion, his books and his pen for companions, and drafted what would remain the quintessential treatise on principles of Japanese taste. Yoshida Kenkō may not have been the first to formulate these principles—some go back to the time of *The Man'yōshū* and others inform *The Tale of the Heike*—but his fluent and engaging commentary helped ensure their long survival.

The prologue to *Essays in Idleness* seems to pick up where *The Pillow Book* left off: "What a strange, demented feeling it gives me when I realize I have spent whole days before this inkstone, with nothing better to do, jotting down at random whatever nonsensical thoughts have entered my head." This parallels the closing passage of Sei Shōnagon's miscellany, in which she explains, "I wrote these notes at home, when I had a good deal of time to myself and thought no one would notice what I was doing." The two works, one by a reclusive Buddhist monk and the other by a gregarious lady-in-waiting, are the twin gems of the *zuihitsu* tradition in Japanese letters (see headnote "Sei Shōnagon," p. 2270). As in *The Pillow Book,* Kenkō's 243 brief entries conform to the informal mode; the only admitted purpose is private satisfaction. Both works lack a unifying theme. Both prefer fragmentary statement to sustained discourse. And both are characterized by an apparently random jumble of reminiscences, anecdotes, narrative fragments, meditations, aesthetic pronouncements, notes, descriptions, and aphorisms.

Yet if Kenkō's essays bear a generic resemblance to the writings of Sei Shōnagon, thereby sustaining the *zuihitsu* tradition, they also diverge appreciably. Their random structure (especially when we deal with representative selections) can be misleading. For a long time it was claimed that Kenkō jotted his thoughts on scraps of paper and pasted them to the walls of his cottage. Supposedly, this whimsical wallpaper was discovered by a later poet, who removed the scraps and sorted them until he had a book. More likely, the entries were arranged by Kenkō (or a subsequent editor) with some attention to a policy of association. Allusive or thematic variations sometimes serve as bridges from one section to the next, and other entries are grouped around a common figure or moral theme.

A more obvious divergence lies in tone. Sei Shōnagon is witty, impulsive, and assertive. Kenkō is withdrawn, apprehensive, and dour. The difference explains itself when one considers their two worlds: Sei Shōnagon's was lit with the radiance of a court society at its summit; Kenkō's was darkened by political uncertainty. As a recluse, he was merely an onlooker; but the further degradation of the imperial court, the precariousness of artistic patronage, and the turbulence that distracted the Japanese and threatened to prevent them from appreciating and preserving their cultural heritage colored everything Kenkō wrote.

Both the physical and spiritual environment impressed on Kenkō the evanescence of earthly life. Time became an obsession. Impermanence and mutability, which had long been among the teachings of Buddhism, in Kenkō's day took on added meaning from the palpable signs of transience in the world. Possible responses included despair, denial, self-indulgence, and many more, but the one Kenkō chose had a considerable intellectual elegance. Transience, he decided, was more than the source of beauty or sorrow; it was the defining quality of life. To appreciate this fact in all its aspects—spring giving way to summer, youth yielding to age—was to understand life. "If a man were never to fade away like the dews of Adashino," he writes, "never to vanish like the smoke over Toribeyama, but lingered forever in the world, how things would lose their power to move us! The most precious thing in life is its uncertainty." Impermanence became something of value. It framed life, and informed it with meaning.

As a corollary Kenkō argued that to expect things to be perfect is to be a victim of illusion:

> In all things it is the beginnings and ends that are interesting. Does love between men and women refer only to the moments when they are in each other's arms? The man who grieves over a love affair broken off before it was fulfilled, who bewails empty vows, who spends long autumn nights alone, who lets his thoughts wander to distant skies, who yearns for the past in a dilapidated house—such a man knows what love means.

Loss thus plays a big part in Kenkō's emotional scheme:

> Are we to look at cherry blossoms only in full bloom, the moon only when it is cloudless? To long for the moon while looking on the rain, to lower the blinds and be unaware of the passing of the spring—these are even more deeply moving.

Longing, nostalgia, an acute sense of the incompleteness of human experience, of mutability, and of the presence of death are the main components of the attitude Kenkō articulates. It is a dark view for a dark time. But the Japanese have continued to appreciate Kenkō's teachings. His transparent style, simple yet poignant, and his compassion help temper the bleakness of the message. And his Japanese admirers have understood that, if the world as he sees it is not the whole of life—joy, for one thing, is missing—it is the part of life we must come to terms with if we are to call ourselves mature.

For a complete translation, with an introduction and annotation, see Donald Keene, *Essays in Idleness: The Tsurezuregusa of Kenkō* (1967). For an interesting study of the connection between Buddhism and Japanese literature at this time, see William R. LaFleur, *The Karma of Words: Buddhism and the Literary Arts in Medieval Japan* (1983). Linda H. Chance, *Formless in Form: Kenko, "Tsurezuregusa" and the Rhetoric of Japanese Fragmentary Prose* (1997), examines a region of contrasts between Japanese and European norms of prose discourse.

PRONOUNCING GLOSSARY

The following list uses common English syllables to provide rough equivalents of selected words whose pronunciation may be unfamiliar to the general reader.

Adashino: *ah-dah-shee-noh* hagi: *hah-gee*

Chuang Tzu: *jwahng zu* Kōyū: *koh-yoo*

Lao Tzu: *low dzu*

mamagodate: *mah-mah-goh-dah-te*

masuho: *mah-soo-hoh*

Tanabata: *tah-nah-bah-tah*

Toribeyama: *toh-ree-be-yah-mah*

Wen Hsüan: *wun shywan*

Yoshida Kenkō: *yoh-shee-dah ken-koh*

zuihitsu: *zoo-ee-hee-tsoo*

FROM ESSAYS IN IDLENESS[1]

1

It is enough, it would seem, to have been born into this world for a man to desire many things. The position of the emperor, of course, is far too exalted for our aspirations. Even the remote descendants of the imperial line are sacred, for they are not of the seed of man.[2] Ordinary nobles[3] of a rank that entitles them to retainers—let alone those who stand in the solitary grandeur of the chancellor—appear most impressive, and even their children and grandchildren, though their fortunes may decline, still possess a distinctive elegance. Persons of lower rank, fortunate enough to achieve some success in keeping with their station, are apt to wear looks of self-satisfaction and no doubt consider themselves most important, but actually they are quite insignificant.

No one is less to be envied than a priest. Sei Shōnagon[4] wrote of priests that they seemed to outsiders "like sticks of wood," an apt description. The clerics impress nobody, even when they flaunt their authority and their importance is loudly proclaimed. It is easy to see why the holy man Sōga[5] should have said that worldly fame is unseemly in priests, and that those who seek it violate the teachings of Buddha. A true hermit might, in fact, seem more admirable.

It is desirable that a man's face and figure be of excelling beauty. I could sit forever with a man, provided that what he said did not grate on my ears, that he had charm, and that he did not talk very much. What an unpleasant experience it is when someone you have supposed to be quite distinguished reveals his true, inferior nature. A man's social position and looks are likely to be determined at birth, but why should not a man's mind go from wisdom to greater wisdom if it is so disposed? What a shame it is when men of excellent appearance and character prove hopelessly inept in social encounters with their inferiors in both position and appearance, solely because they are badly educated.

A familiarity with orthodox scholarship,[6] the ability to compose poetry and prose in Chinese, a knowledge of Japanese poetry and music are all desirable, and if a man can serve as a model to others in matters of precedent and court ceremony, he is truly impressive. The mark of an excellent man is that he writes easily in an acceptable hand, sings agreeably and in tune, and,

---

1. Translated by and with notes adapted from Donald Keene.   2. The imperial family was thought to be descended from the sun goddess.   3. Not of sufficient rank to be eligible for the posts of regent or chancellor.   4. Author of *The Pillow Book* (p. 2270).   5. A high-ranking priest (10th century).
6. Scholarship in the Confucian sense—learning useful in governing a country or of intrinsic moral value.

though appearing reluctant to accept when wine is pressed on him, is not a teetotaler.

3

A man may excel at everything else, but if he has no taste for lovemaking, one feels something terribly inadequate about him, as if he were a valuable winecup without a bottom. What a charming figure is the lover, his clothes drenched with dew or frost, wandering about aimlessly, so fearful of his parents' reproaches or people's gossip that he has not a moment's peace of mind, frantically resorting to one unsuccessful stratagem after another; and for all that, most often sleeping alone, though never soundly. But it is best that a man not be given over completely to fleshly pleasures, and that women not consider him an easy conquest.

7

If man were never to fade away like the dews of Adashino, never to vanish like the smoke over Toribeyama,[1] but lingered on forever in the world, how things would lose their power to move us! The most precious thing in life is its uncertainty. Consider living creatures—none lives so long as man. The May fly waits not for the evening, the summer cicada knows neither spring nor autumn. What a wonderfully unhurried feeling it is to live even a single year in perfect serenity! If that is not enough for you, you might live a thousand years and still feel it was but a single night's dream. We cannot live forever in this world; why should we wait for ugliness to overtake us? The longer man lives, the more shame he endures. To die, at the latest, before one reaches forty, is the least unattractive. Once a man passes that age, he desires (with no sense of shame over his appearance) to mingle in the company of others. In his sunset years he dotes on his grandchildren, and prays for long life so that he may see them prosper. His preoccupation with worldly desires grows ever deeper, and gradually he loses all sensitivity to the beauty of things, a lamentable state of affairs.

8

Nothing leads a man astray so easily as sexual desire. What a foolish thing a man's heart is! Though we realize, for example, that fragrances are short-lived and the scent burnt into clothes[2] lingers but briefly, how our hearts always leap when we catch a whiff of an exquisite perfume! The holy man of Kume[3] lost his magic powers after noticing the whiteness of the legs of a girl who was washing clothes; this was quite understandable, considering

---

1. A crematory on the outskirts of Kyoto, the capital. *Adashino*: a graveyard whose name contains the word *impermanent* (*adashi*), located northwest of Kyoto.   2. Incense was burned in a room until the clothes hanging there were permeated with the scent.   3. A mythical figure capable of flying; he appears in tales dating to the 10th century.

that the glowing plumpness of her arms, legs, and flesh owed nothing to artifice.

12

How delightful it would be to converse intimately with someone of the same mind, sharing with him the pleasures of uninhibited conversation on the amusing and foolish things of this world, but such friends are hard to find. If you must take care that your opinions do not differ in the least from those of the person with whom you are talking, you might just as well be alone. You might suppose that a man who listens in general agreement to what the other person is saying, but differs on minor points—who may contest an opinion, saying, "How can I possibly agree?" or argue, "It's precisely because of *this* that *that* is the case"—would be a great comfort when you were bored, but as a matter of fact, if ever anything is said which might require a word of apology—of course, even when conversing with people who are not of the same mind, differences over the usual insignificant gossip do not matter— one realizes sadly what a great distance separates this man from the true friends of one's heart.

13

The pleasantest of all diversions is to sit alone under the lamp, a book spread out before you, and to make friends with people of a distant past you have never known. The books I would choose are the moving volumes of *Wen Hsüan,* the collected works of Po Chü-i, the sayings of Lao Tzu, and the chapters of Chuang Tzu.[1] Among works by scholars of this country, those written long ago are often quite interesting.

18

It is excellent for a man to be simple in his tastes, to avoid extravagance, to own no possessions, to entertain no craving for worldly success. It has been true since ancient days that wise men are rarely rich. In China there was once a man called Hsü Yu[2] who owned not a single possession. Someone, seeing him use his hands to scoop up water for drinking, presented him with what is known as a "sounding gourd."[3] For a time Hsü Yu hung it on the branch of a tree, but it rattled when the wind blew. "How noisy!" he said, and threw it away. Hsü Yu went back to drinking water scooped up in his hands. What a clean detachment must have been in his heart!

Sun Ch'en[4] slept without a quilt during the winter months. All he had was a bundle of straw that he slept on at night and put away in the morning. The

---

1. Taoist sage from the 4th century B.C. (see headnote "Chuang Chou," p. 832). The *Wen Hsüan* is a collection of Chinese poetry (6th century). Po Chü-i (772–846) was one of the greatest Chinese poets (p. 1393); he had an ardent following in Japan. Lao Tzu (3rd century B.C.), Taoist sage.   2. A famous hermit in Chinese legend.   3. *Narihisago* was a common word for gourd, but the first part, *nari,* suggests "sounding." Gourds were traditionally used as drinking vessels.   4. Chinese man famous for his spartan habits.

Chinese considered these men so notable that they recorded their biographies for the sake of later generations. People in our country would not even think it worth mentioning them.[5]

19

The changing of the seasons is deeply moving in its every manifestation. People seem to agree that autumn is the best season to appreciate the beauty of things. That may well be true, but the sights of spring are even more exhilarating. The cries of the birds gradually take on a peculiarly springlike quality, and in the gentle sunlight the bushes begin to sprout along the fences. Then, as spring deepens, mists spread over the landscape and the cherry blossoms seem ready to open, only for steady rains and winds to cause them to scatter precipitously. The heart is subject to incessant pangs of emotion as the young leaves are growing out.

Orange blossoms are famous for evoking memories, but the fragrance of plum blossoms above all makes us return to the past and remember nostalgically long-ago events. Nor can we overlook the clean loveliness of the *yamabuki*[1] or the uncertain beauty of wisteria, and so many other compelling sights.

Someone once remarked, "In summer, when the Feast of Anointing the Buddha and the Kamo Festival[2] come around, and the young leaves on the treetops grow thick and cool, our sensitivity to the touching beauty of the world and our longing for absent friends grow stronger." Indeed, this is so. When, in the fifth month, the irises bloom and the rice seedlings are transplanted, can anyone remain untroubled by the drumming of the water rails? Then, in the sixth month, you can see the whiteness of moonflowers glowing over wretched hovels, and the smouldering of mosquito incense is affecting too. The purification rites of the sixth month[3] are also engrossing.

The celebration of *Tanabata*[4] is charming. Then, as the nights gradually become cold and the wild geese cry, the under leaves of the *hagi*[5] turn yellow, and men harvest and dry the first crop of rice. So many moving sights come together, in autumn especially. And how unforgettable is the morning after an equinoctal storm!—As I go on I realize that these sights have long since been enumerated in *The Tale of Genji* and *The Pillow Book*, but I make no pretense of trying to avoid saying the same things again. If I fail to say what lies on my mind it gives me a feeling of flatulence; I shall therefore give my brush free rein. Mine is a foolish diversion, but these pages are meant to be torn up, and no one is likely to see them.

To return to the subject. Winter decay is hardly less beautiful than

---

5. That is, the Japanese are too given to display and do not respect simplicity.   1. Kerria, a slender-branched shrub with small yellow flowers.   2. The major Shinto celebration of the year, held in the middle of the Fourth Month. In the lunar calendar, summer began with the Fourth Month. The birthday of the historical Buddha, Prince Siddhārtha, was observed on the eighth day of the Fourth Month; it was commemorated by anointing his statues with perfumed water.   3. On the last day of the Sixth Month (the last day of summer) palace officials sent little boats down the Kamo River. This symbolized the casting off of sins accumulated during the year.   4. A festival celebrated on the seventh night of the Seventh Month to commemorate the annual meeting of the stars Vega, the weaver maiden, and Altair, the herd boy. According to what was originally a Chinese legend, the stars were lovers separated by the Milky Way and could meet only one night a year.   5. A lavender or white flower traditionally associated with the season of autumn rains.

autumn. Crimson leaves lie scattered on the grass beside the ponds, and how delightful it is on a morning when the frost is very white to see the vapor rise from a garden stream. At the end of the year it is indescribably moving to see everyone hurrying about on errands. There is something forlorn about the waning winter moon, shining cold and clear in the sky, unwatched because it is said to be depressing. The Invocation of the Buddha Names[6] and the departure of the messengers with the imperial offerings are moving and inspiring. How impressive it is that so many palace ceremonials are performed besides all the preparations for the New Year! It is striking that the Worship of the Four Directions follows directly on the Expulsion of the Demons.[7]

On the last night of the year, when it is extremely dark, people light pine torches and go rushing about, pounding on the gates of strangers until well after midnight. I wonder what it signifies. After they have done with their exaggerated shouting and running so furiously that their feet hardly touch the ground, the noise at last fades away with the coming of the dawn, leaving a lonely feeling of regret over the departing old year. The custom of paying homage to the dead,[8] in the belief that they return that night, has lately disappeared from the capital, but I was deeply moved to discover that it was still performed in the East. As the day thus breaks on the New Year the sky seems no different from what it was the day before, but one feels somehow changed and renewed. The main thoroughfares, decorated their full length with pine boughs, seem cheerful and festive, and this too is profoundly affecting.

22

In all things I yearn for the past. Modern fashions seem to keep on growing more and more debased. I find that even among the splendid pieces of furniture built by our master cabinetmakers, those in the old forms are the most pleasing. And as for writing letters, surviving scraps from the past reveal how superb the phrasing used to be. The ordinary spoken language has also steadily coarsened. People used to say "raise the carriage shafts" or "trim the lamp wick," but people today say "raise it" or "trim it." When they should say, "Let the men of the palace staff stand forth!" they say, "Torches! Let's have some light!" Instead of calling the place where the lectures on the Sutra of the Golden Light are delivered before the emperor "the Hall of the Imperial Lecture," they shorten it to "the Lecture Hall," a deplorable corruption, an old gentleman complained.

30

Nothing is sadder than the time after a death. During the forty-nine days of mourning[1] the family, having moved to a temple in the mountains or some

---

6. For three days, beginning on the nineteenth of the Twelfth Month, purifying rites were held at the palace, and the names of various Buddhas were invoked.   7. Ceremony that took place on the last day of the year. The next morning, the emperor worshiped the Four Directions and the imperial tombs and prayed for a safe and prosperous year.   8. The last night of the year was one of six times when the dead were believed to return.   1. The period, according to Buddhist doctrine, when the soul remains in an indeterminate existence before the next reincarnation begins. Prayers are offered so that the dead will be reborn in desirable circumstances.

such place, forgathers in large numbers in inconvenient, cramped quarters, and frantically occupies itself with the motions of mourning for the dead. The days pass unbelievably fast. On the final day, all civility gone, no one has a word for anybody else, and each man, with airs of knowing exactly what is to be done, sets about packing his belongings; then all go their separate ways. Once they have returned home, many sad remembrances are sure to afflict them anew.

Sometimes I hear people say on such occasions, "It's bad luck to mention such and such a thing. You should avoid it, for the family's sake." How can people worry about such things in the midst of so great a tragedy? The insensitivity of people still appalls me.

We do not by any means forget the dead, even after months and years have gone by, but, as they say, "the departed one grows more distant each day." We may deny it, but—no doubt because our sorrow is not as sharp as at the time—we talk about foolish things, we smile.

The body is interred in some lonely mountain and visited only at the required times. Before long, the grave marker is covered with moss and buried in fallen leaves. The evening storms and the night moon become the only regular mourners.

As long as people remember the deceased person and miss him, all is still well, but before long those people too disappear, and the descendants, who know the man only from reports, are hardly likely to feel deep emotion. Once the services honoring the dead man cease, nobody knows who he was or even his name. Only the sight of the spring weeds sprouting each year by his grave will stir the emotions of sensitive people; but in the end, even the pine tree that groaned in the storm winds is broken into firewood before it reaches its allotted thousand years, and the old grave is plowed up and turned into rice land. How sad it is that even this last memento of the dead should vanish.

33

When construction of the present palace had been completed, the buildings were inspected by experts on court usage, who pronounced them free of faults anywhere. The day for the emperor to move to the new palace was already near when the Abbess Genki examined it and declared, "The bell-shaped windows in the Kan'in palace[1] were rounder and without frames." This was an impressive feat of memory. The windows in the new palace, peaked at the top, had wooden borders. This mistake was later corrected.

38

What a foolish thing it is to be governed by a desire for fame and profit and to fret away one's whole life without a moment of peace. Great wealth is no guarantee of security. Wealth, in fact, tends to attract calamities and disas-

---

1. An imperial palace in use for approximately one hundred years until it was destroyed by fire in 1259, when the Abbess Genki was thirteen. She was an imperial consort and mother of an emperor who reigned about fifty years before *Essays in Idleness* was written.

ter. Even if, after you die, you leave enough gold to prop up the North Star,[2] it will only prove a nuisance to your heirs. The pleasures that delight the foolish man are likewise meaningless to the man of discrimination who considers a big carriage, sleek horses, gold, and jeweled ornaments all equally undesirable and senseless. You had best throw away your gold in the mountains and drop your jewels into a ravine. It is an exceedingly stupid man who will torment himself for the sake of worldly gain.

To leave behind a reputation that will not perish through long ages to come is certainly to be desired, but can one say that men of high rank and position are necessarily superior? There are foolish and incompetent men who, having been born into an illustrious family and, being favored by the times, rise to exalted position and indulge themselves in the extremes of luxury. There are also many learned and good men who by their own choice remain in humble positions and end their days without ever having encountered good fortune. A feverish craving for high rank and position is second in foolishness only to seeking wealth.

One would like to leave behind a glorious reputation for surpassing wisdom and character, but careful reflection will show that what we mean by love of a glorious reputation is delight in the approbation of others. Neither those who praise nor those who abuse last for long, and the people who have heard their reports are likely to depart the world as quickly. Before whom then should we feel ashamed? By whom should we wish to be appreciated? Fame, moreover, inspires backbiting. It does no good whatsoever to have one's name survive. A craving after fame is next most foolish.

If I were to address myself to those who nevertheless seek desperately to attain knowledge and wisdom, I would say that knowledge leads to deceit, and artistic talent is the product of much suffering. True knowledge is not what one hears from others or acquires through study. What, then, are we to call knowledge? Proper and improper come to one and the same thing— can we call anything "good"?[3] The truly enlightened man has no learning, no virtue, no accomplishments, no fame.[4] Who knows of him, who will report his glory? It is not that he conceals his virtue or pretends to be stupid; it is because from the outset he is above distinctions between wise and foolish, between profit and loss.

If, in your delusion, you seek fame and profit, the results will be as I have described. All is unreality. Nothing is worth discussing, worth desiring.

71

As soon as I hear a name I feel convinced I can guess what the owner looks like, but it never happens, when I actually meet the man, that his face is as I had supposed. I wonder if everybody shares my experience of feeling, when I hear some story about the past, that the house mentioned in the story must have been rather like this or that house belonging to people of today, or that the persons of the story resemble people I see now. It has happened on various occasions too that I have felt, just after someone has said something

2. Refers to a poem by Po Chü-i, containing lines that can be paraphrased, "Even if, by the time you die, you have amassed gold enough to support the North Star, it is not as good as having a cask of wine while you are alive." 3. The expression is from Chuang Chou (4th century B.C.), Taoist philosopher; his works were widely read by Zen monks of Kenkō's time (see p. 832). 4. From Chuang Chou.

or I have seen something or thought of something, that it has occurred before. I cannot remember *when* it was, but I feel absolutely certain that the thing has happened. Am I the only one who has such impressions?

73

Is it because the truth is so boring that most stories one hears are false? People tend to exaggerate even when relating things they have actually witnessed, but when months or years have intervened, and the place is remote, they are all the more prone to invent whatever tales suit their fancies, and, when these have been written down, fictions are accepted as fact. This holds true of skill in the various arts; ignorant men who know nothing about these arts praise the masters indiscriminately, as if they were gods, but the expert gives no credence to such tales. Things known by report always prove quite different when one has actually seen them.

When a man spews forth whatever nonsense comes to his mind, not caring that he may be exposed on the spot, people soon realize that he is lying. Again, if a man, though himself doubting the truth of a story, tells it exactly as it was related to him, with a self-satisfied twitching of the nose,[1] the lie is not *his*. But it is frightening when a man tells a lie convincingly, deliberately blurring the details in places and pretending not to remember exactly what happened, but carefully leaving no loose ends.

Nobody protests very energetically at a lie which redounds to his own prestige.

If, when everyone else is listening with pleasure to some lie, you decide that it would be pointless to be the only one to protest, "That wasn't what happened," and listen in silence, you may even be cited as a witness, and the story will seem all the more authentic.

There's no escaping it—the world is full of lies. It is safest always to accept what one hears as if it were utterly commonplace and devoid of interest.

Stories told by the lower classes are full of startling incidents. The well-bred man does not tell stories about prodigies.[2] I do not mean to suggest, however, that one should not believe wholeheartedly in the miracles of the gods and buddhas, or in the lives of the incarnations.[3] It is foolish to accept popular superstitions uncritically, but to dismiss them as being "most improbable" serves no purpose. In general, the best course is to treat such matters as if they were true, neither giving one's unqualified belief nor doubting or mocking them.

79

A man should avoid displaying deep familiarity with any subject. Can one imagine a well-bred man talking with the air of a know-it-all, even about the matter with which he is in fact familiar? The boor who pops up on the scene from somewhere in the hinterland answers questions with an air of utter

---

1. A twitching nose apparently indicates self-satisfaction, but some commentators believe that the man's face gives the lie away.   2. Refers to the Confucian *Analects:* "The master never talked of prodigies, feats of strength, disorders, or spirits."   3. Buddhas and bodhisattvas who temporarily assumed human form to save deluded human beings.

authority in every field. As a result, though the man may also possess qualities that compel our admiration, the manner in which he displays his high opinion of himself is contemptible. It is impressive when a man is always slow to speak, even on subjects he knows thoroughly, and does not speak at all unless questioned.

81

A screen or sliding door decorated with a painting or inscription in clumsy brushwork gives an impression less of its own ugliness than of the bad taste of the owner. It is all too apt to happen that a man's possessions betray his inferiority. I am not suggesting that a man should own nothing but masterpieces. I refer to the practice of deliberately building in a tasteless and ugly manner "to keep the house from showing its age," or adding all manner of useless things in order to create an impression of novelty, though only producing an effect of fussiness. Possessions should look old, not overly elaborate; they need not cost much, but their quality should be good.

82

Somebody once remarked that thin silk was not satisfactory as a scroll wrapping because it was so easily torn. Ton'a[1] replied, "It is only after the silk wrapper has frayed at top and bottom, and the mother-of-pearl has fallen from the roller that a scroll looks beautiful." This opinion demonstrated the excellent taste of the man. People often say that a set of books looks ugly if all volumes are not in the same format, but I was impressed to hear the Abbot Kōyū[2] say, "It is typical of the unintelligent man to insist on assembling complete sets of everything. Imperfect sets are better."

In everything, no matter what it may be, uniformity is undesirable. Leaving something incomplete makes it interesting, and gives one the feeling that there is room for growth. Someone once told me, "Even when building the imperial palace, they always leave one place unfinished." In both Buddhist and Confucian writings of the philosophers of former times, there are also many missing chapters.

92

A certain man who was learning to shoot a bow aimed at the target with two arrows in his hand. His teacher said, "A beginner should not hold two arrows. It will make him rely on the second arrow and be careless with the first. Each time you shoot you should think not of hitting or missing the target but of making *this* one the decisive arrow." I wonder if anyone with only two arrows would be careless with one of them in the presence of his teacher. But though the pupil is himself unaware of any carelessness, the teacher will notice it. This caution applies to all things.

A man studying some branch of learning thinks at night that he has the

---

1. Poet and antiquarian (1289–1372).   2. Kōyū Sōzu, a little-known contemporary of Kenkō.

next day before him, and in the morning that he will have time that night; he plans in this way always to study more diligently at some future time. How much harder it is to perceive the laziness of mind that arises in an instant! Why should it be so difficult to do something now, in the present moment?

137

Are we to look at cherry blossoms only in full bloom, the moon only when it is cloudless? To long for the moon while looking on the rain, to lower the blinds and be unaware of the passing of the spring—these are even more deeply moving. Branches about to blossom or gardens strewn with faded flowers are worthier of our admiration. Are poems written on such themes as "Going to view the cherry blossoms only to find they had scattered" or "On being prevented from visiting the blossoms" inferior to those on "Seeing the blossoms"? People commonly regret that the cherry blossoms scatter or that the moon sinks in the sky, and this is natural; but only an exceptionally insensitive man would say, "This branch and that branch have lost their blossoms. There is nothing worth seeing now."

In all things, it is the beginnings and ends that are interesting. Does the love between men and women refer only to the moments when they are in each other's arms? The man who grieves over a love affair broken off before it was fulfilled, who bewails empty vows, who spends long autumn nights alone, who lets his thoughts wander to distant skies, who yearns for the past in a dilapidated house—such a man truly knows what love means.

The moon that appears close to dawn after we have long waited for it moves us more profoundly than the full moon shining cloudless over a thousand leagues. And how incomparably lovely is the moon, almost greenish in its light, when seen through the tops of the cedars deep in the mountains, or when it hides for a moment behind clustering clouds during a sudden shower! The sparkle on hickory or white-oak leaves seemingly wet with moonlight strikes one to the heart. One suddenly misses the capital, longing for a friend who could share the moment.

And are we to look at the moon and the cherry blossoms with our eyes alone? How much more evocative and pleasing it is to think about the spring without stirring from the house, to dream of the moonlit night though we remain in our room!

The man of breeding never appears to abandon himself completely to his pleasures; even his manner of enjoyment is detached. It is the rustic boors who take all their pleasures grossly. They squirm their way through the crowd to get under the trees; they stare at the blossoms with eyes for nothing else; they drink saké and compose linked verse; and finally they heartlessly break off great branches and cart them away. When they see a spring they dip their hands and feet to cool them; if it is the snow, they jump down to leave their footprints. No matter what the sight, they are never content merely with looking at it.

Such people have a very peculiar manner of watching the Kamo Festival.[1] "The procession's awfully late," they say. "There's no point waiting in the

1. See n. 2, p. 2331.

stands for it to come." They go off then to a shack behind the stands where they drink and eat, play *go*[2] or backgammon, leaving somebody in the stands to warn them. When he cries, "It's passing now!" each of them dashes out in wild consternation, struggling to be first back into the stands. They all but fall from their perches as they push out the blinds and press against one another for a better look, staring at the scene, determined not to miss a thing. They comment on everything that goes by, with cries of "Look at this! Look at that!" When the procession has passed, they scramble down, saying, "We'll be back for the next one." All they are interested in is what they can see.

People from the capital, the better sort, doze during the processions, hardly looking at all. Young underlings are constantly moving about, performing their masters' errands, and persons in attendance, seated behind, never stretch forward in an unseemly manner. No one is intent on seeing the procession at all costs.

It is charming on the day of the Festival to see garlands of hollyhock leaves carelessly strewn over everything. The morning of the Festival, before dawn breaks, you wonder who the owners are of the carriages silently drawn up in place, and guess, "That one is his—or his," and have your guesses confirmed when sometimes you recognize a coachman or servant. I never weary of watching the different carriages going back and forth, some delightfully unpretentious, others magnificent. By the time it is growing dark you wonder where the rows of carriages and the dense crowds of spectators have disappeared to. Before you know it, hardly a soul is left, and the congestion of returning carriages is over. Then they start removing the blinds and matting from the stands, and the place, even as you watch, begins to look desolate. You realize with a pang of grief that life is like this. If you have seen the avenues of the city, you have seen the festival.

I suddenly realized, from the large number of people I could recognize in the crowds passing to and fro before the stands, that there were not so many people in the world, after all. Even if I were not to die until all of them had gone, I should not have long to wait. If you pierce a tiny aperture in a large vessel filled with water, even though only a small amount drips out, the constant leakage will empty the vessel. In this capital, with all its many people, surely a day never passes without someone dying. And are there merely one or two deaths a day? One some days, certainly, many more than one or two are seen to their graves at Toribeno, Funaoka, and other mountainsides, but never a day passes without a single funeral. That is why coffin makers never have any to spare. It does not matter how young or how strong you may be, the hour of death comes sooner than you expect. It is an extraordinary miracle that you should have escaped to this day; do you suppose you have even the briefest respite in which to relax?

When you make a *mamagodate*[3] with backgammon counters, at first you cannot tell which of the stones arranged before you will be taken away. Your count then falls on a certain stone and you remove it. The others seem to

2. A complex game, sometimes erroneously called Japanese chess, originating in China and employing black and white stones, alternately placed on a board with 361 intersections. The object is to capture the opponent's stones and to secure control over open spaces on the board. 3. A kind of mathematical puzzle. Fifteen white stones and fifteen black stones are so arranged that eliminating the tenth stone, counting in one direction, will result after fourteen rounds in only one white stone remaining. If the count is then resumed in the opposite direction, all the black stones will be eliminated, leaving the one white stone.

have escaped, but as you renew the count you will thin out the pieces one by one, until none is left. Death is like that. The soldier who goes to war, knowing how close he is to death, forgets his family and even forgets himself; the man who has turned his back on the world and lives in a thatched hut, quietly taking pleasure in the streams and rocks of his garden, may suppose that death in battle has nothing to do with him, but this is a shallow misconception. Does he imagine that, if he hides in the still recesses of the mountains, the enemy called change will fail to attack? When you confront death, no matter where it may be, it is the same as charging into battle.

150

A man who is trying to learn some art is apt to say, "I won't rush things and tell people I am practicing while I am still a beginner. I'll study by myself, and only when I have mastered the art will I perform before people. How impressed they'll be then!"

People who speak in this fashion will never learn any art. The man who, even while still a novice, mixes with the experts, not ashamed of their harsh comments or ridicule, and who devotedly persists at his practice, unruffled by criticism, will neither become stultified in his art nor careless with it. Though he may lack natural gifts, he will with the passage of the years outstrip the man who coasts on his endowments, and in the end will attain the highest degree of skill, acquire authority in his art and the recognition of the public, and win an unequaled reputation.

The performers who now rank as the most skilled in the whole country were at the beginning considered incompetent, and, indeed, had shocking faults. However, by faithfully maintaining the principles of their art and holding them in honor, rather than indulging in their own fancies, they have become paragons of the age and teachers for all. This surely holds true for every art.

172

When a man is young he has such an overabundance of energy that his senses are quickly stirred and he has many desires. It is as easy for him to put himself in danger and court destruction as to roll a ball. He likes beautiful clothes and possessions, and spends his fortune on them, only to abandon everything for the shabby black robes of a priest. Or, his abundance of high spirits may lead him to quarrel, only to feel ashamed in his heart and envious of his antagonist; his uncertain whims shift from day to day. Now giving himself to his lusts, now moved by others' kindness, now performing some generous action, he yearns, when he hears stories of men who ruined or even destroyed lives that might have lasted a hundred years, to do the same, and never gives a thought to leading a safe and long life. He is drawn wherever his fancies lead him, and becomes the subject of gossip that lasts even after his death. Youth is the time when a man ruins himself.

An old man's spirit grows feeble; he is indifferent and slow to respond, unmoved by everything. His mind being naturally placid, he engages in no useless activities. He takes good care of himself, is untroubled by worries, and is careful not to be a nuisance to others. The old are as superior to the young in wisdom as the young are superior to the old in looks.

188

A certain man, deciding to make his son a priest, said, "You will study and learn the principle of Cause and Effect, and you will then preach sermons to earn a livelihood." The son, doing as instructed, learned how to ride a horse as a first step towards becoming a preacher. He thought that when people wanted him to conduct a service they would probably send a horse for him, since he owned neither a palanquin nor a carriage, and it would be embarrassing if, because of his awkwardness in the saddle, he fell from the horse. Next, thinking that if, after the service, he were offered some saké and had no social graces to display, the donor would be disappointed, he learned to sing popular songs. When he was at last able to pass muster in these two arts, he felt anxious to attain real proficiency. He devoted himself so diligently to his practice that he had no time to learn preaching, and in the meantime he had grown old.

This priest was not the only one; the story is typical of people in general. When they are young they are concerned about the projects they foresee lying ahead of them in the distant future—establishing themselves in different professions and carrying out some great undertaking, mastering an art, acquiring learning—but they think of their lives as stretching out indefinitely, and idly allow themselves to be constantly distracted by things directly before their eyes. They pass months and days in this manner, succeeding in none of their plans, and so they grow old. In the end, they neither become proficient in their profession, nor do they gain the eminence they anticipated. However they regret it, they cannot roll back the years, but decline more and more rapidly, like a wheel rolling downhill.

In view of the above, we must carefully compare in our minds all the different things in life we might hope to make our principal work, and decide which is of the greatest value; this decided, we should renounce our other interests and devote ourselves to that one thing only. Many projects present themselves in the course of a day or even an hour; we must perform those that offer even slightly greater advantages, renouncing the others and giving ourselves entirely to whatever is most important. If we remain attached to them all, and are reluctant to give up any, we will not accomplish a single thing.

It is like a go[1] player who, not wasting a move, gets the jump on his opponent by sacrificing a small advantage to achieve a great one. It is easy, of course, to sacrifice three stones in order to gain ten. The hard thing is to sacrifice ten stones in order to gain eleven. A man should be ready to choose the course which is superior even by one stone, but when it comes to sacrificing ten, he feels reluctant, and it is hard to make an exchange which will not yield many additional stones. If we hesitate to give up what we have, and at the same time are eager to grab what the other man holds, we shall certainly fail to get his pieces and lose our own.

1. See n. 2, p. 2338.

A man living in the capital has urgent business in the Eastern Hills, and has already reached the house of his destination when it occurs to him that if he goes to the Western Hills he may reap greater advantage; in that case, he should turn back at the gate and proceed to the Western Hills. If, however, he thinks, "I've come all this way. I might as well take care of my business here first. There was no special day set for my business in the Western Hills. I'll go there some other time, after I have returned," the sloth of a moment will turn in this manner into the sloth of an entire lifetime. This is to be dreaded.

If you are determined to carry out one particular thing, you must not be upset that other things fall through. Nor should you be embarrassed by other people's laughter. A great enterprise is unlikely to be achieved except at the sacrifice of everything else.

Once, at a large gathering, a certain man said, "Some people say *masuho no susuki*, others say *masoho no susuki*.[2] The holy man of Watanabe knows the secret tradition of this pronunciation." The priest Tōren, who was present at the gathering and heard this remark, said (it being raining at the time), "Has anyone a raincoat and umbrella he can lend me? I intend to call on this holy man of Watanabe and find out about the *susuki*." People said, "You shouldn't get so excited. Wait till the rain stops." The priest replied, "What a foolish thing to say! Do you suppose that a man's life will wait for the rain to clear? If I should die or the priest passes away in the meantime, could I inquire about it then?" So saying, he hurried out and went to study the tradition. This struck me as a most unusual and valid story.

It is written in the *Analects*[3] that "in speed there is success." Just as Tōren was impatient to learn about the *susuki*, we should be impatient to discover the sources of enlightenment.

190

A man should never marry. I am charmed when I hear a man say, "I am still living alone." When I hear someone say, "He has married into so and so's family" or "He has taken such and such a wife and they are living together," I feel nothing but contempt for the man. He will be ridiculed by others too, who will say, "No doubt he thought that commonplace woman was quite a catch, and that's why he took her off with him." Or, if the woman happens to be beautiful, they are sure to feel, "He dotes on her so much that he worships her as his private Buddha. Yes, that's no doubt the case."

The woman who cleverly manages a household is the least agreeable to her husband. It is exasperating to see the pains and affection she lavishes on her children when they are born; and after her husband has died she will become a nun and look so decrepit that it will be positively shocking.

Living day in and day out with a woman, no matter what she may be like, is bound to be frustrating and the source of irritation. The woman too is likely to feel insecure. The relationship, however, can last unbroken for many years if the couple lives apart, and the man only occasionally visits or stays

---

2. *Susuki* is a variety of pampas grass. *Masuho no susuki* has been identified as *susuki* with a plume about a foot long; *masoho no susuki* as *susuki* with tangled plumes. The ability to make such distinctions was accounted a mastery of the secret arts of poetry, hence the interest of the poet-priest Tōren in the following sentences.   3. The teachings of Confucius (551–479 B.C.), recorded by his disciples (see p. 820).

with the woman. If the man casually visits the woman and remains with her just temporarily, a freshness will cling to their romance.

191

I feel sorry for the man who says that night dims the beauty of things. At night colors, ornaments, and richness of materials show to their best advantage. By day you should wear simple, conservative clothes, but at night showy, flashy costumes are most attractive. This holds true of people's appearance too: lamplight makes a beautiful face seem even more beautiful, and a voice heard in the dark—a voice that betrays a fear of being overheard—is endearing. Perfumes and the sound of music too are best at night.

It is charming if, on a night which is not any special occasion, a visitor arriving at the palace after it has grown quite late appears in splendid attire. Young people, being observant of one another irrespective of the time of day, should always be dressed in their best, with no distinction of formal and informal attire, above all when they are most at their ease. How pleasant it is when a handsome man grooms his hair after dark, or a woman, late at night, slips from an audience chamber and, mirror in hand, touches up her make-up before she appears again.

243

When I turned eight years old I asked my father, "What sort of thing is a Buddha?" My father said, "A Buddha is what a man becomes." I asked then, "How does a man become a Buddha?" My father replied, "By following the teachings of Buddha." "Then, who taught the Buddha to teach?" He again replied, "He followed the teachings of the Buddha before him." I asked again, "What kind of Buddha was the first Buddha who began to teach?" At this my father laughed and answered, "I suppose he fell from the sky or else he sprang up out of the earth."

My father told other people, "He drove me into a corner, and I was stuck for an answer." But he was amused.

NŌ DRAMA

Nō, the classical theater of Japan, is the world's oldest extant professional theater. It is also among the world's gravest and most stylized. Performed on an austere, undecorated stage of polished cypress, with no scenery and virtually no props, the ritual-like poetic dance-dramas of the nō have been described as a theater free of the artifice of stagecraft. But it would be more accurate to characterize the nō as a theater elevating stagecraft to the nth power. The absence of illusory scrims, revolving sets, or cyclorama floodlights is only the absence of the most obvious artifice. The word nō may be translated as "talent," "skill," or "accomplishment." And the ways that "accomplishment" has been cultivated by nō actors (all nō performers are male) demonstrate how fundamental, in fact, artifice, or stratagem, has always been to the tradition of the *nō*.

In Japan's medieval period, when *nō* coalesced from disparate origins—mystery plays, rice-planting rituals, classical poetry, carnival tricks, myth, and Buddhist liturgy—Zeami Motokiyo, master actor, playwright, and critic of the *nō*, analyzed the actor's art in a series of treatises as rigorous and self-conscious as the pronouncements of Stanislavsky, progenitor of the twentieth-century school of "method acting." Zeami's dissection of acting technique reveals both a practical and philosophical command of his craft. It also demonstrates the indissoluble link between *nō* and Zen Buddhism.

Let's begin first with the practical. Because *nō* shunned the trappings of representational theater, the actor's own talent or accomplishment (that is, his *nō*) became paramount. While over time the practice developed of incorporating a chorus and musical instruments to assist the actor, he had nonetheless little but his own artistry to convey the reality of his performance. The stately pace of *nō* drama and its highly conventionalized formal and thematic patterns may distance some audiences today, but the *nō* actor's subtle if stylized stage business can express an astonishing artistry. This artistry rejects theatricality. It also avoids both improvisation and the actor's deployment of personal experience to flesh out or give psychological depth to his characterization. (In fact, as we will see, the Western concept of "characterization" has little utility in the realm of *nō*.)

Instead, in Zeami's conception, the ideal *nō* actor combines a commonsense approach to performing ("If an actor thinks he has attained a higher level of skill than he has reached . . . he will lose even the level he has achieved") with a less-is-more view of art that today sounds curiously modern. "The expression 'when you feel ten in your heart, express seven in your movements,' " he tells us, refers to the necessity of underplaying. "When a beginner . . . learns to gesture . . . he will use all his energies to perform. . . . Later he will learn to move less. . . . No matter how slight a bodily action, if the motion is more restrained than the emotion behind it, the emotion will become the Substance and the movement of the body its Function, thus moving his audience."[*]

To these technical concerns of the impresario Zeami weds some of the more abstruse values of medieval Japanese aesthetics. *Yūgen* is the key criterion, a complex term with a web of meanings: mystery, depth, darkness, but also beauty and elegance, all tinged with the sadness of the ephemeral. The word *yūgen* originated in China (*yu hsüan*), where it described an object concealed from view, something that lay hidden too deep to be either seen or comprehended. *Yūgen* developed in Japan as a poetic principle denoting the profound. Poetry capturing the spirit of *yūgen* expressed emotions so delicate or subtle that they could only be implied. This taste for implication embodied in *yūgen* influenced all the major arts of medieval Japan, not only poetry and drama but also painting, calligraphy, ceramics, and even architecture. In the visual arts, the *yūgen* aesthetic preferred monochrome to color, and the evocative ink landscapes of the fourteenth century—in which a still mountain ridge appears and disappears within the mist, creating from the illusion of vast space a sense of infinity—testify to the fact that a monochromatic work can suggest more than the richest palette. In defining too well, color proves oddly restrictive. But with monochrome, there are no limits to what can be evoked through suggestion.

A famous anecdote about the sixteenth-century warlord Hideyoshi will demonstrate how central the suggestive component of *yūgen* has been to Japanese cultural identity. Hideyoshi was a brute foot soldier who, having risen to unify Japan through prowess and cunning, sought culture under the tutelage of a man of superior taste, Rikyū the tea master. The two men met often to perform the tea ceremony. One afternoon

---

[*] Zeami Motokiyo, *On the Art of Nō Drama*, trans. J. Thomas Rimer and Yamazaki Masakazu (1984), pp. 7, 75.

Hideyoshi asked Rikyū to show him his garden, which was famous for its morning glories. Rikyū demurred, but when Hideyoshi persisted Rikyū invited him to return the following morning. Hideyoshi arrived at the appointed hour, only to find that all the morning glories had been removed from the garden. A man with a hot temper who was accustomed to having his way, Hideyoshi stormed over to the tea hut, where he knew Rikyū would be waiting. He slid back the little door to the hut and entered. Before he could demand an explanation, however, he saw that the tea master had placed a single morning glory in the alcove. The one blossom was the essence of all morning glories. To Hideyoshi it was a revelation.

In the same manner, *yūgen*'s powers of suggestion were for Zeami the apex of the theatrical art of *nō,* what he calls "the art of the flower of mystery." This can by symbolized, he says, by the paradoxical phrase "In Silla* at midnight the sun is bright." Zeami elaborates:

> It is impossible to express in words or even to grasp in the mind the mystery of this art. When one speaks of the sun rising at midnight, the words themselves do not explain anything; thus too, in the art of *nō,* the *yūgen* of a supreme actor defies our attempts to praise it. We are so deeply impressed that we do not know what to single out as being of special excellence, and, if we attempt to assign it a rank, we discover that it is peerless artistry which transcends any degrees. This kind of artistic expression, which is invisible to ordinary eyes, may be what is termed the Art of the Flower of Mystery."†

The profundity of *nō,* according to Zeami, is ineffable. Nō must pierce the brittle surface of everyday reality and reach for the truth that lies hidden underneath. Distilled to its essence, *yūgen* is truth, and *nō*'s quest for the truth marks this theater as the literary progeny of Zen. Both see outward reality as illusory and ultimate reality as beyond words, beyond the senses. Both adhere to the doctrine of karma and the transmigration of souls. All human beings are born into an endless cycle of reincarnation. In this life we sow the seeds for the next. But flawed by our appetite for worldly things, each successive existence is steeped in delusion, suffering, and discontent. There is only one escape: *satori,* or enlightenment, the realization that material phenomena are fancies, not facts. This discovery frees us to let go of illusory attachments, whether love, passion, hatred, ambition, or greed. It is a discovery to be made in our own backyard, as it were. In Zen, enlightenment has nothing to do with cerebration, and everything to do with uncovering the meaning hidden in the particulars of daily experience. Illumination is apt to be sudden, mystical, even accidental.

At the same time, paradoxically, great discipline is demanded of the Zen aspirant, and considerable effort goes into achieving effortlessness. The initiate must submit to the grueling practice of *zazen,* or "meditation sitting," assuming a tortuous yogic position and contemplating an intractable riddle assigned by the Zen master. These riddles vary from seemingly unanswerable questions (What is the sound of one hand clapping?) to gnomic conundrums (A flag waved in the air. Two monks disputed whether the flag was moving or the wind was moving. A third monk retorted, "It is not the wind that is moving; it is not the flag that is moving; it is your mind that is moving!"). Whether such mental exercises strike one as intriguing or exasperating, the persistent meditation of Zen puzzles, when it succeeds, is thought to enable the aspirant to break free of the constraints of logic, to cast off the conceptualization we learn to superimpose on the flow of life's encounters, and thus to experience intuitive insight: enlightenment.

A further refinement of Zen, with important implications for the *nō* theater, was the belief that enlightenment did not occur in a vacuum, that the profane world at

---

* A kingdom in ancient Korea, founded in 57 B.C.   † Donald Keene, *Nō: The Classical Theatre of Japan* (1973), p. 23.

all times intrudes on Zen. The secular arts—archery, *nō*, calligraphy, swordsmanship, and the tea ceremony—were seen as a means of spiritual training. This endeared Zen to the ruling *samurai* class, who were the patrons of the *nō*. Because there was no distinction, or antagonism, between enlightenment and empirical existence and because the anti-intellectual strain in Zen held that an aspirant does not so much ignore the everyday, or the material, as work through it, it was possible for a *samurai* to live the illuminated life within his secular station. Discipline and dedication were required, to be sure, but in the discourse of the times these were already the defining attributes of the *samurai*.

The warrior schooled in the austerities of military training and Zen meditation found the severe aspects of *nō* to his liking. The bare stage, the ritualistic disregard for verisimilitude, the harsh musical accompaniment—hardly melodic and more like a dolorous Gregorian chant, in which the shrill flute and irregular drumbeats seem to puncture the performance more than they accompany it—all were the perfect correlates to the theatrical paring away that is *nō*.

Considering the many dramatic elements that *nō* does not possess, at least from a Eurocentric perspective, one might be forgiven the punning thought that perhaps this is the reason it is called *nō* theater. Where, one might ask, is the conflict that drives a Western play, the touchstone of dramaturgy since Aeschylus? *Nō* plays seldom offer a confrontation between dramatic equals. Instead one figure, the *shite* (literally, the "doer"), dominates the stage. If this is the protagonist, the *shite* lacks any foil with enough dramatic heft to weigh in as a viable antagonist. The other actors, the *waki* ("sideman") and the *tsure* ("companion"), are mere observers. And what they observe can hardly be called the action. That took place a long time ago—in what Hollywood would call the "backstory." To continue in the current idiom, one might characterize present time on stage as the depiction of an obsession precisely about "the action" of the past. The play portrays an emotion, and the *shite* is nothing other than the embodiment of that emotion. Just as the tea master needed only one morning glory to convey the essence of all morning glories, the *nō* play needs only the present moment—stripped of the impedimenta of theatrical realism—to capture the essence of an emotion. At first glance *nō* may appear an abbreviation, but in fact it is a concentration.

The typical play opens with the entrance of the *waki*, often in the role of a priest. He proceeds down the bridge, or runway, at the audience's left, which connects the stage to the greenroom, and announces the circumstances of the play: the season, the place, and the central theme (see illustration, p. 2346). The statement of the theme is repeated in a poem or chant by the chorus of six or eight men, who, together with the "orchestra" of flute player and one or two drummers, have preceded the *waki* on stage. (The musicians sit along the back of the stage under the lone pine tree painted on the wall, the single and unvarying decoration for all *nō* plays. The chorus sits on a veranda at the side of the stage, to the audience's right.) The *waki* moves onto the stage proper and states his name and his intentions. "I am Kumagai no Naozane," declaims the *waki* in *Atsumori*, the first of the *nō* plays printed here, "a man of the country of Musashi. I have left my home and call myself the priest Rensei; this I have done because of my grief at the death of Atsumori, who fell in battle by my hand. Hence it comes that I am dressed in priestly guise. And now I am going down to Ichi-no-Tani to pray for the salvation of Atsumori's soul." As he trails across the stage, intoning a travel song, his slow progress represents his journey. When he reaches the opposite side of the stage, he announces his arrival at his destination, "I have come so fast that here I am already at Ichi-no-Tani, in the country of Tsu." With this, the first, or introductory, movement of the play concludes.

The second, expository, movement opens with the appearance of the *shite*, the principal actor, who is usually followed by his companion, the *tsure*. Advancing down the bridge in slow-motion and making his way onto the stage, the *shite* sings an entrance song that describes his current situation without revealing who he really is.

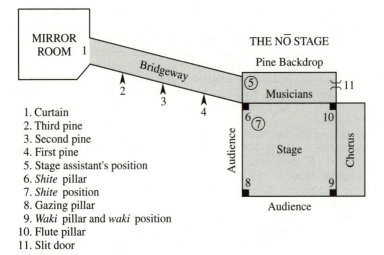

1. Curtain
2. Third pine
3. Second pine
4. First pine
5. Stage assistant's position
6. *Shite* pillar
7. *Shite* position
8. Gazing pillar
9. *Waki* pillar and *waki* position
10. Flute pillar
11. Slit door

The *shite* in *Atsumori* first appears as a young reaper. He and his companion enter chanting,

> To the music of the reaper's flute
> No song is sung
> But the sighing of wind in the fields.

And the *shite* adds,

> They that were reaping,
> Reaping on that hill,
> Walk now through the fields
> Homeward, for it is dusk.

Soon the *shite* encounters the *waki*, who, being a stranger to the region, asks various questions, first about the locality and then about the identity of the *shite*. The chorus elaborates this dialogue in a song of poetic allusion. By now the *waki* begins to realize that there is something odd about the *shite*, and the *shite* tries to evade him. Agitated, the *shite* begins to dance, which in the *nō* is always a sign of emotional excitement. The *shite* implores the priest to pray for him. As the chorus reiterates his plea for help, the *shite* moves onto the bridge and departs, concluding the second movement.

An interlude precedes the third and final movement of the play. An actor identified as a "man of the place" appears to recount the "backstory," which, in this play, would make up the events of Atsumori's death on the battlefield. Note, however, that the translator does not include the entr'acte, since, as he explains, "These interludes are subject to variation and are not considered part of the literary text." Audiences today regard this portion of the play as an intermission, during which they are free to whisper, or rustle through their programs, or slip out for a cup of tea.

After the interlude comes the climax, or *kyū*, a "rushing to the end," which begins with the *waki*'s "waiting song," an admission of willingness to pray for the deliverance of the *shite*. Soon the *shite* reappears, but in a different guise. He has changed his costume and mask to reveal his true self. "Would you know who I am?" asks the *shite*. "Listen, Rensei. I am Atsumori," he says—the very Atsumori whom Rensei, or Kuma-gai, had slain in the wars between the Heike and the Genji, the ghost of a restless spirit unable to free itself from an obsession with past defeat, bound to this world through fixation on the last moments of final battle, incapable of letting go, and so perpetually deprived of enlightenment.

Atsumori now rehearses the elements of his obsession. He recounts the disasters that befell his clan, the Taira, or Heike, whereupon the chorus assists him, as though it were an extension of Atsumori's anxious mind:

> Yet their prosperity lasted but for a day;
> It was like the flower of the convolvulus.
> There was none to tell them
> That glory flashes like sparks from flint-stone,
> And after,—darkness.

But perhaps Atsumori is on the verge of a breakthrough, for he begins to comprehend the darker side of the Taira clan. He admits,

> When they were on high they afflicted the humble;
> When they were rich they were reckless in pride.

Pride led inevitably to war, and war to the trauma that haunts him. As Atsumori revisits the ordeals of war, he works himself into a frenzy, until frenzy bursts into dance. In this final dance, he relives his mortal struggle with Kumagai, narrated by the chorus:

> He looks behind him and sees
> That Kumagai pursues him;
> He cannot escape.
> Then Atsumori turns his horse
> Knee-deep in the lashing waves,
> And draws his sword.
> Twice, three times he strikes; then, still saddled,
> In close fight they twine; roll headlong together
> Among the surf of the shore.
> So Atsumori fell. . . .

But fate seems to have given Atsumori a second chance. He comes out of his dance as from a seizure. The enemy stands before him; revenge is his. Atsumori lifts his sword. Suddenly, however, something strange happens. What he sees is neither a foe nor a warrior, but a priest intoning the name of Buddha. "No," Atsumori understands, "Rensei is not my enemy." The play ends as he asks the priest to pray for him. The audience sits riveted. Slowly, Atsumori makes his final exit. The *shite* glides along the bridge like an apparition fading from sight or a soul on the way to salvation.

Given the subject of *nō*, it should not come as a surprise that many of the plays are peopled by ghosts, for, in the world of *nō*, ghosts represent emotion unreconciled, the mind caught in the spiral of material illusion. Technically, there are five categories of *nō* plays in a repertoire of some 240 dramas: celebratory "god plays," in which the *shite* appears first in human form and later as the deity it really is, performed at New Year's and on other felicitous occasions (the second play included here is an example); plays like *Atsumori*, about the ghosts of warriors doomed to eternal battle, unless a priest will pray to release them from their suffering; "wig plays," in which the *shite* portrays the spirit of an angry woman, often obsessed with unhappy love; "mundane plays" (assuming ghosts are mundane), which make up almost half the repertoire and tend to focus on derangement, a woman driven mad by the loss of a lover or child, or a husband distraught over the death of his wife (the third play printed here belongs to this group); and "demon plays," depicting supernatural creatures, devils in particular, who threaten to overwhelm the forces of good.

Clearly, in the majority of plays, the *shite* embodies the human mind, and this psychological dimension is one of the things that has given *nō* a new lease on life in the present century. While the protagonist of a *nō* play is never a fully wrought character, endowed with a complex temperament or granted realistic substance through individualistic detail, the dramatization of an obsession takes on fresh, contemporary relevance in the wake of Freud and Jung. The psychology of *nō*, combined with its Zen astringency, sloughing off both the decorative and the mimetic, appealed to Yeats, Pound, and other writers of an experimental bent, for whom realism was an outdated bourgeois convention. The very things *nō* lacked were seen by the modernists as its strong suit. Its bold simplicity was a near relation to the new calligraphic line in abstract painting. Its nuanced precision was preferable to traditional Western theater, in which, in the opinion of Pound, "subtlety must give way; where every fineness of word or of word-cadence is sacrificed to the 'broad effect'; where the paint must be put on with a broom." Pound, more than any other, idealized the *nō*, but under his tutorship *nō*'s rich fusion of poetry and prose, creating a compact collage of fragmentary images and complex allusions, helped revivify twentieth-century British and American poetry. We see this particularly in the poetry of Yeats, who drew inspiration from *nō*'s reliance on a single symbol (in *Atsumori*, for example, the flute) to strive for a similar metaphoric unity. Yeats's encounter with the *nō* even led him to write his own brand of *nō* plays, in which he attempted to mine the legends and layered literary traditions of Western culture as Zeami had done with those of Japan.

The three plays offered here are excellent examples of the *nō*. The first two are attributed to Zeami and the third to his grandnephew, Kanze Kojirō Nobumitsu. *Atsumori* demonstrates as well as any play *nō*'s debt to classical Japanese literature, in this case *The Death of Atsumori* from Chapter 9 of *The Tale of the Heike*.

The second play, *Haku Rakuten*, is a curious piece, in which the "obsession" would seem to be Japan's collective national fear of that old bugbear, Chinese influence. *Haku Rakuten* is the Japanese pronunciation of Po Chü-i (772–846), one of the greatest of Chinese poets, whose influence in classical Japan extended even to *The Tale of Genji*. Chinese influence reasserted itself in the fourteenth century, the age of *nō*, and in one of Japan's periodic pendulum swings of reaction, *Haku Rakuten* is a dramatization of cultural, or literary, peril. In the play, Po Chü-i, or Haku Rakuten, is sent by the Chinese emperor to subdue Japan with his superior art. In fact, Po Chü-i never set foot in Japan (see p. 1393). But the Japanese have at times been extremely sensitive about their receptivity to foreign example, and the danger must have seemed real enough at the time. Interestingly, in the play, Haku Rakuten is repulsed by the god of Japanese poetry, who in legend was a reincarnation of the historical figure Sugawara Michizane—one of Po Chü-i's most slavish imitators. A further irony is that Zeami himself was addicted to the poetry of Po Chü-i, if we are to judge by the number of times he quotes Po Chü-i's poems in his plays.

The final play included here, *Dōjōji*, is one of the most dramatic *nō* plays. It is based on a legend included in a collection of Buddhist miracle stories compiled around 1040. In the original tale, a handsome young priest has the misfortune of attracting the attentions of a very lustful widow. He eludes her by departing on a pilgrimage, though not before placating her with the promise to spend the night on his return. When she realizes that he has no intention of keeping his promise, the wrath of the spurned woman is so intense that it transforms her into a serpent. The snake sets off in pursuit of the priest, and the results are not happy.

The *nō* version of this story elicits greater sympathy, and at the same time heightens the drama, by recasting the oversexed woman as a young girl. Now it is her innocence rather than her appetite, combined with her father's careless sense of humor, that precipitates disaster. *Dōjōji* is an unusual *nō* play in several respects. It is one of the few to rely on an elaborate prop: the huge bell that becomes a powerful part of the climax. And *Dōjōji* creates something closer to what we would call a dramatic situation; with more animation on stage than in most plays, the poetry of the text must compete with the spectacle.

Where are we, then, when we are left only with the text and none of the spectacle?

Something is definitely lost. Nō may be spare, but it is highly visual: the rich brocade costumes; the shrinelike atmosphere of the stage; the mad, climactic dances of ghostly characters; the evocative masks worn by the *shite*. And no flute will sound, unless you use your imagination, though, of course, imagination has always been an important part of *nō*. Perhaps this is the key to appreciating *nō* as literature. Imagine yourself as a Zen master. The actors are gone. The chorus is gone. The musicians are gone. The stage is gone. The audience is gone. The words remain—diminishment or essence?

The most accessible introduction to the *nō* is by Donald Keene, *Nō: The Classical Theatre of Japan* (1973), which is also valuable for its photographs. Zeami's theories of drama are available in English in J. Thomas Rimer and Yamazaki Masakazu, *On the Art of Nō Drama: The Major Treatises of Zeami* (1894); they are discussed by Makoto Ueda in "Zeami and the Art of the Nō Drama: Imitation, Yugen and Sublimity," in Nancy G. Hulme, ed., *Japanese Aesthetics and Culture: A Reader* (1998), and Benito Ortolani and Samuel L. Leiter, eds., *Zeami and the Nō Theatre in the World* (1998). Two excellent technical works are P. G. O'Neill, *Early Nō Drama* (1974), and Thomas Blenman Hare, *Zeami's Style: The Noh Plays of Zeami Motokiyo* (1986). Appraisals of the *nō* by Pound and Yeats will be found in a collection of translated plays: Ezra Pound and Ernest Fenollosa, *The Classic Noh Theatre of Japan* (1959). Other collections of translations include Arthur Waley, *The Nō Plays of Japan* (1921); Donald Keene, ed., *Twenty Plays of the Nō Theatre* (1970); Nippon Gakujutsu Shinkōkai, *The Noh Drama* (1973); Kenneth Yasuda, *Masterworks of the Nō Theatre* (1989); and Royall Tyler, *Japanese Nō Dramas* (1992).

PRONOUNCING GLOSSARY

The following list uses common English syllables to provide rough equivalents of selected words whose pronunciation may be unfamiliar to the general reader.

Ariso: *ah-ree-soh*

Atsumori: *ah-tsoo-moh-ree*

Awaji: *ah-wah-jee*

Dōjōji: *doh-joh-jee*

eito: *ay-toh*

eiya: *ay-yah*

Etsu: *e-tsoo*

Haku Rakuten: *hah-koo rah-koo-ten*

Hideyoshi: *hee-de-yoh-shee*

Ichi-no-Tani: *ee-chee–noh–tah-nee*

Juyei: *joo-ay*

Kanze Kojirō Nobumitsu: *kahn-ze koh-jee-roh noh-boo-mee-tsoo*

kotsuzumi: *koh-tsoo-zoo-mee*

Kumagai no Naozane: *koo-mah-gai noh nah-oh-zah-ne*

Matsura: *mah-tsoo-rah*

Michinari: *mee-chee-nah-ree*

Musashi: *moo-sah-shee*

Nihon: *nee-hohn*

nō: *noh*

rambyōshi: *rahm-byoh-shee*

Rensei: *ren-say*

Rikyū: *ree-kyoo*

shite: *shee-te*

Sugawara Michizane: *soo-gah-wah-rah mee-chee-zah-ne*

Sumiyoshi: *soo-mee-yoo-shee*

Tsu: *tsoo*

Tsukushi: *tsoo-koo-shee*

Tsunemori: *tsoo-ne-moh-ree*

tsure: *tsoo-re*

Yamabushi: *yah-mah-boo-shee*

yūgen: *yoo-gen*

zazen: *zah-zen*

Zeami Motokiyo: *ze-ah-mee moh-toh-kee-yoh*

ZEAMI MOTOKIYO
1364–1443

Atsumori[1]

PERSONS

The PRIEST RENSEI (formerly the warrior Kumagai)
A YOUNG REAPER, who turns out to be the ghost of ATSUMORI
His Companion, another REAPER
CHORUS

PRIEST:

> Life is a lying dream, he only wakes
> Who casts the World aside.

I am Kumagai no Naozane, a man of the country of Musashi.[2] I have
left my home and call myself the priest Rensei; this I have done
because of my grief at the death of Atsumori, who fell in battle   5
by my hand. Hence it comes that I am dressed in priestly guise.
And now I am going down to Ichi-no-Tani to pray for the salvation of
Atsumori's soul.
   [*He walks slowly across the stage, singing a song descriptive of his
   journey.*]
I have come so fast that here I am already at Ichi-no-Tani, in the country
of Tsu.   10
Truly the past returns to my mind as though it were a thing of to-day.
But listen! I hear the sound of a flute coming from a knoll of rising
   ground. I will wait here till the flute-player passes, and ask him to
   tell me the story of this place.
REAPERS: [*Together.*]

> To the music of the reaper's flute   15
> No song is sung
> But the sighing of wind in the fields.

YOUNG REAPER:

> They that were reaping,
> Reaping on that hill,
> Walk now through the fields   20
> Homeward, for it is dusk.

REAPERS: [*Together.*]

> Short is the way that leads
> From the sea of Suma[3] back to my home.
> This little journey, up to the hill

1. Translated by and with notes adapted from Arthur Waley.   2. A province in eastern Japan under
Minamoto/Genji control at the time of the war between the Heike and the Genji (1180–1185). Note that
Waley translates the word for "province" as *country* and spells *Kumagai* differently from the translator of
The Tale of the Heike.   3. A coastal town, rich in literary associations. *Kokinshū* poet Ariwara Yukihara
spent time there, Genji is exiled there (in chapter 12 of *The Tale of Genji*), and the decisive battle of Ichi-no-
Tani, where Atsumori dies, is fought nearby (told in *The Tale of the Heike*). This layering of levels of literary
association is an essential feature of *nō* plays. Suma was also known for its production of salt.

And down to the shore again, and up to the hill,—   25
This is my life, and the sum of hateful tasks.
If one should ask me
I too[4] would answer
That on the shore of Suma
I live in sadness.   30
Yet if any guessed my name,
Then might I too have friends.
But now from my deep misery
Even those that were dearest
Are grown estranged. Here must I dwell abandoned   35
To one thought's anguish:
That I must dwell here.

PRIEST: Hey, you reapers! I have a question to ask you.
YOUNG REAPER: Is it to us you are speaking? What do you wish to know?   40
PRIEST: Was it one of you who was playing on the flute just now?
YOUNG REAPER: Yes, it was we who were playing.
PRIEST: It was a pleasant sound, and all the pleasanter because one
does not look for such music from men of your condition.[5]
YOUNG REAPER:

Unlooked for from men of our condition, you say!   45
Have you not read:—
"Do not envy what is above you
Nor despise what is below you"?
Moreover the songs of woodmen and the flute-playing of herdsmen,
Flute-playing even of reapers and songs of wood-fellers   50
Through poets' verses are known to all the world.
Wonder not to hear among us
The sound of a bamboo-flute.

PRIEST: You are right. Indeed it is as you have told me.
Songs of woodmen and flute-playing of herdsmen . . .   55
REAPER: Flute-playing of reapers . . .
PRIEST: Songs of wood-fellers . . .
REAPER: Guide us on our passage through this sad world.
PRIEST: Song . . .
REAPER: And dance . . .   60
PRIEST: And the flute . . .
REAPER: And music of many instruments . . .
CHORUS:

These are the pastimes that each chooses to his taste.
Of floating bamboo-wood
Many are the famous flutes that have been made;   65
Little-Branch and Cicada-Cage,[6]
And as for the reaper's flute,
Its name is Green-leaf;
On the shore of Sumiyoshi

4. Like the literary exiles to Suma.   5. Because the flute was a courtly instrument.   6. The names of
two famous flutes in *the Tale of the Heike.* Little-Branch is the name of a flute of imperial provenance that
Atsumori carried until he died. Cicada-Cage belonged to the son of Retired Emperor Go-Shirakawa (Prince
Mochihito), whose revolt against the Heike precipitated the war between the Heike and the Genji.

2352 / Zeami Motokiyo

> The Korean flute[7] they play.   70
> And here on the shore of Suma
> On Stick[8] of the Salt-kilns
> The fishers blow their tune.

PRIEST: How strange it is! The other reapers have all gone home, but
you alone stay loitering here. How is that?   75
REAPER: How is it, you ask? I am seeking for a prayer in the voice of
the evening waves. Perhaps *you* will pray the Ten Prayers[9] for me?
PRIEST: I can easily pray the Ten Prayers for you, if you will tell me who
you are.
REAPER: To tell you the truth—I am one of the family of Lord Atsu-   80
mori.
PRIEST: One of Atsumori's family? How glad I am!
[*Then the* PRIEST *joined his hands (he kneels down) and
prayed:*—]

> Praise to Amida Buddha!
> "If I attain to Buddhahood,
> In the whole world and its ten spheres   85
> Of all that dwell here none shall call on my name
> And be rejected or cast aside."

CHORUS:[1]

> "Oh, reject me not!
> One cry suffices for salvation,
> Yet day and night   90
> Your prayers will rise for me.
> Happy am I, for though you know not my name,
> Yet for my soul's deliverance
> At dawn and dusk henceforward I know that you will pray."

So he spoke. Then vanished and was seen no more.   95
[*Here follows the Interlude between the two Acts, in which a reci-
tation concerning* ATSUMORI's *death takes place. These interludes
are subject to variation and are not considered part of the literary
text of the play.*]
PRIEST: Since this is so, I will perform all night the rites of prayer for the
dead, and calling upon Amida's name will pray again for the salvation of
Atsumori.
[*The ghost of* ATSUMORI *appears, dressed as a young warrior.*]
ATSUMORI:

> Would you know who I am
> That like the watchmen at Suma Pass   100
> Have wakened at the cry of sea-birds roaming
> Upon Awaji shore?
> Listen, Rensei. I am Atsumori.

---

7. Because Sumiyoshi was where Korean ships docked.   8. That is, wood for the salt maker's fires.
9. Repeat Amida Buddha's name ten times. By invoking the name of Amida (Amitābha in Sanskrit), the
buddha of infinite light, one could achieve rebirth in his paradise, known as the Pure Land.   1. Speaking
for the young reaper, or Atsumori.

PRIEST: How strange! All this while I have never stopped beating my gong and performing the rites of the Law. I cannot for a moment have dozed, yet I thought that Atsumori was standing before me. Surely it was a dream.

ATSUMORI: Why need it be a dream? It is to clear the karma of my waking life that I am come here in visible form before you.

PRIEST: It is not written that one prayer will wipe away ten thousand sins? Ceaselessly I have performed the ritual of the Holy Name that clears all sin away. After such prayers, what evil can be left? Though you should be sunk in sin as deep . . .

ATSUMORI:

> As the sea by a rocky shore,
> Yet should I be salved[2] by prayer.

PRIEST: And that my prayers should save you . . .
ATSUMORI:

> This too must spring
> From kindness of a former life.[3]

PRIEST: Once enemies . . .
ATSUMORI: But now . . .
PRIEST: In truth may we be named . . .
ATSUMORI: Friends in Buddha's Law.
CHORUS: There is a saying, "Put away from you a wicked friend; summon to your side a virtuous enemy." For you it was said, and you have proven it true.
And now come tell with us the tale of your confession, while the night is still dark.
CHORUS:

> He[4] bids the flowers of Spring
> Mount the tree-top that men may raise their eyes
> And walk on upward paths;
> He bids the moon in autumn waves be drowned
> In token that he visits laggard men
> And leads them out from valleys of despair.

ATSUMORI:

> Now the clan of Taira, building wall to wall,
> Spread over the earth like the leafy branches of a great tree.

CHORUS:

> Yet their prosperity lasted but for a day;
> It was like the flower of the convolvulus.
> There was none to tell them
> That glory flashes like sparks from flint-stone,
> And after,—darkness.
> Oh wretched, the life of men!

2. Saved.   3. Atsumori must have done Kumagai some kindness in a former incarnation to account for Kumagai's remorse.   4. Buddha.

ATSUMORI:

> When they were on high they afflicted the humble;
> When they were rich they were reckless in pride.
> And so for twenty years and more
> They ruled this land.   145
> But truly a generation passes like the space of a dream.
> The leaves of the autumn of Juyei[5]
> Were tossed by the four winds;
> Scattered, scattered (like leaves too) floated their ships.
> And they, asleep on the heaving sea, not even in dreams   150
> Went back to home.
> Caged birds longing for the clouds,—
> Wild geese were they rather, whose ranks are broken
> As they fly to southward on their doubtful journey.
> So days and months went by; Spring came again.   155
> And for a little while
> Here dwelt they on the shore of Suma
> At the first valley.[6]
> From the mountain behind us the winds blew down
> Till the fields grew wintry again.   160
> Our ships lay by the shore, where night and day
> The sea-gulls cried and salt waves washed on our sleeves.
> We slept with fishers in their huts
> On pillows of sand.
> We knew none but the people of Suma.   165
> And when among the pine-trees
> The evening smoke was rising,
> Brushwood, as they called it,[7]
> Brushwood we gathered
> And spread for carpet.   170
> Sorrowful we lived
> On the wild shore of Suma,
> Till the clan Taira and all its princes
> Were but villagers of Suma.

ATSUMORI:

> But on the night of the sixth day of the second month   175
> My father Tsunemori gathered us together.
> "To-morrow," he said, "we shall fight our last fight.
> To-night is all that is left us."
> We sang songs together, and danced.

PRIEST:

> Yes, I remember; we in our siege-camp
> Heard the sound of music
> Echoing from your tents that night;
> There was the music of a flute . . .

ATSUMORI: The bamboo-flute! I wore it when I died.

---

5. Or Juei, the year 1183, when the Taira (Heike) evacuated the capital.   6. Literal translation of Ichi-no-Tani.   7. The name of so humble a thing was unfamiliar to nobles like Atsumori.

PRIEST: We heard the singing . . .   185
ATSUMORI: Songs and ballads . . .
PRIEST: Many voices
ATSUMORI:

Singing to one measure.

[ATSUMORI: *dances.*]

First comes the Royal Boat.[8]
CHORUS:

The whole clan has put its boats to sea.
He[9] will not be left behind;
He runs to the shore.
But the Royal Boat and the soldiers' boats
Have sailed far away.

ATSUMORI:

What can he do?   195
He spurs his horse into the waves.
He is full of perplexity.
And then

CHORUS:

He looks behind him and sees
That Kumagai pursues him;   200
He cannot escape.
Then Atsumori turns his horse
Knee-deep in the lashing waves,
And draws his sword.
Twice, three times he strikes; then, still saddled,   205
In close fight they twine; roll headlong together
Among the surf of the shore.
So Atsumori fell and was slain, but now the Wheel of Fate
Has turned and brought him back.
[ATSUMORI *rises from the ground and advances towards the* PRIEST *with uplifted sword.*]
"There is my enemy," he cries, and would strike,   210
But the other is grown gentle
And calling on Buddha's name
Has obtained salvation for his foe;
So that they shall be re-born together
On one lotus-seat.[1]   215
"No, Rensei is not my enemy.
Pray for me again, oh pray for me again."

8. Bearing the child emperor Antoku, fleeing after the rout at Ichi-no-Tani.   9. Atsumori. This passage
is mimed throughout.   1. In Amida Buddha's paradise.

Haku Rakuten[1]

PERSONS

HAKU RAKUTEN (a Chinese poet)
An OLD FISHERMAN, Sumiyoshi no Kami, who in Act II becomes the god of
Japanese poetry
Another FISHERMAN
CHORUS of fishermen

Act I

HAKU: I am Haku Rakuten, a courtier of the Prince of China. There is
a land in the East called Nippon.[2] Now, at my master's bidding, I
am sent to that land to make proof of the wisdom of its people. I
must travel over the paths of the sea.

> I will row my boat towards the setting sun,   5
>   The setting sun;
> And seek the country that lies to the far side
> Over the wave-paths of the Eastern Sea.
>   Far my boat shall go,
>   My boat shall go,—   10
> With the light of the setting sun in the waves of its wake
> And a cloud like a banner shaking the void of the sky.
> Now the moon rises, and on the margin of the sea
>   A mountain I discern.
> I am come to the land of Nippon,   15
>   The land of Nippon.

So swiftly have I passed over the ways of the ocean that I am come
already to the shores of Nippon. I will cast anchor here a little while.
I would know what manner of land this may be.

THE TWO FISHERMEN: [*Together.*]

> Dawn over the Sea of Tsukushi,[3]   20
>   Place of the Unknown Fire.
> Only the moonlight—nothing else left!

THE OLD FISHERMAN:

> The great waters toss and toss;
> The grey waves soak the sky.

---

1. Translated by and with notes adapted from Arthur Waley.   2. Japan, which is written with two characters that mean "source of the sun." The fact that Haku Rakuten is a foreigner is conventionally emphasized by his use of *Nippon*, considered an archaic pronunciation. Note that the Japanese fishermen say
Nihon.   3. Ancient name for Kyūshū, one of the four main Japanese islands, lying to the southwest and
closest to China.

THE TWO FISHERMEN:

So was it when Han Rei[4] left the land of Etsu 25
And rowed in a little boat
Over the misty waves of the Five Lakes.

How pleasant the sea looks!
From the beach of Matsura[5]
Westward we watch the hill-less dawn. 30
A cloud, where the moon is setting,
Floats like a boat at sea,
    A boat at sea
That would anchor near us in the dawn.
Over the sea from the far side, 35
From China the journey of a ship's travel
Is a single night's sailing, they say.
And lo! the moon has vanished!

HAKU: I have borne with the billows of a thousand miles of sea and
come at last to the land of Nippon. Here is a little ship anchored 40
near me. An old fisherman is in it. Can this be indeed an inhabitant
of Nippon?

OLD FISHERMAN: Aye, so it is. I am an old fisher of Nihon. And your
Honour, I think, is Haku Rakuten of China.

HAKU: How strange! No sooner am I come to this land than they call 45
me by my name! How can this be?

SECOND FISHERMAN: Although your Honour is a man of China, your
name and fame have come before you.

HAKU: Even though my name be known, yet that you should know my
face is strange surely! 50

THE TWO FISHERMEN: It was said everywhere in the Land of Sunrise
that your Honour, Rakuten, would come to make trial of the wisdom
of Nihon. And when, as we gazed westwards, we saw a boat coming
in from the open sea, the hearts of us all thought in a twinkling,
"This is he." 55

CHORUS:

"He has come, he has come."
So we cried when the boat came in
To the shore of Matsura,
The shore of Matsura.
Sailing in from the sea 60
Openly before us—
A Chinese ship
And a man from China,—
How could we fail to know you,
    Haku Rakuten? 65

---

4. In Chinese, Fan Li. Having rendered important services to the state of Yüeh (*Etsu*) in ancient China,
Fan Li (Han Rei) went off with his mistress in a skiff, knowing that if he remained in public life his popularity
was bound to decline. The fishermen are groping toward the concept of a visitor from China and the
appearance of his boat. They are not yet consciously aware of the arrival of Po Chü-i (Haku Rakuten).
5. In Kyūshū, located on a bay off the Japan Sea; a likely mooring for boats arriving from Korea or China.

But your halting words tire us.
Listen as we will, we cannot understand
Your foreign talk.
Come, our fishing-time is precious.
Let us cast our hooks,   70
Let us cast our hooks!

HAKU: Stay! Answer me one question.[6] Bring your boat closer and tell
me, Fisherman, what is your pastime now in Nippon?
OLD FISHERMAN: And in the land of China, pray how do your Honours
disport themselves?   75
HAKU: In China we play at making poetry.
OLD FISHERMAN: And in Nihon, may it please you, we venture on the
sport of making "uta."[7]
HAKU: And what are "uta"?
OLD FISHERMAN: You in China make your poems and odes out of the   80
Scriptures of India; and we have made our "uta" out of the poems
and odes of China. Since then our poetry is a blend of three lands,
we have named it Yamato,[8] the great Blend, and all our songs
"Yamato Uta." But I think you question me only to mock an old man's
simplicity.   85
HAKU: No, truly; that was not my purpose. But come, I will sing a
Chinese poem about the scene before us.

"Green moss donned like a cloak
Lies on the shoulders of the rocks;
White clouds drawn like a belt   90
Surround the flanks of the mountains."

How does that song please you?
OLD FISHERMAN: It is indeed a pleasant verse. In our tongue we should
say the poem thus:

Koke-goromo   95
Kitaru iwao wa
Samonakute,
Kinu kinu yama no
Obi wo suru kana!

HAKU: How strange that a poor fisherman should put my verse into a   100
sweet native measure! Who can he be?
OLD FISHERMAN: A poor man and unknown. But as for the making of
"uta," it is not only men that make them. "For among things that
live there is none that has not the gift of song."[9]
HAKU: [*Taking up the other's words as if hypnotized.*][1] "Among things 105
that have life,—yes, and birds and insects—"
OLD FISHERMAN: They have sung Yamato songs.
HAKU: In the land of Yamato . . .

6. Throughout, Haku Rakuten omits the honorific turns of speech that civility demands. The fishermen,
being proper Japanese, speak in elaborately deferential language. Zeami wishes to portray the visitor as an
ill-bred foreigner.   7. The traditional thirty-one syllable poem.   8. An archaic name for Japan.   9. A
quotation from the preface to *The Kokinshū.*   1. The fact that Haku Rakuten continues the quotation
shows that he is under a sort of spell and makes it clear for the first time that his interlocutor is not an
ordinary mortal. From this point onward, the fisherman gradually becomes a god.

OLD FISHERMAN: . . . many such have been sung.
CHORUS:

> "The nightingale singing on the bush,   110
> Even the frog that dwells in the pond——"
> I know not if it be in your Honour's land,
> But in Nihon they sing the stanzas of the "uta."
> And so it comes that an old man
> Can sing the song you have heard,   115
> A song of great Yamato.

CHORUS: [*Changing the chant.*]

> And as for the nightingale and the poem it made,——
> They say that in the royal reign
> Of the Emperor Kōren
> In the land of Yamato, in the temple of High Heaven   120
> A priest was dwelling
> Each year at the season of Spring
> There came a nightingale[2]
> To the plum-tree at his window.
> And when he listened to its song   125
> He heard it singing a verse:
> > "*Sho-yō mei-chō rai
> > Fu-sō gem-bon sei.*"[3]
> And when he wrote down the characters,
> Behold, it was an "uta"-song   130
> Of thirty letters and one.
> And the words of the song—

OLD FISHERMAN:

> Of Spring's beginning
> At each dawn
> Though I come,   135

CHORUS:

> Unmet I return
> To my old nest.
> Thus first the nightingale,
> And many birds and beasts thereto,
> Sing "uta," like the songs of men.   140
> And instances are many;
> Many as the myriad pebbles that lie
> On the shore of the sea of Ariso.[4]
> "For among things that live
> There is none that has not the gift of song."   145

---

2. The priest's acolyte had died, and the nightingale was the boy's soul.   3. Each sound in the nightingale's song is represented in the original text with a Chinese character, and the meaning of the song, when rearranged in Japanese syntax, is as recited below by the Fisherman and Chorus.   4. A place name conventionally linked in Japanese poetry with the words *shore, beach, sand*, and so forth, probably because a pun on the *ari* element in Ariso suggested the verb "have," and thus "having many grains of sand." The wordplay occurred particularly in metaphors depicting love beyond reckoning, usually along the lines of "love as inexhaustible as the grains of sand on a beach."

Truly the fisherman has the ways of Yamato in his heart. Truly, this
custom is excellent.

OLD FISHERMAN: If we speak of the sports of Yamato and sing its songs,
we should show too what dances we use; for there are many kinds.

CHORUS: Yes, there are the dances; but there is no one to dance.   150

OLD FISHERMAN: Though there be no dancer, yet even I—

CHORUS:

> For drums—the beating of the waves.
> For flutes—the song of the sea-dragon.
> For dancer—this ancient man
> Despite his furrowed brow   155
> Standing on the furrowed sea
> Floating on the green waves
> Shall dance the Sea Green Dance.

OLD FISHERMAN: And the land of Reeds and Rushes . . .

CHORUS: The thousand years our land inviolate!   160

Act II[5]

OLD FISHERMAN: [*Transformed into Sumiyoshi no Kami,*[6] THE GOD *of
poetry.*]

> Sea that is green with the shadow of the hills in the water!
> Sea Green Dance, danced to the beating of the waves.
> [*He dances the Sea Green Dance.*[7]]

>> Out of the wave-lands,
>> Out of the fields of the Western Sea

CHORUS:

>> He rises before us,   5
>> The God of Sumiyoshi,
>> The God of Sumiyoshi!

THE GOD:

>> I rise before you
>> The god—

CHORUS:

> The God of Sumiyoshi whose strength is such   10
> That he will not let you subdue us, O Rakuten!
> So we bid you return to your home,
> Swiftly over the waves of the shore!

---

5. The remainder of the play is dance, the words a kind of poetic commentary.   6. The god of poetry,
or as the Chorus calls him, "the god of Sumiyoshi," the historical person Sugawara Michizane (845–903),
a leading political figure and court scholar of his day. He became embroiled in intrigue that led to his exile;
and after his death, when a series of misfortunes in the capital were interpreted as the work of his angry
spirit, he was deified as the god of scholarship, including poetry. Sumiyoshi is the name of a shrine in
Osaka with which the deified Michizane is traditionally associated.   7. Obscure. Recent commentaries
identify "Green Sea Music" (here, *Sea Green Dance*) as a piece in the repertory of *gagaku,* the traditional
music of the Japanese court, but it is without an accompanying dance.

First the God of Sumiyoshi came.
Now other gods[8] have come—   15
  Of Isé and Iwa-shimizu,
  Of Kamo and Kasuga,
  Of Ka-shima and Mi-shima,
  Of Suwa and Atsu-ta.[9]
And the goddess of the Beautiful Island,   20
The daughter of Shakāra[1]
King of the Dragons of the Sea—
Skimming the face of the waves
They have danced the Sea Green Dance.
And the King of the Eight Dragons[2]—   25
With his Symphony of Eight Musics.
As they hovered over the void of the sea,
Moved in the dance, the sleeves of their dancing-dress
Stirred up a wind, a magic wind
That blew on the Chinese boat   30
And filled its sails
And sent it back again to the land of Han.[3]
Truly, the God is wondrous;
The God is wondrous, and thou, our Prince,
Mayest thou rule for many, many years   35
  Our Land Inviolate!

8. They do not appear on stage.   9. These places are all associated with Shinto shrines and, therefore, with native deities.   1. One of the eight great dragon kings: Buddhist deities in dragon form who live in the sea; control wind, rain, and thunder; and protect the Buddhist faith. Although the following line names Shakāra king of the dragons, he is but one among eight.   2. *Hachidairyūō*, usually translated "eight great dragon kings," referring to all of them.   3. The Chinese dynasty (206 B.C.–A.D. 220), used as an archaism for China.

KANZE KOJIRŌ NOBUMITSU
1435–1516

Dōjōji[1]

PERSONS

The ABBOT of Dōjōji
Two PRIESTS of the Temple
Two Temple SERVANTS
A DANCER
The Serpent DEMON
CHORUS

[*As the opening flute is played the* ABBOT, *the two* PRIESTS, *and the* FIRST SERVANT *enter. The* PRIESTS *and the* SERVANT *kneel on the bridgeway, but the* ABBOT *continues on to the stage.*]

ABBOT: I am the abbot of Dōjōji, a temple in the Province of Kii. For many years no bell has hung in the belfry tower of the temple, and

1. Translated by and with notes adapted from Donald Keene.

for a good reason. I have decided lately to restore the ancient custom and at my order a new bell has been cast. In the calendar today is a day of good omen. I have ordered that the bell be raised into 5 the tower and that there be a service of dedication.

[*He calls towards the bridgeway.*]

Servant!

FIRST SERVANT: Here I am, sir.

ABBOT: Today is marked in the calendar as a lucky day, and I want you to hoist the bell into the belfry. 10

FIRST SERVANT: Yes, certainly, sir.

[*As the* SERVANT *stands the two* PRIESTS *enter the stage from the bridgeway and sit at the waki-position² behind the waki. The* SERVANT *leaves the bridgeway but returns shortly with another* SERVANT. *They carry between them on bamboo poles the prop, a huge bell. Two stage assistants help them.*]

FIRST SERVANT: *Ei tō, ei tō.*³

SECOND SERVANT: *Ei ya, ei ya.*

FIRST SERVANT: *Ei tō, ei tō.*

SECOND SERVANT: *Ei ya, ei ya.* 15

[*Groaning under the strain, they lower the bell halfway down the bridgeway.*]

FIRST SERVANT: Let's rest a while.

SECOND SERVANT: A good idea.

FIRST SERVANT: It's certainly a heavy bell.

SECOND SERVANT: Amazingly heavy.

FIRST SERVANT: Well, shall we lift it again? 20

SECOND SERVANT: All right.

[*They lift the bell again.*]

FIRST SERVANT: *Ei tō, ei tō.*

SECOND SERVANT: *Ei ya, ei ya.*

FIRST SERVANT: *Ei tō, ei tō.*

SECOND SERVANT: *Ei ya, ei ya.* 25

[*They reach the middle of the stage.*]

FIRST SERVANT: Let's put it down right here.

SECOND SERVANT: Right you are.

FIRST SERVANT: Everything under control?

SECOND SERVANT: Everything's going fine.

[*With appropriate cries they set the bell down.*]

FIRST SERVANT: Now for hoisting it into the belfry. 30

SECOND SERVANT: Right you are.

[*The two* SERVANTS, *helped by the stage assistants, use poles to thread the rope of the prop through the ring set in the ceiling. Then, with rhythmic shouts they hoist the prop to the appropriate height.*]

FIRST SERVANT: It looks more impressive than ever, now that we've hoisted it up there.

SECOND SERVANT: That's right. It's certainly an impressive sight.

FIRST SERVANT: Let's waste no time in telling the Abbot about this. 35

---

2. Front, stage left, near the chorus.   3. The servants shout rhythmic but meaningless sounds to encourage each other as they carry the big bell.

[*The* FIRST SERVANT *goes before the gazing-pillar*[4] *and addresses the* ABBOT.]

FIRST SERVANT: Excuse me, sir. We've raised the bell into the belfry.

ABBOT: You've raised it, you say?

FIRST SERVANT: Yes, that's just what I said, sir.

ABBOT: Then we will hold the dedication service today. For certain reasons best known to me, women are not to be admitted to the 45 courtyard where the ceremonies are held. Make sure that everyone understands this.

FIRST SERVANT: Your orders shall be obeyed.

[*He goes to the naming-place*[5] *where he addresses people offstage.*] Listen, you people! The new bell of the Dōjōji is to be dedicated today. All who wish to attend the ceremony are welcome. However, 50 for reasons known only to himself, the Abbot has ordered that women are not to be allowed inside the courtyard where the service will take place. Take care you all obey his orders!

[*He goes to kneel before the flute player. The* DANCER *enters. She wears the fukai mask,*[6] *a long wig, a brocade outer robe, an inner kimono with a fish-scale pattern, and a crested garment tied around her waist. She stands at the shite-position*[7] *and faces the area before the musicians.*]

DANCER:

> My sin, my guilt, will melt away,
> My sin, my guilt, will melt away, 55
> I will go to the service for the bell.

[*She faces forward.*]
I am a dancer who lives in a remote village of this Province of Kii. I have heard that a bell is to be dedicated at the Dōjōji, and so I am hurrying there now, in the hopes of improving my chances of salvation. 60

> The moon will soon be sinking;
> As I pass the groves of little pines
> The rising tide weaves veils of mist around them.
> But look—can it be my heart's impatience?—

[*She takes a few steps to the right, then returns to her original position. This indicates she has reached the temple.*]

> Dusk has not yet fallen, the sun's still high, 65
> But I have already arrived:
> I am here at the Temple of Dōjōji.

[*She faces forward.*]
My journey has been swift, and now I have reached the temple. I shall go at once to watch the ceremony.

[*She moves towards the center of the stage. The* FIRST SERVANT *rises.*]

FIRST SERVANT: Stop! You can't go into the courtyard. Women aren't 70 allowed.

---

4. Front, stage right.　5. Rear, stage right, near the bridge, or runway.　6. Worn to portray a woman who has begun to age.　7. Same as the naming-place.

DANCER: But I'm not like other women. I'm only a dancer. I live nearby and I am to perform a dance at the dedication of the bell. Please let me see the ceremony.

FIRST SERVANT: [*To himself.*] A dancer? That's right, I suppose she   75
doesn't count as an ordinary woman. [*To the* DANCER.] Very well, I'll let you into the courtyard on my own, but in return you must dance for me. [*He goes before flute player, picks up a tall court cap lying on the stage, and brings it to the* DANCER.] Here, take this hat.[8] It just happened to be around. Put it on and let's see you dance.   80

DANCER: With pleasure. I'll dance for you as best I can.

[*She retires to stage assistant's position[9] to alter her costume. The* SERVANT *returns to his original place and sits. The* DANCER *puts on the hat and goes to the first pine on the bridgeway. She looks beyond the pillar at the bell, then glides onto the stage to the suddenly stepped-up tempo of large drum. She stops just past the shite-pillar.[1]*]

DANCER: How happy you have made me! I will dance for you. [*She describes her actions.*] Borrowing for a moment a courtier's hat, she puts it on her head.   85

> Her feet already stamp the rhythm.
> Apart from cherry blossoms,
> There are only the pines,
> Apart from cherry blossoms,
> There are only the pines.   90
> When the darkness starts to fall
> The temple bell will resound.

[*She lifts the hem of her robe a little with her left hand, and dances the following passage as if she were climbing step by step up to the bell. This is the famous rambyōshi dance, accompanied by the weird cries and pounding of the kotsuzumi drum.[2]*]

> Prince Michinari, at the imperial command,
> First raised these sacred walls.
> And because the temple was his work,   95
> Tachibana no Michinari,
> They called it Dōjōji.[3]

[*The rhythm of the dance grows more rapid and intense.*]

CHORUS: [*For the* DANCER.]

> To a temple in the mountains
> Now, on this evening in spring,
> I have come, I have seen   100
> The blossoms scattered with the evening bell,
> The blossoms scatter, the blossoms fall.

---

8. It was customary for professional women dancers to wear a tall ceremonial court cap when they performed.   9. Extreme rear corner, stage right.   1. At the corner where the bridge joins the rear stage. In front of the bridge are three potted young pine trees spaced at intervals along a pebble moat. The first pine, where she stands, is toward the end of the bridge nearest the stage.   2. A small hand drum. *Rambyōshi dance:* characterized by slight movements of the feet made in time to single drumbeats at long intervals.   3. The temple of Michinari; the name *Michinari* is pronounced in Sino-Japanese as Dōjō.

DANCER:

> And all the while,
> And all the while,
> At temples everywhere across the land   105
> The sinking moon strikes the bell.
> The birds sing, and frost and snow fill the sky;
> Soon the swelling tide will recede.
> The peaceful fishers will show their lights
> In villages along the river banks—   110
> And if the watchers sleep when danger threatens
> I'll not let my chances pass me by!

[*The* SERVANTS *have become hypnotized by the rhythm of the dance.
The* DANCER *looks at the* ABBOT *and the* PRIESTS. *The* CHORUS
describes her actions.]

CHORUS:

> Up to the bell she stealthily creeps
> Pretending to go on with her dance.

[*She holds her fan and looks at the bell.*]

> She starts to strike it!   115

[*She swings the fan back and forth like a bell-hammer.*]

> This loathsome bell, now I remember it!

[*She unfastens the cords of her hat, then strikes the hat from her
hand with a blow of her fan. She stands under the bell.*]

> Placing her hand on the dragon-head boss,[4]
> She seems to fly upward into the bell.
> She wraps the bell around her,
> She has disappeared.   120

[*At the words, "Placing her hand," the* DANCER *rests her hand on the
edge of the bell, then leaps up into it. At the same moment the stage
assistant loosens the rope and drops the bell over her. The* SERVANTS,
*who have been drowsing, hypnotized by the dance, wake up, startled
by the noise of the bell falling. The* FIRST SERVANT *tumbles in confusion on the stage; the* SECOND SERVANT *falls on the bridgeway.*]

BOTH SERVANTS: [*Variously.*] Ho! Hi! What was that frightful noise?
That awful crashing racket? I'm so frightened I don't know what I'm
doing!

FIRST SERVANT: That certainly was a terrible crash. I wonder where the
other fellow went. [*He sees the* SECOND SERVANT.] Hey there,   125
are you all right?

SECOND SERVANT: How about you?

FIRST SERVANT: I still don't know yet.

SECOND SERVANT: No wonder. We got so carried away by her dance
we dozed off. Then came that awful bang. What do you think that   130
was?

FIRST SERVANT: Do you suppose it was thunder? If it was thunder, there
should have been some sort of warning—a little clap or two before
the big one. Strange, very strange.

---

4. A metal ornament on the bell, in the shape of a dragon's head.

SECOND SERVANT: Yes, you're right. Whatever it was, the earth shook   135
something terrible.

FIRST SERVANT: I don't think it was an earthquake. Look—come over
here. [*He discovers the bell and claps his hands in recognition.*] Here's
what made the noise.

SECOND SERVANT: You're right!   140

FIRST SERVANT: I hung it up very carefully, but the loop must've
snapped. How else could it fall?

SECOND SERVANT: No. Look. The loop's all right. Nothing's broken. It's
certainly a mystery. [*He touches the bell.*] Oww! This bell is scorching
hot!   145

FIRST SERVANT: Why should falling make it hot? [*He too touches the
bell.*] Oww! Boiling hot!

SECOND SERVANT: It's a problem, all right. What do you suppose it can
mean? It's beyond me. Well, we'd better report what's happened. We
can't leave things this way.   150

FIRST SERVANT: That's a good idea. Too bad if the Abbot heard about
it from anyone but us! We've got to do something. But I don't think
I should be the one to tell. You tell him.

SECOND SERVANT: Telling him is no problem, but it would look peculiar
if I went. You tell him—you were left in charge.   155

FIRST SERVANT: That's what makes it so hard! You tell him, please.
      [*He pushes the* SECOND SERVANT *forward.*]

SECOND SERVANT: No, it's not my business to tell him. *You* tell him.
Hurry!
      [*He pushes the* FIRST SERVANT.]

FIRST SERVANT: Please, I beg of you, as a favor. You tell him.

SECOND SERVANT: Why should I? You tell him. I don't know anything   160
about it.
      [*The* SECOND SERVANT *leaves. The* FIRST SERVANT *watches him go.*]

FIRST SERVANT: He's gone! Now I have no choice. I'll have to tell the
Abbot, and it's going to get me into trouble. Well, I'll get it over with.
[*He goes up to the* ABBOT.] It fell down.

ABBOT: What fell down?   165

FIRST SERVANT: The bell. It fell from the belfry.

ABBOT: What? Our bell? From the belfry?

FIRST SERVANT: Yes, Master.

ABBOT: What caused it?

FIRST SERVANT: I fastened it very carefully, but all the same it fell   170
down. Ah! That reminds me. There was a dancer here a little while
ago. She said she lives nearby, and asked me to let her into the
courtyard to see the dedication of the bell. Of course I told her that
it wasn't allowed, but she said she wasn't an ordinary woman, and
that she was going to offer a dance. So I let her in. I wonder if she   175
had something to do with this?

ABBOT: You idiot! What a stupid thing to do! I knew this would happen.
That's why I forbade you strictly to allow any women in here! You
blundering fool!

FIRST SERVANT: Ahhhh. [*He bows to the ground.*]   180

ABBOT: I suppose I must go now and take a look.

FIRST SERVANT: Yes, Master. Please hurry. Help! Help!
[*He exits, still crying for help.*]
ABBOT [*To the* PRIESTS.] Priests, come with me. [*They stand and go to the bell.*] Do you know why I gave the order that no woman was to be permitted to enter the temple during the dedication of the 185 bell?
PRIESTS: No, Master. We have no idea.
ABBOT: Then I will tell you.
PRIESTS: Yes, please tell us the whole story.
ABBOT: Many years ago there lived in this region a man who was the 190 steward of the manor of Manago,[5] and he had an only daughter. In those days too there was a certain *yamabushi*[6] priest who came here every year from the northern provinces on his way to worship at the shrine of Kumano,[7] and he would always stay with this same steward. The priest never forgot to bring charming little presents for the 195 steward's daughter, and the steward, who doted on the girl, as a joke once told her, "Some day that priest will be your husband, and you will be his wife!" In her childish innocence the girl thought he was speaking the truth, and for months and years she waited.

Time passed and once again the priest came to the landlord's 200 house. Late one night, after everyone else was asleep, the girl went to his bedroom and chided him: "Do you intend to leave me here forever? Claim me soon as your wife."

Amazed to hear these words, the priest turned the girl away with a joking answer. That night he crept out into the darkness and 205 came to this temple, imploring us to hide him. But having nowhere else we could hide him, we lowered the bell and hid him inside. Soon the girl followed, swearing she would never let him go. At that time the River Hitaka was swollen to a furious flood and the girl could not cross over. She ran up and down the bank, wild with rage, 210 until at last her jealous fury turned her into a venomous snake, and she easily swam across the river.

The serpent glided here, to the Temple of Dōjōji, and searched here and there until her suspicions were aroused by the lowered bell. Taking the metal loop between her teeth, she coiled herself 215 around the bell in seven coils. Then, breathing smoke and flames, she lashed the bell with her tail. At once the bronze grew hot, boiling hot, and the monk, hidden inside, was roasted alive. [*To the* PRIESTS.] Isn't that a horrible story?
PRIEST: Unspeakable! The worst I have ever heard! 220
ABBOT: I have felt her jealous ghost about here, and I feared she might bring some harm to our new bell. All of our austerities and penances have been for strength in this moment. Pray with all your hearts. Let us try to raise the bell again.
PRIESTS: We will, Master. 225

---

5. Name of the owner of the manor.   6. Mountain ascetic who practiced austerities to attain holy or magical powers.   7. A complex of three Shinto shrines whose local divinities were identified as manifestations of Buddhist deities; they were venerated for prolonging life and assisting rebirth in paradise. The Kumano district, in Kii Province (now Wakayama Prefecture) south of both Kyoto and Nara, is a mountainous area overlooking the sea, long believed the dwelling place of native gods. Kumano was thus a popular site of pilgrimage and the center of the mountain asceticism practiced by the *yamabushi*.

[*The* ABBOT *and the* PRIESTS *stand on either side of the bell, facing it.*]

ABBOT:

Though the waters of Hitaka River seethe and dry up,
Though the sands of its shores run out,
Can the sacred strength of our holy order fail?
[*They pray, their rosaries clasped in their hands.*]

PRIESTS: [*Describing their actions.*] All raise their voices together.

ABBOT: To the East, the Guardian King, Conqueror of the Three   230
Realms;

PRIESTS: To the South, the Guardian King, Conqueror of the Demons;

ABBOT: To the West, the Guardian King, Conqueror of Evil Serpents
and Dragons;   235

PRIESTS: To the North, the Guardian King, Conqueror of Frightful
Monsters;

ABBOT: And you in the Center, Messenger of the Sun, All Holy Immovable One,[8]

TOGETHER:

Will you make the bell move?   240
Show us the power of your avenging noose!
Namaku Samanda Basarada
Senda Makaroshana Sowataya
Un Tarata Kamman
"I dedicate myself to the universal diamond,   245
May this raging fury be destroyed!"[9]
"He who hearkens to My Law shall gain enlightenment,
He who knows My Heart will be a Buddha in this flesh."[1]
Now that we have prayed
For the serpent's salvation,   250
What rancor could it bear us?
As the moon at daybreak

ABBOT: Strikes the hanging bell—

CHORUS:

Look! Look! It moves!
Pray with all your hearts!   255
Pray to raise the bell!

[*They rub their rosaries frantically. The stage assistant lifts the bell a little and the* DEMON *shakes it from within.*]

Here the Priests, joining hands,
Invoke the sacred spell of the Thousand-Handed-One,
The Song of Salvation of the Guardian King,
The Immovable One, the Flaming One.[2]   260
Black smoke rises from their frantic prayers.
And as they pray,
And as they pray,

---

8. These lines are a prayer favored by *yamabushi* priests for invoking the five fierce deities who serve as the guardian kings, messengers of the Buddha's wrath against evil spirits.   9. This mantra is dedicated to Fudō, one of the five guardian kings.   1. Part of the vow of Fudō.   2. All are Buddhist deities.

Though no one strikes the bell, it sounds!
[The DEMON *inside the bell strikes cymbals.*]

Though no one tugs the rope, the bell begins to dance!   265
[*The stage assistant pulls the bell up farther, and the* DEMON *shakes it.*]

Soon it rises to the belfry tower,
Look! A serpent form emerges!
[*The stage assistant lifts the bell completely. The* DANCER, *now transformed into a* DEMON, *wears the hannya mask.*[3] *She has removed her outer brocade robe. When she is clear of the bell she takes up her mallet, then picks up her outer robe in both hands and wraps it around her waist. She stands and tries to drive the* ABBOT *away. The* ABBOT *and* PRIESTS *pray, trying to subdue her. The* DEMON *is driven onto the bridgeway where she drops her outer robe. Then she is forced back as far as the curtain,*[4] *only to turn on the* ABBOT *again, this time compelling him to withdraw. She stands with her back to the shite-pillar,*[5] *throws one arm around it, pauses, and then invades the stage again. She tries to pull the bell down, but the* ABBOT *forces her to the ground with the power of his rosary. The* DEMON *rises again, and during the following passage sung by the* CHORUS, *she and the* ABBOT *struggle.*]

CHORUS:

Humbly we ask the help of the Green-bodied,
The Green Dragon of the East;
Humbly we ask the help of the White-bodied,   270
The White Dragon of the West;
Humbly we ask the help of the Yellow-bodied,
The Yellow Dragon of the Center,
All ye countless Dragon Kings of the three thousand worlds:
Have mercy, hear our prayers![6]   275
If now you show your mercy, your benevolence,
What refuge can the serpent find?
And as we pray,
Defeated by our prayers,
Behold the serpent fall!   280
[*She staggers back under the pressure of the* ABBOT'S *prayers and drops to the ground.*]

Again she springs to her feet,
The breath she vomits at the bell
Has turned to raging flames.
[*She rises and rushes to the bridgeway.*]

Her body burns in her own fire.
She leaps into the river pool,   285
[*She rushes through the curtain.*]

---

3. A female demon mask, which is horned and contorted to suggest a jealous rage.   4. Leading from the bridge into the dressing room, known as the mirror room.   5. The demon has made its way back down the bridge and onto the stage.   6. This is an invocation of the five dragon kings, who in folk belief were each a different color and held sway over a different direction—north, south, east, west, and center. Here, north and south have been omitted.

Into the waves of the River Hitaka,
And there she vanishes.
The Priests, their prayers granted,
Return to the temple,
Return to the temple.   290
[*The* ABBOT *gives a final stamp of the foot near the shite-pillar.*]

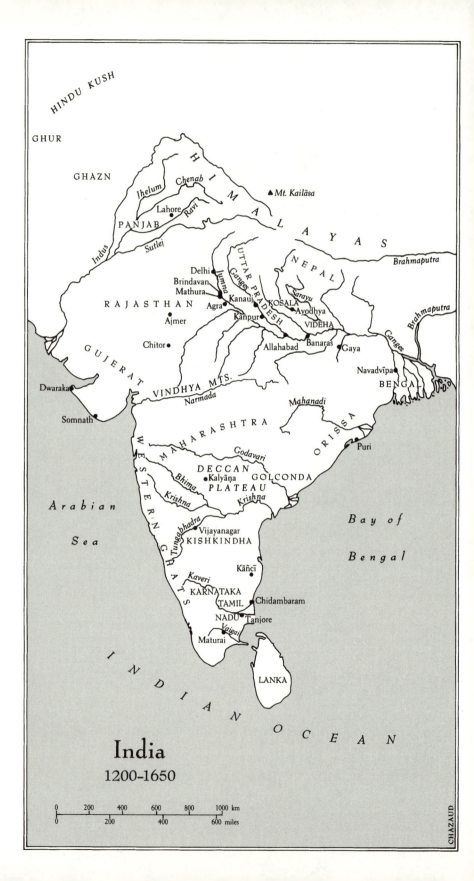

India

1200–1650

Mystical Poetry of India

The eleventh through the eighteenth centuries in India saw the rise of regional kingdoms with distinct identities based on growing differences in language and culture.
While the hegemony of the Tamil kings continued in the south, a succession of Hindu
and Muslim dynasties, the latter mostly of Turkish and Afghan origin, ruled over
various parts of north India. Sizable Hindu and Muslim kingdoms flourished in central India as well. It was during this period that the rapidly evolving regional languages,
including both the Sanskrit-related tongues and the Dravidian languages related to
Tamil in the south, developed their own literary traditions. While these literatures
are as diverse as the languages and subcultures they represent, the quintessential
genre of the medieval era is the lyric poetry of Hindu movements devoted to *bhakti*,
the religion of mystical devotion to God.

The earliest *bhakti* poems preceded the medieval era. These are the Tamil hymns
of the Vaiṣṇava and Śaiva poets (sixth–ninth centuries) who led movements of mystical devotion in the Tamil region, focusing on Śiva and Viṣṇu, the chief Hindu gods.
In the nine hundred years that followed, each of the more than sixteen other major
languages of India acquired a substantial body of *bhakti* poems, devotional songs
associated with regional cults of the worship of Śiva, Viṣṇu in his incarnations as
Krishna and Rāma, the Goddess, and other Hindu deities. The authors of the *bhakti*
lyrics are celebrated as saints, exemplary religious figures, and their poems, preserved
as sacred literature in oral as well as written traditions, are familiar to people from
all walks of life. If the classical period was dominated by masterpieces in the traditional genres in Sanskrit and early Tamil literature, the medieval age in Indian literature is the age of the *bhakti* poet-saints and their lyrics.

While it is not possible to describe here the diverse and complex factors that contributed to the rise of mysticism as a religious ideology in Hinduism, we should note
that *bhakti* religion and literature are essentially popular and populist in character.
Already in the first century, in an attempt to meet the challenge presented by Buddhism and Jainism, rival religions of Hinduism with a more egalitarian cast, the author
of the *Bhagavad Gītā* (p. 1010) had validated the dignity of all the castes and classes
in Hindu society as well as the personal worship of God regardless of social status.
Nevertheless, the *Gītā* is a philosophical text, one written in Sanskrit, the classical
language, by and for the elite classes. Medieval *bhakti* poems, on the other hand, are
lyrics in the spoken mother-tongue, authored by poet-saints who came from low as
well as high castes and classes, and who included women and "untouchables" (persons born into castes that were considered ritually impure). The *Gītā*'s author extols
bhakti as an attitude of devotion, but the medieval poems are genuine expressions of
the mystical love of God by a diverse group of people who practiced this form of
religion in a popular context. Moreover, practitioners of *bhakti* religion believe that
this form of mysticism is the highest path to release (*mokṣa*) from *karma*, and that
their God alone can release them from the chain of birth and death.

Every *bhakti* poem illuminates some aspect of the devotee's love for God. In some
poems, the poet directly addresses God; in others, she or he describes to an implied
audience her/his feelings toward God and the world. Many poems express a wide
range of emotions, from joy and peace to pain and despair. *Bhakti* poems usually end
with a line or verse in which the poet names herself or himself, or uses an expression

or epithet as her or his "signature." Every aspect of *bhakti* poetry bears the stamp of personal feeling and of individual experience. Not surprisingly, the poems of the medieval saints are read as spiritual autobiography.

In *bhakti* mysticism, the metaphors for the saints' relationship with God are drawn from the entire range of human relationships, with the devotee and God playing the roles of son and father or mother, servant and master, friends, lovers, wife and husband. Of the various models for the love of God, none has so captured the imagination of the *bhakti* poets than that of the erotic love between a man and woman. In many *bhakti* poems, the devotee or the human soul is a woman who longs for her lover, and the conventions of classical love poetry are used to portray this mystical love.

Despite the emphasis of *bhakti* religion on the mystical, interior aspects of religious experience, public and social dimensions are integral to *bhakti* poetry. *Bhakti* mystics view themselves as members of a community of devotees, often addressing their songs to their fellow devotees. Not only do women and low-caste poets rank high in the list of *bhakti* saints, but the oppressed and the lowly become models for the highest kind of devotion. Not all *bhakti* poets advocate real social change, but many speak of having defied societal norms in order to practice their religion, while others use metaphors of social transgression to describe the nature of their relationship with God, and all hold out visions of an ideal community of devotees who are equal in the eyes of God. To the audience of these mystical poems, the poet-saints are symbols of social liberation as well as of spiritual perfection. Thus, *bhakti* poems have traditionally served the Hindu masses as instruments with which to question and challenge the very premises of social hierarchy in Hinduism.

Some longer poems, such as the *Rāmcaritmānas*, Tulsīdās's popular Hindi version of the *Rāmāyaṇa* epic, are included in the *bhakti* canon. However, the short lyric is characteristic. Although *bhakti* poems have been preserved in manuscript by the various sects and have attained the status of beloved sacred texts, it is as popular songs that they have gained currency among the common people. All over India, *bhakti* songs are sung by communities of worshipers (*bhakta*) in congregational sessions called *bhajan* or *kīrtan*. *Bhakti* poets use colloquial language and imagery, folksong meters, refrains, and other elements of oral composition in their poems. Some, like Kabīr the weaver, came from humble backgrounds; others, however, were learned men and women who adopted the idiom of simplicity, partly in order to make their songs accessible to the community of devotees, partly because *bhakti* religion idealizes simplicity and humility.

Direct, brief, and passionate, *bhakti* poems have a powerful appeal for Indian audiences of diverse backgrounds. Modern poets of the West such as Robert Bly (who translated Kabīr) and Adrienne Rich (who translated the Bengali Vaiṣṇava poets) have found them equally attractive and accessible. In the final analysis, *bhakti* poems speak to the heart. It is the deep emotion animating works as varied as Appar's ecstatic description of the mystical dance of Śiva, Kabīr's poems of social critique, and Mīrābī's love songs to Krishna that explains their popularity. These mystical poems are powerful because they represent an all-consuming love that crosses the boundaries of the secular and the sacred, a love in which, in Mahādēviyakka's words:

> if you hug
> a body, bones
> must crunch and crumble;
>
> weld,
> the welding must vanish.

Excellent introductions to *bhakti* religion as well as translations of a range of *bhakti* poems in their north and south Indian variants are available in A. K. Ramanujan's *Speaking of Śiva* (1973) and *Hymns for the Drowning* (1981), Indira Viswanathan Peterson's *Poems to Śiva: The Hymns of the Tamil Saints* (1989), and John Stratton

Hawley and Mark Juergensmeyer's *Songs of the Saints of India* (1988). On women poets in *bhakti* literature, see Susie Tharu and K. Lalitha, eds., *Women Writing in India*, vol. 1 (1991), and Margaret Macnicol, *Poems by Indian Women* (1923).

PRONOUNCING GLOSSARY

The following list uses common English syllables and stress accents to provide rough equivalents of selected words whose pronunciation may be unfamiliar to the general reader.

Bhagavad Gītā: *buh'-guh-vuhd geeh'tah*

bhajan: *buh'-juhn*

bhakta: *bhuhk'-tuh*

bhakti: *bhuhk'-tee*

dharma: *dhuhr'-muh*

Kabīr: *kuh'-beer*

karma: *kuhr'-muh*

kīrtan: *keehr'-tuhn*

Krishna: *kreesh'-nuh*

Mahādēviyakka: *muh-hah-day'-vee-*
    yuhk-kuh

Mīrābāī: *meeh'-rah-bah'-yee*

mokṣa: *mohk'-shuh*

Rādhā: *rahd'-hah*

Rāmāyaṇa: *rah-mah'-yuh-nuh*

Rāmcaritmānas:
    rahm'-chuh-reet-mah'-nuhs

Śaiva: *shai'-vuh*

Śiva: *shee'-vuh*

Tulsīdās: *tool'-seeh-dahs'*

Vaiṣṇava: *vaish'-nuh-vuh*

Vīraśaiva: *veeh-ruh-shai'-vuh*

Viṣṇu: *veesh'-noo*

TIME LINE

TEXTS	CONTEXTS
6th–8th centuries Poet-leaders of the south Indian devotional (*bhakti*) movements dedicated to Śiva compose Tamil hymns to him, later collated/compiled as in the *Tēvāram*	
1100–1200 Basavaṇṇa and Mahādēviyakka, leaders of the Vīra-śaiva Hindu religious movement, write poems (*vacanas*) of social criticism and devotion to God in Kannada, a major spoken language of south India	
ca. 1275 Amir Khusrau, a Muslim Sufi (mystic) poet from Deccan in central India, writes poetry in Urdu	
	1288 Venetian traveler Marco Polo visits India
14th–16th centuries Vidyāpati and other poets of the Vaiṣṇava religious sect of Bengal write *bhakti* (devotional) lyric poems in Bengali on the love of the god Krishna and the herdswoman Rādhā	**ca. 1336** Vijayanagar, last major Hindu kingdom in India, is founded in central India
	1350 Thai kingdom of Ayuthia, named after Ayodhya, the capital of the Hindu epic hero Rāma, is established
	1398 Central Asian conqueror Timur (Tamerlane) sacks Delhi
1399 Krittivāsa's version of the ancient Hindu epic *The Rāmāyaṇa* in the Bengali language	
ca. 1400–1448 Mystic poet Kabīr writes poems of social criticism and spiritual quest in Hindi, the major spoken language of north India	**1400** Paper is introduced from Persia
	1498 Portuguese explorer Vasco da Gama arrives in India, signaling the beginning of the European commercial and colonial presence there

Boldface titles indicate works in the anthology.

TIME LINE

TEXTS	CONTEXTS
16th century One of India's most popular poets, Rajput woman saint-mystic Mīrābāī, writes lyric songs of love for the Hindu god Krishna	**ca. 1500** Guru Nanak founds Sikhism, a monotheistic religion synthesizing elements of Hinduism and Islam, in north India
	ca. 1500–1533 Mystical teacher Chaitanya of Bengal spreads the cult of devotion to the Hindu God Krishna in north India
	1510 The Portuguese establish a colony at Goa in western India
	ca. 1526 Central Asian Muslim invader Babar seizes power in Delhi and establishes the Mogul empire in north India
	1542 Jesuit Francis Xavier reaches India
	1556–1605 Jalâluddin Akbar, preeminent Mogul emperor, patronizes miniature painting and translations of texts from Indian languages to Persian, and proclaims Din-e-Ilahi a new universal religion
late 16th century The scriptures of the Sikh religion are compiled in the *Adi Granth*	**1565** The fall of the Hindu kingdom of Vijayanagar
1574 Tulsīdās begins *Rāmcaritmānas* (Sacred Lake of the Deeds of Ram), India's most popular version of *The Rāmāyaṇa*, in a dialect of Hindi	
1580–1588 The Mogul emperor Akbar commissions illustrated Persian translations of the Sanskrit epics *The Rāmāyaṇa* and *The Mahābhārata* and the Sanskrit animal fable collection *Pañcatantra* • Akbar's court poet Abu'l Fazl writes the Persian *Akbar-Nāmā* (The Chronicle of Akbar)	
	1600 Queen Elizabeth grants the British East India Company a charter for trade in India

HYMNS OF THE TAMIL ŚAIVA SAINTS

The 796 Tamil hymns of the Śaiva ("devotee of Śiva") poets Campantar, Appar, and Cuntarar, collected in the anthology known as the *Tēvāram* (Collection of Hymns for Worship), are the earliest *bhakti* poems. The poets, who are canonized saints (Nāyanār) of Tamil Śaivism, are said to have sung these hymns, which were composed in traditional musical modes and with a variety of meters, at more than 260 Tamil temples dedicated to the Hindu god Śiva during the reign of the Pallava Dynasty. Revered as sacred texts, the hymns continue to be sung in private worship and by professional singers (*ōtuvār*) in temple ritual. Written in a Tamil that is highly alliterative and rich in metaphors and imagery, the poems are easily accessible to the modern reader. Each poem consists of ten or eleven verses.

Early Tamil *bhakti* religion was centered on the worship of icons of Śiva (and other gods) in temples and home shrines, a practice that continues in Hinduism today. In their songs, the *bhakti* poets ecstatically visualize and adore Śiva in his many iconic forms, and celebrate the beauty of these forms. Drawing upon the older Tamil tradition of landscape and love poetry (p. 1029), they sing about the physical landscapes of the sacred places in which Śiva dwells. They praise Śiva's glorious deeds as they are narrated in a large number of myths. Above all, they speak of these things in personal, intimate, and emotional terms. Thus, the Tamil saints address Śiva as their Lord and Master, but also as their beloved friend. To them, Śiva is at once awesome and distant, and immediately and concretely present in his icons—a divinity of cosmic stature, but a God who is graciously loving toward his devotees. Appar addresses Śiva as his "Lord sweet as honey" and speaks of "the sweet golden foot" that Śiva raises as he dances his cosmic dance.

An enigmatic god, Śiva combines diverse characteristics in his persona. As Lord of the Animals, he rides on a bull and lives with his consort, the goddess Pārvatī, in the Himalaya mountains. He is also an ascetic, a great *yogi* with matted locks, who dances in the cremation ground with goblins, holding fire in his hand. In his cosmic function as the "Destroyer" god of the Hindu triad, he dances a supreme dance in a ring of fire, orchestrating the destruction of space, time, and all matter at the end of each *yuga* time span (p. 885). This dance, however, is ultimately a dance of creation, and it is Śiva who presides over the new creation that rises out of the ashes of the old universe. In their best-loved poems, the Tamil Śaiva saints eloquently describe their mystical vision of the cosmic dance of Śiva as Naṭarāja (Lord of the Dance), a dance that is associated with the great temple of Chidambaram and celebrated in the beautiful bronze icons of the Cōla period (eleventh–thirteenth centuries).

In *Poems to Śiva: The Hymns of Tamil Saints* (1989), Indira Viswanathan Peterson offers a comprehensive introduction to the *bhakti* religion of the Tamil Śaiva saints, an anthology of translations of the songs of the three major saints, and a history of the performance of these hymns in south Indian temples. David Dean Shulman has translated Cuntarar's 100 songs in *Songs of the Harsh Devotee: The Tēvāram of Cuntaramūrttināyanār* (1990). On the dance of Śiva, see Ananda K. Coomaraswamy, "The Dance of Shiva," in *The Dance of Shiva: Fourteen Indian Essays* (1975), and Paul Younger, *The Home of the Dancing Śivan: The Traditions of the Hindu Temple in Citamparam* (1995).

PRONOUNCING GLOSSARY

The following list uses common English syllables and stress accents to provide rough equivalents of selected words whose pronunciation may be unfamiliar to the general reader.

Ampalam: *uhm'-puh-luhm*

Appar: *uhp'-puhr*

Campantar: *suhn-buhn'-duhr*

Cōla: *choh'-luh*

Chidambaram: *chee-duhm'-buh-ruhm*

Cuntarar: *soohn'-duh-ruhr*

Kaveri: *kah-veh'-ree*	Śaiva: *shai'-vuh*
Nāyaṉār: *nah'-yuh-nahr*	Śiva: *shee'-vuh*
ōtuvār: *oh'-doo-vahr*	Tēvāram: *tay-vah'-ruhm*
Pallava: *puhl'-luh'vuh*	Tillai: *teehl'-lai*
Pārvatī: *pahr'-vuh-tee*	yogi: *yoh'-gee*

CAMPANTAR

sixth–seventh centuries

18[1]

I.16.6, Puḷamaṅkai[2]

He is the king,
a shower of rain for the world.
Pure gold, first being,
living in grove-encircled Puḷamaṅkai
he is my own; he is music, he is   5
like the light of the morning sun.
Ālanturai[3] is the shrine where he abides.

1. Translated by Indira Viswanathan Peterson. In this section, the first number of a work refers to the poem's position in the translation sequence.   2. In this section, these numbers provide the poem's volume number, poem number, and verse number in the *Tēvāram*; the final notation is the name of the sacred place with which each hymn is associated and which is provided in the *Tēvāram* for most hymns.   3. The name of the temple in Puḷamaṅkai.

APPAR

sixth–seventh centuries

20[1]

VI.301.1, Civapuram

See the god!
See him who is higher than the gods!
See him who is Sanskrit of the North
and southern Tamil and the four Vedas!
See him who bathes in milk and ghee,[2]   5
see the Lord, see him who dances, holding fire,
in the wilderness of the burning-ground,
see him who blessed the hunter-saint![3]

1. All selections translated by Indira Viswanathan Peterson.   2. Carified butter, used to anoint Śiva's image during ritual worship.   3. Śiva himself celebrated the extraordinary acts of devotion performed by Kaṇṇappar, a low-caste hunter; Kaṇṇappar is one of the sixty-three saints of the Tamil Śaiva canon.

See him who wells up as honey
in the heart-lotus of his lovers!   10
See him who has the unattainable treasure![4]
See Śiva! See him who is our treasure
here in Civapuram!

From 23

VI.308, Niṉṟa Tiruttāṇṭakam (The Tāṇṭakam Poem of the Lord Who Stands)

1

As wide earth, as fire and water,
as sacrificer and wind that blows,
as eternal moon and sun,
as ether, as the eight-formed god,[1]
as cosmic good and evil, woman and man,   5
all other forms, and his own form,
and all these as himself,
as yesterday and today and tomorrow,
the god of the long red hair stands,
O wonder!   10

3

As rock, as hill, as forest,
as river, as streams and small canals,
as salt marshes by the sea,
as grass, as bush, as plants and herbs,
as the city, as the one who smashed the three cities,[2]   5
as the word, as meaning in the word,
as the stirring of all life,
as the places where life stirs,
as grain, as the earth in which it grows,
as the water that gives it life,   10
the Lord who blazed up as the great flame stands,[3]
O wonder!

26

VI.261.1, Āvaṭuturai

My treasure and good fortune, Lord sweet as honey,
golden flame of heaven, O form of blazing light,

---

4. Release from the chain of rebirth.   1. The five elements plus the sun, the moon, and the patron of the ritual of sacrifice to the gods are the eight forms in which Śiva manifests himself. This poem visualizes Śiva as the divine power pervading the universe.   2. Śiva shot a flaming arrow at the three invincible flying cities built by the demons, thus destroying the cities.   3. When Brahmā the Creator and Viṣṇu the Preserver claimed superiority to Śiva the Destroyer, Śiva blazed up as a cosmic column of light; unable to find the beginning or end of the column, Brahmā and Viṣṇu admitted their inferiority to Śiva.

my friend, my flesh,
heart within my flesh, soul within my heart,
wish-fulfilling tree,[1]   5
my eye, dark pupil in the eye, image that dances within!
Save me from the hidden disease of karma,[2]
bull[3] among the gods, you who live in cool Āvaṭuturai!

29

IV.81.4, Kōyil (Tillai)[1]

If you could see
the arch of his brow,
the budding smile
on lips red as the *kovvai* fruit,
cool matted hair,[2]   5
the milk-white ash on coral skin,[3]
and the sweet golden foot[4]
raised up in dance,
then even human birth on this wide earth
would become a thing worth having.   10

From 166

IV.23, Kōyil/Tillai

1

I can't sing like a true devotee,
O God, great yogi!
How can I worship you?
Do not spurn me, Perfect Being, Primal Lord,
Father who dances in Tillai's Ampalam hall![1]   5
I, your servant,
have come to see your dance.

6

Seeing your dance, I will praise you.
Singing and dancing, I will hail you, crying,
"O Lord, First among the Three!"[2]   10
You who put an end to the misery
of those who sing your praise,

1. A tree in paradise that is said to grant all wishes. 2. Shorthand for the cycle of birth and death from which the pious Hindu seeks release. 3. The bull connotes might and virility. 1. An old name for Chidambaram, the sacred place where Śiva performs his cosmic dance. 2. Śiva's hair, matted since he is a *yogi*, is "cool" because of the waters of the sacred river Ganges, which flows through his locks as it descends to earth from heaven. 3. To remind people of the reality of death, Śiva smears his body with ashes from the cremation ground; his skin is said to be tawny-colored. 4. "Golden" is an expression of endearment in Tamil, but the epithet applies well to the glowing bronze icons of Śiva as Naṭarāja, the cosmic dancer. 1. Śiva dances his cosmic dance in Ciṟṟampalam, the "little hall," at the temple in Chidambaram (Tillai). 2. The triad of great gods in Hinduism (Brahmā, Viṣṇu, and Śiva).

O Dancer in Tillai's Little Ampalam,
even I have come to see your dance.

8

What shall I do, O god with the dark throat,[3]   15
if my mind is confused,
and daily slips from the highest path?
I, your servant, have come
to see all your dances
in the Little Ampalam in Tillai   20
where the Vedas flourish in full glory.[4]

9

Having failed to purify my heart,
and to make me meditate on you as I should,
have you not deceived me, O Lord of the immortals?
And yet, handsome one, you dance,   25
as your soft-spoken lady watches,
in the little hall in Tillai,
town of cloud-kissed groves!

10

Māl who ate earth as a child[5]
and Ayaṉ who has the lotus seat,[6]   30
in vain desired to see
your holy form that pervaded space.[7]
Yet, O Supreme Lord,
you dance to the music of modes[8]
in the little hall of Tillai,   35
home of our abiding wealth![9]

3. When the gods and demons churned the cosmic ocean for the gifts it held, the snake that was their churning rope spewed its venom. But Śiva quickly drank the poison, holding it in his throat, which turned permanently dark.   4. The temple at Chidambaram is famed for its brahmins who recite the Vedas.   5. In his incarnation as the child Krishṇ, Māl (a Tamil name of Viṣṇu) ate dirt in the manner of crawling infants.   6. In an important Hindu creation myth, Brahmā is seated on a lotus that comes out of the navel of Viṣṇu and is ready to perform acts of creation as Viṣṇu sleeps in the cosmic ocean.   7. A reference to Śiva's appearance as the cosmic column of light (see n. 3, p. 2380).   8. Ancient Tamil modal music.   9. Release from *karma* and rebirth.

CUNTARAR
seventh–eighth centuries

148[1]

VII.48, Pāṇṭikkoṭumuṭi

1

Renouncing all my ties,[2] I think
only of your holy feet.

1. All selections translated by Indira Viswanathan Peterson.   2. Worldly concerns and relationships.

Thinking of them, I have achieved
the purpose of my birth.
O good sage of Pāṇṭikkoṭumuṭi shrine   5
in fine Kaṟaiyūr praised by the wise,
even if I should forget you, my tongue
would still say: "Hail Siva!"

2

Friend, the days when I ignored
those who praise your feet,   10
the days on which I myself have failed you,
I think of these as evil days.
O dancer in Pāṇṭikkoṭumuṭi worshipped by the Kaveri[3]
with the garland of her circling stream!
Even if I should forget you, my tongue   15
would still say, "Hail Siva!"

3

I will think of the day on which
I should forget you
as the day of my death,
the day when the senses fail,   20
the day life leaves the body,
the day when I shall be carried away on the bier.
O poet in glorious Pāṇṭikkoṭumuṭi
washed by the Kaveri's cool, swelling tide,
Even if I should forget you, my tongue   25
would still say, "Hail Siva!"

3. An important sacred river in the Tamil region, on the banks of which many major temples of Śiva are located.

POEMS OF THE VĪRAŚAIVA SAINTS[1]

Basavaṇṇa and his younger contemporary Mahādēviyakka are the preeminent poet-saints of the Vīraśaiva (literally, "militant devotees of Śiva") bhakti sect that arose in the Karnataka region in southern India in the eleventh and twelfth centuries. Their poems, known as vacanas ("utterances"), are among the earliest literary works in Kannada, the language of Karnataka. While the colloquial language and the simple rhythms of these brief, epigrammatical poems link them to everyday speech, the bold, often shocking ideas expressed in them, combined with their vivid imagery, place them among the most thought-provoking poems in Indian literature.

Born a brahman, a member of the priestly and learned caste, Basavaṇṇa is said to have been initiated at a young age by a spiritual teacher (guru) into the path of Vīraśaiva bhakti, which rejects mechanical acts of worship and social hierarchies. Although, after a period of wandering, he became a minister of the king of Kalyāṇa, Basavaṇṇa gave his attention not to affairs of state but to building and supporting a community of devotees committed to the ideals of equality and social justice. Basavaṇṇa's more than 900 vacanas bear eloquent testimony to these Vīraśaiva ideals. The

1. All selections translated by A. K. Ramanujan.

poet heaps scorn on all ritualism and show practiced in the name of religion, whether the ritualists are high-caste brahmans or low-caste practitioners of popular cults. His poems are also pervaded by an acute awareness of the domination of the rich over the poor that is implicit in Hindu elite ritualism. With his rejection of gender as a marker of identity, Basavaṇṇa's rejection of social conventions is complete: "O lord of the meeting rivers / I'll make wars for you / but I'll be your devotees' bride."

The -akka in Mahādēviyakka's name makes her "elder sister" to all her fellow devotees, just as the -aṇṇa in Basavaṇṇa's name marks him as an "elder brother" in a spiritual family. Initiated by a Śaiva ("Śiva worshiping") guru at the age of ten, Mahādēvī (or Mahādēviyakka) proceeded to put the principles of her personal religion to practice. This included leaving a royal husband (after he tried to force himself on her); wandering naked in the countryside, pausing only to keep company with the Lord's men and women; and, of course, voicing in beautiful verse her passionate thoughts on God, love, and the world.

In her 350 poems Mahādēvī expresses her conviction that it is only by going against societal norms that she can achieve spiritual fulfillment as a true devotee of Śiva. Total devotion to God means giving up the conventional coverings that society requires for the female body: "When all the world is the eye of the lord, / onlooking everywhere, what can you / cover and conceal?" For her, a woman born into a society in which marriage and chastity are the definitive frames for women's lives, a total relationship with God means rejecting men and declaring: "I'm the woman of love / for my lord, white as jasmine." Mahādēvī's metaphor for the ultimate act of defiance of social taboos is a sexual one: she is determined to "go cuckold my husband with Hara [Śiva] my Lord." In the context of bhakti religion, Mahādēvī becomes a "saint" by doing and fearlessly speaking of precisely those things that are forbidden to ordinary women.

The vacanas of Mahādēvī and Basava (or Basavaṇṇa) are shaped and colored by the specificities of their real-life circumstances, but they have much in common as well. Both poets speak with a provocative directness, their poems luminous with striking images. For Basava, bhakti is like a saw, because "it cuts when it goes / and it cuts again / when it comes." Equally vivid is Mahādēvī's image of worldly desire: "Like a silkworm weaving / her house with love / from her marrow, / and dying / in her body's threads / winding tight, round / and round, / I burn / desiring what the heart desires." In their own ways, both poets give powerful expression to the striving of the self to free itself from the conventional patterns of selfhood.

A. K. Ramanujan, *Speaking of Śiva* (1973), contains fine poetic translations of the poems of Basavaṇṇa, Mahādēviyakka, and other Vīraśaiva poets, along with an introduction to bhakti religion and appendices on Vīraśaivism.

PRONOUNCING GLOSSARY

The following list uses common English syllables and stress accents to provide rough equivalents of selected words whose pronunciation may be unfamiliar to the general reader.

Basavaṇṇa: *buh'-suh-vuhn-nuh*

bhakti: *buhk'-tee*

Kalyāṇa: *kuhl-yah'-nuh*

Karnataka: *kuhr-nah'-tuh-kuh*

Mahādēviyakka: *muh-hah-day'-vee-yuhk-kuh*

Śaiva: *shai'-vuh*

Vīraśaiva: *veeh-ruh-shai'-vuh*

BASAVANNA[1]
1106–1167

125

See-saw watermills bow their heads.
So what?
Do they get to be devotees
to the Master?

The tongs join hands.   5
So what?
Can they be humble in service
to the Lord?

Parrots recite.
So what?   10
Can they read the Lord?

How can the slaves of the Bodiless God,[2]
Desire,
    know the way
    our Lord's Men move   15
    or the stance of their standing?

212

Don't you take on
this thing called bhakti:

    like a saw
    it cuts when it goes

    and it cuts again   5
    when it comes.

If you risk your hand
with a cobra in a pitcher[3]
will it let you
pass?   10

487

Feet will dance,
eyes will see,
tongue will sing,[4]

1. All selections translated by A. K. Ramanujan.   2. Kāma, the Indian love god, whose body was burned by the fiery gaze of Śiva, the destroyer god.   3. Putting one's hand in a pitcher that had a cobra in it was a truth ordeal. That is, a person who spoke the truth would be spared by the cobra.   4. The practice of Hindu devotional religion includes ecstatic dancing and singing in praise of God.

and not find content.
What else, what else   5
shall I do?

I worship with my hands,
the heart is not content.
What else shall I do?

   Listen, my lord,   10
   it isn't enough.
   I have it in me
   to cleave thy belly
   and enter thee

O lord of the meeting rivers![5]   15

494

I don't know anything like time-beats and metre
nor the arithmetic of strings and drums;
I don't know the count of iamb and dactyl.[6]

My lord of the meeting rivers,
as nothing will hurt you   5
I'll sing as I love.[7]

563

The pot is a god.[8] The winnowing
fan is a god. The stone in the
street is a god. The comb is a
god. The bowstring is also a
god. The bushel is a god and the   5
spouted cup is a god.

Gods, gods, there are so many
there's no place left
for a foot.

   There is only   10
one god. He is our Lord
of the Meeting Rivers.

---

5. Basavaṇṇa's signature phrase; an epithet of Śiva at the temple in Basava's birthplace, which was located at the confluence of two rivers. 6. English approximations for metrical units in Kannada poetry. 7. Basavaṇṇa is in favor of spontaneity over discipline and learning. 8. Image worship is an accepted practice, both in elite Hinduism and in popular cults.

703

Look here, dear fellow:
I wear these men's clothes
only for you.

Sometimes I am man,
sometimes I am woman.   5

O lord of the meeting rivers
I'll make wars for you
but I'll be your devotees' bride.

820

The rich
will make temples for Śiva.
What shall I,
a poor man,
do?   5

My legs are pillars,
the body the shrine,
the head a cupola
of gold.

Listen, O lord of the meeting rivers,   10
things standing shall fall,
but the moving[9] ever shall stay.

9. A reference to the wandering devotees of Siva, in contrast to the rich temples (*things standing*).

MAHĀDĒVIYAKKA

twelfth century

17[1]

Like a silkworm weaving
her house with love
from her marrow,[2]
                  and dying
in her body's threads   5
winding tight, round
and round,
            I burn
desiring what the heart desires.

1. All selections translated by A. K. Ramanujan.   2. A variation of the classical Indian image of the spider and her web, representing the soul's self-deception by means of illusory notions.

Cut through, O lord,   10
my heart's greed,
and show me
your way out,

O lord white as jasmine.[3]

114

Husband inside,
lover outside.
I can't manage them both.

This world
and that other,   5
cannot manage them both.

O lord white as jasmine

I cannot hold in one hand
both the round nut
and the long bow.[4]   10

119

What's to come tomorrow
let it come today.
What's to come today
let it come right now.

Lord white as jasmine,   5
don't give us your *nows* and *thens*!

124

You can confiscate
money in hand;
can you confiscate
the body's glory?

Or peel away every strip   5
you wear,
but can you peel
the Nothing, the Nakedness
that covers and veils?

3. This signature phrase is an epithet of Śiva in the temple at Mahadēvī's birthplace.   4. The reference
here is obscure.

To the shameless girl   10
  wearing the White Jasmine Lord's
  light of morning,
  you fool,
  where's the need for cover and jewel?

283

I love the Handsome One:
  he has no death
  decay nor form
  no place or side
  no end nor birthmarks.   5
  I love him O mother. Listen.

I love the Beautiful One
  with no bond nor fear
  no clan no land
  no landmarks   10
  for his beauty.

So my lord, white as jasmine, is my husband.

Take these husbands who die,
  decay, and feed them
  to your kitchen fires!   15

294

O brothers,[5] why do you talk
  to this woman,
  hair loose,
  face withered,
  body shrunk?   5

O fathers, why do you bother
  with this woman?
  She has no strength of limb,
  has lost the world,
  lost power of will,   10
  turned devotee,

she has lain down
with the Lord, white as jasmine,
and has lost caste.

---

5. The men who tried to molest her.

336

Look at
love's marvellous
ways:

if you shoot an arrow
plant it   5
till no feather shows;

if you hug
a body, bones
must crunch and crumble;

weld,   10
the welding must vanish.

Love is then
our lord's love.

THE BENGALI VAIṢṆAVA SAINTS' SONGS OF DEVOTION TO KRISHNA

The poems of the Bengali Vaiṣṇava saints, written in medieval dialects of Bengali, an important language of eastern India, are among the most beautiful *bhakti* songs devoted to Viṣṇu in his popular incarnation as Krishna. Vidyāpati and Chaṇḍidāsa, the major poets of this group, were brahman court poets who lived in the Bengal area in the fourteenth and sixteenth centuries, respectively. Govindadāsa lived in the fifteenth century and belonged to what had by then developed, under the leadership of the charismatic saint Śrī Krishna Chaitanya (1486–1533), into a flourishing devotional sect celebrating Krishna.

No other Hindu god has captured the popular imagination as has Krishna, and the aspect of Krishna mythology most emphasized in *bhakti* literature is the god's love idyll with married herdswomen (*gopīs*), especially with a *gopī* named Rādhā, in the cowherd village of Brindavan in Braj. Current in the Tamil area as early as the sixth century, by the twelfth century the Rādhā-Krishna myth had spread to Bengal and Orissa in eastern India. There it became the central theme of Jayadeva's *Gītagovinda* (Krishna in Song), an extended lyric-dramatic court poem in Sanskrit, and, later, of the short lyric poems of the Bengali Vaiṣṇava saints, in which the poets used Bengali folk-song meters. These songs are still sung in communal sessions called *kīrtan* ("singing of God"). Indeed, according to a popular saying in Bengal, "Without Krishna there is no song."

In the *Gītagovinda* Jayadeva delineates the love affair of Rādhā and Krishna in terms of the conventions of classical Sanskrit love poetry (like Amaru's, p. 1337). After a brief period of happiness, the lovers become estranged because of Krishna's dalliance with other women, but they are eventually reunited with the help of Rādhā's female companion, the *sakhī*. Admired for its exquisite depiction of romantic love and its vivid descriptions of the lovemaking of Rādhā and Krishna, Jayadeva's poem is understood as an allegory of the devotee's separation and union with his or her beloved God.

Influenced as they are by the Sanskrit poet's masterful treatment of the Rādhā and Krishna theme, Vidyāpati and the other Vaiṣṇava poets approach it quite differently. Like Jayadeva, they portray Rādhā and Krishna as courtly lovers, equals engaged in a relationship; not only does Rādhā adore Krishna but he reciprocates her adoration, and both lovers suffer the pain of separation and rejection and are overwhelmed by the bliss of union. However, the Vaiṣṇava poets focus on the adulterous nature of the love affair, a feature implicit in the myth but ignored by Jayadeva. In poem after poem Rādhā speaks of the passion that drives her to leave her husband and family and flee to her cowherd lover Krishna in his forest retreat. She is drawn by his love and enchanted by his beauty and the call of his bamboo flute, and she is ready to face slander and punishment for breaking the rules by which an Indian woman is expected to live.

Why did the allegory of an adulterous liaison between an incarnate god and a herdswoman become the paradigm for the experience of *bhakti* in Bengali Vaiṣṇavism? For one thing, this myth of forbidden love provided the Vaiṣṇava saints with the model for the situation of the human soul in relation to God. At one level, Rādhā is the ideal devotee because her love is spontaneous and sincere and its purity gives her the courage to defy society. Seen from a slightly different perspective, God and the human soul desire each other like Rādhā and Krishna; like the lovers, too, they suffer greatly from inevitable separation, which heightens their passion for each other, deepening at the same time the joy of their moments of union. Finally, far from hindering spirituality, Rādhā and Krishna's sensuous apprehension of each other, as a manifestation of divine love on the physical plane, becomes the devotee's vehicle to a true understanding of God's nature and the fullest experience of a relationship of mutual love with him.

This idea—of the erotic relationship as a way to God—forms the basis of the poetics of the Bengali *bhakti* poems. While the Sanskrit courtly love poems lead the reader to an experience of the erotic mood (*rasa*), a universalized flavor of sexual passion and the emotional states connected with passion, the Bengali Krishna poems plunge the reader/listener into emotion (*bhāva*) itself, with the qualification that "the emotion of sweet delight" that results from savoring the delineation of the love of Rādhā and Krishna is not mundane and the experience of it is the devotee's ultimate goal.

Autobiography is not as important an element in the understanding of the Bengali saints' songs as it is in the Vīraśaiva poems. In the Bengali Krishna poems the quasi-historical identity of the poet is deliberately replaced by a fluid persona that partakes of the emotions of the characters in the drama of Rādhā and Krishna's love. In these poems the *bhakti* framework in which male poets articulate their love of God by identifying themselves with a female self is further complicated by the allegorical structure of the Rādhā and Krishna myth. In some poems the poet speaks in Rādhā's voice, in others in Krishna's, and in yet others as a commentator on the lovers and their love. The songs are addressed variously to Krishna, to the poet's own self, to Rādhā's girlfriend, and to a nameless audience. The greatest complexity is reached in the concluding lines of each poem, which constitute the *bhaṇita*, or "poet's signature." In a song in which Rādhā and Krishna's relationship is described by a series of analogies and that ends with a question voiced by Rādhā—"Mādhava, beloved, / who are you? / Who are you really?"—the *bhaṇita* takes the form of a single line in which the poet's voice "answers" Rādhā's question: "*Vidyāpati says, they are one another.*" Some *bhaṇitas* raise questions or overturn propositions established in the preceding lines; others simply comment on the emotional landscape of the song; but all separate the poet's voice from those that have figured in the dramatic situation in the poem and offer a new perspective on it. This plurality of vision is perhaps the Bengali Vaiṣṇava poets' distinctive contribution to *bhakti* literature.

Edward C. Dimock's collaboration with the poet Denise Levertov has resulted in a slim volume containing the best translations of Bengali Vaiṣṇava poetry to date: Dimock and Levertov, *In Praise of Krishna* (1967). Translations of the poems of Vidyāpati and Chaṇḍidāsa, along with seventeenth- and eighteenth-century miniature paintings on the Rādhā and Krishna theme, may be found in Deben Bhattacharya's

Love Songs of Vidyāpati (1963) and *Love-Songs of Chandidās* (1967). For a fine translation and study of Jayadeva's *Gītagovinda*, see Barbara Miller, *Love Song of the Dark Lord* (1977). W. G. Archer, *The Loves of Krishna in Indian Painting and Poetry* (1957), discusses the Rādhā and Krishna myth.

PRONOUNCING GLOSSARY

The following list uses common English syllables and stress accents to provide rough equivalents of selected words whose pronunciation may be unfamiliar to the general reader.

anchal: *ahn'-chuhl*

bhakti: *buhk'-tee*

bhanita: *bhuh'-nee-tuh*

Brindāvan: *breen-dah'-vuhn*

Chaṇḍidāsa: *chuhn'-dee-dah'-suh*

Gītagovinda: *gee'-tuh-goh-veen'-duh*

Govindadāsa: *goh-veen'-duh-dah'-suh*

Jayadeva: *juh-yuh-day'-vuh*

Krishna: *kreesh'-nuh*

kunja: *koon'-juh*

Mādhava: *mahd'-huh-vuh*

Rādhā: *rahd'-hah*

sakhī: *suhk'-heeh*

Shyāma: *shyah'-muh*

Śrī Krishna Chaitanya: *shree kreesh'-nuh chai-tuhn'-yuh*

tāmbul: *tahm'-boohl*

Vaiṣṇava: *vaish'-nuh-vuh*

Vidyāpati: *veed-yah'-puh-tee*

Viṣṇu: *veesh'-noo*

VIDYĀPATI
fourteenth century

[The girl and the woman][1]

The girl and the woman
bound in one being:
the girl puts up her hair,
the woman lets it
fall to cover her breasts;   5
the girl reveals her arms,
her long legs, innocently bold;
the woman wraps her shawl modestly about her,
her open glance a little veiled.
Restless feet, a blush on the young breasts,   10
hint at her heart's disquiet:
behind her closed eyes
Kāma[2] awakes, born in imagination, the god.

Vidyāpati says, O Krishna, bridegroom,
be patient, she will be brought to you.   15

---

1. All selections translated by Edward C. Dimock and Denise Levertov.   2. The Indian love god.

[As the mirror to my hand]

As the mirror to my hand,
the flowers to my hair,
kohl[3] to my eyes,
tāmbul[4] to my mouth,
musk to my breast,   5
necklace to my throat,
ecstasy to my flesh,
heart to my home—

as wing to bird,
water to fish,   10
life to the living—
so you to me.
But tell me,
Mādhava,[5] beloved,
who are you?   15
Who are you really?

Vidyāpati says, they are one another.

---

3. A cosmetic used as eyeliner.   4. Also known as *pān;* a mixture of nuts, lime, and condiments wrapped in a leaf of the betel plant. It is chewed as a digestive after meals; the juice stains the mouth and lips red.   5. Krishna, suggesting his mighty persona as a slayer of demons.

GOVINDADĀSA
fifteenth century

[O Mādhava, how shall I tell you of my terror?][1]

O Mādhava,[2] how shall I tell you of my terror?
I could not describe my coming here
if I had a million tongues.
When I left my room and saw the darkness
I trembled: 5
I could not see the path,
there were snakes that writhed round my ankles!

I was alone, a woman; the night was so dark,
the forest so dense and gloomy,
and I had so far to go.   10
The rain was pouring down—
which path should I take?[3]
My feet were muddy
and burning where thorns had scratched them.

---

1. All selections translated by Edward C. Dimock and Denise Levertov.   2. Krishna, suggesting his mighty persona as a slayer of demons.   3. This poem builds on a convention of classical Sanskrit love poetry, in which a woman—usually a married woman—braves strange roads and the danger of discovery to meet her lover on a rainy night at a prearranged spot. The rainy season is the time of lovers' union.

But I had the hope of seeing you, none of it mattered,   15
and now my terror seems far away . . .
When the sound of your flute reaches my ears
it compels me to leave my home, my friends,
it draws me into the dark toward you.

I no longer count the pain of coming here,   20
says Govindadāsa.

[When they had made love]

When they had made love
she lay in his arms in the *kunja* grove.[4]
Suddenly she called his name
and wept—as if she burned in the fire of
separation.[5]   5
        The gold was in her *anchal*[6]
        but she looked afar for it!
—Where has he gone? Where has my love gone?
O why has he left me alone?
And she writhed on the ground in despair,   10
only her pain kept her from fainting.
Krishna was astonished
and could not speak.

Taking her beloved friend by the hand,[7]
Govindadāsa led her softly away.   15

[Let the earth of my body be mixed with the earth]

SHE SPEAKS:

Let the earth of my body be mixed with the earth
my beloved walks on.
Let the fire of my body be the brightness
in the mirror that reflects his face.
Let the water of my body join the waters   5
of the lotus pool he bathes in.
Let the breath of my body be air
lapping his tired limbs.
Let me be sky, and moving through me   10
that cloud-dark Shyāma,[8] my beloved.

4. A bower of flowering plants and creepers in the woods, the arena of Rādhā and Krishna's lovemaking.   5. It is the premise of Vaiṣṇava theology as well as of classical Sanskrit love poetry that separation is latent in lovers' union and that brief moments of bliss merely intensify the pain of separation.   6. The free-hanging end of the sari (a garment worn by Bengali and Indian women) in which coins and valuables are carried.   7. Here Govindadāsa takes the part of a *gopī*, one of the herdswomen with whom Krishna dallies as a young man. *Gopīs* are often depicted as witnesses to Rādhā and Krishna's love play. The *beloved friend* is the conventional character of the *sakhī*, the heroine's female friend who acts as a go-between, both in the classical court poetry and in Rādhā-Krishna love poems.   8. Krishna; he has a dark complexion—thus here he is called "the dark one."

Govindadāsa says, O golden one,
Could he of the emerald body[9] let you go?

9. Krishna; another reference to his complexion.

CHAṆḌIDĀSA
sixteenth century

[This dark cloudy night][1]

This dark cloudy night
he'll not come to me . . .
But yes, he is here!
He stands dripping with rain
in the courtyard. O my heart!   5

What virtue accrued in
another life has brought me
such bliss? I who
fear my elders and dare not go out to him?
I who torment him? I see   10
his sorrow and deep love
and I am tormented.
I would set fire to my house
for him, I would bear
the scorn of the world.   15

He thinks his sorrow is joy,
when I weep he weeps.

When it comes to know such depth of love
the heart of the world will rejoice,
says Chandidāsa.   20

[My mind is not on housework]

To her friend:

My mind is not on housework.
Now I weep, now I laugh at the world's
censure.
          He draws me—to become   5
an outcast, a hermit woman in the woods!
He has bereft me of parents, brothers, sisters,
my good name. His flute
took my heart—

1. Both selections translated by Edward C. Dimock and Denise Levertov.

his flute, a thin bamboo trap enclosing me—   10
a cheap bamboo flute was Rādhā's ruin.
That hollow, simple stick—
fed nectar by his lips, but issuing
poison . . .

If you should find   15
a clump of jointed reeds,
pull off their branches!
Tear them up by the roots!
Throw them
          into the sea.   20

Dvija Chandidāsa says, Why the bamboo?
Not it but Krishna enthralls you: him you cannot uproot.

KABĪR
fifteenth century

Born into the low caste of weavers in Benares, the holy city of the Hindus, Kabīr is considered the greatest of the north Indian mystics. His Hindi songs are distinguished by the passion with which he excoriates ritualism, hypocrisy, and social injustice in both Hinduism and Islam. Although the saint's name (*Kabīr*, "the great") is a Muslim one, referring to an epithet of Allah, in his songs Kabīr refers to God by the Hindu name Ram. Kabīr's teachings transcend established boundaries between religions, and his songs express a universal, uncompromising mysticism.

Many legends surround Kabīr's life. In one of these, the generous saint feeds a multitude with the help of a divine miracle; in another, he himself performs miracles, such as walking on water, to overcome challenges posed by jealous brahmin scholars (pundits). In a final miracle, when Kabīr's Hindu and Muslim disciples squabble over whether the saint should be cremated (according to Hindu custom) or buried (according to Muslim custom), a pile of flowers appears in place of Kabīr's body to be divided equally among the disciples.

In Kabīr's mystical religion, which belongs to a stream of *bhakti* called *nirguṇ*, "without qualities," God is beyond name and form, and cannot be apprehended through ritual worship, reading texts, or ascetic practices, which are aspects of organized religious traditions. With the help of a spiritual teacher (*guru*), the mystic seeks God through interior modes of spiritual practice (such as those taught in some schools of Yoga philosophy) and unites with Him in a "spontaneous" experience (*sahaj*). In his poems Kabīr relentlessly ridicules the externally oriented Hindu and Muslim practices. Qazis (Muslim scholars) and pundits (Hindu scholars) are derided for thinking that they can understand God through the study of sacred texts, but *yogis* and ascetics who torture their bodies in an attempt to "reach" God are equally foolish.

Kabīr's songs are treasured for their searing honesty and acerbic wit. The saint also composed enigmatic, riddlelike poems that contain complex mystical imagery reminiscent of the visionary poems of William Blake. His pithy epigrams in the *dohā* couplet form have become household words in north India. Modern poets such as India's nobel laureate Rabindranath Tagore and the American poet Robert Bly have responded to Kabīr's mystical vision with translations of his poems.

For an introduction to Kabīr and his poems, see John Stratton Hawley and Mark Juergensmeyer's *Songs of the Saints of India* (1988). Larger selections of the poems and studies of the life and teachings of Kabīr can be found in *The Bījak of Kabīr*, trans. by Linda Hess and Shukdev Singh, essays and notes by Linda Hess (1986); *Kabīr*, introduced and trans. by Charlotte Vaudeville (1974); and Charlotte Vaudeville, *A Weaver Named Kabīr: Selected Verses with a Detailed Biographical and Historical Introduction* (1993). Translations by modern poets include Rabindranath Tagore, *One Hundred Poems of Kabīr* (1915), and Robert Bly, *The Kabīr Book: Forty-four of the Ecstatic Poems of Kabīr* (1977).

PRONOUNCING GLOSSARY

The following list uses common English syllables and stress accents to provide rough equivalents of selected words whose pronunciation may be unfamiliar to the general reader.

dohā: *doh'-hah*   Qazi: *kah-zeeh'*

Kabīr: *kuh-beer'*   Ram: *rahm*

nirguṇ: *neer'-goon*   sahaj: *suh-huhj'*

[POEMS]¹

[Go naked if you want]

Go naked if you want,
Put on animal skins.²
    What does it matter till you see the inward Ram?

If the union yogis seek
Came from roaming about in the buff,   5
    every deer in the forest would be saved.

If shaving your head
Spelled spiritual success,
    heaven would be filled with sheep.

And brother, if holding back your seed³   10
Earned you a place in paradise,
    eunuchs ⁴ would be the first to arrive.

Kabir says: Listen brother,
Without the name of Ram
    who has ever won the spirit's prize?   15

[Pundit, how can you be so dumb?]

Pundit, how can you be so dumb?
You're going to drown, along with all your kin,
    unless you start speaking of Ram.

---

1. All poem selections translated by John Stratton Hawley and Mark Juergensmeyer.   2. Here and in the following verses, Kabīr ridicules various practices of *yogis* and ascetics, including going naked, wearing animal skins, and shaving the head.   3. Semen; *yogis* and ascetics practice celibacy.   4. Castrated men.

Vedas, Puranas[1]—why read them?
  It's like loading an ass with sandalwood!   5
Unless you catch on and learn how Ram's name goes,
  how will you reach the end of the road?

You slaughter living beings and call it religion:[2]
  hey brother, what would irreligion be?
"Great Saint"—that's how you love to greet each other: 10
  Who then would you call a murderer?

Your mind is blind. You've no knowledge of yourselves.
  Tell me, brother, how can you teach anyone else?
Wisdom is a thing you sell for worldly gain,
  so there goes your human birth—in vain.   15

You say: "It's Narad's command."
  "It's what Vyas says to do."
  "Go and ask Sukdev, the sage."[3]
Kabīr says: you'd better go and lose yourself in Ram
  for without him, brother, you drown.   20

[Hey Qazi]

Hey Qazi,[1]
  what's that book you're preaching from?
And reading, reading—how many days?
  Still you haven't mastered one word.
Drunk with power, you want to grab me;   5
  then comes the circumcision.
    Brother, what can I say?—
If God had wanted to make me a Muslim,
  why didn't he make the incision?
You cut away the foreskin, and then you have a Muslim;   10
  so what about your women?
    What are they?
Women, so they say, are only half-formed men:
  I guess they must stay Hindus to the end.
Hindus, Muslims—where did they come from?   15
  Who got them started down this road?
Search inside, search your heart and look:
  Who made heaven come to be?
Fool,
  Throw away that book, and sing of Ram.   20
    What you're doing has nothing to do with him.
Kabīr has caught hold of Ram for his refrain,

1. Sacred texts of Hinduism.   2. A reference to animal sacrifices.   3. Narad, Vyas, and Sukdev are
ancient sages who wrote works on *dharma*, proper conduct, and morality.   1. A Muslim religious scholar
and teacher.

And the Qazi?
  He spends his life in vain.

[Kabīr is done with stretching thread and weaving]

Kabīr is done with stretching thread and weaving.
He's written on his frame the name of Ram.

His mother steals away and secretly weeps:
"O God, how will these children survive?"

Kabīr says: 5
"Whenever I'd thread the weaver's shuttle
I'd forget to be a lover of Ram;

And listen, Mother, he's the king of all three worlds:
He is the one who provides."

[Why be so proud of this useless, used-up body?]

Why be so proud of this useless, used-up body?
One moment dead, and it's gone.

How nicely you adorn it with sugar and butter and milk:
Once the breath goes out, it's fit to burn.

That head with its turban so artfully arranged   5
Will soon be adorned with the jabbing beaks of crows.

Bones: they burn like tinder.
Hair: it burns like hay.

And still, says Kabīr, people won't wake up—
Not until they feel death's club   10
  inside their skulls.

[Hey brother, why do you want me to talk?]

Hey brother, why do you want me to talk?
Talk and talk and the real things get lost.

Talk and talk and things get out of hand.
Why not stop talking and think?

If you meet someone good, listen a little, speak;   5
If you meet someone bad, clench up like a fist.

Talking with a wise man is a great reward.
Talking with a fool? A waste.

Kabīr says: A pot makes noise if it's half full,
But fill it to the brim—no sound.[1]   10

[That master weaver, whose skills]

That master weaver, whose skills
   are beyond our knowing,
   has stretched his warp
    through the world.
He has fastened his loom   5
   between earth and sky,
   where the shuttlecocks are the sun
    and moon.[2]
He fills the shuttle with the thread
   of easy spontaneity,   10
   and weaves and weaves
    an endless pattern.
But now, says Kabīr, that weaver!
   He breaks apart his loom
   and tangles the thread   15
    in thread.

[EPIGRAMS][1]

[The lean doe]

The lean doe
Avoids the greens
Beside this pond.
Numberless hunters,
Only one life.   5
How many arrows
   can she dodge?

[Kabīr: / My mind was soothed]

Kabīr:
My mind was soothed
When I found the boundless knowledge,

---

1. Typical of Kabīr's style; here Kabīr is using a popular proverb, but the image of the full pot that makes no sound also has mystical significance.   2. Again, the sun and moon are mystical images with esoteric significance.   1. Both epigrams translated by John Stratton Hawley and Mark Juergensmeyer.

And the fires
that scorch the world   5
To me are water cool.

MĪRĀBĀĪ
sixteenth century

Mīrābāī (or Mīrā), a devotee of Krishna who flourished in the sixteenth century, is one of the most popular of the north Indian *bhakti* poets writing in Hindi, and the only woman among them. Born in Rajasthan in western India, Mīrā is said to have achieved fame as a saint during her own lifetime and to have spent the end of her life in the north Indian village Brindavan (the locale of the myths of Krishna's love-making with herdswomen), which had become the principal center of Krishna worship under the leadership of the Bengali saint Chaitanya (p. 2390). The majority of the 1,400 *bhakti* songs attributed to Mīrā are in Brajbhāṣā, a dialect of Hindi, the major language of north India; the rest of the poems are in a form of Gujerati, a western Indian language. Mīrā's songs are sung all over India, including the south, where the dominant languages are not related to Hindi.

Mīrā's poetry and the reception of her songs and life have been profoundly colored by her identity as a woman. According to the traditional biographies, born a princess of one Rajput clan and married into another, Mīrā abandoned her royal husband and family to sing songs about her love for Krishna. For her audience the voice of Krishna's female lover in Mīrā's poetry is no mere persona or metaphor, but Mīrā's own voice. Her songs bring the poignancy and authenticity of a woman's real-life experience to the archetypal *bhakti* myth of the lovelorn woman pining for a beloved God.

The central theme of Mīrā's poetry is that of breaking away from husband and family to engage in an erotic, romantic relationship with Krishna. In many poems Mīrā speaks of her mother-in-law and sisters-in-law tormenting her and of being imprisoned by the king, who may have been her father-in-law or her husband. When the king sends her a cup of poison, she drinks it without being harmed. Mīrā's poems repeatedly evoke trangressions of the rules of modesty, chastity, and seclusion prescribed for married women, especially among the Rajput noble families, whose men considered any infringement of these rules an insult to family honor. The defiant Mīrā speaks of tearing off the veil (*pardā*), which is supposed to help guard her modesty, and of wandering in the streets, singing, in defiance of the custom of female seclusion. In a society in which only courtesans—women who are sexually free—may practice the art of dance, Mīrā dances in public with bells on her ankles, celebrating her love for Krishna. She is "mad" with desire for her God, and she is "colored with the color" of the Lord. In an image that repeatedly appears in her poems, she lies "on the couch of love" with her beloved Krishna as his bride or lover. The distinctly personal sensibility informing the sensuous, subversive language and imagery of Mīrā's poems is quite different from that of the male authors of Krishnaite devotional literature, who evoke the myths of Krishna's love affair with the herdswoman Rādhā or his riotous love play with the herdswomen on the banks of the river Jumna.

An important feature of Mīrā's songs is their closeness to women's songs and folk traditions. Women in north India sing songs to each other at women's festivals and rites throughout the year, especially to mark the cycle of the seasons. In the folk tradition the monsoon season, a time of continuous rainfall, is a time for songs expressing the pain of separation from one's lover, while the songs of Holi, a rite of spring, celebrate the joy of lovers' union. Mīrā's monsoon songs about Krishna share much with women's songs of the rainy season, and her image of being "dyed in Krishna's color" (Krishna has a dark complexion) is taken from the festival of Holi, in which men and women spray each other with colored water or throw colored powder on each other in a carnivalesque frenzy. Many of Mīrā's poems are addressed to a girlfriend or to an implied audience of women, suggesting kinship with the women's song traditions in which, even when an absent lover is addressed, the songs are usually sung to an audience of women. Paradoxically, however, in the context of devotion to Krishna, the feminine sensibility and the language of desire and defiance of social norms that permeate Mīrā's songs are the very qualities that make them speak to men and women alike.

John Stratton Hawley and Mark Juergensmeyer, *Songs of the Saints of India* (1988), offers an insightful discussion of Mīrā's life and excellent translations of her poems. For a larger selection of poems, see A. J. Alston, *The Devotional Poems of Mīrābāī* (1980).

PRONOUNCING GLOSSARY

The following list uses common English syllables and stress accents to provide rough equivalents of selected words whose pronunciation may be unfamiliar to the general reader.

bhakti: *buhk'-tee*

Brajbhāṣā: *bruhj-b-hah'-shah*

Brindavan: *breend-dah'-vuhn*

Chaitanya: *chai-tuhn'-yuh*

Gujerati: *goo-juh-rah'-teeh*

Mīrābāī: *meeh'-rah-bah'-yee*

Murali: *moo-ruh-lee'*

Rādhā: *rahd'-hah*

Rajasthan: *rah'-juhst-hahn*

Rajput: *rahj'-pooht*

37[1]

I'm colored with the color of dusk, oh *rana*,[2]
    colored with the color of my Lord.
Drumming out the rhythm on the drums, I danced,
    dancing in the presence of the saints,[3]
        colored with the color of my Lord.   5
They thought me mad for the Maddening One,[4]
    raw for my dear dark love,
        colored with the color of my Lord.
The *rana* sent me a poison cup:
    I didn't look, I drank it up,   10
        colored with the color of my Lord.
The clever Mountain Lifter is the lord of Mira.[5]
    Life after life he's true—
        colored with the color of my Lord.

1. All selections translated by John Stratton Hawley and Mark Juergensmeyer. 2. King. *Color of dusk:* Krishna has a blue-black complexion. 3. Devotees of Krishna. 4. Here, Krishna; "the one who maddens" is more often the love god Kāma. 5. Mīrā's signature phrase. *Clever:* civilized, gallant. *Mountain Lifter:* a reference to a feat of Krishna's youth, in which he lifted a mountain to shelter the entire cowherd village from torrential rain.

42

Life without Hari[6] is no life, friend,
And though my mother-in-law fights,
    my sister-in-law teases,
    the *rana*[7] is angered,
A guard is stationed on a stool outside,   5
    and a lock is mounted on the door,
How can I abandon the love I have loved
    in life after life?
Mira's Lord is the clever Mountain Lifter:
    Why would I want anyone else?   10

82

I saw the dark clouds burst,
        dark Lord,[8]
Saw the clouds and tumbling down
In black and yellow streams
        they thicken,   5
Rain and rain two hours long.
See—
    my eyes see only rain and water,
    watering the thirsty earth green.
Me—   10
    my love's in a distant land
    and wet, I stubbornly stand at the door,[9]
For Hari is indelibly green,[1]
        Mira's Lord,
And he has invited a standing,   15
        stubborn love.

84

Hey love bird, crying cuckoo,
    don't make your crying coos,
    for I who am crying, cut off from my love,
    will cut off your crying beak
    and twist off your flying wings   5
    and pour black salt in the wounds.

Hey, I am my love's and my love is mine.
    How do you dare cry love?
    But if my love were restored today
    your love call would be a joy.   10

6. Krishna.   7. King.   8. Krishna.   9. Evokes the feelings of a woman waiting for her lover to come to her, the theme of poems about the monsoon season in women's folk songs.   1. One of the meanings of the word *Hari* (a name for Krishna).

I would gild your crying beak with gold
    and you would be my crown.

Hey, I'll write my love a note,
    crying crow, now take it away[2]
and tell him that his separated love   15
    can't eat a single grain.
His servant Mira's mind's in a mess.
    She wastes her time crying coos.

    Come quick, my Lord,
        the one who sees inside;   20
            without you nothing remains.

                        153

Go to where my loved one lives,
    go where he lives and tell him
        if he says so, I'll color my sari red;
        if he says so, I'll wear the godly yellow garb;[3]
        if he says so, I'll drape the part in my hair with pearls;   5
        if he says so, I'll let my hair grow wild.[4]
Mira's Lord is the clever Mountain Lifter:
    listen to the praises of that king.

                        166

Murali[5] sounds on the banks of the Jumna,
Murali snatches away my mind;
My senses cut loose from their moorings—
Dark waters, dark garments, dark Lord.[6]
I listen close to the sounds of Murali   5
And my body withers away—
Lost thoughts, lost even the power to think.
    Mira's Lord, clever Mountain Lifter,
    Come quick, and snatch away my pain.

                        193

Let us go to a realm beyond going,
Where death is afraid to go,
Where the high-flying birds alight and play,

---

2. Modeled on folk songs in which a lovelorn woman speaks to birds and asks them to take a message to her lover.   **3.** The yellow robes worn by monks and nuns in contrast to the red saris worn by Hindu brides.   **4.** The ascetic's matted hair in contrast to the bride's hairstyle adorned with pearls.   **5.** Krishna's enchanting bamboo flute.   **6.** Krishna, who has a dark complexion. *Dark waters:* Jumna River. *Dark garments:* Krishna's cloak.

Afloat in the full lake[7] of love.
There they gather—the good, the true—   5
To strengthen an inner regimen,
To focus on the dark form of the Lord
And refine their minds like fire.
Garbed in goodness—their ankle bells—
They dance the dance of contentment   10
And deck themselves with the sixteen signs
Of beauty,[8] and a golden crown—
There where the love of the Dark One[9] comes first
And everything else is last.

7. A traditional mystical image of pure souls as swans or wild geese and spiritual perfection as a sacred lake.   8. Conventional adornments for a woman.   9. Krishna.

A Note on Translation

Reading literature in translation is a pleasure on which it is fruitless to frown. The purist may insist that we ought always read in the original languages, and we know ideally that this is true. But it is a counsel of perfection, quite impractical even for the purist, since no one in a lifetime can master all the languages whose literatures it would be a joy to explore. Master languages as fast as we may, we shall always have to read to some extent in translation, and this means we must be alert to what we are about: if in reading a work of literature in translation we are not reading the "original," what precisely are we reading? This is a question of great complexity, to which justice cannot be done in a brief note, but the following sketch of some of the considerations may be helpful.

One of the memorable scenes of ancient literature is the meeting of Hector and Andromache in Book VI of Homer's *Iliad*. Hector, leader and mainstay of the armies defending Troy, is implored by his wife Andromache to withdraw within the city walls and carry on the defense from there, where his life will not be con stantly at hazard. In Homer's text her opening words to him are these: δαιμόνιε, φθίσει σε τὸ σὸν μένος (daimonie, phthisei se to son menos). How should they be translated into English?

Here is how they have actually been translated into English by capable translators, at various periods, in verse and prose:

1. George Chapman, 1598:

> O noblest in desire,
> Thy mind, inflamed with others' good, will set thy self on fire.

2. John Dryden, 1693:

> Thy dauntless heart (which I foresee too late),
> Too daring man, will urge thee to thy fate.

3. Alexander Pope, 1715:

> Too daring Prince! . . .
> For sure such courage length of life denies,
> And thou must fall, thy virtue's sacrifice.

4. William Cowper, 1791:

> Thy own great courage will cut short thy days,
> My noble Hector. . .

5. Lang, Leaf, and Myers, 1883 (prose):

> Dear my lord, this thy hardihood will undo thee. . . .

6. A. T. Murray, 1924 (prose):

> Ah, my husband, this prowess of thine will be thy doom. . . .

7. E. V. Rieu, 1950 (prose):

"Hector," she said, "you are possessed. This bravery of yours will be your end."

8. I. A. Richards, 1950 (prose):

"Strange man," she said, "your courage will be your destruction."

9. Richmond Lattimore, 1951:

> Dearest,
> Your own great strength will be your death. . . .

10. Robert Fitzgerald, 1979:

> O my wild one, your bravery will be
> Your own undoing!

11. Robert Fagles, 1990:

> reckless one,
> Your own fiery courage will destroy you!

From these strikingly different renderings of the same six words, certain facts about the nature of translation begin to emerge. We notice, for one thing, that Homer's word μένος (menos) is diversified by the translators into "mind," "dauntless heart," "such courage," "great courage," "hardihood," "prowess," "bravery," "courage," "great strength," "bravery," and "fiery courage." The word has in fact all these possibilities. Used of things, it normally means "force"; of animals, "fierceness" or "brute strength" or (in the case of horses) "mettle"; of men and women, "passion" or "spirit" or even "purpose." Homer's application of it in the present case points our attention equally—whatever particular sense we may imagine Andromache to have uppermost—to Hector's force, strength, fierceness in battle, spirited heart and mind. But since English has no matching term of like inclusiveness, the passage as the translators give it to us reflects this lack and we find one attribute singled out to the exclusion of the rest.

Here then is the first and most crucial fact about any work of literature read in translation. It cannot escape the linguistic characteristics of the language into which it is turned: the grammatical, syntactical, lexical, and phonetic boundaries that constitute collectively the individuality or "genius" of that language. A Greek play or a Russian novel in English will be governed first of all by the resources of the English language, resources that are certain to be in every instance very different, as the efforts with μένος show, from those of the original.

Turning from μένος to δαιμόνιε (daimonie) in Homer's clause, we encounter a second crucial fact about translations. Nobody knows exactly what shade of meaning δαιμόνιε had for Homer. In later writers the word normally suggests divinity, something miraculous, wondrous; but in Homer it appears as a vocative of address for both chieftain and commoner, man and wife. The coloring one gives it must therefore be determined either by the way one thinks a Greek wife of Homer's era might actually address her husband (a subject on which we have no information whatever) or in the way one thinks it suitable for a hero's wife to address her husband in an epic poem, that is to say, a highly stylized and formal work. In general, the translators of our century will be seen to have abandoned formality to stress the intimacy; the wifeliness; and, especially in Lattimore's case, a certain chiding tenderness, in Andromache's appeal: (6) "Ah, my husband," (7) "Hector" (with perhaps a hint, in "you are possessed," of the alarmed distaste with which wives have so often viewed their husbands' bellicose moods), (8) "Strange man," (9) "Dearest," (10) "O my wild one" (mixing an almost motherly admiration with reproach and concern), and (11) "reckless one." On the other hand, the older translators have obviously removed Andromache to an epic or heroic distance from her beloved, whence she sees and kindles to his selfless courage, acknowledging, even in the moment of pleading with him to be otherwise, his moral grandeur and the tragic destiny this too certainly implies: (1) "O noblest in desire, . . . inflamed by others' good"; (2) "Thy dauntless heart (which I foresee too late), / Too daring man"; (3) "Too daring Prince! . . . / And thou must fall, thy virtue's sacrifice"; (4) "My noble Hector." Even the less specific "Dear my lord" of Lang, Leaf, and Myers looks in the same direction because of its echo of the speech of countless Shakespearean men and women who have shared this powerful moral sense: "Dear my lord, make me acquainted with your cause of grief"; "Perseverance, dear my lord, keeps honor bright"; etc.

The fact about translation that emerges from all this is that just as the translated work reflects the individuality of the language it is turned into, so it reflects the individuality of the age in which it is made, and the age will permeate it everywhere like yeast in dough. We think of one kind of permeation when we think of the governing verse forms and attitudes toward verse at a given epoch. In Chapman's time, experiments seeking an "heroic" verse form for English were widespread, and accordingly he tries a "fourteener" couplet (two rhymed lines of seven stresses each) in his *Iliad* and a pentameter couplet in his *Odyssey*. When Dryden and Pope wrote, a closed pentameter couplet had become established as the heroic form par excellence. By Cowper's day, thanks largely to the prestige of *Paradise Lost,* the couplet had gone out of fashion for narrative poetry in favor of blank verse. Our age, inclining to prose and in verse to proselike informalities and relaxations, has, predictably, produced half a dozen excellent prose translations of the *Iliad* but only three in verse (by Fagles, Lattimore, and Fitzgerald), all relying on rhythms that are much of the time closer to the verse of William Carlos Williams and some of the prose of novelists like Faulkner than to the swift firm tread of Homer's Greek. For if it is true that what we translate from a given work is what, wearing the spectacles of our time, we see in it, it is also true that we see in it what we have the power to translate.

Of course, there are other effects of the translator's epoch on a translation besides those exercised by contemporary taste in verse and verse forms. Chapman writes in a great age of poetic metaphor and, therefore, almost instinctively translates his understanding of Homer's verb φθίσει (phthisei, "to cause to wane, consume, waste, pine") into metaphorical terms of flame, presenting his Hector to us as a man of burning generosity who will be consumed by his very ardor. This is a conception rooted in large part in the psychology of the Elizabethans, who had the habit of speaking of the soul as "fire," of one of the four temperaments as "fiery," of even the more material bodily processes, like digestion, as if they were carried on by the heat of fire ("concoction," "decoction"). It is rooted too in that characteristic Renaissance élan so unforgettably expressed in characters such as Tamburlaine and Dr. Faustus, the former of whom exclaims to the stars above:

> . . . I, the chiefest lamp of all the earth,
> First rising in the East with mild aspect,
> But fixèd now in the meridian line,
> Will send up fire to your turning spheres,
> And cause the sun to borrow light of you. . . .

Pope and Dryden, by contrast, write to audiences for whom strong metaphor has become suspect. They therefore reject the fire image (which we must recall is not present in the Greek) in favor of a form of speech more congenial to their age, the *sententia* or aphorism, and give it extra vitality by making it the scene of a miniature drama: in Dryden's case, the hero's dauntless heart "urges" him (in the double sense of physical as well as moral pressure) to his fate; in Pope's, the hero's courage, like a judge, "denies" continuance of life, with the consequence that he "falls"—and here Pope's second line suggests analogy to the sacrificial animal—the victim of his own essential nature, of what he is.

To pose even more graphically the pressures that a translator's period brings, con-

sider the following lines from Hector's reply to Andromache's appeal that he withdraw, first in Chapman's Elizabethan version, then in Lattimore's twentieth-century
one:

Chapman, 1598:

> The spirit I did first breathe
> Did never teach me that—much less since the contempt of death
> Was settled in me, and my mind knew what a Worthy was,
> Whose office is to lead in fight and give no danger pass
> Without improvement. In this fire must Hector's trial shine.
> Here must his country, father, friends be in him made divine.

Lattimore, 1951:

> and the spirit will not let me, since I have learned to be valiant
> and to fight always among the foremost ranks of the Trojans,
> winning for my own self great glory, and for my father.

If one may exaggerate to make a necessary point, the world of Henry V and Othello
suddenly gives way here to our own, a world whose discomfort with any form of heroic
self-assertion is remarkably mirrored in the burial of Homer's key terms (*spirit, valiant,
fight, foremost, glory*)—five out of twenty-two words in the original, five out of thirty-
six in the translation—in a cushioning huddle of harmless sounds.

Besides the two factors so far mentioned (language and period) as affecting the
character of a translation, there is inevitably a third—the translator, with a particular
degree of talent; a personal way of regarding the work to be translated; a special
hierarchy of values, moral, aesthetic, metaphysical (which may or may not be summed
up in a "worldview"); and a unique style or lack of it. But this influence all readers
are likely to bear in mind, and it needs no laboring here. That, for example, two
translators of Hamlet, one a Freudian, the other a Jungian, will produce impressively
different translations is obvious from the fact that when Freudian and Jungian argue
about the play in English they often seem to have different plays in mind.

We can now return to the question from which we started. After all allowances
have been made for language, age, and individual translator, is anything of the original
left? What, in short, does the reader of translations read? Let it be said at once that
in utility prose—prose whose function is mainly referential—the reader who reads a
translation reads everything that matters. "Nicht Rauchen," "Défense de Fumer," and
"No Smoking," posted in a railway car, make their point, and the differences between
them in sound and form have no significance for us in that context. Since the prose
of a treatise and of most fiction is preponderantly referential, we rightly feel, when
we have paid close attention to Cervantes or Montaigne or Machiavelli or Tolstoy in
a good English translation, that we have had roughly the same experience as a native
Spaniard, Frenchman, Italian, or Russian. But *roughly* is the correct word; for good
prose points iconically *to* itself as well as referentially beyond itself, and everything
that it points to in itself in the original (rhythms, sounds, idioms, wordplay, etc.) must
alter radically in being translated. The best analogy is to imagine a Van Gogh painting
reproduced in the medium of tempera, etching, or engraving: the "picture" remains,
but the intricate interanimation of volumes with colorings with brushstrokes has
disappeared.

When we move on to poetry, even in its longer narrative and dramatic forms—
plays like *Oedipus*, poems like the *Iliad* or the *Divine Comedy*—our situation as English readers worsens appreciably, as the many unlike versions of Andromache's appeal
to Hector make very clear. But, again, only appreciably. True, this is the point at
which the fact that a translation is *always* an interpretation explodes irresistibly on
our attention; but if it is the best translation of its time, like John Ciardi's translation
of the *Divine Comedy* for our time, the result will be not only a sensitive interpretation

but also a work with intrinsic interest in its own right—at very best, a true work of art, a new poem. In these longer works, moreover, even if the translation is uninspired, many distinctive structural features—plot, setting, characters, meetings, partings, confrontations, and specific episodes generally—survive virtually unchanged. Hence even in translation it remains both possible and instructive to compare, say, concepts of the heroic or attitudes toward women or uses of religious ritual among civilizations as various as those reflected in the *Iliad*, the *Mahābhārata, Beowulf,* and the epic of *Son-Jara.* It is only when the shorter, primarily lyrical forms of poetry are presented that the reader of translations faces insuperable disadvantage. In these forms, the referential aspect of language has a tendency to disappear into, or, more often, draw its real meaning and accreditation from, the iconic aspect. Let us look for just a moment at a brief poem by Federico García Lorca and its English translation (by Stephen Spender and J. L. Gili):

> ¡Alto pinar!
> Cuatro palomas por el aire van.
>
> Cuatro palomas
> vuelan y tornan.
> Llevan heridas
> sus cuatro sombras.
>
> ¡Bajo pinar!
> Cuatro palomas en la tierra están.

> Above the pine trees:
> Four pigeons go through the air.
>
> Four pigeons
> fly and turn round.
> They carry wounded
> their four shadows.
>
> Below the pine trees:
> Four pigeons lie on the earth.

In this translation the referential sense of the English words follows with remarkable exactness the referential sense of the Spanish words they replace. But the life of Lorca's poem does not lie in that sense. It lies in such matters as the abruptness, like an intake of breath at a sudden revelation, of the two exclamatory lines (1 and 7), which then exhale musically in images of flight and death; or as the echoings of *palomas* in *heridas* and *sombras,* bringing together (as in fact the hunter's gun has done) these unrelated nouns and the unrelated experiences they stand for in a sequence that seems, momentarily, to have all the logic of a tragic action, in which *doves* become *wounds* become *shadows,* or as the external and internal rhyming among the five verbs, as though all motion must (as in fact it must) end with *están.*

Since none of this can be brought over into another tongue (least of all Lorca's rhythms), the translator must decide between leaving a reader to wonder why Lorca is a poet to be bothered about at all and making a new but true poem, whose merit will almost certainly be in inverse ratio to its likeness to the original. Samuel Johnson made such a poem in translating Horace's famous *Diffugere nives,* and so did A. E. Housman. If we juxtapose the last two stanzas of each translation, and the corresponding Latin, we can see at a glance that each has the consistency and inner life of a genuine poem and that neither of them (even if we consider only what is obvious to the eye, the line-lengths) is very close to Horace:

> *Cum semel occideris, et de te splendida Minos*
> *fecerit arbitria,*

> *non, Torquate, genus, non te facundia, non te*
> *restituet pietas.*

> *Infernis neque enim tenebris Diana pudicum*
> *liberat Hippolytum*
> *nec Lethaea valet Theseus abrumpere caro*
> *vincula Pirithoo.*

Johnson:

> Not you, Torquatus, boast of Rome,
> When Minos once has fixed your doom,
> Or eloquence, or splendid birth,
> Or virtue, shall restore to earth.
> Hippolytus, unjustly slain,
> Diana calls to life in vain;
> Nor can the might of Theseus rend
> The chains of hell that hold his friend.

Housman:

> When thou descendest once the shades among,
>   The stern assize and equal judgment o'er,
> Not thy long lineage nor thy golden tongue,
>   No, nor thy righteousness, shall friend thee more.

> Night holds Hippolytus the pure of stain,
>   Diana steads him nothing, he must stay;
> And Theseus leaves Pirithous in the chain
>   The love of comrades cannot take away.

The truth of the matter is that when the translator of short poems chooses to be literal, most or all of the poetry is lost; and when the translator succeeds in forging a new poetry, most or all of the original author is lost. Since there is no way out of this dilemma, we have always been sparing, in this anthology, in our use of short poems in translation.

In this Expanded Edition, we have adjusted our policy to take account of the two great non-Western literatures in which the short lyric or "song" has been the principal and by far most cherished expression of the national genius. During much of its history from earliest times, the Japanese imagination has cheerfully exercised itself, with all the delicacy and grace of an Olympic figure skater, inside a rigorous verse pattern of five lines and thirty-one syllables: the *tanka*. Chinese poetry, while somewhat more liberal to itself in line length, has been equally fertile in the fine art of compression and has only occasionally, even in its earliest, most experimental phase, indulged in verse lines of more than seven characters, often just four, or in poems of more than fifty lines, usually fewer than twenty. What makes the Chinese and Japanese lyric more difficult than most other lyrics to translate satisfactorily into English is that these compressions combine with a flexibility of syntax (Japanese) or a degree of freedom from it (Chinese) not available in our language. They also combine with a poetic sensibility that shrinks from exposition in favor of sequences and juxtapositions of images: images grasped and recorded in, or *as if in,* a moment of pure perception unencumbered by the explanatory linkages, background scenarios, and other forms of contextualization that the Western mind is instinctively driven to establish.

Whole books, almost whole libraries, have been written recently on the contrast of East and West in worldviews and value systems as well as on the need of each for the other if there is ever to be a community of understanding adequate to the realities both face. Put baldly, much too simply, and without the many exceptions and qualifications that rightly spring to mind, it may be said that a central and characteristic Western impulse, from the Greeks on down, has been to see the world around us as something to be *acted on:* weighed, measured, managed, used, even (when economic interests prevail over all others) fouled. Likewise, put oversimply, it may be said that a central and characteristic Eastern counterpart to this over many centuries (witness Taoism, Buddhism, and Hinduism, among others) has been to see that same world as something to be *received:* contemplated, touched, tasted, smelled, heard, and most especially, immersed in until observer and observed are one. To paint a bamboo, a stone, a butterfly, a person—so runs a classical Chinese admonition for painters— you must *become* that bamboo, that stone, that butterfly, that person, then paint from the inside. No one need be ashamed of being poor, says Confucius, putting a similar emphasis on *receiving* experience, "only of not being cultivated in the perception of beauty."

The problem that these differences in linguistic freedom and philosophical outlook pose for the English translator of classical Chinese and Japanese poetry may be glimpsed, even if not fully grasped, by considering for a moment in some detail a typical Japanese *tanka* (*Kokinshu,* 9) and a typical Chinese "song" (*Book of Songs,* 23). In its own language but transliterated in the Latin alphabet of the West, the *tanka* looks like this:

> *kasumi tachi*
> *ko no me mo haru no*
> *yuki fureba*
> *hana naki sato mo*
> *hana zo chirikeru*

In a literal word-by-word translation (so far as this is possible in Japanese, since the language uses many particles without English equivalents and without dictionary meaning in modifying and qualifying functions—for example, *no, mo,* and *no* in line 2), the poem looks like this:

> haze rises
> tree-buds swell
> when snow falls
> village(s) without flower(s)
> flower(s) fall(s)

The three best-known English renderings of this *tanka* look like this:

1. Helen Craig McCullough:

> When snow comes in spring—
> fair season of layered haze
> and burgeoning buds—
> flowers fall in villages
> where flowers have yet to bloom.

2. Laurel Rasplica Rodd and Mary Catherine Henkenius:

> When the warm mists veil
> all the buds swell while yet the
> spring snows drift downward
> even in the hibernal
> village crystal blossoms fall.

3. Robert H. Brower and Earl Miner:

> With the spreading mists
> The tree buds swell in early spring
> And wet snow petals fall—

> So even my flowerless country village
> Already lies beneath its fallen flowers.

The reader will notice at once how much the three translators have felt it desirable or necessary to add, alter, rearrange, and explain. In McCullough's version the time of year is affirmed twice, both as "spring" and as "fair season of . . . haze"; the haze is now "layered"; the five coordinate perceptions of the original (haze, swelling buds, a snowfall, villages without flowers, flowers drifting down) have been structured into a single sentence with one main verb and two subordinate clauses spelling out "when" and "where"; and the original poem's climax, in a scene of drifting petallike snowflakes, has been shifted to a bleak scenery of absence: "flowers have yet to bloom." The final stress, in other words, is not on the fulfilled moment in which snow flowers replace the cherry blossoms, but on the cherry blossoms not yet arrived.

Similar additions and explanations occur in Rodd and Henkenius's version. This time the mist is "warm" and "veil[s] all" to clarify its connection with "buds." Though implicit already in "warm" and "burgeoning," spring is invoked again in "spring snows," and the snows are given confirmation in the following line by the insistently Latinate "hibernal," chosen, we may reasonably guess, along with "veil," "all," "swell," "while," "crystal," and "fall" to replace some of the chiming internal rhyme in the Japanese: *ko, no, mo, no, sato, mo, zo.* To leave no *i* undotted, "crystal" is imported to assure us that the falling "blossoms" of line 5 are really snowflakes, and the scene of flowerlessness that in the original (line 4) accounts for a special joy in the "flowering" of the snowflakes (line 5) vanishes without trace.

Brower and Miner's also fills in the causative links between "spreading mists" and swelling buds; makes sure that we do not fail to see the falling snow in flower terms ("wet snow petals"), thus losing, alas, the element of surprise, even magic, in the transformation of snowflakes into flowers that the original poem holds in store in its last two lines; and tells us (somewhat redundantly) that villages are a "country" phenomenon and (somewhat surprisingly) that this one is the speaker's home. In this version, as in the original and Rodd and Henkenius's, the poem closes with the snow scene, but here it is a one-time affair and "already" complete (lines 4 and 5), not a recurrent phenomenon that may appear under certain conditions anywhere at any time.

Some of the differences in these translations arise inevitably from different trade-offs, as in the first version, where the final vision of falling snow blossoms is let go presumably to achieve the lovely lilting echo and rhetorical turn of "flowers fall in villages / where flowers have yet to bloom." Or as in Rodd and Henkenius's version, where preoccupations with internal rhyme have obviously influenced word choices, not always for the better. Or as in all three versions, where different efforts to remind the reader of the wordplay on *haru* (in the Japanese poem both a noun meaning "spring" and a verb meaning "swell") have had dissimilar but perhaps equally indifferent results. Meantime, the immense force compacted into that small word in the original as both noun and verb, season of springtime and principal of growth, cause and effect (and thus in a sense the whole mighty process of earth's renewal, in which an interruption by snow only foretells a greater loveliness to come) fizzles away unfelt. A few differences do seem to arise from insufficient command of the nerves and sinews of English poetry, but most spring from the staggering difficulties of responding in any uniform way to the minimal clues proffered by the original text. The five perceptions—haze, buds, snowfall, flowerless villages, flowers falling—do not as they stand in the Japanese or any literal translation quite compose for readers accustomed to Western poetic traditions an adequate poetic whole. This is plainly seen in the irresistible urge each of the translators has felt to catch up the individual perceptions, as English tends to require, in a tighter overall grammatical and syntactical structure than the original insists on. In this way they provide a clarifying network of principal and subordinate, time when, place where, and cause why. Yet the inevitable result is a disassembling, a spinning out, spelling out, thinning out of what in the Japanese is an as yet unraveled imagistic excitement, creating (or memorializing) in the poet's mind, and then in the mind of the Japanese readers, the original thrill of consciousness when these images, complete with the magical transformation of snow into the longed-for cherry blossoms, first flashed on the inward eye.

What is comforting for us who must read this and other Japanese poems in translation is that each of the versions given here retains in some form or other all or most of the five images intact. What is less comforting is that the simplicity and suddenness, the explosion in the mind, have been diffused and defused.

When we turn to the Chinese song, we find similarly contesting forces at work. In one respect, the Chinese language comes over into English more readily than Japanese, being like English comparatively uninflected and heavily dependent on word order for its meanings. But in other respects, since Chinese like Japanese lacks distinctions of gender, of singular and plural, of *a* and *the*, and in the classical mode in which the poems in this anthology are composed, also of tenses, the pressure of the English translator to rearrange, straighten out, and fill in to "make sense" for his or her readers remains strong.

Let us examine song no. 23 of the *Shijing*. In its own Chinese characters, it looks like this:

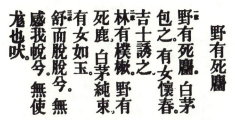

Eleven lines in all, each line having four characters as its norm, the poem seemingly takes shape around an implicit parallel between a doe in the forest, possibly killed by stealth and hidden under long grass or rushes (though on this point as on all others the poem refuses to take us wholly into confidence), and a young girl possibly "ruined" (as she certainly would have been in the post-Confucian society in which the *Shijing* was prized and circulated, though here again the poem keeps its own counsel) by loss of her virginity before marriage.

In its bare bones, with each character given an approximate English equivalent, a translation might look like this:

wild(s)	is	dead	deer	
white	grass(es)	wrap/cover	(it).	
is	girl	feel	spring.	
fine	man	tempt	(her).	
woods	is(are)	bush(es),	underbrush.	5
wild(s)	is	dead	deer.	
white	grass(es)	bind	bundle.	
is	girl	like	jade.	
slow	———	slow	slow.	
not	move	my	sash.	10
not	cause	dog	bark.	

Lines 1 to 4, it seems plain, propose the parallel of slain doe and girl, whatever that parallel may be intended to mean. Lines 5 to 8 restate the parallel, adding that the girl is as beautiful as jade and (apparently) that the doe lies where the "wild" gives way to smaller growth. If we allow ourselves to account for the repetition (here again is a Western mind-set in search of explanatory clues) by supposing that lines 1 to 4 signal at some subliminal level the initiation of the seduction and lines 5 to 8, again subliminally, its progress or possibly its completion, lines 9 to 11 fall easily into place as a miniature drama enacting in direct speech the man's advances and the girl's gradually crumbling resistance. They also imply, it seems, that the seduction takes place not in the forest, as we might have been led to suppose by lines 1 to 8, but in a dwelling with a vigilant guard dog.

Interpreted just far enough to accommodate English syntax, the poem reads as follows:

1. Wai-lim Yip:

> In the wilds, a dead doe.
> White reeds to wrap it.
> A girl, spring-touched.
> A fine man to seduce her.
> In the woods, bushes.   5
> In the wilds, a dead deer.
> White reeds in bundles.
> A girl like jade.
> Slowly. Take it easy.
> Don't feel my sash!   10
> Don't make the dog bark!

Interpreted a stage further in a format some have thought better suited to English poetic traditions, the poem reads:

2. Arthur Waley:

> In the wilds there is a dead doe,
> With white rushes we cover her.
> There was a lady longing for spring,
> A fair knight seduced her.
>
> In the woods there is a clump of oaks,   5
> And in the wilds a dead deer
> With white rushes well bound.
> There was a lady fair as jade.
>
> "Heigh, not so hasty, not so rough.
> "Heigh, do not touch my handkerchief.
> "Take care or the dog will bark."   10

Like the original and the literal translation, this version leaves the relationship between the doe's death and the girl's seduction unspecified and problematic. It holds the doe story in present tenses, assigning the girl story to the past. Still, much has been changed to give the English poem an explanatory scenario. The particular past assigned to the girl story, indeterminate in the Chinese original, is here fixed as the age of knights and ladies; and the seduction itself, which in the Chinese hovers as an eternal possibility within the timeless situation of man and maid ("A fine man *to* seduce her"), is established as completed long ago: "A fair knight seduced her." A teasing oddity in this version is the mysterious "we" who "cover" the slain doe, never to be heard from again.

Take interpretation toward its outer limits and we reach what is perhaps best called a "variation" on this theme:

3. Ezra Pound:

> Lies a dead doe on yonder plain
> whom white grass covers,
> A melancholy maid in spring

                    is luck
                    for   5
                    lovers
    Where the scrub elm skirts the wood
    be it not in white mat bound,
    As a jewel flawless found
                    dead as a doe is maidenhood.   10
    Hark!
    Unhand my girdle knot.
                    Stay, stay, stay
                    or the dog
                    may   15
                    bark.

Here too the present is pushed back to a past by the language the translator uses: not a specific past, as with the era of knights and ladies, but any past in which contemporary speech still features such (to us) archaic formalisms as "Unhand" or "Hark," and in which the term "maid" still signifies a virgin and in which virginity is prized to an extent that equates its loss with the doe's loss of life. But these evocations of time past are so effectively countered by the obtrusively present tense throughout (lines 1, 2, 4, 7, 8, 10, 11, 12, 13, and 15) that the freewheeling "variation" remains in this important respect closer to the spirit of the original than Waley's translation. On the other hand, it departs from the original and the two other versions by brushing aside the reticence that they carefully preserve as to the precise implications of the girl-deer parallel, choosing instead to place the seduction in the explanatory framework of the oldest story in the world: the way of a man with a maid in the springtime of life.

What both these examples make plain is that the Chinese and Japanese lyric, however contrasting in some ways, have in common at their center a complex of highly charged images generating something very like a magnetic field of potential meanings that cannot be got at in English without bleeding away much of the voltage. In view of this, the best practical advice for those of us who must read these marvelous poems in English translations is to focus intently on these images and ask ourselves what there is in them or in their effect on each other that produces the electricity. To that extent, we can compensate for a part of our losses, learn something positive about the immense explosive powers of imagery, and rest easy in the secure knowledge that translation even in the mode of the short poem brings us (despite losses) closer to the work itself than not reading it at all. "To a thousand cavils," said Samuel Johnson, "one answer is sufficient; the purpose of a writer is to be read, and the criticism which would destroy the power of pleasing must be blown aside." Johnson was defending Pope's Homer for those marks of its own time and place that make it the great interpretation it is, but Johnson's exhilarating common sense applies equally to the problem we are considering here. Literature is to be read, and the criticism that would destroy the reader's power to make some form of contact with much of the world's great writing must indeed be blown aside.

MAYNARD MACK

Sources

Brower, Robert H., and Earl Miner. *Japanese Court Poetry*. Stanford: Stanford University Press, 1961.

The Classic Anthology Defined by Confucius. Tr. Ezra Pound. New Directions, 1954.

Kokinshū: A Collection of Poems Ancient and Modern. Tr. Laurel Rasplica Rodd and Mary Catherine Henkenius. Princeton: Princeton University Press, 1984.
Kokin Wakashū: The First Imperial Anthology of Japanese Poetry. Tr. and ed. Helen Craig McCullough. Stanford: Stanford University Press, 1985.
Legge, James. *The Chinese Classics.* Hong Kong: Hong Kong University Press, 1960.
Waley, Arthur. *170 Chinese Poems.* New York, 1919.

A13

Index